BENJAMIN DISRAELI LETTERS: 1865–1867

BENJAMIN DISRAELI LETTERS

The Disraeli Project, Queen's University at Kingston

VOLUME NINE 1865–1867

Edited by

MICHEL W. PHARAND
General Editor

ELLEN L. HAWMAN
Co-editor

MARY S. MILLAR
Consulting Editor

SANDRA DEN OTTER
Consulting Editor

M.G. WIEBE
Editor Emeritus

University of Toronto Press   Toronto, Buffalo, London

© University of Toronto Press 2013
Toronto Buffalo London
www.utppublishing.com
Printed in Canada

ISBN 978-1-4426-4546-2 (cloth)

Printed on acid-free, 100% post-consumer recycled paper with vegetable-based inks.

Library and Archives Canada Cataloguing in Publication

Disraeli, Benjamin, 1804–1881
[Correspondence]
Benjamin Disraeli letters / edited by J.A.W. Gunn ... [et al.].

Vol. 9 edited by Michel W. Pharand ... [et al.]
Includes bibliographical references and index.
Contents: v. 9. 1865–1867.
ISBN 978-1-4426-4546-2 (v. 9)

1. Disraeli, Benjamin, 1804–1881 – Correspondence.   2. Prime ministers – Great Britain –
Correspondence.   3. Great Britain – Politics and government – 1837–1901.   I. Gunn, J.A.W. (John
Alexander Wilson), 1937–   II. Pharand, Michel Walter   III. Wiebe, M.G. (Melvin George), 1939–
IV. Title.

DA564.B3A4 1982   941.081092   c820-941697

The Disraeli Project has received generous funding from the Social Sciences and Humanities Research
Council of Canada. Publication of this volume is made possible by a grant from the Canadian Federation
for the Humanities, using funds provided by the Social Sciences and Humanities Research Council of
Canada.

University of Toronto Press acknowledges the financial assistance to its publishing program of the Canada Council for the Arts and the Ontario Arts Council.

University of Toronto Press acknowledges the financial support of the Government of Canada through
the Canada Book Fund for its publishing activities.

CONTENTS

ILLUSTRATIONS

ACKNOWLEDGEMENTS

We again acknowledge with gratitude our deep indebtedness to the sources of our financial support, both public and private, as listed in previous volumes, especially the continuing support of the Social Sciences and Humanities Research Council of Canada and of Queen's University.

We remain indebted to the individuals and institutions named in the earlier volumes, to which lists we add:

Ben Bakhtiarynia, Queen's University; Georgia Carley, Queen's University; Caitlin Charman, Queen's University; Sheila Cornett, Queen's University; Jim Coyle, British Library Newspapers, London; Jeremy B. Crane, Madison, Wisconsin; Mrs Pat Dallman, Sheffield Local Studies Library; Helen Edwards, International Autograph Auctions Ltd; Chris Fletcher, Bodleian Library; J.A.W. Gunn, Queen's University; Rupert Golding, The National Trust; Rosalind Green, Warwickshire Record Office; Roger Hull, Liverpool Record Office; John Keyworth, Bank of England Museum; Helen Langley, Bodleian Library; Louis Mably, London; Joseph S. Meisel, former Program Officer for Research Universities and Humanistic Scholarship at the Andrew W. Mellon Foundation, now Deputy Provost at Brown University; Mary S. Millar, Queen's University; Arthur Milnes, Queen's University; Anne Morgan, Plymouth and West Devon Record Office; Ana Ramos, British Library Newspapers, London; Alistair Ramsay, Government Office, Douglas, Isle of Man; François Rouget, Queen's University; Professor Frederick M. Schweitzer, Manhattan College, New York City; Paul Weatherall, Manx National Heritage; Judy Williams, University of Toronto Press; Keith Wilson, University of Ottawa; the anonymous assessors of the typescript of this volume and the editors at University of Toronto Press.

Special Acknowledgements

The editors would like to express their gratitude to Ginger Pharand for her efficient management of the Disraeli Project office and especially for her ongoing fundraising skills, and to Dr Mary S. Millar for her indispensable advice during the writing of this volume. The General Editor, Dr Michel Pharand, wishes to convey his indebtedness to the Editor Emeritus, Dr Mel Wiebe, not only for his invaluable assistance with the present volume, but also for his peerless contribution to Disraeli scholarship – eight volumes of *Benjamin Disraeli Letters* published over three decades – and in particular for his personal friendship and mentorship during the last five years.

Research for this volume
was funded by a generous grant
from the Andrew W. Mellon Foundation.

INTRODUCTION

In this volume, covering 1865-7, Derby as prime minister and Disraeli as chancellor of the exchequer – both for the third and last time – manage to pass a landmark franchise reform bill that would expand the electorate in England to an unprecedented extent.

Volume IX contains 837 letters. The main body addresses 153 recipients and is made up of 699 letters, of which 527 have never before been published and 78 published only in part. In addition, 138 for which there is evidence are described at the end of the Chronological List. Appendix I contains 23 letters to 18 correspondents from the years before this volume. Other appendices provide a comprehensive list of the office-holders in Lord Derby's 1866-8 government (Appendix II), Disraeli's resolutions for the 1867 Reform Bill in draft form (Appendix III) and as published in *Hansard* (Appendix IV), Disraeli's detailed memorandum of his 17 February 1867 audience with the Queen (Appendix V), and a selection of Disraeli's memoirs from 1865 with sketches of contemporary personalities (Appendix VI).

Disraeli's acceptance into the social establishment, begun in earnest in the early 1860s (see VIII p xiv), culminates symbolically in this volume with his unanimous election to the Athenaeum Club in 1866, thirty-one years after he had first sought nomination. In conveying the news to Disraeli, Lord Stanhope quoted the club rule that the committee '"will only elect persons who have attained to distinguished eminence"' (**4083**&n3). Disraeli's prestige was further enhanced by the publication of his political pronouncements, with three collections of speeches appearing in three years. The first was a selection of ecclesiastical speeches, *"Church and Queen": five speeches delivered by the Rt. Hon. B. Disraeli, M.P. 1860-1864* (see VIII **3973**&n5). 'I am sure you have done me great honor', Disraeli told editor Frederick Lygon in May 1865 upon receiving a copy of the book from him (**4012**). The second collection, *Constitutional Reform. Five Speeches, 1859-65*, was edited by John F. Bulley (**4187**n3), and the third was an important selection of speeches on reform. For this last book, suggested in late 1866 by publisher Thomas Longman, Disraeli offered to underwrite publication (**4223**&n1). 'They evidently think the subject will revive' (**4187**), he told his new private secretary, Montagu Corry (**4137**n1), a young solicitor who would remain an efficient, loyal confidant until Disraeli's death. Disraeli listed him as editor – 'It might assist yr introduction into public life' – and wrote the book's opening 'Advertisement' (initialled 'M.C.'), where the speeches are described, somewhat effusively, as 'a complete & consistent record of the main opinions of a great party' (**4272**). *Parliamentary Reform: a series of speeches on that subject delivered in the House of Commons (1848-1866)* was published in January 1867 (**4306**&n3).

Disraeli in this volume faces challenges both great and trivial. The latter, for example, include the lack of quality writing paper (**4206**): 'whether it be the ink, the pens, or the paper ... when in office, I never can write like a gentleman. Its a serious nuisance' (**4208**), he complained to Corry; 'my calligraphy has a cheesemongerish look'; 'I seem [to be] writing on stucco' (**4209**, **4237**), he groused, blaming his 'scrawl' on 'the wretched, cheap, huckster's ink, supplied by that miserable Departt., the Stationery office' (**4187**). Disraeli was also beset by incompetence: Sir Fitzroy Kelly, embarking on another anti-malt tax crusade, was a 'knave' (**4073**, **4075**), Sir Emerson Tennent 'a mere club gossip & office lounger' (**4274**) and French economist Louis Wolowski 'a great ass' (**4199**). The Rev Robert Maguire was a 'blundering booby' (**4638**) and Disraeli's butler 'a pompous booby' (**4612**).

More serious challenges abound, however, and Disraeli presciently summed up the theme for the letters in this volume in October 1865, when he warned Lord Lonsdale, 'I foresee tempestuous times, & great vicissitudes in public life' (**4044**). They would be numerous. An uprising in Morant Bay, Jamaica, led to the dismissal (though not the indictment) of governor Edward Eyre for his mishandling of the insurrection (**4150**n2, **4163**nn1-4). There were also Fenian uprisings in England (see below) and in Canada. While in March 1865 Disraeli asked the House not to 'doom Canada to the fate of being absorbed into the United States', in September 1866 he would ask Derby, 'what is the use of these Colonial Deadweights, wh: *we do not govern?*', stressing that it could never be 'our policy, to defend the Canadian Frontier agst the U.S.' (**4216**&n6). He reiterated this view to war secretary Jonathan Peel: 'It would not be wise or generous' to desert Canada when it was 'perhaps on the eve of accomplishing in Confederation a stronger political organisation', but 'if the colonists cannot defend themselves from the mere Fenians, they must be, indeed unworthy of self-government' (**4222**).

In addition, there was ongoing turmoil in Europe. Regular confidential bulletins from Lionel de Rothschild (**4484**&n3, **4513**, **4515**n1, **4550**&n1) kept Disraeli abreast of the political scene across the Channel. At one point Disraeli acted as intermediary between Lord Stanley (foreign secretary as of July 1866) and the Queen, whose opinions differed on the country's role in international affairs. In late 1866, upon learning that Otto von Bismarck, minister-president of Prussia (from 1867 chancellor of the North German Confederation) had suggested 'an arrangement, by which the Southern States of Germany should blend with Prussia, and that France should take possession of Belgium', Disraeli told Stanley he doubted that England 'would see any further glaring case of public violence and treachery with composure. Reaction is the law of all human affairs: and the reaction from non-intervention must, sooner or later, set in' (**4294**). When in April 1867 Bismarck refused to withdraw his troops (installed since 1815) from Luxemburg fortress, the Queen told Derby, '*England* in such a case MUST NOT stand aloof' but 'defend the Independence of Belgium with the whole strength of the British Empire' (**4419**&n3). At Windsor a few days later, Disraeli assured the Queen 'that she was quite under a mistake in supposing that [Stanley] would not act, if necessary' (**4419**). The so-called Luxemburg Crisis would be resolved by the Treaty of London on 11 May 1867 (**4396**n2).

General Grey, the Queen's private secretary, reiterated the Queen's views on foreign policy in July in a twelve-page letter to Disraeli. In light of recent accounts from Paris and Berlin of 'mutual accusations of arming with hostile intentions' and the threat of war in Europe, the Queen had asked whether England, 'adhering to a cold policy of non-interference ... is to continue in her passive attitude, nor make any attempt to avert such a Calamity? Yet she fears that such may be the course which Ld. Stanley, unless some pressure is exercised upon him, may be inclined to pursue'. Disraeli immediately reassured her that Stanley, acting 'under the influence of my reiterated representations, has entirely dropped the phrase, &, I hope, the abstract policy, of what is called "*non-intervention*"' (**4484**&n1). Replying on 5 August, Grey told Disraeli that the Queen felt that if France and Prussia 'were assured that any violation of the Independence of Belgium, or of the neutrality of Luxembourg would certainly bring England into the field ... both Countries wd. probably shrink from being the first to provoke a rupture' (**4484**n5).

War was also being waged on the home front against the cattle plague, an infectious viral disease called 'murrain' or 'rinderpest', which began decimating British livestock in June 1865. The devastation led to the formation of various cattle insurance companies (**4062**, **4067**) and a cattle plague commission (**4051**), and there was protracted debate in Parliament on the Cattle Diseases and Cattle Plague bills in February and March 1866. In September Disraeli noted 'great, & deep, discontent' in Bucks county (**4189**) following an order in council prohibiting the sale of sheep and lambs in markets and fairs. Debate on the importation of foreign cattle continued into 1867 (**4535**&nn1-3).

The numerous animal deaths from the plague, along with demands on the country's 'feeble [bank] balances' and a poor harvest, contributed to what Disraeli, writing to first lord of the admiralty Sir John Pakington in October 1866, called 'an inexorable economy' (**4251**). Moreover, the collapse in May of Overend & Gurney, England's second largest bank (**4125**&n1), had provoked a stock market crash and led to a rise in interest rates to 10%. Disraeli was also 'alarmed' at the 'dangerous condition' of the financial state of the railways, which he feared would result in 'the distress and ruin to many industrial establishments' (**4233**&n5, **4234**). And during protracted negotiations with Portugal for a commercial treaty on importation of wines (**4191**&nn1,2&7, **4196**&n1, **4298**&n6, **4313**&n2), Disraeli denied 'the charge, that we are remitting duties on luxuries [wine], while we leave the articles consumed by the labouring class [beer] untouched' (**4237**). While in September 1866 Disraeli was not 'inclined to run any risk of injuring our revenue' by lowering import duties on wine (**4203**), by January 1867, according to Stanley, he was eager 'to make all the necessary sacrifices of revenue ... £725,000 for the first year: which, though heavy, would be rapidly made good by increased consumption' (**4299**nn1&2). The matter was concluded in December 1867 when Disraeli issued a statement declining proposals for reducing the duties (**4504**n4).

A more serious domestic encumbrance was the continued mismanagement of the navy, Disraeli complaining to Derby of the admiralty's 'feebleness & absurdity' (**4216**), 'mutinous spirit' (**4316**) and 'maladministration, not to say malversation';

rather than build iron ships, for example, it expended 'vast sums ... in cobbling up old wooden vessels' (**4175**&n1). Outlining to Pakington the government's budgetary constraints, Disraeli regretted its inability to purchase a Turkish ironclad, which Pakington found 'vexatious and humiliating ... the most powerful Ship yet designed is to go to Prussia!' (**4251**&n5). Disraeli reassured him that 'in first-class Ironclads, our present position is more than respectable' (**4257**&n1).

Given the country's inexorable economy at this time, it is no wonder Disraeli believed that 'currency is a subject which has made even more people mad than love' (**4181**). Nonetheless, during what would be his last stint as chancellor of the exchequer (6 July 1866 to 29 February 1868), Disraeli succeeded in obtaining financing for a number of very expensive purchases and ventures. Having enthusiastically supported raising funds for a memorial to Prince Albert in 1863 (VIII **3809**&nn1&3), in July 1866 he moved a vote to purchase old gun metal to build it, informing the Queen that 'tho' for a moment menaced, [the vote] was passed, & passed agreeably' (**4159**). In November he authorized the purchase at Paris of the magnificent Blacas Collection of ancient gems and artifacts for the British Museum at a cost of £45,721 (**4269**&n2). For a lavish entertainment for the Sultan of Turkey in July 1867 (**4474**&n4), he obtained £25,000, 'not altogether smoothly, but without a division', he told the Queen (**4493**). And despite 'cavils & petty criticism from secondrate men' (**4592**), Disraeli obtained an astonishing £2,000,000 to finance an expedition to Abyssinia to free a kidnapped British consul (see **4482**&n3, **4518**&n3 and below); he warned Stanley that 'whatever our fate, the Ministry of '67 must not be destroyed by the King of Abyssinia!' (**4521**).

That ministry's struggle with parliamentary reform – as Disraeli had predicted, the subject did revive – forms the topic of the most important and numerous letters in this volume. The political 'inertness & apathy' (VIII **3784**) he had bemoaned in 1863 was now swept away by vigorous debate on the contentious reform question. Boasting to Bucks electors on 20 May 1865 of the recent defeat of a borough franchise extension bill (**4006**&n1), Disraeli hoped that, in future, 'public opinion' would 'legislate in the spirit of the English Constitution, wh: would absorb the best of all classes, & not fall into a democracy, wh: is the tyranny of one class, & that one the least enlightened' (**4013**). (Fear of the rule by the uneducated masses would continue to be the perennial objection to suffrage reform.)

The general election that followed the dissolution of Parliament on 6 July 1865 gave Palmerston's Liberals a substantial majority. 'I have no doubt there were instances on our side of over-confidence', Disraeli told Derby (**4027**), who foresaw – mistakenly, it would turn out – 'no prospect of any state of affairs which shall again place me at the head of a government' (**4030**n1). Disraeli even offered to step down if his retirement would enable Derby to form a coalition with a Whig as leader of the Commons, 'an anti-revolutionary Government on a broad basis' (**4030**). But Derby felt that being merely 'the *nominal* head of a Coalition Government' would be 'personally ... intolerable' (**4033**n1).

Following the death of Lord Palmerston on 18 October 1865 (**4038**&nn7&8), Disraeli wrote to Lonsdale that 'if Johnny [Russell] is the man, there will be a reform bill; very distasteful to the Country' (**4044**&n8). Lord Russell, a frail 74, assumed office on 29 October. 'The reform crisis cannot now be delayed', Stanley had cautioned Disraeli (**4048**n1). On 6 November, replying to Ralph Earle's suggestion to 'try Stanley as Premier & annex [Robert] Lowe', Disraeli predicted that, following some initial 'enthusiasm', 'Stanley after a twelvemonth would be kicked out ... and Gladstone installed as first Minister ... So long as the Whigs are united, the views you describe are a fairy tale' (**4054**&n1). Yet that same day Disraeli told Stanley that 'the Whigs who are gorged & satiated with patronage, will rally round you' and 'the bulk of the Tories ... would accept you as their leader with all your heresies' (**4055**). In the event, Stanley would decline Russell's offer of the Duchy of Lancaster (*ibid* n5).

Stanley was right about reform: Gladstone introduced a Representation of the People Bill on 12 March 1866 and, at a party meeting on the 16th, Conservatives agreed to oppose it (**4083**n2). Disraeli spent the next few months collecting information for use in his speeches, including data on borough limits and populations from his invaluable election agent Markham Spofforth (**4089**nn2&3) and statistics from demographer and electoral analyst Dudley Baxter (**4089**n1, **4093**, **4095**n1), among others. He also worked behind the scenes with Lord Elcho (**4009**nn1&2), Earle and selected 'Adullamites' (**4102**n2) – a group of about forty dissident Liberals led by Elcho and the sardonic Robert Lowe – to bring down Gladstone's moderate measure, which would give the vote to occupiers of property worth £7 per year in rent (down from the existing £10 qualification) in boroughs, £14 per year (down from £50) in counties, and to anyone with at least £50 in the bank for two consecutive years. The bill would create about 400,000 new voters. At second reading on 12 April Lord Grosvenor (an Adullamite), seconded by Stanley, moved a hostile amendment (prepared by Derby) calling for the postponement of the franchise bill until a redistribution measure could also be introduced. On the 27th, after eight days of intense debate, the motion was narrowly defeated 318 to 313, thirty-five Liberals voting with the Opposition.

During May and early June, six Conservative amendments were moved against reform legislation, with Adullamites continuing to play a crucial role. Earle on 20 May sent Disraeli a resolution by Adullamite Edward Bouverie, that the government's 'scheme' was '"not sufficiently matured to form the basis of a satisfactory measure"' (**4098**n3), and on the 22nd Disraeli told him that 'young [Arthur] Hayter must be utilised' and 'the whole of the Adullamites may be counted on' (**4102**). On the 24th Disraeli sent Hayter's notice of amendment to Derby (**4103**) and on the 27th wrote to Earle that he and Derby feared 'a general collapse, and Committee, which would be fatal' (**4105**). In 'an exhausting, & tumultuous, scene' in the House on the 28th, Bouverie's instruction to refer the reform and redistribution of seats bills to the same committee was accepted without debate (**4105**nn1&2) and Hayter's amendment that 'the system of grouping' was 'neither convenient nor equitable' (**4106**n5) was defeated 403 to 2. Disraeli wrote to Lord Grey after 2 *am* on the 29th that 'the situation is critical', predicting that 'a coarser constituency will shake a feebler & more anomalous edifice' (**4106**). 'We ought to strike at once', he told Grey two days later, '& the country will ratify the blow' (**4107**).

By 12 June, Disraeli could assure his wife Mary Anne that 'Affairs look here pretty well ... Lord Dunkellin has given notice of a motion against the government' (**4111**). Selected from among a group of Adullamite peers meeting at Lord Lansdowne's house (**4121**n2), Dunkellin inflicted the fatal blow on 18 June, the eighteenth day of debate, when he moved a hostile amendment (**4111**n1) proposing a borough franchise qualification based on payment of rates (local property taxes) rather than on residential rental value. Its passage – by a mere eleven votes (315 to 304), over forty Liberals voting with the Opposition – quashed the measure Disraeli had feared might 'shatter both Whigs & Tories, & utterly destroy the present Conservative organisation' (**4114**). It also brought about Russell's resignation a week later, the first such resignation of a ministry over reform since 1832.

According to Stanley, Disraeli was now 'sanguine of success, eager for power, and full of his projected arrangements' (**4118**n3). But to everyone's surprise, the Adullamites immediately retreated. According to Grosvenor, they had decided at a council not to guarantee Derby any official support, proposing instead a centrist coalition with Lord Clarendon as prime minister in the Lords and Stanley as leader of the Commons. 'So much for Adullamite co-operation!' exclaimed Derby (**4116**&n1). On 25 June – the day before an embittered Russell resigned in the Lords (**4115**n2) – Disraeli warned Derby that if he refused office a Liberal would be sent for and application made 'to a section of yr party to join the administration ... You *must* take the Government' (**4118**&n1). Derby received the Queen's letter at 10 *am* on the 27th and immediately informed Disraeli, who told Earle that day, '*Nothing can be going on better* ... The formation of Lord Derby's government is *certain*' (**4120**). The next morning, at a meeting at Derby's house of twenty-two of his principal supporters (*ibid* n3), it was agreed that he should form a government. Derby left for Windsor that afternoon to accept the Queen's commission.

Disraeli and Derby soon began discussing the composition of their third (and last) ministry. Disraeli consulted with Derby (**4140**) and Lord Naas (**4141**) on Irish appointments. Some place seekers were turned down (**4129**), while others were offered a position but declined (**4133**). Disraeli thought Lord Shaftesbury would be 'powerful with the religious middle class' (**4121**), but the philanthropist would never hold office. When candidates passed over by Disraeli received from Derby what Disraeli called 'answers of a very different complexion, wh: have created great discontent', Disraeli sent him a memo of a standard reply (to those seeking his interference with Derby) that denied the rumour that Derby was going 'to create a batch of peers & a batch of baronets' (**4146**&n3, **4145**).

Although the Queen had urged Derby to cooperate with sympathetic Liberals – in her words, 'those who have been supporters, or even Members, of the late Government' – and Disraeli believed there was, in his words, 'a good chance' that the new administration would be formed 'on a broad basis' (**4120**&nn2&3), Adullamite desertion resulted in an all-Conservative cabinet. Derby travelled to Windsor on 2 July to present his cabinet appointments to the Queen, who 'has agreed to everything', he told Disraeli (**4123**n1).

Disraeli was again chancellor of the exchequer, Lord Chelmsford lord chancellor, the Duke of Buckingham lord president, Lord Malmesbury lord privy seal, Spencer Walpole home secretary, Lord Stanley foreign secretary, Lord Carnarvon colonial secretary, General Peel war secretary, Lord Cranborne Indian secretary, Sir John Pakington first lord of the admiralty, Sir Stafford Northcote president of the board of trade, Gathorne Hardy president of the poor law board, Lord John Manners first commissioner of works and Lord Naas Irish secretary. There had been no 'Adullamite co-operation': Derby's offers of the foreign office to Clarendon and of cabinet posts to Lowe and Edward Horsman were declined. The only Liberal secured was Catholic moderate Michael Morris, as solicitor-general (and later attorney-general) for Ireland (**4140**&n1).

The new cabinet met for the first time on 9 July and the government's mettle was tested on 23 July when the Reform League (founded in early 1865), headed by its president Edmond Beales, marched peacefully en masse to Hyde Park – despite a ban on the event by home secretary Walpole, who had ordered police to close the park gates. Chaos ensued: some 20,000 protesters swarmed over the railings into the park and police tried to subdue them with truncheons. Forty-two men were arrested and one policeman killed. Disraeli downplayed the rioting to the Queen as 'pure frolic by a knot of laughing boys' (**4155**), but violence escalated the next day, a mob breaking windows of the Athenaeum and of private houses, including Disraeli's home, Grosvenor Gate (**4157**n7). On the 25th a Reform League deputation met with an emotional Walpole (he reportedly broke down), whose 'pathos seems to have melted the multitude' (**4159**), Disraeli told the Queen. 'Public meetings', he assured her, 'are the recognized, & indispensable, organs of a free constitution. They are safety-valves' (**4161**).

Meanwhile, Disraeli on the 20th had proposed to Derby a reform bill that 'would cut the ground entirely from under Gladstone': '£6 *Rating* for Boros: 20£ rating for Counties ... It would prevent all agitation in the Recess' (**4152**). But Derby demurred at the idea of acting too hastily and assemblies and protests continued, many spearheaded by John Bright. On 30 July over 20,000 Reform League members held an 'indignation meeting' in London's Royal Agricultural Hall (**4162**&n2). There were enormous gatherings at Birmingham in August (**4191**&n6), Manchester in September (**4213**&n4) and at Leeds, Glasgow and Dublin. Walpole would resign in May 1867 after issuing a proclamation outlawing a demonstration in Hyde Park (**4416**&n2) and then allowing it to take place (**4498**&n2).

In light of these events, Derby revisited the idea of a reform bill and told Disraeli on 16 September that he was 'coming reluctantly to the conclusion that we shall have to deal with the question of Reform'. He asked Disraeli to consider proceeding by resolutions – outlining the government's broad principles without pledging it to a specific course of action – and enclosed 'a sketch of a Reform Bill' (including a £6 rating borough franchise and £14 occupation county franchise) drawn up by Dudley Baxter. 'We *need* not make the adoption of any of the Resolutions a vital question' (**4202**n4), Derby assured him. But Disraeli's enthusiasm for reform had waned: 'observation, & reflection, have not yet brought me to yr conclusion as to the necessity of bringing in a bill for Parly Reform', he told Derby, who replied from Balmoral that the Queen was 'very anxious' to see the question settled: 'we cannot escape doing something' (**4207**&n5).

Disraeli, still diffident, replied that the issue now occupied his 'almost constant consideration' but suggested, in lieu of legislation, a boundary commission '& supplementary measures, of the same kind, [which] might be deferred till November' (**4216**). Replying from Knowsley on 9 October, Derby dismissed the idea of a commission as impractical ('Our Colleagues are scattered about in all directions') and explained at length the 'great advantages' of resolutions: they would 'put an end to the cry that we are the opponents of all Reform' and his party would be 'less committed to each several Resolution than we should be on the main provisions of a Bill ... If moreover we get the House pledged to our *principles*, we shall be in a much better position for hereafter discussing details: and it will be difficult for the Radicals either to escape from Amendments, or so to frame them as not to clash with the moderate Liberals, and widen the existing breach.' Moreover, Derby concluded, the Queen wished 'the question settled *by us*' (*ibid* n3). Disraeli now came aboard in earnest: 'I shall endeavour to draw up a series of Resolutions in your vein', he replied. 'They must, however, be distinct enough for us to fall back upon, as a clear policy, for the country, in case we are forced to appeal to it, wh: Heaven forefend!' (**4229**).

Disraeli still had reservations, however. Writing from Balmoral on 17 October, Northcote informed him that the Queen had offered to assist Derby in communicating with Russell and Gladstone; she would later write to Derby with that offer (**4247**&n1). Disraeli balked at the idea and told Derby that 'Such sentimental schemes ... come to nothing, or ... convey only to our rivals the impression, that we are alike feeble & perplexed' (**4246**); he also wrote in similar language to Northcote (**4247**&n1). The Queen's proposal was disregarded.

In cabinet on 8 November Derby presented his revised resolutions, which included a royal commission to inquire into constituency boundaries. Disraeli, who considered royal commissions 'an abdication of our duties' (**4216**), sent Derby on the 18th a lengthy 'Memorandum on the present position of the Ministry'; success, he wrote, required 'substantial grounds' for a commission and 'I myself am at a loss to find these grounds' (**4262**). Derby agreed: 'but they *must* be found, as it is, I am convinced, our only chance of escaping Shipwreck' (*ibid* n3). After a cabinet meeting on the 25th, Disraeli had an audience with the Queen, who recorded in her journal that cabinet had been 'unanimous in agreeing that the subject *must* be dealt with by Resolutions, preparatory to a Commission being issued, so that the matter might be settled irrespective of Party'. She thought Disraeli was 'amiable and clever, but ... a strange man' (**4268**n11).

Derby on 2 December sent Disraeli 'a copy of the Resolutions as provisionally agreed to by the Cabinet' (**4274**n3) and a few weeks later came up with a detailed plan 'to extricate ourselves from the Reform Dilemma', which he shared with Disraeli on the 22nd. The commission ('our *Buffer*') could investigate the issue of bribery and polling papers, a 'Savings Bank Franchise' and the effect of a £10 a year lodger franchise, 'and this not numerically only, but as to what *class* of voters it would introduce'. He famously proposed, 'of all possible Hares to start, I do not know a better than the extension of Household Suffrage, *coupled with plurality of voting*' (**4291**n1). Disraeli replied with a list of 'seven wise men' suitable for a bipartisan commission (**4291**). Derby thought Baxter 'invaluable' but found Lord Grey (as president) 'crotchety' (despite 'in the main Conservative' views) and Lord Devon 'very weak'; Sir John Walsh, he wrote, would not know where to 'safely concede, and where to stand firm'; and the 'private and philosophical opinions' of Liberals John Stuart Mill, A.S. Ayrton and Samuel Laing might prove 'subservient to their political interests' (**4291**n5). Disraeli replied on the 29th that the lodger franchise, plurality '& all the cognate expedients for protecting the minority' should be 'specifically referred to the Commission' (**4293**&n7).

The new year began optimistically when, on 10 January 1867, cabinet agreed to proceed by resolutions and the Queen wrote to Derby supporting his course of action. Derby reported to Disraeli, 'we are not only on velvet, but we may look at [the Court] at present as *Partisan*' (**4302**nn1&2). The Queen, still in widowed seclusion, at Derby's request very reluctantly agreed to open Parliament in person on 5 February, '*great, trying,* and *painful* as the exertion will be' (**4302**n2), she warned him. According to *The Times*, 'The Asian mystery was never more insoluble', an allusion to the throne speech's purposefully vague reform paragraph, which hoped for 'the Adoption of Measures which, without unduly disturbing the Balance of political Power, shall freely extend the Elective Franchise' (**4321**n2). Disraeli reported to the Queen that debate on the speech had been 'most serene'; even Gladstone had been 'courteous & considerate' (**4321**). Agreement was reached the following day in cabinet on the resolutions' precise wording.

Events would prove anything but serene. Disraeli's biographer Robert Blake has dubbed the factious reform debacle 'one of the oddest histories of confusion, cross-purposes and muddle in British political history' (456). The first of Disraeli's 'great vicissitudes' occurred only two days after the throne speech, on 7 February, when war secretary Peel threatened to resign: 'his eye lights up with insanity' at the phrase 'household suffrage' (**4323**), Disraeli told Derby. On the 11th, after a hesitant, ambiguous speech lasting over two hours describing (but not presenting) his resolutions (see app III), Disraeli prematurely assured the Queen that the question would be 'comparatively easy', boasting that 'the Opposition will be forced to join issue on the Resolutions'. After learning from General Grey that Disraeli had 'made a great mess of it', the Queen, who had hoped for bipartisan consensus, wrote to Derby that she now feared the resumption of a protracted 'party contest' (**4328**&n3).

After consulting with Cranborne on the 15th Disraeli modified the reform plan and the next day introduced it in cabinet (**4331**n2). Household suffrage safeguarded by plural voting was abandoned and Peel again threatened to resign. The next day Derby sent Disraeli to Osborne to assure the Queen that Derby 'was resolved not to quit the helm, until the settlement was concluded' (see app V). He returned with a letter from the Queen that persuaded Peel to withdraw his resignation: 'the magical letter effected the miracle', Disraeli told her. In cabinet on the 19th, Peel withdrew his objections to Derby's original plan, which had nonetheless been 'modified & mutilated' to please Peel (**4334**&n4). Disraeli on the 23rd wrote that cabinet, which had met that day briefly, was 'unanimous for the great plan' – household suffrage allied with plural (rather than cumulative) voting based on property – for which Dudley Baxter had been busy gathering statistics (**4336**&n2).

The great plan was immediately sabotaged: Cranborne, Carnarvon and Peel resigned. 'This is stabbing in the back!' Disraeli wrote to Derby on Monday the 25th after learning the news from him early that morning. Close scrutiny of the statistics on Sunday had convinced Cranborne that the reform scheme would be (he had told Derby) 'the ruin of the Conservative party' (**4338**&n2) and, as he would tell the House, would 'introduce into the majority of boroughs what was in effect pure and simple household suffrage' (**4359**n1). An emergency cabinet at Derby's house that afternoon (the 25th), a mere ten minutes before the scheduled Conservative party meeting, adopted Stanley's hasty compromise of £6 rating franchise for boroughs (without dual voting) and £20 for counties. (When Pakington on 13 March divulged that cabinet had decided after 'hardly ten minutes' (**4373**&n3), the bill was dubbed the 'Ten Minutes Bill'.) That evening, to a packed House that included peers, ambassadors and the Prince of Wales, Disraeli outlined the four new proposed franchises that he claimed would increase the constituency by 400,000, ironically the same number projected by Gladstone's failed 1866 measure. When Disraeli sat down, 'a storm of indignation burst on his head' (**4340**&nn2&3).

The next day, preempting Gladstone's motion for a withdrawal of the government's resolutions (**4343**n2), Disraeli, as agreed upon in cabinet that morning (**4341**n2), announced that resolutions would be discarded in favour of a bill. Although the House, he reported to the Queen, had been 'agitated & disturbed', he remained 'still confident that ... the solution of the Reform Question will be accomplished' (**4342**&n1). At Court the following day, the Queen found Derby (in her words) 'in terribly low spirits' (**4344**n2) and Disraeli 'much out of spirits' (**4345**n1).

On the 28th there were large party meetings at Grosvenor's house (the Adullamites are for 'Household Suffrage & Plurality – not Duality', Disraeli told Derby) and at the Carlton Club (where most favoured household suffrage with three years' residence and personal payment of rates); the general feeling was, Disraeli told the Queen, that Derby 'ought to be encouraged to fall back on his own policy' (**4346**&nn2,4&6, **4349**). That day the Queen urged Derby to show 'a *bold front* ... to settle this *vexed* and *vital* question of Reform' (**4350**nn1&2). On 4 March Derby duly informed the Lords of his plan to reintroduce his original measure, including 'plurality of votes'; in a 'sulky' House, Disraeli's withdrawal of the 'Ten Minutes Bill' and his proposal to introduce a reform bill on the 18th 'passed without comment' (**4356**&n2), he told Derby. The next day, to an 'agitated and excited' House, he explained the party's return to Derby's original scheme and countered accusations (from the Lords) that reform had been taken up with 'indifference' following a negligent delay (**4359**&n1).

There would be no further delay. Within days Disraeli, Derby and Dudley Baxter had drafted a reform bill. It was discussed in cabinet on the 12th, sent to the Queen (**4370**n4), approved in cabinet on the 14th, explained to a large Conservative party meeting on the 15th (**4372**nn1&3), redrawn that day by legal expert and parliamentary draftsman Henry Thring – Baxter had resigned when he found Thring 'determined to remodel the Bill' (**4369**n3) – and printed during the night for the next day's cabinet. Writing to General Grey from the House after the party meeting, Disraeli detailed the main features of the bill: franchise founded on rating, with borough franchise resting 'on an occupation alone, rated to the relief of the poor, the ratepayer personally paying the rates', and a two-year residence requirement. Under this measure, '700,000 will be *qualified*, or may *qualify* himself, to be a voter ... (my own opinion is that not 50,000 will ever ultimately avail themselves of the provision) ... The principle of his [Derby's] measure is bonâ fide Rating, as distinguished from the fluctuating rental or value of all previous measures'. The measure would have Adullamite support, he wrote, only if 'founded on a real & personal rating, residence, & some compensatory arrangement against the possible influx of Compound Householders, either the dual vote, or some other counterpoise' (**4372**). 'Compounders' were tenants who paid rates via a sum added to their rent and thus did not appear on the rate book (the basis of the electoral register); duality would be abandoned in cabinet on the 23rd (**4380**).

Disraeli introduced the revised bill on the 18th as planned. 'The Ship was launched this evening by the C. of E. not without success', he told the Queen, despite a 'ruthless' speech by Gladstone (**4374**&nn1-7), whose intransigence had begun to alienate even his own colleagues. A few days later, at a Liberal party meeting at Gladstone's house, it was agreed (*contra* Gladstone) not to oppose the bill at second reading but rather to move amendments (**4377**&nn1&3). 'Gladstone is more violent than ever', Disraeli told Derby (**4381**), and although 'there are 100 men' against him, 'they are *moutons*' (**4382**). On the first night (25th) of the second reading, Gladstone's two-hour, statistics-ridden speech was countered by a rousing reply from Gathorne Hardy, who told the House that the government was 'anxious to give a liberal but not an indiscriminate franchise' (**4385**&nn2&3). On the second night (26th), having outlined the inconsistencies of Gladstone's demands, Disraeli invited all members to act 'cordially and candidly ... Pass the Bill, and then change the Ministry if you like'. The second reading passed without a division. The next day an elated Derby told Disraeli, 'you have won our game for us' (**4387**&nn1&3), perhaps a nod to Disraeli's key role during the last few weeks, Derby since the 11th having suffered from chronic fatigue. Sidelined by an attack of gout on the 30th, he would be absent from cabinet meetings in April and leave town mid-month to recuperate at Roehampton (**4413**n1). Disraeli would now be nominally in charge.

But the game was not yet won. Over the next two months Disraeli had to shepherd the bill through committee. He warned Derby of 'rocks a-head' (**4391**) but assured the Queen that though 'the struggle is intense' he would 'make any sacrifice' to secure her 'tranquillity' (**4398**&n1). On 8 April, following a meeting in the Commons tea-room of forty-six dissatisfied Liberals who declined to support an instruction of John Coleridge (**4401**n3) – the so-called 'tea-room revolt' (**4400**n1) – Disraeli informed the Queen that 'a collapse perhaps unequalled in party & political history' had left 'the bill, in all its good & necessary provisions, safe'. She counselled 'moderation in the hour of Victory' (*ibid* &nn2&3). A decisive victory occurred on the last day before Easter recess when, at 1:30 *am* on the 13th, Gladstone's amendment rejecting the principle of personal payment of rates was defeated 310-289 thanks to over forty Liberal votes: 'A smash perhaps without example', wrote Gladstone (**4405**&n1). After writing to the Queen at 2 *am*, Disraeli went to the Carlton Club – where he was famously toasted as 'the man who rode the race, who took the time, who kept the time, and who did the trick' – and then on to Grosvenor Gate, where Mary Anne was waiting with a bottle of champagne and a Fortnum and Mason pie. Disraeli reportedly told her, 'you are more like a mistress than a wife' (*ibid*).

Victories continued when the session resumed, and in early May Disraeli predicted that 'a great encounter – an Armageddon' (**4429**) was at hand. There were in fact two significant encounters. On the 6th, in answer to an amendment by Radical J.T. Hibbert (**4404**n3) that would allow tenants to qualify as voters by paying the reduced rates they had once paid through compounding, Disraeli moved a counter-amendment requiring them to pay full rates (which they could then deduct from their rent) and announced that the government would dissolve Parliament if defeated on this point (**4431**n3). At about 1:30 *am* on the 10th his counter-amendment was carried: 'Majority for Y. M. Government <u>66</u>! ... result overwhelming, & Bill safe', a jubilant Disraeli told the Queen. Although Lowe called the Liberal defeat 'a perfect Waterloo' (**4433**&n2), the counter-amendment never became law.

An even more startling triumph occurred on the 17th when, without consulting Derby or the cabinet, Disraeli accepted an amendment by Grosvenor Hodgkinson that would abolish compounding – all rates would now have to be paid in person – and create nearly 500,000 new voters (**4438**&nn2&8). The clause was carried without a division on the 20th 'amid loud cheers, from both sides of the House', Disraeli told the Queen (**4440**&n1). Writing to her at length on 9 June with 'a general view of the position & prospects of the Reform Bill', Disraeli concluded: 'The Ministry has taken root' (**4448**).

Discussion of boundaries and redistribution of seats continued until the end of June (**4451**&n1, **4452**&n3, **4453**, **4454**&n2, **4456**, **4457**, **4462**nn1&3) and debate on amendments proceeded in July (**4464**&n1, **4465**&n1, **4467**&n1, **4468**&n1). Disraeli on 9 July finally 'carried the Reform Bill thro' Committee ... [to] great cheering from both sides when the Committee closed', he told the Queen (**4469**). The bill passed third reading on the 15th without a division, with Gladstone silent but Lowe accusing the government of 'treachery' and Cranborne also accusing it of 'a political betrayal which has no parallel in our Parliamentary annals'. After refuting their speeches, Disraeli trumpeted to the Queen that he had 'vindicated the course of the Tory Party amid universal sympathy' (**4472**&n1).

The bill had first reading in the Lords the next day and second reading on the 22nd and 23rd. Despite a debilitating attack of gout and rheumatism at the end of June that had left his nerves frayed, Derby managed to speak at great length on the 22nd. There were objections from Lord Grey – a resolution (withdrawn) 'to show that the Bill requires considerable amendment' (**4473**&nn1&2) – but the bill passed second reading on the 23rd and amendments were discussed over five days the following week, until 5 August. At third reading on the 6th, a pale and feeble Derby concluded his ministerial statement with the now-famous pronouncement, 'No doubt we are making a great experiment and "taking a leap in the dark"'. The bill was sent back to the Commons, where on the 8th Disraeli asked the House to consider the Lords' amendments in a 'spirit of prudent but dignified conciliation' (**4491**n3). It received royal assent on the 15th, a 'great and, I believe happy event', he wrote (**4497**).

Although Derby had initiated a reform bill, it was Disraeli who, by accepting various amendments that removed many of the bill's initial safeguards, determined the final shape of the 1867 Reform Act, which trebled the number the bill was originally expected to enfranchise. The Act gave the vote to all householders in boroughs (owners and tenants) who had been resident for one year and who paid rates; lodgers in boroughs paying an annual rent of £10; county residents paying annual rates of £12; and free and lease holders in counties with land valued at £5 a year. The borough electorate was increased by 134%, the county electorate by 46%. Prior to 1867, about 1 in 5 adult males possessed the vote, whereas after the Reform Act about 1 in 3 adult males were enfranchised (see St John 81, 84 and Hawkins 131).

Disraeli's tempestuous times were far from over, however. Beginning in late July and over the next few months – while Derby was disabled by gout so severe that he wrote to Disraeli via Lady Derby (**4526**n1, **4530**n1), their son Frederick (**4545**n3) or his private secretary Lord Barrington (**4492**n4) – Disraeli turned to other matters. One was the selection of members of the Irish Railways Commission (**4503**&n1, **4508**, **4511**, **4532**). Another was the vexing 'Abyssinian mess' (**4522**&n3 and see above), a costly enterprise to be financed, Disraeli reassured Derby, 'out of Army & Navy Votes, & Treasury Chest, without any "misappropriation"' (**4526**&n3). The crisis forced an emergency session of Parliament (19 November to 7 December) during which Disraeli obtained an unprecedented £2,000,000 for 'going to war not to obtain territory', he said, but for 'high moral causes alone' (**4592**&n1).

Disraeli was also busy preparing for a trip to Edinburgh at the end of the month. When he turned down an invitation to attend a grand banquet in Derby's honour on 17 October in Manchester (**4557**&n1), Derby on the 6th informed him that he had heard there was 'great disappointment ... [and] dissatisfaction, at your intended absence' (**4545**n7). Derby's speech to the working classes there would be his last major public address. On 2 November he was again stricken with gout and incapacitated for two weeks. Disraeli also turned down an invitation to Balmoral, regretting that he must 'disobey' the Queen's 'condescending command' (**4556**). Like Derby, he was coming down with gout – from which he had begun to suffer in 1864 (VIII **3894**n1) – and was 'in a state of considerable lethargy' (**4555**): 'my attack is as regular as the trade wind', he told Derby (**4557**).

Nonetheless, the Disraelis travelled to Edinburgh and Disraeli was duly lionized. On the 29th he and Mary Anne attended a Conservative banquet for 1,300 guests (**4556**n2) and the next day Disraeli addressed 2,000 working men. He told them how, during his thirty-year career, thirty-two Acts had been passed, laws affecting the wages, education, working hours and means of self-improvement of the working classes. 'I have always looked upon the interests of the labouring classes as essentially the most conservative interests of the country' (**4563**&n3), he said.

A few weeks after their return to London, Mary Anne became seriously unwell. She had suffered a bronchial attack during most of June 1866 (**4112**, **4113**) and now the Scottish journey had exhausted her. She fell so gravely ill on 15 November (**4574**) that Disraeli delegated Stanley to chair a parliamentary dinner on the 18th (**4577**&nn1&2). Her condition worsened to such an extent over the next few days (**4575**&n1, **4576**, **4577**) that, on the 19th, her doctor thought 'the catastrophe might prove imminent' (**4579**) and Disraeli 'was told to hope no more' (**4580**). That evening in the House, following the throne speech, Gladstone expressed sympathy for Disraeli's 'domestic circumstances' (*ibid* n4). The next day, thanking Gladstone for his consideration, Disraeli reassured him that Mary Anne, who had 'a strong personal regard' for him and valued his 'great gifts & qualities', had begun to rally (**4585**).

During her slow convalescence, however, Disraeli's health again declined. On the 27th he was writing from his bed, 'prostrate – on my back, & positively cannot move witht. agony' (**4593**), and the next day his supplementary budget had to be introduced by treasury financial secretary George Ward Hunt (**4595**&n2). The initial diagnosis was 'Sciatica; wh: frightens me', wrote Disraeli, and *The Times* on the 29th reported he was undergoing a severe attack of lumbago (**4600**&n3). After 'a sleepless night from continuous & agonizing pain', he complained to Mary Anne on 2 December that he was 'irritated at the blundering manner in wh: I have been treated' (**4603**, **4604**). 'It is gout & I always suspected it' (**4605**), he told her. By 11 December, he could report that his wife was 'quite herself again – with all her energy, but she has not yet left her rooms' (**4619**).

Meanwhile, there was Fenian unrest in Canada (**4127**n3, **4216**n7) and Ireland (**4279**n3, **4331**n3, **4444**n3). Fenian violence at home (**4166**n4, **4372**n5) had culminated on 23 November with the hanging in Manchester – despite a petition for clemency to the Queen – of three convicts, the first Fenian executions in England (**4588**nn1,3,4&7). Disraeli and Derby soon began discussing the formation of a secret detective force that would be separate from the police and on 12 December Disraeli wrote to the Duke of Cambridge, commander-in-chief of the military, requesting permission to obtain Colonel William Feilding to head the force (**4621**&nn1&2). And none too soon: the following day, in a failed attempt to free two Fenians from London's Clerkenwell prison, a violent explosion killed a dozen people and injured over one hundred. There was widespread outrage. An appalled Gathorne Hardy, now home secretary, noted in his diary that 'we had been warned *from Ireland* (!)'; even police commissioner Sir Robert Mayne had apparently been told of the plot (**4624**&nn1&2). Disraeli immediately sent government aid to the sufferers – on 26 December he would meet with the Clerkenwell Relief Committee to discuss indemnification (**4636**&n3) – and had told Derby that 'nothing effective can be done, in any way, in these dangers, if we don't get rid of Mayne', with whom Feilding declined to work, fearing Mayne 'would thwart everything' (**4625**, **4628**).

Fenian affairs continued to preoccupy Disraeli until the end of the year. Intelligence of plans to blow up Parliament 'by gunpowder introduced thro' the gas-pipes' (**4628**) led him to suggest to Derby a suspension of *habeas corpus* (already in effect in Ireland). Fearing public unrest at such a drastic measure, Derby countered that for the present 'we must trust to the operation of the ordinary law' (**4629**&n3). When the Queen learned of a plot to assassinate her – the rumour turned out to be a hoax – she wrote to Hardy with the same suggestion. After an emergency cabinet meeting, Derby informed her it had been decided to focus on increasing protection, including 'a separate and secret' detective organization. The Queen replied that even at Osborne she would be 'little better than a *State* prisoner' (**4632**&n4). Following the theft of arms and ammunition from a Martello tower near Cork harbour on 26 December, Disraeli told Corry that 'Fenianism more and more absorbs the public sentiment' (**4641**&n1). It would continue to do so into 1868.

The year 1868 would be Disraeli's *annus mirabilis*. Having weathered the 'tempestuous times & great vicissitudes' of reform, he would complete his long ascent to what he would famously call 'the top of the greasy pole'. On 27 February 1868 Benjamin Disraeli would make political history by becoming England's first and only Jewish prime minister.

EDITORIAL PRINCIPLES

For the complete description of the editorial principles and conventions used in this edition, see VOL I xxvii, reprinted in VOL II vii. Most transcriptions in all volumes published to date were made from and checked against photocopies or, in more recent years, digital images of an original manuscript. The following is an abbreviated list summarizing the main points.

ADDRESSEE: the name is given in the shortest form consistent with clear identifica- *Headnote* tion.

DATE: square brackets indicate the parts of the date not actually in the text or on the cover. A question mark is placed after any parts of the date about which doubt remains (see dating note in EDITORIAL COMMENT).

LOCATION OF ORIGINAL: given in short form: see Abbreviations. A PS indicates a printed source, the MS not having been found (see PUBLICATION HISTORY).

REFERENCE NUMBER: the archival number used by the holder of the original MS, numbers in square brackets added by us if necessary. In the case of a PS, the number refers to the Project's system of reference.

COVER: vertical solidi indicate line divisions in the address. Integral covers and separate envelopes are not distinguished.

POSTMARKS: recorded only if useful for dating; see VOL I xxxiii for illustrations of the most common ones.

PUBLICATION HISTORY: not exhaustive; first and perhaps subsequent important publication, especially in M&B and Blake, are cited.

EDITORIAL COMMENT: *Sic*: list of words and phrases from the text that are incorrect (according to SOED), unusual or otherwise puzzling; includes incorrect, but not omitted, accents and punctuation. *Dating*: cites the logic by which a date has been attributed.

No silent corrections have been made. D's erasures have been noted whenever pos- *Text* sible. Square brackets have been used to add material to facilitate easy reading. When abbreviations ending in periods are thus expanded, the periods have been dropped unless otherwise needed for punctuation. Editorial comments in square brackets are italicized. Catchwords are not repeated or noted, and are given before the page break sign (/). D's insertions are indicated by up and down arrows (↑↓) at the beginning and end respectively of each insertion.

VERTICAL SOLIDI (|) are used to indicate line divisions in the date, address, address-ee and signature sections to allow us to render them in continuous form.

DIAGONAL SOLIDI (/ with space both before and after) indicate page breaks. This is a change from the usage in VOL I and VOL II.

DATE, ADDRESS AND ADDRESSEE, if present in the text, are always given at the beginning of the letter (unless it is a fragment), regardless of where D put them in the MS.

[?] follows any reading on which some doubt remains.

Italics indicate single underlining.

Small capitals indicate multiple underlining.

D's abbreviation of 'the' as 'ye', *ie* using the thorn to represent 'th', has been rendered as 'the'.

Annotations Sources cited are given a short form (see List of Abbreviations and Short Titles) if used more than a few times. Standard reference works (*eg ODNB, EB* XI, *OED*) are cited only if directly quoted. Each name is normally identified by a main note (in bold type in the index) the first time it occurs in the text of a letter, and thereafter only as required for clarification of a letter. Of the material in the appendices, only the pre-1865 letters in Appendix I have been annotated. In transcriptions of MA's writing, we have eschewed the use of '*sic*', despite her unconventional grammar and spelling. We also do not comment on eccentric punctuation.

Index All names in the text and annotation of the letters have been indexed, main notes being indicated by bold type. The subject matter of the letters and notes has also been indexed. All references are to letter numbers, not pages. Except for the pre-1865 letters in Appendix I, the appendices and introductory materials have not been indexed.

DISRAELI CHRONOLOGY 1865–1867

1865

1 Jan	at Hughenden (since 30 Dec 1864)
2 Jan	at Bucks Epiphany Quarter Sessions, Aylesbury
7 Jan	at Gunnersbury (Lionel and Charlotte de Rothschild); news of capture of Savannah
9 Jan	at Hughenden
20 Jan	at Grosvenor Gate
25 Jan	at Burghley House (Lord Exeter)
28 Jan	at Grosvenor Gate
6 Feb	Grosvenor Gate Parliamentary dinner
7 Feb	opening of Parliament
8 Feb	at Derby's Parliamentary dinner
12 Feb	at Boyle Farm dinner for Lord St Leonards's 84th birthday
14 Feb	at Bucks County Rifle Volunteer ball
18 Feb	Grosvenor Gate Parliamentary dinner
22 Feb	at meeting of governors of Wellington College at House of Lords
25 Feb	at Speaker's second Parliamentary dinner
1 Mar	opening of Indo-European telegraph
3 Mar	at Lady Holmesdale's evening party
8 Mar	Grosvenor Gate dinner party
13 Mar	at Queen's second Court at Buckingham Palace
13 Mar	speech on defences of Canada
22 Mar	at Queen's levée at St James's Palace
23 Mar	speech on defences of Canada (army estimates)
29 Mar	at Salisbury's dinner
30 Mar	Grosvenor Gate dinner and reception
1 Apr	receives Bledlow union school deputation
3 Apr	comment on death of Richard Cobden
7 Apr	Grosvenor Gate dinner and reception
8-23 Apr	Easter recess
9 Apr	surrender of General Lee
11 Apr	at Hughenden

1865 *continued*

14 Apr	assassination of President Lincoln
26 Apr	at Grosvenor Gate
28 Apr	Gladstone's budget speech
29 Apr	at Lady Salisbury's evening party
1 May	comment on assassination of Abraham Lincoln (address moved)
3 May	appointed commissioner for Paris Universal Exhibition of 1867; comments on Borough Franchise Extension Bill (2nd reading); at Lady Salisbury's evening party
8 May	speech on Borough Franchise Extension Bill (2nd reading)
10 May	at Frances Countess Waldegrave's and Chichester Fortescue's dinner at Carlton Gardens
11 May	comment on Union Chargeability Bill
12 May	speech on Poor Law Board and High Wycombe Union (motion for papers)
14 May	meets with Sir Lawrence Palk
16 May	at state ball at Buckingham Palace
17 May	at Frances Countess Waldegrave's and Chichester Fortescue's dinner
23 May	at meeting of finance committee of Royal Commission for Exhibition of 1851; comment on Roman Catholic Oath Bill; comment on Leeds Court of Bankruptcy
25 May	at York House dinner (Count and Countess of Paris); at Orleans House ball (Duke and Duchess d'Aumale)
26 May	at Lady Derby's reception
29 May	severe attack of gout
1 Jun	at Prussian Embassy dinner (Count and Countess Bernstorff)
2 Jun	at Norman Court, Hampshire (Thomas Baring)
6 Jun	at Grosvenor Gate
7 Jun	proposes toast at marriage of Evelina and Baron Ferdinand de Rothschild
8 Jun	comment on Princess of Wales – address of congratulation
10 Jun	at Lord and Lady Wilton's dinner
12 Jun	speech on Roman Catholic Oath Bill (clause 1)
14 Jun	at Lady Stanley of Alderley's assembly
17 Jun	at Angela Burdett-Coutts's afternoon party
19 Jun	at Countess Apponyi's dance
21 Jun	at state concert at Buckingham Palace
22 Jun	at Prince of Wales's dinner for Duke and Duchess of Brabant; fall of Navarez ministry at Madrid
24 Jun	at Strawberry Hill (Chichester Fortescue and Frances Countess Waldegrave)
25 Jun	at Grosvenor Gate
27 Jun	at state ball at Buckingham Palace

28 Jun	at Lady Gifford's morning party; at meeting of governors of Wellington College at Palace of Westminster
1 Jul	visits Queen of Netherlands at Claridge's Hotel
3 Jul	comment on Leeds Bankruptcy Court (resolution)
4 Jul	comment on private business of session
6 Jul	Parliament prorogued
12 Jul	at Hughenden
13 Jul	election speech at Aylesbury
14 Jul	at Grosvenor Gate
19 Jul	speech at Newport Pagnell banquet
21 Jul	at Hughenden
24 Jul	at Langley Park (R.B. Harvey)
26 Jul	at Hughenden
1 Aug	privy council orders checks on spread of cattle disease
3 Aug	failure of Atlantic cable
28 Aug	at Grosvenor Gate
31 Aug	at Raby Castle (Duke and Duchess of Cleveland)
7 Sep	at Lowther Castle (Lonsdale)
11 Sep	at Grosvenor Gate
12 Sep	at Hughenden
18 Sep	Fenian arrests in Ireland
20 Sep	speech at annual dinner of Royal and Central Bucks Agricultural Association, Aylesbury
21 Sep	at Ashridge Castle (Lord Brownlow and Lady Marianne Alford)
23 Sep	at Hughenden
26 Sep	at Woburn Abbey (Mr H. and Lady Elizabeth Russell)
30 Sep	at Grosvenor Gate
1 Oct	at Gunnersbury (Lionel and Charlotte de Rothschild)
2 Oct	at Hughenden
10 Oct	at Shardeloes (George T. Drake); speech at annual meeting of Amersham and Chesham Agricultural Association, Amersham
11 Oct	at Hughenden; at inauguration of new Corn Exchange, Aylesbury
16 Oct	at Bucks Michaelmas Session, Aylesbury
18 Oct	death of Palmerston
23 Oct	at Hughenden
11 Nov	dinner party at Hughenden; uprising in Jamaica
13 Nov	declaration of war between Spain and Chile
15 Nov	speech on cattle plague at county meeting, Aylesbury
22 Nov	at Grosvenor Gate
27 Nov	at Wrest Park (Countess Cowper)
30 Nov	at Grosvenor Gate
4 Dec	at Strathfieldsaye (Duke and Duchess of Wellington)

1865 *continued*

8 Dec	at Grosvenor Gate
10 Dec	at Gunnersbury (Lionel and Charlotte de Rothschild); death of Leopold I, King of the Belgians
11 Dec	at Hughenden
20 Dec	at Grosvenor Gate
23 Dec	at Hatfield House (Salisburys)
28 Dec	at Grosvenor Gate
30 Dec	at Gunnersbury (Lionel and Charlotte de Rothschild)
31 Dec	at Grosvenor Gate

1866

1 Jan	at Hughenden
12 Jan	at Grosvenor Gate
1 Feb	speech on choice of Speaker
5 Feb	Grosvenor Gate Parliamentary dinner
6 Feb	opening of Parliament by the Queen
10 Feb	Grosvenor Gate Parliamentary dinner
15 Feb	at Lady Salisbury's first assembly; comments and speech on Cattle Diseases Bill
17 Feb	speech on Habeas Corpus Suspension (Ireland) Bill; numerous arrests for Fenianism in Ireland
18 Feb	at Speaker's Parliamentary dinner
21 Feb	at meeting of governors of Wellington College at Palace of Westminster; Grosvenor Gate dinner party
22 Feb	comment on monument to Palmerston; comment on Princess Helena and Prince Alfred
24 Feb	Grosvenor Gate Parliamentary dinner; at Lady Salisbury's evening party; news of expulsion of Prince Couza of Danubian principalities
28 Feb	at Speaker's Parliamentary dinner
1 Mar	speech on Devonport Election – question
2 Mar	at Lady Holmesdale's dinner and assembly
3 Mar	Grosvenor Gate Parliamentary dinner
7 Mar	comments on Church Rates Abolition Bill
8 Mar	at party meeting at Salisbury's; comments on army estimates – clothing establishment; speech on Parliamentary Oaths Amendment Bill (2nd reading)
9 Mar	comment on Parliamentary Oaths Amendment Bill (2nd reading)
10 Mar	Grosvenor Gate Parliamentary dinner
15 Mar	publishes *Constitutional Reform*; comments on Parliamentary Oaths Amendment Bill – committee
16 Mar	speech at party meeting at Salisbury's
17 Mar	Grosvenor Gate Parliamentary dinner; termination of reciprocity treaty between Canada and United States

1866 *continued*

19 Mar	at Count Bernstorff's dinner party
22 Mar	speech on military savings banks; comment on Ireland – escape of Fenian James Stephens
23 Mar	at Queen's court at Buckingham Palace; at party meeting at Salisbury's; comment on Easter recess – order of public business; comment on cattle plague
24 Mar-9 Apr	Easter recess
28 Mar	at Hughenden
4 Apr	at Grosvenor Gate
5 Apr	at Strathfieldsaye (Duke and Duchess of Wellington)
10 Apr	at Grosvenor Gate
12 Apr	comments on Reform Bill (2nd reading)
16 Apr	attempted assassination of Emperor of Russia
19 Apr	comments on Reform Bill (2nd reading)
20 Apr	speech on Reform Bill (2nd reading); question on electoral returns
23 Apr	comment on Reform Bill (2nd reading)
27 Apr	comment on electoral statistics – petition; speech on Reform Bill (2nd reading)
5 May	at anniversary banquet at Royal Academy
7 May	comments on national debt proposal; comments on Reform Bill
9 May	at party meeting at Derby's
10 May	collapse of Overend, Gurney and Co bank
11 May	question on monetary crisis – panic in the City
12 May	suspension of Bank Charter Act
13 May	at Countess Waldegrave's assembly
14 May	speech on Reform Bill (2nd reading)
17 May	speech on Customs and Inland Revenue Bill (2nd reading)
18-23 May	adjournment of Commons
19 May	at Hughenden; stoppage of European Bank
23 May	stoppage of Bank of London
24 May	at Grosvenor Gate; question on proposed Congress
28 May	at meeting of Derby's supporters at Salisbury's; comment and speech on Reform Bill (committee); stoppage of Consolidated Bank
31 May	comment on Reform Bill
1 Jun	at Angela Burdett-Coutts's dinner; comment on Reform Bills
2 Jun	MA's influenza
4 Jun	comments and speech on Reform Bills
5 Jun	at Buckingham Palace for state ball
6 Jun	stoppage of Agra and Masterman's Bank
7 Jun	at party meeting at Salisbury's; comment on Princess Mary of Cambridge – Queen's message; speech on Reform Bills
8 Jun	speech on proposed Congress – personal explanation

1866 *continued*

11 Jun	comments on Reform Bills
13 Jun	news of Fenian raid in Canada
14 Jun	comments on Reform Bills
16 Jun	declarations of war: Prussia against Hanover and Saxony, Italy against Austria
18 Jun	comments on Reform Bills
19 Jun	at Queen's levée, St James's Palace
25 Jun	meets with Derby
27 Jun	at Buckingham Palace for state ball
28 Jun	at party meeting at Derby's
3 Jul	stables begun at Hughenden; MA recovered from recent illness
5 Jul	at marriage of Princess Helena and Prince Christian at Windsor; Austria's acceptance of Napoleon's mediation for peace
6 Jul	accession of Derby ministry; kisses hands at Windsor; at Mansion House banquet for King and Queen of the Belgians
9 Jul	at Buckingham Palace for Queen's state concert
10 Jul	meets with G.C. Bentinck; meets with Amelia Michell
13 Jul	election speech at Aylesbury, accepting office of chancellor of the exchequer; at Mansion House banquet
14 Jul	at cabinet
16 Jul	receives bank charter deputation from Liverpool; comment on Ireland – medical officers and workhouse schools; speech on Ireland – The Queen's University
18 Jul	at marriage of Lord Sefton and Cecil Emily Jolliffe; meets with governor and deputy-governor of Bank of England; receives deputation from Glasgow Chamber of Commerce regarding inquiry by Royal Commission into Bank Act; comments on Compulsory Church Rates Abolition Bill
19 Jul	meets with governor of Bank of England; comment on Helston election report; comment on Ireland – appointment of Francis Blackburne; comments and speech on outbreak in Jamaica
20 Jul	comment on state of finances
21 Jul	at cabinet
23 Jul	comment on currency and banking; comment on Railways (Ireland) Temporary Advances Bill (2nd reading); speech on supply – supplementary estimates
24 Jul	meets with governor and deputy-governor of Bank of England; speech on reform meeting in Hyde Park
26 Jul	at cabinet; comments on supply – gun metal for monument to the late Prince Consort, National Gallery, completion of HMS *Northumberland*

1866 *continued*

7 Nov	at cabinet
8 Nov	at cabinet
13 Nov	at cabinet
14 Nov	at cabinet
15 Nov	at cabinet
16 Nov	at cabinet; at Lord Mayor's banquet
19 Nov	receives deputation from Incorporated Law Society
20 Nov	at cabinet
21 Nov	at cabinet
24 Nov	meets with Grote; dines with Queen and royal family at Windsor
26 Nov	at cabinet
27 Nov	at Strathfieldsaye (Duke and Duchess of Wellington)
30 Nov	at Grosvenor Gate
4 Dec	death of Evelina, Baroness Ferdinand de Rothschild
6 Dec	meets with Walpole
11 Dec	evacuation of Rome by French troops after seventeen years of occupation
12 Dec	at court of exchequer for Ranelagh's hearing
15 Dec	at Hughenden
27 Dec	at Grosvenor Gate
29 Dec	elected elder brother of Trinity House
30 Dec	at Gunnersbury (Lionel and Charlotte de Rothschild) on visit of condolence
31 Dec	at Hughenden; at Bucks Epiphany Quarter Sessions, Aylesbury

1867

1 Jan	at Hughenden
6 Jan	at Grosvenor Gate; meets with G.W. Hunt, Derby
7 Jan	meets with Stanley; Agra and Masterman's Bank revived
9 Jan	meets with Derby
10 Jan	at cabinet
14 Jan	news of great fire at Yokohama, Japan
15 Jan	at cabinet
16 Jan	meets with Sir John Thwaites and Lord John Manners
19 Jan	*Parliamentary Reform* published
22 Jan	at cabinet
23 Jan	at cabinet
26 Jan	gives £10 to Mansion House colliery relief fund; death of Lady Jersey
29 Jan	at cabinet
30 Jan	at cabinet; at Duke of Buckingham's dinner
31 Jan	at cabinet

1867 *continued*

1 Feb	receives deputation re memorial on search of passengers' luggage at Paris exhibition
2 Feb	at funeral of Lady Jersey at Middleton Stoney, Oxford
3 Feb	meets with G.W. Hunt, Derby
4 Feb	meets with Samuel Graves; Grosvenor Gate Parliamentary dinner
5 Feb	opening of Parliament by the Queen; address in answer to speech from the throne
6 Feb	at cabinet
8 Feb	comment on monetary laws; comment on business of the House
9 Feb	at cabinet
11 Feb	speech on reform (motion for committee); Fenian plot at Chester discovered; Reform League demonstration in London
12 Feb	comment on Metropolitan cabs and hackney carriage trade
13 Feb	excused from serving on election committees because of inconvenience to public service; Fenian raid at Killarney
14 Feb	meets with John Galt and deputation from North American provinces; comment on Jamaica – legal proceedings against officers; comment on reform (resolutions); speech on sugar duties; Fenian riots in south of Ireland
15 Feb	meets with Philip Rose; receives deputation from Birmingham and Leeds re assessment of public buildings to the inhabited house duty; comment on corruption at elections
16 Feb	at cabinet; at Osborne (MA at Portsmouth)
17 Feb	dines with Queen and royal family at Osborne; has audience with Queen
18 Feb	at Grosvenor Gate; comments on reform (resolutions, franchises); comments on supply – Blacas Collection, royal palaces; meets with Derby
19 Feb	at cabinet
22 Feb	comment on Princess of Wales – address to Her Majesty; comment on reduction of the qualification for elective franchise
23 Feb	meets with Dudley Baxter; at cabinet
25 Feb	birth of Coningsby Disraeli; resignations of Lord Carnarvon, Lord Cranborne and Jonathan Peel; meets with Derby; at cabinet ('Ten Minutes Bill'); at meeting of Derby's supporters; speech on Ireland – Lord Mayor's banquet; speech on reform (motion for committee)
26 Feb	at cabinet; comment on reform (resolutions); comment on attorneys &c, certificate duty – leave

27 Feb	at Queen's court at Buckingham Palace; has audience with Queen
28 Feb	meets with Stanley; comment on reports of bribery commissioners; comment on reform (motion for committee)
1 Mar	comment on reform; comment on Scotland (reform)
2 Mar	at cabinet; meets with Derby; resignations presented to Queen; at Lady Derby's reception for the Duke of Cambridge
3 Mar	meets with Derby
4 Mar	comment on reform (borough franchise); ministerial explanations – reform, Criminal Lunatics Bill
5 Mar	comment on Lancaster, Yarmouth &c, commissions; speech on ministerial explanations; comment on public business
6 Mar	meets with Derby; at cabinet
8 Mar	meets with the Reverends D. Wilson, John Rogers, N.M. Brown, R. Black, H. Henderson and C.L. Morell re *Regium Donum* in Ireland; comment on reform (Lancaster, Reigate, Totnes, Yarmouth – ministerial arrangements); comment on Paris Exhibition – search of passengers' baggage
9 Mar	at cabinet; meets with Sir Daniel Gooch, Samuel Laing, Edward Watkin, Sir Stafford Northcote
11 Mar	meets with Stanley; comment on reform (boroughs, statistics); comment on army estimates
12 Mar	meets with John Lambert; at cabinet; comment on reform (statistics)
14 Mar	meets with Derby; at cabinet; dines with Stanley; comment on Scotland – reform; comment on reform (electoral statistics); comment on navy estimates
15 Mar	at party meeting at Derby's; comment on Ireland – railways, Fenianism
16 Mar	meets with Henry Thring; at cabinet
18 Mar	Ralph Earle's resignation; speech and comments on Reform Bill (leave to introduce the bill)
19 Mar	comments on corrupt practices at elections; comment on fire insurance – resolution; comment on Churchward case
20 Mar	at cabinet; at Duchess of Marlborough's dinner
21 Mar	meets with Stanley and Northcote; comments on Reform Bill (forty shilling freeholders); comments on Reform Bill (Ireland and Scotland); comment on railway debentures; comments on Reform Bill (parts of Lindsey)
22 Mar	meets with Derby; comment on Reform Bill (Wednesbury and West Bromwich); comment on Reform Bill (Scotland); comment on Reform Bill (borough franchise); speech on pension to poet Robert Young

23 Mar	at cabinet
24 Mar	at cabinet
25 Mar	meets with Derby; comments on Reform Bill (suffrage to women, West Bromwich, borough franchise, working classes – borough register (2nd reading))
26 Mar	speech on Reform Bill (2nd reading)
27 Mar	at Speaker's Parliamentary dinner
28 Mar	meets with W.G. Anderson; comment on Reform Bill (special franchises)
29 Mar	meets with J.M. Henniker-Major; comment on Reform Bill (Ireland); comments on administration of justice (Ireland) – motion for papers
30 Mar	at cabinet
1 Apr	comment on Reform Bill (question); comment on Easter recess
2 Apr	receives deputations from Reform League and Trades, Friendly, Temperance and other societies; comment on Lancaster Borough; comment on Attorneys, &c, Certificate Duty Bill (2nd reading)
4 Apr	comments on Reform Bill (disfranchised boroughs, arrangement of business); speech on the budget; comment on Tenants Improvements (Ireland) Bill
5 Apr	comment on Reform Bill (voting papers)
6 Apr	at cabinet; receives deputations from the Constitutional Associations of Manchester and other towns in Lancashire re Reform Bill; apprehension of war with Germany on Luxemburg question
8 Apr	receives deputations from Birmingham, Manchester, Leeds and other towns re Reform Bill; Liberal 'tea-room revolt'; comments on Reform Bill – committee; comments on public business; panic on London Stock Exchange from apprehension of war between Austria and Germany
9 Apr	comments on election petitions committees; comment on Landlord and Tenant (Ireland) Bill; comment on London, Chatham, and Dover Railway Company; speech on Offices and Oaths Bill
11 Apr	at cabinet; comments on Reform Bill – compound householders, voting papers, fees of returning officers, Hundreds of Offlow, committee (clause 3); comment on Corrupt Practices at Elections Bill
12 Apr	at cabinet; comments on Tenants Improvements (Ireland) Bill; comments on adjournment for Easter recess; speech on Reform Bill (clause 3)
13-28 Apr	Easter recess
13 Apr	meets with Derby; at cabinet

	comments on Reform (Scotland) Bill; speech and comments on Reform Bill (clause 3 amendment)
14 May	comment on Reform Bill (clause 3 amendment); speech on malt tax
15 May	dines at Count Bernstorff's
16 May	comment on Reform Bill (compound householders, schedule D); comment on Reform (Scotland) Bill; speech on National Debt Acts Bill; comment on Ecclesiastical Titles and Roman Catholic Relief Acts
17 May	comment on Reform (Scotland) Bill; speech and comments on Reform Bill (clause 3 amendment)
18 May	meets with Lord Lonsdale; at cabinet; at Lady Derby's dinner and assembly
20 May	at laying by the Queen of foundation stone of the new Hall of Arts and Sciences; comments on Reform (Ireland) Bill; comments on Reform Bill (clause 3 amendment, clause 4, motion for adjournment); comments on supply – salaries &c of offices of Houses of Parliament, exchequer and audit departments
21 May	comment on new president of Poor Law Board; comment on Ireland – the franchise; comment on adjournment of the House – Derby Day; comment on Ecclesiastical Titles Act
22 May	at cabinet; dines at admiralty (Lord Henry Lennox)
23 May	meets with Bartholomew Woodlock, Catholic University of Ireland; comment on Reform Bill (polling places); comments on business of the House; comment on Reform Bill (clause 4, motion for adjournment)
24 May	meets with Edward Bouverie and Samuel Laing; receives deputation from Swansea; comments on Reform (Scotland) Bill; comments on Reform (Ireland) Bill; comment on supply – inland revenue departments
25 May	at cabinet; state dinner at Grosvenor Gate to celebrate the Queen's birthday
26 May	dines with the Lionel de Rothschilds
27 May	comments on Reform Bill (Tower Hamlets); comment on Ireland – Fenian convict Burke; comments on public business – standing orders; speech and comment on Reform Bill (clause 4, motion for adjournment, clause 34 amendment, clause 34 provisos, clause 35 amendment)
28 May	new morning sittings of Commons begin – sat 9 am to 7 pm; comments on Reform Bill (clause 35 amendment, clause 5, clause 6)
29 May	at Prince of Wales's levée held on behalf of the Queen
30 May	at cabinet; comments on Reform Bill (clause 8 amendment)

31 May	speech and comments on Reform Bill (clause 9)
1 Jun	at cabinet; meets with Irish MPs
3 Jun	comments on Ecclesiastical Titles Act committee; comment on Reform (Scotland) Bill; speech and comments on Reform Bill (clause 9)
4 Jun	meets with Rev A.T. Lee
6 Jun	attempt at Paris to assassinate Emperor of Russia
7 Jun	at cabinet
8 Jun	receives deputation from London and Westminster Working Men's Constitutional Association
11 Jun	speech at Merchant Taylors' annual banquet
12 Jun	at Buckingham Palace for Queen's state concert
13 Jun	speech on Reform Bill (clause 9)
14 Jun	at Downing Street to meet Bishop of Oxford, Bishop of Lichfield, Archdeacon of Buckingham, Canon Hawkins and Vice-Chancellor of University of Oxford; speech on Ireland – petition on Fenianism
15 Jun	at cabinet
17 Jun	comments on boundary commissioners; comments on Reform (Ireland) Bill; speeches on Reform Bill (clauses 10, 12, 15 amendments, clause 14)
18 Jun	at Buckingham Palace for Queen's state concert; comment on boundary commissioners; comment on Reform (Ireland) Bill, 3rd reading; comment on registration clauses (Reform); speech and comments on Reform Bill (clauses 15, 19, 23); comment on Tests Abolition (Oxford and Cambridge) Bill
19 Jun	meets with William Ferrand; dines at Lord Wilton's
20 Jun	30th anniversary of Victoria's accession; receives deputation of Irish peers and MPs re purchase of Irish railways; comment on boundary commissioners; comments on Reform Bill (clauses 24, 29); speech on Reform Bill (clause 29)
21 Jun	comment on boundary commissioners; comments and speech on Reform Bill (clauses 31, 33, 37, 40) motion for adjournment
22 Jun	at cabinet; meets with Rev Dr Taylor of Glasgow and Arthur Laing; speech at Trinity House dinner; at Lady Derby's evening reception
23 Jun	dines with the Mayer de Rothschilds
24 Jun	receives deputation from Scotland re Scotch Reform Bill; meets with Richard Benyon, Lt-Col Loyd-Lindsay and Sir Charles Russell; receives City of London deputation; speeches and comments on Reform Bill (clause 40, clause 42 amendment)
25 Jun	at Buckingham Palace for Queen's state ball; comment on

	Ecclesiastical Titles Act repeal; comments and speech on Reform Bill (clauses 31, 42 amendments, clause 43)
27 Jun	comment on reform (statistics); comments on Reform Bill (clause 31 amendment, additional clause, clauses A, B)
28 Jun	comment on morning sittings of Parliament; comment on Reform Bill (statistics, additional clause); speech on reform (Ireland)
29 Jun	at cabinet
1 Jul	comment on Reform Bill (area of the new borough); comment and speech on public business – morning sittings; speech and comments on Reform Bill (additional clause)
2 Jul	speeches and comments on Reform Bill (ratepaying clause, additional clause)
3 Jul	at cabinet; news of execution of Emperor Maximilian at Queretero, Mexico on 19 June
4 Jul	speeches and comments on Reform Bill (motion for adjournment)
5 Jul	comment on privilege – alteration of notices of questions; comment on business of the House; comment on Reform (Scotland) Bill; speech on Reform Bill (motion for adjournment); comment on privilege – signatures to a petition; comment on case of Fulford and Wellstead
6 Jul	at cabinet; meets with Duke of Leinster, Lord Wilton, Lord Wrottesley, Sir George Clerk and others
8 Jul	comment on foreign postal conventions; comments and speeches on Reform Bill (motion for adjournment)
9 Jul	at dinner given by the Prince of Wales for the Viceroy of Egypt; comments on Reform Bill (redistribution of seats, motion for adjournment, schedules A, B, C, D, preamble)
10 Jul	at Lord and Lady Derby's banquet for Viceroy of Egypt
11 Jul	dinner at Mansion House to meet Viceroy of Egypt; comment on naval review
12 Jul	comments on Reform Bill (consideration of additional clause, clause B amendment, clauses 21, 27, 42, schedules B, C, D, F); arrival of Sultan of Turkey
13 Jul	at cabinet; at state dinner given by Prince of Wales at Marlborough House in honour of Sultan of Turkey
15 Jul	at Buckingham Palace reception for Sultan of Turkey; comment on telegraphic communication; comment on volunteer review; comments on business of the House; speech on Reform Bill (3rd reading)
16 Jul	comment on naval review
18 Jul	at cabinet; at Guildhall reception for Sultan of Turkey; speech and comment on supply – royal palaces

19 Jul	meets with Derby; at Gloucester House dinner for Sultan of Turkey; at India Office state ball for Sultan
20 Jul	at cabinet
22 Jul	statement and comment on business of the House; comment on Reform (Scotland) Bill
23 Jul	comment on admiralty court; comment on purchases at Paris Exhibition; departure of Sultan of Turkey
25 Jul	at funeral of Princess Anne, Mme Musurus
27 Jul	at cabinet; receives deputation from Royal Bank of Scotland
29 Jul	comments on Parks Regulation Bill; speech on s Kensington plan
31 Jul	at cabinet
3 Aug	at cabinet
4 Aug	at Osterley (Lord Jersey)
6 Aug	receives deputation urging adoption of F.S. Corrance's amendment to Contagious Diseases (Animals) Bill
7 Aug	at Lord Mayor's banquet at Mansion House for Her Majesty's ministers
9 Aug	comments on supply – entertainment of Sultan
10 Aug	at cabinet
14 Aug	at cabinet; at ministerial whitebait dinner at the Ship, Greenwich
15 Aug	Reform Bill receives Royal assent
16 Aug	at cabinet
17 Aug	at cabinet
19 Aug	Reform Act issued to the public
20 Aug	at Queen's council at Windsor
21 Aug	meets with Count Lavradio; at cabinet; Parliament prorogued
22 Aug	at Hughenden
28 Aug	government receives tenders for steamers for war against Abyssinia
30 Aug	at Dropmore (Chichester Fortescue); at Hughenden
7-9 Sep	visit from Lord Dalmeny
16 Sep	accepts invitation to Edinburgh banquet
19 Sep	speech at Hughenden harvest home festival dinner
25 Sep	news from Florence of arrest and subsequent escape of Garibaldi
1 Oct	in London; meets with physician Frederic Quin
2 Oct	at Hughenden; panic on the Paris Bourse
5 Oct	receives deputation from Manchester
7 Oct	at Blenheim Palace (Duke and Duchess of Marlborough)
11 Oct	at Grosvenor Gate
15 Oct	meets with Stanley
16 Oct	meets with Stanley; meets with Campbell Swinton

1867 *continued*

21 Oct	news of defeat of Garibaldians in Roman states
22 Oct	receives deputation of Conservative working men of Edinburgh
26 Oct	at Arniston House, Midlothian, Scotland (Dundases)
29 Oct	speech at Conservative banquet at Corn Exchange, Grassmarket, Edinburgh
30 Oct	receives freedom of the City of Edinburgh in Music Hall; receives honorary LLD from the University of Edinburgh in College Library; speaks to working men of Edinburgh in Music Hall
31 Oct	visits Holyrood Palace (Parliament House); dines with lord advocate Edward S. Gordon
1 Nov	at Grosvenor Gate; five Fenians found guilty of murder at Manchester and sentenced to death
2 Nov	at Austrian ambassador's dinner for Austrian prime minister
4 Nov	Garibaldi defeated by papal and French forces and re-arrested by Italian authorities
5 Nov	at cabinet
7 Nov	meets with Derby; at cabinet
8 Nov	meets with Sir H. Bulwer and A. Innes; colliery explosion at Rhondda Valley near Cardiff
9 Nov	at Lord Mayor's banquet at Guildhall
10 Nov	at Windsor; meets with Gen Grey; dines with Queen and royal family
11 Nov	at Grosvenor Gate
12 Nov	at 'Morrow of St Martin'; at cabinet
14 Nov	at cabinet
18 Nov	misses his Parliamentary dinner at Clarendon Hotel because of MA's illness; opening of French chambers with pacific speech by the Emperor
19 Nov	opening of Parliament
20 Nov	at cabinet
23 Nov	at cabinet; executions of Fenians in Manchester
26 Nov	introduces vote of £2 million for Abyssinian expedition
27 Nov	suffers severe attack of lumbago
2 Dec	suffers severe attack of gout
6 Dec	Her Majesty's Theatre burns to the ground
7 Dec	adjournment of Parliament (until 13 Feb 1868)
9 Dec	at cabinet; meets with Derby; meets with Mayo
10 Dec	meets with Archbishop Manning at Grosvenor Gate
11 Dec	meets with Philip Rose
12 Dec	meets with Sir John Pakington
13 Dec	Fenian incendiary explosion at Clerkenwell, London
14 Dec	meets with Gathorne Hardy and Col Feilding; distribution of £500 aid to Clerkenwell survivors

ABBREVIATIONS IN VOLUME NINE

A	denotes an additional letter to be inserted into the sequence
AES	A.E. Scanes, Hughenden papers archivist
Aldous	Richard Aldous *The Lion and the Unicorn: Gladstone vs Disraeli* (2006)
app	Appendix
ARG	Argosy Book Store, New York, NY
BBK	N.M. Bolingbroke-Kent, London
BCP	Lady Beauchamp, collection of (now in BL)
BEA	Belvoir Castle, Lincolnshire
Beeler	John F. Beeler *British Naval Policy in the Gladstone-Disraeli Era, 1866-1880* (Stanford 1997)
Bell *Palmerston*	Herbert Bell *Lord Palmerston* (1936 repr 1966)
BH	*The Bucks Herald*
BHF	Chris Cook and Brendan Keith *British Historical Facts* (1975)
BL	The British Library, London
Blake	Robert Blake *Disraeli* (1966)
BODL	Bodleian Library, Oxford
Bourne	H.R. Fox Bourne *English Newspapers* 2 vols (1887)
BPER	F.W.S. Craig *British Parliamentary Election Results 1832-1885* (1977)
Bradford	Sarah Bradford *Disraeli* (1982)
Bright	John Bright *The Diaries of John Bright* (1930)
BRN	Brandeis University, Waltham, MA
BRS	J.I. Brash, University of West Australia, Nedlands
BUC	Buckinghamshire Record Office, Aylesbury
BUL	Birmingham University Library
CAM	Cambridge University Library, Cambridge
C	Conservative
C of Ex	Chancellor of the Exchequer
CARR	Carrington Collection, Bodleian Library, Oxford
Clergy List	*The Clerical Guide and Ecclesiastical Directory* publ by Rivington, later *The Clerical Directory* publ by Crockford (followed by year of edition)

COR	Cornell University Library, Ithaca, NY
Cowling	Maurice Cowling *1867: Disraeli, Gladstone and Revolution. The Passing of the Second Reform Bill* (Cambridge 1967)
CRA	Jeremy B. Crane, collection of
CUL	Columbia University Library, New York
D	Benjamin Disraeli (and thus 'the DS' = D and MA)
DBP	Derby Papers, 14th & 15th Earls, Liverpool City Libraries
DENL	St Deiniol's Library, Hawarden, Flintshire
DEV	The Duke of Devonshire, Chatsworth, Bakewell, Derbyshire
Dickens Letters	Graham Storey ed *The Letters of Charles Dickens* 12 vols (Oxford 1974-2002)
Disraeli, Derby	John Vincent ed *Disraeli, Derby and the Conservative Party: Journals and Memoirs of Edward Henry, Lord Stanley 1849-1869* (Hassocks, Sussex 1978)
DR	Helen M. Swartz and Martin Swartz eds *Disraeli's Reminiscences* (1975)
DUL	Duke University Library
DUP	Sophie Dupré, Calne, Wilts, England
DURG	Durham University Library (Grey Papers)
EB XI	*Encyclopædia Britannica* Eleventh Edition (1910-11)
ec	Editorial comment section of the headnote
EDE	Maurice Edelman, London
EJM	ex-Jewish Museum (see abbreviations in Volume II)
ESU	East Suffolk Record Office, Ipswich, Suffolk
Feuchtwanger	E.J. Feuchtwanger *Gladstone* (New York 1975)
FIT	Fitzwilliam Museum, Cambridge
Fraser	Sir William Fraser *Disraeli and his Day* (1891)
GLA	John F. Glaser, collection of
Gladstone Diaries	M.R.D. Foot and H.C.G. Matthew eds *The Gladstone Diaries* (1968-94)
GM	*The Gentleman's Magazine*
Greville	Lytton Strachey and Robert Fulford eds *The Greville Memoirs, 1814-60* 7 vols (1938)
GRI	Grinnell College Archives, Iowa
H	The Hughenden papers, Bodleian Library, Oxford
H acc	H WMA 4498 – MA's account book
HAL	Halifax Central Library, Calderdale, Halifax, UK
Hansard	*Hansard's Parliamentary Debates*
Hardy Diary	Nancy E. Johnson ed *The Diary of Gathorne Hardy, later Lord Cranbrook, 1866-1892: Political Selections* (Oxford 1981)
Hawkins	Angus Hawkins *British Party Politics, 1852-1886* (1998)
Hawkins *Derby*	Angus Hawkins *The Forgotten Prime Minister. The 14th Earl of Derby* vol 2 *Achievement, 1851-1869* (Oxford 2008)
HCC	Hampshire County Council
HCR	Hertford County Record Office
HEY	Robert Heyneman, Chapel Hill, NC

HFD	Hatfield House, Hatfield, Herts
H/LIFE	Monypenny papers in H for his *Life of Disraeli*
HOL	David Holland, near Polegate, E Sussex
HUNT	Huntington Library, San Marino, CA
ILLU	University of Illinois, Urbana-Champaign, IL
IAA	International Autograph Auctions, Nottingham
INL	National Library of Ireland, Dublin
JWA	John Wilson Autographs, London
KAN	University of Kansas, Lawrence, KA
KCR	Kent County Record Office, Maidstone
Kebbel	Thomas Edward Kebbel ed *Selected Speeches of the Late Right Honourable the Earl of Beaconsfield* (1882) vols I and II
Kennedy	Padraic C. Kennedy 'The Secret Service Department: A British Intelligence Bureau in Mid-Victorian London, September 1867 to April 1868' *Intelligence and National Security* 18.3 (2003): 100-27
L	Liberal
Law List	*Clarke's New Law List* compiled by S. Hill and later by T. Cockell (followed by year of edition)
LCC	Lowry-Corry Collection
LPL	Lambeth Palace Library, London
LPOD	*London Post Office Directory* (followed by year of edition)
LQVB	George Earle Buckle ed *The Letters of Queen Victoria: A Selection from Her Majesty's Correspondence and Journal between the Years 1862 and 1878* (1926) 2 vols
MA	Mary Anne Disraeli
MAB	Louis Mably, London
Malmesbury	3rd Earl of Malmesbury *Memoirs of an Ex-minister* (1884) 2 vols
M&B	William Flavelle Monypenny and George Earle Buckle *The Life of Benjamin Disraeli, Earl of Beaconsfield* (1910-20) 6 vols
MANN	Université Catholique de l'Ouest, Angers, France (Cardinal Manning Papers)
MARI	National Maritime Museum, London
MC	*The Morning Chronicle*
McCalmont	*McCalmont's Parliamentary Poll Book: British Election Results 1832-1918* (1971)
MCG	McGill University Rare Books, collection of Mrs J.B. Learmont
MH	*The Morning Herald*
MIL	Arthur Milnes, collection of
MOPSIK	The Donald and Delores Mopsik Collection
MP	*The Morning Post*
MPL	Manchester Public Library, Manchester
MTL	Mitchell Library, Sydney, Australia
NLC	National Library of Australia, Canberra

NLF	Northumberland County Record Office, Newcastle
NLS	National Library of Scotland, Edinburgh
NNL	National Library of New Zealand, Wellington
Northcote	Andrew Lang ed *The Life, Letters, and Diaries of Sir Stafford Northcote* 2 vols (1890)
Norton Rose	Andrew St George *A History of Norton Rose* (Cambridge 1995)
NOT	University of Nottingham, Nottingham
NSR	Northamptonshire Record Office, Northampton
NYPL	New York Public Library (Montague Collection)
OCC	Christ Church College, Oxford
ODNB	*Oxford Dictionary of National Biography* (online)
OED	*Oxford English Dictionary*
ph	Publication history section of the headnote
Prest *Russell*	John Prest *Lord John Russell* (1972)
PRO	Public Record Office, London
PS	Printed Source, identified in ph, used when the original MS has not been located
QUA	Disraeli Papers, formerly in the Queen's University Archives, Kingston, Ontario
R	denotes a letter now available from a manuscript or a more complete or reliable printed source replacing a fragmentary letter published in a previous volume (*eg* '**123R**' replaces '**123**')
RAC	Royal Archives, Windsor Castle
RHL	Rhodes House Library, Oxford
RIC	Rice University, Fondren Library, Houston, TX
Ridley *Palmerston*	Jasper Ridley *Lord Palmerston* (1970)
RLF	Royal Literary Fund (housed at BL)
ROG	Dr M.A.T. Rogers, Mount Skippett, Ramsden, Oxford
ROSE	Lady Rosebery, collection of
ROTH	The Rothschild Archive, London
RTC	Lord Rothschild, collection of
Saunders	Robert Saunders *Democracy and the Vote in British Politics, 1848-1867* (Farnham, Surrey 2011)
SBW	Sarah Brydges Willyams
SCR	Somerset County Record Office
Sheahan	James Joseph Sheahan *History and Topography of Buckinghamshire* (1862 repr 1971)
Smith	F.B. Smith *The Making of the Second Reform Bill* (Cambridge 1966)
SRO	Scottish Record Office, Edinburgh
STCL	Strathclyde Regional Archive, Glasgow
Stenton	Michael Stenton *Who's Who of British Members of Parliament: Volume I, 1832-1885; Volume II, 1886-1918* (Hassocks, Sussex 1976, 1978)
Stewart *Writings*	R.W. Stewart *Benjamin Disraeli: A list of writings by him, and*

	writings about him, with notes (Metuchen, NJ 1972). Citations are of item numbers.
St John	Ian St John *Disraeli and the Art of Victorian Politics* (2005)
TCC	Trinity College, Cambridge
TEXU	University of Texas, Austin
TIA	Archives of *The Times*
UO	A source that cannot be divulged for reasons such as requested confidentiality (rarely used)
VER	Sir Ralph Verney, Claydon House, Bucks
VRS	Owen Vernon and Sons, High Wycombe, Bucks
WAR	Warwickshire Record Office, Warwick
Weintraub *Disraeli*	Stanley Weintraub *Disraeli: A Biography* (New York 1993)
Weintraub *Charlotte and Lionel*	Stanley Weintraub *Charlotte and Lionel: A Rothschild Love Story* (2003)
Wellesley Index	Walter E. Houghton ed *Wellesley Index to Victorian Periodicals* 5 vols (1966-89)
Whibley	Charles Whibley *Lord John Manners and His Friends* 2 vols (1925)
WHS	W.H. Smith Archive, Abingdon, OX
WIL	Keith Wilson, Ottawa
WRC	Worcestershire Record Office, Shirehall
WSH	B.D.J. Walsh, London
WSRO	West Sussex Record Office, Chichester
X	denotes an entirely new letter or fragment to be placed in chronological sequence after the corresponding letter number in a previous volume (*eg* '**123x**' follows '**123**')

NO	DATE	TO	PLACE OF ORIGIN	LOCATION OF ORIGINAL
3979	3 JAN '65	JAMES HUNT	HUGHENDEN	QUA
3980	3 JAN '65	PHILIP ROSE	HUGHENDEN	H
3981	5 JAN '65	ARTHUR VERNON	HUGHENDEN	VRS
3982	[10?] JAN '65	PHILIP ROSE	HUGHENDEN	H
3983	10 JAN '65	FREDERICK GEORGE LEE	HUGHENDEN	MCG
3984	10 JAN '65	LEOPOLD DE ROTHSCHILD	HUGHENDEN	H H/LIFE
3985	15 JAN '65	PHILIP ROSE	HUGHENDEN	H
3986	19 JAN '65	JULIANA DE ROTHSCHILD	HUGHENDEN	ROSE
3987	31 JAN '65	SIR HENRY STRACEY	[LONDON]	PS
3988	[EARLY FEB '65]	[WILLIAM?] LESLIE	GROSVENOR GATE	H
3989	4 FEB '65	[LORD] HENRY [LENNOX]	GROSVENOR GATE	MOPSIK
3990	4 FEB '65	PHILIP ROSE	GROSVENOR GATE	H
3991	[1865?]	MARY ANNE DISRAELI	H OF COMMONS	H
3992	28 FEB '65	LORD STANHOPE	BRITISH MUSEUM	KCR
3993	[10 MAR '65]	MARY ANNE DISRAELI	[LONDON]	H
3994	12 MAR '65	WILLIAM W.F. DICK	GROSVENOR GATE	BRN
3995	19 MAR '65	FREDERICK LYGON	GROSVENOR GATE	BCP
3996	20 MAR '65	LORD BEAUCHAMP	GROSVENOR GATE	BCP
3997	24 MAR '65	LORD LONSDALE	GROSVENOR GATE	PS
3998	[4 APR '65]	MARY ANNE DISRAELI	[H OF COMMONS?]	H
3999	[6 APR '65]	MARY ANNE DISRAELI	[H OF COMMONS]	H
4000	11 APR '65	FREDERICK LYGON	GROSVENOR GATE	BCP
4001	17 APR '65	LADY DOROTHY NEVILL	HUGHENDEN	EJM
4002	[1 MAY '65]	MARY ANNE DISRAELI	[H OF COMMONS?]	H
4003	2 MAY '65	FREDERICK GEORGE LEE	GROSVENOR GATE	MTL
4004	7 MAY '65	LORD SHAFTESBURY	GROSVENOR GATE	ARG
4005	8 MAY '65	LIONEL OLIVER BIGG	GROSVENOR GATE	BBK
4006	8 MAY '65	LORD ELCHO	GROSVENOR GATE	SRO
4007	11 MAY '65	MARY ANNE DISRAELI	[H OF COMMONS?]	H
4008	12 MAY '65	PHILIP ROSE	GROSVENOR GATE	H
4009	13 MAY '65	LORD DERBY	GROSVENOR GATE	DBP
4010	14 MAY '65	SIR LAWRENCE PALK	GROSVENOR GATE	PS
4011	14 MAY '65	LORD STANHOPE	GROSVENOR GATE	KCR
4012	14 MAY '65	FREDERICK LYGON	GROSVENOR GATE	BCP
4013	20 MAY '65	ELECTORS OF BUCKS	[LONDON?]	H
4014	[POST-20 MAY '65]	[WILLIAM TAYLOR COPELAND?]	[LONDON?]	H

NO	DATE	TO	PLACE OF ORIGIN	LOCATION OF ORIGINAL
4015	17 JUN '65	[UNKNOWN]	[LONDON]	PS
4016	5 JUL '65	CHARLES CLUBBE	GROSVENOR GATE	RIC
4017	5 JUL '65	LORD SALISBURY	GROSVENOR GATE	HFD
4018	6 JUL '65	C.E.S. (EDWARD) GLEIG	GROSVENOR GATE	NLS
4019	6 JUL '65	ELECTORS OF BUCKS	LONDON	PS
4020	8 JUL '65	ALFRED AUSTIN	GROSVENOR GATE	KAN
4021	10 JUL '65	JOHN DELANE	GROSVENOR GATE	TIA
4022	[MID-JUL '65]	[UNKNOWN]	[LONDON?]	PS
4023	12 JUL '65	WILLIAM H. SMITH	GROSVENOR GATE	WHS
4024	13 JUL '65	ELECTORS OF BUCKS	LONDON	PS
4025	23 JUL '65	MARKHAM SPOFFORTH	HUGHENDEN	H H/LIFE
4026	24 JUL '65	FREDERICK LYGON	HUGHENDEN	BCP
4027	28 JUL '65	LORD DERBY	HUGHENDEN	DBP
4028	28 JUL '65	JOHN POPE HENNESSY	HUGHENDEN	RHL
4029	31 JUL '65	WILLIAM FOLLETT SYNGE	HUGHENDEN	HEY
4029A	31 JUL '65	[JOHN SKELTON]	HUGHENDEN	PS
4030	6 AUG '65	LORD DERBY	HUGHENDEN	DBP
4031	7 AUG '65	HENRY THOMAS RYDE	HUGHENDEN	MOPSIK
4032	10 AUG '65	OCTAVIAN BLEWITT	HUGHENDEN	RLF
4033	14 AUG '65	LORD DERBY	HUGHENDEN	DBP
4034	23 AUG '65	DUCHESS OF CLEVELAND	HUGHENDEN	KCR
4035	23 AUG '65	EDWARD COLEMAN	HUGHENDEN	WSH
4036	25 AUG '65	C.E.S. (EDWARD) GLEIG	HUGHENDEN	NLS
4037	30 AUG ['65]	PHILIP ROSE	GROSVENOR GATE	H
4038	3 SEP '65	LORD DERBY	RABY CASTLE	DBP
4039	3 SEP '65	LORD LONSDALE	RABY CASTLE	MOPSIK
4040	9 SEP '65	LORD HOUGHTON	LOWTHER CASTLE	TCC
4041	10 SEP '65	PHILIP ROSE	LOWTHER CASTLE	H
4042	5 OCT '65	LORD BEAUCHAMP	HUGHENDEN	BCP
4043	13 OCT '65	LORD SALISBURY	HUGHENDEN	HFD
4044	20 OCT '65	LORD LONSDALE	HUGHENDEN	H
4045	21 OCT '65	RALPH EARLE	HUGHENDEN	HOL
4046	[21 OCT '65]	LORD BEAUCHAMP	[HUGHENDEN]	BCP
4047	23 OCT '65	SPENCER WALPOLE	HUGHENDEN	QUA
4048	24 OCT '65	LORD STANLEY	HUGHENDEN	DBP
4049	26 OCT '65	RALPH EARLE	HUGHENDEN	ILLU
4050	27 OCT '65	LORD BEAUCHAMP	HUGHENDEN	BCP
4051	1 NOV '65	JOHN EVELYN DENISON	HUGHENDEN	NOT
4052	1 NOV '65	LORD LONSDALE	HUGHENDEN	MOPSIK
4053	2 NOV '65	LORD STANLEY	HUGHENDEN	DBP
4054	6 NOV '65	RALPH EARLE	HUGHENDEN	PS
4055	6 NOV '65	LORD STANLEY	HUGHENDEN	DBP
4056	7 NOV '65	LORD STANLEY	HUGHENDEN	DBP
4057	15 NOV '65	[LORD BEAUCHAMP]	HUGHENDEN	BCP
4058	15 NOV '65	PHILIP ROSE	HUGHENDEN	H
4059	17 NOV '65	LORD STANLEY	HUGHENDEN	DBP
4060	24 NOV '65	LORD DERBY	GROSVENOR GATE	DBP
4061	27 NOV '65	FREDERICK LYGON	GROSVENOR GATE	BCP
4062	27 NOV '65	R[OBERT?] RIDGWAY	GROSVENOR GATE	PS
4062A	8 DEC '65	[CHARLOTTE DE ROTHSCHILD]	GROSVENOR GATE	CIB
4063	12 DEC '65	LORD HEYTESBURY	HUGHENDEN	MOPSIK

NO	DATE	TO	PLACE OF ORIGIN	LOCATION OF ORIGINAL
4064	14 DEC '65	WILLIAM GLADSTONE	HUGHENDEN	BL
4065	15 DEC '65	SAMUEL SMILES	HUGHENDEN	FIT
4066	20 DEC '65	CHARLES CLUBBE	[HUGHENDEN]	RIC
4067	3 JAN ['66]	CATTLE INSURANCE ASSOC	HUGHENDEN	PS
4068	4 JAN '66	[CONSERVATIVE MPS]	HUGHENDEN	WSRO
4069	[9 JAN '66]	LORD STANHOPE	HUGHENDEN	KCR
4070	9 JAN '66	CHARLES CLUBBE	HUGHENDEN	RIC
4071	10 JAN '66	MARKHAM SPOFFORTH	HUGHENDEN	PS
4072	15 JAN '66	EDWARD COLEMAN	GROSVENOR GATE	WSH
4073	22 JAN '66	SIR FITZROY KELLY	GROSVENOR GATE	H
4074	22 JAN '66	SIR STAFFORD NORTHCOTE	GROSVENOR GATE	H H/LIFE
4075	23 JAN '66	LORD STANLEY	GROSVENOR GATE	H H/LIFE
4076	25 JAN '66	B. HEPBURN	GROSVENOR GATE	MOPSIK
4077	3 FEB '66	EDWARD COLEMAN	GROSVENOR GATE	WSH
4078	10 FEB '66	PHILIP ROSE	GROSVENOR GATE	H
4079	11 FEB '66	PHILIP ROSE	GROSVENOR GATE	H
4080	20 FEB '66	PHILIP ROSE	CHARLES STREET	H
4081	[27 FEB '66]	[LORD DERBY]	CARLTON CLUB	DBP
4082	1 MAR '66	SIR STAFFORD NORTHCOTE	GROSVENOR GATE	H H/LIFE
4083	7 MAR '66	LORD STANHOPE	GROSVENOR GATE	KCR
4084	[POST-8 MAR '66]	[SIR S. NORTHCOTE]	[LONDON]	PS
4085	[9 MAR '66]	LORD DERBY	GROSVENOR GATE	DBP
4086	[POST-16 MAR '66]	ROBERT WATERS	[LONDON]	H
4087	[2 APR] '66	LORD HARTINGTON	HUGHENDEN	DEV
4088	4 APR '66	[UNKNOWN]	HUGHENDEN	BODL
4089	10 APR '66	[MARKHAM SPOFFORTH]	GROSVENOR GATE	PS
4090	[POST-12 APR '66]	DAVID PLUNKET	[LONDON?]	H H/LIFE
4091	14 APR '66	WILLIAM W.F. DICK	GROSVENOR GATE	BRN
4092	14 APR '66	LORD HENRY LENNOX	GROSVENOR GATE	MOPSIK
4093	[22 APR '66]	ROBERT DUDLEY BAXTER	GROSVENOR GATE	QUA
4094	10 MAY '66	CHARLES COLLETON RENNIE	GROSVENOR GATE	NLS
4095	15 MAY '66	ROBERT DUDLEY BAXTER	GROSVENOR GATE	QUA
4096	16 MAY '66	LORD ELCHO	GROSVENOR GATE	SRO
4097	17 MAY '66	JAMES THOROLD ROGERS	GROSVENOR GATE	ROG
4098	19 MAY '66	RALPH EARLE	GROSVENOR GATE	PS
4099	19 MAY '66	PHILIP ROSE	GROSVENOR GATE	H
4100	22 MAY '66	SIR WILLIAM JOLLIFFE	HUGHENDEN	SCR
4101	22 MAY '66	PHILIP ROSE	HUGHENDEN	H
4102	22 MAY '66	RALPH EARLE	HUGHENDEN	PS
4103	24 MAY '66	LORD DERBY	H OF COMMONS	DBP
4104	25 MAY '66	ANGELA BURDETT-COUTTS	GROSVENOR GATE	LPL
4105	[27? MAY '66]	RALPH EARLE	[CARLTON CLUB]	PS
4106	28 MAY '66	LORD GREY	GROSVENOR GATE	DURG
4107	31 MAY '66	LORD GREY	GROSVENOR GATE	DURG
4108	[MAY 1866]	[ALSAGER HAY HILL]	[LONDON]	H
4109	4 JUN '66	CRUIKSHANK COMMITTEE	GROSVENOR GATE	QUA
4110	[8 JUN '66]	MARY ANNE DISRAELI	[H OF COMMONS]	H
4111	12 JUN '66	MARY ANNE DISRAELI	[H OF COMMONS]	H
4112	14 JUN '66	JULIANA DE ROTHSCHILD	GROSVENOR GATE	ROSE
4113	15 JUN '66	JULIANA DE ROTHSCHILD	GROSVENOR GATE	ROSE
4114	15 JUN '66	HENRY LIDDELL	GROSVENOR GATE	PS
4115	17 JUN '66	JOSEPH NEAL MCKENNA	GROSVENOR GATE	ILLU

NO	DATE	TO	PLACE OF ORIGIN	LOCATION OF ORIGINAL
4167	4 AUG '66	MARY ANNE DISRAELI	DOWNING STREET	H
4168	6 AUG '66	QUEEN VICTORIA	[H OF COMMONS]	RAC
4169	8 AUG ['66?]	CHARLES FREMANTLE	[LONDON]	H
4170	13 AUG '66	ANDREW MONTAGU	DOWNING STREET	H
4171	13 AUG '66	LORD STANHOPE	DOWNING STREET	KCR
4172	[MID-AUG '66]	[MONTAGU CORRY]	[DOWNING STREET]	H
4173	15 AUG '66	WILLIAM POWELL	DOWNING STREET	TEXU
4174	17 AUG '66	LORD STANLEY	GROSVENOR GATE	H H/LIFE
4175	20 AUG '66	LORD DERBY	HUGHENDEN	DBP
4176	20 AUG ['66]	CHARLES FREMANTLE	[HUGHENDEN]	H
4177	20 AUG ['66]	[JAMES BAIN]	HUGHENDEN	H
4178	21 AUG '66	LORD NAAS	HUGHENDEN	INL
4179	21 AUG '66	LORD JOHN MANNERS	HUGHENDEN	BEA
4180	[21 AUG '66]	[MARKHAM SPOFFORTH]	[HUGHENDEN]	PS
4181	[21 AUG '66]	[LOUIS WOLOWSKI]	[HUGHENDEN]	PS
4182	23 AUG '66	SIR HUGH CAIRNS	HUGHENDEN	PRO
4183	29 'AUG ['66]	MONTAGU CORRY	GROSVENOR GATE	H
4184	[EARLY SEP '66]	MONTAGU CORRY	[HUGHENDEN]	H
4185	[EARLY SEP '66?]	MARY ANNE DISRAELI	[HUGHENDEN]	H
4186	2 SEP '66	SPENCER WALPOLE	HUGHENDEN	HOL
4187	2 SEP '66	MONTAGU CORRY	HUGHENDEN	H
4188	2 SEP '66	[MONTAGU CORRY]	HUGHENDEN	H
4189	2 SEP '66	DUKE OF BUCKINGHAM	HUGHENDEN	HUNT
4190	4 SEP '66	[MONTAGU CORRY]	HUGHENDEN	H
4191	5 SEP '66	MONTAGU CORRY	HUGHENDEN	H
4192	5 SEP '66	LORD BEAUCHAMP	HUGHENDEN	INL
4193	6 SEP ['66?]	[SIR HENRY EDWARDS?]	[HUGHENDEN]	DBP
4194	6 SEP ['66]	[MONTAGU CORRY]	HUGHENDEN	H
4195	[8 SEP '66]	[MONTAGU CORRY]	[HUGHENDEN]	H
4196	[9 SEP '66]	MONTAGU CORRY	HUGHENDEN	H
4197	10 SEP '66	JOSEPH PARROTT	HUGHENDEN	H
4198	10 SEP ['66]	[MONTAGU CORRY]	[HUGHENDEN]	H
4199	[11 SEP '66]	MONTAGU CORRY	HUGHENDEN	H
4200	12 SEP '66	GEORGE FELL	DOWNING STREET	PS
4201	12 SEP '66	LORD DALMENY	HUGHENDEN	ROSE
4202	14 SEP '66	LORD DERBY	HUGHENDEN	DBP
4203	14 SEP '66	MONTAGU CORRY	HUGHENDEN	H
4204	[16 SEP '66]	[MONTAGU CORRY]	[HUGHENDEN]	H
4205	16 SEP '66	VICTORIA TEMPLE FANE	HUGHENDEN	BODL
4206	[20 SEP '66?]	[MONTAGU CORRY]	HUGHENDEN	H
4207	24 SEP ['66]	LORD DERBY	HUGHENDEN	DBP
4208	25 SEP '66	[MONTAGU CORRY]	[HUGHENDEN]	H
4209	25 SEP '66	MONTAGU CORRY	[HUGHENDEN]	H
4210	27 SEP '66	SPENCER WALPOLE	HUGHENDEN	HOL
4211	27 SEP '66	SPENCER WALPOLE	HUGHENDEN	HOL
4212	27 SEP '66	LORD DERBY	HUGHENDEN	DBP
4213	27 SEP '66	SPENCER WALPOLE	HUGHENDEN	HOL
4214	27 SEP '66	LORD ELCHO	HUGHENDEN	SRO
4215	28 SEP '66	MONTAGU CORRY	[HUGHENDEN]	H
4216	30 SEP '66	LORD DERBY	HUGHENDEN	DBP
4217	30 SEP '66	MONTAGU CORRY	[HUGHENDEN]	H
4218	30 SEP '66	[SIR HENRY BULWER]	[HUGHENDEN]	H

NO	DATE	TO	PLACE OF ORIGIN	LOCATION OF ORIGINAL
4219	1 OCT '66	SPENCER WALPOLE	HUGHENDEN	HOL
4220	[1 OCT '66]	[MONTAGU CORRY]	[HUGHENDEN]	H
4221	2 OCT '66	[MONTAGU CORRY]	HUGHENDEN	H
4222	4 OCT '66	JONATHAN PEEL	HUGHENDEN	H
4223	4 OCT '66	[MONTAGU CORRY]	[HUGHENDEN]	H
4224	5 OCT ['66]	[MONTAGU CORRY]	[HUGHENDEN]	H
4225	8 OCT ['66]	[MONTAGU CORRY]	HUGHENDEN	H
4226	[11 OCT '66]	[MONTAGU CORRY]	DOWNING STREET	H
4227	[12 OCT '66]	MONTAGU CORRY	[HUGHENDEN]	H
4228	12 OCT '66	LORD DERBY	HUGHENDEN	DBP
4229	12 OCT '66	LORD DERBY	HUGHENDEN	DBP
4230	12 OCT '66	[MONTAGU CORRY]	HUGHENDEN	H
4231	12 OCT '66	[UNKNOWN]	HUGHENDEN	QUA
4232	14 OCT '66	CHARLES GREY	HUGHENDEN	DURG
4233	14 OCT '66	[MONTAGU CORRY]	[HUGHENDEN]	H
4234	14 OCT '66	SIR STAFFORD NORTHCOTE	HUGHENDEN	PS
4235	16 OCT ['66]	[MONTAGU CORRY]	[HUGHENDEN]	H
4236	16 OCT '66	[MONTAGU CORRY]	HUGHENDEN	H
4237	16 OCT ['66]	[MONTAGU CORRY]	[HUGHENDEN]	H
4238	17 OCT ['66]	[MONTAGU CORRY]	HUGHENDEN	H
4239	17 OCT '66	LOUISA DE ROTHSCHILD	HUGHENDEN	NNL
4240	18 OCT [66]	MONTAGU CORRY	[HUGHENDEN]	H
4241	18 OCT '66	SIR JOHN DALRYMPLE-HAY	HUGHENDEN	MOPSIK
4242	19 OCT ['66]	[MONTAGU CORRY]	[HUGHENDEN]	H
4243	19 OCT '66	[MONTAGU CORRY]	[HUGHENDEN]	H
4244	19 OCT ['66]	[MONTAGU CORRY]	[HUGHENDEN]	H
4245	[19 OCT '66]	[MARKHAM SPOFFORTH]	[HUGHENDEN]	PS
4246	21 OCT '66	LORD DERBY	HUGHENDEN	DBP
4247	22 OCT '66	SIR STAFFORD NORTHCOTE	HUGHENDEN	PS
4248	22 OCT '66	SPENCER WALPOLE	HUGHENDEN	HOL
4249	23 OCT '66	LORD DERBY	HUGHENDEN	DBP
4250	23 OCT ['66]	[MONTAGU CORRY]	HUGHENDEN	H
4251	23 OCT '66	SIR JOHN PAKINGTON	HUGHENDEN	WRC
4252	23 OCT '66	LOUISA DE ROTHSCHILD	HUGHENDEN	ROTH
4253	24 OCT '66	LORD CARRINGTON	HUGHENDEN	CARR
4254	24 OCT '66	LORD NAAS	HUGHENDEN	INL
4255	25 OCT '66	MONTAGU CORRY	HUGHENDEN	H
4256	30 OCT ['66]	[MONTAGU CORRY]	GROSVENOR GATE	H
4257	30 OCT '66	SIR JOHN PAKINGTON	DOWNING STREET	WRC
4258	1 NOV '66	[LORD STANLEY]	[LONDON]	H
4259	3 NOV '66	LORD STANLEY	GROSVENOR GATE	H H/LIFE
4260	3 NOV ['66]	[MONTAGU CORRY]	[LONDON]	H
4261	16 NOV ['66]	[LORD DERBY]	DOWNING STREET	DBP
4262	18 NOV '66	[LORD DERBY]	[LONDON]	DBP
4263	18 NOV '66	LORD DERBY	DOWNING STREET	DBP
4264	20 NOV '66	MONTAGU CORRY	GROSVENOR GATE	H
4265	[24 NOV '66]	GEORGE GROTE	[LONDON]	H
4266	24 NOV '66	LORD DERBY	[LONDON]	DBP
4267	24 NOV '66	LORD BEAUCHAMP	GROSVENOR GATE	BCP
4268	25 NOV '66	MARY ANNE DISRAELI	WINDSOR CASTLE	H
4269	26 NOV '66	QUEEN VICTORIA	DOWNING STREET	RAC
4270	27 NOV '66	MONTAGU CORRY	GROSVENOR GATE	H

NO	DATE	TO	PLACE OF ORIGIN	LOCATION OF ORIGINAL
4323	[7 FEB '67]	LORD DERBY	H OF COMMONS	DBP
4324	7 FEB '67	SPENCER WALPOLE	GROSVENOR GATE	HOL
4325	[8 FEB '67]	[MONTAGU CORRY]	[LONDON]	H
4326	[8/15 FEB '67]	[PHILIP ROSE]	H OF COMMONS	H
4327	[10 FEB '67]	[MONTAGU CORRY]	[LONDON]	H
4328	11 FEB '67	QUEEN VICTORIA	DOWNING STREET	RAC
4329	14 FEB '67	PHILIP ROSE	GROSVENOR GATE	H
4330	[15 FEB '67]	[MONTAGU CORRY]	DOWNING STREET	H
4331	15 FEB '67	QUEEN VICTORIA	H OF COMMONS	RAC
4332	15 FEB '67	THOMAS KEBBEL	DOWNING STREET	H H/LIFE
4333	[17 FEB '67]	MARY ANNE DISRAELI	OSBORNE	H
4334	19 FEB '67	QUEEN VICTORIA	H OF COMMONS	RAC
4335	22 FEB '67	CHARLES NEWDEGATE	DOWNING STREET	WAR
4336	[23 FEB '67]	[MONTAGU CORRY]	[LONDON]	H
4337	23 FEB ['67]	[PETER MCLAGAN]	DOWNING STREET	H
4338	25 FEB ['67]	[LORD DERBY]	[GROSVENOR GATE]	DBP
4339	[25 FEB '67]	MARY ANNE DISRAELI	DOWNING STREET	H
4340	25 FEB '67	QUEEN VICTORIA	H OF COMMONS	RAC
4341	26 FEB '67	LORD DERBY	H OF COMMONS	DBP
4342	26 FEB '67	QUEEN VICTORIA	H OF COMMONS	RAC
4343	27 FEB ['67]	LORD DERBY	GROSVENOR GATE	DBP
4344	[27 FEB '67]	LORD DERBY	[LONDON]	DBP
4345	[28 FEB '67]	LORD DERBY	DOWNING STREET	DBP
4346	28 FEB ['67]	LORD DERBY	DOWNING STREET	DBP
4347	28 FEB ['67]	LORD DERBY	H OF COMMONS	DBP
4348	[28 FEB '67]	[LORD DERBY]	H OF COMMONS	DBP
4349	28 FEB '67	QUEEN VICTORIA	H OF COMMONS	RAC
4350	1 MAR '67	LORD DERBY	[LONDON]	DBP
4351	[2 MAR '67]	LORD DERBY	[LONDON]	DBP
4352	2 MAR '67	SIR STAFFORD NORTHCOTE	DOWNING STREET	BL
4353	[3 MAR '67]	LORD DERBY	GROSVENOR GATE	DBP
4354	3 MAR '67	LORD DERBY	GROSVENOR GATE	DBP
4355	[4 MAR? '67]	LORD DERBY	GROSVENOR GATE	DBP
4356	4 MAR ['67]	LORD DERBY	GROSVENOR GATE	DBP
4357	[4? MAR '67]	[LORD DERBY]	DOWNING STREET	DBP
4358	5 MAR '67	LORD CRANBORNE	DOWNING STREET	OCC
4359	[5 MAR '67]	QUEEN VICTORIA	[LONDON]	RAC
4360	[6 MAR] '67	[MONTAGU CORRY]	[LONDON]	H
4361	[6 MAR? '67]	[MONTAGU CORRY]	[LONDON]	H
4362	[9 MAR '67]	[MONTAGU CORRY]	[LONDON]	H
4363	11 MAR '67	SIR STAFFORD NORTHCOTE	[LONDON]	H H/LIFE
4364	[12 MAR '67]	[MONTAGU CORRY]	DOWNING STREET	H
4365	[13 MAR '67]	[MONTAGU CORRY]	[LONDON]	H
4366	[13 MAR? '67]	LORD DERBY	GROSVENOR GATE	DBP
4367	[14 MAR? '67]	[MONTAGU CORRY]	DOWNING STREET	H
4368	[14 MAR '67]	[MONTAGU CORRY]	[LONDON]	H
4369	[14 MAR '67]	LORD DERBY	H OF COMMONS	DBP
4370	14 MAR '67	QUEEN VICTORIA	[LONDON]	RAC
4371	[15 MAR? '67]	[MONTAGU CORRY]	[LONDON]	H
4372	15 MAR '67	CHARLES GREY	H OF COMMONS	RAC
4373	[16 MAR '67]	LORD DERBY	GROSVENOR GATE	DBP
4374	18 MAR ['67]	QUEEN VICTORIA	DOWNING STREET	RAC

NO	DATE	TO	PLACE OF ORIGIN	LOCATION OF ORIGINAL
4375	[19 MAR '67]	[MONTAGU CORRY]	DOWNING STREET	H
4376	[20 MAR '67]	LORD DERBY	DOWNING STREET	DBP
4377	21 MAR ['67]	QUEEN VICTORIA	H OF COMMONS	RAC
4378	[22 MAR '67]	[MONTAGU CORRY]	GROSVENOR GATE	H
4379	[22 MAR '67]	MONTAGU CORRY	GROSVENOR GATE	H
4380	[22 MAR '67]	QUEEN VICTORIA	DOWNING STREET	RAC
4381	[24 MAR '67]	LORD DERBY	GROSVENOR GATE	DBP
4382	24 MAR '67	LORD DERBY	GROSVENOR GATE	DBP
4383	24 MAR '67	LADY JOHN MANNERS	GROSVENOR GATE	BEA
4384	[25 MAR '67]	LORD DERBY	H OF COMMONS	DBP
4385	25 MAR '67	QUEEN VICTORIA	H OF COMMONS	RAC
4386	[ABOUT 26 MAR '67]	[MONTAGU CORRY]	DOWNING STREET	H
4387	[26 MAR '67]	[LORD DERBY]	H OF COMMONS	DBP
4388	27 MAR ['67]	QUEEN VICTORIA	DOWNING STREET	RAC
4389	27 MAR '67	LORD LONSDALE	H OF COMMONS	MOPSIK
4390	28 MAR '67	CHARLOTTE DE ROTHSCHILD	GROSVENOR GATE	ROTH
4391	[28 MAR '67]	LORD DERBY	GROSVENOR GATE	DBP
4392	[30 MAR '67]	[MONTAGU CORRY]	DOWNING STREET	H
4393	[30 MAR '67]	[MONTAGU CORRY]	DOWNING STREET	·H
4394	30 MAR '67	RALPH DISRAELI	DOWNING STREET	BL
4395	[APR '67]	[LORD STANLEY]	[LONDON]	H
4396	3 APR '67	LORD STANLEY	GROSVENOR GATE	H H/LIFE
4397	[4 APR '67]	[MONTAGU CORRY]	[LONDON]	H
4398	4 APR '67	QUEEN VICTORIA	[LONDON]	RAC
4399	[5 APR '67]	MARY ANNE DISRAELI	[LONDON]	H
4400	8 APR '67	QUEEN VICTORIA	H OF COMMONS	RAC
4401	9 APR '67	[CONSERVATIVE MPS]	DOWNING STREET	H
4402	[10 APR '67]	[MONTAGU CORRY]	[LONDON]	H
4403	12 APR '67	GATHORNE HARDY	DOWNING STREET	H
4404	12 APR ['67]	LORD DERBY	DOWNING STREET	DBP
4405	[13 APR '67]	QUEEN VICTORIA	H OF COMMONS	RAC
4406	[13 APR '67]	[MONTAGU CORRY]	[H OF COMMONS]	H
4407	[13 APR '67]	[MONTAGU CORRY]	GROSVENOR GATE	H
4408	15 APR '67	RALPH DISRAELI	DOWNING STREET	BL
4409	16 APR '67	HENRY MANNING	GROSVENOR GATE	MANN
4410	17 APR '67	CHARLES FREMANTLE	GROSVENOR GATE	H
4411	17 APR '67	LORD STANLEY	GROSVENOR GATE	H H/LIFE
4412	17 APR '67	CHARLES GREY	GROSVENOR GATE	RAC
4413	17 APR '67	LORD DERBY	GROSVENOR GATE	DBP
4414	18 APR '67	LORD BEAUCHAMP	HUGHENDEN	BCP
4415	[19 APR] '67	MONTAGU CORRY	HUGHENDEN	H .
4416	[20 APR '67]	[SPENCER WALPOLE]	[HUGHENDEN]	HOL
4417	21 APR '67	MARY ANNE DISRAELI	WINDSOR	H
4418	[21 APR] '67	GATHORNE HARDY	WINDSOR	H H/LIFE
4419	22 APR '67	LORD STANLEY	WINDSOR	H H/LIFE
4420	[22] APR '67	[LADY GAINSBOROUGH?]	WINDSOR	EDE
4421	23 APR '67	MR BRIXY	HUGHENDEN	BRN
4422	23 APR '67	[MONTAGU CORRY]	HUGHENDEN	H
4423	27 APR ['67]	QUEEN VICTORIA	[LONDON]	H H/LIFE
4424	30 APR '67	QUEEN VICTORIA	[LONDON]	RAC
4425	[1 MAY '67?]	MARY ANNE DISRAELI	[LONDON]	H

NO	DATE	TO	PLACE OF ORIGIN	LOCATION OF ORIGINAL
4426	[1 MAY '67]	[MONTAGU CORRY]	DOWNING STREET	H
4427	[2 MAY '67]	[MONTAGU CORRY]	[DOWNING STREET]	H
4428	2 MAY '67	QUEEN VICTORIA	H OF COMMONS	RAC
4429	4 MAY ['67]	[LADY GAINSBOROUGH?]	GROSVENOR GATE	MOPSIK
4430	[5 MAY '67]	[MONTAGU CORRY]	DOWNING STREET	H
4431	6 MAY '67	QUEEN VICTORIA	H OF COMMONS	RAC
4432	[8? MAY '67]	[MONTAGU CORRY?]	DOWNING STREET	H
4433	[10 MAY '67]	QUEEN VICTORIA	H OF COMMONS	RAC
4434	11 MAY '67	ALFRED DENISON	GROSVENOR GATE	QUA
4435	[13 MAY '67]	[MONTAGU CORRY]	[LONDON]	H
4436	13 MAY '67	QUEEN VICTORIA	H OF COMMONS	RAC
4437	17 MAY '67	LORD LONSDALE	DOWNING STREET	PS
4438	18 MAY '67	GATHORNE HARDY	GROSVENOR GATE	H H/LIFE
4439	[18 MAY '67]	MARY ANNE DISRAELI	GROSVENOR GATE	H H/LIFE
4440	20 MAY ['67]	QUEEN VICTORIA	DOWNING STREET	RAC
4441	21 MAY '67	HENRY MANNING	[LONDON]	MANN
4442	24 MAY '67	DUKE OF MARLBOROUGH	DOWNING STREET	CAM
4443	[27 MAY '67]	[MONTAGU CORRY]	[H OF COMMONS]	H
4444	27 MAY '67	QUEEN VICTORIA	H OF COMMONS	RAC
4445	[END MAY '67]	[MONTAGU CORRY]	[LONDON]	H
4446	[2 JUN? '67]	[MONTAGU CORRY?]	[LONDON]	H
4447	7 JUN ['67]	[MONTAGU CORRY]	DOWNING STREET	H
4448	9 JUN '67	QUEEN VICTORIA	DOWNING STREET	RAC
4449	11 JUN '67	JOHN WALTER	DOWNING STREET	SRO
4450	[12 OR 26 JUN? '67]	[MONTAGU CORRY]	DOWNING STREET	H
4451	13 JUN '67	QUEEN VICTORIA	DOWNING STREET	RAC
4452	14 JUN '67	LORD DERBY	DOWNING STREET	DBP
4453	17 JUN '67	JOHN WALTER	DOWNING STREET	H
4454	17 JUN '67	QUEEN VICTORIA	DOWNING STREET	RAC
4455	17 JUN '67	CHARLES DICKENS	[LONDON]	MARI
4456	[18 JUN '67]	[LORD DERBY]	[LONDON]	DBP
4457	[19 JUN '67]	[MONTAGU CORRY?]	[DOWNING STREET]	H
4458	20 JUN '67	QUEEN VICTORIA	DOWNING STREET	RAC
4459	[21 JUN '67]	MARY ANNE DISRAELI	DOWNING STREET	H
4460	24 JUN '67	QUEEN VICTORIA	H OF COMMONS	RAC
4461	26 JUN '67	LORD DERBY	DOWNING STREET	DBP
4462	27 JUN '67	QUEEN VICTORIA	H OF COMMONS	RAC
4463	30 JUN '67	[LORD DERBY]	[LONDON]	DBP
4464	1 JUL '67	QUEEN VICTORIA	DOWNING STREET	RAC
4465	2 JUL '67	QUEEN VICTORIA	DOWNING STREET	RAC
4466	[4 JUL '67]	MARY ANNE DISRAELI	DOWNING STREET	H
4467	5 JUL '67	QUEEN VICTORIA	DOWNING STREET	RAC
4468	[9] JUL '67	QUEEN VICTORIA	DOWNING STREET	RAC
4469	9 JUL '67	QUEEN VICTORIA	GROSVENOR GATE	RAC
4470	10 JUL '67	LORD MALMESBURY	DOWNING STREET	HCC
4471	13 JUL '67	MARY ANNE DISRAELI	DOWNING STREET	H
4472	15 JUL '67	QUEEN VICTORIA	DOWNING STREET	RAC
4473	18 JUL '67	[LORD DERBY]	DOWNING STREET	DBP
4474	19 JUL '67	MARY ANNE DISRAELI	H OF COMMONS	H
4475	20 JUL '67	SIR STAFFORD NORTHCOTE	[LONDON]	H H/LIFE
4476	20 JUL '67	SIR THOMAS PHILLIPPS	GROSVENOR GATE	BODL
4477	21 JUL '67	[MONTAGU CORRY]	DOWNING STREET	H

NO	DATE	TO	PLACE OF ORIGIN	LOCATION OF ORIGINAL
4478	[21] JUL '67	LORD DERBY	GROSVENOR GATE	DBP
4479	25 JUL '67	CHARLES GREY	DOWNING STREET	RAC
4480	25 JUL '67	QUEEN VICTORIA	DOWNING STREET	RAC
4481	26 JUL '67	[MONTAGU CORRY]	DOWNING STREET	H
4482	27 JUL '67	LORD DERBY	DOWNING STREET	DBP
4483	[28 JUL '67]	[MONTAGU CORRY]	[LONDON]	H
4484	31 JUL '67	CHARLES GREY	GROSVENOR GATE	RAC
4485	31 JUL '67	LORD DERBY	DOWNING STREET	DBP
4486	[1 AUG '67?]	LORD CAIRNS	[LONDON]	PRO
4487	4 AUG '67	EDWARD COLEMAN	GROSVENOR GATE	WSH
4488	[4? AUG '67]	[EDWARD WATKIN]	[LONDON]	H
4489	5 AUG '67	LORD NAAS	DOWNING STREET	INL
4490	6 AUG '67	LORD NAAS	H OF COMMONS	INL
4491	6 AUG '67	QUEEN VICTORIA	H OF COMMONS	RAC
4492	[8 AUG '67]	LORD DERBY	GROSVENOR GATE	DBP
4493	9 AUG ['67]	QUEEN VICTORIA	DOWNING STREET	RAC
4494	12 AUG '67	LORD DERBY	GROSVENOR GATE	DBP
4495	12 AUG '67	LORD HYLTON	DOWNING STREET	SCR
4496	12 AUG '67	MONTAGU CORRY	DOWNING STREET	H
4497	15 AUG '67	JOHN LAMBERT	DOWNING STREET	H
4498	16 AUG '67	QUEEN VICTORIA	DOWNING STREET	RAC
4499	17 AUG '67	EDWARD COLEMAN	DOWNING STREET	WSH
4500	[20 AUG '67]	[MONTAGU CORRY]	[LONDON]	H
4501	[20 AUG '67]	LORD DERBY	DOWNING STREET	DBP
4502	25 AUG '67	LORD LONSDALE	HUGHENDEN	PS
4503	26 AUG '67	LORD MAYO	HUGHENDEN	INL
4504	27 AUG '67	CHARLES RIVERS WILSON	HUGHENDEN	NYPL
4505	27 AUG '67	MONTAGU CORRY	HUGHENDEN	H
4506	27 AUG '67	WILLIAM LOWTHER	HUGHENDEN	H H/LIFE
4507	27 AUG '67	GEORGE WARD HUNT	HUGHENDEN	NSR
4508	30 AUG '67	LORD MAYO	HUGHENDEN	INL
4509	30 AUG '67	LORD DALMENY	HUGHENDEN	ROSE
4510	[SEP '67]	[MONTAGU CORRY]	[LONDON]	H
4511	1 SEP '67	CHARLES RIVERS WILSON	HUGHENDEN	MOPSIK
4512	1 SEP '67	MONTAGU CORRY	HUGHENDEN	H
4513	1 SEP '67	LORD STANLEY	HUGHENDEN	H
4514	4 SEP '67	LORD DALMENY	HUGHENDEN	ROSE
4515	5 SEP '67	LORD STANLEY	HUGHENDEN	H H/LIFE
4516	5 SEP '67	CHARLES RIVERS WILSON	HUGHENDEN	NYPL
4517	5 SEP '67	PHILIP ROSE	HUGHENDEN	H
4518	8 SEP '67	LORD DERBY	HUGHENDEN	DBP
4519	10 SEP '67	[CHARLES RIVERS WILSON]	HUGHENDEN	NYPL
4520	10 SEP '67	SIR HENRY EDWARDS	HUGHENDEN	HAL
4521	12 SEP '67	LORD STANLEY	[HUGHENDEN]	H H/LIFE
4522	12 SEP '67	SIR STAFFORD NORTHCOTE	HUGHENDEN	H H/LIFE
4523	13 SEP '67	[MONTAGU CORRY]	[HUGHENDEN]	H
4524	13 SEP '67	CHARLES RIVERS WILSON	[HUGHENDEN]	NYPL
4525	13 SEP '67	ROBERT DUNDAS	HUGHENDEN	H
4526	14 SEP '67	LORD DERBY	HUGHENDEN	DBP
4527	15 SEP '67	MONTAGU CORRY	[HUGHENDEN]	H
4528	19 SEP '67	HENRY PADWICK	HUGHENDEN	LCC
4529	22 SEP '67	LORD STANLEY	HUGHENDEN	H H/LIFE

NO	DATE	TO	PLACE OF ORIGIN	LOCATION OF ORIGINAL
4530	22 SEP '67	LORD DERBY	HUGHENDEN	DBP
4531	22 SEP '67	MONTAGU CORRY	HUGHENDEN	H
4532	24 SEP '67	LORD MAYO	HUGHENDEN	INL
4533	24 SEP '67	THOMAS FAULKNER LEE	HUGHENDEN	BODL
4534	25 SEP '67	SIR W. STIRLING MAXWELL	HUGHENDEN	STCL
4535	[25 SEP '67]	CHARLES RIVERS WILSON	HUGHENDEN	NYPL
4536	27 SEP '67	CHARLES RIVERS WILSON	HUGHENDEN	NYPL
4537	29 SEP '67	SIR THOMAS GLADSTONE	HUGHENDEN	DENL
4538	29 SEP '67	SIR MATTHEW RIDLEY	HUGHENDEN	NLF
4539	29 SEP '67	SIR STAFFORD NORTHCOTE	HUGHENDEN	H H/LIFE
4540	29 SEP '67	ALGERNON EGERTON	HUGHENDEN	TEXU
4541	29 SEP '67	CHARLES GREY	HUGHENDEN	RAC
4542	1 OCT '67	MARY ANNE DISRAELI	DOWNING STREET	H
4543	3 OCT '67	[CHARLES RIVERS WILSON?]	HUGHENDEN	NYPL
4544	3 OCT '67	MONTAGU CORRY	HUGHENDEN	H
4545	4 OCT '67	LORD DERBY	HUGHENDEN	DBP
4546	6 OCT '67	[MONTAGU CORRY]	HUGHENDEN	H
4547	6 OCT '67	[MONTAGU CORRY]	[HUGHENDEN]	H
4548	9 OCT '67	JOHN ROEBUCK	BLENHEIM	CUL
4549	14 OCT '67	PHILIP ROSE	DOWNING STREET	H
4550	14 OCT '67	LORD STANLEY	[GROSVENOR GATE]	DBP; H H/LIFE
4551	15 OCT '67	LORD STANLEY	GROSVENOR GATE	DBP
4552	16 OCT '67	LORD ROSSLYN	DOWNING STREET	SRO
4553	[16 OCT '67]	LORD STANLEY	[LONDON]	DBP
4554	[PRE-17 OCT '67]	[E. STRATHEARN GORDON]	[LONDON?]	H
4555	17 OCT '67	MONTAGU CORRY	DOWNING STREET	H
4556	17 OCT '67	CHARLES GREY	GROSVENOR GATE	RAC
4556A	17 OCT '67	JOHN ROEBUCK	DOWNING STREET	IAA
4557	19 OCT '67	LORD DERBY	DOWNING STREET	DBP
4558	21 OCT '67	[CHARLES RIVERS WILSON]	GROSVENOR GATE	NYPL
4559	25 OCT '67	[LORD BARRINGTON?]	DOWNING STREET	BL
4560	[25] OCT '67	LORD DERBY	DOWNING STREET	DBP
4561	4 NOV '67	LORD STANLEY	DOWNING STREET	DBP
4562	4 NOV '67	E. STRATHEARN GORDON	DOWNING STREET	H H/LIFE
4563	4 NOV '67	EMILY DUNDAS	DOWNING STREET	BRS
4564	6 NOV '67	JAMES HARTLEY	DOWNING STREET	BRN
4565	6 NOV '67	LORD DERBY	GROSVENOR GATE	DBP
4566	6 NOV '67	REGINALD STUART POOLE	DOWNING STREET	BL
4567	8 NOV '67	MONTAGU CORRY	[LONDON]	H
4568	[10 NOV '67]	MARY ANNE DISRAELI	WINDSOR	H
4569	[11 NOV '67]	W. COTTER	[WINDSOR]	PS
4570	12 NOV '67	[MONTAGU CORRY?]	[LONDON]	NLC
4571	13 NOV '67	SIR HENRY STRACEY	DOWNING STREET	BUL
4572	14 NOV '67	LORD DERBY	GROSVENOR GATE	DBP
4573	[MID-NOV '67]	[LADY BROWNLOW]	[DOWNING STREET]	H
4574	15 NOV '67	MONTAGU CORRY	[GROSVENOR GATE]	H
4575	[16 NOV '67]	[MONTAGU CORRY]	[GROSVENOR GATE]	H
4576	[17] NOV '67	LOUISA DE ROTHSCHILD	GROSVENOR GATE	ROTH
4577	18 NOV '67	LORD STANLEY	GROSVENOR GATE	DBP; H H/LIFE
4578	[19 NOV '67]	[CHARLOTTE DE ROTHSCHILD?]	DOWNING STREET	ROTH
4579	19 NOV '67	CHARLOTTE DE ROTHSCHILD	GROSVENOR GATE	ROTH
4580	19 NOV '67	QUEEN VICTORIA	DOWNING STREET	RAC

NO	DATE	TO	PLACE OF ORIGIN	LOCATION OF ORIGINAL
4581	20 NOV '67	LORD BEAUCHAMP	GROSVENOR GATE	BCP
4582	20 NOV '67	PHILIP ROSE	DOWNING STREET	H
4583	20 NOV '67	EMILY CLUBBE	GROSVENOR GATE	RIC
4584	20 NOV '67	LOUISA DE ROTHSCHILD	GROSVENOR GATE	ROTH
4585	20 NOV '67	WILLIAM GLADSTONE	GROSVENOR GATE	BL
4586	21 NOV ['67]	PEDRO ROMULO NEGRETE	[LONDON]	BRN
4587	21 NOV ['67]	[PEDRO ROMULO NEGRETE?]	[DOWNING STREET]	BRN
4588	21 NOV '67	QUEEN VICTORIA	DOWNING STREET	RAC
4589	[22 NOV '67]	[PEDRO ROMULO NEGRETE?]	GROSVENOR GATE	BRN
4590	23 NOV '67	CHARLOTTE DE ROTHSCHILD	DOWNING STREET	ROTH
4591	25 NOV '67	JOHN BENJAMIN SMITH	DOWNING STREET	MPL
4592	26 NOV '67	QUEEN VICTORIA	DOWNING STREET	RAC
4593	[27 NOV '67]	MONTAGU CORRY	[GROSVENOR GATE]	H
4594	[28 NOV '67]	GEORGE WARD HUNT	GROSVENOR GATE	NSR
4595	28 NOV '67	LORD BARRINGTON	GROSVENOR GATE	BL
4596	[28 NOV '67]	[MONTAGU CORRY]	GROSVENOR GATE	H
4597	[28? NOV '67]	SIR STAFFORD NORTHCOTE	GROSVENOR GATE	BL
4598	[29 NOV '67]	MARY ANNE DISRAELI	GROSVENOR GATE	H
4599	[29 NOV '67]	MARY ANNE DISRAELI	[GROSVENOR GATE]	H
4600	29 NOV '67	[MONTAGU CORRY]	[GROSVENOR GATE]	H
4601	30 NOV '67	LORD STANLEY	GROSVENOR GATE	DBP
4602	[30 NOV '67]	MARY ANNE DISRAELI	[GROSVENOR GATE]	H
4603	[2 DEC '67]	MARY ANNE DISRAELI	GROSVENOR GATE	H
4604	[2 DEC '67]	[MONTAGU CORRY]	[GROSVENOR GATE]	H
4605	[2? DEC '67]	MARY ANNE DISRAELI	[GROSVENOR GATE]	H
4606	[2? DEC '67]	MARY ANNE DISRAELI	[GROSVENOR GATE]	H
4607	[2? DEC '67]	MARY ANNE DISRAELI	[GROSVENOR GATE]	H
4608	[3? DEC '67]	MARY ANNE DISRAELI	[GROSVENOR GATE]	H
4609	[4 DEC '67?]	[MONTAGU CORRY]	[GROSVENOR GATE]	H
4610	7 DEC '67	LORD DALMENY	GROSVENOR GATE	ROSE
4611	7 DEC '67	SIR HARRY VERNEY	GROSVENOR GATE	VER
4612	7 DEC '67	SIR STAFFORD NORTHCOTE	GROSVENOR GATE	PS
4613	[8? DEC '67]	MARY ANNE DISRAELI	[GROSVENOR GATE]	H
4614	8 DEC '67	HENRY MANNING	GROSVENOR GATE	MANN
4615	9 DEC '67	ELIZA SPENCER	GROSVENOR GATE	GRI
4616	[9 DEC? '67]	MARY ANNE DISRAELI	CARLTON CLUB	H
4617	[10 DEC '67]	[MONTAGU CORRY]	[GROSVENOR GATE]	H
4618	11 DEC '67	PHILIP ROSE	GROSVENOR GATE	H
4619	11 DEC '67	CHARLES CLUBBE	GROSVENOR GATE	RIC
4620	12 DEC '67	SIR JOHN PAKINGTON	GROSVENOR GATE	H
4621	12 DEC '67	DUKE OF CAMBRIDGE	[DOWNING STREET]	RAC
4622	12 DEC ['67]	[MONTAGU CORRY]	[LONDON]	H
4623	13 DEC '67	GATHORNE HARDY	DOWNING STREET	ESU
4624	14 DEC ['67]	[MONTAGU CORRY]	[GROSVENOR GATE]	H
4625	14 DEC '67	LORD DERBY	DOWNING STREET	DBP
4626	[14 DEC '67]	[MONTAGU CORRY]	DOWNING STREET	H
4627	14 DEC '67	LORD MAYO	DOWNING STREET	INL
4628	16 DEC '67	LORD DERBY	[LONDON]	DBP
4629	16 DEC '67	LORD DERBY	DOWNING STREET	DBP
4630	16 DEC ['67]	LORD STANLEY	GROSVENOR GATE	DBP
4631	17 DEC '67	SIR THOMAS PHILLIPPS	DOWNING STREET	BODL
4632	17 DEC '67	LORD DERBY	DOWNING STREET	DBP

4633	[17 DEC? '67]	MARY ANNE DISRAELI	CARLTON CLUB	H
4634	18 DEC '67	LORD STANHOPE	DOWNING STREET	H H/LIFE
4635	21 DEC '67	LORD JOHN MANNERS	DOWNING STREET	BEA
4636	26 DEC '67	GATHORNE HARDY	GROSVENOR GATE	ESU
4637	26 DEC '67	SIR W. STIRLING MAXWELL	DOWNING STREET	STCL
4638	[27 DEC '67]	[CHARLES RIVERS WILSON?]	[GROSVENOR GATE]	NYPL
4639	27 DEC '67	GATHORNE HARDY	GROSVENOR GATE	ESU
4640	27 DEC '67	HENRY MANNING	GROSVENOR GATE	MANN
4641	28 DEC '67	MONTAGU CORRY	DOWNING STREET	H H/LIFE
4642	31 DEC '67	LORD STANLEY	GROSVENOR GATE	DBP
4643	31 DEC '67	MONTAGU CORRY	DOWNING STREET	H
4644	31 DEC '67	JOHN WILLIAM FANE	[LONDON]	COR
4645	['67?]	MONTAGU CORRY	[LONDON?]	H
4646	[JUL '66-FEB '68]	[MONTAGU CORRY]	DOWNING STREET	H
4647	[JUL '66-FEB '68]	[MONTAGU CORRY]	DOWNING STREET	H
4648	[JUL '66-FEB '68]	[MONTAGU CORRY]	DOWNING STREET	H
4649	[JUL '66-FEB '68]	[MONTAGU CORRY]	GROSVENOR GATE	H
4650	['66-8, '74-'80]	[MONTAGU CORRY?]		PS
4651	[FEB '67-AUG '76]	LORD BARRINGTON	[LONDON]	DUL

The following is the available information (source indicated) about Disraeli letters that have not been located, for which no significant portion of the text is available, but which seem to belong to the 1865-7 period, or earlier. Some of them have been used in the notes of this volume, as indicated. The references to items in H are to items from which a specific D letter can be inferred. For pre-1865 letters newly found see Appendix I.

19 Sep '42	To Mrs I.C. Sloper, re death of MA's mother. HD/I/A/119.
Jan '65	To Lady Galway, re Galway's health. H B/XXI/G/48.
before 5 Jan '65	To Lord Exeter, accepting invitation. H B/XXI/E/306.
10 Jan '65	To Lord Stanhope. BRI [3] (cover).
before 15 Jan '65	To Sir Edward Bulwer-Lytton, invitation. H B/XX/LY/152.
before 22 Jan '65	To Lord Stanley, invitation. H B/XX/S/721.
before 11 Feb '65	To George Fell, re repeal of malt-tax. BH (11 Feb 1865).
before 1 Mar '65	To Duchess of Northumberland, re death of Duke. H B/XXI/N/191.
before 8 Mar '65	To George Fell, re prize money. BH (18 Mar 1865).
before 14 Mar '65	To Lord Orford, invitation. H B/XXI/O/36.
before 28 Mar '65	To Lady Salisbury, invitation. H B/XX/S/1424; HC/III/C/307.
before 1 Apr '65	To John C. Stark & Co, re Mount Braddon. H A/V/G/176.
Apr '65	To Lady Georgiana Fane, re universal rating bill. H B/XXI/F/52.
before 10 Apr '65	To Lord Carrington. H B/XXI/C/80a.
before 20 Apr '65	To Lord St Leonards. H B/XXI/S/17.
before 4 May '65	To Markham Spofforth, with enclosure. H B/XXI/S/398.
before 6 May '65	To J. Burnett Stuart, re Mount Braddon. H A/V/G/179.
before 18 Jun '65	To George A. Denison. H B/XXI/D/137.
25 Jun '65	To Rev Thomas Evetts, re Oxford University election. H B/J/D/55.
before 3 Jul '65	To Joseph Trumper. H B/I/D/57.
before 6 Jul '65	To Sir John Dalrymple-Hay. H B/XXI/H/298.
before 8 Jul '65	To Henry Badcock. KAN MS P23A:1. See **4020**&n2.
27 Aug '65	To Lord Lonsdale, re visit to Lowther. H B/XXI/L/280.
before 6 Sep '65	To Lord Henry Lennox. H B/XX/LN/216.
before 28 Sep '65	To Lady Jersey. H A/IV/J/280.

before 30 Sep '65	To Lord Henry Lennox. H B/XX/LN/219.
before 6 Oct '65	To Lady Salisbury, re children's skin condition. H B/XX/S/425.
before 10 Oct '65	To Frederick Lygon. H B/XX/LN/37.
before 15 Oct '65	To Lord Robert Montagu, re his book. H B/XXI/M/472.
before 27 Oct '65	To Lord Beauchamp, invitation. H B/XXI/L/434.
before 28 Oct '65	To Gerard Noel, invitation. H B/XXI/N/100.
before 29 Oct '65	To Edward Bickersteth, invitation. H B/XXI/B/499.
before 31 Oct '65	To William Follett Synge, accepting invitation. H B/XXI/S/749.
before 4 Nov '65	To Lord Cranborne, invitation. H B/XX/CE/5.
before 20 Nov '65	To Frederick Lygon. H B/XX/LN/39.
before 24 Nov '65	To Frederic W. Haydon. H B/XXI/H/381.
before 21 Dec '65	To Lady Salisbury, re visit. H D/III/C/310.
'66	To Jane Ely. H B/XXI/E/130a.
'66?	To Lord St Leonards. H B/XXI/S/19.
before 2 Jan '66	To Lord Stanley, invitation. H B/XX/S/728.
before 4 Jan '66	To Lord Burghley, invitation. H B/XXI/E/314.
before 23 Jan '66	To Sir Edward Bulwer-Lytton, re poems. H B/XX/LY/154.
before 26 Jan '66	To Gerard Noel, re malt-tax meeting. H B/XXI/N/101.
before 1 Feb '66	To Lady Brownlow. H B/XXI/B/1052.
before 4 Feb '66	To Francis Grant, congratulations. H A/IV/M/68.
before 16 Feb '66	To Lady Cremorne, invitation. H A/IV/L/107.
before 20 Feb '66	To Thomas Longman, re indemnification. H E/VII/A.
21 Feb '66	To Edward Ryley. H B/XXI/R/353.
before 27 Feb '66	To Sir Edward Bulwer-Lytton, re poems. H B/XX/LY/157.
before 1 Mar '66	To Edward Ryley. H B/XXI/R/357.
before 30 Apr '66	To Sylvain Van de Weyer, requesting a meeting. H B/XXI/V/5.
before 23 May '66	To Joseph Parrott, re *Bucks Herald*. H B/XX/A/33.
before 1 Jul '66	To Ralph Earle, re a government appointment. H B/XX/E/373.
before 2 Jul '66	To Wentworth Beaumont, suggesting his brother Somerset as D's political secretary. H B/XXI/B/282.
before 9 Jul '66	To Lord G. Gordon-Lennox. H B/XXI/L/130.
14 Jul '66	To J.S. Hubbard, re a meeting. *American Book Prices Current* (1980-1).
before 22 Jul '66	To C.G. Dupré. H B/XXI/D/442.
before 26 Jul '66	To Charles Grey. H B/XIX/D/9.
Aug '66	To T. Bailey, enclosing money. James Tregaskis & Son Catalogue No 886 (1924).
16 Aug '66	To William Powell, enclosing £450. H B/IX/D/3.
before 20 Aug '66	To Lady Jersey. H A/IV/J/297.
21 Aug '66	To Louis Wolowski. See **4181**&n1.
before 9 Aug '66	To Henry Constantine Jennings. H B/VIII/38a.
before 30 Aug '66	To Lord Carnarvon. H B/XX/HE/2.
Sep '66	To Lady Jersey. H A/IV/J/300.
before 3 Sep '66	To Lord and Lady Cranborne, invitation. H B/XX/CE/321. See **4190**&n4.
before 7 Sep '66	To Rev Thomas Evetts, invitation. H B/XXI/E/288.
7 Sep '66	To Lady Clanricarde, invitation. H B/XXI/C/233.
before 8 Sep '66	To Lady Clanricarde. H B/XX/D/348. See **4195**&n3.
before 9 Sep '66	To Lord Arthur Pelham Clinton, invitation. H B/XXI/C/277.
before 10 Sep '66	To Rev Thomas Evetts. H B/XXI/E/289.
before 12 Sep '66	To Duke of Buckingham, invitation. H B/XXI/B/1225.
before 17 Sep '66	To Sir William Jolliffe, invitation. H B/XX/J/99.
before 17 Sep '66	To Count Vitzthum, invitation. H B/XXI/V/85.
before 1 Oct '66	To William Cookesley, re a position. H B/XXI/C/404. See **4211**&n4.
before 1 Oct '66	To Thomas Longman, re D's *Reform Speeches*. H E/VII/A6.

4 Oct '66	To Thomas Longman, re D's *Reform Speeches*. H B/XX/D/17. See **4223**&n6.
4 Oct '66	To Stephen Cave, re bills of T.P. Warlow. H B/XIII/91. See **4222**&n1.
about 8 Oct '66	To Lady Jersey. H B/XX/D/18. See **4225**&n5.
before 11 Oct '66	To Lady Jersey. H A/IV/J/302.
before 11 Oct '66	To Sir John Dalrymple-Hay, thanking him for grouse. H B/XXI/H/302.
before 14 Oct '66	To Lord Carnarvon, re military expenditure. H B/XX/HE/6.
before 24 Oct '66	To Edward Kenealy, turning down his request for a QC. H B/XXI/K/102.
before 25 Oct '66	To Adolphe Barrot, re marriage of his child. H B/XXI/B/131.
before 25 Oct ['66?]	To Lady Galway, re peerage. H C/I/A/38.
before 27 Oct '66	To William Lovell. H A/V/G/207.
before 24 Nov '66	To Lady Salisbury, re a northern friend. H B/XX/S/1432.
before 29 Nov '66	To Lady Brownlow. H B/XXI/B/1053.
about 13 Dec '66	To Thomas Longman, re D's *Reform Speeches*. H B/XX/D/32. See **4282**&n1.
about 21 Dec '66	To Duke of Wellington. H B/XX/D/34. See **4289**&n1.
before 4 Jan '67	To Henry Lancelot Holland, with memorial of Moss & Co (bankers). H B/VIII/59a.
4 Jan '67	To Montagu Corry, re D's *Reform Speeches*. H B/XX/CO/22.
15 Jan '67	To Charles Strange. H B/IX/D/6e.
before 19 Jan '67	To Lord Shaftesbury. H B/XXI/S/133.
19 Jan '67	To William H.P. Gore Langton. Henry Bristow of Ringwood Catalogue No 288.
20 Jan '67	To Montagu Corry, with enclosure. See **4308**&n3.
25 Jan '67	To Robert Andrew Macfie. H B/VIII/36b.
before 28 Jan '67	To Lord Carnarvon. H B/XX/HE/10.
before 13 Mar '67	To Lady Derby, re Derby's health. H B/XX/S/522.
about 13 Mar '67	To Sir Daniel Gooch, refusing assistance. *BH* (6 Apr 1867).
about 14 Mar '67	To Robert Dudley Baxter. DBP Box 146/3. See **4369**&n3.
before 16 Mar '67	To George Ward Hunt. H B/XX/HU/16.
17 Mar '67	To Thomas Baring, re reform bill. H B/XXI/B/69.
before 8 Apr '67	To Lord G. Gordon-Lennox. H B/XI/J/112.
before 17 Apr '67	To Lord G. Gordon-Lennox. H B/XII/L/134.
before 23 Apr '67	To Lady Brownlow. H B/XXI/B/1055.
before 24 May '67	To Arabella Sarah Darby Griffith. H B/XI/J/149.
before 6 May '67	To Count Vitzthum. H B/XXI/V/88.
before 10 May '67	To J.A. Roebuck, accepting invitation.
18 May '67	To Gathorne Hardy. H H/LIFE. See **4439**&n1.
before 12 Jun '67	To Lord Lonsdale. H B/XXI/L/291.
about 21 Jul '67	To Joseph Henley. H B/XX/D/364. See **4477**&n2.
about 21 Jul '67	To William Hutt. H B/XX/D/364. See **4477**&n1.
before 5 Aug '67	To Marcus Moritz Kalisch, thanking him for his *Leviticus*. ROTH.
20 Aug '67	To Joseph N. McKenna. H B/XIII/58. See **4500**&n1.
before 21 Aug '67	To Sir Henry Edwards. H B/XXI/E/71.
before 22 Aug '67	To Lady Brownlow, sending grouse. H B/XXI/B/1057.
24 Aug '67	To John George Dodson. H B/XXI/D/270.
27 Aug '67	To Lord Stanley, re Lisbon. H H/LIFE. See **4506**&n1.
about 1 Sep '67	To Christopher de Gernon. MOPSIK [71]. See **4511**&n7.
before 3 Sep '67	To Lionel de Rothschild. H B/XXI/R/215. See **4515**n1.
12 Sep '67	To George Ward Hunt. H B/XX/HU/22.
before 17 Sep '67	To Lord Mayo. H B/XX/BO/37.

about 18 Sep '67	To George Fell, regrets. *BH* (21 Sep 1867).
before 26 Sep '67	To Lord Stanley, re Abyssinia. *Disraeli, Derby* 318.
before 27 Sep '67	To John Pope Hennessy. H B/XXI/W/405.
about 3 Oct '67	To [William?] Fitzgerald. NYPL Montague [19]. **4543**&n6.
before 4 Oct '67	To Rev Tresham Gregg. H B/XXI/G/346.
before 15 Oct '67	To Fanny Montgomery, re her book. H B/XXI/M/472.
before 17 Oct '67	To John Roebuck, 'a public line to show your friends'. See **4556A**.
before 23 Oct '67	To Lord G. Gordon-Lennox. H B/XII/L/142.
Dec '67	To Juliana de Rothschild, re MA's health. H D/VIII/A/53, 61.
before 9 Dec '67	To Sir Thomas Phillipps, re his library. H B/X/C/2.
before 13 Dec '67	To Charles and Emily Clubbe, re MA's health. H D/III/C/399.
before 16 Dec '67	To William Lovell, enclosing £170. H A/V/G/209.
17 Dec '67	To Lady Derby, re D's and MA's health. H D/VIII/A/45.
before 29 Dec '67	To Sir George Jenkinson. H B/XII/J/32.
before 31 Dec '67	To John Wilson Patten. COR Rare PR 4581 f73+v.2(35). **4644**&n1.

The Derby Cabinet of 1867 by Henry Gates. Watercolour, 1868. © National Portrait Gallery, London. NPG 4893.

THE HONEST POTBOY.

DERBY (aside). *"Don't froth it up this time, Ben. Good measure—the Inspectors have their eye on us."*

'The Honest Potboy' from *Punch* (16 March 1867).

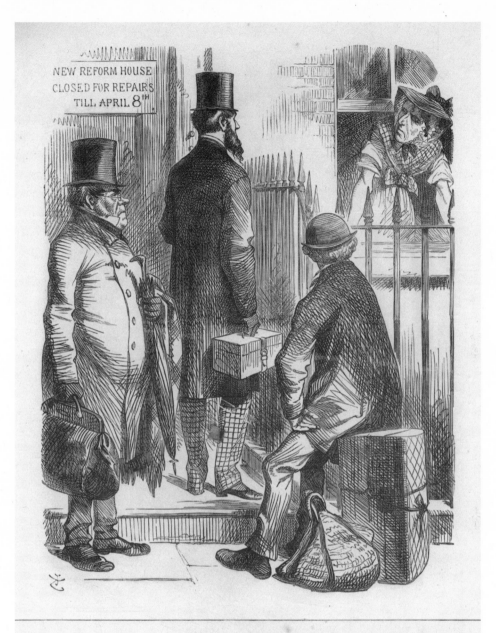

THE "IRREPRESSIBLE LODGER."

Mrs. Dizzy (The Charwoman). "*Well, all I can say is—after the* Eighth of April *I dessay we may be able to accommodate the lot of yer.*"

'The "Irrepressible Lodger"' from *Punch* (6 April 1867).

EXTREMES *MUST* MEET; OR, A BIT OF PRACTICAL SCIENCE.

PROF. D—R—I. "*But you see, to complete the circle, positive and negative* MUST *join hands.*"

'Extremes *Must* Meet; or, A Bit of Practical Science' from *Punch* (13 April 1867).

THE DERBY, 1867. DIZZY WINS WITH "REFORM BILL."

Mr. Punch. "*Don't be too sure; wait till he's* weighed."

'The Derby, 1867. Dizzy Wins with "Reform Bill"' from *Punch* (25 May 1867).

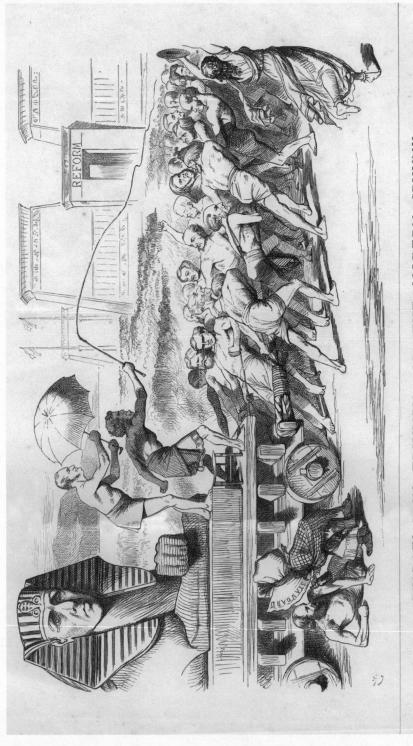

D'ISRAEL-I IN TRIUMPH; OR, THE MODERN SPHYNX.

[*Suggested by* Mr. Poynter's *admirable Picture of " Israel in Egypt."*]

'D'Israel-i in Triumph; or, The Modern Sphynx' from *Punch* (15 June 1867).

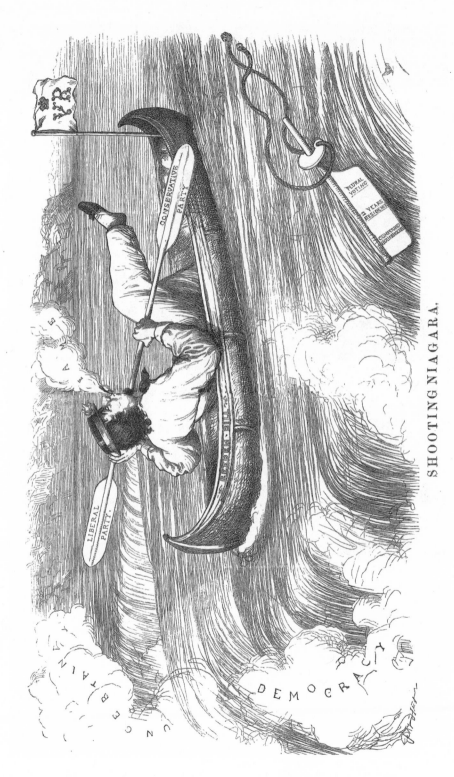

SHOOTING NIAGARA.

'Shooting Niagara' from *Fun* (12 Oct 1867), NS, 6, pp. 50-1.

THE POLITICAL EGG-DANCE.

'The Political Egg-Dance' from *Punch* (29 June 1867).

FAGIN'S POLITICAL SCHOOL.

*" Now, mark this; because these are things which you may not have heard in any speech which has been made in the city of Edinburgh. (Laughter and cheers.) I had—if it be not arrogant to use such a phrase—*TO EDUCATE OUR PARTY. *It is a large party, and requires its attention to be called to questions of this kind with some pressure. I had to prepare the mind of Parliament and the country on this question of Reform."*—MR. DISRAELI'S Speech at the Edinburgh Banquet.

'Fagin's Political School' from *Punch* (9 November 1867).

BENJAMIN DISRAELI LETTERS: 1865–1867

ORIGINAL: QUA 435
EDITORIAL COMMENT: Hughenden paper.

Jany 3 1865

Mr Disraeli presents his Compliments to Dr Hunt,[1] & thanks him for the copy of Professor Vogt's "Lectures on Man", wh: Dr Hunt has had / the great courtesy to forward to Mr Disraeli.

The translation appears to be masterly.

However contrary the conclusions, at wh: the Professor, & Mr Disraeli, have arrived on the main subject, all must admit, that it is one of paramount, & eternal, interest.[2]

ORIGINAL: H R/I/A/181
EDITORIAL COMMENT: Hughenden paper. D has carried over the final word 'me' and the signature block on the first page under the addressee line. *Sic*: sister.

Philip Rose Esqr   Jany 3 1865
My dear Rose,

I enclose a letter just received from the sister of Coulton.[1]

Coulton was a powerful political writer, a true man of letters, & of signal integrity. He was not a / hireling, but wrote from conviction, & was always animated by a high sense of duty. He died in harness, writing the best articles in the "Press" newspaper, wh:, had he lived, would, I think, have been established / as a powerful organ.

It is a case for party interposition.

I wish you would ask Colonel Talbot to place the matter before Lord Derby,[2] as intimated in the enclosed; & afterwards we might take / other steps, &, I hope, efficient ones.

I enclose another letter from a very different writer to the high-minded Coulton. Your name & some of our political friends are mentioned in it as having helped the applicant. I cannot communicate with Ld Clarendon's Mr Birch,[3] but, if he has

---

1 Ethnologist James Hunt (1833-1869), a speech therapist and the author of *Treatise on Stammering* (1854) and *Manual of the Philosophy of Voice and Speech* (1859), was founder (1863) and first president (1863-7) of the Anthropological Society.

2 Hunt had edited *Lectures on Man: his Place in Creation and in the History of the Earth* (1864), the widely read translation of *Vorlesungen über den Menschen, seine Stellung in der Schöpfung und in der Geschichte der Erde* (1863), by German-born Swiss naturalist and physician August Christoph Carl Vogt (1817-1895), a work supporting evolution to which Darwin would refer in his *Descent of Man* (1871). D had famously aired his views on evolution on 25 November 1864 in his 'apes and angels' speech at Oxford: 'I repudiate with indignation and abhorrence these new-fangled theories.' See VIII **3970**n1.

---

1 Sophia Coulton, sister-in-law of David Coulton, former editor of the *Press*, had tried to obtain financial support for his widow since his death in 1857 (see VIII **3607**n1). See n5.

2 For lieut-col Talbot, Derby's private secretary and son-in-law, see VI **2355n2**.

3 For Lord Clarendon and James Birch, editor of the *World*, see V **2178**n4. Clarendon's subsidy to Birch had included £1,700 from secret service funds (eventually repaid), a disclosure that damaged Clarendon's reputation. See A. Aspinall 'The Use of Irish Secret Service Money in Subsidizing the Irish Press' *English Historical Review* 56: 224 (Oct 1941) 639-46 and David F. Krein 'Birth Dates Matter: Generational Voting

any claim on us, & you think I ought to acknowledge it, you may send him a trifle from / me.[4]

Yours sincerely | D.[5]

3981

TO: ARTHUR VERNON   Hughenden [Thursday] 5 January 1865
ORIGINAL: VRS [2]
COVER: Mr Vernon Junr | Land Agent | High Wycomb. | *B Disraeli*
EDITORIAL COMMENT: *Sic*: Wycomb [*cover*].

Mr Vernon Junr.   Hughenden. Jan 5 | :65
Dear Sir,
I conclude, of course, that nothing has been done, or, at least, nothing material, in the matter of Lovett,[1] & that affairs will remain untouched until yr father returns[.] I / merely write this to say, that from something, that has transpired here, I shd. wish to have further consultation with yr. father before any action is taken. Don't trouble him about / this now, as I wish him not to be disturbed while away,[2] and there is no haste, as I shall be here for, at least, a fortnight more.

Yrs ffly | D.

3982

TO: PHILIP ROSE   Hughenden [Tuesday 10?] January 1865
ORIGINAL: H R/I/A/182
EDITORIAL COMMENT: Hughenden paper imprinted 'MAD'. *Dating*: Although the second digit in the date is overwritten and illegible, see n2.

Private   Jany. 1[0?]. 1865
Phil: Rose | Esqr

in the British House of Commons, 1841-1859' *Journal of The Historical Society* 3: 3-4 (Summer/Fall 2003) 373-402.
4 Rose would reply on 5 January, agreeing with D's assessment of Coulton's character and elaborating on Birch: 'He was passed on to me by Lord Malmesbury when he was in office and the acquaintance thus commenced was renewed recently under painful circumstances. He is in an advanced state of Consumption and I had him treated at the [Brompton] Hospital, and have several times relieved him. In doing so I merely looked upon him as a man of letters reduced to a pitiable state of destitution. I know nothing of his party claims beyond his having written in our favor in the Sunday Times. As the poor creature is starving and dying I have taken upon myself to act upon your kind authority and have sent him £5 from you.' Birch would write to D on 9 January acknowledging receipt of the money, calling Rose 'an instrument of Providence' and D 'a Consummate statesman'. H R/I/B/99a; H B/XX/A/166.
5 Sophia Coulton on 28 February would thank D for '£20 received through the medium of Mr Rose ... It relieved us from immediate and pressing difficulties and enabled us to procure many things requisite for two members of our family ... suffering from sickness.' She would write to D on 9 September, 'under our present most urgent distress', reminding D that the £20 had been 'accompanied by the promise that further assistance would be rendered to it.' On 20 December 1866 she would thank D 'for the great benefit you have conferred on Mrs Coulton and her children'. H B/XXI/C/469-70; H R/II/G/57.

---

1 D had received a long letter, dated 29 December 1864, from his steward, George Vernon, urging D to fire Lovett, the Hughenden woodman, for being 'very abusive' to one Mr Cartwright and four other gentlemen who had been rabbit-hunting on D's estate. Claiming to act per D's instructions, Lovett had called on Vernon's son Arthur to draw up 'Notices not to Trespass'; these were served on Cartwright's friends by a police constable and resulted in 'considerable irritation'. Vernon Sr reminded D that D had given Cartwright (but not his friends) permission for 'one day's Rabbit shooting in the Woods.' H A/V/G/20.
2 George Vernon's doctor had recommended a short recuperative holiday to alleviate the 'giddiness or nervousness', and ensuing weakness, brought about by a recent illness. H A/V/G/20.

My dear Rose,

1000 thanks! Be pleased to operate for me immediately.

I have large balances at this moment & shall have / for a month or six weeks. Let me know what you want. I can send you an order for 3 or 4000£.[1]

I shall be in town, about the 20th, for / a few days, on our way to Burghley, where we shall remain until the 28th, & then settle at G. Gate.[2]

I hope this may prove a good year / for all of us, & with my best wishes for you & yours, believe me,

Ever, | D.

TO: FREDERICK GEORGE LEE   Hughenden [Tuesday] 10 January 1865   3983
ORIGINAL: MCG [1]
EDITORIAL COMMENT: Hughenden paper imprinted 'MAD'.

The | Rev: F.G. Lee[1] | a.m.   Jany 10 1865

Reverend Sir,

I am obliged to you for yr courtesy in sending me the current number of the "Union Review".[2] I have / read it with interest, & hope, & must believe, that a publication, conducted with such marked ability, will meet with success, & / effect much good.

faithfully yours, | *B. Disraeli*

---

1 Rose was currently making investments for D. See **3985**.

2 Lady Exeter had written to MA on 10 January 1865 that she was looking forward to seeing the DS at Burghley House on the 25th. The DS would leave Hughenden on 20 January for Grosvenor Gate and, from there, on the 25th for Burghley House, Stamford (to join Lord and Lady Exeter's guests), returning to Grosvenor Gate on the 28th for the season. H D/III/C/733; MP (6 Feb 1865); H acc.

---

1 Anglican theologian Frederick George Lee (1832-1902) was co-founder, with lay Roman Catholic Ambrose Phillipps de Lisle (1809-1878), of the Association for the Promotion of the Unity of Christendom (APUC) (1857-69), which fostered the reuniting of the churches of Rome, England and Russia. In 1870, his research for *The Validity of the Holy Orders of the Church of England maintained and vindicated* would lead him to doubt the validity of Anglican orders. He would be received into the Roman Catholic Church on 11 December 1901. Frederick George Lee Collection, MS no. 212, Pitts Theology Library Archives and Manuscripts Department, Emory University. See **4003**.

2 The APUC was closely associated with the *Union Newspaper*, founded by Lee in December 1856, renamed the *Union Review: A Magazine of Catholic Literature and Art* in 1863 and published monthly. Writing from London on 3 January, Lee had sent D 'the current No. of' the *Union Review* with a letter 'calling [D's] attention to Articles I, IV, and VI'. H B/II/124. Volume III (Jan to Dec 1865) contains Articles I, 'On Doctrinal Developments in the Church' (1-24); IV, 'Early Sentimental Convertism' (52-68), about the fourth-century controversy between Christianity and Judaism, in which the Jews 'appealed to the region of sentiment, and not to that of reflection' and therefore failed to prevail; and VI, 'Mr. Disraeli's Manifesto' (80-7), *ie*, D's 'apes and angels' speech of 25 November 1864 as printed in *The Standard* of 26 November 1864. It praised D as 'a remarkable theoretical politician', drawing attention to the forthcoming publication of D's speech 'as a separate pamphlet' (see **3995**n1) and quoting views about it from the *Daily News*, *Globe*, *Telegraph*, *Star*, *Guardian*, *Churchman* and *Church Times*. It concluded by forecasting that D's speech, 'in towns and cities, in boroughs and counties ... will tend to form a consistent and energetic party, resolved ... to hand down to future generations intact that which has proved so signal a blessing to so many in the past.'

3984 TO: LEOPOLD DE ROTHSCHILD   Hughenden [Tuesday] 10 January 1865

ORIGINAL: H H/LIFE

EDITORIAL COMMENT: From a copy in another hand on paper imprinted 'Ascott Wing, Leighton Buzzard.'

Leopold de Rothschild Esq.   Hughenden Manor | January 10th 1865.

My dear Leopold,

I thought my letter to your father opened your collection very appropriately.[1] A great many changes have happened since it was written, but at any rate, my feelings towards you are the same.[2]

Yours sincerely | *B. Disraeli.*

3985 TO: PHILIP ROSE   Hughenden, Sunday 15 January 1865

ORIGINAL: H R/I/A/183.

Philip Rose | Esq   Hughenden. | Sunday. Jan 15. 65

My dear Rose –

Not hearing from you, I have thought it best to return you the paper signed, tho' it has an awkward mem: on the back,[1] & / an order on L & W.[2] for £2500.

If the paper be inadmissible in consequence of yr confidential mem:, I authorise you to sign another one, to the same effect, for / me – & with 1000 thanks for all the trouble you always take for me, believe me,

Yrs ever, | D.[3]

3986 TO: JULIANA, BARONESS MAYER DE ROTHSCHILD   Hughenden [Thursday] 19 January 1865

ORIGINAL: ROSE [1]

EDITORIAL COMMENT: Hughenden paper imprinted 'MAD'. *Sic*: Wycomb; lossed.

Jany 19 1865

Dear Baroness,

We met the Paté at Wycomb, on our way to Gunnersbury,[1] & I asked leave to acknowledge its arrival, as I principally profit by its delicious contents. I must indeed, have been a / great blunderer to have omitted so pleasing an office, & I can't admit

---

1 Possibly D's first extant letter to Lionel de Rothschild, congratulating him on the birth of his fifth (and last) child, Leopold: 'I hope he will prove worthy of his pure and sacred race' (IV **1451**&n1). Leopold, now nineteen, may have begun collecting letters to his father from notable correspondents.

2 For the Rothschild family, the most significant of the 'many changes' D helped effect had been the passing of the Oath of Abjuration Bill (1858), thanks to which Lionel finally took his seat in the House on 26 July 1858. See VII **3110**n1, **3112**n1 and VIII app VI, *The Progress of Jewish Emancipation Since 1829*, a pamphlet co-written by D and Lionel de Rothschild dated '15 January 1848'.

---

1 Rose's 'paper' has not been found.

2 London and Westminster Bank Ltd.

3 For a possible link to ongoing negotiations for the sale of SBW's former home, Mount Braddon, see **3996**nn3-5.

---

1 The DS had left for Gunnersbury Park on 7 January and returned to Hughenden on the 9th. H acc.

I did so, but I will not quarrel with the circumstances, wh: permit me the gratification of writing / to you again.

I wish you had told us you were quite well: still more, that we might have ocular evidence of yr improvement, but yr handwriting has lossed none of its grace & energy, wh: is / a good sign. We are just going to town, en route to Burghley, & when that visit is over, duty will keep us to G Gate, ↑where I hope we may see you.↓

Mary Anne unites with me in kindest regards to yrself, & the Baron & yr daughter.[2]

Ever yrs | D.

TO: SIR HENRY STRACEY   [London, Tuesday] 31 January 1865   3987
ORIGINAL: PS 805
PUBLICATION HISTORY: Christie's catalogue (4 Nov 1981) item 44, described as 'A.L.S. ... 8vo ... to Sir Henry Stracey, sometime M.P. for Norwich ... 31 January 1865'.

[thanking Sir Henry for a New Year cygnet, he muses] The Swan is the emblem of the County of Buckingham,[1] & I often think your magnificent annual offering is an auspicious omen,[2] that I shall preserve my seat[3]

TO: [WILLIAM?] LESLIE   Grosvenor Gate [early February 1865]   3988
ORIGINAL: H B/XIII/138b
EDITORIAL COMMENT: A printed invitation completed in D's hand. *Dating*: by context; see n2.

[Mr. Disraeli requests the honor of] Mr. Leslie's[1] [company at dinner on] Saturday Feby. eighteen[2] [at] 7½ [o'Clock.]

Grosvenor Gate.   *An early answer will oblige*[.]

TO: [LORD] HENRY [LENNOX]   Grosvenor Gate   3989
                 [Saturday] 4 February 1865
ORIGINAL: MOPSIK [136]
EDITORIAL COMMENT: Grosvenor Gate paper.

            Feb 4 1865

---

2 The Rothschilds' only child, Hannah (1851-1890), upon her father's death in 1874, would inherit Mentmore and become the wealthiest single woman in Britain. She would marry Archibald Philip Primrose, 5th Earl of Rosebery, in 1878.

---

1 One of the white swans on the Bucks coat of arms is in chains, denoting that the swan is bound to the king.
2 D had thanked Stracey on 31 January 1862 for 'a most graceful, present' (presumably a cygnet). VIII **3659**.
3 D would be re-elected MP for Bucks on 13 July. McCalmont.

---

1 Probably William Leslie (1814-1880), MP (C) for Aberdeenshire 1861-6.
2 Leslie is absent from guest lists in MA's account books and in *BH*, which would report the DS' Saturday 18 February 1865 'Parliamentary dinner' as having included Lords Salisbury, Stanhope, Orford and Courtenay, George Boyle, Alexander Baring, Sir Brook Bridges, Sir Thomas Bateson, Sir Henry Stracey, Sir Henry Edwards, Henry Surtees, Davenport Bromley, Morgan Treherne, John Cobbold, Joshua Bond, Henry Paull and Robert Brooks. *BH* (25 Feb 1865).

My dear Henry,[1]
I will be at the Carlton today, about five o'ck.
Yrs ever | D.

3990 TO: PHILIP ROSE   Grosvenor Gate [Saturday] 4 February 1865
ORIGINAL: H R/I/A/184
EDITORIAL COMMENT: Grosvenor Gate paper.

Feb 4 1865

My dear Rose,
This[1] requires an answer, but I can't give it, for I can't annex an idea to it.
Yrs ever | D.

3991 TO: MARY ANNE DISRAELI   House of Commons [1865?]
ORIGINAL: H A/I/A/322
EDITORIAL COMMENT: *Dating*: Although docketed '1865', this note could have been written at any time Parliament was in session. In 1865, it met from 7 February to 6 July.

In my seat | H of Comm: | ½ pt. 7 o'ck

My dearest –
Will you kindly send me an easy pair of boots, my feet, especially my right one, are so much drawn. Let them be neatly packed up.[1]
Your own, | D.

3992 TO: LORD STANHOPE   British Museum [Tuesday] 28 February 1865
ORIGINAL: KCR Stanhope MSS 690(6)2.

Brit: Museum | Feby. 28. 1865

The | Earl Stanhope
My dear Lord,
We had a Building Committee here this morning, & being in the chair,[1] Walpole, Duke of Somerset, & Dundas,[2] wished / me to express to you, their strong opinion, that there shd. be joint action in the two houses on the subject of the Parliamentary petition.

---

1 Presumably Lord Henry Gordon-Lennox.

---

1 Possibly a letter to D of this day (4th) from Joseph Lovegrove stating that he had received Mr Hicks's note (sent by D) and suggesting D offer 'your house No. 5 ... for Sale by *Public* Auction under restrictive Conditions – as for Title &c – The Deeds being with Mr. Rose. I have written him enclosing the Letter and asking him to furnish Mr. Hickes [*sic*] with the extract he asks ànd suggesting as to a Sale as above.' H D/II/B/334.

---

1 D suffered from chronic gout (metabolic arthritis). For a similar request, see **4633**.

---

1 For D's election in 1863 as a trustee of the British Museum, see VIII **3801**&n1.
2 Sir David Dundas (1799-1877), a barrister (Inner Temple 1823), QC 1840, MP (L) for Sutherland 1840-52, 1861-7, sol-gen 1846-8, judge-advocate-general 1849-52, PC 1849 and a trustee of the British Museum 1861-7.

Their attention had been called to yr. notice in / the Lords. Accordingly, Walpole will give notice to day of his intention to present the petition in the Commons on Thursday. But we would, with deference, represent to you our opinion, that it would not be expedient, that you / should accompany the presentation in the Lords with any observations or enquiry, until you had conferred with Mr Walpole generally on the matter, & we co[ul]d contemplate more clearly, than we do at present, the time when the petition can be brought / before the consideration of the Commons.[3]

Perhaps I may have the opportunity of seeing yr Lordship in the Ho: of Lords, but if I fail, I have written this rough note, wh: / I trust you will excuse. It is of the last importance, that the effect of our movement shd. not be diminished by any premature exposition.[4]

Yours sincerely, | *B. Disraeli*

---

to: **MARY ANNE DISRAELI**　　　　　　　[London, Friday 10 March 1865] **3993**
original: H A/I/A/318
editorial comment: Docketed by ma: '1865 March 10th Friday'. *Dating*: by context; see n1.

1½ [*oversize*]
　D.[1]

---

to: **WILLIAM W.F. DICK**　　　　Grosvenor Gate, Sunday 12 March 1865 **3994**
original: brn [37]
editorial comment: Grosvenor Gate paper imprinted 'mad'.

W.F. Dick Esqr[1] | M.P.　　　　　　　　　　　　　　Sunday | Mar: 12 1865
Dear Dick,
I am sorry, that I missed you yesterday, particularly as I cannot have the pleasure of receiving you today.

---

3 In the Lords on Thursday 2 March, a 'Petition of Trustees of the British Museum' and a notice of a motion on that subject would be presented by Stanhope, who would complain that the present building was inadequate and request immediate steps to procure additional space. Many trustees wanted simultaneous discussions in the two Houses. 'The forms of the House of Commons' would prevent Walpole from giving any explanation; he could only present the petition in the usual form and give notice of a future motion. Stanhope would adopt a similar course and would lay the petition on the table. In the Lords on 13 March he would withdraw his motion, the trustees having been recently informed that the Government was preparing a plan for more space; meanwhile in the Commons Walpole decided to postpone his motion, the chancellor of the exchequer (Gladstone) stating that the Government would make a proposal once it received the result of an inquiry by the trustees regarding 'certain questions of internal arrangement in any new building which might be required'. *Hansard* clxxvii cols 956-7, 1530, 1534-5. Construction on a new wing would begin only in 1879; it would open in 1882.

4 Stanhope would reply on 1 March that after conferring with Walpole the previous night they had agreed to speak on the same day; Stanhope had urged him to 'fix some early day ... since otherwise the wind will be taken out of our sails by Mr. [William Henry] Gregory who has already put upon the paper a Notice of Motion referring to the same subject.' kcr Stanhope mss 690(6).

1 The House on 9 March had adjourned at 1:30 *am* on the 10th. *Hansard* clxxvii col 1461.

1 For Dick's name change (from Hume), see vii **2931**n1.

Tomorrow, I am going to Court,[2] & on Tuesday, / I have an engagement with Ld Derby at 12 o'ck: but on any day afterwards, I am at yr service.

You can settle in the House, without troubling yourself to write. /

Yrs sincerely, | D.

3995 TO: FREDERICK LYGON   Grosvenor Gate [Sunday] 19 March 1865
ORIGINAL: BCP [20]; now BL ADD MS 61892
EDITORIAL COMMENT: Grosvenor Gate paper.

Hon: F. Lygon | M.P.   Mar 19 1865

Mon tres cher,

I found today the "missing link"! It is in the "Press", a literal reprint from the "Times".

The Editor of the "Press" has attempted to break the original report into / paragraphs, but with a total absence of discrimination. This requires attention.[1]

I have noted in pencil one or two misprints, as I hastily read it.

Alter anything as you like, & always | believe me | Yours, | D.

3996 TO: LORD BEAUCHAMP   Grosvenor Gate [Monday] 20 March 1865
ORIGINAL: BCP [21]; now BL ADD MS 61892
EDITORIAL COMMENT: Grosvenor Gate paper. *Sic*: a less one.

Private   Mar 20 1865

The | Earl Beauchamp

My dear Beauchamp,

Your letter was most encouraging.[1] I have always been sanguine about you, trusting to yr capital constitution: all that you require is prudence, but that virtue in a large quantity.

The climate of London has / been awful since your departure: I never knew it so cold, & stern, & dark, & cutting.[2]

---

2 The DS would attend the Queen's second Court at Buckingham Palace on Monday 13 March. *MP* (14 Mar 1865); *BH* (18 Mar 1865).

---

1 Lygon was editing for republication five of D's ecclesiastical speeches previously published in *The Times*; see VIII **3973**&n5. Darwin's term 'missing link' in his *Origin of Species* (1859) refers to the discontinuity in the fossil record as evidence for the evolutionary descent of humans from apes. Evidently in the proofs the text of D's speech had been inexplicably paragraphed, and D has found the model the typesetter used. See also **4000** and **4012**.

---

1 Henry Lygon, 5th Earl Beauchamp, had written to D on 17 March from the Royal Hotel, Torquay: 'The climate here suits me better than any I have experienced elsewhere & I have made a decided improvement since we last met.' Upon his return from Torquay on 20 March, Beauchamp's brother Frederick Lygon informed D that 'Torquay has done wonders for my brother's appetite & he is in better spirits than I have seen him for months'. H B/XXI/L/431; XX/LN/32.

2 London weather went from 35 degrees Fahrenheit and 'overcast (dull)' on 16 March down to 27 degrees, with an increase in 'extreme force' winds, on 21 March. From 18 to 25 March there were cold winds from the east 'sometimes approaching the force of a hurricane, and frost during the nights'. *The Times* (17, 22 Mar 1865); *BH* (25 Mar 1865).

If you like to buy Mt. Braddon, you may fix the price. The only condition I make is, that the sum shall be *between ourselves*. My reason: that I have refused a good offer, / & don't want to be laughed at for taking a less one. A weakness perhaps, but still a feeling.[3]

I was advised by my agents to ask 3000 guineas, & take £3000. I was offered immediately by a Mr Davis £2500, free from commission, wh: was equal to £2600; & I refused it.[4] He is watching his opportunity & boasts, that he will now obtain / it for much less. It is a bore to me, because I naturally wish to have the money, & it is an annual expense,[5] & I have no confidence in my agents.

If you look at the Emperors book, read *the last sentence* of the volume.[6] It is worth all the money;[7] & is the secret of his character & career.

Ever thine, | D.[8]

---

3 Beauchamp (n1) had looked at Mount Braddon (former home of sbw), 'a nice little spot, but like most properties that come to one wants money laid out on it to do it justice'.

4 On 18 December 1863 J.W. Murray, an employee of house agent John C. Stark, had written William Lovell regarding an offer of £2,500 for Mount Braddon made 'some time ago' by a 'Rev. W.B. Davies' [*sic*], which was turned down 'because Mr Disraeli thought it might be improved.' Murray had written to MA on 20 January 1864 regretting that £2,500 was not accepted, 'as we fear so much will not be offered again.' Replying to a letter from D (not found) on 1 April 1865, Stark would ask if D would accept 'from our customer a direct offer of £2,500'. Lovell on 12 April would draw D's attention to a 'memorandum at the foot of the agreement' regarding the terms of the sale: '"2000 down and the remaining £500. in 3 months from this date [*4 April*] with interest at £5 per cent,"' the £500 and interest to be secured by 'a promissory note of Dr Stuart'. Receiving no reply, Lovell would write D on 17 April about 'the agreement with Dr Stuart for the sale of Mount Braddon' and ask again if D wished to have Stuart deposit 'the lease and the purchase deed with you as an additional security'. H A/V/G/172a, 157, 176-8. Weston Brocklesby Davis, of The Braddons, Torquay, BA 1851 and MA 1854 St John's College, Cambridge, deacon 1856, priest 1858, had been Senior Curate of St Mary Magdalene, Torquay, in 1856. *Clergy List* (1860).

5 Mount Braddon was plagued with numerous problems. Murray on 8 December 1863 had informed D that thieves had stolen a Bible, a clock and 'five small maltese figures'. D had received a 10 March 1864 bill for £1.5.9 for 'soldering leaks in Roof' and 'repg. the sash cords in conservatory'. On 13 June, Stark had cautioned D that 'The State of the House both internally and externally is much against' accepting a £1,600 offer, suggesting the house be 'Coloured and painted in some parts' to give it 'a very different aspect'. On 23 June he had recommended 'regraining the Drawing Room'. On 26 October, he had posted a notice offering a £2 reward for information about those 'guilty of cutting down and otherwise damaging trees & shrubs in the lawn of Mount Braddon House'. H A/V/G/151, 180aa, 166, 167, 170.

6 Napoleon III had written a two-volume *Histoire de Jules César* (Paris: Plon 1865-6). *The Times* (4 Feb 1865) had announced that vol I 'will be ready in about three weeks' and *MP* (6 Mar 1865) had carried a lengthy review of the book. A *Times* (17 Jan 1865) notice had stated that the Emperor would be overseeing the forthcoming English translation (Cassell, Petter & Galpin 1865). The last sentence of vol I reads: 'Certes César avait foi dans sa destinée et confiance dans son génie; mais la foi est un instinct, non un calcul, et le génie pressent l'avenir sans en deviner la marche mystérieuse.' This would be translated as: 'Certainly, Caesar had faith in his destiny, and confidence in his genius; but faith is an instinct, not a calculation, and genius foresees the future without understanding its mysterious progress.' *Histoire de Jules César* (New York 1865) 391; *History of Julius Caesar* (New York 1866) 463.

7 Vol I of the French edition cost '10s.6d.' *The Times* (4 Feb 1865).

8 Beauchamp would reply on 22 March: 'I have been a wanderer on the face of the earth this year not solely on account of my health but also because my own house is in process of restoration. I hope in the future to be able to live at home, & consequently should not buy a place till I find that my hopes in this respect were illusory. If I thought myself so much of an invalid as to be obliged to come here every year I should accept yr offer, but I am sanguine enough about myself to think it will not be necessary.' H B/XXI/L/432.

3997 TO: LORD LONSDALE   Grosvenor Gate [Friday] 24 March 1865

ORIGINAL: PS 810

PUBLICATION HISTORY: John Wilson Autograph Letters and Historical Documents (1980), described as 'Autograph Letter Signed ('D') to [William Lowther, 2nd Earl of] Lonsdale ... 2 pages 8vo; Grosvenor Gate, 24 March 1865.'

[explaining that Disraeli was about to leave London for Hughenden, but would be returning on the 1st of April] & shall be very glad to talk over the matter in question with you. I don't think that it comes on before the 8th April[1]

3998 TO: MARY ANNE DISRAELI   [House of Commons?, Tuesday 4 April 1865]

ORIGINAL: H A/I/A/319

EDITORIAL COMMENT: Docketed by MA: 'April 4th 1865'.

¼ to 4

My dearest

S. comes & is evidently *most* delighted at being asked.[1]

Yr own | D

3999 TO: MARY ANNE DISRAELI   [House of Commons, Thursday 6 April 1865]

ORIGINAL: H A/I/A/323, 323a

COVER: Mrs Disraeli

EDITORIAL COMMENT: Cover docketed by MA: '1865 March or April'. *Dating*: by context; see n1.

¼ to 9

My dearest

I find things here in great & serious confusion on both sides, & must remain, which I greatly regret. Pray / tell the Baron & Baroness how very sorry, & how very disappointed, I am.[1]

Yrs | D

4000 TO: FREDERICK LYGON   Grosvenor Gate [Tuesday] 11 April 1865

ORIGINAL: BCP [22]; NOW BL ADD MS 61892

EDITORIAL COMMENT: Grosvenor Gate paper. *Sic*: checque.

Hon: Fred. Lygon | M.P.   April 11 1865

---

1 Saturday 8 April 1865 was the first day of Easter recess. For 'the matter in question', see **4017**&n1.

---

1 Lord Stanley, who often signed himself 'S.', was among the dinner guests at Grosvenor Gate on 7 April 1865, along with Count Apponyi (Austrian ambassador), Earl and Countess Percy, Earl of Malmesbury, Earl Beauchamp, Countess of Gifford, Lord Naas, Lord and Lady Robert Cecil, General and Mrs Forester, Mrs Duncombe, Baron Mayer de Rothschild, and Col and Mrs Dudley Carleton. *BH* (15 Apr 1865).

---

1 In the period designated by MA (see ec), the Mayer de Rothschilds held a dinner party at their house in Piccadilly on 6 April 1865. *MP* (7 Apr 1865). On that night, in committee of supply, there was a heated debate on 'Defences of Canada', the House adjourning at 1:30 *am* on the 7th. *Hansard* CLXXVIII cols 793-867.

Cher Camarade!

We are now going to Hughenden,[1] where you can direct to me for the next fort-night[.]

I approve of all yr corrections & / plans.[2]

I want to do something for "Church Times",[3] & shd. like my contribution to be in the shape of advertising yr book; but I will not forward / them a checque till I hear you approve.

Yrs ever | D.

TO: LADY DOROTHY NEVILL   Hughenden [Monday] 17 April 1865 4001
ORIGINAL: EJM [22]
PUBLICATION HISTORY: *Anglo-Saxon Review* IV (1901) 145; Ralph Nevill ed *Leaves from the Note-Books of Lady Dorothy Nevill* (1907) 42, with first paragraph missing and slight variations in punctuation
EDITORIAL COMMENT: Hughenden paper.

April 17 1865

Dear Dorothy,

We were very much obliged to you for your strawberries[1] & for yr letter, & are always for anything, wh: reminds us of one we love so much.

We came down here with our own horses; the first time / for many years. How delightful after Railroads! We baited at Gerrards X, twenty miles from town, & then strolled into Bulstrode Park to see the new house the Duke of Somerset is building in that long neglected, but enchanting, spot. / There, tho' they told us we shd. find nobody but the clerk of the works, we found the Duke & Duchess, who had come down for a couple of hours by rail from Slough, & so they lionised us over all their new creation, wh: is a happy & successful one: a Tudor / pile, very seemly & convenient, & built amid the old pleasaunce, wh: I described, thirty years ago, in "Henrietta Temple", for Bulstrode, then mansionless & deserted, was the origin of

---

1 The DS were at Hughenden 11-26 April. H acc.

2 Lygon on 5 April had sent D proofs of the first sheet of D's ecclesiastical speeches (see **3995**&n1). In his accompanying letter, he had entitled his selection 'Church and King'; this would become *"Church and Queen": five speeches delivered by the Rt. Hon. B. Disraeli, M.P. 1860-1864* (see VIII **3973**n5). 'I have ventured to make one or two corrections required by the imperfections of the reports. I have also endeavoured to arrange the paragraphs so as to give effects to your meanings which the monotony of continuous type tends to obscure.' H B/XX/LN/33. For D's assessment of the book, see **4012**.

3 *Church Times*, founded in 1863 and published by G.J. Palmer & Sons Ltd until 1989, remains the leading Anglican weekly newspaper. It is not listed under D's 'Contributions to newspapers and periodicals' in Stewart *Writings*.

---

1 Lady Dorothy, in a letter to MA on 'Monday' (docketed in another hand 'April 1865'), had promised D some strawberries after Easter (16 April 1865). H D/III/C/1527. See also VII **3083**&n2, VIII **3468**&n1, **3573** and **3919**&n1.

Armine.[2] Excuse this egotism, the characteristic of scribblers, even when they have left off work.

Adieu! dear Dorothy, | D.

4002 TO: MARY ANNE DISRAELI　　　　[House of Commons?, Monday 1 May 1865]
ORIGINAL: H A/I/A/320
EDITORIAL COMMENT: Docketed by MA on the first page: '1865. May 1st'. *Sic*: this morning. *Dating*: by context; see n1.

My dearest –

I never spoke more to my satisfaction, & sate down with great cheering;[1] but I have not heard a single observation from a single person.

Sir George / Grey did very poorly,[2] & I hear that in the House of Lords, *both* speakers quite failed.[3]

I think I may be rather late – 12 o'ck: or so.

Admiral Fitzroy, the / controller of the Storms, cut his throat this morning in a bath,[4] & Mr Prescott, the banker, & head of a great city firm, has just committed suicide,[5] but how I know not.

Your affec | D.

---

2 For D's 1863 visit to Bulstrode Park at Gerrards Cross, twelve miles from Hughenden, see VIII **3850**&n2. As the estate passed through various hands the original house at Bulstrode (built 1686) fell into disrepair until the 12th Duke of Somerset had it demolished in 1860 and a new house erected in the existing 'pleasaunce' in 1862. D's description of the 'Tudor pile' (the house is actually in the Gothic Revival style) resonates with echoes of 'Armine Described', Chapter II of D's *Henrietta Temple* (1836): in the 'neglected' grounds of Armine Place, 'a vast Elizabethan pile', there was not 'a single point in the whole pleasaunce where the keenest eye could have detected a limit.'

---

1 D on 1 May 1865 had seconded Sir George Grey's motion for an Address to the Crown expressing the House's 'sorrow and indignation' at the assassination of Abraham Lincoln on 14 April. *Hansard* CLXXVIII cols 1245-7. *The Times* (2 May 1865) and *BH* (6 May 1865) would report 'Loud cheers'.
2 Following his statement that the Government maintained 'a strict and impartial neutrality' regarding the Civil War, Grey's remark that 'the sympathies of the majority of the people of this country have been with the North' drew '[*Cries of* "No, no!" *and* "Hear, hear!"]'. *Hansard* CLXXVIII cols 1242-3. *The Times* would report that, aside from that 'slight error', the speech was in 'admirable taste' – Grey announced that the Queen had written a letter to Mrs Lincoln conveying the heartfelt sympathy of one widow to another – and concluded to 'Loud cheers'. The language of D's speech would be termed 'carefully and elegantly chosen', D closing with the hope that the 'protracted and perilous struggle' would give way to a renewed 'career of power and prosperity'. *The Times* (2 May 1865); *Hansard* CLXXVIII col 1246.
3 The parallel motion in the Lords on this day (1 May) was moved by Russell and seconded by Derby. *The Times* would bemoan Russell's 'cold and dry manner' as ill suited to the solemn occasion and castigate the 'topics of Lord Derby's speech [as] ill-chosen, the language poor, and the delivery hurried and slovenly ... [reaching] the climax of indiscretion and bad taste when he said that the conduct of the South, if it had authorized this assassination, would have been "worse than a crime – that is, a blunder"', a remark of 'unpardonable levity'. Derby's actual phrase had been 'a gross blunder'. *The Times* (2 May 1865); *Hansard* CLXXVIII cols 1219-28.
4 Vice-Admiral Robert Fitzroy (1805-1865), chief meteorologist for the board of trade, a pioneer in weather forecasting and captain of the *Beagle* during Darwin's second voyage (1831-6), had 'cut his throat' on the morning of Sunday 30 April. *The Times* (2 May 1865).
5 William George Prescott (1800-1865), wealthy London banker and head of Prescott, Grote, Cave & Co., had 'destroyed himself ... by cutting his throat with a razor' on the morning of Saturday 29 April. *The Times* (2, 3 May 1865).

ORIGINAL: MTL [2]
EDITORIAL COMMENT: Grosvenor Gate paper.

May 2 1865

Mr Disraeli, with his Compliments to Mr Lee, could receive him on Thursday next at half past two o'ck:; / & will conclude that appointment is convenient to Mr Lee unless he hears to the contrary.

ORIGINAL: ARG [2]
EDITORIAL COMMENT: Grosvenor Gate paper.

May 7 1865

The | Earl of Shaftesbury | K.G.[1]
My dear Lord,
I am very sorry that I am engaged on Friday the 26th Inst:,[2] &, / therefore, cannot have the great honor of dining with you, & meeting the Deputation from / Canada.
    Ever, my dear Lord, | faithfully yours, | B. Disraeli

ORIGINAL: BBK [2]
EDITORIAL COMMENT: Grosvenor Gate paper.

L.O. Bigg Esqr[1]   May 8 1865
Sir,
Thomas Coward, who wishes to be my coachman, refers me to you for his character.[2]
    I would ask, whether, you consider him capable of the post: whether / you believe him honest, strictly sober, & good tempered: and, lastly, for what reason he quitted your service, in wh:, he assures me, he was / employed four years?[3]
    Believe me, Sir, | faithfully yours, | B. Disraeli

1 This is D's first extant letter to Shaftesbury, who on 6 May had invited D for dinner on the 26th to meet the Canadian deputation. On 20 May, the Prince of Wales, on behalf of the Queen, would hold a levée attended by 'the Hon. George Brown, President of the Executive Council of Canada; the Hon. A.T. Galt, Finance Minister of Canada; the Hon. J.A. Macdonald, Attorney-General of Upper-Canada; the Hon. G.E. Cartier, Attorney-General of Lower Canada; Lieutenant-Colonel Bernard, A.D.C., Secretary to the Canadian Delegates'. H B/XXI/S/118; *The Times* (22 May 1865).
2 On the 26th the Ds would attend Lady Derby's reception at St James's Square. MP (27 May 1865).

1 Attorney Lionel Oliver Bigg (d 1870), originally of Bristol, admitted to practice in 1814. *The Times* (5 Dec 1870); *Law List* (1870).
2 Another hand has recorded in MA's account book that Coward entered D's 'service as Coachman May 16th 1865 To have 30£ per Year Wages 2£ per Year Stable utensils oil Compo &c a fortnights wages or a fortnights warning but no Board Wages 12s per week when on Board Wages one suit of Livery a year & one stable suit a great Coat when wanted'. Signed 'T Coward'. Coachman George Stone, according to MA a 'disagreable man but drove well', would leave the Ds' service on 16 May. The average yearly wage for a coachman in 1865 was £40. H acc; Christopher Hibbert *The English: A Social History 1066 to 1945* (1987) 503.
3 Bigg would reply on 10 May that he had found Coward 'capable, Honest, Sober, & well conducted.' H A/ IV/L/26.

4006

TO: LORD ELCHO   Grosvenor Gate [Monday] 8 May 1865
ORIGINAL: SRO [3]
EDITORIAL COMMENT: Grosvenor Gate paper.

Private   May 8 1865

The | Lord Elcho | M.P.

My dear Lord,

Some day, after the debate,[1] I shd. be very glad to confer with you about the en-closed,[2] wh: I return; but I think it / would be very inexpedient even to hint at its suggestions, until the division is taken on your amendment. I will not weary you with the reasons / for this opinion now.

Yours faithfully, | *B. Disraeli*

4007

TO: MARY ANNE DISRAELI   [House of Commons?, Thursday] 11 May 1865
ORIGINAL: H A/I/A/321.

7 o'ck | May 11 1865

My dearest,

I see before me a heavy & anxious night,[1] & frequent divisions[2] – &, therefore, I

---

1 Second reading of MP (L) Edward Baines Jr's Borough Franchise Extension Bill, proposing to extend the vote from £10 to £6 occupiers, had begun on 3 May and resumed on 8 May, when Elcho in a lengthy rebuttal as an amendment moved the previous question, which the next day would be passed, thus defeating the bill. *The Times* would report that members had been asked to decide whether Baines's 'crude proposal', which would 'transfer the power of choosing our Parliamentary representatives from the better to the worse informed classes', was 'worthy of becoming law. The House of Commons decided, and as we think rightly, that it was not' (by a division of 288-214, Elcho and D voting with the majority). *Hansard* CLXXVIII cols 1372-1450, 1613-1709; *The Times* (10 May 1865). D had spoken briefly on 3 May, urging 'renewal of this debate' (col 1446-9), and at length on this day (8th), cautioning that with 'the re-distribution of seats' comes 'the distribution of power' (cols 1691-1705). For a similar comment, see **4013**. For the Borough Franchise Bills of 1861 and 1864, see VIII **3569**n4 and **3921**n2.
2 Elcho's 7 May letter to D had mentioned 'the Resolution I left with you' that 'would do away with all chance of moderate men pledging themselves to specific measures of Reform.' Elcho's draft contained 'a motion for an enquiry' that was 'the necessary complement to the debate & to your speech especially.' H B/XXI/E/120-1. See **4009**&nn1&2.

---

1 In the House on this day (11th) debate on the Union Chargeability Bill would last nearly seven hours, until 11:30 *pm*, when a motion for adjournment (defeated 174-80) led to raucous disorder. Rising for the first time, D deplored the discreditable scene and agreed it was impossible to proceed further, denying charges that attempts to oppose interruption to the debate originated with the Opposition. The House would adjourn at 12:30 *am* on the 12th. Introduced on 20 February, the bill was 'to provide for the better distribution of the charge for the relief of the poor in Unions.' *Hansard* CLXXIX cols 116-73 (D 172-3); CLXXVII col 468. Under the Poor Law Amendment Act (1834), parishes were grouped into unions to share the cost of building workhouses (one per union). Over the years there had been abuses, and the Union Chargeability Act (passed in June 1865), which required rates to be assessed uniformly, would force wealthier parishes to assist poorer ones.
2 The only other motion (defeated 193-118) was 'an Instruction to the Committee, with a view to render-ing the working of the system of Union Chargeability more just and equal, that they have the power to facilitate in certain cases the alteration of the limits of existing Unions.' *Hansard* CLXXIX col 131.

must give / up going with you to Lady Derby's,[3] wh: I regret, & you can say so, if you have an opportunity.

Ever, dear wife, | D.

TO: PHILIP ROSE   Grosvenor Gate [Friday] 12 May 1865   4008
ORIGINAL: H R/I/A/185
EDITORIAL COMMENT: Grosvenor Gate paper. *Sic*: checque.

P. Rose Esq   May 12 1865

My dear Rose,

It is better, that Evans, the Jobmaster's bill, shd. be paid thro' you.

His time is up on Tuesday, the 16th. & if you / will send for his acct. I will, after examining it, (because there are drawbacks during our residence at Hughenden) send you a checque for the amount.[1]

We shall return / his horses to him on Monday or Tuesday.[2]

Yours ever, | D.

TO: LORD DERBY   Grosvenor Gate [Saturday] 13 May 1865   4009
ORIGINAL: DBP Box 146/1
EDITORIAL COMMENT: Grosvenor Gate paper.

May 13 1865

My dear Lord,

Ld. Elcho acted with my knowledge, but not with my concurrence or sanction.[1]

I had told him, that not only cd. I not hold out a prospect of / my supporting his motion, but that my feeling was, that the party, with whom I acted, wo[ul]d be opposed to such a step.

---

3   MA would attend Lady Derby's 'assembly' in St James's Square this evening (11th). *MP* (12 May 1865).

---

1   On 16 May MA would record a £125.10 cheque from D to Evans. H acc.
2   A jobmaster supplied carriages, drivers and horses for hire.

---

1   Earlier on this day (13th) Derby had written to D that, in reply to a message on the 12th from Elcho about his motion to appoint a franchise inquiry commission, Derby had sent word to him that such a motion would be 'very imprudent'. Not only did Elcho reply, wrote Derby, that he was acting with D's 'entire concurrence', but Derby 'saw with surprise' that morning in *The Times* that Elcho 'has already given his notice. Pray let me know how far he has your sanction'. H B/XX/S/340. Under the heading 'The Parliamentary Franchise', *The Times* on this day (13th) printed Elcho's 12 May notice in Parliament to move for the appointment of 'a Royal Commission to inquire to what extent the wage-paid class of the population is in possession of the Parliamentary franchise, and how far persons in receipt of the same rate of wages as those now possessed of the franchise are excluded from it; to consider generally the changes which have taken place in the relative value of money and property in so far as they bear upon the electoral qualification; and to inquire how without lowering such qualification in boroughs or giving undue preponderance to any class of the population the Parliamentary franchise can be beneficially extended.' A document, probably in Corry's hand, endorsed on the first page 'Notices of Motion. 1865. Page 913.', repeats *The Times* notice nearly verbatim. With it is a note in D's hand: 'whether & what wd. be the consequence of extending the franchise to persons in possession of only a partial occup[ati]on of a tenement;'. H B/XI/J/233a. See **4214**n1.

He replied in return, / that he had resolved to give the notice on his own responsibility, & that his future course wd be influenced by the feeling wh: in time might be / elicited in the House on the subject.[2]

Yrs ever, | D.

4010 TO: SIR LAWRENCE PALK   Grosvenor Gate, Sunday 14 May 1865
ORIGINAL: PS 790
PUBLICATION HISTORY: Meynell II 453, dated 14 May 1865, to Sir Lawrence Palk.

Grosvenor Gate, | Sunday, May 14th, 1865.

Mon Très Cher,

I have seen Lord Stanhope twice, and should like much to see you.[1]

Could you call on me to-day at three o'clock, or to-morrow at twelve?

Yours ever, | D.

4011 TO: LORD STANHOPE   Grosvenor Gate [Sunday] 14 May 1865
ORIGINAL: KCR Stanhope MSS 690(6)4
EDITORIAL COMMENT: Grosvenor Gate paper.

The | Earl Stanhope   May 14 1865

My dear Lord,

My interview, of this morning,[1] was not satisfactory to me. I even declined, at one moment, to place the matter before you; but, ultimately, / in deference to an earnest request, I agreed to leave the matter open, to afford a further opportunity of consulting, & conferring with those deeply interested.

I feel it was / my duty, however, not to lose a moment in apprising you of all this.

Ever, my dear Lord | Sincerely yours, | *B. Disraeli*

4012 TO: FREDERICK LYGON   Grosvenor Gate [Sunday] 14 May 1865
ORIGINAL: BCP [23]; now BL ADD MS 61892
EDITORIAL COMMENT: Grosvenor Gate paper.

The | Hon: Fredk: Lygon | M.P.   May 14 1865

My dearest Editor,

I am sure you have done me great honor; I hope, you may have done some good; by the speeches, wh: you have collected & / by the remarks with wh: you have prefaced them.

It is most agreeable to me, that anything, wh: I have said, should be, thus, con-

---

2 On 11 May Elcho had written to D that he felt 'so strongly on the subject & am so far committed to the reasonable & thoughtful working men whose views I expressed in the Debate & to whom I promised that I would urge inquiry that I must, even if unsupported, at least table a resolution on the subject. The opinion of The House & of the Public upon it would soon be ascertained.' H B/XXI/E/121.

---

1 See **4011**.

---

1 D had planned to see Sir Lawrence Palk on this day (14th); see **4010**.

nected with a companion in public life I so much cherish, / & whom, personally, I
so dearly, & deeply, regard.[1]

Yours ever, | D.

TO: ELECTORS OF BUCKS   [London?, Saturday] 20 May 1865   **4013**
ORIGINAL: H B/I/D/93
PUBLICATION HISTORY: *The Times, MP* and *Standard* (22 May 1865); *BH* (27 May 1865)
EDITORIAL COMMENT: Endorsed in another hand on the first page: 'Hughenden Manor May 20, 1865'.
The pages are numbered consecutively from '1' to '7'. *Sic*: embarassments; developement.

To The Electors of the County of Buckingham
Gentn.,
A dissolution of Parliament being imminent, I beg leave to announce my intention
of soliciting, at your hands, a renewal of that high trust, which, on six previous occasions, you have conferred on me, by sending me as one of your representatives to
the House of Commons.

Although the state of public affairs is, on the surface, little disturbed, the impending appeal to the country involves consequences as momentous, as any recurrence
to its sense by the Crown has perhaps hitherto offered.

Six years ago, Lord Derby, then Minister, proposed a measure on Church Rates,
which while it maintained the principle of a National Church, relieved the conscientious scruples of Dissenters from its doctrines or polity. It was defeated by a large
majority, on / the ground, that nothing short of abolition could be satisfactory.[1]

A month afterwards, anxious to free alike the Crown & the Parliament from the
embarassments in wh: they were placed in reference to the question of the Parliamentary suffrage, he introduced a measure wh: wo[ul]d have greatly extended it
on principles in harmony with the constitution, wh: wisely recognises the electoral
franchise as a privilege, & not a right. This measure was also defeated by a large majority, on the ground, that no extension of the suffrage could be sufficient wh: did
not involve a lowering of the franchise in Boroughs.[2]

In this state of affairs, Lord Derby advised an appeal to the country, & not having
obtained a majority, resigned office; an administration being formed pledged to the
total abolition of Church Rates, & to a measure of Parliamentary reform, wh: should
secure the lowering of the Borough franchise.

Since that period, the parliamentary condition may be generally, but fairly, described as a continued attack on the British constitution in Church & State; if not
always suggested by Her Majesty's ministers, always sanctioned by them, & invariably
originated by the party on whose support their existence, as a Ministry, depends.

---

1 See **4000**&n2 and, for Lygon's preface, M&B IV 353. In sending D a copy of the book on 13 May, Lygon
  had called his preface 'a very inadequate tribute to the orator[,] his abilities & principles.' Publication of
  the 'small pamphlet' would be announced on 20 May. H B/XX/LN/35; *BH* (20 May 1865).

---

1 Derby's Church Rates Abolition Bill had been defeated in the Lords in June 1858. See VII **3076**n1.
2 The Reform Bill of 1858 had formed the basis for D's Second Reform Bill of March 1859, whose defeat
  had brought down Derby's government. See VII **3367**&n1.

The attacks on the Church, commencing with triumphant majorities, have been encountered first with difficulty & defeat, but always with determination & constancy, &, finally, have been signally discomfited. The various schemes to deprive the Church of its constitutional privileges have been withdrawn, & the House of Commons ~~have~~ has resolved, that Church Rates shall not be abolished.

The / attacks upon the ~~est~~ State, never conducted with so much energy, have nevertheless been more prolonged, & it was only a few nights ago, when the House of Commons, impatient of protracted mystification, reflected the candour of the community, & declared by a vast majority, that the franchise in Boroughs should not be lowered, & that the principle, on wh: Lord Derby wished to extend it, was the just one.[3]

The efforts of the Conservative Opposition, during the last six years, have, therefore, ~~not~~ been neither insignificant, ~~nor~~ nor fruitless. They have defeated the measures to carry wh: the present Ministry was formed, & in the course of the struggle, they have educated the public mind to bring to the final solution a decision more matured & enlightened.

The maintenance of a national Church involves the question, whether the principle of Religion shall be an element of our political constitution; whether the State shall be consecrated, or whether, dismissing, the sanctions that appeal to the higher feelings of man, our scheme of government should degenerate into a mere system of police. I see nothing in such a result but the corruption of nations & the fall of empires.

On the extension of the electoral franchise, depends, in fact, the distribution of power. It appears to me, that the primary plan of our ancient constitution, so rich in various wisdom, indicates the source that we ought to pursue in this matter. It secured our popular rights by entrusting power, not to an indiscriminate multitude, but to the Estate, or Order, of the Commons, & a wise government sho[ul]d be careful, that the materials of that Estate should bear / a due relation to the moral & material developement of the country. Public opinion may not, perhaps, be yet ripe enough to legislate on this subject, but it is sufficiently interested in the question to ponder over it with advantage. So, that, when the time comes for action, we may legislate in the ~~aristocratic~~ spirit of the English Constitution, wh: wo[ul]d absorb the best of all classes, & not fall into a democracy, wh: is the tyranny of one class, & that one the least enlightened.

The leaders of the Conservative party, although they will never shrink from the responsibility of their acts, are not obtrusive candidates for office. Place without power may gratify the vain, but can never satisfy a noble ambition. Who may be the ministers of the Queen are the accidents of history: what will remain / on that enduring page, is the policy they recommend, & its consequences on Her people. That will much depend upon the decision & determination of the constituency of the United Kingdom in the ~~e~~ impending general election. Subject to those changes,

3 See **4006**&n1.

wh: the progress of society may demand, & the experience of the nation may sanction, I trust they will resolve on upholding the Constitution in Church & State.

I have &c.[4]

TO: [WILLIAM TAYLOR COPELAND?]   [London?, after 20 May 1865]   **4014**
ORIGINAL: H B/II/125
EDITORIAL COMMENT: Draft copy following a letter from Copeland dated 20 May 1865. As D's writing is
extremely faded, what follows is an approximate transcription. *Recipient* and *Dating*: by context; see n1.

But the experience of first hand has proved that the order & propriety of Life are
best preserved by the citizens of a community. A stated period on [*illeg.*] publickly
[*illeg.*] the allegiance to the fundamental [*illeg.*] & society of wh [*illeg.*] ...[1]

TO: [UNKNOWN]   [London, Saturday] 17 June 1865   **4015**
ORIGINAL: PS 1396
PUBLICATION HISTORY: *Australasia* (23 Sep 1899) 722 dated at Hughenden, 17 June 1865; reprinted from
Literature (London), date unknown
EDITORIAL COMMENT: From a transcript kindly provided by J.A.W. Gunn. Said to be part of a private col-
lection 'recently offered for sale' along with D's instructions for binding some books and sale of others.
Sic: Burnett's, Steven's.

The first, marked B, are for binding, their main contents in calf. Burnett's Lives[1]
and Hamilton's must be renovated in a becoming manner; and the Gibbon[2] must
be put in trim. Mr. Disraeli does not wish the copy to be changed, as he values the
old edition of Gibbon, the references being more correct. Byron's works must be
half bound in red morocco, with gilt tops.[3] The other two cases contain chiefly du-
plicates, which Mr. Disraeli will thank Mr. _____ to dispose of for him, either by
sending them to a sale or in any other way he prefers. There are some good books

---

4 D would paraphrase some of his remarks in two short announcements in *The Times* and MP (7 Jul 1865)
    and BH (8 Jul 1865). See **4019**. D's long letter to the electors of the City of London, written for Thomas
    Baring, would be similarly paraphrased when published, over Baring's signature, in *The Times* (5 Jul
    1865). See H B/II/90.

---

1 The letter by William Taylor Copeland, signed 'a Member of the late Select Committee of Enquiry' and
    addressed 'To the Members of both Houses of Parliament', requested them to examine 'the annexed
    Figures' (a page entitled 'Ecclesiastical Commission') and to 'seriously look at the enormous expendi-
    ture which might be reduced & the Church greatly benefited. Why not sell all Tithes by applying to the
    Legislature to allow a receipt under the Corporate Seal to be the Tithe.' The Ecclesiastical Commission
    (Superannuation Allowances) Bill would be read in the Commons on 8, 12 and 19 June and in the Lords
    on 20, 22 and 26 June, and given royal assent on 29 June. H B/II/125a; *Hansard* CLXXX index.

---

1 Scottish-born theologian and historian Gilbert Burnet (1643-1715) was professor of divinity at the Univer-
    sity of Glasgow 1669, political and spiritual adviser to William III and Mary II 1687 and Bishop of Salisbury
    1689-1715. His books include (in later editions) *Lives of Sir Matthew Hale and John, Earl of Rochester* (1829)
    and *Lives, Characters, and an Address to Posterity* (1833).
2 Hughenden library has *Miscellaneous Works of Edward Gibbon, Esquire. With Memoirs of his Life and Writings,
    composed by himself* ..., edited by John, Lord Sheffield, new edition (1814, 5 vols) in calf.
3 Hughenden library has an edition of Byron's works (1832-3, 17 vols) in half morocco.

in the lot; a [*illegible*] copy of Johnson & Steven's Shakespeare;[4] Warburton's Pope in Cambridge binding;[5] Warton's quarto;[6] Malone's Dryden's prose works,[7] etc.

4016

TO: CHARLES CLUBBE   Grosvenor Gate [Wednesday] 5 July 1865
ORIGINAL: RIC [27]
COVER: The | Revd. C.W. Clubbe | A.M., | Hughenden, | High Wycomb. | *B. Disraeli*
EDITORIAL COMMENT: Grosvenor Gate paper. *Sic*: Wycomb [*cover*].

July 5 1865

Can you help me in this matter?

Yrs ever, | D.

4017

TO: LORD SALISBURY   Grosvenor Gate [Wednesday] 5 July 1865
ORIGINAL: HFD [14]
EDITORIAL COMMENT: Grosvenor Gate paper.

Private   July 5 1865

The | Marq: of Salisbury | K.G.

My dear Lord,

Ld. Lonsdale has launched Ranelagh, with a £1000, for Midd[lese]x: from a belief, after enquiry, that there is a Conservative majority on the Registry of / 700.[1]

I know, from experience, your liberality in all party affairs, & I know also, that, at this moment, you have peculiar claims on your resources.[2] But if you cd. encourage us by your name, & a / moderate subscription, it would have the best effect, & I have been induced to promise to mention this to you.

Pardon me, if I be intrusive, & attribute my indiscretion to the urgency of the occasion, / & not to a deficiency of sincere respect & regard.

Yours ever, | *B. Disraeli*

4 George Steevens (1736-1800) had revised Samuel Johnson's edition of Shakespeare as *The Plays of William Shakespeare with the Corrections and Illustrations of Various Commentators* in 10 vols, 1773, rev 1778, 1785, and (15 vols) 1793.

5 Alexander Pope's editor and literary executor, William Warburton (1698-1779), was author of *The Works of Alexander Pope Esq. In Nine Volumes Complete. ... together with the Commentaries and Notes of Mr. WARBURTON* (1751). Hughenden library has Pope's works in calf (1797, 9 vols), probably the well-known 1797 nine-volume *Works of Alexander Pope* edited by Joseph Warton (1722-1800), as there was no 1797 edition of Warburton.

6 Hughenden library has Warton's *An Essay on the Genius and Writings of Pope* (1782, 2 vols), *Observations on the Faery Queen of Spenser* (1807, 2 vols) and *The History of English Poetry* (1824, 4 vols).

7 Irish scholar Edmond (or Edmund) Malone (1741-1812) edited *The Critical and Miscellaneous Prose Works of John Dryden* (1800, 4 vols).

---

1 Ranelagh would not contest the Middlesex election of 13 July and the two incumbent Liberals would be returned unopposed. See **4044**&n5.

2 Salisbury had much influence in both Hertford borough and in Hertfordshire, where on 11 and 24 July respectively three Conservatives would be returned for the five seats.

TO: C.E.S. (EDWARD) GLEIG   Grosvenor Gate [Thursday] 6 July 1865   4018
ORIGINAL: NLS 4896 ff196-7

EDITORIAL COMMENT: A transcript by Gleig sent to John Blackwood with a request to publish Gleig's address to the electors of Stirling boroughs in *Blackwood's Magazine*. 'That would introduce us to the Carlton Club; and place my interpretation of Disraeli's thought "The corruption of nations and the fall of Empires" before the country'. Gleig was quoting from D's letter to the Bucks county electors. See **4013**.

July 6. Grosvenor Gate. 1865.

My dear Sir,

I have read your address with much interest. It is written with sustained power, and with great strength, both of thought and expression. Its only fault is that you have mentioned me too often and too kindly.[1] I wish I had a vote for the Stirling boroughs.[2] It would certainly be offered you by

Yours sincerely | B Disraeli.[3]

TO: ELECTORS OF BUCKS   London [Thursday] 6 July 1865   4019
ORIGINAL: PS 1469

PUBLICATION HISTORY: *MP* and *The Times* (7 July 1865); *BH* (8 July 1865)

EDITORIAL COMMENT: This typescript is from *BH*.

Hughenden Manor, | July 6th, 1865.

TO THE ELECTORS OF THE COUNTY OF BUCKINGHAM.

GENTLEMEN.

PARLIAMENT being now dissolved,[1] and a new one summoned, I again solicit the honor, which on six previous occasions you have conferred on me, of being your representative in the House of Commons.

It is a distinction which I prize, and which I will endeavour to deserve.

Having recently addressed you at length on the state of public affairs,[2] I will only now remind you, that on the complexion of the new Parliament, the character of our future policy for years, and that of our institutions perhaps for ever, will mainly depend. I fervently pray, therefore, that the country will unmistakeably decide on securing our happy constitution in Church and State.

I remain, Gentlemen, | Your obliged and faithful Servant, | B. DISRAELI.

---

1 C.E.S. (Edward) Gleig had published his lengthy 28 June address in *The Edinburgh Evening Courant* (1 Jul 1865), headed by D's quotation (EC). Gleig had mentioned D many times, decrying 'a degenerated Parliament' and 'the listless attitude and languid inattention' of the senate, and lambasting Gladstone while apotheosizing D with such flourishes as 'the grand self-command of his all-conquering genius.' H B/XXI/G/152.

2 At the 13 July election for Stirling District (Scotland), comprising five boroughs, a Liberal would be returned unopposed.

3 D would advise Gleig not to publish this letter; see **4036**&n1.

---

1 Parliament was dissolved on this day (6th).

2 See **4013**.

4020

Alfred Austin | Esqr[1]   July 8 1865
Dear Sir –
I have written to Mr Badcock.[2] I regret, like him, the retirement of Mr Mills,[3] who was a valuable member of / the House of Commons, but it is a source of much satisfaction to me, that you should have come forward under the circumstances, as I think your talents qualify you for / public life, & I have every confidence in your character & sound political principles.

I heartily wish you success, & should hope, that, if all our friends rally round you, / & yourself do not lack energy & decision, you would, tho' late in the field, succeed.[4]

Believe me, | Very faithfully yours | *B. Disraeli*

4021

J.T. Delane Esq   July 10 1865

1 Austin on 7 July had written to D from the Castle Hotel, Taunton: 'I have, for security's sake, already written to you at Grosvenor Gate, & sent another copy of the accompanying Address. Coming in at the eleventh hour to fill up a gap ... I fight at a great disadvantage ... Mr Badcock, the Banker, whom you doubtlessly remember in consequence of the retirement of Mr Mills, his personal friend, hesitates about giving his vote to Mr Mills's successor. A note from you would ... dissipate his hesitation ... [and] strengthen my position'. Austin's printed address to the electors of Taunton borough is dated 6 July 1865. H B/ XXI/A/243, 243a.

2 D's letter to Henry Badcock (d 1888), of the prominent Taunton banking firm of H[enry], H.J. & D. Badcock & Co (1790s-1872) and who had unsuccessfully stood for Taunton on 4 May 1853, has not been found.

3 Arthur Mills (1816-1898), MP (C) for Taunton 1852-3 and 1857-65, was author of *Systematic Colonization* (1847) and *Colonial Constitutions* (1856).

4 Austin on 9 July would thank D for his 'kind, prompt, & encouraging letter. Tomorrow I shall call on Mr Badcock; & I have no doubt that your note to him ... will have produced the intended effect ... I addressed the Electors again last night, & I believe, with like success.' He assured D he was 'strictly obeying your counsel, & am acting "with energy & decision".' At the 12 July elections at Taunton, Liberals A.C. Barclay (478 votes) and Lord W.M. Hay (470) would defeat Conservatives E.W. Cox (292) and Austin (269). Austin would write to D at length on 13 July that, during the interval between Mills's retirement and Austin's arrival at Taunton, 'so much had been done by the other side & so little by our own, that I soon perceived the acquisition of two seats to be out of the question, & even the retention of one very doubtful.' He went on to discuss the election results and concluded that 'only mismanagement has lost us the Borough ... I shall of course communicate this information to the proper quarters.' H B/ XXI/A/244-5.

Dear Delane,

The Bucks nomination is Thursday next, 13th, in the County Hall, Aylesbury, at /
10 o'ck: *a.m.*[1]

    Yours sincerely, | D.

TO: [UNKNOWN]   [London?, mid-July 1865]   **4022**
ORIGINAL: PS 892
PUBLICATION HISTORY: Winifred A. Myers Autographs catalogue 7 (Spring 1969) item 290: to 'Sir John
(after Sir J.) Neild [*sic*], M.P.'
EDITORIAL COMMENT: The recipients may be Markham Spofforth or Philip Rose as election agents. The
catalogue's text includes the material in square brackets. *Dating*: see n1. *Sic*: Nield.

We are most anxious about Wilts [if Nield advances] he will not be even opposed.
Lord Derby is not less anxious, than myself.[1]

TO: WILLIAM H. SMITH   Grosvenor Gate [Wednesday] 12 July 1865   **4023**
ORIGINAL: WHS Hambleden MSS PS1/44
EDITORIAL COMMENT: Grosvenor Gate paper.

W.H. Smith | Esq[1]   July 12 1865
Dear Sir,

Before I leave town today for my own County,[2] I must express to you my great regret
at the termination of the Westminster / contest, conducted by you with so much
spirit, &, evidently, with such a just expectation of success.[3]

    I hope yet to see you in the House of / Commons; &, in the meantime, I trust you

---

1 'I have sent two excellent reporters to Aylesbury and have no doubt they will do you justice', *Times* editor
Delane wrote to D on this day (10th). H B/XXI/D/78. *BH* would print D's speech on the 14th, *The Times* on
the 13th (under the heading 'From Our Own Reporters'). *The Times* also published a leader stating that
D's speech threw 'little light' upon parliamentary reform and the relations between Church and State,
dismissing his statement that 'the franchise is a privilege, and not a right' – D spoke glowingly of suffrage
as 'a privilege and a trust' – as a 'not very valuable' commonplace. See **4024**&n1.

---

1 See IV **1558**ph,ec&n1 regarding this snippet. Wiltshire N (two members) in 1865 would elect two Liberals,
the first since 1835; Wiltshire S (two members) on 14 July would return one of each in a hotly contested
election in which the second Conservative candidate was defeated. At Chippenham, Wilts (two members), Sir John Neeld would be one of the two Conservatives elected in a contest, on 12 July.

---

1 William H. Smith Jr (1825-1891), head (since 1846) of newspaper agents William Henry Smith & Son,
would become financial secretary to the treasury 1874-7, PC 1877, first lord of the admiralty 1877-80, secretary of state for war 1886-7, and first lord of the treasury and leader of the House of Commons 1887-91.
His appointment to the admiralty would be satirized in Gilbert and Sullivan's *HMS Pinafore* (1878): 'I
thought so little, they rewarded me / By making me the Ruler of the Queen's Navee!'
2 The DS would leave Grosvenor Gate for Hughenden on this day (12th). H acc.
3 Although Smith (L-C) lost the election·on this day (12th) to Liberals R.W. Grosvenor and J.S. Mill, he
would be MP for Westminster 1868-85 and for Strand 1885-91.

may find some dignified consolation & some just pride, in the conviction, that you possess the respect, & the confidence, of / a great party.[4]

I have the honor to be, | Dear Sir, | Your faithful Servt | *B. Disraeli*

4024 TO: ELECTORS OF BUCKS   London [Thursday] 13 July 1865
ORIGINAL: PS 1470
PUBLICATION HISTORY: *BH* (15 Jul 1865).

Hughenden Manor, | 13th July, 1865.

TO THE ELECTORS OF THE COUNTY OF BUCKINGHAM.

GENTLEMEN,

PERMIT me to return you my cordial thanks for the distinction you have conferred upon me, by again placing me in the proud position of member for the County of Buckingham.[1]

I have the honor to be, | GENTLEMEN, | Your very faithful Servant | B. DISRAELI.

4025 TO: MARKHAM SPOFFORTH   Hughenden [Sunday] 23 July 1865
ORIGINAL: H H/LIFE
PUBLICATION HISTORY: Ralph Nevill ed *The Reminiscences of Lady Dorothy Nevill* (1906) 71-2, extracts from the second and third paragraphs
EDITORIAL COMMENT: From a MS transcription with the annotation (in the same hand) referring to D's third paragraph: 'I think D's figures are wrong. My records show this: – In 1857. Conservatives 287. In 1859. Conservatives 305. J.S.S.'

Hughenden Manor | July 23rd 1865.

Dear Mr. Spofforth,[1]

Very many thanks for your polls.

Whatever the result, no one is more conscious & convinced than I am that the contest on the part of the Conservatives has been conducted with admirable ability. I have witnessed your zeal, energy resource & ready information and I have often asked myself where should we have been if these qualities had not been present on our side.

I am sure what I have seen [of] Ld Nevill[2] throughout these affairs has made me often wish that I had such a man by my right hand in public life. I have never known an instance of such fiery energy and perfect self control united with all those personal qualities which make exertion with such an inspiring comrade a labour of love.

---

4 Replying on this day (12th), Smith thanked D for his 'sympathy' and 'kindly feeling'. 'Seeing that I had not identified myself with the party I confess I felt surprise at the warmth and earnestness with which the Westminster Conservatives supported me, and the ready response to our united efforts caused me to be sanguine as to the result.' H B/XXI/S/296.

---

1 D was returned unopposed on this day (13th). His lengthy speech dealt with parliamentary reform, religion, finances, the malt tax, trade, the economy and foreign policy. See **4021**&n1.

---

1 See VIII **3882n1**.
2 See VIII **3969**&**n1**. Spofforth was founder and Nevill chairman of the Junior Carlton Club. D would call them 'the real managers' behind Conservative election gains.

Looking over some old Dods[3] I observe that after Ld Palms dissolution of 1857 we had only 260 Conservatives and after our own of 1859 only 287 returned. Surely this is very pregnant.[4] What really alarms me in this affair is the state of Scotland. If this is irremediable, it is indeed serious.[5]

Yours sincerely | D.

TO: FREDERICK LYGON   Hughenden [Monday] 24 July 1865   **4026**
ORIGINAL: BCP [26]; now BL ADD MS 61892
EDITORIAL COMMENT: Hughenden paper. *Sic*: developement.

Private   July 24 1865

Hon | Fred: Lygon | M.P.

Mon tres Cher,

It never occurred to me, until this moment, that, when we met in the tumult of the Carlton Polling Booth, it was the first occasion, since the University Election, / that historical event, wh:, I believe, to be mainly, if not entirely, owing to your energy & resolution. You must have thought me very cold or stupid, but we live in such a hurried world of events & feelings, / that I fancied at the moment, that we had discussed the catastrophe again & again.[1]

The numerical check at this general Election is really nothing. Lord Derby had only 260 followers after the Disso[lu]tion of –57: after his own in –59 only 287. He will, now, count / above 290:[2] & as the disaffected have all been visited by Providence, we are really a stronger party. What really alarms me is the state of Scotland. Power seems to have slipped from the hands of the proprietors. It may be long leases; it may be *fuars*;[3] it may be / both: but the result is the same. If the Metropolis & Scotland are to be two Liberal recruiting grounds,[4] & nothing more, I do not see how a majority on our principles can ever be obtained, unless some re-construction

---

3 See VI **2369**n8.
4 D would repeat these figures to Frederick Lygon on 24 July and to Derby on 28 July. See **4026**&n2 and **4027**. Figures in official sources vary. For 1857: L 390, C 264; 1859: L 357, C 297. *BPER* 622. For 1857: L 373, C 281; 1859: L 347, C 307. *BHF* 140.
5 See **4026**&n4.

---

1 After holding the University of Oxford seat for eighteen years, Gladstone had been defeated on 18 July by Conservatives Sir William Heathcote and Gathorne Hardy, a 'catastrophe' for Liberals and a personal one for Gladstone, who noted on 17 July, 'At night arrived the Telegram announcing my defeat at Oxford as virtually accomplished. A dear dream is dispelled: Gods will be done.' *Gladstone Diaries* VI 370. For his defeat as 'an event of national significance', see Feuchtwanger *Gladstone* 123-4. *The Times* on 19 July had reported that 'the enemies of the University ... deliberately sacrificed a representative who combined the very highest qualifications, moral and intellectual, for an academical seat to party spirit, and party spirit alone.'
2 D's 'above 290' falls between 288 and 298 in *BPER* 622 and *BHF* 140; see **4025**n4.
3 In Scots law, a *fuar* or *feuar* is a tenant of a *feu*, a piece of land rented annually (*feu* duty).
4 London (City), for example, had been a Liberal stronghold for years, with Lionel de Rothschild regularly re-elected. Following the 1859 elections, Liberals had held sixteen county seats in Scotland, Conservatives fourteen; the figures were now eighteen and twelve. *BHF* 140. 'The boroughs have always been Liberal, and now the Tory dominion in the counties has been attacked with vigour, and in many places overthrown. Never since Scotland has had a real representation – that is, since the year 1832 – has it been so nearly unanimous in its political principles.' *The Times* (19 Jul 1865).

occurs. / However, we live in the age of developement, & shall have, at least, the interesting pursuit of watching the occurrence of some strange events.

G.A. Denison will crow till the end of the year. I am glad we / helped him to such an euthanasia.[5]

I get, occasionally, "John Bull": It is very much improved. I suppose in new hands at last?[6] It is written with briskness & fire. I begin to think we might do something with / it, & write it up. What say you? It is worth thinking off of.

We ought to try, in that case, to get it information, if possible, for its Saturday morning. This attracts attention, & then good writing tells.

Let me hear how you are sometimes.

Yrs ever, | D.

4027   TO: LORD DERBY   Hughenden [Friday] 28 July 1865

ORIGINAL: DBP Box 146/1
PUBLICATION HISTORY: M&B IV 415-16, omitting the first and last paragraphs
EDITORIAL COMMENT: Hughenden paper imprinted 'MAD'. Endorsed by Derby on the first page: 'Ansd Disraeli B'.

Rt Honble | The Earl of Derby | K.G.   July 28 1865

My dear Lord,

I return Vance's letter, scarcely deciphered, but sufficiently read.[1] Apologies, somebody writes, only account for that, wh: they do not alter.[2]

I have no doubt there were instances on our side of over-confidence. There always will be. And I feel sure, that if we had succeeded in forcing a / dissolution last year, we should have done better, but, on the whole, I cannot conceal from myself, that the dissolution took place on fair conditions for the Opposition. The Ministry had no cry, & we had the advantage of six years of unceasing preparation; well employed, for notwithstanding the result, I think the energy, resource, & general

---

5 George Anthony Denison (1805-1896), BA 1827 and MA 1830 Oxford, Archdeacon of Taunton (1851-96), a Tractarian with controversial ritualist views, was firmly opposed to latitudinarianism and liberalism. As editor of *Church and State Review* (1862-5), he had written to D in 1862 thanking him for an article (unlisted in Stewart *Writings*) and would keep D informed about the *Review*'s increasing financial problems. On 9 June 1865 he had announced 'the death of C & S. Review unless some means can be found to prolong its life. ... Meantime I am doing what I can to die peacefully & with becoming dignity[,] but death AFTER the Election, if it must come, would be less damaging than BEFORE it or IN it.' On 30 July he would inform D that the *Review* would cease publication in August, adding in a postscript: 'I have been thirteen years endeavouring to turn out Gladstone, and I rejoice I had a hand at last in doing it. My understanding of his position and of the general position will appear in the leader and other parts of this number of August 1.' H B/XXI/D/136, 138. Denison's brother was House Speaker John Evelyn Denison.
6 Charles Gipps Prowett edited *John Bull* until 1865. See VIII **3507**&n2.

---

1 Derby had received a letter from John Vance, MP (C) for Dublin City since 1852, who had lost at the polls on 17 July, and at his request had sent it to D on the 24th. According to Derby, Vance had hinted at the reason for his defeat, 'which has lost us many more elections: over-confidence, and want of exertion. ... I do not think we shall be much, if at all, weaker than we were six years ago; and the apparent majority of the government will add greatly to their difficulties.' H B/XX/S/334.
2 A source (if there was one) has not been found for 'Apologies only account for that which they do not alter', which D would repeat in the House on 28 July 1871. *Hansard* CCVIII col 413.

efficiency, of Mr Spofforth & / Lord Nevill, who, after all, were the real managers, were truly admirable – not to say unique.[3]

And on paper, affairs look well enough. After Lord P's dissolution in 1857, you had 260 followers in H. of C. After your own dissolution in 1859, you had 287.[4] At present, with what we consider a great check, you will top 290.

But beneath the surface things are not so fair. The / state of Scotland alone is most serious. All influence appears to have slipped away from its proprietors: & if irremediable; if Scotland & the Metrop: districts are to be entirely, & continuously, arrayed against the Conservative cause, the pull of the table will be too great, & no conservative government, unless the basis be extended, will be possible.[5]

The world is so broken up & scattered, that I have no means, at this moment, of getting information. If you are more favored, I am sure you will let me know.[6]

Yrs sincerely | D.

TO: **JOHN POPE HENNESSY**   Hughenden [Friday] 28 July 1865   **4028**

ORIGINAL: RHL Box 2/1 fs 106

PUBLICATION HISTORY: James Pope-Hennessy *Verandah: some episodes in the Crown Colonies 1867-1889* (1964) 43

EDITORIAL COMMENT: The text is taken from a typescript, dated at Hughenden, 28 July 1865, in the Pope-Hennessy papers at Rhodes House Library. We acknowledge the assistance of Dr Andrew Shields in locating this letter.

I have learnt, with the greatest concern, the strange & unexpected conclusion of the contest for Kings County.[1]

By your powers of debate, great information, indefatigable industry & fidelity of conduct, during the six years you were in the House of Commons, you established a parliamentary name – and obtained the confidence of all who acted with you.

It will be a reflection on the sense and spirit of your countrymen, if they do not soon restore you to a position for which by talents & character you are eminently fitted.[2]

Believe me always and faithfully yours.

B. Disraeli.

---

3 For Spofforth and Nevill, see **4025**&n2.
4 D had quoted these figures to Spofforth on 23 July and to Frederick Lygon on the 24th. See **4025**&n4.
5 For the Metropolis and Scotland as Liberal strongholds, see **4026**&n4.
6 For Derby's 4 August reply, see **4030**n1.

---

1 John Pope Hennessy, MP (C) for King's co (Ireland) since 1859, had been defeated (1,240 votes) in the 24 July elections. Sir Patrick O'Brien, MP (L) since 1852, had been re-elected (1,246) and John Gilbert King (C) had won a seat (2,192).
2 After unsuccessfully contesting co Wexford in 1866 (see **4236**n1), Hennessy would hold various colonial governorships until 1889 and become MP for co Kilkenny 1890-1.

4029   TO: WILLIAM FOLLETT SYNGE   Hughenden [Monday] 31 July 1865

ORIGINAL: HEY [5]

EDITORIAL COMMENT: Hughenden paper. Endorsed in another hand on the first page: 'Disraeli' and 'with port.'

W.W. Follett Synge | Esqr[1]   July 31 1865

My dear Sir

Your presence in England permits me to thank you for the very kind manner, in wh: you remembered me in your distant home. / I was much touched by it, & nothing but the distraction of public life would have prevented me from troubling you, ere this, with a letter at Honolulu.

Mrs Disraeli, & / myself, much regret, that our absence from town deprives us of the honor of paying our respects to the interesting visitor, who is under your charge, & of congratulating Lady / Franklin on her Majesty's arrival.[2]

I hope, however, you are going to remain in England some considerable time.[3]

Bélieve me, | faithfully yours, | *B. Disraeli*

4029A   TO: [JOHN SKELTON]   Hughenden [Monday] 31 July 1865

ORIGINAL: PS 1559

PUBLICATION HISTORY: *Contemporary Review* 39 (1881) 975; *Littell's Living Age* 35 (1881) 31. D's letter is quoted in Skelton's essay, 'A Last Word on Disraeli'. Stewart *Writings* 196 (#1441).

Hughenden Manor, July 31, 1865.

My dear Sir,

I am obliged to address you in your mask, for I cannot put my hand upon your letter,[1] and therefore have lost your direction.

Mrs. Disraeli is reading your 'Campaigner at Home,' and gave me last evening a most charming description of it.[2]

---

1   For Synge, consul-general for the Sandwich Islands, see VIII **3607n1**.

2   Synge had arrived on 13 July with Emma Naea Rooke (1836-1885), Queen Dowager of the Sandwich Islands and widow (since 1863) of King Kamehameha IV of Hawaii, whom he was escorting during her visit to England. *The Times* (15 Jul 1865) had quoted the *Panama Star and Herald* on her 'quiet, unassuming benevolence'. Lady Franklin, once a guest of the Hawaiian royal family at Honolulu when seeking information about her husband, Arctic explorer Sir John Franklin, was hosting the queen in London. On 28 July, they had attended a dinner given by the Bishop of London. *The Times* (29 Jul 1865).

3   Replying to D on 15 August from the foreign office, Synge would call his present post 'a terrible place to go back to' and was 'hoping almost against hope for some preferment that will bring me a few thousand miles nearer home.' On 30 October he would become consul-general and commissary judge in Cuba. H B/XXI/S/748.

---

1   This letter by John Skelton (pseudonym 'Shirley', from Charlotte Brontë's novel *Shirley*) has not been found.

2   The fictional work *A Campaigner at Home* 'By Shirley' had been published in late April. See **3924X&n1**.

We brought it with us to the country. I was not surprised at her account, for I am well aware of the graceful fancies of your picturesque pen.[3]

Yours very faithfully, | B. DISRAELI.

TO: LORD DERBY   Hughenden [Sunday] 6 August 1865   4030

ORIGINAL: DBP Box 146/2

PUBLICATION HISTORY: M&B IV 416-17, omitting the first paragraph; Weintraub *Disraeli* 411-12, most of the third paragraph and extract from the sixth

EDITORIAL COMMENT: Hughenden paper. *Sic*: embarassment; indisposed; embarassing.

Private   Augt 6 1865

Right Honorable | The Earl of Derby | K.G.

My dear Lord,

My letter, in reply to one of yours, did not require an answer, &, therefore, I fear, it must have been somewhat clumsily written, to have occasioned you that trouble.[1] / Nevertheless, as we are corresponding, I will take the opportunity of making one or two remarks, wh: will facilitate the future.

You will do me the justice, I hope, to remember, that, when some of your followers, ten years ago, suggested, for the common cause, / you should condescend to take a subordinate office, I utterly repudiated the scheme. It would, then, have been most improper, but, perhaps, not impossible. Now, it would be equally improper, & quite impossible.[2]

With regard to myself, / altho' I am quite aware, that I have had an opportunity in life to wh: I have not been adequate, still, having ~~lead~~ led a portion of the House of Commons for seventeen years, I am disinclined, in the decline of life, to serve under any body / in that assembly, & as no one but yourself would offer me its lead, & as

---

3 D is mentioned twice in *Campaigner*: as one of the men in 'a capital sketch by Richard Doyle – made about the year '48 – which ... represents *Punch* telling the members of the House of Commons "to go about their business"' (p 203) and in a footnote: 'Full justice has not yet been done to the remarkable felicity of Mr. Disraeli's "satiric touch." Putting the famous Rembrandt-like full-length of Sir Robert [Peel] aside (as somewhat overdone), the lightly touched sketches of contemporary statesmen which are to be found in his speeches (Palmerston, Russell, Gladstone, Sir Charles Wood) form a gallery of portraits to which any future historian of our time, who desires to represent these men in their habit as they lived, must turn. The sketches are conceived in a satirical spirit: the form is mocking and ironical: but they never degenerate into caricature, and manifest a rarely delicate, subtle, and imaginative insight into the characters with which they are occupied. They may be compared to Mr. [John] Leech's drawings, which raise a laugh indeed, but from which a truer notion of the English men and women and children of the Victorian era is to be obtained than from all the portraits painted by the Academicians' (pp 40-1).

1 For D's 28 July reply to Derby's 24 July letter, see **4027**. Derby had written to D on 4 August that, given the prevailing 'democratic spirit' in Scotland, 'a purely Conservative government is all but hopeless, until, upon Palmerston's death ... Gladstone tries his hand with a Radical Government, and alarms the middle classes. Then there may come a reaction; but it will probably be too late for my time; and I see no prospect of any state of affairs which shall again place me at the head of a government ... for I think it is a great mistake for any one who has been at the head to take a subordinate post.' Concerning election results, Derby admitted being 'uneasy as to the additional responsibility which may be thrown upon the H. of Lords in resisting measures to which it will be impossible for them to give any but an *enforced* support.' H B/XX/S/335.

2 See VI **2727**n1. John Vincent believes that in 1855 'the picture given by [Stanley's] diary is that it was Derby, not Disraeli, who was decisive in fending off unwelcome mergers.' *Disraeli, Derby* xv.

we both agree, that such a combination would not succeed, I look upon my career in the House of Commons, so far as office is concerned, to have concluded.[3]

But I am not at all / sure, that, at a moment of alarm & embarassment, an influential body of new adherents might not be indisposed to rally round a person, who has so considerable a following in the country as yourself. But this can never happen so long as they understand, as / a condition precedent of such adhesion, that the leadership, in both Houses, is to be appropriated by us. And who can blame them?

What, therefore, I wish you to do, is to take the fitting opportunity to / avail yourself of those confidential connections, wh: you have among the Whigs, & let them clearly understand, that you are free & prepared to form an anti-revolutionary Government on a broad basis. But this sho[ul]d be done in time, not delayed till the crisis arrives, & when other persons / have been hurried into conduct, wh:, had they been aware of the real state of affairs, they would have avoided.

This course involves really no sacrifice on my part. The leadership of hopeless opposition is a gloomy affair, & there is / little distinction when your course is not associated with the possibility of future power.

My retirement from the post would also assist you in another respect. It would be an unanswerable precedent for relieving you from some embarassing / claims, wh: now weaken you in the country.[4]

Believe me, | my dear Lord, | Yours sincerely, | D.[5]

4031 TO: HENRY THOMAS RYDE   Hughenden [Monday] 7 August 1865
ORIGINAL: MOPSIK [166]
EDITORIAL COMMENT: Hughenden paper. *Sic*: T.H.

T.H. Ryde Esqr[1]   Augt 7 1865
Dear Sir,
I did receive a letter, previously to the General Election, respecting the Bucks Herald; but I could not decipher it.[2]

That / charge cannot be brought against your present communication, wh: is very distinct in form & substance.[3]

I wish I could effectually assist you in yr praiseworthy efforts to improve yr position; but / I must frankly tell you, that I know of no party, or person, who is inclined to make any advance to support the journal you mention.

Yours faithfully | *B Disraeli*

---

3 This is not the first time that D offered to step down as leader of the opposition; see, *eg*, VII **3128**.
4 Stanley would soon be touted as a possible new party leader by Ralph Earle (**4054**n5) and, in 1866, by disgruntled Liberals ('Adullamites') proposing a coalition government (**4116**&nn1&2).
5 For Derby's firm rejection of D's offer, see **4033**n1.

---

1 Ryde was founder (1832) and first proprietor of *BH*.
2 In his near-illegible 6 July 1865 letter, Ryde had explained that he had been approached by the firm supplying the paper for *BH* with an offer to edit it, but requiring £1,500. H B/XX/A/31. Previous editor William Lowndes had died in 1864, leaving the paper in considerable debt. For *BH*'s long-standing financial problems, see VIII **3706**&n1.
3 Having received no reply, Ryde had written (legibly) to D on 5 August that, although he had declined the offer, it had been reiterated on 4 August under better financial terms. He again asked D for assistance, pleading 'reduced circumstances'. H B/XX/A/32.

TO: **OCTAVIAN BLEWITT**   Hughenden [Thursday] 10 August 1865
ORIGINAL: RLF M/1077/18 File 609
EDITORIAL COMMENT: Hughenden paper. Endorsed in another hand on the first page: 'Mrs Tinsley's case'.

Oct: Blewitt Esqr[1]   Augt 10 1865
Dear Sir,

Do you know anything of this lady?[2] It seems a sad case. Has anything ever been done for her? Or can anything? Be / so kind as to return me the letter.[3]
    Yours faithfully | *B. Disraeli*

TO: **LORD DERBY**   Hughenden [Monday] 14 August 1865
ORIGINAL: DBP Box 146/2
EDITORIAL COMMENT: Hughenden paper. *Sic*: Windham.

Right Honorable | The Earl of Derby | K.G.   Augt 14 1865
My dear Lord,

I merely send this to acknowledge the receipt of yr letter, as I thought it wo[ul]d be satisfactory to you to know it had duly / arrived.[1]

1 D had asked Blewitt, secretary of the Royal Literary Fund, for help in assisting a female author in 1864; see VIII **3947**.
2 Lancashire author Annie Tinsley, née Turner (1808-1885), began publishing in 1826 with *The Children of the Mist and other Poems*. In 1833 she had married solicitor Charles Tinsley, with whom she had six children. Although her novel *Margaret* (1853) has been likened to Charlotte Brontë's *Villette* (1853), Tinsley's preface denies plagiarism.
3 Blewitt would inform D on 11 August that, over the last forty years, Tinsley had received seven grants and assistance from several private sources. But family illness and 'quarrels with her Publishers' having taken their toll, Tinsley had written to the Queen asking for assistance and was prepared to emigrate if she could raise the funds. Writing from London on 9 August, she had solicited D's help in an eight-page letter describing her family's plight, from the amputation of her son's leg from 'water in the knee' to the 'congestion' of the lungs and brain that had rendered her husband unemployable and debt-ridden. H A/IV/M/92-3.

1 In his long 12 August reply to D's 6 August letter (**4030**), Derby had called D's suggestion 'very generous' but its course 'highly impolitic'. He and D had 'acted together, with perfect cordiality and, I believe, mutual confidence, for more than 17 years. I believe we have been mutually serviceable to each other; my influence with the party has, I hope, served to strengthen your position in the Commons; and I should have looked in vain for anyone in that House, on either side, who would have seconded me with the same ability, faithfulness, and perseverance, which you have exhibited. But my position would be very different if I had a colleague in your place with whom I was politically associated only by a compromise. Such a state of things would leave me the *nominal* head of a Coalition Government, with the lead of the most powerful of the two branches of the Legislature in the hands of one entertaining different views, and, not unnaturally, regarding himself less as a Colleague than as a rival. Such a position would not be politically tenable, and, personally, it would be intolerable. As I can never hold any office but the first, so neither can I be the head of any but a bonâ fide Conservative Government. But even supposing the case which you put, of a sufficient number of moderate Liberals becoming alarmed at the progress of events, and willing to join our ranks to give us a numerical majority', would anyone competent be found to lead the House? 'I remember your saying one day, that our party was too strong to allow of a coalition. How then would it tolerate a coalition in which the lead of the Commons should be in the hands of a Liberal?' Neither he nor D could be members of a government whose leaders and principles were not 'distinctly and avowedly Conservative'. H B/XX/S/336. See excerpts in M&B IV 417-18.

The views, you so clearly urge, had occurred to me, & I had endeavoured to appreciate them: but, I believe, the opposite considerations are weightier. I will / not, however, now touch on them. It would be as long, as the letter of Bolingbroke to Windham.[2]

Yours sincerely, | D.

4034 TO: THE DUCHESS OF CLEVELAND   Hughenden
[Wednesday] 23 August 1865

ORIGINAL: KCR U1590 C502/7 [3]
EDITORIAL COMMENT: Hughenden paper.

Dearest Duchess | of Cleveland,   Augt 23 1865
Persons, who live in profound solitude, are, proverbially, subject to dreams & visions.

Am I haunted by one, when I contemplate, as / I do frequently, that I am to have the inexpressible happiness of being yr guest at Raby on Thursday, the 31st. Inst.?[1] If so, dispel the hallucination as gently, as / you can: but if there be a foundation for my faith, I will not trouble your Grace to write to us, & we shall be sure to come, in person, on / the appointed day, to offer our kindest regards to you, & to the Duke.[2]

Ever yours sincerely | & obliged, | *B. Disraeli*

4035 TO: EDWARD COLEMAN   Hughenden [Wednesday] 23 August 1865
ORIGINAL: WSH [10]
COVER: E.J. Coleman Esqre | Athole Forest, | Blair-Athole. | *B. Disraeli*
EDITORIAL COMMENT: Hughenden paper.

E.J. Coleman | Esqr.[1]   Augt 23 1865
Dear Mr Coleman,
It was very kind indeed, & very neighbourly, of you to remember me, & in so agreeable a manner. I tasted one of / your birds this morning, & I do not think the forest of Athole ever furnished one more tender or succulent. It was first rate.[2]

---

2 From exile in France, 1st Viscount Bolingbroke in 1717 had written a 34,000-word letter to his friend Sir William Wyndham (VIII **3331xn2**). In it Bolingbroke defended his actions since 1710 and attempted to persuade the Tories to abandon the Jacobite cause, which he had fervently espoused until the dismal failure of the First Jacobite Rebellion in 1715. One of his finest compositions, the letter was published in 1753 as *A letter to Sir William Windham ... by the late Right Honorable Henry St John, Lord Viscount Bolingbroke.*

---

1 The DS on 31 August would leave Grosvenor Gate for Raby Castle (Duchess and 4th Duke of Cleveland), remaining until 7 September. H acc.

2 The Duchess on 26 August would reply that the DS 'should travel by the first Northern Express that leaves London at 9 a.m. to Darlington, & thence by the branch line to Barnard Castle, as far as *Winston*, whence you shall find our omnibus.' H B/XXI/C/265.

---

1 Edward John Coleman (1834-1885), a retired stock exchange broker and former owner of a coalmining business, was a staunch Conservative party supporter, a Bucks JP 1870 and high sheriff 1879. In 1878 he would attend the banquet for D and Salisbury upon their return from the Berlin Congress. Peter Pugh *Stoke Park, The First 1000 Years* (Cambridge 2003) 66-7.

2 According to *Baily's Magazine of Sports and Pastimes* 44 (1885) 238-9, of the 130,000 acres of the Forest of Atholl (or Athole) in the Scottish Highlands, '51,000 acres are sacred to the deer, whilst over 83,000 acres may be described as grouse ground.' The town of Blair Atholl is in N Perthshire.

Mrs Disraeli's uncle, the celebrated sportsman William / Scrope, dwelt much in the domain you are now occupying: indeed, I think, his work ~~of~~ on Deerstalking recites his personal experience in yr famous forest.[3] /

Mrs Disraeli unites with me in very kind remembrances to Mrs Coleman.[4]

Yours very faithfully, | *B. Disraeli*

TO: C.E.S. (EDWARD) GLEIG   Hughenden [Friday] 25 August 1865   **4036**
ORIGINAL: NLS 3220 ff7-8
EDITORIAL COMMENT: Hughenden paper.

Major Gleig   Augt 25 1865
My dear Sir

I should recommend you not to publish the pamphlet. Pamphlets, proverbially, are unsuccessful. At all / events, I should wish my letter not to be printed, for reasons too long to trouble you with, altho', in itself, it expressed my real feeling.[1] /

Yours sincerely, | *B. Disraeli*

TO: PHILIP ROSE   Grosvenor Gate [Wednesday] 30 August [1865]   **4037**
ORIGINAL: H R/I/A/186a
EDITORIAL COMMENT: Docketed by AES: '1865'. *Dating*: by context; see nn1-3.

P. Rose Esqr   G. Gate | Aug: 30
My dear Rose

Yours just arrived by post from Hughenden.[1] We are here, en route, tomorrow morning, at 8 o'ck, to Raby Castle, Darlington.[2]

---

3 For William Scrope and *The Art of Deer-Stalking* (1838), see III **801n6** and **864n4**. The 'domain' was Stoke Park, acquired in 1863 (from Lord Taunton for £95,000) by Coleman, who spent over £200,000 to improve the mansion and estate, including restocking the park with red deer in 1865.
4 Gertrude Coleman (d 1898) would marry Robert Bourke, Baron Connemara, in 1894.

---

1 See **4018**&ec. Gleig would reply on 29 August with a seventeen-page letter headed '*This* is long – but READ IT', stating his intention to publish neither his pamphlet ('at any rate at present') nor D's letter. He went on at length with evidence that 'there is *an agency of fraud* in the administration of the finances' of the army and navy. H B/XXI/G/153.

---

1 Rose had written to D on 28 August enclosing a statement of accounts headed 'Turkish loan 1865' (detailing Rose's purchase of £50,000 of shares at £44 each and their sale at £47 and £47.18.10) and a £373.6.10 cheque for D's 'subscription of £10,000'. 'I sincerely wish it had been more ... I had a very successful visit to Constantinople and succeeded in all the main objects of my mission.' Rose was also in Paris in 1865 transacting business with Lewis Merton over the conversion of Turkish Government loans. 'Although Turkish loans had once been popular in London ... and "Turks" remained a favorite for speculation, they were no longer held by Britons for investment (and had not been so since the failure of the 6 per cent loan of 1865).' H R/I/A/186b, B/100; *Norton Rose* 87; D.C.M. Platt 'British Portfolio Investment Overseas before 1870: Some Doubts' *Economic History Review* 33:1 (Feb 1980) 11.
2 D would describe Raby Castle in his 1865 notes as 'a real castle – & vast: & tho' occasionally altered & "improved", not substantially changed in character. The general effect feudal & Plantagenet.' H acc; H A/X/A/75 (*DR* 137).

1000 thanks for all / your kindness – there seems from the enclosed some mistake.[3]

I shd. like much to have seen you on public matters, but all must keep now / till we meet.

I hope Mrs Rose & yourself will find much enjoyment.[4]

Yrs ever | D.

4038   TO: LORD DERBY   Raby Castle [Sunday] 3 September 1865

ORIGINAL: DBP Box 146/1
PUBLICATION HISTORY: Blake 436, the fifth and sixth paragraphs
EDITORIAL COMMENT: Raby Castle paper. *Sic*: Joscelyn [*twice*]; Falloden [*twice*].

Rt Honble | The Earl of Derby | K.G.   Septr 3 1865
My dear Lord,

I will answer a question you asked me, some time ago, in a letter to Hughenden. What they decided on at their first Cabinet?[1] Perhaps, you have learnt / before this, but it is best to let you know what comes to me.

They decided, that the result of the Election necessitated a Reform Bill, & the ardent Reformers in the Cabinet wished, at once, to consider details, but Ld P. wd. not submit to / this, & tho' the resolution to introduce a measure was unanimous, he insisted, that all consideration of details shd be postponed.

My host here,[2] in a confidential stroll, talked to me of £15 for Counties & 8 for Boros. I said nothing, but / it appears to me, that this wd. certainly fail.[3] Gladstone has been ordering returns about Savings Banks, &c, but Palmn. is against "fancy franchises"[.][4]

He told me, that Lady Joscelyn Percy (who had come from *Falloden* to this place)[5] had / mentioned to him a plan talked of, in a certain set, for the Duke of Devonshire to be Premier, to prevent it going to J. Russell; & Gladstone & Stanley to be invited to join: but my host violently repudiated the scheme, & / spoke of the Duke

---

3 D was returning Rose's statement, whose calculations, based on one-fifth of Rose's profits, do arrive at £373.6.10. Rose would reply on 1 September 'very much annoyed at the blunder of my Secretary' and promising to forward 'the right cheque' to D's bank. On 7 September the London & Westminster Bank would advise D that his account had been credited that amount by Rose. H R/I/B/101; H A/V/G [unnumbered].

4 The Roses planned to leave on holiday on 15 September. H R/I/B/100.

---

1 On 24 July 1865, following the general election, Derby had written to D, 'I hear they are to hold a Cabinet on Wednesday. Have you any means of ascertaining what is its object, and what its result?' H B/XX/S/334.

2 D would describe the Duke of Cleveland as 'tall & dignified, but very natural, & tho' not exactly good-looking, a good presence & a good expression of countenance, kind eyes.' H A/X/A/75 (DR 138).

3 Gladstone's 12 March 1866 reform bill would propose to extend the vote to £14 county and £7 borough householders.

4 One of the groups, famously termed by John Bright 'fancy franchises', to whom Derby's failed 1859 reform bill had proposed to extend the vote, included those with deposits of at least £60 in savings banks.

5 Lady Josceline Percy (d 1885), née Margaret Davidson, only daughter of Sir David Davidson, in 1848 as the widow of Sir Robert Grant MP had married Lord Josceline William Percy; his father had succeeded in February 1865 as 5th Duke of Northumberland. Fallodon, Northumberland, 120 km from Darlington, was the birthplace of Charles Grey, 2nd Earl Grey, and the current seat of his cousin Sir George Grey, 2nd Bt.

of Devonshire as a man of no sort of experience in public life.[6] Such a thing cd. not be endured, he said.

The Reformers of the Cabinet, tho' obliged to postpone the consideration of details, console themselves with / the belief, that P. will not be able to meet Parliamt. again.

His bladder complaint, tho' in itself perhaps not fatal, deprives him of his usual exercise, & of sleep, wh: was his forte, & carried him thro' everything.[7]

He / did not say that Lady Joscelyn's news came from Falloden.

Great as the difficulties were, he said a Reform Bill was certain; quite inevitable. Yours sincerely, | D.

P. ~~wd~~ won't go to the Lords as Premier, or otherwise. If anything happen to him, thought J.R. inevitable.[8]

TO: **LORD LONSDALE**   Raby Castle [Sunday] 3 September 1865   **4039**
ORIGINAL: MOPSIK [155]
EDITORIAL COMMENT: Raby Castle paper. *Sic*: past.

Rt Honble | The Earl of Lonsdale   Sept 3 1865
My dear Lord,

On Thursday next, about three o'ck:, we shall arrive at Clifton, ready to avail ourselves of yr thoughtful kindness.[1]

A letter from Wiesbaden[2] tells me, that the marriage of Princess Mary with Prince Ulrich of / Saxe Weimar is arranged.[3] He is very ill-looking, stupid, & can scarcely

---

6 The 7th Duke of Devonshire, chancellor of the University of Cambridge since 1861, was MP from 1829 to 1834.

7 D in a note headed 'Dissolution of 1865 July' similarly wrote: 'The gout, from wh: he [Palmerston] never suffered much, is a pretence. The real complaint is an irritation in the bladder. Probably, there is nothing in itself fatal or dangerous, but its consequences are serious at his time of life in this respect; he is obliged to give up riding; his favorite & principal exercise; & the complaint breaks his faculty of sleep, wh: was his forte, & carried him thro' everything'. H A/X/A/74 (*DR* 137).

8 Palmerston would die on 18 October and Russell would assume office on the 29th.

---

1 Lonsdale had written to D on 1 September enclosing 'the best route' by rail. In an undated letter, he had offered to send his carriage to meet the DS at Clifton Station to take them to Lowther Castle (four miles south of Penrith). The DS would return to Grosvenor Gate on 11 September. H B/XXI/L/281; MOPSIK [158Q]; H acc. See **4044**.

2 This letter has not been found. Wiesbaden, 260 km from Coburg, had long been famous for its thermal springs and spa.

3 Mary Adelaide Wilhelmina Elizabeth (1833-1897), Princess Mary Adelaide of Cambridge, past prime marrying age, unattractive (known as 'Fat Mary') and without income, had been difficult for her cousin Queen Victoria to pair off. Evidently 'Prince Ulrich', too obscure to be identified (possibly the product of a faulty report to D), also escaped being paired with her. Perhaps the rumour was correct and only the name mistaken, as on 12 June 1866 she would marry Prince Francis of Teck (1837-1900), Duke of Teck 1871, whose income was also meagre. Although she would be granted a £5,000 annuity by Parliament in 1866 and receive a supplementary income from her mother, the Duchess of Cambridge, Mary's expensive tastes and extravagant lifestyle would result in large debts. The Queen would refuse her requests for money but provide the future Duke and Duchess of Teck with apartments at Kensington Palace and a country house, White Lodge, in Richmond. The first of their four children would become the future Queen Mary. Francis achieved the rank of captain in the 7th Hussars during the Austro-Prussian War, retiring from the Austrian army in 1866. He would be gazetted a colonel in the British Army in 1882 and promoted to major general in 1893.

articulate, & pennyless – & yet, it is, on the whole, considered a desirable arrangement, after all that has past. A mournful end for an English Princess, whom many
good judges thought once very handsome & / who will have a fair income. She
insists upon living in London: he, on the other hand, has only one passion in the
world; his profession; he is an Austrian soldier.

Many English; the Lansdownes, Cremornes, Alexander Lennoxes, Henry Barings
are at the / baths,[4] & one day the train came in with sixteen Princes & Princesses
from Rumpenheim.[5] Our Prince of Wales incog: jumped out & was soon detected
by 20,000 enthusiastic inhabitants & endless bands.[6]

Yours ever I D.

4040   TO: LORD HOUGHTON   Lowther Castle [Saturday] 9 September 1865
        ORIGINAL: TCC [271]
        EDITORIAL COMMENT: Endorsed in another hand on the first page: 'unable accept invitation'.

The I Lord Houghton   Lowther Septr 9: 65
My dear Lord,
Your very agreeable invitation to revisit Frystone has been forwarded to me here.[1] It
would have given us great / pleasure to have availed ourselves of it, if our stay, in this
part of the world, had been prolonged; but we must return to the South on Monday.

My / wife received from Made. de Rothschild, a not unfavorable account of the
Baron; about ten days ago.[2]

Mrs Disraeli unites with me in kind remembrances to Lady Houghton, & I / am
ever,

My dear Lord, I faithfully yours, I *B. Disraeli*
If this reach you at Hams, remember me, cordially, to yr excellent host.[3]

---

4 Richard Dawson (1817-1897), 3rd Baron Cremorne in the peerage of Ireland, in 1847 had been created
  Baron Dartrey in the UK peerage, but continued to be known by his older title until made Earl of Dartrey
  in 1866. In 1841 he had married Augusta Stanley (1823-1887), second daughter of Edward Stanley, of
  Crosshall, Lancs. Cremorne was LL of co Monaghan, and had been lord-in-waiting to the Queen 1857-66.
  Lord Alexander Gordon-Lennox in 1863 had married Emily Towneley (d 1892), second daughter and
  co-heiress of Charles Towneley, of Towneley, Lancs. Major Henry Bingham Baring in 1854 had married
  secondly Marie de Martinoff (1828-1903) (also Marie Solomonovna Martynov), born at St Petersburg and
  daughter of lieut-col Solomon Mikhailovitch Martynov.
5 Rumpenheim Castle, Cassel, in the Electorate of Hesse, was the summer residence of the Landgrave of
  Hesse.
6 'Of the Royal family only the Duchess of Cambridge and the Princess Mary were absent' for the inauguration on 27 August of a statue of Prince Albert at Coburg, his birthplace. 'They had remained at
  Rumpenheim'. *The Times* (30 Aug 1865). For a detailed account of the ceremonies, see MP (30 Aug 1865).
  Although no report has been found of Edward's incognito surprise appearance at the baths, he did go
  on a shooting expedition with the Duke of Coburg on 31 August. MP (4 Sep 1865).

---

1 On 7 September, Houghton had written to D at Raby Castle inviting the DS to Frystone Hall (which D had
  visited in 1844 and 1853) and inquiring after Lionel Rothschild. H B/XXI/H/681.
2 This letter has not been found. Rothschild, suffering from 'arthritic legs' and fearing it would be 'politically suicidal to campaign in the upcoming General Election in a wheelchair', had had his son Leopold
  speak on his behalf on the hustings; he had been re-elected for London (City) on 10 July. Weintraub
  Charlotte and Lionel 200-1.
3 Hams Hall, N Warwickshire, was the residence of Charles Adderley.

P. Rose Esqr   Lowther Castle | Sept 10. 1865

My dear Rose,

We intend to be at Grosvenor Gate tomorrow (Monday).[1] Let me have a line there, to say what / time it will suit yr engagements to receive me on Tuesday.

As I rise early, I can be with you at ten o'ck or so, if it is more / convenient to you. I shd. indeed prefer it.

Yrs ever, | D.

                              Hughenden | Octr 5. 1865

Lord Beauchamp

You have received a great shock at a moment,[1] when yr friends were happy in the belief of a marked improvement in yr health.[2]

But / you are a philosopher, & will bear this, as we must bear all things, with the dignity of a saddened, but serene, mind.

I shall write to yr brother, who, I fear, will suffer acutely.[3] /

Take care of yourself: your case is one, that only requires care; but care is wisdom, "more precious than rubies."[4] I have lost all the friends, that were the delight of my existence, except / yourself. Do not deprive me, by indifference, of one of the charms of my life.

Ever yours, | D.[5]

---

1 The DS would return to Grosvenor Gate on the 11th. H acc.

---

1 Beauchamp's sister Georgiana (b 1832), Lady Raglan (wife of Richard Henry FitzRoy Somerset, 2nd Baron Raglan), had given birth to her fifth son on 9 August and had died on 30 September 'after a very short illness.' *The Times* (2 Oct 1865).

2 Although D had previously praised Beauchamp's 'capital constitution' (see **3996**), Beauchamp would succumb to consumption on 4 March 1866, aged 37.

3 In his 7 October reply, Beauchamp would tell D that his brother, Frederick Lygon, had 'shown much fortitude, more than I could have expected.' Lygon would thank D on 10 October for his 'touching tribute' and mention 'the numerous proofs which are given of the great regard in which my sister was held.' H B/XXI/L/433; XX/LN/37.

4 Proverbs 3:13-15.

5 Beauchamp (n3) would describe his late sister as 'not of a genial and sympathetic spirit to mine, & always treated me as it appears the Pope would treat a freemason – ... I was always in hopes that time & kindness would modify such narrow & unfortunate notions.' He would respond to D's use of 'indifference' with assurances that 'such a feeling or rather want of feeling could never have place with me towards one whom I have always looked upon with the greatest esteem & regard & from whom I have always received so much kindness & sympathy.'

4043 TO: LORD SALISBURY   Hughenden [Friday] 13 October 1865
ORIGINAL: HFD [15]
EDITORIAL COMMENT: Hughenden paper.

The | Marq: of Salisbury | K.G.   Octr. 13 1865
My dear Lord,
Could you, without inconvenience, send me the printed rules of your "Cattle Insurance" organisation?[1]
    Ever your obliged | & sincere, | D.[2]

4044 TO: LORD LONSDALE   Hughenden [Friday] 20 October 1865
ORIGINAL: H B/II/68
PUBLICATION HISTORY: M&B IV 424, the first two sentences of the last paragraph
EDITORIAL COMMENT: Hughenden paper. There is both a draft and a fair copy of this letter. *Sic*: Wycomb.

Right Honorable | The Earl of Lonsdale   High Wycomb | Octr 20 1865
My dear Lord,
I was glad to see your handwriting.[1]
    The family papers, you mention, must be very interesting, & have a certain unity of subject; inaugurating, as it were, the parliamentary constitution of England, wh: may be said / to commence with Willm. 3rd, tho' only matured by the Hanoverian succession, & illustrating its action under the greatest of our Ministers.[2]

1 Livestock were being decimated since mid-June by the murrain, a viral disease also known as the rinderpest (German for 'cattle plague'), leading to the formation in 1865 of over twenty cattle insurance companies. Salisbury had been instrumental in forming the successful County Cattle Insurance Company of Hertford, whose merits D would extol at Aylesbury on 15 November, explaining that it was '"an insurance association in shares, on the limited liability principle. Every man who insured his stock was supposed to take one-fourth, or 25 per cent. in his shares in the society. For instance, if he insured for £160, he was expected to take a fourth of that in shares, upon which he would pay £1 deposit."' This system also '"allowed the landowners of the county, not having stock to insure, to take shares, so as to augment the fund on which the county might have to fall back."' *BH* (18 Nov 1865). D would elaborate upon the 'sound commercial principles' of the limited liability system on 3 January 1866. See **4058**n2, **4062** and **4067**.
2 Salisbury on 14 October would reply that he was writing 'by this Post to the office to direct our printed Rules to be sent to you. The Insurance C[ompan]y is founded upon principles strictly commercial. We have started it to meet the circumstances of the day which no other Company would do. We believe that our premiums and our capital [£50,000] will meet all exigencies ... You will observe that we take no insurances without requiring the insurer to take shares to the amount of one-fourth of the sum for which he answers ... If you deem the Compy worthy of support you would do well to take some shares one Pound paid up. Your name would do a great deal and induce Buckinghamshire farmers to be large insurers.' H B/XXI/C/146.

---

1 In an undated letter Lonsdale had told D that at Lowther he had forgotten to show him 'some very interesting political correspondence', including 'letters to the first Lord Lonsdale who was one of the prominent men who brought forward Wm the 3d', others from Lord Godolphin and 'a mass of correspondence' from his father's Trinity (Cambridge) friend William Pitt the Younger. H B/XXI/L/282.
2 Dutch Prince of Orange William III (1650-1702), Protestant King of England, Ireland and (as William II) Scotland from 1689 to his death. His Bill of Rights (1689) and the Acts of Settlement (1701) and Union (1707) contributed to the curtailment of the rights of the monarchy and to the establishment of British parliamentary sovereignty, beginning with George I (1714-27) of the House of Hanover. The Germanic royal dynasty of Hanover, which succeeded the House of Stuart in 1714, produced six British monarchs: George I, II, III and IV, William IV and Victoria. Sir Robert Walpole, considered Great Britain's first PM, helped secure the position of the House of Hanover.

I was much pleased with my visit to Lowther, not only because I was glad to see your famous home, & some of its wonders of art & nature,[3] but because I / felt deeply your great kindness in your ceaseless arrangements for our amusement, at a moment, too, when you were still suffering from severe illness.[4] Since I first entered public life, I have experienced from you considerable, & unvarying, kindness, & coming, as it does, from one, who is not merely a grand seigneur, but / a man of vast experience, & great knowledge of character, I am gratified by it, & grateful for it.

I have already attended, as I promised, to the matter of the Middx: election, & am, I fear, involved in a very disagreeable correspondence on the ~~matter~~ subject. Can you conceive, that in only four days, they spent, or allege they spent, upwards of / £3000!![5]

Either there is knavery, or a reckless imprudence even more dangerous: a blunder greater, than a crime.[6] In the whole course of my experience in these matters, wh: is pretty considerable, & yours too, I sho[ul]d think, wh: is even greater, nothing has ever transpired like this. I need / not recommend you to be most careful to have no correspondence with any human being on the subject.

I did not mention yr name, when I made the enquiry; I spoke of two of my friends, who had been among the most considerable contributors. The other was Lady Jersey, who is in for £300:, / & who consults me on these matters.[7]

If Johnny is the man, there will be a Reform Bill; very distasteful to the Country.[8] The truce of parties is over. I foresee tempestuous times, & great vicissitudes in public life. It will be some consolation to me, / in the strife & struggle, to retain your confidence & to be supported by yr counsel.

Believe me, | my dear Lord, | yours sincerely, | & obliged, | *B. Disraeli*

3 The DS had spent from 7 to 11 September at Lowther (H acc), which D would describe as 'a splendid domain: parks & deer, mountains & lakes. The house convenient, & handsome in the interior, but the exterior deplorable, as might be expected from the Gothic of 1800 & [architect] Sir [Robert] Smirke.' H A/X/A/75 (DR 138). Lonsdale's art collection, along with later acquisitions, would be sold by the 6th Earl in 1947 in the largest country house sale of the century.

4 The chronically ill Lonsdale had informed D in March 1862 that he had 'been an invalid for a long time & ceased to partake of the Hospitalities of my friends, but I will make an exception to your invitation', and in late 1863 that 'my state of health has made it necessary for me to decline all invations [*sic*] & I have only made exceptions to you & Lord Derby for the last two years.' On 5 March 1867 he would write to D that he was recovering 'badly' from a 'severe & dangerous illness'. H B/XXI/L/277, 279, 288.

5 See **4017**&n1. Lonsdale (n1) had reminded D of their discussion at Lowther about 'some money' he had advanced for Viscount Ranelagh's election for Middlesex: 'we were not *backed* & Ranelagh retired. The money was advanced by Wolverley Attwood & myself, but no expense was incurred.' *The Times* had reported that on 13 July Ranelagh had told voters he had received '3,500 promises' but that, having been informed by his committee 'that the material support which they had promised him was not forthcoming', he had no alternative but to retire. (14 July 1865). The 'very disagreeable correspondence' included an undated letter (docketed '8 July 65') from 'Edwin' and a long, undated accusatory letter whose signature appears to have been blotted out. H B/XIII/203, 205.

6 Although D may be paraphrasing Derby's remarks of 1 May (see **4002**n3), which had caused a sensation in the Lords, the phrase 'It was worse than a crime, it was a blunder', attributed to Talleyrand, was common currency.

7 Lady Jersey's support may have been a gesture of gratitude for D's painstaking labours, since the spring of 1855, in helping to settle the scandalous financial affairs of her son, Francis Villiers. See VI **2743**n3.

8 Lonsdale (n1) had told D that 'The general impression seems to be that the Queen will send for Johnny.' Following Palmerston's death on 18 October, John Russell would become PM on 29 October. Gladstone would introduce a Representation of the People Bill on 12 March 1866. See *Hansard* CLXXXII cols 18-115. The phrase 'very distasteful to the Country' is not in D's draft.

R.A. Earle Esqr[1] | M.P.   Octr 21 1865

My dear Earle,

I never intended to come up yesterday. It was altogether a blunder between the servants of the two houses. Had it been my intention, I shd. have given it up, as / I hate being in town at a moment of political gossip & excitement, with wh: we have nothing to do.

I was well informed throughout the affair, being acquainted with the hopeless state before his colleagues were apprised, & / hearing on Thursday night, that F.O. was "offered" to Clarendon. I thought the word strange, &, as I have seen no announcement, fancied there might be some hitch. What of Granville? He loses by all this: it was understood, at the time, that the leadership of the Lords was compensation for / not being ↑first↓ Minister.[2]

Why do you consider the arrangement provisional? We were to have gone, beginning of ensuing month, to Wrest, (Lady Cowpers); but, of course, the party is put off.[3] I think, instead, I shall come up to town for a few days; affairs will have then settled.[4]

An autumnal meeting of Parlt., in consequence of the murrain, is quite on the cards.[5]

Write when you can

    Yrs ever | D.

Remember me to Lady Buchan.[6]

1 In light of Palmerston's death on 18 October, Earle had written to D from London on this day (21st) disappointed at not having met him on the 20th and telling him of Clarendon's appointment to the foreign office: 'Why does [Gladstone] not insist upon the F.O. being given to him? Politics will now be very interesting. The new Govt. is only a provisional one I shld. think'. H B/XX/E/347.
2 Despite talk that he would be Palmerston's successor (he had been offered the premiership in 1859), Granville, due to Russell's ill-health, would continue to take the lead in the conduct of business in the Lords.
3 Wrest Park, Bedfordshire, was the residence of Anne Florence de Grey (1806-1880), Countess Cowper, daughter of Thomas de Grey, 2nd Earl de Grey, and widow (since 1856) of George Cowper, 6th Earl Cowper. She had written to D on 8 October reminding him of 'that visit at Wrest which you led me to hope would take place'. MA would reply to Lady Cowper on 22 October; the DS would depart for Wrest on 27 November, remaining until the 30th. H B/XXI/C/553; H D/III/D/150; H acc.
4 D would leave for Grosvenor Gate the following day (22nd) and return to Hughenden on the 23rd. H acc.
5 For the murrain, see 4043n1. Parliament would meet on 1 February 1866. There would be brief discussion on 8 February of 'The Cattle Plague – Day of Fasting and Humiliation' (Hansard CLXXXI cols 188-91) and, throughout February and March, extensive debate on the Cattle Diseases and Cattle Plague Bills.
6 For Earle's aunt, the Dowager Countess of Buchan, see VIII 3362n5. Earle on 23 October would inform D that the foreign office offer to Clarendon had been made 'in very cordial terms, wh: is astonishing', and that he believed Granville was 'really to go to Paris.' H B/XX/E/348.

TO: LORD BEAUCHAMP [Hughenden, Saturday 21 October 1865] 4046

ORIGINAL: BCP [30]; now BL ADD MS 61892

EDITORIAL COMMENT: Paper imprinted with a picture: 'Monument, Hughenden Manor, Buckingham-shire.' *Dating*: by context; see n1.

The | Earl Beauchamp

My dear Beauchamp,

We have been social wanderers all this year, & were going on the 6th. Novr. to Wrest (Lady Cowpers) / but that party is, of course, put off.[1]

We shall be here for a good month, &, therefore, I write to say, how happy we shall be to see you, if it suits your humor.

We are, & shall remain, perfectly alone; & have nothing to offer you, but your / old friends, the Library & the Lady's Walk: you will find some changes in both.[2]

If you feel inclined to vary yr retirement by coming here, let us know at yr convenience. Yesterday, I bought a portrait of an old friend of yours, in a / country town, for sixpence, & so I send it to you in this letter.[3]

Yours ever, | D.[4]

TO: SPENCER WALPOLE Hughenden [Monday] 23 October 1865 4047

ORIGINAL: QUA 37

EDITORIAL COMMENT: Hughenden paper imprinted 'MAD'.

Rt. Honorable | S. Walpole   Octr 23 1865

My dear Walpole,

I was much obliged to you for yr letter from High-Clere, altho' it contained such frightful intelligence.[1] I would prefer the murrain to the meeting / of Parliament.[2]

Have you any further intelligence on the matter, & if the calamity occur, when is it, really, to be?[3]

Pray make my compliments to Mrs. Walpole, & yr circle & / believe me, always,

Yours sincerely, | D.

1 See **4045**&n3&4.

2 MA had planted four dozen Scotch firs in the Lady's Walk (VIII **3747**n2) in December 1862. On 28 September 1863 (VIII **3854**&n3) D had written to Beauchamp that 'yr favorite library [has been] enriched & improved.' For the extensive renovations at Hughenden in 1862-4, see VIII app VIII.

3 D's letter is followed by a *carte de visite* photograph of D by J.E. Mayall. BCP [31Q].

4 Beauchamp would reply on 26 October proposing a 6 November visit. 'I am glad you will have no party as I have neither health or spirits for much society.' H B/XXI/L/434.

1 From Highclere Castle, Hampshire, seat of the 4th Earl of Carnarvon, Walpole on 20 October had informed D that the Cattle Plague Commissioners had completed the first part of a 'very strong' report recommending 'measures, which will probably induce if not compel the ministers to call Parliament together as early as they can in November.' H B/XXI/W/57. See **4051**n4 and **4052**n1.

2 D would use the same comparison on 1 November with John Evelyn Denison and Lord Lonsdale. See **4051** and **4052**.

3 Walpole would reply on 31 October to reassure D that a meeting of Parliament in November was 'more doubtful' and that 'The Commissioners are not unanimous: their Report will be conditional but also late – & it cannot be presented before to-morrow.' H B/XXI/W/58.

4048 TO: LORD STANLEY   Hughenden [Tuesday] 24 October 1865
ORIGINAL: DBP Box 146/1
EDITORIAL COMMENT: Hughenden paper imprinted 'MAD'.

The | Lord Stanley | M.P.   Octr. 24 1865
Dear Stanley,

I catch the post to night, to say we are at home, & quite alone: & shall be delighted to / see you – but not for one night only: that is too much like a commercial travel-ler.[1]

Living in profound solitude, I should hardly be able to collect / my thoughts, or resume my powers of speech, in so brief a space.[2]

You will receive this tomorrow (Wednesday) & we shall be happy to see you to-morrow; if impossible, on Thursday / – but if you come tomorrow, you cd. stay till Friday witht. interfering with yr. Lancashire arrangements.

If you come tomorrow, *telegraph.*

Yrs sincerely | D.[3]

4049 TO: RALPH EARLE   Hughenden [Thursday] 26 October 1865
ORIGINAL: ILLU 25 XB B365b1 Cards 1,2.

R.A. Earle Esqr | M.P.   Hughenden | Oct 26. 65
My dear Earle,

I shd be very glad indeed, if you could come down here on Saturday, & stay two or three days with us. Let me have a / line by return, wh: I hope will arrive here only a few hours before yourself.

Yrs ever, | D.

4050 TO: LORD BEAUCHAMP   Hughenden [Friday] 27 October 1865
ORIGINAL: BCP [28]; now BL ADD MS 61892
EDITORIAL COMMENT: Hughenden paper imprinted 'MAD'.

The | Earl Beauchamp   Octr 27 1865
My dear Beauchamp,

We look forward, with real gratification, to yr coming on the 6th. Novr.[1]

---

1 Stanley had written to D on 23 October that there was 'much to speculate on, perhaps some things to be settled' and had requested to see D 'for one night' on Thursday and Friday, as he would be in Lancashire on Saturday. 'The reform crisis cannot now be delayed: there are at least 50 conservatives on the Whig side. The question is, can we utilise them, and how?' H B/XX/S/722.
2 MA on 26 October would note 'House 1 month no company'. H acc.
3 Stanley on 26 October would record that he had 'found D. and Mrs D. alone. He in good health and excellent spirits. It seems as if the prospect of renewed political life had excited him afresh, and that he had thrown off the lethargy which has been growing upon him for the last year or two.' On the 27th, D would ask him to become his literary executor, 'a trust which I accepted willingly', and show him his correspondence with Derby (see **4030** and **4033**). D 'talked a good deal of Gladstone, puzzled by his per-sistence in High Church opinions ... which it is hard for him to think that a man of so much talent can really hold.' Stanley would leave Hughenden on the 28th. *Disraeli, Derby* 237-8.

---

1 See **4046**&n4.

I hope it will not be a mere visit, but / a residence: that is to say, that you will remain with us as long as you like; a life *sans façon*, & only to be terminated, when you are a little bored.[2]

Yours ever, | D.

TO: JOHN EVELYN DENISON   Hughenden [Wednesday] 1 November 1865   4051
ORIGINAL: NOT OSC 447
EDITORIAL COMMENT: Hughenden paper.

Right Honorable | J. Evelyn Denison. M.P.   Nov 1 1865
Dear Mr Denison,

I must thank you for a most interesting letter,[1] wh:, by its clear & vivid narrative, classically completes my correspondence since the commencement of the / fatal illness of Lord Palmerston, & wh: I shall now seal up – to whet the appetite of some future Lord Stanhope.[2]

The rumor of the meeting of Parliament was scarcely less frightful, than the murrain. Walpole, in the confidence of the Commissioners, / alarmed me some days ago, but, this morning, his letter is more in the tone of yr reassuring suggestions.[3] It seems too, that the recommendations of the Commissioners are not unanimous: their report is to be presented today.[4]

The / only drawback from this more satisfactory state of affairs is, that I shall not so soon have the pleasure of meeting you.

My wife sends you her kind regards, & we both offer our Compliments to Lady Charlotte.

Yours sincerely, | *B. Disraeli*

TO: LORD LONSDALE   Hughenden [Wednesday] 1 November 1865   4052
ORIGINAL: MOPSIK [152]
EDITORIAL COMMENT: Hughenden paper imprinted 'MAD'.

Right Honorable | The Earl of Lonsdale   Nov. 1 1865

---

2 Beauchamp would arrive on 6 November, depart on the 13th and return on the 16th. H acc. D would refer to him as 'an invalid'; see **4055**.

---

1 This letter has not been found, but see **4052**.

2 Stanhope, an avid collector, was president of the Society of Antiquaries from 1846 and would be instrumental in establishing the Historical Manuscripts Commission in 1869.

3 For Walpole's letters of 20 and 31 October, see **4047**nn1&3.

4 *The Times* on 6 October had announced that the Queen had approved a Royal Commission to investigate the cattle plague, with Montague Bernard as secretary. In their *First Report*, presented on 31 October, most of the twelve commissioners had recommended the temporary prohibition of movement of cattle from one place to another. *The Times* (13 Nov 1865). There would be a letter to *The Times* on 25 November about 'Mr. M'Clean, the chief dissentient of the Cattle Plague Commissioners' and his argument that 'the existing panic is unreasonable'. On 16 November, in thanking D for his speech at the Cattle Plague meeting at Aylesbury on the 15th (see **4058**n2), Arthur Helps would send him 'a copy of the Report & of the Evidence which you may like to have.' H B/XXI/H/436. The report would go on sale on the 25th. There would be a *Second Report* on 5 February 1866 and a *Third Report* on 1 May 1866. *The Times* (23 Nov, 15 Feb, 9 May 1866). See Terrie M. Romano 'The Cattle Plague of 1865 and the Reception of "The Germ Theory" in Mid-Victorian Britain' *Journal of the History of Medicine* 52 (Jan 1977) 51-80.

My dear Lord,

There is a rumor abroad, more frightful than the murrain, that Parlt. is to be called togr, in consequence of the recommendation of the Rinder-pest Commission. I don't think it will prove fact, because I hear today, that the report, wh: is / to be presented this morning, is not unanimous.[1]

Besides, nothing could justify such a course, but promptitude of action. Now there must be sixteen days notice in the Gazette: then a week swearing in members. This will consume November; &, then, we can only begin by "leave to bring in a Bill"! /

They opened Ld Palmerston; & on examination of the body, found "all the great organs in a perfect state. There was no trace of disease."[2] Paget, the surgeon, told my ~~informate~~ informant this, who, by the bye, is the Rt Hon: J. Evelyn Denison.

I hope you are not suffering: I suppose you will / soon seek the bland skies of Ventnor.[3]

Yours ever & obliged, I D.

4053 TO: LORD STANLEY   Hughenden [Thursday] 2 November 1865

ORIGINAL: DBP Box 146/1
EDITORIAL COMMENT: Hughenden paper imprinted 'MAD'.

Rt Honble I Lord Stanley   Nov 2 1865
Dear Stanley,

From what reaches me, from a good quarter, I counsel, on your part, the utmost reserve on the subject of reform, in case any minister, or "that sort / of thing", tries to pump you.[1]

All the rest will keep till our next meeting – but I thought it advisable to give you this hint.[2]

Yrs ever, I D.

---

1 Lengthy extracts from the commissioners' report, dated '"31st October, 1865. Montague Bernard,"' would be published in *The Times* on 13 November and *BH* on the 18th. It was signed by Robert Lowe, Lyon Playfair, Richard Quain, E.A. Parkes, Thomas Wormald, Robert Ceeley and Charles Spooner. 'A separate report, signed by [5th] Earl Spencer, Viscount Cranborne, Mr. Read, and Dr. Bence Jones, is appended, stating that these commissioners are unable to join the other members of the commission in recommending the total stoppage of all movement of cattle in Great Britain ... There is also a separate report of Mr. M'Clean, who is opposed to the interference with the traffic in cattle, and who states that the evils arising from it would be greater than those arising from the disease itself.'

2 See **4051**. Palmerston had died of pneumonia on 18 October, two days before his eighty-first birthday, after catching 'a severe chill while out of doors during the recent sudden change in the temperature.' *The Times* (20 Oct 1865) quoting the *Globe*.

3 For Lonsdale's health, see **4044**n4. Ventnor was a fashionable health resort on the south coast of the Isle of Wight.

---

1 Stanley on 28 October had written to D that Clarendon, who had discussed reform at length with Russell the previous night, had described Russell as '"oppressed with his responsibility and afraid of being thought to betray his former principles."' On 4 November he would ask to know D's 'reasons for wishing that nothing should be said' about reform. 'You write as if in possession of some new facts'. H B/XX/S/723-4.

2 D would expand upon his 'hint' on 6 and 7 November; see **4055** and **4056**.

TO: RALPH EARLE   Hughenden [Monday] 6 November 1865   4054

ORIGINAL: PS 1528

PUBLICATION HISTORY: M&B IV 425.

Hughenden, Nov. 6, 1865

Who are the moderate men of all parties who are to form this new Government?[1] Opposite to us there is, certainly, Mr. Lowe. He could not join us alone, or, if he did, he would be fruitless.

As for the movement in *The Times*, the same organ, and probably the same pen, agitated as vigorously in favor of our Reform Bill, yet all the Whigs voted against us, and Mr. Lowe, then a six-pounder, among them.[2]

So long as the Whig party hold together, nothing can be done.

The name of Stanley would at first produce some excitement, even an appearance of enthusiasm. The great towns would no longer growl; the great employers of labor would smile; Bass would pay us public compliments, and Peto embrace us in the lobby.[3] But when the new Government were formed, if such a thing were possible, "the great Liberal party" would, as usual, reconstruct in Opposition, and Stanley after a twelvemonth would be kicked out, like his father,[4] though with a little more respect, and Gladstone installed as first Minister, with a stronger bench of colleagues, and some spoil among the Liberal outsiders, who are now bawling for Stanley.

So long as the Whigs are united, the views you describe are a fairy tale.[5]

TO: LORD STANLEY   Hughenden [Monday] 6 November 1865   4055

ORIGINAL: DBP Box 146/1

EDITORIAL COMMENT: Hughenden paper imprinted 'MAD'. *Sic*: ricketty; its clear.

Private   Nov 6. 1865

Right Honorable | The Lord Stanley

Dear Stanley,

My letter was oracular, because I had reason to believe the hint was urgent, & had

---

1   D addresses issues raised in two letters by Earle: one of 23 October urging D to 'try Stanley as Premier & annex [Robert] Lowe' and claiming the 'articles in the Times are attributed *by the Govt.* to Lowe. Ld. R[ussell] has, I am told on very good authority, a reform Bill cut & dried'; and one of 4 November stating that 'The necessity of reconstruction is in every Conservative mouth & the idea of an amalgamation of moderates under Stanley is talked of in places where one is least accustomed to look for new party confirmations ... I really think that after our defeat at the Elections, & under the apprehension of a Reform Bill, the Tories wd accept Stanley, with all his heresies.' H B/XX/E/348-9.

2   Lowe, who had voted with his party on the 1860 Reform Bill, with its £6 franchise, wrote an average of three leading articles a week for *The Times* from 1851 to 1868 and had become a zealous opponent of franchise reform.

3   For entrepreneurs Bass and Peto, see **4055n3**.

4   Derby had resigned in June 1859 following a no confidence vote.

5   Earle had called for 'a new platform' headed by Stanley, who 'would find all the support he requires from a Parliament, elected by the present constituencies. ... The *coup d'état* should be made before the meeting of the new Parliament, in order that new members may be saved from contracting party ties & obligations.' H B/XX/E/349.

no time to enter into long details, wh: I thought, wd. keep till we met. Things have marched / more rapidly, than I had anticipated.[1]

I believe the position of affairs is most ricketty,[2] & from all I can hear, & think, I am of opinion, that if you take an opportunity, before the meeting of Parliamt.; it would be desirable before Xmas; to make some public declaration of yr policy; / to this effect; that altho' there are many things to be done in many departments of administration, a minister in earnest to do them would find all the support he requires from a Parliamt: elected by the present constituencies, the thing wd. fall to pieces, & you / wd. be master of the situation.

Your name is the only one, wh: could inspire faith in such language: they would not heed it from yr father, or myself. As regards both of us, certainly as regards myself, the country would be unjust – but that does not signify; we have to deal with facts. / You alone can marry the finality, wh: the country desires in the way of the franchise, with the progress & movement, wh: it expects in other directions.

It will not do to postpone such a declaration until the occasion offers in Parliamt:, for one of its objects is to save the new members from contracting party ties & / obligations.

I believe if you take this course, the mass of the Whigs who are gorged & satiated with patronage, will rally round you; the great towns will rally round you; the great employers of labor, the Bass' & the Petos, will rally / round you,[3] & it is my firm opinion, that the bulk of the Tories, our own people, humbled by their defeat on the hustings, & frightened by the threatened reform Bill, would accept you as their leader with all your heresies.[4]

With / these views, I need not add, what I think shd. be yr tone & language with the Minister.[5] I shd., unequivocally, announce my general policy; I shd. avoid all details, & not attempt, by entering into them, to facilitate his course by expressing the concessions wh: ↑you may be prepared to↓ make in the / House of Comm:. It will always be in yr power to make those, if it be ultimately necessary to assist them in passing their bill. Be frank & explicit as to your general view: most reserved as to all expedients, concessions, compromises. Let / the "moderate party" in the Cabinet, wh:, so far as I can collect, includes every member of it, infer their chances of yr support from the expression of yr general policy: from nothing else.[6]

---

1 In his 4 November letter (4053n1), Stanley had called D's 2 November letter, with its 'hint' at 'the utmost reserve on the subject of reform', an 'oracular warning'. H B/XX/S/724.

2 On 3 November, Stanley had recorded that Derby 'has alienated personal friends, and is less popular with the party than at any former time.' *Disraeli, Derby* 239.

3 Under Michael Thomas Bass (1799-1884), MP (L) for Derby 1848-83, the Bass & Co. Brewery, established by his grandfather in 1777, became the largest brewery in the world. For railway contractor and MP (L) Sir Samuel Morton Peto, see VII **3360n3**.

4 D is repeating Ralph Earle's 4 November comment about Stanley. See 4054n1.

5 Russell had requested a 10 November meeting with Stanley: 'Of course this means an offer. Indeed I have had private hints to that effect.' H B/XX/S/724. See 4053. On 3 November, Stanley had noted that one of 'the objections to its acceptance' was that he 'could not honourably abandon Disraeli without cause'. *Disraeli, Derby* 239; see 240 for an account of the 10 November meeting and Stanley's reasons for declining Russell's offer of the Duchy of Lancaster.

6 Stanley (n1) had told D that their 'best course would be to strengthen the hands of the moderate as opposed to the thorough-going reformers.'

I write this on a Nov[embe]r / morning with a frozen hand, but I hope its clear enough; I stand in no man's way; least of all in yours. But you know all this.

I shd say, that in case you want to see me, there is no necessity of giving any notice. I am / always at home, & yr room is always ready.

Poor Beauchamp, at his own wish, comes today, but he is an invalid, rarely out of his room, & would not, under any circumstances, interfere with us.[7]

Yrs ever, | D.

TO: LORD STANLEY   Hughenden [Tuesday] 7 November 1865   4056
ORIGINAL: DBP Box 146/1
EDITORIAL COMMENT: Hughenden paper imprinted 'MAD'.

Private   Novr. 7 1865
Rt Honble | Lord Stanley
Dear Stanley,

I wrote yesterday as you wished – & fully.[1] ↑It shd. have reached you this morng.↓

One or two points have subsequently occurred to me.

When Peel, in Decr 1845, relinquished his scheme of repealing the corn-laws, / & John Russell was sent for by the Queen, he endeavoured to obtain from Peel an undertaking to support the Whig measure for the same object. Peel declined, on the ground, that he co[ul]d give no opinion of / any measure, unless he saw it in the shape of a bill, brought into the H of Comm: Upon wh:, Lord John, after all the vaunting taunts of the Edinburgh letter, & his ostentatious journey to town, resigned.[2]

I think you might extract / a profitable hint from this souvenir.

It is worth considering, whether, while you think you are strengthening the "moderate party" in the Cabinet, you are only extricating a body of impostors, who are all in / a funk, out of a scrape, into wh: they have fallen from their total want of principle in their opposition to our bill of 1859. Remember yr own reminder to him of the Appropriation clause in that debate, & of the prophecy I ventured to make as to his position in my closing observations before the division.[3]

I / can't hear, that there is any "immoderate party"[.]

The present state of affairs forcibly illustrates the truth, that I have so frequently

---

7 See **4050**.

---

1 See **4055**.

2 See IV xxx-xxxi, **1204**&nn1-3, **1452**n3 and **1454**n5. In his celebrated letter of 22 November 1845 advocating repeal of the corn laws, Russell had urged abolishing 'a system which has been proved to be the blight of commerce, the bane of agriculture, the source of bitter divisions among classes, the cause of penury, fever, mortality, and crime among the people.' See Prest *Russell* 425-8.

3 Following the defeat of the 1859 Reform Bill (see VII **3323**&n1), the Conservatives had fallen and been replaced by Palmerston's Liberals. D's 'prophecy' occurs near the end of a long speech on the seventh night of debate, 31 March 1859: 'And I tell the noble Lord [Russell] that when he goes to the hustings, of which he talks, and brandishes this Bill, he will find the minds of his constituents full of another matter, and that they will demand from him the reasons for the course he has adopted.' See *Hansard* CLIII cols 1157-1264 (D 1230-57).

pressed upon Ld. Derby: that no government can stand with the Prime-Minister & /
the Foreign Secy both in the House of Lords.

Yrs | D.[4]

4057 TO: [LORD BEAUCHAMP]   Hughenden [Wednesday] 15 November 1865
ORIGINAL: BCP [29]; now BL ADD MS 61892
EDITORIAL COMMENT: Hughenden paper imprinted 'MAD'.

Nov 15 1865

We shall be delighted to see you.

The summer of St Martin continues here, but, every day, fairer. Now, the wind is
due west, the sky cloudless, & the sun brilliantly warm.[1] All I hope is, that it will continue so during yr stay, wh: will complete yr cure.

We do not leave this, until Wednesday the 22nd:; & hope you will remain in yr
nest till then – or longer, if you like.[2]

Yours ever, | D.

4058 TO: PHILIP ROSE   Hughenden [Wednesday] 15 November 1865
ORIGINAL: H R/I/A/188
EDITORIAL COMMENT: Hughenden paper imprinted 'MAD'.

Phil: Rose Esqr   Nov 15 1865
My dear Rose,

I shall be in town in a few days, more or less, & be there for a week.[1] I shall see you
directly, & more than once, I / hope. I should, indeed, have come up yesterday, or
Monday, but for this County Meeting on the Cattle Plague, wh: takes place to day.[2]

---

4 Stanley would reply to D's 6 and 7 November letters on the 8th, promising to be 'cautious and reserved'
with Russell on the 10th while admitting that D's 'altered view' perplexed him, as they had just three
weeks ago agreed on 'a very small bill' and 'now you are against any bill.' H B/XX/S/725.

---

1 St Martin's Summer is a brief period of unusually mild weather often occurring around 11 November, St
Martin's Day. The weather on 15 November had 'again become fine, with moderate westerly winds, and
high barometric pressure.' *The Times* (16 Nov 1865).
2 See **4050**n2. Beauchamp would arrive at Hughenden on 16 November. H acc.

---

1 The DS would arrive at Grosvenor Gate from Hughenden on 22 November and would leave for Wrest
Park on the 27th. H acc.
2 The high sheriff of Bucks had convened a county meeting at Aylesbury at noon on this day (15th).
According to *BH*, 'Numerically speaking the meeting was a signal failure'. One of the resolutions put
forward was that foreign cattle should land at certain specified ports, be immediately slaughtered, and
'their skins and offal ... disinfected or destroyed' before being sent to various markets. D had (he said)
'very grave objections' to it, regretting that no measures had been taken in June, when the disease had
first appeared, 'such as preventing the moving of cattle about the country, or preventing the importation of foreign cattle', and predicting that 'these violent measures will probably have no effect on the
plague, while they may have a very injurious effect on your interests as traders.' The motion was carried,
D among six voting against the 'large majority'. *BH* (18 Nov 1865). For D's account this day of the success
of Hertfordshire's cattle insurance association, see **4043**n1. The Duke of Buckingham, in attendance on
this day, would preside at two meetings at the Buckingham town hall: one on the 28th ('for the purpose
of forming a limited liability company for protection against loss of cattle by the rinderpest') and one on
the 29th (see **4062**&n3). *BH* (25 Nov 1865).

This kept me, / & now some other things have happened, wh: make me, for a few days, adscriptus glebæ.[3]

Yrs ever, | D.

TO: **LORD STANLEY** Hughenden [Friday] 17 November 1865 **4059**
ORIGINAL: DBP Box 146/1
EDITORIAL COMMENT: Hughenden paper imprinted 'MAD'. *Sic*: St James'.

Right Honble | Lord Stanley Nov. 17 1865
Dear Stanley,

I shall be in town on Wednesday morning until the following Monday, when we go to Wrest.[1] I cannot, therefore, have the great pleasure / of receiving you here, but, I much trust, we shall have an opportunity of talking over affairs together in St James' Square.[2] It is difficult, & wearisome, to both of / us, to write on such large & fine questions. Conversation is the touchstone, that exhausts a subject.

I count on seeing you.

Yrs ever, | D.

TO: **LORD DERBY** Grosvenor Gate [Friday] 24 November 1865 **4060**
ORIGINAL: DBP Box 146/1
PUBLICATION HISTORY: M&B IV 426, beginning at 'If the Government' in the third paragraph
EDITORIAL COMMENT: Grosvenor Gate paper. *Sic*: Göschen; embarass; mâlaise; whom they deem.

Private Nov. 24 1865
Right Honble | The Earl of Derby | K.G.
My dear Lord,

Your letter, by second post on Wednesday, caught me in the train.[1]

---

3 'belonging to the land'; a serf.

---

1 The DS would be at Wrest Park 27-30 November. H acc.
2 Stanley on 16 November had written from St James's Square requesting to see D the following week and alerting him to 'the leading article of the *Star* ... announcing a reform bill. This is evidently an authorised indiscretion.' On the 22nd he would record a 'long talk with [D] on affairs', with D showing him 'a letter just received from Ld D. on the subject of the Irish church'. H B/XX/S/726; *Disraeli, Derby* 241. For Derby's 21 November letter and D's 24 November reply, see **4060**&n1.

---

1 On Wednesday 22 November D was en route to Grosvenor Gate from Hughenden. Derby's 21 November letter had discussed recent post-election changes among the Liberals, mostly 'patchwork among themselves' but also two 'significant' new appointments: 'Göschen, a very clever man, but an advanced Radical', and Fortescue in Ireland, the latter 'especially indicative of their Irish policy; and they, who were always charging us with the Ultra montane alliance, have, it is clear, bribed the R. Catholics with the promise of a Catholic University, probably to be largely endowed by the state, and, I think, the sacrifice of the Irish Protestant Church. ... I only hope that no members of the English branch will look upon [the matter] as heavy top hamper which it is wise to throw overboard to lighten the ship. They may rely upon it that the two are so closely tied together, that the one in sinking will drag the other with it. But it is quite possible that hatred of our own Church may lead even Protestant Dissenters to connive at R. Catholic Endowment, and if they and the R. Catholics unite, with the influence of Government in their favour, I own I look with great apprehension to the result.' H B/XX/S/337.

I did not put on the two appointments the same interpretation, as yourself. Göschen[2] takes the programme of the London / Committee, but that body is essentially Whig, & never wish their advanced representatives to embarass a Whig Govmt. G. also is a high churchman of the improved type: Puseyite ceremonies, & neologian opinions: & I have no doubt has entirely identified his career / with Gladstone's: he sits behind the C of Exr, & not below the gangway.

Fortescue's appointment I look upon as rather social than political;[3] tho', of course, he is well adapted to maintain the position, wh: the Ministry assumed, on Irish / affairs, at the end of last Sess: A charter for the Cath: Univy. I take for granted, tho' hardly with endowment. If the Government bring forward any specific measure respecting the Irish Ch:, it is possible, that it may be effectively resisted, because it would not be difficult / to pick holes in it, & of various kinds & sizes; but I do not think, that any general resolution respecting the Irish Church could be successfully withstood in the present Parliamt. It is a very unpopular cause, even with many of our best men.[4]

So far as I can learn, the difficulties of the existing Cabinet are so serious, that / it would at once break up, if there were a successor, but there is none – at least this is the opinion of Lord Taunton & that class of men. I think, however, myself, that it will not last very long, & for two reasons:

1st. Because the Prime Minister & the For: Secy[5] are both in the House of Lords, wh: I hold to be fatal to / any Cabinet under any circumstances, & wh: is really the proximate cause of the present mâlaise.

2ndly. Because all the younger portion of the Liberal party, including ↑those in↓ the Ministry, think that, by getting rid of Ld. Russell, they will obtain more, & higher, place under one, whom they deem immediately, or / at a short interval, must be his successor, vizt the present leader of the House of Commons.[6]

---

2 George Joachim Goschen (1831-1907), 1st Viscount Goschen 1900, from adolescence 'intoxicated with the ideas of free trade, free markets, and free enterprise', was a director of the Bank of England 1858-65 and vice-president of the board of trade and paymaster-general 1865-6. He would be president of the poor law board 1868-71, first lord of the admiralty 1871-4 and 1895-1900, chancellor of the exchequer 1887-92, rector of the University of Edinburgh 1890-3 and chancellor of the University of Oxford 1903-7. He was MP (L) for City of London 1863-80, Ripon 1880-5 and Edinburgh E 1885-6, and author of the very successful *The Theory of the Foreign Exchanges* (1861). *ODNB*.

3 Samuel Chichester Fortescue would be chief secretary for Ireland from 7 December 1865 to 26 June 1866.

4 On 20 June 1865, Daniel O'Donoghue had moved for an address to the Queen 'that conscientious objections to the present system of University education in Ireland prevents [*sic*] a large number of Her Majesty's subjects from enjoying the advantages of a University education, and praying that such steps may be taken as will remedy this grievance.' He pointed out that, 'while there was a University for 600,000 Protestants, and special arrangements for the Presbyterians', the 4,500,000 Roman Catholics had 'no recognized University'. After long debate, the motion was withdrawn. Debate on the motion of 28 March 1865 that 'the present position of the Irish Church Establishment is unsatisfactory' would resume on 10 April 1866. The Catholic University of Ireland in Dublin, established in 1854, with John Henry Newman as rector, had no state charter to confer degrees. The University Education (Ireland) Act of 1879 would establish the Royal University of Ireland, chartered 27 April 1880 and dissolved in 1909 with the establishment of the National University of Ireland and Queen's University Belfast. *Hansard* CLXXX cols 541-90; CLXXVIII cols 384-455; CLXXXII cols 973-1070.

5 Lords Russell and Clarendon.

6 Gladstone, who had succeeded Palmerston.

The alternative they contemplate is, that you will decline to take the reins, or that, if you do with the ancient regime, you must speedily fail. I think they would prefer the latter course, because they could make better terms, & / arrange & consolidate their resources better in opposition. In either case, Gladstone will declare, that he never will take the second post again.[7]

With these views, I cannot refrain from again calling yr attention to the suggestions I made respecting the party, & its prospects, at the end of the summer.[8] Some / new combination must be formed, or considerable changes will occur both in Ch: & State, wh: neither the necessities of the country require, nor its feelings really sanction.

Believe me, my dear Lord, I sincerely yours I D.

TO: **FREDERICK LYGON**   Grosvenor Gate [Monday] 27 November 1865   **4061**
ORIGINAL: BCP [32]; now BL ADD MS 61892
EDITORIAL COMMENT: Endorsed in another hand on the first page: 'Cheque £30. Nov' and on the fourth page: '*161*. Disraeli. £30. Nov: 27. 1865.'

Grosvenor Gate I Nov. 27. 1865

Hon: Fred: Lygon I M.P.
My dear Lygon,
The enclosed from Hubbard[1] will save me troubling you with too long a letter. It is a dreadful thing to have to pay £90 for / such a wretched fellow as Mr Adams, & such a dead thing as his low newspaper, wh: I shall never see again.[2]

We, however, gained on two points. We prevented the death of the C. & S. before the / Oxford Election, & we spared the feelings, & saved the dignity, of Geo. Anthony, who, with all his indiscretions, deserved our consideration.[3]

Adams has [*illegible deletion*] dunned me so intolerably, that I referred him to my solicitor, who said payment / was not due to Decr. It is £30. a-piece – i.e. six months at £15.

We shall have a good deal to talk about when we meet.
    Yours ever I D.

TO: **R[OBERT?] RIDGWAY**   Grosvenor Gate [Monday] 27 November 1865   **4062**
ORIGINAL: PS 1549
PUBLICATION HISTORY: *The Times* (30 Nov 1865); BH (2 Dec 1865).

Grosvenor Gate, Nov. 27, 1865.

---

7 Only while PM himself would Gladstone serve as chancellor of the exchequer (1873-4, 1880-2).
8 See **4027** and **4030**.

---

1 MP (C) John Hubbard, director of the Bank of England.
2 Possibly William Edwin Adams (1832-1906), ultra-radical journalist and editor of the *Newcastle Weekly Chronicle* 1864-1900.
3 For George Anthony Denison and the *Church and State Review*, see **4026**.

Mr. R. Ridgway, Cattle Association, Buckingham.[1]

SIR, – Your letter reaches me as I pass through town.[2] I regret that my absence from the country will prevent my attending the Buckingham meeting.[3] I see no mode of meeting the plague, in case it ravages our herds, in an effective manner, except by following the example of the county of Hertford.[4] There, they have established an insurance company on the joint stock principle, with limited liability. Their capital is £50,000 in shares: £1 per share called. Every insurer to take 25 per cent of the amount insured in shares. By this scheme, founded on a true commercial principle, every landlord, who has no stock to insure, by taking a certain number of shares, may contribute to the support of his neighbours in their emergency, in a manner agreeable to their feelings and his own. The shares would be so distributed that in case of repeated or even complete calls, the burden would not be overwhelming or even distressing, while between the amount of the subscribed capital and that of the premiums, a fund would be at command that would greatly alleviate the general loss upon the county. At the county meeting the other day I gave to Mr. Rose, of Eythrope,[5] and Mr. Fowler,[6] all the papers of the Hertford society, which Lord Salisbury had sent me, otherwise I would have forwarded them to you. I trust you will be able to comprehend this very hurried letter, but I am only in town for a few hours, and have a great pressure of business.

– Yours, faithfully, | B. DISRAELI

1 Most likely Robert Ridgway, born 28 November 1843 in Tingewick, eldest child of Benjamin Ridgway (born at Thornborough, Bucks *ca* 1819/20 and died at Tingewick, Bucks 29 Dec 1893) and Eliza Smith of Tingewick (d 1864). 1851 and 1881 Tingewick censuses. See n3.
2 This letter has not been found.
3 The Duke of Buckingham on the 29th would preside over 'a numerously attended meeting' at the Buckingham town hall. After reading D's letter to Ridgway, the Duke cited recent statistics showing 'a very considerable increase' in cattle deaths nationally and also mentioned local cases such as those 'on the farm of Mr. Ridgway, at Thornborough.' He advised his audience to 'carefully consider the opinion so clearly expressed by Mr. Disraeli; and when it comes to the fact that the societies which have adopted the form of registration have worked well, it will be a question whether a merely voluntary set of rules can be properly enforced.' After further discussion, 'a society on the limited liability principle was established, and a committee was formed to carry on the operations.' *The Times* (30 Nov 1865).
4 See **4043**&n1.
5 For the 15 November county meeting, see **4058**&n2. One W. Rose of Eythrope, a hamlet in Waddesdon parish, Bucks on 9 August had presided over a 'densely crowded' meeting of agriculturists at the Crown Hotel in Aylesbury that had concluded with a memorial to the Privy Council 'signed in the room by owners of stock representing an aggregate of 5,000 head of cattle'; it demanded 'stringent measures ... to prevent further introduction of any diseased stock' into Bucks by means of 'compelling all vessels laden with cattle entering the ports of the United Kingdom to undergo a sufficient quarantine to enable the Government inspector to ascertain whether the animals are infected.' Rose was appointed chairman of a committee to draw up the rules of a 'society for the mutual assurance against loss of cattle by the new disease.' *The Times* (10 Aug 1865). The 1841 census of Waddesdon, Bucks lists a William Rose of Eythrope, age 35, born in the county.
6 Speaking at length on 15 November (n5), one J.K. Fowler had urged 'that all fat animals should be slaughtered at the ports at which they land' but 'a sort of *cordon* ... placed round those ports, and lean stock be subjected to a considerable quarantine before being allowed into the country ... I cannot go quite so far as to say that all animals should be slaughtered immediately on their arrival, unless as food for the people.' *BH* (18 Nov 1865). John Kersley Fowler of Prebendal Farm, Aylesbury, was an authority on duck breeding and rearing; he would write *Echoes of Old Country Life: Being Recollections of Sport, Politics, and Farming in the Good Old Times* (1892), *Recollections of Old Country Life: Social, Political, Sporting and Agricultural* (1894) and *Records of Old Times: Historical, Social, Political, Sporting and Agricultural* (1898). He would later be a member of the Royal Agricultural Society of England.

TO: [CHARLOTTE, BARONESS LIONEL DE ROTHSCHILD]

Grosvenor Gate [Tuesday] 8 December 1865

ORIGINAL: CIB [3]

EDITORIAL COMMENT: Grosvenor Gate paper imprinted 'MAD'.

Dec 8 1865

Dear Baroness,

We have just returned, from Strathfieldsaye,[1] & find yr agreeable note. We shall have / great pleasure in being yr guests tomorrow at dinner, but must return at / night.

Ever yours, | D.

TO: LORD HEYTESBURY   Hughenden [Tuesday] 12 December 1865 **4063**

ORIGINAL: MOPSIK [88]

EDITORIAL COMMENT: Hughenden paper. *Sic*: accomodated.

The | Lord Heytesbury[1]   Decr 12 1865

Dear Lord Heytesbury,

Charles Newberry is a good servant, & I can recommend him to you in every respect. /

I regret, that he leaves my service, but there seems to have been some quarrel in our absence, between him & the housekeeper, wh: could not be / accomodated.[2]

faithfully yours, | *B. Disraeli*

TO: WILLIAM GLADSTONE   Hughenden [Thursday] 14 December 1865 **4064**

ORIGINAL: BL ADD MSS 44408 ff207-8

EDITORIAL COMMENT: Hughenden paper.

Decr. 14 1865

Dear Mr Chancellor | of the Exchequer,[1]

Be so kind as to inform me, at yr convenience, when will be the Speech day after the meeting of Parliament.[2] /

I don't ask this information, in order to move, as at present advised, an amend-

---

1 The DS had been to Wrest Park (Countess Cowper) and to Strathfieldsaye (Duke and Duchess of Wellington). *BH* (9 Dec 1865).

---

1 William Henry Ashe à Court-Holmes (1809-1891), 2nd Baron Heytesbury 1860, MP (C) for the Isle of Wight 1837-47.

2 MA on 13 December would record that 'Charles Newberry, under butler left our service Monday after a great quarrel with Mrs Cripps during our absence (by his own desire)'. H ACC.

---

1 Gladstone would retain this office until 26 June 1866.

2 Parliament would convene on 1 February 1866 and the throne speech would be read in the Lords on the 6th. *Hansard* CLXXXI cols 21-6.

ment to the Address, but in order to arrange about another / ceremony, wh: we shall, probably, both be fulfilling at the same time.[3]

I hope Mrs Gladstone is quite well.[4]

faithfully yours, | *B. Disraeli*

4065   TO: SAMUEL SMILES   Hughenden [Friday] 15 December 1865
ORIGINAL: FIT MS 101-1947
EDITORIAL COMMENT: Hughenden paper imprinted 'MAD'.

Samuel Smiles | Esqre.   Decr. 15 1865
Sir,

On my return to Hughenden, I found your "Lives of Boulton & Watt", by the presentation of wh: I feel honored.[1]

I / have, since, been gratified by reading the work.

The subject is of vast & enduring interest, & you have treated it in a style bearing some resemblance to the great invention it / celebrates: with condensed & unceasing vigor, combined with a management of details complete & felicitous.[2]

Yours faithfully,

B. Disraeli

4066   TO: CHARLES CLUBBE   [Hughenden, Wednesday] 20 December 1865
ORIGINAL: RIC [31]
COVER: The | Revd: C.W. Clubbe A.M. | Vicarage | *B. Disraeli*
EDITORIAL COMMENT: *Recipient:* see cover.

Dec. 20. 1865

Let me know, when I return,[1] what is the complete sum for wh: they propose to contribute.[2]

Yrs | D.

---

3 Gladstone would reply on 16 December that it was 'doubtful whether swearing in would be sufficiently advanced' to proceed with business on the 6th, the cabinet having fixed the 8th for the Queen's speech. 'You will thus be enabled to fire a long shot at your guests.' He would write on 30 December to say that the speech would be given on 6 February and that there would be 'no difficulty in getting the swearing in sufficiently forward.' H B/XXI/G/105-6. In the Commons, the oaths would be taken on 2, 3, and 5 February.

4 Gladstone would reply on 16 December (n3): 'My wife has been busy in winter festivities.'

---

1 Samuel Smiles (1812-1904), MD Edinburgh 1832, editor of the *Leeds Times* 1838-44 and secretary of the Leeds and Thirsk (1845-54) and South Eastern (1854-66) railways, was a prolific author of self-help books, including the extremely popular *Self-Help* (1859), and of biographies of leaders of industry, such as *Lives of the Engineers* (3 vols 1861-2, 5 vols 1874). *Lives of Boulton and Watt* (1865) celebrates the firm of [Matthew] Boulton (1728-1809) & [James] Watt (1736-1819), formed in 1775 at Smethwick, near Birmingham, which made steam engines until 1895.

2 The Smethwick Engine, the first to use expansive steam force and a vacuum simultaneously, would revolutionize steam engine design. It pumped water back up the Smethwick locks, often twenty-four hours a day, from 1779 to 1891.

---

1 The DS would leave Hughenden on this day (20th) and return on the 28th. H acc.

2 See **4070**n1.

Hughenden [Wednesday] 3 January [1866]

ORIGINAL: PS 1465

PUBLICATION HISTORY: *BH* (13 Jan 1866)

EDITORIAL COMMENT: A paraphrase of D's letter read at Windsor on 13 January by F. Buckland, honorary secretary, to 'a committee of landowners and agriculturalists from Berks, Bucks, and Middlesex', D's being one of many communications. It was then 'resolved that the association should be called "The Windsor Mutual Cattle Insurance Association".'

Hughenden Manor, Jan. 3.

[Mr Disraeli, after expressing the gratification he always felt at co-operating with his constituents in any measure for the public welfare, observed that he had great doubts as to whether the mutual association proposed would be able to bear the burden of the pressure which would be put upon it if the pestilence should fall upon the heads of its members. The county of Buckingham ought to have established at the outset an assurance association upon the principle of limited liability, with a capital of £50,000, in 5,000 shares, £1 to be paid on each share. Every owner of stock ought to pay a regular premium on his policy, and take shares to the amount of 25 per cent, on the sum insured. These conditions would ensure prudence. Thus the landed proprietors might take any number of shares they liked, the £1 per share paid being an immediate contribution to the fund, while the policies would represent their amount of guarantee to the community. Again, fifty shares would represent an immediate subscription of £50, and a guarantee of £450.[1] These suggestions were based upon sound commercial principles. Premiums would be received, a dividend shared, and shares distributed, and the amount of premiums being considerable, there would be a large and efficient capital for purposes of compensation. When the nature of the calamity was first known he proposed to hold a county meeting, when he would have brought forward for adoption some plan of the kind; but, unfortunately, the graziers and the farmers in the Vale with whom he communicated believed for a time that the government would interfere. The letter concluded with some other observations upon the subject of local mutual assurance associations.]

TO: [CONSERVATIVE MPS] Hughenden [Thursday] 4 January 1866 4068

ORIGINAL: WSRO Mitford Archives MS55 f61b f29

PUBLICATION HISTORY: *BH* (13 Jan 1866)

EDITORIAL COMMENT: A copy to Sir William Stirling Maxwell of this facsimile of D's original has been found; the draft is H B/II/76E. *BH* publication is preceded by: 'The members of the Opposition have received the usual circular.'

Hughenden Manor | Jany. 4. 1866.

Sir,

The meeting of Parliament is fixed for the first of next month, when the members

---

1 See **4043**, **4058**n2 and **4062**.

of the House of Commons will proceed to elect / their Speaker,[1] &, then, to take the oaths.

Her Majesty's speech will be delivered on Tuesday, the 6th. Feby:; & I beg leave to request your attendance, in your place, on that day, / as business of great importance may be under consideration.[2]

I have the honor to remain, | Sir, | your faithful Servt. | *B. Disraeli*[3]

4069 TO: LORD STANHOPE   Hughenden [Tuesday 9 January 1866]

ORIGINAL: KCR Stanhope MSS 690(6)5
EDITORIAL COMMENT: Paper imprinted with a picture: 'Monument, Hughenden Manor, Buckinghamshire.' Endorsed in another hand: 'January 9, 1866'. *Dating*: by context; see n1. *Sic*: Göschen; Wycomb.

To | The Earl Stanhope
My dear Lord,
The literary Treasury of Chevening is rich, & this is not the first time, that / I have profited by it, thru' yr enduring, & always esteemed, kindness.[1]

What do you say of / Mr Göschen now?[2]

    Yours sincerely | D.
I bought this sheet, at Wycomb for a penny.[3] It may recall to you one of yr youthful haunts. I wish, I could induce / you, some day, to revisit it, with Lady Stanhope, & yr beauteous daughter.[4]

4070 TO: CHARLES CLUBBE   Hughenden [Tuesday] 9 January 1866

ORIGINAL: RIC [33]
EDITORIAL COMMENT: Hughenden paper.

The | Rev. C.W. Clubbe | A.M.   Jany 9 1866

---

1 John Evelyn Denison would be unanimously re-elected Speaker for a third term.
2 Among other matters, the Queen's speech would mention treaties with Japan and Austria, an inquiry into the Morant Bay rebellion in Jamaica, the Fenian uprising in Ireland, the cattle plague and franchise reform. *Hansard* CLXXXI cols 21-6.
3 Markham Spofforth would write to D on the 5th that 'The circular is in the proper hands and will be sent out on Monday or Tuesday unless orders to the contrary from Col Taylor are received.' H B/XXI/S/405.

---

1 Despite this letter's putative date (see ec), D appears to be thanking Stanhope for his *Catalogue of the Library at Chevening* (1865), sent to D with a letter dated 'May 21' and docketed by the archivist '?1865'. Stanhope hoped that the Ds would allow him 'the pleasure of showing you the collection itself' some day. H B/XXI/S/490.
2 On 9 January 1866, under the heading 'Mr. Göschen in the Cabinet', *The Times* reprinted an article from the *Globe* praising (and justifying) Russell's upcoming appointment of G.J. Goschen: 'His present promotion to the Cabinet is unexampled in point of rapidity, but because it is thus bold and unprecedented the public will not think it the less wise ... The accession of such a man to the Cabinet at the age of 34 is a startling deviation from our general rule by which public men are put forward so slowly that they only arrive at the leading posts in the Government when age has given them warning to retire from active life altogether.' As of 26 January, Goschen would be chancellor of the Duchy of Lancaster. See **4071**&n2.
3 For the memorial to Isaac D'Israeli, see ec and VIII **3707**&n3.
4 Lady Mary Catherine Stanhope (1844-1876) would become Countess Beauchamp in 1868 upon her marriage to 6th Earl Beauchamp.

Dear Mr. Clubbe,

I return you the Priv: Counc: Letter.[1]

The Jany. numbers of last year, (1865), are wanting in my Livraisons of the "Revue / des Deux Mondes." Could they, by any chance, be among yr papers?[2]

Yrs sincerely | D.

TO: MARKHAM SPOFFORTH   Hughenden [Wednesday] 10 January 1866   4071
ORIGINAL: PS 1547
PUBLICATION HISTORY: *The Times* (2 Sep 1931).

Confidential.

Hughenden Manor, Jan. 10, 1866.

Dear Mr. Spofforth, – ... I think the precipitate promotion of Mr. Goschen[1] a great party mistake. Ld. Russell was no doubt reconciled to Mr. Gladstone's scheme by the arrangement affording some promotion for the officials, who had been so strangely, & so unwisely, passed over in the first instance: but, tho' it may thus soothe the feelings of one or two individuals, the evil consequences to the Government must be extensive.[2]

I have, however, long resolved not to move in this affair unless we have the certainty of an extensive reconstruction. From what I hear, & observe, that is not impossible, but it will require, for its successful fulfilment, the utmost courage & discretion. I shall myself trust no one in its management, & particularly beg that you will, for the future, be most cautious in intimating nothing, as to the quarter with wh: you are communicating, to any one but myself. I am always accessible to you.

With respect to your correspondent the prospect is I fear that he will be regained, but I hope not:[3] because to a certain extent he wd. be a representative man in this

---

1 The Fondren Library, Rice University, has copies of three 1865 letters from Clubbe, headed 'Hughenden Natl. School' (see VIII **3725**&n3), to the Secretary of the Education Department, Privy Council Office: 27 October, concerning repair of school fences; 24 November, enclosing 'the Agreement shewing the conditions upon which the land has been let'; and 21 December, requesting a cost estimate for 'building a house with all the requisite outbuildings &c so as to satisfy the requirements of the Committee of Council on Education.' Clubbe was replying to Council letters dated 24 October, 20 November and 5 December 1865. RIC [28Q, 29Q, 32Q].

2 Tome 55 (Jan and Feb 1865) of *La Revue des deux mondes* included a two-part article on 'Les crises commerciales et monétaires': 'I. le money-market en ANGLETERRE depuis 50 ans' and 'II. la fuite de l'argent et la hausse de l'escompte'.

---

1 See **4069**n2.

2 As Goschen had been in Parliament only three years, his promotion was arousing hostility. 'The Whigs in the Cabinet were furious that Russell should try to out-manoeuvre them, and that the Marquis of Hartington should have been passed over ... The promotion only damaged party morale for the [reform] crisis ahead.' Smith 61-2.

3 Spofforth on 5 January had sent D a note (not found), to 'be destroyed as soon as read', from Edward Hugessen Knatchbull-Hugessen (1829-1893), BA 1851 and MA 1854 (Oxford), MP (L) for Sandwich (Kent) 1857-80, lord of the treasury 1859-66, under-sec of state for the home office 1866, 1868-71 and for the colonies 1871-4, PC 1873. Shortly after being created 1st Baron Brabourne (1880), he would become a Conservative and join the Carlton Club. A second letter (in another hand but signed by Spofforth), dated 9 January and headed 'private & confidential', had informed D that Knatchbull-Hugessen had told Spofforth that morning 'that he *had resigned the office of whip* to the Government but *had been induced to*

matter from his ancient family, their former connection with the Tory Party[4] & the freemasonry with wh:, alike from his official experience and his landed connection, he could communicate with the independent *gentlemen* of his party.

The Government must be sore pressed, & very vacillating in their course of policy, if it be true, as I am assured on the highest authority, that Mr. Lowe was recently offered Lancaster & the Cabinet.

Yours faithfully, | D.

4072 TO: EDWARD COLEMAN   Grosvenor Gate [Monday] 15 January 1866
ORIGINAL: WSH [9]
EDITORIAL COMMENT: Grosvenor Gate paper.

E.J. Coleman | Esqre.   Jany 15 1866
Dear Mr Coleman,
You have announced to me your return to the South in as magnificent a manner, as you did your / arrival in the North.[1]

Pray accept our cordial thanks for so much kindness.

We have just arrived in town for the season, but envy you in Stoke Park on such a brilliant / morning.

Mrs Disraeli unites, with me, in very kind remembrances to Mrs Coleman, who, I hope, is as well & bright, as when we last had the pleasure of seeing her.

Yours sincerely, | *B. Disraeli*

4073 TO: SIR FITZROY KELLY   Grosvenor Gate [Monday] 22 January 1866
ORIGINAL: H B/II/69a
EDITORIAL COMMENT: A draft in D's hand on Grosvenor Gate paper. In another draft, H B/II/69c, dated 20 January, D replaces 'crusade' with 'agitation' and omits 'not to say ruin'. *Sic*: embarassment.

Sir Fitzroy Kelly | M.P.   Jany 22 1866
Dear Sir Fitzroy,
I regret very much to hear, that you have again embarked in an Anti-Malt Tax crusade.[1] It can only lead to great embarassment, not to say ruin, to the party, / &

---

retain his office at the Treasury "out of personal regard for Lord Russell" *for the present* and that he was attending to financial matters in that department. He told me that it was *possible* Lord Russell might offer him a higher position under his Administration than he at present held, and that if he did so he should accept it, provisionally, but that his acceptance of such office would not guarantee his support to any material reduction of the Franchise against which he was decidedly opposed.' Knatchbull-Hugessen had also 'expressed his opinion pretty freely on Mr Goschen having been pitchforked into the Cabinet laying it entirely upon the fact of his worshipping Mr Gladstone, saying it was Mr Gladstone's doing entirely'. H B/XXI/S/405-6. In fact, Russell had insisted on the appointment, while Gladstone had advised against it. Saunders 191.

4 Knatchbull-Hugessen's father, Sir Edward Knatchbull, had been Tory MP for Kent 1819-31 and E Kent 1832-45.

---

1 Coleman apparently had sent the DS some game, perhaps from the Scottish Highlands. See **4035** and **4499**.

---

1 For the contentious malt tax issue, see VII **3095**&n2 and VIII **3890**&nn1-4. Kelly on 19 January had written to D for advice on how to proceed, asserting that 'the inescapable arguments for the repeal are at last

discomfiture to yourself. The grave & determined opinion of the country is against you, & you are only supported by a section of the landed interest, wh:, when united, is no longer irresistible.

There are particular circumstances also, wh:, at / this moment, render this course, on your part, unfortunate & disastrous.

↓G↑

I have not read Mr. Smee's pamphlet on the Malt Tax, but I have read another financial lucubration of his – & that was enough.[2]

Yours sincerely, | *B. Disraeli*

T.O. /

~~I ought to add, that, far from~~ Insert G. sanctioning yr course, it will, I fear, be my painful duty actively to resist your movement.[3]

TO: **SIR STAFFORD NORTHCOTE**   Grosvenor Gate   4074
[Monday] 22 January 1866

ORIGINAL: H H/LIFE

EDITORIAL COMMENT: From a typescript headed: 'D. to Sir S. Northcote. Grosvenor Gate. Jan. 22, 1866.' What are most likely paragraph markers ([) have been inserted manually before sentences three, four, six and eleven. Following the typescript is a transcription of part of Northcote's 23 January reply; see n7.

My dear N,

When are you coming to town? I found the plot thickening so much, & so quickly, that I deemed it prudent to come up, & I am here permanently. The state of affairs requires the greatest courage & the greatest discretion. To add to my troubles read the enclosed from Kelly, & my reply.[1] Steps must be taken by the Whips, who, of course, are not here, to make the monster meeting a fiasco – Last year, many

felt by the radical free-traders and the working classes' and alerting D to 'another monster-meeting in London on the eve of the Queen's speech, followed by a deputation to Gladstone'. *The Times* had called Kelly a 'political quack' who had gone 'beyond the bounds of common sense'. On 17 April his motion for the 'immediate reduction and ultimate repeal' of the malt duty would be defeated 234-150; no vote is recorded for D. H B/II/69b; *The Times* (26 Dec 1865); *Hansard* CLXXXII cols 1509-76.

2 Kelly (n1) had written: 'A pamphlet lately published, (Smee's) of which I'll send you a copy, makes the thing worse still, and shows that beer would be 2d. a quart instead of 4d. & 6d. if there were no malt-tax.' *The Malt Tax* (1865) by William Ray Smee (1816-1877) had gone to five editions by 1866. Smee's 'financial lucubration' included *The Income Tax; its extension at the present rate proposed to all classes; abolishing the malt-tax, etc. With observations on the Tea-Duties* (1846), *A Proposal to Increase the Smaller Salaries under Government* (1860), and *Three Letters to the Chancellor of the Exchequer* (1861), on silver and gold prices, joint stock and post office savings banks.

3 Kelly on 9 February would reply that he knew 'the result of the meeting at Free-Mason's Hall, & of the interview with Gladstone' (see **4074**n2). 'Your letter of January seems almost to identify me personally with this movement. I would, therefore, beg you to lay aside at once all considerations personal to myself. I have no personal views or interests in relation to the question.' Pressing D to tell him 'explicitly what your views are ... upon the question itself, and upon the line of conduct to be adopted in relation to it in the House of Commons', Kelly reassured D that 'no form that this question could assume need ever put a government in peril, of which you & Lord Derby are the chiefs.' H B/XXI/K/69. D would share his misgivings about Kelly with Northcote on this day (22nd) and with Stanley on the 23rd. See **4074** and **4075**.

---

1 See **4073**&n1.

members attended it, who were not obliged, but who thought, they were serving us.[2] I met Stephenson[3] at dinner at Panizzis on Saturday (Lowe also there) – He was singularly cordial, & unusually frank with me, afterwards. He said a wise Minister would do away with the Income Tax. Is Gladstone meditating this?[4] And if he is not, and is going to fritter away millions of surplus by the means announced in the "Sunday Gazette" yesterday,[5] I am not sure, in the probable temper of the House of Commons, his budget might not be upset. Lowe says, that the Reform Bill must be opposed on the second reading, & that there is a clear majority against it now, whatever its nature. But I think, in that case, it must be met by a resolution.[6]

Yours sincerely D.[7]

4075   TO: LORD STANLEY   Grosvenor Gate [Tuesday] 23 January 1866

ORIGINAL: H H/LIFE

PUBLICATION HISTORY: M&B IV 427, the sixth and seventh paragraphs; *Disraeli, Derby* 244, excerpts

EDITORIAL COMMENT: From typescripts headed 'D. to Ld. Stanley, Grosvenor Gate, Jan. 23. '66.' Endorsed in the margin: '1 Stanley had forwarded a report that "the next best morning journal to *The Times*" was in the market' and '2 Wood resigned the India Office & was succeeded by Lord de Grey, Milner Gibson' and in another hand '*solid*' twice. There are slight differences between the typescripts, the first one ending at the second sentence of the sixth paragraph. Our text is the complete one.

Dear Stanley,

The paper is, no doubt, the "Morning Post".[1] It has been brought before me by

2 Kelly had spoken at the Central Anti-Malt-Tax Association's 'monster meeting' (D quotes Kelly's term) in Ipswich on 26 December 1865, attended by MPs George Tomline, Clare Sewell Read, Lord Augustus Hervey, John Chevallier Cobbold and Major William Parker. The Association would meet again on 5 February at the Freemasons' Tavern in London, Council chairman P.S. Punnett moving a resolution (carried unanimously) that the malt tax was 'a grievous burden upon the consumers of our national home beverage, especially the working classes'. Kelly would point out that while duty on foreign wines ('the luxury of the rich') had been reduced, the tax on malt and beer ('one of the necessaries of life to millions of the humble and labouring classes') had been increased. On 7 February Gladstone would tell a deputation of Association members and 29 MPs that he was 'not unduly given to the relief of mere class interests', cautioning them that 'nothing except a very magnificent surplus can serve to raise for immediate purposes the question of the malt-tax.' *The Times* (26 Dec 1865, 6 and 8 Feb 1866).

3 Sir William Henry Stephenson (1811-1898), KCB 1871, Peel's private secretary 1843-7, was chairman of the inland revenue commission 1862-77.

4 As chancellor of the exchequer, Gladstone had steadily reduced the income tax: from 9 pence in 1861 to 7 in 1863, 5 in 1864 and 4 in 1865. In the House on 9 February he would state that 'the present system of assessing and collecting the Queen's taxes is a most defective one' and would call for a re-examination of the subject. L.C.B. Seaman *Victorian England: Aspects of English and Imperial History, 1837-1901* (1973) 183-4; *Hansard* CLXXXI cols 308-9.

5 Stanley on 4 February 1866 would note that 'Delane and Lord Russell seem to have quarrelled, and Lord R. gives whatever information he has to give to a new journal called the *Sunday Gazette*, which is in his interest.' *Disraeli, Derby* 245.

6 The Representation of the People Bill would have its first reading on 12 March and protracted second reading on 12, 13, 16, 19, 20, 23, 26 and 27 April. It would be discussed together with the Redistribution of Seats Bill on 28 and 31 May and 1, 4, 7, 8, 11, 14 and 18 June. Both bills would be withdrawn on 19 July.

7 On 23 January (see ec), in returning Kelly's letter and D's reply, Northcote cautioned D 'to avoid false moves of all kinds. The Government appears to be in great difficulties, & if we are quiet I think they are not unlikely to break down.'

---

1 On 21 January Stanley had written to D enclosing an 18 January letter from Samuel Lucas, first editor in 1853 of the Conservative weekly *The Press* (see VI **2498**&n1), which he edited for a year, and reviewer for

two or three persons. My opinion is, that a formal connection between journals and leaders is advantageous to neither parties. In the present instance, your correspondent would like much to call on Ministers of State, or leaders of opposition, and lounge and gossip, and occasionally dine. He is not without some brilliancy: but there's no practice in him, and his vanity and conceit reach almost to insanity. We gave him a place of £1,000 per ann:, when we were in office, which he rejected, because he wanted to reside in the Metropolis, and be a permanent U.S. of State.[2]

A weekly organ, to give the tone to the Press generally, might be useful: I dare say it will come when it is wanted.

Wood remains, tho' he came up to town to resign. At the last moment, it was discovered that Milner Gibson expected the office, and would resign if he did not receive it.[3]

Johnny, smarting still under the Goschen fiasco,[4] could not face this, which would certainly have induced the immediate resignation of Charles Villiers. It seems, that Gibson has been, for some time, discontented, and declares, that he is heartsick of the B. of Trade.[5]

Johnny, who really wished to bring Bright into the Cabinet, could not bring himself to make a Secretary of State out of a man, whose proper province in life was to have been a counter jumper at Swan and Edgars.[6]

I have been here some days, and, pretty well, know everything. The whole affair is utterly rotten; quite ruined; the blow will be struck from the other side. The appointment of Goschen precipitated the resolution. It was the first nail in their coffin, according to Milner Gibson, but the sound of the undertaker in the house has been heard ever since. But what then? The present plan, I hear, is to meet the 2nd. Reading of the Reform Bill adversely. In that case, I should think, it would be wise to

The Times 1855-65. Stanley had asked D which newspaper Lucas meant when writing about 'an opening for a Liberal Conservative paper, as the next best morning journal to the Times is now in the market. You will doubtless guess the Journal I allude to, but as yet its name must not be mentioned until the negotiations for its purchase are completed. The terms asked by the intending sellers are £30,000'. Lucas's 'rich friends', who were 'resolved to raise the capital', wanted Stanley's advice 'as to the direction which such a Journal should take.' Fitzroy Kelly had brought the paper to D's attention on 19 January: 'Could not we seize upon the Morning Post? It's floating about without helm or compass. We're miserably off with the press, & such a paper would help much to set us up.' H B/XX/S/727, 727a; II/69b.

2 Lucas had been appointed stamp distributor under Derby in 1858. See VII **3250**n4.

3 Stanley (n1) believed 'Wood will retire – he is really damaged in health by his accident'. On 7 February *The Times* would announce Wood's 'sudden retirement' (following a hunting accident) as secretary of state for India and his replacement by Lord de Grey, noting wryly that 'India is the land of official crotchets and unsound theories, and the anomalies of its administration have often warped the minds of the most clear-headed men.' De Grey would remain in office only from 16 February to 26 June, when the Government would fall. Meanwhile, Gibson remained president of the board of trade.

4 For George Goschen's swift promotion, see **4069**n2 and **4071**&n2.

5 That Gibson was 'heartsick' is evidenced by a comment on this day (23rd) to his constituents at Ashton-Under-Lyne (in an otherwise uplifting and positive speech) that the board of trade had more 'important business ... than I have ability and physical power to look well after'. *The Times* (24 Jan 1866).

6 In December 1868 Bright would become the first Quaker cabinet minister when, after declining India, he accepted an appointment as president of the board of trade. Swan and Edgar Ltd, 49 Regent Street, Piccadilly, specialized in fine wools and silks. 'Counter jumper' is a derogatory term for a shopkeeper or shopkeeper's assistant. Bright's father Jacob, a cotton spinner and manufacturer, had founded a cotton mill at Rochdale in 1823.

meet it by a resolution; but, at present, I shall leave them to themselves. The other side will do the business.

That knave, Sir Fitzroy [Kelly], is recommencing his mischievous agitation about the Malt Tax. He has arranged for a monster meeting in London, and then has the impudence to ask for my counsel. I have given him such a duster in reply, that he has gone, I believe for his health, to Torquay.[7] I am taking measures to prevent our men unnecessarily going to his meeting, which many did last year, thinking they were aiding us. Far from sanctioning him, I have told him I shall oppose him actively and personally. He may do immense mischief.

I suspect that Gladstone is going to terminate the Income Tax.[8]

Yours ever, I D.[9]

4076

TO: B. HEPBURN   Grosvenor Gate [Thursday] 25 January 1866
ORIGINAL: MOPSIK [108]
EDITORIAL COMMENT: Grosvenor Gate paper imprinted 'MAD'.

Private   Jan 25 1866

B. Hepburn[1] I Esqr

Dear Sir,

Can you receive me, Saturday morning next, at eleven o'ck:?

Yrs flly I D.

4077

TO: EDWARD COLEMAN   Grosvenor Gate [Saturday] 3 February 1866
ORIGINAL: WSH [8]
EDITORIAL COMMENT: Grosvenor Gate paper imprinted 'MAD'.

Private   Feb: 3 1866

E. Coleman Esqr

Dear Mr Coleman,

I signed your nomination, at the Carlton, on Thursday; I am not, myself, on the / Committee, but I will take ↑care↓ to mention, to some of its members, my particular wish, that you shd. be selected.[1]

My / compliments to Mrs. Coleman.

Yours sincerely, I *B. Disraeli*

---

7 For D's 'duster', replying to Kelly's 19 January letter (n1) headed 'Torquay', and Kelly's reply, see **4073**&n3.

8 Following a meeting with D on 30 January, Stanley would record that D 'has also got an idea that Gladstone means to sweep away the income-tax, replacing it by a tax on capital exclusively – this he seems to have picked up from one of the Rothschilds.' *Disraeli, Derby* 245.

9 Stanley on 24 January would thank D 'for a very curious & interesting letter.' H B/XX/S/729.

---

1 Possibly John Buchan-Hepburn (1806-1874) of Clune, Fife, brother of Sir Thomas Buchan-Hepburn (1804-1893), 3rd Bt, of Smeaton-Hepburn, co Haddington, MP (C) for Haddingtonshire 1838-47.

---

1 Coleman would become a member of the Carlton Club.

Grosvenor Gate [Saturday] 10 February 1866 **4078**

ORIGINAL: H R/I/A/190

COVER: Philip Rose Esqre | 59 Rutland Gate. | *B. Disraeli*

EDITORIAL COMMENT: Grosvenor Gate paper imprinted 'MAD'.

Private Feb 10 1866

Phil: Rose Esqr

My dear Rose,

Your letter of the 26th. Ulto.[1] was only delivered at the Carlton yesterday! I went down immediately to Mr Harvey,[2] but he was not in town.

I wish everything to be done / as arranged: the two things to be dropped, & the money to be paid to you. It was down in my mem[oran]da "anytime before the 14th. Feby"[.]

However, I can do it when I see you, wh: I hope to do very soon, as I wish to consult you on / a matter of some interest & importance.

I have appointments today until four o'ck: but cd. call on you afterwards.

I cd. see you tomorrow, or any morning, in your way to yr office: except Tuesday, as we shall have a debate that / night,[3] & I don't want to be distracted with private affairs.

Yours ever, | D.

Grosvenor Gate [Sunday] 11 February 1866 **4079**

ORIGINAL: H R/I/A/191

COVER: Philip Rose Esq | 59 Rutland Gate | *B. Disraeli*

EDITORIAL COMMENT: Grosvenor Gate paper.

P. Rose Esqr Feb 11 1866

My dear Rose,

I return the Californian letter.[1] It seems, to me, more than a coincidence!

Yrs ever | D.

Charles Street [Tuesday] 20 February 1866 **4080**

ORIGINAL: H R/I/A/192

EDITORIAL COMMENT: Paper imprinted: '26, Charles Street, St. James', London, S.W. _____ 186__.' (office of solicitor William Lovell). Following this letter is a note in another hand: 'The Policy is for £2500. No. 11762 and dated 30 August 1856. Mr. Rose's letter to the Clerical is dated 12 Jany 1863.'

P. Rose Esqr Feb 20 [186]6

---

1 This letter has not been found.

2 Possibly estate agent William Henry Harvey.

3 The House would meet very briefly on Tuesday 13 February, mostly to discuss the Parliamentary Oaths Bill, from 4 to 5:30 *pm*. *Hansard* CLXXXI cols 447-60.

---

1 This letter has not been found. The San Francisco weekly *The Californian* (founded 1864) published poetry, satire and political essays.

My dear Mr Rose

There is a hitch in some policies, wh: I am surrendering, in consequence of a letter written by you three years ago to the "Clerical,"[1] thro' some / mistake, originating from the similarity of name betn. Mr Lovell & Mr Lovegrove of Gloucester, & there being two policies in the same office.[2] The / Gloucester one was surrendered long ago, as you know [.] What we want is, that you shd. withdraw, & immediately, the notices you gave the "Clerical" in 1863.

Yours sincy | *B. Disraeli*

4081   TO: [LORD DERBY]   Carlton Club [Tuesday 27 February 1866]
ORIGINAL: DBP Box 146/2
EDITORIAL COMMENT: Carlton Club paper. Endorsed in another hand on the first page: 'Feb. 27' and on the fourth page: 'Disraeli B'. *Dating*: by context; see n1.

¼ to one o'ck:
My dear Lord,

Ld. Russell resigned the day that Phipps died. He was with the Queen when the telegram arrived, informing / H. M. of the decease. The Queen showed it to Lord Russell & said "this must be postponed: I ~~cons~~ can attend to no public business now." / This has occasioned the delay.[1]

This may be depended on. | D.

4082   TO: SIR STAFFORD NORTHCOTE Grosvenor Gate [Thursday] 1 March 1866
ORIGINAL: H H/LIFE
EDITORIAL COMMENT: From a typescript headed: 'D. to Sir S. Northcote. Grosvenor Gate. March 1. 1866.'

My dear N,

I think it would be advisable that you should fall in with Lord Carnarvon today,[1] and prevent his connecting his future with the *Retrograde* party.[2]

Yours, D.

1 Neither Rose's 12 January 1863 letter to the 'Clerical' (perhaps an insurance company) nor D's £2,500 policy of 1856 has been found.
2 D's solicitor William Lovell, from whose office D is writing (see ec), had been D's creditor and financial agent; attorney Joseph Lovegrove was agent of D's Gloucester properties (see V **2001**n1).

———

1 Sir Charles Phipps, keeper of the Queen's privy purse since 1849, had died of bronchitis on 24 February 1866. *The Times* on the 26th had noted that, due to his death, the Queen had postponed her 27 February court to 9 March. D likely refers to the 'delay' in announcing Russell's resignation. Although he would not resign until 26 June, *The Times* on 28 February would report the rumour that 'Lord Russell has asked Her Majesty to relieve him from duties which have proved too irksome for him, and has begged permission to resign once more the office of First Minister of the Crown.'

———

1 In the Lords on this day (1 March), Carnarvon would propose that the 'thirty-six different Railway Bills affecting the metropolis at present before Parliament', and involving great inconvenience and injustices particularly to the displaced poor and working classes, be monitored by a committee, as had been the case in 1863-4 when 'an almost equally large number of railway schemes were launched'. *Hansard* CLXXXI cols 1275-9.
2 Carnarvon, with a reactionary approach to issues such as parliamentary reform about to be brought up in the Commons, was difficult to keep within the confines of party policy. He would resign abruptly on 5 March 1867; see **4358**&n1.

ORIGINAL: KCR Stanhope MSS 690(6)6

EDITORIAL COMMENT: Grosvenor Gate paper imprinted 'MAD'.

The | Earl Stanhope   March 7 1866

My dear Lord,

Notwithstanding morning sittings,[1] & party meetings,[2] I must thank you for your letter.[3]

    No one does so many kind things as Lord Stanhope, & in so kind a manner!

    Yours most sincerely,| D.

TO: [SIR STAFFORD NORTHCOTE] [London, after Thursday 8 March 1866] **4084**

ORIGINAL: PS 1532

PUBLICATION HISTORY: Blake 439; Bradford 260, omitting the fragment and first sentence; Northcote I 251, 'Salisbury' replaced by a long dash

EDITORIAL COMMENT: *Recipient* and *Dating*: by context; see n1.

dreams of princesses in fairyland. Lady Salisbury wants Stanley to take a leading place. It won't do. W.E.G. and S. sound very well. One is a man of transcendent ability; the other, though not of transcendent ability has considerable power. But neither of them can deal with men. S. is a mere child in such matters. The other, though more experienced, is too impetuous and wanting in judgment to succeed as a leader.[1]

1 The 7 March sitting of the House, from noon to 5 *pm*, had been taken up by the second reading of the Church Rates Abolition Bill. *Hansard* CLXXXI cols 1632-95 (D 1690).

2 Lord Salisbury would host meetings of the Conservative party on 8 and 16 March. On the 8th it would be resolved that 'no opposition should be offered to the introduction of the Reform Bill on Monday next, but that during the interval between its introduction and the second reading ... the party would consider what course should be pursued'. Later that day, at a secret meeting, D, Walpole, Heathcote, Northcote and Cranborne would agree to speak in support of the Liberal rebels; this appears to have been done without Derby's knowledge. Saunders 197. On the 16th, from 2 to 3 *pm*, with D speaking in Derby's absence (from gout) to over 200 members, it would be agreed to oppose the bill. *The Times* (9, 19 Mar 1866).

3 Stanhope had written on 6 March announcing D's election that afternoon to the Athenaeum Club, quoting the rule that the committee '"will only elect persons who have attained to distinguished eminence"' and welcoming D to 'a very agreeable resort. One meets here accomplished men of all parties; & there is an excellent collection of 30,000 volumes'. In H is the official letter to D, dated 6 March 1866, announcing his unanimous election to the Athenaeum. H B/XXI/S/491; H A/IV/M/3. For D's 30 January 1835 letter to Stanhope seeking nomination (stressing 'the utmost importance to me to become a member of the Athenaeum Club, on account of its library') and Stanhope's reply, see II 371&nn2&5 and 372&n1.

---

1 Northcote on 8 March 1866 records that he had told D of Lady Salisbury's views, 'which he treated as the "dreams of princesses in fairyland," and quite unpractical.' Northcote I 251. According to Blake (439), it was 'a plan of Lady Salisbury that Stanley should take office under Gladstone at the head of a Conservative-Liberal alliance.'

4085

TO: LORD DERBY   Grosvenor Gate, Friday [9 March 1866]
ORIGINAL: DBP Box 146/1
EDITORIAL COMMENT: Above the salutation Derby has inserted 'Mar 9'. *Dating*: by context; see nn2&4.
Sic: Torquamada.

Rt Honble | The Earl of Derby | K. G.   Friday G Gate

My dear Lord

I am obliged to go out of town this morning, & shall hardly get up for House of Comm: wh: is the reason I cannot call.[1]

The affair was very successful in the House, & the Govt., Monsell told / me, would take our oath, on both points.[2]

The truth is, there is a majority for us in the House: the Scotch members cheered me much.

Bowyer told me, if we were firm, we should / win, but said he cd. do nothing for us, & dare not speak. He showed me a letter from Manning worthy of Torquamada![3] I'll tell you about it when we meet, & other things.

I propose to call tomorrow after Brit: Mus: / wh: will suit you, I hope; three ock:[4]

I propose to have the oath ready for Monday, & read it to the House when I give notice. Will you, therefore, draw it up in the complete form.

My hand is frozen – but I hope you can read this.

Yrs | D.

4086

TO: ROBERT WATERS   [London, after 16 March 1866]
ORIGINAL: H B/II/128b
EDITORIAL COMMENT: A draft reply in D's hand to a letter from Robert Waters dated 16 March 1866. *Sic*:
commited.

Sir,[1]

I have to acknowledge yr letter of the 16. Inst informing me that you have not been

---

1 In the House on Friday 9 March 1866 Sir Henry Barron would ask D when he would table the amendments to the Parliamentary Oaths Amendment Bill (see n2), D replying that he would table 'the terms of the oath which I mean to propose in a complete form' on 14 March. *Hansard* CLXXXI col 1808.

2 In the House on 8 March 1866 the second reading of the Parliamentary Oaths Amendment Bill had been carried 298 to 5. Although D would 'cheerfully consent' to the second reading, he had two 'grave objections' to the oath: that it was 'an oath of allegiance to the Queen alone, and not to her heirs and successors', and that 'it makes no reference to the supremacy of the Crown' in the country's law courts. He concluded by assuring members that he would 'place on the table an uniform oath, constructed to meet the two great points which I have endeavoured to impress on the attention of the House'. The bill would be discussed in committee on 15 March, passed on 19th and debated in the Lords on 20 March and 16, 19, 20 and 23 April. The Lords' amendments would be agreed to on 26 April and the bill given royal assent on 30 April. *Hansard* CLXXXI cols 1712-36 (D 1712-21); CLXXXII cols 289-314 (D 297-8, 300-1, 307-8), 509-18, 1322-55, 1616-28, 1759-60, 1865, 2176.

3 MP (L) Sir George Bowyer and Archbishop Henry Edward Manning were Catholic converts. Spanish Dominican friar Tomàs de Torquemada (1420-1498) was the first Inquisitor General (or Grand Inquisitor) 1483-98.

4 Derby on 9 March 1866 would reply from St James's Square: 'I am glad to hear that all passed off so well yesterday, and that the prospects for the future are so good. I shall be happy to see you at 3 o'Clock tomorrow. When you come, will you bring with you a print of the Govt. Bill? I have not one by me.' H B/ XX/s/342.

---

1 Robert Edmond Chester Waters, a barrister (Inner Temple 1852) who had stood unsuccessfully for Nor-

elected a member of the J.C. Cb. & calling on me as "leader of the party" to secure for you a diff[eren]t result[.] / I am ↑commited to be↓ one of the Trus of J.C. Cb., but I do not interfere in its management, wh: is entrusted to a Comm[itt]ee ~~who alone~~ of gentlemen & with ~~their~~ whom ↑alone↓ must depend the decision of questions that wh: you have put under my notice.

TO: LORD HARTINGTON   Hughenden, Monday [2 April] 1866   **4087**
ORIGINAL: DEV 340.248
EDITORIAL COMMENT: Hughenden paper. Endorsed in another hand on the second page: 'Rt. Hon. B. Disraeli MP 3rd April/66. Pte Sadler's Effects Case Ansd 7/4/66.' *Dating*: Easter Monday was 2 April in 1866.

Hughenden Manor | Easter Monday 1866

Right Honorable | The Lord Hartington | M[.]P.[1]

Dear Lord Hartington,

Pray, at your leisure, read the enclosed letter from the Vicar of Turville.[2]

    I confess, I think the / matter requires sifting.

        Yours faithfully, | *B. Disraeli*

TO: [UNKNOWN]   Hughenden [Wednesday] 4 April 1866   **4088**
ORIGINAL: BODL Ms. Autogr b.8 f698
EDITORIAL COMMENT: A fragment in D's hand on Hughenden paper.

April 4 1866

Mr Disraeli presents [*the rest of the leaf has been cut off; verso*] so obliging as to present to Mr

wich in 1865, had written to D on 16 March 1866, indignant that his name, having been proposed by Markham Spofforth and T.E. Taylor for membership in the Junior Carlton Club, had been withdrawn by Taylor 'on my being opposed from personal spite by an old schoolfellow'. Claiming early assurances that 'my election was secure', Waters demanded his name 'be replaced for immediate ballot' and appealed to D not to 'allow this grievance to remain without remedy'. H B/II/128a. For Derby's fears that the Club might create jealousies through exclusivity, see VIII **3841**n3 and **3882**n3.

---

1 Lord Hartington, former under-secretary for war, had been secretary for war since 16 February.
2 Richard Wallace Deane, BA 1841 and MA 1842 Oxford, deacon 1843 and priest 1844 by the Bishop of Ely, was chaplain to the Bedford Infirmary and to the Bedford Union. *Clergy List* (1860). Deane, now vicar of Turville, Bucks, had written to D on 14 March about the plight of a parishioner, William Sadler, whose son (not named), a private in the 19th Regiment of Foot, had died in India in August 1863. The Sadlers had duly applied to the War Office for their son's £15, held (as of May 1863) in the Regimental Savings Bank. After a two-year delay and the death of the father, the mother (now remarried) had received a letter addressed to her deceased husband with 'the sum of One Pound and one Penny' and 'an intimation that he was to look for no more.' Deane asked D whether the case required 'some more satisfactory explanation than persons in a private station can very easily obtain.' In H there is an undated synopsis of Deane's letter in D's hand. H B/II/127a,b.

4089

TO: [MARKHAM SPOFFORTH]   Grosvenor Gate [Tuesday] 10 April 1866

ORIGINAL: PS 1542

PUBLICATION HISTORY: *The Times* (2 Sep 1931), headed 'Disraeli to an agent' and sub-headed 'Markham Spofforth'.

Private   Grosvenor Gate, April 10, 1866.

My dear Sir, –

What amount of the inhabitants of the great Boros lives without the Parliamentary line, is of the utmost importance to ascertain. Is there any parl[iamentar]y return of Boundaries? I fear not. Could you obtain from our agents, for my purposes, information in half-a-doz: cases?[1] So that I could get it in time for my speech, it wd. do. That might be this day week. I would suggest Birmingham, Brighton, as I believe these are very illustrative, & two or three others you may fix on. Thank you for what you sent.[2]

Yours ffy,

D.[3]

4090

TO: DAVID ROBERT PLUNKET   [London? after 12 April 1866]

ORIGINAL: H H/LIFE

EDITORIAL COMMENT: From a MS copy headed: '*Wynyard* | Dr Mahaffy. | D. to D. Plunket when a new member from Ireland (Mr. Pim) made a speech'. *Dating*: by context; see n1.

I have observed that the members you send us from Ireland are generally either gentlemen or ruffians. This one appears to be neither.[1]

1 Electoral analyst Dudley Baxter would send D on this day (10th) 'a copy of a pamphlet I have today published [*most likely* 'The Redistribution of Seats and the Counties' (37 pp)]. I am searching for the information for which you wrote to Mr Spofforth. Our agents in large Boroughs all say that enlargement to include part of the County will be a double advantage to us, first by modifying the deeper Radicalism of the present Constituencies & secondly by taking a large number of Town voters out of the Counties. The small boroughs vary in opinion, but generally the same view is held, especially in Boroughs now Radical.' On the 11th Baxter would send D a 'List of Boroughs in Lancashire and Yorkshire, which have Manufacturing populations close by their boundary, and which ought to be enlarged to include that population.' H B/XI/D/18, 21. See **4093**n3.

2 Spofforth had written to D on this day (10th): 'I have written to our agents and am having the Parliamentary returns carefully looked through to see if there be anything likely to answer your purpose. I send for your assistance a complete Copy of the Boundary Reports by which the present limits of the Boroughs (as settled in 1832) and Counties are defined. I have underlined in the enclosed returns those Boroughs from which I hope to receive the information.' H B/XXI/S/412.

3 Spofforth on the 11th would send a 'private & *confidential*' letter to Grosvenor Gate: 'Dr Guy, who you will remember was very useful in preparing statistics for your Reform Bill of 1859 [*see* VII **3295**&n2] has been good enough to make extracts from the Population Returns with regard to the Boroughs enumerated in the enclosed Paper. You will see that the Parliamentary Borough is in Brighton, Birmingham[,] Manchester[,] Birmingham [*a lapsus for* '*Buckingham*'], Calne and High Wycombe, larger than the Municipal. I quite understand that you want to get the inhabitants whether within or without the *Municipal* but Dr Guy's general impression from these Returns is that the Parliamentary Limits are larger than the Municipal. When the real Returns come in from the agents I will make a tabular statement and furnish it to you, I hope by Saturday.' The two-page enclosure lists statistics for Chipping Wycombe, Brighton, Birmingham, Manchester, Ashton under Lyne, Buckingham and Calne. H B/XXI/S/413, 413a.

1 MP (C) David Robert Plunket (1838-1919), an Irish barrister 1862, QC (Ireland) 1868, sol-gen for Ireland 1875-7, PC 1880, first commissioner of works 1885-6 and 1886-92, would unsuccessfully contest Dublin City in 1868 but sit for Dublin University 1870-95. Draper and textile manufacturer Jonathan Pim (1806-1885),

Confidential   April 14 1866

W.F. Dick | Esqr. M.P.

My dear Dick,

Laing told my informant yesterday, that, counting everyone, the Govt. would have a majority of *10*.[1]

Had the wild Irish gone / tolerably right, the game, therefore, might be won.

But you observed, of course, that Maguire moved the adjournment of the debate, & it was clearly understood by the Speaker, in favor of the Government.[2] /

Most private

You may have heard rumors, but this may be relied on tho', so far as I am concerned, *secret* – Ld. Clanrickarde has declared against the Govt. &

Ld. Dunkellin[3]

Gregory

Morris[4]

&

Blennerhassett[5]

vote / with us – but the least said about this the better.

Yrs ever | D.

то: LORD HENRY LENNOX   Grosvenor Gate [Saturday] 14 April 1866   **4092**
ORIGINAL: MOPSIK [110]
EDITORIAL COMMENT: Grosvenor Gate paper imprinted 'MAD'.

Lord H. Lennox   April 14 1866

---

author of *The Condition and Prospects of Ireland* (1848), was MP (L) for Dublin City 1865-74 and the first Irish Quaker to sit in Parliament. In his speech at the second reading of the Representation of the People Bill on 12 April 1866, Pim expressed 'great difficulty in refusing his support to the Government' and 'felt that he ought not to be led blindfold into a course of which he could not approve.' *Hansard* CLXXXII cols 1186-92. Sir John Pentland Mahaffy (see ec), ordained 1864, was a historian and littérateur.

---

1   On 12 April Grosvenor had tabled a now-famous amendment (see **4098**n1) that would be discussed over several nights. The debate would conclude on the 27th with a division that would give the government a majority of 5, widely viewed as a moral defeat.

2   The previous day (13 April), after a second night of long debate on the Representation of the People Bill, John Francis Maguire had moved to adjourn at 12:30 *am*. *Hansard* CLXXXII cols 1227-1321.

3   Ulick Canning de Burgh (1827-1867), Lord Dunkellin, eldest son of Lord Clanrickarde, had been aide-de-camp to the LL of Ireland 1846-52, ensign 1846 and lieut-col 1854-60 in the Coldstream Guards and military secretary to Lord Canning in India 1856. He was MP (L) for Galway borough 1857-9 and co Galway 1865-7. On 18 June Dunkellin would move the amendment that would bring about Russell's resignation; see **4111**n1.

4   William Morris (1811-1877), a banker, JP for Carmarthen co and borough, high sheriff 1858 and MP (L) for Carmarthen district 1864-8.

5   Sir Rowland Blennerhassett (1839-1909), 4th Bt 1849, MP (L) for Galway borough 1865-74 and co Kerry 1880-5, inspector of reformatory and industrial schools 1890-7 and president of Queen's College, Cork 1897-1904. He would found a weekly newspaper, the *Chronicle*, whose early support for Irish home rule made it short-lived: 23 March 1867 to 13 February 1868.

My dear Henry,

I am sorry I cannot receive you tomorrow, but I have, at this moment, my time entirely occupied. I / am sure from yr talents & H of Comm: experience, you will say the right thing.[1]

Yrs ever | D.

4093 TO: ROBERT DUDLEY BAXTER Grosvenor Gate, Tuesday [22 April 1866]

ORIGINAL: QUA 61

EDITORIAL COMMENT: Endorsed in another hand on the fourth page: 'Letter April 1866. for information for Speech on Reform – April 27'. *Dating*: by context; see nn2&3.

Private Grosvenor Gate: | Tuesday

R.D. Baxter | Esqr[1]

Dear Sir

I must have precise information respecting Rochdale.[2] The blue book says there are no, or rather very few, workmen on the / registry, because they live without the boundary of the Boro.

Is there without the Boundary a continuous urban population, & of considerable

---

1 Lennox on 28 April would preside over a dinner of the Artists' Benevolent Fund Society and give 'a very humourous [*sic*] speech'. *The Times* (30 Apr 1866).

---

1 Robert Dudley Baxter (1827-1875), who had joined his father's firm (Baxter, Rose & Norton) in 1865, was a statistician, demographer and electoral analyst. He would act as special adviser to Derby and D on franchise reform and draft the 1867 Reform Bill (redrafted by the home office draftsman); see **4368**&n1. His works include *The Budget and the Income Tax* (1860), *The Franchise Returns and the Boroughs* (1866), *Railway Extension and its Results* (1866), *The National Income* (1868), *Results of The General Election of 1868* (1869), *The Taxation of The United Kingdom* (1869) and *History of the English Parties and Conservatism* (1870). *Norton Rose* 62-3, 78. Among D's political papers are two 1866 pamphlets by Baxter: *The New Reform Bill. The Franchise Returns Critically Examined, with a table of the future constituency, and proportion of the working classes in each borough* (44 pp) and *The Redistribution of Seats and the Counties* (37 pp). H B/XI/F/26-7. *The Times* on 18 May would praise Baxter's *Redistribution* pamphlet, which showed that 'The Counties overpower the Boroughs in population, in electors, and in rental, and yet they are wofully [*sic*] deficient in members.'

2 Baxter on the 24th would reply, 'You shall have the Rochdale information by Thursday.' On Friday 27th he would send D 'the following papers. 1 Rochdale Boundaries & Cooperative Societies. 2. Ashton under Lyne Copy Petition and papers. 3 Stoke on Trent (Burslem) Copy Petition & papers. 4 Ashburton. Letters as to Working Men. 5 Memorandum as to Working Men. 6. Lowering the Franchise. Also two petitions (tied together) 1 Ashton under Lyne (Parchment) 2 Stoke upon Trent (Paper.) ... Also Map of Rochdale ... I hope you received at the House last night a Petition from Rochdale and a paper on Lowering the Franchise with a Table, which I left with the doorkeeper ... I have the list of the Rochdale Working Men Voters if it is of any use to you.' There are in H some undated papers about Rochdale (Lancashire), a Liberal stronghold represented by Thomas B. Potter 1865-95: 'Rochdale is an exact circle of three quarters of a mile from the centre of the Town and a very large population resides just outside the circle ... A curious circumstance is that in 1832 the Reform Bill as originally drawn included the whole of Rochdale Parish with two Members. The Radicals knowing that this would be adverse to them came up to London and got the Bill altered to the ¾ mile boundary now existing, thus restricting it to the most Radical portion.' H B/XI/D/37, 39; F/10-16.

amount? I must have a distinct reply to this. / If I get it on Friday morning, it would do. The debate closes on that day, & on that day I shall speak. D.V.[3]

 Yours faithfully, | D.[4]

TO: CHARLES GARTH COLLETON RENNIE   Grosvenor Gate   **4094**
                                          [Thursday] 10 May 1866

ORIGINAL: NLS 966 f100
EDITORIAL COMMENT: Grosvenor Gate paper imprinted 'MAD'.

May 10 1866

Mr Disraeli presents his Compliments to Mr Colleton Rennie,[1] & thanks Mr Rennie for his interesting paper.[2] /

 Mr. Disraeli regrets extremely, that he is so much engaged at this moment, that / he cannot make an appointment to see Mr Rennie, but he wd be extremely obliged to Mr Rennie to / send him further information;[3] & in time for Monday's debate, when he will require it[.][4]

---

3 One of the three petitions D would present in the House on Friday 27 April was from the electors of Rochdale. Noticing 'that the number of the working classes upon the Parliamentary register' in their borough had been stated in the Government returns to be only 68, they had inquired into the number of working men 'that came within the instructions of the Poor Law Board' and 'found the number in one township to be 68, in another 53, and in a third 105', a total of 226 not counting 'overseers, superintendents, or foremen, not employed in daily manual labour.' *Hansard* CLXXXIII col 4.

4 Spofforth on 10 April had made similar inquiries at D's behest (see **4089**&nn1-3), as evidenced by the 14 April reply from an informant in Brompton (Chatham borough) providing information on 'the number of Inhabitants living without the Parliamentary Boundary & within the Parish.' H B/XI/F/22.

---

1 Charles Garth Colleton Rennie (1837-1893), son of civil engineer Sir John Rennie, MA 1863 Trinity College (Cambridge), a barrister (Inner Temple 1863). Joseph Foster *Men-At-The-Bar* (1885) 389.

2 Rennie on 7 May had sent D 'statistics on the Reform question ... sufficient to show that an universal and all important movement is in progress, which cannot be overlooked in connection with Reform. They show, 1st That a far greater number of operatives are in possession of the county franchise than is generally supposed, perhaps equal to one fourth of the whole[.] 2nd That this population is rapidly increasing. 3rd That operatives have already a means of obtaining the franchise, of which they most eagerly avail themselves. 4th That the small number of operatives on the register of the great Northern boroughs is due to their preferring to build their own freeholds without the borough boundaries to renting houses within them.' Rennie had asked to meet D and offered to send him 'further explanation or information'. H B/XI/D/46. The 'interesting paper' may have been Rennie's *Reform considered in connection with the government bill* (1866, 47 p).

3 Rennie on 14 May would send D 'some of the statistics [D] required'. He believed 'the present bill is aimed almost exclusively at the county constituency' and was 'one of the most dangerous & factious schemes ever laid before parliament.' H B/XI/D/52.

4 In the House on 14 May most of the debate would be taken up by the second reading of the Redistribution of Seats Bill. *Hansard* CLXXXIII cols 874-921 (D 874-901). In reporting D's speech, *The Times* on 18 May would note that while he repudiated 'the argument on behalf of increased representation of Counties', D had formerly asserted that 'whether tried by the test of wealth, of population, or of electoral numbers, the County members bore a less proportion to the members for Boroughs than they ought.' *BH* on 19 May would summarize the speech, noting D's 'doubt and suspicion' at the government's proposed 'plurality of voting', which would add representatives to places already represented and result in 'an enfeebled and imperfect local representation.' To preserve the distinctive character of county constituencies, D had urged Gladstone to form a commission to visit all boroughs and report on their boundaries. The Government declined to act upon D's advice.

4095   TO: ROBERT DUDLEY BAXTER   Grosvenor Gate [Tuesday] 15 May 1866

ORIGINAL: QUA 63

EDITORIAL COMMENT: Grosvenor Gate paper imprinted 'MAD'. Endorsed by D on the *verso* of the last page: 'R. Dudley Baxter Esqr D.'

May 15 1866

Dear Sir,

I fear this may not be all, but I can't put my hand on any others at this moment – Let me know, if necessary [.][1]

Yrs ffly | D.

4096   TO: LORD ELCHO   Grosvenor Gate [Wednesday] 16 May 1866

ORIGINAL: SRO [8]

EDITORIAL COMMENT: Grosvenor Gate paper.

The | Lord Elcho | M.P.   May 16 1866

My dear Lord,

I thank you much for your letter, wh: I highly appreciate.[1]

I return the "state paper", wh: is / an interesting record of the views, feelings, & circumstances, wh: have mainly led to the present political position, & wh: may have a permanent effect on the state of / parties. I am obliged to you for permitting me to read it.

My impression daily is stronger that the amendment shd. be moved, if possible, from the right of / the Speaker's chair.[2]

My own opinion is, but I offer it with diffidence, that the amendment, as drawn by you, shd. be confined to the first paragraph. The House of Commons, I have often observed, is / shy of long & complicated amendments, fearing they may be entrapped into admissions, wh:, afterwards, they may regret. I think, also, the reference to the relative position of / urban and county constituencies will necessarily lead to controversy, wh: it wd. be wise to avoid in a resolution, tho' it may be convenient & politic in a speech.[3]

We / will talk over all this, however, in the little room today.[4]

Yours always, | with sincere regard, | D.

---

1 Baxter on this day (15th) had written to D: 'I have an intimation from the Times that they will be glad of any remarks of mine on the Redistribution or Franchise Bills. I think of writing a short summary of their grouping scheme ... If you are not using the letters from the grouped boroughs, & do not think it unadvisable, would you kindly lend them me? The publication just before the Whitsun holidays may supply our friends facts for use in the Country.' 'The Principle of Grouping', Baxter's lengthy letter to the editor dated 'May 21', would appear in *The Times* on 23 May. Baxter had written to D about the grouping question on 12 and 14 May. H B/XI/D/50-1, 55.

---

1 Elcho on 15 May had congratulated D on his 'most excellent & convincing speech – quite unanswerable' (see **4094**&n4) and enclosed a paper (not found) written 'at the request of a member of the Cabinet.' H B/XXI/E/122.

2 For Arthur Hayter's 28 May amendment, see **4106**n5. The government sits to the Speaker's right.

3 D had commented on county constituencies in his 14 May speech; see **4094**n4.

4 D would also meet Elcho on 24 May; see **4103**.

TO: JAMES THOROLD ROGERS   Grosvenor Gate [Thursday] 17 May 1866   **4097**
ORIGINAL: ROG [1]
EDITORIAL COMMENT: From a transcription by John Matthews. Grosvenor Gate paper.

James E. Thorold Rogers | Esq.[1]   May 17 1866.
Dear Sir,

I feel honored by the presentation of your volumes.[2]

I think you will be mistaken in your estimate of their reception / by the public. I have yet been able, from the great pressure of public business, only cursorily to examine them, but I have seen enough to assure / me, that we have the commencement of a work of profound interest, a national subject, treated in a learned and masterly manner, and in a style / becoming the gravity and greatness of the theme.

Yours sincerely, | and obliged, | B. Disraeli

TO: RALPH EARLE   Grosvenor Gate [Saturday] 19 May 1866   **4098**
ORIGINAL: PS 1524
PUBLICATION HISTORY: M&B IV 435-6
EDITORIAL COMMENT: *Sic*: Prince's.

Grosvenor Gate, May 19, 1866

Write immediately to Lord Grosvenor,[1] who lives, I think, at 28, Prince's Gate,[2] and place yourself at his disposal. He expects this, and Lord Elcho requests that you will do it.

---

1 James Edwin Thorold Rogers (1823-1890), BA 1846 and MA 1849 Oxford, classical examiner at Oxford 1857-8, was Tooke Professor of statistics and economic science at King's College, London, 1859-90, Drummond Professor of political economy at All Soul's College, Oxford, 1862-7 and MP (L) for Southwark 1880-5 and Bermondsey 1885-6. His *Education in Oxford* (1861) propounds a free-market system of teaching. A clergyman of the Church of England, Rogers would relinquish orders to enter Parliament, becoming the first beneficiary of the Clerical Disabilities Act of 1870.

2 Rogers had written to D from Oxford on 5 May 'forwarding you by my publisher a copy of the two volumes which I have just now completed'. H B/XXI/R/124. These were vols 1 and 2 of *A History of Agriculture and Prices in England from 1259 to 1400*. Vols 3 and 4 (1401-1582) would be published in 1882, 5 and 6 (1583-1702) in 1887 and 7 (1703-1793), completed by his son, Arthur, in 1902.

---

1 Hugh Lupus Grosvenor (1825-1899), Earl Grosvenor, eldest son of 2nd Marquess of Westminster and himself 3rd Marquess 1869, 1st Duke of Westminster 1874, had been educated at Eton College 1839-43 and Balliol College, Oxford 1843-7, leaving without a degree to enter Parliament as MP (L) for Chester 1847-69. 'In 1866 Grosvenor the socialite and back-bencher transformed himself into a serious politician with his moderate but unyielding opposition to Gladstone's Reform Bill.' ODNB. At second reading of the bill on 12 April, Grosvenor had moved the ingeniously phrased amendment that it was 'inexpedient to discuss a Bill for the reduction of the franchise in England and Wales until the House has before it the entire scheme contemplated by the Government for the amendment of the representation of the people.' *Hansard* CLXXXII col 1156. On 21 March, the day after Grosvenor had given notice of his motion, *The Times* had stated that the amendment 'seems to prove the hopelessness of expecting that this partial measure can become law'.

2 The houses at Princes Gate, Knightsbridge, built by Charles James Freake in 1857, were known for their many professional and titled occupants, including Earl Grosvenor (at no. 28).

You will continue to consult with Lord Grosvenor as to the best means to adopt in the present exigency. . . .[3]

4099   TO: PHILIP ROSE   Grosvenor Gate [Saturday] 19 May 1866
ORIGINAL: H R/I/A/193
EDITORIAL COMMENT: Grosvenor Gate paper imprinted 'MAD'.

Private   May 19 1866

Phil: Rose Esqre

My dear Rose,

I am sorry to leave town witht. seeing you. I shall be back, I think, on Wednesday.[1]

I fear, / I have rather pressed on yr good offices about advances, but I have been so pressed by affairs, that I have not been able to attend to / private business, or reach you, in whom I confide under all circumstances.

Yrs ever, | D.

4100   TO: SIR WILLIAM JOLLIFFE   Hughenden [Tuesday] 22 May 1866
ORIGINAL: SCR DD/HY C/2165 [72]
EDITORIAL COMMENT: Hughenden paper.

Right Honorable | Sir W.H. Jolliffe | Bart M.P.   May 22 1866

My dear Jolliffe,

Your letter of friendship reached us this morning.[1] It gave my wife, & myself, hearty satisfaction.

We wish our favorite / Cecil all the happiness she deserves: & that would be illimitable. She has every charm & virtue to ensure it, & I never heard of Sefton anything, but what was good. I / know him, myself, to be the merriest of spirits, & I doubt not his heart is as good, as his taste.

Embrace Cecil for me, & give her my love. 'Tis for the last time, / & I hope, therefore, she will not reject it.[2]

Yours ever, | D.

---

3 In a letter marked 'Sunday night' (docketed in another hand '20 May 1866') Earle would reply that 'G' (Grosvenor) would call upon him 'tomorrow' (21st) at noon. Earle, MP (C) for Maldon, had spent the morning with Edward Pleydell Bouverie, who had helped him 'concoct another version of his own resolution', which he enclosed for D and which specified that the Government's 'scheme' for the redistribution of seats was '"not sufficiently matured to form the basis of a satisfactory measure".' H B/XX/E/359, 359a.

---

1 On this day the DS would leave for Hughenden at 5 *pm*, returning on Thursday afternoon (24th). H acc.

---

1 Jolliffe on 19 May had written from Merstham to announce that his fifth daughter, Cecil Emily, was engaged to William Philip Molyneux (1835-1897), 4th Earl of Sefton 1855, ensign 1854 and capt 1857 Grenadier Guards, LL of Lancashire 1858-97. 'It is an affair that has been a long time thought about & from all I have seen & heard I have as much reason as I can have, to be satisfied with the pangs I must feel at parting with her.' The DS would attend the 18 July wedding at St George's Church, Hanover Square, where they had wed on 28 August 1839. H B/XX/J/98; *The Times* (19 Jul 1866).
2 Cecil Jolliffe, in a letter of 3 July 1866 endorsed by MA with a description of a 'Turquoise necklace', would thank MA for her 'lovely present'. H D/III/C/1070.

TO: PHILIP ROSE   Hughenden [Tuesday] 22 May 1866   4101
ORIGINAL: H R/I/A/194
EDITORIAL COMMENT: Hughenden paper.

Philip Rose Esqr   May 22 1866
My dear Rose,

I shall be in town on Thursday, & shall endeavour to catch you, if I can in these busy times.

I want to see you on some private business, / about this estate & some other things.

Vernon tells me, he wrote to you, or consulted you, about a small purchase. I believe it must be made, & I can manage / it, if I am not pressed to complete before the Midsum[me]r dividends.[1]

    Yrs ever | D.

TO: RALPH EARLE   Hughenden [Tuesday] 22 May 1866   4102
ORIGINAL: PS 1525
PUBLICATION HISTORY: M&B IV 436.

Hughenden, May 22, 1866

Yours just received very satisfactory[1] – as it shows that Grosvenor has not got over his original repugnance to the lowering of the franchise, and that, when a final effort is to be made, the whole of the Adullamites may be counted on.[2]

    At present I am clearly of opinion that the young H[ayter][3] must be utilised; and it may do the business if sanctioned by G[rosvenor].

1 Although Britain had changed from the Julian calendar (old style) to the Gregorian calendar (new style) in 1752, 'The old style is still retained in the accounts of Her Majesty's treasury. This is why the Christmas dividends are not considered due until Twelfth Day, nor the midsummer dividends till the 5th of July'. *The Times* (16 Feb 1861).

1 In a letter marked 'Monday' (and docketed in another hand '21 May 1866') Earle had written to D that he had seen Grosvenor, who did 'not like Elcho's resolution & will not vote for it' but would vote for Earle's, 'altho' he would have preferred some allusion to the reduction of the franchise, which was his great objection to the Govt: scheme.' H B/XX/E/360.

2 In a speech on 13 March 1866, the second night of the first reading of the Representation of the People Bill, John Bright had referred (derisively) to fellow Liberal Edward Horsman as 'the first of the new party who has expressed his great grief by his actions – who has retired into what may be called his political Cave of Adullam – and he has called about him every one that was in distress and every one that was discontented.' *Hansard* CLXXXII col 219. The Adullamites, a dissident Liberal anti-reform faction numbering around forty and led by Robert Lowe and Lord Elcho, were most commonly referred to as 'the Cave' (see **4116**n1). David, having fled Saul's jealous rage at David's popularity following his triumph over Goliath, had sought refuge in the cave of Adullam and had assembled there 'every one that was in distress, and every one that was in debt, and every one that was discontented' and 'became a captain over them' (1 Sam 22:1-2).

3 Arthur Divett Hayter (1835-1917), 2nd Bt 1878, Baron Haversham 1906, educated at Eton and Oxford (classics), Grenadier Guards 1856-66, would be lord of the treasury and junior whip 1880-2, financial secretary to the war office 1882-5 and PC 1894. He was currently MP (L) for Wells 1865-8 and would represent Bath 1873-85 and Walsall 1893-5, 1900-5.

He must give notice of his resolution on Friday, and Lord D. must pledge the party to support it on Monday.[4] If you can discreetly modify the language, well and good. It will, however, be looked upon as his father's, and so gain confidence.[5]

As to the seconder, that is more serious. . . . . It should be a popular man; no harm if from our side, though that is not indispensable. Would Anson[6] do it? . . .[7]

4103 TO: LORD DERBY   House of Commons [Thursday] 24 May 1866
ORIGINAL: DBP Box 146/2
EDITORIAL COMMENT: House of Commons paper.

Rt. Honble | The Earl of Derby | K.G[.]   May 24 1866

My dear Lord,

I returned from Hughenden this afternoon, & shd., have called on you, but had to see Ld. Elcho on my / arrival.

I enclose the copy of notice of amendment given, this evening, by Captain Hayter,[1] the son of the old whip, & drawn up under his father's inspiration.[2] I / think it will do.

I am to see, at two o'ck: tomorrow, a personage of parliamy. importance on these matters: a dark horse;[3] but intend, & hope, to see you before I get / to the House.

Yrs ever | D.

---

4 On Friday 25 May, 'Forty Members not being present at Four o'clock, Mr. Speaker adjourned the House till *Monday* next.' Hayter on Monday 28 May would move an 'Amendment to the Instruction to be moved by Mr. [Edward Pleydell] Bouverie'. *Hansard* CLXXXIII cols 1289, 1348. See **4106**n5.

5 Sir William Goodenough Hayter had been Liberal chief whip 1850-8. Earle had told D (n1) that 'Young Hayter ... [had] read me a letter from his father, criticizing the bill severely & advising him to vote against it at every stage ... [Hayter] says he has ample materials for a speech & feels confident of being able to do the thing well.' On 23 May, Earle would tell D that Hayter 'has received another letter from his father, entirely approving your line & assuming that you wd. move resolutions in accordance with it. He tells him, if *necessary*, "to enter the Cave."' H B/XX/E/362. See also **4103**.

6 Earle (n1) had asked D: 'Who shall Hayter's seconder be?' Augustus Henry Archibald Anson (1835-1877), son of 1st Earl of Lichfield, had entered the army in 1853 and in 1857, as captain in the 84th Regiment of Foot, had received the VC at Lucknow during the Indian Mutiny. He was MP (L) for Lichfield 1859-68 and Bewdley 1869-74. For his speech seconding Hayter's amendment, see *Hansard* CLXXXIII cols 1360-6.

7 Earle would write to D on 23 May (n5) that Grosvenor 'does not think he can vote against going into committee. I agree with Heathcote & Elcho in thinking this very bad behaviour. *We are now in a far worse position than if we had never divided* against the second reading ... I think it possible that he [Hayter] may bring 10 men, but ... we can only expect some 12 or 15 Adullamites! ... I don't think we can ever get better materials for success than on this resolution of Hayter's for the redistribution bill is a dead failure & very unpopular.' Earle had also suggested 'it wd. perhaps meet the views of the Adullamites & of all parties, if you were to move that the Bills be committed to a "Select Committee". It is not a very forcible move but it is plausible & wd. suit the cowards. It would stand as an amendment to Bouverie.' See **4105**nn1&2.

---

1 Hayter's amendment follows D's letter in DBP.

2 See **4102**&nn4&5.

3 Possibly Lord Grey; see **4106**. Although 'dark horse' was first used in 1822 in the *Edinburgh Advertiser*, D's use of the phrase in chapter 5 of *The Young Duke* (1831) is the first instance given in the OED.

ORIGINAL: LPL MS 1381 ff49-50

EDITORIAL COMMENT: Grosvenor Gate paper imprinted 'MAD'.

May 25 1866

Dear Miss Burdett | Coutts,

I returned to town yesterday, only in time for the House, & received yr note this morning.[1] I am, at this moment, / greatly pressed with affairs, &, literally, have not an instant at my command. I will enquire today about Mr Cardwell's bill.[2] I should think there is / very little prospect of its being introduced at present, or at any rate proceeded with, as the Reform struggle recommences on Monday next.[3] / However, I will ascertain, & take care to confer with you in due time, being

     Most sincerely yours, | *B. Disraeli*

ORIGINAL: PS 1526

PUBLICATION HISTORY: M&B IV 436, dated 'Carlton Club [? *May* 27]'

EDITORIAL COMMENT: *Dating*: by context; see nn1&2.

Carlton Club

I shan't be able to see you again to-day. Lord D. says that W. Martin comes on before Knightley and Sandford,[1] and also that if it were the reverse, and either of their

---

1 Angela Burdett-Coutts, whose note has not been found, would spend her vast fortune on philanthropic causes, from founding in 1847 (with Charles Dickens) Urania Cottage, a home for the rehabilitation of London's prostitutes, to financing the first archaeological survey of Jerusalem in 1864 (to improve sanitation) and helping Turkish refugees of the 1877 Russo-Turkish War. A benefactor of the Church of England, she built and endowed numerous churches and church schools.

2 Colonial secretary Edward Cardwell's Colonial Bishops Bill – 'to remove doubts as to the effect of Letters Patent granted to certain Colonial Bishops, and to amend the Law with respect to Bishops and Clergy in the Colonies' – which sought to broaden the rights of clergymen ordained in the colonies, had passed first reading on 15 May but would be withdrawn at second reading on 17 July. In the Lords on 13 July there would be discussion of Burdett-Coutts's petition recording (in her words) '"my most emphatic protest against my endowments [of several colonial bishoprics] being appropriated to any kind of bishopric other than such as Her Majesty's letters patent purposed when the respective Bishops received their consecration."' The Bishop Colenso scandal of 1863 (see VIII **3741**&n4) and its aftermath explains Burdett-Coutts's desire for accountability. See **4137**n3. *Hansard* CLXXXIII cols 1032-4; CLXXXIV cols 916, 787-810.

3 For the 28 May reform debate, see **4106**&nn2&5.

---

1 In the House on 28 May, Philip Wykeham Martin (1829-1878), BA 1850 Oxford, MP (L) for Rochester 1856-78, Rainald Knightley and George Sandford would speak, in that order. *The Times* on 28 May would record that Martin had 'an amendment also on the paper relative to the proposed disfranchisement of dockyard workmen, which, in point of form, may stifle the more formidable proposal of Captain Hayter.' In the event, he would defer to the wishes of the House, give way to Hayter and withdraw his motion. Knightley's instruction to the committee '"that they have power to make provision for the better prevention of bribery and corruption at Elections"' was carried by the Opposition by ten votes (248-238), D voting with the majority. Knightley had drafted his motion with Earle and his instruction made the bill a great deal more vulnerable, as legislation against corruption lengthened and complicated the bill, making it nearly impossible for the Government to carry it in one session. Twenty-six nominal Liberals would vote with the Opposition. Smith 102-3. Sandford (until 1866 known by his birth name, Peacocke) would inveigh against the grouping of small boroughs, those 'nurseries in youth and the refuge in age of our public men ... None but the very richest would be able to stand for any one of the proposed groups ... In

motions were negatived, we might altogether be shut out, and find ourselves in the Committee in a jiffy.

This is a result which he, most of all, fears. Then he says that, if the veto be exercised (of which, by the bye, he never heard before), Hayter's amendment could not be moved at all, because it does not refer to the Franchise Bill.

This is serious. What we most fear is a general collapse, and Committee, which would be fatal. If Hayter can be brought on *à propos* to Bouverie's resolution, we must contrive a long debate.[2]

4106　TO: LORD GREY　　　　　　　　　　Grosvenor Gate, Monday 28 May 1866

ORIGINAL: DURG Earl Grey Papers, 3rd Earl: Beaconsfield [2]

EDITORIAL COMMENT: Grosvenor Gate paper. D has written '*confidential*' at the top of the fifth page and 'confidential' at the top of the ninth page. Endorsed (by Lord Grey?) on the twelfth page: 'Mr Disraeli May 28/66 Ansd M 31st'. *Sic*: inartificial.

Monday night | May 28 1866

Right Honorable | The Earl Grey | K.G.

My dear Lord,

Lord Elcho told me to night, in the Ho: of Comm:, that you were not disinclined to have some conversation with me on the state of affairs, & there is no / one with whom, at any time, it gives me more satisfaction to confer, than yourself; as you well know. But I shall not be able to reach you early tomorrow, & a late hour, he tells me, wd. not suit you. On Wednesday, / at noon, or a little before, I could call on you, & will, unless I hear to the contrary.[1]

I shd. have been glad, if I cd. have ↑had↓ the advantage of seeing you sooner, for the situation is critical. Excuse me, therefore, if / I jot down a few rough thoughts & suggestions, & excuse also their inartificial garb, for the hour is very late, & I have come from an exhausting, & tumultuous, scene.[2]

It does not seem to me possible to mould the present measures of the / Government into a satisfactory form. There is no philosophy in it; no real politics. It is not,

short, the measure was an organized system of confiscation and corruption'. *Hansard* CLXXXIII cols 1319 (Martin), 1320-1 (Knightley), 1384-90 (Sandford). See **4106**&n2.

2 Earle would reply in an undated letter docketed '? May 1866': 'Unfortunate I cannot see you, but I think I see my way. Hayter must give his notice on going into committee on Distribution of Seats Bill, for wh: at present *no Amendment stands*, but this we must keep secret lest others should interfere as Martin did on Franchise Bill. In the meantime, we must organize Scotch point & get some one to object to Bouverie's motion. Do you understand?' Edward Bouverie's instruction on 28 May that the Representation of the People and Redistribution of Seats Bills be referred to the same committee would be accepted without debate. The bills would be discussed jointly (in committee) on 31 May and 1, 4, 7, 8, 11, 14 and 18 June. H B/XX/E/365; *Hansard* CLXXXIII cols 1319-20.

---

1 D and Grey would meet on Wednesday 30 May. See **4107**&n1.

2 About the narrow government defeat on Rainald Knightley's motion (see **4105**n1), *The Times* on 29 May would report that 'The victory was magnificent, but nothing will come of it ... The debate was short and spirited; the House hot, eager, excited; the enthusiasm over the victory immense, and all about a motion to which few attached any real importance, save such as it might possess as a straw to show the current of the stream.' It dismissed the 'skirmish' as having 'no effect whatever on the result of the campaign' for franchise reform.

in my mind, even a temporary settlement; not for ~~one~~ a generation, or even the remainder of our careers. It is founded on the Census of 1861, & it will be impugned / by the census of 1871, when, if carried, a coarser constituency will shake a feebler & more anomalous edifice. The effect of the arrangements on the just influence of the landed interest will be vast. The anomaly of 162 county / members representing more than a moiety of the population, while 330 Boro' members represented the remainder,[3] has hitherto *worked*, because there were about ninety ↑Boro'↓ seats, wh: were appended to the landed interest: 47 of these are disfranchised by / the present Bill.[4] I say nothing about the amount, & nature, of the franchises, a subject of wh: you are master. Nothing can be more coarse & indiscriminate, than the scale.

What, however, most alarms me, is the conviction, that this bill / must go to the House of Lords, & without any considerable modification, if the present opportunity, afforded by Captain Hayters amendment,[5] is lost.

Against a common object, the Bill itself, the united effort of the Conservative ↑party↓ can ~~with~~ be directed: but the moment we get / into Committee, that united effort can no longer be depended on. The Boro' members are jealous of the County members: the County members have, imprudently, let the former feel, that if the Counties cd. make good terms, or what are called good terms, for themselves, they / would not much bestir themselves for the victims. Then, there are great differences among the County members themselves. And various other causes & sources of dissension & discord.

It is my deliberate opinion, that no essential change can be effected in / Committee.

This is very serious, & I commend the circumstances to your earnest consideration. If I have the pleasure of seeing you on Wednesday, I will say more, but it is now ½ past 2 o'ck:, & I will ↓therefore↑ only add, that I am

    sincerely yours ǀ D.

3 *The Times* (23 Mar 1866) had given similar figures for England and Wales of '162 county members and 334 borough members.'

4 For the names of the forty-one boroughs to be grouped, eight towns under 8,000 left ungrouped and twenty-three seats 'distributed as one extra seat to each of the counties and divisions of counties with over 150,000 population', see Smith 257.

5 On this day (28th) Hayter had proposed an amendment to add the words '"this House, while ready to consider the general subject of a Re-distribution of Seats, is of opinion that the system of grouping proposed by Her Majesty's Government is neither convenient nor equitable, and that the scheme is otherwise not sufficiently matured to form the basis of a satisfactory measure."' Bemoaning the lack of discussion on 'the principle of the complete measure' for 'the improvement of the representation of the people', D had said the amendment had not been given enough notice. It would be defeated 403-2 on 4 June, after protracted debate and a failed attempt to withdraw it, amidst great confusion and chaos, with members stampeding to and from the chamber, the House adjourning at 2:30 *am* on the 5th. *Hansard* CLXXXIII cols 1319-1407, 1913-16 (Hayter 1348-60, D 1397-1402), 1798-1920 (D 1900-13). For events leading up to Hayter's disastrous amendment, see Smith 98-102.

4107

TO: LORD GREY   Grosvenor Gate [Thursday] 31 May 1866

ORIGINAL: DURG Earl Grey Papers, 3rd Earl: Beaconsfield [3]

EDITORIAL COMMENT: Grosvenor Gate paper.

Right Honble I The Earl Grey KG   May 31 1866

My dear Lord,

I return you the paper,[1] & am obliged to you for permitting me to read it. If we had the opportunity of constructing ~~the~~ a / Reform Bill, there is much in it, that might be very serviceable; but if the House of Commons goes into Committee on the Governmt measure, I am convinced it will pass thro' the ordeal / with no material alteration. The Conservative party, after the impending election by the new Constituency, will not count 200; & it will then be too late to combine for the / maintenance of the present Constitution.

We ought to strike at once, & the country will ratify the blow.

This is quite consistent with my endeavouring to effect the conciliatory arrangement you suggested yesterday.

Yrs very faithfully I D.

4108

TO: [ALSAGER HAY HILL]   [London, during or after May 1866]

ORIGINAL: H B/II/126

EDITORIAL COMMENT: A draft in D's hand on the verso of a letter from Alsager Hay Hill dated 22 January 1866. *Dating*: by the preface to *The oratorical year book for 1865* (see n1) dated 'The Temple, May, 1866.'

You[1] must allow an old acq[uaintance] whom you have dist[inguished?] by the happy ~~delightful~~ exercise of yr delightful art to congratulate you on an event ~~wh:~~ wh: ↑might be a source of pride to any one &↓ I am sure, judging from my own feelings, must deeply gratify all ~~who have~~ ↑yr friends & [*illegible deletion*] admirers↓ ~~the g great pleasure of being~~ known to you[2]

---

1 There is in DURG an eighteen-page handwritten document headed (in another hand) 'Enclosure in letter Disraeli to Grey 31 May 1866 (Beaconsfield file) [Memorandum by 3rd Earl Grey]'. The concluding paragraph reads: 'The above is a very rough & hasty sketch of the chief changes which appear to me to be required in the Govt Reform bill. I have no doubt a more careful & deliberate examinatn of the measure wd suggest to me many others. G. May 23/66.' There follows, in darker ink, 'N.B. This memorandum was written for Ld Elcho at his request in consequence of a conversatn I had with him after dinner in his own house on the evening of the 18th of May. I also that eveng in consequence of the same conversatn wrote him a long letter ... explaining to him very fully my reasons for thinking that no oppositn shd be offered to going into Comm[itt]ee on the Govt Bill. – I kept no copy of this letter. – On now sending the paper over I perceive that I have omitted to notice in it one of the amendments I consider to be most essential viz. the introductn of a clause repealing the law which makes the acceptance of a Parlty Office vacate the seat of a member of the H. of C. I got this paper back from Ld Elcho & it was shown to Mr Disraeli on the 30th of May.' DURG [10Q].

---

1 Social reformer Alsager Hay Hill (1839-1906), LLB 1862 Cambridge, a barrister (Inner Temple 1864) and poet (*Footprints of Life* 1857, *A Scholar's Day Dream* 1870), would devote himself to poor law and labour issues. *Our Unemployed* (1867) and other pamphlets advocate a national system of labour registration.

2 Hill on 22 January had asked D's permission to include 'any speeches of your own which may seem to us appropriate' in an annual collection ('"The Oratorical Yearbook"', to be edited by Hill) of 'the most conspicuous speeches of the past year.' H B/II/126. The 'event' D mentions is most likely the publication

ORIGINAL: QUA 239

EDITORIAL COMMENT: Grosvenor Gate paper. *Sic*: Cruickshank.

June 4 1866

Mr Disraeli much regrets, that the great pressure of public business has prevented his previously / acknowledging the circular of the Cruickshank Committee.

    Mr Disraeli will be happy to insert his *name in the list*.[1]

TO: MARY ANNE DISRAELI   [House of Commons] Friday [8 June 1866] **4110**

ORIGINAL: H A/I/A/324, 324a

COVER: Mrs. Disraeli | Grosvenor Gate | *B. Disraeli*

PUBLICATION HISTORY: M&B IV 437, dated 8 June, the third paragraph

EDITORIAL COMMENT: Docketed by MA on the cover: '1866 June 8' and 'June 8th'. *Dating*: by context; see n3.

Friday

My dearest, darling Wife

I hope you are a little better – & have taken some sustenance.[1]

    The Clarendon affair went off very / well.[2]

of *The oratorical year book for 1865: being a collection of the best contemporary speeches delivered in Parliament, at the bar, and on the platform* (1866). Under 'Speeches Delivered in Parliament During the Session of 1865' are D's speeches on the defence of Canada, the death of Richard Cobden (D would be a signatory to a petition, in *The Times* on 20 June 1866, to place Cobden's bust in Westminster Abbey), the assassination of Lincoln and the extension of the borough franchise. Also included are speeches by Gladstone (five), Bright (five), Palmerston (three), Lowe (three), Stanley (two) and Derby (one). This volume appears to be the only one published in the proposed series.

---

1 This is presumably an effort to assist graphic artist George Cruikshank (1792-1878), the principal satirical caricaturist and book illustrator of his day. Art dealer and collector Charles Augustus Howell 'initiated the first of several "testimonials" intended to supply [Cruikshank] with money, reawaken interest in his art, and, in some instances, obtain his archive for public collection. None of these efforts by Howell or by others paid off.' ODNB.

1 MA had suffered a 'bronchial attack' on 3 June 1866 and would suffer 'extreme debility' for some weeks. See **4111**, **4112** and **4113**.

2 In the House on 4 June 1866 D had attacked foreign secretary Clarendon for his 'great want of resource' in failing to prevent the Crimean War, accusing him of having, at the 1856 Congress of Paris, 'forfeited all the maritime rights of England' and of entering 'into a conspiracy to put down the free press of Europe.' In the Lords on 5 June Clarendon had countered the conspiracy charge by pointing out that he and fellow diplomats had condemned only 'certain newspapers published in Belgium by French exiles with the intention of their being smuggled over the frontier and disseminated among the lower classes and the army of France, and preaching not only revolutionary doctrines, but the assassination of the Emperor.' He quoted his own remarks in two excerpts from the conference Protocols to the effect that '"the Plenipotentiaries of England ... cannot associate themselves to measures of coercion against the Press of another State."' *The Times* of 6 June had reported Clarendon's repudiation of D's charges and on 8 June D justified his allegations by also quoting from the Protocols to show there had indeed been 'a combination, or conspiracy, or whatever phrase you may wish to apply to it' of diplomats regarding 'the excesses' of the Belgian press. He concluded by asserting that his previous remarks had therefore been 'neither unjustifiable nor reckless.' *Hansard* CLXXXIII cols 1911-12, 1921-3; CLXXXIV cols 27-31.

Our troops are a little dispirited after the two battles of yesterday[3] – but I think of you, wh: always sustains me, & I know we / shall find many sources of happiness without politics – if it comes to that.

There is no news, at least I have heard none: you are / better off than I am, for, I dare say, you have read the evening papers.[4]

Your affectionate, | D.

4111   TO: MARY ANNE DISRAELI   [House of Commons, Tuesday] 12 June 1866
ORIGINAL: H A/I/A/325
PUBLICATION HISTORY: M&B IV 437-8, the second paragraph
EDITORIAL COMMENT: Docketed by MA at the top of the fourth page: '1866'. *Sic*: Clanrickarde.

June 12 1866

My dearest Wife,

It made me quite unhappy to leave you, & so I write you this little line to say I hope you are already better.

Affairs look here pretty / well. Lord Clanrickarde has quite joined the Opposition, & brings five votes, & his son, Lord Dunkellin, has given notice of a motion against the / government.[1] Grosvenor seems also active, so far as talking & writing to men.

Be so kind as to have an extra blanket put on my bed, as I am suffering a little from / incipient cold, & don't wish to catch the *grippe*, which Bulwer has, & can't

---

3 In the House on 7 June 1866 there had been two divisions in the debate on the Representation of the People and Redistribution of Seats bills: one on Stanley's motion (given without prior notice to the government) that the fourth clause, to reduce the county franchise from £50 to £14, be postponed (287-260), and one on Walpole's amendment to change the £14 to £20 (297-283), D voting with the minority in both. Stanley's motion had been an attempt to put off a vote on the franchise clauses while taking up the remainder of the session in technical divisions on which the government could not possibly dissolve. Gladstone would note, 'The folly of the Opposition not unmingled with unscrupulousness gave us an early victory 287:260, which told upon the later one 297:283.' Prior to the second division, D had bemoaned the government's ignorance of the nature of the county population, which in his view amounted to half the nation and 'ought surely to be secured a fair and legitimate enjoyment of the franchise if you invest them with that great privilege.' *Hansard* CLXXXIII cols 2042-2133 (D 2115-22); *Gladstone Diaries* 441-2. See n4.

4 *The Times* on 7 June had published much of the debate (including D's speech) and, briefly reporting the proceedings on this day (8th), concluded that it was 'impossible not to connect the summary defeat of Mr. Walpole's Amendment with the imprudent, if not impudent, attempt of the Opposition to catch a victory on an unexpected issue earlier in the evening.'

---

1 In the House on 18 June, during the committee stage of the Redistribution of Seats Bill, Dunkellin would move the now famous amendment (in his words, 'the effect of which would be to substitute the principle of a rating franchise for that of net rental') whose passage by a 315-304 division – 42 to 51 Liberals (estimates vary) voting with the Opposition – would bring about Russell's resignation at the end of the month, the first such resignation of a ministry over reform since 1832. *Hansard* CLXXXIV cols 536-644. For the crucial differences between rating value and rental value, see pp 584-6 of Robert Saunders 'The Politics of Reform and the Making of the Second Reform Act, 1848-1867' *Historical Journal* 50.3 (2007) 571-91.

come to the House. We want him to second Lord Dunkellin, & Earle has gone up to see him.[2]

Adieu, dearest, dearest wife | Your affec | D.

TO: **JULIANA, BARONESS MAYER DE ROTHSCHILD**   Grosvenor Gate   **4112**
[Thursday] 14 June 1866

ORIGINAL: ROSE [2]
EDITORIAL COMMENT: Grosvenor Gate paper imprinted 'MAD'.

June 14 1866

Dear Baroness,

Mrs Disraeli has never left her room since the 3rd. of this month: a severe, but, I / still hope, not a dangerous, bronchial attack. There is, however, I fear, little chance of her seeing much of her friends this season. / There is none she will more miss than you.

This is the reason, why we cannot have the gratification of / being your guests on the 17th.[1]

I am so occupied with public affairs, that I never leave her on any day of rest. Yours sincerely | D.[2]

TO: **JULIANA, BARONESS MAYER DE ROTHSCHILD**   Grosvenor Gate   **4113**
[Friday] 15 June 1866

ORIGINAL: ROSE [3]
EDITORIAL COMMENT: Grosvenor Gate paper.

June 15 1866

Dear Baroness,

I am sitting with Mrs Disraeli, the House of Comm: having fortunately expired[.][1]

We both of us thank you very much for your kind thoughts & words. My wife is / suffering from extreme debility, &, I fear, will require many days before she is better.[2]

She is much touched by your kindness: you send her the most delightful presents: / flowers & fruit; & she desires her love to Hannah.

---

2 Earle would write to Bulwer-Lytton on '*Tuesday night*' (presumably 12 June) that he had called upon him 'this afternoon at the Express request' of D, who 'would BE VERY MUCH OBLIGED if you would kindly undertake to second' Dunkellin's motion. 'He believes that there is no one, who could *so discreetly* widen the issue & make it one to interest the house & the country.' On 18 June Stephen Cave would second the motion, Bulwer-Lytton voting with the majority in the division. HCR [26Q]; *Hansard* CLXXXIV cols 546-50, 639-43.

---

1 This invitation has not been found.
2 For D's reply to the baroness's reply (not found), see **4113**.

---

1 The House had sat only briefly on this day (15th), adjourning at 7:45 *pm*. D did not speak. *Hansard* CLXXXIV cols 465-501.
2 *MP* (3 Jul 1866) would report that MA had recovered from her 'recent indisposition'.

I fear the steel pen of a sick room may be almost unintelligible.[3]

Ever, dear Baroness, I Your obliged & fl I D.

4114   TO: HENRY LIDDELL   Grosvenor Gate [Friday] 15 June 1866

ORIGINAL: PS 812

PUBLICATION HISTORY: Christie's catalogue (20 July 1977) item 295: 'A.L.S., *Grosvenor Gate* ... 15 June 1866, to [Sir Henry] Liddell ... *marked "Confidential"* ... *4pp.* 8vo', extracts; Bradford 261.

If the Reform Bill passes, the aristocratic settlement of this country will receive a fatal blow from wh: it will not easily recover.[1] Many of the Whigs, now, feel this, as keenly as we do, & Lord Dunkellin's motion for Monday,[2] fatal to the Bill, will be carried if our friends are united ... It is our only chance of defeating a measure wh: will shatter both Whigs & Tories, & utterly destroy the present Conservative organisation.[3]

4115   TO: JOSEPH NEAL MCKENNA   Grosvenor Gate [Sunday] 17 June 1866

ORIGINAL: ILLU F162 [34]

PUBLICATION HISTORY: *Daily Chronicle* (26 July 1897)

EDITORIAL COMMENT: The newspaper article is headed: 'Disraeli and Ireland. The Story of a Compact. Toryism and Irish Finance.'

Grosvenor-gate, June 17, 1866.

J.N. McKenna, Esq., M.P.[1]

My dear Sir, –

Mr. Earle, who possesses my entire confidence, informs me this morning that he had the pleasure of seeing you to-day, and of conferring with you on public affairs. The situation is most critical, as I believe there is now no doubt that if the Ministry are defeated, they will give up both the Bill and their posts.[2] I am very sensible of

---

3 D's hand is no less intelligible than usual.

---

1 Stanley had recorded on 10 June that 'the political excitement among the upper classes is greater than it has been for the last seven or eight years'. On 18 June, following the division that would quash the bill, he would note that 'The exultation of the country gentlemen is unbounded'. *Disraeli, Derby* 252-3.

2 See **4111**n1.

3 Henry Liddell (VI **2849n1**) on this day (15th) wrote to D expressing 'great difficulty *now* in regard to my vote upon Dunkellins Motion [on the 18th], if I go with my party, which I am anxious to do if possible, it must be upon the broad ground of opposition to the whole Bill, & here again I have *grave misgivings as to the wisdom of that line of policy*. I will however think well over the whole matter and give Taylor a positive answer to-night.' H B/XXI/L/163. In the House on the 18th Liddell and D would vote with the majority.

---

1 Joseph Neal (or Neale) McKenna (1819-1906), educated at Trinity College, Dublin, an Irish barrister (1848), Kt 1867. He was DL for co Cork, JP for Cork and Waterford counties, chairman of the National Bank of Ireland, and MP (L) for Youghal 1865-8, 1874-85 and for Monaghan s 1885-92. 'He took a leading part in the agitation which has been set on foot from time to time during the last quarter of a century against the alleged over-taxation of Ireland.' *The Times* (17 Aug 1906).

2 The Representation of the People and the Redistribution of Seats bills would be defeated on 18 June and withdrawn on 19 July. In the Lords on 25 June Russell would announce that 'Her Majesty's Ministers tendered their resignations to Her Majesty', Gladstone that day making a similar statement in the Commons; they would make their official resignation speeches on the 26th. 'The Ministerial Crisis' would be

the valuable support that I have had the honour of receiving from you during the present Parliament, and I shall feel personally anxious to prove to you that I fully appreciate it.[3] – Believe me, dear sir, yours very faithfully,

B. DISRAELI.[4]

TO: LORD DERBY   Grosvenor Gate [Saturday] 23 June 1866 **4116**

ORIGINAL: DBP Box 146/2
PUBLICATION HISTORY: M&B IV 440
EDITORIAL COMMENT: Grosvenor Gate paper.

Right Honorable | The Earl of Derby | K.G.   June 23 1866
Dear Lord Derby,

The terms intimated by Lord Grosvenor, in his letter to Lord Wilton,[1] are not consistent with the honor of the Conservative party, & are framed in ignorance, & misconception, of its elements, & character.

I am, &, as you know, ever since the last general election, have been, prepared to withdraw from the leadership of that party in the House of Commons, with the / view, & the hope, of seeing it re-constructed on a broader personal basis: but I have only been ready so to act on two conditions:

1stly: that, whether in or out of office, you should be the chief:

discussed at length over many days, and in the Lords on 9 July Derby would deliver his 'Ministerial Statement' as 'the First Minister of the Crown'. *Hansard* CLXXXIV cols 650-60, 684-92, 726-44.

3 McKenna on 17 June would reply that he had 'complete confidence' in Earle and assured D he could count on his vote. McKenna, who had given his maiden speech in the House on 16 April, would vote with D and the majority at the 18 June division. H B/XI/D/71; *Hansard* CLXXXII cols 1395-9, CLXXXIV col 642.

4 McKenna would be interviewed in 1897 about evidence in support of his 'published statement that he co-operated as a leading Irish Member in defeating the Russell-Gladstone Reform Bill of 1865, pursuant to a private alliance with the then Conservative leader on the subject especially of Irish financial relations.' He would explain that the late Ralph Earle had said he had been 'commissioned' by D to see McKenna 'to bespeak his co-operation in influencing certain Members who had already voted for the second reading to accept his views on the question. To this he [McKenna] replied that he could only enter upon a canvas of other members, British or Irish, on getting satisfactory assurance from the Conservative leader in the House of Commons that the Conservatives on their return to power would do better for Ireland financially than the Liberals had done since 1853. Furthermore, he thought Mr. Earle should get his character as envoy verified by Mr. Disraeli in writing. The note [D's *above letter*] came without delay'. *Daily Chronicle* (26 Jul 1897).

1 In an undated letter to D (in M&B IV 439-40, dated '? *June* 22 *or* 23') Derby had quoted from a letter from Grosvenor to his uncle, Lord Wilton: '"after a long conference the opinion expressed was that we could not guarantee Lord Derby the support (in its strict sense) of the Cave – that a Government under a Whig in the H. of Lords such as Lord Clarendon, would be most desirable on all accounts, with Stanley leader in the H. of Commons; that if such an arrangement could be effected, there would be every reason for believing that a very strong Government could be formed under those auspices. Present at the meeting: Ld. Lansdowne, Lowe, Elcho, Horsman, Gregory, G. Heathcote, A. Anson." So much for Adullamite co-operation!' Elcho, who had hosted the meeting on 21 June, that night had written to D summarizing the proceedings and thanking D for his and Derby's 'readiness to join in any combination or arrangement' that would 'resist Gladstone and democracy.' H B/XX/S/350; XXI/E/126.

& 2ndly, that, in the event of / your declining the post, you shd. be succeeded by Lord Stanley.[2]

Ever yours sincerely, | *B. Disraeli.*

4117 TO: LORD DERBY   Grosvenor Gate [Saturday] 23 June 1866
ORIGINAL: DBP Box 146/2
EDITORIAL COMMENT: Grosvenor Gate paper.

Private   June 23 1866

Rt. Honble | The Earl of Derby | K.G.

My dear Lord,

Since I wrote to you this morning, I have heard a good deal about the movements & views of the gentlemen who / communicated with you,[1] & would come on to you at once, only that the Duke of Buckingham is coming here about County matters. The moment he has left / me I shall come on to St Jas Sqr, & hope to be with you by ½ past two o'ck.

Yours ever | D.

4118 TO: LORD DERBY   Grosvenor Gate [Monday] 25 June 1866
ORIGINAL: DBP Box 146/2
PUBLICATION HISTORY: M&B IV 440, omitting the last sentence; Blake 445, omitting part of the sixth paragraph and the last two sentences; Bradford 262, extracts
EDITORIAL COMMENT: Grosvenor Gate paper.

Right Honorable | The Earl of Derby | K.G.   June 25 1866

My dear Lord,[1]

The amiable & spirited Elcho has played his unconscious part in a long matured intrigue.[2]

---

2 Stanley on this day (23rd) recorded: 'Conversation with Ld D. after breakfast. He tells me that the Adullamites have held a council, that the result is they decline to join him, and that consequently there is now no question of his attempting to form a govt. Their wish is for a coalition under some Whig chief of which I should be leader in H.C. (this Ld D. told me.) But as they are 40 at the utmost, the Conservatives 280, this claim does not appear altogether reasonable.' *Disraeli, Derby* 254. See **4119**n3.

---

1 See **4116**.

---

1 This appears to be a reply to an undated letter by Derby (docketed '1866') written from St James's Square at '7 P.M.': 'I have just had a long conversation with Elcho, who called to give me an account of the state of the Adullamites, which appears to be one of complete disorganization. I am afraid we cannot look to any official support from any of them; and he cannot answer even for the votes of more than ten or a dozen; but in his view the only mode of obtaining numerical strength from the moderate Liberals would be a junction with some of their present Officials, which, from their hatred and fear of Gladstone, he thinks might be effected. On consideration, I think I had better see you before I go down to Windsor, as I am led to believe I shall certainly be sent for, but not, I suppose, before tomorrow afternoon. Could you call here at any time between 11 & 2? I should like to confirm with you as to the language I should hold to the Q.' H B/XX/S/397. Derby would be sent for on 28 June; see **4120**&n3.

2 Elcho had written to D at length about reform on 7, 11 May 1865; 15, 22, 25 May and 2, 21 June 1866. H B/XXI/E/120-6.

The question is not Adullamite: it is national.

You *must* / take the Government: the honor of yr house, & the necessity of the country, alike require it.

What is counted on, & intended, (not by the Court) is, that you shd. refuse; that a member of the late Governmt. shall then be sent for, &, then, that an application shd. be made to / a section of yr party to join the administration; wh: ↓application↑ will be successful, for all will be broken up.

There is only one course with the Queen: to kiss hands.

And the effect will be this: in four & twenty hours, all, Lansdowne, Granville (if you want him) Clanricarde, / who thought yesterday you wd. not have an "application", but who will think very differently tomorrow, will be at yr feet.[3]

Nothing can prevent yr winning, if you *grasp* the helm.

I propose to call at ½ past 11 tomorrow, & take my chance of seeing you.

Yrs, | D

TO: LORD DERBY   Grosvenor Gate [Monday] 25 June 1866   **4119**
ORIGINAL: DBP Box 146/2
EDITORIAL COMMENT: Grosvenor Gate paper.

Rt Hono[ra]ble | The Earl of Derby | K.G.   June 25 1866
My dear Lord,
Many thanks for both letters.[1]
I will be with you in good time this morning; ½ past 2 to 3 o'ck: & with the last information I can get. I / can't, at all, agree with the opinion that the confidence resolution[2] is a trifling matter, & can be triflingly treated. But I will say no more, until we have its language in the House, & its reception there. It can neither be / in its character, ↓nor↑ its career, a matter of course[.]

The person you conferred with yesterday, must have been "got at" since Thursday, when his tone was different; very. Somebody has been at him, perhaps Lord Halifax, the moment the / confidence resolution was in petto. He is looking out for the chance of a Granville, or Clarendon, re-arrangement,[3] & has made his book

---

3 Lansdowne would die on 5 July and neither Granville nor Clanricarde would be in the new government. On 21 June Stanley had recorded that 'Disraeli called, sanguine of success, eager for power, and full of his projected arrangements, which he had been discussing with Ld D[erby]. They all turn on the supposition that a considerable number of the Adullamite Whigs, or followers of Lowe, will join us – which is doubtful.' *Disraeli, Derby* 253.

---

1 These letters have not been found.
2 Stanley on this day (25th) recorded that for three days, expectation had been 'that a vote of confidence in the ministry would be proposed by some friends of theirs, which being carried would set them on their legs again ... It now appears that they reject all such offers to extricate them from the awkwardness of their position, and the scheme is therefore dropped.' *Disraeli, Derby* 255.
3 The Adullamites had 'hoped to produce a situation in which, if Derby failed to form a government, one of them, or Clarendon or Granville, would be asked to do so instead.' Since resigning in January, Halifax 'had been trying to stop Gladstone and the Cave destroying the Liberal Party between them' and 'was almost certainly conducting a rescue operation which the Liberal conflict had made necessary.' Maurice Cowling 'Disraeli, Derby and Fusion, October 1865 to July 1866' *Historical Journal* 8.1 (1965) 31-71 (see 62-3).

for it. When it has failed, wh: it will, he will come back to you. All these interviews & offers do good.

    Yours ever, | D.

4120   TO: RALPH EARLE   [London, Wednesday] 27 June [1866]
ORIGINAL: H H/LIFE
PUBLICATION HISTORY: M&B IV 441, dated 27 June 1866, the second paragraph
EDITORIAL COMMENT: From a typescript dated '1866' headed: 'D. to Mr. R.A. Earle, June 27. – '. *Dating*: by context; see nn2&3.

Nothing can be going on better.[1] but it is most difficult to give information to our friend at this particular moment. Lord Derby was summoned by H.M. this morning at 10 o'clock, General Grey personally delivering the letter and conferring with him. The result is, that Lord Derby will not wait on the Queen until tomorrow at noon.[2]

    The formation of Lord Derby's government is *certain*; but there is a good chance of its being on a broad basis, with elements, that will command general approbation and support.[3]

    Yours, D.

4121   TO: LORD DERBY   Grosvenor Gate [Wednesday] 27 June 1866
ORIGINAL: DBP Box 146/2
PUBLICATION HISTORY: M&B IV 442
EDITORIAL COMMENT: Grosvenor Gate paper.

Private   June 27 1866

Rt Honble | The Earl of Derby | K.G.

My dear Lord,

What do you think of utilising Lord Shaftesbury? The suggestion reaches me from

---

1 In an undated letter, Earle had written to D: 'I thought you might like to send the enclosed [*not found*] to Ld. D, before he goes to Windsor.' H B/XX/E/378. The Liberal government had resigned and D and Derby had begun forming a new one. For Gladstone's 26 June resignation speech and Derby's 9 July 'Ministerial Statement', see *Hansard* CLXXXIV cols 684-92, 726-44.

2 In a letter docketed by MA '1866 June 27th' Derby had written to D that he had 'just received, by C. Grey, the Queen's letter. It is important that I should see you *at once.*' The Queen on the 27th had written to Derby 'as to the only person whom she believes capable of forming such an Administration as will command the confidence either of the country or herself, and have the best chance of permanency.' She also urged him 'to obtain the assistance of some, at least, of those who have been supporters, or even Members, of the late Government.' Derby would reply on the 27th that he would 'go down to Windsor by the 2 p.m. train to-morrow.' H B/XX/S/346; *LQV*B I 342-3.

3 On 28 June at 11 *am*, before leaving for Windsor, Derby would gather at his house twenty-two of his principal supporters, including D. According to Derby's 28 June memorandum to the Queen, it would be agreed to 'attempt to form the Government on an enlarged basis, seeking the co-operation of supporters, and even Members of the late Government, and of those Members of the Liberal party who had seceded from them on the late occasion'. *LQV*B I 344-5. In the event, the new cabinet would be made up exclusively of Conservatives: Derby (first lord of the treasury), D (chancellor of the exchequer), Lord Chelmsford (lord chancellor), Duke of Buckingham (lord president), Earl of Malmesbury (lord privy seal), Spencer Walpole (home secretary), Lord Stanley (foreign secretary), Carnarvon (colonial secretary), General Peel (war secretary), Cranborne (Indian secretary), Sir John Pakington (first lord of the admiralty), Sir Stafford Northcote (president of the board of trade), Gathorne Hardy (president of the poor law board), Lord John Manners (first commissioner of works) and Lord Naas (Irish secretary).

Lord Beauchamp, tho' a keen partizan, a very high Churchman. Lord / Shaftesbury wd. be a representative of Palmerstonian sympathies & influences; powerful with the religious middle class; &c, &c.[1]

He dined with Lord Lansdowne.[2]

The latter, whom you / may yet gain in a personal interview, could not join you alone: Lord Shaftesbury would remedy that.

It is an adhesion, that, I think, would bring strength at Elections.

Yours sincerely, | D.[3]

TO: **LORD JOHN MANNERS**   Grosvenor Gate [Monday] 2 July 1866   **4122**
ORIGINAL: BEA [90]
PUBLICATION HISTORY: Whibley II 136n2
EDITORIAL COMMENT: Grosvenor Gate paper. Endorsed in another hand on the fourth page: 'Mr. Disraeli. Preparatory to offer of Lord Lieutenancy of Ireland. July 2d: 1866.'

Monday ½ past 2 ock | July 2 1866

Right Honble. | Lord Jno. Manners
My dear John
You must come to me immediately, or as soon as you possibly can. Nothing must prevent you.

I am remaining, & / shall remain, at home until you arrive.

Yrs ever, | D.
Nothing bad.[1]

TO: **LORD DERBY**   Grosvenor Gate [Monday] 2 July 1866   **4123**
ORIGINAL: DBP Box 146/2
EDITORIAL COMMENT: Grosvenor Gate paper. *Sic*: plate.

Confidential   July 2 1866
Rt Honble | The Earl of Derby | K.G.

---

1 Philip Rose on 27 June 1866 had written to Ralph Earle that he believed Shaftesbury 'would be glad to act under Lord Derby if office were offered to him', and to D that he 'would not object to serve under Lord Derby if the Chance were offered him. The Connection would have moral might in the Country and I therefore send you the hint.' Like Palmerston (an advocate of toleration, especially of Catholics), Shaftesbury, although an anti-ritualist, held conciliatory (if evangelical) religious views and had influenced many of Palmerston's church appointments. H B/XX/E/367; H R/I/B/104.
2 Shaftesbury's name is one of thirty-two on an undated document, in D's hand on Grosvenor Gate paper, headed '*Confidential*' and entitled 'List of Peers whom Ld Lansdowne thinks of inviting to Lansdowne Ho: for conference on the present state of affairs.' H B/XX/S/345a. It was at this meeting of dissident Liberals that Dunkellin had been chosen to move his amendment (see **4111**n1). For the list, drawn up by D and chief whip T.E. Taylor and sent to Derby (who returned it to D with annotations), see Smith 108.
3 In a letter to D, docketed by MA '1866 June 27th', Derby writes: 'I had thought of Shaftesbury, and though I do not think he would accept, he would probably be pleased by an offer. But it would be premature till I shall have received the Q's permission to form a government.' Invited to join the cabinet on previous occasions, Shaftesbury would never hold office, preferring to devote his energies to social reform (efforts to improve working conditions in mines, mills and factories). He would be associated with over thirty philanthropic associations in his lifetime. H B/XX/S/347.

---

1 See **4123**&nn1,3&4.

My dear Lord,[1]

Still in communication with Lord S. who asks for another hour. I will write instantly I receive his ultimatum.[2]

J. Manners is only deterred / by fear of expence, & his want of resources.

But if he tries it for a year, & finds it beyond his means, we could give him an embassy: also, these are the six inexpensive months; & / "*entertaining*" is very much exaggerated always:[3]

also, he has no great places to keep up in England. ↑There is Beauchamp's plate, if his brother won't help him.↓[4]

If Ld. S. accepts, I *strongly recommend* you to take Peel on / his terms.[5] He can't do much harm – & it will give the appearance of a great & organised adhesion.

I strongly recommend you ↑also↓ to offer Secy. of Admy to *Sir R. Knightley*[6] – & I beg for *special reasons*, that you will not distribute any other subordinate offices till you see

Yr faithful, D.

4124   TO: LORD DERBY   Grosvenor Gate, Tuesday [3 July 1866]

ORIGINAL: DBP Box 146/2

EDITORIAL COMMENT: Grosvenor Gate paper. Endorsed in another hand on the eighth page: 'July 3 Disraeli Right Honble B. July 3 concerning Sir R. Peel Mr Henley Lord Salisbury D of Buckingham arrangements in forming Govt'. *Dating*: by endorsement and context.

Tuesday morning 6 o'ck: a.m.

Right Honorable | The Earl of Derby | K.G.

1 Derby wrote to D twice on this day: first to inform him that 'Devon refuses Ireland; and altogether the prospect there appears so unpromising, and the Post is so important at this moment, that I am not without my apprehensions that on this rock we may ultimately make shipwreck'; and again upon returning from Windsor (where he had presented his cabinet appointments to the Queen), at '7.20 PM', hoping to find a note from D 'to say that you had made it all right with J. Manners, and right (or wrong) with Shaftesbury. On the first of these everything depends. The Q. has agreed to everything, Peerages, Baronetcies and all ... I have to send her a detailed list tomorrow, so far as we can complete it. We shall be at home and alone if you can look in this Evening. It is well to strike while the iron is hot.' H B/XX/S/353-4.

2 For Lord Shaftesbury, see **4121**&nn1-3.

3 Earle on 1 July had written to D that if 'Manners were raised to the Peerage he wd make an excellent Ambassr. at Vienna'. H B/XX/E/373. Having accepted the lord lieutenancy of Ireland, Manners would persuade Derby to release him after finding himself named in *The Times* of 3 July as an 'unfortunate' choice and an 'amiable but unprogressive nobleman' for 'an appointment which we cannot bring ourselves to discuss seriously ... Ireland will be a difficulty to the new Government.' Lord Abercorn would be appointed Irish LL while Manners, as in 1852 and 1858-9, would be first commissioner of works.

4 The word 'plate' (overwritten by D) must be read as 'place' for the sentence to make sense. 'Beauchamp's place' could refer to his position as a lord of the admiralty in the previous Conservative government (Mar-Jun 1859) now unavailable to him because of his succession to his title (in March 1866), or to his houses at 13 Belgrave Square, London, and Madresfield Court, Great Malvern. John Manners lived at 6 Cumberland Terrace, Regent's Park, and his brother, the Duke of Rutland, owned Bute House, Camden Hill, Kensington, and several county seats including Belvoir Castle.

5 Jonathan Peel would be war secretary as of 6 July.

6 Knightley, who would sit for Northamptonshire s until 1892, would write to Derby on 3 July that he had '"not sufficient confidence in Mr Disraeli to justify my accepting office in any administration of which he is the leader in the House of Commons".' Qtd in Maurice Cowling 'Disraeli, Derby and Fusion, October 1865 to July 1866' *Historical Journal* 8.1 (1965) 31-71 (p 65). Lord Henry Gordon-Lennox would be first secretary of the admiralty as of 16 July.

My dear Lord,

I have slept over the matter, & feel convinced, that it wo[ul]d be wise to take Peel on his own terms.

An appeal to Henley, very courteous, & even more, to / serve you & the party, at this moment, by taking a seat in the Cabinet without office, I think would succeed: after so great an offer, wh:, of course, must be made well known.[1]

Peel is still a great name / in the country: besides, in society, there is an impression, that ↑t↓he ↑present representative of it↓ always joins the winning side.

You must be careful to *communicate* with Ld. Salisbury before you name his successor.[2] I suppose Malmesbury's old scheme of making him / a Duke has not occurred to you? There is nothing in your objection, made at the time, that Salisbury was the junior branch of the House of Cecil. That is true: but Salisbury is an *older* marquisate than Exeter;[3] so there is a precedent in the very case.

The / Duke of Buckingham is rather a difficult man to find in a hurry, & you want him now in a hurry.

He may be at Wootton, Aylesbury

or

Stowe, Buckingham

or

Langley Park, Slough.[4]

Telegrams to Stowe are / generally longer than the post: & I doubt, whether Wootton is much better.

If news of him can't be had at the Carlton, I would suggest, that Talbot shd. take the matter in hand, & work all the / places, as you want an immediate result.

I shall be with you at 11 o'ck: & send, herewith, Achitophel's final refusal.[5]

Yrs ever, | D.

TO: RALPH EARLE   Downing Street [Wednesday] 4 July 1866   **4125**
ORIGINAL: H H/LIFE
EDITORIAL COMMENT: From a typescript headed: 'D. to Mr. R.A. Earle, C. of E., Downing St. July 4. '66.'

I suspect, that Rose is quite wrong. He represents the distressed Shareholders.[1]

---

1 Joseph Henley would not be in Derby's cabinet.

2 Salisbury had been lord president of the council in the 1858-9 cabinet.

3 The marquisate of Exeter was created in 1801 and that of Salisbury in 1789. The first title in the Exeter branch of the Cecil line was created in 1571, of the Salisbury line in 1603.

4 Buckingham, who would be appointed lord president of the council, had three Buckinghamshire residences: Wootton House, Stowe House and the manor at Langley Park.

5 Shaftesbury; see **4121**. An allusion to John Dryden's political verse satire 'Absalom and Achitophel' (1681-2), about the rebellion of Absalom (the Duke of Monmouth) against his father King David (Charles II). Absalom's advisor was Achitophel (Anthony Ashley-Cooper, 1st Earl of Shaftesbury).

---

1 In one of the worst financial disasters in British history, on 10 May 1866, the second wealthiest bank in the country (after the Bank of England), Overend, Gurney and Co, had collapsed. In June it had gone into liquidation, owing about £11 million to some 2,300 shareholders and the public. Overend, which specialized in buying and selling bills of exchange at a discount, had gone public in the summer of 1865 but ruined themselves through ill-judged railway and shipping speculations. The repercussions

Rothschild told me, on Sunday, that the quantity of English paper held at Paris, where it has aggregated from all parts of Europe, and indeed the world, exceeds, far exceeds, all his experience. His House, in a very brief space, has discounted 2 millions, and it comes in shoals every day. Money is cheaper in France, than in England, because there is more money there.

We are now paying the penalty of our enormous commitments during the last two years.....[2]

4126

TO: LORD LONSDALE   Grosvenor Gate [Wednesday] 4 July 1866
ORIGINAL: MOPSIK [154]
EDITORIAL COMMENT: Grosvenor Gate paper.

Confidential   July 4 1866
Right Honorable | The Earl of Lonsdale
My dear Lord,
G[eorge] B[entinck] shall not be forgotten. I hope, some day, to push him on for his own sake: but, now, it shall be for yours.[1]

He must remember, that / we are three in a bed, & not expect much. The thing is to get into the saddle.

I would have called on you, but every moment has been occupied; & the absence of the Court from London, & / the preparations for the wedding,[2] wh: engross the Queen, render the labors of forming a government, always vast, unusually severe & prolonged.

Your obliged & faithful | friend, | D.[3]

---

were catastrophic: Parliament suspended the Bank Charter Act of 1844, and when the Bank of England suspended production of banknotes and, for over three months, raised its base lending rate to 10%, domestic securities and shares depreciated while foreign trading in English currency increased due to lower interest rates abroad. *The Times* (11, 12, 14, 24 May 1866). See **4171**n2 and **4172**nn1&3.

2 Companies had grown at a terrific pace, from 409 in 1860 to 1,014 in 1865; following the Overend panic, their number fell to 754 in 1866 and to 469 in 1867. During the mid-1860s, railway expansion had peaked and the shipping industry was undergoing a transition from wood and sail to iron and steam. 'Loanable funds all over Europe grew scarce ... bonds sold at a heavy discount, and companies quickly exhausted their borrowing powers without filling their capital requirements. But it was necessary to continue construction; so they issued notes, frequently renewed, circulating on the security of their own shares, which contractors pledged with banks for more advances.' Leland Hamilton Jenks *The Migration of British Capital to 1875* (1938) 238, 251-3.

---

1 Lonsdale had written to D on this day (4th) 'anxious to see you to recommend my nephew G. Bentinck, if anything could be done for him.' H B/XXI/L/286. George Bentinck would be parliamentary secretary to the board of trade (1874-5) and judge advocate-general (1875-80) in D's second administration.

2 Princess Helena would marry Prince Christian of Schleswig-Holstein-Sonderburg-Augustenburg at Windsor Castle on 5 July. *The Times* (4 Jul 1866).

3 Lonsdale on 8 July would reply that D's letter had been 'so satisfactory & reassuring that I must confess I built strong hopes upon it of seeing him [Bentinck] appointed. As you are no doubt aware he is a very active & zealous Politician as well as a sound and steady debater & moreover than this he is not at all afraid of work. I see that all the places are now filled up except the Secretaryship of the Admiralty & I should be glad to have the gratifying intelligence that he had received this appointment.' MOPSIK [157Q]. See **4133**&n1 and **4263**n3.

TO: ELECTORS OF BUCKS   Grosvenor Gate [Friday] 6 July [1866]   **4127**
ORIGINAL: PS 1466
PUBLICATION HISTORY: *BH* (14 Jul 1866).

Grosvenor-gate, July 6.

TO THE ELECTORS OF THE COUNTY OF BUCKINGHAM.

Gentlemen, –

Her Majesty's Ministers having, as they allege, lost the confidence of the House of Commons, have resigned their offices to the Queen; and Lord Derby, by her Majesty's command, has formed a new Administration.[1] Her Majesty having been graciously pleased this day to entrust to me the seals of Chancellor of the Exchequer,[2] my seat in the House of Commons has become vacant, and I now solicit the honour of your electing me, for the eighth time, your representative in Parliament. Although the state of affairs, both at home and abroad, is not free from anxiety,[3] I have every expectation that, with prudence and firmness on the part of her Majesty's advisers, this country, under Divine favour, may continue to enjoy prosperity and peace. – I have the honour to remain, gentlemen, your obliged and faithful servant, B. DISRAELI.

TO: SIR THOMAS GLADSTONE   Grosvenor Gate [Sunday] 8 July 1866   **4128**
ORIGINAL: DENL Glynne-Gladstone MSS 403 [4]
EDITORIAL COMMENT: Grosvenor Gate paper.

Private   July 8 1866

Sir. T. Gladstone | Bart:

Dear Sir Thomas,[1]

Mr Howes' qualities are fully recognised, & I inserted his name in the list, wh: Ld. Derby requested me to furnish him with, of those members of the Ho: of Commons, who by their official / aptitude, skill in debate, or parliamentary influence, were qualified to assist him in the administration of affairs.

When, however, I tell you, that after deducting those appointments, wh: were almost a matter of course, there were only seven / offices respecting wh: Lord Derby could exercise his judgment on the claims of very numerous candidates,[2] I hope his

---

1 See **4120**n3.

2 At Windsor on 6 July 1866 D and the other new ministers 'received their seals of office and kissed hands on appointment'. *The Times* (7 Jul 1866). D's third and last term as chancellor of the exchequer would run from 6 July 1866 to 29 February 1868.

3 The cattle plague continued to destroy British livestock (see **4043**n1); the Austro-Prussian War (or Seven Weeks War) had begun on 15 June and would end on 23 August (see **4153**nn1-6); and in June Fenians had begun attacking British targets in Canada to pressure England into withdrawing from Ireland.

---

1 Gladstone on 5 July had written to D proposing his brother-in-law Edward Howes (1813-1871), a JP and MP (C) for Norfolk E 1859-68 and Norfolk S 1868-71, for preferment: 'He stands high as a working member of the House & as a man of considerable talents.' H B/XXI/G/137.

2 D's list has not been found, but Derby, with an undated ('Wednesday 7 PM.') letter, had sent D 'a list of the offices (H. of C) still vacant; and a list of names out of which perhaps you might fill them up ... Look over the lists [*not found*] and let me have them when we meet tomorrow.' H B/XX/S/400. For D's similar letters to Alexander Baillie-Cochrane and Lord Lonsdale, see **4129** and **4133**.

friends will not deem their omission from his arrangements as arising from want of sympathy or appreciation.

If / the Government take root, I have little doubt Mr Howes will soon be engaged in the public service.

Pray believe me, | dear Sir Thomas, | faithfully yours, | *B. Disraeli*

4129   TO: ALEXANDER BAILLIE-COCHRANE

Grosvenor Gate [Sunday] 8 July 1866

ORIGINAL: H B/XIII/47

EDITORIAL COMMENT: A draft in D's hand.

Private   Grosvenor Gate | July 8. 1866

My dear Cochrane,

I am grieved that you are disappointed – but yet, I hope, that on reflection you may feel that you have not been neglected.[1]

When Ld D. was called upon to form a ministry, he / requested me to furnish him with the names of those, ↑in mem of the H of C↓ who from official aptitude, ~~parliament influence~~ [*illegible deletion*] skill in debate, or parliamentary influence were qualified to assist him. I forwarded him a list in wh: yr name was included.

When however you consider, that after ↑deducting↓ the Privy Councillors offices, wh: were engaged by the Cab or by them who on previous occasions had held high offices, the professional offices, the offices in the Household wh: are / also confined to a class; ↑the two Lds of the Treasy wh. are claimed by Ireland & Scotland↓ ~~& after leaving only~~ ↑the↓ two offices ~~for the~~ ↑wh: were scarcely sufft portions of the↓ gentlemen who as Whips had worked so long & so arduously for the party, ~~there were only the 2 Lords of the Treasy wh: are claimed by the Ireland & Scot:~~ there were ↑really↓ only seven places ~~at our~~ his disposal, I ~~hope our~~ ↑earnestly↓ trust his friends ~~will~~ may not ascribe their omission to want of sympathy ~~on his part or want of~~ or appreciation. ~~of their claims~~

Ld. D. had to perform one of the most difficult & painful tasks wh: ↑can↓ well devolve on a public man – & the only consider[ati]ons wh: sustained him in / its discharge ~~was~~ were the conviction that he made no ~~recommenda~~ selection wh: he did not believe was best for the party, & the belief, that if the govt take root he will be able in due time to gratify the fair ambition of all his supporters.

I hope therefore you will give a kind consider[ati]on to their cir[cumstan]ces & believe me to be sincerely yrs

D.[2]

---

1 Honiton borough, for which Baillie-Cochrane had sat since 1859, would be disenfranchised in November 1868. Although Cochrane would never hold a government post, D in 1868 would offer him the governorship of Cape Colony shortly before the government fell. D would make him 1st Baron Lamington in 1880.

2 In an undated letter to Col Taylor, forwarded by Taylor to D on 28 February with another letter dated 27 February 1868, Cochrane would write that 'there is no appointment [admiralty secretary] that would please me more and what [*sic*] my feelings will be if I am again passed over.' H B/IX/F/39a-c.

TO: **LORD BEAUCHAMP** Grosvenor Gate [Sunday] 8 July 1866 **4130**
ORIGINAL: BCP [33]; now BL ADD MS 61892
EDITORIAL COMMENT: Grosvenor Gate paper.

July 8 1866

The | Earl Beauchamp
When I see the shade of the departed, I am, in some degree, consoled for his loss, by the recollection, that the inheritor of his name is my beloved friend![1]
   D.

TO: **LOUISA, LADY ANTHONY DE ROTHSCHILD** Grosvenor Gate **4131**
[Monday] 9 July 1866

ORIGINAL: PS 813
PUBLICATION HISTORY: Sotheby's catalogue (28 Oct 1980) item 816: 'A.L.s., *3 pages 8vo. Grosvenor Gate, 9 July 1866*, to Lady [Anthony] de Rothschild ... *envelope*'.

[informing her that, as the High Sheriff can postpone the nomination for an hour, allowing him to leave town at 9.00 o'clock and reach County Hall in time, he need not stay with her] tho' I shall not now be your guest, I shall ever be your obliged friend.[1]

TO: **GEORGE CAVENDISH BENTINCK** Downing Street [Monday] 9 July 1866 **4132**
ORIGINAL: NOT PWM 94
EDITORIAL COMMENT: 11 Downing Street paper.

G.C. Bentinck Esqr | M.P[.] July 9 1866
Dear Bentinck,
If you be disengaged, I wish you would call here tomorrow, at three o'ck: that we may / have an opportunity of talking over, together, your letter to Ld. Derby, & its subject.[1]
   Yours faithfully, | *B. Disraeli*

TO: **LORD LONSDALE** Downing Street [Monday] 9 July 1866 **4133**
ORIGINAL: H B/XIII/48
EDITORIAL COMMENT: A draft in D's hand on 11 Downing Street paper.

Private July 9. 1866
Right Honorable | The Earl of Lonsdale

---

1 On 7 March 1866, Frederick Lygon (6th Earl Beauchamp since the death on 4 March of his only brother, Henry) had written to D that he had not forgotten D's 'wish of having some memento of your departed friend; & I have instructed Dickerson to prepare a replica of a picture wh: you may remember to have seen in Grosvenor Place. I fear it will take some weeks to execute'. H B/XX/LN/46.

---

1 Lady Anthony de Rothschild lived at Aston Clinton House, Aston Clinton, near Aylesbury. D would address the electors of Aylesbury on 13 July. *The Times* (14 Jul 1866).

---

1 See **4133**&n1.

My dear Lord,

I am very sorry about Mr Bentinck's decision, & I have requested him to call upon me tomorrow on the subject.[1]

After deducting the Privy Councillors / ↑offices↓, reserved for the Cabinet & a few others, who have already filled high ~~office~~ posts; after deducting the professional places in the Law & the Navy; after deducting the places in the Household ↑wh: are↓ confined to a class; after deducting only two places for / the gentlemen, who, as whips, have passed so many years of arduous & anxious service; after ~~allotting, as is the custom~~ deducting, one Lordship of the Treasury ↑allotted as is the custom↓ to Scotland, & ~~one~~ ano[the]r to Ireland; there ~~also~~ remained to Lord Derby ↓absolutely↑ only six places[2] on which he could exercise his discretion as to the claims / of the numerous candidates[.]

You will see, therefore, what immense difficulties we had to encounter in attempting to respect yr wishes.

In my opinion, it is wise to get into the saddle; ~~if only when if promoted you shd. have something to give away~~ – you have then something to give away when promotion offers.

I shd. certainly, for yr sake, have taken the earliest oppor[tunit]y of advancing the views of G. B.

4134   TO: JAMES HANNAY   Grosvenor Gate [Monday] 9 July [1866]
ORIGINAL: BRN [5]

EDITORIAL COMMENT: Endorsed in another hand on the first page: 'June 9th/43 [sic]'. Dating: Only in 1866 was D making government appointments in July.

Mr. Hannay[1]   Grosvenor Gate July 9
Sir –

I have ↑again↓ represented, as you wished, the claims of your friend, Mr William Ford,[2] to promotion; & have been promised, that they / shall be considered; but I regret, that at present, it is not in my power to give you any more specific information. / It will give me pleasure, should you ultimately succeed.

I have the honor to be, Sir, | Your fl Servt | B Disraeli

---

1 Lonsdale on 9 July 1866 had written to D that his nephew, George Cavendish Bentinck, had told him he had 'been offered a court appointment by Ld Derby. I fear from this that my application on his behalf has been quite misunderstood, as his desire was to hold some office in which politically he might have advanced the interests of his party, whereas the post now offered him would, were he to accept it, altogether nullify his services. I believe his zeal & activity in the H of Commons are well known & generally recognized & I had hoped from your letter to me on the subject [4126] that some place ought [to] have been found for him where he could have efficiently exercised his energies in the service of the Present Administration ... P.S. I need hardly say that Mr Bentinck has under the circumstances declined Ld Derby's offer.' H C/II/A/17. See 4132.

2 The previous day D had told Alexander Baillie-Cochrane and Sir Thomas Gladstone that there had been seven available places. See 4128 and 4129.

———

1 For James Hannay, see VIII 3752n1.

2 Perhaps William Ford, messenger, Custom House, Comptroller General's Office. LPOD 1860.

ORIGINAL: DBP Box 146/2

EDITORIAL COMMENT: Endorsed in another hand on the fourth page: 'Disraeli Right Honbl B. July 9.' and (in a third? hand) on the fourth page: 'with regard to the appt. of an Irish Lord of the Ty. recom Mr Whitmore to be appd.' *Dating*: by endorsement and context; see n1.

Grosvenor Gate | Monday morning

Rt Honble | Earl of Derby | KG.

My dear Lord,

Mr Childers, the present Secy. of the Treasury, a high authority, says there is no sort of compulsion, that there shd. be a↑n↓ ~~Lord~~ Irish, or a Scotch, Lord of the Treasury.

An Irishman & a Scotchman are / required at the Treasury, to attend to the local interests & arrange judiciously the patronage.[1]

He says it is absurd, if we want the place for others, to give it necessarily to an useless Irish member, when Taylor is Secretary.[2] The Scotchman is necessary, because, / altho' we have few Scotch members, we have all the patronage of the Country, &, if judiciously distributed by a person acquainted with the local interests, it will, of course, strengthen our party.

Ld. Palmerston had no Irish Lord of the Treasury: but / he had an Irishman, Luke White, M.P. for Kidderminster.[3]

I mentioned, that I thought the matter was referred to in Statutes. He replied, that, altho' he had no doubt about the matter, he would examine into it, & report to me in writing, wh: he has done.

I can't send you the letter because / it is at my office, & I thought this matter was pressing. Mr. Childers' letter is the same as his conversation.

Under these circumstances, assuming that Bingham[4] refuses, I most earnestly recommend you to appoint Whitmore.[5] The case of a Whip is not like that of a follower, who / formerly, for a brief space, held Parliamentary office. It is continuous service. Here are 14 years of continuous service — & if not very effective, at least

---

1 Hugh Childers, financial secretary to the treasury under Palmerston, had written to D on 7 July that he had found 'nothing in any Act of Parliament' relative to the nationality of the lords of the treasury, nor 'any case of a Board of Treasury containing no Irishman since the Reform Bill, but several where there was no member for an Irish constituency, or a Scotch constituency. Col White was M.P. for Kidderminster ... As to the Private Secretaries I find that you set the precedent in 1858 of the Chancellor of the Exchequer having a 2nd Secretary, and that the minute recited the additional business in the House of Commons. You gave a salary of £150 to the 2nd Secretary, and Mr Gladstone never gave more than £300 between his two Secretaries. The rule is laid down in a minute of 1806, under which the 1st Lord and the C of the Exchequer only have one Secretary each, at £300 a year. Ld Liverpool broke into this in 1813 by appointing a 2nd at £300 a year, and I see no reason why any arrangement you think right should not be made.' H B/XXI/C/213.

2 Col Taylor, MP for co Dublin, would be parliamentary secretary to the treasury as of 14 July.

3 Eton-educated Luke White (1829-1888), 2nd Baron Annaly 1873, 13th Light Dragoons 1847-53 (retired as capt) and lieut-col Longford Rifles 1857, had been elected MP (L) for co Clare 1859 but was unseated on petition. He represented co Longford 1861-2 and Kidderminster 1862-5, was a junior lord of the treasury 1862-6 and would be state steward to the LL of Ireland 1868-73.

4 George, Lord Bingham (1830-1914), 4th Earl Lucan 1888, capt and lieut-col in the Coldstream Guards 1848-59, MP (LC) for co Mayo 1865-74.

5 Henry Whitmore would be a junior lord of the treasury as of 12 July.

honorable, loyal, & sincere. We put him in the place, or at least our Representative, Jolliffe, did, & we are bound to guard / him from unnecessary mortification.

Taylor is prejudiced against him: I am not prejudiced in his favor: but I think, on the whole, for the honor and interests of the party, it is expedient he shd. be appointed.

You might appoint him / subject to his giving up the Post when the contemplated improvements in the organisation of the Treasury require his resignation, ⌐& the presence of a Lord of financial aptitude & attainments.⌐

I hear from Taylor Hunt[6] wants Howes[7] appointed, but Hunt is not aware, that he is to be assisted by Cave.[8]

Yrs ever, | D.

4136   TO: AMELIA MICHELL   Grosvenor Gate [Tuesday] 10 July [1866]
ORIGINAL: QUA 279
COVER: Mrs Michell
EDITORIAL COMMENT: Grosvenor Gate paper. *Dating*: by context; see n1. Endorsed by D on the fourth page (integral cover): 'Mrs Michell'.

                                                                                July 10

Dear Madam,[1]
It is, I regret, impossible for me to have the pleasure of seeing you now — & I am greatly engaged the whole day / — but if you can call in Downing St. to day, at four o'ck:, I will make every endeavour to see you.

Yrs ffly | D.

4137   TO: MONTAGU CORRY   [London] Wednesday [11 July? 1866]
ORIGINAL: H B/XX/D/324
EDITORIAL COMMENT: C of Ex paper, seal crossed out. *Dating*: by context; see nn1&2. *Sic*: Montague.

                                                                            Wednesday

My dear Montague,[1]
The weather seems better,[2] & I would recommend you to go out of town at once.

---

6   George Ward Hunt would be financial secretary to the treasury as of 14 July.
7   See **4128**&n1.
8   Stephen Cave would be vice-president of the board of trade as of 10 July.

---

1   Amelia Michell, née Blair, in 1841 had married classicist Richard Michell, 'a leading manager of the tory party in Oxford', where he enjoyed a distinguished teaching career. *ODNB*. Richard Michell had written to D from Oxford on 7 July 1866, enclosing (with D's permission) information on his son: '*Edward Blair Michell* B.A. of Magdalen College Oxford was born on the 6th of Decr. 1842 ... His principles are Conservative, and he is an active member of the Canning Club in this university.' H B/XXI/M/363.

---

1   Montagu William Lowry Corry (1838-1903), Baron Rowton 1880, BA 1861 Cambridge, a barrister (Lincoln's Inn 1863), CB 1878, KCVO 1897 and PC 1900. D had observed Corry on 31 August 1865 at Raby Castle and had told him, '"I think you must be my impresario."' *ODNB*. On 29 June 1866 Corry had written D 'with much hesitation ... most anxious to get a start in political life ... though I can scarcely presume to ask for the honour of being Private Secretary to yourself'. On 11 July he had written to tell D 'how deeply I value the confidence which you have reposed in me, and to assure you, that it will be owing to no neglect on my part, if I fail to prove myself worthy of it.' H B/XX/CO/1, 2.
2   'During the first seven days of July the large amount of 2.76 inches of rain fell, and the weather was cold

You are probably suffering, / like myself, & many others, from the relaxing & influenzaish atmosphere[.]

yrs, | D.

I think you might condense Rose's mem: about the Bishop, & send it from me to Ld Carnarvon at once.[3]

TO: RALPH EARLE   Downing Street [Wednesday] 11 July [1866] **4138**
ORIGINAL: MOPSIK [131]
EDITORIAL COMMENT: C of Ex paper. *Dating*: by context; see n1.

R.A. Earle Esqr | MP.   July 11

Will you inform the Stationery office, that I cannot use the materials with wh: they supply me. I request, that I shd. have, at least for / my own use, writing paper stamped of the quality I am in the habit of using of wh: I inclose a specimen.[1]

Yrs evr | D.

TO: LORD STANLEY   Downing Street [Thursday] 12 July 1866 **4139**
ORIGINAL: H H/LIFE
EDITORIAL COMMENT: From a typescript headed: 'D. to Ld. Stanley, 11, Downing St., July 12. '66. Endorsed: "Observations on Lord Cowley's letters."'

What a crisis![1]

All you have done turns out quite right.[2]

---

and ungenial. On the 9th it changed [to] the almost Indian temperatures we have had to endure', with a mean temperature of 70.88. *The Times* (18 Jul 1866).

3 Although Philip Rose's memorandum to the Bishop of London, Archibald Campbell Tait, and Carnarvon's reply have not been found, D's letter is evidently related to the Colonial Bishops Bill (see **4104**n2). In the Lords on Friday 13 July the Bishop would move an address to the Queen to obtain specific information on foreign and colonial bishoprics (appointment dates, revenues and their sources, number of clergymen and churches under each bishop). Recently appointed colonial secretary Carnarvon would reply that if the motion were withdrawn (it was) 'he would take care that it should be brought in in a shape which would enable the Colonial Office to give the Returns.' *Hansard* CLXXXIV col 811.

---

1 1866 is the only year in which, on 11 July, D was chancellor of the exchequer (since 6 July) and Earle both an MP and D's secretary. Earle on 12 July would become secretary of the poor law board; Montagu Corry would assume Earle's duties and remain D's loyal and devoted private secretary until D's death; he would not marry. According to M&B (IV 528) when Earle continued to 'frequent the secretaries' room and expect to be treated as if he were still one of them, Disraeli gave Corry and [Charles] Fremantle [D's other secretary; *see* **4169**n1] distinct instructions that matters of confidence should not be imparted to him. Earle marked Corry's rapid advance to a degree of intimacy to which he had never himself attained; his feelings were deeply wounded.'

---

1 Stanley on this day (12th) had written to D: 'I send you [British ambassador to France Earl] Cowley's private letters. Also drafts of mine to him. The Emp. [Napoleon III] has got into hot water. He jumped at the position which the Austrian offer of Venice gave him, and forgot the difficulties in his way. These are great & increasing: Words will not stop Prussia: and he is not ready to go to war. We are well out of it. The language I hold is that while generally favoring peace, we maintain an attitude of reserve, and do not pledge ourselves to any specific proposals. I think the Prussians will begin again, and reach Vienna. Farther I don't see.' Stanley on the 13th would comment at length about the political situation in his journal. H B/XX/S/734; *Disraeli, Derby* 259.

2 Stanley had been re-elected MP for Lynn Regis on 11 July and, at King's Lynn that day, remained circum-

I go to my election to-morrow,[3] but I congratulate you on being again an M.P.
Yours ever, D.

4140   TO: LORD DERBY   Grosvenor Gate [Thursday] 12 July 1866

ORIGINAL: DBP Box 146/2

EDITORIAL COMMENT: C of Ex paper, seal crossed out on the first sheet and 'G. Gate' written in. Endorsed in another hand on the eighth page: '"July 12 | Disraeli B | *Put by* D | July 17 | Irish Legal | appointments".' *Sic*: Arundel.

Rt Honble | The Earl of Derby | K.G[.]   G. Gate | July 12 1866

My dear Lord,

You need not trouble yourself about Mr Morris this morning, as I suggested yester-day: as he would not take office under Whiteside, nor / would indeed any other R. Cath.[1]

I suggest one or two modes of extricating ourselves from this extreme difficulty.

Would Whiteside take the C. Justiceship with / a Peerage?[2]

Plunket, I think, did.[3]

Whiteside is sixty, & childless.

With Whiteside Chancellor, we can expect no allies.

Or could you send Rolt / to Ireland as Chancellor?

You will say, he will be wanted in England, perhaps, for the Attey Genlsp.[4]

spect in his acceptance speech, published in *The Times* on 12 July, as to his role as foreign secretary (as of 6 July). He felt compelled to observe 'reticence and reserve', called France 'our friendly competitor for the first place in the civilization of the world' and assured his audience that 'our sole interest lies in the return of a peace ... the consequence of which will be the comparative disarmament of Europe.' *The Times* on 13 July would praise Stanley's speech while wishing for 'a more exact and more substantial account of our political relations with our Continental neighbours.'

3 D would be re-elected MP for Bucks at Aylesbury on 13 July and his acceptance speech summarized in *The Times* and *BH* on the 14th. While commending D on his 'strong opinions in favour of British neutrality' (England ought merely to exercise '"moral influence"' upon those making European quarrels and be ready to mediate if called upon to do so), on his foreseeing '"no difficulty"' in dealing with parliamentary reform, *The Times* noted wryly that 'whoever raises expectations raises difficulties.' D also spoke on Irish emigration (a haemorrhage to be staunched) and stated that it was no more in his power to regulate the rate of interest than to regulate the direction of the winds.

---

1 Michael Morris (1827-1901), 1st Bt 1885, Baron Morris of Spiddal 1889, 1st Baron Killanin 1900, a Roman Catholic, an Irish barrister 1849, high sheriff 1849-50 and recorder 1857-65 of Galway and QC 1863, would become lord justice of Ireland in 1887. MP (L-C) for Galway borough 1865-8, 1874-80, Morris would become a Conservative when made solicitor-general for Ireland on 3 August 1866, a post he relinquished when appointed attorney-general for Ireland on 1 November. For former attorney-general for Ireland James Whiteside, see V **2137n7**, n2 below and **4141n7**.

2 It had been rumoured that Whiteside had been offered the choice of LC of Ireland or chief justice of the Queen's Bench for Ireland (he would become the latter). He would feel slighted at being passed over for the chancellorship, an office 'generally considered rightfully to be his, but his association with the extreme tory and protestant wing of the Conservative Party would not allow Derby thus to elevate him, since the prime minister wished to form a broad-based Irish executive.' *ODNB*.

3 William Conyngham Plunket (1764-1854), 1st Baron Plunket 1827, an Irish barrister 1787, KC 1797, sol-gen for Ireland 1803-5, att-gen for Ireland 1805-7, 1822-7, chief justice for Ireland 1827 and LC for Ireland 1830-41.

4 John Rolt (1804-1871), a barrister (Inner Temple 1837), a JP, QC 1846, Kt 1866, MP (C) for Gloucestershire w 1857-67, lord justice of appeal 1867-8, would succeed Sir Hugh Cairns as attorney-general on 29 October 1866 and be knighted in November.

But the pressing difficulty is the greater one.

Rolt has done nothing to prove he would be an efficient Parly. officer. / Would he be better than Baggallay,[5] who, if R went to Ireland, would probably be your Solicitor?

The ↑Private↓ Secretary to the Ld. Lieutenant is a place of great importance – & it is said to be not filled up. Suppose Lord Abercorn offered / it to Lord Arundel of Wardour?[6]

The offer alone would be a *coup.*

Yrs ever | D.

TO: LORD NAAS   [London, Friday 13 July 1866]   4141

ORIGINAL: INL Mayo Papers MS 11,144

EDITORIAL COMMENT: Written on Naas's stationery. Endorsed in another hand on the first page: 'Disraeli July 13/66'. From a transcription by Andrew Shields. *Sic*: Brown; thing.

---

confidential[1]

I give this to yr dear wife.[2]

I have had a very important communication respecting the Irish Govt. wh: might produce / good effects for us — but I will not open my mouth, till I have seen you.

In the meantime, say, / or write, nothing about the materials of the Irish Ministry.

On second thoughts, it is best to give you the outline to think over. If a Govt. is formed thus: /

Brewster Chanr[3]

Walsh Att Genl[4]

Morris }

now in} Sol Genl.[5]

the House}

---

5 Richard Baggallay (1816-1888), BA 1839 and MA 1842 Gonville and Caius College, Cambridge, a barrister (Lincoln's Inn 1843), a JP, QC 1861, Kt 1868, MP (C) for Hereford 1865-8 and Mid-Surrey 1870-5, lord justice of appeal 1876-85, would become solicitor-general on 16 September 1868 and attorney-general in 1874.

6 As of 13 July Abercorn would be LL of Ireland (1866-8, 1874-6). John Francis Arundell (1831-1906), 12th Baron Arundell of Wardour 1862, was from an ancient Roman Catholic Anglo-Norman family.

---

1 Naas on 6 July had written to D from Cockermouth (his constituency) 'in great haste': 'Brewster Chr. Walsh atry Genl are excellent – Morris has hardly – Professional position.' H B/XX/BO/20.

2 D's enclosure to Lady Naas has not been found.

3 Abraham Brewster (1796-1874), BA 1817 and MA 1847 Trinity (Dublin), an English 1817 and Irish 1819 barrister, QC 1835, was legal adviser to the LL of Ireland 1841, Irish att-gen 1853-5, PC 1853, lord justice of appeal July 1866 and LC 1867-8. The new LC would be Francis Blackburne. Derby's undated letter to D, written during this period, proposed his 'old friend' Blackburne, to whom he would write accordingly. 'This will give time to deal with both Whiteside & Brewster. This is, I think, the best possible solution.' H B/XX/S/395.

4 John Edward Walsh (1816-1869), BA Dublin 1837, an Irish barrister 1839, QC 1857, would be MP (C) for Dublin U from 30 July 1866 until October, when he would be appointed master of rolls in Ireland. He would be Irish attorney-general from 25 July to 1 November 1866.

5 For Morris, see **4140**n1.

a great effect in our favor wd. take place in Ire: I think Ld. John Brown wd then be a Lord of the Treasury.[6]

The person at work in this is Ed: of the Mail,[7] our whilom [?] foe. I thing poor Longfield shd. be Castle Adviser.[8]

D.

4142   TO: LORD DERBY   Grosvenor Gate [Sunday] 15 July 1866
ORIGINAL: DBP Box 146/2

EDITORIAL COMMENT: C of Ex paper, seal crossed out and 'Grosr Gate' written in. Endorsed by Derby on the fourth page: 'Note Apptmts. for Tuesday at 4 D.'

Rt Hono[ra]ble | The Earl of Derby | K.G.   Grosr Gate
July 15 1866

My dear Lord,

I think Mahon an excellent idea, if, unlike most families, the branches are on good terms.[1]

Lord Clanricarde has written to me to receive him, / & one or two others, about the Irish Railway Loan — but adds, that it wd. be gratifying, if you were present.[2]

I think it would be as well to please him, as he is very friendly.

Would Tuesday do? We shall / have a morning sitting in H of C. on Thames

---

6 Lord John Thomas Browne (1824-1903), eldest surviving son of 3rd Marquess of Sligo, would be 4th Marquess of Sligo 1896. A JP and MP (L) for co Mayo 1857-68, he would not be in the new government.

7 The appointments of Brewster, Walsh and Whiteside had been discussed in *The Times*: an 11 July report from Dublin quoted the *Dublin Evening Mail* to the effect that Whiteside's '"intense personal animosities, his nepotism, his deplorable want of discretion and self-restraint, his habitual and offensive indulgence in language which touches the verge of Parliamentary toleration, indicate him as politically the most mischievous person whom Lord Derby could place in that delicate and onerous trust [of LC] ... The appointment of Mr. Brewster, on the other hand, will admittedly strengthen Lord Derby."' *The Times* (12 Jul 1866).

8 Robert Longfield (1810-1868), an Irish barrister 1834, QC 1852, had been MP (L-C) for Mallow, co Cork 1859-65. *The Times* on 22 October 1866 would report that Longfield, 'owing to impaired health, has signified his wish to retire from the Incumbered [*sic*] Estates Court', and on 19 November that he was acting as 'law adviser to the Castle' in connection with the trial of Fenian agitator Denis Dowling Mulcahy.

---

1 Derby on 14 July had written to D enclosing a letter from Sir Edward Kerrison: 'I am inclined to suggest to Sir E.K. his own Nephew Ld Mahon, who wants to come into Parliament. Stanhope is very angry at being passed over; his Son is a sure and steady vote; and if Sir E.K. should not approve of the selection, the knowledge by Stanhope (or rather the Stanhopes, for she is as angry as he) might serve to put them on terms of Christian charity with me – which at present they are not.' H B/XX/S/355. Arthur Philip Stanhope (1838-1905), eldest son of 5th Earl Stanhope and his wife Emily Harriet (Kerrison's sister), Visct Mahon 1855, 6th Earl Stanhope 1875, Grenadier Guards 1858-69, war instructor of musketry 1863-68, JP for Kent, would be MP (C) for Leominster 1868 and Suffolk E 1870-5, junior lord of the treasury 1874-6, first church estates commissioner 1878-1905 and LL of Kent 1890-1905.

2 D on 16 July would send Clanricarde's letter (not found) to Derby; see **4146**. Gladstone on 18 May had met with a 'deputation of noblemen and gentlemen' led by Clanricarde, who had made 'a statement showing the present depression of Irish railway property, and recommended that Government should, at a fair rate of interest, make advances to the companies to meet their debentures as they fell due.' On 14 June Clanricarde and a deputation from the Irish Railway Directors' Conference had met with financial secretary to the treasury Childers and would meet with D on 17 July. D (chancellor of the exchequer as of 6 July) on 23 July would move the second reading of the Railways (Ireland) Temporary Advances Bill

Navigation,³ but I cd. come up — and↑, if so,↓ at what hour? Three or four ↑o'ck:↓ perhaps?

Yrs ever, | D.

TO: [MONTAGU CORRY?]   [between Monday 16 July 1866 **4143**
                                        and Sunday 12 August 1867]
ORIGINAL: H B/XX/D/316

EDITORIAL COMMENT: A note in D's hand on verso of 11 Downing Street paper. Beneath the address and crossed out by a diagonal line: 'Naas to see Hunt after seeing Lord Derby.' *Recipient*: Corry became D's secretary on 16 July 1866. *Dating*: D was C of Ex on 6 July 1866 and Naas succeeded as Mayo on 12 August 1867. *Sic*: Wycomb.

Write to

H. Wanklyn Esq J.P.

Slough¹

that C of Exr. earnestly recommends to his kind consideration the case of Mr Collett of Wycomb Station.²

D.

TO: EDITOR OF *THE TIMES*   Grosvenor Gate [Monday] 16 July [1866] **4144**
ORIGINAL: PS 674
PUBLICATION HISTORY: *The Times* (17 Jul 1866); *BH* (21 Jul 1866).

---

*TO THE EDITOR OF THE TIMES*¹   Grosvenor-gate, July 16.

Sir, –

I refrain, as a general rule, from troubling you with corrections of reports, but I beg leave to say that I did not state on the hustings that there was no difficulty in dealing

to provide, in D's words, 'a sum of not more than £500,000 for a period of three months ... [at] not more than 4 per cent', the situation being so critical that 'there was every prospect of the general railway communication in Ireland being stopped.' The bill would be discussed in committee on 27 July and given royal assent on 10 August. *The Times* (22 May, 15 Jun, 18, 24 Jul 1866); *Hansard* CLXXXIV cols 1361-3 (D 1361), 1625-34 (D 1631), 2154.

3 In the House on 17 July the Thames Navigation Bill would be discussed briefly in committee, most of the sitting being taken up with a motion for a royal commission 'to inquire into the present condition of the Seamen of the Mercantile Marine' (withdrawn) and another to curtail 'corrupt' election practices by 'an experiment' with anonymous voting (defeated 197-110), the House adjourning after 12:30 *pm*. D did not speak. *Hansard* CLXXXIV cols 933-7, 943-96.

---

1 One 'Wanklyn, Edward, Esq., Fulmer, Gerrards Cross' is listed under 'Justices – Residing within the County' in James Joseph Sheahan's *History and Topography of Buckinghamshire* (1862) online. Under 'West London Extension' one 'Edward Wanklyn, Esq., Fulmer Place, Slough' is listed as a director of the Great Western Railway in *Bradshaw's Railway Manual* (1867) 351 online.

2 Collett has not been identified.

---

1 *The Times* on 14 July had published a short editorial on D's 13 July speech (accepting the chancellorship of the exchequer) at Aylesbury and printed the speech a few pages later. The *Times* reporter had written that D had been 'surprised, if not angry, that any one should think Parliamentary Reform "is the difficulty of the present Ministers, and will be their stumblingblock." No such thing. He is quite of a different opinion. "I see no difficulty in the matter at all, and if we stumble rest assured we shall not stumble over Parliamentary Reform."' According to *The Times* and other sources (see n2) D had in fact said those words, including 'I am of quite a different opinion' and 'The Great Reform Bill of 1832 was mainly devised by Lord Derby, and it was entirely carried by his energy'.

with the question of Parliamentary Reform, which I acknowledge to be, perhaps, the most difficult of all public questions. What I maintained was, there was no difficulty in the question peculiar to the Conservative party, and I argued that they were as free and as qualified to deal with it as any other party in the State.

What I wished to express respecting Lord Derby's connexion with the Act of 1832 was exactly what I said this year in the House of Commons – that the Act of 1832, if not devised by Lord Derby, was, at least, carried mainly by his energy.

Your faithful servant,

B. DISRAELI[2]

4145

TO: [UNKNOWN]   Downing Street [Monday 16 July 1866]

ORIGINAL: DBP Box 146/2

EDITORIAL COMMENT: C of Ex paper. Endorsed in another hand on the fourth page: 'Disraeli Rt Honbl B. July 16 as to Honors – V[ery] P[rivate]'. Also on the fourth page in another hand: 'as to distribution of Peerages & other honors'. *Dating*: by endorsement and context.

Mem: as to Honors.

"I shall, with pleasure, lay your wishes before Lord Derby, but I ought to tell you, in confidence, that there is no foundation, whatever, in the rumor you refer to, that he is about to create a batch of peers & a batch of baronets.[1] /

If his Government, as I hope & believe it will, take root, & he finds himself in the confirmed exercise of an assured majority, I know, that it is the intention of Lord Derby to consider the claims of his supporters, & / I am sure, that it will be gratifying to him to meet every fair & just expectation.

The honors, wh: he has advised Her Majesty to confer on his friends at present, have been recommended for two reasons: to facilitate the formation of the Ministry, & to fulfil ex promises, wh: were made in the Ministry of 1858-9, & wh: its abrupt termination rendered it, at the time, impossible to accomplish."[2]

2 On 16 July, *The Times* commented on D's 'superficial' and 'unsound' view 'that Reform is a matter of no difficulty at all ... If Reform be after all so easy a thing, there is not much honour to be got by accomplishing it, and a great deal of disgrace to be incurred by failing in it.' In the 18 July issue, 'The Reporter' (as he signed himself), quoting from D's 16 July correction, would reply: 'I have nothing to do with the meaning which the right hon. gentleman attaches to the language of his speech; but, as he seems to impugn the accuracy of two passages which appeared in the report published in *The Times*, I beg to enclose for publication the same passages as they were given in the five London papers which, besides *The Times*, were represented at Aylesbury on the occasion, in two of the Manchester papers which also had reporters there, and in a paper published in Mr. Disraeli's own county. This is not a case in which there was any omission of words which could affect the context; for every sentence uttered by the right hon. gentleman was given in the report which appeared in *The Times*.' There followed nine near-identical versions of the two disputed passages (see n1) quoted from *The Times, Morning Herald, Daily News, Morning Star, Morning Post, Daily Telegraph, Manchester Guardian, Manchester Courier* and *Bucks Chronicle*.

---

1 See **4146**&n3.

2 The names on the Roll of the Lords would increase from 452 (1864) and 454 (1865, 1866) to 462 in 1867, when three peerages would become extinct and the new names include Sir Charles Wood, created Viscount Halifax; Sir Edward Bulwer Lytton, Lord Lytton; Sir William Jolliffe, Lord Hylton; Sir Hugh Rose, Lord Strathnairn; Colonel Pennant, Lord Penrhyn; and the Earl of Caithness, representative peer for Scotland, a peer of the UK as Baron Barogill; Irish peers made peers of the UK included Lord Clermont, Lord Athlumney (Lord Meredyth), the Earl of Dunraven (Lord Kenry), Lord Monck, Lord Henniker (Lord Hartismere) and Viscount Boyne (Lord Brancepeth). By D's death in 1881, the number would reach 511. *The Times* (16 Feb 1864, 17 Feb 1865, 22 Feb 1866, 16 Feb 1867, 27 Jan 1881).

ORIGINAL: DBP Box 146/2

PUBLICATION HISTORY: Blake 448, the fourth (omitting the last sentence) and fifth paragraphs

EDITORIAL COMMENT: C of Ex paper. Endorsed by Derby on the first page: 'Put by Very Private — I have seen the Ch. of Exch. D.' Endorsed in another hand on the last page: 'July 16/66 D'israeli B. as to distribution of Peerages & Honors'. *Sic*: St James'.

Rt Honble | The Earl of Derby | K.G.   July 16 1866

My dear Lord,

I have fixed, for the Clanricarde appointment, Tuesday 4 o'ck:, at the *Treasury*, as there seems impropriety in your attending the Chanr. / of Exr.

I enclose his letter, that you may observe the point, wh: interests him.[1] Perhaps, you will give directions to have the Mem[oran]dum & the Minute at hand.

I enclose also a / Mem: of the reply, wh: I have given to those, who have requested my interference with you on the subject of honors.[2] I think, the position taken up is a sound one, & I have found, generally speaking, that it was, ↑considered↓ satisfactory.

But, / unfortunately, the very individuals, who have received this sort of reply from me, have received, subsequently, from you, or by your authority, answers of a very different complexion, wh: have created great discontent. There are one or two instances respecting wh: I / must speak to you with[ou]t loss of time.[3]

I doubt whether the leader of a party, even with a majority, can ever afford to give point-blank refusals to applications for honors. I have reason / to believe, that Sir Robert Peel never did, altho' he had a large majority, &, practically, was very parsimonious in the distribution of dignities.

Yrs ever, | D.

I am obliged to be early at my office today to receive a Bank Charter Deputation from Liverpool[4] — but will call at St James' Sqre in my way.

---

1 See **4142**&n2.

2 See **4145**.

3 For instance, J. Edward Walcott on 14 July 1866 had sent D a letter he had written to Derby on the 9th 'on seeing in the Newspapers that Col. Edwardes and other Members were to be selected for Baronetcies.' After telling Derby that 'It is rumoured very generally that it is your intention to raise some of your supporters to the dignity of the Baronetage on your coming into office', Walcott went on to ask one for himself. H C/II/A/18a, b.

4 There is no record of a 16 July 1866 meeting between D and a deputation from Liverpool, which, like other major commercial centres, continued to be affected by the monetary crisis of 10 May (see **4125**&n1). D would meet on the 18th with members of the Glasgow Chamber of Commerce to discuss the appointment of a royal commission on the 1844 and 1845 Bank Charter Act and British law affecting currency and banking. D would tell the deputation, 'What I think we are suffering from is not so much a want of currency as a want of capital. I do not think there is any banking arrangement that could relieve us from the embarrassments we are now daily experiencing ... I do not conceive that any very great benefit would be obtained by a roving commission [to investigate the question at Glasgow, Liverpool and Manchester], should we decide upon the expediency of an inquiry.' *BH* (21 Jul 1866). The text of the Glasgow deputation's memorial would be published in *The Times* on 19 July.

4147

TO: MONTAGU CORRY   [London, Monday 16 July? 1866]
ORIGINAL: H B/XX/D/323
EDITORIAL COMMENT: C of Ex paper. *Dating*: conjectural; see n1.

Mr M. Corry[1]
Don't stay at the office for me, as I am pretty sure to go straight to the House – & you will lose yr place, if / you don't go in time.
     You have done all I want.
          D.

4148

TO: QUEEN VICTORIA   Downing Street, Monday 16 July 1866
ORIGINAL: RAC B22 86
PUBLICATION HISTORY: M&B IV 448-9, omitting the last two paragraphs
EDITORIAL COMMENT: C of Ex paper.

                                                        Monday night | July 16. 1866
The Chancellor of the Exr with his humble duty to Yr Majesty.
The House of Commons met this evening after a month's abeyance.[1] Nearly the whole evening has been taken up by an / animated, & interesting, debate on the charter to the Queen's University (Ireland); brought on by Sir Robert Peel.[2] It was, with the exception of a clear, but technical, speech on the part of Sir Hugh Cairns, confined to / the Opposition.[3] It was occasionally rather warm, & Mr Gladstone concluded with a vindication of passion & fire[4] – but it was generally felt & observed, that he left the House in doubt, whether he / was in favor of Mixed Education or not.[5]

1 The formal address may indicate a letter early in D's relationship with Corry, whose appointment as one of D's private secretaries was announced in *The Times* on 16 July 1866.

---

1 Although the House had met several times since then, in his first extant letter to the Queen as newly appointed chancellor of the exchequer, D is alluding to the watershed defeat on 18 June of the franchise bill. For the debate on this day (16th), see *Hansard* CLXXXIV cols 819-917 (D 906-10).
2 The Queen's University of Ireland, comprising colleges at Cork, Galway and Belfast, was a non-denominational institution open to Catholics and Protestants (so-called 'mixed education') that served as an alternative to Dublin's Trinity College, which was Anglican. See **4060**n4. Targeting Gladstone, Peel (n1) had discussed the late government's introduction of a supplemental charter (see n3) which had been signed by the Queen without consultation with Parliament (as would have been proper) and which contained alterations 'of the gravest possible character'.
3 Attorney-general Cairns (n1) had argued that, whereas under the original charter Queen's University could confer degrees only on students who had passed through one of the Queen's Colleges (students being obliged to reside three years at a college before graduating), the supplemental charter stipulated that a young man who had lived at home without attending one of the Colleges might obtain a degree at Queen's University by passing the minimum examination, 'a complete subversion of the whole system of education' at the Queen's Colleges. Cairns objected that the supplemental charter had been sealed when the executive Government, in Gladstone's phrase, was '"in abeyance,"' and when, therefore, the Government had no right to affix the seal.
4 Although he could not 'adopt the strong expressions' of Joseph Henley, who had called mixed education 'fatal to faith and morals', Gladstone (n1) had stated that 'they are not the wisest friends, who would seek to stamp [the Queen's Colleges] with the character of a public monopoly, maintained at the expense of the State ... invested with ... severe prohibitions imposed on others, who are excluded from the natural and ordinary advantages which crown an educational career for the purpose of fostering an odious monopoly.'
5 D paraphrases his own comments (n1) following Gladstone's speech: 'I am at this moment in ignorance

The House is now in Estimates, & making progress.[6]
There is to be a Morning Sitting tomorrow for the Thames Navigation Bill.[7]

TO: THOMAS BAYLEY POTTER [London, Wednesday] 18 July 1866 **4149**
ORIGINAL: PS 503
PUBLICATION HISTORY: *Catherine Barnes Catalogue* 6 (1988) item 29: 'Autograph Letter Signed to Thomas B. Potter, London, 18 July 1866. 2 pp., 8vo, on Chancellor of the Exchequer stationery.'

I have long been obliged to decline writing autographs, but I cannot refuse so slight an attention to an old acquaintance, whose courtesy, at Manchester, I always remember with kindness.[1]

B. Disraeli.

TO: [MONTAGU CORRY] [Grosvenor Gate] Thursday [19 July 1866] **4150**
ORIGINAL: H B/XX/D/317
EDITORIAL COMMENT: C of Ex paper. The illegible word below (in D's parentheses) may be 'Gurney'. *Dating*: by context; see n2. *Place*: Despite C of Ex paper, D evidently writes from Grosvenor Gate.

Thursday 10:30

See Mr Adderley,[1] & say I have not yet received the Memorandum of Mr Russell Gurney,[2] wh: he / ↑ (*illegible*) ↓ promised, referring to Mr Mills questions. This evening.[3]

---

as to whether he is in favour of mixed education or not. I only say this to illustrate the inconvenience of treating these vast questions in a manner so unexpected, so occasional, and so desultory.' D also addressed Bernal Osborne's objections to the recent Irish appointments of Francis Blackburne ('eighty-five — the shadow ... of his former self') as LC and of Joseph Napier ('as deaf as a post') as lord justice of appeal. *The Times* on 17 July would note that D's remarks had elicited much laughter.

6 Discussion in committee of civil service estimates had occurred near the end of the sitting, the House adjourning at 1:15 *am* on the 17th.

7 See **4142**&n3.

---

1 Thomas Bayley Potter (see ph) (1817-1898), a JP £ was MP (L) for Rochdale 1865-95, succeeding his friend Richard Cobden. Potter was much engaged in Manchester's radical politics (especially universal suffrage), which D had dubbed in 1846 'the school of Manchester' (see IV **1472**n1), and in May 1866 had founded the Cobden Club, a stronghold for advocates of free trade. See IV **1326**&nn1&3.

---

1 Presumably colonial under-secretary Charles Bowyer Adderley.

2 This memo has not been found. Russell Gurney (1804-1878), BA 1826 Cambridge, a barrister (Inner Temple 1828), QC 1845, recorder of London 1856-78 and MP (C) for Southampton 1865-78, had been one of three commissioners sent to Jamaica in December 1865 to investigate governor Edward Eyre's handling of an insurrection. Resentment among the impoverished peasantry had driven several hundred protesters, led by black deacon Paul Bogle (who had been ordained by wealthy mulatto politician and radical Baptist George William Gordon), to march into Morant Bay on 11 October 1865 to petition Eyre. When militia killed seven protesters, riots ensued and black rebels roamed the countryside, killing eighteen planters. British retaliation had been fierce: fearing an uprising of the 350,000 blacks against the 13,000 whites, Eyre had imposed martial law for a month, Bogle and over four hundred rebels were hanged and a thousand homes burned. Gordon, a virulent opponent of Eyre's policies, despite having been in Kingston during Bogle's uprising, had been charged with high treason and hastily tried and hanged. Although Eyre was dismissed following an inquiry (the Report of the Jamaica Royal Commission had been released on 18 June 1866), subsequent efforts to indict him would fail. See **4163**&nn1-4.

3 In the House on this day (19th) J.S. Mill, who had recently replaced Charles Buxton as chairman of the Jamaica Committee set up to prosecute Eyre, would ask D if 'any steps had been or will be taken to bring

If the Mem: can be with me at Grosvenor Gate by one o'ck: well & / good: afterwards, I shall be in D.S., as I meet Governor of Bank at two o'ck:[4]

But the sooner I can have the Mem: the better, or I shall have little / time to digest it, otherwise, before meeting of the House.

D.

4151   TO: QUEEN VICTORIA   Downing Street [Thursday] 19 July 1866
ORIGINAL: RAC B22 87
PUBLICATION HISTORY: M&B IV 449
EDITORIAL COMMENT: C of Ex paper.

July 19 1866

The Chr of the Exr with his humble duty to Yr Majesty:

Lord Cranborne brought forward the Indian Budget, to night, in a speech, wh: interested / the House.

The manner was vigorous, & showed a mastery of his matter, wh:, considering his short experience of office, evidently surprised the House.[1]

Persons of weight, / in private, of both parties, spoke of the effort with approbation.

The Chr of the Exr much regrets that, from want of habit, he omitted to send a report on Tuesday night. / It was not an eventful one: a discussion on the Ballot, very insipid. The House recoiled from the subject.[2]

Yesterday the Church Rates a higher tone, but the House wearied.[3]

to trial' those responsible for the floggings, burning of homes and 'numerous unlawful executions' during the insurrection and also Eyre 'for complicity in all or any of the above acts' and, if not, whether the Government 'are advised that these acts are not offences under the Criminal Law'. D would reply that Mill's ten questions were phrased 'beyond the boundaries of Parliamentary precedent, because in putting questions in which opinions are expressed, we are trespassing in some degree upon the liberty and freedom of discussion.' After 'nine inquiries, throughout which the conduct of certain individuals is assumed to be illegal,' the tenth asked whether the 'Government, after inquiry, are of opinion that such conduct and proceedings were illegal'. There was 'extreme irregularity and inaccuracy' in the questions because Mill seemed 'entirely oblivious' that the proceedings 'took place during the existence of martial law [under which] there can be no irregularity in the constitution of the courts ... This being the state of the case, I am not prepared to offer any further information'. *The Times* (10, 30 Jul 1866); *Hansard* CLXXXIV cols 1064-9.

4 Henry Lancelot Holland (*c* 1808-1893), governor of the Bank of England 1865 to March 1867 and then a director, was a director of the Pelican Life Insurance Company 1847-92. *The Times* (10 Jun 1847, 24 Nov 1866, 23 Nov 1892, 27 Jan 1893).

---

1 In the House on this day (19th) the East India Revenue Accounts had been discussed in committee with Cranborne, secretary of state for India only since 6 July, who quoted from various studies an array of financial statistics. He had ended by stating that the policy to be followed was 'to push on the public works ... [and] increase the immense means she [India] possesses for the production of commodities'. *Hansard* CLXXXIV cols 1079-1146. For Gladstone's speech on this day, see **4152**n1.

2 See **4142**n3 and *Hansard* CLXXXIV cols 971-96.

3 Gladstone's Compulsory Church Rate Abolition Bill had first been read on 8 May. Debate on the second reading of 18 July would resume on 1 August, when the bill would be withdrawn. *Hansard* CLXXXIII cols 619-36, CLXXXIV cols 1029-52 (D 1031-2), 1847-85.

TO: LORD DERBY   Grosvenor Gate [Friday 20] July 1866 4152

ORIGINAL: DBP Box 146/2

PUBLICATION HISTORY: M&B IV 452-3; Smith 133, omitting the first paragraph; Aldous 166

EDITORIAL COMMENT: Grosvenor Gate paper. *Dating*: by context; see n1. M&B date the letter 29 July but Smith dates it the 21st (as does Aldous, following Smith), referencing Gladstone's speech in the House on the 19th. D appears to have mistakenly conflated '20' and '19'.

Confidential   July 29 1866

Rt Honble | The Earl of Derby | K.G.

My dear Lord –

I would not trouble you with things when you are dealing with persons, but things may affect persons.

This is, I think important: it is the result / of my reflections, this day, on what Gladstone said yesterday.[1]

Suppose, instead of discharging the order of the Day on the reform Bill, you took up the measure, where it stops? £6 / *Rating* for Boros: 20£ rating for Counties, ↑to be brought up on Report:↓ the northern Boros to be enfranchised; no disfranchisement of any kind.

You cd. carry this in the present House, & rapidly. It would prevent / all agitation in the Recess: it would cut the ground entirely from under Gladstone: & it would smash the Bath Cabal,[2] for there wd. be no dangerous question ahead.

Think of this

  Yrs ever, | D.

TO: QUEEN VICTORIA   Downing Street [Friday] 20 July 1866 4153

ORIGINAL: RAC B22 88

PUBLICATION HISTORY: M&B IV 449, omitting the second and third paragraphs

EDITORIAL COMMENT: C of Ex paper.

                                                                   July 20 1866

The Cr of the Exr with his humble duty to Yr Majesty:

An interesting discussion on foreign affairs[1] opened by Mr Laing, in a colorless, non-intervention, speech.[2]

1 As the House had not sat on 28 July 1866 ('yesterday'), it is likely that D is writing on the 20th, the day after Gladstone, during the sitting of the 19th but early on the 20th (in his words, 'two hours past midnight'), had made a very short speech withdrawing the Representation of the People and Redistribution of Seats Bills, the House adjourning at 2:30 *am* on the 20th. He had challenged the Opposition 'to deal with this question in an effectual manner', promising to 'support any measure which we may deem to be at once prudent and effectual ... to settle a great Imperial question' but cautioning that his party would 'resist to the utmost of our power any illusory or reactionary measure.' On the 19th he had noted: 'H of C 4½-7¾ and 11½-2¼. Made the little dying speech on Reform.' *Hansard* CLXXXIV cols 1143-45; *Gladstone Diaries* VI 452.

2 The Bath Cabal, a group of 'ultra-Tories' led by 4th Marquess of Bath, was opposed to Derby and 'had long despised Disraeli as a Jewish upstart'. Aldous 166.

1 For the protracted debate on foreign policy on this day (20th), the House adjourning at 1:30 *am*, see *Hansard* CLXXXIV cols 1217-58. Discussions had centred on the Austro-Prussian War (begun 15 June), specifically on Austria's recent ceding to France of the Venetia region (under Austrian rule since 1797). See **4139**nn1&2 and below nn3&5.

2 Samuel Laing had asked the Government to keep in view the general principles of non-intervention and

Mr Horsman followed, a very studied oration, of ability, / but too much like highly-finished newspaper articles.[3]

Then came Sir George Bowyer with gentlemanlike tirades, less fierce than the Marquis de Boissy, but scarcely less absurd.[4]

A considerable oration from / Mr Gladstone, wh: covered the subject. Though glowing & earnest, it was conciliatory, & fair & courteous to the Government.[5]

It produced less sensation, than it otherwise would have done, for the House was / anxious to hear the ↑new↓ Minister, & Mr Gladstone was long, & ↑too↓ academical.

The new Secretary of State afforded a great contrast to him. Lord Stanley was never more characteristic — at the same time, clear, cautious, & candid. He pleased the House, wh: evidently gave him, on both sides, its confidence.[6]

4154   TO: LORD DERBY   Downing Street [Monday] 23 July 1866
ORIGINAL: DBP Box 146/2
EDITORIAL COMMENT: C of Ex paper. *Sic*: see.

Rt Honble | The Earl of Derby | K.G.   July 23 1866

above all to avoid mediation, the 'most dangerous form in which intervention could be disguised', asking foreign secretary Stanley for his assurance to take no step that might commit Britain to intervene in the war without giving Parliament the opportunity to express its opinion. See n6.

3 Edward Horsman, regretting that 'the policy of France has been avowedly and ostentatiously the policy of intervention, which England repudiates and condemns', asked Stanley if the Government had 'expressed its readiness to concur with that of France in recommending Austria to accept the two conditions proposed by Prussia and Italy as to the surrender of Venetia, and Austria ceasing to be a member of the Germanic Confederation.' See n6.

4 D is plagiarizing Gladstone's comment about George Bowyer having 'delivered a tirade against the Emperor of the French of such a nature and character that I cannot help thinking intelligent Frenchmen, when they read the report of what has fallen from him in the columns of the English newspapers, will regard his remarks with somewhat of the same feeling with which we peruse the speeches of the Marquis de Boissy.' French senator Hilaire Étienne Octave Rouillé de Coudray (1798-1866), marquis de Boissy, was a caustic orator famous for his perennial opposition to parliamentary regulations and his violent attacks on England. A typical speech of his 'hurries from one subject to another, regardless of any relation between them.' *The Times* (13 Feb 1866). Bowyer's speech had been similarly wide-ranging.

5 Gladstone had urged an examination of Britain's role in promoting 'the well-being and happiness of Europe', averring that the British Government and people considered 'a united and strong Italy ... an element of immense power added to the guarantees of European order.' He deeply regretted Austria's 'great error' of ceding Venetia to France, 'a transaction without example, parallel, or precedent of any kind that in a state of war one of the belligerents should hand over a territory, which is part of the matter in question, to an indifferent party, not engaged in the war, for the purpose of raising some artificial barrier against the enemy.'

6 Although Stanley had assured Laing of the Government's 'policy of observation rather than of action', he could not discount the possibility of 'intervention in the shape of friendly advice tendered by a neutral Power'. If solicited, advice should be given 'under a deep sense of moral responsibility' while avoiding 'involving ourselves or the country in any responsibility for the results of following that advice in a matter where no English interest is concerned.' He had also answered Horsman that it was 'premature ... to express an opinion on the abstract question as to what conditions might or might not be accepted' by Austria and concluded by saying that he did not believe that 'the establishment of a strong North German Power ... would be to us any injury, any menace, or any detriment'.

My dear Lord,

What is Hardy doing to the Roman Catholics?[1] I thought, he had see Manning.[2] But I find them all a-blaze, & that "if / he (Hardy) will not make the amendment, Lord Ed: Howard (who is anxious to support us) will divide against us, & we shall lose all prospect of support from / the English Catholics."[3]

What does it all mean? I can't come on to you, having a load of business tonight.[4]

But I am told, in the / same letter, you are to receive a deputation today.[5]

I am sure you will put it all right.

Don't trouble yourself to reply to this.[6]

Yrs ever, I D.

TO: QUEEN VICTORIA   Downing Street [Monday] 23 July 1866   4155
ORIGINAL: RAC F14 74
EDITORIAL COMMENT: C of Ex paper.

July 23 1866

The Chancellor of the Exchequer with his humble duty to Yr Majesty.

Yr Majestys servants ↑to night↓ have made considerable progress with the Estimates, & it is more than / possible, the Committee of Supply may be closed on Thursday.[1]

---

1 Gathorne Hardy, president of the poor law board as of 12 July, would note on the 24th that on this day (23rd) he had had 'a busy time what with papers & interviews with Lord Derby & others. The R. Caths. were urgent & we agreed to a clause [see n3] wh. is fair & may I hope satisfy them until legislation is effected.' *Hardy Diary* 20.

2 Henry Manning, archbishop of Westminster since June 1865 and head of the Catholic Church in England and Wales, had presided over a public meeting 'for the extension of education among the Catholic poor' on 14 June. *The Times* (14 Jun 1866).

3 In the House on 26 July the Poor Law Amendment Bill would be discussed in committee, Lord Bingham moving 'the insertion of a new clause providing for the education of pauper children in the religion to which they belong ... to do a simple act of justice to a large section of their Roman Catholic fellow-countrymen, many children belonging to whose faith were at present, there was good reason to suppose, brought up in London workhouse schools as Protestants.' Lord Edward Howard (L) would object that 'the clause was not all that Catholics could wish', as 'the conductors of a certified Catholic orphanage had requested twenty-one unions in London to allow Catholic children to be taken into its schools, but the answer in every case was a refusal.' Hardy, while giving the clause 'hearty assent', had not 'thought it right to make the proposal himself, inasmuch as it would have the effect of placing in his hands a power different from that possessed by his predecessors in office.' The clause was accepted in a division of 67 to 8 and, after 'words were introduced to the effect that proof should be given of the religion of the child', added to the bill. *Hansard* CLXXXIV cols 1581-7.

4 D would introduce a supplemental budget early in the evening on this day (23rd), the House adjourning at 1:45 *am* on the 24th. *Hansard* CLXXXIV cols 1278-1364 (D 1286-90).

5 This letter has not been found. Derby did meet on this day (23rd) with a Roman Catholic deputation; see nn1&6.

6 In a letter to D docketed '24 July 1866' Derby would write: 'I made it all right with the R.C.s yesterday – I see Bingham is to move the [Poor Law] Amendment, which we must support as a Govt. We must also take up the question broadly next Session.' H B/XX/S/356.

---

1 In the House on this day (23rd) there had been two discussions in committee of supply (at the beginning and end of the sitting) on supplementary estimates. The first was D's critique of the former chancellor of the exchequer's financial statement (Gladstone responding at length), D advocating 'a prudent and economical management of our finances ... in an epoch like the present – which is an epoch of speculative armament; of discoveries, of experiments and of rapid vicissitudes of practice'. The second, prior

The House after six o'ck: was very thin, all the members having repaired to Hyde Park[2] – but tho' thin, it was not dull, / but, on the contrary, was agitated.

As the evening drew on, the most alarming rumors circulated, wh: soon became circumstantial; but wh:, eventually, turned out to be gross exaggerations, &:, / in many instances, pure fiction.

Sir Brook Bridges[3] told the Cr. of the Exr, that he saw the first rails of the Park pulled down, wh: was pure frolic by a knot of laughing boys, who seemed astonished at their own exploit.[4]

4156   TO: GEORGE ALEXANDER HAMILTON   Downing Street

[Tuesday] 24 July 1866

ORIGINAL: H B/XIII/50d
EDITORIAL COMMENT: C of Ex paper.

Private   July 24 1866

G.A. Hamilton Esqr. | Treasury

My dear Hamilton,

I am interested in the case of Mr Bayly[1] of the Privy Council office. He seems to have been hardly / treated in the recent re-organisation of that office.

---

to the House adjourning at 1:45 *am*, concerned expenditures relative to 'arming our soldiers with good breech-loading weapons' (General Peel) and to public education in Great Britain. The committee of supply would close on 27 July following a brief discussion of the previous evening's vote on the purchase of old gun metal for the Albert Memorial (see **4159**&n2). *Hansard* CLXXXIV cols 1286-1302 (D 1286-90), 1338-60, 1604-6 (D 1605-6).

2 Members of the Reform League (founded 23 February 1865) were planning a large meeting in Hyde Park on 23 July. On 18 July London Metropolitan Police commissioner Sir Richard Mayne had sent League president Edmond Beales a copy of a public notice forbidding that meeting. *The Times* on 20 July had published Beales's 19 July reply quoting Mayne's notice, first, '"that such a meeting, being in-consistent with the purposes for which the park is thrown open to and used by the public, is illegal." ... What law, or what statute, declares such a meeting, when held in the park, to be illegal?'; and secondly, '"that such a meeting is calculated to lead to riotous and disorderly conduct, and to endanger the public peace." ... I positively and emphatically repudiate this charge as most odious and unjustifiable'. On this day (23 July) Beales had led demonstrators to Hyde Park and found it blockaded by over a thousand 'foot and mounted police'. Around 8 *pm* 'a company of the Grenadier Guards and a troop of the Life Guards entered the Park, but it was then too late to prevent the influx of people' who were already storming the Park after pulling down the iron railings. 'After leaving the Park, gangs of ruffians broke the windows in Great Cumberland-street. At 1 o'clock in the morning 200 or 300 were engaged in this work of dev-astation.' *The Times* on 25 July would publish a list of forty-two 'prisoners charged with rioting and with assaulting the police on Monday evening.' *The Times* (20, 24, 25 Jul 1866). See **4157**nn3-7 and n4 below.

3 Sir Brook Bridges (1801-1875), 5th Baronet, Baron Fitzwalter 1868, BA 1822 and MA 1827 (Oxford), DL of Kent, capt East Kent Yeomanry Cavalry 1830-53, was MP (C) for Kent E 1852, 1857-68.

4 Aside from police barricades, 'the only obstacle to the entry of the crowd is an old rusty railing resting on a dwarf wall, and a few prises of a lever are sufficient to throw down several yards of it ... The great majority of the people in the crowded streets were the usual slouching, shambling man-boys who con-stitute the mass of the ordinary London multitude.' Derby would tell the Lords on 24 July that 'a great portion of those who assembled in Hyde Park last night were boys and young men, who had no serious views with regard to the demonstration, but joined in it merely for the purpose of assisting in any row or disturbance that might take place.' *The Times* (24, 25 Jul 1866).

---

1 Following her death in 1867, Lady Jersey would leave her nephew Charles Bayly £1,000, her 'personalty being sworn under 300,000£.' *The Times* (1 Jun 1867) quoting the *Illustrated London News*. Lady Sarah Vil-liers (d 1852), sister of 5th Earl of Jersey, in 1800 had married Charles Nathaniel Bayly.

He is a nephew of our excellent friend, the Dowager Lady Jersey.
I wish you would look / in to his case.
Mr Helps is favorable, I believe, to his claim.²
    Yours sincerely, | D.

TO: QUEEN VICTORIA   House of Commons [Tuesday] 24 July 1866   **4157**
ORIGINAL: RAC F14 77
PUBLICATION HISTORY: M&B IV 449-50
EDITORIAL COMMENT: House of Commons paper.

                                           July 24 1866

The Cr of the Exchequer with his humble duty to Yr Majesty –
The discussion in the House tonight, on the affairs of the Park, was highly, & unexpectedly, satisfactory.¹ /

    Tho' introduced by a speech from Mr Ayrton,² & from some others, in a very full house, wh: appealed rather to the malevolent ~~op~~ passions of a popular assembly, the reply of Mr Walpole was so dignified, / so full of good feeling & supported by so much adequate knowledge, that a very favorable reaction soon was visible.³

    This was clenched by an animated speech from Sir George Grey, than wh: nothing could / be more complete, more gentlemanlike & generous.⁴

2 Arthur Helps was clerk of the privy council.

---

1 See *Hansard* CLXXXIV cols 1385-1416 (D 1412-14), the House adjourning at 1:45 *am* on the 25th, and **4155**&nn2&4.

2 Ayrton (n1) had noted the ambiguities surrounding legitimate use of public parks with examples of how 'the people are deeply impressed with the idea that they have a right to use this public property for their own particular purposes and objects.' He asked Walpole to produce Sir Richard Mayne's notice (placed on the Hyde Park gates the previous day), 'one of certainly an extremely disagreeable description, because it suggested that the meeting proposed to be held was one calculated to lead to a disturbance and a breach of the peace ... No army in this country ought to be used as an agent of Government.' Acton Smee Ayrton (1816-1886), a barrister (Middle Temple 1853), MP (L) for Tower Hamlets 1857-74, would be treasury secretary 1868-9, PC 1869, chief commissioner of works 1869-73 and judge-advocate-general 1873-4. See n6.

3 Spencer Walpole (n1), home secretary since 6 July, had been conciliatory yet firm, insisting that the notice had been issued only to prevent meetings 'likely to create political excitement or to cause religious agitation'. While repudiating the use of force, he cautioned that, 'if the law is likely to be violated, and if the public peace is likely to be endangered, it is a very great responsibility ... for any person occupying the position I hold, should he not have the moral courage to take measures for the preservation of order.' To Bernal Osborne, who had asked what instructions had been given by the home office to Mayne, Walpole replied that the police had been instructed to 'temperately and forbearingly warn' anyone disobeying the notice and not to use force unless 'absolutely necessary'; he had also heard that the military had taken no 'measures of severity or coercion'. He believed ordering the gates of the Park to be locked a 'wise course' and hoped that 'it will be perceived that there is really no ground of complaint against the Government for the manner in which they have discharged a most painful but a most imperative duty.' Despite 'very favorable reaction' to the speech, Laurence Oliphant did not see how Walpole 'could escape serious blame' and believed the effect of the riots had been 'to impair very seriously the authority of the Executive, to bring the police into contempt, and to lessen the prestige of the military', while A.H. Layard called the Government's actions 'injudicious and foolish' and an invitation to 'roughs and pickpockets'.

4 Former home secretary Sir George Grey (n1), who had dealt with earlier Trafalgar Square disturbances, had read to the House the 2 July letter he had instructed Mayne to send to Beales (warning of police

When Sir George rose, nearly a dozen members, of the extreme party, rose at the same time, but when he sate down, the feeling of the House was so / decided, that none of these gentlemen attempted to follow him. Among these, was Mr Bernal Osborne, who had risen twice.

The Cr of the Exr hoped, that all was over, & over well, but Mr Cowper / would make a speech, chiefly on his flower beds.[5] This gave breath to the extreme party, & Mr Mill rose, & delivered a speech hardly worthy of a philosopher, but / rather more adapted to Hyde Park.

The Cr of the Exchequer ventured to tell him this,[6] & then the matter died off: the general result being, that the leading authorities in the House / discountenanced entirely the criticism on Mr Walpole's conduct.

The accounts, this evening, are, that the chief leaders of the mob are now active in their efforts to terminate the disturbance.[7]

intervention following a breach of the peace) and Beales's 3 July reply (blaming the disturbances on '"the work of a few boys, as the great bulk of those assembled dispersed quietly to their several homes"'). As Grey had told Mayne to intimate that the Hyde Park meeting 'would not be permitted', he accepted 'a full share of responsibility for having acted on the opinion that it is inexpedient that meetings of a political character should be held in Hyde Park.' Grey, on the scene the previous night, thought the police had acted with 'firmness and moderation' but regretted the destruction of the railings and 'of those beautiful borders of flowers from which the public have derived so much pleasure.'

5 William Francis Cowper (n1), former chief commissioner of works (an office assumed by John Manners on 6 July), had offered Walpole as proof that 'the Parks were appreciated by the people ... the fact that the crowds who on the previous evening had torn down the railings, even in the excitement of the moment and their anxiety to baffle the police, did not forget the flowers whose beauty had afforded them so much pleasure, but carefully avoided interfering with the beds.' *The Times* on 25 July would report that 'Between the Marble Arch and Grosvenor-gate the railings were entirely demolished and the flower beds ruined. Between the Grosvenor and the Stanhope gates, moreover, not a railing remained erect, those not actually levelled being forced considerably out of the perpendicular. This had been done out of mere wantoness [*sic*], after ingress had been effected at other points, as was evident from the fact of the flowers and shrubs having escaped damage.'

6 D (n1) had called John Stuart Mill's impassioned defence of the people's right to hold meetings in Hyde Park 'a sample ... of the rhetoric which will prevail at those periodical meetings we are promised [in the Park].' To Mill's assertion that all public parks 'assuredly must be held to belong to the public', D had countered that it was a standing rule that no public meeting should be held in public parks 'for any political or religious discussion.' However, D regarded 'public meetings, properly held, at the proper time and in the proper place ... as one of the great political safety-valves to which we should trust.' Addressing Ayrton, D said: 'What we [the Government] said was that a meeting of this kind would tend possibly and probably to riot – and has it not? They may be going on even at this moment.'

7 There had been further rioting also on this day (24th). Crowds in Hyde Park had 'again attacked the police with stones and brickbats. They tore up the shrubs, broke off branches from the trees ... As night approached the attack on private houses was resumed. The windows of the Athenaeum Club were smashed ... In other streets near the Parks similar outrages were committed.' *The Times* (25 Jul 1866). Corry had written to D from Grosvenor Gate at '6:40' *pm* a note docketed by MA 'July 24th 1866' and, in another hand, 'Sent to the House of Commons': 'No mob outside your house now; ... The Inspector in charge at Gros. Gate tells me that while the crowd was at its worst here, your house was never mentioned as obnoxious – though the houses of Mr Walpole and Lord Elcho and others have come in for some threats. The soldiers have moved away to the M[arble] Arch, and Mrs Disraeli wishes me to add that the people in general seem to be thoroughly enjoying themselves: and I really believe she sympathizes with them.' Charlotte de Rothschild on 30 July would write to her son Leopold that 'Ten of Mr. Disraeli's windows were broken by the mob'. H B/XX/CO/2; ROTH.

TO: MARY ANNE DISRAELI   Downing Street, Thursday [26 July 1866]   **4158**
ORIGINAL: H A/I/A/326
PUBLICATION HISTORY: M&B IV 452, prefaced by 'He [D] wrote to his wife on July 26 [1866]:', the second
paragraph
EDITORIAL COMMENT: C of Ex paper. Docketed by MA 'July 26th/66'.

Thursday

My dearest

I write, because I promised, tho' I have nothing worth your reading.

I hope with energy & prudence, we / may overcome the difficulties,[1] but it is very obvious to me, that the affair is encouraged by our opponents underhand, with / the view of upsetting the Government. I think they will fail.

Yours ever, | D.

TO: QUEEN VICTORIA   Downing Street [Thursday] 26 July 1866   **4159**
ORIGINAL: RAC F14 84
PUBLICATION HISTORY: LQVB I 361
EDITORIAL COMMENT: C of Ex paper, seal crossed out and 'Ho: of Comm:' written in.

Ho: of Comm: | July 26 1866

The Cr of the Exr, with his humble duty to Yr Majesty.

All goes well: the House entirely rallies round Yr Majesty's servants with respect to the Park meetings[.] The / Cr of the Exr confesses he was a little nervous, when he first heard of Mr Secretary Walpole's movements, but he is bound to say, that they ♭ appear to be successful. His pathos seems to have melted the multitude, who suppose / a Secretary of State, particularly if connected with the Police, must be an Ogre.[1]

---

1 Apparently the Hyde Park riots; see **4157**n7.

---

1 *The Times* on this day (26th) had noted 'the conception which brawling and ignorant patriots had formed during the last few days of Mr. Walpole as a dark and insidious enemy of the people'. It found 'inconceivable' that Walpole, at his 25 July meeting (at 2:00 *pm*) with a deputation from the Reform League, should have granted it (as had been reported) 'permission to hold a meeting next Monday subject to no supervision but that of Mr. Beales himself, and subject to no guarantee of order but his undertaking.' This rumour may have prompted Derby to write to D on this day (from St James's Square): 'I am very anxious to see you about this fiasco of Walpole's. I believe you have a morning sitting of the House. If so, pray call here on your way down. The matter is serious & pressing.' H B/XX/S/357. The 'pathos' D mentions alludes to Walpole's emotionalism at his meeting with the deputation, when he 'was said to have shed tears' (M&B IV 452). His remarks to them were published in *The Times* on 26 July and would provoke animated debate between Russell and Derby in the Lords on 3 August. In the House on this day (26th) Walpole had noted the 'misconception of a most extraordinary kind' of his behaviour, explaining that he had received Beales's letter asking permission to hold a meeting in Hyde Park on 30 July only 'near six o'clock yesterday afternoon, while the notices that the meeting was to be held with the sanction of the Government must have been printed' by then. Beales had arrived at the park on the 25th after 5 *pm* and notices had then been posted announcing the meeting for '"Monday afternoon next [30 July] at 6 o'clock."' Walpole read Beales's letter to the House and also his own reply of 26 July denying permission to hold meetings 'in the Royal Parks'. *Hansard* CLXXXIV cols 1537-40, 1984-92. According to Stanley, writing on this day (26th), Walpole had also been 'on the point of bursting into tears' in the House, thus creating 'an impression of weakness. It is a mixture of pathos and solemnity quite uncalled for, and almost ludicrous.' *Disraeli, Derby* 261.

The Cr of the Exr informs Yr Majesty, with great satisfaction, that the vote for the National / ↑Memorial↓, tho' for a moment menaced, was passed, & passed agreeably.[2]

4160   TO: MARY ANNE DISRAELI   Downing Street [Friday] 27 July [1866]
ORIGINAL: H A/I/A/327
EDITORIAL COMMENT: C of Ex paper. Docketed by MA: '1866'. *Dating*: by context; see nn1&2.

July 27

My dearest,

I think General Grey's letter, enclosing Gladstone's,[1] must be at my writing table, Grosr Gate.

If / you find it, about my blotting paper, send it by messenger, who brings this.

They tried to oppose the Royal Vote / on report, but I defeated them. It is now finished.[2]

Your own, | D.

4161   TO: QUEEN VICTORIA   House of Commons [Friday] 27 July 1866
ORIGINAL: RAC F14 86
PUBLICATION HISTORY: M&B IV 450, omitting the first paragraph; Weintraub *Disraeli* 438, brief extracts
EDITORIAL COMMENT: C of Ex paper, seal crossed out and 'H of Comm:' written in.

H of Comm: | July 27 1866

The Chanr of the Excheqr with his humble duty to Yr Majesty:

2 In the House in committee on this day (26th) D had moved a vote of £4,970 'for the purchase from the War Department of gun metal to be employed in the construction of the [Albert] memorial – namely, seventy-one tons at £70 per ton.' Asked by Ayrton if that amount was 'in addition to the £50,000 which the House had voted for the memorial three years ago' (see VIII **3809**n1) and if it 'would have to vote sums of money from time to time' for the monument's completion, D had replied that the larger sum had been intended as 'the extreme and only sum this House should ever be called on to vote towards the memorial, ... the Government of the day' having promised seventy-one tons of old gun metal for the bronze work. The Queen replied on this day (26th) expressing 'great satisfaction at the manner in which [D] had carried the vote for the gun-metal for her dear, great Husband's Memorial. She knows how truly he appreciated him!' H H/LIFE has typed transcriptions of two documents relating to the application to purchase gun metal: a 'Private Sec's précis' dated '14th July 1866' and an extract from a 'July 17, 1866' letter (presumably to D) from Northcote. *Hansard* CLXXXIV cols 1551-2; H B/XIX/A/27. See **4160**n2.

— — —

1 General Grey on 26 July 1866 had written to D that 'before you present the Estimate tomorrow, I wish to put you in possession of what Gladstone says on the subject. I thought it right to tell him that the Comm[itt]ee wishes to press for the fulfilment of Ld. Palmerston's promise, & the same messenger that brought your very satisfactory note [*not found*], brings this most *un*satisfactory one from him. We ought not to run the risk of unpleasant remarks. But I feel that the matter is in very safe hands with you, & that you will do what is right. The Gun Metal *is* much wanted – & wanted as soon as we can get it ... Pray let me have Gladstone's letter again.' H B/XIX/D/9.

2 On this day (27th) MP (L) Charles J. Monk had objected to the previous day's resolution of a vote of £4,970 to purchase old gun metal for construction of the Albert Memorial (see **4159**n2), citing no 'unanimous agreement on the part of the late Government with regard to this gift'. After repeating some of his remarks of the previous evening, D had asserted that Palmerston, not only in the House and in cabinet but also 'in a letter I have seen', had indeed agreed to purchase the gun metal. 'I am sure the House will feel that it would be proceeding in a captious spirit to turn round now, when Lord Palmerston is no longer here to uphold his engagement, to rescind that agreement'. The vote was agreed to. *Hansard* CLXXXIV cols 1604-6.

Morning & evening, a very busy ~~session~~ sitting: a great deal of business transacted; the Reformatory Bill, the Public / Health bill, & so on. The Cr. of the Exr calculates, that the Session may be brought to a ~~clos~~ close on the 8th. August.[1]

The general rumor, & understanding, in the House, to night, is, / that all attempts at tumultuous meetings are now definitively relinquished, & that Monday will be quite tranquil.[2]

It is said, that no effort will be made to hold a public / meeting in Victoria Park any more, than in Hyde Park. The principle, that they are Royal Parks, is to be fully recognised.

If this be true, as the C of E. hopes, & believes, he ventures to think, that the / whole question of the localities of public meetings deserves the serious consideration of your Majesty's servants.

Public meetings are the recognised, & indispensable, organs of / a free constitution. They are safety-valves.[3]

It is desirable, it would seem, that, when the occasion offers, some act shd. be passed, recognising & regulating the rights & privileges of Yr Majesty's Parks enjoyed, / thro' Yr Majesty's gracious sanction, by all classes of Yr Majesty's subjects, &, at the same time, that there shd. be some public places provided where the great body of / the people, like the Comitia of the Romans, shd. have the right to assemble, & discuss, & express, their opinion.[4]

Yr Majesty will, perhaps, deign to consider these suggestions.

TO: QUEEN VICTORIA   Downing Street [Monday] 30 July 1866   4162

ORIGINAL: RAC F14 88

PUBLICATION HISTORY: Weintraub *Disraeli* 439, the last two paragraphs

EDITORIAL COMMENT: C of Ex paper. *Sic*: Belzhazzar.

July 30 1866

The Cr of the Exr with his humble duty to Yr Majesty:

A great deal of business has been transacted this evening. The public Health bill passed thro' / Committee after a long ordeal of several days. This would, at all times, be an important measure: at the present moment, it is of paramount importance, / & would alone redeem the Session from the imputation of being fruitless.[1]

---

1 Among the bills discussed on this day (27th) were the Reformatory Schools Bill, Railways (Ireland) Temporary Advances Bill, Landed Estates Court, &c., (Ireland) Bill and Public Health Bill, the House adjourning at 1:45 *am* on the 28th. *Hansard* CLXXXIV cols 1603-53. The session would close on 10 August.

2 For the proposed meeting of the Reform League in Hyde Park on 30 July, see **4159**n1. Aside from a question to John Manners (n1) as to whether the monies 'to repair the ravages recently committed in the Parks' would come from the Metropolis or from taxpayers (to which he replied 'that is a question that will be taken into the consideration of the Government'), the riots were not otherwise mentioned on this day.

3 D had used this expression in the House on 24 July. See **4157**n6.

4 Speakers' Corner in Hyde Park would be officially sanctioned by the Royal Parks and Gardens Regulation Act 1872. The four Roman *comitia* (assemblies) – *calata*, *curiata*, *centuriata* and *tributa* – included all citizens and possessed legislative and judicial powers, including the election of magistrates.

---

1 Amendments to the Public Health Bill had been discussed on this day (30th) and the bill would receive third reading on 2 August and royal assent on 7 August. It rendered 'the power of nuisance [*health hazard*] authorities more summary and complete': they could now maintain 'carriages for the conveyance

All the accounts from the various public meetings, up to 10 o'ck:, indicate a / perfectly orderly state.

The meeting in the Agricultural Hall was very full. It is said that it holds 30,000 persons![2] A hall of Belzhazzar![3]

Mr. Bright was not there, / & no notable except Mr Mill, who, after having voted against the Ballot a few weeks ago, attended a monster meeting, one of the principal objects of wh: was to support the Ballot.[4]

Mr / Mill entered the House this evening about ten o'ck. & then I knew the great meeting was really over. He had not been seated ten minutes before he sank into profound slumber, from wh: nothing / could rouse him. It was a great contrast to his usual demeanour: his bright, ultra-vigilant face, with almost too much tension of interest, & air of unflagging duty.

A / philosopher, who, ~~passed~~ past middle life, becomes member for Westminster, & attends monster meetings at Islington, may be pardoned if, for a moment, he confesses the weakness of exhausted nature.[5]

4163   TO: QUEEN VICTORIA   [London, Tuesday] 31 July 1866
        ORIGINAL: RAC B22 94.

July 31 1866

The Cr of the Exr with his humble duty to Yr Majesty:

An interesting & well sustained debate on the Jamaica affairs.[1] Begun with some violence, / as it proceeded, the good effects of parliamentary discussion were shown

---

of persons suffering under infectious diseases' and were authorized to take them to hospital. 'But, above all, it provides a steady means of compelling local authorities to do their duty.' The Sanitary Act, 1866 (as it would be termed) was an especially important piece of legislation because it improved upon the 1848 Public Health Act by providing more stringent measures to deal with sewers, drainage and overcrowding, and by empowering the home secretary to intervene if local authorities failed to remove nuisances. *Hansard* CLXXXIV cols 1679-87, 1905-10, 2126; *The Times* (10 Aug 1866).

2 The Reform League on this day (30th) had held 'an Indignation Meeting' in the Royal Agricultural Hall, Islington. Opened in 1861 and capable of holding 50,000 people, it was the largest building of its kind in London and one of the largest exhibition halls in the world. *The Times* (30 Jul 1867).

3 The Babylonian king Belshazzar gave 'a great banquet for a thousand of his nobles'. Daniel 5:1-4.

4 Over 20,000 had gathered for the 8 *pm* meeting. Although 'the assemblage was, on the whole, decent, quiet, and tradesmanlike', the crowd's 'steady hum, sometimes deepening into a roar' in the cavernous venue rendered Edmond Beales inaudible. J.S. Mill, 'who ought to have been the lion of the evening ... could not get a hearing' and left midway through his address. He and John Bright were among the MPs on the official program, and a banner depicted Bright 'carried in triumph by the Clerkenwell branch of the Reform League.' Activist Charles Bradlaugh moved a resolution for a petition to the House (see n5) and charged Derby's government with 'illegal conduct'. *The Times* (31 Jul 1866).

5 Sixty-year-old J.S. Mill had been MP (L.) for Westminster since 12 July 1865. On 2 August he would present 'the petition adopted at the meeting in the Agricultural Hall, complaining of the exclusion of the public from Hyde Park on Monday week [23 July], and praying the House to institute an inquiry into the conduct of the Chief Commissioner of Police [Sir Richard Mayne], and of the Police generally.' *Hansard* CLXXXIV col 1905.

---

1 In the House on this day (31st) there had been two very long debates: 'Currency and Banking', a motion for a royal commission to investigate the recent financial crisis (see **4125**&n1), and 'Disturbances in Jamaica' (see **4150**n2), the House adjourning at 2:30 *am* on 1 August. Anti-slavery advocate Charles Buxton, first chairman of the Jamaica Committee, had moved four resolutions: deploring 'the excessive punishments which followed the suppression of the disturbances'; 'that grave excesses of severity on the part

in its increased candor & information; till, at length, the lucid remarks of the Attorney General,[2] & / an ample & discreet speech from Mr Cardwell,[3] vindicated the cause of common sense.

At the close of the debate, the Recorder rose, & made his maiden speech — & / with great effect & success.

Certainly, he will never be able again to address the house, when he was so completely master of his subject, wh: is the foundation of eloquence; but his voice was fine; & his manner impressive, & yet natural.[4]

TO: [MONTAGU CORRY] [London, end of July 1866] 4164
ORIGINAL: H B/XX/D/320
EDITORIAL COMMENT: *Dating*: by context; see n1.

Is there no answer about the Duke of Wellington rê Ld. Walden & Cte. Kielmansegge's Plate?[1]

D

of any Civil, Military, or Naval Officers ought not to be passed over with impunity'; that compensation be awarded to those whose property was destroyed and 'to the families of those who were put to death illegally'; and that since over 1,000 had been 'executed or severely flogged ... all further punishment on account of them ought to be remitted.' *Hansard* CLXXXIV cols 1705-1845 (D 1838-9).

2 Attorney-general Sir Hugh Cairns (n1), while objecting to resolutions two ('a prejudging the question ... of grave excesses of severity' by island authorities) and three (a 'loose, vague principle of compensation to be awarded in a manner' left unexplained), approved the first resolution's use of the word 'punishment', as 'it assumes the legality and necessity of the acts of authority at the time when these were committed.' D would argue that 'because the use of the term "punishment" is an acknowledgement that it was the result of a legal act', it would not 'be possible to take this Resolution as the groundwork of an impeachment of Governor [Edward] Eyre.' This resolution would be carried and the others withdrawn.

3 Former colonial secretary Edward Cardwell (n1) had defended Eyre as having acted with 'vigour and promptitude' and in 'the real belief that he was discharging his duty'. In his opinion, compensation should be made not only to 'the poor people' but also 'magistrates, landed proprietors and others, whose property was destroyed'. He concluded with an apotheosis of Jamaica and of its prosperous future under new governor Sir John Grant.

4 Although Russell Gurney had not changed his opinion about radical George William Gordon (who had been hanged for high treason) – quoting (n1) from the Jamaica Royal Commission Report that there was not '"sufficient proof either of his complicity in the outbreak at Morant Bay or of his having been a party to a general conspiracy against the Government"' – he was careful to distinguish Gordon's crime from his 'very questionable speeches and writings ... that might possibly have subjected him to an indictment for sedition'. He asked the House not to ignore 'the danger which had to be encountered by the whole white population, and the difficulties which beset those in authority at the time of the outbreak', and concluded by asking if, since 'very recently the power to declare martial law had been given in other parts of the West Indies', the House could examine 'with what safeguards' that power 'may best be exercised.'

---

1 The Duchess of Wellington was the sister of Arthur Hay (1824-1878), Viscount Walden, 9th Marquess of Tweeddale 1876, who in 1857 had married Hélène Eleanore Charlotte Augusta de Kielmansegge, daughter of Count Kielmansegge. Walden, who had had a distinguished career in the Grenadier Guards 1841-63 (retiring as colonel), was a noted ornithologist and fellow of the Linnean Society 1866, president of the Zoological Society of London 1868 and FRS 1871. On 21 July 1866 he had written to Wellington that Kielmansegge some twenty years ago had brought to England a large quantity of plate which, however, he had taken back to Germany two years ago. Upon his death (in June), Lady Walden had inherited the plate, but the treasury insisted it could not be re-imported without incurring duty. Walden asked for this unprecedented case to be assessed by the customs board. On 23 July Wellington had asked D to intervene, saying Kielmansegge had claimed no return of duty when exporting the plate, indicating that he had intended to send it back to his daughter in England. A note in H (probably in Corry's hand) states

Shall be at the office before Cabinet when you can tell me.

D

4165   TO: RALPH EARLE   Downing Street [end of July 1866]

ORIGINAL: H H/LIFE

EDITORIAL COMMENT: From a typescript headed: 'D. to Mr. R.A. Earle, C. of E., Downing St.' *Dating*: by context; see n1.

.... You must not pay too much attention to the Irish howls of either side.[1]

If Napier had not been appointed, Brady, the late Chancellor[2] must have been. Such is the law!

This would have been too absurd....

4166   TO: QUEEN VICTORIA   Downing Street [Thursday] 2 August 1866

ORIGINAL: RAC B22 97

PUBLICATION HISTORY: M&B IV 451, omitting the first clause of the first sentence and the last paragraph

EDITORIAL COMMENT: C of Ex paper.

Augt 2 1866

The Cr of Exr with his humble duty to Yr Majesty.

After making considerable progress with some important bills,[1] & sending them to the Ho: of Lords, the evening has been taken up with a dreary debate on the Habeas / Corpus Suspension Act in Ireland.[2]

Mr Bernal Osborne, at one moment, promised some relief in a very elaborate speech & evidently, from several allusions, long matured – but it was old-fashioned & out of tune & time, & fell very flat.[3]

---

that the plate was 'now on its way to England' and that Walden's letter had been 'Forwarded to Custom House. – Answer from Mr Goulburn saying duty must be paid.' H B/XXI/W/179, 179a.

---

1 In an undated letter (docketed by AES '? July 1866'), Earle had told D that he feared Joseph Napier's appointment as the new Irish lord justice of appeal was 'irrevocable' and enclosed a letter (dated 'Sunday') from William Monsell objecting to the 'scandalous & profligate' appointment; 'a Bar meeting to protest against it on the ground of his nearly complete deafness is under consideration.' There is in H a clipping from *The Irish Times* of Saturday 14 July 1866 calling Napier's rumoured appointment 'an act of suicidal fatuity indeed on the part of the Government ... a deaf judge to hear appeals!' H B/XX/E/390, 390a. Napier accepted Derby's offer but then withdrew it in a letter dated 28 July 1866 which would be read by Naas in the Lords on 30 July and published in *The Times* on the 31st.

2 Maziere Brady (1796-1871), 1st Bt 1869, BA 1816 and MA 1819 Trinity College (Dublin), an Irish barrister 1819, sol-gen 1837 and att-gen 1839 for Ireland, chief baron of the court of exchequer 1840, LC of Ireland 1846-52, 1853-8 and 1859-66.

---

1 The Public Health and Reformatory Schools bills.

2 In the House on this day (2nd) Lord Naas had moved second reading of the Habeas Corpus Suspension (Ireland) Act Continuance Bill. *Hansard* CLXXXIV cols 1910-83. D did not speak.

3 Among other topics, Bernal Osborne (n2) had inveighed against habeas corpus ('Are the Irish such an incorrigible nation that they are only to be weighted and kept in order by measures of coercion?'), Fenianism ('its objects are pillage, confiscation, and murder'), the Ecclesiastical Titles Act (which should be repealed) and the office of Lord Lieutenant of Ireland (a 'mode of governing ... vicious in principle and mischievous in practice'). He closed by quoting from D's 1844 speech calling for the reconstruction

The new Attorney General / for Ireland made his maiden speech, & showed much vigor, tho' wanting refinement. He will speak better next time, for he was unnecessarily loud, as men often are, from being nervous, & seemed dictatorial, when he was only frightened. / He is, however, likely to be an accession to the House.[4]

TO: MARY ANNE DISRAELI   Downing Street [Saturday] 4 August 1866   **4167**
ORIGINAL: H A/I/A/328
EDITORIAL COMMENT: C of Ex paper.

Private   Augt 4 1866
My dearest love,
The communication[1] was with respect to a plot against the Government, wh: has been revealed to her by a Roman Catholic workman. / I could not stay long eno' to X examine her. But Lord Derby, to whom alone I mentioned it, wishes me to see her again, wh: I shall do tomorrow.[2]

    It / must be kept quite secret.

    We have had a long Cabinet.[3]

    Yours ever | my dearest Wife, | D.

TO: QUEEN VICTORIA   [House of Commons, Monday] 6 August 1866   **4168**
ORIGINAL: RAC B22 106
PUBLICATION HISTORY: M&B IV 451.

                           Augt 6. 1866
The Cr of the Exr with his humble duty to Yr Majesty:

---

of Ireland's social system: '"They had a starving population, an absentee aristocracy, an alien Church, and, in addition, the weakest Executive in the world. That was the Irish question. What would gentlemen say, on reading of a country in that position? They would say at once, the remedy is revolution (not the suspension of the Habeas Corpus Act)."' Since D had said that the duty of a minister was '"to effect by his policy all those changes which a revolution would do by force"' Osborne now called upon him to initiate such a policy and 'inscribe his name on the rolls of his country as the regenerator of a people.'

4 John Edward Walsh, attorney-general for Ireland since 25 July, thought the bill under discussion (n2) absolutely necessary, citing 'gaols filled with 320 prisoners charged with Fenianism', most of them not 'industrious fellow-countrymen' but 'adventurers and strangers' from America and such towns as Manchester and Birmingham. He feared the worst if these 'desperadoes' were 'turned out upon the country to create bloodshed and commit murder, with no power existing to arrest them.' Ireland's salvation, he concluded, 'lay in comprehensive measures, which would encourage industry and direct the energies of the people to that which they lacked – a patient, persevering, peaceful use of the great blessings which Providence had conferred upon them.'

---

1 This communication has not been found.
2 This incident appears to be related to the ongoing Fenian uprisings. Reasons for Roman Catholic opposition to Fenianism included its use of violence but also its challenge to the Church's authority as the representative of the Irish people.
3 Stanley on this day (4th) recorded a 'Cabinet in afternoon, settling the Queen's speech'. The speech, of which almost one-third dealt with the suspension of habeas corpus in Ireland, would be read at prorogation on 10 August and published on 11 August in *The Times*, which would note the conspicuous absence of any mention of the reform debate. *Disraeli, Derby* 263; *Hansard* CLXXXIV cols 2155-60.

The Extradition Treaty Act passed, but with a limitation to one year[.][1]

We defeated all attempts / to exclude "political offences", wh: wd. have included everything, but thought it best to accept the condition of time: as nothing could / have prevented the discussion next year: the question must be reproduced, &, under any circumstances, the opinion of the House will be taken.[2]

Time / brings everything – consolation & catastrophe, & it is hoped it may help Yr Majesty's servants in this matter.

The House meets again tomorrow, but only for a few minutes. Its pulse is very low; but extreme unction will not be administered↑, I believe,↓ until Friday.[3]

4169 TO: CHARLES FREMANTLE   [London, Wednesday] 8 August [1866?]
ORIGINAL: H B/XX/D/368
EDITORIAL COMMENT: *Dating*: the earliest possible date; see n1. *Sic*: Bushey.

Mr Fremantle[1]   Aug 8
Have the kindness to tell them to send me one buck here from Bushey.[2]
    D.

4170 TO: ANDREW MONTAGU   Downing Street [Monday] 13 August 1866
ORIGINAL: H B/XIII/51
EDITORIAL COMMENT: A draft in D's hand on C of Ex paper.

Confidential   Augt 13 1866
Andrew Montagu | Esqr
My dear Montagu,
I have been so very much engaged these last two months, & indeed during the whole year, that I have a hundred times relinquished / my intention of writing to you.

---

1 The Extradition Treaties Act Amendment Bill, amending the 1843 Extradition Treaty Act between England and France, would be given royal assent on 10 August. Stanley in the House on this day (n2) had suggested that the bill's duration 'be limited to one year from the 1st of next September.'
2 In the House on this day (6th) Sir Francis Goldsmid had moved (but later would withdraw) a clause that, in his words, 'was not only necessary to the vindication of the honour of this country and the preservation of the right of asylum, but ... would tend to maintain rather than endanger our friendly relations with foreign Powers.' The clause stipulated that nothing in the act '"shall be construed to authorize the extradition of any person in whose case there shall be reasonable grounds for belief that his offence, if any, had for its motive or purpose the promotion or prevention of any political object"'. Dissenters had included Sir George Bowyer (were the clause adopted, the country would 'be forced to sanction murders committed for a political purpose') and A.S. Ayrton, who objected that 'the clause was so worded as to appear to give some moral right to murder people for political differences.' D did not speak. *Hansard* CLXXXIV cols 2107-24.
3 The House would meet briefly on 7 August, adjourning at 6:45 *pm*, and on Friday 10 August to prorogue Parliament until 25 October. *Hansard* CLXXXIV cols 2133-52, 2160-6.

---

1 Charles William Fremantle (1834-1914), third son of former Tory MP for Bucks Sir Thomas Fremantle, a JP for London, Middlesex and Westminster, KCB 1890, comptroller of the Royal Mint 1890-4 and British representative on the board of the Suez Canal Company 1896-1903. Fremantle was one of D's private secretaries (with Corry) from July 1866 to December 1868.
2 Bushy Park was gifted in 1529 by Cardinal Wolsey to Henry VIII, who walled it and created a deer chase. At 1,100 acres it is the second largest (after Richmond Park) of the eight royal parks and home to over three hundred free-roaming deer.

The greatest gratification one can experience in the possession of power is, that it may give one the opportunity of showing to your friends how much you regard them. /

If the Ministry of Lord Derby take root, as I hope, & as many believe, he will, in due course, lay before the Queen the names of some gentlemen, whom he will recommend Her Majesty to raise to the Peerage.

Blood, / fortune, & the possession of many virtues, indicate you as one eminently entitled to the distinction, & it would be most agreeable to me, who ~~have ever~~ counted you ↑as↓ one of his best & dearest friends, to mention my wishes in that respect to Ld. Derby.[1]

TO: LORD STANHOPE   Downing Street [Monday] 13 August 1866 4171
ORIGINAL: KCR Stanhope MSS 690(6)7
EDITORIAL COMMENT: C of Ex paper.

The | Earl Stanhope   Augt 13 1866
My dear Lord,
I will appoint any two names, wh: you will recommend to me. The Gallery was yr happy creation, / & no one so well qualified to call into being its trustees.[1]

I am detained in town by the monetary pressure, wh: is very serious, tho' I / think, we have seen the worst.[2]

I envy you your retirement in your classic groves.[3]

    Ever yours most | sincerely, | D.

TO: [MONTAGU CORRY]   [Downing Street, mid-August 1866] 4172
ORIGINAL: H B/XX/D/319
EDITORIAL COMMENT: C of Ex paper. *Dating*: conjectural; see nn1&3. *Sic*: Watkins.

---

1 Writing on 17 August from Hurst, Sussex, Montagu would thank D for his 'kind & friendly letter', explaining that 'an *offer* would be an undoubted compliment to me personally ... but ... a heavy blow & great discouragement to certain Whig Houses in Northern Counties whose political antipathies are fiercely established against me. The difficulty on my part would be as to *accepting*, in as much as I am really more of a confirmed invalid than anything else & incapable of mental exertion, and can only assist my Party by *deputy*.' H B/XXI/M/410.

---

1 Stanhope would reply on 14 August: 'I thank you much for your very kind offer, but I had really rather not suggest any names to you on this occasion. The interests of the National Portrait Gallery are I know quite safe in your hands.' KCR Stanhope MSS 690 (6) 8. Montagu Corry on 3 September would inform D that 'Lord Stanhope wishes me to tell you that he highly approves of your choice of Trustees for the National Portrait Gallery.' H B/XX/CO/5. *The Times* on 8 September would announce the appointments of 'Alexander James Beresford Beresford-Hope, Esq., M.P., and Sir Coutts Lindsay Bart.' See also VII **3298**n1.

2 D on 11 August had met with a deputation to discuss 'the reduction of the Bank rate of discount' and on this day (13th) with the governor of the Bank of England. On the 17th *The Times* would note that D had left for Hughenden. *The Times* (14, 15, 17 Aug 1866). See **4125**&n1.

3 Chevening House, Kent, is set amidst a 3,500-acre park.

For Mr Corry

Enquiry was made by Mr Watkins M.P. on the eve of the adjournment of Ho: of Comm: respecting the Govt letter to the Bank.[1]

Look this up & let me have a precis of Mr Gladstone's answer[2] when I come to the office[.][3]

D.

4173   TO: WILLIAM POWELL   Downing Street [Wednesday] 15 August 1866
ORIGINAL: TEXU [41]
EDITORIAL COMMENT: 11 Downing Street paper.

Wm. Powell | Esqr   Augt 15 1866
My dear Sir,

I enclose order for £450 – being my guarantee of £300: & £150: from the Duke.

I shall propose to my colleagues, when the / occasion offers, to supply the arrears, now not very considerable, by a rate in aid.[1]

Yrs faithfully | D.

4174   TO: LORD STANLEY   Grosvenor Gate [Friday] 17 August 1866
ORIGINAL: H H/LIFE
PUBLICATION HISTORY: M&B IV 468
EDITORIAL COMMENT: From a typescript headed: 'D. to Ld. Stanley, Grosvenor Gate, Aug. 17. '66.' 'Mosier' is a misreading of D's 'Morier'. *Sic*: Mosier, Elliott.

Dear Secretary,
I have read Cowley's letters with much interest.[1]

1 In the House on 31 July 1866 MP (L) Edward Watkin (IV **1374n1**) had moved an address to the Queen for a royal commission to investigate '"the causes which have led to the late severe and protracted pressure in the money market, and to the continuance, for a long period, of a minimum rate of discount of 10 per cent at the Bank of England; and also to investigate the Laws at present affecting Currency and Banking in the United Kingdom"'. He noted the press's 'complaint and remonstrance' and quoted the *Economist* (on 30 June): '"It is alleged that the Bank Directors do not reduce the rate because 10 per cent was fixed in the Treasury letter, and because they are still held to that letter ... it is a matter of grave regret, that owing to the present interregnum we cannot search into this matter at once, or discuss it, or obtain upon it the judgment of Parliament."' Watkin withdrew his motion on 6 August; Parliament was prorogued on the 10th. *Hansard* CLXXXIV cols 1706-61 (D 1761), 2124-5.

2 Although Gladstone (n1) thought Watkin's speech 'eminently satisfactory', he believed 'we ought never to ask a Government to undertake a function which it is impossible for them to perform with any approach to satisfaction', and that the result of a commission, 'so far as it related to causes and principles ... would not weigh with this House.' He called the present banking system 'entirely at variance with the spirit and intention of the [Bank] Act of 1844 ... [and] with the laws which ought to regulate our currency.'

3 D on the 13th received deputations from the Joint-Stock Banks and from the Birmingham Chamber of Commerce to discuss the reduction of the 10% discount rate (in effect since 11 May). *The Times* (13, 14 Aug 66).

---

1 D appears to be wrapping up his expenses (from his previous month's election) with William Powell, one of his political agents in Bucks. 'The Duke' is presumably Buckingham and the 'colleagues' the other Conservative members for Bucks, George Caledon Du Pré and Robert Bateson Harvey.

---

1 Stanley, with a letter dated 'Aug. 16.', had sent D 'confidentially, the letters we talked of. Cowley's have

Bloomfield's, both handwriting and matter, are those of a green-grocer:[2] Loftus should be the foreign Editor of the Morning Herald.[3]

Mosier, as ambassador, is "high life below stairs."[4]

Elliott, a partisan.[5]

Mem: None of your people address you rightly in their public despatches. They should be addressed to

Secretary The Right Hon: The Lord Stanley, M.P.

As the Venetians, who were great authorities in their day, used to say, "Punctilio is the Soul of Diplomacy".[6]

Yours ever, D.

TO: LORD DERBY   Hughenden [Monday] 20 August 1866 **4175**

ORIGINAL: DBP Box 146/2

PUBLICATION HISTORY: M&B IV 474-5, omitting the fifth, sixth and seventh paragraphs; Blake 454, extracts; Beeler 69-70, extracts.

Confidential   Hughenden Manor. Augt. 20. 1866

Right Honorable | The Earl of Derby, K.G.

My dear Lord,

The maladministration, not to say malversation, of the Admiralty has struck deep into the public mind, & is, at this moment, the predominant feeling of the nation.[1]

---

most in them. The rest are of less interest. Please return them when done with.' Lord Cowley had been ambassador to France since 1852. Stanley on the 11th had noted the receipt of a 'long and curious letter from Cowley, which makes it plain that Napoleon is ill, nervous, disappointed', and on the 17th that 'Cowley writes that the Emperor's weak and nervous state makes him "an object of pity": that it is questioned whether his illness has not affected his mind.' H B/XX/S/739. *Disraeli, Derby* 265-6. See **4182**&n2.

2 John Arthur Douglas Bloomfield (1802-1879), 2nd Baron Bloomfield 1846 (Ireland) and 1871 (UK), PC 1860, had held diplomatic posts at Lisbon 1824, Stuttgart 1825 and Stockholm 1826, had been envoy to Russia 1844-51 and Prussia 1851-60, and was ambassador to Austria 1860-71. On 11 December 1868 Stanley would note 'some points touched on between Ld Clarendon and me: ... Diplomatists: get rid of Crampton and Bloomfield – both worn out'. *Disraeli, Derby* 338.

3 Lord Augustus Loftus had been appointed ambassador to Prussia in February 1866. In 1857-9 D had noted that Loftus 'was not fit to be resident at a third rate German Court – & was quite despised & disregarded by that of Vienna. He was a pompous nincompoop – & of all L. Malmesbury's appointments the worst – & that's saying a good deal.' VII app IV. MH (founded 1780) would fold in 1869.

4 Robert Burnett David Morier (1826-1893), chargé d'affaires at Vienna 1853-8, the Grand Ducal Court of Hesse-Darmstadt 1866-71 and Munich 1871-5, minister-plenipotentiary at Lisbon 1876-81, ambassador at St Petersburg 1885-93, CB 1866, KCB 1885, PC 1885, GCMG 1886 and GCB 1887. Possessed of 'a copious, declamatory, slangy prose style', Morier was 'impulsive, argumentative, and even rude ... too excitable and self-centred for consummate diplomacy.' ODNB. Stanley on 21 August 1867 would call him 'very clever, very hard-working: something of a dreamer, full of German ideas.' *Disraeli, Derby* 316. In the popular *High Life Below Stairs: A Farce in Two Acts* (1759) by James Townley, servants ape nobility at a party during their master's absence.

5 Henry George Elliot (1817-1907), younger brother of 3rd Earl of Minto and Lord Russell's brother-in-law, had been a diplomatist since 1841 and British envoy at Florence since 1865. In July 1867 he would be appointed ambassador at Constantinople (and sworn PC), and at Vienna 1877-84.

6 A possible source for D's idea is a discussion of 'punctilio' (court etiquette) in 'The Diary of a Master of the Ceremonies', in Isaac D'Israeli's *Curiosities of Literature* (1866 edition, 248-52): 'One of the most subtle of these men of *punctilio*, and the most troublesome, was the Venetian ambassador; for it was his particular aptitude to find fault, and pick out jealousies among all the others of his body' (251).

---

1 Frederic Haydon on 14 August had written to D a letter (docketed in another hand 'ackd. with thanks Aug.

If dealt with vigorously, it will divert opinion from Parliamentary Reform: if neglected, it may precipitate great political changes.

Some few years ago, when I endeavoured to draw the attention of our party, but not as successfully as I wished, to this subject,[2] I was guided by the information & advice of Mr. Laird, M.P. for Birkenhead.[3] Before I left town, that gentleman requested an / interview with me, of wh: the object was to offer, if I wished it, to resume the reports & counsels, that he had previously given me.

Mr. Laird attributes the deplorable administration of the Admy., mainly, to two causes:

1stly. The expenditure & waste, wh: are occasioned by the accumulation of stores; thus illustrated.

There are about 18000 workmen in the Royal Yards. The value of the Stores, when the accounts were made up in 1864, was five mill: sterling: for 1865, 4 mill: 800,000 sterling. The accounts for 1866 are not yet made up. But we may take it, in round numbers as five mill: for 18,000 men.

In Mr Laird's yard, wh:, in its functions, more nearly resembles a Royal / establishment, than any other private yard,[4] there are 4000 men, more than 1/5th. of the total Admiralty establishment, & the value of the stores is £60,000, beyond wh: waste begins.

If we estimate the necessary stores in the Royal yards at this rate, £300,000 would

15') suggesting that 'mal-administration at the admiralty, & the neglect of the Poor might be made two forceful subjects of attack against the Liberal Government for the Autumn & Winter.' H C/II/C/2a. Navy administration was a perennial problem. A royal commission formed on 21 August 1860 had inquired into the management of the dockyards, including '"the purchase of materials and stores, the cost of building and repairing, altering, fitting, and refitting the ships of your Majesty's navy"'. It had ascribed the inefficiency of the management of the dockyards to four causes: '"1st. The constitution of the Board of the Admiralty. 2d. The defective organization of the subordinate departments. 3d. The want of clear and well-defined responsibility. 4th. The want of any means, both now and in times past, of effectually checking expenditure, from the want of accurate accounts."' *The Times* (23 Mar 1861). *The Times* on 11 August 1866 had published a letter (dated 9 August) signed 'O.' complaining that navy administration would likely 'absorb a large share of public attention for some time to come. Having spent upwards of 70,000,000*l.* on the Navy during the last seven years, we find ourselves utterly destitute of ships adapted for coast and harbour defence, we have not yet succeeded in producing a serviceable naval gun, and now the First Lord of the Admiralty informs us that the state of the ships in the Reserve is such that "the Admiralty have great difficulty in finding relief for the ships that return from foreign service."' *The Times* on 14 August had reported the Admiralty's first annual inspection of Portsmouth Dockyard by Sir John Pakington and the other lord commissioners, including 'vessels under repair or outfit in the reserves and in commission', of which 'a number of wooden screw gunboats ... may be set down as *nil* in the item of our national defences, but with the cost of their maintenance as of a very serious character.' See also **4202** and **4216**&n14.

2 For D's views on the admiralty and his previous efforts to reform its administration, see VII **3213**&nn6-8, **3239**n2 and VIII **3891**&n1.

3 John Laird (1805-1874), after training as a solicitor, in 1828 had entered his father's Birkenhead ironworks business (founded 1824), eventually becoming a highly successful shipbuilder (J. Laird Sons & Co) and one of the first to use iron in ship construction. He had retired in 1861 (his three sons taking over the business) to become Birkenhead's first MP (C) 1861-74.

4 There were, however, significant differences. Laird's responsibility for ships ended when they were delivered, while the navy maintained up to 250 ships in commission while readying more as replacements. Naval shipyards kept, in readiness for war, huge amounts of stores and also manufactured their own supplies for repair – factors necessitating a large workforce. Beeler 70.

be sufficient, but double, or even treble, them, put them even at a million, the contrast is startling.

Mr. Laird is of opinion, that the surplus stores should be sold, & consisting mainly of timber, iron, & copper, he believes they may be disposed of at half price. This would place a large sum at the disposal of the Admiralty.

The second cause of mal-administration was pointed out by him to me some years ago, & is now still more enforced: vizt: the obstinacy with wh: the Admy. has declined building iron ships, & the vast / sums, wh: they have vainly expended in cobbling up old wooden vessels.[5]

These are the two principal causes of the present condition of the Navy, wh:, if encountered in a masterly manner, may be a source of strength & reputation to your government: if neglected, may lead to public disaster.

Mere increased expenditure will aggravate, not cure, the disease.

I refrain from having any communication with Sir John Pakington on this subject.[6] All extraordinary motion in the great Departments shd. come from you. It confirms your authority, & it prevents jealousies. But I earnestly beg you to give your personal attention & energy to this matter.[7] A first Lord is surrounded by the criminals, & it requires intellectual grasp, & a peremptory firmness, to ~~ded~~ deal with them.

Yours ever, | D.

TO: CHARLES FREMANTLE   [Hughenden] Monday 20 August [1866] 4176
ORIGINAL: H B/XIII/89a
EDITORIAL COMMENT: Docketed in another hand on the first page: '1866'. *Dating*: by context; see nn1&2.

C.W. Fremantle | Esq   Monday | Aug. 20
Be so good as to make a copy of the enclosed letter to Lord Derby, & then forward the original to him from me, in a ~~b~~

box.[1]

Write "*private*" over / his name ↑in the label.↓

Take great care of the copy, & of all copies of my letters generally, as I never trouble my secretaries to do much work, unless they are on matters of great / importance & confidence.

Never let such copies be lying about yr office: &, generally speaking, be very care-

---

5 In 'Wooden or Iron Ships', a 21 May 1859 letter to *The Times* (published 24 May), Laird had outlined 'the advantages of substituting iron for wood in the construction of ships for war purposes', warning that 'if the construction and re-construction (as it is now called) of wood vessels is persevered in, millions of money will be thrown away which might be saved by the immediate adoption of iron'. In any event, 'the policy of "cobbling up" old wooden vessels was to a great extent the consequence of naval funding that was often insufficient to permit major overhauls, much less the construction of new vessels.' Beeler 70.
6 D would write to Pakington, first lord of the admiralty since 12 July, on 23 October; see **4251**.
7 Derby would write to Pakington on 15 September; see **4202**n4.

---

1 For D's 20 August 1866 letter to Derby, see **4175**. Fremantle's copy differs slightly from D's original: 'mill:' is 'million', 'vizt:' is 'viz:', 'Admy.' is 'Admiralty'; and 'gentleman', 'administration', 'yard', 'government', 'criminals' and 'first' are capitalized. H B/XIII/89b.

ful not to let your papers be seen by / any chance visitor, or looker in. I have known inadvertence in such matters cause much mischief.

D.[2]

4177　TO: [JAMES BAIN]　　　　　　　Hughenden [Monday] 20 August [1866]

ORIGINAL: H B/XIII/59

EDITORIAL COMMENT: *Dating*: docketed in another hand '? 1866-7'; D was not at Hughenden on this day in 1867.

Hughenden | Augt. 20

Private

Mr Bain[1] is requested to send down by the messenger Ld Stanhope's history bound, or Life of Pitt.[2]

4178　TO: LORD NAAS　　　　　　　Hughenden [Tuesday] 21 August 1866

ORIGINAL: INL Mayo Papers MS 11,144

EDITORIAL COMMENT: Black-edged paper. Endorsed in another hand on the first page: 'V' and on the fourth page: 'Disraeli Rec Aug 22/66 Master of Rolls'.

Right Honorable | Lord Naas MP.　　　　　　Hughenden Manor | Augt 21 1866
My dear Chief Secy.[1]

I fear a too casual hint to Fremantle[2] has given you trouble, wh. you might have been spared, but I am always glad to hear from you.

I don't pretend to give opinions on Irish affairs, but I furnish you with such hints, as reach me. I agree with you, / that it would be imprudent to proceed more in that direction at present.

I didn't even know that Fitzgerald was a Tory.[3]

---

2 Fremantle would reply to D on 21 August 1866 that he had copied D's letter to Derby and sent the original. 'You may rely upon my taking the greatest care of any confidential Papers which you may entrust to me, and that no indiscretion on my part shall make me unworthy of the complete confidence which I am proud to think you are so good as to repose in me.' H B/XXI/F/265.

---

1 London bookseller James Bain (IV **1244n2**).
2 Stanhope had written *The History of the War of Succession in Spain, 1702-1714* (1832), *The History of England from the Peace of Utrecht to the Peace of Versailles, 1713-1783* (7 vols, 1836-53) and *Life of the Honourable William Pitt* (4 vols, 1861-2); Hughenden Library has the 4th ed (1867) of *Pitt*.

---

1 Naas had written to D from Dublin Castle on 17 August that he had received 'Freemantle's [*sic*] letter about Baron [of the Irish exchequer Henry G.] Hughes – If we appointed a Political Opponent and an R.C. to the Mastership of the Rolls, [Rickard] Deasy ought to be his Man. His professional position is much higher than that of Hughes and he is I am told very much disposed towards us. But I own that we cannot go too fast ... Baron Fitzgerald is the first equity Lawyer (with the exception of [Jonathan] Christian) among the Puisne Judges. I think we must promote him and put [MP (C) for Wexford John] George in his place. I am anxious to get George out of Wexford.' H B/XX/BO/21.
2 Possibly Sir Thomas Francis Fremantle, chairman of the board of customs and father of D's secretary Charles Fremantle.
3 Francis Alexander Fitzgerald (1806-1897), a barrister (Middle Temple 1832), an Irish barrister 1834, practised in equity, QC 1849, had been appointed Baron of the Irish exchequer in 1859. F. Elrington Ball *The Judges in Ireland, 1221-1921* (1926) 362.

I hope things are going / on well with you: we shall have a good harvest in England. 'Tis finished in these parts.[4]

My kind regards to your wife.

Ever yours, | D.

TO: LORD JOHN MANNERS   Hughenden [Tuesday] 21 August 1866   4179
ORIGINAL: BEA [92].

Hughenden Manor | Augt. 21. 1866

Right Honorable | Lord John Manners[1]

My dear President.

Suppose you, & Lady John, come down & pay us a visit before you go to Scotland? It wd. be delightful. When? When you like.

    I / agree to yr suggestion about Banks & Barry.[2]

      Yrs ever, | D.[3]

TO: [MARKHAM SPOFFORTH]   [Hughenden, Tuesday 21 August 1866]   4180
ORIGINAL: PS 1543
PUBLICATION HISTORY: *The Times* (2 Sep 1931), dated 21 August 1866, to Markham Spofforth.

What you have done about the *Globe* is capital.[1]

---

4 Land agent H.J. Turner, who wrote regularly on agricultural matters in *The Times*, had forecast a lingering harvest that would be a fortnight later than the one in 1865. Presiding at a dinner at the Hughenden parish harvest festival on 12 September, D would tell the two hundred guests that they 'were met to celebrate ... an event more important than the existence or formation of a Ministry ("Hear," and a laugh), and that was the ingathering of the harvest'. *The Times* (27 Aug, 14 Sep 1866).

---

1 Manners, first commissioner of works since 6 July, had written to D on 18 August from Cadland, Southampton: 'If you see no objection I propose to entrust the reconstruction of the wings of Burlington House for the learned Societies, to Banks & Barry, to whom we gave the commission in 1859, and who prepared a block plan for us. I return to town for a week or ten days on Monday, and shall be glad to put them in communication with the Academy's architect without delay in order that, so far as is possible, the various works on the Burlington House site may proceed simultaneously.' H B/XX/M/136.

2 Architects Robert Richardson Banks (1812-1872) and Charles Barry, Jr (1823-1900) were in partnership 1847-72.

3 Manners would reply on 22 August declining D's invitation: 'every day until we go to Edinburgh I have deputations and appointments, and at Edinburgh my officials are waiting for me before they take their holyday.' H B/XX/M/137.

---

1 Spofforth on 18 August 1866, in a letter marked 'Private,' had informed D that 'we have completed the purchase of the Globe newspaper for Mr Wescomb of Exeter a friend of ours who has successfully established the Exeter Gazette and Maidstone Journal making them both paying properties. He will do the same by the Globe bringing it gradually over to the Conservative Interest. The price will after Michaelmas be reduced to 2d.- and energy and capital will make it a valuable organ for your administration.' H B/XXI/S/415. See **4245**&n2.

4181   TO: [LOUIS WOLOWSKI]   [Hughenden, Tuesday 21 August 1866]

ORIGINAL: PS 1553
PUBLICATION HISTORY: *La Revue des deux mondes* (1 Sep 1866) 209
EDITORIAL COMMENT: *Dating*: by context; see n1.

I believe currency is a subject which has made even more people mad than love.[1]

4182   TO: SIR HUGH CAIRNS   Hughenden [Thursday] 23 August 1866

ORIGINAL: PRO 30/51/1 ff1-2.

The | Attorney General   Hughenden Manor | Augt 23. 1866
My dear Mr Attorney,
It gave me great pleasure to be remembered by you, & in so agreeable a manner.[1]

I hope you are having good / sport, & greatly enjoying yourself; gaining health & establishing your strength, so that the foe may feel the renovated vigor of yr ever-puissant arm.

The French Emperor has / been, & is, very ill, but I hope not going to die.[2] His death may let loose the French democracy, & Bismarck's[3] electoral law[4] the German: if so, we shall have stirring times.

I trust Lady Cairns / is quite well, to whom I beg you to give my compliments.[5]
Yours sincerely, | D.

---

1 Extract from a letter by D (not found) to Louis Wolowski quoted by him in 'La crise financière de l'Angleterre. II. L'*ACT* de 1844 et la liberté des banques', *La Revue des deux mondes* (1 Sep 1866); the sentence appears in French translation on pp 208-9 and in English on p 209 (note 1) dated 'Le 21 août 1866.' Louis François Michel Raymond Wolowski (1810-1876) (Ludwik Franciszek Michat Reymond Wolowski), a Polish jurist, banker and economist, had studied in France in 1823-7 and became a naturalized Frenchman in 1834. He was founder in 1834 of the *Revue de législation et de jurisprudence*, chair of industrial legislation at the Conservatoire des Arts et Métiers 1839-71, member of the Académie des Sciences Morales et Politiques 1855, elected to the legislative assembly 1848 and to the national assembly 1871, senator for life 1876. Among his works are *La banque d'Angleterre et les banques d'Écosse* (1867) and *L'or et l'argent* (1870). Wolowski on 16 August 1866 had written to D to say he had sent him two of his books, *Les finances de la Russie* (1864) and *La question des banques* (1864), drawing D's attention to his recent article on the financial crisis in England in *La Revue des deux mondes* (15 Aug 1866). H C/XI/32.

---

1 Cairns may have sent D a gift, perhaps game. His letter (if there was one) has not been found.
2 The Paris *Moniteur* on 10 August had reported: '"By the advice of the doctors His Majesty gave up the course of treatment he was following at Vichy. The Emperor is much better in health since his arrival at St. Cloud."' *The Times* (11 Aug 1866). Napoleon III, who suffered from gout, arthritis and chronic kidney, bladder and prostate infections, would die in 1873 from kidney failure during an operation to fragment a bladder stone.
3 Otto Eduard Leopold von Bismarck (1815-1898), Graf von Bismarck-Schönhausen 1865, Prince of Bismarck 1871 and Duke of Lauenburg 1890, minister-president of Prussia 1862-90, would be chancellor of the North German Confederation 1867-71, established by a treaty signed at Prague on this day (23rd), and of the second German empire 1871-90.
4 *The Times* on 17 August 1866 had published the preamble to and summary of the thirteen clauses of 'The New Prussian Electoral Law'. The preamble stated that '"the King's Government submits to the Diet the electoral law of April 12, 1849, with some indispensable modifications, as the electoral law for the Parliament of the Confederation of Northern Germany, reserving to itself the right of issuing regulations governing the details of voting."' The first clause stipulated that '"Every Prussian who has completed his 25th year is an elector."'
5 Cairns in 1856 had married Mary Harriet McNeile (d 1919), eldest daughter of John McNeile of Parkmount, co Antrim.

ORIGINAL: H B/XX/D/1

EDITORIAL COMMENT: Docketed in another hand on the first page: '1866'. *Dating*: speculative; but see D's similar instructions to Corry in **4187**. *Sic*: decypher.

Montagu Corry | Esq   G. Gate. Aug 29

Dear Montagu,

I must see the circulation boxes: there were one, or two, things, in that wh: I have just examined, wh: I wd. not have missed / on any account.

It is, however, quite absurd to send special messengers to Hughenden with such cold meat. I wd. suggest, as, probably none of my colleagues at / this irregular period of the year (or, at least, very few) open these boxes, & as they come to me, practically, first, you might allow ~~they~~ them to accumulate at our / office at discretion, & then, occasionally, send me down a bevy of boxes: so that, on the whole, so far as this portion of our business is concerned, you need not send more / than one messenger a week, & not, necessarily, even that.

Understand, I don't want these boxes for *news*: that is all anticipated by telegrams.

I hope you / will be able to decypher this.

  Yours sincerely | D.

ORIGINAL: H B/XX/D/347

EDITORIAL COMMENT: Docketed in another hand on the first page: '? Sept. 1866'. *Dating*: by context; see n2.

Mr *Corry*

Can you tell me who are [the] Duke of Hamilton's Trustees?[1]

  If you dont know, some Scotchman in town, Sir Jas Fergusson, might.[2]

  D.

ORIGINAL: H A/I/A/330

EDITORIAL COMMENT: *Dating*: from location in H following 1866 letters to MA and before 1867.

1 William Alexander Louis Stephen Douglas-Hamilton (1845-1895), 12th Duke of Hamilton 1863 and 8th Earl of Selkirk 1886 (SCT), 9th Duke of Brandon 1863 (UK) and 2nd duc de Châtellerault 1864 (FR), Kt 1878, was commandant 1866-82 and hon col 1882-95 of The Queen's Own Royal Glasgow and Lower Ward of the Lanarkshire Regiment of Yeomanry Cavalry, col of the 1st Royal Lanarkshire Militia 1878-81 and hon col of the 3rd Battalion of The Highland Light Infantry 1881-95.
2 Corry on 3 September would write to D that 'No one in this neighbourhood can tell me who are the D. of Hamilton's Trustees', and on the 7th, 'I am told by the Duke of Hamilton's lawyer that during the Duke's minority, the Duchess acted as his guardian and Trustee, guided by the advice of the Duke of Buccleuch and Lord de Tabley – and M. Alexander Oswald (of Green Street) was Trustee of the Suffolk Estates: but all this has come to an end since he has attained his majority. Did you ever hear that the Duke died without signing his will, which was drawn up, and by which he devised the Suffolk Estates to the Duchess?' H B/XX/CO/5, 6.

My dearest,

I corrected the address – all right.[1]

I am glad to hear good news of a footman.

What you ↑can↓ do in pensions &c. / is made out, & you will know tomorrow.

Yr affec I D.

4186 TO: SPENCER WALPOLE   Hughenden [Sunday] 2 September 1866
ORIGINAL: HOL [9]
EDITORIAL COMMENT: Black-edged paper.

Right Honble I Mr Secy Walpole   Hughenden Manor I Sept 2 1866
Dear Walpole,

We are very anxious, that Cooke Q.C. shd. be made Recorder of Oxford now vacant.[1] Mr Cooke / has served us well: he is a clever fellow, full of energy, leading, with exception of Huddleston,[2]

on his own circuit.

These men shd be / rewarded when we can – & Mr Cooke has, more than once, been neglected by us. It does not encourage exertions in a class, wh: he represents, & / wh: is very useful to a party.

Yours sincerely, I D.[3]

4187 TO: MONTAGU CORRY   Hughenden [Sunday] 2 September 1866
ORIGINAL: H B/XX/D/2
PUBLICATION HISTORY: M&B IV 464, the first three paragraphs and part of the fourth, and M&B IV 480, the last two paragraphs
EDITORIAL COMMENT: *Sic*: Montague.

Montague Corry I Esq   Hughenden Manor I Sept. 2. 1866
Longmans want me to publish all my speeches on "Parliamentary ~~vot~~ Reform" in an 8vo vol: They evidently think the subject will revive, & that it may be, in every respect, / expedient & advantageous, that the collected views of one, who has taken an active part in the question, shd. be before the country in a portable form.

I shall not consent, if I do / at all, until I have made further observations on the public humor with respect to this question.

---

1 Possibly related to the misdirected letter inviting Lady Cranborne to Hughenden on 17 September 1866. See **4187**.

---

1 *The Times* on 2 October would report the appointment of William Henry Cooke (1811-1894), a barrister (Inner Temple 1863), QC 1863, county court judge 1868-88, DL and JP for Herefordshire and JP for Norfolk. *The Times* (22 Oct 1894).

2 John Walter Huddleston (1815-1890), educated at Trinity College (Dublin) 1836, a barrister (Gray's Inn 1839), QC 1857, had acquired extensive criminal practice on the Oxford circuit and at the Old Bailey. He was MP (C) for Canterbury 1865-8, judge-advocate of the fleet 1865-75 and Kt 1875.

3 Walpole would reply on 3 September requesting 'that The Recordership shall not be filled up until they have fixed a salary for the office ... from what I hear, they are going to recommend some one for the place. Of course I am not *bound* to attend to any recommendation of theirs ... I shall do all I can to forward your wishes'. H B/XXI/W/62.

But I may, eventually, have to act with promptitude, &, therefore, I wish to be prepared for the occasion. /

I wish, therefore, (not having "Hansard" at Hughenden) that you wd. make me a list of my speeches on Parly. Ref: & count the number of columns, (*not pages*) in Hansard, wh: they comprise. /

The first speech, of any moment, on the subject made by me, was shortly after my being appointed Leader of the Opposition. Start from this.

I became Leader of the Opposition, (after the death of Ld. G. Bentinck) at the commencement of the year *1849*[.] /

The speech on P.R. would probably be in 1850: on a motion of Mr Hume.[1] After this, I doubt whether there is anything of moment until the introduction of our bill in 1859, & then it is plain sailing: the speeches that year; on the introduction of Lord John Russell's in 1860: & / on Baines ⌐annual⌐ motions; & then the bill of 1866.[2]

I want a list of the speeches at yr convenience, & of the number of columns they contain.[3]

A memorandum I wrote for you about Lady Cranborne's letter was left behind, but I have no doubt your tact / guided you to do the right ⌐thing⌐; wh: was to get her husband, if he were at his office, to take it to her – if not, that you shd. obtain her country direction; somewhere in Hants.[4]

I send back the £500,000 minute signed, & also the papers / connected with it, wh: shd. be kept as a record of the transaction, in case we ever have to refer to it.[5]

Also the papers respecting the rate of interest for the new issue of Exr bills; & for the same reason.[6] /

1 See **4194**&n4.

2 For D's 1859 Reform Bill, see VII **3301**n1; for Russell's 1860 Reform Bill, see VIII **3456**n6. Edward Baines Jr had introduced private members' bills in 1861, 1864 and 1865.

3 Corry would reply to D on 3 September: 'Your directions as to your Speeches on Reform shall be promptly carried out.' H B/XX/CO/5. See also **4194**. Longmans, Green, & Co would publish *Parliamentary Reform: a series of speeches on that subject delivered in the House of Commons (1848-1866)*, edited by Corry, 478 pages, in 1867. Earlier in 1866, Saunders, Otley & Co had published D's *Constitutional Reform. Five Speeches, 1859-65*, edited by John F. Bulley. *The Times* (15 Mar 1866).

4 Neither D's memorandum to Corry nor his letter to Lady Cranborne has been found. Lady Cranborne (1827-1899), as Georgina Caroline Alderson, in 1857 had married Lord Robert Cecil (Viscount Cranborne as of 14 June 1865). Corry (n3) would inform D that Charles Fremantle had forwarded D's letter to Lady Cranborne. See **4190**, **4191** and **4195**&n1.

5 William George Anderson (auditor of the civil list as of 28 August), writing to D from the treasury on 31 August, had discussed with Sir Alexander Spearman (comptroller-general of the national debt) 'the best means of strengthening the balance before the 30th. Septr.' by the sale of £500,000 of New Zealand bonds 'taken, in the Budget Estimate, in aid of the Revenue Receipts of the current financial year'. He had enclosed copies of a letter by Spearman to Henry Lancelot Holland, governor of the Bank of England, and the latter's reply (agreeing to the transaction). 'As we know that the Bank is willing to take these Bonds, the time for official action has arrived; and I send you herewith an official letter to the Governor and Deputy Governor for your signature if you should approve.' H B/VIII/58a, b.

6 Anderson (n5) had written: 'As to Exchequer Bills we have only sold in the last fortnight £79.000 out of the £865.000 which we have to place out; but as times are improving I hope we may sell more before the close of the quarter.' Spearman and Holland had also discussed the bills, Holland stating that they were 'not popular ... and it will take a little time to run off any large amount, but, with the change in the rate of interest which is now going on, there is every chance of an improved demand for them on the part of the Public.' The *London Gazette* on 4 September would report that the treasury had given notice 'to

I send, with deep regret, an order for the wretched Goodwin.[7]

When letters come from my colleagues marked "private", it is unnecessary to ·
open ↑them,↓ as no action can be taken on them until / they are forwarded to me.
Nothing therefore is gained by the process, wh: is not necessary, & wh: my correspondents, under such circumstances, dislike.

My hand is, by no means, as bad as my handwriting wd. imply: the / scrawl is the
consequence of the wretched, cheap, huckster's ink, supplied by that miserable Departt., the Stationery office[.][8] \

Yours, | D.

4188   TO: [MONTAGU CORRY]   Hughenden [Sunday] 2 September 1866
       ORIGINAL: H B/XX/D/3
       EDITORIAL COMMENT: *Sic*: £299.000.

Hughenden Manor | Sept. 2. 1866.

The figures in the two Compares under the head "Excise" perplex me, & I request
an explanation.[1]

The year from 1st Apl to 25th. Aug:, 1866 gives an increase of £339,000.

The / same item, from 1st. Apl. to 1st. Sept 1866, gives an increase only of £299.000:
altho' the week shows an additional increase to Excise of £20,000.

Let the two Compares / be returned to me with an explanation of this apparent
discrepancy.

D.

Enquire of Mr Anderson[2]

4189   TO: DUKE OF BUCKINGHAM AND CHANDOS   Hughenden
                                                     [Sunday] 2 September 1866
       ORIGINAL: HUNT STG Box 119 (28)
       EDITORIAL COMMENT: Black-edged paper.

Hughenden Manor | Septr. 2 1866

His Grace | The Duke of Buc[kin]gham & Chandos[1]

---

the holders of Exchequer bills issued under the authority of the Act, 24th of Victoria, cap. 5, and dated
March 11, 1862, that ... the interest of such Exchequer bills for the following half-year, to March, 1867,
will be at the rate of 4*l.* per centum per annum.' *The Times* (5 Sep 1866).

7 This individual has not been identified.

8 See **4208**.

---

1 'Compare' is shorthand for 'weekly revenue returns', printed for the use of the treasury. Stanley on 29
August had recorded that Derby had shown him 'the weekly revenue returns, which are sent to him:
they are accurately made up, and give at a glance the power of comparing the present year with the last.'
Disraeli, Derby 268. Stanley would write to D on 4 September requesting D's own weekly revenue returns.
See **4191**&nn1&4.

2 See **4187**nn5&6. Corry would reply on 3 September: 'Anderson is away for 3 days. I enclose the explanation [*not found*] as to the "compares", which his locum-tenens sends me. The unusually large payments
in the week ending Sept. 2 1865 account for what, at first, seems very perplexing.' H B/XX/CO/5.

---

1 The Duke was lord president of the privy council, which oversaw the Cattle Plague Office. The Cattle

My dear Duke,

There is great, & deep, discontent in the County about the Order of the 8th. Ulto:, which practically, prohibits markets / being held in this County.² Our best friends complain, not only that the restrictions are unnecessarily severe, but, that they are not impartially extended.³

I can / assure you, there is a very bad feeling about.

Yours sincerely, | D.⁴

TO: [MONTAGU CORRY] Hughenden [Tuesday] 4 September 1866 **4190**
ORIGINAL: H B/XX/D/4.

Hughenden Manor | Sept 4. 1866.

I enclose a letter from Mr Fitzgerald, U. Secy. for F. Aff: in the Government of 1858-9.¹ It would be a great thing to open Parliamt with a Spanish Commer: Treaty. / Don't let the matter sleep.²

I have had no answer from Lady Cranborne – &, I fear, therefore, Fremantle must have forwarded the letter to her London residence, where, / in all probability, it

Diseases Prevention Act Amendment (No. 2) Bill had been given royal assent on 10 August 1866. *Hansard* CLXXXIV col 2154.

2 *The Times* on 13 August had printed a circular letter, dated 10 August, sent to the lords-lieutenant of counties by H.D. Harness and enclosing '"a copy of an Order of Council, passed on the 8th inst., which directs the use of a more precise form of licence for the removal of animals, and also extends the restrictions on sales and movement in several counties to sheep"'. On 24 August it had reported the new order as 'prohibiting the sale of sheep and lambs in open market and fairs in certain counties'. See n4.

3 These views had been expressed to D by Joseph Parrott in a 31 August letter (see **4197**n1) that most likely was the impetus for D's present letter to the Duke.

4 In the first of two letters dated 'Sept. 4. 1866', the Duke would inform D: 'The fairs & market are no doubt practically stopped to the great but I consider *unavoidable* loss of the townspeople but there is nothing to prevent farmers from selling their own stock – nor from buying other stock from farmers – nor from going to Wales or Scotland or to any other uninfected place & buying sheep or cattle & bringing [them] to their farms. I think the present state of the disease is such that the restrictive order may be taken off except in certain districts at the end of the month – provided that the experiment now making in Scotland – of freeing their Markets & fairs for their own stock proves successful & that the local authorities exert themselves – the extent of disease amongst sheep has been unfortunately little known & is not believed – the returns as sent in by the inspectors are in some cases quite delusive as regards sheep.' In his second letter, the Duke would call 'complaints & remonstrance' against further restrictive measures 'only natural – I believe the danger was great & imminent and the restrictions necessary – I do not see that there can be any formulation for a charge of partiality against the Cattle department ... The difficulty of ascertaining the existence & state of disease is extreme – local authorities & inspectors in many cases ignoring or concealing it ... I enclose herewith the particulars of infected places on Aug. 20th'. He also enclosed a long handwritten 'Memo respecting Order 8th August restricting movement of Sheep'. H B/ XXI/B/1223-4. See **4198**&n2.

---

1 William Seymour Fitzgerald had written to D from the Hotel de Paris, Madrid, on 29 August saying that on the 25th he had mentioned to Stanley that Manuel Alonso Martinez, then Spanish minister of finance, in November 1865 had asked Fitzgerald to approach Clarendon about a commercial treaty with Britain. Fitzgerald thought the new minister would also favour such a treaty and believed it would, in opening Spain to British trade, 'do more for us than fifty Reform bills.' It would require equalization of wine duties to 1s, with a probable loss of £500,000 which, however, would be balanced by trade in British goods to an 'incredible' amount. H B/IX/E/8. See **4198**&n1.

2 See **4191**n7.

137

remains: for I know, from experience, it is a household, that has no order in these matters.

Will you ask the messengers where my / letter went to, & if taken to Mansfield St,[3] regain it, & direct it on, with explanations to ~~them~~ ⌐her present⌐ residence somewhere in Hants.[4]

D.

4191   TO: MONTAGU CORRY   Hughenden [Wednesday] 5 September 1866
ORIGINAL: H B/XX/D/5
PUBLICATION HISTORY: M&B IV 480-1, paragraphs one, two, four, five and six.

Montagu Corry | Esq   Hughenden Manor | Sept 5 1866
Dear Montagu,
I enclose you Lord Stanley's letter.[1]

In the first place, obtain, immediately, for me the answer of the Board of Trade referred / to.[2] Be pleased also to tell the Board of Trade – I suppose it will be Mr Cave,[3] as Sir Stafford [Northcote] is absent – that I wish copies of all correspondence &c, that may take place between the Board ⌐respecting commercial Treaties⌐ & the F.O., to be forwarded / immediately to me. The Treasury is the chief, & controlling, department of the State, & it is perfectly absurd, that in matters, wh: cannot be carried into operation without sensibly influencing the Revenue, we should not / have the best information at the earliest date.

I think it would be best for you to take a copy of Lord Stanley's letter to keep with your other papers respecting the Commercial treaties; Portugal & Spain. Return

---

3 Lady Cranborne's London address was 20 Arlington Street (*LPOD* 1865).
4 See **4195**n1.

---

1 Stanley on 4 September had written to D: 'You will have seen the Board of Trade answer to [Portuguese ambassador Count de] Lavradio's proposal. It is well done, and to my thinking, quite sound. We cannot abolish the alcoholic test, but it is a question whether we might not modify it without considerable loss to the exchequer. What occurs to me is as follows: (1) Admit all wines under the one shilling duty up to 30 degrees alcoholic strength instead of 26 as at present. (2) Reduce duty above that strength to two shillings from two and sixpence, the present rate. By the first change the loss would be, as near as I can reckon, £200,000, not allowing anything for recovery. By the second, I have no means of estimating which it would be, but £100,000 would be a large allowance. No present action is possible, but you might ascertain, if so disposed, what these alternatives would cost, and what the Board of Customs have to say to them. Am I taking a liberty in asking to see, confidentially, the weekly revenue returns? They interest me much, and I know that you have them in print. European affairs have been less interesting during the last three weeks: but I will make up a bundle of letters for you shortly.' H B/XX/S/743. See n4.
2 There is in H a copy of a very long letter from the 'Office of Committee of Privy Council for Trade', dated 'Whitehall 1st September 1866' and signed by Louis Mallet, to Edward Egerton (foreign office undersecretary as of 6 July) instructing him to inform Stanley that the Lords of the committee 'are of opinion that a reduction in the present high Custom's tariff of Portugal would have a powerful effect in encouraging trade, and would be very beneficial to both countries ... They have prepared Memoranda showing the results which have attended the reduction of Custom's duties in this country and in some others. Some of these have already been communicated to the Portuguese Government, but it may be convenient to place the whole of them in the hands of Count Lavradio'. Mallet stated their 'conclusion that it is now rather the interest of Portugal to reduce her own import duties, than the interest of this country to enter into a treaty of reciprocity with her. England, indeed, has already done her part.' H B/IX/E/1.
3 Stephen Cave was vice-president of the board of trade as of 10 July.

to me the original as / it contains suggestions, wh: I must have at hand; on second thoughts, I shall send this up in a bag, as I have an accumulation of those machines. It was intended as a letter[.]

Observe what Ld. S. says about the "compares."

As / there is, & has ever been, an entire alliance between us, I wish particularly that his request shd be complied with.

But I don't want it to be known in the office. Do this: tell the office that, in future, I wish *two* copies of the "Compare" to / be sent to me. It will be your duty to send one immediately to Lord Stanley in a packet marked "private," with C of E. in the corner.

I have sent him enclosed my last "compare" as I thought you might not have one at hand; & I have / told him, that you would send him also the whole collection since we have been in office, tho', I fear, I shd. have to trouble him, in due course, to return them, as I was not sure I could obtain copies of the back numbers[.][4] /

The "letters," wh: he refers to in his last sentence, are the private letters of the chief Ambassadors to him: not the public despatches wh: are circulated.

No letter from Lady C[ranborne], wh: much disturbs our / domestic arrangmts.

The D of Buckingham & Chandos is furious, & I think justly, that Col. Office never even sent to Privy Council Office to say Ld. Derby was in town, the day of the Canadian Council. The Duke was at the Privy Coun: Office the whole / of the day till seven o'ck![5]

Enquire of the H.O., whether they have any official acct. of the number, that attended the Birmingham meeting.[6] They ought to have had a military eye there in plain clothes: an eye accustomed to ~~calcu~~ estimate numbers.

Yours, | D.[7]

TO: LORD BEAUCHAMP   Hughenden [Wednesday] 5 September 1866 **4192**
ORIGINAL: INL O'Hara Papers MS 20,346 (8).

Hughenden Manor | Sept 5. 1866

The | Earl ~~of~~ Beauchamp

---

4 D's 'last "compare"' has not been found. Corry would write to D in a letter docketed '? 9th Sept 66': 'I have sent, & will in future send the "compares" to Lord Stanley.' H B/XX/CO/7.

5 The Duke of Buckingham had written to D on 4 September: 'I was much annoyed at the Colonial Office not sending to the Council Office the other day for the meeting as to Canadian reinforcements – I was there the whole day till nearly 7. in the ev[enin]g and never heard of the meeting till next day.' H B/XXI/B/1223. *The Times* on 6 September would report that 'despatches were received yesterday at the Colonial-office from the Governors of Canada and Labuan.'

6 On 27 August a 'great Reform meeting' had been held at Birmingham, with John Bright addressing a crowd estimated at 70,000, 150,000, 200,000 and 500,000. *The Times* (28 Aug, 1 Sep 1866). See **4213**.

7 Corry on 7 September would reply to D that, although it had been suggested that Spain and Portugal would be satisfied by admitting wines up to 40° proof, both Inland Revenue and Customs disapproved of such a move. He enclosed two reports which concluded that the reduced duties would considerably affect revenues, notably by decreasing consumption of spirits. He doubted that the proposed concessions would satisfy Spain or Portugal. He would write to D again on 9 September that, since Stanley's suggestions (n1) differed from the proposal they had been considering, he would obtain more information from Customs. H B/XX/CO/6, 7.

My dear Beauchamp,

If you be disengaged, will you come to your old haunts, & visit yr old friends, on Monday the 17th. Inst:? I hope so.[1]

    yrs e[ve]r, | D.[2]

4193   TO: [SIR HENRY EDWARDS?] [Hughenden, Thursday?] 6 September [1866?]
ORIGINAL: DBP Box 146/2
EDITORIAL COMMENT: A small black-edged card located on the microfilm between two letters (1869 and 1879) to Sir Henry Edwards. *Recipient, Place* and *Dating*: conjectural; see n1.

                                              Septr 6.

All right, my dear Baronet.[1]

    D.

4194   TO: [MONTAGU CORRY]   Hughenden [Thursday] 6 September [1866]
ORIGINAL: H B/XX/D/6
EDITORIAL COMMENT: *Dating*: by context; see nn1&2.

                                        Hughenden. Sep. 6

I wish, very much you would carefully look over the New Forest Case. The memorial is as good as a brief.[1] It is a case on wh:, as a lawyer & a man of the world, you are well qualified to / form an opinion. Don't hurry yourself, & don't be at all influenced by the opinion given by Ld. by Ld. Derby. Decide entirely on the merits, & by your own judgment.[2]

---

1 See **4195**&n2.
2 Beauchamp on 7 September would reply that he was unable to accept D's 'agreeable invitation' because 'To my very great regret I am condemned to stay with a local Conservative Esquire from the 17th to the 19th'. H B/XX/LN/52.

---

1 Edwards was created a Baronet on 3 August 1866. The DS were at Hughenden from 17 August to 29 October 1866.

---

1 This 'memorial' may be related to the 1858 *Register of Decisions on Claims to Forest Rights*. Corry on 10 September 1866 would write to D, 'I have read, and am digesting my New Forest brief.' H B/XX/CO/8.
2 In the Lords on 4 June 1866 there had been a motion (withdrawn) for papers relating 'to the Value of the New Forest if leased for shooting Purposes; and as to the best Mode of dividing the same for the Purposes of public Tender'. *Hansard* CLXXXIII cols 1792-3. (A New Forest Association would be formed in 1867 to halt further enclosure and defend the rights of commoners.) Corry on 14 September 1866 would write to D: 'I cannot see that the old licence-holders in the New Forest have any legal cause of complaint, on the ground that the fee annually payable is to be increased: on the other hand, – after what occurred in the House of Lords, which Lord Derby says is correctly set forth in the Memorial, and after the subsequent "express bargain" with the office of Woods that "all reference to a money consideration for licences" should be expunged from the clause, (as alleged in the Memorial), – it seems to me to be rather sharp practice to demand 20 times the former fee for such licences. I assume, when I say this, that the office of Woods *did* agree, as alleged by Lords Malmesbury, Nelson & the other memorialists. They, however, it would appear, would be content if the fee were lowered to £10, in lieu of the £20, demanded; and, as a shooting man, I think their demand is very fair. The office asks £20 x 80 (£1600) for the right of shooting, *to be shared by 80 persons*, over 50,000 acres of not very good ground; whereas I should have thought that sum a large rent to pay for the *sole* right. As you have done me the honor of asking my opinion, I should say – grant licences at £10, as that seems to be a sufficient reduction to satisfy them – grant free licences

I am much obliged to / you for yr mem: as to the speeches, wh: will guide me, a good deal, as to the amount of matter.[3] I am of opinion however, that there is, at least, one speech omitted, wh: must have been delivered between 1847 & 52. It was, as I recollect, on / Mr Hume's annual motion, & must have been of considerable length, as it was published by itself at the time by Conservative Societies.[4]

There was a quotation in it, on wh: there was a controversy, at the time, betn Sir Jas Graham & myself, whether it was / in Juvenal or Horace. I turned out to be right, but what the quotation was, & whether it were Juvenal or Horace, I can't, at this period of time, say.[5]

Send papers enclosed to Mr E. Egerton.[6]

The Anti-Tea Pot Review, / wh: is always sent me, I have ever ~~always~~ looked upon as the most self complacent piece of idiocy afloat – & how such things can float, I wonder.[7]

Now, we know ~~how~~ who the Editor is: a fussy & intrusive person evidently, who / wishes to bring himself into notice by great schemes, wh: require men of the utmost experience & influence to manage. You must answer his letter however, & inform him that it will not be in my power to attend any meeting &c.[8]

D.

to the tenderer's and Crown lessees, as Mr Howard proposes and for the same reasons, – while as to the Ex-Master Keepers I can see no reason, why they should not pay as the others. There can be no doubt that there is a great deal of irritation in Hampshire on this subject, – and that among the most considerable men in the county. Is it worth while to stir up so much ill feeling for so few hundred pounds? M.C. They *want* these papers, and, if possible, your decision on the case, on Monday.' H B/XX/CO/9. See **4204**.

3 See **4187**.

4 D's two speeches (20 June 1848 and 25 March 1852) on Joseph Hume's motions (see V **1657**n2 and VI **2262**n1), both entitled 'On Mr Hume's Motion on National Representation', would be included in Corry's edition (1-31, 56-80). The Church and State Gazette Office had published in 1848 'The New Parliamentary Reform. Mr. Disraeli's speech. In the House of Commons, on Tuesday, June 20, 1848, on Mr. Hume's motion' (16 pp). Stewart *Writings* item 618.

5 Corry on 7 September would write to D that Hume's motion had been given 'on June 21. 1848. – Hansard Vol. 99. Page 944. 22 columns long. "Rhetor, grammaticus, geometres, pictor, aliptes | Augur, schenobates, medicus, magus –." I have no doubt that Juvenal so wrote. I dont think Horace could have made up his mind to use the word "schenobates."' H B/XX/CO/6. The passage is from Juvenal's third Satire; see **4196**.

6 These papers have not been found.

7 'The Anti-Teapot Review (Politics, Literature, and Art), edited by Members of the Universities ... was established in 1863, and circulates among the upper classes of society in Great Britain, the continent, and the colonies.' *The Times* (28 Oct 1867). The anonymous writers of the satirical *Anti-Teapot Review* (1863-9), printed at Oxford, belonged to the Anti-Teapot Society of Europe and considered tea-drinking a symbol of hypocritical class pretension.

8 The editor's letter has not been found. The annual dinner of the Anti-Teapot Society of Europe had been announced for 3 February 1866 in London. *The Times* (27 Jan 1866).

4195 TO: [MONTAGU CORRY]   [Hughenden, Saturday 8 September 1866]

ORIGINAL: H B/XX/D/348

EDITORIAL COMMENT: Endorsed in another hand: 'Sep 8/66'. *Dating*: by context; see nn3&4.

I have got Lady C's answer,[1] & I am making up a party here for the 17th.[2]

Mrs Disraeli hopes, that you will give us the pleasure of yr. company also, & visit the Chiltern Hills.

Its rather awkward about business, but I think, with a / little management, we might arrange it. Its Monday the 17th. That day, you can come down to dinner; we might crib all Tuesday; & on Wednesday, you might, if necessary, go up, & reconnoitre, & return for dinner.

Take care that Lady C[lanricarde] gets this by the first post. I think she is at Beaumonts, but they will tell you in Stratton Street.[3]

D.[4]

4196 TO: MONTAGU CORRY   Hughenden, Sunday [9 September 1866]

ORIGINAL: H B/XX/D/7

PUBLICATION HISTORY: M&B IV 481, dated 9 September 1866, the second and third paragraphs.

Montagu Corry | Esq   Hughenden. Sunday

My dear Montagu,

I received, by this post, the Board of Trade Despatch.[1] It is very weighty, & when [*illegible deletion*] I have read & digested it, I will send it on to you, that / you may deposit it with the other papers, after having mastered it. By that time, you will, I think, understand the subject, as well as Mallet.[2]

---

1 Lady Cranborne on 3 September had written from Headley, Liphook, Hants accepting D's invitation, 'that is, Cranborne certainly will & I too if you are really in earnest about bearing the dreadful infliction of a baby in your house.' H B/XX/CE/320. The 'baby' was her sixth and youngest child, Edgar Algernon Robert, born 14 September 1864.

2 MA on 17 September would record: 'Dined here Vist & Viscou[ntes]s Cranborne Lord Henry Lennox Count Vitzthum [von Eckstaedt] Mon[sieu]r [Peter Alexandrovich] Sabouroff Mr Montague.[*sic*] Corry & Mr Clubbe'; a few pages later, she writes: 'One month no company exception dinner party of 8 (with ourselves) from the 17th of Aug to 17 of Sep'. The Duke of Buckingham would write to D on 12 September: 'I have just received yours – I am afraid the Duchess will not be able to accept Mrs Disraeli's invitation having some friends staying with her who do not I think leave until Thursday in next week.' H acc; H B/XXI/B/1225.

3 Lord Clanricarde in 1825 had married Harriet Canning (1804-1876); Wentworth Beaumont in 1856 had married their daughter Margaret Anne. The Clanricardes resided at 17 Stratton Street, Piccadilly. Lady Clanricarde on 7 September had replied from Allenhead to D's letter of that day (not found) turning down his invitation because of an imminent trip to Scotland. H B/XXI/C/233.

4 Corry would reply on 9 September accepting D's invitation, adding that 'Lady Clanricarde is at "Allenhead, near Carlisle," whither I have sent your letter.' H B/XX/CO/7.

---

1 Although this despatch has not been found, see **4191**n2. Northcote on 9 October would send D 'a despatch respecting the duties on Portuguese wine ... It would undoubtedly be of great importance to us if we could conclude a good treaty of commerce with Portugal ... I think Mr. Mallet should be furnished with instructions and sent to Lisbon with a view to collect information and to bring the matter to a point.' H B/IX/E/13.

2 Louis Mallet (1823-1890) was private secretary to the president of the board of trade 1848-52 and 1855-8, CB 1866, Kt 1868, council of India 1872-4, permanent under-secretary of state for India 1874-83 and PC

I am not surprised B of T. rather demurs at / having to work in September, wh: is unnatural, but it will give them a lesson, & teach them wh. Department is at the head of the Governm[en]t.

You, also, have not found the Secretariat quite / as much of a Sinecure, as we expected – but you have done yr work very well, & it will season you for the impending struggle.

The passage is in Juvenal: 3. Sat.[3]

I had hoped to have cleared my business in this bag, but the post has brought me an urgent box from Ld Stanley, ↑& not an agreeable one,↓ wh: prevents my doing so.[4]

Yrs D.

TO: JOSEPH PARROTT   Hughenden [Monday] 10 September 1866   **4197**
ORIGINAL: H B/XIII/90
EDITORIAL COMMENT: An incomplete draft in D's hand.

Private   Hughenden Manor | Sept 10. 1866

Jos: Parrott | Esqr
Dear Sir,

Since I received your letter[1] I have ↑been↓ in communication with the Privy Council Office. The state of the country, with respect / to the sheep disease appears to me to have rendered the order of the 8th. Ulto. imperative, & with the applica[tio]ns & appeals before me to connect such an order ↑merely↓ with the circ[umstanc]es of the disease appearing at / Brill is not less than absurd.

The Council were influenced in their course by the ~~concep~~ belief that stringent measures adopted in time might ensure that relax[ati]on at Mich[ael]mas is necessary for the breeding & change of stock[2]

1883. His appointments as assistant commissioner for trade treaties with France 1860-5 and Austria 1865-7 led to some sixty commercial treaties in Europe and a promotion to assistant secretary and head of the commercial department 1867-72. He was at this time 'the principal authority on commercial policy, and ... chief adviser to the British government in matters of commercial foreign policy.' ODNB. On this day (9th) Corry reassured D that 'Mr Mallet (who was Mr Gladstone's right hand man in his Commercial Treaties) is taking much interest in this question [*wine duties*]. He seems to be a very able man.' H B/XX/CO/7.

3 See **4194**&n5.
4 Stanley on 8 September had asked D 'to look at the papers sent herewith – which please return. The subject is not a pleasant one, inasmuch as it seems that political considerations have led our government to involve itself in a debt to the Chinese of rather considerable amount. We did not allow the Chinese to sell their own ships lest they should be bought by Confederates, and so increase our American difficulties. I fear in equity we are bound to make good the loss. Tell me what you think ... I have heard with regret from Sir F[rederick] Bruce that the Alabama claims will be revived!' H B/XX/S/746.

1 Aylesbury solicitor Joseph Parrott, one of D's chief election agents, had written a '*Private* & Confidential' letter to D on 31 August about his recent correspondence with the privy council on the Cattle Diseases Prevention Act (see **4189**&nn1-4). He felt that the act virtually prevented markets by restricting the transport of sheep. Local farmers' reaction to the restrictions had made the Duke of Buckingham extremely unpopular in the county, and Parrott had asked D to try to moderate the Duke's severity. H B/XXI/P/121.
2 Parrott would reply on 16 September saying he understood the privy council's reasons for severe restrictions but thought they should not apply to the entire county in a case where disease affected only one area. H B/XXI/P/122.

4198
TO: [MONTAGU CORRY]   [Hughenden] Monday 10 September [1866]
ORIGINAL: H B/XX/D/8
EDITORIAL COMMENT: Endorsed in another hand on the first page: '?1866'. *Dating*: by context; see n2.

Monday Sept. 10

Put Lord Stanley's private letters in a box with "private" written on the label, & forward them to F.O.

I had forgotten S. Fitzgerald, to whom I have written a few lines,[1] lest he shd. feel, in his adversity, / he was neglected.

Lords Stanley, Cranborne, & Carnarvon, shd. be impressed with the duty of providing for Fitzgerald. He is a man of talents, has served us well, &, had it not been for losing his seat, & his private misfortunes, / would have been, justly, in an eminent post. He wd. make a good Plenipo: Governor, &c.

Send to the Duke of Buck[in]gham in a box the list of the infected places,[2] & send the letter with it, if his Grace is in town, ⌐or expected that morning.⌐ Otherwise let / it be forwarded to him at by post: I conclude Stowe, Buckingham – but they will tell you at P[rivy] C[ouncil] O[ffice].

Yours | D.

You have Fitzgeralds letter. I think direction

    Hotel de Paris

    Madrid.

But if no delay of importance, it had better go with F.O. bag.

    D.

4199
TO: MONTAGU CORRY   Hughenden, Tuesday [11 September 1866]
ORIGINAL: H B/XX/D/9
PUBLICATION HISTORY: M&B IV 481, dated 11 September 1866, paragraphs two, three and four; Blake 400, extract
EDITORIAL COMMENT: Docketed in another hand on the first page: 'Sep 11/66'. *Dating*: by context; see n1. *Sic*: publickly; Walowski.

Montagu Corry | Esqr   Hughenden Manor | Tuesday

Write to Mr Isham,[1] that I shall be glad if it be in my power, as I hope, to give his son another chance, but let him understand, that there are many claimants on my influence, & that I took care to give him / the earliest, & the best, chance.

---

1 D's letter, most likely a reply to William Seymour Fitzgerald's letter of 29 August (see **4190**n1), has not been found. Fitzgerald, elected MP (C) for Horsham, had been unseated in July 1865. His wife Maria Triphena had died in 1865. See **4229**&n5.

2 *BH* on 8 September had published a 'List of "Infected Places"' in Buckinghamshire. *The Times* on 7 September had published a list of 'Counties Reporting Attacks' (with the number of cases per county) and towns in '26 petty sessional divisions of England' where the cattle plague had been reported during the previous week. Since the beginning of the outbreaks, 253,324 cattle and 6,831 sheep had been reported as attacked. See **4189**n2.

---

1 Possibly the Rev Arthur Isham. Corry on 10 September had sent D 'Mr Isham's letter [*not found*] knowing that you took some interest in his Son's nomination.' H B/XX/CO/8.

Read the enclosed letter from Mr Wellings, a clergyman of Shropshire.[2] The youth referred to ~is~ was the godson of ↑the late↓ Mrs. Brydges Willyams, who, about three years ago, made me her heir. She left this lad £3000:[3] & / requested me, if I had the opportunity, of planting him in life. I never saw him, nor wish to see him, but I shd. like, very much, to forward his interests: particularly as he does not seem to want much.

The Mr Lovell referred to / is the lawyer to the Brydges Willyams ↑estate↓, who has communicated with all the legatees, but this matter shd. not be left to Mr Lovell any further.

I don't want the boy to be unnecessarily plucked, & therefore, I wd. wish you to write to his uncle, & enquire, whether he is / prepared to pass the preliminary examination &c &c & generally put things in train.[4]

I remember once seeing Mr Strutt, & a more dreadful person I have seldom encountered.[5]

The late D of Buck[in]g[ha]m had the talent of inspiring ruffians with enthusiasm, of charming creditors, & / of taking swindlers in. He played the same comedy, wh: he practised on Strutt, on all the bill-discounters in London, & generally gulled them: he was so great an artist in their own way.[6]

2 *The Times* on 23 December 1868 would report that 'The Queen has been pleased to present the Rev. Edward Penwarne Wellings, B.A., to the vicarage of Stanford-in-the-Vale, in the county of Berks, and diocese of Oxford.' Wellings, rural dean of the vale of White Horse deanery 1877-87, had written to D on 29 August 1866: 'Having been informed by Mr Lovell that I am at liberty to address you on the subject of my Nephew's nomination for a Civil Service appointment, which you have kindly promised to accord him, I have to state that he will be 18 years of age on the 30th. of next October: that his name is Arthur Mendez da Costa Penwarne Wellings, & that I believe him qualified for a situation in either of the following departments of the Service. Audit Office – Board of Trade – Paymaster General's Office – India Office – Exchequer or Tithe Commissioners Office.' H C/II/C/4a.

3 Two of the names on an undated list in D's hand of SBW's legatees include 'Geo. Aug. Penwarne W. 100' followed by 'Arth. P. da M.P. [*sic*] 3000'. RTC [489Q]. See VIII **3877**&n3.

4 E.P. Wellings would write to Corry on 20 September 1866 thanking him for his letter of 15 September, assuring him that his nephew could pass 'French, History, Arithmetic & Précis writing ... this Autumn ... If he fails the first time will he be allowed a second trial?' He would write to C.W. Fremantle on 17 October asking him to thank D 'for having so kindly procured a nomination for my Nephew' and on 22 October asking if D could '*retain the nomination till about the middle of next month*' so as to enable his nephew 'to master the book keeping'. H C/II/C/4b,c,d. Arthur Wellings would fail the examination for a clerkship in the Paymaster General's Office in mid-December 1866 (see **4295**&n3) and again in early August 1867 (H C/II/C/4i). William Lovell would write D on 28 August 1868 (enclosing a 24 August letter from E.P. Wellings): 'You will perceive that he has at length given up the hope that his nephew would be able to pass an examination.' Wellings had asked Lovell to convey to D his 'grateful acknowledgements for his endeavours to benefit my Nephew, & my regrets that his kind efforts should have proved unsuccessful.' He then asked Lovell to intercede with D, who had 'great Church Patronage', on his own behalf: 'My failing health makes me dread lest I shall have to resign my appointment here in the [Ludlow] Grammar School'. He described himself as 'a moderate Churchman ... & in Politics a Conservative' whose mother was SBW's 'oldest & dearest friend'. H A/V/G/210, 210a.

5 Most likely the John Strutt reprimanded by the House in 1851 for election fraud; see V **2146**n1. William Lovell would write D on 27 October acknowledging D's letter 'enclosing Mr Strutts communication' and recommending that D see Strutt 'and treat him as being desirous of giving up a letter, by the improper use of which a dishonest Solicitor had abused the confidence of his Employer; and therefore to accept his offer to give the letter up. Mr Strutt is himself a certificated Solr., so he will be cautious in what he does.' H A/V/G/207.

6 See IV **1579**n1. Such were the 'folly, extravagance, and breathtaking incompetence' of the 2nd Duke of

Strutt, I believe, was not only a bill discounter, but / a bawdy-house keeper, a broken attorney & common cut throat. I leave him in your hands.

I don't understand about the conscience ꜛmoneyꜜ. When did the halves arrive? You have omitted in yr letter the word, wh: wd. have informed / me. Did they arrive ꜛin D.S.ꜜ before ~~us~~ we did? and has their receipt never been acknowledged in the "Times"; & ~~&~~ if not, why not?[7]

I have signed the letter.[8] We can't be too strict about such matters – & it is a question, whether they shd. not [*illegible deletion*], even now, be / specially & publickly acknowledged.

I fear this awful weather[9] will play the deuce with our northern, & our Irish, harvest. There has never been so wet a harvest since 1841, when I was canvassing Shrewsbury, amid the cries of "cheap bread"[10] & / when I remember, in the same year, in Normandy, the grain out in the fields in October.[11]

I know Walowski, who sends me all his works.[12] He is a great ass. Being a bullionist, he cannot talk much nonsense, even on currency, but / he has no tact, or discrimination, & makes a ~~go~~ sound cause ridiculous by his commonplace exaggeration. There's nothing in him. He wrote to me the other day,[13] & wanted to entrap me into a controversy on "issues", wh: I declined & told him something, wh:, to my surprise, he has quoted / in a grave dissertation.[14] You'll find it where the page is turned down. You can keep his things, as they are only reprints from ~~his~~ the Revue des Deux Mondes, to wh: I am a subscriber.

Yrs, | D.

Keep Strutts letter in our archives.

Buckingham and Chandos, who had died bankrupt in 1861, that by 1847 he had accumulated 'debts of nearly £1.5 million ... with annual interest payments of at least £66,000 and an annual income of at most £61,000'. ODNB.

7 *The Times* on 8 September had reported that 'The Chancellor of the Exchequer acknowledges the receipt of the first halves of banknotes for 740*l.* from "A. B.," for unpaid income-tax; the first half of a 5*l.*-note from "Siga," for unpaid tax on armorial bearings; and of a 5*l.*-note from "Fides," for unclaimed property-tax.' On 10 September, it had reported D's 'receipt of a 10*l.*-note from "Bricks and Mortar," and of the second halves of bank-notes for 740*l.* from "A. B.," for unpaid income-tax.' According to John Keyworth, curator of the Bank of England Museum, it was not unusual for banknotes sent through the post to be cut and the halves sent separately, an anti-theft ploy dating from the seventeenth century. An additional safeguard was to wait until receipt of the first half had been acknowledged before remitting the second.

8 This letter has not been found.

9 'Strong north-westerly gales [on 11 September] continue to blow on the Irish coasts, and the weather is very strong in the Irish Sea and English Channel. Barometers in the north have again fallen considerably. Cautionary telegrams were sent yesterday to the western coasts of England; our eastern and northern coasts have been cautioned this morning.' *The Times* (12 Sep 1866).

10 Following the formation (in 1839) of the Anti-Corn-Law League, cries of 'free trade', 'big loaf' or 'little loaf' and especially 'cheap bread' became commonplace, in particular during the general election of 1841.

11 The DS had 'been wandering in Normandy, much pleased' in October 1841. III **1192**.

12 See **4181&n1**.

13 This letter has not been found.

14 Corry (n1) had told D that 'Every body is writing and talking about Mr Wolowski's articles in the "Revue des deux Mondes" on our Crisis. I forward the 2[è]me Partie which has been sent you from abroad.' Tome 65 (1 Sep 1866) of *La Revue des deux mondes*, pp 176-211, had carried Wolowski's 'La crise financière de l'Angleterre. II. L'*ACT* de 1844 et la liberté des banques.'

TO: GEORGE FELL   Downing Street [Wednesday] 12 September 1866 **4200**
ORIGINAL: PS 1472
PUBLICATION HISTORY: *BH* (22 Sep 1866)
EDITORIAL COMMENT: Written by Montagu Corry at D's request.

George Fell, Esq.   11 Downing-street, Whitehall,
Wednesday, September 12, 1866.

Sir, –

I am directed by the Chancellor of the Exchequer to express to you, as Secretary to the Royal and Central Bucks Agricultural Association, his great regret that he will be unable to attend the annual dinner of the association on Thursday, the 20th inst.[1] He is prevented so doing by the fact that during the whole of next week he will have a party of friends staying with him at Hughenden.[2] – I have the honour to be, sir, your obedient servant,

    MONTAGU CORRY.

TO: LORD DALMENY   Hughenden [Wednesday] 12 September 1866 **4201**
ORIGINAL: ROSE [37] Dalmeny House Collection
EDITORIAL COMMENT: Black-edged paper.[1] *Sic*: Wycomb.

The | Lord Dalmeny   Hughenden Manor | High Wycomb. Sept 12/ | 66
Dear Dalmeny,[2]

Where are you? In Europe? In England? In town?

   If in England, or in the south, or about, / pray come & see us, Monday the 17th, or the 18th.[3]

   Line: Paddington; Station: H. Wycombe; whence, only ten minutes / to our gates.

   Yours, | D.[4]

---

1 *BH* on 22 September would give full coverage of the event's exhibitions, prizes and dinner speeches: 'The show of sheep, pigs, roots, &c.' would not be as successful as on previous occasions, 'the horned stock being for the second year interdicted, the committee deeming it inadvisable to have an exhibition of horned cattle during the prevalence in neighbouring counties of that fearful scourge, the rinderpest.'
2 See **4195**n2.

---

1 MA was in mourning for her cousin and close friend, Emma Phipps Scrope, who died in 1866; former chancellor of the exchequer Lord Northbrook had died on 6 September 1866 (*The Times* 8, 10 Sep 1866).
2 Archibald Philip Primrose (1847-1929), 2nd Lord Dalmeny 1851, 5th Earl of Rosebery 1868, Viscount Mentmore, Baron Epsom and Earl of Midlothian 1911. In 1854 his mother, Wilhelmina, Baroness Dalmeny, had married secondly 4th Duke of Cleveland. Educated at Eton 1860-5 and matriculating at Christ Church, Oxford in January 1866, Dalmeny would be sent down without a degree at Easter 1869 for refusing to sell his racehorse. He would become a prominent Liberal, serving as foreign secretary Feb-Aug 1886, 1892-4 and (succeeding Gladstone) PM 1894-5. In 1878 he would marry Hannah de Rothschild, whose death from typhoid fever in 1890 would devastate him.
3 See **4195**n2.
4 Dalmeny would reply from Raby Castle on 15 September: 'I only got your letter an hour ago. I should like of all things to come to Hughenden as you may guess but I see no chance of it as I am not free till the 8th of October ... You will see by this that I am neither in Europe or town but at the extremity of a third continent i.e. my room at Raby ... P.S. The reason for my not getting your letter was my being away from home.' H B/XXI/R/135.

4202

TO: LORD DERBY   Hughenden [Friday] 14 September 1866

ORIGINAL: DBP Box 146/2

EDITORIAL COMMENT: Black-edged paper. Endorsed by Derby on the first page: 'Ansd'.

Confidential   Hughenden Manor | Sepr. 14. 1866

Right Honorable | The Earl of Derby | K.G.

My dear Lord.

I enclose letter from Cranborne:[1] I have not heard from Henry Lennox.[2] For the reason, mentioned in / my letter about naval affairs to you,[3] I entirely avoid communicating directly with the Admiralty, but I agree with Lord Cranborne, that its condition, &, to a certain extent, its management, / is, in the present state of the public mind, not merely a departmental question. I hope, therefore, you will exercise yr supreme authority, & prevent any step being taken, as that, / apparently, contemplated, without the previous deliberation of the Cabinet.[4]

Yrs ever, | D.

1 Lord Cranborne on 11 September had written a '*Private*' letter to D: 'Just before the prorogation [junior naval lord] Sir John Hay told me that the Admiralty, he feared, would insist on repairing their old wooden ships ... Today [first secretary of the admiralty] Henry Lennox writes me word that [senior naval lord Alexander] Milne is pressing that view in the teeth of the Comptroller of the Navy [Robert Spencer Robinson]: that Pakington is inclined to yield: & that the decision has only been postponed – for a week at his Henry Lennox's request. In this dilemma he writes to me. Probably he has written to you. In case he should not have done so, I trouble you with this letter. On the merits of the question I do not offer an opinion – for it is hardly my business. But what I would urge, most earnestly, is that if you make an opinion you should make it practically felt, without loss of time: for you will undoubtedly have to defend in Parliament the course that is being taken. Might not Pakington be urged to hang the question up till the Cabinet shall have considered it? ... Anyhow the question is too important both in the higher & the lower regions of politics – both to the nation at large, & to us as a party, to be left to the decision of an old Admiral.' H B/XX/CE/9.

2 Lennox, first secretary of the admiralty, had written to D on 10 September that he 'should be glad to have a few words' with him. He would write on the 17th accepting MA's invitation to visit Hughenden on the 18th. H B/XX/LX/242, 243.

3 See **4175**.

4 Derby would reply on 16 September with a letter headed '*Private*': 'I have anticipated your wishes as expressed in the letter received this morning. I did not like to trouble Pakington while he was engaged in his tour of inspection (little importance as I attach to such flying visits) but I wrote to him at great length yesterday, urging upon him the importance of minimizing, first by diminishing the amount of repairs upon our old ships, 2d by reduction in the amount of stores, 3d by selling off a number of our old wooden ships, ... and 4th by improving the system of superintendence at the Dockyards: when the Officers appointed to that duty have so much indoor work to do that they cannot possibly have their eyes upon the waste and peculation which I have no doubt goes on to a vast extent. I also suggested that the best use to which some of our old Line of Battle ships could be put would be to cut them down, and fill them with armour and Turret guns for Harbour defence alone. The expense of this would be borne by sales of ships & stores. I will however write again, without naming you, to urge that nothing should be done in the way of repairs of old wooden Vessels, till he has had an opportunity of conferring with his Colleagues. I am coming reluctantly to the conclusion that we shall have to deal with the question of Reform. I send you a Memorandum, which I will thank you to return, containing a sketch of a Reform Bill drawn up by R.D. Baxter, who has the whole question at his fingers' ends. Some of his suggestions are very good. But I wish you would consider whether, after all the failures which have taken place, we might not deal with the question in the shape of Resolutions, to form the basis of a future Bill. We *need* not make the adoption of any of the Resolutions a vital question: which, if we should be beaten on some great leading principle, we should have a definite issue on which to go to the Country. This is worth turning in your mind; and I should be glad to hear what you think of it ... I go to Balmoral on Wednesday, to remain till the 1st of October.' H B/XX/S/364. See **4207**.

Montagu Corry | Esqr   Hughenden Manor | Sept. 14. 1866

I returned your boxes yesterday – but retained one from Lord Stanley, containing his dr[af]t reply to the Portuguese Govt, & other papers connected with the proposed treaty; among them a copy of the / reply of the Board ↑of Trade↓, with wh: you had previously furnished me.[1] After looking at these papers, return them in a box to Lord Stanley F.O.

The difficulties in this matter are no doubt very great, & I am not, myself, / inclined to run any risk of injuring ɫ our revenue for the sake of a Portuguese expansion of our commerce. But Spain is another matter, &, to secure that market, would justify some hazard & / prompt much invention in encountering difficulties.

I don't exactly know where Ld. Derby is: I suppose, at Knowsley: but he might be coming up the day you receive this. Take care he has the enclosed promptly.[2]

I hope you will bring sunshine on Monday [.][3]

Yrs | D.

EDITORIAL COMMENT: Docketed in another hand on the first page: 'Sep 16/66'. *Dating*: by context; see n5.

Sunday

What a Day! I fear our Malt Tax will suffer terribly. With fine weather, it wd. have been immense this year.

Your train is 5 o'ck: that will land you here by ½ pt. 6. or so.

How many lines in a Hansard / column?[1]

I have written up all my paper, & used almost all my pens. Send me a lot pr. post.[2] It need not be in mourning, as I shall be out of that in a few days.[3]

I fear there has / been an unfortunate delay in the N. ~~Fre~~ Forest papers.[4] They must be again referred to Lord Derby, as you will see. The facts were not correctly set forth in the original papers, wh: he referred to me, & wh:, unfortunately ↑without↓ examining, I handed over to you. It was not your / fault, but it required special H of Comm: knowledge, wh: it is my duty to supply.

---

1 See **4191**&n2.
2 See **4202**.
3 The weather on Monday 17 September 1866 at 8 *am* would be reported as follows: 'This morning the winds have veered to north-west and moderated, with fine weather.' *The Times* (18 Sep 1866).

---

1 There are about sixty lines in one *Hansard* column, slightly more depending on quoted matter (in smaller font).
2 See **4208**.
3 See **4201**ec&n1.
4 See **4194**&nn1&2.

I hope, however, he may have returned from Knowsley, & so may be able to finish it off hand.[5]

I trust you will contrive not to have to go to town during yr visit here.[6]

Yrs ever | D.

4205
TO: VICTORIA TEMPLE FANE   Hughenden [Sunday] 16 September 1866
ORIGINAL: BODL MS Top Oxon b217 ff115-16
EDITORIAL COMMENT: *Sic*: Wormesly.

Hughenden Manor | Septr 16 1866

Dear Mrs Fane,

It will give us very great pleasure indeed, if you, & our good friend, the Colonel,[1] will dine with us on Tuesday next, the 18th, & meet Lord & Lady Cranborne, & some of my colleagues.[2]

We also beg, that you will not think of returning to Wormesly at night, but that you will rest under our roof. Your rooms / are ready & waiting you.

We dine at ½ pt. 7 o'ck: precisely.

Yours sincerely, | *B. Disraeli*

4206
TO: [MONTAGU CORRY]   Hughenden, Thursday [20 September 1866?]
ORIGINAL: H B/XX/D/12
EDITORIAL COMMENT: Hughenden paper. *Dating*: *cf* **4204** re paper. *Sic*: Stevens [*twice*]; *Stephen's*; *Martins*.

Thursday

While this is too austere, I think the Grosvenor Gate paper is too much like compo:[1] Lord Foley's house, just after its annual restoration.[2] I think a bluer paper ~~with~~ of a superior texture / might be desirable. The pen does not fly on any of these papers. Ld. Derby's letter had better go by bag, if one goes tomorrow night, but there must be no delay, & if no bag, send it by post to Balmoral. /

---

5 Derby would write to D from Knowsley on 18 September 1866: 'I have returned to the Treasury your Memorandum on the Crown Forests question, together with a Minute, which I should wish you to see, adopting your proposed compromise, which might be even modified by making the reduced rate of payment applicable only to those who held licenses at the passing of the Act, and on whom it imposes an unexpected hardship. I have recorded the circumstances under which the Act was passed.' H B/XX/S/365.
6 On 9 September, accepting D's invitation for a 17 September visit to Hughenden, Corry had written (on 11 Downing Street paper), 'I can easily "run up" here if necessary.' H B/XX/CO/7.

---

1 For the Fanes, see VIII **3499**n3.
2 Although there is no record of a Hughenden dinner on 18 September 1866, there would be one on the 17th (see **4195**&n2). MA on the 22nd would note that 'The larder looked like a butcher shop. The cook Mrs. Rogers discharged on 17th of October.' H ACC.

---

1 Given the context (n2), D is using 'compo:' (abbreviating 'composition' or 'composite') to denote 'a mixture of whiting, resin, and glue, used instead of plaster of Paris for wall and cornice ornamentation.' *OED*.
2 Thomas Henry Foley, 4th Baron Foley, had purchased a town house at 26 Grosvenor Square (in the DS' neighbourhood) in 1840. The stucco may have needed touching up every year.

Could you find out what influences the "Times" in urging the policy & necessity of our bringing in a Reform Bill? It might throw light on the state of parties.[3]

Mrs Disraeli has just brought me some "Stevens" / blue-black ink. It is a relief. I have tried it on the Govt Compo: & even there it is an improvement. It is very well on this austere paper. The pen runs.

This last paragraph is all Stevens: it is quite delightful *"Stephen's Blue Black 18 St. Martins le Grand"*[.][4]

TO: LORD DERBY   Hughenden [Monday] 24 September [1866]   **4207**
ORIGINAL: DBP Box 146/2
PUBLICATION HISTORY: M&B IV 454, the fourth paragraph, beginning with 'observation'
EDITORIAL COMMENT: C of Ex paper, seal crossed out. *Dating*: by context; see nn1-8.

Hughenden Manor | Septr. 24

Right Honorable | The Earl of Derby K.G.

My dear Lord,

A box from Walpole, wh: I am to send to you,[1] & only ten minutes allowed, so I cannot write now at any length on any matter. /

I agree with you as to yr view of the Telegraph Rewards. You must do them all.[2]

I take this opportunity of returning Pakington's letter[3] – & Baxters Memorandum.[4]

They both require long comment. I will only say, / now, as to the latter, that observation, & reflection, have not yet brought me to yr conclusion as to the ne-

---

3 *The Times* on 8 September 1866 had published a leader stating: 'No Reform Bill can escape opposition, but no opposition in the present day could succeed against a good Reform Bill. In whatever tactics the necessity of Reform may have originated it is a necessity now, not only because a question thus far opened must needs be settled, but because until this settlement is accomplished all other legislation remains impracticable.'

4 Dr Henry Stephens (1796-1864), an apothecary and surgeon, had invented 'blue-black writing fluid' in 1832 and founded Stephens Ink Ltd, a very successful business manufacturing indelible ink. See **4208** and **4209**.

---

1 Spencer Walpole on 22 September 1866 had written to D that he had informed Derby that he would 'make enquiries as to the different persons, whom he proposes to recommend to the Queen for Baronetcies & Knighthoods: that I hope to be able to do this by & by Monday morning: and that I will send the information on to you, so that you may be able to forward it on without delay.' On this day (24th) he had sent D at Hughenden 'the result of my enquiries ... by messenger, that he may bring back the box in time to post it by Mail Train tonight.' H B/XXI/W/63, 64.

2 Derby on 27 September would reply from Balmoral with a letter headed '*Confidential*': 'On the receipt of your Box and Walpole's letter, entirely confirming my previous impressions, I submitted to the Queen my recommendations for Honors connected with the Atlantic cable: to the whole of which H. M. gave a ready assent. I have accordingly written to the parties concerned, and Northcote will announce all of them at a "Banquet" at which he is to preside on Monday at Liverpool.' The first transatlantic telegraph cable had been laid in 1858 but operated for only one month. After several attempts, lasting connections between Ireland and Newfoundland had been achieved on 27 July 1866. *The Times* would report the banquet honouring 'the layers of the Atlantic Cables'. H B/XX/S/366; *The Times* (28 Jul, 2 Oct 1866).

3 See **4202**n4. Derby had written to D on 18 September enclosing 'a long letter from Pakington in answer to one which, as I told you, I had written him a few days ago. I think you ought, and would wish, to see it: but I should be glad to have it returned at your leisure.' H B/XX/S/365.

4 See **4202**n4.

cessity of bringing in a bill for Parly Reform: but, I hope, I say this with becoming diffidence.[5] /

I conclude, from what I hear, that Ld. Exeter is in extremis. The party never had a better friend, & his personal qualities were engaging. Still, with such accumulated honors, it is some consolation, that / they do not fall to the Whigs.[6]

I have heard, that the Duke of Newcastle would formally & completely join you for the Garter. That is his object.[7]

With respect to the two / Lord Lieutenancies, it might be well for you to consider, whether that of Rutlandshire might not be conferred on Ld. Gainsboro', to whom we owe much.[8]

But it is rather impertinent, / perhaps in my interfering in such matters.

Yrs ever, I D.

4208 TO: [MONTAGU CORRY] [Hughenden, Tuesday] 25 September 1866

ORIGINAL: H B/XX/D/12a

PUBLICATION HISTORY: M&B IV 481

EDITORIAL COMMENT: D has written on a sheet of C of Ex paper: '*Stephen's Blue-Black* | *Montagu Corry* | *Montagu Corry*'; and on a sheet of Hughenden paper: 'Hughenden | Montagu Corry | What do you think | of the ink they | sent.' *Sic*: wooly.

Sept. 25/66

What do you think of the ink they give us? Is it detestable? Or is it this fat, wooly paper, wh: they think is fine?

The ink is not so bad on my own paper, of wh: I enclose a specimen: but it soon

---

5 Derby would reply (n2) that 'the Reform question requires very mature consideration. There is considerable difference of opinion among our own friends upon the policy: but I think the general feeling is that we cannot escape doing something. The Queen spoke to me about it the other day. She said she was very anxious to see it settled, and that if she could do anything personally to bring opinions together, she would most readily do it. On the other hand the violence of Bright's language is, I think, in our favour; not in favour of resisting all Reform, for which I believe that there is a genuine demand now, however it may have been excited, but in favour of the acceptance of a moderate & Conservative measure. But I still think that Resolutions, on which the sense of the House might be taken separately, and on which defeat on one or two might not be fatal, afford many advantages. I wish you would consider this question seriously before we meet.'

6 Derby (n2) could not 'bear to think of Lord Exeter's death. He is a very old friend of mine, and a very good friend to the party; but when I saw him last in Lords, I felt sure I had seen him for the last time, and all my accounts, public and private, are such that I open the paper every morning in expectation of seeing his death recorded. It is however quite necessary that we should be prepared for the political consequences. I have had some conversation with the Queen on the subject and have obtained from her, by anticipation, an absolute veto on Cardigan for the Ld. Lieutenancy of Northamptonshire ... I have however a very good man in store in Southampton; whose influence has done a great deal for us in the County, and who has never asked for any thing!'

7 Henry Pelham Alexander Pelham-Clinton (1834-1879), 6th Duke of Newcastle-under-Lyne 1864, MP (L) for Newark 1857-9 (as Earl of Lincoln) and provincial grand master of the Nottinghamshire Freemasons 1865-77. Derby (n2) believed he could not 'offer the Garter to the D. of Newcastle. It will not do to bring new friends at the risk of alienating old ones. I think the choice will be between the D. of Beaufort & Lord Vane. I incline to the latter, as he will have immense influence, and was much disappointed at not being made Lord Steward.'

8 Derby (n2) 'had all along intended to offer Rutland to Ld. Gainsborough, despite his deafness. He has a good property, is a good friend, and will be the only R.C. Lord Lieutenant in England.'

gets so – I can't think / it is the pens. Bad stationery adds much to the labor of life – & whether it be the ink, the pens, or the paper, it seems to me, when in office, I never can write like a gentleman. Its a serious nuisance.

D.[1]

TO: MONTAGU CORRY [Hughenden, Tuesday] 25 September 1866 **4209**
ORIGINAL: H B/XX/D/13
PUBLICATION HISTORY: M&B IV 481-2, misdated 26 September 1866, paragraphs one, two, five and six
EDITORIAL COMMENT: Grosvenor Gate paper. D has written the last two sentences upside down on the first page. *Sic*: yesterday.

Montagu Corry | Esqr   Sept 25 1866

My dear Montagu,

We must not make another mistake about our paper. I observe the "Hughenden" sheet, wh: I sent you yesterday,[1] is part of a lot, wh: I did not much approve of at the / time. ~~Now~~ I thought it too austere.[2]

Now I write on some "Grosvenor Gate" paper, wh:↑, I think,↓ perfectly satisfied me in town, but whether it be the office ink, or the office pens, my calligraphy has a cheesemongerish look. /

I enclose another sheet for you to consider.[3]

Is this what I sent as a model to the Stationery Office?

The whole subject will employ yr vacant hours till I return to town, as I shall, certainly, lose my temper, / when real business commences, if my tools are not first-rate.

You do your business very well, & I am always glad to hear from you.

Obtain for me a list of our settlements on the West Coast of Africa, & their annual cost.[4]

I am anxious about the Elections. Who is the Irish Master of the Rolls?[5]

Yours D.

I don't much like this paper. The ink is, undoubtedly, horrid.

---

1 See also **4206**&n4 and **4209**.

---

1 See **4208**&ec.

2 See **4206**.

3 This sheet has not been found.

4 Charles Bowyer Adderley on 21 February 1865 had moved 'for a Select Committee to consider the state of the British Establishments on the Western Coast of Africa' – Sierra Leone, the Gambia, the British Gold Coast and Lagos territory – which he called an 'unhealthy spot ... costing this country nearly £1,000,000 a year'. The motion was agreed to and a committee would be nominated on 3 March. D would tell Derby on 30 September that giving up the settlements would 'enable us to build ships & have a good budget' (see **4216**). *Hansard* CLXXVII cols 535-59.

5 The *London Gazette* on 30 October would announce the appointment on 27 October of John Edward Walsh as 'Keeper or Master of the Rolls and Records of the Court of Chancery in Ireland.' *The Times* (31 Oct 1866).

4210 TO: SPENCER WALPOLE   Hughenden [Thursday] 27 September 1866
ORIGINAL: HOL [20]
EDITORIAL COMMENT: Hughenden paper.

Private   Sept 27 1866

Right Honble. | Mr Secretary Walpole
My dear Walpole,
    I return you Ld Derby's letter, having followed yr instructions, as to Balmoral.[1]

    As to a peerage for a friend of ours, mentioned in yr previous letter, I hope he will not / be precipitate in quitting the Ho: of Commons.[2]

    The peerages, conferred on Ld. Derby's accession to office, were either to assist the formation of his Ministry, or to complete engagements made previous to the General Election of / 1859, wh: from the abrupt termination of the Ministry, Ld. Derby could not with comfort to himself fulfil.

    If his Ministry take root, no doubt Lord Derby will show his sense of the support, wh: he has received / from several eminent members of the Ho: of Commons, who have not, from various causes, formed part of his Administration.
    Yours sincerely, | D.

4211 TO: SPENCER WALPOLE   Hughenden [Thursday] 27 September 1866
ORIGINAL: HOL [10]
EDITORIAL COMMENT: C of Ex paper, seal crossed out and 'Hughenden' written in.

Mr Secy. Walpole   Hughenden | Sep 27 1866

---

1 Walpole had written to D from the home office on 22 and 24 September: 'The Enclosed letter will explain itself. I have written to Lord Derby to say that I will make enquiries as to the different persons, whom he proposes to recommend to The Queen for Baronetcies & Knighthoods; that I hope to be able to do this by Monday morning; and that I will send the information on to you, so that you may be able to forward it on without delay.' With his second letter Walpole had enclosed 'the result of my enquiries. I send by messenger, that he may bring back the box in time to post it by Mail Train tonight. I send you a label of direction inside that the Messenger may take it straight from Hughenden to The Post Office.' H B/XXI/W/63-4.

2 Walpole on 3 September had written to D from the home office that Sir William Heathcote was 'very anxious' to retire. 'After a long life as County Member first of all, and as [Oxford] University Member afterwards; & true to his party through all the struggles they have had to pass through I think there is no one more entitled to a Peerage than he is.' H B/XXI/W/62. Heathcote would retire in 1868.

My dear Walpole,

The enclosed is a dreadful letter.[1] Surely with your Ecclesiastical connections,[2] you can help this poor fellow![3]

Yrs scy | D.[4]

TO: LORD DERBY   Hughenden [Thursday] 27 September 1866   **4212**

ORIGINAL: DBP Box 146/2
PUBLICATION HISTORY: M&B IV 444, undated, the fourth sentence
EDITORIAL COMMENT: Hughenden paper. *Sic*: an Irishmen.

Private   Septr 27 1866

Right Honorable | The Earl of Derby | K.G.

My dear Lord,

Cranborne writes to me about Bombay & Naas,[1] & says he has communicated with you, wh: is always the best thing to do.

I hope the idea, that Naas wants Bombay, is only an ancient tradition / of yr government of 1858.[2] He has now the Cabinet, wh: makes a great difference in a man's position, views, & feelings. I have a high opinion of Naas: I think him eminent for judgment; a quality rare, in any degree, in an Irishmen, & eminent judgment, with a complete knowledge of Ireland, is / a [*illegible deletion*] ↑choice↓ combination for a chief Secretary.[3]

---

1 William Gifford Cookesley, vicar of St Peter's, Hammersmith since 1860, had written to D on 12 September that 'unless some hand be stretched out to save me, I must sink ... every conceivable distress has fallen on me ... [the] rector of Tempsford, Bedfordshire, is dying. The living is in the gift of the crown. If it *should* fall vacant, will you consider whether you can recommend me as the person to fill it?' In his 'dreadful letter' of 24 September, Cookesley had reiterated that his life was 'a mere variety of distress & affliction': his eldest son had died in China, another had returned from Canada 'a hopeless cripple' and a daughter was 'completely broken in health'. As a result, he was suffering from 'the heaviest pecuniary difficulties' and asked D to apply to Derby on his behalf. 'If I could get a crown living which would set me free from my present anxieties & embarrassments, I should indeed be grateful.' H B/XXI/C/402-3.

2 Walpole had served in 1857 on an ecclesiastical commission with the Archbishop of Canterbury and three archdeacons. At a 31 May 1865 dinner, to discuss 'The Revision of the Liturgy', his fellow guests had included five bishops and the Archbishops of York and Dublin. *The Times* (4 Apr 1857, 1 Jun 1865).

3 Walpole would reply on 3 October: 'Poor Cookesleys letter is indeed a sad one. He is coming down to dine & sleep at my House to-night, when I will take the opportunity of talking the matter over with him: but it is really an extremely difficult matter to help him. Between ourselves, I fear he has been too much his own enemy; certainly he was so, when a Tutor at Eton. Nevertheless I should be heartily glad if something could be done for him.' H B/XXI/W/65. See also VI **2268A**&n1.

4 Cookesley on 1 October would thank D 'for your kind letter [*not found*] – so worthy of your generous heart. I can only assure you that I am deeply sensible of your affectionate expressions of willingness to serve me.' H B/XXI/C/404. In 1868 the Crown would appoint Cookesley to the vicarage of Tempsford, where he would remain until his death in 1880.

---

1 This letter has not been found.

2 See VII **3294**&n1.

3 As of 10 July, Naas was chief secretary for Ireland (a post he had held in 1852 and 1858-9 but without being in cabinet). He would become viceroy of India in 1868. Derby on 9 October would write to D that he had 'heard nothing of any wish on Naas's part to go to Bombay; and should be very sorry to send him there'. H B/XX/S/367.

If Gregory were his successor, it would be impossible to put him in the Cabinet,[4] & that wo[ul]d weaken yr Irish Government, wh: promises to be a success.

I hope, therefore, you will exercise yr influence with Naas to retain a post, in wh: / he may gain great distinction, & wh: may last longer than some think. Perhaps, yr interference will be unnecessary, for I can hardly think a man of heart & spirit wd. leave you at this moment.

Yrs ever | D.

If Naas really wants a permanent appointment, he had better take the Irish Mast[er] ship of the Rolls; too long vacant.[5]

4213   TO: SPENCER WALPOLE   Hughenden [Thursday] 27 September 1866
ORIGINAL: HOL [22]
EDITORIAL COMMENT: C of Ex paper, seal crossed out and 'Hughenden' written in.

Right Honorable | Mr Secy: Walpole   Hughenden | Septr 27 1866
My dear Walpole,

I have written to you twice, before this, today.[1]

When you were at Balmoral, I sent to the H.O. to enquire, whether they had any official account of the / numbers at the Birmingham Meeting, & received an idiotic reply,[2] that they had not, but that they cd. get, no doubt, some authentic information[.]

The reason I sent was, that, while the country was electrified by statements in the "Times", endorsed of course by Pall-Mall Gazettes, & all that sort of thing, that / there were 200,000 persons assembled &c &c,[3] I had been informed by a commercial traveller, of sense & observation, that he calculated there were not 20,000.

The H.O. has been very deficient in not having a trustworthy agent present at all these meetings, so that the Governmt. shd. have authentic information in their / possession.

I have reason to suspect, that the Manchester meeting was very inferior to the Birmingham & yet the "Times", for some sinister purpose, talks of 200,000 present,[4] when even the "Star" speaks only of half. The "Times" wants to force a Ref: Bill.[5]

---

4 William Gregory, a long-time L-C, had formally joined the Liberal party in 1865, following the death of Palmerston.
5 See **4209**n5.

---

1 See **4210** and **4211**.
2 Although this official reply has not been found, see **4191**&n6.
3 See **4191**&n6.
4 On 24 September there had been a reform meeting in Manchester at Campfield, 'a fine open plot of ground, well paved and drained ... [of] about 220,000 square feet ... Perhaps at no period of the meeting were there more than 80,000 to 100,000 in the square at once, but ... the total number present at various times did not fall much short of 200,000.' *The Times* (25 Sep 1866).
5 See **4206**&n3.

If the H.O. had been awake, this mischief might have been prevented. Cannot we get rid of Waddington?[6]

Yrs | D.

TO: LORD ELCHO   Hughenden [Thursday] 27 September 1866   **4214**

ORIGINAL: SRO [5]

EDITORIAL COMMENT: Hughenden paper.

The | Lord Elcho | M.P.   Septr 27 1866

My dear Lord

Your letter, from various reasons, has only just reached me.[1]

I thank you very heartily for it, & I can, sincerely, assure you, / that any suggestion, made by you to me on public affairs, & especially on a subject, wh: you have so mastered, as that, wh: formed the topic of yr communication, will always be received / by me with the utmost regard & respect.

Ever sincerely yours, | D.

TO: MONTAGU CORRY   [Hughenden] Friday 28 September 1866   **4215**

ORIGINAL: H B/XX/D/14

EDITORIAL COMMENT: C of Ex paper, seal crossed out. *Sic*: checque.

Montagu Corry Esqr   Friday. | Sept. 28 1866

My dear Montagu,

Will you have the kindness to send me £100 in 5£ notes, & use the balance of the checque for the two small accts. enclosed; one to be paid by a P.O. / to Aylesbury.[1]

I forgot, in my letter to Ld. Derby yesterday,[2] to enquire whether he wd. come from Balmoral to town, or go to Knowsley again. Enquire of George Barrington,[3] & ascertain, whether Ld Derby keeps ↑on↓ his villa at / Roehampton, as I see, by the papers, that Lady Webster's villa there, wh: was the one, I understood he had engaged ↑for 2 years,↓ is for sale with immediate possession.[4]

---

6 Horatio Waddington (1799-1867), BA 1820 and MA 1823 Trinity College, Cambridge, a barrister (Lincoln's Inn 1825), PC 1866, was permanent under-secretary of state for the home office from 1848 until his resignation (due to failing health) in 1867. *GM* (July 1867) 687-8. Corry on 9 September had informed D that 'Mr Waddington has no official estimate of the numbers of the Birmingham gathering; but could soon procure an estimate from a competent person.' H B/XX/CO/7.

---

1 Elcho on 19 September had written to D 'humbly to suggest the policy of appointing a Commission at once to verify the returns that were presented last Session & to obtain such further information bearing upon the franchise, present or proposed, in Town & County, as may form the basis of sound legislation upon the subject.' He reassured D that this 'would in no way commit your Govt. to any course of action' and that 'in any case you would have obtained accurate and reliable data for legislation for the use of yourself & others.' H B/XXI/E/129.

---

1 Among D's financial papers are receipts for payments to *BH* of £1.8.6 (1 October 1866) and to the South Bucks Agricultural Association of £3 (2 October 1866). H B/A/V/G/[unnumbered].

2 See **4212**.

3 George Barrington, elected MP (C) for Eye in July 1866, was Derby's private secretary while the latter was premier. *Disraeli, Derby* 379n7.

4 For Lady Webster, see I **169n14**. *MP* on 6 August had announced that 'The Earl and Countess of Derby

I am very anxious to see Ld. Derby, & I cannot go to Knowsley. Ld. D. said in his last letter, that he / shd. leave Balmoral on the 1st Octr,[5] so I don't care to write to him again there.

Yrs | D.

Irish affairs look very bright.[6]

4216

TO: LORD DERBY   Hughenden [Sunday] 30 September 1866
ORIGINAL: DBP Box 146/2
PUBLICATION HISTORY: M&B IV 476-7, paragraphs twelve to seventeen; Blake 454-5, snippets
EDITORIAL COMMENT: C of Ex paper, seal crossed out on all sheets and 'Hughenden Manor' written in on the first page. *Sic*: developement; made.

Hughenden Manor | Sept 30 1866

Right Honorable | The Earl of Derby | K.G.

My dear Lord,

I received your interesting letter from Balmoral[1] this morning.

You need not impress upon me the expediency of considering the best modes, whether by Resolution or otherwise, of bringing the Reform Question before the attention / of Parliament, in case you decide upon such appeal. The subject occupies my almost constant at consideration, & I shall endeavour to be prepared on all the points connected with it, when we meet: but it is really too vast, & difficult, to write about.

The immediate difficulty / I feel in the matter is this:

If we decide upon dealing with Reform, we shall have to introduce the subject almost immediately when Parliament meets: after an announcement of our purpose, the H of C. won't brook delay:

If, on the other hand, we decide against immediately dealing with the question, then, / we ought to be laying ground for future action, & give the House, if it wishes one, an opportunity to support us on the ground principle that information, wh: was generally acknowledged to be wanted, will be duly supplied.

Elcho has written to me about his Royal comm: I enclose his letter,[2] / wh: have the kindness to return.

---

have taken the villa formerly belonging to the late Sir Henry Webster at Roehampton, in order that the noble earl may, in the urgency of public business, be in the vicinity of town.' *The Times* on 22 September had advertised the following: 'In the choice and favourite Neighbourhood of Roehampton. – A capital Mansion, charmingly situate, with extensive lawns, pleasure grounds, gardens, paddocks, stabling, farm buildings, &c., extending over upwards of 18 acres, freehold, with immediate possession; late the residence of Lady Vassall Webster, deceased.' See **4413**&n1.

5 Derby had written on 18 September that if D had anything 'to send to me up to Saturday the 29th my address will be Balmoral, whither I go tomorrow.' H B/XX/S/365.

6 *The Times* on this day (28th) carried a report (dated the 26th) from Dublin stating that long-time MP (L) for Tipperary Laurence Waldron had 'surprised the public not a little' by coming 'forward as a supporter of the present Government.' He would be defeated at the 17 October elections. See also **4212** and, for D's less optimistic prognoses, **4209** and **4226**.

---

1 See **4207**&nn2-7.
2 See **4214**n1.

I rather shrink from R[oyal] C[ommission]s, as an abdication of our duties: but there might be other modes of enquiry, & of obtaining, ↑that↓ information, wh: we have, always, maintained was wanting; e.g. commissions about Boundaries, & so on.

But, if this is done, there shd. be no delay. If we / meet in Novr. & consider these things, & resolve to issue commissions, in December probably, it will be too late. It will look only like subterfuge.

Without troubling yourself to come up from Knowsley & holding a Cabinet, could you communicate with yr colleagues, & issue a Boundary / Commission? This would be a bonâ fide move, if taken at once, & supplementary measures, of the same kind, might be deferred till November.[3]

I know to do this wd. be difficult.

I agree in everything you say about the D. of Newcastle, but I wished you to know his views. By the bye, his brother might be in the Household.[4]

Until / the American Elections have taken place,[5] there will be no chance of anything like sense or moderation in Amer: politics; but there will be a chance then.

3 On 9 October, in a letter headed '*Confidential*', Derby would tell D that he could not undertake to act upon D's suggestion. 'Our Colleagues are scattered about in all directions; and even if I could satisfy myself as to the precise object and terms of the Commission, it would be a considerable time before I could collect their opinions, even if it were possible to do so satisfactorily in writing ... I come myself more and more to the conclusion that, in some shape or other, we must deal with it, and that immediately; but considering the great difficulty which every Government has found in framing a Bill, and the admitted fact that the question can only be settled by compromise, I see great advantages in dealing with it by Resolutions. In the first place, by introducing them, we put an end to the cry that we are the opponents of all Reform; no inconsiderable advantage if we should be driven to appeal to the Country. In the next place, there will, I think, be less likelihood of the necessity for such an appeal; and the House of Commons will not be sorry for an excuse which will postpone, at least for a year, a dissolution and a general Election. Then we are less committed to each several Resolution than we should be on the main provisions of a Bill; and whatever may be the point, if of sufficient importance to justify us in dissolving, the issue will be plain and simple, and the Opposition will have the credit of doing their best to obtain legislation. If moreover we get the House pledged to our *principles*, we shall be in a much better position for hereafter discussing details: and it will be difficult for the Radicals either to escape from Amendments, or so to frame them as not to clash with the moderate Liberals, and widen the existing breach. I think also that the issue of a Commission, with definite objects, under the sanction of a Parliamentary vote, will have advantages which will far more than compensate for the delay; and it seems to me that the *immediate* issue of a Commission, without such a sanction, would virtually pledge us to act, at the first possible moment, upon its recommendations. I have, with these views, and the better to explain my meaning, drawn up a very rough outline of such Resolutions as I think might be submitted, and which, if carried, would place us in velvet. You will see that I have adopted, in reference to the enquiries of the Commission, very much the view taken by Elcho, whose letter I return ... I ought to say that while I was at Balmoral the Queen expressed to me very strongly her wish to see the question settled *by us*; and told me that if She could in any way contribute to bring about an understanding between us and the moderate Liberals, we might depend on Her to do it. She is very friendly – very hostile to J. Russell and very much annoyed and disappointed, as well as displeased, with Gladstone's course. If it be thought desirable to enter, in the Resolutions, into more detail, it would be easy to do so: I only send you the enclosed as illustrating the course of proceeding which, as far as I am at present advised, seems to me the safest and best.' H B/XX/S/367. For an outline of the contents of Derby's enclosure ('a very rough outline' of resolutions), see Hawkins *Derby* 321.
4 The 6th Duke of Newcastle had three brothers: Lord Edward William Pelham-Clinton (1836-1907), Lord Arthur Pelham-Clinton (1840-1870) and Lord Albert Sidney Pelham-Clinton (1845-1884). On 24 September, Derby had mentioned that there would 'be a vacancy in the Household; if Burghley becomes a Peer', listing the names of nine possible candidates. H B/XX/S/366.
5 At the American congressional elections on 5 November 1866, Republicans would win by a landslide: 173 seats to the Democrats' 47.

Then, also, we must seriously consider our Canadian position, wh: is most illegitimate. An army maintained in a country, wh: does not permit us even to govern it! What an anomaly!

It never can be our / pretence, or our policy, to defend the Canadian Frontier agst the U.S.[6] If the Colonists can't, as a general rule defend themselves agst the Fenians, they can do nothing.[7] They ought to be, & must be, strong enough for that. Power & influence we shd. exercise in Asia; consequently in Eastern Europe, / consequently also in Western Europe, but what is the use of these Colonial Deadweights, wh: *we do not govern?*

I dont regret what we did the other day about Canada,[8] because the circumstances were very peculiar. A successful raid of the Fenians was not off the cards, wh: wd. / have upset your untried ministry, & might have produced an insurrection in Ireland – & it was not fair to the Canadians, when, at the last, they were making some attempts at self-defence, to allow them to be crushed in the bud of their patriotism. But the moment the American Elections are over, / we shd. withdraw the great body of our troops,[9] & foster a complete developement of self-government.

Leave the Canadians to defend themselves; recall the African Squadron;[10] give up the settlements on the W. coast of Africa; & we shall made a saving, wh: will, at the same time, enable us to build ships & / have a good budget.

What is more we shall have accomplished something definite, tangible for the good of the country. In these days, more than ever, the people look to results.[11]

6 D's views were not always thus. Speaking on the 'Defences of Canada' on 13 March 1865, he had stated that 'if at a moment like the present – a moment of revolution in North America – we find English colonies asserting the principle of their nationality, ... I cannot doubt that the course we should pursue is to assist in placing our North American provinces in a state of proper defence.' On 23 March, prior to voting with the majority (275-40) against a motion that '£50,000, for the Improvement of Defences at Quebec, be omitted from the proposed Vote', D had asked: 'why are we to doom Canada to the fate of being absorbed into the United States or becoming a mere dependency on some American republic?' *Hansard* CLXXVII cols 1570-8; CLXXVIII cols 154-60, 175.

7 D would reiterate this idea to war secretary Jonathan Peel on 4 October; see **4222**. The Fenian Brotherhood, founded in the United States in 1858 by expatriate Irishman John O'Mahony, sought to overthrow British rule in Ireland. The *Toronto Globe* would publish a detailed 'Fenian Plan of Campaign' predicting that the 'hundreds of Fenians hanging around Canadian cities at the present moment' would 'make a rising' and gain a foothold in Canada, which would 'then be thoroughly captured, a Fenian provisional Government ... established, local rulers appointed, and the people taxed for the support of the new order of things.' *The Times* (1 Oct 1867).

8 The government at this time was 'on the alert and in earnest in their desire to counteract or prevent the mischievous Fenian movement both at home and abroad. In addition to the numerous troops and military stores which have already been sent out to Canada, others in considerable numbers are about to follow immediately.' *The Times* (26 Sep 1866).

9 Britain would withdraw its troops from Canada only in 1871.

10 The Royal Navy, West Africa Squadron (formed in 1808 following passage of the 1807 Slave Trade Act), patrolled the coast and captured slave ships.

11 D in this letter has cribbed wholesale from a long letter to him by Ralph Earle (headed '*Private*') of 21 September: 'How *could* we send more troops to Canada? *That* policy is quite exploded. To guarantee Canada against the States is impossible. To protect themselves against the Fenians, the Colonists ought to be strong enough. Power & influence we should exercise in Asia, consequently in Eastern Europe, consequently also in Western Europe, but what is the use of these Colonial deadweights, wh: *we do not govern?* Leave the Canadians to defend themselves, recall the African Squadron, give up the settlements on the West Coast of Africa & you will have made a saving, wh: will enable you to build ships, &, at the same time, to make a good budget. What is more, you will have accomplished something definite, tangible for the good of the Country. In these days, more than ever, our people look to results.' H B/XX/E/398.

What we have done about Canada is perfectly defensible, if it is not looked upon as a permanent increase of / our Canadian establishm[en]ts. According to my accounts from the Continent, Hartington mentioned at more than one place, that our recent despatch of troops is to be made the great point of attack on the part of the Opposition.[12] May they long enjoy that venerable name, wh: I never yet read, or hear / without thinking there is something personal.

I thought the French circular a tissue of maladroit & contradictory humbug.[13]

Yours ever, | D.

Pakingtons letter wh: / I returned in the box, tho' long & clear, does not touch the real questions. They are two. The prodigality of our stores, wh: he says he has not investigated. The question of reliefs, wh: is a question of policy. The maintenance, or the reverse, of the African Squadron, for instance, wo[ul]d greatly, indeed mainly, affect it[.]

It is, therefore, utterly absurd in / his talking about Gladstone's popularity-hunting budgets, to wh: the efficiency of the Navy has been sacrificed, when he has not come to any conclusion ⌈about⌋, or has not completely mastered, the two points on wh: all hinges.

The more I see & hear about the Admy., the more I feel the feebleness & absurdity / of the administrative scheme of that Department.[14] Power is exercised there by individuals, who have no responsibility. If something is proposed, Sir A. Milne will resign, I am told, or Sir John Hay, if the proposition is insisted on. Fancy [*two lines of words crossed out*] / a Secy. of the Treasury, or an U. Sec: of State, threatening to resign because he did not approve of his Chief's policy! The Admy. shd. be remodelled on the general scheme: a Secy. of State with Under-Secretaries.

D.

TO: MONTAGU CORRY   [Hughenden, Sunday] 30 September 1866   4217
ORIGINAL: H B/XX/D/15
EDITORIAL COMMENT: C of Ex paper.

My dear Montagu,   Sep 30 1866

You need not hurry yourself about the cost of the African ports.[1] It will do after Blenheim, I mean[.][2]

---

12 D would also mention this to Peel (n7); D's 'accounts' came from Berlin, where former war secretary Hartington was staying.

13 Although this document has not been found, D may refer to 'The Imperial Circular', dated 16 September at Paris and published in *The Times* on the 18th, 'addressed by the French Government to its representatives in foreign countries' and signed '"Lavallette."' For French foreign minister La Valette, see **4294n4**.

14 The lords commissioners of the admiralty in 1866 were Sir John Pakington (first lord), vice-admiral Sir Alexander Milne (first sea lord), vice-admiral Sir Sydney Colpoys Dacres (second sea lord), rear-admiral George Henry Seymour (third sea lord), rear-admiral Sir John Dalrymple-Hay (fourth sea lord) and Charles Du Cane (civil lord). Blake (ph) replaces 'feebleness' with 'fecklessness.'

---

1 See **4209**&n4.

2 As great-grandson of 4th Duke of Marlborough (his mother, Lady Harriet Anne Ashley-Cooper, was the daughter of 6th Earl of Shaftesbury and granddaughter of 4th Duke of Marlborough), Corry may have visited Blenheim occasionally. Activities at this period included the Marlboroughs 'entertaining a select

I don't like the enclosed despatch for Lord Derby[3] to go unnecessarily by post. I heard / from him this morning, & this is my answer. I send it to you, with the hope, there may be a bag going to him this evening from D.S.[4] but if not, you must send this by post: only, in that case, seal it / with the office seal.

D.

4218

TO: [SIR HENRY BULWER]   [Hughenden, Sunday] 30 September 1866
ORIGINAL: H B/XXI/B/1339a
EDITORIAL COMMENT: C of Ex paper, seal crossed out.

The answer of the Chr of the Excheqr to Sir. H. B.   Sept 30. 66
My dear B.
I am quite unable to answer yr letter at this moment.[1] It requires a knowledge of circumstances with wh: I have no immediate acquaintance, & / I think it would be inconvenient, & more than inconvenient, to correspond with any of my colleagues on such matters. I am now in the country, & it is not improbable [I] may not be able to see / those, with whom I shd. wish to confer, for a month.[2]

I will take care, however, to bear your letter in mind.

Yrs sincerely, I D.

4219

TO: SPENCER WALPOLE   Hughenden [Monday] 1 October 1866
ORIGINAL: HOL [11]
EDITORIAL COMMENT: C of Ex paper, seal crossed out and 'Hughenden Manor' written in. In the fourth paragraph 'Mr' has been written over 'Re'. *Sic*: Horsenden, Brazenose.

Private   Hughenden Manor I Oct 1 1866
Right Honorable I Mr Secretary Walpole
My dear Walpole,
I am sorry to have to trouble you about little matters, when, I doubt not, both of us have plenty to do with great ones – but / a strong county pressure forces me, again, to introduce to your notice↑, the name↓ of the Reverend William Edwards

---

party' on 20 September and the annual harvest home festival on the 27th. Foxhunts were organized at Blenheim regularly. *MP* (20 Sep, 1 Oct 1866).
3 See **4216**.
4 Corry on 1 October would reply that Derby's letter 'is to go in his bag.' H B/XX/CO/10.

---

1 Bulwer on 22 September had written to D from the British Embassy in Paris an obsequious letter headed 'Private & confidential'. Retired as ambassador to Constantinople since 1865, he told D, 'my mind does not counsel me to indefinite idleness' and asked whether he (Bulwer) should communicate with the foreign office. He went on at length to describe 'where I think I could be usefully employed.' In light of the imminent vacancy of the post of French ambassador, he stressed his familiarity with France as well as his 'general acquaintance with European affairs' and suggested Vienna, 'supposing Paris disposed of.' H B/XXI/B/1339.
2 *The Times* on 21 September had reprinted from the *Scotsman* an announcement that D would be the guest of the Earl of Lonsdale at Lowther Castle in October, and that 'the Conservative party in Carlisle are understood to be already arranging for a grand banquet, to which Mr. Disraeli will be invited.' Aside from a brief visit to Highclere Castle (26-8 October), the DS would spend most of October at Hughenden.

Partridge, of Horsenden House, as a Candidate for ↑an↓ Inspectorship of Prisons.[1]

I introduced his name to / you in 1858↑, with the same object↓.[2]

All I can say is, he is most competent for the office, having been, for many years, one of our most active magistrates, & having devoted his time & thought to prison discipline. If, therefore, you had an Inspectorship, & did / not exactly know what to do with it, you cd. not appoint a better man.

Mr Partridge is of Brazenose, & is a man of some estate, as well as holding the small living of his parish, to wh: he preferred himself.

Yours sincerely, | D.[3]

TO: [MONTAGU CORRY]   [Hughenden, Monday 1 October 1866]   **4220**

ORIGINAL: H B/XXI/H/301a

EDITORIAL COMMENT: C of Ex paper. Endorsed by Corry: 'Shall I answer as below? M.C.', beside which D has added: 'Yes D.'. Docketed by Corry: 'Oct 1/66', beneath which he has written 'Answered. Oct 11/66'. Beneath this, someone has written 'Sir John Hay.' *Dating*: by context; see n1.

Report to me on the enclosed letter of Sir J.D. Hay.[1] I know nothing of the affair.[2]

D

---

1 William Partridge had written to D from Horsendon House, Bucks, on 28 August 1866: 'During my interview with you at Hughenden last week I ventured to solicit your interest with Mr Walpole as a Candidate for an Inspectorship of Prisons and Reformatory Schools. You then requested me to address a letter to you stating my qualifications, which though well known to yourself would be necessary for his Information ... I went to Brasenose College Oxford and took my B.A. degree in 1831 ... In 1840 I was made a Magistrate by Lord Lyndhurst ... In 1845 the Duke of Buckingham presented me to the Rectory of Horsendon ... and though I have never before made any application for Preferment, yet I feel desirous of obtaining more active Employment. I have taken much interest in the working of the Reformatory system and the question of Secondary Punishment, and the noble President of the Council will recollect my being frequently associated with himself in carrying out Prison work at Aylesbury.' H B/XXI/P/132.

2 See VII **3196**&n1.

3 Walpole would reply on 3 October that although he would place Partridge's name on the list of candidates, 'I ought to tell you that the vacancies are few, and that there are one or two Candidates, already down – one especially recommended by The Lord Chancellor, whom I could hardly pass by.' H B/XXI/W/65.

---

1 Sir John Dalrymple-Hay, as a public works loan commissioner, had written on 1 October asking D to expedite the settlement of 'the postal subsidy for the Portpatrick Railway' (Scotland), which the treasury had promised ten years ago. 'Government also promised to complete Portpatrick harbour for the transmission of the mails by Steamers ... Government failed to complete Portpatrick harbour & they have as yet refused to arrange for the conveyance of the Mails ... The Limited Mail runs to Castle Douglas a small town on the system & there the Limited Mail stops short & refuses to run over the railway made under a Government guarantee which is still unfulfilled. The practical result is this – My letters leave London at 8:40 at night reach Castle Douglas at 6 am and are not delivered here until 1 PM – whereas they should be here by 7.30 am. I thus can not answer my letters the same day. Now what must this be to men of business and the great community of Belfast, who also could save the day if this arrangement were carried out ... If you could signify to me that the consideration of this matter would soon terminate favourably, it would be an act of justice & politically very useful both here and at Belfast.' H B/XXI/H/301.

2 Someone (most likely G.W. Hunt) has written beneath D's signature: 'We have called for a Report from the Post Office on the subject of the Portpatrick & Donaghada communication[;] until we receive such report the matter is not ripe for decision. GWH 9/10'. On 15 March 1867 a delegation (including Dalrymple-Hay) would meet with Derby to discuss 'the mail service to Belfast and the north of Ireland *viâ* Portpatrick and Donaghada.' In the House on 14 July 1868 in committee of supply there would be a vote of £20,000 'for compensation to the Portpatrick Railway Company'. *The Times* (16 Mar 1867, 15 Jul 1868); *Hansard* CXCIII col 1210.

ORIGINAL: H B/XX/D/16
PUBLICATION HISTORY: M&B IV 482, omitting the last sentence; the name 'Anderson' appears as 'A——'
EDITORIAL COMMENT: C of Ex paper, seal crossed out and 'Hughenden' written in.

Hughenden | Oct 2 1866

What you write about Mr Anderson sending the "Compare" regularly to Mr Gladstone is distressing.[1]

It appears to me a proceeding highly irregular, & fraught with injurious consequences, while, at the same time, I feel reluctance / in interfering, where Mr Gladstone is concerned.

If Mr Gladstone, on the ground alleged, as I understand by Mr Anderson, had asked me for this privilege, considering his eminence & services, howr. reluctant to do so, I shd not have hesitated to have accorded / it; but there is a great difference in such a proceeding sanctioned by me, & a communication, wh: has the appearance of being clandestine, between a permanent officer of the Government & an ex-head of his Department.

I do not know of any precedent for such a course, & / Mr Anderson has, certainly, no right to make one.

Where is the line to be drawn between communications between Mr Anderson & a late Chanr. of the Exchequer? Why shd. they not refer to future Bulg Budgets, as well as to past?

Such a proceeding has a / tendency to destroy that complete confidence, wh: ought to exist betn. me & an officer in Mr Anderson's position.

I should wish that you should have conferred on this matter, with Sir Stafford Northcote who, from being a friend of / Mr Gladstone, would have considered the circumstances witht prejudice agst him, but Sir S. is at Balmoral.[2]

In the meantime, consult Mr. Hamilton confidentially on the matter, & report to me.[3]

1 Corry had written to D on 1 October: 'Is this proper? Mr [William George] Anderson [auditor of the civil list] sends Gladstone a copy of the "compare" weekly; – and has given as his reason to one of the Treasury clerks that he thinks it fair that an outgoing Chancellor of the Exchequer should be kept informed of the working of his Budget till the end of the Financial year!!' H B/XX/CO/10. On a separate page Corry would write in 1903: 'There was a row! & I dont think Mr Anderson ever spoke to me again R/03.'
2 Northcote had arrived at Balmoral on Saturday 6 October as Minister in attendance upon the Queen. *The Times* (10 Oct 1866).
3 Corry would reply on 4 October: 'I have seen [treasury secretary] Mr [George Alexander] Hamilton who shares your feeling as to the impropriety of sending the "compares" to Mr Gladstone. He undertakes to speak to Mr Anderson on the subject when he returns and forbid the continuance of the habit. I hear today that Mr Anderson makes no secret of the matter, and that he even on one occasion asked one of the Clerks to *copy out* the compare on Saturday, – being the day on which it is sent to you, – our printed copies not arriving here till Monday afternoon. The Clerk refused, knowing it was for Gladstone. As the affair is known to nearly all the office, Hamilton will be able to rebuke Anderson without mentioning his informant, which probably you would prefer. It is a good feature in the case that he did not make any secret of his sending the compares.' Corry would inform D on 6 October that 'Hamilton *at once*, and *proprio motu*, expressed his strong disapproval of the fact I informed him of: and it was not till he had declared his determination to interfere that I mentioned your name. He spoke to me again yesterday on the subject, saying that he, as head of the office, would desire that the practice should be discontinued, as being an infringement of the regulations.' H B/XX/CO/11, 13.

Mr Anderson writes to me, that he himself has gone to Scotland, & will be absent, probably, three weeks.[4]

D.

TO: JONATHAN PEEL   Hughenden [Thursday] 4 October 1866   **4222**

ORIGINAL: H B/XIII/91

EDITORIAL COMMENT: A copy by Montagu Corry; see **4223**.

Hughenden Manor. Private. | Oct 4. 1866

Rt Honble | Secy Lt General Peel.

My dear General,

I have authorized by this post the Pay-Master General[1] to honor the bills of Capt. Warlow to an amount not exceeding £60.000, as the War Office wishes.[2] I must, however, impress upon you the great importance of avoiding if possible, a supplementary estimate on this matter, on the meeting of Parliament. I hear from Berlin / where Hartington has been staying, that the opposition mean to make our Canadian Policy their cheval de bataille on the reassembling of our House.[3] No doubt, under ordinary circumstances it is liable to much imputation; as the maintenance by the mother country of a vast and expensive force in a Colony wh. does not condescend to be governed by us, is absurd and indefensible at the first glance: – but the / peculiar circumstances of the present case, which possibly involved not merely

---

4 This letter has not been found.

---

1 D's letter to paymaster-general Stephen Cave has not been found.

2 Captain T.P. Warlow, RA, was assistant superintendent of the Royal Small Arms Factories, Birmingham. LPOD (1865). Peel would tell D in a '*Private*' letter on 6 October that he had been in Scotland when Warlow was sent to the United States to purchase arms under instructions from the colonial secretary; 'but the instant I heard of it I wrote to Carnarvon to say that if I was to be responsible for the expenditure the instructions must proceed from me and Capt Warlow must report what he was doing to me and not to the Colonial Office who had nothing to do with it. I enclose a copy of the letter I directed to be written to Capt Warlow and he was further written to privately to say that he was not to go and lay out 60,000£ merely because he had got authority to do so – but that he was only to purchase such arms as were absolutely required ... I have seen a private letter from Capt Warlow in which he says he had re[ceive]d a telegram from [gov gen of the Province of Canada] Lord Monk [*sic*] saying that 5000 rifles would be sufficient and that he had purchased them and I hope he is now on his road home and I trust that he will not have spent more than 30,000 including the ammunition but the instant we hear from him I will let you know the exact sum and I will endeavour to pay it out of the Supplemental vote for converting arms, as I do not think the Contractors would be able to make all their deliveries within the financial year.' The 7 September 1866 letter from war under-secretary the Earl of Longford instructed Warlow that 'no new engagement should be entered into which will not admit of the Arms purchases being delivered by the date specified', and that he was to return to England 'with the least possible delay'. H B/XXI/P/154a, b.

3 Peel (n2) did 'not think that there is any chance of the late Government making an attack upon us on account of what we have done for Canada.' He had received 'rather a cool private letter from Lord Russell in which he expressed a hope that I would excuse him for urging our sending as many of the very best arms as we possibly could to Canada in consideration of the great loyalty the Canadians have displayed. I thought it cool considering the total number of breechloaders his Government handed over to me was 12 and that they never proposed to have any more until November ... I do not think Canada will be the battlefield selected by either the Fenians or the late Government.' Corry would reassure D on 5 October: 'I suppose you do not seriously fear Hartington's attack on your Canadian policy; I hear nothing but approval of it from both sides.' H B/XX/CO/12.

a successful invasion of Canada, but a consequent insurrection in Ireland, I think, justified the course we resolved on.[4]

There are also at this moment other considerations not of an ordinary character, of which we must not lose sight.

The impending election struggle in the U.S. attracts the emulous and / hostile spirit of both parties to our American Colonies. It would not be wise or generous ostentatiously to desert them at such a moment, when they are making, apparently, a sincere effort to organise their self defence, and are perhaps on the eve of accomplishing in Confederation a stronger political organisation.[5] Under ordinary circumstances however, which, after the American elections, will, I trust reassert themselves, / it would, I conceive, not be our policy, in the event of a war with the U.S. to undertake the defence of the Canadian frontier; while, certainly, if the colonists cannot defend themselves from the mere Fenians, they must be, indeed unworthy of self-government. I hope therefore when the elections are over, which will be before the meeting of Parliament, we / shall begin to consider about the withdrawal of our forces from Canada. I trust we shall be able to meet Parliament with a clear and definite policy on the subject.

A supplementary estimate will, however, precipitate the opposition move by giving them an immediate opportunity, which, otherwise they could only obtain / with difficulty and delays.

What is your impression as to Public feeling respecting Parliamentary Reform?[6]

Yrs sincerely | D.

4223 TO: [MONTAGU CORRY]   [Hughenden, Thursday] 4 October 1866
ORIGINAL: H B/XX/D/17
PUBLICATION HISTORY: M&B IV 464, sentences two to seven and the sixth paragraph
EDITORIAL COMMENT: C of Ex paper. The context suggests D is at Hughenden but has neglected to cross out the seal; *cf* **4225**.

October 4. 1866

Be careful to date your notes.

Longman is pressing me about the speeches.[1] Have you confidence in the list you sent me?[2] For example, on acceding to office in 1852, I had to / speak on a Reform

4 See **4216**&nn6-9.
5 The 1864 Charlottetown (1-9 September) and Quebec (10-27 October) conferences would lead up to the London Conference of December 1866 and the drafting of the British North America Act, which would be presented to the Queen on 11 February 1867 and given royal assent on 29 March. The Act, uniting the Province of Canada with New Brunswick and Nova Scotia into the 'Dominion of Canada', would come into effect on 1 July 1867.
6 Peel (n2) would tell D that 'The only expression I hear of public feeling with regard to Reform is that Mr Bright's Speeches are alarming everybody – and that if he would only make one a week Ld Derby might remain in office as long as he liked.'

---

1 Thomas Longman had written to D on 1 October 1866 on Farnborough Hill, Hants. paper, the address crossed out and 'Pater Noster Row' (Thomas and his brother William had their offices at 39 Paternoster Row) written in: 'It will give me much pleasure to publish your speeches on Parliamentary Reform, and as you are so good as to propose to guarantee the cost, I will accept that obliging proposal. I wait your further directions'. H E/VII/A6.
2 This list has not been found.

motion – probably one of Hume's, in wh: I took occasion to observe, that, in any future change, the claims of the working class ought to be considered. They had been unwisely dealt with, & neglected, in the measure / of 1852.[3]

My recollection, faint, is that my observations were brief. They occasioned much discontent, I remember, & particularly at Court.[4] Events have proved they were just, & I felt they were in accordance with true Tory principles. Is / this the speech described in yr list as Mar 25. 1852 v. 120. p 136 – because it seems longer (16 cols.) than I supposed? Or, by any chance, have you passed it over? There shd. be no mistake about it. Let me know[.][5]

D.

On second thoughts, I have written to Longman[6] with a flying / zeal, so that you may insert the list, after revision.

Beg him to direct the printer to send the proofs to D.S. so that you can regularly forward them to me.

I think it worth / consideration, whether you might not figure in the title-page as Editor. It might assist yr introduction into public life. We can think about this.[7]

I must trouble you / to copy this letter to Genl. Peel,[8] & then seal & forward it to W[ar] O[ffice].

Longman, who is a great swell, is at his Country seat,[9] but you had better send your letter to Paternoster Row, & by messenger.[10]

D.

3 Corry would reply on 5 October that he had 'found the Speech you mention; – April 27, 1852. – 3 columns. The importance thereof shows me the necessity of revising the list even more carefully than I intended, and I think it possible that I may find that I have omitted one or two other short speeches, which I may have passed over on account of their brevity, but which may be as pregnant as that you today mention. You need fear no omissions in the list which I shall tomorrow send to Longmans; – I cannot today complete it to my satisfaction.' H B/XX/CO/12. D's 27 April 1852 speech, 'On Mr Locke King's Motion on the County Franchise', would be included in Corry's edition.
4 See VI **2279**&n1.
5 See **4194**n4.
6 This letter has not been found.
7 Corry (n3) would tell D he would be proud 'to figure on the title page, as Editor of the Reform Speeches of one, of whom I have this week heard two political enemies say, – "Mr Disraeli knows more about Reform than any other man in England."'
8 See **4222**.
9 Architect Henry Edward Kendall had completed Farnborough Hill for Thomas Longman in 1863. The magnificent country house is characterized by turrets, gables, chimneys, stone friezes and ornate woodwork.
10 Corry would write to D on 8 October: 'I found it necessary to go to Longman's today, and see the regent for the time being. He asks for a copy of the requisite vols. of Hansard, at the same time warning me that the printers will probably soil them to a very great extent. He also assumes that, beyond mere errors of the press, you will wish to revise some parts of the Speeches, and points out that doing so after the type is set up, may almost double the cost of publishing ... I have detected another omission. viz two Speeches on "Parliamentary Voters (Ireland) Bill" – one of 7, the other of 4 columns. anno 1850. I conclude you would wish them inserted. Longmans will print for you as fast as you can correct the press, and promise, when once the matter is in hand, to have it out almost as soon as you may choose to name, – certainly in less than a month. M.C. He is considering the best form of type & page.' H B/XX/CO/14. The two speeches (25 February and 10 May 1850) would not be included in Corry's edition.

4224

TO: [MONTAGU CORRY]   [Hughenden, Friday] 5 October [1866]

ORIGINAL: H B/IX/D/6a

EDITORIAL COMMENT: A memo in D's hand. *Dating*: by context; see n1.

This case requires attention.

Perhaps you will lay it officially before the authorities, so that I may have a reply to show to the father.

At the same time, I wish the matter to be strongly represented privately – there is a general impression in this part of the world, that the interests of our fellow subjects in India, who die there, are much neglected.[1]

I brought, in the last Sess:, the case of a ↑Bucks↓ soldier before the House of Commons – Hartington's reply was not deemed satisfactory here.[2]

D. | Oct 5

4225

TO: [MONTAGU CORRY]   Hughenden [Monday] 8 October [1866]

ORIGINAL: H B/XX/D/18

EDITORIAL COMMENT: C of Ex paper, seal crossed out and 'Hughenden Manor' written in.

Octr 8 | Hughenden Manor

It is not impossible I may be in town tomorrow for an hour or so – &, in that case, I shall be, probably, in D.S. about 4 or 5 o'ck: when I hope to see you.

I think Sir John Hay's direction is

    Dunragit

    Glenluce

but you have his letter.[1]

See Hamilton about the Aberdeen University, & tell him that I do not wish the settlement, wh: I / made in 1858 9 to be departed from.[2]

The Scotch shall never have any favors from me, until they return more Tory

---

1 Charles Strange on 4 October 1866 had written to D from High Wycombe for assistance in obtaining information about the cause of his son Charles's sudden death (in India on 3 October 1865) and to have his personal effects forwarded to him. Unanswered letters to the Indian authorities led Strange in May 1866 to contact the India Office. At their suggestion he had written to the administrator-general of Bengal at Calcutta but had received no reply. Strange's letter to D is docketed (perhaps by Corry) 'ansd as within sending Memo. C. of E. will do all he can Oct. 20.' H B/IX/D/6a. See **4238**n15.

2 On 22 May 1865, Darby Griffith (L-C) had presented the case of Lieut-Col William Gregory Dawkins (1825-1914), Coldstream Guards, of Over Norton, Chipping Norton, Oxfordshire. Dawkins had been imprisoned without trial for eleven days in 1860 for not shaking the hand of Lord Rokeby, but merely saluting. Griffith called the secret proceedings of the first court of enquiry (July 1864), after which Dawkins was forced to relinquish his duties, 'pure despotism'. The Marquess of Hartington, then under-secretary of war, admitted not having read the proceedings and refused 'to give any pledge that the subject shall receive any further consideration.' On 26 May Griffith, via an amendment, proposed an address to the Queen requiring that all correspondence relating to the first enquiry and up to the second (January 1865) be tabled. Hartington replied at length, concluding: 'I decline to lay the papers on the table ... I decline to enter into the other charges that have been raked up.' The amendment was defeated. In 1871 Dawkins would charge Rokeby with libel and slander, but his appeal would be dismissed, with costs. *Hansard* CLXXIX cols 641-63, 879-905, 1336-7; *The Times* (29 Jun 1875).

---

1 See **4220**n1. The address is that of Sir John Dalrymple-Hay's seat.

2 For the Universities (Scotland) Act of 1858, see VII **3160**&n3.

~~Conservative~~ members to the H of C.,[3] & of all / parts of Scotland, the most odious are the Universities. They have always been our bitterest & most insulting foes. Of course, I have not said this to the D. of R.[4]

Lady Jerseys letter to Berkeley Sqre to be forwarded.[5]

D.

TO: [MONTAGU CORRY]   Downing Street, Thursday [11 October 1866]   **4226**

ORIGINAL: H B/XX/D/19

EDITORIAL COMMENT: C of Ex paper. *Dating*: by context; see n1.

Thursday

I go by 5 o'ck: train.[1] Your Irish news is Rash.[2]

I fear the Ultra-Montane party[3] as Dub: Ev. Mail calls them, i.e. the Real Irish Cats have prevailed on Rome – & / may carry White.[4] Very vexatious.

I can't sanction the Irish job. It is too gross, & I am glad to save our menaced balances. Tell Hunt, however, to / hold back his decision, if possible, until the Elections are over.[5]

D. Baxter will be with me in a few minutes. I have a long despatch from Ld. Derby[6] this morning, / wh: comes very apropos.

Yours | D.[7]

---

3 Elected Scottish Liberals invariably outnumbered Tories at general elections: 1832 (43-10), 1841 (31-22), 1857 (38-15), 1865 (41-12). McCalmont xxii.

4 Charles Henry Gordon-Lennox, 6th Duke of Richmond, had been named chancellor of the University of Aberdeen (a life appointment) in 1861.

5 This letter has not been found. Lady Jersey would die at home at 38 Berkeley Square on 26 January 1867. See **4312**&n1.

------

1 D would return to Hughenden on this day (11 October 1866) by the 5 *pm* train. H acc.

2 Corry on 5 October had written optimistically to D that 'Ld Lismore has written to [Laurence] Waldron giving him his support; his neutrality seemed more than we could hope for at first. In other ways things are looking very well in Tipperary, and there is a fair prospect of a walk-over. Falmouth is at best quite an "outside chance" for us; [Jervoise] Smith has both money and manners. He is much too good a fellow to be a Radical, I should have thought. [Junior treasury lord] Gerard Noel says the registrations generally are in our favor.' On 6 October he had told D: 'We do not yet know if Charles White will accept the Tipperary invitation. I am inclined to think he will not.' H B/XX/CO/12, 13.

3 Adherents of Ultramontanism emphasize the supremacy of the Pope, who lives *ultra montes*, 'beyond the mountains' (the Alps).

4 At the 17 October Tipperary by-election, Charles William White would defeat Laurence Waldron (L-C) 3,419 to 2,865. White (1838-1890), fifth son of 1st Baron Annaly, was a captain in the Scots Fusilier Guards and MP (L) for Tipperary 1866-75. *The Times* on 6 October had carried a report from Dublin stating that 'the contest will be full of interest' because White, 'though a Protestant, will be supported by the Roman Catholic Archbishop, Dr. [Patrick] Leahy, and his clergy; while Mr. Waldron, a Catholic gentleman connected by property with the county and personally held in the highest estimation, will be opposed with all their influence.' In March 1867, the results would be challenged by petitions charging White with 'intimidation, violence, and undue influence', Waldron claiming that 'divers of the Roman Catholic clergy' had compelled electors to vote for White. *The Times* (26, 29, 30 Mar and 1, 2, 4, 5, 6 Apr 1867). See **4254**&n2.

5 Possibly related to Irish railway loans. See **4373**&n2.

6 For Derby's 9 October letter, see **4216**n3.

7 See also **4236**.

4227

4227   TO: MONTAGU CORRY   [Hughenden, Friday 12 October 1866]
ORIGINAL: H B/XXI/K/100
EDITORIAL COMMENT: A note from D written at the bottom of a letter from Edward Kenealy dated 12 October 1866.[1]

This is a troublesome fellow, who once dedicated to me a poem:[2] genus irritabile. Mr Kenealy – must not, altogether, ↑be neglected.↓ Consult the Lord Chancellor's Secy. – & report to me.[3]

     Yrs D

4228   TO: LORD DERBY   Hughenden [Friday] 12 October 1866
ORIGINAL: DBP Box 146/2
EDITORIAL COMMENT: C of Ex paper, seal crossed out and 'Hughenden Manor' written in. *Sic*: its'.

Hughenden Manor | Oct. 12 1866

Right Honorable | The Earl of Derby | K.G.
My dear Lord,
On my return to this place last night from town, where I had been up mainly to see Mr Dudley Baxter,[1] I found yr letter of the 10th.,[2] too late to reply by / return of post, &, therefore, I send this up to town ↑this morning↓ by my servant, so that, I trust, you will receive it, as soon, as if the post had not been missed.

---

1 Edward Kenealy had heard 'that some of my *Juniors* on the circuit are applying to the Chancellor for rank as Queen's Counsel' and, wishing 'not to be passed over', had enclosed a copy of his letter to the Chancellor (Lord Chelmsford), hoping that D would 'kindly send his Lordship a line in my favour.' H B/XXI/K/100, 100a. See **4243**&n1.
2 See VIII **3745**&nn1-3. Kenealy had dedicated his 570-page *A New Pantomime* (1865) 'To The Right Hon. B. Disraeli, M.P. ... the first and kindest of Critics on this Poem in its fragmentary form' and 'the most illustrious living Orator and Statesman ... one who also as a Writer ranks with the highest on the roll of Fame. For these rare qualities the world admires you; but for my own part, I value more that noble candour and majestic integrity of soul which win from all who approach you love and attachment ... That you are now misunderstood by many is but the fate which unites you with all who achieve; but history will do justice to one of the truest, brightest, and most disinterested public characters that ever illuminated our country's annals.'
3 Corry would write to D on 16 October: 'I know Kenealy, – he being on my Circuit. He is not held in high repute, though reckoned very clever, and deservedly so in some ways. There is no better advocate on the Circuit, for a man whose case is nearly desperate, and who is not scrupulous as to the mode of extricating himself. I have heard him make some splendid defences.' H B/XX/CO/16.

---

1 See **4226**.
2 Derby on 10 October had written to D a letter marked '*Confidential*' enclosing a letter, received that morning, from Sir Hugh Cairns. 'I will thank you to return it without loss of time, as I will defer answering it till I hear from you; though we have really no alternative but to accept his resignation. It will however be a very heavy loss to us, and you will feel the want of him much in the House of Commons; but the grounds on which he places it, and in which he has long placed it, are such that we cannot refuse him. The matter presses also for immediate decision, as the same post has brought me a letter from the Lord Chancellor, announcing that Lord Justice [Sir James] Knight Bruce has actually sent in his resignation, and desires it may take place on or before the 22d of this month! As soon therefore as I hear from you, I will write both to Cairns and to [John] Rolt, to offer him the Attorney Generalship, in pursuance of the arrangement to which [William] Bovill gave his assent on his appointment. It is desirable that he should have early notice, on account of its vacating his County. Should he decline, which however I hardly expect, we must make Bovill Attorney. We could not put any one else over his head. I am as much annoyed as I know you will be by this contretemps – but there is no help for it.' H B/XX/S/368.

It is a great blow, & comes to me unexpectedly,[3] for I wd. not believe it, & always thought something wd. occur to save us. He was / my right arm in a great struggle,[4] & if he had only a little imagination, & a little heart, would have been, by far, the first man in the House of Commons. Indeed, if he had had only a little imagination, & a little heart, he wd. not have deserted / you at this great crisis, wh: may be historic.[5]

I agree with you not a moment shd. be lost in communicating with Rolt, but, I fear, he will not accept the post, from the insecurity of his seat, wh:, locally, I have bad accounts of.[6] / If he refuses, Bovill cannot be again passed over;[7] he is a sharp man in little things, but in great debate, quite useless. But if we did pass him over, wh: is impossible, what better man have we? Who indeed for a Solicitor?

I will write on / no other matters at this moment.

I only received yr interesting despatch on Reform: in the course of the day I will endeavour to respond to its' contents.[8]

Yrs ever, | D.

TO: LORD DERBY   Hughenden [Friday] 12 October 1866 4229
ORIGINAL: DBP Box 146/2
PUBLICATION HISTORY: M&B IV 454-5
EDITORIAL COMMENT: C of Ex paper, seal crossed out and 'Hughenden Manor' written in. *Sic*: to be; forefend.

Confidential   Hughenden Manor | Oct 12 1866
Right Honorable | The Earl of Derby | K.G.
My dear Lord,[1]

I had no idea, when you first wrote to be about "Resolutions", that you contemplated the possibility of not legislating the Session they were passed. If we can / succeed in that, we ~~are~~ shall, indeed, be on velvet. This view throws quite a new light on our position, &, therefore, I will not trouble you, now, with any remarks on the

---

3 Stanley on 1 November would note that Cairns, attorney-general only since 10 July, had 'made it a condition of accepting office that he should be allowed so to retire if the occasion presented itself: we have therefore nothing to complain of though the loss to us in debate is serious.' *Disraeli, Derby* 269. Cairns would succeed Sir James Knight-Bruce as lord justice of appeal. See **4234**&n2.
4 The defeat of the Russell-Gladstone reform bill in June. See also, *eg*, VII **3115**&n1. Cairns would tell D on 16 October that he had learned from Derby about 'some of the kind expressions you had used to him, as indeed you had formerly used to me, of regret at the loss of my aid in the Ho of C.' He most regretted 'the idea that the Governmt, & you as the leader in the Ho of C, can suffer inconvenience by the step I have taken', and would thank D 'warmly & gratefully, may I say affectionately, for the many friendly words & acts I have had from you in our long & hard fought battles.' H B/XX/CA/9.
5 For similar comments by D about Cairns to Sir Stafford Northcote and Montagu Corry, see **4234** and **4238**.
6 John Rolt would succeed Cairns as attorney-general on 29 October, be knighted on 10 November and be returned unopposed for Gloucestershire W on 15 November.
7 Sir William Bovill would succeed Sir William Erle as chief justice of the common pleas in November 1866, Sir John Karslake replacing Bovill as solicitor-general.
8 For Derby's 9 October letter, see **4216**n3; for D's reply, see **4229**.

---

1 D is replying to Derby's 9 October letter (**4216**n3).

comparative advantages of Bills or Resolutions, in / case, as I now conclude, the Cabinet resolves on acting.

It will, I think, be quite unnecessary to have Cabinet Committees of preparation, as of yore; there is so much previous knowledge, now, on the main subject, that these preliminary investigations are / unnecessary, while they tend to jealousy.

The time for meeting will quite suit me.[2]

I shall endeavour to draw up a series of Resolutions in your vein.[3] They must, however, be distinct enough for us to fall back upon, as a clear policy, for the / country, in case we are forced to appeal to it, wh: Heaven forefend!

I came down yesterday in company ~~of~~ with a Bucks gentleman, who had been staying on a visit ~~with~~ to the Duke of Somerset. His Grace was very sore & indignant about / Pakington's statement respecting the Reserves of the Navy,[4] wh: the Duke said was the most rash & unfounded declaration ever made by a Cabinet Minister. But the Duke added, that it was, nevertheless, his / determination to support Lord Derby.

I think you have decided wisely about Fitzgerald. The morale of a party is injured, when any individual who has been encouraged to take a prominent part, is neglected in the hour of triumph. He was also personally popular among the / rank & file. Our Stanley never thinks anybody in the Ho: of Commons is equal to anything: & I am not sure he is not right. But the world cannot be governed by this inexorable estimate of human qualities – & the political circle generally will agree, that a man, who, if in Parlt., would probably have ~~to~~ been a Cabinet Minr, is not unfit to be an E. I[ndian]. President.[5]

Ever yrs | D.

4230 TO: [MONTAGU CORRY]   Hughenden [Friday] 12 October 1866
ORIGINAL: H B/XX/D/361
EDITORIAL COMMENT: C of Ex paper, seal crossed out and 'Hughenden Manor' written in.

Hughenden Manor | Oct 12 1866

The enclosed[1] must be sent to Ld Derby by this nights post: by his bag, of course, if he have one.

D.

---

2 Derby (n1) had proposed to 'summon a Cabinet from Wednesday Novr. 1 [*sic*] when our first subject of discussion should be the Reform question.' Thirteen cabinet members would meet on Wednesday 31 October; absent would be Naas and the Duke of Buckingham. *The Times* (1 Nov 1866).

3 There is in H a document in D's hand headed 'Resolutions' and endorsed by Montagu Corry: 'Altered in Cabinet Wed. Feby 6. M.C.' This is accompanied by a note in Corry's hand: '*1867 Reform Resolutions*. C. of E's draft. alterations of Cabinet Feby 6. & the final amendments in Cabinet Feby 9.' H B/XI/J/204a-b.

4 For Sir John Pakington's claim of (in D's terms) 'the prodigality of our stores', see **4216**. Pakington had succeeded 12th Duke of Somerset as first lord of the admiralty.

5 Derby (n1) had told D that 'I have advised Cranborne to adopt your suggestion of [William Seymour] Fitzgerald. Stanley, I do not know why, does not think him equal to it; but we owe him something, and I do not know that we could place him better elsewhere.' See **4198**&n1. Fitzgerald would be appointed governor of Bombay in November.

---

1 D's letter to Derby (**4229**).

ORIGINAL: QUA 50
EDITORIAL COMMENT: C of Ex paper, seal crossed out and 'Hughenden Manor' written in.

Hughenden Manor | Octr. 12 1866.

If Mr Montagu Corry be not in Downing St., the bag is to be opened by *Lord Derby's Secretary*.[1]

    D.

ORIGINAL: DURG Earl Grey Papers, 3rd Earl: Beaconsfield [7]
EDITORIAL COMMENT: C of Ex paper, seal crossed out and 'Hughenden Manor' written in. *Sic*: événmens [*twice*].

Private   Hughenden Manor | Octr. 14 1866

M. General | The Hon: Charles Grey

My dear General,

Whether in, or out of, office, you may rest assured, that I shall never omit any opportunity of testifying my affectionate devotion to the memory of that / rare & admirable person, with whom it was your choice fortune to enjoy so long & confidential an intimacy, & mine to form an acquaintance, too brief, but which has left an indelible impression on / my heart & mind.[1]

What can immediately be done, in the matter to wh: you refer, must depend greatly on the state of the finances at the close of the year; the financial year, I, of course mean.[2]

The first half, just / concluded, nearly realizes my predecessors estimate, but then his estimate left an only nominal surplus.[3] I had counted on a considerable increase in the current & concluding ↑halfyear,↓ in consequence of what seemed, in the spring & / early summer, a matchless crop of barley. This would have poured in an immense malt tax. But all this is unhappily changed: a bad harvest, & particularly a bad barley-harvest.[4]

However, the great point you mention shall be / always borne in mind; & we must hope the best.

I had a very curious letter, from a highly-authentic quarter in France, this morn-

---

1 Either W. Patrick Talbot or George Barrington.

1 Grey had served as private secretary to Prince Albert from 1849 to Albert's death in 1861.

2 This communication by Grey, possibly about the Albert Memorial, has not been found.

3 In the House on 23 July, in presenting his supplemental budget, D had pointed out that when Gladstone 'brought forward his Financial Statement, he estimated the revenue at £67,013,000' and 'his expenditure at £66,727,000 ... The result of that Estimate of revenue and expenditure left a surplus of £286,000.' *Hansard* CLXXXIV cols 1286-1302 (D 1286-90).

4 *The Times* on 8 September had reported that the barley crop 'has this season well rewarded the farmer's labour. Almost equal in England in bulk and yield to the great crop of 1864, it will nearly balance the deficiency of last year's crop.' On 16 October, however, it would report that the northern barley crop 'is in many cases discoloured, and therefore disqualified for malting purposes, but otherwise its condition will not be much deteriorated.'

ing, wh: gives a detailed account of the first interview between the Emperor & Moustier at Biarritz.⁵ It says that / the new Minister enjoined the Emperor "se tenir strictement dans la ligne du statu quo absolu; conseiller et soutenir constamment la Porte, *qui tiendra pour le moins encore pendant plusieurs generations*; ne contribuer, en rien, à créer des événmens dans l'Empire Turc, et, si les événmens arrivent, les *apaiser*, les étouffer, ou les laisser tomber d'eux mêmes, et pour tout celà, *se lier en particulier avec l'Angleterre*, et effacer les dissidences avec elle, vu qu', au fond, elle a la même politique conservatrice en Orient que la France, et ne demande pas mieux que de se [*word torn out*] au Gouvernement de l'Empereur en tant ce qui regarde les affaires de la Turquie."⁶

My informant says, that the Emperor has entirely ratified these views, & that their ~~por~~ promulgator, who was coldly received by the Empress, has, already gained / her good opinion.

You know more about these things, than I do, but, as this reached me only this morning, & from a first-rate quarter, I thought, perhaps, it was as well to send it you.

Yrs sincerely, | D.

4233 TO: [MONTAGU CORRY] [Hughenden, Sunday] 14 October 1866
ORIGINAL: H B/XX/D/20
EDITORIAL COMMENT: C of Ex paper. The context (n1) suggests D is at Hughenden but neglected to cross out the seal.

Octr 14 1866

I shall be going to Quarter Sess: tomorrow morning early, & not return till too late for post.¹

Take care Genl. Grey gets his letter.² I generally send to Buckingham Palace, & they forward on – but let / our messenger take care there is no mistake about ↑it↓, & ascertain that it goes tomorrow night by the Royal bag – if no bag, you can send it to Balmoral by post.

---

5 This letter has not been found. Napoleon III had arrived at Biarritz on 21 September looking 'pale and tired'. *The Times* (25 Sep 1866). Lionel Désiré Marie François René, 5th Marquis de Moustier (1817-1869), French ambassador to Berlin 1853-9, Vienna 1859-61 and Constantinople 1861-6, had been appointed minister of foreign affairs on 1 September. *The Times* on 17 October would report that the 'settlement of the Turco-Roumanian difficulty is ascribed to the diplomatic exertions of the Marquis de Moustier'.

6 Moustier had enjoined the Emperor '"to adhere strictly to the absolute status quo; to continuously advise and support the Porte, *which will stand for at least many generations*; to have no part in creating events in the Turkish Empire, and, if events arise, to *quell* them, smother them, or to let them collapse naturally, and for all of this *to ally onself especially with England*, and obliterate whatever dissidence exists between us, as she basically shares with France the same conservative policy in the Orient and wants nothing better than to [*word torn out*] itself to the Emperor's Government regarding Turkish affairs."'

———

1 Topics discussed at the Bucks Michaelmas session at Aylesbury on 15 October would include a new rule requiring prisoners to sleep on extremely uncomfortable plank beds, 'the object being to deter people from frequently coming into prison, or, indeed, at all.' D would suggest that its use should be left '"to the discretion of the Gaoler in a great measure."' A resolution would be agreed to '"That the Visiting Justices may in their discretion direct the Gaoler to require any convicted criminal prisoner to sleep on a plank bed without a mattress for any period not exceeding fourteen consecutive nights."' *BH* (20 Oct 66).

2 See **4232**.

Write to
> Thos: Moxon Esq[3]
> 3 Copthall Court
> Threadneedle Street /

& thank˙him from me for his confidential paper,[4] wh: I will carefully consider. Tis on the present ↑state↓ of our Railway Finance – wh: is in a dangerous ~~state~~ condition.[5] He is a first-rate authority.

Send me in bag some foolscap paper: a / little ↑plain↓ note-paper↑; i.e,↓ witht. stamp.

Some good blotting paper and a few bands.

adieu!

Let me know how yr sister is getting on.[6]

TO: SIR STAFFORD NORTHCOTE   Hughenden [Sunday] 14 October 1866   **4234**
ORIGINAL: PS 1529
PUBLICATION HISTORY: M&B IV 479.

... I am anxious, and rather alarmed, about the financial systems of our railway companies.[1] So far as I can judge, from the information that reaches me, nearly the

---

3 'Thomas Moxon, Esq., Old Broad-street' is listed in 1845 as one of several individuals to whom 'applications for shares and prospectuses' for The Great North and South of France Railway Company should be made. *The Times* (9 Jul 1845). London's Threadneedle and Old Broad streets meet. Moxon (1792-1869) was a stockbroker.

4 James Disraeli on 8 October 1866 had written to D that 'Moxon wants me to send you some papers to read about railways & as he values them very much he wishes me to forward them to you ... *Can I send them to Downing Street to be forwarded.* The great line has gone˙ & *four more* must go according to him and his papers are a plan to save them, & if it can be carried out would be one of the most popular things ever carried out. Moxon is a stockbroker of long standing very hard *headed & very safe* and perhaps on getting the papers you could drop him a line as he has been very useful & very kind to me during the Panic.' Although Moxon's paper has not been found, in H is a document, most likely in Corry's hand, headed 'Precis of Mr Thomas Moxon's Plan for dealing with the Railway debt of the United Kingdom' and docketed 'Oct 1866'. It was Moxon's 'firm opinion that finance system of Railways will very soon collapse. Govt will be called upon for assistance. Suggests that, if collapse does not arrive before Parliament meets, power be taken to make advances to R. Companies "under certain conditions, & that any Govt advances should be a *first* mortgage over each Railway Co[mpan]y that accepts advances from Govt from time to time."' After outlining those conditions, the précis concludes that 'Mr M. expects the L[ondon] & N[orth]W[estern] R[ailway] & others of the lines in good credit will fall in with this scheme. Mr M. names 5% for the Railways to pay because he thinks that, the companies pay, all costs included, more or at all events never less than that sum Pr. ann. on their Bonds.' Along with the précis is an anonymous eight-page pamphlet, dated '15*th November* 1866' and entitled 'CONFIDENTIAL. Railway Companies Arrangements. Heads of Proposed Bill, with Observations'; across the title page D has written 'Remember to give me this before the Cabinet D.' H A/I/D/26; H B/IX/C/25b, 25a.

5 The troubled financial state of the country's railway system had led to the appointment in 1865 of a Royal Commission on Railways, whose report would be published in May 1867. The first reading by Sir Stafford Northcote of the Railway Companies' Arrangements Bill, 'to make better provision for the arrangements of the affairs of Railway Companies unable to meet their engagements', would take place on 7 February 1867. *The Times* (5 Apr 1865, 18 May 1867); *Hansard* CLXXXV cols 89-108.

6 Alice Charlotte Mary Lowry-Corry (1839-1885), Corry's 'frail unmarried sister', would usually live with him at 71 South Audley Street after 1873. ODNB.

---

1 See **4233**&n5.

whole of them will collapse; the distress and ruin to many industrial establishments will be great, but the effect on the condition of the working classes, at a moment when there are elements of discontent abroad, would be very serious.

Is it possible for the Government to interfere? It would be a great affair. Between bonds and debentures we should have to deal with more than a hundred million. This is one of the subjects over which we must talk together....

Our great misfortune at present is the acceptance by Cairns of the Lord Justice-ship, vacant by the resignation of Knight Bruce.[2] It is an irreparable loss, and falls with peculiar severity on myself, for in debate he was my right arm.

If Cairns had had only a little heart and a little imagination, he would have been by far the first man in the House of Commons; and if he had had only a little heart and a little imagination, he would not have deserted Lord Derby at such a crisis, which may be historic....[3]

We are victims of Patronage. Never was such a shower, especially of legal posts.

4235   TO: [MONTAGU CORRY]   [Hughenden, Tuesday] 16 October [1866]

ORIGINAL: H B/XX/D/21
PUBLICATION HISTORY: M&B IV 464, dated 16 October 1866, the first, second, fourth and fifth sentences
EDITORIAL COMMENT: C of Ex paper. D is at Hughenden but neglected to cross out the seal. *Dating*: by context; see **4187**n3.

Oct 16

I see that Longmans have advertised your volume: in the Sat[urda]y Review, I think, I saw it. "Speeches on Parliamty Reform by Rt Hon B. D. M. P. C of Er &c" a horrid title, it will do for the moment, but when we advance a / little, & real advertising begins, there shd. be something more condensed & simpler. What do you think of this?

~~8vo~~

~~Parliamentary Reform~~

I hate Rt. Hons. & M.P.s & all that. C of Es *must* be R[t]. H[on]s. & M. Ps & so on, as a matter of course. /

8vo

PARLIAMENTARY REFORM:

a series of speeches on that subject, delivered in the House of Commons by

     The Chanr of the Exr.

     1848 to 1866

Edited by

     Montagu Corry A.M. (or whatr you may be) of &c.

     Longmans & Co

This would make a good title page.[1]

---

2 Sir James Lewis Knight-Bruce (1791-1866), a barrister (Lincoln's Inn 1817), KC 1829, MP (C) for Bishop's Castle 1831-2, DLC University of Oxford 1834, PC and Kt 1842, first lord justice of appeal 1851-66, would die on 7 November.

3 *Cf* **4228** and **4238**.

---

1 The published title page, following '(1848–1866).', reads: '*REPRINTED (BY PERMISSION) FROM HANSARD'S DEBATES.* EDITED BY MONTAGU CORRY, B.A. OF LINCOLN'S INN, BARRISTER-AT-LAW.' See **4306**.

ORIGINAL: H B/XX/D/22
PUBLICATION HISTORY: M&B IV 482-3, the third and fourth paragraphs
EDITORIAL COMMENT: C of Ex paper, seal crossed out and 'Hughenden Manor' written in. The letter is incomplete. *Sic*: Hennessey [*twice*]; Mansell; Mansel; Arundel.

Confdl   Hughenden Manor | Oct 16. 1866

I enclose a letter from Hennessey.[1] I shan't answer it, nor do I wish you to notice it – but I thought, as you had some knowledge of his proceedings, you shd. be kept *au fait*. /

Take care of his letter, & keep it in yr archives, as he is a slippery customer.[2]

I assume, that, after all our experience, now of many years, of Roman Cath: influences & interests in Ireland, men like Naas & Taylor,[3] & especially the former, who is a most / able, sensible, & enlightened man, are taking the right course – & I will not interfere with them in any way. They know my Irish policy; & any observations of mine are unnecessary.

As for Hennessey running with ↑us↓ & Cullen[4] & Co., ↑(Cullen is a mere Whig)↓ at the same time, it / is plainly impossible, that he can succeed in such an adventure. The Tipperary election will show whether there be any substance in Mansell's views of a national R. Cat: party in Ireland.[5] I confess, I am not sanguine.

The "Evening Mail" wh: was always attacking me for my Ultra-montane views / & truckling to the Irish priests, fell into the mistake, wh: clever, provincial, minds are apt to do. Mansel never saw ~~hi~~ farther than his nose, & never believed, that ~~there~~ H.M. had any ↑other↓ Rom: Cat: subjects except Irishmen.

My Roman Cat: policy, as / distinguished from my Irish policy, has always mainly been shaped with reference to the Eng: Rom: Cats. a most powerful body: & naturally Tories. They have behaved admirably to us, & have much influenced the Eng: Elections in our favor. They are generally / speaking Ultra-montane – but we never

---

1 John Pope Hennessy on 13 October had written to D from New Ross, co Wexford, a letter headed '*most confidential*': 'In July last at the request of the Government I retired in favor of Mr Ram. I wrote to Mr Ram sending him a paragraph for insertion in the local Catholic paper' stating he did not intend opposing Ram, '"but, if Mr. Ram retires from the contest, Mr. Hennessy will avail himself of the invitation he has received and offer himself as a candidate for the County." ... Mr. Ram has retired and in obedience to a summons received from the leading Catholics ... I have come to the County & resumed my canvass ... In this state of things the Irish Government have thought it fit to start an opposition to me, in the person of a County Carlow protestant conservative Mr. Kavanagh (a man who has neither legs or arms, & who is extremely unpopular with the Catholics). I must add that the very unpleasant position of affairs in Tipperary ought to have warned your friends here. Had I been started instead of Mr. Waldron I should have been supported by the Bishops & priests, & returned.' H B/XIII/194a.
2 Hennessy – 'pushy, arrogant, ambitious, manipulative, ... a careerless, disreputable adventurer' – had lost the 1865 King's co (Ireland) election by six votes because, having not paid his debts from the 1859 election 'to the King's county jaunting-car owners; they refused to work for him, so he could not transport rural voters to the polls.' He would be governor 1867-71 of 'swampy, unhealthy, backward, and impoverished' Labuan, a small island off Borneo. ODNB.
3 Thomas Edward Taylor had become parliamentary secretary to the treasury in the new government.
4 Archbishop of Dublin Paul Cullen had been created cardinal by Pius IX on 22 June 1866.
5 Most likely zealous Irish Roman Catholic William Monsell, vice-president of the board of trade and paymaster-general March-July 1866.

had, ↑& we have not,↓ better friends than Sir Robert Gerard, Lord Gainsbro', Lord Denbigh, Arundel of Wardour,[6] & many others of that class.

25 R. Caths. ↑(an Ultra Mont. movement)↓ voted agst Ld Palmn. on the Danish Division: my motion;[7] & / if our own men had been firm, the game was won, & we shd. have acceded to office in a house with 310 of our own – besides the R.C. defection. Under such circumstances, a dissolution↑, in time,↓ wd. have given ↑us↓ a real majority. Now, we may have to run that chance with only 290 of our own. The whole difference

---

4237   TO: [MONTAGU CORRY]   [Hughenden, Tuesday] 16 October [1866]
ORIGINAL: H B/IX/E/15
EDITORIAL COMMENT: C of Ex paper, seal crossed out. *Dating*: which establishes the year and the recipient; see n1.

Octr 16

With regard to the Port: Treaty, I have written to Sir S.N. on the matter.[1] ↑Before his letter of today reached me.↓[2]

The case is simply this: we must not allow any feeling about Malt Tax to prevent the legitimate commercial development / of the country. But if the question involves a reduction of the spirit duties, ↑which is not impossible,↓ it assumes a new character. We must do justice to the landed interest, tho' it wd. be folly to yield to ↑its prejudices; & especially to↓ the prejudices of a / section ↑only↓ of the landed interest, & ↑so↓ baulk a beneficial policy.

There is nothing in the charge, that we are remitting duties on luxuries, while we leave the articles consumed by the labouring class untouched.

Everyone knows our object in dealing with the Wine duties, is not to render wine / cheaper, but to increase our markets; & that is the main interest of the labouring class.

---

6 Sir Robert Gerard, 12th Bt; Charles George Noel, 2nd Earl of Gainsborough; Rudolph William Basil (1823-1892), 8th Earl of Denbigh; John Francis Arundell, 12th Baron Arundell of Wardour.
7 For the 8 July 1864 non-confidence division, see VIII **3933**n1.

---

1 D's letter to Northcote of 14 October 1866 (**4234**) does not mention the Portuguese treaty. D replies here to Corry's letter of 11 October: 'A long memorandum [*not found*] has just come in to the Board of Trade, since the enclosed papers [*not found*], on the proposed treaty, have been sent to me. Neither Mallet or I can see what leads Sir Stafford Northcote to conclude that "nothing short of an uniform rate of duty up to a certain point" would be satisfactory. We think that (say) 1d per degree above 25 would be an acceptable modification. The Board of Trade will send you the mem. soon; – meanwhile the plan of having a conference on the subject seems the only way to solve the question. I should say that, since I last wrote to you on this subject, Mallet has procured information which seems to make the Treaty possible.' H B/XX/CO/15.
2 Although a 16 October 1866 letter from Northcote has not been found, he had written to D at length about a commercial treaty with Portugal on the 9th and 13th, cautioning D on the 13th that 'if we bind ourselves by treaty to reduce the wine duty to a certain point, and if we find by actual experience that it does lead to illicit distillation, we have left ourselves no alternative but to reduce our Spirit duty. I am inclined to think that in prudence we should reduce the Spirit duty to 8d. a gallon at the same time that we reduced the duty on Strong wine; – but how about the revenue? and how about malt?' H B/IX/E/13, 14.

But above all, is the Revenue question. We must have ↑more↓ precise information as to the effect of these contemplated, or contingent, changes, than we have.

I hope you will be able to make this out: I seem [to be] writing on stucco: but it will do till I come / to town.

D.

I have the greatest confidence in Mallet.

TO: [MONTAGU CORRY]   Hughenden [Wednesday] 17 October [1866]   **4238**
ORIGINAL: H B/XX/23
PUBLICATION HISTORY: M&B IV 480, undated snippet from the seventh paragraph; Blake 455, undated extracts from the sixth and seventh paragraphs
EDITORIAL COMMENT: *Sic*: Hennessey.

Hughenden Octr 17

I think the page will do very well.[1]

According to the united estimates of yourself & Longman, it would be a vol. of 440 p: about: quite enough. Especially as it may be necessary, as appendix, to reprint the Bill of 1859.[2] /

There must be some heading to each speech, stating the occasion, motion, date &c: perhaps even the names of the preceding speakers. Look at some published speeches: Cannings[3] for / example; & see about this.[4]

Gladstone's volume of finance speeches[5] wd. hardly be a guide as, probably, they are all financial statements, witht. previous discussion.

Look well at a letter enclosed from a Mr Ryley.[6] He is a R. Cath: / a Tory, much trusted by the Eng: Caths: who, in Journalism, are mainly represented by "The Tab-

---

1 Corry on 16 October had sent D 'a specimen page. I dont think there will be above 310 columns, but I cannot yet speak for certain, as I am completing my revision slowly, reading on the way. It will, however, be ended, before they require the list.' H B/XX/CO/16.

2 There is no appendix to Corry's 478-page volume.

3 The most comprehensive edition is *The Speeches of the Right Hon. George Canning, with a Memoir of his Life*, 6 vols (1836), ed Roger Therry.

4 Corry would reply on 19 October proposing 'as a heading to the Speeches, merely to give the terms, in full, of the Motion, and the names of the chief Speakers, pro and con, who preceded you; not touching upon the matter in any particular speech, unless your remarks thereupon seem to make it necessary. This is the system adopted in the editions, I have looked into, of the speeches of Windham, Peel, Wellington, Sheridan, Pitt[,] Huskisson and others. The introductory remarks in "Cannings Speeches", seem to me needlessly diffuse. Would it not be well to print, in an appendix, the Bill of last Session, as well as yours of /59? All this will make nearly 500 pages, I imagine.' H B/XX/CO/17.

5 Three such compilations by Gladstone had appeared in 1865: *The Financial Statement of 1865*; *The Budget of 1865, or, The facts and fallacies of finance examined*; *The Financial Statements of 1853 and 1860, to 1865: To which are added, a speech on Tax-Bills, 1861, and on Charities, 1863*. See **4256**. D in 1862 had published two of his own speeches (24 February 1860 and 8 April 1862) as a 41-page booklet: *Mr. Gladstone's Finance, from his accession to office in 1853 to his budget of 1862, reviewed by the Right Hon. B. Disraeli*.

6 Edward Ryley, who had begun corresponding with D on 23 June 1865, had written on 16 October (his last extant letter to D) requesting an interview to discuss 'the state of Ireland', to ask D's help in doing 'something for Mr. J.P. Hennessy, who may perhaps be called a personal follower of yours' and to 'lay before you a suggestion for getting rid of the Malt tax – or at least of so increasing another source of revenue as to make you to do so if you please.' H B/XXI/R/362. Ryley (d 3 April 1896 aged 84) had been 'one of the ablest and most zealous of Cardinal Wiseman's lay coadjutors in obtaining equal rights for Catholics in prisons, workhouses, and the Army.' With Wiseman's death in 1865 'his connexion with purely Catholic

let", ⌐the Editor, Ryley's friend⌐.[7] He was, for several years, trying to connect himself with me, but I always fought shy. However, of late, I was obliged to see him. Only once. I have no / reason to doubt his sincerity to us, from all I have heard of his antecedents – but I suspect him to be a Jesuit, & I think it as well, that, without hurting his selflove, I shd. keep him at arm's length. Earle knows him, & all his entourage, & cd. give you advice if you / require it.[8] You had better write to Mr Ryley & give him an appointment; the great pressure of affairs on me at the present moment rendering it quite impossible &c &c, but expressing my desire, that, he shd. always communicate confidentially with yourself.[9] /

If Kenealy's business in his profession justifies it, I think it wd. be as well, that the Ld Chanr. shd. recognise his claim;[10] but I don't want to ask anything of the Ld Chanr. as I have always snubbed him, & I believe he knows that I recommended Ld. Derby not to re-appoint him,[11] & if ~~Cairns~~ / Cairns had had the spirit of a louse, he wd not have been re-appointed.

Only think of Cairns asking for the Lord Justiceship! It is a great blow for the party, & mainly for myself. For he was my right arm in debate, & with him, I was not afraid to / encounter Gladstone & Roundell Palmer.[12] Now I have got them both, without the slightest assistance. If Cairns had had a little heart & a little imagination, he wd. have been, by far, the first man in the House of Commons; but if he had / these qualities, he wd. not have deserted Ld Derby at such a crisis.[13]

D.

This does not seem bad paper.

What Ryley says about Hennessey is quite true. He came into Parlt., / tho returned by the Priests, as an avowed Conservative & mentioned in his address, that

---

matters almost ceased; for Mr. Ryley ... was not a *persona grata* with Cardinal Manning. He, however, continued for some years to devote himself to bringing back the English Catholics to Tory principles.' One of his 'chief successes' occurred in 1866, when 'he persuaded some Irish members to vote against Earl Russell's Government, and others to abstain.' He had been a 'constant contributor' to *The Tablet* (see n7). *The Times* (15 Apr 1896).

7 *The Tablet*, a weekly first issued on 16 May 1840 in London but published from Dublin as of 1849, was edited by Frederick Lucas (1812-1855), a barrister (Middle Temple 1835) and Quaker who had converted to Catholicism in 1839 and had been MP (L) for co Meath 1852-5. His ultramontane and pro-Irish views placed him in opposition to powerful sections of his own religious community. His younger brother was Samuel Lucas. In H there is a 'Reprint from a Leading Article of the TABLET (an influential Roman Catholic Newspaper) of March 10, 1866.' It suggests that the Ecclesiastical Titles Bill and certain provisions of the Emancipation Act be repealed; that 'Catholics in England should be allowed to claim exemption from the payment of church-rates for the support of the English Protestant State Church'; and that Catholic archbishops of England and Ireland be made 'peers of Parliament'. H B/XXI/R/358a.

8 Ryley had written to Ralph Earle on 25 April 1866 concerned at how certain MPs would vote at the second reading of the reform bill. H B/XXI/R/359.

9 In H is a note in Corry's hand dated 'Oct 22.': 'C. of E. regrets press. of business prevents. Will Mr R. call on M.C. on 24 or 25 inst.?' On the 23rd Ryley would write Corry from 'the conviction, founded I acknowledge on grounds which would not appear entirely to warrant such a conclusion, that my communications are useless, and not agreeable to those to whom I make them.' Apologizing for troubling D, he begged 'to be excused from prosecuting the attempt to make my views known to him.' H B/XXI/R/363.

10 See 4227&n3.

11 Frederic Thesiger, 1st Baron Chelmsford, Lord Chancellor 1858-9, had been reappointed in July 1866.

12 Cairns had succeeded Sir Roundell Palmer as attorney-general.

13 *Cf* 4228 and 4234.

the public ↑man↓ whom he wd. indicate as ↑representing his general views,↓ ↑as↓ holding his confidence, was myself.[14]

He has served us well, & ought to be well rewarded.

T.O. /

Write to Mr Strange as you suggest, & even say, that I have directed you to keep the business in mind.[15]

TO: LOUISA, LADY ANTHONY DE ROTHSCHILD   4239
Hughenden [Wednesday] 17 October 1866

ORIGINAL: NNL [1]

EDITORIAL COMMENT: C of Ex paper, seal crossed out and 'Hughenden Manor' written in.

Hughenden Manor | Octr 17 1866

My dear Lady de Rothschild,

My wife, engaged in colossal works, has given me some instructions so hastily, that I do not clearly comprehend them – but, I am sure, I am not / making a mistake, when I say, that we shall be most happy to see your brother & his wife, if you could come here as she hoped.[1]

I don't know, whether she has given you any / clue as to our movements; but they are these. On Friday, the 26th, we go to Highclere, & shall return on Monday,[2] but it is very probable that we may, then, have *immediately* to repair to / London, & remain – &, I hope, you may visit us before.

Ever yours, | D.[3]

14 'At King's County nineteen priests came out publicly in favour of Hennessy, the only Catholic candidate openly standing as a Conservative ... In his address Hennessy announced a policy of general support for "the party of Disraeli" on all imperial issues. To universal astonishment he was returned at the head of the poll, displacing the Protestant Liberal, Loftus Bland.' K. Theodore Hoppen 'Tories, Catholics, and the General Election of 1859' *Historical Journal* 13.1 (March 1970) 48-67 (p 57).

15 Corry (n1) had enclosed 'the India Office Mem. [*not found*] on Mr [Charles] Strange's case, and will answer him in accordance therewith, when you return it to me.' W.H. Benthall (at the India Office) on 15 October had written to Corry returning Strange's 4 October letter to D (**4224**), which he had shown to Lord Cranborne. 'His lordship desires me to send you the enclosed Memorandum on the case, and to say that enquiries shall be made from India respecting it by the next Mail.' Benthall would receive a reply (dated 'Calcutta 7th Decr/66') to his 15 October letter to administrator-general of Bengal, Charles Swinton Hogg. Having received no communication from Strange, Hogg would 'wind up the Accounts and remit the balance' to Strange 'with an Account of the Estate if he will in the meantime furnish me with a statement in writing that the deceased was his lawful son and that he has left no widow or children surviving him.' Benthall on 12 January 1867 would send Corry Hogg's reply, and Strange would write to D on the 15th acknowledging D's letter (not found) and Hogg's. 'Agreeably with your instructions' Strange had forwarded to Hogg the necessary particulars and thanked D for his 'kind intercession on my behalf'. Strange on 4 September would send D 'the final a/c & Settlement' of his late son's estate and thank him for his intervention. H B/IX/D/6b-f.

1 MA's account books do not record a Rothschild visit to Hughenden at this time. Louisa de Rothschild (née Montefiore) had two brothers: Joseph Mayer Montefiore (1816-1880), who in 1860 had married Henrietta Francisca Sichel (1837-1915), and Nathaniel Mayer Montefiore, who in 1850 had married Emma Goldsmid.

2 The DS would leave for Highclere Castle on 26 October, returning on the 29th. H acc.

3 For Lady de Rothschild's reply, see **4252**n1.

4240 TO: MONTAGU CORRY   [Hughenden] Thursday 18 October [1866]
ORIGINAL: H B/XX/D/362
EDITORIAL COMMENT: C of Ex paper, seal crossed out. *Dating*: by context; see n1.

My dear Montagu,   18 Octr
Send me, if you please, £100 as before.[1]
   D.

4241 TO: SIR JOHN DALRYMPLE-HAY   Hughenden [Thursday] 18 October 1866
ORIGINAL: MOPSIK [14]
EDITORIAL COMMENT: C of Ex paper, seal crossed out and 'Hughenden Manor' written in.

Sir J.D. Hay Bart | M.P.   Hughenden Manor | Oct 18 1866
My dear Sir John,
You are too magnificent!
   Your birds are as good, as yourself[.][1]
   Remember me most / kindly to the Squire of Addington.[2]
      Yours sincerely, | D.
Cairns is a terrible loss.[3]

4242 TO: [MONTAGU CORRY]   [Hughenden, Friday] 19 October [1866]
ORIGINAL: H B/XX/D/24
EDITORIAL COMMENT: *Dating*: by context; see n1. *Sic*: Henessey.

Octr 19

Here is another insolent & indiscreet letter from Henessey.[1]
   He criticises our Electioneering tactics, but the only instance, in wh: he had the direction of affairs in that way, the famous ↑C[oun]ty↓ Cork Election, in wh: he

1 On 19 October 1866 Corry would send D 'twenty £5 notes, – Nos. 82261-80.' MA would note the transaction that day as 'One hundred pounds by Dizzy from London.' H B/XX/CO/17; H acc.

1 Dalrymple-Hay on 1 October had written to D that he had 'come down for a little shooting & fishing & have been tolerably successful' and had 'ordered a box of grouse to your address.' On the 11th he had written from Dunragit (Scotland) to thank D for his 'kind note' (not found), 'glad to find that our Galloway Grouse are not despised in a Buckinghamshire larder. I have again despatched you a box which will I hope reach you in good Condition'. This second box is apparently the one for which D is thanking him. H B/XXI/H/301-2.
2 John Gellibrand Hubbard had bought the old Addington manor house and park at Winslow, Bucks, in 1854 and in 1857 had erected a mansion on the property. Dalrymple-Hay on 11 October (n1) had written that 'Next week I hope to have the Hubbards with me, to enjoy such fare as our country affords.'
3 See **4228**&n2.

1 Hennessy's letter to D of 17 October 1866 from New Ross, co Wexford, was headed '*Private*': 'My letter, of four or five days ago, will have I trust produced some result before now upon our friends in Dublin Castle; I mean my letter to you [*see* **4236**n1], for I venture to assume that you have given them a hint as to the great blunder they were committing. They are always wrong about their electioneering; Waldron was to have had a walk over, & they were perpetually saying Ram was quite safe ... Would you have any objection to write me a line, which I could show privately, to any of the great conservative landlords during my canvass?' H B/XIII/195a.

induced ↑the present↓ Lord Gainsboro' to / be the Candidate under his management, he made the greatest *fiasco* on record: not only lost a seat, wh:, otherwise,
might have been won, but nearly ruined Lord Gainsboro' by the wildest, most reckless, / & most foolish, expenditure, in wh: a candidate was ever involved.[2]

I fear his professional status wd. not justify an Indian Judgeship, but if so, it wd. be
as well thus, when we can, to provide for him.

D.[3]

TO: [MONTAGU CORRY]   [Hughenden, Friday] 19 October 1866   **4243**
ORIGINAL: H B/XX/D/25.

Octr 19. 1866

Here is another wild letter from Kenealy.[1] I can't write to him, even if I felt inclined,
as he wd. publish my letter, wh: he did in a literary case, when he dedicated to me
his poem.[2]

As you know him, I think / you might ask him to call on you, & recommend him,
at my desire, to take all the means in his power, & wh: he says are alike easy & irresistible, to obtain the object he desires; & not in any way to trust to my influence, ↑if it
exists↓, wh: I have / no wish to exercise in the quarter to wh: he refers.

Beg him also to understand, that I am not the virtual Prime Minister.

And that his claim can only be decided on by the considerations wh: usually influence such appointments.

You / can tell him, if you think proper, that I had already written to you indirectly

---

2 Wishing to build on the success of the Catholic-Tory alliance of the 1859 general election, Hennessy had
pushed Conservative Viscount Campden (Lord Gainsborough from 1866) to stand for Cork co in an 1860
by-election against newly appointed Irish attorney-general Rickard Deasy. Campden, a Catholic convert
and thus 'a suspect figure to Irish Conservative opinion', had lost to Deasy by some 2,000 votes. Andrew
Shields *The Irish Conservative Party, 1852-68: Land, Politics and Religion* (Dublin 2007) 185. *The Times* on 10
March 1860 had reported: 'Every one is asking the delicate question who is accountable for Lord Campden's election expenses. Cork county cannot be fought with less than 5,000*l*. or 6,000*l*. a-side.' *The Times*
on 25 July 1860 had announced, under the heading of 'The Great Campden Controversy', that Hennessy
had been ordered to pay £1,000 '"for the balance of expenses incurred on behalf of Lord Campden at
the recent election"'.
3 Hennessy on 20 October would write to D boasting that his 'success in Wexford & New Ross has increased
the popular feeling, & the meeting which took place here today in the open air adopted me with even
greater enthusiasm than my previous one ... The organ of the protestant & conservative interest in the
County has come out this morning with an article most friendly to me, & leaving the road open for Mr.
Kavanagh to retire.' On the 21st, he would complain to D that 'the manner in which Lord Naas took
him [Kavanagh] up against me has made the clerical party indignant.' On the 23rd, he would write that
Naas's 'management of Tipperary was the greatest wisdom & success compared to Wexford electioneering.' H B/XXI/H/486, H B/XIII/197a, 198. Arthur Macmorrough Kavanagh would be elected MP (C) for
co Wexford on 15 November, with 2,641 votes to Hennessy's 1,882.

---

1 Having written to D on 12 October (**4227**n1), Edward Kenealy had reiterated on the 18th how deserving
he was of a QC: 'to be passed over is a species of professional extinction: to me it would be a loss of at least
£1500 a year ... I am so clearly *entitled* to it from my standing & business ... You, who are virtually Premier,
will I hope bear me in mind in this most important juncture.' H B/XXI/K/101. Appointed QC in April
1868, Kenealy would be disbarred in 1874 for professional misconduct.
2 Kenealy's dedication includes no quotation from a D letter. See **4227**&n2.

to assist his views – but the recommendation of the Lord C.J. of England, who, is friendly to him,[3] would be far more effective.[4]

D.

4244

TO: [MONTAGU CORRY]   [Hughenden, Friday] 19 October [1866]

ORIGINAL: H C/II/C/3b

EDITORIAL COMMENT: *Dating*: by context; see n3. *Sic*: Colonel Viney.

Oct 19

My wife's brother, Colonel Viney,[1] was a very good-looking man, & apparently of a very amorous disposition, as he appears to have left an Elvira in every colony & station where the 29th., wh: / he ultimately commanded, was quartered.[2]

Write to this person,[3] as silence wd. probably, only occasion you ulterior trouble, that I regret it is not in my power to interfere in his affairs. I don't / know him, &, so far as I can recollect, never heard of him.

Colonel Viney died in 38 – or 39, young & rather suddenly. He only left debts, being heir to an estate – of his uncle Sir James Viney,[4] – wh: thus / went out of the family.

My wife, who had bought his Commission, also paid his debts – & I think she has done eno'.

Yrs D

I don't mention this to her as it wd. only revive sorrows.

3 The lord chief justice of England, Sir Alexander Cockburn, had praised Kenealy's *Pantomime* effusively in 1862; see VIII **3745**nn2&4.

4 Kenealy would write at length to Corry on 24 and 26 October, indignant at D's acknowledgement, which 'my friends say, is the usual stereotype form of *refusal* ... I have asked no *favour* from the Chancellor: I have solicited only a *right*: and a right, which if withheld I shall suffer great wrong.' Clearly 'the Chancellor has not up to the present consulted [judges] with reference to my claims, position &c, &c ... I therefore hope that ... *you*, the real Master of the ministry will interfere to prevent a great wrong, & a great scandal.' H B/XXI/K/102-3.

1 John Viney Evans, lieut-col in the 29th Regiment of Foot, had died intestate at 48 in 1839, possibly of malaria; his last posting had been at Mauritius. See III **804n4**, 946n1.

2 An allusion to the seduced and then abandoned Donna Elvira in Mozart's *Don Giovanni* (1787). There are several letters from an Elvina le Bourgeois at Port Louis, Mauritius, in 1838 bewailing Evans's departure, requesting money and sending the children's love. Also at Port Louis that year an Elisa Richard thanks Evans for having sent money. MA on 23 June 1831 had reprimanded Evans about a woman at Mauritius: 'For God's sake, shake off this disgraceful connection, any other man might have purchased this woman as you, her heart having nothing to do with it. And you are laugh'd at & called romantic for supposing otherwise & for having bought her & spending so much on such a person.' H D/I/F/96-104, 158; c/103.

3 James Avin had written to D (addressing him as 'My Grace' and 'Your Grace') on 27 August 1866 from Port Louis enclosing a letter (not found) from Evans (n1) to Avin's mother. Avin claimed Evans had 'protected my infancy. He provided for my education together with that of my sister Mary ... he died in 1839. From that moment the allowance which had until then been served on my family by Mr. T.M. Campbell, his agent in Mauritius, was withdrawn ... from 1865 to the beginning of the present year, I lost everything I possessed ... The only prospect I could look for is to obtain a Government situation in the Mauritius office.' H C/II/C/3a.

4 For Sir James Viney, see III **806n1**.

TO: [MARKHAM SPOFFORTH] [Hughenden, Friday 19 October 1866] **4245**

ORIGINAL: PS 1544

PUBLICATION HISTORY: *The Times* (2 Sep 1931), dated at Hughenden, 29 October 1866

EDITORIAL COMMENT: *Dating*: *The Times* appears to have misdated D's letter (perhaps misreading '19' as '29'), whose tenor and language would date it prior to 23 October; see n2.

Private

The *Globe* is sent here, & I read it regularly.[1] I am much pleased with it. I shd. like to know what is the ulterior plan as to price. Is it to be lowered? and if not, what is the circulation at the high price that cd. be depended on? Has that circulation increased under the new management? Hardly yet, I suppose? Or is the increase wh: may have been obtained by better management counterbalanced by some defection in consequence of the new political position it occupies? I shd. like to know all about this. It seems to be conducted with great spirit, & I hope may ultimately prove, what it deserves to be, a great success.[2]

TO: LORD DERBY Hughenden [Sunday] 21 October 1866 **4246**

ORIGINAL: DBP Box 146/2

EDITORIAL COMMENT: *Sic*: proceed; seperation.

Private Hughenden Manor | Octr 21 1866

Right Honorable | The Earl of Derby | K.G.

My dear Lord,

I return you Northcote's letter,[1] by post, tho' I dont like that conveyance, but, between our homes, I fancy, it makes the difference of a day.

---

1 Spofforth had written to D on 18 October enclosing a *Globe* article (annotated by AES, 'on decline of Conservatives in Scotland') '1 to shew you how Wescombe [*sic*] is managing the paper & 2 to enable you to judge whether it may be possible to effect any change in the views of the Scotch electors. I hope you see the Globe if not I will have it sent to Hughenden.' H B/XXI/S/416.

2 Spofforth would write to D on 24 October enclosing a copy of a letter from Exeter schoolmaster (1840-55) turned newspaper proprietor Charles Wescomb (1821-1869), who had asked Spofforth 'by his letter ... to answer [D's] queries. – Wescombe [*sic*] is a man of energy ... I got him to revive a declining paper called the Maidstone Journal & this he has made a commercial as well as political Success.' Wescomb had written to Spofforth on the 23rd thanking him for mentioning the *Globe* to D. 'It is very curious that the Chancellor should not have seen the notice over the first leader, which has been inserted every day since I bought the paper to the effect that the price will be reduced to 2d. on the 1st of November. I am going to lay out several hundreds of pounds in advertising the reduction at about one hundred stations for twelve months & in announcing the reduction I also announce that the paper may be obtained at those stations on the evening of publication. My object is to increase the circulation and thereby to aid the Conservative cause. With reference to the present circulation I am very pleased to state that we have suffered no diminution, but on the contrary the publisher informs me that we are issuing rather more papers than when I purchased. I cannot tell whether the old Whig party are giving up taking the paper ... but it is very satisfactory to me to find that whatever number is given up, it is more than counterbalanced by the orders which they have received – whether from our own party or from the general public I cannot state.' H B/XXI/S/417, 417a. See **4180**&n1.

---

1 Derby had written to D on 19 October enclosing a letter from Northcote (not found) received that morning. 'The message from Ld. Grey is important; but I think a Commission to frame a measure both inexpedient and impracticable. One for information, following up Resolutions of principle, I should think very desirable; but with that object we should not require to appoint Privy Councillors.' H B/XX/S/369.

I do not think Lord Grey's scheme, at any period, & / under any circumstances, could have been accepted, but at the present time, & in the existing state of affairs, it is like listening to the murmuring of children in a dream.[2]

The Court Plan, too, of gracious interference, is a mere phantom.[3] Such sentimental schemes please the / vanity of a Court without substantial power, but, in practice, we know they come to nothing, or if they do anything, convey ↑only↓ to our rivals the impression, that we are alike feeble & perplexed. Our future, &, in some ~~future~~ degree, the future of the country, depends on our own / course. That is too deep & vast a theme to write about, but I look forward, with interest & anxiety, to conversation with you about it. That should proceed, I think, a Cabinet Council; it wo[ul]d be inconvenient to meet for / the first time, since our seperation, in that scene.

Assuming, therefore, that your plans are unaltered, I propose to be in town also by the 29th., & shall hold myself in readiness to call on you on the 30th:,[4] at such place, & at such time, / as may be convenient to you.

These are our movements: on Friday, the 26th., we go to Highclere, & remain until Monday. I intend, at present, to start for London from Highclere. This on the assumption, that you also arrive on the 29th. In case, therefore, there / be any change in your plans, I shd. feel obliged by yr informing me, as, in such event, I shd. return from Highclere to Hughenden.

Yours sincerely, | D.

4247   TO: SIR STAFFORD NORTHCOTE   Hughenden [Monday] 22 October 1866
ORIGINAL: PS 1530
PUBLICATION HISTORY: M&B IV 456-7; Blake 452, brief extracts.

I was much obliged to you for your interesting despatch,[1] and I appreciate the entire fidelity which I have always experienced from you, and on which I have ever, rightly, counted. Lord Derby also forwarded to me your letter to him, on Saturday last.[2]

---

2 D would repeat almost verbatim the second and third paragraphs of the present letter in a 22 October letter to Northcote (**4247**).
3 See **4247**n1.
4 Derby would allude to having recently seen D, perhaps on 30 October, in a letter of that day from St James's Square. H B/XX/S/372.

---

1 Northcote on 17 October had written to D from Balmoral that General Grey had brought him a note from the Queen stating her eagerness to settle the reform question and offering to assist Derby in communicating with Russell and Gladstone. Northcote had then written Grey that although such a communication '"might strengthen his [Derby's] hands to be thus made aware of her readiness to support him ... a formal offer might be embarrassing, as, if the Cabinet ultimately decided that it was inexpedient that any communication should be made to the Liberal party leaders, it might be awkward to have to decline Her Majesty's gracious proposal ... I told the General that I thought there would be very little practical use in communicating with Lord Russell or Gladstone; that they would only give vague promises of candid consideration, which would lead to nothing."' The Queen would write at length to Derby on 28 October, following his visit to Balmoral, offering '"to make a personal appeal to Lord Russell and Mr. Gladstone, and other leading members of both Houses"'. M&B IV 455-8.
2 D had returned Northcote's letter to Derby on 21 October; see **4246**&n1.

I am much gratified by your successful visit to Balmoral.

I doubt myself whether Lord Grey's scheme, at any time or under any circumstances, would or could have been accepted, but at the present moment, and in the existing state of things, it is the murmuring of children in a dream.

The royal project of gracious interposition with our rivals is a mere phantom. It pleases the vanity of a Court deprived of substantial power, but we know, from the experience of similar sentimental schemes, that there is nothing practical in it, or, rather, that the only practical result is to convey to our rivals that we are at the same time feeble and perplexed.

Our future, and in some degree the future of our country, depends on the course we shall chalk out for ourselves; and that must be the result of anxious, grave, and profound deliberation.... The first question for the Cabinet to decide will be, 'Shall we act in the matter of Reform?'[3] I think the discussion of that question will occupy entirely our first meeting, and will facilitate our subsequent councils, in case we decide on action....

P.S. – I have not room to tell you how entirely I approve and admire the wisdom with which you parried the royal proposition. It was worthy of Hyde,[4] and you tell it as well.

TO: SPENCER WALPOLE   Hughenden [Monday] 22 October 1866   4248
ORIGINAL: HOL [12]
EDITORIAL COMMENT: C of Ex paper, seal crossed out and 'Hughenden Manor' written in.

Rt Honorable | Mr Secy. Walpole   Hughenden Manor | Octr 22 1866
My dear Walpole,

I have sanctioned the publication of the Syllabus of the Fœdera,[1] approving very much of the labors of the Master / of the Rolls in this respect.[2]

Are we not entitled, as "great officers of State,"[3] to copies of these calendars &

---

3 *Cf* **4229**n2.
4 Edward Hyde (1609-1674), 1st Earl of Clarendon, eminent statesman and adviser to both Charleses.

---

1 Thomas Duffus Hardy (1804-1878), deputy keeper of the public record office, in 1857 had established the Rolls Series (funded by the treasury and published under the direction of the master of the rolls), which would include *Syllabus of Rymer's 'Foedera'* (1869-85). *Foedera, Conventiones, Literae, et Cujuscunque Generis Acta Publica*, edited by historiographer royal Thomas Rymer, is a collection of medieval diplomatic treaties, agreements and letters between English monarchs and European kingdoms.
2 Sir John Romilly (1802-1874), second son of Sir Samuel Romilly, BA 1823 and MA 1826 Cambridge, a barrister 1827, MP (L) for Bridport 1832-5, QC 1843, sol-gen 1848, Kt 1848, att-gen 1850, PC 1851, master of the rolls 1851-73, had been created 1st Baron Romilly, of Barry, co Glamorgan (peerage of UK) on 3 January 1866. In H there is a letter dated '1 Oct. 1866' to Walpole from Romilly, who had enclosed a copy of his letter to the treasury 'on the subject of making Rymer's Foedera really accessible to the literary world', and in which he urged Walpole to persuade D to 'look favorably on the scheme.' Walpole had forwarded Romilly's letter to D on 3 October, hoping D would add to his 'reputation for Literature as a Patron no less than an author.' H B/XXI/W/65, 65a.
3 Actually, D and Walpole were not entitled to this designation, which describes crown ministers who had inherited their positions or been appointed to exercise largely ceremonial functions.

other publications? Are there no perquisites left to soothe our cares, & lighten our responsibilities? / No "cakes & ale"?[4]

Yours ever, | D.

4249   TO: LORD DERBY   Hughenden [Tuesday] 23 October 1866
ORIGINAL: DBP Box 146/2
EDITORIAL COMMENT: C of Ex paper, seal crossed out and 'Hughenden Manor' written in.

Hughenden Manor | Oct 23 1866

Rt Honble | The Earl of Derby | K.G.

My dear Lord,

I received your letter, & enclosures,[1] by second post yesterday, &, this morning, have written to Sir John Pakington.[2] I inclose you / a copy of my letter to him, & also return his letter to you.

I had, by a previous post, written to you on other matters.[3]

I trust, that the paragraphs in the Journals, that Rolt is / the Attorney, are correct.[4]

Yrs sincerely, | D.[5]

4250   TO: [MONTAGU CORRY]   Hughenden [Tuesday] 23 October [1866]
ORIGINAL: H B/XX/D/26
EDITORIAL COMMENT: C of Ex paper, seal crossed out and 'Hughenden' written in.

Hughenden Oct 23

Immediately on the receipt of this bag, let a copy be made of my letter to Sir John

---

4 'Dost thou think, because thou art virtuous, there shall be no more cakes and ale?' Sir Toby Belch in *Twelfth Night* II.3.115-16.

---

1 Derby had written to D on 21 October enclosing 'by Pakington's desire, a letter, with its enclosure, which I have received this morning. Large as the sum is, yet if the Chief Construction certifies that it is not extravagant – if another Power is willing to give it – and if it be true that we shall thus obtain "the most powerful Ship yet built by any Country", I think we should be open to some censure if we allowed it to slip through our hands. Of course it must go in deduction of other building operations which would have been undertaken during the year; and I do not see, if the Turkish Government, being unable to fulfill their contract, agree to transfer it to us, why we are to pay an extra £30,000. If you concur with me, you will perhaps write to Pakington – if you have a doubt, it may stand over till we meet next week.' H B/XX/S/370. See **4251**&n5.

2 See **4251**.

3 See **4246**.

4 *The Times* on 24 October would report, 'We believe it is now certain that Mr. Rolt, Q.C., will be the new Attorney-General.'

5 Derby would reply on 25 October acknowledging receipt of D's answer to Pakington. 'I am disappointed at your report of our financial position, in which however you are quite right in insisting on the strictest economy. I do not however give up the hope that Pakington may be able to retrench on other heads so as to enable us to obtain the Turkish Iron-clad. It would not look well to have her bought over our head by Prussia! I did not write to tell you of Rolt's acceptance of the Attorney Generalship, as you knew, at the time, of the arrangement with Bovill, and that it was to be offered to him. He will have no difficulty about his re-election; but he will not make up to us for the loss of Cairns! My plan remains unaltered for going up to London on Monday; and I shall be happy to see you at any time most convenient to yourself, after 11 on Tuesday. I have directed a Cabinet to be summoned at 3 o'Clock on Wednesday. The D. of Buckingham will not be able to be in London before the Evening of the 2d.' H B/XX/S/371.

Pakington,[1] & then let the original, & enclosure, be sent to the / Admy., without loss of time.

The open despatch to Ld. Derby[2] will go in the evening, but be careful to inclose in it a copy of my letter to Sir John Pakington; keeping / one, of course, for our own use. It, probably, will be wanted[.]

With regard to your movements, it is impossible for me to reply definitely to yr enquiry.[3]

You must not neglect yr Shropshire home,[4] / &, as Fremantle has returned, there can be no insurmountable difficulty to yr visit. I am, howr, inclined to think, that it wd. be better for you to decide on making yr visit at the beginning of the second week of Novr. – It might be / awkward for you to be absent, or on the point of departure, on my arrival in town.

That will be on the 29th.: & my arrangements are these.

We go to Highclere on Friday, / the 26th, & shall stay ⌈there⌋ till Monday, coming up to town without revisiting Hughenden, as was our first plan.

My post, therefore, must be directed on Friday, Saturday, / & Sunday, to me at
>   Highclere Castle
>   Newbury.

I hope to be at D.S. on Monday afternoon,
>   D.

TO: SIR JOHN PAKINGTON Hughenden [Tuesday] 23 October 1866 **4251**
ORIGINAL: WRC 705:349 BA 3835/7(ii)21
PUBLICATION HISTORY: M&B IV 477-8, omitting the first and last paragraphs
EDITORIAL COMMENT: C of Ex paper. D has written the catchword 'supplementary' instead of 'supplemental' on the ninth page. *Sic*: Milnes.

Confidential   Hughenden Manor | Octr 23 1866
Right Honorable | Sir John Pakington | G.C.B.
My dear Pakington,
Lord Derby has forwarded me your letter to him of the 20th Inst:, & the enclosure of Sir A. Milnes, wh: latter I now return.[1]

If / your proposition involves a second naval supplemental estimate, & a consequent charge on the balances of the present financial year, I must, at once, express my inability to provide for it.

Our financial position is not satisfactory. I have been obliged to borrow largely

---

1 See **4251**.
2 See **4249**.
3 Corry's letter, to which D replies, has not been found. Corry had told D on 19 October that he had 'been sleeping at Frognal [Hampstead, London] all this week.' H B/XX/CO/17.
4 Rowton Castle, Shropshire, would pass to Corry in 1889 upon the death of his aunt, Lady Charlotte Lyster, whose husband Henry had named Corry as his heir in 1863. Corry would be created Baron Rowton of Rowton Castle in 1880.

---

1 For Derby's comments on Pakington's letter, see **4249**&n1. The enclosure by first naval lord Sir Alexander Milne has not been found.

from / the Bank for the payment of the recent dividends, & tho', by the last return, the 20th Inst:, these advances have been satisfied, still that result has been accomplished by appropriating the revenue of nearly three weeks of the new quarter, / & our balances in the Bank are under one million. They ought to be between three & four millions.

But that is not all. On these feeble balances, the demands are great & unusual. Claims for the advances, agreed upon, in respect to Cattle compensation, Irish railways, & Cheshire distress,[2] are now pouring in.

Altho', notwithstanding the financial pressure & the bad harvest, the revenue has wonderfully maintained itself, it, as yet, scarcely realizes the estimate of my predecessor; &, you may remember, ~~that~~ in / that estimate, virtually, no surplus was provided.[3]

When we acceded to office, the magnificent crop of barley, then in the fields, gave me reason to believe, that the second half of the financial year would have been buoyant from the increased malt- / tax, then anticipated. But all these hopes have been, since, dashed to the ground.

Under these circumstances, it will be one of my first duties, when the Cabinet re-assembles, to call its attention to our financial position, & discarding every other consideration but / that of an inexorable economy, to request its sanction to a proposal, that no department of the State shall exceed the amount of the estimates of 1866-7 – with a hope, that they may not reach them: ↑otherwise, we shall get into a scrape.↓

I ought to observe, with respect to second supplemental / estimates, on the ground of good administration alone so very objectionable, that I have communicated with General Peel on this head, & he has promised me, that the increased expenditure for Canadian small arms[4] shall be defrayed / out of the supplemental vote of this year.

This is our condition; which renders me powerless to assist you. I regret it, for I am of opinion, that it would, otherwise, have / been prudent to have purchased the Turkish Ironclad.[5]

Believe me, | my dear Pakington, | sincerely yours, | B. *Disraeli*

2 According to *The Times* of 20 April 1866, 'The number of animals attacked by the cattle plague in Cheshire had attained on April 7 the frightful total of 50,954, or nearly one-fourth the whole number of attacks in England, Wales, and Scotland.' On 19 February 1867, to a question about 'compensation for cattle which has been slaughtered in consequence of the plague', Sir Stafford Northcote would reply that, although 'the inhabitants of Cheshire had suffered a very severe calamity', compensation would not be forthcoming. *Hansard* CLXXXV cols 586-7.

3 See **4232**&n3.

4 See **4222**&nn2&3.

5 Pakington would reply on 25 October in a letter headed '*Confidential*': 'I cannot deny the force of what you say, but the result is vexatious and humiliating in no ordinary degree. Turkey cannot afford to build – England cannot afford to buy! – So the most powerful Ship yet designed is to go to Prussia! – This ought not to be, and I shall go to London tomorrow morning, to ascertain whether any financial arrangements are practicable, within our own estimates, to which you would be able to consent. With regard to the Estimates of my Department for next year, it would be premature for me now to enter into the subject – I can only say to you, as I have already said to Lord Derby, that I do not wish to ask for a shilling which the Cabinet does not agree to be really required for the honour of the Country, and the credit of the

Hughenden [Tuesday] 23 October 1866

ORIGINAL: ROTH BK I Loose
EDITORIAL COMMENT: C of Ex paper, seal crossed out and 'Hughenden Manor' written in.

Hughenden Manor | Octr 23 1866

Dear Lady de Rothschild,[1]
I delayed thanking you, for your magnificent specimen of the preserves of Aston, because I lived in the hope, that I might have the gratification of doing so personally; but / your letter, just received, has destroyed that pleasing illusion. Let me, therefore, thus express to you, how gratified I am, that you remember us so often, & so kindly!

Ever yours, | D.

ORIGINAL: CARR [21]
EDITORIAL COMMENT: C of Ex paper, seal crossed out and 'Hughenden Manor' written in. Carrington is also spelled Carington.

Private   Hughenden Manor | Octr 24 1866
The | Lord Carington
My dear Lord,
I learnt, with deep regret, from Sir Thos Fremantle, that your Lordship contemplated retiring from the Chairmanship of the Court / of Quarter Sess:, by accepting wh: post, & your admirable performance of its duties, you have so much contributed to raise the tone, & general character, of our County proceedings.

I am still in some hopes, that the Justices may / not lose the distinction of being presided over by their Lord Lieutenant, but, in the event of its, unfortunately, becoming necessary to consider who shd. be his successor, I would suggest, that Fremantle himself is the person, who most happily combines the qualities calculated to fulfil the duties, & maintain the decorum & harmonious feeling, of our Court.

I shall not take any steps in this matter without yr sanction, &, indeed, feel, that it would be both graceful & proper, that you shd, virtually, indicate yr successor.[1]

Government.' In February (1866) the Thames Ironworks and Shipbuilding Company had received from Turkey an order for 'a second iron-clad frigate of greater strength and size, and equal, if not superior, in offensive and defensive power to any ironclad yet designed.' In fact 'four 6,400-ton seagoing ironclads had been built by English firms for the Turkish navy during the 1860s ... The Turks, moreover, ordered five additional ironclads from foreign shipbuilders during the late 1860s and the 1870s', three of which ended up wearing British colours. H B/XX/P/79; *The Times* (24 Feb 1866); Beeler 195. See **4257**&n1.

---

1 Lady de Rothschild had written to D from Aston Clinton on 21 October: 'I deferred thanking you for your very kind note [**4239**] in the hope of being able to say that we could take advantage of the amiable and tempting invitation it contained but an old friend having come down here as well as my brother and sister in law I find that it would be quite impossible for us to leave Aston Clinton before the 26th.' H D/III/C/2029.

---

1 Carrington's 'delayed answer' of 14 December is headed '*Private*': 'When I wrote to Sir Thos Fremantle I felt that I could not satisfactorily to myself perform the duties required from me at the Sessions.' Car-

I trust Lady Carington is quite well, to whom I beg leave to present my Compts. & am,

My dear Lord, Ever sincerely Yours | *B. Disraeli*

4254 TO: LORD NAAS   Hughenden [Wednesday] 24 October 1866

ORIGINAL: INL Mayo MS [36]
EDITORIAL COMMENT: C of Ex paper, seal crossed out and 'Hughenden Manor' written in. Endorsed in another hand on the first page: 'Ld. N. Oct 30' and on the eighth page: 'Disraeli Oct. 31/66 Elections'.

Private   Hughenden Manor | Oct 24 1866

Right Honorable | Lord Naas

My dear Naas,

I take quite yr view of the Tipp[erar]y Election & never was more hopeful as to Irish affairs.[1]

Its a great thing, that elections shd. no longer be questions betn. Prots: & Cats:, & still greater, / that we can support a Rom: Cath: gentleman without having Ultramontanism thrown in our face.

I hope everything will be done to show Waldron,[2] that his spirited conduct is appreciated by the aristocracy. That, I take it, to be his point. He may have faults, but he wd. be a capital candidate, / on another occasion.

I wish, for yr sake, we had won, because it wd. have given great lustre to yr Irish administration, wh:, however, seems a great success. I hear, even in Buckinghamshire, of the splendor, tact, & popularity of yr Ld. Lieut: never was so good an appointment.[3] / As Lady Jersey (the Dow[age]r) said to me, with her usual social tact: "His very family make a Court"[.][4]

I fear Pope Hennessy is playing terrible tricks. He has written to me many letters, & appeals, to none of wh: have I given the slightest answer, tho' I / have forwarded them all to Montagu Corry, for future use if required. Hennessy, what[eve]r happens, can't very well join the Whigs – but, I fear, he has endangered Wexford.[5]

---

rington had received letters from so many justices and members of the bar 'expressing their desire that I shd take time to see whether I shd not recover my voice that reluctantly I thought it right on my part to listen to those wishes & I will make the trial once more. From what I can gather your view will not be unacceptable to the Justices if I am constrained to retire. Much difference would be kindled if the proposed Vice Chairman be either a Clergyman or a gentleman farmer – in opposition to such appointments I should actively join. It is very desirable that on appointments connected with the administration of justice canvassing & voting shd be avoided, & I will cordially assist any arrangement which may obviate this inconvenience.' H B/XXI/C/81. Carrington would remain LL of Bucks until his death in 1868.

---

1 This communication from Naas to which D appears to reply has not been found.
2 Laurence Waldron (1811-1875), an Irish barrister 1840 (ceased to practise 1842), high sheriff of Lough 1860, a JP for Tipperary and co Dublin, a DL for co Dublin, MP (L) for Tipperary 1857-65. See **4226**n4.
3 The LL of Ireland was James Hamilton, Lord Abercorn.
4 Lord and Lady Abercorn had thirteen children; all seven daughters would marry peers.
5 A 22 October report from Dublin on the Tipperary elections had stated that Hennessy was 'not likely to resign his claims. In case he does not, Wexford will present the same sort of anomaly as Tipperary – a Roman Catholic will appear on the hustings, backed by the Protestant landlords, as the supporter of a Conservative Government; while the priesthood, leading a fierce democracy, will fight for the Protestant candidate.' *The Times* (23 Oct 1866).

Never mind, whatever happens – I am certain we are at last on the right / line, so far as Irish politics are concerned.

And I am not very much afraid about English.

Not knowing what sort of man Waldron was, & thinking he might, in a huff, publish my letter, I didn't like to write / to him, or I wd. have done so, to have thanked him for his spirited effort.[6]

We go to HighClere on Friday, &, from thence, on Monday to town, where we shall now fix our headquarters.

I think our first Cabinet will, / probably, be summoned for the 1st. Novr. I hope you will be there.[7]

Yrs ever | D.

Give my love to your wife.

TO: MONTAGU CORRY   Hughenden [Thursday] 25 October 1866   **4255**
ORIGINAL: H B/XX/D/363
EDITORIAL COMMENT: C of Ex paper, seal crossed out and 'H' written in.

Montagu Corry Esq.   H | Octr 25. 1866
Pray give directions, that my newspapers are sent to Highclere, ↑Newbury↓. Tomorrows evening papers, for example, to begin with.

Yrs | D.

TO: [MONTAGU CORRY]   Grosvenor Gate [Tuesday] 30 October [1866]   **4256**
ORIGINAL: H B/XX/D/27
PUBLICATION HISTORY: M&B IV 465, dated 30 October 1866, the first two paragraphs
EDITORIAL COMMENT: Endorsed in another hand on the first page: '1866'. *Dating*: by context; see n2.

Octr. 30

I send Gladstone's book, wh: I found on my arrival at G. Gate with the Publishers Comp[limen]ts[.][1]

It is a sorry looking volume: more of a reprint of the speeches of last year, with no evidence of matured & continuous policy. /

---

6 Naas on 30 October would write to D a letter headed '*Private*': 'I have written the handsomest letter I could pen to Waldron thanking him for the gallant fight he made and telling him that I hope he will be able to point to our *measures* as a gratification for the course he took – when he next addresses the Tipperary Constituency ... We think the best thing to be done in Wexford is to keep Henessy [*sic*] and Kavanagh going on a little. This policy has been so far successful that no Whig has yet come forward. [Liberal MP] Sir J[ohn] Gray who is now the wire puller of the Radicals and Place hunters here does not know what ticket to take up in Wexford. If Kavanagh retires he must raise the "Moderate" flag against Henessy to catch the Cork Protestants and the Whigs – if Henessy retires – he must raise the Catholic Flag agst Kavanagh – however I am very nervous about it ... I hope to see you in a few days and will have a good talk with you over Irish affairs which were never more interesting and never so difficult – Abercorn does right well. He is not only a splendid Pageant but a very sensible and tractable man of business – he made quite an oration at the Q[ueen']s University last Week.' H B/XX/BO/23.

7 Naas on 29 October would send D a note saying he would be unable to 'get over for the 1st Cabinet – I hope however to be there for the second.' H B/XX/BO/22.

---

1 See **4238**&n5.

I hope yours will be much more business-like & impressive: ↑both in matter & in form:↓ but the sooner you get it out the better.

I send you also f a very curious letter from yr friend, Ld. Arthur![2]

D.

4257 TO: SIR JOHN PAKINGTON Downing Street [Tuesday] 30 October 1866
ORIGINAL: WRC 705:349 BA 3835/7(ii)22
EDITORIAL COMMENT: C of Ex paper.

Confidential October 30 1866

Right Honorable | Sir Jno. S. Pakington Bart | G.C.B.

My dear Pakington,

Your letter,[1] addressed to Hughenden, only reached me last night.

The proposal of a second supplemental estimate is so highly irregular, that it can only / be justified by an emergency.

I cannot bring myself to believe, that the circumstances, wh: you allege, reach that character.

I do not see, to us, either the disgrace, or the inconvenience, involved in the purchase of the / Ottoman iro ironclad by Prussia. If we purchase it, Prussia will, of course, order another of the same build; perhaps half a dozen. What then?

If we want such a ship, why should we not build it ourselves? By / purchasing the Turk, we shd. gain, perhaps, twelve months. In the present state of foreign affairs,

---

2 Lord Arthur Pelham-Clinton on 28 October 1866 had written to D that his 'ambition is to be in office' and would D 'use your influence in my favour'. A letter to Derby had led to 'a most kind answer, promising when in his power to accede to my wishes.' Pelham-Clinton had enclosed a clipping from the *Irish Times* 'thinking it may interest you. It is written in defence of Mr [Laurence] Waldron, from the villainous attacks made upon him, "& The Conservative Party," by most of the Irish papers.' H B/XXI/C/277. Lord Arthur Pelham-Clinton (1840-1870), son of the Duke of Newcastle and MP (L) for Newark 1865-8, was lover of cross-dresser Ernest ('Stella') Boulton (whose visiting cards read 'Lady Arthur Clinton'). Boulton and his companion Frederick William Park would be arrested on 28 April 1870; Pelham-Clinton would die (an apparent suicide) on 18 June, the day after receiving a subpoena for the trial.

———

1 See Pakington's letter of 25 October (**4251**n5). With his 26 October letter, headed '*Confidential*', he had enclosed a 'paper from the Accountant General's Office – I think the estimated surplus is reliable to the full extent stated, because the men are now sufficiently below the vote to make it probable that the surplus on vote 1 for the last six months of the year, will be at least equal to that on the First – On the other hand I am very sorry to hear there is an excess of £170,000 on the Transport vote. But this has really nothing to do with Naval Expenditure, & has been caused by the late sudden demand for troops from Canada. I have talked the matter over with Sir A. Milne, & he feels very strongly with me that both in fact, & in effect out of doors, the purchase of this remarkable Turkish Ship by Prussia, would be greatly to be deplored. He also tells me that although we find the instalments strictly due to the Contractors within the financial year will be rather more than I stated as a conjecture, in my letter to Lord Derby, he has no doubt we can make a bargain with the Contractors if we agree to take the ship, to limit the payments within the financial year to £100,000, and to accept for the ship completed, the price agreed upon with the Turkish Government. The question I have therefore to submit for your consideration is whether you will consent to our entering into negotiation for the purchase & completion of the ship, on the understanding that not more than 100,000£ is to be paid to the Contractors before April – Thus leaving a surplus of £60,000 towards the excess which has been incurred on the Transport vote. P.S. – Since writing the above I have been informed by the Accountant General that the excess upon vote 17 will be £149,000 instead of 170,000£.' The 'paper', headed 'Memo 26 Oct 1866 Surplus roughly estimated on Estimates 1866/67', lists a total 'Probable Saving' of £160,000. H B/XX/P/80, 80a.

twelve months are not so valuable as £420,000, wh: might be expended on those classes of vessels, in wh: we are notoriously deficient; whereas / in first-class Iron-clads, our present position is more than respectable; indeed, so far as I can collect, quite adequate to the occasion.[2]

I hope, therefore, you will not press me again[3] to sanction a step, / wh: not only the state of the Exchequer, but general policy, does not, I think, justify.

Ever yours sincerely, | D.

TO: [LORD STANLEY]　　　　　　　　　[London] Thursday 1 November 1866　**4258**
ORIGINAL: H B/XIII/21
EDITORIAL COMMENT: A note in D's hand.

Nov. 1. 1866

What about the "Tornado"?[1]

TO: LORD STANLEY　　　　　　Grosvenor Gate [Saturday] 3 November 1866　**4259**
ORIGINAL: H H/LIFE
EDITORIAL COMMENT: From a typescript headed: 'D. to Ld. Stanley, Grosvenor Gate, Nov. 3. '66.'

Dear Stanley,

I see, by the papers, that you have appointed Harcourt to a post of great authority: it may not be true; it probably is.[1]

---

2 The Royal Navy in 1866 had numerous classes of armoured warships: eight floating batteries, fourteen broadside ironclads, four armoured sloops, three turret ships, two central battery ships and one armoured gunboat. Prussia had two ironclads. See **4550**n3.

3 The next extant letters in H from Pakington to D are from 3 and 4 December and concern other topics.

---

1 Stanley has replied beneath D's query: 'Nothing new. I think the Spaniards have very strong grounds of suspicion against her. We can only hasten the trial, & watch the case. S. Her sister ship the Cyclone is supposed to have got away and to be now in the Chilian service.' A letter by captain Edward M. Collier, dated 31 October at Cadiz and published in *The Times* on 9 November, related how his screw steamship, the *Tornado*, having put in at Madeira for coal and provisions on 21 August, had set sail on the 22nd and was soon boarded by the Spanish frigate *Gerona*. Collier's crew 'were forced on the poop, like so many pigs' and his ship ransacked. On the 26th they arrived at Cadiz 'and although we have been about ten weeks detained as prisoners of war, I am quite ignorant of the charges made against my ship's crew.' According to *The Times* on 15 January 1867 (reprinting from the *Observer*) a decree of 15 December 1866 had declared the *Tornado* '"a good prize of war," and ordered the proceeds of her sale (she cost 75,000*l.*) to be divided amongst the crew of the frigate Gerona, which captured her. The crew (57 of whom are British subjects) are declared to be "Chilian prisoners of war," and as such are to remain in prison until the close of the war between Spain and Chili.' The crew had endured months of 'inquisitorial examinations by the secret tribunal' and the Spanish court had 'pronounced the sentence on the grounds that the *Tornado* was '"a Chilian privateer"'.

---

1 William George Granville Venables Vernon Harcourt (1827-1904), BA 1851 Cambridge, a barrister (Inner Temple 1854), QC 1866, would be MP (L) for Oxford City 1868-80, Derby 1880-95 and Monmouthshire W 1895-1904. He would be professor of international law at Cambridge 1869-87, sol-gen 1873-4, Kt 1874, home secretary 1880-5, PC 1880 and chancellor of the exchequer 1886 and 1892-5. In favour of strict neutrality in the American civil war, Harcourt had published his *Times* articles as *Letters by Historicus on some Questions of International Law* (1863) and *American Neutrality* (1865). In 1866 he declined D's offer of a safe Conservative seat in Wales.

I think, I am as free from personal rancor, as most men, and hope I take a large, and charitable, view of the excesses of political writing. But there is a line, which ought not to be passed, even in times of fiercest controversy, and there are statements, and expressions, which ought never to be forgiven.

I think, that the author of "Public Morality" ought not to be preferred by a Ministry, of which your father is the chief, and in which I still continue his scandalous Lieutenant![2]

There is also another reason, which should make you hesitate before sanctioning such an appointment.

Mr. Harcourt is the author of a long continued series of personal, and malignant libels against Malmesbury. They were avowedly written "to drive him out of the Foreign office and to prevent him from re-entering it."[3]

The successor of Lord Malmesbury[4] ought not to place himself in confidential communication with his malevolent, and now successful, accuser.

Yrs. D.[5]

4260   TO: [MONTAGU CORRY]   [London] Saturday 3 November [1866]
ORIGINAL: H B/XIII/1
EDITORIAL COMMENT: C of Ex paper, seal crossed out. Docketed beside the date in another hand '66'.
Dating: by context; see n1.

Nov. 3

Write to Sir Geo: Bowyer Bart: M.P. & say, that H.M. Governm[en]t intend to issue a Royal Commission to consider the best mode of making a Digest of the Statute / Law, &, that, if it would be agreeable to him, I will recommend his name to be inserted in the Commission.[1]

---

2 In his anonymous 48-page pamphlet (by 'An Englishman'), *The Morality of Public Men. A letter to the Right. Hon. the Earl of Derby* (1852), Harcourt alludes to D as Derby's '"scandalous ally"' (p 40). He would also publish *The Morality of Public Men. A second letter to the Right. Hon. the Earl of Derby* (1853).

3 These 'libels' and D's quotation have not been traced.

4 Malmesbury had been foreign secretary in 1852 and 1858-9.

5 Stanley would reply on 3 November 1866: 'Your letter is reasonable and just, but it applies to a state of things which does not exist. You have been misled by some newspaper report which I have not seen. I have not named Vernon Harcourt to "a post of great authority" or to any post of authority small or great. What I have done is this. I have formed a commission to enquire into and report upon the state of our neutrality laws generally. This commission consists of twelve persons, mostly lawyers. Cranworth, Cairns, several of the judges, are members of it. The list was approved by Lord Derby, and made out by me in consultation chiefly with Cairns. The commission is unpaid, and its sole function is that of enquiry. On this commission I have placed the gentleman to whom you refer. As he took the most active and prominent part in the long discussions on the American claims, and is one of the very few lawyers who have mastered international questions, I could not well have excluded him. He gets nothing for the service: nor does it give any increase of position to a Q.C. who is making from £8000 to £10,000 a year at the parliamentary bar. I cannot help thinking from your letter that you must [have] got hold of some story very different from the fact.' H B/XX/S/751.

---

1 On the letter's last (blank) page, Corry has written, 'Wrote to Sir G.B. according to instructions.' Bowyer on 5 November 1866 would thank D 'for proposing to put my name in the Statute Law Commission. It is a subject in which I take a great interest & I shall be glad to give my services.' Bowyer would not be listed among the members of the Statute Law Committee. H B/XXI/B/715; *The Times* (20 Dec 1878). See **4261**n2.

TO: [LORD DERBY] Downing Street [Friday] 16 November [1866] 4261
ORIGINAL: DBP Box 146/2
EDITORIAL COMMENT: C of Ex paper. *Dating*: by context; see n2.

See Cairns note[1] Nov 16

There is great want of a Treasury Draughtsman & the Treasury have mentioned the name of Mr Reilly,[2] of whom I / do not know, whether he is the same gentleman who sketched our bill of yesterday[.]

The Treasury is pressing, as the bills are / thickening daily[.]

D.

TO: [LORD DERBY] [London, Sunday] 18 November 1866 4262
ORIGINAL: DBP Box 146/2
PUBLICATION HISTORY: M&B IV 459-61, omitting the first line and the next two paragraphs
EDITORIAL COMMENT: Docketed in another hand on the last page: 'Mr. Disraeli. Novr. 6/66'. *Sic*: embarassed.

MEMORANDUM on the present position of the Ministry: Nov. 18. 1866

It is probable, that the general deliberations of the Cabinet may conclude on Wednesday next, & it is scarcely desirable, that our colleagues shd. disperse without another meeting on Parliamentary Reform.

It becomes, therefore, necessary that a precise conception / of our situation shd. prevail.

We are entirely unpledged upon the subject.

But if no notice is taken of it in the Queen's Speech,[1] or no subsequent announcement of measures is made by the leader of the Ho: of Commons, it is probable, that an amendment of a general character may be carried, wh: / will replace the question in the hands of the late Government, & they return to power not more embarassed by the Radicals than before.

It is not probable, that a dissolution, even if granted, would, under these circumstances, help us.

---

1 This note has not been found.
2 Francis Savage Reilly (1825-1883), educated at Trinity College, Dublin, a barrister (Lincoln's Inn 1851), author of *Parliamentary Drawing and Conveyancing* (1880), in 1882 would be named counsel to the Speaker of the House of Commons, QC and KCMG. During January and February 1867, Reilly would prepare several drafts of the British North America Bill (introduced in the Lords on 12 February) and is most likely the one who replaced, at the last moment, 'Welfare' (well-being) with 'Order' in the now-famous phrase 'Peace, Order and good Government'. In the Commons on 1 March 1867 D would state: 'I regret to say that at the Treasury at the present moment there is no equity draughtsman who can assist the Government in that respect [*in the preparation of the proposed reform bill*]. There ought to be one; and I made an offer this year to one of the most distinguished men in the profession; but so great is the reward which first-rate professional talent now commands, that the application of the Government was fruitless, and I did not think myself justified, though the sum offered was considerable, in increasing that offer.' In 1868 Reilly would serve on the Statute Law Committee nominated by Cairns to revise the Statutes, whose fifteenth and last volume would be published in December 1878. Richard Gwyn *John A.: The Man Who Made Us* (Random House Canada 2007) 400-1; *Hansard* CLXXXV col 1235; *The Times* (20 Dec 1878, 17 Aug 1880, 18 Apr 1882, 28 Aug 1883).

---

1 See **4321**n2.

It would seem, therefore, we must act.

How?

1st. / By the introduction of a Bill?

2nd. By resolutions leading to a Bill?

3rdly By resolutions leading to Enquiry?

It seems probable, that no measure of Parliament[ar]y Reform could be passed by a Conservative Govt., except in a Parliament where they have essentially a majority.

Resolutions, / as the basis of a bill, tho' not so immediately dangerous as a proposal of direct legislation, would ultimately lead to defeat.

There remains, therefore, to be considered the case of Resolutions, wh:, tho' laying down a complete scheme, should end in a Royal Commission.

If the difficulty to wh:, in a moment, I will advert, could be removed the / chances are, that this would be a successful course.

It may be assumed, that the Ho: of Commons is really opposed to any violent reform, & to any reform of any kind wh: is immediate; & the longer the decision of its opinion can be delayed, the more likely it will be in favor of moderation & postponement[.]

If the first week of / March was fixed for the introduction of the Resolutions, the discussion on them need not commence until the 1st. week in April.

If the House, then, gets involved in the discussion, the Liberal Party will, probably, be broken up.

If, as is more likely, Mr. Gladstone meets the ministerial motion by a general resolution in favor of immediate legislation, it is not impossible / he may be defeated, wh: will establish the Government.

But if he succeed, it will, probably, be only by a narrow majority, & the dissolution would, then, take place on an issue between Bright's policy & our programme.

But to ensure the success of such a campaign, one condition is necessary: that there should be substantial grounds for / a Royal Commission; & this is the difficulty to wh: I referred.

I myself am at a loss to find these grounds, & this is the point on which the thought of the Cabinet sho[ul]d be concentrated.

If the Resolutions at present in yr portfolio were adopted, there wo[ul]d be substantial grounds, in a great degree arising from the necessary Re-settlement / of the boundaries of the smaller Boros': but reflection persuades me, that this proposal would not, on the whole, be a wise one; because one of our leading principles sho[ul]d be to enlist, as far as possible, the sympathies of the small Boros', & they perhaps, would deem an alteration of their boundaries only second, as a disaster, to their total / disfranchisement.

The settlement of the boundaries of the Northern Boros' is not ample enough for a Royal Commission issued under such circumstances. Means to effect such an end might have been adopted in the Recess.

It has been suggested, that the subject of Bribery might be, among those referred to the R.C., & this deserves consideration, but if it were / practicable, there is still not a dignus nodus.[2]

2 'Dignus vindice nodus' (Horace): literally, a knotty point worthy of being made a civil action.

The substantialness of the Royal Commission is the key of the position, & I, therefore, bring it under yr deep consideration.[3]

D.

TO: LORD DERBY   Downing Street [Sunday] 18 November 1866   **4263**
ORIGINAL: DBP Box 146/2
EDITORIAL COMMENT: C of Ex paper.

Right Honble | The Earl of Derby | K.G.   Novr 18 1866
My dear Lord,
Depend upon it, Mr Macaulay is not susceptible of any management.[1]

He will resign, tho' it may be prudent for you, / or me, to see him.

I rather apprehend he is legally entitled to his full abolition pension: morally, certainly, for tho' a commissioner only a year, he was Secretary for / twelve.

If he go, wh: he will, I really do not know a more competent successor than Montagu, who really understands the business.

---

3 Derby would write to D on 'Monday' (19 November): 'I am at a loss to imagine from what source you derive the happy delusion that our present Cabinet may probably terminate on Wednesday next. For my part, I should be too happy to think that we had been able to put our own preliminary measures en train by Wednesday *week*: and I do not look forward to my own release before the middle or latter end of that week: We have not yet touched upon the very difficult Irish questions, such as Landlord & Tenant, R.C. Charter, and National Education, which cannot be satisfactorily disposed of under, if in, two days deliberations. Then I quite agree with you that we must have another discussion on the Reform Question. The difficulties of finding sufficient reason for a reference to a Commission are very just; but they *must* be found, as it is, I am convinced, our only chance of escaping Shipwreck; and, from what I hear, it is a very good one. Such at least, I have reason to know, is the opinion of our Opponents, as it certainly is my own. I should much like to talk this matter over with you – but take my word for it you must discard all notion of seeing Hughenden this week.' H B/XX/S/375.

---

1 Charles Zachary Macaulay (1814-1886), a barrister, was a commissioner of audit from 2 May 1865 to 1 April 1867. Derby had written to D on 18 November: 'I had actually written, but fortunately had not sent a letter to [Lord] R[obert] Montagu, when I received the accompanying papers from [permanent financial secretary to the treasury] G[eorge] Hamilton. It seems to me that whether Macaulay goes or stays, the Act will require Amendment; and that as it stands at present, we could not appoint Montagu; for we are restricted to appointing "one of the Com[missione]rs. of Audit"; and if Macaulay, for whom it was intended, declines to accept, neither of the others are competent to do the duty. Sir W[illiam] Dunbar, who is at the head, is, I am told, absolutely inefficient; so that even if the legal difficulty could be got over, the whole of the duty would really devolve on a new and inexperienced man. I have not the Act before me, and can therefore express no opinion as to the justice of Mr. Macaulay's criticisms; but the late Government were, it seems, aware of his objections, and ought not to have allowed the Bill to pass, leaving unsettled a matter which lay at the root of the whole scheme. I must have some conversation with you and G. Hamilton before we take any step: Of course I have left back the letter to R. Montagu; but the Pall Mall Gazette of Friday announced his intended appointment! You will see [financial secretary to the treasury George Ward] Hunt's & Hamilton's notes in the 2d. Packet of Papers. *If* we are obliged to accede to the request, it must be on the same condition as the Irish grant, of a local Subscription in aid, and to an equal extent. I doubt its being passed on such terms.' H B/XX/S/376. The Exchequer and Audit Departments Act, 'to consolidate the duties of the Exchequer and Audit Departments, to regulate the receipt, custody, and issue of public money, and to provide for the audit of the accounts of the same', was scheduled to come into effect on 1 April 1867. *The Times* (7 Nov 1866).

The police Magistrate is dead.[2] Malmesbury said Ld. Lonsdale seemed / to like the idea, but little Bentinck[3] was away.

Secure Walpole about it.

I will send on the Scotch papers tomorrow. My "memorandum",[4] wh: you have returned, was only drawn up for / yr own consideration[.] By returning it to me, it wd. seem you thought I intended it for a circular, wh: I shall not make it – even if there were / time, wh: there is not.

Yrs ever, | D.

4264   TO: MONTAGU CORRY   Grosvenor Gate [Tuesday] 20 November 1866
ORIGINAL: H B/XX/D/28
EDITORIAL COMMENT: C of Ex paper, seal crossed out and 'G. Gate' written in. *Sic*: Montague [*twice*].

Montague Corry | Esqr.   G. Gate | Nov 20 1866

My dear Montague,

You must not, on any account, return to town till you are quite yourself.[1]

I enclose two proofs, wh:, as the second contains a great blunder / that will stop the way until it is rectified, you had better forward to the Printer by return, if possible.

I, wd. say, myself, that there was little hope of getting the volume out / before Xmas.[2]

We had better bow to our fate & not vex ourselves, wh: will only retard yr recovery.

It must be a New Year's gift, instead of a Xmas box.[3]

When / the speeches are official, I am convinced that the speaker shd be described as I have corrected it. It is of vast importance, that the opinions expressed shd be received, as much as possible, as of a *party*, & not a mere *personal*, character.

Besides the C of Er / has no personal name in the H of C., differing in this respect

---

2 Edward Yardley (1805-1866), a barrister (Lincoln's Inn 1834) and a magistrate at Marylebone police court, after a lengthy illness had died at 6 *pm* on this day (18th). *The Times* (20 Nov 1866).

3 Presumably George Bentinck – cousin of the late Lord George Bentinck, known as 'Big Ben' and so-called by Derby – for whom his uncle, Lord Lonsdale, had tried to find government employment (see **4126**&nn1&3 and **4133**&n1). Bentinck, MP (C) for Whitehaven 1865-91, was apparently being considered to replace Yardley.

4 See **4262**.

---

1 The letter from Corry to which D appears to reply has not been found.

2 Thomas Longman had written to D on 19 November 1866 from Paternoster Row apologizing for the delay in printing D's speeches on parliamentary reform: 'Mr Corry has had considerable difficulty in procuring copy to print from of which probably you are not aware ... The printer has copy for the whole, excepting 3 or 4 speeches in a volume of Hansard Debates for which application has been made to Mr Corry. Should there be no delay the printer will undertake to have all in type by the end of the second week in December ... the quick return of proofs will be essential for publication by Xmas.' H E/VII/A7.

3 *Parliamentary Reform* would be published in January 1867. A *Times* leader would note that D had furnished 'his friends with a body of doctrine, his enemies with an arsenal where they may find weapons hereafter to be used against him.' Another would comment that the speeches' most 'striking characteristic ... is their completeness and consistency.' William Longman would write to Corry on 4 February 1867 that 'we are selling a good many copies of Mr D'Israeli's Speeches. On the 25th January we had on hand 279[,] on the 29th 201 and today (Feb 4) 153.' *The Times* (22, 23 Jan 1867); H B/E/VII/A8.

from all other Ministers. It is not merely an office but a title, & on all the ↑daily votes on↓ proceedings of the House & on Committees & on every occasion his surname is never used.

Yours | D.

TO: **GEORGE GROTE** [London] Saturday [24 November 1866]   **4265**
ORIGINAL: H B/XXI/G/369
EDITORIAL COMMENT: Docketed by MA on the fourth page: '1866 Novbr. 24th Mr. Grote'.

Geo: Grote | Esqr¹   Saturday

Dear Mr Grote,

I am very sorry, indeed, to give you the trouble of calling on me again – but could you do me the honor of calling / *here* at two o'ck: today?

Yrs faithfully | D.²

TO: **LORD DERBY** [London, Saturday] 24 November 1866   **4266**
ORIGINAL: DBP Box 146/2
EDITORIAL COMMENT: C of Ex paper, seal crossed out. Endorsed in another hand on the fourth page: 'Ansd. Encl retd. D' and in a third hand: 'Nov. 24. Disraeli Right Honbl B. as to an Appt. Ecclesiastical History Chair at Oxford Letter from Ld. Beauchamp'.

Confidential   Nov 24 1866

Right Honorable | The Earl of Derby | K.G.

My dear Lord,

I am scrupulous in never attempting to interfere in the distribution of yr patronage, except when it affects the peculiar department, you have entrusted to / my care – the Ho: of Commons; when it is always my duty to offer you my counsel without reserve – & I shall reply, by this post, in that spirit, to the writer of the enclosed,¹ / recommending him to address himself to the Prime Minister. – but as he is a very powerful, & a very *sensitive*, individual, I think, on reflection, it is best, that I shd forward / you his letter, tho' I shall not admit that to him.

Yrs ever, | D.²

---

1 D may be consulting eminent classical historian George Grote, a member of the council of University College, London, regarding the appointment of the regius professor of ecclesiastical history at Oxford. See **4266**&n2.
2 Grote would endorse D's letter on the third page: 'most certainly – I will call here at *two* I am much obliged by the appointment *G.G.*' H B/XXI/G/369.

———

1 Beauchamp's letter to D (see ec) has not been found. See **4267**.
2 Derby would return Beauchamp's letter to D on 24 November: 'You need not give yourself the trouble of recommending him to apply to me, as he has done so already. I received from him this morning a letter very nearly the duplicate of that which he has written to you, which of course I shall answer. I am quite aware of the importance of keeping him in good humour, and I shall be glad if I can meet his wishes: but the post is a very important one, and especially so in the eyes of the University; and Candidates are coming in in numbers. I must take him before I decide among them.' H B/XX/S/377. The Rev Walter Waddington Shirley, canon of Christ Church, Oxford and regius professor of ecclesiastical history, had died on 20 November 1866. He would be succeeded in January 1867 by the Rev Henry Mansel. *The Times* (22 Nov 1866, 9 Jan 1867).

4267 TO: LORD BEAUCHAMP   Grosvenor Gate [Saturday] 24 November 1866

ORIGINAL: BCP [34]; now BL ADD MS 61892
PUBLICATION HISTORY: M&B V 59n1, the first paragraph
EDITORIAL COMMENT: C of Ex paper, seal crossed out and 'Grosvenor Gate' written in. *Sic*: entres.

The | Earl Beauchamp   Grosvenor Gate | Nov 24 1866
My dear Beauchamp,

I will do my utmost, & immediately, to forward yr wishes[1] – but, entres nous, I don't think my interference, in matters of that kind, is much affected – at least, I fancy so. I asked for a deanery, the other day, for / Mansel, but he is not a Dean.[2]

However you may rely upon my always doing my best – at least for you.

Yours ever, | D.

4268 TO: MARY ANNE DISRAELI   Windsor Castle [Sunday] 25 November 1866

ORIGINAL: H A/I/A/329
PUBLICATION HISTORY: Weintraub *Disraeli* 441, extracts from the fifth and sixth paragraphs
EDITORIAL COMMENT: Windsor Castle paper. *Sic*: Wycomb; ¼ to.

Nov 25 1866

My darling Wife,

Your handwriting this morning cheered me.[1]

When I arrived here, a page appeared, who sd. "you are to dine with the Queen, Sir, at ½ pt 8 o'ck:"

After that, General Grey came, & talked over many affairs with / me. He had just come from a visit to Ld. Macclesfield,[2] & stopped at Wycomb on the railroad[.] "The scene of our first acquaintance" he said.

At ½ pt 8, I found I was to dine with the Queen at a little round table, with ½ a dozen guests. The Prince & Princess Christian,[3] the / Duke of Edinburgh,[4] the Princess Louise,[5] Lady Caledon[6] & Col. Genl Grey: a most agreeable party: general conversation in wh: the Queen joined much & sustained. Much merriment.

---

1 See **4266**ec.
2 Henry Longueville Mansel (1820-1871), BA classics and mathematics 1843 Oxford, deacon 1844, ordained 1845, Waynflete professor of moral and metaphysical philosophy 1859-66 at Magdalen College, regius professor of ecclesiastical history and canon of Christ Church 1866-8, would be Dean of St Paul's Cathedral 1868-71.

---

1 This letter from MA has not been found. According to Charlotte de Rothschild, writing to her son Leopold on 26 November 1866, MA was proud that D had been invited to Windsor for two days, 'whereas the other ministers have not spent more than one day' there. ROTH.
2 Thomas Augustus Wolstenholme Parker (1811-1896), 6th Earl of Macclesfield 1850, MP (C) for Oxfordshire 1837-41.
3 Prince Frederick Christian Charles Augustus (1831-1917) of Schleswig-Holstein-Sonderburg-Augustenburg had married the Princess Helena on 5 July 1866. See **4126**n2.
4 Prince Alfred had been created Duke of Edinburgh, Earl of Kent and Earl of Ulster on 24 May 1866.
5 Princess Louise Caroline Alberta (1848-1939), sixth child of Queen Victoria, Marchioness of Lorne 1871 and Duchess of Argyll 1900. In 1871 she would marry the Marquess of Lorne, whom D would appoint governor-general of Canada in 1878. Beautiful and outspoken – the Queen reacted 'with some annoyance and alarm towards her daughter's feminism and liberalism' – she would become an able painter and sculptor. ODNB.
6 The Dowager Countess of Caledon in 1845 as Lady Jane Frederica Harriot Mary Grimston (1825-1888),

I sate next to the Princess Christian – very good looking, & vivacious. "It's a great many years since / we met" she said to me.

"Nay, Madam; only recently; a very interesting occasion" "Ah! yes!" she sd "you saw me then: I didn't see you. I meant old days: I was one of the little girls, who always had to knock, when you were talking with my father, & dinner was waiting"[.] /

The Duke of Edinburgh talked to me much after dinner, & said, that there was a vacancy in the Brotherhood of the Trinity House,[7] & that as he was Master, having succeeded the Prince Consort, he intended to propose me. This is a very great distinction indeed, & you wear the / Windsor uniform.[8]

After dinner, the Queen & Princesses disappear: after some conversation, the Princes, who go & smoke, & you see them no more. Genl. Grey & myself went to a Drawing Room, where we found again Lady Caledon, all the maids of Honor &c. & equerries, Alfred / Paget,[9] Lord Crofton,[10] &c &c – who now, as I gather, never dine with the Queen or see her scarcely.

The Queen talked to me when she rose from dinner, when there was a little circle, wh: lasted ¼ to an hour – & said she shd. see me today on affairs; / & I have since been informed I am to have an audience at six o'ck.[11]

One of my worst nights: quite shattered, but I don't go out, & shall repose all day. Adieu! my best beloved! | D.

TO: QUEEN VICTORIA   Downing Street [Monday] 26 November 1866   **4269**
ORIGINAL: RAC B22 125
EDITORIAL COMMENT: C of Ex paper.

Nov 26 1866

The Chanr of the Exchequer with his humble duty to Yr Majesty.
On arriving in town, the C of E. had the satisfaction of finding a telegram, followed /

---

fourth daughter of 1st Earl of Verulam, had married James Du Pre Alexander, 3rd Earl of Caledon, deceased 1855.

7 See VI **2308n3**, **4286**&n4 and **4293**&n2.

8 Introduced by George III in 1779 and modified by George IV in 1820, the Windsor uniform includes elaborate gold embroidery on the front of the coatee and at the cuffs. On 19 December 1866, Charles Fremantle would inform D that 'your Tailors have a proper sense of their responsibilities, and will have accomplished the Trinitarian Costume in good time.' H B/XXI/F/273.

9 Lord Alfred Henry Paget, a younger son of the late 1st Marquess of Anglesey, enjoyed a long career in the royal household as equerry 1837-41, chief equerry and clerk marshal 1846-52, 1852-8 and 1859-74, remaining clerk marshal until his death.

10 Edward Crofton (1806-1869), 2nd Baron Crofton 1817, a representative peer (Ireland) 1840 and lord in waiting 1852, 1858-9, 1866-8, in 1833 had married Lady Georgiana Paget, third daughter of 1st Marquess of Anglesey.

11 The Queen on this day (25th) recorded in her journal: 'Saw Mr. Disraeli after tea, who spoke of the great Reform meeting on the 3rd, also of Reform in general. He said only two Cabinets had been held upon it, that the members were unanimous in agreeing that the subject *must* be dealt with by Resolutions, preparatory to a Commission being issued, so that the matter might be settled irrespective of Party. Then he talked of the army, and of the great importance of having an Army of Reserve, which was dearest Albert's opinion. He was amiable and clever, but is a strange man.' *LQVB* I 378.

by the enclosed letter,[1] informing him, that the celebrated Blacas Collection[2] had been purchased on behalf of Yr Majestys Government.

The collection is not / only rare, but unique.

It is extremely rich in choice gems, in wh: our national collection is deficient; & wh: ~~cann~~ could not, otherwise, be supplied, as almost all / the fine gems are now in Royal, or Imperial, Collections. The head of Esculapius in marble is said to be the finest of ancient sculptures remaining: being of the best period, & in a condition so / complete, both in form & color, that it would seem as if it had ~~just~~ just left the atelier.

The complete toilette of a Roman Lady, all of precious materials, would, / it is said, fill the cases of a small room.

The cameos singularly fine: one of Augustus of great size & beauty.

There is nothing in the collection, wh: is not of a / very high: &, in many instances, of an unique character.

This magnificent acquisition will compensate for the loss of the Campana Collection,[3] wh:, after much hesitation & lost / opportunity on our side, was obtained by France, to our shame & unceasing regret.

This purchase, too, ↑will↓ facilitate the plans of the Cr. of the Exr., next Session, for / the separation of the National collections, & the establishment of the Museum of Natural History at Kensington.[4]

1 Charles Thomas Newton (see n5) had sent D a telegram dated 25 November 1866: 'Contract signed for blacas [sic] museum price forty eight thousand pounds.' With a letter of that same day from Paris, informing D of ongoing negotiations for the purchase of the Blacas Collection (n2), Newton had enclosed a copy of the contract, dated 25 November 1866 and signed by himself and the comte Stanislas de Blacas. He told D, 'I propose to begin packing the gems tomorrow.' H B/XIV/A/21C, a.

2 The British Museum would acquire the magnificent collection of antiquarian Pierre Louis Jean Casimir, duc de Blacas. The Greek, Roman and Egyptian artifacts included a 'precious collection of ancient gems, in intaglio and cameo', including the 'celebrated cameo of Augustus'; the 'celebrated toilet service of a Roman bride, consisting of a large casket and many cases, small figures, personal ornaments and trappings, all of silver-gilt, and covered with mythological reliefs, embossed and chased'; and 'a colossal head of Aesculapius ... with a votive inscription addressed to Aesculapius and Hygeia'. The House in committee of supply on 18 February 1867 would vote £45,721 to purchase the collection. After explaining its value (in particular that of some of the artifacts mentioned above), D concluded that 'this country has acquired this celebrated collection upon terms which it never will regret.' The Times (5 Dec 1866); Hansard CLXXXV cols 491-512 (D 491-5).

3 The priceless Etruscan, Greek and Roman antiquities in this collection are listed in Susanna Sarti, Giovanni Pietro Campana, 1800-1880: The Man and His Collection (Oxford 2001). Convicted of embezzling public funds in 1857, Campana had been exiled in disgrace and his collection dispersed to various museums. The Times on 16 April 1861 had published a report (dated 9 April) from Rome: 'The agent lately sent to Rome by the British Museum to buy parts of the Campana collection has returned to England without effecting any purchase. It is understood that the sum he was authorized to expend was quite insufficient to give him a commanding position in the negotiation ... It is said that the French particularly want the terracottas, which is just what the Museum wants particularly.' France purchased the Campana collection for £192,000. The Times (10 Jun 1861).

4 The British Museum, lacking space to house its collections, added 96,751 specimens to its Natural History department in 1866 alone. Construction on a new building in South Kensington would last from 1873 to 1880. The 'British Museum (Natural History)', its official name until 1992, would open on 18 April 1881, the day before D's death. The Times (11 May 1867, 16 Apr 1881).

When Mr Newton's report[5] is received, to prepare / wh: he was now at Paris (for the sudden purchase~~d~~, authorised on his private letters~~)~~ was a coup d'etat, or a coup de main,) the Chanr will forward it immediately to Yr / Majesty. In the meantime, he humbly congratulates Yr Majesty on this splendid addition to the treasures of Yr Majesty's Museums.

TO: **MONTAGU CORRY** Grosvenor Gate [Tuesday] 27 November 1866 **4270**
ORIGINAL: H B/XX/D/29
EDITORIAL COMMENT: C of Ex paper, seal crossed out and 'G.G.' written in.

Montagu Corry Esq G.G. | Nov 27 1866

I have sent you, among other things, Mr Major's paper,[1] & Rose's long threatened manifesto.[2] I fear the objections, urged by the Economist,[3] & other journals are scarcely encountered by it, / but I have only glanced over its pages.

I have returned all the proofs – keeping the Revises (3) by me.[4]

I shall probably hear from you before we leave this wh: will be at ½ past 3.[5]

Yours | D.

5 Archaeologist Charles Thomas Newton (1816-1894), BA 1837 and MA 1840 Oxford, had worked in the antiquities department at the British Museum 1840-52 and, after consular postings at Mytilene 1852, Rhodes 1853 and Rome 1859 (involving excavation and acquisition of antiquities for the Museum), was keeper of Greek and Roman antiquities at the Museum 1861-85, obtaining grants in 1864-74 to purchase the Farnese, Pourtalès and Blacas collections. Author of numerous guidebooks to the Museum's collections and of *Essays on Art and Archaeology* (1880), Newton would become a DCL Oxford 1875, LLD Cambridge and PHD Strasbourg 1879, CB 1875, KCB 1887 and in 1889 would receive the royal gold medal of the Royal Institute of British Architects. See **4275**&n2.

---

1 Mr Major has not been identified, nor his paper found.
2 Philip Rose on 24 November 1866 had written to D: 'I am anxious not to have sent you the accompanying observations [*not found*] before this. I hope you will kindly read them and allow me to see you on the subject. I am sure the importance of the subject cannot be exaggerated & it is one that you will be *obliged* to deal with. The Representatives of the principal Railways are pressing me to organize a deputation to you on the subject.' H R/I/B/107.
3 The anonymous author of 'The State of the Money-Market', reprinted in *The Times* on 13 August 1866 from the *Economist*, had objected to the raise by the Bank of England of its lending rate to 10% following the collapse of the Overend bank in May; a lower rate 'would have better regulated the foreign exchanges.' 'Why "Overend's" Failed', reprinted in *The Times* on 26 November 1866 from the *Economist*, detailed the background to the collapse of the bank, listing figures that 'reveal a kind of money dealing which no prestige, no credit, no immense deposits, no accumulated wealth, could make anything save ruinous ... Why Mr. John Henry Gurney, who soon showed himself alive to the evil consequences of irregular transactions, should have permitted the continuance of those transactions must remain a mystery. Mr. Disraeli justly remarks that it is "very difficult for people at the summit of life to believe in the possibility of ruin." ... But we believe that shareholders will fail in their present resistance to their creditors. They must pay their debts, however they may have been induced to incur them.' According to D, Philip Rose represented 'the distressed Shareholders'; see **4125**&n1.
4 Corry was still editing D's speeches on parliamentary reform; see **4187**n3.
5 The DS would leave for Strathfieldsaye (Wellington's estate) on 27 November, returning to Grosvenor Gate on the 30th. H acc.

4271

TO: MONTAGU CORRY   Strathfieldsaye [Wednesday] 28 November 1866
ORIGINAL: H B/XX/D/30
EDITORIAL COMMENT: *Sic*: Montague [*twice*].

Montague Corry Esq   Strathfieldsaye | Nov 28 1866

My dear Montague,

The post arrives here by 8 o'ck: :so I was very glad this morning, when I stepped into my dressing room, to find yr bag.

I return the proofs, & should have been glad to have seen the revise, wh: one looks at, now & then, / & finds slots wh. had escaped us.

I shall not be up till Friday. I find I can't get away without causing great disappointment, & breaking up some social plans.

The Cabinet is called on a merely technical point, & perhaps, wont sit ¼ of an hour.[1] Of course, if there had been real business, / I shd. not have hesitated a moment in finding myself at No. 11 D.S., wh:, between ourselves, suits me much ~~bea~~ better than country houses.

Yrs ever | D.

I am very much amused with the speeches, several of wh: I had quite forgotten.

4272

TO: MONTAGU CORRY   Strathfieldsaye [Thursday] 29 November 1866
ORIGINAL: H B/XX/D/31
COVER: *Private* | Montague Corry Esq | D.S. | *Chr of Exchequer*
PUBLICATION HISTORY: M&B IV 465-6, the first two paragraphs and the full text of the 'Advertisement'
EDITORIAL COMMENT: *Sic*: Montague [*cover*].

M.C. Esq   Strathfieldsaye | Nov 29. 66

My dear Editor,

I send you the two proofs, & begin to see daylight.

Herein, also, is a rough sketch of an advertisement, or preface, wh: you may, not only, alter in any way you like, / but even reconstruct, or altogether put aside.

I made it as a memorandum for yr guidance, & think it indicates the purport & value of yr volume.

Yrs ever | D.

[H B/XX/D/31b]

Advertisement

These speeches commencing at a period even antecedent to the desertion of the principle of Finality by Lord John Russell,[1] & ending with the last Session, were made by a member of Parliament, who, during the whole interval, was either Leader of the opposition, or principal Minister / of the Queen in the House of Commons.

They represent, therefore the opinions of a party, & we have the highest authority for stating that, scarcely with an exception, the views, wh: they represent, were, after

---

1 D is not listed among those present in cabinet on 29 November. *The Times* (30 Nov 1866).

---

1 For the origin of Russell's nickname, 'Finality Jack', see VII **3289**n3.

due deliberation, adopted by every eminent man, who has since sate in the councils of Lord Derby, & by every leading country gentleman of the time. /

So long as the Whig party were firm in upholding the settlement of 1832, the Tory party, tho' not insensible ~~of~~ to some injustice in that measure, resolved to support its authors against all attempts at further change in the constitution of the House of Commons. But when the Whigs yielded their position, their political opponents determined to assert / the principles wh:, in their opinion, shd guide any future re-construction, & wh:, from that time, have, consequently, been placed before the country in the following speeches with an amplitude of knowledge & a vigor & versatility of argument & illustration, wh: have been acknowledged.

These speeches then, form a complete & consistent record of the main opinions of / a great party in the State during the important period in wh: a further change of the constitution of the Ho: of Commons has been in agitation: & the Country, therefore, will now be enabled to ǰ see with what justness it has been asserted, that the Tory party are disqualified from dealing / with the most difficult of modern political questions ~~by~~ ↑in consequence of↓ their constant & unvarying hostility to any attempt to improve our popular representation[.]

London   M.C.
Dec. 1866²

TO: ANTHONY PANIZZI   Grosvenor Gate [Saturday] 1 December 1866   **4273**
ORIGINAL: TEXU [43]
EDITORIAL COMMENT: C of Ex paper, seal crossed out and 'Grosvenor Gate' written in.

Grosvenor Gate | Dec 1 1866

Alas! my dear Panizzi, after a few days work, I go out of town, & shall not return from Hughenden | until after Xmas!¹

Yrs sincerely, | D.

TO: LORD DERBY   Grosvenor Gate [Monday] 3 December 1866   **4274**
ORIGINAL: DBP Box 146/2
PUBLICATION HISTORY: Blake 324, the seventh paragraph
EDITORIAL COMMENT: C of Ex paper, seal crossed out on the first page and 'G. Gate' written in. Endorsed on the eighth page by D 'Confidential for Lord Derby D.' and by Derby 'Put by Confidential D.'. *Sic*: Tennant; embarassing.

Private   G. Gate | Dec 3 1866

The constitution of the Board of Trade is weak, &, in an important division, it is feebly manned.

---

2 The published 'Advertisement' (pp V-VII), dated 'London: *January* 1867.', is identical to D's 'rough sketch', with minor exceptions: 'we have' is 'there is', 'scarcely with an exception' is 'with scarce exceptions', 'sate' is 'sat' and 'universally' has been added before 'acknowledged.' See also **4282**.

---

1 The letter from Anthony Panizzi to which this appears to be a reply has not been found. The DS would leave for Hughenden on 15 December, returning to Grosvenor Gate on 27 December. H acc.

On the other hand, its duties are, every Session, increasing, & from a mere consultative committee, it has become a / Department.

I approve of this scheme of renovation: with some reserve.

The conversion of the V. President, into a Parliamentary Secretary, shd. be postponed until Mr Cave is otherwise placed.[1] / He is a very valuable official, & fully realizes our expectations. Notwithstanding his anomalous position, as long as Northcote remains President, there is no doubt Mr Cave will have the opportunity of serving the Government with / effect, & will not feel any disinclination in that respect.

The real difficulty is with Sir Emerson Tennant. You appointed him in 1858 at my suggestion.[2] I thought it a good opportunity to relieve you from an embarassing claimant, / ~~consideration~~ & I sincerely believed, that his talents, experience, & particular aptitude, would have eminently qualified him for the post.

I have been much disappointed.

He has turned out to be one of the most inefficient, / & useless, of our public servants: no business in him: no sound information: his department in a disgraceful state: & himself a mere club gossip & office lounger.

I shd. like to know from / Northcote how he proposes to provide for him, for, of course, he cannot be sheerly superseded.

D.

I duly received the Resolutions,[3] for wh: my thanks.[4]

4275 TO: CHARLES THOMAS NEWTON   Downing Street
[Wednesday] 5 December 1866

ORIGINAL: H B/XIV/A/25
EDITORIAL COMMENT: A draft in D's hand on C of Ex paper.

C.T. Newton | Esqr   Decr 5 1866

1 The office of board of trade vice-president, held at this time by paymaster-general Stephen Cave, would be replaced in 1867 with a parliamentary secretaryship.
2 In 1852 (not 1858) D had written to Derby (see VI **2387**) suggesting James Emerson Tennent as 'perfectly qualified for the office' of permanent secretary to the board of trade, which he would retain until retiring on 2 February 1867.
3 Derby on 2 December had sent D 'a copy of the Resolutions as provisionally agreed to by the Cabinet. You need not return it. Nos. 9 & 10 will require amendment; and I think it was understood that the three last might be dropped.' H B/XX/S/378. There is in H an undated document in D's hand entitled 'RESOLUTIONS', a draft of 'THE RESOLUTIONS *referred to by the Chancellor of the Exchequer, on the 11th February*' containing ten resolutions; the version published in *Hansard* CLXXXV (Feb-Mar 1867) has thirteen. See app IV and V.
4 Derby would reply on this day (3rd) with a letter headed '*Private*': 'I will return Northcote's papers – I agree with you in approving the general outline of his plan, and also that the change from Vice President to Secretary must be deferred till we can place Cave elsewhere. In the mean time he will discharge the same duties which he would as Secretary, but the pecuniary saving must be postponed. What he refers to as to my expression about "a scheme to make the office more considerable" was a scheme for giving to the V. President certain definite functions, apart from those of the President, which had, I believe, been marked by the late Government. Emerson Tennent is a great difficulty; and unless he retire voluntarily, I do not see how we can move him. If there is to be only one permanent Secretary instead of two, he might naturally say, let the Junior be reduced; which would not answer the purpose. Subject to this difficulty, I think Northcote might be instructed, after the communications which he wishes to have with the Heads of his office, to prepare a Bill, to be at once introduced, if sanctioned by the Cabinet when we meet in January.' H B/XX/S/379.

Sir, I have recd. &c

Before the ~~Treasury~~ Govt can give the order for the payment of the ~~sum due to~~ purchasemoney of ~~for the Collection of~~ the ↑Duc de↓ Blacas ↑Collection↓,[1] a formal / application must be made to ~~it~~ the Treasury by the ~~authorities~~ Trustees of the Brit: Museum, – ~~wh: they have neglected to do~~ This application has not yet been made, but ~~I have given directions that / Mr Winter Jones shall be applied to immediately on this head.~~

When ~~that has been done~~ the necessary official steps have been taken wh: will no doubt be [*illegible word*] you will be empowered to draw on the Pay Master General & / the ~~money~~ claim will be ~~paid~~ discharged at once.

In the meantime, you may, if you please, give this to the ~~Comte~~ representatives of the D. de Blacas as my guarantee for the payment.

It is my intent to be present at the meeting of the Trustees on the 8th.[2]

TO: **WILLIAM FORSYTH**   Downing Street [Thursday] 6 December 1866   **4276**
ORIGINAL: QUA 91
EDITORIAL COMMENT: C of Ex paper. *Sic*: Forsythe.

W. Forsythe Esqr[1]   Decr. 6 1866
My dear Sir,
Your life of Cicero is a valuable addition to my shelves.[2]

As an author, you may be deemed *felix*: for you have selected a / subject of inexhaustible interest, & treated it in a manner not unworthy of it.

Yours faithfully, | *B. Disraeli*

TO: **[SPENCER WALPOLE]**   Downing Street, Thursday 6 December [1866]   **4277**
ORIGINAL: HOL [13]
EDITORIAL COMMENT: C of Ex paper. '1866' has been added in another hand. *Dating*: by context; see n1.

Thursday Dec 6 | 10 min: to 3.

1 See **4269**&nn1-5.
2 There is in H a hand written document, signed by J. Winter Jones, principal librarian of the British Museum, which reads: 'At a Standing Committee of Trustees of the British Museum, 8th December, 1866, It was Resolved, That the thanks of the Trustees be tendered to the Right Honourable the Chancellor of the Exchequer for his recent conspicuous act of liberality to the British Museum and regard towards the interests of Art in England in authorising the purchase of the Blacas Collection at Paris, as well as for that promptitude of decision, which enabled Mr Newton to secure for the nation a Collection of such superlative value.' H B/XIV/A/27.

---

1 William Forsyth (1812-1899), BA 1834 and MA 1837 Cambridge, a barrister (Inner Temple 1839) and JP 1857, standing counsel to the secretary of state for India 1859-72, had been elected MP (C) for Cambridge borough in 1865 but had been unseated in April 1866 on the ground that his office of standing counsel was one of profit and disqualified him from sitting in Parliament. He would be MP (C) for Marylebone 1874-80.
2 Forsyth on 4 December 1866 had written to D asking him to accept a copy of the second edition of his *Life of Marcus Tullius Cicero* (2 vols, 1864). H A/IV/L/172.

I am here – & will come on to you at once, or see you here, as you like.[1]

D.

4278 TO: SPENCER WALPOLE   Grosvenor Gate [Friday] 7 December [1866]
ORIGINAL: HOL [14]
EDITORIAL COMMENT: Black-edged paper.[1] Endorsed in another hand on the fourth page: '7th. Dec. 1866'.

Secy | Rt Hon: S. Walpole   Decr 7 G Gate.

My dear Walpole,

Your first box was returned to you early this morning – but to D.S., or rather the Home Office.[2] I am ashamed / to say I was not aware you were in town.

I shall be glad to meet in D.S. at three o'ck: to day. The more I think of the matter, the more I / am convinced, that Lord S.[3] is right.

Yrs ever | D.

4279 TO: SPENCER WALPOLE   Downing Street [Saturday] 8 December 1866
ORIGINAL: HOL [15]
EDITORIAL COMMENT: C of Ex paper.

Mr Secy Walpole   Dec 8 1866

I have been to the Brit: Mus: & was in the chair,[1] wh: is the reason I cd. not send the papers before.[2]

I see nothing in / Naas' letter,[3] wh: alters, or modifies, my opinion of yesterday.

Yrs ever | D.

---

1 Walpole on this day (6th) had written to D from the home office: 'I have sent on a box, containing some important Irish Papers [*not found*], through General Peel & Pakington, to you. It seems to me that we ought to have Lord Derby's opinions upon them; but before I forward them to him, I should like to confer with you upon them. When & where can we meet today?' With this letter in H is a piece of paper inscribed (in D's hand) 'Decr. 1866 Right Hon: S. Walpole' and beneath it (in another hand) '*Fenianism*'. H B/XXI/W/66, 66a. See **4278**.

---

1 Evelina, Baroness Ferdinand de Rothschild (b 1839), second child of Lionel and Charlotte de Rothschild, had died in childbirth on 4 December 1866, her child stillborn.
2 See **4277**n1.
3 Foreign secretary Stanley; see **4279**&n4.

---

1 See **4275**.
2 In a postscript to his 8 December 1866 letter (n3), Walpole had asked D to 'return the Papers when done with'.
3 Walpole on 8 December 1866 had sent D 'Naas' box that you may see how matters now stand. Two things are evident – one that the Irish Government was on the eve of breaking up, if they could not Carry their point with [commander-in-chief in Ireland] Lord Strathnairn – The other that a sort of Compromise will be effected by means of the two additional Regiments which were yesterday ordered. The facts which Naas mentions or refers to, do not seem to warrant the extreme Panic with which the Government & the Country have been thrown; more I fear from the Bluster of [Fenian leader James] Stephens, than from any thing tangible upon which we can rest. Preparation, strict preparation was certainly necessary: but I am rather apprehensive that we have created the alarm, which it is now very difficult to appease. However that may be, the clear Policy for us to pursue, is to keep the Civil & Military authorities as much at one

They need not be sent to Stanley[.]⁴

TO: QUEEN VICTORIA   [London, Monday] 10 December 1866   4280
ORIGINAL: RAC C78 79.

Decr 10 1866

The Chancellor of the Exchequer with his humble duty to Yr Majesty.

He has investigated the circumstances respecting the post of *Private Secretary to the Sovereign*,¹ & the method, hitherto adopted, of remunerating / that officer.

It appears, that, under King William 4th., Sir Henry Wheatley² received £1500 pr annm:, as Keeper of the Privy Purse, paid out of that fund:

And Sir Herbert Taylor,³ at the same time, the same salary, from the same / source; really as Private Secretary to the Sovereign, but without that office being indicated.

Although the office of Sir Henry Wheatley was not indicated, the Chancellor of Exchequer, ↑is of opinion,↓ that there is no constitutional objection to the public recognition of / that office; in which belief he is confirmed by the practice, hitherto observed by the House of Commons, of annually voting specific salaries for the private Secretaries of Yr Majesty's ministers.

Under ordinary circumstances, therefore, the / Chancellor of the Exchequer would be prepared to propose to the Ho: of Commons a specific salary, on the estimates, for Yr Majesty's private Secretary: but it is to be noted:

1°: That the Opposition is aware, that the salary of Sir Herbert Taylor was a charge / on the Privy Purse, & that point will, doubtless, be urged; & though the C of Er. might reply, that the Privy Purse was now sufficiently, & even heavily, charged, it appears there is, & has been for some time, an annual saving on the Civil List, wh: is / paid over to the Privy Purse. Last year,

£7000 was so paid over.

There is no doubt the Opposition would point to this surplus as the fund, from

---

as we can – and I hope we may succeed. Indiscriminate arrest however will never do: and the statement I see in the Daily News to-day that fifteen arrests have been made at Belfast, all of whom were brought before the resident Magistrate & discharged, must tend to shake confidence in any Government.' H B/ XXI/W/68.

4 In a second 8 December 1866 letter, Walpole told D he had received 'a telegraph from Lord Derby, stating that he has received my box; that he will write to N[aas]: & that he will let me know – When he does I will forward on his letter to you.' On the 9th Walpole would send D 'another letter from Naas, received last night, which as it concerned Stanley I have sent on to him'; and on the 10th he would send D Derby's letter to Naas, with a request to 'send it on to Stanley, Pakington & Peel.' H B/XXI/W/67, 69, 70.

1 General Charles Grey had been the Queen's private secretary since 1861.
2 Maj-gen Sir Henry Wheatley (1777-1852), privy purse 1830-47 to William IV, Bt 1847. GM 37 (May 1852) 519.
3 Sir Herbert Taylor (1775-1839), KCH 1819, the first to hold the office of private secretary to the sovereign, in addition to a distinguished military career (2nd Dragoon Guards, 9th West India Regiment and Coldstream Guards), had been aide-de-camp, military secretary and private secretary to Lord Cornwallis 1798-9, and private secretary to the Duke of York 1799-1805, King George III 1805-11, Queen Charlotte 1811-18, William IV 1830-7 and Victoria 1837-9.

wh: the Private Secy. of Yr Majesty might find remuneration; & make a question of it; probably with success.

These circumstances are / humbly submitted to Yr Majesty, by the Chanr. of the Exr, from no wish to avoid the ultimate solution of the difficulty, but rather to indicate to Yr Majesty the obstacles to the contemplated course, wh: must not be disregarded.

The Cr. of the Exr will not permit the matter to escape his attention, & trusts that in this, as in all affairs, wh: concern Yr Majestys personal convenience & happiness, he shall never be wanting in grateful devotion.

4281 TO: THOMAS FRANCIS FREMANTLE

Downing Street
[Wednesday] 12 December 1866

ORIGINAL: BUC [4]
EDITORIAL COMMENT: Black-edged 11 Downing Street paper.

T.F. Fremantle[1] | Esqre.   Dec 12 1866
Dear Fremantle,
I thanked your father,[2] yesterday, for a kind recollection of me, for wh: I find, with pleasure, that I was indebted to you.

The / birds, Sir Thomas tells me, flew from the classic ground of Encombe.[3] I hope you had good sport.

With my best compliments to Lady / Augusta,

believe me | Very truly yours, | *B. Disraeli*

4282 TO: MONTAGU CORRY   Downing Street [Thursday] 13 December 1866

ORIGINAL: H B/XX/D/32
EDITORIAL COMMENT: 11 Downing Street paper. Endorsed in another hand on the first page: 'As to Advertisement (Reform Speeches)'. *Sic*: Montague [*three times*].

Montague Corry Esq   Decr. 13. 66
My dear Montague,
I enclose you a letter from Longman.[1]

I answered, of course, that I approved of the sheets being sent: indeed, if only as an advertisement, the notice wd be invaluable.

But / I said also, that Mr Montague Corry had shown me, before he left town, a short preface, or rather advertisement,[2] wh: he proposed to prefix to the volume, wh: so tersely, & clearly, indicated the character of the book, & the purpose of its publication, that I shd. be sorry, if Mr Reeve[3] / did not *also* see that.

---

1 Thomas Francis Fremantle (1830-1918), 2nd Baron Cottesloe 1890, MA Balliol, a barrister (Inner Temple 1855), JP, DL and MP (C) 1876-85 for Bucks, had married in 1859 Lady Augusta Henrietta (1836-1906), second daughter of 2nd Earl of Eldon.
2 Sir Thomas Francis Fremantle, Bt, 1st Baron Cottesloe 1874.
3 The 1st Earl of Eldon in 1806 had purchased Encombe House, in Dorset, now the seat of the 3rd Earl.

---

1 Thomas Longman's letter and D's reply have not been found.
2 See **4272**&n2.
3 Most likely journalist and editor Henry Reeve, whose 'mania for independence and impartiality extended to printing harsh reviews of works by friends, and of publications by Longman, his employer.' *ODNB*.

I shd. think you could have no difficulty in so arranging.

I hope to hear that you are well, or, at least, better.[4]

Yours sincerely, | D.

TO: GATHORNE HARDY   Downing Street [Friday] 14 December 1866   **4283**
ORIGINAL: GLA [3]
EDITORIAL COMMENT: C of Ex paper.

Right Honorable | G. Hardy   Dec 14 1866
Dear Hardy,

I am going to Hughenden tomorrow, & therefore have little chance of seeing you[.]

It is possible, that we *may* find it necessary / to deal with the London question.[1] I wish you wd. look at it a little, if you have time, so that the Cabinet may have it discussed, when we re-assemble. /

I have spoken to Earle fully about the matter, & he will give you explanations.

Yrs sin[cerel]y | D.[2]

TO: [MONTAGU CORRY]   [London?, 15? December 1866]   **4284**
ORIGINAL: H C/II/C/6
EDITORIAL COMMENT: Written on the verso of a letter from Percy Greg dated 13 December 1866 (see n1). Endorsed in another hand: 'ansd. as endorsed Dec. 15'. The DS left for Hughenden on 15 December 1866 (H acc). *Dating*: by context; see n2.

I never mentioned his father to my knowledge – who is a Radical, always abusing me in the "Economist".[1] What can we do for this gentn.[2] You must tell him that I have no personal patronage of any kind, that if he is a candidate for office in the gift of

---

4 Charles Fremantle would write to D on 3 January 1867: 'Our poor M. Corry does not shake off his affection of the throat – the Surgeons say it is in a tooth, the Dentists that it is only the gland that is to blame – but both agree that it may lead to a disagreeable result, if he catches cold. He ought to stay quietly at Tunbridge Wells now that he is there, & lay up.' H B/XXI/F/277.

---

1 Ralph Earle had written to D on 28 November: 'I am still very strongly in favor of a Commission upon the improvements of London, dwellings of the Poor, & sites for Gvt. Offices'. H B/XX/E/403. Earle was secretary and Hardy president of the poor law board. For their Metropolitan Poor Bill, see **4370**&n3.

2 Hardy would reply on the 16th: 'I expect Earle here tomorrow & will talk over with him "the London question" – It is a very puzzling one and I fear we cd hardly be prepared to solve it next session. The Committee of the last do not seem to have taken any definite line about it – A number of municipalities would hardly vary from the Vestries wh. are the local governments in many cases justly complained of and it is to them that [John Stuart] Mill and others appear to look as a remedy for existing evils. I will however get what information I can on the subject in view of the possible discussion in the Cabinet. It is pretty certain to be brought on in the House by some independent member.' H B/XX/HA/3.

---

1 William Rathbone Greg, a leading essayist, reviewer and political and social commentator, was a regular contributor to the weekly *Economist* and for a while its manager. Articles in the *Economist*, subtitled 'a political, literary, and general newspaper', were usually unsigned. The only one about D in 1866, 'Mr Disraeli's Case', was on his 14 May speech, whose argument 'fails to inspire intellectual confidence' and whose 'merest party-views are disguised in the language of abstract principle and broad generalisation.' *Economist* (19 May 1866) 585-6.

2 Journalist Percy Greg (1836-1889) had written to D on *MH* paper on 13 December 1866 as 'the son of a gentleman whom you have honoured with most complimentary mention in your place in the House of

any of my colleagues, I will support his claim; or that if he will indicate any definite object, I will consider his wishes. At present all is vague &c.[3]

    D.

4285

TO: [MONTAGU CORRY?]   [Hughenden, after 17 December 1866]
ORIGINAL: H B/XIII/57
EDITORIAL COMMENT: A note in D's hand on the first page of a letter from Dunbar J. Cother[1] to MA dated 17 December 1866.

---

a most impudent letter.[2] never was ↑at↓ Gloucester, but one day, when we dined with our agent Mr Lovegrove: ↑probably↓ "my father" was also a guest, but have no sort of recollection of him[.][3]

    D.

4286

TO: [CHARLES FREMANTLE]   Hughenden [Thursday] 20 December 1866
ORIGINAL: H B/XX/D/33
EDITORIAL COMMENT: C of Ex paper, seal crossed out and 'H.' written in. Endorsed in another hand on the first page: 'Wrote Major D. & infd. Robert Murray Decr. 21' and on the fourth page: '20. Decr. 1866 I Major Dickson I appt. of Mr. Churchward as J.P. at Dover.'

                                        H. I Dec 20 1866

I was very remiss in not telling you, that I came across the Ld. Chanr. & settled Churchward's affair.[1] He has been a Magistrate these ten / days, tho' he mayn't know it.[2]

Commons; Mr. W. Rathbone Greg, the present Comptroller of H.M. Stationery Office.' Having written for six and a half years for the MH and *Standard*, 'I have to eke out my income by working for other papers; & this with the work of the Parliamentary session, is very trying to my health, which is far from strong.' Greg was now seeking 'some place among those which may fall vacant, & are in your gift: by preference, one which I could hold while continuing to serve the party, to the best of my ability, by writing for this paper.' H C/II/C/6.
3 Greg would continue to seek D's patronage in letters to D's secretary Charles Fremantle (19, 26 Dec 1866; 4 Apr, 8 May 1867) and to D (15 Oct, 29 Jul 1867). H C/II/C/7, 8, 9a-d.

---

1 Dunbar John Cother (b 1819), BA 1840 and MA 1842 Oxford, a barrister (Inner Temple 1845), had published *Suggestions for the Amendment of the Lunacy Laws: in a letter to the right honorable the Lord Chancellor of England* (1861), 13 p.
2 'Madam [,] Twenty years ago I once had the pleasure of meeting you at my late Father's house at Gloucester ... My poor Father on his death bed told me if I needed advancement, and applied to you, that he thought you would use your influence with the now Chancellor of the Exchequer to secure me some appointment. I am engaged to be married to a young Widow with a small income but mine is not sufficient to justify me in taking such a step.' For her sake Cother was acting 'on what were almost my poor Father's dying words to me sixteen years ago, and if you can aid me, as he suggested, two grateful hearts will ever thank you.' H B/XIII/57.
3 William Cother had died on 22 February 1850 at Sandhurst (near Gloucester) in his 64th year. *The Times* (25 Feb 1850).

---

1 Charles Fremantle had written to D on 19 December: 'The Churchward agitation continues. Col. Taylor thinks that his appointment as J.P. at Dover would *not* be the subject of attack in the House of Commons – but he will be glad of your opinion whether, if it were to be commented upon unfavorably in Parlt, the comments would be such as wd. be likely to do harm to the Govt.– Meanwhile, I have not heard from the Lord Chancellor's Secretary in answer to my note, and I think I had better not write to him again.' H B/XXI/F/273.
2 Joseph George Churchward (d 1900), a JP and mayor of Dover 1867-8, was agent for the contractors for

You may tell him, & Major Dickson,[3] if you like.

I must be in town on Friday week – & prob[abl]y Thursday. It shows / a great ignorance of English manners in the Trinitarians to have an inauguration in Xmas week.[4] Their name ought to have taught them better.

D.

TO: SIR STAFFORD NORTHCOTE   Hughenden [Friday] 21 December 1866   **4287**
ORIGINAL: H H/LIFE
EDITORIAL COMMENT: From a copy, partly manuscript and partly typescript, headed: '*To Sir Stafford Northcote*. Hughenden Dec 21. 1866.'

.... I enclose you a matter of a different kind, that appears to me to require, & deserve, our attention. It's a great affair, that, tho' difficult, it appears to be sound & solid.[1]

The official papers have not yet come before me, and this Report has been given me behind the curtain. I wished to know where the 2 or 3 millions were to come from? Mr Scudamore[2] replies from the 8 millions of the Savings Bank. Could this be done? ....

TO: LORD DERBY   Hughenden [Friday] 21 December 1866   **4288**
ORIGINAL: DBP Box 146/2
EDITORIAL COMMENT: Black-edged 11 Downing Street paper, imprinted address crossed out and 'Hughenden' written in. Endorsed in another hand on the fourth page: 'Dec. 21. Disraeli Mr. sends Reform Resolutions'.

Hughenden | Decr 21. 1866

Right Honorable | The Earl of Derby K.G.

---

the Dover to Calais mail packet service. In 1863 the renewal (to 1870) by the admiralty of his contract had been awarded but then revoked following his attempt to intervene in an election on behalf of the Conservative candidate, a lord of the admiralty, and in 1865 he had lost his suit for contract payments since 1863. In March 1867 a motion to remove him as JP for Dover would be narrowly defeated, D voting with the majority. *The Times* (22, 25 Nov 1865, 20 Nov 1866, 21 Mar 1867); *Hansard* CLXXXV cols 1914-15, CLXXXVI cols 167-207; Alpheus Todd *On Parliamentary Government in England: its origin, development, and practical operation* vol 1 (1887) 772-6.

3 Alexander George Dickson (1834-1889), maj 13th Hussars 1860, capt Royal East Kent Regiment of Mounted Rifles Yeomanry Cavalry 1863, a director of the London, Chatham and Dover Railway and MP (C) for Dover 1865-89, would become chairman of the Crystal Palace Company. On 22 December 1866 Dickson would ask Charles Fremantle to thank D 'for his kind attention to my wishes in regard to the appointment of magistrates at Dover.' H B/XX/D/33a.

4 Fremantle had written to D on 17 December: 'I am afraid the enclosed Summons from the Trinity House may break in upon your holidays. I feel that I ought to send your Tailor down to Hughenden at once!' H B/XXI/F/272. See **4268** and **4293**&n2.

---

1 D's enclosure has not been found. The 'great affair' may be the nationalization of the telegraph companies; see **4293**&n4.

2 Frank Ives Scudamore (1823-1884) had joined the post office in 1840, becoming assistant secretary 1864 and second secretary 1868. The projects he sponsored, making him 'arguably the most important civil servant in the entire government by the late 1860s', included the establishment in 1861 of government-operated savings banks. *ODNB*.

My dear Lord,

I send you a Xmas Box – some raw material, wh: may be not unuseful.[1]

Also the compliments of the Season, / & my best wishes, that many a Xmas may find you Prime Minister[.]

Yours sincerely, I D.

4289   TO: [MONTAGU CORRY]   Hughenden [Friday] 21 December 1866
ORIGINAL: H B/XX/D/34
PUBLICATION HISTORY: M&B IV 483, the third and fourth paragraphs
EDITORIAL COMMENT: *Sic*: patronage [*repeated as catchword*].

Hughenden I Dec 21. 1866

It has just occurred to me, that the D of W. may be in town. Try, therefore, at Apsley Ho: first, before you post enclosed.[1]

If Sir Northcote is still in Paradise,[2] send him the note & Report[3] in / box, marked "confidential" & if he have departed for Devon,[4] enclose it in a cover, marked accordingly. I have none here large eno'.

I think the time has arrived, when the patronage / Secy. of the Treasury[5] (of all men in the world!) shd. at least learn the office wh: his master fills ↑& his due title↓. Give him, ↑& his due titles↓ at the earliest opportunity, a gentle educational hint. Somebody has instructed Hunt; long ago; I suppose Hamilton. The / manners of D.S. are getting quite American. The tradition of the old etiquette must be gradually revived.

We ought to have made the F.O. Press print all their labels over again & I think you had better order the circ[ular] one. I did insist upon it in the case of "Earl Derby!" I dare say Col. Taylor addresses the Lord Chancellor as Lord Chelmsford!

Yours I D.

4290   TO: CHARLES FREMANTLE   Hughenden [Saturday] 22 December 1866
ORIGINAL: QUA 99
EDITORIAL COMMENT: Black-edged paper. Endorsed by Fremantle on the fourth page: '18. Decr. 1866 I Mr. J.W. Randolph I Mad.'

Hughenden I Dec 22

Dear Fremantle,

Notwithstanding Blomer,[1] I send you another mad letter.[2]

---

1 See ec; perhaps the 'Resolutions' referred to by Derby at **4291**n5.

---

1 This enclosure, evidently for the Duke of Wellington, has not been found.
2 The Queen often called Balmoral her 'paradise in the Highlands'.
3 For D's note and report, see **4287**.
4 Northcote was MP (C) for N Devonshire. His seat was Pynes, near Exeter.
5 Col T.E. Taylor, parliamentary secretary to the treasury since 14 July 1866.

---

1 D may be referring to the case of '*In re* [Charlotte] Bloomar, *a lunatic*', heard in Chancery on 22 December 1857. *Law Journal Reports* (1858) vol 27 (n.s.) 173-5, with summary in the index at XVI.
2 This letter (see ec) has not been found. Although J.W. Randolph has not been identified, there are several mentions in *The Times* between 18 March 1844 and 10 February 1866 of a James Randolph of Milverton, Somerset co, a solicitor.

It seems very hard, that a man shd. be locked up, because he thinks he has "first rate abilities". If this were acted on generally, what lacunae in social life, to say nothing of the H of C.! All the men who / have not office.

I shall be in town on Thursday afternoon, & walk down to the sacred spot[3] – I shall, ↑of course,↓ be very glad to see you, but I beg you will not let this interfere with any holiday arrangements you may / have made.

Yrs sin[cere]ly, | D.

I stumbled over these two cards,[4] wh: reminds me, that we must begin to put our house in order.

I didn't quite settle the day for the meeting of Parlt with Ld Derby, but I think it was to / be Thursday the 7th. Feby;[5] if there be such a day in 1867, but I have not even yr friend Chas Knight's almanach here – wh: we could not trust, by the bye.[6] Will talk over the matter when we meet[.]

D.

TO: LORD DERBY   Hughenden [Monday] 24 December 1866   **4291**
ORIGINAL: DBP Box 146/2
EDITORIAL COMMENT: Black-edged paper.

Hughenden | Decr 24. 66

Right Honorable | The Earl of Derby | K.G.
My dear Lord,
Our confidential despatches[1] crossed. Mine went viâ D.S., but I send this straight to Knowsley, as tomorrow is Xmas Day, & there will, probably, be no one at our / offices.

---

3 Trinity House; see **4293**&n2.
4 These two cards have not been found.
5 Parliament would reconvene on Tuesday 5 February 1867.
6 Charles Knight (1791-1873) had been joint proprietor (with his father) in 1812 and sole editor (until 1827) of the *Windsor and Eton Express*, the borough's first newspaper. He had published the *Working Man's Companion* (1830-2), *Quarterly Journal of Education* (1831-5) and the popular *Penny Magazine* (1832-45). The latest edition of his *British Almanac* (first published 1828) was *British Almanac of the Society for the Diffusion of Useful Knowledge: for the year of our Lord 1866*.

---

1 Derby on 22 December 1866 had written to D from Knowsley a letter headed '*Confidential*': 'I have been considering anxiously, as I do not doubt you have also, how we are to extricate ourselves from the Reform Dilemma; and I agree with you that the key of our own position is the substantiality of our Commission. It seems to me that we have no alternative but to entrust it with some powers more than those of mere enquiry. If the statistics of last year are to be at all depended on, they furnish materials for estimating the probable effect of any particular figure upon the future Constituency; but it is clear that we cannot prepare any such figure without exposing ourselves to all but certain defeat from one side or the other. We must therefore have a Commission for our *Buffer*. Mere revision of the Statistics of last year may serve as a make-weight, but can be nothing more. Then there is the question of boundaries; to which you object that by an extensive enlargement the small Boroughs will be virtually swamped, and that such a proposal would enlist them against us as much as actual disfranchisement. Otherwise you admit that this is work for a Commission. Now I agree with you if you keep the minimum for a single member as high as 10,000; but as that is the point below which we propose that no Borough should have *more than one*, it seems unreasonable to insist on the same amount for those which are to have only one. Now if from these last you take the figure of *7000*, there will still be 30 Boroughs to be raised to that number by new Boundaries, ·

I am much in favor of the question of plurality of voting being included in the labors of the Commission, & I only did not mention it in the sketch I sent to you, because I fancied that, in the first / place, it might be expedient, that the desire for its investigation shd. originate in the House – but I am not, at all, strong on this point, &, perhaps, it wd. be more straightforward, that, tho' not, by any means, prepared to propose / a resolution on the subject, I shd., in my preliminary statement, wh: must review all the difficulties of the case, advert to this rising & new opinion, & mention it as one, that required, deserved, very calm & / deliberate research.

I still approve of Lord Grey being the President of the Commission, & the seven wise men have occurred to me in this wise:

Lord Grey

Lord Devon

Mr. Laing

Mr / Mill,

Mr. Ayrton,

Sir John Walsh,

&

Mr Dudley Baxter.

As you can't put on Lowe, I suggest Laing, by far the ablest of the Adullamites: Mill is in favor of plurality.

Ayrton, M.P. for Tower Hamlets, the largest of the / most popular constituencies in England, hates the mob – & is a man of immense political acquirement, & of a very subtle mind.

If you were to take these, it wd. be necessary, that there shd. be, at least, one commoner from our benches; / & there's the difficulty, because, of course, all our men competent for such duties are, generally speaking, in office.

and at the same time comparatively few of them will have a very great increase. If therefore we adopt the figure of 7000 Pop. for the single Boroughs, we shall to a great extent remove their objections, and still give the Commission some work to do. But I would also suggest as a subject of enquiry for them that which has never been touched: the effect which would be produced by a Lodger franchise, say of £10 a year, which is equivalent to about 4s a week, and this not numerically only, but as to what *class* of voters it would introduce; and how far the effect, in both senses, would be modified by requiring a *two years'* continuous residence. The same enquiry might extend to the Savings Bank Franchise; and of all possible Hares to start, I do not know a better than the extension to Household Suffrage, *coupled with plurality of voting.* You may add, if you please, Bribery, and Polling Papers; and the advantage of multiplying such questions is that we do not bind members to the adoption of any, but afford an opportunity for feeling the pulse of Parliament and the Country on all, and showing how many doubtful points there are to be cleaned up before Parliament commits itself to so great and irrevocable a change. If you can suggest any better mode of escape from our difficulties, I should be very glad to hear your opinion. If you adopt my view, it will be necessary most carefully to consider the composition of our Committee. We talked at one time of asking Lord Grey to preside over it; and if you are still of opinion that it would be desirable, and think that he might be seconded, there is at this moment an excellent opportunity for doing so, as Genl. Grey is at Howick we have till about the 8th or 9th of next month. He, as you know, is very friendly. R. Montagu, who has not a halfpenny, refuses the Assistant Comptrollership, and takes the same ground as Macaulay, the insignificance to which the Office was reduced by the changes made in the Bill in the H. of Commons. Sir W. Dunbar has not sent in (so far as I know) his answer to Macaulay's letter; but I suppose the latter will resign, and we shall have to look out for a good man to fill his place. I suppose Emerson Tennent would neither take it, nor be equal to it. The Salary is the same as his present office. I have offered him a K.C.B. He wants a Baronetcy, but I must say he does not make any difficulties.' H B/ xx/s/380.

Sir Wm. Heathcote is too timid & too churchy:[2] Sir Phil: Egerton I don't know much about but, I / fancy, too scientific.[3] Sclater Booth, who has an excellent head, has not position enough: Sir John Walsh has been long in Parliament, has great political culture, & is, I think firm. He was in H of Comm: before the Reform: has written on / that subject, & with some reach & grace, & power of generalising;[4] It co[ul]d be advantageous to get Dudley Baxter on, if we cd. venture it. For so young, & new, a man, he stands well, almost high, in public opinion.

These / are my views: perhaps, all this time, you have seven wiser men ready.

Have you settled the day for the meeting of Parliament?

And when do you propose, that the Cabinet shall re-assemble? /

There are several matters on wh: I must communicate with you – but this will do at present.

Yours sincerely, | D.[5]

2 The ultra-conservative and deeply religious Heathcote was a staunch Anglican and Tractarian.
3 Sir Philip de Malpas Grey Egerton (1806-1881), 10th Bt 1829, BA 1828 Oxford, MP (C) for Chester 1830-1, Cheshire s 1835-68 and Cheshire w 1868-81, was a DL of Cheshire and lieut-col Cheshire Yeomanry Cavalry. A palaeontologist and fellow of the Geological Society 1829 and the Royal Society 1831, he was a trustee of the British Museum and the Royal College of Surgeons. His collection of fossil fish, described in his *Alphabetical Catalogue of Type Specimens of Fossil Fishes* (1871), would be acquired by the British Museum (Natural History).
4 The many pamphlets by Sir John Benn Walsh include *On Reform of Parliament, Popular Opinions on Parliamentary Reform, Observations on the Ministerial Plan of Reform* (all 1831) and *The Practical Results of the Reform Act of 1832* (1860).
5 Derby would reply on 27 December 1866 in a letter headed '*Private*': 'Not to run the risk of our letters crossing again, I delayed for a few days noticing the receipt of your Resolutions [*not found*]. I have now before me your letter of the 24th on which, and on them, I will say a few words. I think that the Resolutions, on the whole, are very judiciously conceived; and if they should be adopted, even partially, by the House, there will be no ground for complaint that enough work is not provided for the Commission. I do not, of course, stop to notice a few verbal amendments which might be advantageously introduced; but confine myself to the substance. I am quite satisfied with what you say on the plurality of votes question, which I only wish introduced as one mode by which the Franchise may be carried lower than would otherwise be safe. I think however you will have to allude to it in your introductory speech, as a subject deserving consideration. Then it seems to me that two objections may be raised to the scheme, as a whole, one by our side, the other by the other. The first is that it is a mere reduction of amount; and that no notice is taken of any franchise founded, or to be founded, on any other basis than the value of the tenements occupied: This I think must be met, either by a substantive Resolution (which on the whole I should prefer) or by an addition to the Instructions to the Commission, which might come in toward the end of the first Paragraph of Nr. 10. Then the scheme makes an allusion to any increase in the Population of the very smallest Boroughs, and this will be a reasonable ground of objection on the "Liberal" side, that Arundel, for example, and Calne, and others of the same class, will retain undiminished influence from their very scanty population and voters. I would suggest that your last Paragraph should read something in this way: "To revive the Boundaries &c and to prepare schemes, for the consideration of Parliament, for new and enlarged Boundaries, so that all Boroughs retaining the right of returning a Member to Parliament should include a population of not less than (7000) and that provision should be made for admission to the franchise of that portion of the population which, in Boroughs now represented, may have outgrown the limit. &c and, subject to such consideration &c.["] But I am afraid you have gone too far in enquiring into the boundaries (which will be interpreted as pledging us to the enfranchisement) of all Boroughs above 10,000 Pop. This, unless I am mistaken, will include not less than 41 Boroughs – which is more than we shall be able to provide for by disfranchisement. If you take 12000, you will reduce the number of claims to 32, which I think we should just be able to satisfy. These are the questions which seem to me to deserve your consideration, so far as the Resolutions are concerned. But by far the most important question is the composition of the Commission to which we are about to delegate so large an authority: and on that point I am not at ease. I do not object to Ld. Grey as the Chairman, if he will undertake it.

TO: LORD CRANBORNE   Hughenden [Wednesday] 26 December 1866
ORIGINAL: OCC BPD 6164 ff3-4
PUBLICATION HISTORY: M&B IV 463, the second, third and fourth sentences.

PRIVATE   Hughenden Manor | Dec. 26 1866
Right Honble | Secy Ld Cranborne[1]
My dear Cranborne,
I suppose, from what you say, that my Denison is Denison of the Clock,[2] wh: had
not occurred to me: & justifies yr conclusion. I have, / throughout, been against
legislation, & continue so. Lord Derby, about the time you were here, thought it
inevitable, but, as you know, his views are now modified.

It's a difficult affair, but, I think, we shall pull thro': / the Whigs are very unanimous in wishing the question "settled" – but you & I are not Whigs.

Yrs ever, | D.
I return G.B.

He is crotchety, and will make himself very disagreeable, but his views are in the main Conservative, and
he will not want firmness to maintain them. But your three Liberal Members alarm me. I do not know
enough of Laing's opinions to say much about him; but though Mill may be in favour of plurality, and
Ayrton may "hate the mob", we must not forget that they represent two Radical Constituencies, and have
avowed the most extreme principles; and I fear that practically their private and philosophical opinions
will be found subservient to their political interests. At any rate, if you have them, you will want some
strong men on our side to counter-balance them; and these I do not think you have got. Lord Devon is a
member of the Government, though not in Cabinet; and I think he is very weak. I should have no confidence in him; and I would far rather put on such a man as Hylton (Jolliffe) who is liberally inclined, and
yet would understand where to make a stand. Baxter would be invaluable; and his perfect acquaintance
with all the details of the subject would quite justify putting him on. I do not think Walsh would be a good
selection. He knows something of the subject, and is highly respectable; but I do not think he would be
found practically useful. He would not know where he might safely concede, and where to stand firm. It
is very difficult to suggest another name, but what should you say to old Henley? I think he is at all events
worth consideration. But, after all, is it necessary at once to decide on the Members of our Commission?
If the principle be accepted, may it not be made matter of negotiation? And will not the solution itself
be influenced by the temper in which our scheme is received, and the readiness of Liberals to meet us
fairly, or the reverse? I have decided that Parliament should meet for the despatch of business on Tuesday the 5th of February. That is about the usual time, and it will be fixed at the Council tomorrow. I shall
be in Town on the 8th of Jany and will summon the Cabinet for Wednesday the 9th or the following day,
as you may think best. Perhaps Thursday may be soon enough – it will give our idlers another day, and
you and I ought to have ample time for consultation before we meet them. Let me know which day you
would prefer, as I should like to give ample notice. May the New Year be prosperous for all of us!' H B/
XX/S/381.

1 Lord Cranborne on 24 December 1866 had written to D a letter headed 'Private': 'I return your Xmas
  box with many thanks – & send you what *I* have received this morning. Which prophet are we to believe?
  I am bound on George Bentinck's behalf to say this. Last winter we met in the street – he alludes to it in
  his letter –, & discussed the then impending Reform Bill. I was very gloomy. I said, with a majority of 75
  it must pass the Commons – & the Lords will be our only chance. He was very earnest the other way. He
  said he knew that there was a large section of Whigs bitterly opposed to it. "You will not be able to throw
  it out on second reading" he said, "but they will help you to stifle it in Committee". I cite this because
  the issue confirmed his anticipation so signally: & gives a certain weight to his present prediction. On
  the other hand Denison is a man who has been in trouble of some sort half his life & is I think generally
  esteemed a wrongheaded man ... Let me have G.B.'s letter back.' H B/XX/CE/11.
2 House Speaker John Evelyn Denison in 1864 had presented a weight-driven eight-day clock (made by
  George and Francis Cope of Nottingham) to Ossington Holy Rood, the church built alongside Ossington
  Hall by his great-uncle Robert Denison as a memorial to his brother William, who had died in 1782. The
  clock was installed in the church tower.

TO: LORD DERBY   Downing Street [Saturday] 29 December 1866   4293

ORIGINAL: DBP Box 146/2

PUBLICATION HISTORY: M&B IV 461-2, omitting the first and last three sentences

EDITORIAL COMMENT: Black-edged 11 Downing Street paper.

Confidential   Decr 29 1866

Right Honorable | The Earl of Derby K.G.

My dear Lord,

Your letter reached me,[1] last night, from Hughenden. I have been most inconveniently summoned to town, in the midst of Xmas, to be sworn in, today, a brother / of the Trinity House.[2] Those of my brethren, who are also country gentlemen, must think such a disturbance of a holy festival, on the part of such a body, very strange, & indeed scarcely orthodox.

I / shd. like the Cabinet not to be summoned till Thursday, as there are many points of great importance on wh: consultation is desirable before we meet in formal council. Work thickens. The army question[3] must be grappled with. Then the Portuguese Treaty of / Commerce is assuming a practical shape, & a plan of the Post Office for the purchase of all the private telegraphs of the country[4] demands our decision. These are all heavy affairs – & the latter two fall entirely on the Treasury. /

With respect to Reform: I agree with you, that it is quite premature to trouble ourselves about the materials of the Royal Commission: tho', I think Lord Hylton ↑ an admirable suggestion & infinitely preferable to Lord D.

I have / not the dr[af]t of the Resolutions at hand, but I [*word crossed out*] ↑suspect↓, you will find, on reference to them, that the Resolution pledges the House to "Extension" not "reduction["], of the franchise; & "extension" wd. include everything.[5]

We must be careful not to commit ourselves ↑both↓ to reduction, & "fancy" franchises:[6] if / it be true, as I now hear, that the lodger franchise in the way of extension, & especially among the wage-paid class, would produce incredible results.[7]

1 See **4291**n5.

2 *The Times* on 31 December 1866 would report that 'His Royal Highness the Duke of Edinburgh, Master of the Corporation of Trinity-house, presided at a Court held at their house on Tower-hill on Saturday afternoon, when the Right Hon. Sir Stafford H. Northcote, President of the Board of Trade, and the Right Hon. B. Disraeli, Chancellor of the Exchequer, were elected Elder Brethren of that ancient corporation, in the room of Lord Northbrook and Admiral Sir W. Parker, deceased.'

3 Issues involving the army dealt with during the 1867 session would include the appointment of a select committee 'to inquire into the duties performed by the British Army in India and the Colonies', the Recruiting Commission of 1866 and flogging. *Hansard* CLXXXV cols 1032-64, 1768-99, 1951-91.

4 In 1865 postmaster-general Lord Stanley of Alderley had commissioned Frank Ives Scudamore 'to study the condition of the privately owned telegraph companies, and to consider the possible results of nationalization.' In 1869 Parliament would allocate '£7 million for telegraph purchase costs and capital improvements ... The average price of a telegram fell by 6*d.* to 1*s.*1*d.* During the first year of government management, the number of telegrams sent increased by 3 million to almost 10 million.' ODNB.

5 Derby (n1) had feared there would be objections to the franchise 'scheme' as 'a mere reduction of amount'.

6 For the so-called 'fancy' franchises, see **4038**n4.

7 Although the 1867 Reform Act would introduce a lodger franchise giving the vote to male lodgers paying £10 rent a year for unfurnished accommodation, the scheme would prove almost inoperative in practice; see Charles Seymour *Electoral Reform in England and Wales* (New Haven 1915) 284-5, 364-5.

Indeed, I think that particular franchise shd. be specifically referred to the Commission, & indeed I am rather inclined to refer Plurality also, & all the cognate expedients for protecting / the minority.

I don't ~~think~~ believe the Liberals are in favor of extending the boundaries of small Boro[ugh]s.

As to 10000,[8] I wished to put a figure wh:, accepting the estimates of the Census – as wd. virtually apply to towns of not less than 20,000 pop: at present, I wd., therefore, suggest the insertion of 10,000.

These are only rough notes to remind us what to consider when we meet.

Sincerely yrs, | D.

[*added at the top of the first page:*] I shall return to Hughenden on Monday D.

4294   TO: LORD STANLEY   Grosvenor Gate [Sunday] 30 December 1866
ORIGINAL: H H/LIFE
PUBLICATION HISTORY: M&B IV 469, the first four paragraphs
EDITORIAL COMMENT: From a typescript headed: 'D. to Ld. Stanley, Grosvenor Gate, Dec: 30. '66.' *Sic*: Thuilleries.

Right Hon'ble Sec: Lord Stanley.
Dear Stanley,
I have just heard, from a first-rate quarter,[1] that, at the last Cab: Council at the Thuilleries,[2] a proposition, from Bismarck,[3] suggesting an arrangement, by which the Southern States of Germany should blend with Prussia, and that France should take possession of Belgium, was absolutely brought forward, and favored by several of the Ministers: principally by Lavalette.[4] It was opposed by the Minister for F. Aff's.[5]

Can this be true? And if so, or if there be any foundation for it – what are Bismarck's relations with us? Have you heard anything from our Goosey Gander at Berlin,[6] a pretty instrument to cope with the Prussian Minister! And Mr. Fane,[7] what does he say? And what shall we say?

The Emperor[8] is like a gambler, who has lost half his fortune and restless to recover: likely to make a coup, which may be fatally final for himself.

I doubt, whether this country would see any further glaring case of public vio-

---

8 Derby (n1) had feared D had 'gone too far in enquiring into the boundaries (which will be interpreted as pledging us to the enfranchisement) of all Boroughs above 10,000 Pop.'

---

1 Lionel de Rothschild. The DS visited Gunnersbury on this day (30th). ROTH. See **4297**.
2 The Council of State had met on 27 December 1866 at the Tuileries 'under the presidency of the Emperor' to discuss a 'project for the reorganization of the army ... one of the most unpopular measures that have been proposed since the Empire.' *The Times* (29 Dec 1866).
3 Bismarck was minister-president of Prussia.
4 Charles Jean Marie Félix (1806-1881), marquis de La Valette, French ambassador to the Ottoman Empire 1851-3 and foreign minister from 1 September to 2 October 1866. On 16 September he had issued a 'circular representing the Prussian triumph as advantageous to France by its division of Germany into three slices – North Germany, South Germany, and Austria.' *The Times* (20 Sep and 5 Oct 1866, 4 May 1881).
5 The Marquis de Moustier.
6 For D's low opinion of Lord Loftus, see **4174**n3.
7 Julian Fane was first secretary and acting chargé d'affaires at Paris 1865-7.
8 The mercurial Napoleon III. See n11.

lence and treachery with composure. Reaction is the law of all human affairs: and the reaction from non-intervention must, sooner or later, set in. I would rather, however, try to prevent mischief – i.e, as long as we can.

I go to Q. Sess: to-morrow morning, and in the evening to Hughenden, where I shall remain till the 8th.[9]

Write to me there if you have anything to say: and about Crete?[10]

Yours ever, D.[11]

TO: [CHARLES FREMANTLE]　　　　　　　　　Grosvenor Gate　**4295**
[Sunday] 30 December 1866

ORIGINAL: QUA 100

EDITORIAL COMMENT: Black-edged 11 Downing Street paper, imprinted address crossed out and 'G. G.' written in. *Recipient*: by context; see n3.

G. G. | Decr. 30 1866

I don't know Mr Crewe, tho' he "My dear Sirs" me.[1] But as he is a Bucks Rector, he must be *acknowledged*.[2]

I don't care a straw about either of the claimants, who are unknown / to me.

Young Wellings has made a mess.[3] I wish to give him another chance, if it be possible, but I wish to make a great favor of it.

---

9 D would attend the Bucks Epiphany Sessions at Aylesbury on 31 December 1866 and return to Grosvenor Gate on 7 January 1867. *BH* (5 Jan 1867); H acc.

10 A Cretan uprising against Ottoman rule had been officially proclaimed on 21 August 1866 and would be suppressed in early 1869. There would be a second, decisive insurrection in 1897, leading the Ottoman Empire to declare war on Greece and to the expulsion of Ottoman forces from the island in November 1898.

11 Stanley would reply on 31 December 1866 in a letter headed '*Confidential*': 'In Napoleon's position, which though not quite as bad as your friends described it, is unsatisfactory enough, there is no saying what he may or may not do. But nothing that is known here encourages the supposition that there is any understanding between him and Bismarck. That Bismarck offered him Belgium during the war is certain; and it is equally certain that he rejected the proposal with some warmth, probably thinking it a trap. The feeling in southern Germany, though divided, points in general to union with Prussia: that is to close alliance offensive and defensive. There is a report that secret treaties to that effect have been entered into by Baden and Wurtemberg: which seems likely enough, but not certain. But this alliance is directed expressly against France, and is certainly not made with her consent, if it is made at all.' Stanley could 'hardly believe in a deliberate proposal to annex Belgium, though like many other wild ideas, it may have passed through the Emperor's brain. The Cretan question is likely to give trouble. Up to this point we are perfectly uncommitted and free to act, if we act at all, as events may lead us. Moustier has got a plan of some sort which he will communicate shortly. I do not know its purport.' Also on 31 December Stanley would note in his journal that 'Disraeli has got hold of a wonderful story to the effect that it is decided at the Tuileries that Napoleon shall take Belgium, allowing Prussia to annex southern Germany as an equivalent. I have written this to Fane that he may find out what he can, but I have told him at the same time I do not believe a word of it.' H B/XX/S/759; *Disraeli, Derby* 282.

---

1 This letter has not been found. Henry Harpur Crewe (1828-1883), BA 1851 and MA 1855 Trinity College, Cambridge, deacon 1856, priest 1857, curate of Drinkstone (near Woolpit, Sussex) 1858-9 and rector 1860-83 of Drayton Beauchamp, a civil parish within Aylesbury Vale district, was also a naturalist with a keen interest in entomology, botany and horticulture. *Clergy List* (1857, 1859, 1860).

2 Fremantle's letter (if he wrote one) has not been found.

3 Fremantle had been informed on 14 December 1866 that Arthur Wellings (see **4199**&nn2-4) had failed 'the test examination for Clerkships in the Paymaster General's Office, and that he is therefore ineligible to compete for an appointment under the Treasury.' H C/II/C/4e.

Write to Mr Lovell, that I / am much disappointed by his not passing, but that I will consider the matter &c.

Send me to Hughenden Mr Mallet's Report:[4] I don't want the *"pieces justi[fi]cat-ives"*.[5]

Yrs | D.

4296   TO: [MONTAGU CORRY?]   Downing Street [Monday] 31 December 1866

ORIGINAL: BRN [39]
EDITORIAL COMMENT: C of Ex paper.

Decr. 31. 1866

Two letters for the Messenger to take: & three boxes to
Secy. Lord Stanley
Secy. Genl Peel
    &
Mr. Fremantle
    D

4297   TO: CHARLOTTE, BARONESS LIONEL DE ROTHSCHILD
                              Hughenden [Wednesday] 2 January 1867

ORIGINAL: ROTH RFAM C/2/6 RAL 000/848
EDITORIAL COMMENT: 11 Downing Street paper, imprinted address crossed out and 'Hughenden Manor' written in.

Hughenden Manor | Jan: 2 1867

Dearest Baroness,

I had no conception, when I departed for Q. Sess: on Monday morning,[1] that, on the preceding eve, our carriage had been laden with luxuries, wh:, I really believe, are / only to be found at Gunnersbury: some delicacies wh:, certainly Apicius[2] never tasted, & a pine-apple, wh: was worthy of the desserts of Paul Veronese![3]

Accept our thanks, unceasing, for kindnesses, wh: are as constant!

Tell / Lionel, that my friend was entirely sceptical as to the Paris rumors: all his information having another tendency. But, he said, he should write immediately, & communicate with me. Nothing has, as yet, reached me.

---

4 For Louis Mallet, see **4196n2**; for the proposed Portuguese Treaty, see **4191**&nn1,2&7. Corry had outlined Mallet's report (not found) for D on four pages, the first dated 'Dec 20/66' and headed 'P.T. – *Mallet's report*'. Corry summarized the 'effect on Spirits, threefold objection. I Chance of redistillation. II Strong wines wld compete with Spirits. III On ground of "Fiscal Equity" ... *Conclusions of my Lords* 1. Treaty desirable 2. Loss of revenue involved of £730.000'. H B/XX/CO/19.

5 *Pièces justificatives* (French): supporting documents.

---

1 See **4294**n9.
2 There were three Romans of that name: Apicius (1st cent BCE), a lover of luxury; Marcus Gavius Apicius (*c* 25 BCE-*c* 37 CE), a decadent gourmet attributed with the authorship of *Apicius*, a collection of recipes compiled in the late 4th or early 5th centuries; and Apicius (2nd cent CE), the emperor Trajan's cook.
3 In Paolo Veronese's painting *The Wedding at Cana* (1563), quinces (a yellow, pear-shaped fruit) are served as dessert. *Apicius* (n2) gives recipes for stewing quinces with honey.

The stupid Turks have / made a sad mess of the Cretan business:[4] but in all Levantine politics, I have great confidence in M. de Moustier, for he thoroughly understands them.

My love to all; especially to Baby.[5]

Yours ever, | D.

TO: LORD DERBY   Hughenden [Thursday] 3 January 1867   **4298**
ORIGINAL: DBP Box 146/3
EDITORIAL COMMENT: 11 Downing Street paper, imprinted address crossed out and 'Hughenden Manor' written in. *Sic*: a-head.

Confidential   Hughenden Manor | Jan: 3 1866[7]

Right Honorable | The Earl of Derby | K.G.
My dear Lord,

I have now been entirely thro' the affair of the Portuguese treaty of Commerce,[1] & am convinced, that we can do the business. It is not a mean affair in itself; / but with reference to its probable effect on the commercial policy of Spain, may be, in its results, & value, only second to the French Treaty.[2]

Subject to yr approbation, I shall signify this to Stanley,[3] as the great point with the Portuguese / Government is to be armed with the announcement for the impending Cortes.[4]

The letter from the Board of Trade to the Treasury has arrived, & been forwarded to me here.[5] It is a formidable document; but / I cd. tell you the results viva voce in our Wednesday conference; wh: promises to be a long one, for we must then decide on our Reform movements, or, otherwise, I see anarchy a-head. There are many other great matters pressing, but that is paramount.[6]

Yrs ever, | D.

---

4 For the 'Paris rumors', D's 'friend' (Stanley) and the 'Cretan business', see **4294**&nn1,10&11.
5 Possibly a granddaughter. Charlotte's first daughter Leonora and her husband Alphonse (of the Paris Rothschilds) had two daughters: Bettina (1858-1892) and Charlotte Beatrix (1864-1934). D's consideration may arise from the tragic death on 4 December 1866 of her second daughter, Evelina, in childbirth. See **4278**n1.

---

1 See **4191**&nn1,2,7, **4196**&n1 and **4313**&n2.
2 Following the Anglo-French treaty of commerce of 1860 (see VIII **3448**n2), the value of British exports (mainly manufactured goods) to France more than doubled during the 1860s and the importation of French wines also doubled. Sir Llewellyn Woodward *The Age of Reform 1815-1870* (Oxford 1962) 179 n1.
3 See **4299**&nn1&2.
4 The Portuguese king had opened the *cortes* (legislature) on 2 January at Lisbon with a throne speech 'of unusual length'. *The Times* (4 Jan 1867).
5 This letter has not been found.
6 Derby would reply on 6 January asking D to call on him Wednesday at noon (or earlier) or in Downing Street around 4 *pm* (after his 3 *pm* appointment). 'I am glad to hear from Stanley as well as from you, that we have a good prospect of making an advantageous Commercial Treaty with Portugal, which must tell also on our Commerce with Spain. There is, I presume, nothing in the French treaty to prevent our dealing as we think fit, with the Alcoholic test. We shall meet with opposition, I suppose, from the Spirits Trade; and I conclude you have calculated on the amount of loss to be expected on that branch of Revenue. I have a letter from Naas which leads me to fear that we shall have serious difficulty with respect to Irish Education. I write to desire him to circulate the papers at once.' H B/XX/S/401.

4299
ORIGINAL: H H/LIFE
EDITORIAL COMMENT: From a typescript headed: 'D. to Ld. Stanley, Hughenden, Jan. 3. '67.'

Dear Stanley,

I am more than favorably disposed to the P[ortuguese] Treaty,[1] and will settle the business with you on Monday next,[2] which, I hope, will be in time for the Cortes, should we decide favorably, as I anticipate....

4300
TO: CHARLES FREMANTLE   [Hughenden, Friday] 4 January 1867
ORIGINAL: H B/XIII/219a
EDITORIAL COMMENT: C of Ex paper. The draft enclosure is in D's hand. *Place of origin*: the DS were at Hughenden until 7 January. H acc.

Jan 4. 1867

Dear Fremantle,

It is cruel work, when I have only two real days of business left to me, to be disturbed, at such a moment, by such a disgusting epistle as the enclosed.[1] It must, however, be / answered, & I have hatched a reply – tho' perhaps you had better see Rose, who is a prof[e]s[siona]l man, as well as acquainted with the business, before you send it ↑but do as you like↓.[2]

     Yrs, | D.

---

1 Stanley had written on 2 January from the foreign office inquiring if D had come to a decision regarding the wine duty: 'The Portuguese are pressing for an answer, and the B. of T. seems more favorable to a larger reduction than was to be expected. They have not supplied me with the estimate of loss by an extension of the shilling duty up to 40° (which would cover all the Portuguese demand, and even more); but remembering that the whole duty is only about £1,400,000; that if the whole of this were on the 2s.6d. scale, the reduction to 1s would be but £840,000; and that in fact, the reduction will only apply to a part of the duty, not to the whole: I suppose I may assume that the loss will not exceed half a million, the recovery on which will necessarily be rapid. My fear was for the spirit duties, but as to these the B. of T. does not seem to apprehend danger. I should like to consult with you on reform before we meet in Cabinet. The scheme of an enquiry does not appear to find favor with the public, but I own I despair of a bill, and have nothing better to propose.' H B/XX/S/762.

2 Stanley on Monday 7 January would record, 'Called on Disraeli: discussed with him Portuguese treaty and wine-duties, as to which he is willing, and even eager, to make all the necessary sacrifices of revenue. It is estimated that to do away with the alcoholic test altogether, and reduce the duty in all cases to 1s., would involve a sacrifice of £725,000 for the first year: which, though heavy, would be rapidly made good by increased consumption. We have not yet heard from Paget what the Portuguese will be ready to concede. We talked over the budget: D. opposes increased armaments, but thinks that some increase of expenditure will be necessary, as recruits cannot be got without additional inducements.' *Disraeli, Derby* 283.

---

1 Solicitor Edward Letchworth (1833-1917), Junior Carlton Club member, chief steward of manors to the Queen 1860, a freemason 1875, Kt 1902 and grand secretary of the United Grand Lodge of Freemasons 1892-1917, had written from Enfield, Middlesex on 3 January. Addressing D as 'one of the Guarantors of the funds to meet the expenses of Lord Ranelagh's contest for this County', Letchworth recounted how, as Ranelagh's agent, he had defrayed the latter's election expenses ('not one farthing of which I have been able to recover') in light of funds allegedly 'provided, or guaranteed, by yourself, & other noblemen & gentlemen belonging to the Carlton Club'. Mentioning that he had a judgment for the funds against Ranelagh (see n2), he threatened 'further proceedings' (in which he would regret connecting D's name with the transactions) and asked D to deny any involvement in the matter. H B/XIII/219b.

2 D on 12 December 1866 had been at the court of exchequer for the hearing for an action against Ranelagh, who had expected his party to pay his election expenses. When they declined to do so, a verdict was

[*enclosure*.]
drt.   D.S.

E. Letchworth Esq
Sir,

I am directed by the C of E. to acknowledge the rect of yr letter of the 3rd Inst:, & ~~to~~ ↑in↓ reply to the enquiries, contained in it, to state: that Mr Disraeli never promised to ~~contribute~~ provide, or guarantee, any funds to meet the expenses of Ld. R[anelagh]'s ↑candidature or↓ election for Middx, & that, altho' Mr D. is not a member of the Committee of the Carlton ↑Club,↓ or ever interferes in / its management, he is authorised to say, that no person or persons, who, by any ~~intre~~ interpretation, cd. be looked upon as representing the CC., ever had any communication either with Ld. Ran:, or his agents, on the subject.

~~Some private friends of Ld. R; some of whom were members of the C.C., did secure the payment of "the preliminary expenses", the maximum amount of wh: was specifically ~~defined~~ defined, & the C of E. is assured, that sum, though considerable, has not only been discharged, but exceeded.~~

I am &c

TO: SIR STAFFORD NORTHCOTE   Downing Street   4301
                                              [Friday] 11 January 1867

ORIGINAL: BL ADD MS 50015 f177
EDITORIAL COMMENT: Black-edged 11 Downing Street paper.

The R.H. | Sir S.N.   Jany. 11 1867
My dear N,

This is the paper, wh: I shd. like you to see, & give me your opinion on, & wh:, I think, has not been seen even by Ld. Derby.[1]

Yrs | D.

---

given against him for £96, for which he was sued by Letchworth. *BH* (15 Dec 1866). For Ranelagh and the July 1865 Middlesex elections, see **4017**&n1.

---

1 Northcote on 16 January 1867 would write to D critiquing the paper (not found) that D had sent him. He agreed with Cranborne 'that the preamble is not in harmony with the resolutions as they now stand; but ... the amendment which is requisite to make them agree should rather be in the resolutions than in the preamble.' The House would not consider 'resolutions which do not show upon their face that we contemplate a reduction of the borough franchise ... We might defend a policy of absolute inaction, tant bien que mal, but not a policy of giving carte blanche to a Commission to settle principles as well as details.' He suggested household suffrage as 'a stand-point' and proposed 'an amendment in the 10th resolution, – and would have the second paragraph run thus: – "To enquire to what extent the occupation franchise must be reduced (either generally or in particular cases) so as to admit the Labouring Classes to a direct and substantial share in the representation; and what conditions, as to plurality of votes or otherwise, can beneficially be adopted for the purpose of preventing a numerical majority of the population from acquiring an undue preponderance in the representation."' H B/XX/N/1.

4302 TO: LORD DERBY   Grosvenor Gate [Sunday] 13 January 1867

ORIGINAL: DBP Box 146/3

PUBLICATION HISTORY: M&B IV 487, the fourth sentence

EDITORIAL COMMENT: Grosvenor Gate paper. Endorsed in another hand on the first page: 'Jan. 13. Disraeli Mr. returns the Queen's & Genl. Grey's letters.'

Private   Jany 13 1867

Right Honorable | The Earl of Derby K.G[.]

My dear Lord,[1]

I return you the letters,[2] & thank you, much, for permitting me to see them.

They are very encouraging. I entirely / agree with you, that no action shd. take place until after the statement. The more I think over it, the more complete seems to me the conclusion, that proceeding by resolutions is / the parliamentary, & constitutional, consequence of the conduct of the Ho: of Comm: itself upon the question of Parly. Ref: The H of C. first disturbed the settlement of 1832: & the House of C. has defeated the / measures, taken in consequence of that disturbance, of *five* ministries.

The other point is the difficulty.[3]

Tomorrow, as I understand, on Naval Estimates, with you at ½ past 3 o'ck: D.S.

Yrs ever, | D.

4303 TO: [CONSERVATIVE MPS]   Downing Street [Thursday] 17 January 1867

ORIGINAL: PS 1552

PUBLICATION HISTORY: MP (21 Jan 1867); BH (26 Jan 1867)

EDITORIAL COMMENT: A circular letter.

Downing-street, Jan. 17, 1867.

Sir, –

The meeting of Parliament has been fixed for Tuesday, the 5th. February, when

---

1 Derby had written to D a '*Confidential*' letter from St James's Square on 'Saty Night' enclosing three letters (see n2) 'received this Evening': 'we are not only on velvet, but we may look at it [the Court] at present as *Partisan*; and we can have their intervention when, and as, we choose. I think nothing ought to be said till the day after you have made your statement. Do not say anything as to the Queen's opening Parliament in person, till She herself announces it. I shall not hesitate to assure her that we will put no pressure on her *in future years*!' H B/XX/S/468.

2 On 12 January the Queen had replied to a 10 January letter from Derby, who had written at length summarizing the afternoon's cabinet council, at which it had agreed to proceed 'by way of Resolutions, which should embody the principles on which the future Parliamentary Representation should be founded.' One resolution 'will pray your Majesty to appoint a Royal Commission ... to report upon the probable effect of certain changes in the electoral body, and of alteration of boundaries of boroughs, etc. etc.' Although Derby welcomed the Queen's support (she had offered to communicate 'with the Leaders of the moderate Liberal party'), it was 'of the utmost importance that nothing should transpire as to the course to be pursued' until after the opening of Parliament, which he entreated her to open in person. The Queen replied that she entirely approved of Derby's course of action ('dictated by common sense') and would not use her influence until told by Derby 'that the time for doing so has arrived'. She would open Parliament in person, '*great, trying*, and *painful* as the exertion will be to her', only with the understanding 'that she is *not* to be expected to do it as a *matter* of *course*, year after year ... [and] *not* be asked to make a similar exertion next year'. LQVB I 388-91.

3 Derby had closed his letter (n1): 'I wish we could calculate on the "Patriotism" of the Leaders of Opposition with as much confidence as the Queen does – but it may do them some good to be made aware of H. M's feelings.' H B/XX/S/468.

the House of Commons will immediately proceed to the consideration of business of the highest importance. I therefore take the liberty of earnestly requesting your presence on that day. – I have the honour to remain, Sir, your faithful servant, B. DISRAELI.'[1]

TO: [MONTAGU CORRY?] Downing Street [Saturday] 19 January 1867 **4304**
ORIGINAL: H B/XI/J/1
EDITORIAL COMMENT: C of Ex paper. *Sic*: Regents Park [*twice*]; Regents St.

---

confidential   Jany 19: 67

Mr Secretary Walpole has received a report from Sir R. Mayne[1] of what was decided last night ↑in council of Ref: League↓ as to the demonstration for Monday the 11th:.

It is to be on the / greatest scale & to parade London: from the Regents Park, down Oxford St: to cross the Park (I think) by Coopers Road, from Victoria Gate to Queens Gate: then by Kensington, Knightsbridge, / Piccadilly, Pall Mall, all Regents St. to Regents Park again, where resolutions will be passed.[2]

Now for the Memorials.[3]

 D.

TO: LORD DERBY Downing Street [Saturday] 19 January 1867 **4305**
ORIGINAL: DBP Box 146/3
EDITORIAL COMMENT: C of Ex paper. *Sic*: publickly.

Confidential   19 Jany: 67

Right Honorable | The Earl of Derby | K.G.

My dear Lord,

This from Walpole – to go on to you. We will consider it when I call – about ½ past two, or so, today.

I was so alarmed with the imbecility of the / Home Office, when I called there the other day, on the matter of the enclosed paper,[1] that I took private steps to get up

---

1 See **4321**.

---

1 Sir Richard Mayne (1796-1868), BA 1818 Trinity College, Dublin, MA 1821 Trinity College, Cambridge, a barrister (Lincoln's Inn 1822), CB 1848 and KCB 1851. He had been joint commissioner (with Col Charles Rowan 1829-50 and Capt William Hay 1850-5) of Sir Robert Peel's Metropolitan Police Force (formed 1829) and sole commissioner since 1856. His resignation was twice refused (following the June 1866 Hyde Park riots and the December 1867 Clerkenwell explosion) on the grounds of long public service.
2 The 11 February 1867 Reform League demonstration would go off 'in perfect order ... nothing occurred to mar the perfect harmony of the gathering or disturb the good order and good temper with which it was carried on throughout.' Its 'most circuitous' route went 'from Trafalgar-square, by Pall-mall, St. James's-street, Piccadilly, Regent-street, Langham-place, Portland-place, Park-crescent, Euston-road, Pentonville-road, to the Agricultural Hall, Islington', which it would enter shortly after 6 *pm*. *The Times* (12 Feb 1867).
3 See **4305**&n2.

---

1 Neither Walpole's letter nor this paper, forwarded by D to Derby, has been found. Walpole would write to D on the 21st: 'I hope I have now done what you wish. My object is to refer to the Comm[on]s nothing but the ascertainment of *facts*, & to reserve for The House the ultimate decision.' H B/XXI/W/71.

Memorials, & I have reason to believe, that one, / ~~signed~~ originated by Trollopes the great builders[2] is, this morning, circulating confidentially among the chief London Tradespeople. When signed by them, it will be publickly circulated – & then, / I think, shd. be published in the papers with all the signatures.

Yrs ever | D.

I have ~~just~~ also received your box – & this answers it.

4306

TO: MONTAGU CORRY   Grosvenor Gate [Saturday] 19 January 1867
ORIGINAL: H B/XX/D/35
EDITORIAL COMMENT: 11 Downing Street paper, imprinted address crossed out and 'Grosvenor Gate' written in.

Montagu Corry Esq   Grosvenor Gate | Jany 19 1867
My dear Montagu

I enclose a letter to Mr Longman,[1] wh: read, & forward, ↑(tomorrow)↓ if you approve of it, but not without. Time is so valuable, that we cannot afford to cancel / the obnoxious title,[2] but let us anticipate we may have the occasion.

Your note was most successful, & it deserved to be so. The volume is much admired, for its type & / general getting up.[3]

I have sent you Kebbel, wh: read at yr convenience. I cd. not get it into any box.[4]

I have got the Edinbro', & shall read it today.[5]

Yrs ever, | D.

---

2 George Francis Trollope (1817-1895) was head of George Trollope and Sons (builders). Memorials were being gotten up by London merchants against reform demonstrations, which cost businesses valuable custom and blocked off traffic routes.

---

1 This letter has not been found.

2 See **4235**&n1.

3 *The Times* on 23 January would call *Parliamentary Reform* 'a crucial test of the speaker's powers ... the editor has been audacious, and possibly at the same time discreet, in reprinting these Speeches just as they were delivered ... The most striking characteristic of these Speeches is their completeness and consistency. They extend over a period of eighteen years, and it would almost seem that from the commencement Mr. Disraeli had thoroughly studied the subject, and had arrived at definite conclusions upon it.' The *London Review* on 9 February would find D's speeches 'singularly dull ... ingenious and elaborate, but ... cold and lifeless' and lacking 'high eloquence or generous thought', and the *Church and State Review* on 27 April would lament the absence of 'a well-digested index, with sub-headings to each page'. Gladstone would read *Parliamentary Reform* on 13 February and 6 March. *Gladstone Diaries* IV 500, 504.

4 The most recent book by Thomas Edward Kebbel (VIII **3467n1**), *Essays upon History and Politics* (1864), 407 pp, included (at pp 326-62) 'Mr. Disraeli, May, 1860.' See **4332**.

5 In H/LIFE, adjacent to a typed excerpt from **4305**, is an undated clipping from the *Edinburgh Evening Courant* which begins: 'Mr Disraeli has for many years been the best-abused public man in England. A less able man must long ago have gone down before the persistent and vehement abuse with which he has been assailed by the Liberal and Radical parties, and by journals which seem to have mainly existed for the purpose of attacking him. He has paid little heed, however, to the vocabulary of foul language discharged at his head.'

Montagu Corry | Esq   Jan 19 1867

My dear Mr Editor,[1]

Lord Derby has sent to me to be with him today, in St Ja[me]s Sqr, at ½ past two or three, & I may / be with him a very long time.

Pray make my apologies to Mr Mellor, if I do not arrive in time to give him the interview I promised.[2]

If / he will communicate freely with you, he will oblige me. He will speak to one, who possesses my entire confidence.

Yrs, | D.

Monday 21 Jan.

Not a single box here, tho' I have pressing need of several. Send some up directly.

Also the Queen's speech after the panic of 1847.[1] I am not clear at this moment, whether there / was an autumnal Sess: in 1847.

Send, also, the vol: of Hansard (I think 1848 commencement of Sess:) when Ld. John Russell proposed great increase of armaments & income tax; all of wh: he / was obliged to with draw.[2]

I shall not be at the office today.

Send up quickly.

Yr | D.

I sent to you yesterday at / Grosvenor St. enclosing a letter &c[.][3]

---

1 On this day (19th) Corry would write to MA: 'I am very happy to be able to send you (at last) a copy of "Parliamentary Reform." I am not a humble Editor. I am proud of my child. The outside is good: the contents are *perfect*.' H D/III/C/467.

2 Possibly cotton manufacturer Thomas Walton Mellor (1814-1902), MP (C) for Ashton-under-Lyne (1868-80), or John William Mellor (1835-1911), a barrister (Inner Temple 1860), eldest son of Sir John Mellor.

---

1 Following the collapse of the financial markets on 23 October 1847, the Bank of England had requested a suspension of the Bank Charter Act. Parliament opened on 23 November 1847 and the Queen's speech was read in the Lords by the Marquess of Lansdowne. Although she had '"seen with great Concern the Distress which has for some Time prevailed among the Commercial Classes"', the Queen expressed '"great Satisfaction in being able to inform you ... that the Pressure on the Banking and Commercial Interests has been mitigated."' However, she viewed with deep anxiety both '"the Recurrence of severe Distress in some Parts of Ireland, owing to the Scarcity of the usual Food of the People"' and the occurrence, in some Irish counties, of '"atrocious crimes ... and a Spirit of Insubordination ... leading to an organized Resistance to Legal Rights."' *Hansard* XCV cols 11-14.

2 In the House on 18 February 1848, in committee of ways and means, Russell had proposed 'a temporary increase of an existing direct tax, in the face of circumstances of almost unparalleled difficulty which have occurred during the last year.' *Hansard* XCVI cols 900-26.

3 Corry's father, Henry Thomas Lowry-Corry, lived at 71 Grosvenor Street 1862-8. D's letter has not been found.

4309　TO: [MONTAGU CORRY]　　　　[Downing Street] Monday [21 January 1867]
ORIGINAL: H B/XX/D/38
EDITORIAL COMMENT: C of Ex paper. *Dating*: by context; see **4308**.

Monday

You must have sent me Hansard *1860* by mistake. The other ↑vol↓ was right.

What I want is that wh: contains the statement of Lord John Russell / at the beginning of a Sess: (I think 1848) when he proposed a considerable increase in our naval & military expenditure, in consequence of the alarming state of Europe, / *& a proportionate increase in the Income Tax.*[1] The House wd. not have the scheme at any price; they wd. not wait for the C of E (Cha[rle]s Wood) to bring forward his Budget; but made the / Government at once ᴡ give up their scheme, & recast & reduce the Estimates accordingly.[2]

Find & send me this.

D.

Probably 1848.

4310　TO: GEORGE BARRINGTON　　　Grosvenor Gate [Saturday] 26 January 1867
ORIGINAL: BL ADD MS 58210 f1
EDITORIAL COMMENT: 11 Downing Street paper, imprinted address crossed out and 'Grosr Gate' written in.

Private　　　　　　　　　　　　　　　　　Grosr Gate | Jany 26 1867

Hon: Geo Barrington | M.P.

Dear Barrington,

Pray let me know exactly how the Chief is – as I am nervous & distressed about him. Tell me the truth.[1]

I shall also call in my way to D.S: about / three o'ck: & ask to see you.

Yrs sincerely, | D.[2]

4311　TO: [MONTAGU CORRY]　　　Downing Street [Tuesday 29 January 1867]
ORIGINAL: H B/XX/D/64
EDITORIAL COMMENT: 11 Downing Street paper. Endorsed by AES on the first page: 'Sir Edward Kerrison's resignation of seat'. *Dating*: by context; see nn1&2.

Do what is necessary for the enclosed, keeping it very quiet.[1] Perhaps it is not necessary to do anything immediately.

---

1 See **4308**&n2.
2 On 28 February 1848 D had ridiculed a speech by Sir Charles Wood. See V **1632**n1 and *Hansard* XCVI cols 1392-1450 (D 1431-9).

---

1 Malmesbury on 22 January had sent D a letter (of the 21st) from Lady Derby, who said Derby was 'unable even to turn himself in bed ... and I am afraid this attack will be a rather long one.' H B/XX/HS/132.
2 A reply from Barrington has not been found. Derby had suffered 'a slight attack of gout. It promises to yield to treatment, but it is necessary that he should as much as possible remain in the same temperature.' *The Times* (29 Jan 1867).

---

1 Sir Edward Kerrison on 29 January 1867 had written from Oakley Park, Norfolk, with 'the first intelli-

Taylor will return on Thursday night.[2]

    D.

TO: [FREDERICK VILLIERS]   [London, Wednesday 30 January 1867]   4312

ORIGINAL: H B/XIII/97a (first three paragraphs) and H B/XIII/97b (fourth paragraph)

EDITORIAL COMMENT: A draft in D's hand. The word 'life' in the fourth paragraph is 'hope' in H H/LIFE. *Dating*: by context; see n1.

I am much gratified by the wish you express & I shall follow ~~with some feeling of~~ ↑not witht↓ solace the remains of a much-loved & most interesting friend.[1]

    She was so vital, that I really never ↑cd↓ contemplate~~d~~ ↑that↓ we shd ↑ever↓ lose her, & to me the shock ↑was quite↓ that of a sudden & unexpected death / notwithstanding the liveliness of her mind & the gaiety of her heart, she had a depth ↑of judgment,↓ & ↑a↓ steadiness of ~~mind &~~ purpose ↑for↓ wh: the world did not give her credit.

    I cd trust her with anything, & often did, & sometimes, received counsels from her wh: her immense experience & unswerving tact rendered invaluable. She was a great woman as ~~indeed~~ well as a charming one & had the most unflagging spirit I ever knew[.]

    I knew her in great sorrows,[2] but I was happy in thinking ~~that the~~ ↑her↓ latter ~~part of her life~~ years were soothed & more serene. This was greatly owing to yr goodness to her, ↑wh: was admirable &↓ on wh: she rested as a rock – & in some degree in the life she cherished ↑& wh: I earnestly trust will be ~~fulfilled~~ accomplished↓ that Jersey wd. fulfil his duty to his [*illegible deletion*] ↑home↓ & his country[.][3] [*illegible words*]

    D.

Monday & Tuesday next are the only days on wh: it cd.[4]

---

gence of my intended resignation.' Having been ill the previous year and not yet fully recovered, he was 'therefore for the present determined to quit Parliament ... If the secret of my resignation is kept until Saturday, & the writ moved on Tuesday, I see no fear of serious opposition. I believe it is to you I should apply "formally" for the Chiltern hundreds. Please make the necessary arrangements so that the writ may be moved for, on Tuesday the 5th by Taylor.' H B/XXI/K/115.

2 In the House on 5 February, on the motion of Col Taylor, a writ would be ordered for the election of a new member for E Suffolk to replace Kerrison, who had accepted the Chiltern Hundreds. *Hansard* CLXXXV col 43; *The Times* (6 Feb 1867).

1 Villiers on 29 January 1867 had informed D that he would receive an invitation to attend the funeral of his mother, Lady Jersey, who had died on the 26th at 38 Berkeley Square. H A/IV/J/317.

2 Lady Jersey had been pre-deceased by her husband and their other six children.

3 Victor Albert George Child-Villiers (1845-1915), 7th Earl of Jersey 1859, Kt 1890, GCB 1900, eldest son of Frederick's brother George Child-Villiers, 6th Earl of Jersey, had entered Balliol College, Oxford, in 1864 but left in 1867 without taking a degree. Lord Jersey, principal proprietor of the banking firm of Child & Co, would be a DL of Warwickshire, a JP for Warwickshire and Oxfordshire, lord-in-waiting to the Queen 1875-7, LL of Oxfordshire 1887-1915, paymaster-general 1889-90, governor of New South Wales 1891-2 and chairman of the Light Railways Commission 1896-1905.

4 Villiers on this day (30th) would thank D for his 'most kind letter. It is a very soothing recollection to find that the memory of my dear Mother, is so well honoured & cherished by such a friend as you have always shown yourself to be, & I feel deeply grateful for your affectionate sentiments. I trust the invitation has properly reached you, & it will be a great satisfaction to me to see you with us at Middleton on Saturday.' Although D's 29 January invitation had 'miscarried' (leading to a letter of apology to D on the 31st), D

TO: [MONTAGU CORRY] Downing Street [Friday] 1 February [1867]

ORIGINAL: H B/XX/D/40

EDITORIAL COMMENT: C of Ex paper. *Dating*: by Lady Jersey's funeral (n5) on 2 February 1867.

Feb 1 /

Tell yr father immediately, that I will sanction the increased Educ[ati]on Estimate. He wants to get out of town.[1]

———

Vide Ld Stanley's note. & / attend to it.[2] I hope myself, that nothing will be done at present, but after what has occurred, it is of importance, that Portugal shd not think we have been trifling with her. /

I am not satisfied as to our position about the luggage question.[3] I shd like much

———

would attend the funeral on Saturday 2 February at Middleton Stoney, Oxfordshire. Villiers on 1 March would send D some malachite items and Lord Jersey's watch 'left by my Mother to be given to you.' H A/ IV/J/318; H B/XXI/J/55, 55a; *The Times* (5 Feb 1867); H A/IV/J/320.

———

1 Stanley on 31 January 1867 had noted a 'cabinet in the afternoon, where discussed ... a plan of Corry's for improving the revised code, about which I have doubts, but it is a small matter.' *Disraeli, Derby* 287. Henry Thomas Lowry-Corry, vice-president of the council on education, on 28 February would table a privy council minute containing provisions that, he admitted, 'would ultimately lead to a considerable increase in the Educational Vote'. After assuring the House that 'the Minute contained nothing at variance with the principles of the Revised Code' and 'did not cancel a single article' in it, he outlined his plan and explained that although the 'Estimate of 1867-8 for the increased rate of grants was only ... a total of £15,200 ... in future years the cost would be much more considerable. The Estimate for 1868-9 would probably not fall short of £40,000; and eventually, in the course of three or four years, when the scheme would be in full operation, the annual increased expenditure calculated on the present number of schools would probably exceed £60,000, or might amount to £70,000.' *Hansard* CLXXXV cols 1147-58.

2 Stanley on 31 January 1867 had written to D from the foreign office: 'I understand that you can spare about £400,000 for the Portuguese treaty; but in this office I have no means of knowing how far that sum will go in the way of reductions; and the question which the Portuguese will ask is, what rate of duty do we mean to fix? I understand that a uniform rate of 1s would in round numbers, cost £700,000, and leave £700,000 as receipt instead of £1,400,000, the present amount: this we cannot afford: a reduction of the 2s.6d. duty to 2s is within our means, but would satisfy nobody: circumstances therefore point to some such rate, for wine above 26°, as 18d, 20d, or 21d: which would be a substantial concession. Can you obtain from the Customs an estimate of what the loss would be at these respective rates; or in other words, how much reduction can we afford, with a loss not exceeding £400,000? I have no data here for such a calculation.' H B/IX/E/16.

3 On 10 January, Edward William Watkin had sent D a copy of a memorial (published in *The Times* on the 11th) signed 'by 127 peers, and 318 members of the House of Commons praying for the suspension of the offensive and unnecessary practise of searching Passengers' Baggage on the route between London and Paris during the 7 Months of the Great French Exhibition' of 1867. It begged D to consider 'substituting Custom House surveillance through detective or other Officers for the practice of individual and personal search of baggage at the Ports and in London, in the case of travellers by Railway between London and Paris'. The issue would be discussed in the House on 8 March, Alexander Beresford-Hope moving a resolution (withdrawn) to suspend baggage searches of passengers arriving from France during the 1 April-31 October Exposition Universelle. According to Beresford-Hope, a few weeks earlier D had met with a deputation about the matter, 'heard their case, shook his head, and sent them off with a Papal *non-possumus*.' Without searches, treasury secretary Hunt predicted 'an organized system of smuggling spirits and tobacco' and Hugh Childers (citing figures) that 'revenue would suffer considerably.' Watkin refuted Hunt's 'hobgoblin argument', while Gladstone favoured an arrangement with the French government of keeping suspicious parcels under surveillance during transit. D closed the discussion by asserting that 'the real question' was 'is the House of Commons prepared to support Her Majesty's Government in their attempt to defend the revenue of the country?' H B/VIII/23a; *Hansard* CLXXXV cols 1581-96 (D 1594-6).

to have ↑Sir↓ Fremantles reply to Watkin.[4] Several of my colleagues, evidently, think the Treasury case bad. /

I hope to see you today, as I have several things to tell you, & tomorrow I am sorry to say I must go down to Middleton, for Lady Jersey's funeral.[5] I shall return in the evening.

The speech will not be printed, & you had better see Mr Barrington about our copy.[6]

D.

TO: [CONSERVATIVE MPS] [London, before Saturday 2 February 1867] 4314
ORIGINAL: PS 1538
PUBLICATION HISTORY: *BH* (2 Feb 1867), with minor variations
EDITORIAL COMMENT: A circular letter. *Dating*: see ph.

The Speaker of the House of Commons will be the guest of the Chancellor of the Exchequer on Monday the 4th. Febry. & meet the Mover[1] & Seconder[2] of the Address & the Members of the Government in the House of Commons. Covers will be laid for forty.[3]

TO: MONTAGU CORRY [Downing Street] Saturday [2 February 1867] 4315
ORIGINAL: H B/XX/D/334
EDITORIAL COMMENT: C of Ex paper. *Dating*: by context; see n1.

Saturday morning

Montagu Corry

I find *we* must supply Gladstone with the speech.[1] He sent it to me last year.

---

4 Sir Thomas Fremantle, chairman of the board of customs, on 28 January had informed D that one of the commissioners for the Fishery Convention (a Mr Goulburn, possibly Frederick Goulburn, a future chairman of the board of customs), writing from Paris, had told him that the Directeur Général des Douanes of France was adamantly against suspending baggage searches, as (quoting Goulburn) '"there would be no possibility of re-imposing restrictions, if once taken off." ... I will let you have a memorandum in reply to Mr Watkins' extravagant & incorrect assertions.' H B/VIII/23b. See **4432**&n1.
5 See **4312**&n4.
6 Stanley on 4 February 1867 would record, 'Dined Disraeli's [*see* **4314**n3], the usual official party. [The throne] Speech read, and seemed to be approved by those who had not heard it before.' *Disraeli, Derby* 287. See **4321**nn1&2.

---

1 Thomas de Grey (1843-1919), 6th Baron Walsingham 1870, FRS 1887, BA 1865 and MA 1870 Trinity College, Cambridge, MP (C) for W Norfolk 1865-70, lord in waiting to the Queen 1874-5, high steward of the University of Cambridge 1891 and the borough of King's Lynn 1894. An amateur lepidopterist and president of the Entomological Society 1889-90, de Grey in 1910 would donate his vast collection to the British Museum (Natural History).
2 Samuel Robert Graves (1818-1873), a Liverpool merchant and shipowner, chairman of the Liverpool Shipowners Association and of the local Marine Board 1856, mayor of Liverpool 1860-1, was MP (C) for Liverpool 1865-73.
3 Denison (the Speaker), de Grey and Graves would be among thirty-one guests at a parliamentary dinner at Grosvenor Gate on 4 February 1867. *The Times* (5 Feb 1867).

---

1 The 5 February throne speech, which would be read at D's parliamentary dinner on the 4th. On that day Gladstone would note: '9-11 P.M. Meeting at Lord Russell's on the Speech.' *Gladstone Diaries* VI 497. See **4313**&n6.

Lord Palmerston used to send it to me, / but it was as Leader of the House of Comm:, not as Prime Minister.

You must make, therefore, I fear two / copies, but you have good assistance.

yrs | D

4316

TO: LORD DERBY   Grosvenor Gate [Saturday] 2 February 1867
ORIGINAL: DBP Box 146/3
PUBLICATION HISTORY: M&B IV 478; Blake 454, extracts; Beeler 72, extracts
EDITORIAL COMMENT: Black-edged paper.

Grosvenor Gate | Feby. 2. 1867

Right Honorable | The Earl of Derby, | K[.]G.

My dear Lord,

The Admiralty is beyond the control of a Chanr. of the Exr, or any other subordinate Minister. It is the Prime Minister, that can alone deal with that / department.

If the Admiralty want more guns, they must proportionately diminish their contract expenditure.

It is useless to attempt to reason with them: you must command. The whole system of administration / is palsied by their mutinous spirit. Not another four & twenty hours ought to elapse without the estimates being settled. Several acts of great policy: the formation of the / army of reserve, & the Portuguese treaty, depend upon the programme on wh: we agreed, & wh:, so far as the Admy. is concerned, gives it more than ½ mill: of excess.

Yrs si[ncere]ly, | D.[1]

---

1 Derby had written to D twice on this day (2nd), first from St James's Square ('*Confidential*'): 'I return the Papers you left with me. They are conclusive to my mind that without plurality of voting we cannot propose Household Suffrage, which would give the Working Classes a majority of nearly 2:1 ... What do you say to the enclosed letter from Pakington? I doubt whether we can sufficiently recognize the Adullamites as a Party to send them the Speech, and especially as they might misconstrue the Reform Paragraph.' Pakington on 1 February had informed Derby that Augustus Anson (L) had suggested giving Grosvenor 'some intimation of our intended course, as he is to have an *Adullamite dinner* on Monday'; he had asked if Derby 'would think it proper' to send him the speech. Derby's second letter ('*Private*') was headed 'Saturday 6.30 P.M.': 'I have just received the enclosed unsatisfactory note from Hunt [*see below*] ... With regard to the guns, it was clearly understood that their demand on the War Office should not exceed that of last year – and that £170,000 must be knocked off. But I understood Pakington to undertake that the excess of his Estimate should not be more than £600,000, or thereabouts, against which if he were allowed to set the proceeds of his Ships & Iron, the *net* excess would not be over £300,000, and to this arrangement I understood you to accede. If I am right in this, he has done (setting the guns aside) more than he promised. Let me know what you think about letting Grosvenor have a copy of the Speech ... Ld. Russell ... hopes I will send him the Speech, which of course I will do.' Treasury secretary Hunt on 2 February had alerted Derby to 'a very great difficulty respecting the Navy Estimates – The original Sketch Estimates were £1,329,989 in excess of those of 1866-7 (including the Supply Est. of nearly £50,000). The Revised Estimates have come to me unofficially today – Mr. Disraeli has not seen them. They show an excess over last years Est. (including as before) of £*510,880*. But there is also an excess of about £170,000 on account of the Admiralty demands upon the War Office for Guns for her service, making nearly £*700,000* excess in all for the Navy – To meet the Chancellors financial requirements there ought to be a further reduction of £450,000 for he told me that not more than £250,000 could be allowed to the Admiralty over last years Estimates, Guns included.' Hunt felt it was vital that the coming year's expenditure 'be met without additional taxation or making use of the relief to the Exchequer that will arise by the falling in of the Deadweight Annuity – (without availing ourselves of which the Portuguese Commercial Treaty would have to be abandoned).' H B/XX/S/404-7.

TO: [LORD DERBY] Grosvenor Gate, Sunday [3 February 1867] **4317**
ORIGINAL: DBP Box 146/3
EDITORIAL COMMENT: Black-edged 11 Downing Street paper, imprinted address crossed out and 'G. Gate' written in. Docketed in another hand on the first page: '10 o'ck'. *Dating*: by context; see n1.

G. Gate | Sunday

I don't think it would be expedient to send the speech to Lord Grosvenor.[1]

I heard yesterday of a curious conversation on the state of affairs / with Lord Grey.

Lord Grey, much perplexed, holds, after deep & ~~bo~~ long reflection, that "cumulative voting" is the best solution.

I / have no doubt that "cumulative voting" is very conservative, & on the whole, it is not improbable, that, in a party sense, it might ultimately be advantageous – but we must remember, that / its primary effect would, without doubt, be to disturb our friends in their counties, & ~~that~~ this has always made me feel we cd. not entertain it.[2]

D.

I hope you will break the line of the Adm[iralt]y to day.

TO: LORD DERBY Grosvenor Gate, Sunday [3 February?] 1867 **4318**
ORIGINAL: DBP Box 146/3
EDITORIAL COMMENT: Black-edged 11 Downing Street paper, imprinted address crossed out and 'Grosvenor Gate' written in. Endorsed in another hand on the third page: 'Mr. Disraeli *Jany 3.67* describing a conversation by Ld Grey in which he expresses himself in favour of Cumulative Voting.' *Dating*: conjectural; see **4317**. 3 January 1867 was a Thursday. *Sic*: Sunday Jan 3.

½ pt. 11. Grosvenor Gate | Sunday Jan 3 67

My dear Lord,

I propose to be with you about a quarter past three to day.

I have Hunt &c., with me at two, & ½ past.

The enclosed about Ld. / Grey was in a box for you before I received yr note.[1]

Yrs sin[cere]ly | D.

---

1 See **4316**n1 and **4321**&n1.
2 In the House on 31 May D would speak against 'schemes which depend upon the allocation of a third Member to certain constituencies. One of these plans is cumulative voting – that any constituent may give his three votes in favour of one person ... There is no place which needs to be represented by more than two Members. In this age of rapid communication, both personally and by post, if we were to choose between three Members and one, I should certainly be in favour of one Member.' *Hansard* CLXXXVII cols 1416-22. There were two forms of cumulative voting proposals: 'In the most conservative form, when coupled with duality or other sorts of plural voting, it involved specially qualified voters (e.g. property owners or possessors of educational qualifications) being given two or more votes in a constituency and being entitled to cast all of them for one candidate in a three-member constituency. In the less conservative form (as Cairns formulated it in March and as he succeeded, from the House of Lords, in interpolating it into the [Reform] Act in the summer of 1867) it merely entitled electors to cast all their votes for a number of candidates one fewer than there were seats to be elected to (i.e. they could vote for only two candidates in a three-cornered constituency, etc.).' Cowling 421n6. In 1867 Archibald Smith published *What is the Best Form of Cumulative Voting? Considered in a Letter to Thomas Hughes, Esq., M.P.* (8 p).

---

1 D's enclosure and Derby's note have not been found.

4319 TO: [MONTAGU CORRY]   Downing Street [before Monday 4 February 1867]
ORIGINAL: H B/XX/D/65
EDITORIAL COMMENT: 11 Downing Street paper. *Dating*: by context; see n1. *Sic*: De.

The announcement in our contemporaries respecting ~~the movement of~~ the Address ↑in answer to the Queen's speech↓ in the ↑Ho: of↓ Commons,[1] is incorrect.

The Address in answer to the speech will be moved by the Hon Thos De Grey, member for Norfolk / & sec[o]nded by Mr Graves, member for Liverpool.[2]

4320 TO: LORD DERBY   Downing Street [Monday] 4 February 1867
ORIGINAL: DBP Box 146/3
PUBLICATION HISTORY: M&B IV 490-1, omitting the third sentence
EDITORIAL COMMENT: Black-edged 11 Downing Street paper.

Confidential   Feby. 4 1867
Right Honorable | The Earl of Derby | K.G.
My dear Lord,
Walpole is very much against "plural voting".[1] He says, he has only heard but one opinion of it since Horsman's suggestion[2] "And / is this all the Adullamites have invented!" Walpole says, he thinks the defeat of the proposition will be crushing – the old story, finesse, & giving with / one hand & taking away with the other.

He says, there is but only one course, if we legislate – household suffrage founded on residence & rating, wh: he is convinced is most conservative – no / compound-householders on any account.

So far as he has spoken with our friends, he has heard no difference on the point; that fighting about 1 or 2 £ ridiculous, & probably will give us a worse constituency.

Mr. Graves, the M.P. for / Liverpool, has just left me. He was delighted with the Reform Parag: in the Speech:[3] an immense relief to him: only one opinion out of doors: settlement of the question.

But what settlement? "Oh! a moderate settlement.["] But / what do you call moderate?

"Oh! I shd. say for myself, household suffrage founded on rating.[4] Thats the real thing; rating is better than any money qualification. There are 10,000 Parly. voters ↑now↓ in Liverpool, who / do not pay their rates – & never will. Its the Distribution of Seats that is the difficulty; not the Franchise."

Yrs ever, | D.

---

1 See **4321**.
2 See **4314**&nn1&2.

---

1 Resolution 5, read by D on 11 February, reads: 'That the principle of Plurality of Votes, if adopted by Parliament, would facilitate the settlement of the Borough Franchise on an extensive basis.' See app IV.
2 Horsman proposed a mixture of household suffrage and plural voting (on the Prussian model), such that working, middle and upper classes would each secure one-third of the representation.
3 See **4321**n2.
4 Resolution 4 (n1) reads: 'That the Occupation Franchise in Counties and Boroughs shall be based upon the principle of Rating.'

TO: QUEEN VICTORIA   Downing Street [Tuesday] 5 February 1867 **4321**

ORIGINAL: RAC B23 18

PUBLICATION HISTORY: *LQV*B I 391-2, omitting the last three paragraphs

EDITORIAL COMMENT: 11 Downing Street paper. *Sic*: De.

Feb 5 1867

The Chr of the Exchequer, with his humble duty to Yr Majesty:

The first night of this critical Session has been most serene: the effect of the Speech from the Throne.[1] The / House was full: but the announcement of great measures & subjects, & the paragraph on Reform,[2] had so influenced, & mitigated, the spirit of the House, that it was at once apparent, that all immediate / hostility was out of the question.

Mr Gladstone did graceful justice to the general character of Y.M's speech, & was courteous, & considerate, to the Ministry.[3]

All now depends on Monday next, when the / C of E. brings forward the Resolutions.[4] Altho' they cd. not be debated until, probably, the 4th. March, still, in the present state of affairs, it will not be difficult to form an opinion on the probable / result, parties not being severely divided, & much communication taking place between individual members.

If Mr Gladstone be forced to divide against the resolutions in / favor of immediate legislation, the C of E. thinks he would be defeated: & if once the Ministry got a majority on an issue of that importance, it would be like the India Bill, all wd. proceed smoothly & / even rapidly.[5]

The Address, in answer to the Gracious Speech, was moved by Mr. De Grey, in a style [*illegible deletion*], & general tone & intelligence, wh: much pleased the house.

His voice sweet & / flexible: his manner simple, yet with grace: & in the expres-

1 In the Lords on this day (5th) the Queen had attended the reading of the Speech from the Throne. Topics included the war involving Prussia, Austria and Italy, post-Civil War United States, the war between Spain and the republics of Chile and Peru, the insurrection in Crete, '"a more intimate Union of the Provinces of *Canada, Nova Scotia*, and *New Brunswick*"', the famine in India, the '"treasonable Conspirators abroad"' (Fenians), the cattle plague, pure water supply, army expenditures, reform (see n2), an inquiry into trade unions, better regulation of workshops employing women and children, the Mercantile Marine, the end of exemptions from shipping charges between Britain and France, railway companies, relief of metropolitan poor and landlord-tenant relations in Ireland. *Hansard* CLXXXV cols 1-8.

2 '"Your Attention will again be called to the State of the Representation of the People in Parliament; and I trust that your Deliberations, conducted in a Spirit of Moderation and mutual Forbearance, may lead to the Adoption of Measures which, without unduly disturbing the Balance of political Power, shall freely extend the Elective Franchise".' *Hansard* CLXXXV col 6.

3 Gladstone had remarked that only a few of the announcements in the Queen's speech sufficed 'to make any candid and well-judging man reluctant to see dissension introduced into this debate.' He called the language in the reform paragraph (n2) 'in some degree enigmatical; but I do not think it will be fair to make that circumstance a subject of complaint.' He closed with the hope of removing 'this obstacle ... [that] threatens to become ... a standing discredit to Parliament and the institutions of the land.' *Hansard* CLXXXV cols 67-74.

4 See **4328**&n1. Stanley on the 6th would record a 'Long and important cabinet on the reform question. It was virtually decided to drop the idea of asking for delay, to go on as proposed by way of resolutions, but to make these resolutions preliminary to a bill.' *Disraeli, Derby* 287.

5 The India Act (1858), which transferred the rule of the British East India Company to the Crown (see VII **3177**n1), had set a precedent in being introduced by resolutions and passed by consent. M&B IV 492-3.

sion of his own opinions, he broke from routine, & yet was not arrogant or conceited; but ingenuous, & sufficiently modest:

A success.[6]

4322   TO: LORD DERBY   Downing Street [Thursday] 7 February 1867
ORIGINAL: DBP Box 146/3
PUBLICATION HISTORY: M&B IV 491-2
EDITORIAL COMMENT: Black-edged 11 Downing Street paper. *Sic*: it tis.

Confidential   Feb. 7 1867

Right Honorable | The Earl of Derby K.G.

My dear Lord,

Besides urging all the considerations, to wh: you so properly referred, as to the impossibility of carrying on affairs, if mutual concessions / are not made, & so on – this suggestion might relieve us.

I – Our great anxiety not to lose his services,[1] would make you agree to recast, & modify, the Resolution in question, wh: you / also might take the occasion of making him understand was your own particular policy, & wh: you had deeply & carefully considered.

"That the principle of Plural voting, if adopted by Parliament, ~~ĭe~~ might / lead to the adjustment of the Borough Franchise on a safe & permanent basis."[2]

The House ~~wd~~, & the Country ↑(more important)↓, would understand this.

If the Resolution be / adopted, we cd. do without Peel: if rejected, we shd. have to fall back on a moderate reduction of the franchise, coupled with fancy safety valves for the working class.

With such a resolution, / Peel could honorably remain until we attempted to carry it into action ↑according to our interpretation of it↓: & if the House did not sanction our doing so, then, of course, he need not budge. /

But you ought to make him understand, that it tis yr personal appreciation of his value &c, that makes you consent to a change, wh:, in yr opinion, enfeebles yr / policy.

It wd. be a great thing, if the resignation co[ul]d be postponed.

Pardon these crude suggestions of a much-vexed, but faithful, colleague.

D.

---

6 De Grey's motion (agreed to) had been followed by supporting speeches from Gladstone and D, the latter assuring the House that reform would be discussed 'fully' on 11 February. *Hansard* CLXXXV cols 43-76 (D 74-6).

---

1 According to M&B IV (491) General Peel had begun to threaten resignation between 5 and 11 February. He would threaten to resign at a cabinet meeting on 16 February and would do so (with Carnarvon and Cranborne) on the 25th. See **4331**n2 and **4340**.

2 In the final version of Resolution 5, plural voting 'would facilitate the settlement of the Borough Franchise on an extensive basis'; see **4320**n1.

TO: LORD DERBY   House of Commons, Thursday [7 February 1867]   **4323**
ORIGINAL: DBP Box 146/3
PUBLICATION HISTORY: M&B IV 492, dated '*Thursday [Feb.* 7, 1867]', omitting the first two sentences and 'Since my box to you'; Blake 456, the fourth sentence
EDITORIAL COMMENT: House of Commons paper. *Dating*: by context.

Rt Honorable | The Earl of Derby | KG.   Thursday

My dear Lord,

Thank you for yr box. Very good.

Since my box to you, I have sent you a note to House of Lords,[1] telling you of / ↑my interview with↓ Peel – & of its general success.

The words I gave you wd. entirely satisfy him – but I have not committed *you* to them: & if you can devise, with / him, more suitable ones ↑for yr purpose↓, you can.

You will find him very placable, except on the phrase "Household Suffrage" when his eye lights up with insanity.[2]

He evidently annexes / no definite idea to the phrase – but told me, that the whole of our back benches wd. rise & leave us, as one man, if the phrase remained.

I believe, in three months time, they will unanimously call for it.

But I soothed him, & *it is all right.* You will give the finishing touch.

  D.

TO: SPENCER WALPOLE   Grosvenor Gate [Thursday] 7 February 1867   **4324**
ORIGINAL: HOL [16]
EDITORIAL COMMENT: Black-edged 11 Downing Street paper, imprinted address crossed out and 'Grosr Gate' written in.

Confidential   Grosr Gate | Feb 7 :67

My dear Walpole,

What does this mean?

  I ~~me~~ allude to what is said of Lowe.[1]

  I hope we are all right.

    Yrs | D.

TO: [MONTAGU CORRY]   [London] Friday [8 February 1867]   **4325**
ORIGINAL: H B/XX/D/39
EDITORIAL COMMENT: Docketed in another hand on the first page: '?1867' and 'Feby 8'. *Dating*: by context; see n1.

Friday

---

1 See **4322**.

2 According to D's memorandum of his 17 February 1867 audience with the Queen at Osborne, after reviewing the resolutions, Peel would return them to D on the 8th 'with a dry note; identical with one addressed, at the same moment, to Lord Derby; announcing that he could not support Household Suffrage'. That afternoon D would propose 'that the line shd. be drawn at a £5 nominal rating. The General said he was perfectly satisfied.' See app V.

---

1 Walpole on this day (7th) would reply: 'I cannot conceive what the reference to Lowe alludes to. The only thing I have heard of him is that he is against our dealing with the subject of reform at all. But I have never heard what he would do himself, or what course he intended to take.' H B/XXI/W/72. See **4340**n4.

I don't think it advisable, that the Cabinet shd. have any more papers at present, than those I directed to be sent round. They must digest those first.[1]

  D.

4326 TO: [PHILIP ROSE] House of Commons, Friday [8 or 15 February 1867]

ORIGINAL: H R/I/A/196

EDITORIAL COMMENT: House of Commons paper. *Recipient*: in Rose papers of H. *Dating*: by context; see nn1&2.

Friday

I can't leave the house *well* at five today.[1]

  I don't go tomorrow to Ashridge in consequence of Lord Brownlow's illness.[2]

  Will / tomorrow do at ½ past four o'ck:?

    Yrs ever | D

4327 TO: [MONTAGU CORRY] [London] Sunday [10 February 1867]

ORIGINAL: H B/XI/J/48

EDITORIAL COMMENT: *Dating*: by context; see n1.

Sunday

Send me tomorrow morning the technical title of the Reform Act of 1832

  (2&3 William 4:

  Cap: __ ?)[1]

4328 TO: QUEEN VICTORIA Downing Street [Monday] 11 February 1867

ORIGINAL: RAC F15 11

PUBLICATION HISTORY: *LQVB* I 395

EDITORIAL COMMENT: C of Ex paper.

Feb 11. 1867

The Chanr of the Exchequer with his humble duty to Yr Majesty:

  The Chr: proposed, to night, the course of the Govt. respecting Parliamentary Reform.[1]

---

1 Corry on 11 February would reply: 'Thank you for your note much; I will go early to the House. No copy of the Resolutions shall go out of my hands before 6. P.M.' H B/XI/J/3.

---

1 On Friday 8 February 1867 the House adjourned at 9:45 *pm*; on Friday 15 February 1867 at 8:45 *pm*.
2 Ashridge Castle (see VII **2976**n5) was the seat of Lord Brownlow, who would die on 20 February 1867, having 'long been in delicate health.' *The Times* (22 Feb 1867).

---

1 Corry on 10 February 1867 would reply from Downing Street: 'I trust you are better today, & in nerve for the great tomorrow ... The "Act to amend the Representation of the People in England and Wales" is 2 & 3 Will IV. Cap. *45.*' H B/XI/J/2. In the House on the 11th D would refer many times to the 1832 Reform Act; see **4328**&n1.

---

1 In the House on this day (11th) D had spoken at length on the resolutions (see app III) which 'will be, I hope, in the hands of Members to-morrow morning', and moved for a committee of the House to ex- amine them on the 25th (see **4340**&nn3&4). He had assured members that the Government intended

His / statement was listened to with interest.

The general feeling of the House may be summed up as that of – curiosity.[2]

Until the Resolutions have been seen & / considered, / it wd. be difficult &, perhaps, presumptuous, to foresee the result. The Chanr, however, is inclined to believe, that the Opposition will be forced to join issue on the Resolutions, / & that they will be defeated.

In that case, the progress of the Ministry with the question would, with management, be comparatively easy.[3]

TO: PHILIP ROSE Grosvenor Gate [Thursday] 14 February 1867 **4329**
ORIGINAL: H R/I/A/199
EDITORIAL COMMENT: C of Ex paper, seal crossed out and 'G.G.' written in. *Sic*: checque.

Confidential   G.G. | Feby 14 1867
Phil: Rose Esq
My dear Rose,

I was very sorry to miss you yesterday, as I am anxious to see you.

Between ½ past two tomorrow & three, I / cd. give you half an hour. At three o'ck: I have deputations.[1]

Bring a mem: of the amount of yr balance & I will give you a checque. / I want no details. I am ashamed so to have ↑so↓ delayed settling it, but I quite understand now, why Ministers of state neglect their private affairs. /

Yrs ever, | D.[2]

'to re-construct this House on the principles of the English Constitution' and that 'the elective franchise must be regarded as a popular privilege, and not as a democratic right.' Stanley noted that D's speech was 'generally thought a failure, being tedious, ambiguous, and not much to the purpose'. According to Charlotte de Rothschild, during his speech D reportedly had quaffed six glasses of water fortified with spirits. *Hansard* CLXXXV cols 214-49 (D 214-43); *Disraeli, Derby* 289; ROTH.

2 Gladstone, the only one to comment on D's speech (n1), believed the House had been placed 'in a somewhat peculiar position' and that D's opinions had 'somewhat departed from the principles of the British Constitution.'

3 General Grey on the 12th would inform the Queen that D had 'made a great mess of it' with an injudicious speech that unnecessarily recounted previous reform bills, accused Russell of having brought 'a Party spirit into discussion on Reform' and inadequately explained government proposals. He recommended the Queen read only the *Times* summary. She would write to Derby on the 13th expressing her 'fear as to the prospects of a settlement of the Reform question. Mr. Disraeli, in a short account of what passed in the House on Monday, says the Opposition will probably be forced to "join issue" on the Resolutions. Thus, then, the party contest, which the Queen had *hoped* and *understood* it was the object of this mode of proceeding to avoid, is to recommence.' *LQVB* I 395-6; M&B IV 494.

---

1 D on 15 February would meet with George Dixon, mayor of Birmingham, aldermen Hawkes and Ryland of Birmingham, councillor Price and the Borough Treasurer of Leeds to discuss 'the assessment of public buildings to the inhabited house duty.' *The Times* (18 Feb 1867).

2 In a lengthy letter to D on 15 February Rose would detail Ralph Earle's visit to him late on this day (14th) and the 'very painful scene' of Earle 'brooding over what he has taken as slights & want of appreciation.' Although 'more than satisfied' with the office D had obtained for him, Earle complained that D's 'altered demeanour, snubbing him before subordinates, excluding him from confidences ... has made his position intolerable.' Rose had pointed out to Earle 'the fatal consequences' of 'overt opposition or of private hostility', since his ingratitude would affect his reputation. He strongly urged D to meet with Earle and 'throw a little oil upon his wounded spirit ... I attach the greatest importance to your seeing him and letting him frankly tell you all he feels ... I shall see you this afternoon.' H R/I/B/110a. See **4414**&nn2&4.

4330 TO: [MONTAGU CORRY]   Downing Street, Friday [15 February 1867]
ORIGINAL: H B/XX/D/325
EDITORIAL COMMENT: C of Ex paper. *Dating*: by context; see n2.

Friday

Put off the Audit commissioners[1] as I am going to Osborne tomorrow.

Ascertain for me also what are the trains tomorrow to Portsmouth, & / the best Hotel at Portsmouth.[2]

Sir Jno. Pakington, or some one at the Adm[iralt]y wd tell you.

D

4331 TO: QUEEN VICTORIA   House of Commons [Friday] 15 February 1867
ORIGINAL: RAC F15 18
EDITORIAL COMMENT: House of Commons paper.

Feb 15 1867

The Chanr of the Excheqr with his humble duty to Yr Majesty:

He is informed, on authority, that the Opposition has relinquished all intention of / a general resistance to the Resolutions.[1]

If the Cabinet, tomorrow, adopt the Chanr of the Exchequer's views as to the mode by wh: those Resolutions shd be applied, & authorise him, / on the 25th, Inst:, to make a statement accordingly, his belief is, that the Reform Bill will pass with as much ease, as the India Bill.[2]

A telegram just / arrived from Lord Naas, says "From sub-Inspector at Killarney, troops returned from wood, saw 13 or 14 Fenians, could not catch them, found

---

1 At this time and until the audit commission (established 1785) terminated on 1 April 1867 (when its functions would be transferred to the comptroller and auditor general), the commissioners were Sir William Dunbar (chairman), Richard Vaughan Davis, William Leader Maberly, Charles Zachary Macaulay and William George Anderson. Dunbar would be appointed comptroller and auditor general and Anderson assistant comptroller and auditor general.

2 See **4333**&n1.

---

1 Returning D's letter to the Queen on the 16th, General Grey would state (in the third person) that 'he does not believe the Opposition had ever formed any intention of making a general resistance to the Resolutions. He has heard from Lord Halifax who says on the contrary that tho no decision cd. be taken as to the course the Opposition wd pursue till they know what the Gov. is going to say in answer to the questions that have been & will be put, it was pretty well "determined to make no move wh. cd. put the Govt. if beaten, under the necessity of resigning."' RAC F15 19.

2 Stanley would summarize the two-hour 16 February cabinet meeting proceedings that same day: 'Disraeli brought forward his plan of plural voting, including a savings bank franchise, an educational franchise, and one founded on direct taxation, so that, these being added to the existing franchise, the same individual might have four votes ... Peel objected to every plan by which the suffrage should be lowered ... [and] expressed his intention to resign rather than concur in the scheme proposed.' Malmesbury, also on the 16th, would outline D's reform plan in his memoirs: 'Four franchises, namely – 5*l*. rated house; 50*l*. in savings bank; an educational franchise; and direct taxation, supposed, in its result, to give 680,000 voters to property and 360,000 to democracy. General Peel positively objects.' *Disraeli, Derby* 289-90; Malmesbury II 365. For D's statement to the House on 25 February, see *Hansard* CLXXXV cols 937-52. For the India Bill, see *BDL* vol VII index.

some arms & ammunition, & saddle / of shot orderly: measures taken to pursue & intercept"[.][3]

TO: THOMAS KEBBEL   Downing Street [Friday] 15 February 1867   **4332**
ORIGINAL: H H/LIFE
PUBLICATION HISTORY: *Standard* (14 Aug 1906); T.E. Kebbel *Lord Beaconsfield and other Tory Memories* (1907) 62
EDITORIAL COMMENT: From the *Standard* series "Some Beaconsfield Recollections," number VII. The final instalment (VIII) would appear on 15 August 1906.

Downing-street,.Feb. 15, 1867.

Dear Mr. Kebbel, –

I have been, and am, so continuously engaged that it has been quite out of my power to reply to your letter,[1] and I would not address you on such a subject by the hand of another.

The moment I acceded to office, I mentioned your name to two of my colleagues, who, I thought, would have the power and opportunity of forwarding your views, and expressed the strongest feeling on my part that they should be advanced and gratified.[2]

I make no doubt that they will take the earliest occasion to forward my wishes. But, unhappily, I learn from Mr. Corry that my assumption, the foundation of all my efforts, that you could accept professional office and employment, is not warranted, and that I must consider your case as that of one without a profession.

This throws immense difficulties in my way, not to say insurmountable ones – for there is scarcely an office which does not require a professional qualification, but I will watch and do my best for you.

I have given your book[3] to read to Mr. Corry, and you may communicate with him, either personally or by letter, without reserve. He is almost as anxious to serve you as

Yours sincerely, | D.

---

3 On Wednesday 13 February a Killarney (co Kerry) coastguard station had been sacked and the town threatened by gangs of armed men. A 'mounted orderly of the constabulary force, named Duggan', carrying despatches, had been shot in the hip, 'the rebels seizing his horse and arms.' Amidst the panic many residents had sought refuge in local hotels guarded by soldiers who had arrived from Cork that night. Home secretary Walpole had informed the House on the 14th that Irish secretary Naas had left for Dublin that morning. By Friday morning (15th) the Fenian raid had been stopped and the insurgents 'believed to have taken to the mountains'. Troops scoured Toomies Wood 'to discover a party of about 50 Fenians' but no arrests were made and 'the rebels are supposed to have entirely dispersed.' On this day (15th) Walpole had reassured the House that 'the present movement in the south-western part of Ireland is completely arrested.' *The Times* (15, 16, 18 Feb 1867); *Hansard* CLXXXV cols 335-6, 400-1.

1 This letter has not been found.
2 According to Kebbel, one of those colleagues 'was Lord Cairns, and I understood that a county court judgeship might be mine if it suited me to take it. But, though called to the Bar, I had never practised, never held a brief, never even sat in court.' Moreover, when D spoke to Cairns 'he did not know that I had never practised at the Bar.' *Standard* (14 Aug 1906). About 1877 D would appoint Kebbel receiver of fines and penalties at the treasury, a civil service position he would hold until his death in 1917.
3 See **4306**&n4.

4333

TO: MARY ANNE DISRAELI   Osborne, Sunday [17 February 1867]

ORIGINAL: H A/I/A/332, 332a

COVER: Mrs. Disraeli | Queen's Hotel | *Southsea* | *Chr of Exchequer*

EDITORIAL COMMENT: Osborne paper. Docketed by MA on the first page: '1867: Febry ~~17th~~ ~~18th~~ 17th Sunday' and on the cover: 'Sunday 1867 Febry ~~18th~~ 17th'. *Dating*: by context; see n1.

Sunday

My dearest,

I think the ~~boat~~ yacht for Portsmouth will leave this at nine o'ck: tomorrow morning: & I calculate we / shall be at the Hotel by 10 o'ck: about.

In that case, we might return to town by the 10:25 train.

If not, it must be / by the 12:20 – but some people here are to go by the 10:25 & they will cross with us.

If we do, ~~you must a carriage ready~~, you must be ready, & have paid / yr bill.

The carriage we come in will take us also to the Railway.[1]

I have just arrived: luncheon finished – but I had some delicious mutton broth, & wd. take nothing else.

My audience at 7 ock:[2]

Your own | D.

4334

TO: QUEEN VICTORIA   House of Commons [Tuesday] 19 February 1867

ORIGINAL: RAC F15 24

EDITORIAL COMMENT: House of Commons paper.

Feb 19 1867

The Chanr of the Exchequer with his humble duty to Yr Majesty:

On arriving in town, he was obliged to go immediately to the Ho: / of Commons, where he was detained until ½ past nine,[1] but reached Lord Derby at that hour, & remained with him until midnight, having conveyed to Lord Derby fully & adequately, he / hopes, Her Majesty's views & pleasure.

The instant the C of E arrived in town, Genl. Peel received his box.[2]

Lord Derby was greatly animated & encouraged by the Chr of the Exchequer's report of / his visit to Osborne, & of your Majesty's unbounded kindness, & determination to support Your Majesty's ↑Ministers↓ at this critical moment.

---

1 The DS and footman James Foote had left for Osborne on Saturday 16 February via Portsmouth, overnighting at the Queen's Hotel, Southsea. D and Foote had continued on to Osborne on this day (17th) and would depart on the 18th. Charlotte de Rothschild had noted on the 16th that the Queen 'invites her ministers frequently, but leaves their better, or worse halves at home.' H acc; *The Times* (19 Feb 1867); ROTH.

2 For D's 'Memorandum' of his audience with the Queen, see app V.

---

1 D had returned from Osborne on the 18th; see **4333**&n1. The House on this day (19th) had adjourned at 11:30 *pm* after protracted debate on a resolution on the inefficient management of the dockyards; D did not speak. *Hansard* CLXXXV cols 583-654.

2 The box contained a letter from the Queen that would persuade Peel to withdraw his resignation. General Grey had shown the letter to D, with the Queen's instructions for him to 'suggest any alteration'; D thought it 'both in conception & expression, perfect.' See app V for the 'precis' (mentioned at the end of the present letter) of D's visit to Osborne.

Lord Derby reviewed his position in every light, & prepared for every contingency; much / encouraged & cheered by the report given of Yr Majesty's approval of the possible re-arrangement of offices.

But all these precautions were unnecessary; the magical letter effected the / miracle. Early this morning, the General called on Ld. Derby, withdrew his resignation, & said that, under the circumstances, he was prepared to support any measure, which Lord Derby deemed necessary & / advantageous for the country.[3]

As there was a Cabinet at one o'ck:,[4] Lord Derby took advantage of the occasion, addressed his colleagues with much, & unusual, fire & feeling: said there were / three causes wh: encouraged him, & made [him] feel confident of success; 1. The return ↑of the General:↓ 2. The tone of the House of Commons last night, wh: was very favorable to us:[5] & 3rd., & chiefly, the gracious favor of Yr Majesty & the deep personal interest, / wh: Yr Majesty took in the settlement of the question[.]

The Cabinet finally adopted Lord Derby's original plan, wh: was modified & mutilated to please General Peel, who now / made not the slightest remonstrance.

The general opinion of the political world is, that we shall carry a large, popular, & thoroughly conservative measure: & no doubt it will be greatly owing to Your Majesty's energetic / interposition on Sunday last.

The Chr of the Exchequer thought the letter would be irresistible. If he might presume to say so, he would dare to observe, that he never read any ~~letter~~, appeal, wh:, / both in conception & expression, more completely realized what he had desired.

The C of E. is obeying Yr Majestys commands about the precis: at this moment.

TO: CHARLES NEWDEGATE   Downing Street [Friday] 22 February 1867 4335
ORIGINAL: WAR B.6337A
EDITORIAL COMMENT: C of Ex paper.

C.N. Newdegate | Esqr M.P.   Feb 22 1867
Dear Mr Newdegate,
Your note has only, this moment, reached ↑me↓, as I was preparing to go down to the House.[1]

---

3 Derby, in an undated note, had informed D, 'I have this instant seen Peel. He *consents* and *remains*!' H B/ xx/s/460.

4 In cabinet at 1 *pm* on this day (19th), wrote Stanley, 'the plan of Saturday was provisionally adopted, with the limitation of votes to two', although he doubted 'the principle of double voting will be accepted by the House, but it is worth a trial.' *The Times* (19 Feb 1867); *Disraeli, Derby* 290.

5 In the House on the 18th A.S. Ayrton had placed a notice on the paper asking D '"whether it will be necessary to proceed with the Committee on the Representation of the People if he receives sufficient assurances that no obstacle will be interposed to his proceeding to a Committee on his intended Bill for amending the Laws relating to the representation of the People."' To Ayrton's request that the government 'dispense with long debates on the abstract question, and on hypothetical grounds', D had replied that there would be no 'ultimate postponement or procrastination' and that ministers would 'not desist from the work unless arrested in their labours by the House, or until the field is tilled.' Although Gladstone said he did not 'refuse ... to entertain the method of procedure by Resolution', he wished for 'prompt and effectual progress in dealing with this question.' *Hansard* CLXXXV 480-91 (D 484-6).

---

1 The House on this day (22nd) would sit from 4 *pm* to 1:30 *am* on the 23rd. *The Times* (23 Feb 1867).

The / question you propose to ask me is very important, & I shd feel obliged by yr giving notice of it for Monday next.[2]

Yours sincerely | *B Disraeli*

4336   TO: [MONTAGU CORRY]   [London, Saturday 23 February 1867]
ORIGINAL: H B/XI/J/S
PUBLICATION HISTORY: M&B IV 498, dated Saturday 23 February 1867
EDITORIAL COMMENT: Docketed in another hand on the first page: 'Feby 23./67.' *Dating*: by context; see nn1&2.

The Cab: unanimous for the great plan.[1] Baxter must stop to see me.[2]

    D.

4337   TO: [PETER MCLAGAN]   Downing Street, Saturday 23 February [1867]
ORIGINAL: H B/IX/D/2i
EDITORIAL COMMENT: A draft in D's hand on 11 Downing Street paper. *Recipient* and *Dating*: by context; see n1.

Saturday Feby 23.

---

2 In the House on Monday 25 February Newdegate would ask D whether, given Cardinal Cullen's comments at the inaugural banquet of the Lord Mayor of Dublin on the 20th (as reported in *The Times* on the 21st), 'it is consistent with the Laws of this Country, or with International Law, that an ecclesiastic should, in the capacity of a Cardinal Legate from the Court of Rome, be permitted ... to interfere on public occasions of an official character, by advice or otherwise, with matters touching the Government of the United Kingdom?' D would reply: 'Besides the Lord Lieutenant [Lord Abercorn], there was no other Peer present, and therefore, according to the rules of social etiquette, Cardinal Cullen, who is recognized as a Roman Prince, took merely the same precedence to which he would be entitled in any assembly in England, public or private. I believe he appeared on that occasion in no diplomatic capacity.' D was also 'doubtful whether he is really what is called a Cardinal Legate from the Court of Rome' and reminded Newdegate that 'a Cardinal is not necessarily an ecclesiastic.' *Hansard* CLXXXV cols 933-6 (D 934-6). *The Times* had remarked that 'the appearance of the head of the Irish Roman Catholic Church at the same social board with the Queen's representative ... seems to augur an era of reconciliation and union in Ireland.' Cullen had assured the assembly that 'he had the promise of the Lord-Lieutenant that, as far as lay in his power, he would contribute and confer every possible advantage on Ireland ... All should, therefore, unite, determined to promote in every possible way any work of interest that could tend to the honour, glory, and prosperity of the country. If the rulers of the country but assist and lead the way, the people but follow and act in a spirit of obedience, he [Cullen] had no doubt that Ireland would become what it was in the bright vision of the poet [Thomas Moore], but not in reality – "First flower of the earth, and first gem of the sea."'

---

1 In cabinet at 3 *pm* on this day (23rd), Derby had pushed through his proposal for household suffrage allied with plural voting based on property. Stanley on this day noted their discussion of a 'plan for redistributing 30 seats, and effects of the new franchise proposed ... Cranborne made objections, but all the rest assented without difficulty: and indeed as to the seats, if we are to do anything we cannot well do less.' Hawkins *Derby* 298; *Disraeli, Derby* 290.

2 Corry had written to D on 'Friday Feby 22. | 5.20': 'I have just come from Dudley Baxter's, after consultation with whom I can safely promise you that, on your arrival at Downing St tomorrow, you shall have full and definite calculations of the members that will be admitted under each franchise, and of the total increase of Electors in the Upper & Lower Classes. We have gone very carefully through them all, and he appears quite satisfied with his conclusions. He will however give his mind to the subject again tonight, & therefore perhaps it will be best for me not to attempt to give you any statement now, but to leave him to explain his own figures to you at *1* tomorrow, the time you have appointed.' H B/XI/J/4. See **4368**n1.

Sir,

↑I have received your letter of the 21st instant.↓¹ Without troubling you with ~~the whole of~~ all the communications ~~w~~ add[ressed] by Mr D. M. to the C. of E. I select to send ~~to you~~ ↑for your perusal↓ the enclosed letter / dated Jan. 8/67, wh: will I think sufficiently explain why that gentleman has received no reply from this office.² The Chr of the E has ↑between Augt. & Jany last↓ had the advantage / of receiving 5 in all 5 letters from Mr D. M.³ – ~~all of~~ wh:, tho' differing in lengths & matter, ~~have presented a~~ possess certain ~~analogy, affinity~~ similarity to each other, ~~and vie with each other~~ & are not, as I think you will admit ~~in rendering it impossible which~~ [*illegible deletion*] ~~that they are not of~~ of a character to entitle them to any attention of ~~the hand of~~ / [*illegible deletion*] ~~as I~~ [*illegible deletion*] ~~have no doubt you will admit, for as I~~⁴

TO: [LORD DERBY]   [Grosvenor Gate] Monday 25 February [1867] 4338
ORIGINAL: DBP Box 146/3
PUBLICATION HISTORY: M&B IV 500 and Blake 458, dated (by context) 25 February 1867, Blake omitting the two clauses beginning with 'but'
EDITORIAL COMMENT: C of Ex paper. *Dating*: by context; see n2.

Monday | Feby 25

This is stabbing in the back!¹

I will come on to you as soon as possible – but I am not up, being indisposed – but I shall rally immediately in such dangers.

1 Peter McLagan had written to Montagu Corry on 21 February: 'I have a letter from Mr. Duncan McFarlane [*sic*] Jr. who writes that he sent a letter to Mr. Disraeli between October 1866 & Jany 67 on Foreign affairs to which he has not yet received any reply. He is afraid from this that his letter has not been received by Mr Disraeli. You will oblige me by informing me whether the letter referred to ever reached your office.' H B/IX/D/2f. Peter McLagan (1823-1900), educated at the University of Edinburgh, was a JP for Edinburgh and Linlithgow counties, vice-lieut for Linlithgow and MP (L) for Linlithgowshire 1865-93. He had been appointed a royal commissioner to inquire into the law relating to the 'Landlords' right of Hypothec in Scotland' in 1864.
2 Little is known about Duncan Macfarlane, but according to his letter to D of 15 October 1866 (n3) from Bathgate, Linlithgowshire, he had been in India in 1854, Bengal in 1859 and a soldier in the English army in 1863. He had written to D on 8 January 1867 from Bathgate a rambling letter about what he termed 'a charge of shabbiness' brought against him in connection to the Princesses Alice and Helena, asserting that 'altho I don't care a b[lood]y sixpense [*sic*] for princesses or Queens either ... yet rather than be considered shabby in a matter where ladies are concerned I "*would*" marry a Princess if I got a Guarantee along with her of £40.000 ay & made Governor General of India –' H B/IX/D/2d.
3 Macfarlane had written to D on 15 August, 15 October, 3 December 1866, 8 and 29 January 1867. He would write again on 3, 21, 27, 30 June, 3 and 4 July 1867, and 31 March and 5 April 1868. H B/IX/D/2a-e,g,h,j-o.
4 On the last page of D's draft is a note from Corry: 'Mr. D's hand – They [*the five letters*] are entirely at your service, should you wish to inspect them, and I will only venture to request that you will do me the favor to return the enclosed at your convenience. M.C.' McLagan's reply to Corry is mutilated (including the date): 'I have just received your letter of this date, & one of Mr. D McFarlane's which I now return. His letter quite confirms the opinion I was beginning to entertain of him, that he was *non compos* ... I would not have troubled you with my previous letter, if McFarlane had not called upon me with a letter of introduction from the parish clergyman of Bathgate of whose congregation he was a member. I am only sorry that under the circumstances I should have put you to the trouble of writing your letter to me.' H B/IX/D/2p.

1 There is in H a note, most likely in Corry's hand, dated 'Monday Feby 25. 1867.': 'On this day, being that

It seems like treachery.[2]

D

4339 TO: MARY ANNE DISRAELI   Downing Street [Monday 25 February 1867]
ORIGINAL: H A/I/A/333
PUBLICATION HISTORY: M&B IV 500, dated (by context) 25 February 1867, omitting with the salutation, valediction and the word 'but'
EDITORIAL COMMENT: C of Ex paper. Docketed by MA on the first page: 'Monday 25th Febry 1867' and on the second page: '1867 Febry 25th'. *Dating*: by context; see n1.

---

confi[dential]
My dearest,
I am now going down to the House. The ship floats – but that is all.[1] –
     Thine own | D.

4340 TO: QUEEN VICTORIA   House of Commons [Monday] 25 February 1867
ORIGINAL: RAC F15 32
EDITORIAL COMMENT: House of Commons paper, one sheet black-edged.

Febry. 25 1867

The Chancr of the Exchequer with his humble duty to Yr Majesty:

     He was summoned this morning early to Lord Derby & found / affairs in a state of chaos: Lord Cranborne having tendered his resignation, & apparently induced Lord Carnarvon to / take the same step.

     General Peel followed.[1] He had sacrificed everything for an united Cabinet – but as there was not an united / Cabinet, he was not prepared to make a sacrifice.

on wh. the C. of E. was about to introduce the large scheme of Reform adopted by the Cabinet, early in the morning Ld D received the resignations of Lds Cranborne & Carnarvon & of Gen. Peel. – forwarded with this note to the C. of E.' The 'note' was a scrawl by Derby headed '8.45 AM.': 'My dear D. The enclosed [*see n2*], just received, is utter ruin! What on earth are we to do?' H B/XX/S/410.

2   Cranborne had written to Derby at length on the 24th ('*Sunday evening*'): 'I find, on closely examining the scheme which Mr. Disraeli brought to the notice of the Cabinet five days ago, that its effect will be to throw the small boroughs almost, and many of them entirely, into the hands of the voter whose qualification is lower than £10.' After careful study of the statistics, Cranborne had been unable 'to concur in this scheme' and therefore asked Derby 'to summon a meeting of the Cabinet before the meeting of the party to-morrow. Lord Carnarvon, to whom this evening I showed the figures, concurs with me in this request ... I think the abandonment of the policy under which the Queen's Speech was framed was a disastrous step ... I am convinced that [the scheme] will, if passed, be the ruin of the Conservative party.' M&B IV 499-500. Derby on the 25th would inform the Queen that after receiving at 8:30 *am* a letter from Cranborne and at 8:45 *am* one from Carnarvon, he had 'instantly despatched a messenger' to D, 'who came down at once.' *LQVB* I 399-401.

---

1   See **4338**&n1. Montagu Corry would reassure MA on this day (25 February 1867) at 9:20 *pm*: 'Clouds always pass away at last, and that terrible one of today already looks less dense. In spite of the unexampled trial he has gone through, the Ch. of the Exch: made an admirably clear and forcible statement, which, on the whole was well received ... I have seen him since the debate – decidedly in better spirits – while at this moment he is at dinner with Lord Stanley, and by the time you see him depend upon it he will be himself again.' H B/XI/J/6. See **4340**&nn3&4.

---

1   See **4338**&n1.

Ld. Derby had to address the whole ↑Conservative↓ party at two o'ck: & the Chr. of Exchequer the House of Commons two / hours afterwards.

A Cabinet was summoned at Lord Derby's *private* residence, but it cd. not be collected until 1 o'ck: & the last member who arrived was / Lord Cranborne.

Notwithstanding the absolute ruin that seemed inevitable, the Cabinet was rallied together on a modified scheme & *pledged* itself individually / to stand by it.[2]

The Cr of Exr had to reconstruct the whole of his observations, but they were not unsuccessful.[3]

Bitter opposition from Mr / Lowe & Mr Bright, but this, tho' it sounded terrible, has done no harm.[4]

Lord Grosvenor says the moderate Whigs will take the Government Bill.

TO: LORD DERBY   House of Commons [Tuesday] 26 February 1867   **4341**
ORIGINAL: DBP Box 146/3
PUBLICATION HISTORY: M&B IV 504-5
EDITORIAL COMMENT: House of Commons paper.

Confidential   Feb 26 1867

My dear Lord,

I have requested Taylor to furnish you, without loss of time, with two reports:

1.° The general result of the effect on the small / Boros of yr plan:

2.° A special report, from every member of a small Boro, on our side, of ~~their~~ his individual feelings & wishes. /

Sir Henry Edwards & Mr Waterhouse,[1] for example, who have just been with me,

---

2 Prior to addressing, from 2:10 to 3:15 *pm* at Downing Street, 230 supporters (whose names would be listed in *The Times* on the 26th), Derby on this day (25th) had held a cabinet at St James's Square at 12:30 *pm*. He later informed the Queen that '*at the last moment*, and to prevent a discreditable break-up, the Cabinet was compelled to assent to a measure far less satisfactory and comprehensive than that which had been proposed.' What D calls here a 'modified scheme' was a hasty compromise proposed by Stanley for a £6 rating franchise for boroughs and £20 for counties. Adopted a mere ten minutes before the party meeting, it would be famously dubbed the 'Ten Minutes Bill'. On the 26th John Manners (who disliked the scheme) would tell Malmesbury, 'We are in a very broken and disorganised condition.' *LQV*B I 400; Malmesbury II 367. See **4373**n3.

3 At 4:30 *pm*, to a packed House – 'members even sitting on the floor, the galleries and the bar crowded with peers, ambassadors, and other distinguished strangers, headed by the Prince of Wales' – a dispassionate D had presented 'proposals for which he had no particular affection'. When he sat down, 'a storm of indignation burst on his head.' M&B IV 500-1. D had outlined the four new proposed franchises – educational, savings bank, property and direct taxation (20s a year) – and explained their effect (and that of the readjustment of the occupation franchise in boroughs to a £6 rating basis) on the constituency, which he said would increase by 400,000. He had reassured the House that the bill he hoped to introduce would contain no 'attempt to disfranchise any voter.' *Hansard* CLXXXV cols 937-93 (D 937-52, 989-91). D's motion for the House to go into committee to discuss the resolutions (see app IV and V) was withdrawn by leave.

4 Robert Lowe ridiculed D's resolutions (n3) as 'mere hungry and empty abstractions' whose consideration in committee would be 'absolutely useless and worthless.' John Bright stated that, 'under this Bill, a ratcatcher who keeps four dogs would pay a direct tax to the amount of 20s., and, of course, would come into that new constituency, which the right hon. Gentleman says is to save this country from destruction.' Stanley believed that Lowe, Bright and Gladstone 'had the best of the argument, as they well might, for in fact the resolutions have served their purpose, and may be dropped.' *Disraeli, Derby* 291.

---

1 Samuel Waterhouse (1815-1881), who in 1840 had married Charlotte Lydia Edwards, sister of Sir Henry

are members for small Boros. They are absolutely for the great plan.[2] Is that feeling general – or universal? /

I dined alone with Walpole, who thinks, that our fall now is only an affair of a little time, assuming that, in our present feeble position, all the sections will re-unite for a vote against / us wh: it would be absurd to appeal to the country. *That* he thinks is Gladstone's tactic; to play with us, till we are contemptible.[3]

As Sir Lawrence Palk says, "till he comes / in with household suffrage, wh: is getting riper every moment."

At present, the House expects "compensation."

I tried Walpole hard as to regaining our position. He thought, / if certain persons left, & you re-organised yr Ministry, that it wd. not be looked upon as changing our front, but that, with a frank & obvious explanation, it wd. / do us good & strengthen us in the country.

It was evident, that he was contemplating the old story of a reconstruction with the Adullamites. I don't think that can / be brought about: what we must think of is the country, not the Ho: of Commons.

But it would never have done, as Pakington proposed, to have thrown ourselves on / the House of Commons with three Secretaries of State in abeyance[4] – a policy must be supported by a *complete* Cabinet.

Rather than die in a ditch, think of this, / if the worst comes.

The Duke of Buckingham vice Carnarvon

The Duke of Richmond vice Buc[kin]gham

Pakington v. Peel

Corry v. Pakington

Northcote v. Cranborne

Cave without Cabinet v. / Northcote.

At the same time, I must tell you, that I have since heard from Noel,[5] that a meeting at the Carlton will probably take place,[6] & some memorial will be signed by the party to Cranborne, Peel / &c. – to show them they have completely misapprehended the feeling & spirit of the party.

This, of course, would be good.

Yrs | D.[7]

Edwards, was JP and DL for the West Riding of Yorkshire, a major in the 2nd West Yorkshire Yeomanry Cavalry and MP (C) for Pontefract 1863-80.

2 In cabinet on this day (26th) Derby, supported by Disraeli and Pakington, had urged withdrawal of their resolutions in favour of a reform bill. Stanley on this day noted that he did not attend but had written to D 'urging the immediate withdrawal of the resolutions, with a view to anticipate any motion that might be made on the subject. This I found afterwards had been done, and I suppose everyone was agreed: there was in fact no alternative.' Hawkins *Derby* 338; *Disraeli, Derby* 291. See **4342**&n1.

3 See **4343**n2.

4 Carnarvon (colonies), Cranborne (India) and Peel (war).

5 Junior treasury lord Gerard Noel had written to Montagu Corry on 'Tuesday 6 oc' that he had heard 'a general wish expressed that Peel should be brought back into the Cabinet ... I am also sure it would be advisable to make overtures to Cranbourne [*sic*]. He would not accept, but it would please the Party.' H B/IX/F/69.

6 See **4346**&nn2,4&6 and **4349**.

7 Derby on this day (26th) would reply at '10 PM' with a '*Confidential*' letter enclosing one from General Grey inviting him to Buckingham Palace at 1 *pm* on the 27th. 'I think it would be well that I should not

TO: QUEEN VICTORIA   House of Commons [Tuesday] 26 February 1867   **4342**

ORIGINAL: RAC F15 36

PUBLICATION HISTORY: *LQVB* I 401-2

EDITORIAL COMMENT: House of Commons paper. *Sic*: Ridey; Bankes.

Feby. 26 1867

The Chr of the Exchqr with his humble duty to Yr Majesty:

So far as he can form an opinion, there is a general, almost / an universal, feeling of annoyance, almost of indignation, among the Conservative benches, that Lord Derby shd. have been, as it were, forced to / surrender his policy, wh: no doubt had, alike, all the elements of security, popularity, & permanence.

The Cr of the Exr has had difficulty in preventing / gentlemen of great eminence on the Tory side, Sir Matthew Rid[l]ey, Sir Lawrence Palk, Mr Bankes Stanhope, for example, from moving in the same sense as / that of ↑the↓ supposed policy of Ld. Derby.

General Peel, & Lord Cranborne, have acted in a complete ignorance, & misapprehension, of the real feeling of the Conservative party, & / of the Country generally, for the Conservative party, tho' slow, is always accurate in the long run.

The House is agitated & disturbed, but the Cr of the Exr. is still confident, that Her Majesty will not / be disturbed. Lord Derby has troubles awaiting him, but, with discretion & firmness, they will be overcome, & the solution of the Reform Question will be / accomplished.[1]

TO: LORD DERBY   Grosvenor Gate [Wednesday] 27 February [1867]   **4343**

ORIGINAL: DBP Box 146/3

PUBLICATION HISTORY: M&B IV 506-7, dated 27 February 1867, the first seven paragraphs

EDITORIAL COMMENT: Black-edged 11 Downing Street paper, imprinted address crossed out and 'Grosvenor Gate' written in.

Confidential   Grosvenor Gate | Feb. 27

Right Honorable | The Earl of Derby K[.]G.

My dear Lord,

I think Gladstone's position, & even tone, seem changed since the declaration of our definite policy.[1] Altho' there may not be, probably is not, any compact alliance

---

see Cranborne till after my audience. Not that I think he is a man to be swayed by the Queen's opinion, but that if, after hearing what she thinks, a movement in the Carlton such as you suggest might have a great effect upon him. I will not enter into the details of your proposals as to changes of office in the event of the necessity of a reconstruction. Some I think excellent, others inadmissible. But for these we have ample time.' H B/XX/S/411. For D's reply to this letter, see **4343**.

---

1 In the House on this day (26th) D had asked to proceed no further with the resolutions but be allowed to introduce a bill 'on the earliest practical opportunity.' Gladstone had replied that D's was the most advantageous course and read his previously submitted motion (withdrawn) that 'a discussion of the Resolutions now before [the House] must tend to delay the practical consideration of the question, and that it will be for the public advantage that the plan of Her Majesty's Government should be submitted to the House in a definite form.' *Hansard* CLXXXV cols 1021-8 (D 1021-2). For the withdrawn amendment, see **4343**n2.

---

1 See **4340**n3 and **4342**&n1.

yet, he has nevertheless succeeded in getting / the party together, & even in combining ↑them↓ in an united action: the assault on the Resolutions.[2]

Lord Russell, Bright, Grosvenor, all under the same roof![3]

He will proceed slowly, & feel his way: but I little doubt, that, by the time we get / into Committee on our Bill, he will be prepared to try 5 against 6: & probably succeed.

What shall we do then? He will count on our giving up the bill, with nothing to go to the country on.

I will not, however, trouble you now with all / these various considerations, but, if you wish it, will call upon you anywhere after the Court.

If Gladstone have these views, it wd. hardly seem, that the Queen cd. interpose with any advantage.[4] The most he wd. offer, wd. be, that you shd. go on with / the bill as amended by the House, but even if, from a sense of duty, you might be inclined to do this, the malcontents in the Cabinet would leave you, &, therefore, you wd. be forced to resign, or reconstruct.

If there is to be / reconstruction, I think it shd. be at once. I cd. not see Northcote yesterday: a wise head: & Stanley was away.

What I believe to be the malaise in the Opposition ranks is, that Lord Russell has pledged himself / to put Bright in the Cabinet, & the Whigs will not stand it.

Gladstone wd. throw Bright over.[5]

This is why, I apprehend, they want a change of leaders.

You / can tell me at the Court, if you wish me to call on you this afternoon & where.

Yours ever, I D.

4344 TO: LORD DERBY   [London, Wednesday 27 February 1867]
ORIGINAL: DBP Box 146/3
PUBLICATION HISTORY: M&B IV 507, dated '[*Feb.* 27]', omitting the closing sentence
EDITORIAL COMMENT: Black-edged C of Ex paper, seal crossed out. *Dating*: by context; see n1. *Sic*: embarassed.

Confidential
Right Honorable I The Earl of Derby I K G
I had not read the "Times" when I wrote early this morning.

2 On 26 February from 2 to 4:20 *pm* Gladstone had held a party meeting (289 members attended) at his house. He had counselled moderation but condemned the resolutions and proposed 'to set them aside by an amendment [*see* **4342**n1] which he read and submitted to the meeting.' He considered D's 'sketch of the Government measure ... inadequate with respect to the franchise and the distribution of seats ... On the whole ... those present went away highly approving the judicious manner in which Mr. Gladstone, without compromising the Liberal party, had advocated the necessity of assisting the Government by every means in its power to pass a substantial measure of Reform.' *The Times* (27 Feb 1867).
3 At Gladstone's meeting (n2) Russell had stressed 'the momentous nature of the crisis'; Bright had said Gladstone 'must eventually adopt a sterner course. No good could come of supporting the proposed Bill'; and Grosvenor thought D's bill 'more unsatisfactory even than that of last Session.'
4 Derby on the 26th (**4341**n7) had asked D: 'Should the Queen sound Gladstone as to the possibility of an agreement? She would be only too happy to attempt it.' H B/XX/S/411.
5 Bright would serve as president of the board of trade in Gladstone's cabinet from December 1868 to January 1871.

If you follow the course there indicated,[1] they will censure your government immediately the Bill is passed & you / will not be able to appeal to the Country, as the new constituency will not be registered.

It appears ↑to me↓, that Gladstone has committed himself in a manner, wh: may extricate you.

He is for £5 rating: you / can truly say, that is no better settlement than 6£ – worse, & therefore you can revert to your original scheme in preference. If they throw out the bill on the 2nd Reading, or defeat yr Boro' qualification, / you cd. dissolve with honor, & a prospect of success, & meet Parlt, at any rate with a powerful party.

I conceive, that Gladstone has weakened / & embarassed his position by his programme.

But no doubt, with this prospect, you must ~~co~~ reconstruct at once if / the malcontent colleagues will not, on reflection, see they are only cutting the throat of the party by not supporting you.

Yrs | D. /

I hold myself at your service after the Court.[2]

TO: **LORD DERBY**   Downing Street [Thursday 28 February 1867]   4345
ORIGINAL: DBP Box 146/3
PUBLICATION HISTORY: M&B IV 505, dated 27 February 1867, the first two paragraphs
EDITORIAL COMMENT: C of Ex paper. Docketed in another hand on the sixth page: '1867 Feby 28 Mr. Disraeli'. *Dating*: by context; see nn1&2.

My dear Lord,

I had my audience, wh: was long & animated. She said she did not like to see you dispirited. I replied you were, naturally, / chagrined at such incidents, but I saw a marked improvement in your countenance since your audience to day. She said, & repeated, she wd. do anything.[1]

Still more important was my interview with Stanley,[2] who exhausted the subject

---

1 *The Times* on this day (27th) had given details of the Liberal party meeting on the 26th (see **4343**nn2&3) and then proffered advice on the reform issue. 'The Government will do well to enlarge their views of enfranchisement in the interval before their Bill is laid on the table ... It is, however, vain to suppose that the county occupation franchise can be fixed at a rating of 20*l*., and the Ministry had better at once propose the limit of 14*l*., adopted by the House of Commons last year. They may then expect to encounter only a formal objection to the substitution of a rating for a rental qualification. In the same way it will be true wisdom to anticipate opposition by proposing at once a 5*l*. rating franchise in boroughs ... The policy of subdividing the present county constituencies is a device for increasing territorial influence, which ought not to be adopted without discussion.'

2 The Queen on this day (27th) would hold a Court at Buckingham Palace attended by the Derbys and the Ds. Derby, D and Carnarvon on that day had separate audiences with the Queen, after which she would record in her journal that Derby had been 'in terribly low spirits', and that she had urged he 'part with the 3 Ministers who were causing all this trouble, and reproduce the original measure'. *The Times* (28 Feb 1867); *LQV*B I 402-3. For D's audience with the Queen, see **4345**&n1.

---

1 The Queen, following D's audience on the afternoon of the 27th, recorded in her journal that D was 'much out of spirits, but thought nothing ought to be done in a hurry, and that there should be time given to reflect.' *LQV*B I 403.

2 Stanley on the 28th would record, 'Serious talk with Disraeli about the state of the reform question: the matter to be decided being, can we get back to the plan originally proposed, which is evidently the safer,

in the most logical manner, & concluded there was only one thing to be done; &, that was to recur to / our original position; but how was that to be done?, he added – "Only by the pressure of the party".

I hear, that a meeting is called at the Carlton tomorrow at twelve o'ck: by / a circular signed by thirty leading men.[3]

You will get, probably, a memorial well signed before you go to Windsor[.]

I have not succeeded in seeing Northcote.

Yrs, | D

4346 TO: LORD DERBY   Downing Street [Thursday] 28 February [1867]
ORIGINAL: DBP Box 146/2
PUBLICATION HISTORY: Blake 460, dated 28 February 1867, the third and fourth paragraphs
EDITORIAL COMMENT: C of Ex paper. *Dating*: by context; see nn1&6.

Feby 28

My dear Lord,

There is nothing in D.B's mem:[1] these results were always known. I have a list of every ~~one~~ ↑Boro↓ under the conditions in / question.

What are called the "working classes" in small Boros are those, who are under the patronage of the Upper Classes, & depend on them for / employment & existence.

In great towns, the "working classes" are powerful trades formed into Unions, & the employers are dependent on them. /

The meeting at the Carlton,[2] described to me by Mr Dick, was very numerous, &

as well as the more popular of the two? The £6 rating would be well enough if it could be adhered to, but the House will certainly change it to £5, and this Conservatives cannot accept with honour, while to dissolve on so small a difference is not expedient: and if we resign, the bill will be equally carried. On the other hand, the secession of three members of the cabinet is a serious matter: and there is an appearance of vacillation in making a second change of plan within a few days.' *Disraeli, Derby* 292.

3 See **4346**&nn2,4&6. For the background to the movement in favour of household suffrage, begun at the Carlton Club and spearheaded by Samuel Robert Graves, see M&B IV 502-3.

---

1 Dudley Baxter on this day (28th) had sent D 'the Table respecting Boroughs under 10,000 inhabitants asked by Col. Taylor; and a Memorandum [*not found*]. I have sent Lord Derby the principal results, but very briefly, and have mentioned to him the possibility of introducing into the Bill a less stringent form of the former Ratifying Clause and of enacting that the Small Tenements Act should be confined below £6; so as to base the Bill consistently upon a Ratepaying principle; which might obtain the support of the Adullamites.' This letter in H is followed by an 8-page letter of 28 February from Baxter to Derby (see n6). H B/XI/J/73-4.

2 John Manners on this day (28th) wrote to Malmesbury summarizing the Carlton Club meeting: 'Sir M.W. Ridley in the chair; between 120 and 150 present. Much difference of opinion, no resolutions passed, but a general disposition evinced in favour of rated residential household suffrage *v.* 6*l.* rating and an equal division of new seats between the counties and boroughs. An anxious desire expressed that we should fix upon the franchise we thought best and then stick to it, declining to carry our opponents' measures.' *Malmesbury* II 368. Alexander Beresford-Hope on 11 March would write that at the 'now rather notorious meeting ... at which I was present' there had been 'no conclusion whatever' on household suffrage; 'motions and counter-motions approving or disapproving household suffrage were suggested and withdrawn ... [which] sufficiently disproves the impression that the feeling of the meeting was in favour of household suffrage.' *The Times* (12 Mar 1867).

he gave me a memorandum since drawn up by his son-in-law Mr Long,[3] ↑one not too much inclined to us.↓ I enclose it.[4]

There was a meeting / at Lord Grosvenor's, I am assured today, & numerously attended for a Cave meeting – & they resolved they wd. support neither us, nor the Government, but assert their own opinions / – & they are Household Suffrage & Plurality – not Duality. ↑The old story they are 80! on this.↓

But they came, I am informed, to a resolution to communicate frankly with the Government on this ground.

Mr Hume[5] mentioned / to me the universal opinion of the party, that Gladstone & Co. only wished to use ↑us↓ for their purpose, & then discard us with ignominy. Our friends were unanimous agst our yielding from any line wh: we / determined on in our bill.

I confess I see nothing to change the resolution at wh: we had arrived.

Yrs ever | D.[6]

3 William W.F. Dick and his wife Margaret-Bruce Chaloner had one daughter, Charlotte Anna, who in 1853 had married Richard Penruddocke Long (1825-1875), son of former Tory MP Walter Long, capt Royal Wiltshire Yeomanry 1848, MA Cambridge (Trinity 1852), JP for Wiltshire, JP and DL for Montgomeryshire, high sheriff for Montgomeryshire 1858 and MP (L-C) for Chippenham 1859-65 and Wiltshire N 1865-8. Long supported '"any measure which would admit to the privileges of the franchise the steady, sober, and intelligent portion of the working classes."' Stenton.

4 A copy of an undated 11-page memo (the first page on 11 Downing Street paper) initialled 'RPL' summarizes the meeting. Sir Matthew White Ridley presided, with 'over 120 present' (19 of them named in the memo), of which '4 fifths' were in favour of household suffrage. 'It was *strongly* felt that whatever characteristic touches the Bill received shld. be MADE BY GOVT, not accepted from opponents. And Household suffrage, thus protected, especially with the power of Cumulative voting, was urged as a *Conservative* measure, on the ground that it offered the best means of resisting farther & wilder changes. And if the Opposn. were to accept the offer yet try to knock away the *checks*, that wld. enable Govt. to dissolve & appeal *as Conservatives* to the country ... But if Govt. cannot make up their minds ... & frankly announce ... that they have remoulded their Bill with a view of offering a just, comprehensive & statesmanlike measure *as a* SETTLEMENT *of the question* – including a larger extension of the suffrage than that offered by Gladstone & Earl Russell last year – if they cannot do this & so *obtain the credit* of the future Reform Bill they had far better give up their task & resign. This was strongly felt & urged by several – though more in conversation than in speeches.' The memo is accompanied by a 4-page document (the first page on Carlton Club paper) 'signed Richard P. Long': 'A decided majority of the party is cordially in favor of Household Suffrage in Boroughs with 3 years' residence and personal payment of rates. To this a small & not very influential minority objects. Therefore no *unanimous* resolution could be carried. But it is abundantly clear that if Ld. Derby & Mr. Disraeli are willing to go that length – as the best means of resisting farther changes & obtaining a lasting settlement – they will be supported by a majority of the Conservative party as well as by sufficient Liberals to carry their Bill. A strong expression also made in favor of the *cumulative vote*. Good feeling generally towards Ld Derby & Mr. Disraeli as representing the progressive element in the Cabinet. It is suggested that a meeting of the party be at once called, & the final decision of the Cabinet announced or taken afterwards as a consequence of such meeting.' H B/XI/J/205, 205a.

5 Apparently D's lapsus: William W.F. Hume had assumed the name Dick (n3) in 1864.

6 Derby on this day (28th) would reply, 'My report of the Carlton Meeting, brought to me by Ridley and B[anks] Stanhope, corresponds in the main with yours, but is hardly as favourable. According to them there were *150* present, of whom about 2/3 were in favour of Rated Residential Suffrage, with *three* year residence. They came to no distinct resolution; and the only point on which they seem to have been agreed was that whatever we proposed we should stand by, and not accept amendments dictated by Gladstone. They would take a £5 franchise, if proposed by us. They admitted that if we proposed £6, and we were beaten, we could not, on such an issue, go to the Country; and they would, in such a case, prefer our resignation to assent. If this is the general feeling (and they represent it as universal) and we cannot propose £5, I think it is a strong argument in favour of meeting our fate on the bolder line; but I am afraid, especially if there is a secession, that our own party will not be united in our support. Probably you

4347

TO: LORD DERBY   House of Commons [Thursday] 28 February [1867]

ORIGINAL: DBP Box 146/3

PUBLICATION HISTORY: M&B IV 508, dated 28 February 1867 (by context), the first sentence; Weintraub *Disraeli* 444, the first sentence

EDITORIAL COMMENT: House of Commons paper. *Dating*: by context; see ph.

Rt Honble | Earl of Derby K.G[.]   Feb 28

My dear Lord,

All I hear & observe more & more convinces me, that the bold line is the safer one, &, moreover, that it / will be successful.

The ↑Tory↓ member for Cheltenham has given notice of a question to me tomorrow, the object of wh:, I am told, is to show, that rating franchise is / quite conservative enough without checks:[1]

and on Monday, the Radical member for Norwich is to beg me to re-consider our determination, & to / revert to dual voting & rating-franchise.[2]

These are straws, but they show &c.

As for Baxter's beer barrel influence I see no harm in it, & I think he is a puritanical prig to presume to make such observations to a Prime-Minister.[3]

Yrs D.

4348

TO: [LORD DERBY]   House of Commons, Thursday [28 February 1867]

ORIGINAL: DBP Box 146/3

PUBLICATION HISTORY: Blake 459, dated 28 February 1867, the second paragraph

EDITORIAL COMMENT: House of Commons paper. Docketed in another hand on the fourth page: 'Feb. 28'. *Dating*: by context; see **4349**&n1.

Thursday –

You shd know that Horsman has given notice of a Bill, wh: is to be introduced

---

are quite right in your estimate of the distinction between the lower classes in the small and large Boroughs: but I fear there is too much truth in Baxter's view of the probable prevalence of the "Beer barrel" influence.' H B/XX/S/412. Baxter's 28 February letter to Derby (n1) closed with: 'Whether the Working Classes in these boroughs would be Conservative or Liberal, nobody knows. But every agent I have ever seen says that they would be highly venal, and that douceurs and beer barrels would be the indispensable requisites of success.'

---

1 Charles Schreiber (1826-1884), BA 1850 and MA 1853 Cambridge, a classical scholar and fellow of Trinity College 1852-5, was MP (C) for Cheltenham 1865-8 and Poole 1880-4. In the House on 1 March he would ask if D 'could inform the House of the number of male occupiers resident in the boroughs and cities of England and Wales who would be placed upon the register for the election of Members of Parliament, by a household suffrage, accompanied by a three years' residence and the personal payment of rates?' *Hansard* CLXXXV cols 1270-1.

2 Edward Warner (1818-1875), MA 1844 Oxford, a barrister (Lincoln's Inn 1850), was a JP and DL for Essex, MP (L) for Norwich 1852-7, 1860-8 and author of *The Representation of the Working Classes* (1860). In the House on 4 March he would ask if D would be willing 'to discuss, as a possible basis of Borough Representation, the following or some similar proposition: – Occupiers who for two years have been rated to the poor, and not excused on the ground of poverty, to have one vote for each Member to be elected; Residents in the Borough who for two years have been assessed to House Tax or to Property or Income Tax upon the full scale to have one vote for each Member to be elected; Persons entitled under both qualifications to vote under both?' D would reply with a request 'to answer that Question at another time.' *Hansard* CLXXXV col 1306.

3 See **4346**n6.

the day after ours / as a substitute & proposing Household Suffrage & Plural Voting.

The thing gets riper every hour, tho' I don't think it / would have been so ripe, if we had originally proposed it – I must confess that.

D.

TO: QUEEN VICTORIA   House of Commons [Thursday] 28 February 1867 **4349**
ORIGINAL: RAC F15 43
PUBLICATION HISTORY: *LQVB* I 403-4
·EDITORIAL COMMENT: House of Commons paper.

Feby. 28 1867

The Cr of the Exr with his humble duty to Yr Majesty:

Mr Horsman, after a meeting at Lord Grosvenor's, has, tonight, given / notice, that, on the day following the introduction of the Reform Bill by the Cr of the Exr, Mr Horsman will ask leave to introduce / another bill with the same object, & wh: will recommend a rated & residential house franchise in Boros, accompanied with plural voting: that / is to say, speaking generally, Lord Derby's original plan.[1]

There was a great meeting of M.Ps at the Carlton today,[2] more than 150 – no person in office being invited. / There was only one feeling, that Lord Derby ought to be encouraged to fall back on his own policy – & that the measure he seemed forced to introduce was / not equal to the occasion.

Sir Alexander Hood, Sir Edward Kerrison,[3] & other country gentlemen of that calibre, have written up from the / country this evening, in the same vein: saying that the question must be settled, & that there is only one opinion, in the most conservative circles, / that Lord Derby should not have been forced to change his front.

The Chanr of the Exchequer believes, that the Reform Question will yet be / settled this year: but he feels quite certain, that there will not be a May crisis, & that Yr Majesty's Highland Home will not be / disturbed.

TO: LORD DERBY   [London, Friday] 1 March 1867 **4350**
ORIGINAL: DBP Box 146/2
PUBLICATION HISTORY: M&B IV 509, the first three paragraphs
EDITORIAL COMMENT: Black-edged 11 Downing Street paper, imprinted address crossed out.

Confidential   Mar. 1 1867
Rt Honble | The Earl of Derby K G

---

1 General Grey on 1 March would write to the Queen: 'This [*D's letter*] seems satisfactory, & Genl. Grey quite shares Mr. Disraeli's belief. He had not noticed Mr. Horsman's notice, but it will doubtless make it much easier for the Govt. to revert to their original plan.' RAC F15 44.
2 See **4346**&nn2,4&6.
3 No letters to D at this time from Kerrison or Hood have been found. Sir Alexander Bateman Periam Fuller-Acland-Hood (1819-1892), 3rd Bt 1851, a DL of Somerset 1852 and MP (C) for W Somerset 1859-68, on 27 February had written to Col Taylor, 'I wish Ld Derby had stuck to his own opinion and proposed household suffrage.' H B/XI/J/72.

My dear Lord

Gen: Grey, *au fond,* is trying to carry Gladstone's franchise bill of last year. He thinks it the best way to settle the question: it will settle you, & your party.

He / has, unceasingly, impressed the Queen, since Wednesday, with the expediency of yr not receding from yr £6. position – &, therefore, you will find a change in the Queen's mind, for wh: it is well, that you should be / prepared.[1]

She will not, however, recede a jot from her engagements to you, if she finds you firm & confident.

Understand, that, as ↑the bill is at↓ present arranged, the franchise question wd. / not come before the House of Comm: until the month of June, & if you were, wh: is not likely, defeated on your proposal, you would be defeated with a great fund of popular / sympathy at yr back: it would be unnecessary to resign, & so far as I can judge, unless you wished it, to dissolve.

The question would rest in your keeping, & you would be looked upon / as the statesman, who wd. settle the question in a large spirit[.]

There would be no fear, therefore, or rather there is no fear of a summer crisis & H. M. being disturbed in her Highland Home: her great horror. /

Yours | D.[2]

4351   TO: LORD DERBY   [London] Saturday [2 March 1867]
ORIGINAL: DBP Box 146/3
EDITORIAL COMMENT: C of Ex paper, seal crossed out. Docketed in another hand on the first page: 'March 2'. *Dating*: by context; see n2.

Confidential   Saturday night

The Earl of Derby

My dear Lord,

What do you think of this?

Pres[iden]t of Board of Trade & Cabinet, for Lord Percy. He was yr Vice Prest. in 1859. His / manner is certainly not fascinating, but after a frank understanding as

---

1 General Grey had written to the Queen twice on the 27th and twice on the 28th of February. On the 28th he had enclosed a letter he proposed to send to D and suggested the Queen write to Derby 'a short line ... to tell him not to be discouraged' and to assure him of her support. In his long letter to D Grey had stressed that 'the Queen thinks your course a very plain one: namely, to adhere, in all its essential features, to the measure as you have described it, till you have ascertained, not by the gossip of the streets or the Clubs, but by a vote of the H. of Cs., that it will not be accepted ... But there seems every advantage in your adhering, in the first instance, to the £6 rating. In the first place it will probably avert further unpleasant discussions in the Cabinet – & in the second it will avoid the appearance of weakness ... inseparable from frequent changes of plan.' RAC F15 37-40.
2 In a letter dated 'Friday Morng.' and docketed in another hand '[1 March 1867]', Derby would reply, 'There is no doubt that Grey has been working on the Queen in favour of the £6. but the enclosed, recd. last night, will show just how fully we may rely on Her support.' He enclosed a 28 February letter from the Queen, who advised that 'it might be wisest and best, *if possible*, to *adhere* to the measure as announced by Mr. Disraeli to the House ... The Queen feels *sure* a *bold* front must be shown, and the country will then see that the Government is sincere in trying to settle this *vexed* and *vital* question of Reform.' H B/ XX/S/415; M&B IV 509.

to Parly. Reform, he might be depended on, being a very honorable / man, & far from devoid of feeling.[1]

At such a moment, bringing forward a great liberal measure, the marked adhesion ↑to you↓ of such a house & / interest, would affect the opinion, & imagination, of the country.

Yrs ever, | D.

There is nothing in the impending act to prevent this arrangement.[2]

TO: SIR STAFFORD NORTHCOTE Downing Street [Saturday] 2 March 1867 4352
ORIGINAL: BL ADD MS 50015 f217
PUBLICATION HISTORY: Northcote 268, the last sentence
EDITORIAL COMMENT: C of Ex paper.

Confidential   Mar: 2 1867

Right Honorable | Sir Stafford Northcote

My dear Northcote,

Lord Derby desired me to see you & to say, that he shall be happy, if you will accept the / office of Secretary of State for India.

He is now writing to the Queen, & has so much to do, that he thought you wd excuse receiving this offer from me, instead / of himself.[1]

But, send yr. answer to him – & at once.

Yrs ever | D.

---

1 Algernon Percy, Earl Percy since 1865, as Lord Lovaine had been vice-president of the board of trade in Derby's second ministry from 3 March to 18 June 1859. Upon his father's death on 21 August 1867, Percy would succeed him as 6th Duke of Northumberland.

2 Derby on 3 March would reply from St James's Square with a letter headed '*Confidential*': 'I do not think Lord Percy would be a good, or a popular, appointment, besides which, he is not in Parliament; and, if he were, his father's death might move him any day to the H. of Lords, where I do not think it desirable that the Prest. of the Bd. of Trade should be. Could you call here towards 4 o'Clock this afternoon? I will do nothing in the Bd. of Trade matter till I see you. Have you considered the effect of the residential qualification on the £10 (& upwards) voters? As far as they are concerned it will be a restriction. Certainly there ought to be a provision that those already on the register should not lose their votes by reason of a shorter period of residence than three years. While I have been writing this note Taylor came in, and I asked him in confidence what he thought of Ld. Percy's appointment. He shook his head, and said it would give us neither strength nor popularity. I have just sent him with a note to Peel to ask him to move the Army Estimates tomorrow. He will still be Secy. of State, if Pakington is not actually appointed; and there is no time to lose.' H B/XX/S/416. The Duke of Richmond would be appointed president of the board of trade on 8 March.

---

1 On this day (2nd) at 6 *pm* Derby wrote to the Queen 'to place at your Majesty's feet' the resignations of Cranborne, Carnarvon and Peel. General Grey replied at 10 *pm* giving Derby the Queen's 'entire approval of your at once proceeding to fill up the places of the retiring Ministers'. *LQVB* I 404-5. Northcote would replace Cranborne as Indian secretary on 8 March. The resignations would be followed by a reversion to the original scheme of household suffrage.

TO: LORD DERBY   Grosvenor Gate, Sunday [3 March 1867]
ORIGINAL: DBP Box 146/3

EDITORIAL COMMENT: 11 Downing Street paper, imprinted address crossed out and 'G. Gate' written in. Docketed in another hand on the last page: 'March 3. Disraeli Rt. Hnbl. B.' *Dating*: by context; see **4351**&n2.

Rt Honble | The Earl of Derby KG   G. Gate | Sunday
My dear Lord,
I will call towards four – Ld. Ripon, in Lord Grey's Governmt., was Prest. of B. of T.[1]
Yrs | D.

TO: LORD DERBY   Grosvenor Gate [Sunday] 3 March 1867
ORIGINAL: DBP Box 146/3

EDITORIAL COMMENT: Grosvenor Gate paper.

8 o'ck: | March 3 1867

Right Honorable | The Earl of Derby | KG
My dear Lord,
I have just returned home, having missed Hunt, but finding a long letter from him.[1]

I think there is much in what he says, / & never much liked the plan in question – but I write to you, because if, as I think, it is wisest to give up the moving of the Estimates by the General, / no time shd. be lost in yr sending him a line, as I heard from his son today, that his father was going to sit up all night for / the business.[2]

This is most vexatious, but I think it wisest to decide as Hunt suggests.[3]

Ever yrs, | D.

1 Under 2nd Earl Grey, PM from November 1830 to July 1834, George Eden, 1st Earl of Auckland, had been president of the board of trade from 22 November 1830 to 5 June 1834 and Charles Poulett Thomson, 1st Baron Sydenham (1841), from 5 June to 14 November 1834. Frederick John Robinson, 1st Earl of Ripon (1833), had been secretary of state for war and the colonies from 22 November 1830 to 3 April 1833, when he succeeded Lord Durham as lord privy seal.

1 Hunt on 3 March had written: 'Understanding that it is arranged that General Peel is to move the Army Estimates tomorrow I have seen Lord Derby and suggested to him that there may be some risk of an objection being taken on constitutional grounds to a Member who has virtually ceased to be a Minister moving the Estimates. He thought if such an objection were made it would be factious but said if I had a strong opinion on the subject I had better see you. My impression is that it is exactly the point which Gladstone would take up and as we cannot say that we have a majority in the House I venture to think that it would be an unsafe thing to attempt. If we had to give it up, we should weaken our position in the House which at the present moment is very undesirable. It would no doubt be most convenient for General Peel to do as proposed but it is by no means indispensable – there is plenty of time before Easter to pass the two Mutiny Bills ... Sir J. Pakington might move the Navy Estimates on Thursday next – then get reelected & move the Army Estimates on the 14th. I cannot help thinking this would be a more prudent course than the one proposed, as no exception would be taken to it.' H B/XX/HU/15.

2 Peel had four surviving sons (of five): Edmund Yates (1826-1900), lieut-col in 85th Foot and 12th Regiment of Turks; Archibald (1828-1910), MA Oxford, DL of co Denbigh and JP Herts; John (1829-1892), lieut-gen in the army and Kt of the Medjidie; and, the one most likely to have written to D, William Augustus (1833-1899), a local government board inspector.

3 Derby on 'Sunday *at Dinner*', presumably on this day (3 March), would reply: 'I confess I do not agree with Hunt. I think the anticipated objection would be very captious; and that there would be an immense advantage in having the Army & Navy Estimates respectively moved by the only man who can explain

TO: LORD DERBY   Grosvenor Gate, Monday [4 March? 1867]   4355

ORIGINAL: DBP Box 146/3

EDITORIAL COMMENT: Black-edged 11 Downing Street paper, address crossed out and 'G. Gate' written in. *Dating*: by context; see n1.

Right Honorable | The Earl of Derby | KG   G. Gate | Monday

My dear Lord,[1]

What I fear is, that for the sake of obtaining comparatively slight results, you are endangering yr position – & that the / House of Commons will not stand the Reform Bill being put off for a fortnight by a mutilated administration.[2]

If our ranks had been announced as complete, they wd. have taken our proposition without a murmur – but for the sake of the Estimates, I very much fear you ~~will~~ may find you will have to / encounter an address to the Crown for the formation of a strong Govt, & be forced to appeal to the present Constituency, wh: will not support you.

Yrs | D.

TO: LORD DERBY   Grosvenor Gate, Monday 4 March [1867]   4356

ORIGINAL: DBP Box 146/3

PUBLICATION HISTORY: M&B IV 513-14, dated Monday 4 March 1867, omitting the last two paragraphs

EDITORIAL COMMENT: C of Ex paper, seal crossed out and 'G. Gate' written in.

            G. Gate | Monday Mar: 4

Right Honorable | The Earl of Derby | KG

My dear Lord,

We have had a bad night in the Ho: of Comm: They wd. let Peel do nothing. He has put off his business till Thursday; they / will let him do nothing then.[1]

them: but the arrangement of business in the H. of Commons is so much more your business than mine, that I leave the decision in your hands. Only, I asked Peel *as a favour* to move the Estimates, and hardly like to change the course which I recommended.' H B/XX/S/467. See **4357**&n1.

---

1 This appears to be a reply to **4354**n3.

2 For the resignations of Cranborne, Carnarvon and Peel, see **4338**nn1&2 and **4352**n1.

---

1 In the House on this day (4th) Peel was about to make his army estimates statement when MP (L) Arthur John Otway objected, 'as certain rumours were afloat' and the House might surmise that Peel's successor 'might not agree with him as to the proper number [of men] to be voted for the year's service.' Peel had replied that there would be no use in bringing forward the estimates 'unless we were to take the Vote for the number of men, of which, I trust, I shall be able to give a very good explanation. I am sure the House will acquit me of any wish to deceive them ... but if there is the slightest wish I will postpone my statement.' D spoke briefly on the reform bill (the cabinet 'having resolved to recur to their original policy with respect to the borough franchise and to establish it, in their belief, upon a sure, extensive, and permanent basis'), which he said would be introduced on the 18th. He mentioned Peel's 'readiness and personal wish' to explain 'to the House those Estimates and that policy which ... his Colleagues ... have adopted and sanctioned.' Peel's lengthy explanation on 7 March would be followed by protracted debate. On 15 March, following the army estimates votes on account in committee of supply, when asked 'up to what period these Votes on Account would last,' Sir John Pakington (who would succeed Peel on 8 March) would reply: 'with one or two exceptions, they were one-third of the total amount of the Army Estimates.' *Hansard* CLXXXV cols 1308-10 (D 1309-10), 1448-1510, 1991-2. See **4357**n1.

Nothing can be more insolent, bullying, & defiant, than they are.

I am confident they will not let Pakington move the estimates. ↑and he himself, says, it is not of the slightest importance.↓

The sooner we get / out of this mess the better.

If we had moved the writs, they wd have been daunted.

The House, too, is sulky now, because there has been an explanation in the Lords, & not in the Commons.[2] /

The proposal for the introduction of the Bill ↑for the 18th.↓ passed without comment, but I shall be surprised if, tomorrow, some adverse move is not hatched by them. The fear of a Dissolution may check them; but that is all.

As / some explanation must take place in the Commons tomorrow,[3] had you not better communicate with Cranborne, whose mouth is at present sealed.

I said exactly what was / settled with you & him: & cd. not have said more, when he was in enforced silence.[4]

Yrs sincerely, I D.

4357   TO: [LORD DERBY]   Downing Street [Monday 4? March 1867]
ORIGINAL: DBP Box 146/3
EDITORIAL COMMENT: C of Ex paper. *Dating*: by context; see n1.

Then we will agree, that the General shall move the Estimates[.][1]

Yrs ever I D.

---

2 Bernal Osborne had bemoaned that 'The secret with regard to the Bill which ... ought to have [been] communicated to us in the first place, ... has been let out in "another place,"' where Derby had communicated 'the original policy of the Government' and Carnarvon stated his reasons for resigning. Osborne admonished D for maintaining an obstinate silence, D replying that there would be opportunity for 'frank communication to the House' and that he was unaware of what had transpired in the Lords. In the Lords on this day (4th) Derby had provided background to his original resolutions, including the fifth one 'which, though it has not been formally communicated to your Lordships' House, was, I may mention, to the effect that the introduction of a system of plurality of votes might allow us to reduce the franchise lower than could be done under other circumstances, and to establish it on a firm and durable basis.' Carnarvon had explained that while he 'recognized the importance of admitting so many of the unenfranchised classes ... we should not admit [the working classes] in such proportions, and under such conditions, as would place them in absolute pre-eminence and control over all other constituents. I shrink from a class government of whatever kind ... I saw great reason to fear that the results of the measure would effect an enormous transfer of political power'. *Hansard* CLXXXV cols 1323-4 (D 1324), 1284-91. *The Times* on 5 March would call Derby's 'confession ... the most extraordinary that the Legislature has listened to in our time. He tells the House of Lords that he and his colleagues were in the painful position of choosing between what they "believed to be the more desirable and more extensive measure of Reform," with the loss of three Secretaries'. Derby's plan to reintroduce his original measure was deemed to contain 'an element of absurdity ... which almost saves it from indignation.'
3 For D's 'Ministerial Explanations' on 5 March, see **4359**&n1.
4 Derby on 5 March would reply with a letter headed '*Confidential*': 'I have taken on myself to absolve Cranborne from secrecy if he should find it necessary. As the Queen has given *me* permission, it cannot be withheld from my Colleagues. But I have asked him previously to communicate with you. I said no more, though at greater length, than you did; Carnarvon went more into detail than I should have done, and did himself no good. Richmond accepts. The Queen comes to Town tomorrow to stay till Saturday; and I think we shall be ready for a Council, & for moving this writ, by Friday.' H B/XX/S/418. See **4358**&n1.

---

1 See **4356**&n1. In the House on 7 March, in committee of supply and with the consent of the ministry, General Peel would move the army estimates: '"That the number of Land Forces, not exceeding 139,163

TO: LORD CRANBORNE Downing Street [Tuesday] 5 March 1867 **4358**
ORIGINAL: OCC BPD 6164 ff7-8
PUBLICATION HISTORY: M&B IV 515
EDITORIAL COMMENT: C of Ex paper. *Sic*: disembarass.

Confidential Mar: 5 1867

Right Honorable | Visct Cranborne, M P.

My dear Cranborne,

Lord Derby has written to me what has taken place between you.[1]

I shall say something when the House meets. It / will not displease you, tho' it will only feebly express my sense of yr services & loss – & I hope it will disembarass us all of the difficulties inseparable from our position.[2]

Ld. Derby says you / are to consult with me what you are to say, ↑I mean as to Cabinet secrets,↓ but I have such confidence in you, in every respect, that such previous communication is quite unnecessary.

Yours ever, | D

TO: QUEEN VICTORIA [London, Tuesday 5 March 1867] **4359**
ORIGINAL: RAC F15 56
EDITORIAL COMMENT: Docketed in another hand on the first page: 'Mar 5/67'. *Dating*: by context; see n1.

The Chanr of the Exchqr, with his humble duty to Yr Majesty:

The House tonight, during the explanations of the Ex-Ministers, was agitated & excited. The / general feeling, as to the impending measure, one of suspense & curiosity.[1]

It is expected, that the measure, in a printed form, will be submitted to the Cabinet / on Saturday for revision.[2]

---

men ... be maintained for the Service of the United Kingdom of Great Britain and Ireland from the 1st day of April 1867, to the 31st day of March 1868, inclusive.'" The vote would be agreed to. *Hansard* CLXXXV cols 1448-1510.

---

1 Derby had written to D from St James's Square a letter dated 'Monday' (docketed in another hand '4 March 1867'): 'I send you a letter received this morning by Post from Cranborne, with my answer, which, after you have read it I will thank you to send on in a box by my messenger who will wait for it ... A similar application from Carnarvon has just arrived, which I shall answer more shortly. I shall of course see you at the Levée where we shall have an opportunity of finally settling what we shall say this Evening ... Return me Cranborne's letter.' H B/XX/S/417.

2 See **4359**&n1.

---

1 In his 'Ministerial Explanations' to the House on 5 March D had called 'not accurate, not just' criticism that he had not been justified the previous day in stating that the three cabinet resignations had taken place 'in consequence of the majority of the Cabinet having arrived at a decision in favour of our original policy, because no original policy had been intimated to the House.' Ranking such incidents 'among the calamities of life', he countered accusations in the Lords that reform had 'been taken up by us without sufficient thought, with indifference, and after a delay, characterized, probably, by negligence.' Peel and Cranborne then defended their resignations, both with reference to what Peel termed 'that fatal fifth Resolution', one which Cranborne (after reviewing the statistics) believed would 'introduce into the majority of boroughs what was in effect pure and simple household suffrage.' *Hansard* CLXXXV cols 1339-70 (D 1339-45, 1354, 1361).

2 Attending the cabinet meeting on Saturday 9 March would be D, Derby, Chelmsford, Walpole, Stanley, Manners, Lowry-Corry, Hardy, Pakington (succeeding Peel), Northcote (succeeding Cranborne), Buck-

The first copy, that comes to the hands of the C of Exr, will be forwarded to Her Majesty.

4360 TO: [MONTAGU CORRY]   [London] Wednesday [6 March] 1867
ORIGINAL: H B/XI/J/41
EDITORIAL COMMENT: *Dating*: Ash Wednesday was 6 March in 1867.

Ash Wednesday 1867

I shall be at D.S. about three – unless Ld Derby keeps me ↑wh: I don't expect↓ [.] I must see Baxter to day, & finally settle everything.[1]

    D.

4361 TO: [MONTAGU CORRY]   [London, Wednesday 6 March? 1867]
ORIGINAL: H B/XI/J/42
EDITORIAL COMMENT: 11 Downing Street paper. *Recipient* and *Dating*: by context; see **4360**.

Most important

I shall probably be at the office at one or ½ past one o'ck:, & it is absolutely necessary, that you shd be there to receive me – *& Baxter if possible.*

    D.

4362 TO: [MONTAGU CORRY]   [London] Saturday [9 March 1867]
ORIGINAL: H B/XI/J/37
EDITORIAL COMMENT: *Dating*: by context; see nn1&2.

Saturday

A Cabinet must be called for Thursday at one o'ck:[1] & a copy (marked confidential) of Mr Lamberts Mem:[2] must be sent to every Cab. Minister.

    D.

ingham (succeeding Carnarvon), Marlborough and Richmond. Stanley on the 9th would note that D was 'anxious to get rid of the double vote plan, and fall back on a rated household suffrage pure and simple. All opposed this, though Ld D. wavered a good deal.' There is in H a note in Corry's hand: 'Written by Ld D. in cabinet Sat March 9 1867 to the C. of E. who was pressing Mr H. & Mr W. to give up the "Dual vote."': 'If we do not take care, we shall have another break-up. Duality will defeat us, abandonment of it will destroy us.' *The Times* (11 Mar 1867); *Disraeli, Derby* 294; H B/XX/S/419.

---

1 See **4368**&n1.

---

1 See **4370**&n5.
2 There is in H a three-page manuscript document, initialled 'J.L.' and dated Wednesday 'March 13. 1867', entitled 'Memorandum As to Compound Householders above £10.' It ends with an estimate of the number of 'Total Compound Householders at and over £10' of 84,806. H B/XI/L/3. John Lambert (1815-1892), KCB 1879, PC 1885, a Salisbury solicitor 1836-57 and mayor 1854 (the first Roman Catholic mayor of a cathedral city since the Reformation), was a poor law inspector 1857, a statistician for the 1865 and 1867 Reform Bills, receiver of the metropolitan common poor fund under the Metropolitan Poor Act 1867 (which he helped draw up) and a member of the 1867 boundaries commission. Gladstone would send him to Ireland in 1869-70 to gather information in connection with the Irish church and land bills. He would be first permanent secretary of the new local government board 1871-82 and chairman of the boundaries commission 1884-5. His works include *Modern Legislation as a Chapter in our History* (1865) and *Vagrancy Laws and Vagrants* (1868). See **4364**.

TO: SIR STAFFORD NORTHCOTE [London, Monday] 11 March 1867 4363
ORIGINAL: H H/LIFE
PUBLICATION HISTORY: M&B IV 516
EDITORIAL COMMENT: From a manuscript copy headed: 'D. to Sir S. H. Northcote Mar 11 '67.'

We must watch & hope. Things are not so dark as they seemed[.][1]

TO: [MONTAGU CORRY] Downing Street, Tuesday [12 March 1867] 4364
ORIGINAL: H B/XI/J/51
EDITORIAL COMMENT: C of Ex paper. Docketed in another hand on the first page: '?1867'. *Dating*: by context; see n1.

Tuesday
I am disappointed at not receiving the printed dr[af]t of Lamberts Resol[uti]on.[1] I hope the Cabinet have got it.

I wish to see him at 3 o'ck: today.
D.

TO: [MONTAGU CORRY] [London] Wednesday [13 March 1867] 4365
ORIGINAL: H B/XI/J/9a
EDITORIAL COMMENT: 11 Carlton House Terrace paper. Endorsed in another hand on the first page: '12 or 13 Mar 1867' and 'Pray let me have the promised numbers.' *Dating*: 13 March was a Wednesday in 1867. The Gladstones lived at 11 Carlton House Terrace, where MA on the evening of 13 March 1867 attended Mrs Gladstone's assembly. MP (14 Mar 1867).

Wednesday
See the Lord Advocate[1] on the enclosed.[2] I cannot give him an appointment at present. He will tell you all.
D.

---

1 Stanley on this day (11th) recorded a 'Short talk with Disraeli, who talks of probable, though not certain failure in the House, and consequent dissolution, but he does not wish it to be at once, thinking that to gain time may be an advantage. Dined Arlington St where much friendly talk with Lord Salisbury as to the situation. He thinks (I am afraid) that Disraeli has done himself great injury with the country by his management of the reform business.' *Disraeli, Derby* 294.

1 Apparently John Lambert's 'Memorandum' at **4362**n2.

1 Edward Strathearn Gordon (1814-1879), Baron Gordon of Drumearn 1876, LLB Edinburgh 1835, a barrister (Scotland) 1835, capt 1859, lieut-col 1867 and hon col 1873 in the 1st Edinburgh Rifle Volunteer Corps, sol-gen for Scotland 1866, lord advocate 1867-8 and 1874-6, dean of the faculty of advocates 1868-74, QC 1868, PC 1874, lord of appeal 1876-9 and MP (C) for Thetford 1867-8 and for Glasgow and Aberdeen Universities 1869-76. Gordon had written to D on 12 March asking to see him at his house (1 New Street, Spring Gardens) on the 13th 'in reference to Reform as applicable to Scotland, which the Lord Advocate observes is to form the subject of a question by Colonel Sykes in the House of Commons on Thursday.' H B/XI/J/9b.

2 Possibly a handwritten, three-page 'Memorandum for the Chancellor of the Exchequer in reference to Questions to be put by Colonel Sykes on Thursday *14th March*' asking the same questions that would be posed (slightly differently) by Sykes: 'Whether a Reform Bill for Scotland is to be brought in this Session?'; 'Whether the principles of Representation applied to England will be applied to Scotland?'; and 'Whether more members are to be given to Scotland in proportion to its present population & wealth?' The memo also includes statistics on the Scottish reform bills of 1852, 1860 and 1866, and states that 'it

4366 TO: LORD DERBY — Grosvenor Gate [Wednesday 13 March? 1867]

ORIGINAL: DBP Box 146/3

EDITORIAL COMMENT: *Dating*: conjectural; see n1 and **4370**n5. *Sic*: serener.

Rt Honble | The Earl of Derby | K G.   G. Gate

My dear Lord[1]

Too late: our bill will secure his object.

I have had a good conference with Northcote & Hardy, & tomorrow at / yr house, we shall, I think, be able to arrive at a final conclusion.

I feel serener in my mind, & not altogether with[ou]t hope. /

Yrs ever, | D.

4367 TO: [MONTAGU CORRY] — Downing Street, Thursday [14 March? 1867]

ORIGINAL: H B/XI/J/36

EDITORIAL COMMENT: 11 Downing Street paper. Docketed in another hand on the first page: 'Reform 1867'. *Dating*: conjectural: see n1.

Thursday –

Mind – I have no copy of the Bill. Let one be ready for me. I will try to look in before Cabt.[1]

D.

4368 TO: [MONTAGU CORRY] — [London] Thursday [14 March 1867]

ORIGINAL: H B/XI/J/7

EDITORIAL COMMENT: Docketed in another hand on the first page: '? March 1867'. *Dating*: by context; see n1.

Thursday

The Cabinet has decided that Mr D. Baxter shall put himself *immediately* in communication with Mr Thring, & that they / shall together settle the Bill.[1]

---

is expedient that a few members should be added to Scotland'. D in the House would reply to Sykes that such a bill would be introduced, although it was not in his power to say when; that its principles would be 'the same as those we shall recommend for the representation of England,' with the necessary 'alterations'; and that the question of 'increasing the representation of Scotland' would be decided 'upon its merits.' H B/XI/M/12; *Hansard* CLXXXV cols 1801-2 (D 1802).

1 Derby on 'Wednesday 6.15' had written to D: 'On my return home I found the enclosed from Grosvenor: and though I am sorry to interrupt your conference with Hardy, I think you had better see it. I propose to tell him that in my opinion the time for Resolutions is gone by: and that we must introduce our Bill & stand by it. His Resolution mem[oran]dum is hardly intelligible. My messenger will wait for your answer.' The 'enclosed' is probably a letter of 6 March 1867 from Grosvenor to Derby accompanying draft resolutions urging an extended franchise and plural voting. H B/XX/S/463; Derby papers 164/9.

---

1 The Reform Bill would be discussed in cabinet at noon on 14 March 1867; see **4370**n5.

---

1 The Reform Bill, which had been drafted by D, Derby and Dudley Baxter, had been discussed in cabinet on 9 and 12 March, approved in principle on Thursday 14 March and would be explained to a party meeting on the 15th. That day, on Derby's instructions, it would be redrafted by parliamentary draftsman Henry Thring, printed that night in preparation for cabinet discussion on the 16th and approved on the

I am obliged to go up t with Ld. Derby, & therefore write, that you may see Mr D. B.

D

TO: LORD DERBY   House of Commons, Thursday [14 March 1867]   4369
ORIGINAL: DBP Box 146/3
PUBLICATION HISTORY: M&B IV 518, dated 14 March 1867
EDITORIAL COMMENT: House of Commons paper. Docketed in another hand on the first page: 'March 14/67'. *Dating*: by context; see n1. *Sic*: Bankes.

Right Honorable | The Earl of Derby | K.G.   Thursday
My dear Lord,[1]

It was painful: but decision was absolutely necessary. I decided for Thring. He will sit up all night,[2] &, I believe, we / shall have the bill printed for the Cabinet on Saturday.

I have written myself to Baxter.[3]

Much depends on tomorrow.[4]

Grosvenor has established a / newspaper – "the Day" – & has engaged Kebbel, an Oxford man, well acquainted with the press, but a fine writer, & a scholar, for Editor.[5]

18th. Cowling 169. Henry Thring (1818-1907), a barrister (Inner Temple 1845), counsel to the home office 1860, parliamentary counsel to the treasury 1869, KCB 1873 and 1st Baron Thring 1886, would serve on the Statute Law Committee 1868-1907. His major contributions include the Succession Act 1853, Merchant Shipping Act 1854, Companies Act 1862, Irish Land Act 1871 and Army Act 1871. The introduction to his *Practical Legislation* (1877) describes his part in drafting the 1867 Reform Bill. See **4369**&nn2&3.

---

1 Derby on this day (14th) had written to D: 'What have you done re Thring v. Baxter? It is very important; for the Def[endan]t has done all the work, and the Pl[ainti]ff has all the real knowledge and experience on his side. But if Baxter refuses to communicate with Thring, I do not see on what ground we can support him. Thring is a very safe man, a good draftsman, and a fair politician; and as he is employed on all other Government Bills, I do not see how we can set him aside, without pledging ourselves to all the points of difference which may come between him & Baxter, in which it is quite possible that he may have the best of it. Your success over Gladstone, or rather Gladstone's blunder, was very satisfactory, & I hear H. Lennox, once admitted, did well.' H B/XX/S/421. See **4370**n1.

2 Thring would work on Friday 15th with two shorthand writers from 10 *am* to 6 *pm* to complete the draft, which would be printed during the night. M&B IV 518n1. See **4368**n1.

3 Baxter on this day (14th) wrote what is evidently a reply to D's letter (not found): 'Allow me to explain that in my interview with Mr Thring in the presence of Mr Corry I found him determined to remodel the Bill, and animated by no conciliatory spirit towards myself,: so that it was hopeless to think of our being able to act together. Mr Rose & my father, whom I consulted on the subject, were thoroughly agreed with me on the course to be taken. I only hope that the Government may not find their Bill completed on principles at variance with those on which it has been drawn, and not in harmony with the wants and wishes of the Conservative party. I did not seek the responsibility which you so flatteringly laid upon me, and until today no intimation was given of the least desire to subordinate me to any officer in carrying it out. In retiring altogether from the service of the Government as regards the question of Reform, may I thank you for your uniform kindness to me during its continuance'. H B/XI/J/89.

4 See **4372**&n1.

5 *The Day*, backed by leading Adullamites, was a moderate Liberal journal, part of an attempt to realign the party with Palmerstonian liberalism. Due to insufficient funding only 41 numbers (19 March to 4 May) would be published. Bourne II 273.

Grosvenor & ~~L~~ Elcho were / with Kebbel today, giving him his final instructions: he asked them, ~~as to~~ for his general government, to let him know what they really thought wo[ul]d be the result.

Grosvenor said, that if / our policy was what he understood it to be: ↑household suffrage; –,↓ – absolute rate-paying, & compensatory arrangement against compound householders, they had ascertained they cd. pull the Government / thro', *provided our men went straight.*

That is the question.

Bankes Stanhope has written to Taylor, that real rating will unite the party to a / man, or something like it. ↑But there is Hotham, Cecil, & Co.↓[6]

Gladstone's great fight is against real rating. That is ascertained.[7]

Yours ever, | D.

At dinner, Stanley said, he / thought we had a good chance; at any rate, a policy; & no minister was ↑ever↓ more justified in going to the country.

4370 TO: QUEEN VICTORIA   [London] Thursday 14 March 1867
ORIGINAL: RAC B23 33

Thursday | Mar: 14 1867

The Chr of the Exchequer with his humble duty to Yr Majesty:

In the absence of Mr Corry, Lord Henry Lennox moved the Navy Estimates with distinguished / ability.[1]

The Attorney Genl. introduced the new Bankruptcy Bill, wh: promises to be a success.[2]

Mr Hardys Bill on the London Work-houses passed the House amid / cheers from all sides. This is one of the most popular & successful measures, that has been introduced into Parliament for many years.[3]

---

6 This letter from Banks Stanhope to Taylor has not been found. Lord Hotham was MP (C) for East Riding, Yorkshire 1841-68; Lord Eustace Cecil was MP (C) for s Essex 1865-8. Although Hotham, Cecil, Thomas Baring, Henry Baillie, Sir Brook Bridges, Baron Dimsdale, Sir Rainald Knightley, James Lowther, George Bentinck, Lord Henry Scott and his brother, the Earl of Dalkeith, 'at various moments between March 18 and April 12 all thought of voting against the bill, none of them did so.' Cowling 176-7.

7 D on the 15th would summarize to Charles Grey the principle of Derby's measure as 'bonâ fide Rating', *ie* personal payment, to the exclusion of compound householders; see **4372**.

---

1 In the House on this day (14th) admiralty secretary Lennox had moved the navy estimates in committee of supply, after which D asked 'not to press this Vote to-night, and we can report Progress ... a telegram has arrived from Ireland, informing us that the election of the First Lord of the Admiralty (Mr. Corry) will take place on Tuesday, and not on Thursday, so that my right hon. Friend will probably be in his place on Thursday, to go on with these Estimates.' A vote on account for £2,900,000 would be agreed to in committee of supply on 15 March. *Hansard* CLXXXV cols 1824-57 (D 1854-5), 1992. Stanley on this day (14th) noted that Lennox had done 'very well: complimented on all sides.' *Disraeli, Derby* 294.

2 The first reading on this day (14th) of 'a Bill to consolidate and amend the Acts relating to Bankruptcy in England' had been given by Sir John Rolt. *Hansard* CLXXXV cols 1867-87. This complicated piece of legislation would lead to the Bankruptcy Act of 1869.

3 The Metropolitan Poor Bill of Gathorne Hardy and Ralph Earle had been introduced (by Hardy) on 8 February 1867, given second reading on the 21st and passed at third reading on this day (14th). Its full title was 'Bill for the establishment in the Metropolis of Asylums for the Sick, Insane, and other classes of

The Ch of the Exr had / the honor of receiving, last night, General Grey's letter written by command of Your Majesty.[4]

He will reply to it tomorrow morning, & shd. have done so to day, but the Cabinet / met this morning at twelve o'ck: & from that hour until this midnight, he has not had a moment to himself,[5] so that he cd. forward to Yr Majesty a calm & / correct view of the situation of affairs.

TO: [MONTAGU CORRY]   [London] Friday [15 March? 1867] **4371**
ORIGINAL: H B/XI/J/39
EDITORIAL COMMENT: *Dating*: conjectural; see **4364**&n1.

Friday

I shall be at D.S. at ¼ pt. 2 o'ck: Let Lambert be there. I am much indisposed.
  D.

TO: CHARLES GREY   House of Commons, Friday 15 March 1867 **4372**
ORIGINAL: RAC F15 62
PUBLICATION HISTORY: *LQVB* I 407-9, omitting the last two paragraphs
EDITORIAL COMMENT: Black-edged 11 Downing Street paper. *Sic*: Bankes; Kendal [*twice*]; developes.

M Genl | The Hon: Chas Grey   Friday *Mar: 15* 1867
My dear General,
The principle of the Reform Bill is that the franchise shd be founded on Rating, & as no test of value seems at all permanent, & / new propositions in respect to it are made every year, we arrived at the conclusion, that we would not connect the Boro' franchise with value, but that it shd. rest on an occupation alone, rated to the relief / of the poor, the ratepayer personally paying the rates. We looked upon

---

the Poor, and of Dispensaries; and for the distribution over the Metropolis of portions of the charge for Poor Relief; and for other purposes relating to Poor Relief in the Metropolis'. Hardy modestly ascribed its popularity to 'the great grievances which were suffered by the poor, the great injustice which was done to the ratepayers in expending money in other objects than those intended ... This is an attempt on my part to make a beginning to redress those evils.' *Hansard* CLXXXV cols 150-79, 746-80, 1861-6. The new act empowered the poor law board to raise contributions from London's unions and parishes for a Common Poor Fund used to finance new hospitals. It would lead to the establishment in June of a Metropolitan Asylums Board that would set up (between 1867 and 1930) around forty health-related institutions.

4 In a letter dated 'March 13/67' and headed '*Draft Private*', Grey had thanked D for the copy of the reform bill he had sent the Queen. She had observed that D proposed 'to go much farther in your reduction of the Borough Franchise than was contemplated last year', and, unable to 'shut her eyes to the fact that many most distinguished Members of both Parties have expressed great alarm at the possible consequences of the proposed reduction', the Queen, wrote Grey, wished to know 'approximately, the numbers of the Working Classes that will be added to the Constituencies.' She had also asked what D thought his prospects were 'of carrying the second vote to the Payers of Assessed Taxes – & if carried what you calculate will be its effect as a counterpoise to mere numbers; & whether you will consider its rejection as fatal to the Bill.' RAC F15 61. For the full text of Grey's letter, see *LQVB* I 405-6; for D's reply, see **4372**.

5 Stanley on this day (14th) recorded: 'Cabinet: finished details of reform bill, which it is clear to me will not pass, but I am nearly alone in that opinion, and indeed there is no reason why I should obtrude it, having nothing better to propose ... Short talk with Disraeli, who [is] evidently despondent, though he does not admit it in so many words.' *Disraeli, Derby* 294.

these conditions, coupled with an ascertained term of residence, vizt. two years, ar as adequate to secure regularity, / & general trustworthiness, of life.

The number introduced on these conditions will not be so great as the number proposed last year, & proposed on no principle whatever.

The figures are instructive, & / I give them from the last, & most authentic, return of the Poor Law Board.

There are in the Boros of England & Wales 1,367,000 Householders of wh: 644,000 already are enfranchised.

There / remains, therefore, 723,000, who have not a vote.

Our proposition, that every householder, ↑shd. have a vote,↓ who is rated, & pays his rates, in respect of a house, wh: he has inhabited for two years, would *qualify* 237,000, of whom, after making the necessary & customary deductions for / migratory habits, pauperism, &c., would remain

115,000,

wh: would be our addition to the Constituency, but that Constituency would be founded on a principle.

There would remain 484,000 householders, who / are not personally rated, but for whom their landlords pay the rates compounding with the Parishes.

Our principle being that the enjoyment of a public right shd. depend on the performance of a public duty, & wh: is the best security for regularity of / life, we do not give votes to these compound householders, but we provide, that anyone of them who, by virtue of the small Tenements Act, & other Rating Acts, has his rates paid, or alleged to be paid, by his Landlord, may, by the powers of our / measure, claim to be rated & pay his rates, & then he will accede to his constitutional privilege, & be placed on the Parliamentary Register[.]

So under our measure, everyone of these 700,000 will be *qualified*, or may *qualify* himself, to be a voter. /

As there is great, but, I think, unfounded, fear of the numbers, that may avail themselves of this privilege (my own opinion is that not 50,000 will ever ultimately avail themselves of the provision,) we have proposed, that one, / & one only, of the new franchises shall have the privilege of a double, or rather second, vote: that is to say: any payer of a certain sum of direct taxation shall be a voter for a Boro', but he shall not be disfranchised because he happens to be a householder & / also pays rates. ↑He votes therefore in respect of taxes, & of rates.↓

Lord Derby will not consider this a principle of the Bill: but this must only be known to Her Majesty & ourselves; he cannot venture to say that, as yet, even to his colleagues; but the course of the debate will / prove the wisdom of his determination.

The principle of his measure is bonâ fide Rating, as distinguished from the fluctuating rental or value of all previous measures, & in wh: there is no settlement.

There has been a meeting of his followers to / day, when he addressed ↑them↓ at great length & with great spirit. There were 240 present,[1] & I was glad to see Ld

---

1 On this day (15th) Derby had met at Downing Street with 195 MPs, 43 others having sent 'letters of adhesion to the Government.' M&B IV 519. *The Times* on the 16th would publish 'as nearly as possible, a correct list' of those present.

Cranborne among them. He was silent. Sir William Heathcote was the only person, who at all demurred. Mr Henley spoke strongly in favor of the measure & / produced a great effect. Sir John Trollope, Sir John Walsh, Mr Bankes Stanhope, Mr. Laird of Birkenhead, Mr Graves of Liverpool, Mr Kendal of Cornwall, in the same vein. These are all representative men. Mr Kendal represents the National Club & the high Protestant / party.[2] I think after this meeting, that it may fairly be held, that Lord Derby's party will support him as a mass.[3]

Lord Grosvenor has communicated confidentially with us, & says, that if our measure be founded on a real & personal rating, residence, & some compensatory arrangement / against the possible influx of Compound Householders, either the dual vote, or some other counterpoise, he will answer for himself & his friends, & he believes that there is sufficient to carry the Government thro', / if their own party stick to them. Our utmost efforts are now given to this end.

With regard to ~~disfranchisement~~ the distribution of seats, our proposition is moderate, & tho' we propose to take away one member from 23 Boros, still in the scheme of / last year, these Boros were totally disfranchised, & so far as we can judge, they seem, on the whole, to think they have made a good bargain.

I do not count at all on the support of the Radicals, the measure has really no spice of Democracy. It will be assailed by them as "re-actionary" more likely. /

I think we shall be able to make a satisfactory arrangement about the Scotch seats, but I found it impossible to mix them up with the English ones. If we have the opportunity, H. M. may rest assured, that Her wishes in this respect shall be well considered / & attended to.[4]

I am writing this in a ~~the~~ Gallery of the House of Commons much disturbed with telegrams from Liverpool,[5] & anxious & bustling members, but I hope I have con-

---

2 Nicholas Kendall (1800-1878), BA 1830 Oxford, a JP and DL of Cornwall, chairman of the Board of Guardians of the Bodmin Union, capt in the Duke of Cornwall's Rangers 1826, special Dept Warden of the Stannaries 1852, patron of two livings, was MP (C) for Cornwall E 1852-68, a police magistrate of Gibraltar 1868-75 and a member of the National Club (IV **1519**&n2).

3 According to M&B IV (519), Derby (n1) had been perfectly candid that household rating suffrage would form the basis of borough franchise, with the two essential conditions of payment of rates and two years' residence. He had explained that compound householders (whose landlords paid a composition for the rates and charged the amount in the rent) would obtain the vote by assuming personal payment themselves. Joseph Henley called household suffrage, with payment of rates, 'the true basis of the right to vote'. Heathcote, the sole dissenter, thought 'the measure would destroy the influence of rank, property, and education, by the force of numbers.'

4 General Grey on 13 March had informed D that the Queen regretted 'that the important Commercial & Seaport towns of Scotland have not come in for their share of consideration – & that they must either be left inadequately represented in comparison with English, & even Irish towns of the same Class, or that an inconvenient addition must be made to the total numbers of the H. of Cs.' RAC F15 61.

5 On this day (15th) D had told the House, 'What the Fenian movement is I do not at this moment understand, although in the course of the day I receive several telegrams on the subject, and give them very anxious consideration.' Measures had been taken to contain what *The Times* on this day called an 'Anticipated Fenian Rising in Liverpool ... one of the principal centres of the Fenian movement.' These included four steamers manned by seamen and marines at the docks, and the arrival of the ironclad *Lord Clyde* and of three companies of the 54th Regiment. In the event, the 17th (Saint Patrick's Day) would be 'perfectly quiet', authorities believing that Fenian leaders had been 'effectually cowed by the preparations which have been made.' *Hansard* CLXXXV col 1950; *The Times* (15, 18 Mar 1867).

veyed to you, & thro' you, to our Gracious Mistress, some / clear idea of the situation, & will write again as it varies & developes.

After Monday, we shall see clearer. I don't like to be sanguine; but I still am of opinion, that a "Crisis" is / not impending.

Yours ever, I D.

4373   TO: LORD DERBY   Grosvenor Gate, Saturday [16 March 1867]
ORIGINAL: DBP Box 146/3
EDITORIAL COMMENT: Black-edged 11 Downing Street paper, imprinted address crossed out and 'G Gate' written in. Docketed by Derby: 'March 16/67'. *Dating*: by context; see nn2&3.

Rt Honble I The Earl of Derby I KG.   G Gate I Saturday
My dear Lord,

I have got to receive Thring, at one o'ck: today, in D.S. & go thro' the Bill, previous to the Cabinet. It will be an affair of hours.[1]

I have had an / almost sleepless night from Hunt's affair. Lord Barrington has, doubtless, told you all about it. I was away from the House during the debate, working in Taylor's Room at our measure, when I was sent for / by an alarmed party, wh: was on the point of being disgracefully defeated. I yielded to the urgency of the Whip & some of our colleagues, who were present, & threw Hunt over.

He is our best man, & / thinks his influence at the Treasury destroyed.

He can't be more vexed than I am. I have apologised to him without restriction, &, personally, I hope he is soothed.

But, officially, he may, from a sense of duty, / be inexorable.

His retirement wd. at this moment destroy the Govmt:

I hope, therefore, he may relent; but yr influence can alone prevail on him. I can do nothing, being the criminal – but I am, at least, penitent.[2]

---

1 There is in H a 21-page pamphlet, dated 16 March 1867, entitled 'Reform. Draft of a BILL Further to amend the Laws relating to the Representation of the People in England and Wales.' A line has been drawn through the word 'Reform' and, above it, D has written 'Repres[entati]on of the People.' In the 'Franchises' section there are a few corrections in two hands (one of them D's) on p 2 and in D's hand on p 3. Deletion lines have been drawn across clause 17, 'Joint Occupation in Boroughs' (p 6), and clause 33, 'For the Purposes of and in relation to any Franchise conferred by this Act a County shall be deemed not to include a Borough although such a Borough be geographically situated within its Limits' (p 11). Adjacent to this pamphlet is an undated 78-page document headed 'SECRET. *Printed Solely for the use of the Cabinet*', an expanded version of the draft pamphlet with numerous corrections and deletions in D's hand. H B/XI/H/24, 25.

2 On the previous day (15th) John Aloysius Blake (L) had proposed an amendment (later withdrawn) to the Railway Companies (Ireland) Temporary Advances Act 1866 '"directing that the period within which temporary advances should be made be extended to the maximum period allowed by the Act."' He explained that the Irish railway companies were to borrow £500,000, of which £300,000 'remained undisposed of, the greater portion of the debenture debt being due at periods beyond the three months' after the passing of the act. Application had recently been made to the treasury 'to exercise the powers vested in it to grant loans for debts falling due beyond the period within which the Loan Commissioners were empowered to act. To the surprise, however, of the applicants, the Treasury refused to exercise their powers for the purpose.' In a short speech, treasury financial secretary Hunt had stressed the change in circumstances since the passing of the act: the 'derangement in the money-market ... had entirely passed away, and ... the monetary considerations which had induced the Government to introduce the Bill had entirely disappeared.' Moreover, 'other applications about to be made' made it seem as if 'the

I think he exaggerates the result. Nothing rests on the public mind at present while the great / impending problem is unsolved.

If we win, it will be utterly forgotten: if we lose, it does not signify.

He shd. take into consideration all our difficulties & troubles. / After all, it can't be more annoying to him, than Pakington's speech is to us.[3] But that is borne, & in 9 days will be forgotten.

I trust in you – in this & in all things[.]

D.

TO: QUEEN VICTORIA   Downing Street, Monday 18 March [1867] **4374**
ORIGINAL: RAC F15 69
PUBLICATION HISTORY: *LQVB* I 410-11, dated '*18th Mar.* [1867].'
EDITORIAL COMMENT: C of Ex paper. *Dating*: by context; see nn1-7.

Monday Mar. 18

The Cr of the Exchequer with his humble duty to Yr Majesty:

The Ship was launched this evening by the C. of E. not without success. He scrupulously / followed, or endeavoured to follow, Yr Majesty's instructions.[1]

Mr Gladstone then rose, & having had the advantage, thro' Ld. Derby's & Sir

Government were a great "Credit Company," bound to find money for all persons who could not get it elsewhere, or to lend it at a lower than the current rate of interest in the market.' Speaking after Liberals Lawson, McKenna, Childers, Synan, Barron and Smith – during whose speeches (most finding fault with Hunt's justifications) he had most likely been summoned – D had stated adamantly that he wished to carry out 'the policy of our predecessors ... in its integrity. I do not want to change it. I do not propose to change it, and I will not sanction any change in it. If the Irish railways can come forward and give us good security it will be the duty of the Government ... candidly to consider their claims. They will be considered, I must fairly tell them, with the severity that becomes the office which I hold.' *Hansard* CLXXXV cols 1937-51 (D 1949-50).

3 Consequent upon his appointment as war secretary on 8 March, Pakington had stood for re-election (unopposed) for his borough of Droitwich, in Worcestershire. In his speech there on 13 March he had disclosed to his electors the proceedings of the 25 February cabinet meeting (**4340**n2), whose members had been 'driven to a decision which they really had hardly ten minutes to think of ... For myself I deeply felt that the course taken had been a mistake, and that was the unanimous feeling of the Cabinet after they met together.' He had also disclosed details of the reform bill to be introduced by D on the 18th (**4374**), which he said 'would be in point of numbers an enormous concession to the working classes.' (According to Blake 459, Pakington's speech was the source of the notorious 'Ten Minutes Bill' tag.) *The Times* on 15 March had made much of Pakington's indiscretions: not only had he discussed 'the deepest secrets of State' and 'the minute and circumstantial account of the backsliding and repentance of the Ministry,' but he had confided to his electors 'the secrets which Lord Derby will confidentially impart to his faithful followers to-day [**4372**&nn1&3], and which the Chancellor of the Exchequer ... will retail to the House of Commons next Monday evening.' In the House on the 18th Pakington would be castigated for his breach of confidentiality. *The Times* (14, 15 Mar 1867); *Hansard* CLXXXVI cols 78-9.

---

1 General Grey on this day (18th) had informed D that the Queen was (in her words) '"very anxious & nervous about the H. of Cs ... Mr. D. & Ld. Derby ought to bring forward their measure as a thing they *wished & intended* to carry, if possible – & not leaving it open to be altered according to the feeling of the H of Cs., whatever alteration they might afterwards be disposed to consent to. At the same time that he is firm, Mr. Disraeli ought to be *conciliatory.*"' Also on this day D had introduced the Representation of the People Bill, the House adjourning on the 19th at 1:30 *am*. For a summary of D's speech, which outlined the main principles and features of the bill, see M&B IV 519-21. H B/XIX/D/18; *Hansard* CLXXXVI cols 6-94 (D 6-25, 89-94).

John Pakington's speeches,[2] of a complete knowledge / of the subject, he made the speech wh: he, otherwise, wd. have made on the second reading. He never spoke more ably; it was ruthless.[3]

Mr Lowe, Sir W. Heathcote, & others, excited / by his success, all against the bill – & except Mr Henley, who, however spoke with great authority,[4] not a word was said ↑for it.↓

Things looked very black: but as the evening advanced, they mended. / Mr. Roebuck spoke, & with great moderation & good sense, on the folly of allowing any party feeling to throw out the bill.[5] I observed, for the first time, all / the independent Liberals cheered him: then, not long after, Mr Bernal Osborne absolutely said, that the Bill ought to be read a second time – altho', he added, / it would almost seem that Mr Gladstone did not originally mean, that it shd. be read ↑even↓ a first time: i.e. in Parliamentary language, be even introduced. This also / was cheered, &, then, a murmur went about the House, that "Gladstone had gone too far".[6]

After that everything went right, & the Chr. of the Exchequer may / even presume to say that he was fortunate in his reply, & rallied the Party.[7]

4375   TO: [MONTAGU CORRY]   Downing Street, Tuesday [19 March 1867]
ORIGINAL: H B/XI/J/31a
EDITORIAL COMMENT: 11 Downing Street paper. Docketed in another hand on the first page: '? 1867'. *Dating*: by context; see **4378**&n1.

Tuesday

Let me have, when I arrive, distinctly & accurately, the residential qualific[ati]on in the bill of 1854., & the proviso as to the 10£ voters[.]

2 Gladstone (n1) had stated, 'I am not one of those who believe the Constitution of the country is dependent upon the suffrage as absolutely as the Earl of Derby, who spoke the other night of an extended suffrage involving the destruction of the British Constitution.' For Derby's 15 March speech, see **4372**nn1&3; for Pakington's 13 March speech, see **4373**n3.

3 Gladstone (n1) had attacked the bill for being both too wide and too full of checks: he opposed the reduction to household suffrage but also the restrictions on it (personal rating and the dual vote, the latter 'a gigantic engine of fraud') and demanded a lodger franchise. See **4383**&n1.

4 Joseph Henley (n1) believed that the bill should be based on 'payment of rates, which should constitute the ground for the borough franchise', and favoured the principle 'that in towns those who bear the burden of the poor rates, whatever be the amount of the tenement, shall have a vote', the advantage being that 'it does not take in all one class down to a hard line.' He called dual voting 'unmixed mischief.'

5 After disparaging Gladstone's speech as 'disingenuous' and 'inconsistent', John Roebuck (n1) had urged the House to pass 'the best Bill we can pass at this time, and let us leave it to posterity to settle its own affairs.'

6 Although Bernal Osborne (n1) was in favour of a second reading, he felt 'very certain that if the re-distribution is as you have announced it to-night it is no settlement of the question at all, and I shall feel myself called upon to move a Resolution, unless some greater changes are made and the re-distribution Bill be altogether separated from the franchise Bill.'

7 Most of D's closing remarks (n1) had addressed Gladstone's speech, which he dismissed as 'half alarm, half derision – alarm at the revolutionary proposal, derision at the petty consequences it will produce.' Corry on this day (18th) at 11:15 *pm* had written to MA that D's 'reply has just been described to me as "the most magnificent piece of oratory ever heard." His opening statement was most clear and statesman-like. – the fire being reserved for the reply ... Gladstone's attack was most violent – too violent to serve his object, I think.' Corry wrote to D at 11:45 *pm*: 'Your reply is *universally* acknowledged to be the finest thing ever heard. Gladstone's invective told at the moment: but his partial and premature criticism is being severely commented on in the lobbies by men of both sides.' H B/XI/J/10, 11.

ORIGINAL: DBP Box 146/3

EDITORIAL COMMENT: C of Ex paper. *Dating*: by context; see nn3-6.

Rt Hono[ra]ble | The Earl of Derby | K.G Wednesday

My dear Lord,[1]

Little George Bentinck[2] has so committed himself, in private conversation with / Lowe & others about Reform, that he has not courage to take the office,[3] fearing the contumely, wh: our Adullamites have / lavished on the hapless Robert Montagu.[4] But he is *delighted* with the offer, & so is Lord Lonsdale, & he will, in future / work loyally & heartily with us[.] He can vote for us, but not in office.

Public opinion points strongly to Sclater / Booth, & Hardy writes to suggest him for consideration, tho' very modestly.[5]

I have ventured, therefore, to see him & / say, that I shall recommend his name to you for the post.

Some think it advisable, that his appointment shd be announced in the / papers tomorrow. This shall be done if you approve of his appointment.[6]

Yrs | D.

1 With an undated note (headed '5 P.M.') Derby had sent D a resignation letter (dated 18 March) from Ralph Earle, 'which I will not answer till I have seen or heard from you.' Following the Cranborne, Carnarvon and Peel resignations, Earle had apparently approached D for promotion. In an undated letter headed '*Confidential*', he asks D for a post abroad: 'EVERY ONE I meet expects that I shall receive some acknowledgement of my devotion & *sufferings* for the Party'. H B/XX/S/422, 422a; XXI/E/406. See n5 and **4414**&n2.

2 George A.F.C. Bentinck.

3 Lonsdale on this day (20th) had written to D that he believed George Bentinck's opinion on reform and household suffrage 'so strong, that he could not accept office without such a sacrifice of his political principles', which he was 'disinclined to make.' This was not from 'any want of loyalty to his party ... but from high motives which you will appreciate & though he cannot form one of the Government, he will support them as heretofore to the utmost of his power.' H B/XI/J/75.

4 Montagu had recently been sworn in as PC and appointed vice-president of the council on education, an office he would hold until 1 December 1868. *The Times* (20 Mar 1867).

5 In a 15 March letter headed '*Private*', poor law board president Hardy had told D that he had received a letter from Earle informing him of his resignation from the board 'on the ground that he cannot support the policy of the Government on the Reform question! He gives no further reason ... It is not for me to do more than suggest a successor but Sclater-Booth may be worth consideration.' H B/XX/HA/4.

6 Derby on this day (20th) would reply that 'G.B.'s declining is, under the circumstances, autant de gagné for us. I cordially assent to the proposal of Sclater-Booth, who, I think, though I do not know him personally, is likely to be by far the better man of the two. But it will not be right to announce his appointment till the Queen has been informed of it. I will write by Her Messenger tomorrow morning, and request to have an answer by Telegraph: which will be before the meeting of the House tomorrow. He will not have to vacate his seat.' Derby on the 21st would inform D that he had received the Queen's approval of Sclater-Booth's appointment, 'which may therefore be announced as soon as you please.' H B/XX/S/423, 424. *The Times* on 22 March would announce Sclater-Booth's acceptance of 'the office of Parliamentary Secretary to the Poor Law Board, vacant by the resignation of Mr. Earle. His acceptance does not involve the necessity of resigning his seat.'

4377 TO: QUEEN VICTORIA   House of Commons, Thursday 21 March [1867]

ORIGINAL: RAC F15 76

PUBLICATION HISTORY: *LQVB* I 412-14, dated '21st Mar. [1867] (*Thursday*)'

EDITORIAL COMMENT: C of Ex paper. D has numbered some of the pages; the fourth, fifth and sixth pages are black-edged. *Dating*: by context; see nn1-7. *Sic*: man.

House of Comm: | Thursday Mar: 21

The Chr of the Exchequer with his humble duty to Yr Majesty:

At the meeting of the Liberal party to day,[1] Mr Gladstone addressed them, & gave / twelve reasons, why the Bill shd be thrown out on the second reading.

The moment he mentioned this, there was a murmur, & scuffling of feet. He started, / but continued his address, & spoke with great energy & emphasis, concluding that there never was any thing so clear for a party, than their duty & interest to vote / against the second reading.

There was revived the same murmur of dissent & disapprobation, & cries of "Bright" – who did not, however, advance.

Then a Mr Cogan[2] / rose, & supported Mr Gladstone's view, &, afterwards, another (or two) obscure man.

The same disapprobation in the meeting, but singular, that no one rose & expressed their feelings / – but continued cries of "Bright".

Then a pause – the cries renewed – & then Mr Bright came forward. He supported Mr Gladstone with great fire & fervor, but / with the candor, & want of tact, wh: distinguish him, he recognised the feeling of the meeting; & that they were averse to taking the step recommended by Mr / Gladstone. He ended by saying "If Mr Disraeli were here he would say, the Lord has delivered you into my hands"[.]

Previously, he had shown, that if the House once went into / Committee, the Bill must be passed, there wo[ul]d be *cross* voting, & the Government wd. remain the masters of the situation.

All ↑this↓ from an eye witness, & may be depended / on.

There is a hope, this evening, among ↑some of↓ the Liberal party, to regain their lost position, by moving some resolution, after the second reading, & before the / Speaker leaves the chair, declaring that no settlement can be satisfactory, &c. with *personal* rating, & duality of votes.[3]

---

1 *The Times* on 22 March would list the 278 members present on the 21st at Gladstone's Carlton House Terrace residence, where Gladstone's preferred strategy of opposing the reform bill immediately on second reading was not accepted, but the decision of opposing the bill deferred until after his speech on second reading. Grosvenor and Elcho did not attend the meeting, which went from 2:30 to 3:30 *pm* – 4 *pm* according to Gladstone, who on this day (21st) noted, 'I spoke near an hour: the end as good as I could hope.' *Gladstone Diaries* VI 508.

2 William Henry Ford Cogan (1823-1894), MA Trinity, Dublin, an Irish barrister 1845 (but relinquished practice), JP for Wicklow, Kildare and Carlow, MP (L) for Kildare 1852-80, would be a commissioner on the Irish board of national education 1880-94.

3 Stanley on this day (21st) recorded that at Gladstone's 'it was agreed not to divide against the second reading, but to move amendments on the Speaker leaving the chair. As these will be in a liberal or rather radical sense, we must oppose them, and the question will be brought to an issue in a most satisfactory way. Gladstone and Bright were both for immediate war, but were overruled by the general feeling of their party.' *Disraeli, Derby* 295.

They might rally round this.

Personal rating by / itself would not do, but combined with Duality, it might pass.[4]

Personal rating is really popular in the country.

It comes to this: if the Cabinet will be wise & bold, & relinquish Duality on the second reading, / & take a bold stand on personal rating, their honor wd. be saved entirely by that, the opposition wd. be completely baffled, the Bill wd. pass, & the prospect of a strong & permanent government / not impossible.

Mr. Bright said today, the Liberal party would never, perhaps, recover the passing of the Bill.

The Chanr of the Excr. has felt the pulse of the Cabinet, & brought the matter incidentally before / them yesterday morning.[5]

The Duke of Marlboro' spoke with much ability on the point, & adjured his colleagues to take the step of necessary boldness.

The Duke of Richmond / supported him.

Lord Derby did not conceal his feelings. Lord Stanley, Sir S. Northcote, the Duke of Bucks & Mr Hardy, clung to Duality, of wh: they did not approve, / as a point of honor.

But this, in the present state of affairs, is mere foolishness & euphuism.

The Chr. of Exr has, this afternoon, seen Lord Stanley & N̶ Sir S. / Northcote, & they are now right.

He will see Ld. Derby tomorrow morning.

He has no apprehension now except about the Duke of Bucks & Mr Hardy.[6]

Everything shall be / done not to give Yr Majesty trouble, but everything shd. be done to pass the Bill, & it may be necessary, that the personal authority of Yr Majesty sho[ul]d be invoked, & that the thunder of Olympus shd. sound! /

The Chr of the Exr will keep Your Majesty *au courant* to everything, & he believes it is only with Yr Majesty's aid, that Yr Majestys Ministers can succeed, / but he feels persuaded that the business can be done, &, everything depends on it.

He humbly apologises for this long report, but he knows Yr Majesty loves / truth & detail, & that your ↑Majesty's↓ inexpressible, & unwearied, graciousness, will pardon him if he has exceeded his duty.[7]

---

4 'Personal' rating applied to individuals who paid their rates (local taxes) in person, as opposed to 'compounders', who paid them to a landlord as part of their rent (landlords receiving a discount on their own rates) and thus did not appear on the rate book, which was the basis of the electoral register. Blake 461. For 'duality', a type of 'plural' voting, see **4317n2**.

5 Stanley on 20 March had noted that in cabinet on that day 'it was agreed to make no changes or concessions on the second reading of the reform bill, but to reserve to ourselves the right of consenting to such or not when it goes into committee if it does so.' *Disraeli, Derby* 295.

6 Stanley on 24 March would note 'Fears of the D of Buckingham resigning, but he wrote to Ld D. to say that though reluctantly, he had made up his mind to accept the bill and go on. Hardy, who had been in doubt, had at the cabinet expressed the same opinion.' *Ibid.*

7 In forwarding D's letter on 22 March, General Grey would write to the Queen at length: 'When Mr. Disraeli says (using rather extraordinary expressions) that Your Majesty's assistance will be indispensable, he means probably, that without Your Majesty's intervention, the Duke of Buckingham, Mr. Hardy, & possibly also Sir S. Northcote, will resign rather than give up a proposal to which they consider their honour pledged.' RAC F15 77.

TO: [MONTAGU CORRY]   Grosvenor Gate, Friday [22 March 1867]

ORIGINAL: H B/XI/J/8

EDITORIAL COMMENT: C of Ex paper, seal crossed out and 'Grosvenor Gate' written in. Docketed in another hand on the first page: 'March /67'. *Dating*: by context; see n1.

Grosvenor Gate | Friday

With reference to what we were talking over last night, two points occur to me. Would a stiff residential test assist the case of the smaller Boros? If so, notwithstanding Mr / Hardy's opinion, that it wd. not be attended to by the overseers, we ought to insert it.

And with respect to the great objection that it wd. make an invidious distinction between / the old & new voters, remember there is a precedent for that distinction in Lord John Russell's Bill of 1854: a £5 rating qualific[ati]on with three years residence.[1]

Ascertain how, in / that bill, the different rights, in this respect, of the old & the new voters, were proposed to be regulated.

Ascertain also, from Mr Baxter, whether a clause can be devised making / the payment of rates by the elector absolutely personal – so that no election agent shd. have the power of paying rates for persons who really had no knowledge of / them thus attaining their privileges.

And ask him, whether any other plan can be devised for this object.

D. /

I shd. be glad if you cd. generally report to me on this before I go to the H of C. where I shall be able to consult with Mr Hardy.

TO: MONTAGU CORRY   Grosvenor Gate, Friday [22 March 1867]

ORIGINAL: H B/XI/J/152

EDITORIAL COMMENT: C of Ex paper, seal crossed out and 'Grosr Gate' written in. *Dating*: by context; see n1. *Sic*: De.

Friday | Grosr Gate

Montagu Corry | Esq

Mon tres cher,

Affairs very critical, but not bad.

I am now going to Lord Derby – & shall be at the office early.

---

1 In the House on Thursday 21 March 1867, Gladstone had asked D whether voting conditions in boroughs would be the same for occupiers of £10 and upwards and those under £10, and whether 'the occupying franchise in Boroughs, which now depends upon the occupation of "any house, warehouse, counting house, shop, or other building," is henceforward to depend upon the occupation of dwelling houses exclusively'. D had replied that the current residence qualification was one year and would be two years 'for the new house-holders proposed to be enfranchised ... We follow in that precisely the precedent set in the Bill of 1854, brought in by Lord John Russell [which] proposed a considerable reduction in the amount of the borough qualification. It was proposed to reduce to a £6 rental. There was a proviso ... that the rights and privileges under the Act of 1832 should not be impugned or affected by that arrangement ... The reason why we have limited franchise in the Bill to the occupation of dwelling-houses is because there are no warehouses, counting-houses, and scarcely shops at a rating which the Bill particularly deals with ... Therefore, we have resolved that it should be a *bonâ fide* household qualification.' *Hansard* CLXXXVI cols 284-8.

Ld. Stanley, who wants to speak, wants a / brief – *as to facts* – he said a ~~paper~~ memorandum wh: might be sent round to the Cabinet.

Think of this: but there is no time to lose.

The Solr. General who will speak on Monday[1] / wants somebody to talk the matter over with him at the House of Commons this evening. Who shall it be? Yourself?

Think of all this & a 1000 other things after / De Grey,[2] Mr[3] & Sir Beach[4] come at three o'ck today in the same errand.

Yours I D.

TO: **QUEEN VICTORIA**   Downing Street, Friday [22 March 1867]   4380
ORIGINAL: RAC F15 78
EDITORIAL COMMENT: C of Ex paper. Docketed in another hand on the first page: '22. March'. The word 'understood' has been added in another hand. *Dating*: by context; see n1.

Friday.

The Cr of the Exchequer with his humble duty to Yr Majesty:

He has the gratification to report, that he has reason to believe, that the Cabinet will / be unanimous tomorrow in agreeing to give up the principle of Duality, provided the Second Reading of the Reform Bill is agreed to, as understood.[1]

TO: **LORD DERBY**   Grosvenor Gate, Sunday [24 March 1867]   4381
ORIGINAL: DBP Box 146/3
PUBLICATION HISTORY: M&B IV 529, dated '*Sunday* [? *April* 7]', the first two paragraphs
EDITORIAL COMMENT: Black-edged 11 Downing Street paper, imprinted address crossed out and 'Grosvenor Gate' written in. Docketed by AES: '[March 17, 1867]? M & B says April 7'. *Dating*: by context; see **4382**.

Confidential   Grosvenor Gate I Sunday

Rt Honble I The Earl of Derby I K.G.

My dear Lord,

Gladstone is more violent than ever – & the Independents, who baffled him the

---

1 See **4385**&n5.
2 Thomas de Grey.
3 William Wither Bramston Beach (1826-1901), BA 1849 Christ Church, Oxford, capt Hampshire Yeomanry Cavalry 1858, PC 1900, MP (C) for N Hampshire 1857-85 and Andover 1885-1901.
4 Sir Michael Edward Hicks Beach (1837-1916), 9th Bt 1854, 1st Earl St Aldwyn 1915, MP (C) for E Gloucestershire 1864-85 and W Bristol 1885-1906, parliamentary secretary to the poor law board and undersecretary for the home office 1868, Irish secretary 1874-8 and 1886-7, PC 1877, colonial secretary 1878-80, president of the board of trade 1888-92 and chancellor of the exchequer 1885-6, 1895-1902.

---

1 According to Stanley, cabinet on 23 March 1867 'lasted three hours: reform the chief subject.' *Disraeli, Derby* 295. General Grey would inform the Queen, in his third letter to her on 23 March, that 'this evening' he had spoken with Northcote about the meeting. Northcote, Manners, Hardy and others 'had doubted how far they could creditably give up the dual vote on the Second Reading, at all events without a strong expression of opinion in favour of their doing so from their own side of the House – but he understood that such an opinion would be unmistakably expressed, & in that case, he led Genl Grey to believe ... that there wd. be no difficulty in the fact of any of the Gvt. in acquiescing in the course proposed.' RAC F15 81. For the second reading of the Reform Bill on 25 and 26 March, see **4385**&nn1-5 and **4387**&nn1&2.

other day,[1] have had a council, at wh: / it was discussed, whether some communication shd. not be opened with Mr Henley, & Colonel Wilson Patten, in order to assist the Government, & pass the Bill: the names / even were mentioned of Managers of the Conference on the part of the Independent Liberals: *Mr Whitbread & Mr Clay.*

It is said, that whatever / statement is made by us, Gladstone means to propose to his party an abstract Resolution on the Speaker leaving the chair, to the effect that no settlement &c. can be satisfactory wh: / recognises in electoral rights a distinction between Rich & Poor[.][2]

You may rely on all this, as it comes from the fountain head.

It was impressed upon me, that you must on / no account resign, as if Gladstone were to entrap his party into an abstract resolution, not probable, the House wd. never push things on further.

I will tell you more about / contemplated tactics on both sides when we meet.

We are counselled to maintain the debate, & not go into Committee before Easter.

I was sorry to hear from Taylor, that the / Duke of Bucks. seems still wrong.[3]

You ought to be prepared for everything: if you are prepared, & act with promptness, ~~it will~~ his secession will do rather good than harm: as the Country will see / that you are determined to pass yr Bill[.]

You have a first rate man for Board of Trade (Duke of R. going to Colonies) if you like – Hunt – ↑(and a mere Mr. *wh: is something*)↓[.] He stands high with the / House & with everybody. He is one (not a few) who have made reputations during ~~the~~ your Governm[en]t.

He wd. be a great loss at the Treasury – but the work is done for the Sess; & he / wd. keep his eye on affairs, & coach Sclater Booth, who, with a little time & ~~with~~ experience, wd. rank with the best of that class.[4]

Yrs ever | D.

4382   TO: LORD DERBY   Grosvenor Gate [Sunday] 24 March 1867

ORIGINAL: DBP Box 146/3

PUBLICATION HISTORY: M&B IV 522, the first, second and tenth paragraphs

EDITORIAL COMMENT: Grosvenor Gate paper. D has numbered the second and third sheets and has superimposed a '6' over a '5' in '1867' in the first sentence. *Sic*: that is.

Confidential   Mar: 24 1867

Rt. Honble | The Earl of Derby | K.G.

---

1 See **4377**n1.
2 See **4385**n2.
3 Buckingham remained at odds with the government on the reform question. In an letter from St James's Square marked '*Confidential*' and docketed 'Sunday' (dated 10 March 1867 by Hawkins *Derby* 343), Derby had informed D that he had seen Buckingham and that 'I am afraid I have made no impression on him. He says, if the Dual vote is withdrawn, he does not see how he can support the Bill.' H B/XX/S/459.
4 On 8 March 1867, Richmond had succeeded Northcote as president of the board of trade and Buckingham had succeeded Carnarvon as colonial secretary. George Sclater-Booth, secretary to the poor law board as of 1 March 1867, would succeed Hunt as treasury secretary in 1868, Hunt succeeding D as chancellor of the exchequer.

My dear Lord,

It is very trying, & no doubt, we shall, both of us, always remember the year 1867.

But there is more than hope.

Since I wrote to you,[1] / I have learnt, that Mr Gladstone, on the meeting of the House ↑tomorrow↓, or, rather, I shd. suppose, on our motion for the second Reading, means to rise &, while announcing his / assent to 2nd Reading, declare, that [it] is on only certain understandings, or conditions, to wit, you know what – & that if not agreed to, the battle is to be fought on the Speaker's / leaving the Chair – wh: cd. not be greatly postponed: to that day week at the utmost: if he succeed in preventing, as he wishes, & counts on, a debate.[2]

I / might answer him & reply:

Expressing, what we have before, that this question ought not to be a question of party, for party has failed to solve it; & that it cannot be settled witht. / the assistance of the House; & that, in our course, we wish to be influenced by opinion of the House; that having failed, by the way of Resolutions, to obtain that opinion, we have / brought forward a Bill; nevertheless, we wish to be guided, as much as possible, by the opinion of the House; that still, under the circumstances of bringing forward a / bill, there must be certain principles announced wh: are fundamental; that personal rating, & an adequate residence, are much in our mind; that with ~~ex~~ regard to others, dual voting for / example; on wh:, of course, he has spoken much; it is a means, not an end, but if the end can be ~~obt~~ otherwise obtained, we are ready to consider, in ~~any~~ committee, any such proposition – that all / we desire is, to secure a general representation witht. preponderance of class, &c &c.[3]

This might not satisfy him, or the bulk opposite, but it wd. keep our men together, & Gladstone / wd. then on Monday, the 1st. April, bring forward his abstract resolution.[4]

As it wd. virtually be a debate on the whole question, the division wd. not take place until the / eve of the Holidays.

It wd. not be a resolution, ↑if carried,↓ that requires immediate attention.

I shd. adjourn the House, fixing the Committee for the 2nd. ~~Apr~~ May, & during that time, we shd. have had an opportunity / of considering our position.[5]

I must tell you, that there are 100 men, on the other side, against Gladstone, but they are *moutons*; there is nobody who can / speak – against him.

At the meeting, there was no one, tho' the feeling was so strong, that by murmuring, round robins, & scuffling of feet, they controlled "iracundus Achilles".[6]

---

1 See **4381**.

2 See **4385**n2.

3 In the House on the 25th D would make only a few brief interventions during Gladstone's speech; see **4385**&n1.

4 In the House on 1 April, replying to a question by Gladstone, D would state that he would on this night 'put on the Paper a Notice' to 'move the omission of Clause 7 – that is, the clause which proposes to give a second vote'. This would be the only reform-related matter in a long debate devoted to the Mutiny Bill and Navy Estimates. *Hansard* CLXXXVI cols 907-8, 912-74.

5 In the House on 12 April, following the division, the committee would report progress and agree to sit again on 2 May. *Hansard* CLXXXVI col 1703; see **4428**&n1.

6 See **4377**n1. Horace describes Homer's Achilles as 'impiger, iracundus, inexorabilis, acer': indefatigable, irascible, ruthless, fierce (or violent). *Ars Poetica* lines 120-2.

They / won't have Ayrton,[7] because he is not a Swell: & tho' inclined to follow Osborne, because he married a territorial heiress,[8] they say he is so ignorant, & particularly of the distinctions between / rating & rental, that he is sure to break down.

What an opportunity! and the occasion, therefore, does not always, produce the man!

I will call tomorrow: in the meantime, the Cabinet remains.

Yrs | D.

4383   TO: LADY JOHN MANNERS   Grosvenor Gate [Sunday] 24 March 1867
ORIGINAL: BEA [165]
EDITORIAL COMMENT: Black-edged 11 Downing Street paper, imprinted address crossed out and 'Grosvenor Gate' written in.

The | Lady John Manners   Grosvenor Gate | March 24 1867
Dear Muse!
I delayed responding to your lyric burst,[1] because I wished to acknowledge it in a more sympathetic manner, than / "tumbling down to prose",[2] but amid the present

---

7 For staunch reformer Acton Smee Ayrton (L), see **4157n2**.
8 Ralph Bernal Jr on 12 August 1844 had legally changed his name to Ralph Bernal Osborne prior to his marriage on 20 August to Catherine Isabella Osborne, daughter of Sir Thomas Osborne (9th Bt) and Catherine Rebecca Smith.

---

1 Lady John Manners had written to D from 6 Cumberland Terrace, Regent's Park, on 'Thursday': 'I just scribbled off my indignant impression of Gladstone's speech [of 18 March 1867], and think you may possibly consider there is some truth in the sketch, – as I saw the scene from Lady Charlotte's gallery.' She had enclosed the following poem, to whose date another hand (after 'March') has added '1867'. H B/ XX/M/297, 297a. See **4374**&nn2,3&7.

'After hearing the Debate – Monday 19 March!

The Chief has raised his war cry now!
With quivering lip, with scowling brow,
Once more he summons to the fight
His legions – Potter, Beales, and Bright,
Invoking too, the aid of Lowe,
To wreak his vengeance on his foe!
Straightway to number he begins
That Foe's past, present, future, sins

Then with a roar, records his vow,
His time is come for vengeance now. –
He tears the passion all to rags!
Certain unsympathetic wags,
Declare, the orator of late,
Has passed some time in Billings-gate,
And there has learnt the war to wage,
Thersites-like, with wordy rage.'

2 'I've half a mind to tumble down to prose, / But verse is more in fashion – so here goes.' Byron *Beppo: a Venetian Love Story* (1817).

struggles of my life, the shell will not sound, & instead of being inspired, I / can only sign myself

Your grateful | D.[3]

TO: **LORD DERBY**   House of Commons [Monday 25 March 1867]   **4384**
ORIGINAL: DBP Box 146/3
EDITORIAL COMMENT: House of Commons paper. Endorsed by Derby on the fourth page: 'Disraeli Right Honble B. on Hardy's Speech. 2nd Reading of Reform Bill – /67'. *Dating*: by context; see n1.

½ pt 9

My dear Lord,
A hurried note: Hardy, a great success.
    The party quite rallied.
    Gladstone elaborate / & too committeeish – no effect, or a bad one.
    Things look very well.
    Amberley / up.[1]
        Yrs | D.

TO: **QUEEN VICTORIA**   House of Commons [Monday] 25 March 1867   **4385**
ORIGINAL: RAC F15 82
EDITORIAL COMMENT: House of Commons paper.

Mar: 25 1867

The Chr of the Exchequer with his humble duty to Yr Majesty:
    A very good report. The first night of the Debate very successful, / & the general tone never more hopeful.[1]
    Mr Gladstone made an elaborate speech of detail & wearied the House.[2]
    When / the Bill was introduced, he made a speech suited only to the Second Reading: & on the Second Reading, he made a speech suited only / to Committee.
    He was answered by Mr Hardy in a speech full of sense & spirit, wh: entirely rallied the House, & the Conservative party.[3]

---

3 Lady John Manners had written a letter to MA on 'Monday night' (docketed by MA '1867 March 18th'): 'I did so wish you had been in the house this evening. Disraeli was sublime ... Oh, it was most beautiful and his voice so proud & pathetic ... You should have cried if you had been there, with admiration ... Even the women were quite hushed and wrapt in attention.' H D/III/C/1348.

---

1 For Hardy's and Gladstone's speeches in the House on 25 March 1867, see **4385**&nn2&3. Amberley (L) would object that he failed to see the difference between personal ratepayer and compound household-er 'which makes it proper that the personal ratepayer shall vote and the compound-householder shall not.' *Hansard* CLXXXVI cols 529-34.

---

1 The second reading of the Reform Bill was moved on this day (25th), the House adjourning at 12:30 *am* on the 26th. *Hansard* CLXXXVI cols 472-558 (D 479-80, 484, 491, 558).
2 Gladstone, in a two-hour speech (n1), had cited figures and statistics in relation to compound house-holders, payment of rates, the Small Tenements Act and what he termed the 'enfranchising part' of the bill, which he believed admitted 'a principle of needless breadth' and whose own provisions defeated its application. He concluded that the quantity of the enfranchisement was 'insufficient' and the quality 'defective.'
3 After countering a number of comments by Gladstone (n2), Hardy (n1) had concluded by stating that

The / next speech of the evening was Mr Roebucks, wh: was very effective, & much influenced the House.

He was strongly for the Bill, but very constitutional / & conservative in tone.[4]

The Solicitor General closed the debate in a very clear & closely argued speech, wh: touched all the points.[5]

Mr / Roebuck admonished the Government to be firm & constant, & the Bill would pass. He mentioned this also to Mr Walpole privately.

It is said, that there / are 100 members on the Opposition side, who really wish the question settled – Mr Hastings Russell,[6] Mr Whitbread,[7] among them & very active: & in this in spite of Lord Russell's remonstrance.[8]

the Government was 'anxious to give a liberal but not an indiscriminate franchise', and that the basis of their measure, 'a household residential rating, with personal payment and continued residence', was a better one than any measure thus far introduced. 'If the Government are met in a reasonable spirit ... they will be liberal in the enfranchisement of the people, while not allowing it to be unlimited and without discrimination.' Hardy on the 26th would note that on this day (25th) at 3 pm Derby had asked him to follow Gladstone: 'I had nothing prepared & did not attempt more than to collect my thoughts & discuss his speech. Mine was well received & Disraeli & my Colleagues much gratified. Lord Derby has written me a very kind letter of thanks.' Derby would write to D on the 26th that 'Hardy has quite vindicated our selection of him, and has placed himself in the front rank *as a Debater*.' *Hardy Diary* 34-5; H B/XX/S/425.

4 Roebuck (n1) had distinguished between that portion of the labouring class having 'character, probity, intelligence, sagacity' from 'that body who are not educated, who are vicious, who are unfit to have in their hands the government of mankind.' The real question, he believed, was how to admit into suffrage 'the worthy and intelligent portion of the working class and ... shut out the unworthy, and those to whom it could not be confided without danger.'

5 Sir John Burgess Karslake (n1) had countered at length charges that the bill was 'without principle', asking the House 'to accede to the principle that a person who occupies a house for a certain length of time, and who pays his poor rates, shall be entitled to be admitted to exercise the franchise.' Karslake (1821-1881), a barrister (Middle Temple 1846), QC 1861, Kt Jan 1867 and PC 1876, was sol-gen 1866-7, att-gen July 1867-Dec 1868 and Feb-Apr 1874, MP (C) for Andover Feb 1867-Dec 1868 and Huntingdon 1873-6, accepting the Chiltern Hundreds in 1876.

6 Francis Charles Hastings Russell (1819-1891), 9th Duke of Bedford 1872, Scots Fusilier Guards 1838-44, major Bedford Militia 1849 and lieut-col 1st battalion Bedfordshire Rifle Volunteers 1860. He was DL of Bedford 1861, MP (L) for Bedfordshire 1847-72 and would be president of the Royal Agricultural Society 1879, KG 1880 and LL of Huntingdonshire 1884-91.

7 Samuel Whitbread (1830-1915), great-grandson of brewer Samuel Whitbread, educated at Rugby and Cambridge, DL of Bedfordshire 1852, a lord of the admiralty 1859-63 and MP (L) for Bedford 1852-95. He would make brief interventions during the reform bill debates on 11 April, 9 May and 8 July. *Hansard* CLXXXVI cols 1499-1500; CLXXXVII cols 312-15; CLXXXVIII cols 1234-5.

8 In the Lords at the opening of Parliament on 5 February, Russell, after disparaging the effects of the 1832 reform bill's so-called Chandos clause – moved by the Duke of Buckingham and Chandos, it enfranchised tenants-at-will paying £50 in annual rent (tenants typically voted with their landlords, usually Tory supporters) – had criticized the Government's handling of the reform issue to date. *The Times* had noted his 'extraordinary assertion that all past and present agitation for Reform' was due to the Chandos clause. 'We know not whether to marvel more at the obstinacy of Lord Russell's resentment or at the limited view of the reasons for Reform implied in this assertion.' *Hansard* CLXXXV cols 26-35; *The Times* (6 Feb 1867).

ORIGINAL: H B/XI/J/33
EDITORIAL COMMENT: C of Ex paper. Docketed in another hand on the first page: '?1867'. *Dating*: conjectural; see nn3&4.

The Armenian[1] shd. get from my room in H of C. the box (not a Queen's box) wh: contains my interleaved copy of / bill. It was too late to send it to D.S. last night.

Think of 1 & 2 ff. of 14 & 15 Vic: c. 14[2] & see if there is anything in Gladstone's (Morning / Posts) objection.[3]

D.

Let me have Times' Report of Civ: Eng: Dinner of last year in my room when I arrive.[4]

TO: [LORD DERBY]   House of Commons, Tuesday [26 March 1867]   4387
ORIGINAL: DBP Box 146/3
EDITORIAL COMMENT: House of Commons paper. *Dating*: by context; see n1.

Tuesday

I am going to speak, &, therefore, can't write at length.[1]

Rolt was flat: Palmer not as good as usual.

Nothing very important / has happened – but the tone is hardly as good as yesterday – but this may be imaginary.

---

1 Corry on 21 April 1867 would write to D from Rowton Castle: 'The Armenian sends me all the Journals. Even the 19 which have reached me today throw little light on coming events'. H B/XI/J/21.

2 The Compound Householders Act 1851. See **4443**n3.

3 *MP* on 26 Mar 1867 had published the lengthy speech made by Gladstone on the 25th, the first night of the second reading of the reform bill. Many of his remarks concerned compound householders. He wished to do away with the 'vexatious distinctions ... between compound-householders in a condition of life and society that are recognized by law as fitting them for the franchise, and those persons of the very same condition not being compound-householders. This Bill does not do away with these distinctions; on the contrary, it introduces new ones.' *Hansard* CLXXXVI cols 472-505. See **4385**&n2.

4 D is not listed among the guests at the 9 May 1866 dinner of the Institute of Civil Engineers (speakers included the Prince of Wales and Robert Lowe) but would speak at their 8 May 1867 dinner. Both were held at Willis's Rooms, St James's. *The Times* (10 May 1866, 9 May 1867).

---

1 D is writing from the House on 26 March 1867 during the second night of the second reading of the Reform Bill, which would be passed without a division. Derby on this day (26th) had asked D to 'be as short and pithy as possible, striking the Key-note which I understand to have been agreed upon between us, of willingness to consult the opinion of *the House*, but refusal to submit to the dictation of *one assumed* Leader of a Party.' After famously declaring that Gladstone's 'manner is sometimes so very excited and so alarming that one might almost feel thankful that Gentlemen in this House who sit on opposite sides of this table are divided by a tolerably broad piece of furniture', D outlined the inconsistencies in Gladstone's demands and closed on a bipartisan note by inviting all members to assist him in carrying the measure. 'We will not shrink from deferring to your suggestions so long as they are consistent with the main object of this Bill ... which is to preserve the representative character of the House of Commons. Act with us, I say, cordially and candidly, [and] you will find on our side complete reciprocity of feeling. Pass the Bill, and then change the Ministry if you like.' John Bright thought D's speech 'amusing but not statesmanlike'. Stanley would call it 'admirable in point of temper, tact, humour, and even argument: though the last is not generally his forte ... D. before delivering this speech was in a state of nervousness and depression almost painful to witness'. H B XX/S/425; *Hansard* CLXXXVI cols 569-665 (D 642-65); Bright 299; *Disraeli, Derby* 296. For the main points of D's speech see M&B IV 524-6.

Percy Wyndham spoke / against us, having asked us to interfere for him, & Butler Johnstone made a nonsensical speech, wh: seemed against us, tho' I hear it was not so intended.²

Yrs | D.³

4388   TO: QUEEN VICTORIA   Downing Street, Wednesday 27 March [1867]
ORIGINAL: RAC F15 83
PUBLICATION HISTORY: *LQVB* I 414, dated '27*th Mar.* 1867 (*Wednesday morning*)'
EDITORIAL COMMENT: Black-edged 11 Downing Street paper. Docketed in another hand on the first page: 'March 27/67.' D has written 'Mar: 27' at the end of the letter. *Dating*: by context; see n1.

Wednesday Morning | Mar: 27

The Chr of the Exchequer with his humble duty to Yr Majesty:

The bill was read a second time early this morning: a great fact.¹

The / prospect continues hopeful.

4389   TO: LORD LONSDALE   House of Commons [Wednesday] 27 March 1867
ORIGINAL: MOPSIK [153]
PUBLICATION HISTORY: Weintraub *Disraeli* 446, the first sentence
EDITORIAL COMMENT: House of Commons paper. *Sic*: Folkstone.

Confidential   Mar: 27 1867

Rt Honble | The Earl of Lonsdale

My dear Lord,

If you could soften Jem Lowther, you would greatly serve us. All that he fears will disappear / in Committee, with a little tact & patience.¹ The business is in our hands, & the stronger we are, & the more united / our friends, the more satisfactory will be the solution. Rest assured, that it will not be one, that you will disapprove of.

---

2 Attorney general Sir John Rolt (n1) had examined objections to the manner, mode and conditions for the franchise, while Sir Roundell Palmer had criticized at length remarks made the previous day (25th) by Hardy, showing that he was not 'master of this Bill which he is here to advocate.' Percy Scawen Wyndham (1835-1911), MP (C) for Cumberland W 1860-85, wanted 'to see a very wide measure of the re-distribution of seats based upon philosophical principles' rather than the 'Utopian' ones of Henry Butler-Johnstone, who considered the position of Robert Lowe and others 'perfectly unassailable' and who claimed that the bill, if unamended, would 'ruin the constitution.'

3 Derby on the 27th would write from St James's Square offering D 'cordial congratulations on your splendid achievement of last night. I hear from all quarters that it was the finest speech you ever made; and you seem to have carried the House bodily away with you. In fact you have won our game for us; and in writing to the Queen this morning to announce your "triumphant success," I told H.M. that I now, for the first time, entertain a sanguine hope of carrying a Bill through in the course of the present Session ... The most dangerous rock I now see ahead is the proposal for a £5 rating, and excluding those below the line from the option of claiming to be rated ... I have summoned a Cabinet for Saturday as usual: shall you be prepared to give the outline of your financial scheme by that time? Stanley has a serious question to bring forward, threatening a rupture (not very alarming, but unpleasant) with Spain.' H B/XX/S/426.

---

1 The House had sat on the 26th and adjourned at 1:15 *am* on the 27th. See **4387**&n1.

---

1 James Lowther (1840-1904), BA 1863 and MA 1866 Trinity College, Cambridge, a barrister (Inner Temple 1864), a JP, DL and alderman for the North Riding of Yorkshire, would be parliamentary secretary to the poor law board Aug-Dec 1868, under-secretary for the colonies 1874-8, chief secretary for Ireland 1878-80

Lowther is however very violent, &, with such / a name, does infinite harm.[2]
I hope you are gaining health & strength at Folkstone,[3] & I am
Ever yours | obliged | D.

TO: CHARLOTTE, BARONESS LIONEL DE ROTHSCHILD | 4390
Grosvenor Gate [Thursday] 28 March 1867

ORIGINAL: ROTH RFAM C/2/7
PUBLICATION HISTORY: Weintraub *Charlotte and Lionel* 215, dated 28 March 1867
EDITORIAL COMMENT: Black-edged 11 Downing Street paper, imprinted address crossed out and 'Grosr Gate' written in.

Grosr Gate | Mar: 28 1867

Dearest Baroness,[1]
Amid the struggles of my life, the sympathy of those we love is balm; & there is no one I love more than you.
your affectionate | D.

TO: LORD DERBY | Grosvenor Gate, Thursday [28 March 1867] | 4391
ORIGINAL: DBP Box 146/3
EDITORIAL COMMENT: Black-edged 11 Downing Street paper, address crossed out and 'Gros: Gate' written in. *Sic*: a-head. *Dating*: by context; see nn1&3.

Rt Honble | The Earl of Derby | K.G. | Gros: Gate | Thursday
My dear Lord,
Many, many thanks for yr letter, wh: was most kind.[1]

---

and PC 1878. He would be MP (C) for York 1865-80, N Lincolnshire 1881-5 and the Isle of Thanet division of Kent 1888-1904. At second reading of the Reform Bill on 25 March, Lowther had explained the reasons that 'compelled him to entertain fears' about a measure that, 'in its present shape, and still more after the introduction of a compound householder franchise,' would give 'undue preponderance to one class' and lead to 'the utter annihilation of the Constitutional party.' *Hansard* CLXXXVI cols 544-5.

2 'As Lord Houghton (Monckton Milnes) reported to his wife [in May or June 1867], "There is a *mot* of James Lowther's going the round of the town, that he did not see how he could meet his constituents after having refused a moderate measure from a good Christian [Gladstone] and taken an extreme measure from a bad Jew."' Weintraub *Disraeli* 446, 682. Lowther was Lonsdale's kinsman.

3 Lonsdale on 5 March had written from Folkestone that following five weeks of 'a severe & dangerous illness' he was gaining strength and wished to see D upon his return to London. Although he had written to D from Carlton Terrace on the 14th reiterating his wish, he had apparently returned to Folkestone. H B/XXI/L/288, 289.

---

1 Charlotte de Rothschild had written to D on the 27th congratulating him 'with my whole heart on the brilliant success of your beautiful speech [4387n1]. I rejoice to know that it was received with enthusiastic cheers by the unanimous admiration of the House of Commons. Those who had the good fortune to hear you assure me that no triumph was ever more complete and that tories, conservatives[,] whigs, liberals, radicals and nondescripts were equally spell-bound. Lionel thought you looked anxious on Sunday, but he had no misgivings, and both he & I fondly hoped and believed that your marvellous talent in combination with courage & energy still more marvellous would enable you – while making ample concessions – to win a great & glorious victory.' H B/IX/F/83.

---

1 See 4387n3.

I am dying to have a conference with you, & talk over the rocks / a-head – but the budget demands every instant.² I am to see Anderson at D.S. to day at three o'ck: for the final touch – & / shall, certainly, be able to put it before the Cabinet on Saturday.³

But it ought first to be submitted to you – tho' when I cannot say or see.

For tomorrow at three o'ck: / I have some malt-tax figures to talk over.⁴

Yrs ever | D.

4392

TO: [MONTAGU CORRY]   Downing Street, Saturday [30 March 1867]
ORIGINAL: H B/XI/J/14a
EDITORIAL COMMENT: 11 Downing Street paper. Docketed in another hand on the first page: '30 Mar '67'. *Dating*: by context; see n1.

Saturday ½ pt 11

Lord Stanley will receive the Deputation on Tuesday with me.¹ They must not be disappointed. See Lord Barrington about it.²

D.

4393

TO: [MONTAGU CORRY]   Downing Street, Saturday [30 March 1867]
ORIGINAL: H B/XI/J/43
EDITORIAL COMMENT: 11 Downing Street paper. *Dating*: by context; see nn1&2.

Saturday

2 For D's budget speech on 4 April, see **4398**&n1.
3 D would attend a cabinet on Saturday 30 March but Derby, still ill with the gout, would not. Stanley that day would record: 'Cabinet: settled the budget, which deals chiefly with a modification of Gladstone's scheme for the payment of debt: the available surplus is in round numbers £1,250,000. We read and passed a draft despatch of mine, calling on the Spanish govt to make reparation in the case of a vessel called the *Victoria*, seized illegally more than a year ago, and in regard to which they have hitherto disregarded all appeals for justice.' *The Times* (1 Apr 1867); *Disraeli, Derby* 297.
4 In the House on 14 May MP (C) Walter Barttelot would introduce a motion (agreed to) '"That a Select Committee be appointed to inquire into the operation of the Malt Tax."' *Hansard* CLXXXVII cols 526-57 (D 551-5).

---

1 At Downing Street on Tuesday 2 April at 3:30 *pm* Stanley and D would receive a deputation 'from the Reform League, and from Trades, Friendly, Temperance, and other Societies'. Their objections to the proposed reform bill included 'the rate-paying and residential conditions attached to household suffrage', 'the invidious distinctions which the Bill drew between the wealthier householders and the compounders', and 'all the "fancy franchises," including the 20s. direct taxation suffrage.' Replying that the speakers were 'professors of extreme opinions', D called for 'mutual forbearance, mutual concession, mutual conciliation, and mutual compromise.' When dissatisfaction arose following his references to 'a Bill which is based on popular principles' and to a House animated by 'patriotic sentiments', D reassured the deputation that 'when there is a better understanding between the House of Commons and assemblies like the present those murmurs of disapprobation will cease.' *The Times* (3 Apr 1867). Stanley on 2 April would record that Edmond Beales had made 'a long pompous speech with very little in it: I thought him a charlatan ... I saw among the deputation very few faces expressive of fanaticism: they were an ordinary gathering of artisans. Being over 300 in number, and crowded together, the room was intolerable before the meeting ended. – I attended at Ld D.'s request, in his place.' *Disraeli, Derby* 297-8. See **4415**&nn6&7.
2 Presumably D wished Derby to be kept abreast of events via his private secretary, Viscount Barrington (as of 9 February, succeeding his father).

See Gladstone's Questions for Monday.[1] Consult with Fremantle about them.
Did you say Thring was drawing any clauses?[2]
D.

TO: RALPH DISRAELI   Downing Street [Saturday] 30 March 1867   **4394**
ORIGINAL: BL ADD MS 59887 ff93-4
PUBLICATION HISTORY: Bradford 285
EDITORIAL COMMENT: Black-edged 11 Downing Street paper.

30 March 1867

Ralph Disraeli Esqr
My dear Ralph,
I congratulate you; & shall be happy to comply with your request: in person if I can,
/ & if I be alive, wh: is rather doubtful, if the present struggle goes on.[1]
Yours ever, | D.

TO: [LORD STANLEY]   [London, April 1867]   **4395**
ORIGINAL: H B/XIII/22
EDITORIAL COMMENT: An undated note in D's hand docketed in another hand '? April 1867'. *Dating*: by
context; see n1.

All the powers have representatives at Dresden, & the German ~~Constitution~~ ↑Parlia-
ment↓ has decided that the "allied" German Sovereigns are to have an independent
diplomacy, do you mean to do anything?[1]

TO: LORD STANLEY   Grosvenor Gate [Wednesday] 3 April 1867   **4396**
ORIGINAL: H H/LIFE
PUBLICATION HISTORY: M&B IV 470, omitting the last sentence
EDITORIAL COMMENT: From a typescript headed: 'D. to Ld. Stanley, Grosvenor Gate, April 3. '67.'

My dear S.,
Rothschilds have received information, that the Emperor has definitely informed

---

1 In the House on Friday 29 March Gladstone had given notice of a question for D to be asked on 'Monday': whether the Government intended 'to make any alteration in the arrangements or provisions'
of the reform bill prior to discussing its clauses in committee, and whether D was willing to table 'the
Reports or other Documents from which he quoted on Tuesday the opinions of the late and present
Chairmen of the Board of Inland Revenue, with respect to the proposed taxing Franchise?' D on Monday
1 April would reply that he had no intention of tabling 'the communications from which I read freely ...
the other night, but which were strictly of an informal character ... With regard to the other and more
important Question ... to-night I shall put on the Paper a Notice that in Committee of the Whole House
... I shall move the omission of Clause 7 – that is, the clause which proposes to give a second vote'. *Hansard* CLXXXVI cols 819, 907-8.
2 For Henry Thring, see **4368n1**.

---

1 Ralph Disraeli had evidently asked D to stand as godfather to his son Coningsby, born on 25 February.
See **4408**&nn1&2.

---

1 Stanley has replied beneath D's query: 'Wait. S'. Stanley's journals for April 1867 mostly record European
events, in particular developments in Prussia. See *Disraeli, Derby* 297-306, **4541**n1 and **4550**&n5.

Bismarck, that the arrangement between himself and the King of Holland is concluded, and that he shall act at once on it.[1]

What have you heard?[2]

D.

4397 TO: [MONTAGU CORRY]   [London] Thursday [4 April 1867]
ORIGINAL: H B/XI/J/45
EDITORIAL COMMENT: 11 Downing Street paper. *Dating*: by context; see n1.

Thursday

With reference to S Wm Hutts enquiry, I must know, definitively, when I arrive at
D.S. whether the *clause* or *clauses* respec[t]ing Comp: / Householders, will be ready
for the paper tomorrow: whether it be one clause, or more.[1]

Tell Fremantle to *have his* Resol[uti]ons *ready.*

D.

4398 TO: QUEEN VICTORIA   [London, Thursday] 4 April 1867
ORIGINAL: RAC B23 42.

April 4 1867

The Chr of the Excheqr with his humble duty to Yr Majesty:

The Budget was introduced to night, & with complete success. / It was unfolded

---

1 *The Times* on 30 March had announced that 'negotiations between the French Government and that of
the King of the Netherlands have advanced a stage. Holland ... gives up to France her outlying territory
for a consideration of 100,000,000f.' Stanley on this day (3rd) had informed D that 'The Dutch government are willing to sell, if they can get the consent of Prussia. Bismarck says positively that the feeling
of Germany makes it impossible for him to give way. [Prussian minister] Bernstorff has been here this
morning. He expects war – and asks whether we will join! If the Emperor moves, it will be war. At least I
think so.' H B/XX/S/769. William III (in financial straits) had accepted France's offer on 23 March. At
Bismarck's adamant refusal to cooperate, Napoleon III had demanded only the withdrawal of the Prussian garrison (installed at Luxemburg since 1815), but had threatened war if Prussia did not comply.
2 Stanley on 4 April would write to D from the foreign office (at '2.30') that according to Bernstorff, whom
he had met that morning, William III had 'withdrawn from his offer, and the Luxembourg question is at
an end. What dirt for the Emperor to eat! I am not bound to secrecy, and shall make the thing public in
answer to any question that may be asked. I think there can be no doubt of the truth of his story; it is an
official telegram; but I have telegraphed to Cowley for confirmation.' H B/XX/S/770. The so-called 'Luxemburg Crisis' would be resolved by the Treaty of London, which reaffirmed the personal union between
Luxemburg and the Netherlands under the House of Orange-Nassau and demanded the demolition of
Luxemburg City's extensive fortifications (which would take sixteen years). The treaty would be signed
on 11 May 1867 by nine countries (Stanley representing England) and would remain in effect until 1890.
See 4419&nn1,3&5.

---

1 In the House on Thursday 4 April 1867 Sir William Hutt (L) would ask D if, prior to 8 April, 'he will lay
before the House, in a printed form, all the alterations' which the government wished to introduce into
the reform bill. D would reply that he 'did not know of any Government that ever existed which could
tell all the alterations that might be introduced into such a Bill. At present the modifications introduced
by the Government were not so much alterations as additions, and they had reference chiefly to a series
of clauses as to the modes by which the right of compound-householders to claim the franchise should
be established.' D hoped 'to be able to lay them before the House to-morrow, and in the hands of hon.
Members by Saturday.' *Hansard* CLXXXVI col 1105.

in a speech less than an hour; & whether it were that unusual circumstance, or its intrinsic merits, the House, at once, / adopted it; almost with enthusiasm.[1]

The Chr. is impartial in these observations, as he is guilty of having, in 1852, made the / longest Budget speech on record, on wh: Yr Majesty was graciously pleased to send him a letter of condescending approbation.[2]

Since then, there / have been many, & very long, Budget speeches, but he thought the hour, the inevitable hour of Reaction, had arrived / – & he ventured to pay off 24 Mill: of the National debt, &, ↑otherwise,↓ to relieve the commerce of the Country – in fifty minutes. – /

Lord Derby, having apprised Yr Majesty of these details, the C of Exr will not dwell on them.

With regard to the greater business; the struggle is intense.

It / is understood, that Mr Gladstone will certainly move some instruction, or some Resolution, on Monday next, which will be what is called "a trial of strength".[3]

If this movement be / defeated, & the Bill go into Committee, there is no doubt, it will pass, however modified; & the question will be settled.

For / the sake of the Country, & especially for Your Majesty's serenity, it is hoped, that this will be the case.

The Chanr will / keep Yr Majesty as well informed on these matters, as he possibly can, & he will never hesitate to make any sacrifice, consistent / with personal honor, to secure Your Majestys tranquillity.

TO: MARY ANNE DISRAELI   [London] Friday [5 April 1867] **4399**
ORIGINAL: H A/I/A/334
EDITORIAL COMMENT: Docketed by MA on the first page: 'April 5th/67'.

Friday

My dearest Love,

I am detained with much business,[1] & send you this to say, how sorry I am not / to be your guest.

Your own, | D.

---

1 In the House on this day (4th) D had introduced his budget, which had included a proposal to cancel £24,000,000 of the national debt 'by granting Terminable Annuities which shall cease in 1885'. This, he admitted, was 'a simpler description than that recommended to our notice last year by [Gladstone]; but to the merits of which ... the right hon. Gentleman is solely entitled.' After explaining in detail how this would be effected, D had been cheered. According to Stanley, following 'a short confused discussion ... on the whole D.'s plan was approved by the House.' *Hansard* CLXXXVI cols 1110-59 (D 1110-24); *Disraeli, Derby* 298. See **4418**&n2.
2 See VI **2281**&n1. Gladstone had given the longest continuous budget speech on 18 April 1853 (four hours and forty-five minutes); the shortest was by D on this day.
3 See **4400**&n2.

---

1 The session in the House on this day (5th) would adjourn at 1:15 *am* on the 6th. D had stated his intention to retain in the Reform Bill the clause for the use of voting papers, which he hoped would be adopted by the House and in Ireland. *Hansard* CLXXXVI cols 1165-1259 (D 1174).

House of Commons [Monday] 8 April 1867

ORIGINAL: RAC F15 87

PUBLICATION HISTORY: *LQVB* I 414-15; Weintraub *Disraeli* 447, the first sentence of the last paragraph up to 'safe'

EDITORIAL COMMENT: House of Commons paper.

April 8 1867

The Chr of the Exchequer, with his humble duty to Yr Majesty:

One of the most important nights since Yr Majesty's happy / accession.

The House of Commons met under the impression, that one of those great party fights, that decide the fate of Ministries, & / sometimes change the fortune of Empires, was about to take place.

On Sunday, the authentic rumors were, that the Ministry was to be / defeated by a majority of, at least, 45.

About noon, to day, there was a whisper, that a party revolution was at hand, &, about an hour before the Ho: of Comms: met, / a body of members, representing 107 men, & all sections of the Liberal party waited, by their Chairman & other Representatives, on Mr / Gladstone, to inform him, that they must decline to support his motion.[1]

Then a collapse perhaps unequalled in / party & political history, & the result is Your Majesty's government is not only immensely strengthened, but with no fear of subversion: the bill, in all its good & necessary provisions, safe;[2] / & this, in a great degree, nay, mainly, owing to Your Majesty's determined support of Yr Majestys advisers in their difficult enterprise.[3]

---

1 On this day (8th), following a meeting of forty-six dissatisfied Liberals (spearheaded by James Clay) in the Commons tea-room, seven MPs had proceeded to Carlton House Terrace to see Gladstone, who later noted: 'At 3¼ came a Deputation from the conventicle at the H. of C. After them a conclave of members of the late Govt. They were unanimous, & some disposed to go a little beyond me in concession. We went then to H of C. and I saw Coleridge & Osborne: the retreat was effected, perhaps "as well as could be expected".' *The Times* (10 Apr 1867); *Gladstone Diaries* VI 512. For the important repercussions of this so-called Liberal 'tea-room revolt', see **4405**n1.

2 Stanley on this day (8th) recorded that fifty Liberal MPs had met 'to consider what they should do as to Coleridge's (which is in fact Gladstone's) amendment. They decided not to support it: and sent him word accordingly. He thereupon decided to withdraw: saving appearances by retaining the first line of the proposed instruction [that the committee have the power to alter the law of rating], which is quite harmless – indeed, we should probably have moved it ourselves. As this *dénouement* was unforeseen, the surprise on one side, exultation on the other, and perplexity of those who had prepared to take part in a great fight, were ludicrous to see. The causes of this unhoped-for success have been – dislike of Gladstone among his supporters – wish to get the question settled anyhow – and above all, fear of a dissolution.' *Disraeli, Derby* 300. See also *Hansard* CLXXXVI cols 1268-1317 (D 1269-70, 1272, 1276, 1282, 1290-1), the House adjourning at 10 *pm*. For Coleridge's motion, see **4401**n3.

3 General Grey on 9 April would inform D that the Queen was hoping for 'a satisfactory settlement of this question ... for H.M. wd not have you to assume from what happened last night, that a spirit of Conciliation, & a readiness to concede (where Concession is possible without the abandonment of principle) are less necessary than they have been. A single false movement wd. unite a large Majority agst you. – In fact, it was, in all probability, the suspicion that Gladstone was seeking the means of destroying the measure altogether, that caused the defection from him, & any want of conciliation on the part of the Govt., might operate equally injuriously agst. them. Your best policy, H.M. is sure, will be to show moderation in the hour of Victory.' RAC F15 88.

ORIGINAL: H C/XI; identical to Mitford Archives MS 55 f479a f30, of which there is a draft in H B/II/184
PUBLICATION HISTORY: *The Times* (10 Apr 1867), headed 'Mr. Gladstone's Amendments'; *Hansard* CLXXXVI col 1942 (3 May 1867)
EDITORIAL COMMENT: An original for duplication. The published version (see ph) is preceded by 'The Chancellor of the Exchequer has issued the following circular to the supporters of the Government:'.

Downing Street | April 9. 1867

My dear Sir,

Mr Gladstone has given notice of a series of Amendments,[1] wh: he proposes to move, in Committee on the Reform Bill, on Thursday next.[2]

These / amendments are Mr Coleridge's relinquished Instruction in another form.[3]

The first of them relates to the vital question of Residence; & if any one of them be adopted, it will be impossible for / the Government to proceed with the Bill.

I shall, therefore, feel particularly obliged by your attendance in the House of Commons on that evening.[4]

I have the honor to remain, | faithfully yours, | *B. Disraeli*

---

1 *The Times* (see ph) would list Gladstone's amendments: '"In Committee on Representation of the People Bill. Mr. Gladstone, – Clause 3, page 2, line 5, leave out 'two years' and insert 'twelve months.' Same line, leave out 'an inhabitant,' and insert 'the.' Line 6, leave out 'dwelling-house within the borough and,' and insert 'house, shop, or other building, being either separately or jointly with any land within such borough occupied by him as owner, or occupied by him as tenant under the same landlord.' Line 8, leave out from 'has' to 'and,' in line 11, and insert 'such premises must be of the yearly rateable value of 5*l.* or upwards.' And, after the last-named words, insert: – '4. Such occupier must have resided in the borough, or within seven statute miles of some part of the borough, for the six months immediately preceding the said last day of July in such year.'"'

2 In the House in committee on Thursday 11 April Gladstone would 'move in Clause 3 [*Occupation Franchise for Voters in Boroughs*], page 2, lines 3 and 4, after "and 2," to insert, "whether he in person, or his landlord, be rated to the relief of the poor."' *Hansard* CLXXXVI cols 1509-25 (D 1521). This important amendment, one of the key battles of the reform crisis, was intended to admit compound householders on the same terms as personal ratepayers.

3 On 8 April D had informed the House of J.D. Coleridge's 'intention to move the following Resolution: – "That it be an Instruction to the Committee that they have power to alter the law of rating ... And to provide that, in every Parliamentary Borough, the occupiers of tenements below a given rateable value be relieved from liability to personal rating, with a view to fix a line for the Borough Franchise at and above which all occupiers shall be entered on the rate book, and shall have equal facilities for the enjoyment of such Franchise, as a residential occupation Franchise."' The second part having already been withdrawn (as per **4400**n2), D (in his words) had nonetheless 'devoted no inconsiderable time' to it and 'hitherto been unable to put any definite meaning upon it.' *Hansard* CLXXXVI cols 1268-72 (D 1269-70, 1272). John Duke Coleridge (1821-1894), 1st Baron Coleridge 1874, a barrister (Middle Temple 1846) until 1864, recorder of Portsmouth 1855-65, QC 1861 and MP (L) for Exeter 1865-73, Kt 1868, would be sol-gen 1868-71, att-gen 1871-73, DCL (Oxford) 1877, LCJ of Common Pleas 1873-80 and LCJ of England 1880-94.

4 Edward Horsman on 3 May would read the present letter to the House and call attention to two expressions – 'that the provision as to two years' residence is a vital provision, and that if the term be diminished by carrying an Amendment to substitute twelve months, it would be impossible to proceed with the Bill' – and would ask D if his letter was 'authentic' and 'written with the knowledge and sanction of the Cabinet.' D would reply that 'as the author of that letter ... my opinion is that the letter did express the sentiments of my Colleagues, many of whom I had the opportunity of consulting individually before I wrote it.' *Hansard* CLXXXVI cols 1942-5. See **4428**n4.

4402 TO: [MONTAGU CORRY]   [London, Wednesday 10 April 1867]

ORIGINAL: H B/XI/J/16

EDITORIAL COMMENT: Docketed in another hand on the first page: 'Wed. April 10/67'. *Dating*: by context; see nn1&2.

Confidential

The ↑Secret↓ Cabinet tomorrow ↑(Thursday)↓ will be held at the house of Lord Barrington 19 Hertford St. at one o'ck:[1]

 The Law officers shd. be there – not later than ½ pt one.[2]

  D.

4403 TO: GATHORNE HARDY   Downing Street [Friday] 12 April 1867

ORIGINAL: H H/LIFE

PUBLICATION HISTORY: M&B IV 531, undated, omitting the last sentence

EDITORIAL COMMENT: From a typescript headed: 'C. of E., April 12. '67.'

Right Honorable Gathorne Hardy.

My dear Hardy,

You will follow Bright, assuming he follows Roebuck.[1]

 Permit me to intimate, that, without, in the slightest degree, compromising your convictions, it is expedient not to make an unnecessarily uncompromising speech to-night:[2] and with regard to the question on which the Cabinet was so divided this

---

1 Barrington on this day (10th) had written to D from 19 Hertford Street: 'Malmesbury says that it is desirable to have the Cabinet as secret as possible tomorrow, so I have suggested that it *sho[ul]d* take place *here* – He argues that it will be less conspicuous than if you all go to [19] Stratford Place [*Malmesbury's house*] – I have written to each Minister to be *here* at 1-o'clock.' H B/XX/BA/4.

2 Stanley on Thursday 11 April would note a 'Cabinet called to consider a proposal from a large number of the independent Liberals, [John] Hibbert being their spokesman: what they ask is that the person who claims a vote on personal payment of rates shall be liable to pay the reduced rate only, as though he were a compounder. If this were conceded, they would support the principle of personal rating and the limitations as to residence. Pakington and Malmesbury were for yielding, all the rest – and I among the strongest – for refusing all farther concession. So it was settled.' Hardy on 13 April would write about 'the "Secret" meeting wh. I was sorry shd be secret. All but Ld Derby attended. I stated my views on the point for consideration & they were adopted. The debate began on Gladstone's amendment and kept us late.' Hardy had 'insisted on full personal payment of rates by a voter, i.e. that Hibbert's proposals be rejected.' *Disraeli, Derby* 301; *Hardy Diary* 36&n7.

---

1 In the House on this day (12th) Roebuck would speak first and Hardy (see n2) after Horsman and before Bright (see n4), D and Gladstone. Hardy the next day would note, 'I was to have answered Bright but he did not rise and I went home to dine. After I got back Horsman rose & I was tempted to follow him & certainly never was so enthusiastically applauded as I was throughout & the expressions of satisfaction from our friends afterwards were overwhelming.' *Hansard* CLXXXVI cols 1599-1703 (D 1675-88); *Hardy Diary* 36-7. See **4405**&n1.

2 After speaking forcefully against Gladstone's proposed amendment ('to insert the words "whether he in person or his landlord be rated to the relief of the poor"') to Clause 3 (Occupation Franchise for Voters in Boroughs), Hardy (n1) would inveigh against Gladstone's 'tone of contempt ... It is not merely the mellifluous tone of the speaker, but the language, and the meaning, and the bearing of the Gentleman who uses that language that should be borne in mind ... and as for the sordid motives which hon. Members have not thought it unbecoming to impute to those who sit upon this Bench, I repudiate them with all the scorn which Parliamentary language is capable of expressing.'

morning,[3] it seems to me unnecessary to touch on it. It is not really under discussion, and Bright, who will be only declamatory, will scarcely bring it in, or anything like business.[4]

Yours sincerely, D.

TO: **LORD DERBY**   Downing Street, Friday 12 April [1867]   4404
ORIGINAL: DBP Box 146/3
EDITORIAL COMMENT: C of Ex paper. *Dating*: by context; see n3.

Right Honorable | The Earl of Derby | K.G.   Friday | April 12
My dear Lord,

The Cabinet was equally divided, &, as it was a point on wh: absolute union was requisite, of course the matter / ends.[1]

We must rest on my answer to Mr Hibbert[2] last night, wh: fortunately cannot be recalled.[3]

I have prepared our Colleagues tomorrow for / a Cabinet in St Ja[me]s Sqr. at three o'ck:.[4]

Yrs ever, | D.

TO: **QUEEN VICTORIA**   House of Commons, Saturday [13 April 1867]   4405
ORIGINAL: RAC F15 91
EDITORIAL COMMENT: House of Commons paper. Docketed in another hand on the first page: '*13. April*'.
Dating: by context; see n1.

Saturday morning | 2 o'ck:

---

3 The cabinet, which had met on the 11th (see **4402**&n2), had met at noon on this day (12th) and would meet at St James's Square on the 13th. See **4404**nn1&4.
4 John Bright (n1) would close his speech by stating that if D were to settle the reform question 'for the next fifty years upon a broad and generous foundation ... it will make amends for the many mistakes of his political career, especially of the last twenty years.'

---

1 Apparently the cabinet held this day (12th) 'to reopen what had been settled the day before'. *Hardy Diary* 36.
2 John Tomlinson Hibbert (1824-1908), BA 1847, MA 1851 St John's College, Cambridge, a barrister (Inner Temple 1849), a JP 1855 and DL 1870 for Lancashire and MP (L) for Oldham 1862-74, 1877-86 and 1892-5, would be parliamentary secretary to the local government board 1871-4 and 1880-3, under-secretary of the home department 1883-4, financial secretary to the treasury 1884-5 and 1892-5, admiralty secretary 1886, PC 1886 and KCB 1893. He would serve on three commissions (sanitary 1868, boundary 1877 and Welsh Sunday closing 1890) and help pass the Execution Within Gaols Act 1868, Married Women's Property Act 1870, Clergy Disabilities Act 1870 and Municipal Elections Act 1884.
3 Hibbert, who had given notice of an amendment to Clause 3 (Occupation Franchise for Voters in Boroughs), in the House on 11 April had asked D if the government were prepared to accede to his proposition that 'compound-householders [be given] every facility to acquire votes by enabling them to place their names upon the register on paying or tendering the amount of the composition rate upon their houses.' D had replied that although he would gladly entertain suggestions 'as long as those propositions are consistent with the principles ... of personal payment of rates and of adequate residence', it was impossible to give a definite answer. *Hansard* CLXXXVI cols 1486-7 (D 1486-7). See **4431**n3.
4 At Hemsted on 16 April Hardy would note that he had got away 'at 6.15 on Saturday [13th] having been on the point of starting at 2.20 when summoned to a Cabinet.' *Hardy Diary* 37.

The Chr of the Exchequer with his humble duty to Yr Majesty:

He has the satisfaction / to report to Yr Majesty, that in a House of 600 members, Yr Majestys servants / have a majority of 21 –

310 Govt:

289 Opp:[1]

4406

TO: [MONTAGU CORRY]   [House of Commons, Saturday 13 April 1867]
ORIGINAL: H B/XI/J/46
EDITORIAL COMMENT: 11 Downing Street paper. Endorsed in another hand on the first page: 'April 13'. *Dating*: by context; see **4404**&n4.

1 o'ck

I shall expect him at four o'ck – at the latest. I am going to Ld. D. now.

4407

TO: [MONTAGU CORRY]   Grosvenor Gate [Saturday 13 April 1867]
ORIGINAL: H B/XI/J/47
EDITORIAL COMMENT: Endorsed in another hand on the first page: 'April 13'. *Dating*: by context; see **4404**&n4.

G Gate | 2 o'ck:

Returned from Ld D., find there is a Cabinet at his House at three, today. I must see you HERE: so come at / ½ past four, & if I have not returned wait for yr friend.
D.

4408

TO: RALPH DISRAELI   Downing Street [Monday] 15 April 1867
ORIGINAL: BL ADD MS 59887 ff95-6
PUBLICATION HISTORY: Bradford 285-6, the second and third paragraphs
EDITORIAL COMMENT: Black-edged 11 Downing Street paper.

R. Disraeli Esqr   April 15 1867
My dear Ralph,
I thought over our matter yesterday, the first day, that I have really been able to consider it for a moment.[1]

---

1 A long debate in committee on 12 April on Clause 3 (Occupation Franchise for Voters in Boroughs) had ended in a division, at 1:30 *am* on the 13th amidst 'extraordinary excitement', on Gladstone's amendment rejecting the principle of personal payment of rates (defeated), the House adjourning at 2:15 *am* until 2 May. Gladstone called the division 'A smash perhaps without example' and Stanley noted that, 'of Liberals, 45 voted with us, 18 being Adullamites, and 27 supporters of the late govt: 27 stayed away: of Conservatives, there voted against us only 6: how many stayed away is not clear, but I am told about 14 or 15.' Stopping at the Carlton Club – where Sir Matthew Ridley proposed his now famous toast, '"Here's to the man who rode the race, who took the time, who kept the time, and who did the trick"' – D would refuse offers to stay for supper. He walked to Grosvenor Gate, where MA was waiting with champagne and a Fortnum and Mason pie: 'Why, my dear', D supposedly told her, 'you are more like a mistress than a wife.' The Queen would write to Derby on this day (13th) that D 'deserves great praise for the temperate and judicious way in which he has conducted the very difficult discussions in the House of Commons during the past fortnight.' *Hansard* CLXXXVI cols 1599-1703 (D 1675-88); *The Times* (13 Apr 1867); *Gladstone Diaries* VI 513; *Disraeli, Derby* 301; M&B IV 533; Kebbel 40; *LQVB* I 418.

---

1 See **4394**&n1. Ralph Disraeli on 13 April had written to D: 'Will you now be able to give the young Con-

I feel, that for the sake / of the future, it is highly expedient, that nothing should be done without the knowledge & approbation of Mary Anne, & I have never yet had an opportunity of speaking to her on the subject; wh: / cannot be done hurriedly.

I think, therefore, that it will be best for you not to postpone the ceremony. I shall, of course, be gratified, tho' not present, in being a sponsor, & I / trust my god-child may prove a credit to the family.[2]

Yours ever, | D.

TO: **HENRY MANNING** Grosvenor Gate [Tuesday] 16 April 1867 **4409**
ORIGINAL: MANN A619

EDITORIAL COMMENT: Black-edged 11 Downing Street paper, imprinted address crossed out and 'Grosvenor Gate' written in.

Private Grosvenor Gate | April 16 1867

His Grace | The Arch Bp of Westminster[1]

My dear Lord,

I am honored, & gratified, by the receipt of yr Grace's Pastoral,[2] wh: I shall read, especially on the subject, you mention, of / Fenianism, with still greater interest, since I have had the pleasure of becoming acquainted with the writer.[3]

Believe me, with great | consideration | Your faithful Servt, | *B. Disraeli*

---

ingsby his name & be introduced to Dolly & Sybil. It will be all to ourselves, & the hour must be after twelve o'clock, as next week there will be daily service, but I will look to the arrangement when you settle.' H A/I/E/76. The brothers had apparently discussed the possibility of D 'making Coningsby his heir, but Disraeli felt that Mary Anne, being childless and naturally sensitive on the subject, might find such a formal acknowledgement of her failure to bear a child hard to accept.' Bradford 285.

2 Coningsby Ralph Disraeli (1867-1936) would be MP (C) for Altrincham 1892-1906, Royal Berks Hussars 1900-21 (retiring as major), a DL and JP for Bucks, high sheriff 1931-2 and chairman of Governors of the Royal Grammar School in High Wycombe 1911-36 and of the Bucks Archaeological Society. The only Disraeli male heir, he would inherit Hughenden in 1881, marrying Marion Grace Silva in 1897; they would have no children. *The Times* (1 Oct 1936).

---

1 This is D's first extant letter to future cardinal (1875) Henry Edward Manning, who had written on 13 April: 'I should not trouble you with the inclosed [*see* n2] if Lady Gainsborough had not expressed the wish that you may know how we express ourselves about Fenianism. I cannot overstate my anxiety on this subject. Nothing will lessen it but a large & adequate policy for Ireland. I hope you will have the rest of a quiet Easter after the strain of the last days.' H B/XXI/M/160.

2 Manning's 'A Pastoral Letter to the Faithful of the Diocese of Westminster' (1867), paginated 121 to 130 and dated 'Feast of S. Patrick, 1867', countered statements made in a paper published on 16 March and 'addressed especially to my [*Manning's*] Flock in London'. He called 'erroneous and false' its propositions '1. That Fenianism is not condemned by name, and is therefore not condemned at all. 2. That the condemnation of the Church applies to "*oath-bound* societies," and that it therefore does not apply to Fenianism. 3. That Fenianism is not opposed to Catholicity, and is therefore not condemned.' However, Manning expressed sympathy with Irish Catholics: 'many who have become entangled in this sinful rising have done so in full belief that it was a holy cause ... unconscious of doing wrong, misled ... and overpersuaded by evil voices and the false principles I have here exposed ... I grieve for those who are misled by an affection which England counts one of its chief virtues, the love of our country. But the words of our Divine Lord are clear: "All who take the sword shall perish with the sword."' H B/XXI/M/160a.

3 For a fuller treatment of Manning and Fenianism, see Jacqueline Clais-Girard 'The English Catholics and Irish Nationalism 1865-1890: A Tragedy in Five Acts' *Victorian Literature and Culture* 32.1 (March 2004) 177-89, according to which (p 179) Manning also sent his pastoral letter to Gladstone.

4410 TO: CHARLES FREMANTLE   Grosvenor Gate [Wednesday] 17 April 1867
ORIGINAL: H B/XX/D/48
EDITORIAL COMMENT: C of Ex paper, seal crossed out and 'G.G.' written in. *Sic*: Freemantle.

Chas Freemantle | Esq   G.G. | Apr 17 1867
My dear Ftle.
I am now going to Hughenden,[1] & shall always be happy to hear from you.

European Circulation Boxes must be sent down as a general rule: / but America, N. & S., & Japan &c, as a general rule, not: but all this, of course, subject to yr inspection & discretion.

These foreign boxes are generally sent to / G.G. Give yr orders accordingly ↑for the nonce.↓

Yrs | D.

4411 TO: LORD STANLEY   Grosvenor Gate [Wednesday] 17 April 1867
ORIGINAL: H H/LIFE
EDITORIAL COMMENT: From a typescript headed: 'D. to Ld. Stanley, Grosvenor Gate, April 17. '67.' Endorsed by Monypenny in the margin: 'Luxemburg'.

Right Hon'ble Sec: Lord Stanley.
I like Beust's scheme: it would satisfy everybody, if, as appears, Prussia sanctions.[1] Let me have a line to Hughenden, where I am now going, if you think there is anything in it. Your approval, perhaps, would help.[2]

Ever, D.

4412 TO: CHARLES GREY   Grosvenor Gate [Wednesday] 17 April 1867
ORIGINAL: RAC B23 46
EDITORIAL COMMENT: C of Ex paper, seal crossed out and 'Grosvenor Gate' written in.

Genl | Hon: Chas Grey   Grosvenor Gate | April 17 1867
My dear General,
Your letter frightened me. A new vote for Gun Metal!
No vote wanted. See enclosed.[1]

---

1 The DS would be at Hughenden later on this day (17th). H acc.

---

1 Friedrich Ferdinand von Beust was Austrian minister-president as of 7 February 1867. Stanley on 16 April had recorded: 'Telegram from Vienna. Beust has proposed to Prussia that Luxemburg should be ceded to Belgium, Belgium giving up to France an equivalent amount of territory. This proposition is said (I suppose by Beust) to have been well received at Berlin. But it is in direct contradiction to the dispatch read me by Bernstorff yesterday!' In that dispatch, 'Bismarck states that Germany cannot afford to give up Luxemburg on any conditions whatever. This if true would almost of necessity lead to war: but who can tell whether Bismarck means what he says?' *Disraeli, Derby* 301.
2 Stanley would reply on this day (17th) from the foreign office: 'I like Beust's scheme too: but you and I are alone in our taste. Bismarck declared to me through Bernstorff, on Monday, that on no condition whatever would Prussia consent to give up her right of garrison: and the K. of the Belgians on the other hand affirms that nothing shall induce him to consent to the proposed exchange. This does not look like a settlement.' H B/XX/S/771. See **4419**.

---

1 For the vote to purchase old gun metal for the construction of the Albert Memorial, see **4159**&n2. D's

I am off, at this moment, for Hughenden, most happy / to see, once more, my woods, & in a tolerably serene state of mind.

Did Lord Derby ever write to you about the Priv: Sec:? And your contemplated / announcement in the journals?[2]

His severe illness has perhaps made him neglect this. I will write to him.[3] ~~again~~ I spoke to him before, & he seemed / to apprehend no diff[icult]y: but took yr letter from me to consider.

Yrs ever, | D.

TO: **LORD DERBY** Grosvenor Gate [Wednesday] 17 April 1867 **4413**
ORIGINAL: DBP Box 146/3
EDITORIAL COMMENT: C of Ex paper, seal crossed out and 'G. Gate' written in.

G. Gate | April 17 1867

Right Honorable | The Earl of Derby | K.G.
My dear Lord,
I hope Roehampton will be a talisman.[1]
I return H.M's letter.[2]
Did you ever settle anything about General Grey & the Priv. / Secty.?[3]

enclosure has not been found. Grey on 13 April had written to D from Windsor Castle a letter headed '*Private*': 'A doubt has been expressed whether as the whole of the Gun Metal was not actually drawn during the financial year in wh. it was voted, a fresh vote wd. be required for what was left. – I shd imagine not myself – for it seems that is merely a question of where certain material purchased by the Country, was kept till it was wanted. But it is as well to have it ascertained.' H B/XIX/D/20.

2 The Queen on 26 February 1866 had written to Lord Russell that 'General Grey's position should be a *recognised one* – as her Private Secretary,' Grey 'having been the Prince's Private Secretary for twelve years and acted as hers for more than four years – it is absolutely necessary that his position should *now* be recognised'. She had told her equerry Lord Charles FitzRoy on 2 March 1866 that she wished to create 'two distinct offices: her Private Secretary to transact the official business and her Privy Purse for financial duties and those of a more domestic nature.' She had written on 4 March 1866 to Russell that although she accepted his arrangement (Grey and Sir Thomas Biddulph as Joint Keepers of the Privy Purse), 'she would have been better satisfied ... if the *honest* course had been adopted by giving the proper name to the duties which it is admitted that General Grey or someone else *must* perform.' Derby on 25 April 1867 would write to Grey from Roehampton that D had shown him 'some time ago ... a letter from you in which, waiving the question of salary altogether, about which there might be a difficulty, you wished to be recognised as the Queen's Private Secretary. I cannot but think the objection to the appointment the merest pedantry; and if her Majesty desires that a notification of the appointment, subject to that understanding, should be inserted in the Gazette, I will give immediate directions for it.' Grey would reply on the 26th that the Queen was 'much pleased' at Derby's consent to allow his (Grey's) and Biddulph's positions 'to be properly defined ... all that would be required, as it seems to me, would be that some correction of the Gazette as it then appeared should now be made.' *LQVB* I 301-2, 304, 421-2. *The Times* on 1 May would reprint an advertisement from the *London Gazette* of 30 April announcing the appointment of Grey as private secretary and Biddulph as keeper of the privy purse.

3 See **4413**.

---

1 Derby had left St James's Square on 16 April to recover from gout (see n4) at a villa in Roehampton whose rental had been negotiated in August 1866 (see **4215**&n4). Stanley on 18 April would record his first visit to the 'pleasant old-fashioned house, with large grounds well shaded with trees, and a good large garden'. Hawkins *Derby* 346; *Disraeli, Derby* 302.
2 Perhaps the Queen's letter of 13 April; see **4405**n1.
3 See **4412**&n2.

You took the letter he wrote to me on the matter, & on wh: I was to consult you. I have never seen the notification, he contemplated, in the / journals: & perhaps, the business may have escaped yr recollection amid so many cares, & so much suffering.[4]

I hope, for the future, you will have less / of both.

I am now going to Hughenden.

    Ever yours, | D.

Sir John Duckworth wants to be a Commissioner.[5]

4414

TO: LORD BEAUCHAMP   Hughenden [Thursday] 18 April 1867

ORIGINAL: BCP [35]; now BL ADD MS 61892

PUBLICATION HISTORY: M&B IV 528, beginning at the fourth sentence and omitting the last two sentences; Bradford 269; Blake 468, the fourth paragraph and the three first sentences of the fifth paragraph

EDITORIAL COMMENT: Hughenden paper. H B/XIII/139 is a copy of an extract (beginning at the fourth sentence and omitting the last sentence) from this letter on Madresfield Court paper endorsed on the first page: 'Extract from letter of ~~Lo~~ Mr Disraeli to Lord Beauchamp'; and (in a different hand) on the fourth page: 'Mr D. first met Ralph Earle in Paris, where he held some post in the English Embassy.' Docketed in another hand on the fourth page: 'B. Jan 1903'. *Sic*: a-head.

Private   April 18 1867

The | Earl Beauchamp

Dearest Beauchamp,

It gave me great pleasure ↑to hear↓ from you, & so cordially. You always live in my heart.[1]

I long to talk matters over with you. / There are, no doubt, breakers yet a-head – but I feel great hope of overcoming them, & of realizing the dream of my life, & re-establishing Toryism on / a national foundation.

The only black spot in this great business, & wh: I wd. not notice to anyone but yourself, is the treason of Earle![2]

I have known him / for ten years, &c, tho' warned, from the first, by the Cowleys,

---

4 *The Times* on 1 April had noted Derby's absence from Parliament since 28 March 'owing to a slight attack of gout' and on 9 April 'the indisposition which confined [him] to his bed.'

5 Sir John Thomas Buller Duckworth (1809-1887), 2nd Bt 1817, BA 1829 Oriel College, Oxford, major 1st Devon Yeomanry Cavalry 1844, a JP and DL for Devon and sheriff of Devon 1861, had been MP (C) for Exeter 1845-57. For the boundary commission (to which Duckworth would be appointed), see **4448**&n7.

---

1 Beauchamp had written on 16 April from 13 Belgrave Square: 'I have arrived this afternoon in London (having left Rome on Thursday,) & cannot deny myself the pleasure of congratulating you most sincerely on your great Victory of Friday. To triumph with a majority is a task which some have found difficult; it has been reserved for you by tactics most skilful to manipulate at your pleasure an adverse majority & to save the House of Commons from universal ridicule. I have not yet given up sighing after the happy days when I was in the House of Commons & proud to act as one of your humblest lieutenants.' H B/XX/LN/53.

2 Ralph Earle had resigned on 18 March, Hardy noting on the 20th that his 'grievance is not Reform but some quarrel with Disraeli. Each is bitter against the other.' *Hardy Diary* 34. Earle told Sir William Fraser: '"Disraeli and I have quarrelled, as you know: the quarrel is absolutely hopeless: it can never be made up under any circumstances"'. Fraser 365. Earle's 'treason' had occurred in the House on 12 April, when he had voted against his party. On the 11th he had made what would be his only intervention on the reform debate: If the government, he had said, 'addressed themselves to the Conservative party in the country, were they to say with the Chancellor of the Exchequer that popular privileges were not democratic rights,

whom he had treated as he has treated me, I utterly disregarded their intimations, & ascribed them all to prejudice & misapprehension.[3]

I have worked for / his welfare more earnestly than for my own – & do not believe, that I ever, even in the most trying times, gave him a hasty, or unkind, word. I loaded him with favors, & among them, / introduced him to you. I am ashamed of my want of discrimination. But we will not dwell on a disagreeable theme. May we soon meet, & meet often / – & may there ever exist between ↑us↓ those feelings of real ↑sympathy &↓ affection, wh: bind us together.[4]

D.

TO: MONTAGU CORRY   Hughenden, Friday [19 April] 1867   **4415**
ORIGINAL: H B/XI/J/20
PUBLICATION HISTORY: M&B IV 535, dated 'Good Friday', the ninth sentence
EDITORIAL COMMENT: Hughenden paper. Endorsed in another hand on the first page: 'To Rowton Castle' and 'April 19?' *Dating*: by context; Good Friday was 19 April in 1867. D's 'a letter' may mean 'a long letter'. *Sic*: Odgers.

Montagu Corry Esq   Good Friday 1867
Mon ami!
Your letter reached me yesterday afternoon, & gave me great pleasure. Your friends, here, will receive you with open arms; whenever you arrive.[1]

My own prospect of / repose is soon disturbed, as I have just received a telegram from Windsor, summoning me there tomorrow, to stay till Monday. Our gracious Mistress seems in high good humor.[2]

The weather, here, / enchanting, but everything very backward. The beechwoods, &, of course, the oaks, like skeletons, & even the chestnuts are but slightly sprinkled.

---

or with the Secretary for India [Northcote] that household suffrage was a fancy franchise?' The 'great question before them' was whether 'they should leave it to fluctuate according to the caprice of municipal cabals, by adding to the normal constituency a sort of constituency of reserve, which at any moment might be called under arms by the competition of opulent candidates, the violence of political passions, or the corrupt manoeuvres of organized agitation.' *Hansard* CLXXXVI cols 1574-5, 1699.

3 The few extant letters to D from Cowley, ambassador to Paris until July 1867, and his wife, do not mention Earle, who had written to D on 1 June 1857, '"If we cannot reward friends, it is something, at any rate, to be able to punish enemies ... I am very anxious that Ld. Cowley shd. be undone ... If his salary were cut down, he wd. probably resign."' H B/XX/E/17.

4 Beauchamp on 27 April would reply: 'I thoroughly enter into your feelings about Earle. His conduct has bewildered me, & it is no satisfaction that his ingratitude to you has not only injured his prospects now but excited a very strong feeling against him even out of political circles, against which he will probably find it hard to contend hereafter.' H B/XX/LN/54.

---

1 Corry on 17 April had written from Rowton Castle: 'The result of the Parliamentary Sadowa [*see* **4405**] of last week seems likely to be greater than I (in my ignorance) had thought possible. In these remote parts the victory is accepted as decisive, while the prevailing feeling seems to be largely in favour of the Government and the Bill. The tone of the London Newspapers is remarkable, also, the latter part of the first article in the Daily News of yesterday especially – there, you are indeed recognised as master of the situation, which you are and ought to be ... I hope to have the great pleasure of paying a visit to Hughenden on this day week.' H B/XI/J/18, 19.

2 D would be at Windsor Castle on Saturday 20th and return to Hughenden on Monday 22nd. *The Times* (22, 23 Apr 1867); H acc.

It would be mournful, were it not for the forest of young larch, wh: / is very green, & tenderly bright.

I really believe, that Pope Hennessy is Governor of Labuan![3]

I am sorry to say, the Compound Householder has forced his way to Hughen[den], introduced by Lord Cairns.[4] Vale! Illud cognosces profecto, mihi te neque, cariorem, neque jucundiorem, esse quemquam.[5]

D. /

P.S.

I shall count on a letter to welcome me on my return, on Monday, from Windsor.

I see Beales (M.A)[6] is abusing me for saying that I asked questions of the Reform Deputation about the Lodger franchise, & they answered me &c.

He is right: I never asked any question, & never said so in the Ho: of Comm: / It was a blundering report of the "Times" & did not appear in any other paper – I believe.[7]

Had we not a shorthand Report of our own? The statement was made by Odgers,

3 John Pope Hennessy on 17 April had written from London to thank D for speaking to the Duke of Buckingham, which 'has made him think more of my slender claims than all the other friendly hints and letters he got put together.' He would write to D on 25 April: 'The day I got the Duke's letter I wrote to him accepting Labuan. My application was for Queensland; and I trust that you may be able to give me some hope that I may get a better post than Labuan when the vacancies which are expected in the Autumn occur ... the more I find out about Labuan the less I like it. – I now hear that ... the few white inhabitants (about 40 in all) are constant victims to the jungle fever.' He closed with the hope of receiving 'some assurance that Labuan is not to be my ultimate fate'. H B/XXI/H/490-1. *The Times* on 11 May would cite the *Cork Examiner*'s indignation at Hennessy's banishment to 'remote and savage' Labuan, where he would be governor 1867-71.

4 Cairns (Baron Cairns of Garmoyle as of 27 February) on 17 April had written to D about 'the great difficulty, viz. of the Landld being retained as surety for the rate, & being certain therefore to charge the tenant, in the shape of rent, for this suretyship. Hunt admitted to me yesterday that he cd. see no answer to this, if the liability of the Ld.Ld were retained.' H B/XX/CA/13. 'Compound householders' arranged with their landlords to have their property taxes ('rates') included in their rent; see **4431**&n3. Corry (n1) hoped D had been able to dismiss from his thoughts 'our great friend the compound householder. I am sorry to say that I have brought him here with me and that he sometimes rather annoys me in my dreams.'

5 Cicero, *Epistolarum ad Familiares – Letters to Friends* (62-43 BCE) – Book II, the closing sentence of the third letter to C. Scribonius Curio: 'But there is one thing which you will assuredly discover – that nobody in the world is dearer and more delightful to me than yourself.' W. Glynn Williams trans *Cicero. The Letters to his Friends* vol I (1927) 99.

6 Edmond Beales (1803-1881), BA 1825 and MA 1828 Trinity College, Cambridge, a barrister (Middle Temple 1830), had been an equity draftsman and conveyancer and a revising barrister for Middlesex 1862-6. President of the Reform League since March 1865, he would resign on 10 March 1869, the league dissolving formally on the 13th. He would unsuccessfully contest Tower Hamlets in 1868 and in 1870 would be appointed county court judge of circuit 35, comprising Cambridgeshire and Huntingdonshire.

7 *The Times* on 3 April had reported that at D's 2 April meeting with the reform deputation (see **4392**n1), Beales had stated that D 'had claimed to be the father of the lodger franchise. They trusted he would not be so unnatural as to abandon his own offspring. (A laugh.) At all events, without that franchise, they were compelled to say that the Bill could not be made acceptable to the country, and that ... it would be a fruitful source of illwill and discord between different classes.'

who was introduced as one, who cd. speak on the Lodger Franchise.[8] It might be important to get his words; he being a Representative man on the matter.[9]

TO: [SPENCER WALPOLE]   [Hughenden, Saturday 20 April 1867] **4416**
ORIGINAL: HOL [18]

EDITORIAL COMMENT: Docketed in another hand (possibly Walpole's) 'April 1867'. *Dating*: by context; see n1.

I must go,[1] but, of course, you will not publish any proclam[ati]on with[ou]t another Cabinet.[2]

 D

---

8 *The Times* on 8 March 1866 had reprinted from *Punch* a poem, 'What Lord Russell May Be Saying', that included the following: 'Clay's plan, and Hare's plan, / Take them, O working man, / Take them to Beales and to Odgers; / One thing I will do, / Slip in a clause or two, / Giving the franchise to lodgers.' 'Odgers' is London shoemaker and trade unionist George Odger (1813-1877), secretary of the London Trades Council 1862-72, president and then chairman of the council of the International Working Men's Association (founded 1864) until 1871, editor of *Commonwealth* (formerly the *Workman's Advocate*) 1866-7 and one of the best-known speakers and activists of the Reform League.

9 Corry on 21 April would reply from Rowton Castle that D's name was 'in the mouth of every labourer, who without knowing what "Reform" means, or caring, hears that Mr. — has won a great victory. I leave the blank, as it is impossible to express the Protean variety, which a name, revered and cherished by me, here assumes. My private opinion is that my Aunt's carpenter who "heard say that Mr. Disraeli had laid Mr. Gladstone on his back," thinks that you really knocked that godly man down. I have too much jealousy for your fair fame to undeceive him ... I will attend to Odgers at once. We had a short-hand writer there, luckily. To him I will refer.' H B/XI/J/21.

---

1 D on this day (20 April 1867) left Hughenden for Windsor. *The Times* (22 Apr 1867).

2 Walpole on 25 April 1867 would inform D that 'with the concurrence of Lord Derby, & indeed almost at his instigation I have summoned a Cabinet, of which you will receive notice, for Saturday next at 3 o'clock, to consider what steps ought to be taken with reference to the intended meeting in Hyde Park. I am sorry to break in on your repose: but the matter will hardly admit of delay.' H B/XXI/W/73. Stanley on Saturday 27th would record a 'Cabinet at 3 p.m. to consider what shall be done if the reform league persist in holding their meeting in Hyde park, contrary to law. We agreed to issue a proclamation declaring any such meeting illegal, but farther steps were left for consideration.' *Disraeli, Derby* 304. The proclamation (dated 1 May) would be published on 2 May in *The Times*: 'Whereas it has been publicly announced that a meeting will be held in Hyde Park on Monday, the 6th day of May, for the purpose of political discussion; and whereas the use of the Park for the purpose of holding such meeting is not permitted, and interferes with the object for which Her Majesty has been pleased to open the Park for the general enjoyment of her people; now all persons are hereby warned and admonished to abstain from attending, aiding, or taking part in any such meeting, or from entering the Park with a view to attend, aid, or take part in such meeting. S.H. Walpole.' On the same page was an account of the previous day's meeting of the Reform League, at which police had distributed copies of the proclamation (which was read aloud by Edmond Beales); the chairman had entreated members to come to the park '"as loyal, peaceful, and orderly citizens, enemies of all riot and tumult"' while pointing out that the fault for any disturbance 'would lie with those who employed force to prevent the peaceful exercise of a right.' In the adjacent column was a letter (dated 1 May) by Beales questioning the announcement (on 30 April) in another paper that the Government would '"take active and strenuous measures for the suppression"' of the 6 May meeting. He thought this an inexplicable measure, given that no such official announcement had been made and especially in light of Walpole's 'admirable conduct' on 25 July 1866 (see **4158**n1 and **4498**&n2).

TO: MARY ANNE DISRAELI   Windsor [Sunday] 21 April 1867
ORIGINAL: H A/I/A/335
EDITORIAL COMMENT: Windsor Castle paper.

April 21 1867

My dearest Wife,

We had a very agreeable dinner yesterday of eight: H.M. the Princess Louise, next to whom I sate, Prince Christian,[1] Prince Arthur,[2] a lady in weeds to whom I was / presented, but whose name I cd. not catch, Genl. Grey & Lady Churchill. There was so much conversation, that between talking & listening, I got nothing to eat, & woke in the night very hungry. H.M. was most gracious & congratulated me on all / that had happened, & said she wd. give me an audience today, after Church.

I had a good night. The Princess Louise had been to see the Blacas Collection, of wh: she was very full. She likes Mr Newton, who seems to be / known to the Royal family.[3]

Prince Arthur intelligent, well-bred – & has travelled a great deal – in Asia Minor, where he visited Cnidus, wh: Mr Newton excavated, tho' Mr N. was not there then.[4]

I write this early, as I have many despatches from Ld. Stanley wh: must be returned immediately: affairs very critical.[5]

Your own, | D.

4418 TO: GATHORNE HARDY   Windsor, Sunday [21 April] 1867
ORIGINAL: H H/LIFE
EDITORIAL COMMENT: From a typescript headed: 'Windsor Castle, Eáster Sunday, '67.' *Dating*: Easter Sunday was 21 April in 1867, and by context; see n1.

Right Honorable Gathorne Hardy.

..... Foreign affairs are very queer. I sometimes fear the worst is at hand.[1] It is very

---

1 Frederick Christian Karl August (1831-1917), Prince Christian of Schleswig-Holstein, was the son of Christian August, Duke of Schleswig-Holstein-Sonderburg-Augustenburg and of the Countess Louise Sophie of Danneskjold-Samsøe, now Duchess Louise. Prior to his marriage on 5 July 1866 to the Princess Helena, now Princess Christian, the Queen had granted him the qualification of 'Royal Highness'. A KG 1866 and PC 1894, he was maj-gen 1866, lieut-gen 1874 and gen 1877 in the British Army. In 1897 he would become the Queen's personal aide-de-camp.
2 Arthur William Patrick Albert (1850-1942), 1st Duke of Connaught and Strathearn and Earl of Sussex 1874, the Queen's third and favourite son, entered the Royal Military Academy at Woolwich in 1867. He would be commander-in-chief of the Bombay army 1886-90 and inspector-general of the Forces 1904-7, marrying the Princess Louise Margaret of Prussia in 1879 and serving as governor-general of Canada 1911-16.
3 For the Blacas collection and C.T. Newton, see 4275&n2 and 4269&nn1&5. *The Times* on 8 February, describing the collection, had praised D for having shown 'an appreciation of the claims which archaeology and objects of classical art have upon the Treasury, which other Chancellors, not less accomplished, have certainly not with equal readiness acknowledged.'
4 The Greek city of Cnidus (or Knidos) in Anatolia (now Tekir in Turkey) had been excavated by Newton in 1857-8.
5 These despatches most likely included Stanley's 17 April letter; see 4411n2.

---

1 Hardy on 25 April would record that 'War threatens abroad & Disraeli in a letter to me uses very ominous language on the subject. I hope it may not be after all for it will be no easy matter to keep out of it.' *Hardy Diary* 37.

lucky, or, let us say, it was very wise, that we took off no taxes this year, and established our credit, in case we have to go into the Market as borrowers.[2]

My compliments to Mrs. Hardy.[3]

Yours sincerely, D.

TO: LORD STANLEY   Windsor, Monday 22 April 1867 4419
ORIGINAL: H H/LIFE
PUBLICATION HISTORY: M&B IV 470-1, omitting the last three paragraphs
EDITORIAL COMMENT: From a typescript headed: 'D. to Ld. Stanley, Windsor Castle, Easter Monday, April 22.' *Sic*: Brunow; Torren's.

My dear Secretary,

My visit here has tumbled me into the midst of the Luxembourg business; and I have had all the despatches, and all the private letters of all the cousins, submitted to me: and you know all the rest.[1]

I assured our Royal Mistress, and most sincerely, that she was quite under a mistake in supposing that you would not act, if necessary, and that, I knew, you had well considered all the eventualities about Belgium; that you would never act without determination and constancy; and that anything you did, or said, would have double the effect of the old stagers with their mechanical interference; sometimes bluster and sometimes blundering.

I told Her Majesty also, that we were not really half a Government until the division of last Friday,[2] and that a hint from you could, and would, do more now, than reams of despatches a month ago.

I think she understood all this: and I think I did good.

I pointed out also, that, so far as matters went, the question of Belgium was really not on the tapis. This, after reflection, she agreed to: but still thought that, in confidential conversation, our people might let it be known at Berlin and Paris, that the violation of Belgian neutrality should not pass with impunity.[3]

---

2 In the House on 4 April, in introducing his budget, D had dealt with taxes at length, emphasizing that, with the exception of the malt tax, there was no particular tax 'that unduly interferes with the industry of any portion of the community, or which from its severe and unequal pressure demands our immediate attention ... I maintain that, generally speaking, there is no particular tax ... which demands, before any other, special consideration or immediate attention.' *Hansard* CLXXXVI col 1114. See **4419**.

3 Hardy on 29 March 1838 in Ireland had married Jane Orr (d 1897), third daughter of James Orr of Holywood House, co Down. She would be styled Viscountess Cranbrook of Hemsted in 1878 and Countess of Cranbrook in 1892. Eight of their eleven children would survive to adulthood.

---

1 The Queen on 17 April had recorded in her journal that her cousin Leopold II, King of the Belgians, had sent her 'two most anxious letters', according to which 'the Emperor was very conciliatory and most anxious to meet Prussia halfway, if only she would evacuate the fortress [of Luxemburg]. The Emperor wanted *no* territory. The thing would be to press Prussia, and *we* ought to do that. Leopold was likewise most anxious that it should be *clearly* understood that England would fight for Belgium, if attacked. I promised to do all I could.' On this day (22nd) she recorded that she had written to the King of Prussia 'urging him to be as conciliatory as France was, and not let the whole responsibility of a cruel war fall on Prussia.' On the 25th Derby would write to General Grey that Stanley had shown him a copy of the Queen's letter; 'I greatly fear, however, that even her Majesty's intervention will be unsuccessful.' *LQVB* I 418-21.

2 The House had last met on Friday 12 April (see **4405**&n1) before adjourning for Easter recess.

3 The Queen on 19 April had written to Derby 'most anxious at the danger which appears to be impending

At present it seems the pressure should rather be put upon Berlin, than on the ancient capital of Julian the Apostate.[4]

Two things seem to me clear: that France is not prepared, and that Bismarck lies to everyone. His explanations prove his perfidy.[5]

I think, myself, as old Brunow says, "it is time for a little re-action", and that we might begin to dictate a little to Europe. Gladstonism is at a discount.[6]

It's very lucky, however, we didn't take off any taxes: and that by paying off some debt, we shall be able to borrow any amount at a very moderate price. That is to say, in case we want it.[7] Nevertheless, as nothing happens which one expects, I begin to believe you will turn out a regular Chatham.[8]

As for domestic affairs, we ought to carry our Reform now in a canter, if all I hear be true.

We can't take Torren's Lodger: and I doubt whether the House will take him at any rate or rent.[9]

I wish, in the interval of settling the affairs of Europe, you would get up an Anti-Lodger speech, or a speech on the subject either way;[10] as I think our debates want a little variety, and the House will get wearied of the eternal partridge[11] of

over Belgium ... Though *all* the *other* Powers should stand *aloof,* England in such a case MUST NOT stand aloof.' England was '*determined* to fulfil her obligations, and (*even single-handed* if need be) to defend the Independence of Belgium with the whole strength of the British Empire.' She felt '*very* strongly on the subject, and will not, if she can help it, be a party to the national disgrace that England would incur, if she stood by passively, while *such* an act of violence as the seizure of Belgian territory by France, was perpetrated.' *LQVB* I 419-20.

4 Flavius Claudius Julianus (331-363), the last non-Christian Roman emperor (360-3), known as Julian the Apostate because he rejected Christianity in favour of neoplatonic paganism, was proclaimed emperor in Lutetia (Paris).

5 Bismarck had stated recently that he would make no concession with regard to Luxemburg, or consent to its neutralization, or withdraw his troops from the fortress, or admit that the question was open to negotiation. *The Times* (19 Apr 1867).

6 Baron Philip von Brunnow was Russian ambassador in London. D appears to be using 'Gladstonism' as shorthand for a reluctance to get involved in international disputes.

7 See **4418**&n2.

8 William Pitt the Elder, 1st Earl of Chatham, was secretary of state 1756-61. See **4513**.

9 In the House on 6 May Torrens would move 'a franchise for lodgings which would let unfurnished for the sum of £10 yearly. He did not ask the House to go lower in amount than the Chancellor of the Exchequer went when he proposed a £20 furnished franchise, as, on an average, furnished lodgings were worth about twice as much as lodgings not furnished.' *Hansard* CLXXXVII cols 28-32. According to Smith (193), D 'initiated a secret conference with Torrens to seek a compromise at £15. But Torrens held to £10, for he knew that he could outbid Disraeli for the freebooters' votes.' William Torrens McCullagh Torrens (1813-1894), BA 1833 and LLB 1842 Trinity College, Dublin, an Irish barrister (King's Inns 1836), commissioner of the Irish Poor Inquiry 1834 and co-founder of the first Irish mechanics' institute in Dublin, was (radical) MP (L) for Dundalk 1848-52, Yarmouth 1857 and Finsbury 1865-85. His works include *The Industrial History of Free Nations* (1846) and *Our Empire in Asia: How we Came by it: a Book of Confessions* (1872).

10 Stanley on 23 April would reply from the foreign office with a letter headed '*Private.*': 'Thanks for your letter ... We must carefully consider what we do about the lodger franchise. I am so deeply pledged to the principle that I cannot speak against it; but we may fix the limit where we please. I think £15 would do no harm. It would swamp only constituencies which are already as radical as they well can be. – I think our bill, or at least a bill, is safe.' H B/XX/S/772.

11 For the origins of the French expression '*perdrix, toujours perdrix*' ('partridge, always partridge'), too much of the same thing, see *Brewer's Dictionary of Phrase and Fable* (1970) 821-2.

Your affectionate Colleague, | The Chancellor of the Exchequer.[12]

TO: [LADY GAINSBOROUGH?] Windsor [Monday 22] April 1867 **4420**
ORIGINAL: EDE [1]
EDITORIAL COMMENT: From a transcript made by J.P. Matthews. *Recipient*: see **4429**&n1. *Dating*: 'April 20'
may be a transcription error, as D left Windsor on the 22nd; see **4415**&n2.

Private Windsor Castle | April 20 1867

I could not call again, as I left town on Wednesday morning.

I earnestly hope you are better.

My hopes, and plans, of a little repose, have been, hitherto, baffled, for / I had scarcely reached Hughenden, when I was summoned here – however, I shall return home this afternoon.

External affairs are very critical indeed.[1] I hope, now, we shall be / able to settle our domestic ones – at least with the aid of yr. prayers – and, then, we may give our mind earnestly to foreign matters.

It is impossible, that Gladstone can be acting / from pique, it must be a ruse to revive, or to create, some enthusiasm. I doubt its success.[2]

I shall be in town in less than a week, and shall try to see you very soon.

Your servt | D.

TO: MR BRIXY Hughenden [Tuesday] 23 April 1867 **4421**
ORIGINAL: BRN [40]
COVER: Mr Brixy | Grosr Gate.

For Mr Brixy | Grosvenor Gate. Hughenden Manor | Apl 23. 1867

---

12 Stanley (n10) would tell D that it 'is satisfactory to see that even the dulness of a Windsor visit has not affected your spirits. H.M. has written to the K. of Prussia in the strongest terms that can be used, deprecating war and advising him to give way. The Belgian influence has helped to bring about this interference: Leopold thinks that if a war were to break out, it would very probably end in France getting Belgium and Prussia Holland. I am ready to go as far as may be necessary in support of Belgium, short of giving an absolute pledge to fight for its independence. Suppose we gave such a pledge, that France and Prussia came to an understanding, Russia and Austria standing aloof, where should we be? But I say nothing in an opposite sense, lest we should lose our influence. The neutralisation of Luxemburg is the one indispensable condition of peace. If that can be obtained from Prussia, arrangements of detail may be easily made. Bismarck has chosen this time of all times to go off into the country. He returns tomorrow, when Loftus will see him. The French say they can put 40,000 men into the field. Our reports give them from 300,000 to 350,000. Excitement at Paris very great.'

1 On this day (20th) *The Times* observed that Prussia was determined not to evacuate Luxemburg under any circumstances, and Stanley noted that Moustier 'urges strongly that we should interfere, thinks the maintenance of peace may depend on it.' *Disraeli, Derby* 303.

2 D may have heard rumours of Gladstone's new agenda following the 12 April division (see **4405**&n1), when many of his party voted against his amendment. *The Times* on the 22nd would publish a letter from Gladstone, dated 18 April, stating that he would '"not proceed with the amendments now on the paper in my name, nor give notice of other amendments such as I had contemplated."' *The Times* asked 'whether the resolution to abstain from interference be due to the despondency incident on defeat or to pique at the desertion of a section of his followers.' Stanley on the 21st would note the rumour that Gladstone 'has cast in his lot with the extreme party, and is little concerned at the prospect of a rupture with the old Whig families.' *Disraeli, Derby* 303.

This is the case of Razors you gave me just before I left town.[1]
Neither of them will cut in the least: I am very much inconvenienced.
D.

4422   TO: [MONTAGU CORRY]   Hughenden [Tuesday] 23 April 1867
ORIGINAL: H B/XX/D/41
EDITORIAL COMMENT: Hughenden paper.

April 23 1867

We count on embracing you tomorrow.[1]

I had a most interesting visit to Windsor, & returned with signal marks of Royal favor, wh: you will look at with / interest on yr arrival here – no less, than a copy of the Memoir of the Prince Consort written under the immediate super-intendence of the Queen, & greatly by / her own pen. It is a splendid volume, very richly illustrated, & extremely interesting.[2]

There are only 100 copies printed, & it is specifically mentioned, that they are reserved for the various members of / the Family & for the Queen's "personal friends."[3] I have so much to talk about, that I will not attempt to write.

D.

I am obliged to send you some letters wh: must be answered imme[diate]ly – ~~they~~ the rest will keep.

D

4423   TO: QUEEN VICTORIA   [London, Saturday] 27 April [1867]
ORIGINAL: H H/LIFE
EDITORIAL COMMENT: From a MS copy on paper imprinted 'Windsor Castle' and headed: '1866-67 D. to the Queen.' *Dating*: by context; see n1.

April 27

---

1 D had left Grosvenor Gate ('town') for Hughenden on the 17th. Mr Brixy may be the Grosvenor Gate valet or butler.

---

1 Corry planned to visit Hughenden on the 24th; see **4415**n1. Writing on the 21st from Rowton Castle (see **4415**n9), he had told D, 'It is probable that I shall tomorrow send you a budget from Downing St. where I shall arrive at about 3. P.M. I trust your visit to Her Most Gracious Majesty has been in every way agreeable & satisfactory to you.' H B/XI/J/21.

2 *The Early Years of His Royal Highness the Prince Consort, Compiled Under the Direction of Her Majesty the Queen* (1867) by Charles Grey. A leader in *The Times* on 27 July, announcing the book's publication and printing lengthy extracts, would describe the volume as 'containing the most unreserved description of the life and character of the Prince, and even laying open to us, in great measure, the private thoughts and feelings of the Queen herself during the period over which the volume extends.' Hughenden Library has the Smith, Elder & Co edition published in 1866 for private circulation.

3 In a letter to the Queen prefixed to his book, Grey had written: '"As I believe your Majesty intends to limit the circulation of this volume to your Majesty's own children and family, or, if it goes beyond them, to a very small circle of personal friends, I have not thought it necessary to omit any of the very interesting and private details contained in your Majesty's memoranda, or to withhold the touching expressions of your Majesty's feelings as given in your Majesty's own words."' *The Times* (27 Jul 1867).

France desires peace.[1] I do not feel [the] same conviction as to Bismarck![2]

TO: QUEEN VICTORIA   [London, Tuesday] 30 April 1867   **4424**
ORIGINAL: RAC B23 51.

April 30 1867

The Chanr of the Exr with his humble duty to Yr Majesty:

The motion of Mr Trevelyan (son of Sir Chas Trevelyan)[1] for / terminating the Purchase System in the Army, was defeated, this evening, by a sufficient majority.[2]

The division was called at the dinner hour, when the House was / thin, but the numbers were 75 to 116: tho' a surprise was attempted.

Just before the division, affairs were nervous.

Mr Trevelyan made an able speech: a young man, clever but conceited: but, / perhaps, everyone has a right to be conceited – until he is successful.

Mr. Stanley (Ld. Derby's son)[3] made his maiden speech: against purchase.[4] It was neither clever, nor conceited: a stick.[5]

1 One report (24 April) from Paris had noted 'that while Paris is full of rumours of wars, the French Foreign-office exhibits the utmost serenity, and seems to scout the notion of peace being disturbed'. Another (26 April) had called attention to an article in the *Constitutionnel*, signed by the editor but 'evidently of official origin, and there are even traces of the hand of the Emperor himself,' stating that France's 'feeling from the very outset has been, and still is, a policy of peace and conciliation.' *The Times* (25, 27 Apr 1867).
2 See **4419**&n5.

---

1 George Otto Trevelyan (1838-1928), who would succeed his father as 2nd Bt in 1886, was MP (L) for Tynemouth 1865-8, Hawick district 1868-86 and Bridgeton division of Glasgow 1887-97, when he would accept the Chiltern Hundreds. He would be a civil lord of the admiralty 1868-70, secretary to the admiralty 1880-2, chief secretary for Ireland 1882-4, chancellor of the Duchy of Lancaster 1884-5, secretary for Scotland Jan-Mar 1886 (resigning over home rule) and 1892-5, PC 1882, LLD Edinburgh 1883, DCL Oxford 1885 and OM 1911. Trevelyan's works include *Cawnpore* (1865), *Life and Letters of Lord Macaulay* (1876, 2 vols), *The Early History of Charles James Fox* (1880) and *The American Revolution* (1909, 4 vols).
2 In the House on this day (30th), during debate on 'Army – Purchase of Commissions', Trevelyan had moved that 'the system of purchasing Commissions in the Army tends greatly to diminish the efficiency of our Military Force.' He had closed by stating that in England's small army 'every officer should be zealous, intelligent, and skilful in his profession; and this result will never be produced until our officers owe their promotion, not to pounds, shillings, and pence, but to zeal and intelligence, and professional experience and skill.' *Hansard* CLXXXVI cols 1787-1825.
3 Derby's second son, Frederick Arthur Stanley (1841-1908), Baron Stanley of Preston 1886 and 16th Earl of Derby 1893, JP for Lancashire and Westmoreland, Grenadier Guards 1858-65, col of 3rd and 4th battalions of the King's Own Royal Lancaster regiment and of the 1st volunteer battalion of the Liverpool regiment, was MP (C) for Preston 1865-8 and Lancashire N 1868-85. He would be a civil lord of the admiralty 1868-70, financial secretary of war 1874-7 and of the treasury 1877-8, secretary of state for war 1878-80, GCB 1880, colonial secretary 1885-6, president of the board of trade 1886-8, gov-gen of Canada 1888-93, lord mayor of Liverpool 1895-6, KG 1897 and LL of Lancaster 1897-1908. Stanley would abolish flogging in the army by the Army Discipline Regulation Bill 1879. In 1892, at a sports banquet in Ottawa, he would state his intention to donate a bowl to be awarded annually to the best amateur hockey team in Canada. The Stanley Cup would be presented for the first time in 1893.
4 Frederick Stanley (n2) had suggested that increasing 'promotions from the ranks' would ensure that a large number of officers 'would be fully conversant with the wants and habits of the men under them' and that 'a higher standard of military knowledge would be, as it were, forced into the profession.' He closed with the hope that 'the army would cease to be the only service in which responsible positions could be purchased for a sum of money.'
5 Oratory was not Stanley's forte. On 6 August 1875 D would write to Cairns that 'F. Stanley [is] a stick – at least at speaking, & an Irish Secy shd have the gift of the gab.' PRO Cairns 30/51/51 ff123-6.

4425

TO: MARY ANNE DISRAELI   [London, Wednesday 1 May 1867?]

ORIGINAL: H A/I/A/331

EDITORIAL COMMENT: *Dating*: conjectural; see **4426**&n2.

My dearest,

It is Levée Dress – or Trinity.

    In haste[.]

      Yrs ever | D.

4426

TO: [MONTAGU CORRY]   Downing Street [Wednesday 1 May 1867]

ORIGINAL: H B/XI/J/34

EDITORIAL COMMENT: C of Ex paper. Docketed in another hand on the first page: '1867'. *Dating*: by context; see nn1&2. *Sic*: leveé.

See if you can prepare a memdum for tomorrow as regards "residence" how the bill would exactly act as to precise term[inology]: how in / the existing law? &c. &c.[1]

    D.

I will hope to see you betn. leveé & Cabinet.[2]

4427

TO: [MONTAGU CORRY]   [Downing Street, Thursday 2 May 1867]

ORIGINAL: H B/XI/J/49

EDITORIAL COMMENT: A note by D written at the end of a note, on C of Ex paper and dated Thursday 2 May, from Montagu Corry, endorsed in another hand on the first page: '? 1867'. *Dating*: by context; see n1.

I will see you in the little room for an instant[.][1]

    D.

4428

TO: QUEEN VICTORIA   House of Commons [Thursday] 2 May 1867

ORIGINAL: RAC F15 97

EDITORIAL COMMENT: House of Commons paper.

May 2 1867

The Chanr of the Exchqr with his humble duty to Yr Majesty:

    Your Majestys Governmt was defeated this evening, by a large majority, / in Committee, on the Reform Bill: on the question of Residence, as part of the qualification for a Borough Vote.[1]

---

1 See **4428**&nn1&4.

2 On 1 May 1867 D would attend the Queen's levée and a cabinet. *The Times* (2 May 1867).

---

1 Corry's note (see ec) reads: 'I am about to return to Thring, unless you want me, and shall be here in less than an hour. We are preparing all necessary notes. M.C.'

---

1 In the House in committee on this day (2nd) independent radical A.S. Ayrton had moved an amendment to Clause 3 (Occupation Franchise for Voters in Boroughs) 'to leave out the words "two years," and insert the words "twelve months," as the period of residence for compound-householders.' D spoke only once, immediately following the division (278-197): 'After the grave decision at which the Committee has

The point, tho' not / unimportant, was not vital; & was so treated, & understood.[2]

The Chr of Exr. has summoned a Cabinet tomorrow,[3] when Y. M. Ministers will / decide upon some communication to be made to the House of Commons at four o'ck:[4]

TO: [LADY GAINSBOROUGH?]   Grosvenor Gate, Saturday 4 May [1867]   **4429**

ORIGINAL: MOPSIK [133]

EDITORIAL COMMENT: C of Ex paper, seal crossed out and 'G.G.' written in. *Dating*: by context; see n1.

G.G. | Saturday May 4

Dear Saint![1]

Things are not so bad as they seem. I cannot come, scarcely write – & only to you. I have not time for sleep or / food.[2]

The division of Thursday, (tho' it seem strange ↑to say so↓,) is rather working in our favor. It was not the real battle, wh: is at hand. On Monday, or / Thursday next, or about those days, there will be a great encounter – an Armageddon – & if we win, we may, &, probably, shall, be established for years.[3] / The chances are not bad – tho' most critical. Now is the time for our friends to aid ↑us↓.

arrived, it is not in my power, without consultation with my Colleagues, to proceed with the Bill. Therefore, I beg to move that the Chairman report Progress, and ask leave to sit again.' *Hansard* CLXXXVI cols 1879-1912 (D 1912).

2 General Grey, writing on 4 May from Osborne, would inform D˙that the Queen 'was very sorry to hear of the defeat of the Govt. by so large a Majority, though rejoiced to find that you did not consider the point on which you were beat, vital.' She hoped that D would avoid 'the mistake made by the late Govt., & should further amendments be carried against you, in a way to show that they are in accordance with the feeling of the House & of the Country, that you will not refuse to accept them, & thus again postpone the settlement of this question, as Lord Russell did, the Queen thinks, so unnecessarily, last year.' H B/ XIX/D/24.

3 Stanley on 3 May would attend a cabinet meeting from 1 to 2:30 *pm* 'on reform and the threatened Hyde Park riot: agreed to have a meeting of the party on Monday, the situation being critical.' *Disraeli, Derby* 306.

4 In the House on 3 May D would express regret at the previous day's 'misconception ... not merely on one side of the House with regard to the character of the qualification as to residence,' whose merit 'depends upon the principle, not of numbers, but of locality.' Although they deferred to the opinion of the House, his colleagues wished 'to establish a borough franchise upon the principle of *bonâ fide* rating and *bonâ fide* residence.' D thus proposed to insert two clarifying phrases in the third and fourth sections of Clause 3. *Hansard* CLXXXVI cols 1939-45.

---

1 Most likely Lady Adelaide (Ida) Harriet Augusta, Countess of Gainsborough, who would die on 22 October 1867. Her daughter, Lady Blanche Noel, would write to D on 25 October: 'You used to call my darling mother, your *patron Saint*, if I remember right – think of her now as your guardian angel ... she died like a saint, she is lovely as a saint now ... Remember how fond she was of you!' In an undated letter (docketed '?1867') Lady Gainsborough had written to D: 'I have just returned to London, & am deeply grieved by the bad news of last night [*see* **4428**]. I tremble for the fate of our Government, & scarcely know *what* to pray for, or what to hope. May God help, guide & lead you ... I hope I shall see you soon.' H B/ XXI/N/152; G/37.

2 On this day (4th) D attended a cabinet, received (with Derby) a deputation from the University of Glasgow and spoke briefly at a Royal Academy banquet. MP (6 May 1867); *The Times* (6, 7 May 1867).

3 See **4431**&n3 and **4433**&n1.

Ld. Derby has summoned his friends for Monday at one o'ck to address them.[4]
Your Servt | D.

4430   TO: [MONTAGU CORRY]   Downing Street, Sunday [5 May 1867]
ORIGINAL: H B/XI/J/32
EDITORIAL COMMENT: C of Ex paper. *Dating*: by context; see nn1&3&4.

Sunday

Mon Ami!

Call on me today, if you can conveniently, at three o'ck:[1] as I am anxious to hear your bulletin as to Comp: Hous:[2]

I ~~saw~~ met Ld Cairns at the / Academy dinner,[3] & he spoke of you with great praise.

I hope you have not made an appointment with the Lord Adv: tomorrow, for Ld Derby's / meeting is at one o'ck:, wh: I had forgotten[.][4]

D.

I met Dalglish at the dinner, & had a confidl convers[ati]on with him.[5]

4431   TO: QUEEN VICTORIA   House of Commons [Monday] 6 May 1867
ORIGINAL: RAC F15 104
PUBLICATION HISTORY: *LQVB* I 424
EDITORIAL COMMENT: House of Commons paper.

May 6 1867

The Chr of the Exchequer with his humble duty to Yr Majesty:[1]

He has had a long, & most earnest conversation with Lord Stanley, this / evening, & has great hopes, that the Secy. will accept the proposition of General Guarantee.

---

4 Gathorne Hardy on 7 May would note that the previous day's meeting at St James's Square had begun 'threateningly & people even said we must go out. He [Derby] explained the Hyde Park affair pretty well to their satisfaction & the compound householder also.' *The Times* would note 'the usual busy rumours' at the meeting: 'The Government had resolved, it was whispered, on self-immolation, and was rather grateful than otherwise for the chance of being delivered from an onerous task.' 225 members attended. *Hardy Diary* 38; *The Times* and *MP* (7 May 1867).

1 Corry on this day (5th) had written to D: 'These clauses are the result of yesterday's consultation, printed for your consideration. I shall hope to find you at home, earlier than last Sunday.' H B/XI/J/24.
2 See **4431**&nn1&3.
3 D and Cairns on Saturday 4 May 1867 had attended the anniversary banquet at the Royal Academy, where D had paired the Academy and the Commons as 'ancient institutions' that had been 'very much criticized ... [and] occasionally reformed. (Loud cheers and laughter.)' but that remained 'among the most flourishing and popular institutions of the country.' *The Times* (6 May 1867).
4 For the meeting at St James's Square on Monday 6 May, see **4429**n4.
5 Robert Dalglish (1808–1880), educated at the University of Glasgow and head of the Glasgow calico printing firm of R. Dalglish, Falconer and Co, was MP (L) for Glasgow 1857-74. He was 'an independent Radical, in favour of extension of the franchise, vote by ballot, [and] a more equal distribution of electoral districts.' Glasgow Digital Library.

1 General Grey on 5 May had written to D from Osborne that the Queen feared D was 'preparing for yourself a probable, if not a certain, defeat, by the way in which you propose to deal with the Compound Householders; and if the hope of preserving Peace by means of a Conference is disappointed owing to the refusal of England to join in the Guarantee of the neutrality of Luxemburg which the other

The Chr of the Excheqr impressed upon him, that / he misconceived public feeling, & that both the House of Commons, the City of London, & Society generally, were in favor of Peace / at the price of general guarantee.[2]

The Chr of Exchequer has also the gratification to inform H.M. that his solution of the Compound / Householder difficulty was received with great favor by the House – at least, by all independent sections of the Opposition, & the general / opinion is, that the Reform Bill is now safe.[3]

TO: [MONTAGU CORRY?]   Downing Street, Wednesday [8? May 1867]   **4432**
ORIGINAL: H C/II/A/32b
EDITORIAL COMMENT: C of Ex paper. *Dating*: by context; see n1. *Sic*: has suspended.

Wednesday

Read Watkiniana & see Rose.[1]

W. was in the 2nd. Batch – for next Council – probably the 17th:[2] – & therefore was / not omitted, as he thinks. But his name, tho' recommended by me & approved by Ld. Derby has been objected to: & I have only prevented rejection / by withdrawing it, & treating the affair has suspended.

You must tell Rose the real reason.

Yrs | D

Powers are willing to enter into, a very heavy responsibility will rest upon this Country. H.M. cannot understand the hesitation on this point. We are already Parties to the Guarantee of Belgian neutrality & Independence, & to extend the guarantee of neutrality to Luxemburg does not seem to entail upon us any great additional responsibility.' The Queen had 'every confidence in your deciding for the best.' H B/XIX/D/21.

2 Stanley on 5 May had noted that Berlin was insisting 'on neutralisation of the Duchy [of Luxemburg], and collective guarantee.' *Disraeli, Derby* 307.

.3 In the House on this day (6th), in answer to Hibbert's amendment (**4404**n3), which allowed tenants to qualify as voters by paying the reduced rates they had once paid through their landlords (*ie* through compounding), D had moved 'a counter-amendment requiring them to pay the *full* rates, which they could then deduct from their rents, and announced that the Government would dissolve Parliament if defeated on this point.' *Hardy Diary* 38n7. According to Blake (470), D's counter-amendment 'would in practice almost certainly have been either legally meaningless or administratively unworkable.' It would be carried on 9 May (**4433**&n1) but would not become law. *Hansard* CLXXXVII cols 15-56 (D 15-20, 43-8, 52-3, 56).

---

1 The Grand Trunk Railway (begun 1853) was deeply in debt by 1861 when Edward W. Watkin was sent to Canada to confederate the five British provinces into a dominion and to plan railways designed to bring Quebec within easier reach of other parts of Canada. The ambitious and irascible Watkin had been president of the Grand Trunk Railway of Canada 1861-3. On Saturday 4 May he had sent Philip Rose a note (not found) from George-Étienne Cartier (who in 1852 had introduced a bill to create the GTR Company of Canada) 'in wh. you will see he thanks me on his own behalf: & on that of Canada'. Underscoring his contribution to 'the Intercolonial Railroad' and his role as 'the head of the largest enterprise in the Provinces (1340 Miles of Railway)', Watkin assured Rose that he had been told by Cartier that he 'had received influential communications urging that my "great services" should be suitably acknowledged.' H C/II/A/32a. See **4488**.

2 Although there would be a cabinet on 18 May (*The Times*, 20 May 1867), D may refer to a meeting of the privy council.

4433 TO: QUEEN VICTORIA   House of Commons, Friday [10 May 1867]

ORIGINAL: RAC F15 109

EDITORIAL COMMENT: House of Commons paper. Docketed in another hand on the first page: '10 May 1867.' *Dating*: by context; see n1.

Friday morning | 10 min: past one[1]

The Chancellor of the Exchequer with his humble duty to Yr Majesty:

Majority for Y. M. Government <u>66</u>!

Numbers /

For	Agst
322	256

A fine debate – Mr Lowe broke down: lost his thread of thought. ↑Mr↓ Bright, good – but / result overwhelming, & Bill safe.[2]

4434 TO: ALFRED DENISON   Grosvenor Gate [Saturday] 11 May 1867

ORIGINAL: QUA 301

EDITORIAL COMMENT: Grosvenor Gate paper. *Sic*: Furzecotte.

Alfred Denison | Esqre[1]   May 11 1867

My dear Sir,

The collapse of the House yesterday[2] prevented my asking Mr Speaker to do me the favor of admitting a gentleman to hear the debate / next Monday;[3] & there are reasons, wh: make me much regret this.

Could you arrange this for me? I shd. be personally obliged, if you cd. do so. The name of the gentleman is / Furzecotte[4] who I wish to be permitted to sit under the Gallery, or otherwise enter[.]

Yours faithfully | *B. Disraeli*

---

1 After protracted debate on 9 May 1867 the House adjourned at 1:45 *am* on this day (10th) shortly after the division (322-256) carrying D's amendment (**4431**n3) to Clause 3 (Occupation Franchise for Voters in Boroughs). *Hansard* CLXXXVII cols 266-361 (D 330, 347-56).

2 According to Robert Lowe, 'The practical result of the Bill would be that the landlord would be fined, and would therefore have an interest in limiting the extension of enfranchisement'. John Bright's argument 'was based chiefly on the unequal and unjust treatment of the 170 boroughs where compounding prevailed compared with the other 29 boroughs, and ... with the whole of Scotland and Ireland, where Household Suffrage would practically be established.' Lowe would call the division 'a perfect Waterloo, a rout complete and hopeless'; Bright went home on this day (10th) disturbed by 'so many men on our side deserting their party and their principles.' *The Times* (10 May 1867); W.A. Gardner (Baroness Burghclere) ed *A Great Lady's Friendships* (1933) 124; Bright 304; *Hansard* CLXXXVII cols 323-9 (Lowe), 330-42 (Bright).

---

1 Alfred Robert Denison (1816-1887), BA 1839 Christ Church, Oxford, was younger brother of and private secretary to John Evelyn Denison, Speaker of the House.

2 The House on 10 May had convened shortly before 4 *pm* but, due to the unexpected postponement of the army estimates by Sir John Pakington, 'members interested in the other business were not in their places, and the sitting came to a sudden termination at 20 minutes past 5 o'clock.' *Hansard* CLXXXVII cols 369-77 (D 371, 373, 375-6); *The Times* (11 May 1867).

3 The main topic of debate in the House on Monday 13 May would be reform. *Hansard* CLXXXVII cols 442-75 (D 452-3, 465-7, 472-5).

4 Samuel Furzecott of Notting Hill was MA's hairdresser.

[London, Monday 13 May 1867] **4435**
ORIGINAL: H B/XI/M/13
EDITORIAL COMMENT: A memo in D's hand on the verso of a note, in another hand, headed 'Scotland 1861.' *Dating*: by context; see n1.

Let me have 2 cop[ie]s of this for the Newspapers Times & Stan[dard.][1]

TO: **QUEEN VICTORIA**   House of Commons, Monday 13 May 1867 **4436**
ORIGINAL: RAC F15 111
EDITORIAL COMMENT: House of Commons paper.

Monday | May 13 1867

The Chr of the Excheqr with his humble duty to Yr Majesty:
The Scotch Bill introduced, & with much approbation[1] – it is not yet printed, or / rather only roughly. The first copy, perhaps tomorrow, will be sent to Yr Majesty. It will not be in the hands of the House for several days. /
The English Bill went into Committee, & considerable progress was made in it. All promising.[2]
2 o'ck. a.m.[3]

TO: **LORD LONSDALE**   Downing Street [Friday] 17 May 1867 **4437**
ORIGINAL: PS 815
PUBLICATION HISTORY: John Wilson catalogue (n.d.) item 41/18, described as 'Autograph Letter Signed ('D.') to [William Lowther, 2nd Earl of] Lonsdale, ... 3 pages 8vo; Office of the Chancellor of the Exchequer, Downing Street, 17 May 1867.'

[expressing his pleasure at having heard from Lonsdale][1] in good heart & condi-

---

1 The note (see ec) lists statistics for Scotland in 1861 on population (burghs 1,244,106, counties 1,818,188), electors (burghs 55,515, counties 49,979), annual value (burghs £4,700,000, counties £8,700,000) and number of members (burghs 23, counties 30). In the House on 13 May 1867 D cited the 1861 Scottish census statistics in introducing the Representation of the People (Scotland) Bill; see **4436**&n1.

---

1 In the House on this day (13th) D had introduced the Representation of the People (Scotland) Bill, D describing the borough franchise proposed for Scotland as 'identical in spirit, if not absolutely in form, with the borough franchise in England', with payment of rates and an adequate period of residence as qualifications in both countries. The bill would increase the number of Scottish representatives from 53 to 60: two new members to the universities, one to Glasgow, one to a new group of burghs and one each to Lanarkshire, Ayrshire and Aberdeenshire. D believed it would double the existing constituency, and as it 'does not much exceed 50,000 or 55,000, I cannot conceive that these are numbers that ought to alarm any one.' *Hansard* CLXXXVII cols 399-441 (D 399-407, 434-40).
2 In committee on this day (13th) George Denman had proposed an amendment to Clause 3 (Occupation Franchise for Voters in Boroughs) to insert 'the words – in reference to the payment of rates by the occupier claiming the franchise – "and which have been duly demanded of him by the overseer, collector, or other officer appointed for that purpose."' D had objected to the phrase 'duly demanded' on the grounds that 'it would affect the new and not the old constituency, and would be about as blundering a piece of legislation as could well be conceived.' The debate had ended in two divisions: one in favour of the government (208-145) and one in favour of the chairman reporting progress (235-48). *Hansard* CLXXXVII cols 442-75 (D 452-3, 465-7, 472-5).
3 D is writing on the 14th, the House having adjourned at 1:45 *am* on that day.

---

1 Lonsdale on 16 May had written from 15 Carlton Terrace wishing to congratulate D 'on your present prospects & would gladly accommodate my time to yours.' H B/XXI/L/290.

tion [and announcing his intention of calling at Carlton Terrace the following day] on my way to the Cabinet²

4438

TO: GATHORNE HARDY   Grosvenor Gate [Saturday] 18 May 1867

ORIGINAL: H H/LIFE

PUBLICATION HISTORY: M&B IV 540-1; Alfred E. Gathorne-Hardy *Gathorne Hardy, First Earl of Cranbrook: A Memoir* (1910) I 208-11; Smith 199-200, lengthy extracts

EDITORIAL COMMENT: From a typescript. M&B (ph) replaces 'residence' with 'franchise' in the tenth paragraph.

Right Honorable Mr. Secretary Hardy.   Grosvenor Gate, May 18. '67.

My dear Hardy,

I have had great difficulties about the Reform Bill since we parted, and have terribly missed your aid and counsel.

On Thursday night, Dalglish[1] gave notice of a motion for Committee on [Comp. *written in*] Householders, which, if carried, would have "hung up" the Bill, and which, as it was to be supported by all the Independent Liberals and many of our own men, would certainly have been carried. I prevailed on him, yesterday morning, to give this intention up, but he informed us at the same time, that he, and all his friends, and many of ours, as we knew, must support Hodgkinson's amendment for repeal of Small Ten: Act.[2]

I sent off to you, but you had gone to Osborne:[3] Lord Barrington told me, however, that you had mentioned to him, that you were not unfavorable to the Repeal in itself.

I sent for Lambert[4] who, after long consultation with myself and Thring, said, if required, he could effect the repeal of the Rating Bill in five clauses, and was in favor of it.

Two months ago, such a repeal was impossible: but a very great change had occurred in the public mind on this matter.

Two months ago, Gladstone would have placed himself at the head of the Vestries

---

2 See **4438**&n9.

---

1 For Robert Dalglish, see **4430n5**.

2 In the House in committee on 17 May Grosvenor Hodgkinson had moved an amendment to Clause 3 (Occupation Franchise for Voters in Boroughs) – '"no person other than the occupier shall ... be rated to parochial rates in respect of premises occupied by him within the limits of a Parliamentary Borough"' – which would repeal the Small Tenements Act and abolish compounding; it was passed without a division. *Hansard* CLXXXVII cols 708-56 (D 720-6, 729-30, 733, 749-53, 755-6). Grosvenor Hodgkinson (1818-1881), a solicitor 1839-70 and a JP for Nottinghamshire, was MP (L) for Newark 1859-74. For the repercussions of D's startling acceptance (see n8), without prior consultation with Derby or cabinet, of an amendment that would create nearly 500,000 new voters, see Blake 471-2 and especially Cowling 267-86. See also Saunders 250-2.

3 On the evening of the 17th Hardy had recorded: 'Just got back from Osborne with the seals. Walpole, Malmesbury, Marlborough & self had a rapid run down ... H.M. was looking very well but might have saved us the journey as she comes to Windsor tomorrow & to London on Monday when there is a function at the Hall of Science wh. I have to attend in Levée dress.' *Hardy Diary* 40.

4 See **4362n2**.

and "Civilization":[5] now, we were secretly informed, he intended to re-organize on the principle of Repeal of Local Acts.

In this state of doubt and difficulty, I went down to the House: and about nine o'clock, being quite alone on our bench, and only 45 men on our side, some of whom were going to vote for Hodgkinson, the amendment was moved, and, as I had been led somewhat to believe, Gladstone got up, (his benches with about 100 men,) and made his meditated coup, which you will read.[6]

I tried to get up some debate, or rather I waited for it, for I could do no more, but it was impossible.

This [His *written in margin*] "appeal" to me prevented anyone, but Bass & Co., speaking, and they were for Hodgkinson.[7]

I waited until the question was put, when, having revolved everything in my mind, I felt, that the critical moment had arrived, and when, without in the slightest degree receding from our principle and position of a rating and resident'l residence [(sic) *written in*], we might take a step which would destroy the present agitation, and extinguish Gladstone & Co. I, therefore, accepted the spirit of H's amendment.[8]

It was most painful, truly grievous and annoying, to act, in such a matter, without your personal and immediate countenance: and I can't conceal from myself, tho' I felt the pulse of many in the course of the morning, feeling that some crisis, which required decision, might arrive – I say, I cannot conceal from myself, that this course may excite some discontent: but if you stand by me, all will go right.

I have no reason to doubt the adhesion of the Cabinet, with the exception of the Duke of Bucks., whom I have not seen. If the Cabinet is united to-day, all will go right, and no further opposition to the Ref: Bill will take place.[9]

I had always, from our frequent conversations on the subject, inferred that, in theory, you were opposed to the Rating Bills, but were of opinion, as I was myself, that it was unwise, not to say impossible, for us, to touch them. But if the Opposition originated the move, that was a great difference.

I inferred also, from what Barrington impressed on me, that you were not insensible to the change of public opinion on this subject.

---

5 In the House on 18 March, following D's introduction of the reform bill, Gladstone had remarked sarcastically that the substance of D's speech had been 'that the existence of a class of lodgers is a necessity of our modern civilization.' He had also made much about the power of vestries and 'the will, exclusively I may say, of the propertied classes in the parish', to affect the franchise: 'Is that state of things to form a basis for our legislation?' *Hansard* CLXXXVI cols 37-46.

6 In the House on 17 May, after affirming his 'uncompromising hostility' to the reform bill as it now stood, Gladstone had spoken forcefully in favour of Hodgkinson's amendment (n2). *Hansard* CLXXXVII cols 712-19. So certain was Gladstone that the amendment would be defeated that he had left immediately after speaking, just as Disraeli began to speak.

7 Michael Bass (**4055n3**) thought (n2) compounding 'had not a single social or economical advantage' and in fact 'caused expense.' He believed 'the Amendment would help to get rid of all odious inequalities and invidious distinctions'.

8 D had stated (n2) that 'as far as the spirit, not of the Amendment, but of the proviso of the hon. Gentleman is concerned, Her Majesty's Government can have no opposition whatever to it.'

9 Stanley on this day (18th) would note a 'Long cabinet, chiefly on reform: but all agreed, which I did not expect. Some objections were made by me, but not pressed.' *Disraeli, Derby* 309.

I have written all this off to you, curr: cal:,[10] that you might fully understand all I feel at this moment.

It is a critical one which requires alike courage and conciliation for all. I hope you may, on the whole, not disapprove of my course, but I feel confident, that if you do not entirely, you will for the sake of the party, and perhaps a little for mine, support a colleague, who has endeavoured to do his best, in great difficulties.[11]

Yours ever, D.

4439 TO: MARY ANNE DISRAELI   Grosvenor Gate [Saturday 18 May 1867]
ORIGINAL: H H/LIFE
PUBLICATION HISTORY: M&B IV 542, dated 'the morning after the concession'
EDITORIAL COMMENT: From a typescript headed: 'D to Mrs D. Thursday Grosvenor Gate.' *Dating*: by context; see n1.

Dearest,

Come to me, when you are up & breakfasted, as it is necessary to confer on affairs before you go into the world....[1]

4440 TO: QUEEN VICTORIA   Downing Street, Monday 20 May [1867]
ORIGINAL: RAC F15 112
EDITORIAL COMMENT: C of Ex paper. *Dating*: by context; see n1. *Sic*: suceeding.

Monday May 20

The Chr of the Exchequer with his humble duty to Yr Majesty:

The Borough Franchise Clause in the Reform Bill / was, at length, carried this evening amid loud cheers, from both sides of the House.[1]

The real difficulties of the question were involved / in this Clause – & the Chr of the Exchequer anticipates no serious difficulties in the suceeding portions. It is,

---

10 Abbreviation of 'currente calamo' (Latin), 'with a running pen'; fluently, without making a rough copy.
11 Hardy on this day (18th) would reply that D had taken 'the logical & consistent course with respect to the Reform Bill ... and though the change may now be more rapid than we anticipated I do not see upon what principle we can object to enabling all who pay their rates to come upon the register. I dislike the compounding acts in themselves and have no objection to their disappearance.' H B/XX/HA/8.

---

1 M&B (IV 542) notes that D 'was greatly relieved to receive [MA's] reply: "All right; Mr. Hardy highly approves."' In H H/LIFE D's letter is followed by an undated typed note initialled 'M.C.': '(Note) The day after accepting Hodgkinson's [17 May] amendment, Mr D wrote that night to Hardy who had been absent.' This is followed by a typescript note: '*Mr Hardy highly* approves. All right of course you have seen the Times. Yrs. M.A.D.' See **4438**&n2.

---

1 In the House on this day (20th), following a long, sarcastic peroration by Robert Lowe – who believed the 'idea' of the reform bill was to ensure that new voters would be 'as poor and ignorant as possible' – and some shorter speeches, Clause 3 (Occupation Franchise for Voters in Boroughs) had been agreed to without a division. An amendment to Clause 4 (Occupation Franchise for Voters in Counties) by J.S. Mill, extending suffrage to women (by replacing the word 'man' with 'person'), had been defeated 196 to 73; D did not vote. The House adjourned at 1:45 *am* on the 21st. Hansard CLXXXVII cols 779-852 (D 779-80, 850-1).

now, merely an affair of time, / temper, & labor, & he contemplates the bill reaching the Ho: of Lords, about the 10th. July.[2]

TO: HENRY MANNING   [London, Tuesday] 21 May 1867   4441
ORIGINAL: MANN [2]
EDITORIAL COMMENT: C of Ex paper, seal crossed out.

Private   May 21 1867
His Grace | The Arch Bp of Westminster
My dear Lord,
I fear you may have thought me neglectful, wh: I have not been.
    Lord Naas would be happy to / talk over the matter, of our last conversation, with you, & ~~you~~ with yr friend, if he be still in England.
    Would Thursday, at two o'ck: suit you? and / at this house, Grosvenor Gate.
    Ever, my dear Lord, | with sincere regard, | Yours, | D.[1]

TO: THE DUKE OF MARLBOROUGH   Downing Street   4442
                                             [Friday] 24 May 1867
ORIGINAL: CAM ADD 9271/3/10
EDITORIAL COMMENT: C of Ex paper. *Sic*: Marborough.

His Grace | The Duke of Marborough   May 24 1867
My dear Lord President,
Your Grace has enriched my library, at Hughenden, with a work, which I have always most desired to / possess, & which I never expected to acquire.
    But what makes its presence on my shelves still more gratifying is, that it is the gift of a colleague, whom, / personally, I much regard, & on whose courage & counsel I rely with confidence, amid circumstances of no ordinary difficulty.[1]

---

2 The Reform Bill would be introduced in the Lords on 16 July and be given second reading on 22 and 23 July. *Hansard* CLXXXVIII cols 1615, 1774-1872, 1916-2033.

---

1 Manning on 4 May had informed D that Bartholomew Woodlock (1819-1902), rector of the Catholic University of Ireland 1861-79 and Bishop of Ardagh and Clonmacnois 1879-95, had been authorized by Cardinal Cullen to approach the government to obtain a charter for the university, 'or failing this a fairer & more just recognition of the only Catholic University in Ireland.' Manning on 11 May had thanked D for agreeing to see Woodlock, who had requested an interview for the 12th with any government member. Manning on this day (21st) would reply that Woodlock was still in London and would accept D's Thursday 23 May appointment, assuring D that 'any favourable proposal ... would not only encounter no opposition, but would be assisted,' including the granting of a charter. 'I can add that the "Chief" I conferred with ... fully recognizes the need of removing the Catholic Education of Ireland from the turbulent region of politics.' H B/XXI/M/161-3.

---

1 The Duke of Marlborough on 21 May had written from 10 St James's Square asking D to 'accept a copy of the Blenheim Gems which after the fine [Blacas] collection you have added to the National possessions may be of some little interest to you.' H B/XX/CH/4. Hughenden library has a copy of 'Gemmarum Antiquarum Delectus; Du Cabinet du Duc de Marlborough' in half morocco, 2 vols, n.d. There had been editions of *Gemmarum antiquarum delectus ... Choix de pierres antiques gravées du cabinet du duc de Marlborough* by George Spencer, 4th Duke of Marlborough, in 1780, 1783 and 1795. 'In 1781-90 the duke had printed for presentation two folio volumes with 100 plates of the finer and more interesting examples drawn

Pray accept my / grateful thanks, & believe me, ever, my dear Lord President, |
Your sincerely obliged, | *B. Disraeli*

4443 TO: [MONTAGU CORRY] [House of Commons, Monday 27 May 1867]
ORIGINAL: H B/XI/J/35
EDITORIAL COMMENT: *Dating*: by context; see n1.

It is very probable that the 34 Cl: will be on in a very short time.[1]

The Atty-Genl, who is alone here to aid me, wants the point raised / by *Lambert*,[2] that Clay's Act cl: 1 & 2 referred, as the bill is now drawn, to both the old & the new constituencies.[3]

D.

4444 TO: QUEEN VICTORIA House of Commons [Monday] 27 May 1867
ORIGINAL: RAC F15 113
PUBLICATION HISTORY: M&B IV 543
EDITORIAL COMMENT: House of Commons paper.

May 27 1867

The Chanr of the Exchequer with his humble duty to Yr Majesty:

The Reform Bill makes good, & even great, progress.

We / have had a most important, & successful, night, & the feeling of the House is excellent.[1]

We meet again tomorrow morning, & shall, at the least, have / four sittings pr week.[2]

The Chr of the Exr takes even a sanguine view of affairs, & counts on sending the Bill up to the Lords in the earlier part / of July.

The House received the announcement of the remission of the capital punishments of the traitor-convicts with dignified satisfaction.[3]

---

by Cipriani and engraved by Bartolozzi ... A reprint, in which the old plates were used, was published in 1845, but it was an exceedingly unsatisfactory production in every respect.' The 7th Duke would sell his collection of 739 antique and Renaissance engraved gems and cameos in 1875. *The Times* (25, 29 Jun 1875, 10 Apr 1899). See John Boardman *The Marlborough Gems: Formerly at Blenheim Palace, Oxfordshire* (Oxford) 2009.

---

1 In the House on Monday 27 May 1867 in committee D had introduced an amendment (agreed to) to Clause 34 (Occupier may claim to be rated in order to require the Franchise), 'in line 29, after the word "rated," to insert, "at the time of the passing of this Act to the poor rate."' *Hansard* CLXXXVII cols 1176-9. See **4444**&n1.
2 Attorney-general Sir John Rolt and statistician John Lambert.
3 Clay's Act – 14 & 15 Vict. ch. 14 (Compound Householders Act 1851) – was named after Sir William Clay. It had been mentioned numerous times in the House on 9 May; see **4433**&n1.

---

1 The House in committee on this day (27th) had discussed Clauses 4 (Occupation Franchise for Voters in Counties) and 34 (see **4443**&n1), and divided on amendments by Hardy (carried 255 to 254) and by MP (L) Sir Edward Colebrook (defeated 264 to 254, D voting with the majority). *Hansard* CLXXXVII cols 1135-91 (D 1135-42, 1163-4, 1176-8, 1182-3, 1188-91).
2 The House would meet on 28, 29, 30 and 31 May.
3 In Dublin on 2 May Fenians Patrick Doran and Thomas Burke had been found guilty of high treason and

ORIGINAL: H B/XI/J/38
EDITORIAL COMMENT: *Dating*: by context; see n3. *Sic*: Moncrieff.

I think he had better write nothing. If he is to meet Moncrieff,[1] Baxter & Bouverie,[2] they will eat him up!

At any rate, they will / be witnesses to his statement, that he is entirely ignorant as to the distribution of seats the Govt will propose in consequence of the vote on Baxter's Motion.[3]

I / shall be at the office by 2 o'ck: & Ld. Ad:[4] can call on me after his interview.
D

TO: [MONTAGU CORRY?] [London, Sunday 2 June? 1867] 4446
ORIGINAL: H B/XI/J/152a
EDITORIAL COMMENT: A note in D's hand scribbled on an envelope addressed to 'The Chancellor of the Exchequer' marked 'Private | J Walsh.' *Dating*: by context; see n1.

? whether Sir John has not adopted County popul[ati]ons witht. deduction of Boro' pops.?[1]
D.

---

were to be executed on 29 May. Stanley on the 22nd had noted that cabinet that day had been divided: Naas, Walpole, Marlborough and Stanley against execution, the rest in favour. On the 25th Derby had met at St James's Square with a deputation of MPs requesting clemency: Sir George Bowyer feared that 'The infliction of death for a purely political offence would be a scandal and disgrace to the country' and J.S. Mill that the convicts would become 'martyrs in the eyes of their misguided countrymen'. Derby agreed to discuss their petition that day in cabinet. D, when asked if the government had recommended clemency (n1), had replied in the affirmative, expressing 'fervent hope – I would almost say my belief – that this act of most gracious clemency on the part of Her Majesty will be one which Her Majesty will never regret, and that the exercise of this prerogative on the present occasion will be looked back to by her subjects with perfect satisfaction.' *The Times* (2, 27 May 1867); *Disraeli, Derby* 309-10.

1 James Wellwood Moncreiff (1811-1895), Baron Moncreiff 1874, 11th Bt of Tulliebole 1883, a Scottish barrister 1833, sol-gen for Scotland 1850-1, lord advocate 1851-8, 1859-66 and 1868-9, a DL of Edinburgh 1854, dean of the faculty of advocates 1858-9, rector of Edinburgh University 1868-71, MP (L) for Leith 1851-9, Edinburgh 1859-68 and Glasgow and Aberdeen Universities 1868-9. He would be lord justice-clerk and president of the second division of the Court of Session 1869-88.
2 William Edward Baxter (1825-1890), a DL of Forfar, admiralty secretary 1868-71, joint-secretary to the treasury 1871-3 and PC 1873, was MP (L) for Montrose Burghs 1855-85. Edward Bouverie was MP (L) for Kilmarnock.
3 In the House in committee on 30 May 1867 William Baxter's amendment to Clause 8 (Disfranchisement of certain Boroughs), that the boroughs of Great Yarmouth and Lancaster retain one member each, was passed 325-49, D voting with the majority. *Hansard* CLXXXVII cols 1301-27 (D 1323-4).
4 Lord advocate Edward Strathearn Gordon.

1 Former Irish attorney-general Sir John Walsh on 2 June had written to D 'at very great length': 'In compliance with the wish you expressed, I will proceed to state the principal grounds on which I support my proposed amendment of that part of Mr Laings plan, which gives a second member to Boroughs having a population of 50,000. I propose extending the operation of this Clause to Counties. The practical effect of my motion would be to give an additional member to each of the seven Welsh Counties of Anglesea, Brecon, Cardigan, Carnarvon, Flint, Montgomery, and Pembroke ... I enclose some tables, extracted from the Electoral Return[,] to show that these seven Counties are quite upon a par with a considerable number of English Counties, & Divisions of Counties, returning two members, in point of population, and property.' H B/XI/J/152.

4447 TO: [MONTAGU CORRY] Downing Street, Friday 7 June [1867]

ORIGINAL: H B/XI/J/156a

EDITORIAL COMMENT: A note in D's hand on 11 Downing Street paper. *Dating*: by context; see n2. *Sic*: McClaren.

Friday | June 7

See McClaren's[1] Return.
  Leaders in M. Star[2] & Daily News. & Report thereon.

4448 TO: QUEEN VICTORIA Downing Street [Sunday] 9 June 1867

ORIGINAL: RAC F15 114

EDITORIAL COMMENT: C of Ex paper. *Sic*: Boundary Commissioner.

Jun 9 1867

The Chanr of the Exchequer with his humble duty to Yr Majesty:

He is now prepared to give Yr Majesty a general view of the position & prospects of the Reform Bill on wh:, he ventures to / think, Yr Majesty may rely.[1]

Yr Majesty will recall, that, on Monday last, the first portion of the Bill, relative to the Franchise, was passed by the House of Commons: some of its provisions may be / safely modified in the Ho: of Lords, tho' its character cannot be substantially changed.

The vote of the House of Commons, wh: increased the number of seats for re-distribution, has required, & occasioned, great / deliberation, but Yr Majesty's Government have prepared a scheme, wh: they trust will be satisfactory to Yr Majesty, & wh:, of the forty-five seats to be appropriated, will secure, from twenty five to thirty, for the / County representation.[2]

It was only last night, that a definite communication was received from a powerful body of Whig gentlemen, including Lord Enfield, Mr Hastings Russell, & Mr Bouverie, & others of / that calibre, that they would support Yr Majestys Government in such a proposition.[3]

---

1 Duncan McLaren (1800-1886), a draper, was JP and DL of the county and city of Edinburgh from 1836, city treasurer 1837, lord provost 1851-4, president of the chamber of commerce from 1862 and MP (L) for Edinburgh 1865-81. In 1848 he had married John Bright's sister, Priscilla. McLaren, a Free Churchman, was 'anti-drink, anti-establishment, anti-trade union, and anti-home rule.' ODNB.

2 Adjacent to D's note in H is a letter from McLaren dated 7 June 1867 calling D's attention 'to an article on the Distribution of seats, from the *Star* of this day, written by myself ... Please also to notice how Edin[burgh] stands so high on all the points of comparison. There is one sentence which, when printed, looks rather disrespectful, but nothing beyond fair discussion was intended, and I hope it will be read in this spirit. It is only because of the candid spirit in which you listened to my remarks last night that I have used the freedom of writing you on the subject.' H B/XI/J/156b.

---

1 Writing from Roehampton on this day (9th) Derby informed D that 'in a letter received a day or two ago, the Q. expressed great surprise that She had not heard from you about the late division. Which, H.M. did not say.' H B/XX/S/434.

2 In the House in committee on Monday 3 June, during debate on Clause 9 (Certain Boroughs to return one Member only), D had referred to the vote (on 31 May) that had added 'a considerable number of seats ... to those which we propose to appropriate by the present measure' and that created the need 'to consider how to distribute forty-five seats instead of thirty, as originally contemplated.' *Hansard* CLXXXVII col 1532.

3 Lord Enfield represented Middlesex, Hastings Russell, Bedfordshire and Edward Bouverie, Kilmarnock.

As the Conservative party is united on the subject to a man, the Chanr of the Exchequer cannot doubt, that he will / be able to carry this highly satisfactory arrangement, wh: he will introduce on Thursday next on the re-assembling of the House, asking for the decision on the following Monday.[4]

The debates on this / portion of the Bill may probably proceed until the end of the month. The miscellaneous clauses may require one week.

On the whole, the Chanr of the Exchequer thinks it not an unreasonable estimate to assume, that / the Bill may reach the Ho: of Lords by the 12th., or 15th, of July.

It will be necessary to nominate five Commissioners for the Boundaries, who shd. be persons whose names would inspire general / ↑confidence↓ & prove to the world that no mere party interests will be considered.[5]

Lord Eversley has expressed his readiness to act on this Commission.[6]

Sir John Duckworth would be a good man: a very temperate Tory, long a / member of the Ho: of Commons, &, at present, fulfilling the difficult office of Assessor to the Speaker on private Bills.[7]

There shd perhaps be a military Engineer on the Boundary Commissioner, & if he were thus qualified, Sir Henry Storks would be / a good appointment.[8]

If Members of the Ho: of Commons were on the Commissioner, perhaps the Recorder,[9] representing the Government side, & Mr Hastings Russell [,] that appointment would inspire, & command confidence.

On all matters, generally in the House, the Chanr. can give a good report. The Ministry has taken root.

TO: JOHN WALTER   Downing Street [Tuesday] 11 June 1867   **4449**
ORIGINAL: SRO NRA(S)2950/1960/1-3
EDITORIAL COMMENT: C of Ex paper.

John Walter Esqre   June 11 1867

---

4 See **4451**&n1 and **4454**&nn2&4.
5 D had told the House (n2) that the government had 'to choose five gentlemen who, from their high character and from their accomplishments, will command universal respect, and whose position in life will enable them to give the necessary time to the duties they will be called on to perform.'
6 Lord Eversley would chair the commission.
7 In the House on 20 June D would announce Duckworth as one of seven proposed boundary commissioners; the others were Eversley, John Walter, Thomas Bramston, Edward Bouverie, Russell Gurney and Lord Penrhyn. In committee on the 21st D would recommend Duckworth as 'a very able and competent man of business, and of very temperate views', D's wish being that 'no individual, with strong political or party opinion, or who is very much mixed up with our party struggles, ought to be appointed on this Commission.' Duckworth on 16 August would attend the commission's inaugural meeting, along with Eversley, Gurney, Walter and Sir Francis Crossley. *Hansard* CLXXXVIII cols 176, 281-4; *The Times* (19 Aug 1867).
8 Sir Henry Knight Storks (1811-1874), son of Henry Storks, a career army officer since 1828, lieut-col 1848, col 1854, maj-gen 1862 and lieut-gen 1871, was KCB 1857, GCMG 1860, GCB 1864 and PC 1866. He had been assistant adjt-gen at the Cape 1846-7, assistant military secretary at Mauritius 1849-54, the last high commissioner of the Ionian Islands (succeeding Gladstone) 1859-63 and governor of Malta 1864-5 and Jamaica 1865-6. At the war office he had been secretary for military correspondence 1857-9 and would be controller-in-chief and under-secretary from December 1867 to June 1870 and surveyor-gen of the ordnance 1870-4. He would be an MP (L) for Ripon 1871-4.
9 Russell Gurney.

Dear Walter,

It would be very satisfactory to H.M. Government, & very agreeable to me person-ally, if you wd. permit me to insert your / name among those of the five Boundary Commissioners, whom we have, now, to appoint.[1]

Lord Eversley, & Sir John Duckworth, have accepted the office, & / I wish to present names to Parliament, wh: will command the entire confidence of the Coun-try.

I trust, therefore, you will accede to my request.

Pray, / present my Compliments to Mrs Walter,[2] & believe me,

sincerely yours, | *B. Disraeli*

4450 TO: [MONTAGU CORRY]   Downing Street, Wednesday [12 or 26 June? 1867]
ORIGINAL: H B/XX/D/365
EDITORIAL COMMENT: C of Ex paper. Docketed in another hand on the first page: '1867'. *Dating*: by context; see n1. *Sic*: Gabbetas.

Wednesday

What Mrs Disraeli wanted was standing room, for two humble country friends, to see the ladies go *to the Drawing Room*.[1] /

It is too slight a matter to trouble you about: Gabbetas[2] ought to be able to get these tickets from Ld. Chan's office[.]

D.

4451 TO: QUEEN VICTORIA   Downing Street [Thursday] 13 June 1867
ORIGINAL: RAC F15 115
EDITORIAL COMMENT: C of Ex paper.

June 13 1867

The Chanr of the Exchequer with his humble duty to Yr Majesty.

He stated to the House of Commons, tonight, the new plan for the re-distribution of the increased / number of seats.[1] It seemed to be received with favor – but the

---

1 For John Walter, chief proprietor of *The Times*, see **4453**.
2 A widower since 1858, Walter in 1861 had married secondly Flora MacNabb (d 1917), third daughter of James Monro MacNabb of Highfield Park, Hampshire.

---

1 In 1867 Drawing Rooms were held on behalf of the Queen by Princess Alice on 15 and 27 June. *The Times* (17, 28 Jun 1867).
2 At the treasury, H. Gabbitas (as of 2 July 1860) was messenger to the chancellor of the exchequer and John R. Gabbitas (as of 2 June 1859) a messenger (second class). LPOD (1865). See **4510** and **4511**.

---

1 In the House in committee on this day (13th) D had 'explained his new plan for the redistribution of the forty-five seats given by the adoption of the 10,000 population limit. Nineteen were to go to towns, mostly new boroughs, and twenty-five to counties, and there was one University seat.' M&B IV 544. D, in his words, had 'no wish to invite discussion to-night, and I do not expect it ... The schedules, in which this plan is in greater detail explained, will be in the hands of hon. Gentlemen, I hope, to-morrow.' He recommended the committee 'give well-defined but really large powers to the Boundary Commission-ers', who would review the schedules in view of producing a boundary bill. *Hansard* CLXXXVII cols 1776-85 (D 1776-80, 1784-5).

House, as is not unusual on re-assembling after holidays, was thin.[2]

TO: LORD DERBY   Downing Street [Friday] 14 June 1867   **4452**
ORIGINAL: DBP Box 146/2
EDITORIAL COMMENT: C of Ex paper.

Private   June 14 1867
Right Honorable | The Earl of Derby | KG
My dear Lord,
You will perceive by my statement, last night,[1] that I was obliged to depart a little from the arrangement / agreed on for the seats.

This was very disagreeable, but inevitable.

I passed three days in receiving deputations from the various localities,[2] & settling the / schedules. But the tri-partition of Durham was impossible, & in order to keep up the number of County seats as high as we ~~possible~~ could, this led, eventually, / to the change about E. Surrey.[3]

I did not decide on these points until yesterday morning, when Hardy arrived in town, & went into the / whole matter with me, & he was clearly of opinion, that it was a case, in wh: we were not only justified in acting on our own / responsibility, but were bound to do so.

I will not trouble you with details, but will bring the matter before the Cabinet tomorrow,[4] / when I hope you will be satisfied, that in a difficult, & pressing, position, we took the right course.

Yrs ever | D.

TO: JOHN WALTER   Downing Street [Monday] 17 June 1867   **4453**
ORIGINAL: H B/XIII/49
EDITORIAL COMMENT: C of Ex paper. *Sic:* publickly.

Confidential   June 17 1867
John Walter Esqr
My dear Walter,
I must throw myself on your most generous kindness of feeling & interpretation of my conduct.

---

2 The House had last met on Friday 7 June, after the Whitsun recess.

---

1 See **4451**&n1.
2 On 8 June D had met with a deputation from the London and Westminster Working Men's Constitutional Association. *The Times* (10 Jun 1867).
3 Derby on 9 June had written to D from Roehampton, returning the papers D had given him the previous day and stating that 'if Luton *must* be admitted, and the political reasons for it are strong, I see no mode of doing it but by sacrificing E. Surrey: though, if there is any mistake as to the Parliamentary paper ... the whole County would have a better claim to 2 additional members than either Durham or Derbyshire ... It is quite necessary that we should have the question of the E. Surrey population cleared up'. H B/xx/s/434. The Reform Act 1867 would divide East Surrey into East and Mid Surrey. At the November 1868 elections two Liberals would be elected to East Surrey, two Conservatives to Mid Surrey.
4 Cabinet would meet on 15 June at 4 *pm. The Times* (14 Jun 1867).

I have just received / a letter informing me, that Lord Eversley objects to preside over the Boundary Commission unless his liberal Colleague is a member of the Ho: of Commons.

That liberal colleague is / yourself.

I have proposed, to make of my fellow-labourers with whom I have been able to communicate, that they should permit three liberal members to / sit upon the Commission, for they, like me, entirely value your services & are like me convinced that you would perform them with admirable impartiality. But they have expressed to / me their conviction that the arrangement would be misconceived in the country & lead to great heart-burnings, misapprehensions, & bad feeling.

Your name has not / been publickly announced, tho' it was unanimously accepted & sanctioned by the Cabinet.

I can do nothing but throw myself on your good heart, for I / cannot, & wish not, to conceal from you, that I am deeply mortified & distressed in requesting yr. com permission not to announce yr name in the commission.[1]

I / indulge the ardent hope that in future plans of co-operation we may be more fortunate.

Ever yours ↑sincerely,↓ | D.

4454 TO: QUEEN VICTORIA   Downing Street [Monday] 17 June 1867

ORIGINAL: RAC F15 116

PUBLICATION HISTORY: *LQVB* I 431-2

EDITORIAL COMMENT: C of Ex paper. *Sic*: Inkermann; lossed.

June 17 1867

The Chanr of the Exchequer with his humble duty to Yr Majesty:

This has been a very remarkable day.

For more than ten days, it has been known / by the Government, tho' most strictly & secretly arranged, that an attack, contemplated as fatal, would be made on the Reform Bill.

It was a "*conspiration / des salons*" – but powerfully equipped. When all was ripe, "The Times" thundered.[1]

The issue decided on, which, if successful, would have entirely subverted the Government plan of / re-distribution, was popular & plausible: merely to give a few members to a few great towns.[2]

---

1 See, however, **4448**n7.

---

1 Possibly a leader beginning, 'The demerits of the Government scheme of Redistribution become more apparent the more it is examined ... Its apparent advantages are superficial, and disappear the moment any attempt is made to investigate the true character of the plan.' *The Times* (15 Jun 1867).

2 The House in committee on this day (17th) had debated Clause 10 (New Boroughs to return One Member each). Samuel Laing's amendment (apparently D's '*conspiration*'), to '"return three members instead of two"' to boroughs with a population of over 150,000 (Birmingham, Bristol, Leeds, Liverpool, Manchester, Sheffield), had been defeated by only eight votes (247 to 239), D voting with the majority and the House adjourning at 1:30 *am* on the 18th. *Hansard* CLXXXVII cols 1942-2006 (D 1955-60, 1968, 1976-7, 1981-4, 1987, 1989, 1991-2, 2001-5).

It was an affair of Inkermann,[3] &, for a moment, the result seemed doubtful, tho' the Chanr of the Exchequer, as the grey of the morning dispersed, & the position of the assailants developed, never lossed heart.

The Ladies Gallery was full of fascinating conspirators; all / the stormy petrels of politics; all the statesmen out of place; revisited the House of Commons, & hovered about the Peers' tribune; Mr Gladstone spoke with former fire; Mr Bright warned us with / mild denunciation, & Lord Cranborne denounced.

But Yr Majesty's Governmt was in a majority of 8! – & tho' that figure may seem small, it represents a much greater force than / it indicates: for all the other issues, of the combined attack, were at once given up.[4]

TO: CHARLES DICKENS   [London, Monday] 17 June 1867 4455
ORIGINAL: MARI [1]
PUBLICATION HISTORY: *Dickens Letters* (vol 11) 379n4
EDITORIAL COMMENT: C of Ex paper, seal crossed out. *Sic*: Stansfield. Our thanks to the executors of Mrs Henrietta Walton and the National Maritime Museum.

Chas Dickens Esqr   June 17 1867
Dear Mr Dickens,[1]
It is a duty to serve the case of Stansfield,[2] & it is a pleasure, & always my pleasure, to oblige you.
 I / will put the matter in train, & let you know the result.
  Yours sincerely, | D.[3]

3 See VIII **3595**n2.
4 There had been protracted debate on 'other issues' following the division (n2), with Laing complaining that, had discussion occurred prior to the vote, 'the minority might have been converted into a majority.'

---

1 Dickens on 16 June had written to D from Gad's Hill Place, Kent, enclosing a letter, received that morning, from the widow of 'my late dear friend the great painter' Clarkson Stanfield, who had died on 18 May. 'I honestly believe that you will be glad to do this thing, if you can, for the son of such an Artist.' Mrs Stanfield had asked Dickens for 'help in obtaining for her youngest son, Herbert, a supplementary clerkship in the Treasury or, failing that, in the Board of Trade: the career Stanfield had wished for him.' *Dickens Letters* (vol 11) 379-80&n3.
2 Clarkson Stanfield (1793-1867), RA 1835, after being apprenticed to a painter in Edinburgh, had run away to sea in 1808, joined the navy in 1812 and served on various ships until 1816. He became decorator and scene-painter at the Royalty Theatre 1816-22 and Drury Lane Theatre 1823-34, where 'he achieved a legendary reputation as a creator of romantic landscape scenery,' most notably with his vast moving dioramas (land and seascape panoramas). 'Stanfield painted over 550 scenes in more than 170 productions in his scenic career' and between 1820 and 1867 showed 135 paintings at the Royal Academy. He and Dickens had been great friends since 1837; *Little Dorrit* is dedicated to him. In *All the Year Round* on 1 June Dickens had described Stanfield as '"the soul of frankness, generosity and simplicity."' ODNB.
3 Dickens on 28 June would inform D that he had 'received an official letter to-day from Mr. Fremantle, which I have duly acknowledged. But I must beg to thank you, privately and personally, for your prompt and generous response to my appeal in behalf of Stanfield's son. I use no form of words when I assure you that I shall never forget it.' D's secretary Charles Fremantle had written offering Herbert Stanfield 'a test for a clerkship in the National Debt Office.' Stanfield would acknowledge receipt of the 'official papers relating to the vacancy' on 2 July. He would become branch manager of an insurance company. H B/XXI/D/261; *Dickens Letters* (vol 11) 384&n2.

4456 TO: [LORD DERBY]   [London] Tuesday [18 June 1867]
ORIGINAL: DBP Box 146/3
EDITORIAL COMMENT: *Dating*: conjectural; see nn1&2.

Tuesday

Thursday, the 20th. at 3 o'ck: I will attend you.[1]

Last night very good.[2]

Bouverie told me, confidentially, that / he thought the Whigs would back us up in a good distribution for Counties: and we heard, from another source, that / they were in favor of division, & not third members.

I found that yr. Distribution Committee was for *this* morning at twelve o'ck.

D.

4457 TO: [MONTAGU CORRY?]   [Downing Street] Wednesday [19 June 1867]
ORIGINAL: H B/XI/J/50
EDITORIAL COMMENT: C of Ex paper. *Dating*: by context; see n1.

Wednesday

C of Er. will be at D.S. about ½ past five – wishes to see Mr Corry on Reform Bill:

concludes that clause / as to Boundary Comm[isso]ners has been presented to-day.[1]

4458 TO: QUEEN VICTORIA   Downing Street, Thursday 20 June 1867
ORIGINAL: RAC F15 117
EDITORIAL COMMENT: C of Ex paper.

Thursday night | June 20 1867

The Chr of the Exr with his humble duty to Yr Majesty:

The whole evening has been occupied with a discussion on the subject of "Voting Papers"[.]

The Government proposal, as was contemplated, was defeated – by a majority of 38.[1]

The result does not at all signify.

The / debate was interesting, & well sustained: the most notable speeches on

---

1 On Thursday 20 June at 3 *pm* Derby, D, Hedges Eyre Chatterton and Lords Abercorn, Naas and Barrington would meet with a deputation of MPs and Irish Peers 'relative to the purchase of the Irish railways by the State with a view to their consolidation and better management.' *The Times* (21 Jun 1867).
2 See **4454**n2.

---

1 In the House on Tuesday 18 June, when asked when the clause appointing the boundary commissioners would be presented, D had replied he hoped to table it 'in the course of the morning'. On 20 June he stated that 'since the Chairman last reported progress I have laid on the Table the Clause which describes the powers of the Boundary Commissioners'. *Hansard* CLXXXVIII cols 17, 176. See **4448**n7.

---

1 In the House in committee on this day (20th) debate on Clause 29 (Electors may Vote by Voting Papers) had ended in a division of 272 to 234 (D voting with the minority), the House adjourning at 1:15 *am* on the 21st. *Hansard* CLXXXVIII cols 177-238 (D 179-80, 220-5).

either side – those of Lord Cranborne & Mr Ayrton. The former said all that could be urged in / vindication: the latter exhausted attack.[2]

TO: **MARY ANNE DISRAELI**   Downing Street, Friday [21 June 1867]   **4459**
ORIGINAL: H A/I/A/352
EDITORIAL COMMENT: C of Ex paper. Docketed in another hand on the first page: '?1867'. *Dating*: conjectural, but see n1. *Sic*: Meyer.

Friday

My darling,
We will dine with the Meyers on Sunday – with great pleasure.[1]
   I will see what I can do about Hart.[2]
      Your own | D.
I am very well.

P.T.O. /

TO: **QUEEN VICTORIA**   House of Commons [Monday] 24 June 1867   **4460**
ORIGINAL: RAC F15 118
EDITORIAL COMMENT: House of Commons paper.

June 24 1867

The Chanr of the Excher with his humble duty to Yr Majesty:
   A very successful night, Yr Majesty's Government having been triumphant in three important divisions.[1] /

---

2 In replying to W.T. McCullagh Torrens, who had moved to omit Clause 29 (which he predicted would give rise to a 'magnitude of ... evils') (n1), Cranborne had outlined the advantages of the voting papers system and concluded by stating that if the House rejected the clause, it would be guilty of 'a conservatism of all that is barbarous and inconvenient ... stupid and absurd.' Among the objections raised by Ayrton were the expense of the 'traffic and barter' by agents gathering voting papers and the introduction of 'the practice of manufacturing votes, which would end in pulling down the whole of the existing electoral system.'

---

1 There is in H a letter to MA from Juliana, Baroness Mayer de Rothschild dated 'Tuesday' on 107 Piccadilly paper and docketed by MA '1867 June': 'We were charmed to see you and Mr. Disraeli here on Sunday & it is very good of you to speak so kindly of the little party. I may congratulate [you] on last nights votes [*see* **4460**&n1] may I not? The bill will now pass through the House rapidly I should think. We have a most courteous letter from Mr Corry with the gratifying news of Mr. Hart's appointment [*see* n2]. Will you thank Mr Disraeli most sincerely from me. We will write to Mr Corry of course in answer to his letter.' H D/III/C/1925.

2 Historical genre painter Solomon Alexander Hart (1806-1881), ARA 1835, RA 1840 (the first Jew to be so honoured), was professor of painting at the Royal Academy 1854-63. As RA librarian 1864-81 he expanded its collection by over 2,000 volumes. Charlotte de Rothschild had written to her son Leopold on Monday 27 May hoping D's intercession (among that of many others) 'may have obtained from Mr. [Henry Lowry-] Corry [first lord of the admiralty] the curatorship of the Painted Hall at Greenwich for Mr. Hart.' On the 28th she would note that Hart had been appointed curator at £150 per annum. ROTH. The Painted Hall was known as the National Gallery of Naval Art from 1824 until the 1930s, when its contents were transferred to the National Maritime Museum. There is in H a letter to MA from Charlotte de Rothschild (n1), docketed by MA '1867 March': 'I enclose a note from Mr. Hart the *R.A.* who wished to do the honour of [showing] the Royal Academy Library to you ... It will only take you half an hour & will highly gratify Mr. Hart, who is an old friend of ours.' H D/III/C/1921.

---

1 The House in committee on this day (24th) had adjourned at 2:15 *am* on the 25th following four divisions

The situation of affairs continues very favorable.

4461 TO: LORD DERBY   Downing Street [Wednesday] 26 June 1867
ORIGINAL: DBP Box 146/3
EDITORIAL COMMENT: C of Ex paper.

Right Honorable | The Earl of Derby | K.G.   June 26 1867

My dear Lord,

I have examined strictly into this affair, & can state, that the allegations of Mr Ferrand are perfectly correct.[1]

The post is Registrar of Births, deaths &c, at / Devonport.[2]

I should feel obliged to you, if you would take an early opportunity to bring the matter before the attention of Lord Devon,[3] as it excites great discontent & indignation / in our ranks.

Yrs e[ve]r, | D

4462 TO: QUEEN VICTORIA   House of Commons [Thursday] 27 June 1867
ORIGINAL: RAC F15 122
EDITORIAL COMMENT: House of Commons paper.

June 27 1867

The Chanr of the Exchequer with his humble duty to Yr Majesty:

The Reform Bill made considerable progress this evening, &, / so far as the clauses are concerned, was gone through.[1]

There remain some new clauses, ↑to be↓ proposed by independent members, wh: will, probably / be disposed of tomorrow morning.[2]

Then come the Schedules, but altho' great difficulties & struggles were once

---

– 106-98, 171-151, 256-230, 200-179 – on Clause 40 (General Saving Clause) which, as amended, had been agreed to. *Hansard* CLXXXVIII cols 430-86 (D 430-7, 448-51, 454, 466-9, 485-6).

1 The last extant letter of William Ferrand to D, dated 'June 19', is a request to meet D 'at home' that day prior to Ferrand's interview with one 'Wilson'. H B/XXI/F/145. For previous elections involving the quarrelsome Ferrand, former MP (C) for Devonport, see VII **3331**n1 and VIII **3787**n2. He would be defeated on 23 July in a by-election at Coventry. See VI **2326**&n1, **2327** and VII **3260**&n3.
2 Richard Bennett Oram (1804-1886), a conveyancer, was superintendent registrar of births, marriages and deaths from 1857. R.N. Worth *History of the Town and Borough of Devonport* (1870) 42.
3 The 11th Earl of Devon, as Lord Courtenay, had been MP (C) for s Devonshire 1841-9.

---

1 In the House on this day (27th) debate begun on the 25th had resumed on Clause 31 (Inclosure Commissioners to appoint Assistant Commissioners to examine Boundaries of New Boroughs), which, after brief discussion, had been agreed to as amended, the House adjourning at 2 *am* on the 28th. *Hansard* CLXXXVIII cols 609-47 (D 610, 612-13, 616-17, 624, 645-7).
2 New clauses had been discussed (n1), including five by D: 'providing for the increase of polling places ... the hire of rooms for polling places, the delivery of lists and the commencement of registers for voters, the disfranchisement of persons in the receipt of parochial relief, and the amendment of the oath to be taken by the poll-clerk.' *The Times* (28 Jun 1867). Further clauses would be proposed on 28 June and 1 July. *Hansard* CLXXXVIII cols 668-703 (D 681-2, 692-4, 696-7, 702-3); cols 782-844 (D 783, 791, 793-4, 807-8, 832-8, 843-4).

anticipated about these, the appointment of the Boundary Commission, to whom great powers are entrusted,[3] has already mitigated the mutterings of the Tempest.[4]

TO: [LORD DERBY] [London, Sunday] 30 June 1867 **4463**
ORIGINAL: DBP Box 146/3
EDITORIAL COMMENT: C of Ex paper, seal crossed out. *Sic*: lossed.

June 30 1867

My dear Lord,

I was so seized upon after the Cabinet,[1] that I lossed the occasion of writing to you, as I had intended.

The Cabinet were unanimous about giving an / additional member to the four towns,[2] & on withdrawing the intended boon from Luton & Keighley – but demurred to touching the County arrangement, wh: I proposed they shd consider. /

Ultimately, Lord John Manners suggested, that the additional members to Salford & Merthyr shd be withdrawn, wh: met with general acceptance.

I think, under the / circumstances, Salford may be managed, but Merthyr will die hard.

If they carry an additional member to Merthyr ag[ain]st one of the new Boros, Gravesend for example, we must submit. I hope to hear a good Bulletin.[3]

Ever, | D.

TO: QUEEN VICTORIA Downing Street [Monday] 1 July 1867 **4464**
ORIGINAL: RAC F15 123
EDITORIAL COMMENT: C of Ex paper. *Dating*: D is writing in the early morning of Tuesday 2 July.

July 1 1867

The Chanr of the Exchequer with his humble duty to Yr Majesty:

The Chanr of the Exr made a compromise this evening on the subject of the increased representation of the great / northern towns; offering an additional member to Manchester, Birmingham, Leeds, & Liverpool.[1]

---

3 In the House on 24 June D had justified at length the appointment of the boundary commissioners (three Liberals, two Conservatives), the government having endeavoured, he said, 'to select men from both sides of the House ... of moderate principles and temperate views.' *Hansard* CLXXXVIII cols 430-6. See **4448**nn5&7.

4 Perhaps an allusion to 'the morbid distrust previously expressed' about the boundary commission. *The Times* (25 Jun 1867).

---

1 Lady Derby, writing from St James's Square on 28 June, had informed D that her husband was 'confined to his bed both by gout and rheumatism' and invited D to visit Derby on the 29th 'any time before the Cabinet.' H B/XX/S/436.

2 See **4464**&n1.

3 D's redistribution scheme of 13 June (**4451**&n1) had recommended that of the 45 seats 19 should go to boroughs; these were to be absorbed by giving one member each to the new constituencies, among them Luton, Keighley and Gravesend, and an additional member each to Salford and Merthyr Tydvil. *The Times* (14 Jun 1867).

---

1 In the House in committee on this day (1 July) Thomas Horsfall had moved a new clause that would

He has reason to believe, that this arrangement will be generally accepted in the spirit / of conciliation in wh: it was offered, & that the progress of the Bill will be expedited in consequence.

The Committee meets again tomorrow, or rather this morning, at / two o'ck:[2]

4465

TO: QUEEN VICTORIA   Downing Street [Tuesday] 2 July 1867
ORIGINAL: RAC F15 124
EDITORIAL COMMENT: C of Ex paper.

July 2 1867

The Chr of the Exchequer with his humble duty to Yr Majesty:

The House decided, by a very large majority, in favor / of the plan, brought forward last night by Yr Majesty's government, for the distribution of seats: & the division is generally considered / conclusive on all matters.[1]

The Chr of the Exchequer has received assurances from a great number of gentlemen on the Liberal Benches, announcing / their determination, that in future, so far as the Bill is concerned, they will always vote with the Ministers.

It is thought, that Mr Gladstone & Mr Bright cannot rally more than 120 men.

4466

TO: MARY ANNE DISRAELI   Downing Street, Thursday [4 July 1867]
ORIGINAL: H A/I/A/336
EDITORIAL COMMENT: C of Ex paper docketed by MA on the first page: 'July 4th 1867'. *Dating*: by context; see nn1&3.

Thursday

My dearest Love,

It is most vexatious, but you must give it up.[1]

M. C.[2] has gone up to you again. I am so busy, that I / can't write anything worth reading.

---

give three members to boroughs with a population of over 250,000. D had agreed, he said, 'to make such changes in the Schedule as would give an additional representative to each of these four constituencies ... in the spirit of compromise, in the spirit of mutual and reciprocal concession ... with the sincere hope that we shall by this means advance and expedite the cause of the great measure now under our consideration.' *Hansard* CLXXXVIII cols 782-844 (D 783, 791, 793-4, 807-8, 832-8, 843-4).

2 The House had adjourned at 1:45 *am* on 2 July. See **4465**n1.

---

1 In the House in committee on this day (2nd) two amendments had been proposed to D's amendment (to insert the words 'the City of Manchester, and the Boroughs of Liverpool, Birmingham, and Leeds, shall each respectively return three Members to serve in Parliament') to Thomas Horsfall's clause (see **4464**n1): to insert the words 'and Sheffield' (defeated 258 to 122) and the words 'and the City and County of Bristol' (defeated 235 to 136). The clause, as amended by D, was agreed to and added to the bill. *Hansard* CLXXXVIII cols 857-99 (D 868-70, 879-81, 885, 887-8, 892).

---

1 Having learned (via telegrams on 2 and 4 July) that her cousin, Emperor Maximilian I of Mexico, had been executed by firing squad on 19 June, the Queen decided to postpone her review of troops scheduled for 5 July in Hyde Park. MA's morning party, announced for 5 July, 'is postponed till the day which may be fixed for holding the Review in Hyde Park.' In the House on this day (4th) D announced that 'the Review has been postponed; but only for a few days'. *LQVB* I 440; *The Times* (2, 5 Jul 1867); *Hansard* CLXXXVIII col 985.

2 Presumably Montagu Corry.

The Queen sent to command an announcement from me to the H of Comm:; she says "*in a few days*", she will ~~holds~~ hold / the Review. I think of you every moment, & sympathise with you in this great annoyance more than I can say.[3]

Your own | D.

TO: QUEEN VICTORIA   Downing Street [Friday] 5 July 1867   **4467**
ORIGINAL: RAC F15 125
EDITORIAL COMMENT: C of Ex paper.

July 5 1867

The Chancellor of the Exchequer with his humble duty to Yr Majesty:

This morning, the long expected question of / Cumulative Voting, or the defence of the Minority, was decided in the House of Commons, & a clause in its favor proposed by Mr Lowe, was rejected / in a very full house by an overwhelming majority, wh: supported Your Majesty's Ministers.

The debate, wh: had been adjourned from / the preceding night, was brilliant & interesting.[1]

TO: QUEEN VICTORIA   Downing Street, Monday 8 July 1867   **4468**
ORIGINAL: RAC F15 126
EDITORIAL COMMENT: C of Ex paper. *Dating*: D is writing at 12:15 *am* on Tuesday 9 July.

Tuesday ¼ past 12. | July 8 1867

The Chancellor of the Exchequer with his humble duty to Yr Majesty:

It may be now considered, that the Reform / has virtually passed. The only two dangerous questions remaining; one a motion by Mr Gladstone to increase the representation / of South Lancashire; was settled by his retiring without a division, announcing, that he would concentrate all / his opposition on the succeeding motion, vizt, to disfranchise four more small Boroughs, & in this, in a House of more / than four hundred members, he was beaten by a majority of *29*.[1]

---

3   Charles Fremantle had written to MA on 27 June 1867: 'I send you an amanuensis to help you in your labours. He is a "Supplementary Clerk" in the Treasury, thoroughly correct and trustworthy, for whom we have all a great regard'. On Saturday 27 July at 10 *am* there would be a review of the 1st battalion Coldstream Guards and 2nd battalion Scots Fusilier Guards in Hyde Park 'opposite Grosvenor-gate' lasting about two hours. H D/III/C/794; MP (29 Jul 1867).

---

1   In the House in committee on 4 July, Robert Lowe, in order (in his words) 'to give to the minority of a constituency an opportunity of being better heard at an election', had moved a new clause that he claimed was 'founded on no undue or unfair attempt to give a minority an advantage they are not entitled to exercise': that '"At any contested election for a county or borough represented by more than two members, and having more than one seat vacant, every voter shall be entitled to a number of votes equal to the number of vacant seats, and may give all such votes to one candidate, or may distribute them among the candidates as he thinks fit."' The clause had been defeated 314-173 on this day (5th), D voting with the majority. *Hansard* CLXXXVIII cols 990-1045 (D 990-3, 1006-7, 1022-3, 1029, 1033-4, 1036); 1068-1124 (D 1109-15). See **4481**n1.

---

1   In the House in committee on 8 July Gladstone had moved '"That the southern division of the county of Lancashire be divided into two divisions, and that each division be represented by three Members."'

The Chanr of the / Exchequer expects to proceed with his Schedules tomorrow morning, & anticipates, that they will run thro' very / quickly.²

4469 TO: QUEEN VICTORIA   Grosvenor Gate [Tuesday] 9 July 1867
ORIGINAL: RAC F15 128
EDITORIAL COMMENT: Grosvenor Gate paper.

July 9 1867

The Chancr of the Excheqr with his humble duty to Yr Majesty:

He has the gratification to inform Yr Majesty, that, / following up the great successes of last night, he has, this morning, carried the Reform Bill thro' Committee, & closed the Committee.

It reports its / labors to the Speaker on Friday morning, & in all human probability, the Bill will be read a third time in the House of Commons on / Monday next, & passed.¹

There was great cheering from both sides when the Committee closed.

4470 TO: LORD MALMESBURY   Downing Street [Wednesday] 10 July 1867
ORIGINAL: HCC 9M73/461/13
PUBLICATION HISTORY: Malmesbury II 371-2, omitting the last paragraph; M&B IV 567 (from Malmesbury II), omitting the last paragraph
EDITORIAL COMMENT: C of Ex paper.

Right Honorable | The Earl of Malmesbury G.C.B.   July 10 1867

My dear Malmesbury,¹

The Constitution of this Country is a Monarchy, modified, in its action, by the coordinate authority of Estates of the Realm: An / Estate is a political order, invested with privileges for a public purpose.

The clause was negatived. Richard Gilpin had moved '"That the four Parliamentary Boroughs next above ten thousand inhabitants ... now returning two Members each, shall only return one member; and that Luton, Keighley, Barnsley, and St. Helens, shall each return one Member to serve in Parliament."' The clause was rejected 224-195. The House would adjourn on 9 July at 2:30 *am. Hansard* CLXXXVIII cols 1193-1250 (D 1197, 1199-1200, 1201-5, 1208, 1210-12, 1221-6, 1228, 1243-6).
2 See **4469**&n1.

---

1 In the House on this day (9th) the reform bill as amended had passed through committee at 6:30 *pm* and would be reported on Friday 12 July at 2 *pm. Hansard* CLXXXVIII cols 1264-92 (D 1272-5, 1280-6, 1290-1); 1439-82 (D 1447, 1451-4, 1457-8, 1460-2, 1475-6, 1479-81); *The Times* (10 Jul 1867). See **4472**&n1.

---

1 Malmesbury on this day (10th) had written to D a letter marked '*Private*': 'I was much struck at what you said last night in defence of Proxies altho' I did not catch the point as clearly as I shd wish. As I am on the Committee wh is considering the subject I shd be most obliged to you to put on paper yr argument. Granville who is on this Committee has brought forward the question of privilege wh [he] jealously maintains as it is now by the Commons impedes much business. He says he has spoken to Gladstone on the subject who is willing to restrict this jealousy to the *public* taxation of the country, & to waive it in respect to *local* payments, & that if you take the same view a Committee in both Houses could effect this change in feeling & proceedings. Our Committee charged me to ask your opinion & lay it before them.' H B/ XX/HS/136.

There are three Estates: the Lords Spiritual, the Lords Temporal, & the Commons[.] The / Estates of the Lords Spiritual & Temporal, being very limited in number, their members can easily meet in their own Chamber.

The Estate of the Commons being, on / the contrary, very numerous, choose, for convenience, Representatives, instead of holding general meetings, like the Polish Diets[.]

The House of Commons is / not an Estate of the Realm: its members are only the Proxies of an Estate.

The Lords, in using Proxies, possess ↑& exercise↓, the same privilege as the Commons: no more: & / if it is not convenient for them to attend the meetings of their Orders, they have the right to choose their Representatives.

I think the monetary privilege of the House of Commons shd. / be confined to public Taxation, & am prepared to co-operate in any attempt to place it on that defined footing.[2]

Yours sincerely, | D.

TO: MARY ANNE DISRAELI   Downing Street [Saturday] 13 July 1867   **4471**
ORIGINAL: H A/I/A/337
EDITORIAL COMMENT: C of Ex paper.

July 13 1867

My dearest,

It is the *very fullest dress* today; breeches & white silks. The Prince said so to Ld Derby.[1]

Your own, | D.

TO: QUEEN VICTORIA   Downing Street [Monday] 15 July 1867   **4472**
ORIGINAL: RAC F15 129
PUBLICATION HISTORY: *LQVB* I 445
EDITORIAL COMMENT: C of Ex paper.

July 15 1867

The Chancr of the Exchequer with his humble duty to Yr Majesty:

The English Reform / Bill passed the House of Commons without a division. House full: the evening began with great bitterness in speeches from Mr Lowe / & Ld Cranborne, but the C. of Exr. vindicated the course of the Tory Party amid uni-

2 Malmesbury on 13 July would thank D for his 'lucid diagnosis of Proxies' and would write in his *Memoirs* that D's letter had been 'elicited, at my request, by the motion of the late Lord Stanhope in the House of Lords, abolishing the use of Proxies. It never was debated on really constitutional grounds, but merely on that of convenience, and the Peers appeared to have no idea of their origin, and that the custom was not a peculiar privilege or anomaly in the Constitution.' H C/II/A/35; Malmesbury II 372n1.

---

1 One style of formal court dress for men at this time included a white or cream silk waistcoat and white silk stockings. On this day (13th) D would attend a state dinner for the Sultan of Turkey given by the Prince of Wales at Marlborough House. *MP* (15 Jul 1867).

versal sympathy[1] & Mr. Gladstone, who had / been taking copious notes, refrained from replying.[2]

4473   TO: [LORD DERBY]   Downing Street [Thursday] 18 July 1867
ORIGINAL: DBP Box 146/3
EDITORIAL COMMENT: C of Ex paper.

---

confidential[1]   July 18 1867

Lord Grey made a proposition, that the Bill shd not be permitted to pass this year, & that the Lords shd carry alterations wh: / the Commons cd. not accept – so "that the Country shd. have the opportunity of considering the state of affairs,"[2] but Lord / Granville opposed this, & is for carrying the Bill.

---

1   On this day (15th) the reform bill had had its third reading, the House adjourning at 2:15 *am* on the 16th. Speaking first, Cranborne had lamented the disappearance of all the 'precautions, guarantees, and securities' in the bill's second reading and inveighed against what he famously termed 'a political betrayal which has no parallel in our Parliamentary annals.' Next came Lowe, accusing the government of 'treachery' in a diatribe that had ended with a plea for a man to rise and give voice to 'the shame, the rage, the scorn, the indignation, and the despair with which this measure is viewed by every cultivated Englishman who is not a slave to the trammels of party, or who is not dazzled by the glare of a temporary and ignoble success.' After numerous other speeches, D (speaking last) refuted Cranborne's accusations at length and ridiculed Lowe's speech as 'the production of some inspired schoolboy'. He also gave an account of the evolution of the bill and ended with an assurance that England was 'safe in her national character, in her fame, in the tradition of a thousand years, and in that glorious future which I believe awaits her.' *Hansard* CLXXXVIII cols 1526-1614 (D 1599-1614). For synopses of the debate, see M&B IV (547-9) and Smith (208-9), who claims that D 'sat smiling through the abuse.'
2   Gladstone on this day (15th) recorded: 'A remarkable night. Determined at the last moment not to take part in the debate: for fear of doing mischief on our own side.' *Gladstone Diaries* VI 536.

---

1   Derby on this day (18th) had written to D from St James's Square a letter marked '*Confidential*': 'Lord Grey has placed his Amendment to the 2d. Reading of the Reform Bill on the table this Evening. I have immediately sent out as strong a Whip as possible against it. But I know that the whole of the Opposition will support him, and he has been tampering, and, with the aid of Carnarvon, not unsuccessfully, with our people. It is therefore quite on the Cards that we may be left in a minority; in which case it is very important not only that we should consider our course of proceeding, but that I should know the language which I must hold at a meeting of our Party which is summoned for tomorrow at 3 o'Clock. The tenour of the Motion is to declare that the Bill, as at present framed, cannot be accepted – but that it is urgently necessary to pass the 2d. Reading, in order that such Amendments may be made in Committee, as would render it possible for the House of Lords to accept it. Now there are two modes of meeting this Amendment, either to treat it as virtually disposing of the Bill, or as an opinion of the House to which effect could only be given in Committee; and which, being obviously intended to combine votes which could not concur in any specific Amendment, was a mere factious proceeding which we would not allow to interfere with our attempting to carry out a measure which, as a whole, had received the *unanimous* approval of the H. of Commons. As far as the House of Lords is concerned, the second would be the obvious course; but what I want to know, is what you think I ought to say to our *friends* tomorrow [at a meeting at St James's Square]? If they incline to think that Grey's success (which is not improbable) will be fatal to the Bill, they may stand by us and carry us through – but we must then be prepared to meet the consequences, *and resign*: if, on the other hand, I have an impression that, notwithstanding the vote, we shall go on with the Bill, damaged as it will have been by an anticipated condemnation, we shall expose ourselves to a furious storm of invective, and the Bill itself to no little risk ... It is *essential* that I should see you.' H B/XX/S/438. See **4474**.
2   In the Lords on 16 July Grey had told Derby that although he did 'not intend to oppose the second reading ... it is my intention before the Bill is read a second time to move a Resolution ... to show that the Bill requires considerable amendment.' On 22 and 23 July there would be protracted debate on

All "Young Whiggery", & those who think they have a future, are with / Ld Granville – but Ld Grey has supporters. There are two parties in the Opposition camps.[3]

D.

TO: MARY ANNE DISRAELI   House of Commons [Friday] 19 July 1867   **4474**

ORIGINAL: H A/I/A/338

EDITORIAL COMMENT: C of Ex paper, seal crossed out and 'H of Comm:' written in. *Sic*: Sultann [*twice*].

H of Comm: | July 19 1867

My dearest wife,

My interview with him was satisfactory as to the *great point* – but he fears the Bill will be defeated.[1] Never mind: / it will pass another time.

The Sultann comes to the House of Commons, with some state, at six o'ck: today.[2]

Some correspondence / is going on, at this moment, betn. Duke of Cambridge & his guests as to the course today.[3]

We are to be at the Ball to receive the Sultann & this cannot / be arranged unless we leave the Duke before His Imp: Majesty.[4]

Grey's amendment (see n1), which Derby would call 'absolutely incomprehensible ... the most gratuitous interposition between the introduction of a measure and the passing of a particular stage that ever was attempted in a deliberative assembly.' The amendment would be rejected, the original motion agreed to and the bill read a second time and committed to a committee of the whole House on 29 July. *Hansard* CLXXXVIII cols 1616, 1774-1872, 1916-2033.

3 Granville, former Liberal leader in the Lords, was considered 'a great whig magnate'. Stanley on the 19th would note, 'Much talk about a coalition between the Whig opposition in the Lords, and the malcontent Conservatives, to support some amendment to the reform bill, which, as they calculate, will compel the ministry either to resign or withdraw the bill. Grey, Carnarvon, Cranborne, Lowe, are actively engaged in this project, and they appear to have secured the support of the *Times*.' ODNB; *Disraeli, Derby* 314.

---

1 See **4473**n1.

2 Abdul Aziz Khan (1830-1876), who had succeeded his brother as Sultan of Turkey in 1861, was the first Ottoman sultan to visit Europe. He would be deposed on 30 May 1876 and two weeks later found dead, 'trustworthy medical evidence' attesting to suicide. *EB* XI. He would modernize the Ottoman navy and establish the first Ottoman railroad network. In the House on this day (19th) Henry B. Sheridan would question Northcote (who declined to reply) about the selection process for the 2,600 guests who would attend the '"State Entertainment" so-called' for the Sultan later on this day (see n4). In committee of supply he would move for a guest list and an account of the reception's expenses, which he felt had been 'most wantonly and culpably' increased by the erection of temporary wooden structures. Henry Fawcett would raise the more embarrassing issue of the reception having been financed in part by 'heavy taxation in India'. *Hansard* CLXXXVIII cols 1726-7, 1759-64. See **4493**&n2.

3 On this day (19th) the Sultan would dine with the Duke of Cambridge at Gloucester House at 8 *pm* ('Covers were laid for 32'). Guests would include Lord Raglan and major-general Nelson Hood, 'especially appointed by the Queen to attend on his Imperial Majesty', D and Derby. The Sultan would proceed to India House (see n4) shortly after 10 *pm*. *The Times* (20 Jul 1867).

4 On this day (19th) the Sultan would be given a lavish state reception at India House, with guests arriving at 9:30 *pm* and the DS 'among the first to take their places on the dais'. A temporary roof (with twenty chandeliers) had been built over the opulent inner courtyard of the newly constructed (but unfinished) building, converting it into a ballroom whose temporary floor had been 'planed and polished to the smoothness and equality of a billiard-table.' The India Council Room, for which 'all the treasures of Windsor and Buckingham Palace had been ransacked to lend [it] additional splendour', had been set aside for the reception and supper, which would begin at 12:30 *am* on the 20th. *Ibid.* Charlotte de Rothschild on the 23rd would report that MA 'goes about London rhapsodizing about the Grand Turk's beautiful eyes and sweet smile – and she is overjoyed at having dined off pure gold.' ROTH. See **4475**.

Lady Newport & Lady Tankerville did not get home till 3 o'ck this morning & then in a strange carriage.[5]

Yrs | D.

4475   TO: SIR STAFFORD NORTHCOTE   [London, Saturday] 20 July 1867
ORIGINAL: H H/LIFE
PUBLICATION HISTORY: M&B IV 567-8, 'event' replaced with 'scene'
EDITORIAL COMMENT: From a manuscript copy with a note at the bottom of the page: 'Ball in honour of the Sultan.'

July 20, 1867

My dear Northcote

I can't refrain from congratulating you on the brilliant success of your fête,[1] one of the most striking festivals of the century; if indeed ever exceeded at any time. The space, the proportion, beauty of form and color, & the glittering guests, produced a coup d'oeil unrivalled; brightened by the occasion so strange & picturesque.

The admirable arrangements so perfect and so unusual, & wh. put every one at their ease were worthy of the historic event.

Yours ever | D.

4476   TO: SIR THOMAS PHILLIPPS   Grosvenor Gate [Saturday] 20 July 1867
ORIGINAL: BODL MSS Phillipps-Robinson [2]
PUBLICATION HISTORY: Alan Noel Latimer Munby, *The Dispersal of the Phillipps Library* (Cambridge 1960) 10, omitting the first paragraph
EDITORIAL COMMENT: Grosvenor Gate paper.

Sir Thomas Phillipps | Bart: July 20 1867
Dear Sir Thomas,

I find, that you did me the honor of writing to me a letter, in the midst of the Reform pressure, to wh: one of my Secretaries / replied, but wh: ought to have been acknowledged by my own hand.[1]

You are right in assuming, that my father greatly respected you & your pursuits, &

5 From 7 to 11 *pm* on the 18th the Sultan had been entertained at Guildhall by the Lord Mayor. 'After 5 o'clock seats were with difficulty obtained by any comers. Mr. Disraeli was among the earliest arrivals, and was warmly received.' Guests had included the Countess of Tankerville and the Countess of Bradford, formerly Lady Newport (until 1865, when her husband succeeded as 3rd Earl of Bradford). *The Times* (19 Jul 1867).

1 Northcote was Indian secretary and president of the Council for India as of March 1867. See **4474**&n4.

1 According to Munby (ph), the eccentric and obstinate bibliophile Sir Thomas Phillipps was planning to endow his collection of 40,000 printed books and 60,000 manuscripts 'as a permanent institution' at his Cheltenham home, Thirlestaine House. He had recently consulted D, most likely in a letter (not found), 'on how best such a legacy might be freed from the provisions of the Mortmain Act'.

I have often heard him say, that he believed your name & / collections would, some day, rank with those of the Bodleys[2] & the Cracherodes.[3]

I have inherited all that consideration for you, & I beg to assure you, on the part of H. M. Government, that they will be happy, in any way, to assist in forwarding your noble intentions.

If an act of Parlt. is necessary, I will myself undertake to carry it thro' the House of Commons.[4]

Believe me with esteem | Your faithful Servt | *B. Disraeli*

TO: [MONTAGU CORRY]   Downing Street [Sunday] 21 July 1867   **4477**
ORIGINAL: H B/XX/D/364
EDITORIAL COMMENT: C of Ex paper.

July 21 1867

I have no pens:

no envelopes:

no blue note paper:

   D.

Letters to Hutt[1] & Henley[2] to be sent immediately.

TO: LORD DERBY   Grosvenor Gate [Sunday 21] July 1867   **4478**
ORIGINAL: DBP Box 146/3
PUBLICATION HISTORY: M&B IV 550-1, an extract from the last paragraph
EDITORIAL COMMENT: C of Ex paper, seal crossed out and 'Grosvenor Gate' written in. Endorsed by Derby on the first page: 'Ansd'. *Dating*: D appears to have misdated his letter '20' instead of '21'; see n1. *Sic*: July 20.

Grosvenor Gate | July 20 1867

Right Honorable | The Earl of Derby K.G.

---

2 Sir Thomas Bodley (1545-1613), Kt 1604, BA 1563 Oxford, fellow of Merton College 1564, lecturer in Greek 1565, MA 1566 and junior proctor 1569, was MP for Portsmouth 1584. After serving as foreign diplomat for Elizabeth I 1585-97, he began refurbishing the University of Oxford library: acquisitions, cataloguing, classification, binding, preservation and fund-raising (much of it from his own purse). The new Bodleian Library reopened on 8 November 1602 with about 2,000 volumes. Bodley willed the greater part of his fortune (£7,000) to the Bodleian.

3 Clayton Mordaunt Cracherode (1730-1799), BA 1750 and MA 1753 Christ Church, Oxford, a trustee of the British Museum 1784, FRS 1785 and FSA 1787. A Bucks bibliophile, he willed his collection of 4,500 books, seven portfolios of drawings and 100 portfolios of prints to the British Museum.

4 See **4631**&nn1-3.

---

1 Sir William Hutt on 17 July had sent D a letter he had written on that day to Northcote complaining of his exclusion from the entertainment to be given the Sultan on the 19th (see **4474**&n4). 'As Lady Hutt & I are always included in the Court Invitations I felt & feel that the Govt has shown me gratuitous incivility in passing us over on this remarkable occasion.' Hutt had told Northcote, 'I did not mean to ask for a ticket, but only an explanation of what seemed to me a public discourtesy. You say that no slight was intended me by the Govt. The sarcasm – for in effect it is one – may be just ... I suspect it will appear that I am the only Privy Counsellor ... against whom the Govt has thought fit to close the doors of this national entertainment.' H B/XIX/Adds [unnumbered].

2 D's letter to Joseph Henley, perhaps a reply to Henley's letter of 19 July (see **4478**n2), has not been found.

My dear Lord,

Returning home, at 8 o'ck:, I found yr letter.[1]

I can't make out, that there are more, than 25 new County seats / proposed.

And yet my nerves are fluttered, for it seems impossible, that you, & especially on such matters, could make a mistake.

South Lancashire – have / you counted that *two?*

Henley must remain, until you have five minutes.[2]

According to Lord Stanhope, the Grey move has quite collapsed.[3] Ld. Grey told Lord Bristol, coming / out of Church, that he would divide.

Lord Stanhope votes against him; also Lord Carnarvon, & most others.

There is, however, no doubt, that Lord Russell &c. encouraged him: / but my original informant seems to be right, that the younger generation, Granville, Argyll[4] & Co., shrank from the too ridiculous climax / – of a Reform Bill in 1867 opposed by Ld. Grey & the Whigs.[5]

Yrs sin[cere]ly, | D.

1 Derby had written to D from Roehampton a letter marked '*Confidential*' on 'Sunday' (presumably 21 July): 'In looking over the papers preparatory to my statement tomorrow [at the second reading of the reform bill], I have discovered an extraordinary oversight in connexion with the Reform Bill. You have considered that you had 45 seats to dispose of; and have given 26 of them to Counties, and 19 to Boroughs, overlooking the fact that you had given a seat to the London University. How am I to deal with this? I have looked at the papers over & over again, and feel very confident that I am not mistaken. The result is an increase of one to the English Representation. It will be impossible to conceal the blunder.' H B/XX/S/439.

2 Derby (n1) had told D that 'Henley has sent me, through Stanley, I know not why, a letter a copy of which he tells me he has sent to you as to some statement said to have been made by you of what passed in the Cabinet of 1859. I cannot answer him until I hear from you, and probably you will yourself have an explanation with him.' Joseph Henley on 19 July had written D enclosing 'a copy of a letter to Lord Derby asking his permission to state what may be necessary if any question turns up as to what passed while I was a member of the Government of 1858. I may be questioned by my Constituents.' Henley's 19 July letter to Derby includes two quotations from D's speech to the House on 15 July (the third reading of the reform bill) on the need to establish the borough franchise on the principle of household suffrage. H B/XXI/H/472, 472a.

3 See 4473nn1&2.

4 George Douglas Campbell (1823-1900), 8th Duke of Argyll 1847, had made his maiden speech in the House in May 1848 supporting the removal of Jewish disabilities. He was chancellor of the University of St Andrews 1851-1900, rector of Glasgow University 1854-6, president of the Royal Society of Edinburgh 1860-4 and of the Highland and Agricultural Society of Scotland 1862-6, postmaster-general 1855-8, secretary of state for India 1868-74 and lord privy seal 1852-55, 1859-66 and 1880-1. His works include *The Eastern Question* (2 vols 1879), *The New British Constitution and its Master Builders* (1888), *Irish Nationalism: an Appeal to History* (1893) and *Our Responsibilities for Turkey: Facts and Memories of Forty Years* (1896).

5 Derby on 22 July would write to D from St James's Square: 'I am sorry to have alarmed you by a mares nest which I discovered when too late. The Bill is all right. Strange to say, I was misled by Lambert, who sent me a Memorandum of Redistribution in which he says 13 Counties, 2 each, 26, and omits the University. It was stupid in me not to recollect that S. Lancashire only counts for one seat. I am very nervous about what I have to do tonight, though Grey appears to have collapsed – and if it were any one else, I should say he would not divide.' H B/XX/S/440.

Genl | Hon Chas Grey　　　　　　　　　　　　　　　　　　　　July 25 1867
My dear General,[1]
The matter was not really postponed at the instance of the jackanapes in question; but, in truth, it is not in a satisfactory position, & the Secy. of the Treasury was / embarassed.

There is no doubt if the House were properly dealt with, & led, on the subject, the affair would be carried & pushed on – but it has, hitherto, not been grappled with. /

The House of Commons wants the plot to be decided on: it wants plans to be laid before it, as in the case of the Palacee of Justice[2] & National Gallery; &, if bills are / necessary for the separation of the Collections, it wishes them to be introduced, & enforced with all the power & influence of the Government. I am going to bring the / whole question before the Cabinet on Saturday,[3] & shall insist on the establishment of the Kensington Museum being made one of the principal measures / of the Government, & introduced immediately on the re-assembling of Parlt. by myself.[4]

I have not yet decided on the postponed vote.

Yrs ever, | D.

July 25 1867
The Chancellor of the Exchequer with his humble duty to Yr Majesty:
Sir John Pakington carried his vote this / evening for the "Army of Reserve." It

---

1 Grey on 22 July had written to D from Osborne a letter marked '*Private*': 'You have always shown such an appreciation of the Prince's great plans for South Kensington that the Queen feels she can always turn to you with Confidence in any matter affecting the future progress of the Museum ... H.M. has heard with much regret that in consequence of objections raised by two of the most inveterate enemies of South Kensington, who said that the vote for the erection at S. Kensington of the proposed Natural History Museum ought to have been preceded by a Bill authorising the removal of the Collection from the British Museum, the vote was at once postponed. There has already been so much delay in this matter, that the Queen hopes you will interpose your authority to prevent a further delay of another year. – It is really time that something was done to give effect to a plan wh. wth. the exception of Messrs. C. Bentinck, D. Seymour &c &c, has met with general approval.' H B/XIX/D/28.

2 Presumably the Courts of Justice Building Act 1865. Construction on the Royal Courts of Justice, contracted to architect George Edmund Street in 1868, would begin in 1873 and the building be opened by the Queen on 4 December 1882.

3 See **4482**&n1.

4 D on 29 July would assure the House (in committee of supply) that 'at an early period of next Session' he would lay before it a course to be adopted. 'A Bill would probably be necessary to insure the separation of the collections', he said, lamenting that rich collections in private hands 'which might become part of a national collection were not so, because there was not space or order to justify or encourage those gifts.' *Hansard* CLXXXIX cols 342-53 (D 347-9).

was coldly, & even captiously, received; but only on the ground that the scheme was not sufficiently extensive[.][1]

4481

TO: [MONTAGU CORRY]   Downing Street [Friday] 26 July 1867
ORIGINAL: H B/XX/D/42
EDITORIAL COMMENT: C of Ex paper.

July 26 1867

I want a paper on cumulative Voting, Representation of the Minorities &c. (against the system) that appeared in Saty. Rev: (a few weeks ago) for / a friend in the H. of Lords.[1]

Have the goodness to look over the numbers, wh:, I hope, are filed at the office; & find it for me, if you can – & let / me have it when I arrive.

D.

I have not a box left.

4482

TO: LORD DERBY   Downing Street [Saturday] 27 July 1867
ORIGINAL: DBP Box 146/3
EDITORIAL COMMENT: C of Ex paper.

Private   July 27 1867

Right Honorable | The Earl of Derby | K.G.

My dear Lord,

We went thro' all the amendments, & satisfactorily. I think, our friends will be fairly coached.[1]

Then, / I brought forward, the question of the Kensington Museum & the separation of the collections in the Brit: Museum.[2]

---

1 In the House on this day (25th) in committee of supply on 'Army Estimates' there had been protracted discussion of a scheme (Pakington called it essentially that of his predecessor, General Peel, who had introduced it on 7 March) for the formation of an army of reserve. *The Times* on 27 July would outline the scheme for two reserves: the first of 30,000 militiamen (to be drafted into the regular army in the event of war) and some 20,000 soldiers having completed two-thirds of their first term of service who 'might elect to commute each remaining year of service in the Line for two years' service in the Reserve'; the second of 30,000 'Enrolled Pensioners' and 'soldiers in their second term of service in the Line who might be willing to exchange into the Reserve upon the terms already stated.' There were numerous objections. Three votes were agreed to: £63,250 (Increase of Pay to Non-Commissioned Officers and Men of the Militia), £20,000 (Additional Pay to the Army Reserve Force) and £50,000 (Increase of Pay to Non-Commissioned Officers and Privates, Royal Marine Corps). *Hansard* CLXXXV cols 1448-1510; CLXXXIX cols 87-103, 118-40.

---

1 MA's clippings file includes numbers 610 and 611 of *The Saturday Review* containing three essays discussing D: 'The Government and the House' (which makes fun of Lowe's 'proposal to give a cumulative vote to three-cornered constituencies') and 'The Difficulties of Reform' (both 6 July) and 'The Reform Bill as it Was and as it Is' (13 July). H G/VI/[unnumbered].

---

1 Cabinet had met on this day (27th). *MP* (29 Jul 1867).
2 See **4479**&n1.

The Court is pressing / much on this matter, &, I hope, I have placed it in a better position, & one wh: will be soothing to H. M.

Afterwards, Abyssinia, wh: begins to alarm me.[3] / Northcote was instructed to telegraph to Bombay, & the Cabinet is to meet on Wednesday next at 4 o'ck,[4] when he will have received his answer.

Yrs ever, | D. /

I spoke to Stanley about Queen's Advocate: he said, he knew no one, & that Phillimore was thoroughly inefficient. Judging from / popular opinion, he was in favor of Travers Twiss, who has a public reputation, & not confined to this country: & who must / be a man of learning.[5]

TO: [MONTAGU CORRY]   [London, Sunday 28 July 1867]   4483
ORIGINAL: H B/XXI/60
EDITORIAL COMMENT: A note in D's hand on the fourth page of Malmesbury's letter docketed in another hand (possibly Corry's): 'July 28 /67. Ld Malmesbury. asks C. of E. to attend at meeting of Lords in Cabinet on Reform.'

If at the office in time, let Ld. M.[1] know you are in attendance at my request. I am engaged.[2]

D.

---

3 Emperor (and King of Kings) Tewodros II of Abyssinia, a temperamental but progressive Coptic Christian, in late 1862 had asked the new British consul, Captain Charles Duncan Cameron, to deliver a letter to the Queen. The foreign office having instructed Cameron to post it, the letter duly arrived but was filed and forgotten. When in January 1864 Tewodros imprisoned Cameron, his staff, some missionaries and their families, the foreign office sent a reply to his letter which arrived only in January 1866. Tewodros freed the prisoners but then had them intercepted on their way to the coast and imprisoned again in July. Although Stanley on 1 November 1866 had called their rescue one of the 'chief questions under discussion at the F.O.', on 11 May 1867 the cabinet had decided not to send an expedition. In the House on 26 July Henry Seymour had moved an address to the Queen to rescue the prisoners and proposed an ultimatum: release them or face an expedition. Dissenters included Stanley, who said 'it would be madness to throw a British army into an unknown country ... without a full previous investigation as to the means of moving, feeding, and keeping them in health'. The motion was withdrawn. *Disraeli, Derby* 269, 308; *Hansard* CLXXXIX cols 232-55. See **4518**&n3 and **4521**n4.
4 Cabinet would meet on Wednesday 31 July at 4 *pm. The Times* (31 Jul 1867).
5 Sir Robert Joseph Phillimore, author of *Commentaries upon International Law* (4 vols, 1854-61), on 23 August would be succeeded as Queen's advocate-general by Travers Twiss, a civilian jurisprudence and international law scholar whose major work is *The Law of Nations Considered as Independent Political Communities* (1861-3). Twiss would be knighted on 4 November 1867.

---

1 Malmesbury (see ec) had informed D on 'Sunday' that 'The 3 Dukes & I are to make a Cabinet Committee at the Treasury tomorrow at 12 to be crammed by Lambert. I hope you will look in for ¼ of an hour just to give us confidence & advice.' On the 29th he would note that Derby was 'still confined to his bed, and I have to conduct the Reform Bill through Committee in the House of Lords. This is no easy work, especially with many of our men against me.' H B/XIII/60; Malmesbury II 373.
2 In the House on the 29th D would oppose a motion by John Locke (L) to shelve the Parks Regulation Bill. *Hansard* CLXXXIX cols 382-404 (D 396-8). See **4498**&n1.

TO: CHARLES GREY   Grosvenor Gate [Wednesday] 31 July 1867

ORIGINAL: RAC 148 30

PUBLICATION HISTORY: *LQVB* I 455-6

EDITORIAL COMMENT: C of Ex paper, seal crossed out and 'Grosvenor Gate' written in. Endorsed by D on the fifth page: '*Confidl*' and in another hand on the first page: 'Germany'.

---

confidential   Grosvenor Gate | July 31 1867

Lt Genl: | Hon: Chas Grey

My dear General,

I received your packet last night, or rather early this morning, on my return home.

With my humble duty / to H. M., you may assure the Queen of the entire confidence in wh: I receive the intimations contained in your letter, & of my constant efforts to sustain H. M's policy.[1]

Lord Stanley, of late, / acting I hope, in some degree, under the influence of my reiterated representations, has entirely dropped the phrase, &, I hope, the abstract policy, of what is called "*non-intervention*," & during the last few / weeks has held to this language, when pressed by the French Government to join in some representation to Prussia: that he considered that Prussia had been somewhat unduly pressed in the / matter of Luxembourg, & that he was unwilling to convey to that power an impression, that England unduly favored France. I think the general bias of Lord

---

1 Grey on 29 July had sent D from Osborne a 12-page letter marked '*Private*.' Recent accounts from Paris and Berlin of 'mutual accusations of arming with hostile intentions' and 'a state of continual preparation for war', he wrote, posed an imminent danger of war in Europe. The Queen wondered whether England, 'adhering to a cold policy of non-interference or rather to one of total abstention from all concern in the affairs of the Continent, is to continue in her passive attitude, nor make any attempt to avert such a Calamity? Yet she fears that such may be the course which Ld. Stanley, unless some pressure is exercised upon him, may be inclined to pursue.' She felt strongly that 'our true policy, in the interest of peace, would be ... to let it be clearly understood, that certain contingencies wd bring England, inevitably, into the field. A war cannot take place between France and Prussia, without, in all probability, bringing not only the neutrality of Luxembourg, but the Independence of Belgium, into question; & no possibility of doubt shd exist of the determination of England to maintain her own engagements, & to insist on other Powers maintaining theirs on both these questions. Ld. Stanley is quite right in saying that we are equally bound by ties of alliance and friendship, both to France & Prussia, & that we should "hold the balance even" between the two countries, & do nothing, unnecessarily, to endanger our peaceful relations with either ... While, therefore, we cultivate the most friendly relations with all other Powers, including France, the *principle* of our Foreign Policy, (& this was also the opinion of the Prince Consort) should be a thorough understanding, for mutual support in the interest of Peace, with North Germany ... Prussia is not likely to violate either the neutrality of Luxembourg or the Independence of Belgium ... *unless she sees reason to believe that England means her guarantee of both these objects to remain a dead letter, in which case she might think it her interest to come to an agreement with France fatal to the Independence of the rest of Europe.* – France is much more likely to disregard the Engagements into which she has entered, for in all the questions which threatened the peace of Europe during the past year, she put herself, as the Queen views it, clearly & unmistakably in the wrong. She can have no right to interfere in the internal organization of Germany, & certainly had none to demand the evacuation of the Citadel of Luxembourg by its German garrison ... H.M. would therefore strongly urge the necessity of your giving your best attention to our whole system of Foreign Policy, so as to secure to England the respect & influence which is due to her as the Power who, above all others, can have no ambitious views of her own, nor any interest but in the preservation of Peace ... I need hardly say that this letter is meant strictly for yourself.' Beneath the last sentence the Queen had written: 'General Grey has *quite* understood the Queen's views & she *entirely* approves of all that is contained in this letter.' H B/XIX/D/30.

Stanley's mind / is to lean towards Prussia, & I have always encouraged & enforced that tendency.

But I do not gather the actual state of affairs from your letter. I apprehend it to be this.

On Sunday last, I / received information from a first-rate channel, that France, greatly disappointed by Lord Stanley's refusal to join in a representation to Prussia respecting the Schleswig question, had made an overture to / Russia, who consented to make a joint representation ↑with France↓ at Berlin, & that it ↑joint appeal↓ had succeeded; & removed all causes of disagreement.[2]

I could not manage to see Lord Stanley until Monday, when we / met at the House of Commons, & I told him this.[3] It was unknown to him, but he was greatly interested ↑by it↓ – but he told me, that from something wh: had reached him during the / last 8 & 40 hours, he was convinced that France did not contemplate war: he believed she never had. Her action was all restless & mortified vanity, but she was neither / able, nor willing, to go to war. He distinctly told me, that in declining joint action with France some little time previously, he had not touched on "noninterference", but clearly / said we reserved to ourselves to take such a course as the interests of Europe & England required.[4]

This is written currente calamo, but you will not esteem it less for being unstudied.[5]

Ever yrs sin[cere]ly, | D.

2 In a note to Denmark dated 18 June 1867, Prussia had requested "'guarantees for the protection and security of the national institutions'" of Germans residing in Prussian-occupied North Schleswig. Denmark in mid-July had replied that its liberal laws 'afford ample protection to German residents. Special guarantees, therefore, are not required.' Rumours had circulated for weeks that the French government had sent a note to Prussia on the subject of North Schleswig. Despite numerous denials in the French press, Prussian journals, wrote the *Times* correspondent in Paris on 29 July, insisted on 'the existence of a document which was described as an unwarrantable interference in Prussian affairs.' Such a note, he believed, would 'be a pretext for an open breach with Prussia'. The animosity would climax in the Franco-Prussian war of 1870-1. *The Times* (1, 19, 25, 29, 30 Jul 67).

3 Stanley on Monday 29 July had noted, 'Disraeli tells me that the Rothschilds [D's 'first-rate channel'] are confident of peace, and consider the Danish question as being virtually settled.' *Disraeli, Derby* 314.

4 Yet Stanley on 9 August would tell Grey unequivocally that 'If war does break out, we have only one course; that of a rigidly impartial neutrality.' *LQVB* I 458.

5 Grey on 5 August would reply that the Queen was glad that D 'coincided in the policy she recommended, & still more to hear what you said of Lord Stanley's tendency to lean towards Germany rather than towards France.' She felt that 'if England stood passively by,' France and Prussia, 'after a battle or campaign or two, might ... make up their quarrel at the expence of the Independence of the rest of Europe.' She feared Stanley 'might go too far in expressing a determination, under no circumstances to allow England to be mixed up in the disputes of the two countries ... Still if the Aggressor were to know that, in such a quarrel, the moral, &, in certain cases, the material support of England would be given to the other side – that is: that England would not ... maintain a dogged neutrality – it might prevent steps being taken on either side that must lead to war.' If both countries 'were assured that any violation of the Independence of Belgium, or of the neutrality of Luxembourg would certainly bring England into the field ... both Countries wd. probably shrink from being the first to provoke a rupture'. Grey on 6 August would add a lengthy summary of a letter to the Queen from the Queen of Prussia, who had related that France's 'continued *military* preparations ... have so impaired public confidence, that the trade & prosperity of Germany are daily suffering, & People begin generally to say that it wd be better to have war at once, than to continue in a position which, under the name of peace, produces all the evils of war.' H B/XIX/D/31.

TO: LORD DERBY Downing Street [Wednesday] 31 July 1867
ORIGINAL: DBP Box 146/3
EDITORIAL COMMENT: C of Ex paper. *Sic*: embarass.

Confidential July 31 1867

Rt Honble Earl of Derby | K.G.

My dear Lord,

The Cabinet just up, having considered the Abyssinian question, Irish Railways & P.O. Packets.[1]

Then, / we discussed state of affairs in H. of L. as to Reform Bill.

Duke of Buck thought both Grey & Lyvedens amendments wd. be carried. / There was ~~a ge~~ a rather general feeling, that, if Grey's amendment, as to the 12 seats, were carried, it might be accepted & utilized. John Manners, / however, opposed the idea, saying we were pledged to the 12000 Boro' men, & Hardy supported his view.[2]

Naas gave it as his opinion, that if we began / altering our Redistribution scheme, the whole thing wd. fall to pieces.

There was a universal opinion expressed, that if Cairns gave notice / of an amendment against tri-section of Counties, & advocating unicorn divisions instead, all our men wd. support him – they being quite demented – & / it was earnestly hoped, that you wd. see Cairns & expostulate with him.[3]

He did say to Malmesbury, that, tho' favorable to Grey's plan, / he was disinclined to vote for it, lest it might embarass the Government.

Stanley was for Grey's plan, so far as the 12 seats were concerned, but strongly recommended we / shd. not accept what they persist in calling the "cumulative vote".[4]

Walpole was for accepting.

I gave no opinions, as I thought such expression / was premature, but I did not discourage their remarks.

Gerard Noel[5] suggests from H of C. that Grey shd. be accepted / & the 12 seats apportioned to

Inns of Court	2
The omitted Boros	} 4
& Unicorns	
for Suffolk	}
Cornwall & S. Lancas[hire]	} 6
	12[6]

---

1 Derby had not attended this day's (31st) cabinet. In the House on 1 August there would be long debate on Irish Railways and, in committee of supply, on a vote (agreed to) for '"£507,428, to complete the sum for Post Office Packet Service."' *The Times* (1 Aug 1867); *Hansard* CLXXXIX cols 606-29, 658-704.

2 In the Lords on 1 August Lords Grey and Lyveden would move amendments to Clause 15 (Certain Boroughs to return One Member only). Grey's – '"to leave out ("Ten thousand") and insert ("Twelve thousand"),"' – would deprive twelve boroughs of one member each, Grey explaining that 'none of [those boroughs] are of such importance or of such a character that they would not be adequately represented by a single Member.' It would be adopted by a division of 98 to 86. Lyveden's motion, that '"every Borough which had a less population than Five thousand at the said Census shall cease to return any Member to serve in Parliament"', would be defeated 93 to 37. *Hansard* CLXXXIX cols 526-95.

3 So-called unicorn divisions were represented by three members. For Cairns's amendment, see **4491**n3.

4 See **4317**n2.

5 Gerard Noel was a lord of the treasury.

6 For a list of boroughs disfranchised between 1832 and 1867, see McCalmont 333-44.

/ Finally an opinion of Naas, backed up by Walpole was unanimously approved: that ~~if~~ Grey shd. be resisted, but if carried, progress shd. be immediately reported.

My hand is so cold, I cannot write.

D.

TO: LORD CAIRNS   [London] Thursday [1 August 1867?]   4486
ORIGINAL: PRO 30/51/1 ff60-3
EDITORIAL COMMENT: C of Ex paper. *Dating*: by context; see nn4&5.

Thursday

Right Honorable | The Lord Cairns

My dear Cairns,

I received your letter.[1]

It seems, that we must have the meeting of the party on Friday the 9th.[2] Inst. Now, / the ~~resolutions~~ amendments must be previously submitted to, & sanctioned by, the Council, who assembled before at Grosvenor Gate.[3] Therefore, there is no time to lose; tho' if I / can count on receiving the dr[af]t amendments from you on the 5th. or 6th.,[4] & having, at the same time, a conference with you, the Council might be appointed for / the 7th. or even 8th. & the general meeting could be held on the following Friday.

It will not do to have general meetings on a Saturday or Monday, & if the notice of the amendments is postponed until Tuesday the / 13th. Inst, there will be complaints from the Government of not sufficient time to consider &c.[5]

I think of asking Lord Lonsdale to allow the general meeting at / his house, wh: is spacious & central.[6]

Yours ever | D.

TO: EDWARD COLEMAN   Grosvenor Gate [Sunday] 4 August 1867   4487
ORIGINAL: WSH [7]
EDITORIAL COMMENT: C of Ex paper, seal crossed out and 'Grosvenor Gate' written in.

E.J. Coleman Esqr   Grosvenor Gate | Augt 4 1867

---

1 This letter by Cairns, 1st Baron Cairns (UK) as of 27 February 1867, has not been found.

2 There is no record of a Conservative party meeting on Friday 9 August 1867. The House that day met from 2 *pm* to 3:15 *am* on the 10th; until 2:10 *am* according to *The Times* (10 Aug 1867). *Hansard* CLXXXIX cols 1217-91.

3 This may have been a secret council meeting, as there is no evidence of such a meeting at Grosvenor Gate during this time.

4 On Tuesday 6 August the reform bill would be given third reading in the Lords (with protests from Lords Ellenborough and Selkirk) and be sent to the Commons, where D would 'move that the Amendments of the Lords be printed and taken into consideration on Thursday' 8 August. *Hansard* CLXXXIX cols 930-53, 1002.

5 The Commons' amendments to the Lords' amendments would be discussed in the Lords on Monday 12 August, with a motion that a committee be appointed 'to prepare Reasons to be offered to the Commons for the Lords insisting on the said Amendments: The Committee to meet *forthwith*.' *Hansard* CLXXXIX cols 1306-26.

6 Lonsdale had lived at 15 Carlton Terrace since 1840 and in 1845 had taken over number 14, occupying both houses until his death.

Dear Mr Coleman,

I must thank you for your ever kind recollection of us, wh: reminds me, also, of your beautiful park.[1] Alas! it is long, since I / visited such scenes, & have never seen my woods in foliage this year! I long for sunny shades!

Pray give for us a thousand kind words, / & thoughts, to Mrs. Coleman.

Yours sincerely, | D.

4488   TO: [EDWARD WATKIN]   [London, about Sunday 4 August 1867]

ORIGINAL: H C/II/A/32f

EDITORIAL COMMENT: A draft in D's hand. *Recipient* and *Dating*: by context; see n1. *Sic*: embarassing.

Dear Sir,

I have had the honor of receiving yr letter of the 2nd. Inst.[1] in wh: you ~~state~~ refer to ~~a public statement that it was~~ the ↑supposed rumoured↓ int[enti]on of ~~the~~ ↑H.M↓ Govt to recommend your name to the Q for the honor of Knighthood in consider[ati]on of yr services ~~in common~~ ↑connected↓ with the Inter Co[ntinenta]l Railway & ~~its~~ ↑the↓ influence of that undertaking on the Union of the B.N.A. Prov[inces]: ~~& your fear~~ & in wh. you state yr appreh[ensi]on that ~~the~~ such ~~discontent~~ ↑an↓ in[tenti]on ~~might~~ in consequence of / the recent intelligence ↑from Canada↓ with respect to the [*illegible deletion*] distrib[uti]on ↑of honors↓ ~~might~~ ↑might↓ prove embarassing to the Govt.

Under ~~these such an assumption~~ ↑that impression↓ you have in a manner, highly creditable to y[our]s[el]f & most considerate to the Govt., ~~expressed~~ stated that you shd not "feel yourself slighted or aggrieved" if the int[enti]ons ↑views↓ of the government towards yourself were not proceeded with pending such an unfortunate feeling in Canada.

It is ~~very~~ quite true that it was the intention of H.M. Govt. to recommend / to H.M. to confer the honor of knighthood upon you in consider[ati]on of yr services in question, thereby, ↑as they believe,↓ fulfilling the intentions of the late D. of N. when Secy of State for the Colonies,[2] but H.M. Govt appreciates your motives in the suggestion you have made, are of opinion, that it may be expedient to suspend for a time conferring a distinction on you wh: under the peculiarities of the case might occasion ~~an in~~ ↑a painful tho'↓ unfounded ↑feeling of↓ jealousy.[3]

---

1 Stoke Park; see **4035**&n3.

---

1 Watkin had written to D from London on 2 August to thank him for having proposed his name to the Queen for knighthood but with reservations, having recently learned that 'the French-Canadian population' looked upon the 'recent distribution of honors' to George-Étienne Cartier and Hector-Louis Langevin with 'dissatisfaction, wh. arises at the very inopportune moment of the birth of the "new dominion."' Not wishing to aggravate that feeling, Watkin would not feel 'slighted or aggrieved should your kindness proceed no further.' On 3 August he had sent Rose his 2 August letter for transmission to D, stating that he felt D '*might* be embarrassed, if, at this moment, he conferred upon me the honor proposed', closing with 'P.S. Do you think me Quixotic. I only want to do as I would be done by.' H C/II/A/32c,e. See **4432**&n1.

2 Watkin had pointed out (n1) that 'my late most kind & indulgent friend – the Duke of Newcastle – suggested some time before his death [in 1864], an even higher reward for the services which he, alone, knew the full extent of – but, at my request it was postponed until all the manifold difficulties being, one by one, cleared away'.

3 Watkin would be knighted in 1868 for his 'service in the British cause in Canada.' ODNB.

ORIGINAL: INL Mayo Papers MS 11,150
EDITORIAL COMMENT: C of Ex paper. *Sic*: Mansel.

Confidential   Augt 5 1867

Right Honorable | The Lord Naas

My dear Naas,

I complain very much of the disagreeable position in wh: you have placed me with respect to Mr Mansel,[1] who is here, / an applicant for Government employment, & who has come over to England in consequence of the expectations, wh:, under your sanction, I held out to him.[2]

I asked you, when we last / talked over the matter, to tell me fairly, that the Irish government meant to do nothing for him, if that were really their decision – & I shd. act accordingly & close the matter.

You assured me, that / was not the case, & that, altho' in the instance under discussion you cd. not meet his views, nevertheless you were far from saying, or thinking, that an opportunity with a different, or rather contrary, result might not / occur.

He has, therefore, been fed with hope; & as everything is known in Dublin, if he supports the Government, it is said, that he has been promised a place, & if he criticises their / conduct, that he has been refused one.[3]

The man, therefore, is injured by our shilly-shallying, & it is better, that he shd. be told distinctly, that he is never to have anything, than that he shd be left in this equivocal condition. /

You must be a better judge of what he is worth, than I am; but in a country governed by newspapers so much as Ireland is, I should have thought an experienced & trenchant pen, / the writer of wh: has apparently a large political connection, was worth securing.[4]

Yours ever, | D.

---

1 Henry Maunsell (1806-1879), MD 1831 University of Glasgow, had been chair of Midwifery 1835-41 and of Hygiene and Political Medicine 1841-6 at the Royal College of Surgeons in Ireland (Dublin) and was the author of *The Dublin Practice of Midwifery* (1834). In 1860 he had purchased a leading Tory newspaper, *The Dublin Evening Mail*, which he would edit until his death.

2 Maunsell on 28 June had written to Montagu Corry from Morley's Hotel (Charing Cross) that he had been informed by Ralph S. Cusack (see n4) of three possible vacancies: master of the exchequer, master of the Queen's bench and registrar of deeds. Maunsell had written to Corry from Dublin on 5, 11, 15, 24, 29 and 31 July (twice). In his first 31 July letter he reiterated that D 'had authorised you [Corry] to say that he was desirous of serving me & would not refuse any opportunity that might occur for offering me a place ... I must request that you will be so kind as to place this letter before Mr Disraeli.' In the second he stated his intention to be in London on 2 August and see Corry the following day. He would write to Corry on 7 and 14 August ('I am returning today to Ireland & will bore you no more, for the present at least.') and ten times from Dublin between 19 August and 23 December. H B/XXI/M/258-78.

3 Maunsell on 15 January 1868 would send Corry two pages headed '[Printed for Convenience–not for Publication.]' containing seven letters (6 to 10 January) between Maunsell and Gustavus Lambart that placed him 'in the cruel position which Mr Disraeli foresaw & stated in his letter to Lord Mayo [*Naas would become Earl Mayo on 12 August*] the contents of which you mentioned to me by his desire – I am represented as a disappointed & vindictive place hunter'. H B/XXI/M/279, 283.

4 Naas would reply to D on 7 August with a letter marked '*Confidential*': 'I am really very sorry that you should imagine that I have placed you in a disagreeable position with regard to Dr Maunsell. The Irish

TO: LORD NAAS   House of Commons [Tuesday] 6 August 1867
ORIGINAL: INL Mayo Papers MS 11,150
EDITORIAL COMMENT: C of Ex paper.

Right Honorable | The Lord Naas   H of Comm: | Augt 6/1867

My dear Naas,

I am very nervous about your legal appointments.[1] Is Harrison settled? I hear nothing in his / favor: they say, a hot Orangeman, & of little talent?

What of Purcell? Is he not a Conservative? Is he a R. Catholic? I have heard him well spoken / of professionally.[2]

I am entirely against preferring R. Caths: if they are not bonâ fide on our side – but if we can legitimately prefer a ~~Rath~~ R. Cath: lawyer / who is also a Tory, it wd. surely be very wise.

Yrs | D.

TO: QUEEN VICTORIA   House of Commons [Tuesday] 6 August 1867
ORIGINAL: RAC B23 95
EDITORIAL COMMENT: C of Ex paper, seal crossed out and 'House of C.' written in. *Sic*: both ... both; Schelswig.

House of C. | Augt 6 1867

The Chancellor of the Exchequer with his humble duty to Yr Majesty:

The motion on the Simla Court Martial has / just been defeated by 66 to 48![1]

Govt were asked but for one office for him which was on his suggestion was [*sic*] to be obtained in a round about way. The present clerk of the Hanaper was to be made Master of the Court of Exchequer and Maunsell was to be appointed clerk of the Hanaper. I never did more than listen to this proposal and never held out any hope to him or Cusack on the subject. It was however discovered that the appt. of Cusack would be contrary to the Statute as the Master of the Exchequer must be either a practising Barrister or a Solicitor a qualification which Mr Cusack does not possess. Cusack and Maunsell are both perfectly aware of this so he has no excuse for troubling you on this matter. However the Lord Chancellor has settled the affair by agreeing to a Clause proposed by Ld Cranworth which takes away the Patronage of this office from the Crown – altogether ... I am not aware that there has been any office vacant in the Gift of the Irish Govt since we have been in office which he could have accepted.' H B/XX/BO/31.

---

1 A report of 17 August from Dublin would tell of a 'keen controversy' over the appointment of a new solicitor-general for Ireland. Among the three candidates were Michael Harrison, of the North Circuit Bar, 'whose claims are most strongly supported by the Ulster Conservatives', and Mr Purcell, QC, 'a very respectable barrister, who has abated but little of his high Protestant principles, but is also popular with the moderate Liberals.' *The Times* (19 Aug 1867).

2 Michael Harrison (1823-1895), BA Dublin University 1846, an Irish barrister (Lincoln's Inn 1849), QC 1863, sol-gen 1867, would be appointed a judge of the bankruptcy court 1868 and justice of the common pleas division 1878 and of the Queen's bench division 1888. Francis Elrington Ball *The Judges of Ireland, 1221-1921* (New York 1927) 373. It would be reported in 1868 that 'Mr. Purcell, Q.C., is likely to obtain the law-advisership at the [Dublin] Castle, now held by Mr. Charles Shaw.' *The Times* (30 Nov 1868).

---

1 In the House on this day (6th) there had been two motions for an address to the Queen in the case of the sentence by the court martial of Captain Ernest Scott Jervis, 106th regiment (Bombay light infantry): one by William Brett, MP (C) for Helston, '"to reinstate that Officer in his rank in the Army and in his Regiment"' (withdrawn) and one by Arthur Otway, MP (L) for Chatham, '"to give effect to the recommendation to mercy"' (defeated 66 to 48), the House adjourning at 1:30 *am*. Jervis in June 1866 had been tried at Simla for misappropriating funds and goods belonging to General Sir William Mansfield,

It was very near, & it is very difficult to get men together at this moment. They / are scraped up from every corner. Nevertheless, if the motion had been carried, it wd. have been serious.

The Reform Bill came down from the / House of Lords today,[2] & the Chancr of the Exchequer has fixed Thursday next to consider the Lords' Amendments. Some good judges think, that both the *soi disant* cumulative vote, / & the voting papers, will both be carried.[3]

Lord Stanley told the C. of Er. today (they dined together at the House) that Prussia troubled / him very much: that he was convinced of the sincerity of France in desiring peace: but that Prussia, as fast as one difficulty was / removed, revived the old story, that war was inevitable: "sooner or later"[.] Mr Canning ~~used~~ ↑was wont↓ to say, when he heard this phrase used, "then, I prefer later" – but / Prussia seems to prefer "sooner."

Stanley said "that tall latte", to day, when I noticed that both the Luxembourg & the Schelswig difficulties had been successfully encountered, / said "I feel we must have war; it is in the air; it cannot be avoided"[.] Stanley rated him very severely, & pressed him for his reasons: he / had none: but Stanley ↑said↓ this was the way with all the Prussians at the present moment.[4]

TO: **LORD DERBY**　　　　　　　Grosvenor Gate [Thursday 8 August 1867]　**4492**
ORIGINAL: DBP Box 146/3
EDITORIAL COMMENT: Grosvenor Gate paper. *Dating*: by context; see nn3&4.

Confidential

Right Honorable | The Earl of Derby | K.G.

My dear Lord,

I wanted to get to you this morning but can't.

We owe much to Henley in this great struggle. I said so to Lord Abingdon the other / day, who had mentioned the subject to me.

---

commander-in-chief of India, to whom Jervis was aide-de-camp. Although Jervis had been found guilty of insubordination but acquitted of fraud, Mansfield, disregarding the court martial's recommendation of mercy, had sentenced him to dismissal from the service (the sentence for fraud). Brett claimed Jervis 'was driven to these acts of insubordination by false charges made under circumstances of the greatest provocation.' *Hansard* CLXXXIX cols 1004-40.

2 Amendments to the reform bill had been discussed in the Lords on 29, 30 July and 1, 2, 5 August. The bill had passed at third reading on this day (6th) and was sent to the Commons. *Hansard* CLXXXIX cols 256-328, 405-73, 526-95, 705-52, 821-42, 930-52.

3 On Thursday 8 August D would move that the Commons consider the Lords' amendments in a 'spirit of prudent but dignified conciliation', the House adjourning at 2:15 *am* on the 9th. There would be protracted debate on Cairns's amendment (providing for the representation of minorities in three-membered constituencies, the so-called 'unicorns') to Clause A (Restriction as to Number of Votes in certain Counties and Boroughs), which would be agreed to 253-204, D voting with the majority. D's own amendment to Clause C (Power to Vote by Voting Paper), 'after the word "County" to leave out the words "or Borough"', would be agreed to, but the clause rejected 258-206, D voting with the minority. *Hansard* CLXXXIX cols 1108-99 (D 1108-13, 1118, 1185-6, 1192, 1197-8).

4 Bismarck (nearly six feet three inches tall) was not in London at this time. Stanley's '"tall latte"' is most likely Count Albrecht von Bernstorff, former Prussian minister and since July 1867 ambassador of the North German Confederation. See **4396**n1. 'Latte' (German) is 'sapling' but also 'pole', 'rod' and 'staff'. For the Schleswig difficulties, see **4484**&n2.

I was under an impression, that Henley, who wd. ask for nothing, wanted something for his eldest son.[1]

It is not so, but for / a younger, & a clergyman.[2]

It shd. not be less than £400. per ann: I wish we cd. do it "handsome".

I can't speak to the Lord Chanr, for I lose my temper with him. / With prodigious patronage, he does nothing for the party, & is so insensible of his great obligations to you, & his own demerits![3]

Yrs ever | D.[4]

4493   TO: QUEEN VICTORIA   Downing Street, Friday 9 August [1867]

ORIGINAL: RAC B23 98

EDITORIAL COMMENT: C of Ex paper. *Dating*: by context; see nn1&2. *Sic*: Sultann.

Friday Augt 9

The Chanr. of the Excheqr with his humble duty to Yr Majesty:

He passed the vote for the entertainment of the Sultann[1] this evening: / not altogether smoothly, but without a division; & in a manner, he trusts, on the whole, not displeasing to Your / Majesty.[2]

1 The eldest of Joseph Henley's four sons was Joseph John Henley (1821-1910), CB 1892. Educated at Eton and Christ Church, he had served in the 1st Royal Dragoons and was JP and DL for Oxfordshire. He was private secretary to his father when president of the board of trade and general inspector of the local government board 1867-92. *The Times* (14 Oct 1910).

2 Henley's second son was the Rev Francis George Henley (*c* 1827-1898), rector of Lydlinch, Blandford, Dorset. *The Times* (2 Jul 1898). Abingdon on 8 August 1867 had written to D enclosing a letter of 6 August from Joseph Henley and suggesting that D communicate with him. 'The living, his son is holding of mine, is a good £400 per a. & he has about 3 or 4 years to run – it is Cumnor near Oxford his name is Frank.' Henley had informed Abingdon, 'It is pleasant to hear that my former Colleague D'Israeli thinks I have been of use to the Government, & wishes to do me service ... You know my Son Frank, is a good man in a country parish, & I should be glad if he can get a permanency as good, as that, which by your kindness he enjoys for a time.' H B/XX/S/444a,b.

3 Lord Chelmsford, who had spoken repeatedly in the House against the removal of Jewish disabilities, who was 'a poor debater' and 'no asset in council' and 'whose views on patronage enraged' D, would be summarily set aside by D in 1868 (in favour of Cairns) and go into retirement 'muttering angrily that some people became "dizzy" with promotion'. Blake 487-8, 390.

4 Barrington on 8 August would write to D on Derby's behalf, returning D's letters (n2) and expressing Derby's gratitude for Henley's assistance 'to the Conservative Party, and especially during the last Session, on the momentous question of Reform.' However, since taking office Derby had had only 'two livings to dispose of, the value of which was over £400 a year. One of these was the Living of Kew, which was immediately secured by the Duchess of Cambridge. Lord Derby can therefore, at present, do no more than have Mr Henley's wishes in mind, with a sincere hope that at some future time, he may be able to satisfy him.' Abingdon on 3 January 1868 would write to D: 'I return Ld. Barringtons letter, which I forwarded to Henley, who writes that Ld. B. had just offered him *another* living which his son is going to see.' H B/XX/S/444; XXI/A/68.

---

1 See 4474&nn2-5.

2 In the House on this day (9th) in committee of supply there had been a motion '"That a sum, not exceeding £25,000, be granted to Her Majesty, to defray the Charge which will come in course of payment during the year ending on the 31st day of March 1868, for the Entertainment of Foreign Potentates."' To A.S. Ayrton's demand for an explanation of this request for 'an excessive expenditure', D had replied that 'the late occasion was one of a very rare and extraordinary character, and the expenditure was of a particular kind ... This was in every respect a national visit, and it should be a national reception, and a national expense.' He had also emphasized that the vote was in no way connected 'with the expenditure of the Civil List.' *Hansard* CLXXXIX cols 1246-60 (D 1246, 1248-9, 1253-6).

Grosvenor Gate [Monday] 12 August 1867 **4494**

ORIGINAL: DBP Box 146/3

EDITORIAL COMMENT: Grosvenor Gate paper imprinted 'MAD'.

R.H. | The Earl of Derby | K.G.   Aug 12 1867

My dear Lord,

I don't think you can count on proroguing before Tuesday.[1] If an idea gets about, that / you are pressed for time, it will be all up with the Parks Bill, on wh: we commence tomorrow / morning.[2]

   I will call.
      Ever | D.

TO: LORD HYLTON   Downing Street [Monday] 12 August 1867 **4495**

ORIGINAL: SCR DD/HY C/2165 [73]

EDITORIAL COMMENT: C of Ex paper. *Sic*: Wolf.

Private   Aug 12 1867

Right Honorable | The Lord Hylton

My dear Hylton,

Our friend, Rose, from the negligence of a partner, is in great difficulty about a bill in your house, & / on wh: you report today.[1]

---

1 Parliament would be prorogued on Wednesday 21 August to Wednesday 6 November 1867. *Hansard* CLXXXIX col 1649.

2 Spencer Walpole on 3 May had introduced the Meetings in Royal Parks Bill, which would forbid meetings in any of the royal parks in the metropolis without the Queen's permission and carry a maximum penalty of £10 or two months imprisonment. Discussion of the Parks Regulation Bill (as it was now called), begun on 29 July, would resume on 13 August. *Hansard* CLXXXVI cols 2024-6, CLXXXIX cols 382-404, 1453-87, 1571-91. See **4498**&n1.

---

1 Margaret Rose on this day (12th) had written from 59 Rutland Gate asking D's help in 'a matter in which my Husband thinks his honor and interests are *deeply* concerned, but in which he is unable to act for himself being completely *prostrate* in Mind and Body by all over strain and mental pressure. It is a matter that admits of no delay as it has to be decided in the House of Lords tomorrow.' Hylton on the 13th would write to D from Merstham a letter marked '*Private*': 'I was extremely sorry yesterday to find myself powerless to do anything that would rectify the mistake which Rose's Firm appears to have made in dealing with this Chatham & Dover Railway Bill, which has been 21 days before a Committee of the Commons, & for 10 days before our Committee ... but I did all in my power to get the promoters of the Measure to agree to take their proposed Clause, at the last moment though it could not according to the Rules of the House come regularly before Us ... This is not the only case in which my Friends have been involved in the affairs of the Roguish Railway we had under our consideration & I never had a business cast upon me which was so great a bore.' H B/XX/R/27, 27b.

Sir Drummond Wolf will explain the matter to you.[2] I am most anxious to serve Rose, & shall / feel personally obliged to you if you will aid him.[3]

Yrs ever, | D.[4]

4496 TO: MONTAGU CORRY Downing Street [Monday] 12 August 1867
ORIGINAL: H B/XX/D/43
EDITORIAL COMMENT: C of Ex paper. *Sic*: coniferist; là Fontainbleau.

Montagu Corry | Esq   Augt 12 1867

Mon très Cher,

Your letter arrived this morning, & I was much pleased at receiving it.[1] I should like to have had some slight description / of the forest, for I love forests, & have never seen Savernake,[2] that my dear friend, D'Orsay, always told me was unequalled in England.

What is its size? Is it flat or undulating? what / tree most abounds? its soil, whether coniferist or ferny? for it cd., scarcely, be both. Are there vistas à là Fontainbleau? glades of green delight?

Genl. Knollys (he is a chevalier)[3] sent for the / accounts yesterday. I said I cd. not

---

2 Margaret Rose (n1) had told D that 'Sir Henry D. Wolff has most kindly undertaken to do what he can in the matter, if you will kindly hear what he has to say, and give him the assistance he requires & will fully explain to you.' Wolff on 13 August would write to D from 15 Rutland Gate: 'Lord Bateman will on Thursday on the 3rd reading move the insertion of a clause & Lds Hylton & Cadogan will support it. If a word could be said to Lord Colville to get Peers to vote for it the house is not likely to be full & we may carry it. Poor Rose is so very affected by it that I should not be surprised to hear of some unfortunate seizure.' H B/XXI/W/482.

3 In the Lords on Thursday 15 August Lord Redesdale would explain how the London, Chatham, and Dover Railway Company 'had on the same day [*21 February 1866*] ... mortgaged the same property to two different parties [the Imperial Mercantile Credit Company and the General Credit Company] ... one of the most disgraceful transactions which had ever taken place in the affairs of any company.' Clause 36a, which solved the problem by a scheme of government intervention, was added to the bill, which was passed and sent to the Commons. *Hansard* CLXXXIX cols 1536-9. In H are two printed documents: 'London, Chatham, and Dover Railway (Arrangement) Bill. STATEMENT On behalf of The General Credit Company in support of the Clause to be proposed for insertion in the Bill on 3rd Reading, which stands for Thursday, 15th August, 1867' and the clause itself. On the title page, above another printing of the 'STATEMENT', D has written '*This is urgent*'.

4 Rose on 15 August would write to Corry from Rayners thanking him and D for extricating him 'from a position of great difficulty in which my good partner Baxter had inadvertently involved me.' In H is a note to Corry signed 'HDW' (Henry D. Wolff), docketed in another hand 'Aug 15 /67': 'The question is in no wise settled so pray do not let the Peers off. It was a mistake of Spofforths.' H B/XX/R/27e, 27d, 27c. See **4517**n1.

1 This letter has not been found.

2 The 4,500-acre Savernake Forest, Wiltshire, is over one thousand years old and the only privately owned (14th Earl of Cardigan) forest in England. When Capability Brown built his famous Grand Avenue of beech trees through the heart of the forest in the late 1790s (at 3.9 miles the longest avenue in Britain), the Savernake had 40,000 acres.

3 Sir William Thomas Knollys (1797-1883), KCB ('chevalier') 1867, PC 1871, educated at Harrow and Sandhurst, had entered the 3rd (later Scots) Guards in 1813, becoming adjutant 1821, lieut-col 1844, regimental col 1850 and maj-gen 1854. He was lieut-gov of Guernsey 1854-6, the first commander of Aldershot military camp 1854-60, president of the council of military education 1861, treasurer and comptroller of the household of the Prince of Wales 1862-77 and gentleman usher of the black rod 1877-83.

give them in your absence, but your colleague[4] replied immediately he could get them! And sure eno' he did. I hope he has not broken into yr. sacred muniments!

Ever, | D.

TO: JOHN LAMBERT   Downing Street [Thursday] 15 August 1867   **4497**
ORIGINAL: H C/II/B/297C
EDITORIAL COMMENT: A copy in John Lambert's hand sent to George Sclater-Booth on 26 December 1876 as attesting to his worthiness to be made a KCB (received 1879).

John Lambert Esq   Downing Street | Augt. 15. 1867
My dear Sir,

The Reform Bill has this moment received the Royal Assent, and that great and, I believe happy event makes my memory recur to one, who by his intelligence, knowledge, prudent counsel, and happy resource assisted me so effectually in my labours; and, that too, with a patience, and pleasantness of temper, which mitigate and soften the exertions of public life.

Let me, therefore, my dear Mr. Lambert, thank you sincerely for all your kind and valuable aid to me in this vast enterprise. I shall always cherish the recollection of your cordial cooperation.[1]

I hope before I leave Town[2] to have the pleasure of seeing you.[3]

Yours sincerely | (signed) B. Disraeli

TO: QUEEN VICTORIA   Downing Street [Friday] 16 August 1867   **4498**
ORIGINAL: RAC B23 101
PUBLICATION HISTORY: M&B IV 566-7, omitting the fourth, fifth and seventh paragraphs
EDITORIAL COMMENT: C of Ex paper.

Augt 16 1867

The Chanr of the Exchequer with his humble duty to Your Majesty:

He has now virtually brought the business of the House of Commons to a conclusion, & it will / only meet on Monday to complete the business of the House of Lords.

He regrets, that H.M. Government were obliged to relinquish the Parks Bill yesterday, after / a division, wh: showed, that the House was desirous of legislation on the subject, but it was impossible to proceed with the Bill without considerably lengthening the / Session.[1]

---

4 Presumably Charles Fremantle.

---

1 In H there are over two dozen reform-related memos and letters from John Lambert to D in 1866-7. H B/XI/J/143, 174-8, L/2-21.
2 See **4500**&n2.
3 Lambert on 16 August would reply that he would treasure D's letter 'not only as a proof of your friendship and consideration, but as an historical document of surpassing value to myself and my children in connexion with the final stage of one of the greatest and wisest measures of our day ... I shall most gladly avail myself of the privilege of seeing you before you leave Town'. H B/XI/J/174.

---

1 In the House in committee on 15 August an amendment by MP (L) George Denman to the Parks Regulation Bill had been rejected 86-31. Hardy, in light of continued opposition from some members and

The truth is, that the whole dealing with this subject, from the commencement, has been a series of errors, originating in a fundamental one. The / matter was originally treated by Y. M. Government without sufficient knowledge & sufficient thought.[2]

They depended on Mr Walpole; Mr Walpole depended on / Sir George Grey; & Sir George Grey depended on Mr. Waddington, the permanent U. Secy. of State.[3]

Mr Waddington was wrong / in his law & alike headstrong & feeble in his policy; but Mr Waddington was, once, a man of strong character, & still of high reputation, & he ruled the late Government, / & Mr Walpole, with unresisted authority, from a superstitious conviction of his infallibility.

It will require great tact & temper to bring all this right, but it will be done. /

Lord Stanley seems to have increased, & increasing, confidence in the maintenance of European peace: although Lord Stanley, is of a reserved & rather / morose temper, & will not go out of his way to confess, that he has been in error, he is really *au fond* truthful & impartial; & / if convinced, that he has erred, or miscalculated, is never blind to the result, &, often unavowedly, to a certain degree, perhaps, unconsciously, will / assuredly modify his conduct. So, in the present state of affairs, it is far from improbable, that Lord Stanley will, ultimately, be the Minister, who will destroy, & shatter to pieces, the decaying theory & system of non-interference.[4]

4499   TO: EDWARD COLEMAN   Downing Street [Saturday] 17 August 1867
ORIGINAL: WSH [6]
EDITORIAL COMMENT: C of Ex paper.

E.J. Coleman Esqr   Augt 17 1867
Dear Mr Coleman,
You are always remembering us, & always kindly. The venison of Bucks, & the birds of Shrop-shire! Your / gifts are choice![1]

'yielding ... to the obstinate minority who will not allow me to go on in the ordinary course', withdrew the bill. *Hansard* CLXXXIX cols 1571-91.

2 After outlawing the Reform League demonstration held in Hyde Park on 6 May 1867 by a proclamation signed by home secretary Spencer Walpole, the cabinet on 4 May had decided (in Stanley's words) 'not to stop the meetings if peaceable'. Although more than 10,000 police and military troops had been assembled to quell any disturbance, the demonstration and Reform League speeches went off 'with the quietness and good order of a temperance meeting.' Stanley on that day (6 May) had noted that 'Walpole's conduct in first announcing that the meeting was forbidden, and then allowing it, is generally blamed. We are all equally responsible, but he is the minister in whose department the matter lay, and from his somewhat weak and vacillating character there is a tendency to assume that it was his personal doing.' *The Times*, reporting Walpole's resignation on 10 May, had called him an 'excellent, amiable, and honourable man, but with little judgment, and with a sensitiveness now hardening into obstinacy, now melting into feebleness'. He would remain a member of cabinet without portfolio until 1868. *Disraeli, Derby* 307; *The Times* (6, 7, 10 May 1867).

3 Walpole had succeeded home secretary Sir George Grey, who had worked closely with permanent undersecretary Horatio Waddington, who had recently resigned and whose position had been assumed on 14 August by Adolphus Liddell. Waddington would die in early October. *The Times* (16 Aug, 9 Oct 1867).

4 For Stanley's policy of non-intervention, see **4484**&nn1,4&5.

---

1 See **4035** and **4072**.

I trust, notwithstanding all we hear, your sport is worthy of your gun.

With very kind remembrances to Mrs / Coleman.

Yrs sincerely, | D.

TO: [MONTAGU CORRY] [London, Tuesday 20 August 1867] **4500**

ORIGINAL: H B/XIII/58

EDITORIAL COMMENT: A note by D written on the verso of a letter from Joseph Neal McKenna. Docketed by Corry on the same page: 'Aug. 19. /67 M Kenna M.P. Knighthood Aug 20 Ansd by C. of E.' *Dating*: by context; see nn1&2.

I will answer this[1] after the Council today.[2]

D.

TO: **LORD DERBY** Downing Street, Tuesday [20 August 1867] **4501**

ORIGINAL: DBP Box 146/3

EDITORIAL COMMENT: C of Ex paper. *Dating*: by context; see nn1&2. *Sic*: *miseres*; etat.

Right Ho[nora]ble | The Earl of Derby | KG Tuesday

My dear Lord,

I am sorry to trouble you about such *miseres*: but I have got a letter from our Irish Knight,[1] who is / much perplexed, having heard nothing.[2]

---

1 Joseph McKenna had written to D at Grosvenor Gate on '19th August' about 'the offer so graciously made through Lord Mayo accepted by me a few weeks since. I am committed to a confidential statement of the fact, to certain political friends which in effect forbids my returning to Ireland should I require to explain any delay.' He congratulated D on 'those *alliances* your policy secured – that policy in face of many difficulties I did my part to promote. Ireland is to be dealt with next year – you will find I continue able to deal with the opposition *there*, who simply seek to play a Whig game with the aid of a Seditious Contingent.' H B/XIII/58. D's reply (see ec&n2) has not been found.

2 At Windsor on 20 August at 3 *pm* the Queen would hold a council attended by D, Derby, Stanley and the Duke of Marlborough, D and Derby would have audiences with the Queen and McKenna would be knighted. On that day he would thank D for his 'announcement and congratulation – I feel the honor conferred on me by the Queen ... is much enhanced by the consciousness of your friendship which has procured me the distinction.' *The Times* (21, 22 Aug 1867); H B/XXI/M/48.

---

1 Joseph McKenna; see **4500**&nn1&2.

2 Derby on 19 August 1867 had written to D from St James's Square a letter marked '*Private*': 'It is all right about the Knighthoods. I received yesterday Evening the Queen's assent to both of them, accompanied by a "grumble" at the trouble given Her on the day on which She was to begin Her journey [*see n3*]. I have written to console H.M. by saying that I hoped we should take up very little of H.M's time, and that as the new Knights had not been summoned, She would not have that duty to discharge. The result will be an increase of "Fees" on Knighthood by Patent, which the Sheffield man will not care for, and I hope the Irishman will make up his mind to. She gives the C.B. (Civil) to Major Grey for the part he took in the suppression of the Fenian outbreak at Chester; & the Civil K.C.B. to W. Rose (Strathnairn's Brother) on the recommendation of Sir J. Lefevre (!) under whom he has acted for very many years in the same capacity as Sir T. May in your House. We shall meet tomorrow on our way to Windsor, where I shall have one or two other subjects to talk to you about. I have, very much contre coeur accepted an invitation, sometime in October, to a Conservative "Banquet" in Manchester!! and I am threatened with another in Liverpool. You will of course be invited; and I hope that if you come over, as I hope you may, you and Mrs. Disraeli if she accompanies you, will remember that Knowsley is within easy distance, & that we shall be most happy to receive you.' H B/XX/S/445.

I conclude it is not necessary, that the benighted should attend tomorrow ????[3]

The last batch did: they went to / Osborne.

I would not, for the world, have any mistake in this Irish business, as the whole South has been informed, in confidence, of the / impending coup d'etat.[4]

Tell your Hall Porter to reply to this.

Yrs | D.

4502 TO: LORD LONSDALE Hughenden [Sunday] 25 August 1867

ORIGINAL: PS 816

PUBLICATION HISTORY: John Wilson catalogue (1980) item 42/30, described as 'Autograph Letter Signed ('D.') to [William Lowther, 2nd Earl of] Lonsdale ... 4 pages 8vo ... Hughenden Manor, 25 August 1867'.

[reminiscing about their friendship of more than forty years, explaining that Disraeli had just arrived at Hughenden Manor and would be unable to visit Lord Lonsdale at Lowther] If anything could have tempted one to quit the scene of some pleasures & many duties, it would be to visit Lowther, for I delight in your country, & often remember the brightness of your lakes, & the renovating breezes of your moors. It would have been pleasant to have talked over many things with an old friend and colleague ...[1]

4503 TO: LORD MAYO Hughenden [Monday] 26 August 1867

ORIGINAL: INL Mayo Papers MS 11,150

EDITORIAL COMMENT: Hughenden paper. *Sic*: Wycomb.

Right Honorable | The Earl of Mayo[1] Augt 26 1867

---

3 D presumably means McKenna's attendance at Court on Wednesday 21 August, but there would be no Court on that day, the Queen having left for Scotland on Tuesday evening. *The Times* (23 Aug 1867).

4 For D's efforts (via a secret agent) during the 1868 election to uncover evidence that Gladstone had agreed to disestablish the Church of Ireland in return for the Vatican's promise of Irish Catholic votes, see Padraic C. Kennedy '"Underhand Dealings with the Papal Authorities": Disraeli and the Liberal Conspiracy to Disestablish the Irish Church' *Parliamentary History* 27:1 (2008) 19-29.

---

1 Lonsdale on 21 August had written from Lowther suggesting that, 'now the Parliamentary campaign is over for this Session & the horrors of Political strife & warfare at an end for a time, I think perhaps you may be induced to seek some repose after your late fatigues & anxieties. I shall remain here for another month & if Lowther can afford you relaxation, or the surrounding hills with their bracing qualities add further inducement I should be delighted to receive you any day or time that suits you.' H B/XXI/L/292.

---

1 Lord Mayo (which Naas had become at his father's death on 12 August) on the 24th had written to D: 'What have you done about the Railway Commission? I think if you could secure John Fowler[,] Anderson and Christopher Johnson [*sic*] of the Caledonian Railway we should do well. We might then wonder whether we ought not to add two more and make the Commission consist of five members. A first rate Parliamentary Lawyer such as Mereweather [*sic*] and an Irishman of high Standing such as [Robert Dillon, 3rd Baron] Clonbrock or a leading merchant such as [textile manufacturer John] Mulholland ... We should however start it at once. For Secretary I should recommend Dr Neilson Hancock a Statis[ti]cian of much eminence and an Irishman[.] Clanricardes 2d Son is to start for Galway. He will enter Parlt under the names of Canning Burke! Heavens what names to be borne by a creature who as [*sic*] all the appearance and manners of a French dancing Master without his activity ... I have good hopes that Fenianism is gradually dying out[.]' H B/XX/BO/33.

Mon tres cher –

I enclose you Fowler's letter:[2] it will be rather late to begin in October? will it not?[3] I spoke to him of a Treasury Commission, but it is, really, a statutory commission. /

I have seen Sir Alexander twice. He is getting, & is looking, old – & fears physical exertion; but he will do what I desire – I see that.[4]

Ever yours, | D.

My post town

High Wycomb

& my county is

Bucks

not

Berks!!!

Where were you educated! Counties, however, need not be mentioned in England: probably necessary in Ireland, where there are no towns.[5]

TO: CHARLES RIVERS WILSON   Hughenden [Tuesday] 27 August 1867   4504
ORIGINAL: NYPL Montague [17]
EDITORIAL COMMENT: Hughenden paper.

Private   Augt 27 1867

C. Rivers Wilson Esqr[1]

Read a letter from Lord Stanley.[2] I am not myself particularly anxious about the

---

2 This letter has not been found. John Fowler (1817-1898), 1st Bt 1890, Kt and KCMG 1885, had worked as an engineer since 1841 for a number of railway companies and was the youngest-ever president of the Institution of Civil Engineers 1865-7. His most important work includes Pimlico Bridge (1860), the first railway bridge over the Thames, the Metropolitan District Line (which would open in stages from 1868) and the Forth Bridge in Scotland (1890), the first all-steel bridge.

3 Mayo on 29 August would reply that October would be 'rather late to begin the Railway Commission but I do not see how it can be avoided for every public man is now over worked and the month of Sepr. seems to be accepted by all as a general Holiday ... we must have Fowler. He is worth waiting for.' H B/ XX/BO/34. See **4508**nn1&6.

4 Sir Alexander Spearman, comptroller-general of the national debt, would be 84 in September.

5 Mayo, who had clearly directed his letter to 'Berks.', would reply on 29 August: 'I could not for the life of me recollect your Post Town and I was working in a great hurry but I do happen to know that you are Member for Bucks. which you must have read without Spectacles.' H B/XX/BO/33a, 34.

---

1 This is D's first extant letter to Charles Rivers Wilson (1831-1916), BA 1853 Balliol College, Oxford, KCMG 1880 and GCMG 1895, who had served in the treasury in 1856 as secretary to financial secretary James Wilson and to permanent under-secretary G.A. Hamilton 1858-68. From August 1867 Wilson would be private secretary to D for seven months, becoming secretary to Robert Lowe 1868-73, comptroller-general of the national debt 1873-94, a government director of the Suez Canal Company 1876-96, finance minister of Egypt 1877-9, a director of the Alliance Life & Fire Assurance Company 1880 and president of the Grand Trunk Railway of Canada 1895.

2 Stanley on 24 August had written to D from Knowsley that Portuguese minister Lavradio 'is at me again about his commercial treaty. He is most anxious, he says, to get the question decided one way or the other before next year. Can you meet his wishes? Weeks ago, we asked the B. of T. to make experiments on the subject of illicit distillation to see whether the risk was as great as it is represented. I don't know whether they have done anything. Will you stir them up?' H B/IX/E/27.

Portuguese Treaty, but it is necessary to give some reply ↑& keep the affair a little alive.↓ I saw Cte. Lavradio / just before I left ↑town↓; but I did not say much to him, tho' he said a good deal to me.

I rather think Mr Montagu Corry may look in at D.S. tomorrow. If so, you might consult / him on this matter, as he knows all about it.[3]

I send you, also, a handful of letters. They are of that class that, probably, require no answer; but if any do, they are of that / class, that shd. not be answered by myself. Some seem to refer to previous correspondence, wh: has, very properly, not been shown to me.

Roehampton must be delicious in this weather.

D.

When you next write, throw a handful of bands into yr bag.[4]

4505   TO: MONTAGU CORRY   Hughenden [Tuesday] 27 August 1867
ORIGINAL: H B/XX/D/44
EDITORIAL COMMENT: Hughenden paper. *Sic*: Chatellaine; Stephens'; Brookes'.

Montagu Corry | Esqr   Augt 27 1867
Mon tres cher,
I was delighted with your letter, tho' hardly satisfied with the length of your visit to Rowton.[1] It seems too short, where there is so much at / stake, & so much passionate feeling in the Chatellaine.[2]

I am beginning to enjoy Hughenden.[3] I always suffer the first week: a mysteri-

---

3 See **4191**&nn1&7.

4 Wilson on 30 August would inform D that there had 'been some delay in setting on foot the experiments for testing the possibility of distilling spirit from wine at a profit, but I have stirred up the Inland Revenue authorities and the Persons to whom the operation has been entrusted and a commencement will be made at *once*. I have written to Ld. Stanley's Private Secretary to beg that he will inform Lord Stanley.' On 14 September he would tell D that the experiments, now terminated, 'are *not* very favorable to the advocates of the low rate of duty who deny that any risk would accrue to the Revenue.' On 31 December *The Times* would publish a statement, signed by Wilson, dated 30 December at 11 Downing Street: 'I am desired by the Chancellor of the Exchequer to acquaint you that Her Majesty's Government have, after deliberation and inquiry, felt it their duty to decline the proposals for reducing the duty on Portuguese wines imported into Great Britain which have been submitted by the Portuguese Government as a basis for the negotiation of a commercial treaty between this country and Portugal.' H B/XXI/W/395, 400.

---

1 Corry on 25 August had written to D from Rowton Castle: 'I rejoice to think you must be well and in spirits; since the air and woods of Hughenden greet you when you leave the house, and the Reform *Act* smiles upon you as you enter your study. I keep a copy of it in my bedroom here, so that I never want something to remind me of the glorious past and the great future ... I have heard from Andrew Montagu, who begs you to advance the interests of Mr B. Webster junr, Barrister at Law, & Son of Benjamin Webster of the Adelphi. I have written him a civil answer ... I leave this on Wednesday & shall visit Downing St on that day; on Thursday, I propose to join my Father at Devonport. I trust my vice-regent has given you every satisfaction. I hear today from him that Fremantle has finally quitted Downing St, and resigned all keys etc.' H B/XI/J/30.

2 Corry's aunt, Lady Charlotte Barbara Ashley-Cooper (1799-1889), was the daughter of 6th Earl of Shaftesbury and Lady Anne Spencer Churchill, and sister of philanthropist 7th Earl of Shaftesbury. The matter 'at stake' may have been the Wellington and Market Drayton Railway, a branch line of the Great Western Railway, which would open on 16 October, with a stop at Rowton Halt.

3 The DS had arrived at Hughenden on 22 August. H acc.

ous languor & depression always seize me in 4 & 20 hours after / a recurrence to my native bowers. Charles Fox used to say, that "he had not health enough for the country". No doubt, the reaction from the double excitement of St Stephens' / & Brookes': politics & play, must have been severe & trying to him.[4]

The enclosed is from Lady Bisshopp, the second wife of the late Walter Long.[5] Will you show it to your father from me – & ask what I am to say?[6]

Adieu! | D.

TO: **WILLIAM LOWTHER**   Hughenden [Tuesday] 27 August 1867   **4506**
ORIGINAL: H H/LIFE
EDITORIAL COMMENT: From a copy by Monypenny purportedly preserving all the features of the original, which was on Hughenden paper.

Private   Augt 27 1867
William Lowther Esq
Dear Lowther,

I pass a portion of my life in asking for appointments for you – but I don't grudge it as I think your claims are considerable, and those of your family not to be told. / I have written, this morning, to Lord Stanley, who is at Knowsley, about Lisbon.[1]

Your aunt, the Duchess of Cleveland, told me the other day that Buenos Ayres was about to be vacant and that you would like it.[2] I saw Lord Stanley next / day at the Cabinet,[3] and asked for it, but he replied, that he had heard of no such vacancy.

Yours sincerely, | D.

TO: **GEORGE WARD HUNT**   Hughenden [Tuesday] 27 August 1867   **4507**
ORIGINAL: NSR WH220
EDITORIAL COMMENT: Hughenden paper.

G.W. Hunt Esqr | M.P.   Augt 27 1867

---

4 Whig politician and celebrated orator Charles James Fox, an overweight immoderate drinker, had often faced opponents in St Stephen's Chapel (the debating chamber of the House in the old Palace of Westminster) and had also incurred enormous losses at the gaming tables in Brooks's Club.
5 Mary Anne Bickerton Hillyar (1817-1891), daughter of rear-admiral Sir James Hillyar and widow of the Rev Sir Cecil Augustus Bisshopp, 10th Bt, in 1857 had married secondly Tory MP Walter Long, who had died on 31 January 1867. D is distinguishing her (he should properly call her 'Mrs Walter Long') from Lady Bisshopp, wife of Sir Edward Cecil Bisshopp, 11th Bt. Her letter has not been found.
6 Corry on 30 August would write to D from aboard HMS *Enchantress* at Devonport: 'My father's secretary assures me that Capt. Hillyar is certain to have a ship, before his time is up. Of course my Father cannot promise, but you may safely say that you hope from what you hear, that your request will be of avail.' H B/XX/CO/24. Mrs Walter Long's younger brother, Henry Shank Hillyar, would become captain of the ironclad frigate *Royal Oak* on 14 December 1867.

1 This letter (not found) is most likely a reply to Stanley's letter of the 24th; see **4504**n2.
2 William Lowther, nephew of 2nd Earl of Lonsdale, would be minister plenipotentiary to Argentina 1867-8. See **4529**n1.
3 Cabinet had met on 16, 17 and 21 August. *The Times* (17, 22 Aug 1867).

My dear Hunt,[1]

The objections of the H of Comm:, &, I think, of the general public, against connexion with the French Company are two-fold:[2]

1st. On grounds of general impolicy, / particularly as regards India.

2ndly. On the ground of the impossibility of establishing any fair competition with an Association, wh: receives from its Government an alleged subsidy of 20/ pr mile. /

So far as I can read opinion, I think it would be dangerous to hanker after the French arrangement. I would, therefore, terminate all negotiations with France, & give our undivided attention to the establishment of / some at least temporary arrangement, wh: would, at any rate, secure us a fair chance of negotiation with the P. & O., or even, ultimately, altogether supersede its agency.[3]

Yours sincerely, | D.

---

1 Hunt on 26 August had written to D a letter marked '*Private*': 'Mr Rivers Wilson of the Treasury wrote about ten days ago to [French minister of state] Mr [Eugène] Rouher (in accordance with what you expressed to me) that the question of our making use of the French Service for our China postal communications must be considered in abeyance at present. I promised to let him hear further before long. There were two modes of making use of the French line under consideration. 1. That the Messageries [Impériales] should by permission of the French Government make a tender for a Service once in 4 weeks. 2. That we should have no direct dealing with the Messageries but that we should arrange with the French Government that it should undertake to convey our Mails once in 4 weeks under this contract with the Messageries a reciprocal arrangement being made as regards the conveyance of these Mails by our contractors once in the alternate fortnight. I think we might now inform the French Government that we abandon proposition 1. but that after the tenders are received (due on the 16th Sept) we will consider whether we shall be able to reopen the consideration of proposition 2. I may observe that we now have a Convention with France by which we can require each other to carry our mails at a rate named – but the terms are too high for us to make regular use of their Company's service in substitution for our own subsidized line. We are I think bound to let the French Government hear before the time comes for sending in tenders and after what took place in the House we could hardly I think safely make a contract directly with the Messageries. I should be sorry to put an end altogether to the prospect of a reciprocal arrangement before we learned by the tenders on what terms we can get the China Service performed independently of the French.' H B/XX/HU/18.
2 In the House on 1 August MP (L) Robert Crawford had protested 'in justice to our own companies' against the ships of the Messageries or of any other foreign companies 'being employed in the conveyance of our Eastern mails ... Such a course of proceeding would be Free Trade gone mad.' There would also be the threat to England's 'political and social relations with India, in the event of our being unfortunately engaged in hostilities with the country whose people the contract has been entered into.' Moreover, as the Messageries were already under contract with the French Government, 'they would not relinquish [it] for the purpose of taking up one with us.' Hunt on 15 August had refuted rumours that the Government would 'hand over the whole of the services to India and China if the French tender was lower than the English.' There had been only 'semi-official communications' with the French Government to come to 'an amicable arrangement ... by which the vessels of each country should convey the mails in alternate fortnights', thus relieving 'both nations from the necessity of paying a high subsidy.' *Hansard* CLXXXIX cols 658-704, 1561-4.
3 Hunt (n2) had stated that, given the 'exorbitant' terms of the Peninsular and Oriental [Steam Navigation] Company – a subsidy of 10s per mile at the rate of £280,000 a year, 'in addition to the present subsidy' – the Government would 'continue their efforts to make a temporary arrangement' elsewhere. See **4570**&n1.

ORIGINAL: INL Mayo Papers MS 11,206 (4)
EDITORIAL COMMENT: Hughenden paper.

Right Honorable | The Earl of Mayo　　　　　　　　　　Augt 30 1867

My dear | Irish Governor,

What are you thinking of? Sir Alexander means Sir Alexr Spearman, whom yourself suggested, / that I shd address. He will serve, if I insist on it.[1]

Choose any Railway manager you like. I know nothing of Seymour Clarke[2] or any other. It was Fowler,[3] / who proposed S. Clarke.

I approve of Mulholland.[4] We must have an Irishman: perhaps we shd. have two, if you really could find two Irishmen, who / wd. not job, & who possessed, at the same time, the necessary qualifications.

My bag is gone, & I have just got yr letter returning from Dropmore at sunset.[5]

Yrs ever | D.[6]

1　See **4503**n4. In his 29 August reply to D's letter of the 26th (the 'letter' D mentions below), Mayo had written, 'I suppose you mean *Sir Wm*. Alexander – well – he is old crotchety and conceited but has had great experience of R[ailwa]y Rogues & he will do – I would rather have had Merewether – Seymour Clarke is one of the cleverest of the Railway managers. But I would rather take Christopher Johnson [*sic*] of the Caledonian Railway as being more likely to do what we want. Though the other is the best known, we must have Fowler he is worth waiting for. I want one Irishman to represent the commercial and industrial Public and I suggest Mulholland the first of the Belfast Merchants, a very able man – and who will I hope be our next member for Belfast. The Commission would stand very well thus – Sir W. Alexander[,] John Fowler[,] Seymour Clarke[,] Anderson[,] Mulholland. You could hardly get a stronger Commission – & Pray settle it at once and let us announce it as the Public are getting fidgety at the delay.' H B/XX/BO/34.

2　Seymour Clarke (1814-1876), principal engineering assistant on Isambard Brunel's Great Western Railway, superintendent of its London to Swindon line in 1840-50 and general manager of the Great Northern Railway (opened 1848) 1850-70, would become vice-president of the Great Western Railway in Canada in 1874. He served on the Railways (Ireland) Commission.

3　See **4503**n2.

4　John Mulholland (1819-1895), 1st Baron Dunleath of Ballywalter 1892, proprietor in 1851 of the York Street Flax Spinning Company (which would become the world's largest integrated flax-spinning and flax-weaving business), would be high sheriff for co Down 1868 and co Tyrone 1873, JP for co Antrim and co Down, DL for co Antrim, LLD (hon) 1881 Trinity College, Dublin, and MP (C) for Downpatrick 1874-85 until the seat was abolished.

5　Lady Grenville had died childless in 1864, leaving her estate, Dropmore House, Bucks, to her late husband's nephew, George Matthew Fortescue.

6　Mayo on 31 August would reply that he was 'much relieved by finding that your Alexander is the right man – I only know Seymour Clarke by reputation, as an able manager of one of the honestest lines, the Great Northern. But I am ignorant of his politics, his character or his inclinations. However I should be inclined to trust to Fowler's opinion and take him – The second Irish man is a puzzle[;] on the whole I would be inclined to suggest Longfield the late Judge of the Landed Estates Court. He is an able man but Crotchety – though Honest. However he is a good Lawyer and has much experience of Irish property. The Comm[issio]n would then stand thus Fowler[,] Spearman[,] S Clarke[,] Mulholland[,] Longfield. Shall I therefore write to Mulholland and Longfield? ... Neilson Hancock would make an excellent Secretary and he is quite with me on the question – will you appt him?' H B/XX/BO/35. The Railways (Ireland) Commissioners (Spearman, Mulholland, Fowler, Clarke and Christopher Johnstone, with Hancock as secretary) would meet on 22 and 26 October. *The Times* (28 Oct 1867).

Hughenden [Friday] 30 August 1867

ORIGINAL: ROSE Dalmeny Collection [32]

EDITORIAL COMMENT: Hughenden paper. *Sic*: develope.

The | Lord Dalmeny   Augt 30 1867

My dear Dalmeny,

I was very glad to hear from you, & always shall be. If I do not always reply, you must not ascribe my apparent neglect to / an ⱥ unwillingness to have you as a constant correspondent.[1]

Raby, as you, at present, describe it, seems more calculated to develope your poetic, rather than ↑your↓ political, nature: a sort of "Mysteries of Udolpho".[2]

When your domestic visit is over, I hope you will come & see us. I calculate, from what you say, about the middle of next month:[3] not a very bad time; before the / equinox & the fall of the leaf.

I was at the inauguration of the Wynyard Museum[4] – my last visit there – not my last visit to Frances Anne in the County Palatine: that was three years ago,[5] but / it was to Seaham, where we slept in what was originally the principal saloon of the old Noel-Milbanke mansion, & in wh: Byron was married. The certificate of that momentous ceremony / was one of the amusements there, & the Parish Register used to be sent for after dinner to charm & astound visitors.[6]

When you next have a political controversy, or / conversation, with Vane's agent, make him define his terms. What does he mean by pure democracy?[7]

1 Lord Dalmeny on 27 August had written to D from Raby Castle: 'At last you are all broken up, and sent home with tolerably good characters. La Reyne le veult, and those who don't must lump it. It is lucky that no one has denounced Lord Derby's epithalamium on the bill becoming wedded to the law of England. "Taking a leap in the dark" ought to go down to posterity with the flesh and blood argument as instances of unhappy audacity ... Are you in your woods at Hughenden? I am going to be here for three weeks with my family. The house is a trifle large for a parti carré. I and my brother [Everard Henry Primrose] live in one tower, my mother & the Duke in a second, & my sister [Mary Catherine Primrose] in a third. The other forty and odd bedrooms are vacant. I met the wife of your Kneller picture & one of your three Graces – the Duchess of Marlborough. Lady Cornelia Churchill & I are desperately jealous of each other's friendship with Mrs Disraeli. I hear you are going to Blenheim. Please tell Mrs Disraeli to treat Lady Cornelia with chilling coldness, or else I shall "splash," as the expression goes ... Please remember me affectionately to Mrs Disraeli'. H B/XXI/R/136.

2 *The Mysteries of Udolpho* (1794) by Ann Radcliffe.

3 See **4514**&n1.

4 Dalmeny (n1) had visited 'the house of your majestic friend Frances Anne, and have been much edified with the inscriptions on the house & the collection of Lord Londonderry's inexpressibles, which is very large & kept in a separate room. Have you ever seen it?' Although a fire on 19 December 1861 at Wynyard Hall (see VIII **3638**n10) had caused extensive damage, a 'splendid marble room, appropriated to the monumental armour, trophies, and military remains of the late Marquis, and a suite of rooms superbly furnished and most richly decorated ... with the valuable pictures they contained' had been spared. *The Times* (21 Dec 1861).

5 D's last recorded visit to Seaham Hall, Durham (one of England's three palatine counties), had been on 29 November 1861 (VIII Chronology), but he may have returned in late 1864 to see Frances Anne, the Dowager Marchioness of Londonderry, prior to her death there on 20 January 1865. *The Times* (23 Jan 1865).

6 See VI **2735**&n4.

7 Dalmeny (n1) had spoken 'to Lord Vane's agent about the bill, as he finds it. It increases Lord Vane's interest, but he disapproves of the bill, as he thinks that it puts an end to everything except purely democratic government. But he & all who agree with him will not see that it does not *necessarily* do so, but puts

My wife commands me to send you her love.

If our kind regards are / welcome to the Lord & Lady of your castle,[8] & all around your hearth, distribute them plenteously, even prodigally – for they are sincere.[9]

Ever yours, I D.

TO: [MONTAGU CORRY]   [London, about September 1867] **4510**
ORIGINAL: H B/XX/D/332
EDITORIAL COMMENT: The second page is written on the verso of C of Ex paper. *Dating*: conjectural; see **4511**&n6.

I want paper.

D.S. mourning *note*

Blue D.S. *note*

Foolscap:

Quarto letter paper

and *pens.*

Be particular that the last are good: not / split up &c. and tell Gabbitas & Co. to cut the feathers off half way – by wh: they will travel in the box more safely – & suit me better.

D.

TO: CHARLES RIVERS WILSON   Hughenden [Sunday] 1 September 1867 **4511**
ORIGINAL: MOPSIK [71]
PUBLICATION HISTORY: Weintraub *Disraeli* 455-6, snippets
EDITORIAL COMMENT: Hughenden paper. *Sic*: Gabbetas.

Private   Sept 1. 1867

C. Rivers Wilson Esq

I am very much obliged to you about arranging the transfer of Lieut. Vaughan. I hope you cd. find time to send Loftus a line.[1]

You did well, also, in writing to Lord Stanley's Secy. / about the Distillation ex-

---

the aristocracy on their good behaviour. Reform is the result of railways, and it produces the same effects – it must jumble up people. If the aristocracy, by which I mean more especially the aristocracy of educa- tion, are not the lots that spring first from the helmet, they are not the aristocracy in fact & must go to the wall to make way for a better. England is a country which needs an aristocracy, but it must be one in fact or the new constituency will look for another & find another.' The agent for Earl Vane has not been identified.

8 The Duke and Duchess of Cleveland.

9 Dalmeny on 1 September would tell D: 'It was very good of you to answer my letter which did not deserve an answer. Many thanks for it.' H B/XXI/R/137.

---

1 Wilson on 22 August had sent D a letter from Loftus 'asking you to procure the removal of Lieutenant Vaughan from one Brigade of the Artillery to another.' Wilson on the 30th had informed D that he had arranged the transfer; 'The Horse Guards will move him before January next.' H B/XXI/W/392, 395. Loftus is presumably Lord Augustus Loftus, ambassador to Prussia, and Vaughan is possibly Edward Courtenay Vaughan (1841-1876), son of Ernest Augustus Vaughan, Earl of Lisburne, lieut and later capt 4th Battalion Rifle Brigade.

periments,[2] &, bet[wee]n ourselves, I hope the matter may now rest. Abyssinian campaigns[3] will hardly comport with financial experiments, were there no other objections to / the Portuguese treaty at the present moment.

If anything arrives of interest about the Irish Railways, you had better send it to the Irish office, & let it be forwarded to Lord Mayo, / who is at the Castle at Dublin, & is, at this moment, de jure as well as de facto, (he always is the latter) the Government of Ireland, for Lord Abercorn has retired to his palatial retreat at Baronscourt, the Chancellor has gone / to Scotland, the Atty. Genl to Switzerland, & the U. Secy. is dead, or nearly so, of Fenianism[.] I have had some active correspondence with Lord Mayo, & I hope he may be able to settle the Irish Commission on the Railways early in / this month.[4]

I fear we must have five members. Fowler will do, for nobody will really work in the month of Septr, &, I hope, Sir A. Spearman will accept – I'm sure he will if I press him – for tho' old, / his name, as a Treas[ur]y name, is high; I think Mulholland will be a good Irish man.[5]

I find this domestic paper very austere to write on[.] I wish you would throw into the bag now & then, ~~haff~~ half / a quire, or so, of Downing St. notepaper, stamped blue – some that was made for myself (Gabbetas will tell you)[6] not the usual stuff, wh: is infamous & tinny: also some pens, also made for me, & wh: are very good. /

I am not going to Ireland – but I didn't like to tell yr friend Mr De Gernon so, so I have not yet replied to his letter[.] I think, the rumor, that Stanley & myself are going to Ireland, does good, & occupies / an imaginative people.[7]

By the bye, his letters marked "private" are not to be opened. You must not misapprehend me. I have confidence in you, but it is a reserve wh: Lord Stanley requires & has / a right to expect. The ~~note~~ letter enclosed is not a despatch, but a private letter intended only for the eye of the Secretary of State – & would not be seen even by my colleagues.[8]

I fancy Fremantle & / the Boundary Commissioners perspiring at their work in this sultry weather![9]

D.

2 See 4504n4.

3 Preparations for an Abyssinian campaign had begun and it had been reported recently that 'the expense will be borne by Imperial funds.' *The Times* (29 Aug 1867). See 4482n3, 4515 and 4518&n3.

4 Mayo on 29 August had written to D that 'The Attorney Genl. is gone to Switzerland. The Chancellor to Scotland. The Under Secretary is done up and must go away for a month. The Fenians have nearly killed *him*. The Ld. Lt. retires to Palatial Barons Court next week.' H B/XX/BO/34.

5 Wilson on 2 September would inform D that 'Sir A. Spearman accepts to serve on the Irish Railway Commission. He thinks you understand him as having consented. He only makes it a condition that he is not to go to Ireland, for which I imagine in his case there can be no necessity.' H B/XXI/W/397.

6 See 4450n2.

7 The LL of Ireland in 1860 had appointed Christopher Joseph de Gernon, former sub-inspector of constabulary at the Curragh (co Kildare), resident magistrate. His letter to D has not been found. On 9 September Wilson would send D 'another hospitable invitation from Ireland which you will probably wish to answer yourself.' *The Times* (2 Apr 1856, 13 Aug 1860); H B/XXI/W/398.

8 Wilson (n5) would tell D that 'The Private letter from Lord Stanley came in a Box – not as a letter nor in an Envelope – and I hesitated about sending it down by special messenger.' For Stanley's 30 August letter and D's reply, see 4513&n1.

9 Wilson (n5) would inform D that 'The Boundary Commissioners – or rather their staff – have had a few

Be pleased to send me, also, a few long covers, with the Royal arms in blue. I'm afraid you will think I mistake [*illegible*]¹⁰

TO: MONTAGU CORRY   Hughenden [Sunday] 1 September 1867   4512
ORIGINAL: H B/XX/D/45
EDITORIAL COMMENT: Hughenden paper. *Sic*: Edgecombe.

Montagu Corry Esq   Sept 1 1867
Mon tres Cher!

I leave the whole Scotch business to your discretion, in wh: I have almost as much confidence, as in yr friendship.¹

This / morning has brought the invitation from Manchester, (from Algernon Egerton) Octr 17th: Even if the Scotch business do not come off, I should / not like to go to Manchester.²

I am not as well as I could wish. Change of air always knocks me up at first, but I shall acclimatize, & count on being quite well / when I embrace you here.

I know well your late delightful scene³ – having paid a visit to Mt. Edgecombe,⁴ & also having passed some delightful days with the Normanbys, when they rented the Winter Villa.⁵

Ever D.

---

very hard days work – Fremantle reports that with the exception of one – Sir F. Crossley – who is not very sympathetic with his colleagues – the Commissioners are perfectly harmonious.' The temperature in London had been 62° in the shade. *The Times* (31 Aug 1867). See **4516n4**.

10 Wilson (n5) would promise to send D 'a more complete supply of long envelopes tomorrow. I find, too late, that Fremantle has almost exhausted the Downing St. store for his Boundary Commission.'

---

1 Corry on 30 August had written to D from HMS *Enchantress* at Devonport that a letter from the lord advocate had informed him that the Duke of Buccleuch 'will be glad to join in inviting you to a dinner at Edinburgh to celebrate your success' on 29 October. Corry had replied that this would be too late, 'seeing that the Cabinets are to resume their sittings early in November ... I think the Duke's adhesion is a guarantee for the complete success of the dinner, still, I have suggested to him that the names of other magnates should be collected, who mean to be present, before a formal invitation be sent to you ... I trust you are well in every way.' H B/XX/CO/24.

2 This letter by Algernon Egerton of Worsley, Manchester, has not been found. D would not attend the banquet in Derby's honour at Manchester on 17 October. See **4540**&n1.

3 Corry (n1) had written that 'Most of the [Admiralty] Board fly to their wives tomorrow, leaving the First Lord & Henry Lennox to represent the Admiralty on Tuesday ... Henry is most official, and has already, of course, loaded with grievances to lay before you. Have you ever been here? If so, you can envy me; for it is indeed a lovely place.'

4 The 4th Earl and Countess of Mount Edgcumbe had their seat at Mount Edgcumbe House, near Plymouth.

5 For the DS' visit to the Normanbys at the Mount Edgcumbes' Winter Villa in Stonehouse, Plymouth, in January 1863, see VIII **3766**&n4. Constantine Henry Phipps (1797-1863), Viscount Normanby 1812-31, 2nd Earl of Mulgrave 1831-8, 1st Marquess of Normanby 1838, MA 1818 Trinity College, Cambridge, PC 1832, GCB 1847 and KG 1851, had been MP (C) for Scarborough 1818-20, Higham Ferrers 1822-6 and Malton 1826-30, governor of Jamaica 1832-4, lord privy seal 1834, LL of Ireland 1835-9, secretary for war and the colonies 1839, home secretary 1839-41, ambassador at Paris 1846-52 and minister at Florence 1854-8. In 1818 he had married Maria Liddell (1798-1882), eldest daughter of Thomas Henry Liddell, 1st Baron Ravensworth, who would partly inspire the character of Berengaria, Lady Montfort, in D's *Endymion* (1880).

4513 TO: LORD STANLEY   Hughenden [Sunday] 1 September 1867

ORIGINAL: H B/XIII/95

EDITORIAL COMMENT: Hughenden paper. *Sic*: Bismark [*twice*].

Private   Septr 1 1867

Right Honorable | Secy. Lord Stanley
Dear Stanley,

I return Fane's letter, with many thanks.[1]

I have heard nothing from the R[othschild]s. I observe, they never write, & only talk, indeed, on these matters in a corner & / a whisper.

To form a judgment of the present state of affairs, one must be greatly guided by our ↑knowledge of the↓ personal characters of the chief actors. There are four: The Emperor, Gort[chako]ff, Beust & Bismark.

The Emperor will / never act alone; Bismark wants peace; & Beust, tho' vain, is ~~st~~ shrewd & prudent.

Gortch[ako]ff is the only man who could, & would, act with the Emperor, in order to gain his own ends, but if the Emperor combines with him, he will so disturb, / & agonize, Austria by the ↑impending↓ C[ontin]ental anarchy, that he would ~~at once create~~ ↑throw her into the arms of Prussia & force↓ an united Germany, ~~in order~~ ↑if only↓ to arrest his course.

I think affairs will trail on, at least for a time, & the longer the time, the stronger will be your pos[iti]on. In such a balanced state of cir[cumstan]ces you will be the master. I expect you to become the greatest f. m. since Ld. Chatham[.]

4514 TO: LORD DALMENY   Hughenden [Wednesday] 4 September 1867

ORIGINAL: ROSE Dalmeny House Collection [39]

EDITORIAL COMMENT: Hughenden paper. *Sic*: Chatellaine.

The | Lord Dalmeny[1]   Sept 4 1867

My dear Dalmeny,

We shall be very glad to see you on Saturday – but hope you will not make us so short a visit – but perhaps, you will be / able to pay us another visit in the middle of the month, & keep our Harvest Home.[2]

---

1 Stanley on 30 August had written to D from Knowsley a letter marked '*Private*' enclosing a letter from Julian Fane, first secretary and acting chargé d'affaires at Paris, which 'tells all the little that is known to me of what has passed at Saltzburg. The Emperor's speeches, and the tone of the French press, are reassuring on the whole: the press of Berlin on the other hand is using the most offensive language, defying the French. "We know you would fight us if you dared, but you dare not." Whether this is only stupidity, or a premeditated purpose of forcing on a quarrel, the result is the same. What do the Rothschilds say? I don't forget Lowther, but nothing has turned up.' H B/XX/S/776. For D's reply, see **4515**.

---

1 Lord Dalmeny on 1 September had written to D that he would be going to St Anne's Hill on 'Wednesday next' and wanted to know if he might visit Hughenden 'on Saturday till Monday ... We can then discuss what I wrote to you about [on 27 August], or more cheerful subjects. I or Lord Vane's agent used the expression "pure democracy" very loosely, but I will try & explain what I think he meant if I see you. Would you or Mrs Disraeli send one line to "St Anne's Hill Chertsey"?' H B/XXI/R/137.

2 Hughenden parish on 19 September would celebrate its third annual Harvest Home, with D attending for the second time. His speech would be published in *The Times* on the 20th.

I wish you could induce the charming Chatellaine of St Anne's / Hill[3] to accompany you.

↑Try!↓

Yrs sincerely, | D.[4]

TO: LORD STANLEY   Hughenden [Thursday] 5 September 1867 **4515**

ORIGINAL: H H/LIFE

EDITORIAL COMMENT: From a typescript headed: 'D. to Ld. Stanley, Hughenden, Sept. 5. '67.'

Right Honorable Sec'y. Lord Stanley.

Dear Stanley,

I took your hint and wrote to R. and not receiving an answer, rather regretted it; but, this morning, the enclosed came.[1]

There is not much in it, but he is a man, who never dresses up a tale, and always understates.

It is as well, too, that you should have the power of comparing accounts and impressions from quarters of equal, and first-rate, authenticity. I shall, therefore, encourage him.

I hope the Abyss: news is true.[2] It will be another feather in your cap.[3]

Yours ever, | D.

---

3 A mansion on the southern slope of St Anne's Hill, Chertsey, Surrey (22 miles sw of London), former residence of Charles James Fox (son of 1st Baron Holland), was now the home of Lady Holland, widow of Henry Edward Fox, 4th Baron Holland. *The Post Office Directory of the Six Home Counties* (1874) 1923.

4 Lady Holland on 11 September would write to MA from St Anne's Hill: 'One of you has sent me a lovely rose, & the other some excellent grouse!' H D/III/C/1044.

---

1 Lionel de Rothschild on 3 September had replied to D's letter (not found) from New Court (St Swithin's Lane, London) that 'our friends also have been travelling about and have not written to us as regularly as they usually do. I am therefore not able to answer yr kind letter as I should like. Mayer came back this morning from Paris; he heard that the Austrian Minister had said, his Emperor would not join in any action against Prussia. A well informed person told me that at Vienna the court party are still very Antiprussian and therefore for a French alliance; but that the public generally are decidedly against such an alliance and for remaining quiet. Letters from the different German watering places are full of complaints about the haughty manner of the Russians, and of the increased taxation, but they add, all parties would immediately unite against the slightest move on the part of the French ... It appears to me that the Emperor of the French must be aware of the wishes of all parties to remain quiet and that all the world would be against the one who should be the first to disturb the present state of things; I quite agree with you in thinking that Peace will be maintained but at Paris, there is no confidence and opinions are very much divided. Here in the city we have not been particularly gay. We live in hope of better times.' H B/XXI/R/215.

2 *The Times* on 13 September, under the heading 'The Abyssinian "Canard"' (see n3), would publish a letter by the editor of the *Levant Herald* tracing the source of a report (published in his paper on the 4th) claiming that, thanks to the intercession of the Armenian Bishop, '"King Theodore has liberated the Consul [Charles Duncan] Cameron and his companions in captivity. We have made inquiries regarding this rumour, but have not yet been able to authenticate it."' Items sceptical of the alleged release would appear in *The Times* on the 6th and 7th under the headings 'The Abyssinian Captives.' Cameron would not be released until April 1868 following a British military expedition. See **4521**n4.

3 Stanley, after visiting Balmoral from 31 August to 7 September, on 9 September would reply to D from the foreign office, returning Rothschild's letter: 'My intelligence is not positive as to what passed at Saltzburg, but all peaceable as far as it goes. Read a despatch of Paget's on Italian finance and the church-

TO: CHARLES RIVERS WILSON   Hughenden [Thursday] 5 September 1867
ORIGINAL: NYPL Montague [13]
EDITORIAL COMMENT: C of Ex paper, seal crossed out and 'Hughenden' written in.

Private   Hughenden | Sept 5 1867
C Rivers Wilson Esqr
Before the Cabinet separated, a ↑Cabinet↓ Comm[itt]ee on Scotch Education was appointed, of wh: the Duke of Marlboro' was to be Chairman.[1]

I / think, therefore, you had better forward Mr Weir's letter[2] to His Grace, with all the documents, at my desire, & marked for his private attention.

I am going to / Blenheim at the beginning of next month,[3] & I shall be glad of ↑the opportunity of↓ talking the subject over generally with the Duke &, especially if I have to attend some meeting / in Scotland, late in the autumn, wh: is not altogether impossible.

I hope Sir Crossley will prove a tame elephant in the custody in wh: we have placed him.[4]

D.

TO: PHILIP ROSE   Hughenden [Thursday] 5 September 1867
ORIGINAL: H R/I/A/200
EDITORIAL COMMENT: C of Ex paper, seal crossed out and 'Hughenden Manor' written in.

Philip Rose Esq   Hughenden Manor | Sept 5 1867

lands: it is interesting. – I found the great lady [the Queen] in good spirits living out of doors in all weathers; not a word said of home affairs, nor much of any business: I don't see that she has at present any political idea, except the old one of supporting Prussia against France, which is not practical, and quite harmless. La valette [*sic*] holds language as regards Crete &c entirely opposed to that of Moustier, and it looks as though the French policy was going round again. What fellows they are, not knowing their own minds for six months together. You will have learnt before now that the Abyssinian tale is a *canard*. Worse luck!' *Disraeli, Derby* 316-17; H B/XX/S/777.

---

1 Marlborough on 10 October would send D ten pages of 'impressions as regards the Scotch Education scheme; they seem to be the *Salient* principles which should guide us.' The *Education Commission (Scotland). Second Report* had been discussed in the House on 21 June 1867. H B/XX/CH/5; *Hansard* CLXXXVIII cols 303-49. See R.D. Anderson 'Education and the State in Nineteenth-Century Scotland' *The Economic History Review* N.S., 36.4 (Nov 1983) 518-34.
2 This letter has not been found. Alexander Campbell Weir, appearing before the royal commission on 10 December 1864, had identified himself as 'a sessional schoolmaster in the parish of St. George's, Glasgow.' *First Report ... Schools in Scotland* (Edinburgh 1865) 271-82. Weir was author of *Primary education considered in relation to the state: reply to the address of the Right Hon. Robert Lowe, M.P., on 1st November 1867*, a lecture before the Edinburgh Association of the Educational Institute of Scotland on 15 February 1868 (Edinburgh 1868).
3 See **4547**n1.
4 Sir Francis Crossley (1817-1872), 1st Bt 1863, an important carpet manufacturer in Halifax, Yorkshire, was JP and DL for the W riding of Yorkshire, JP for E Suffolk, mayor of Halifax 1849-50 and MP (L) for Halifax 1852-9, W riding of Yorkshire 1859-65 and the W riding, northern division of Yorkshire 1865-72. Crossley was a philanthropist (twenty-one almshouses, a park, an orphan home and school), a benefactor to the London Missionary Society and the Congregational pastors' retiring fund and a boundary commissioner (see **4511**n9). *The Times* on the 3rd had noted the importance of elephants in 'pushing and clearing a way' for the Abyssinian expedition.

My dear Rose,

You have made me a magnificent, & most interesting, present.[1]

But what I value most is, that it is offered to me by one, whom I / have known from his boyhood, & who, during an interval of five & thirty years, has, invariably, shown so much ability, such high principle, & such good feeling, that he has obtained the most distinguished place in my esteem & regard.

I / shall ever take the greatest interest in the welfare of yourself, & of your family, & if I can contribute, in any way, to that end, I shall receive one of the best rewards of public life: & that is advancing the wishes / of a faithful & admirable friend.

Yours ever, | B. Disraeli

TO: LORD DERBY   Hughenden [Sunday] 8 September 1867   4518
ORIGINAL: DBP Box 146/3
PUBLICATION HISTORY: M&B IV 568-9
EDITORIAL COMMENT: C of Ex paper, seal crossed out. On the fifth page D has written 'Hughenden' above the crossed-out seal.

Confidential   Sept 8 1867

Right Honorable | The Earl of Derby | K.G.

My dear Lord,

So long as there was a wild chance of the captives being released, I would not trouble you, but, now, when that hope seems / over, I must call your consideration to the difficult & dangerous position to wh:, it seems to me, your government is drifting.[1]

We are carrying on a / war, & an expensive war, without the sanction of Parliament.

I feel persuaded that this is exactly a condition of affairs wh: in February next, the whole "liberal" party / will resent, & they will do it under the leadership of Gladstone, who, from the line, wh: he pursued in the instance of the Persian war, will advance, in this case, with additional / authority[.][2]

---

1 Rose on 4 September had written from Rayners: 'I am very sorry that I am unable to accompany Mrs Rose to Hughenden today to thank you in person for the great kindness and consideration you lately shewed me and which was so effectual in relieving me from a position of difficulty [*see* **4495**&n1] as well as for your kindness in calling here so promptly after your arrival in the County to enquire after me ... I hope soon to see you and thank you in person. Mrs Rose is the bearer of a little Box containing an inkstand which is interesting from its previous associations and which I venture to ask you kindly to accept and if you will allow it a place on your table and make use of it and permit it [to] remind you sometimes of our early acquaintance commencing upwards of 35 years ago and our more intimate relations during the last 20 years & of all the kindnesses I have received from you in the interval and of my deep personal interest in your high career I shall be very proud and happy.' The catalogue listing D's possessions to be sold at auction 'by Messrs. Christie, Manson & Woods' on 13-15 July 1881 includes six inkstands (items 51, 117, 215, 244, 279, 296). H R/I/B/111; H A/XI/C/9/1.

---

1 See **4511**n3.

2 In the House on 17 July 1857 a vote of £500,000 had been agreed upon 'to repay to the Indian Government one half of the extraordinary expenses' of the Anglo-Persian War of 1856-7 (see VII **2947**n2). Gladstone had stated that 'the view which her Majesty's Government have taken of the Persian war has been that it was mainly a war to maintain the independence of the town of Herat ... It is only because of our possessions in India that the town of Herat is of importance to us.' *Hansard* CXLVI cols 1730-67.

I see only one mode of extricating ourselves from this impending peril, & that is a very disagreeable one. Parliament ought, in my opinion, to be / called together as soon as practicable. The refusal of the Ultimatum, & the act of war consequent thereon, would be the logical occasion.[3]

The earlier the Houses are summoned, the / more anxious they will be to get away again.

At present, the contemplated expedition is popular with the country, & the expenditure, already incurred, would not only / be condoned, but might, under the peculiar circumstances, be justified.[4]

Yrs ever, | D.[5]

4519   TO: [CHARLES RIVERS WILSON]   Hughenden
                                                         [Tuesday] 10 September 1867

ORIGINAL: NYPL Montague [14]
EDITORIAL COMMENT: C of Ex paper, seal crossed out and 'H' written in.

H | Sept 10 1867

Mrs Disraeli, who has an *abonnement* to "All the Year aRound": has never received any of her numbers since our residence – & the Housekeeper at Grosr / Gate[1] says she has always given them to the Messenger that they might be forwarded.

Will you ask about this great question?

What is more important is, that I have never received my Revue des Deux Mondes for 1st of the month.[2]

There seems therefore some screw loose.[3]

Yrs | D.

---

3 At the opening of Parliament by commission in the Lords on 19 November, the first item in the Queen's speech would address the continued refusal of King Tewodros II to release his captives: '"The Sovereign of *Abyssinia*, in violation of all international Law, continues to hold in captivity several of My Subjects ... and his persistent Disregard of friendly Representations has left Me no Alternative but that of making a peremptory Demand for the Liberation of My Subjects, and supporting it by an adequate Force. I have accordingly directed an Expedition to be sent for that Purpose alone ... [and] directed that Papers on the Subject shall be forthwith laid before you.'" *Hansard* CXC col 3.

4 G.W. Hunt on 9 September would inform D that he had sent for the *Hansard* volumes 'with the debate on Roebucks resolution respg. the Persian War – & on the Vote in Supply. After reading it I am the more persuaded that it will be prudent to summon Parliament. In the case of the Persian War the Imperial Exchr. only laid half the expense, it is to bear the whole in the case of Abyssinia. In the case of the former if Parlt. had been officially summoned, it would only have met earlier than usual by a very short time – vide Palmerston's speech – In the latter it will be a matter of 3½ months.' H B/XX/HU/20.

5 For Derby's reply to this letter, see **4526**n1.

---

1 Most likely Mrs Cripps.

2 The weekly *All the Year Round* (1859-95), founded by Charles Dickens in 1859, would be edited by him until his death in 1870. The monthly *La Revue des deux mondes*, founded in 1829 by Prosper Mauroy and P. de Ségur-Dupeyron, would be edited by François Buloz from 1831 until his death in 1877.

3 In *La Revue des deux mondes* 70 (pp 1061-3), in a contribution dated 14 August 1867, Eugène Forcade had praised D's skill and courage in having passed the reform bill, calling 'unjust' the charge that D had returned to the 'tendances radicales de sa jeunesse et ... abandonné la cause conservatrice' (radical tendencies of his youth and abandoned the conservative cause).

ORIGINAL: HAL [2]

EDITORIAL COMMENT: C of Ex paper, seal crossed out and 'Hughenden Manor' written in.

Sir Henry Edwards | Bart: M.P.   Hughenden Manor | Septr 10 1867

My dear Edwards,

I have now found out, why there are no grouse in Yorkshire: they have all fled into the County of Bucks![1]

You are too magnificent!

Pray / give my kindest remembrances to Lady Edwards, & believe me

Ever yours, | D.

TO: LORD STANLEY   [Hughenden, Thursday] 12 September 1867   4521

ORIGINAL: H H/LIFE

EDITORIAL COMMENT: From a typescript headed: 'D. to Ld. Stanley, Sept. 12. '67.' *Sic*: Saturday last.

Right Honorable Sec'y. Lord Stanley.[1]

I believe we have, on the part of the Treasury, established as complete and efficient a check as is practicable under the circumstances.[2]

That is not the part of the business, that disturbs me. My anxiety arises from the fact, that we are carrying on a war, and an expensive war, without the sanction of Parliament, and I cannot resist the conviction, that if we do not, with becoming energy, extricate ourselves from this dangerous position, the House of Commons, in February, will resent our course, and that, too, under the leadership of Gladstone, whose recorded opinions on the subject of the Persian War, will allow him to advance, in this case, with additional authority.

There is no way out of the difficulty except calling Parliament together at the earliest opportunity.[3]

The reply of Theodore,[4] assuming a refusal, would be the occasion.

---

1 Edwards had written from Pyenest House in Yorkshire on 21 August to thank D for his 'kind note [*not found*]. *No one* but *yourself* shall taste a grouse killed on my moors this year if I know it.' H B/XXI/E/71.

---

1 Stanley on 11 September had written to D from the foreign office a letter marked '*Private*': 'I cannot avoid the conviction founded on all that I hear and read that the India Office are making a mistake in the scale of their preparations for this detestable Abyssinian campaign. It is not my business, in a departmental point of view: it is yours. Are you keeping any check upon the outlay, or if not, don't you think it is time you should?' H B/XX/S/778.

2 C. Rivers Wilson on 18 September would send D a minute, drawn up by G.W. Hunt and G.A. Hamilton, 'arranging the scheme of financial arrangements as regards the Abyssinian Expedition.' Hunt 'wished me to forward it to you tonight in the hope that you may be able to return it to us with your signature tomorrow.' H B/XXI/W/402a.

3 The Abyssinian question would be discussed at length in both houses when Parliament reconvened on 19 November. See **4518**n3.

4 Tewodros II (*ca* 1818-1868), born Kassa Haile Giorgis, Emperor of Ethiopia 1855-68. His rule ended the so-called Era of the Princes, two centuries of warlords vying for power and control, and benevolent treatment of his subjugated regions gained him popular support. He would commit suicide during a siege when some 13,000 British and (mostly) Indian troops, led by Sir Robert Napier, stormed and burned the fortress at Magdala on 13 April 1868 to free the captive British consul and his staff. See **4482**n3 and **4511**n3.

I wrote to your father on this affair on Saturday last,[5] and Hunt, who has been down here on the business generally, forwarded him some important papers from town, about the same time. Lord Derby's most unfortunate indisposition is, of course, the reason, why I have not heard from him in return. Indeed, it is possible, that our communications may have brought on the attack. I'm sure it was a sufficient cause.

We must exert ourselves: whatever our fate, the Ministry of '67 must not be destroyed by the King of Abyssinia!

Yours ever, | D.

4522   TO: SIR STAFFORD NORTHCOTE   Hughenden
                                                  [Thursday] 12 September 1867

ORIGINAL: H H/LIFE
EDITORIAL COMMENT: From a typescript headed: 'D. to Sir Stafford Northcote. Hughenden Manor. Septr 12. 1867.' *Sic*: 'ratting' (presumably a mistranscription of 'rattling'); Saturday last.

My dear Northcote,

I have been in hopes, that I might have received a confidential line from you about this Abyssinia mess. Is it so bad? I wrote to Lord Derby on Saturday last, as to whether we should call Parliament together, but I have heard nothing from him. I suppose the unfortunate gout is the cause: perhaps, my letter may have given it him. Cause enough.[1] I have gloomy letters from Stanley, but he does not seem to be aware of the Parliamentary difficulty.[2] He is frightened by the newspapers, & thinks, & talks, only of your awful India expenditure without check, but that is all nonsense, I presume. The ratting of the "Times" and its systematic writing down the expedition is rather ominous.[3] Let me hear from you.

Yours ever, D.

4523   TO: [MONTAGU CORRY]   [Hughenden, Friday] 13 September 1867
ORIGINAL: H B/XX/D/46
EDITORIAL COMMENT: C of Ex paper, seal crossed out.

I have not heard of you for a very long time: I wrote last.[1]

---

5   See **4518**.

---

1 D had written to Derby on Sunday 8 September (**4518**). Derby's reply of the 10th (**4526**n1) would be forwarded to D on the 13th by Frederick Stanley, whose father (he told D) remained 'entirely disabled' by gout. 'I fear the last few days of Reform have something of this to answer for, as he was not half cured when he went down to his place in the House. It was, however, a worthy occasion for that amount of risk.' H B/XX/S/447.

2 Stanley, who had written to D on the 9th (**4515**n3) and 11th (**4521**n1), would address the 'Parliamentary difficulty' in a letter to D on the 17th (**4529**n1).

3 *The Times* on the 11th had reported that 'The Topographical Department of the War Office has collected a mass of information concerning the practicable routes in Abyssinia, in the hope, apparently, of diminishing the anxiety with which the expedition has been regarded. It has not been very successful.' It went on to describe the country's inaccessibility ('Europeans can only enter at the peril of their lives') and to quote from reports complaining of scarcity of water and a climate like 'a "suffocating Pandemonium".'

---

1 D's previous extant letter to Corry is **4512**.

I suppose you are now approaching England; perhaps you are there. Could / you come & see us now?

On the 18th.? *Before* if you like. On the 19th, we have our Harvest Home, & you cd. help me very / much.[2]

If Claud J. Hamilton is passing thro' town, bring him down with you.[3]

Yr | D.

This is the *good* paper; / but it seems to me like writing on plaster of Paris.

TO: **CHARLES RIVERS WILSON**   [Hughenden, Friday] 13 September 1867   **4524**
ORIGINAL: NYPL Montague [15]
EDITORIAL COMMENT: C of Ex paper, seal crossed out.

C.R.W. Esqr   Sept 13 1867

I think, we must begin to remember, that there are such things as Circulation Boxes. Have you a good stock assembled?

Ld / Stanley, in a recent letter, refers to a despatch of Paget on Italian finance, wh: he wants me to consider.[1]

Boxes on South America: & indeed, on / North America, need not be sent – nor boxes on Japan. They may be passed, crossing out my name.[2] But I shd. like to see the European boxes now.

Can't they be sent by post? / In old days, there used to be leathern covers wh: carried them safely – at least despatch boxes, not perhaps circulation boxes. But I leave it to yr tact.

Yrs | D.

TO: **ROBERT DUNDAS**   Hughenden [Friday] 13 September 1867   **4525**
ORIGINAL: H B/XIII/94
PUBLICATION HISTORY: *MP* (20 Sep 1867); *The Times* (21 Sep 1867); *BH* (28 Sep 1867)
EDITORIAL COMMENT: C of Ex paper, seal crossed out and 'Hughenden Manor' written in.

Robert Dundas Esqre   Hughenden Manor | Septr 13 1867

---

2 Corry, having returned to London on the 14th, would decline D's request due to 'an old engagement to spend a week with the D. and Dss of St Albans.' H B/XX/CO/25.
3 According to Corry (n2) Hamilton was 'not in England. He is drinking the waters somewhere.' Lord Claud John Hamilton (1843-1925), PC 1917, second son of James Hamilton, 2nd Marquess (1st Duke) of Abercorn, MP (C) for Londonderry City 1865-8, King's Lynn 1869-80, Liverpool 1880-5, Liverpool West Derby 1885-8 and s Kensington 1910-18, would be a lord of the treasury 1868 and aide-de-camp to the Queen 1887-97.

---

1 Although Stanley's last extant letter (**4521**n1) does not mention a despatch, his 9 September letter does; see **4515**n3. Sir Augustus Berkeley Paget (1823-1896), CB and KCB 1863, PC 1876, a career diplomatist, had held posts at Madrid 1843-6, Paris 1846-52, Athens 1852, Egypt 1852-3, The Hague 1854-7, Lisbon 1857-8, Berlin 1858-9 and Copenhagen 1859-66. In July 1867 he had been appointed to Italy as envoy-extraordinary and minister-plenipotentiary to Victor Emmanuel. He would be ambassador at Rome 1876-83 and at Vienna 1884-93. Wilson on 14 September would reply to D that Paget's despatch 'was not sent here, but I have procured it from the F.O. and forward it.' H B/XXI/W/400.
2 Wilson (n1) would inform D that 'One solitary Circulation Box has arrived during your absence – and as it held papers relating to the United States and Japan I have, to day, passed it on.'

Dear Sir,

I feel deeply honored by the invitation of my friends in Scotland to dine with them in their beautiful, & famous, Capital;[1] & / ↑par[ticu]larly↓ by the medium, thro' wh: the invitation has been conveyed.

And on the 29th. October, as proposed, I count on the gratification of finding myself / their guest.

Believe me, dear Sir, to remain with great consideration,

Your faithful | & obliged Servt | B. Disraeli[2]

4526   TO: LORD DERBY   Hughenden [Saturday] 14 September 1867

ORIGINAL: DBP Box 146/3

PUBLICATION HISTORY: M&B IV 569, the last paragraph

EDITORIAL COMMENT: C of Ex paper, seal crossed out and 'Hughenden' written in.

Right Honorable | The Earl of Derby K.G.   Hughenden | Septr 14 1867

My dearest Lord,

I was most distressed when I found my letter had troubled you, when you were ill.

Your reply, tho' dated the / 10th.,[1] has only just reached me, with an explanatory line from the Hon: Member for Preston.[2]

---

1 *The Times* on 14 September would publish an announcement from *The Scotsman* that 'at a meeting of Scotch Conservative gentlemen' it had been resolved to invite D 'to a banquet in Edinburgh about the end of October ... the committee only awaits his answer to proceed with the arrangements for an event which altogether, irrespective of its political bearing, will naturally excite much curiosity and interest in Scotland.'

2 Robert Dundas of Arniston (1823-1909), 1st Bt 1898, JP for Midlothian and Fife and DL for Midlothian, would reply on 16 September: 'The banquet committee will receive your answer to their invitation with much satisfaction ... it will give Mrs Dundas and myself great pleasure if you and Mrs Disraeli will do us the honor of being our guests at Arniston at the time of the Banquet.' H B/X/A/37. The DS would arrive at Edinburgh on 26 October. See 4527&n1, 4544&nn1&2 and, for the banquet, 4556n2.

---

1 Derby on the 10th had written from Knowsley (via amanuensis Lady Derby) a letter marked 'Confidential': 'Hunt's Memorandum, received last night with the accompanying Documents, and your letter of this morning [4518], have arrived at an unfortunate time – for I have been since Friday last confined to my bed, in which I am unable to turn myself without assistance, by one of the severest and most painful attacks of gout that I have had for years ... I agree with you that we have no alternative except the very disagreeable one of an autumnal Session. The same motives however which induced us to abstain from sending down a Message to Parliament must still operate until we shall have received Theodore's refusal of our Ultimatum. But it is by no means clear when that refusal may reach us, and we may have to contemplate the case of his not deigning to send any answer, and still keeping the prisoners in confinement. In that case, we should, I think, have a vindication for postponing to the last moment consistent with the safety of the expedition, the formal announcement to Parliament of a Declaration of actual war. Parliament now stands prorogued to the 6th. of November; and I am not sure what circumstances would enable us, if we desired it, to anticipate that period. I believe we must also give ten days notice of the Meeting of Parliament for the dispatch of business and that Notice can only be founded, either upon the receipt of a refusal, or the efflux of time. And my own private opinion is that it would be no humiliation to us, and would effectually turn the flank of our Opponents, if we frankly stated all the circumstances to Parliament, and applied ourselves for an Act of Indemnity for any technical violation of its privileges. I do not believe they would dare to refuse it, nor that, if they did, they would be supported by the Country. I shall be glad to hear from you again as soon as possible, as we ought not to lose time in making up our minds. I see that Northcote is to be in attendance on the Queen from the 28th Inst, and he will be able to ascertain how soon, and where, the Queen can hold a Council, if it should be necessary, for the Meeting of Parliament for dispatch of business.' H B/XX/S/446.

2 Derby's son Frederick Stanley.

It is some satisfaction, that the delay allows him to say you are better. Yet / I would not trouble you again, if I did not think my letter might rather relieve you at this moment, & I, therefore, send a servant up with it / to London, as we have no post here today.

This morning, I heard from Hunt,[3] that he had taken Anderson down to Wadenhoe (his place)[4] to go with / him thoroughly into the question of how the expense of the Abyssinian Expedition is to be provided for.

Anderson had written a rather morose paper on the subject, wh:, / I believe, was forwarded to you, & said we ought to have taken a vote of credit, wh: was impossible, without a declaration of war.

He now states, that all the preparatory expenditure / can be provided for in a constitutional manner, & is working out in detail the technical arrangements necessary to enable us to make good our payments, for the present, out of / Army & Navy Votes, & Treasury Chest, without any "misappropriation".

I will, therefore, no longer doubt, that we can make everything square with the Appropriation Act, so far as our Ways & Means go.

/ I thought this would, in some degree, relieve your mind; as we shall, at all events, meet Parliament, if we are obliged to summon it, with an erect front; &, I assume certainly, / now, not before the 6th. Novr.

I think Willoughby wd. soon break down, even were he to accept the post. Brownlow I know well, & tho' young, quite equal, by his training & disposition, to the ~~post~~ office.

But what about Lord Exeter?[5] /

I am selfish in hoping you will not quit public life, as my career will terminate with

3 G.W. Hunt on 12 September had written to D from Wadenhoe House: 'I have got Anderson to come down here and to go with me thoroughly into the question of how the expense of the Abyssinian Expedition is to be provided for. He entirely concurs in the view I took of the question in the Memdum. I sent to Lord Derby & which I had previously expressed to you at Hughenden that we shall be able to provide in a constitutional way for the expenditure incurred in the way of preparation but that if we go to War we should call Parliament together & propose a Vote of Credit. He is working out for me in detail the technical arrangements necessary to enable us to make good our payments for the present out of Army & Navy Votes & Treasury Chest without any "misappropriation", and I see no reason to doubt, that we can make every thing square with the Appropriation Act, so far as our Ways & Means go. When you have come to a decision as to summoning Parlt. in case of war I should like to know.' Hunt on the 13th had also replied to D's letter of the 12th (not found): 'I have already answered it by anticipation ... If the Expedition is starved and failure ensues we shall be justly blamed. Let us provide for every emergency & contingency and if we fail we shall not be able to reproach ourselves.' H B/XX/HU/21-2.
4 Wadenhoe House (near Oundle, Northants), a magnificent Jacobean house built in 1617 by the Earl of Westmorland, was extensively remodelled by Hunt.
5 Derby (n1) had heard from Lord Aveland about the vacancy of the lord-lieutenancy of Lincolnshire (previously held by Aveland's father, who had died on the 6th): 'Can you suggest to me a fit and proper person? The natural person would be the present Lord Willoughby, but I am not sure whether his physical position would not incapacitate him. What would you say to the young Lord Brownlow?' Alberic Drummond-Willoughby (1821-1870), 21st Baron Willoughby de Eresby and 3rd Baron Gwydyr 1865. Adelbert Brownlow-Cust (1844-1921), 3rd Earl Brownlow (since February 1867), PC 1887, GCVO 1921 and MP (c) for Shropshire N 1866-7, would be LL of Lincolnshire from 4 December 1867 until his death, parliamentary secretary to the local government board 1885-6, paymaster general 1887-9 and under-secretary of state for war, 1889-92. For Lord Exeter, see v **1692n6**.

yours: but it is not for that reason, that I beg you will let me know how you are getting on, by "the ready & / confidential pen", to wh: I offer my sympathies & kindest regards.[6]

Ever yrs, | D.

I go to Edinburgh on the 29th. Octr as at present arranged.

4527   TO: MONTAGU CORRY   [Hughenden, Sunday] 15 September 1867
ORIGINAL: H B/XX/D/47
EDITORIAL COMMENT: C of Ex paper, seal crossed out. *Sic*: Wycomb.

Montagu Corry Esq   Septr 15 1867
My dear Montagu
I have only time to say I accepted the invitation for the 29th:[1]

When I saw Dundas of Arniston at the end / of the letter, I knew all was right.

I am glad you are going to the St. Albans. It will be agreeable & amusing.[2]

Yrs ever | D.

Will you ask Rivers Wilson to be so kind, as to send pr post Ritual Comm[issi]on Report & Evidence[3] to

Revd. C. W. Clubbe A.M.[4]

Hughenden Vicarage

High Wycomb

6 Derby (n1) had cautioned D that 'if the increasing frequency of these attacks is to continue, I feel that the time cannot be far distant when I must seek for restoration to health in an absolute withdrawal from the public service ... Do not scruple writing to me, though I cannot answer you myself, for I have, as you see, a ready and confidential pen at my disposal.'

---

1 Corry on the 14th had written at length about D's plans for the Edinburgh banquet ('Evidently a great & valuable demonstration and expression of good-will is in store for you'), requesting a decision by return post so that he could inform Edward Gordon, the Lord Advocate, whose letters Corry had enclosed. H B/XX/CO/25.

2 See 4523n2. William Amelius Aubrey de Vere Beauclerk (1840-1898), 10th Duke of St Albans 1849, LL of Nottinghamshire, capt yeomen of the guard 1869-74, had married, firstly, Lady Sybil Mary Grey (1848-1871), granddaughter of 2nd Earl Grey, on 20 June 1867. In 1874 he would marry Ralph Bernal Osborne's daughter Grace. *The Times* (11 May 1898).

3 The Royal Commission on Ritualistic Practices in the Church of England (or 'Ritualistic Commission'), chaired by the Archbishop of Canterbury (Charles Thomas Longley), had been appointed on 3 June. Its purpose and scope had been outlined and the names of its commissioners listed in an official document (dated 3 June 1867) signed by Gathorne Hardy and published in *The Times* on 24 June. The commission's findings had been discussed at length on 10 September in *The Times*, which had noted that the commissioners had 'met 19 times, only eight of which were occupied in receiving evidence ... the last 10 were wholly occupied in deliberating their report.' The first report, signed by the 29 commissioners and dated 19 August 1867, would be summarized in *The Annual Register ... for the year 1867* (1868) 253-4. It had found that while the vestments worn by the ministers of the United Church were regarded by some as 'symbolical of doctrine ... they are by none regarded as essential, and they give grave offence to many. We are of the opinion that it is expedient to restrain in the public services of the United Church of England and Ireland all variations in respect to vesture and we think this may be best secured by providing aggrieved parishioners with an easy and effectual process for complaint and redress ... We have placed in the Appendix the evidence of the witnesses examined before us' and other documents.

4 See V 2149n1.

to: HENRY PADWICK   Hughenden [Thursday] 19 September 1867 **4528**

ORIGINAL: LCC LC.1 Item 9

EDITORIAL COMMENT: Hughenden paper imprinted 'MAD'.

confidential   Sept 19 1867

Henry Padwick | Esqr

My dear Sir,

I have received your letter,[1] & will make a note of it. But about the person princi-pally interested / in it?

Is it his personal wish?

Is he aware, that it is an office, not merely of great rank, & authority, but of great responsibility? /

Lord Lieutenants receive a great number of letters, & they must reply to them, in the majority of instances, & in all important cases, personally.

Habits of business are absolutely required for / such an office, & great discretion in many matters, especially in the selection of Magistrates.

Considerable residence in the County, & very decorous residence, are indispen-sable.[2]

Let me hear further.[3]

   D.

---

to: LORD STANLEY   Hughenden [Sunday] 22 September 1867 **4529**

ORIGINAL: H H/LIFE

EDITORIAL COMMENT: From a typescript headed: 'D. to Ld. Stanley, Hughenden Sept. 22, 1867'.

Right Honorable Secretary Lord Stanley.[1]

---

1 Henry Padwick Sr had written to D on 14 September, on 'Palace Hamilton' (Lanarkshire, Scotland) stationery that the LL of Lanarkshire, Lord Belhaven, was 'in great danger, & ... not likely to recover', suggesting as his successor the Duke of Hamilton, 'a good staunch ally so far as politics are concerned ... [who] would carry out his duties properly, and would unquestionably strengthen your hand in every way in his power.' H B/XXI/P/13. Hamilton would not succeed Belhaven, who would live until December 1868.

2 The young Duke of Hamilton, who had a predilection for fast living, had escaped financial ruin in March when his horse, Cortolvin, won the Grand National Steeplechase. *The Times* (7 Mar 1867).

3 Padwick on 25 September would reply that, although 'the past, & perhaps present career of the Duke, is not exactly what one would desire, he is yet daily exhibiting more wisdom and shaking off the compan-ionship of those who have encouraged him in mischief. In this neighbourhood be assured he is most popular and a month's residence and a little attention to the neighbouring Country gentlemen, would restore him to all he would, or could desire ... he would feel most bitterly being passed over ... You might fully rely on his proper dispensation of Patronage'. H B/XXI/P/14.

---

1 Stanley on 17 September had written to D from the foreign office: 'I incline to think with you that an early summoning of parliament is inevitable, in the event of Theodore not giving way, and of the expedition having to proceed. But we cannot decide upon that for at least a month to come. The sitting need not be before the 1st of Dec. as it is confined to the consideration of a single question. I see much contin-gent inconvenience in the impossibility of having measures ready by that time: but that is a less evil than spending millions without sanction. All quiet in Europe. Bismarck gives up the Prussian F.O. but retains the chief direction of affairs. I fancy the change is only on grounds of health. I have been long expecting to hear of Moustier's retirement; but he seems to have got a new lease. I am trying to arrange so that

Dear Stanley,

The death of Bruce, I fear, is a great blow.[2] Who, on earth, is fit for such a post; now the most difficult we have?[3]

It should be a man not only of abilities, but of experience – and great experience of the world, and knowledge of character, and tact. I declare, that Julian Fane seems to me to be the only competent person, and, I think, he would charm the Yankees, particularly, if he would tell Seward the story of the Diligence of Bordeaux. Did he ever tell it to you? If you do ever send him across the Atlantic, make him tell it you before he goes.[4]

Yours ever, | D.

4530 TO: LORD DERBY   Hughenden [Sunday] 22 September 1867
ORIGINAL: DBP Box 146/3
EDITORIAL COMMENT: C of Ex paper, seal crossed out and 'Hughenden' written in. Endorsed by Derby on the first page: 'Ansd'. *Sic*: burthern.

Right Honorable | The Earl of Derby | K.G.   Hughenden | Septr 22 1867
My dear Lord,

I fear it will be impossible to reach you on the 28th:, & that I have inextricable engagements about that time. I am grieved, because / not only I naturally wish to confer with you, but because it would have gratified me to have assisted you, however slightly, in bearing the impending burthern.[1]

Lowther shall go to Buenos Ayres, but cannot answer for success. Fane must have the first offer of the vacancy, but I am trying to make him refuse: and I think he will. I have filled up Rio from B. Ayres, with a view to this arrangement. If Fane takes the place, I can at any rate move Lowther to Paris, which is a gain every way for him.' H B/XX/S/779.

2 Sir Frederick William Adolphus Bruce (1814-1867), CB 1858, KCB 1862 and GCB 1865, was the youngest son of 7th Earl of Elgin. A distinguished diplomatist, he had held positions at Hong Kong, Newfoundland, Bolivia, Uruguay, Egypt and China before being appointed envoy to Washington on 1 March 1865. He had died on 19 September in Boston of diphtheria. *The Times* (21 Sep 1867).

3 See **4550**n6.

4 Julian Fane was first secretary and chargé d'affaires at Paris and William Seward was American secretary of state. 'The Bordeaux Diligence' (anonymous) is found in *Lord Halifax's Ghost Book: A Collection of Stories of Haunted Houses, Apparitions, and Supernatural Occurrences* (1936), compiled by Charles Wood, 2nd Viscount Halifax, and published after his death by his son Edward. It tells the enigmatic story of how a French widower is inexplicably sentenced to seven years in the penal colony at Cayenne (French Guiana) for asking at what time the Bordeaux diligence departs.

---

1 Derby on 20 September had written to D (via amanuensis Lady Derby) from Knowsley a letter marked 'Confidential': 'That restless woman, the Queen of Holland, has invaded England for ten days, three of which, from the 28th to the 1st. of next month, she has intimated her intention of bestowing upon me ... I know that her great wish is to meet the celebrities, and especially the Male celebrities, of the Country. And you could not do me a greater kindness than assisting me to bear a portion of Her Majesty's exuberant friendship, to the entire weight of which, in my present weak state, I am wholly unequal. Seriously, I should be very desirous of seeing you here, if you could spare a few days, as it appears inevitable that we must now have a November Session – and that although I hope it may not last long, we must be prepared to lay our Programme before Parliament. We can have, I believe, a Council for the Prorogation by Saturday the 2nd. but we shall require either ten or twelve days, I forget which, for the summons for the Despatch of business. We must therefore have our scheme arranged, and our Speech prepared, by about

But / you talk of a Programme.

What Programme?

Surely, it is not necessary to have a real Queen's speech in Novr?

Is it necessary, from the Throne, to ~~no~~ notice anything, / but the matter of pressing moment? Cannot we treat the sitting as a complete Session? In that case, there would be a Prorogation, & we sho[ul]d meet again in Feby. with / another, & the real Queen's, speech.

If we were to meet in Novr., & then only *adjourn*, the programme for the entire Session would have to be put in the Queen's speech. But by observing the distinction / betn. prorogation & adjournment, it seems to me, that we might save ourselves from this difficulty.

But I write without any books to consult, Hansard, Hatsell, or May,[2] & ♭ no one to whom I can apply for advice. /

The Red Deer has just arrived. I am very much obliged to you, not only for remembering me, but in so agreeable a manner, for I know, from experience, it is excellent food.[3]

I / hope you will every day get better.

Yrs sincerely, | D.

TO: MONTAGU CORRY   Hughenden [Sunday] 22 September 1867   4531
ORIGINAL: H B/XX/D/49
EDITORIAL COMMENT: Hughenden paper imprinted 'MAD'.

Montagu Corry Esq   Sept 22 1867

My dear Montagu,

Don't let the thought of Hughenden interfere with yr arrangements at this moment.[1] My own movements are most unsettled. / Last night, I got a letter from Ld Derby,[2] *pressing very much* my ↑immediate↓ presence at Knowsley, a visit wh:, at this juncture, wd. be most inconvenient, not / to say impossible, for me – yet something must be arranged – in the course of the next two or three days.

Adieu! Mon tres Cher! | D.

---

the 12th. of November, before which time it is absolutely necessary that you and I should have some personal communication. I am still, as you will see, unable to write, and am indeed only able to be on my sofa for a couple of hours in the day, but I hope that my acute attack has at last subsided. I sent you a day or two ago a haunch of Red Deer venison, which I hope will arrive safely.' H B/XX/S/448.

2 For John Hatsell, see VI **2752n1**. Thomas Erskine May (1815-1886), 1st Baron Farnborough 1886, a barrister (Middle Temple 1838), CB 1860, KCB 1866, PC 1885, was clerk assistant 1856-71 and clerk 1871-86 of the Commons. He would see his *A Practical Treatise on the Law, Privileges, Proceedings and Usage of Parliament* (1844), the authoritative work on parliamentary procedure (known as *Parliamentary Practice* or 'Erskine May'), through eight editions. Hughenden library has the 6th (1868); the 23rd was published in 2004.

3 See **4545**.

---

1 Corry on 20 September had requested a short visit to Hughenden 'about Thursday next', following his proposed visit to Christopher Sykes at his new house, Brantingham Thorpe. H B/XX/CO/26.

2 **4530**n1.

TO: LORD MAYO   Hughenden [Tuesday] 24 September 1867
ORIGINAL: INL Mayo Papers MS 11,206 (4)
EDITORIAL COMMENT: C of Ex paper, seal crossed out and 'Hughenden' written in. Endorsed in another hand on the first page of the MS: 'VN Sept 25' and on the fourth page: 'Disraeli 28. Sept 67 Railway Commission'.

Right Honorable | The Earl of Mayo   Hughenden | Septr 24 1867
My dear Mayo,

Seymour Clarke writes, this day, that his Chairman permits him to accept.[1]

The Treasury don't like / the idea of Judge Longfield. They deem him wrongheaded.[2]

If you wish another Irishman, what do you think of Smith at the head of the Ra[ilwa]y Office, Dublin, who either / just has retired, or is about to retire.[3] He was about three years (appointed temporarily) doing duty at the Ray Office in London in Fosters place, when F. went to / Turkey. Anderson[4] had a high opinion of him. I only know him by report, but I shd. think strong in the investigation of accounts.

　Yrs ever, | D.

Let me know[.][5]

TO: THOMAS FAULKNER LEE   Hughenden [Tuesday] 24 September 1867
ORIGINAL: BODL MS Top Bucks c1 ff180-1
EDITORIAL COMMENT: Hughenden paper. *Recipient*: see n1. *Sic*: LLD.

Private   Sept 24 1867
The | Revd. T.F. Lee | LLD.[1]

Dear Sir,

I have no separate book plate of my father, whose arms wd. be the same as the en-

---

1　This letter by Seymour Clarke has not been not found.
2　Samuel Mountifort Longfield (1802-1884), Irish PC 1867, an Irish barrister 1828, MA 1828 and LLD 1831 Trinity College, Dublin, first holder of the Whately Chair of Political Economy 1832-6, regius professor of feudal and English law 1834-84 and QC 1842, had been a judge of the Irish landed estates court 1858-67 and was law adviser at Dublin Castle. He had recently declined 'the mastership of the Court of Exchequer, which had been vacant for five months and keenly competed for', and in December would relinquish his position as law adviser to become chairman of Galway county. ODNB; *The Times* (7 Sep, 19 Dec 1867).
3　John Chaloner Smith (1827-1895), BA 1849 Trinity College, Dublin, was resident engineer of the Waterford and Limerick Railway 1853-7, engineer of the Waterford and Kilkenny Railway 1857-61 and on 27 February 1868 would be appointed engineer (later chief engineer) of the Dublin, Wicklow and Wexford Railway. He would be president of the Institution of Civil Engineers of Ireland 1893-4. His *British Mezzotinto Portraits* (4 vols, 1871-82) is a descriptive catalogue of his collection, parts of which would be purchased by the Dublin National Gallery.
4　Possibly the Anderson mentioned by Mayo in **4503**n1.
5　Mayo on 28 September would reply from Dublin Castle with a letter marked 'Private & Confidential': 'Do not think of Smith. He is an empty headed conceited ass and owes his position to his toadyism of a Treasury Offr. one of whose daughters it was expected he would marry – ! His position in the Service is the wonder of every one who knows him – I think 4 would do very well. Fowler. Spearman. S Clarke. Mulholland ... Dr Hancock *ought* to be Secretary –'. H B/XX/BO/39.

1　Probably Thomas Faulkner Lee (d 1875), BA 1848, MA 1851, BD 1860 and DD 1866 Queen's College, Cambridge, deacon 1848, priest 1849, incumbent of Christ Church, Lancaster 1857, headmaster of Royal

closed shield[2] (Spanish) except the bunch of grapes, wh: I quarter ↑impale↓ as in /
right of my wife, who was the heiress of the Vineys of Gloucestershire[.][3]

Thank you for the books.

yours faithfully, | D.

TO: SIR WILLIAM STIRLING MAXWELL   Hughenden   **4534**
[Wednesday] 25 September 1867

ORIGINAL: STCL 17/20
EDITORIAL COMMENT: Hughenden paper. *Sic*: Anne.

Private   Sept 25 1867
Sir Wm. Stirling Maxwell | Bart: M.P.
My dear Stirling,
A most kind letter from you![1]

To pay a visit to Keir, & to visit, in his cedar library,[2] its accomplished Lord, who
has contributed such / treasures to all other libraries, was one of the social pleasures, wh: I had always counted on, & cherished – &, now, it seemed, that it was to be
realized, & under the most agreeable / circumstances!

But alas! I know not where we are. I have scarcely a doubt, that Theodore of Abyssinia[3] will call Parlt. together early in November, & tho' I may visit Edinburgh, / I
fear I must renounce every other pleasure, & that it will be the length of our tether.

My wife joins with me in offering our kind complts to Lady Anne.[4]

Yours sincerely, | D.

I am most gratified, that you take the chair[.][5]

Grammar School, Lancaster 1850, chaplain to Penny's Hospital, Lancaster 1851, 2nd master of the St
Albans Grammar School 1848-50, and author of *A Short Account of the Abbey of St Albans* and of papers on
archaeological subjects. *Clergy List* (1860).

2 D's coat of arms, on what appears to be a bookplate (included with this letter), matches the description
at VII **3390**n1, with the exception that the shield has been halved and the right half contains a bunch of
grapes. The *Edinburgh Evening Courant* on 30 October 1867 would describe D's armorial bearings: 'Quarterly in saltire, 1st, Gules, a tower proper; 2nd and 3d, Argent, a lion rampant gules; 4th, Or, an eagle,
displayed, sable. Impaled with, Argent, a bunch of grapes proper. Motto – Forti nihil difficile.'

3 See III **806**n1.

---

1 Stirling Maxwell on 19 September had written from Keir, near Dunblane, inviting the DS to visit while in
Scotland at the end of October. H B/XXI/M/293.

2 Among Stirling Maxwell's alterations to Keir House, the family seat since the fifteenth century, was a
magnificent cedar-lined, two-storey library that included his collection of some 1,200 emblem books
(now in Glasgow University Library).

3 See **4521**n4.

4 Stirling Maxwell in 1865 had married Lady Anna Maria Leslie-Melville (1826-1874), daughter of vice-
admiral David Leslie-Melville, 10th Earl of Leven, and Elizabeth Anne, née Campbell.

5 Stirling Maxwell, chairing the Conservative banquet in Edinburgh on 29 October, would ascribe the passing of the Reform Bill to D's 'energy, patience, tact, and genius'. *The Times* (30 Oct 1867). See **4556**n2.

4535 TO: CHARLES RIVERS WILSON

Hughenden [Wednesday 25 September 1867]

ORIGINAL: NYPL Montague [16]

EDITORIAL COMMENT: Paper imprinted with a picture of the Hughenden monument. Docketed in another hand on the first page of the MS: 'Sept. 26, 1867' and in a third hand: 'C. Rivers Wilson Esq 26/9/67'. The last part of the final sentence is written across the bottom of the first page. *Dating*: Despite the two docketed dates, the context indicates 25 September 1867; see nn1&2. *Sic*: Marboro'.

Private[1]

It is quite out of my power to come up tomorrow to this absurd Council – & were I there, / I could not presume, off hand, to decide such a question.

If the Duke of Marboro', who, I conclude, has had it much in his mind, hesitates, as to his course, he ought to bring the question / before the Cabinet.

I think Ld. Robert is right in his general view as to the relations betn. the Govt & the H of Comm:, but they were formed during the last days of the Session & with a Whip of country- / gentlemen, & he shd., therefore, proceed with the utmost degree of compromise, in the application of his policy, possible.

I enclose Helps' letter[2] for yr private guidance as I have no time to write to him: so give him, from me, a very civil message. Can't they postpone their ultimate decision, till the Cabinet meets wh: may be sooner, than they expect?[3]

D.

4536 TO: CHARLES RIVERS WILSON   Hughenden [Friday] 27 September 1867

ORIGINAL: NYPL Montague [18]

EDITORIAL COMMENT: C of Ex paper, seal crossed out and 'H' written in. *Sic*: Millenium.

C. Rivers Wilson Esqr   H Sept 27 1867

In consequence of the "Millenium," I think you had better strike the son off the list,

---

1 Wilson on 25 September had written to D: 'I do not know if Mr. Helps will be able to make out a case for the necessity of your presence at the Council tomorrow, but so much importance appears to be attached to it by Ld. Robert Montagu that I cannot refuse to send down a messenger to you, altho' I do so most reluctantly. I know that I cannot myself see the urgent necessity of your being actually a party to the Cattle Plague discussion that is to take place, or that the ordinary members of the Council are not quite competent to mark out the limits of the Port of London. As for defending their measures in Parlt, you do not I should imagine require to have been present for that purpose, and the vice President of the Council or Home Secretary would be the proper persons to speak on the subject – I apprehend there is a dread of responsibility.' H B/XXI/W/403.

2 Arthur Helps, clerk of the privy council, in response to a memorandum by D, on 13 September had sent D (via Wilson) an 11-page letter on cattle plague matters (specifically the admission of foreign cattle) that he hoped would enable D 'to speak forcibly and safely at the Royal Bucks Agricultural Association' meeting on the 18th (which D would not attend). Helps called the subject 'a detestably thorny one, and requires to be handled with great caution, to speak at all authoritatively about it.' H B/XXI/H/437, 437a.

3 Montagu on 26 September would attend a privy council meeting 'on the subject of the cattle plague' and receive a deputation 'on the subject of the importation of foreign cattle.' Wilson on 26 September would inform D that the council had 'agreed to postpone till the 15th October the operation of the provisions of the consolidated order of 20 Aug/67 relating to the landing of Foreign Cattle.' In H is a printed cutting with the manuscript heading 'General Consolidated Order / 20th August 1867.' *The Times* (27 Sep 1867); H B/XXI/W/404, H/437d.

if you ever put him there.[1] I scolded you for / sending me Bradshaw. I *prefer* Bradshaw: it is much less perplexing.[2]

I think you had better offer Bletchley to
    Sir Pauncefort Duncombe Bart:[3]
    Great Brickhill Manor
    Bletchley Station /

Lowndes is the proper man, because he lives at hand, & knows the people: but if
you offer it to him again, you must rap him over the knuckles for the blunder he has
made, & all the consequent trouble / he has caused.[4]
    D.

TO: SIR THOMAS GLADSTONE   Hughenden [Sunday] 29 September 1867   **4537**
ORIGINAL: DENL Glynne-Gladstone MSS 403 [6]
EDITORIAL COMMENT: Hughenden paper imprinted 'MAD'. Docketed in another hand on the first page:
'B. D'Israeli Sep 29/67 end Oct.' *Dating*: D's date can be read either as 27 or 29.

Private   Sept 29 1867
Sir Thos Gladstone Bart:
Dear Sir Thomas,
Your charming invitation[1] – for I shd. have been most happy to have paid you a visit,
& also the beeches of Fasque,[2] wh: / a lady told me, the other day, were superior to

---

1 Wilson had closed a 26 September letter to D with: 'The Book of Poetry is from Mr Edmund Carrington
  [son of Sir Codrington Edmund Carrington] who wrote the other day for an appointment for his son
  [*unidentified*]. I have acknowledged it with thanks.' H B/XXI/W/404. The book is probably Edmund Frederick John Carrington's millenarian work *The Victoriad; or, The New World: An Epic Poem Illustrative of the
  Spirit of Progress and the Victorian Era* (1861).
2 Wilson on 9 September had written to D that 'Bradshaw was a special attention on the part of the Downing Street messengers who persuaded me that it was forwarded regularly – tho' they did not explain for
  what special object.' H B/XXI/W/399. George Bradshaw (1801-1853), a Quaker engraver and printer, had
  published the world's first compilation of railway timetables, *Bradshaw's Railway Time Tables and Assistant
  to Railway Travelling* (1839); the title was changed (and the book expanded) in 1840 to *Bradshaw's Railway Companion*. 'Bradshaws' were issued from December 1841 as *Bradshaw's Monthly Railway Guide*, their
  yellow wrapper becoming famous worldwide. Bradshaws were also synonymous with incomprehensibil-
  ity for their numerous footnotes and addenda in minuscule type. Alternatives (presumably even more
  'perplexing') included *The A B C or Alphabetical Railway Guide* (from 1853, subtitled '"Easy as ABC."') and
  the many volumes of Sir George Measom's Official Railway Guides, which had first appeared in 1852 and
  by 1867 covered the entire railway network.
3 Sir Pauncefort Duncombe was JP and DL of Bucks.
4 Bletchley railway station (built 1847) was an important node on the London and North Western Railway
  line. Wilson (n1) had asked D: 'Shall I offer the nomination for the Railway Messengership at Bletchley to
  Mr. Richard Lowndes (letter from P.M. Genl. enclosed)? He nominated Kempson who has declined the
  appointment.' Richard William Selby-Lowndes (1848-1914) of Fenny Stratford (near Bletchley), son of
  Richard William Selby-Lowndes (1811-1892) of Elmers, Bletchley, was JP of Bucks. James Joseph Sheahan,
  History and Topography of Buckinghamshire (1862).

---

1 Gladstone on 17 September had invited D to visit him while in Scotland. 'We are about 5 or 6 hours North
  of Edinburgh; & perhaps you might be able to combine us with other friends in this direction – Fasque is
  on the Line of Rlway to Aberdeen from Edin[burg]h.' He would write on the 29th ('as I have not heard
  from you') reiterating his invitation. H B/XXI/G/138-9.
2 Fasque, in Kincardineshire (now Aberdeenshire), is a Georgian mansion completed in 1809 and purchased in 1829 by Sir John Gladstone, upon whose death in 1851 it had passed to his eldest son, Thomas.

my own – yr charming invitation found me in a state of great difficulty, wh: time has not removed, altho' I waited in / hope.

I fear my visit to Scotland will be limited to Edinburgh, & to a day, & that I must renounce all those agreeable propositions of hospitality, wh: the kindness of my / friends has bestowed on me – at least, if it be true, that ↑the↓ King of Abyssinia intends to call Parlt. together at the beginning of November. The newspapers say so, & I suppose they always speak truth.[3]

Yours sincerely, I D.

4538　　TO: SIR MATTHEW RIDLEY　　　　Hughenden [Sunday] 29 September 1867
ORIGINAL: NLF ZRI 25/89
EDITORIAL COMMENT: Hughenden paper imprinted 'MAD'.

Private　　　　　　　　　　　　　　　　　　　　　　　　　　　　Sept 29 1867

Sir M.W. Ridley I Bart: M P.

My dear Sir Matthew,

I often liken my choice friends to choice wine, &, strange to say, I put you down as Cote Rotie, wh: you so temptingly, / & hospitably, offer me.[1]

Alas! Alas! I must renounce all my pleasant visits to the North, among wh: that to Blagdon wd., I am sure, not have [been] the least interesting, / except my visit to Edinbro'; & that will be only for a day.

I say this, because the newspapers tell me that King Theodore of Abyss. means to call Parliamt together at / the beginning of Novr, & newspapers, I suppose, always speak truth.

Yrs sincerely, I D.

4539　　TO: SIR STAFFORD NORTHCOTE Hughenden [Sunday] 29 September 1867
ORIGINAL: H H/LIFE
EDITORIAL COMMENT: From a typescript headed: 'D. to Sir Stafford Northcote. Hughenden. Sept. 29th 1867.'

My dear Northcote,

I never thanked you for your letter,[1] which was all that I could wish, but I have been in a sort of lethargy since I came down here, and am only slowly emerging from it. One of its forms is a great inability of letter-writing. However the epistolary epoch is near at hand again, &, therefore, I try my prentice pen on you – but I have nothing to say, which you don't know, for I am sure you are well acquainted, that I am,

Yours sincerely D.

3　*The Times* on 24 September, quoting from the *Pall Mall Gazette*, had reported that, 'unless by some happy but improbable circumstance the necessity of a war with Abyssinia should cease, Parliament will be assembled to vote supplies during the month of November.' Parliament would reconvene on 19 November.

1　Ridley on 23 September had written from Blagdon, Northumberland, inviting the DS to visit on their trip to Edinburgh and offering to serve them 'some very old & fine Cote Rotie'. H B/XXI/R/88. Côte-Rôtie is a wine from France's northern Rhône region.

1　This letter has not been found.

TO: ALGERNON EGERTON   Hughenden [Sunday] 29 September 1867   **4540**
ORIGINAL: TEXU [26]
EDITORIAL COMMENT: Hughenden paper imprinted 'MAD'. *Sic*: embarassing.

Private   Septr 29 1867

The | Hon: Alg: Egerton | M.P.

Dear Algernon Egerton,

I must begin by offering you a thousand apologies – & then, I must repeat them.

Your letter, of the 30th. Ulto:,[1] duly reached me, but it found me, / as regards the request it contained, in an embarassing position. After due reflection, I meant to have consulted Lord Derby on the matter, but before I could do so, I heard of his severe illness, & / then it was impossible to recall his thoughts to a subject, wh: must have been to himself one of the most nervous anxiety. So time went on, & was lost!

I highly appreciate the honor of the invitation you have forwarded me from Manchester, but I am under / the necessity of saying, that I cannot have the gratification of availing myself of it.

I console myself by the conviction that it is much better, that the Banquet shd. be given to the Prime / Minister alone & not with his colleagues: better for himself, & better for the Party.

     With sincere regard.

        Yours, | D.

TO: CHARLES GREY   Hughenden [Sunday] 29 September 1867   **4541**
ORIGINAL: RAC 148 55
EDITORIAL COMMENT: Hughenden paper imprinted 'MAD'. *Sic*: Princesses'.

Lt. Genl. | Hon Chas Grey   Septr 29 1867

My dear General,

I return you the Princesses' letter.[1] Stanley was to have been with me here yesterday, /

---

1 Egerton's letter (not found) evidently reiterated his earlier invitation (see **4512**&n2) for D to attend Derby's banquet at Manchester on 17 October. In proposing his toast to Derby, Egerton (in the chair) would mention 'the brilliant manner in which the work in the Lower House had been managed by Mr. Disraeli.' *The Times* (18 Oct 1867). See **4557**&n1.

---

1 Grey on 24 September had written to D enclosing a letter (not found) 'received this morning from Princess Christian. When, after the arrangement between Prussia & Saxony which took from the latter the direction of her own foreign relations, or at least placed them under the control of Prussia, Lord Stanley proposed the withdrawal of the British mission from Dresden, the Queen strongly objected to what appeared to H.M. both an unnecessary & uncourteous proceeding. Lord Stanley, however, argued [on 31 October 1866] with much justice that after the surrender made by Saxony of the direction of her Foreign Affairs, it would be a burlesque on Diplomacy to maintain the farce of a Mission to a Court which had no power to decide any question that might arise. – Her Majesty yielded to his strongly expressed opinion, tho' still feeling deeply the apparent unkindness & discourtesy of such an act, to a sovereign who was the Head of the Family to which She herself belonged. This feeling was much increased, when it appeared that England was the *only* Power which had taken this step – Prussia herself continuing her Minister at Dresden. H.M. in consequence, brought the subject again under the consideration both of Ld. Derby & Lord Stanley, in the hope that something might be devised which would have the effect of showing the King of Saxony that no slight had been intended towards him; & it was, I believe, determined that a Chargé d'Affaires, to be attached, however, to the British Embassy at Berlin, should still be maintained at

had we not been, both, summoned to Knowsley, to assist in receiving that restless Lady, the Q. of Holland.[2]

I could not go: but / I lost my guest, to whom I cd. have spoken very naturally, as I had a letter from poor Vitzthum on my table.[3]

I will not neglect / H. M's wishes, she may rest assured.[4]

Yours sincerely, | D.

4542   TO: MARY ANNE DISRAELI   Downing Street [Tuesday] 1 October 1867
ORIGINAL: H A/I/A/339
EDITORIAL COMMENT: C of Ex paper. *Sic*: arch-ideot; Audubon.

Oct 1 1867

My dearest Love,

I saw Quin, who was himself ill in bed,[1] but very interested about my case, & gave me an hour, very critical & crossexamining. I am to see him again tomorrow, / but, still, shall manage, I think, to be with you by the early train: ¼ to 2, or whatever you wrote down.

He says, that all his remedies, from the first, were to work on / the liver, as much as ↑on↓ the nervous system, but they have been counteracted by a cause he cannot penetrate: he will have, it must be *local*: he still harps on *water*! /

I have seen Corry, who is not asked to Blenheim.[2] He is full of the Scotch business.[3] The Duke of Hamilton *is* to be one of the Stewards.[4]

The Reform banquet was a ludicrous failure.[5] Lord Carnarvon's brother, that / arch-ideot, Audubon Herbert attended & made a suitable speech![6]

Adieu! my dearest Wife. | D.

Dresden ... That the King was *deeply* hurt, the Queen has long known & lamented, & the enclosed letter will show you how deeply the wound still rankles ... I am sure you will give your best consideration to the means of giving effect to the Queen's wish that something shd be done to soothe the King's wounded feelings ... Pray return the Princess's letter.' H B/XIX/D/33.

2 Queen Sophie of the Netherlands had arrived in England on 18 September 1867 on the Dutch war steamer *Falk*. Derby on the 28th had told D, 'I am mending, though very slowly, and by no means up to receiving my Royal visitor today.' Stanley and his brother Frederick had gone to Huyton on the 28th to receive the queen and on 1 October would return to Huyton to see her off. She would leave Southampton that evening for Cherbourg. *The Times* (19 Sep 1867); H B/XX/S/449; *Disraeli, Derby* 318-19.

3 Count Carl Friedrich Vitzthum von Eckstaedt, Saxon minister in London 1852-66, had written to D from Dresden on 6 May 1867, in reply to D's letter (not found), and again on 31 August ('I heard nothing from you since May'). H B/XXI/V/88-9.

4 See **4550**&n5.

---

1 Homoeopathic physician Frederic Quin suffered from chronic asthma and arthritis.

2 See **4546**&n1.

3 Corry was helping to organize D's visit to Edinburgh at the end of October; see **4556**&n2.

4 No evidence has been found that the 12th Duke of Hamilton was a steward at D's Edinburgh banquet. D may have mistaken him for Charles Baillie-Hamilton, who would attend the banquet. MP (30 Oct 1867).

5 The day-long 'Reform Fête' (celebrating the passing of the reform bill) at the Crystal Palace on 30 September had included 'grave historiographers, who recited the misdeeds of the Tories in lists as extensive as Leporello's catalogue of Don Giovanni's intrigues', an orchestra, military sports, the acrobatic 'Benizoug-zoug Arabs' and fireworks. Covers had been laid for 1,000 but only 500 or 600 had attended the grand banquet at 7:15 *pm*. Letters of regret by Gladstone and Bright were published in *The Times*, which called the event 'an egregious failure', as more than half of the 20,000 present 'were ordinary visitors, having no connexion whatever with the incongruous business of the day.' *The Times* (1 Oct 1867).

6 Auberon Edward William Molyneux Herbert (1838-1906), brother of Henry Herbert, 4th Earl of Carnar-

ORIGINAL: NYPL Montague [19]

EDITORIAL COMMENT: C of Ex paper, seal crossed out and 'H' written in. Docketed in another hand on the fourth page: '15/10/67'. Wilson (?) has made large check marks through the two addresses in the body of the letter. *Sic*: Mann; rê.

H | Oct 3 1867

Write to

Editor of Manx Sun,

Douglas,

Isle of Mann

& thank him, from me, for the numbers of his paper, wh: he sent me. There are some very vigorous articles / in defence of the Govt., rê Reform, & especially myself, in them[.][1]

Corry writes about a vacancy in the Admy.[2] We have a candidate: I have written a line to Fremantle about it, as / the candidate, Clayton, is his cousin[3] & he will tell you all about it.

Write to

J.W. Hamersley Esqr

255 Fifth Avenue

New York

& thank him, from me, for ~~his~~ ↑a↓ copy of ↑his Edit: of↓ Abbadie on the Eucha-

von, BCL 1862 and DCL 1865 Oxford, lieut 7th Dragoons 1859 (retired 1862), MP (L) for Nottingham 1870-4, was at this time private secretary to Northcote. At the banquet (n5), 'Mr. Eldon ... proposed "A free Press, a free Parliament, and a free People, the safeguards of Liberty and Progress." The Hon. Auberon Herbert responded.' *MP* (1 Oct 1867). Herbert, a future disciple of Herbert Spencer, would originate the libertarian and (according to some) anarchist philosophy known as voluntaryism, whose ideas he expounded in *The Right and Wrong of Compulsion by the State* (1885), *The Free Life* (a newspaper he would edit 1890-1901) and a collection of articles, *The Voluntaryist Creed* (1908).

---

1 The editor in 1867 of the Isle of Man's Conservative newspaper, the *Manx Sun* (1821-1906), was engraver and copper-plate printer Harriet Curphey (d 1881 at 74), printer to the Manx Society and publisher of the Statutes of the Isle of Man. She had taken over the business from her late husband Peter in 1858 and at her death her son (also Peter) would run it until 1887. The *Manx Sun* was published on Wednesday and Saturday in the Summer, Wednesday in Winter. William Thwaites *Isle of Man: Its Civil and Ecclesiastical History* 1863 (online); William Cubbon *A Bibliographical Account of Works Relating to the Isle of Man* vol 2 (1939) 1155.

2 Edward Giffard, senior clerk in the admiralty secretary's department, had died on 1 October. G.H. Hill Carrington would be appointed to an admiralty clerkship in December. *The Times* (12, 19 Oct, 26 Dec 1867).

3 These letters from Corry to D and from D to Charles Fremantle have not been found. Corry on 5 October would inform D that 'Fremantle is enjoying a 10 days holiday in Paris; so I have taken young Clayton in hand, and will take action tonight, when I shall see my Father at Tunbridge Wells. I believe he has only promised one nomination, – to young Northcote.' H B/XX/CO/28. Fremantle's mother Louisa, daughter of Sir George Nugent, Bt, of Waddesdon, Bucks, had a sister, Maria Amelia, who in 1832 had married Rice Richard Clayton of Hedgerley Park, Bucks. They had four sons (Fremantle's cousins): Richard Nugent Clayton (1833-1914), George Augustus Clayton (1840-1918), Francis Edmund Clayton (1844-1905), Arthur John Clayton (1846-1922).

rist[.]⁴ / Be so kind as to send this to poor Campbell.⁵ I have written in the strongest manner to Mr Fitzgerald to soften his position by attention, &, if possible, aid him in his enterprise.⁶

D.

4544   TO: MONTAGU CORRY   Hughenden [Thursday] 3 October 1867
         ORIGINAL: H B/XX/D/50
         EDITORIAL COMMENT: C of Ex paper, seal crossed out and 'Hughenden Manor' written in. Endorsed in another hand on the fourth page: 'To Rowton Castle.'

Montagu Corry | Esq   Hughenden Manor | Octr 3 1867
My dearest M.

The Arnistons have cut the Gordian knot & have asked us to come to them on the previous Saturday, so that I may / ↑have↓ a couple of days rest. This is considerate.¹

There is a train, they say, 10 in the morning, & 9 at night, brings us to their station – 4 miles – so that will do. But we / shall have to change at Carlisle, where I have no doubt I shall lose my servants & luggage.²

Quin did me a great deal of good, but / I am again withering in this poisonous Paradise.

Yrs | D.

4 Treatises by Jacques Abbadie (1654-1727), a Protestant divine, include *Traité de la religion chrétienne* (1684) and *Réflexions sur la Présence réelle du Corps de Jésus-Christ dans l'Eucharistie* (1685), translated as *Chemical Change in the Eucharist. In four letters shewing the relations of faith to sense* (1867) by American lawyer John William Hamersley (1809-1889), who would die at his Fifth Avenue residence. *New York Times* (8 Jun 1889).

5 Possibly Church of Scotland minister John McLeod Campbell (1800-1872), DD (hon) 1868 Glasgow University, a leading (and controversial) theologian who had retired in 1859 due to poor health. His *Christ, the Bread of Life* (1851, rev 1869) is a study of the holy communion (which he considered 'a protestant answer to the Roman Catholic doctrine of transubstantiation') and *The Nature of Atonement* (1856) is his most important work. ODNB.

6 D's letter (not found) may have been to William Fitzgerald (1814-1883), BA 1835, MA 1848 and BD and DD 1853 Trinity College, Dublin, where he was professor of moral philosophy 1847-52 and ecclesiastical history 1852-7. Deacon 1838, priest 1847, bishop of Cork, Cloyne and Ross 1857 and of Killaloe 1862, Fitzgerald held moderate, broad-church views and was author of numerous works on controversial topics, including *Episcopacy, Tradition and the Sacraments Considered in Reference to the Oxford Tracts* (1839), *Thoughts on Present Circumstances of the Church of Ireland* (1860) and *The Athanasian Creed* (1875).

---

1 Robert Dundas's wife Emily Louisa Diana, née Knox (1825-1881), on 30 September had written to MA suggesting she and D arrive on 26 October to give D 'Sunday and Monday on which to rest ... The train which leaves Euston Square at ten in the morning arrives at Eskbank five miles from this [*Edinburgh*], at 9.8 in the evening, changing carriages at Carlisle.' H B/X/A/36-7.

2 Dundas on 18 October would inform Corry that 'the North British Railway Superintendent has agreed to stop the express train at *Gorebridge* on the 26th; and to avoid the usual change of carriage at Carlisle he has written to the authorities at Euston Square to ask them to allow one of their carriages to run over the North British Waverley line to Gorebridge ... the train ought to arrive there at nine oclock, and I shall have the carriage waiting and a cart for the luggage.' H B/X/A/14. See **4559**n2.

ORIGINAL: DBP Box 146/3

EDITORIAL COMMENT: C of Ex paper, seal crossed out and 'Hughenden' written in. *Sic*: embarassing.

Right Honorable | The Earl of Derby | K.G.   Hughenden | Octr 4 1867
My dear Lord,

I was nearly throwing the enclosed into my waste basket: instead of that, I send it to you.[1] Pray read it, & tell one of your Secretaries / to return it to me – at yr convenience.[2] I hope you are getting on well. It is a sad thing you shd. have such a local strain upon you with an impending meeting of / Parliament; wh: seems to me inevitable.[3]

    Lord Belhaven, I am told, is very bad – dropsy; & the Duke of Hamilton has appealed to me to recommend you to consider him as Ld. Lieut: of the County. This / is embarassing, & I hope that Ld Belhaven may be tapped, & go on, till you have time for consideration[.][4]

---

1 A near-illegible sixteen-page letter from John Gould Avery, writing on 1 October from Belsize Park, London, has been endorsed by AES as follows: 'Ireland. From a large Landowner & popular Landlord. Results of extensive observations on Journey thro' "the Country" & intercourse with all classes. Though prosperous, discontented. Why, and suggesting remedies. A visit from the Queen would create an enthusiasm such as would inaugurate a new era. Permanent residence for one of Royal family.' H B/XX/S/450.

2 Replying to D on 6 October from Knowsley with a letter marked '*Private*', Derby would return the letter. 'I do not know him personally, though if he is the owner of a great part of the Town of Cashel [co Tipperary], his property must immediately adjoin an outlying portion of mine. I must say that there is a great deal of truth and good sense in what he says; and there is no doubt but that a very great effect would be produced on the Irish mind, IF the Queen, or the Prince of Wales, could be induced occasionally to take up residence there. The former is out of the question; the latter would be not unwilling to do so, if a suitable residence were found for him. (He could not afford to buy one, as you well know.) I had some conversation last year on the subject with Mr. Gore of the Woods & Forests, when Tom Conolly's property near Carton, with about the best house in Ireland, was for sale; but he would not look at an Irish Investment on the part of the Crown ... The other remedial measure, suggested by your Correspondent, of *compelling* all the Landlords to buy up the Title Rent charge, and lending them money to do it, will, I think, meet with no acceptance in any quarter; and I incline very much to the opinion that the less we meddle with Ireland, the better.' H B/XX/S/451.

3 Replying to **4530**, Derby on 28 September had written to D (via amanuensis Frederick Stanley) from Knowsley that he, Northcote and Lord Stanley had 'reluctantly, but I think unanimously' decided that if Parliament were to be called together 'it will be impossible to confine their attention to the single question of Abyssinia. I cannot find any authority or precedent for such a meeting as you suggest, followed by an immediate Prorogation, and a new Session held at the usual time. Some speech from the Throne must in any case be delivered, and I think that one which should be confined to a single subject ... would lay the ground for very unpleasant discussion. I apprehend that in no case would it be advisable, even if it were possible, to call Parliament together before the middle of November ... and as I do not think that the House will be anxious for a prolonged Session, we shall probably have no difficulty in arriving at an adjournment by the first week in December.' H B/XX/S/449. Derby (n2) would tell D that 'I look upon an Autumn Session as inevitable; but I hope we shall have no difficulty in confining it within a very narrow compass. Walpole writes me word that there must be 14 clear days' notice for calling Parlt. together; and as the Queen returns on Saturday the 2d, and has signified her readiness to hold a Council on Monday the 4th I think we may look on Tuesday the 19th as the day for meeting. I shall be in Town on the 4th and, if you approve, I propose to summon a Cabinet for the following day.'

4 Lord Belhaven, LL of Lanarkshire since 1863, would die on 22 December 1868 after a long illness and be succeeded as LL on 27 January 1869 by Sir Thomas Edward Colebrooke. A letter of appeal to D from the Duke of Hamilton has not been found. Derby (n2) believed Hamilton 'could neither be appointed, nor passed over, in safety.' *The Times* (24 Dec 1868, 28 Jan 1869).

The Red-deer was admirable: tender & succulent as the dish of Esau.[5] I will tell you its fate when we meet, for I believe it unprecedented.[6]

Yrs, | D.[7]

4546 TO: [MONTAGU CORRY] Hughenden [Sunday] 6 October 1867

ORIGINAL: H B/XX/D/52

EDITORIAL COMMENT: C of Ex paper, seal crossed out and 'H' written in.

H | Oct 6 1867

I am very glad to hear we shall meet tomorrow.[1] Pray let the Irish Ry. Commission be pushed on.

Write to the /   Master Cutler

↑Cutlers Hall↓

Sheffield

& regret I cannot have the honor of dining with him, & the Corporation, on Thursday 31 Oct, as / I shall be in Scotland.[2]

D.

4547 TO: [MONTAGU CORRY] [Hughenden, Sunday] 6 October 1867

ORIGINAL: H B/XX/D/51

EDITORIAL COMMENT: C of Ex paper, seal crossed out.

Octr 6 1867

I have sent up another bag with the Abyss: papers, so that they may be ready in town when wanted, as we shall / not return here at present.

---

5 'Esau came from the field, and he was faint ... Then Jacob gave Esau bread and pottage and lentils'. See Genesis 25:29-34.

6 Derby (n2) would be 'glad that the Venison was approved: but what "unprecedented" fate a haunch can have met with passes my comprehension.'

7 Derby (n2) had seen 'reports of Ld. Russell having had a fit, and being in a precarious state; but I am inclined to think it is probably only one of the fainting fits to which he has been subject for many years. There is, as you will have learnt from Algernon Egerton, great disappointment, and I am afraid I must add dissatisfaction, at your intended absence from the "Banquet" on the 17th. You would receive a positive "Ovation" if you could come down; and I must wish that it were possible for you to do so.' See **4540**&n1.

---

1 Corry on 4 October had informed D that he had received an invitation to meet him at Blenheim and would arrange for all letters arriving at 11 Downing Street to be taken there on the morning of the 8th. 'The messenger can be back with answers in time for post.' Corry on the 7th would take the 4:50 *pm* train from Paddington. H B/XX/CO/27-8.

2 D had been invited (letter not found) to attend the annual Cutlers' Feast (since 1625) in the Cutlers' Hall, Sheffield (built 1832, extended 1865-7 and 1888). The 31 October 1867 feast would inaugurate a new banqueting hall accommodating 350 persons. Sheffield steel manufacturer Mark Firth (1819-1880), recently elected Master Cutler, would be a founder of the Iron and Steel Institute 1869 and mayor and alderman of Sheffield 1874. In 1875 he would donate £20,000 towards building Firth College (opened 1879), one of three institutions that would merge into the University College of Sheffield (1897), the future University of Sheffield (1905). John Roebuck would write to D on 19 August 1869, on Firth's behalf, inviting D to that year's feast and mentioning D's inability to accept Firth's previous invitation in 1868. H B/XXI/R/108. See **4548**.

Be so good, as to announce, that we have left this place for Blenheim Palace on / a visit to &c.,[1] for yesterday a Deputation of 3 gentlemen from Manchester came here – & the day before some one / else.

D.

TO: JOHN ROEBUCK   Blenheim [Wednesday] 9 October 1867   4548
ORIGINAL: CUL MS Coll Disraeli [5]
EDITORIAL COMMENT: Blenheim Palace paper. *Sic*: Edinbro'.

J.A. Roebuck | Esqr M.P.   Octr 9 1867

Dear Roebuck,

I quite agree with you about Sheffield, & should like to have made the visit very much:[1] but / it is physically impossible, as I have a great function to perform, I believe, the very day, at Edinbro'.

I hope you are well, & that some trumpet / sounds from the Cutlers Hall will soon assure me of the fact.[2]

Always yours, | D.

I have answered the card.

TO: PHILIP ROSE   Downing Street [Monday] 14 October 1867   4549
ORIGINAL: H R/I/A/201
EDITORIAL COMMENT: C of Ex paper.

Philip Rose | Esq   Octr 14 1867

My dear Rose,

The Cardiff interest has been paid into Drummonds.[1]

Yrs ever | D.

TO: LORD STANLEY   [Grosvenor Gate, Monday] 14 October 1867   4550
ORIGINAL: DBP Box 12/3/38; H H/LIFE
EDITORIAL COMMENT: The first part of the letter, as indicated below, is from a typescript in Monypenny's papers headed: 'D. to Ld. Stanley, Oct. 14. '67. Grosvenor Gate. (Preceding: "The information of the Secret Treaty &c.)"'. C of Ex paper (in DBP), seal crossed out.

[H H/LIFE:]

---

1 The DS would leave Hughenden for Blenheim on the 7th and return to Grosvenor Gate on the 11th. H acc; *The Times* (8, 12 Oct 1867).

---

1 The letter from Roebuck to which D is replying has not been found, but see **4546**&n2.

2 At these lavish feasts, held amidst much pageantry, toasts are heralded by a trumpet fanfare. Roebuck would write to the Master Cutler 'to exonerate him from his promise to attend the Cutlers' Feast, in consequence of a painful and weakening attack of illness', whose effects made 'him fear the consequences of the long and cold journey from Dorsetshire, where he is at present residing.' *The Times* (28 Oct 1867).

---

1 MA's business interests in Wales included a railway company (III **1078**n1) and a colliery (VIII **3565**n2). In addition, Cardiff solicitors and bankers regularly remitted money from Wyndham Lewis's investments, property rentals and mortgages. See also VII **3420**n1.

Dear Stanley,

I thought it wise to reconnoitre, and called on our friend yesterday.

He said the Emperor was no longer master of the position, and repeated this rather significantly.

In time, I extracted from him, that they had information from Paris, that there was a secret treaty between Prussia and Italy.[1]

I rather expressed doubts about this, and hinted that it seemed inconsistent with what had reached us, that there was an understanding between France and Italy, that the Emperor should give notice of his course &c.

He was up to all this, and showed, or rather read, me a telegram, I should think of yesterday, in precisely the same words as you expressed, so I inferred the same person had given the news to Fane and his correspondent. Probably Nigra himself.[2] /

[DBP:] The information of the secret treaty had arrived infrequently, & he stuck to it, & evidently believed it.

I give no opinion, but as I cd. not see you to day till late, & might / interfere with your railroad, I thought it best to write this.

The Berlin Ministry have consulted another member of the family about Ironclads. They are / going to expend 1½ mill: sterling immediately thereon, & told him they thought of having the order executed in America, as, in case of war with France, the ships would not be allowed to depart if / they were constructed in England.[3]

He told me a good many other things, that may wait, as I am very busy this morning.

Poor Vitzthum, who is going to publish something,[4] still moans over our non-representation at Dresden where all powers are represented, except us, & wh: he says is the focus of German information & intrigue.[5]

P.S.

I forgot to say, that the appointment of Thornton is highly approved of in the City.[6]

---

1 Stanley on this day (14th) would record that D had written 'from [Lionel de] Rothschild's information, that the Emp. is no longer master of the position, that there is a secret treaty between Italy and Prussia'; on the 19th he would note, 'Nothing is known, at least nothing is avowed, as to any secret understanding between Prussia and Italy.' *Disraeli, Derby* 319-20.

2 Julian Fane was first secretary at Paris. Costantino Nigra (1827-1907), Count Nigra 1882, senator 1890, had studied law at the University of Turin and was Italian minister-plenipotentiary to Paris 1860-76. He would be ambassador at St Petersburg 1876-82, London 1882-5 and Vienna 1885-1903. He was also a poet, classical scholar, translator and an authority on Gaelic language and literature. *EB* XI; *The Times* (2 Jul 1907).

3 Prior to 1867, Germany (including Prussia) had only two ironclads (built 1865); 11 would be purchased between 1867 and 1878. England had 30 (built 1855-66) and would purchase 42 between 1867 (five that year) and 1882. Recently ironclads had been built for the Prussian Government in the United States and England. 'Foreign Ironclads, 1855-1880' online; *The Times* (18 Mar, 20 Aug 1867).

4 Vitzthum was the author of *Maurice, comte de Saxe, et Marie-Josèphe de Saxe, dauphine de France. Lettres et documents inédits des archives de Dresde* (Leipzig: L. Denicke 1867).

5 Sir Charles Augustus Murray, minister at the court of Saxony (at Dresden) since 1859, had been appointed to Copenhagen in June 1866 and replaced by John Savile Lumley (formerly at St Petersburg). A few months later the mission was withdrawn.

6 Edward Thornton (1817-1906), CB 1863, KCB 1870, PC 1871, GCB 1883, BA 1840 and MA 1877 Pembroke College, Cambridge, had held diplomatic posts at Turin 1842, Mexico 1845, Montevideo 1854, Buenos

The art: in the "Times"[7] was a Kimberley move:[8] he told me so. I am not myself a votary of the ultra-professional spirit in dip: appointments: but the system certainly ought not to be broken into in favor / of a violent partizan on the wrong side, & who, according to my personal judgment of him, is vain, shallow, & incapable.[9]

D.

TO: LORD STANLEY   Grosvenor Gate [Tuesday] 15 October 1867   **4551**
ORIGINAL: DBP Box 12/3/39
EDITORIAL COMMENT: C of Ex paper, seal crossed out and 'Grosvenor Gate' written in.

Grosvenor Gate | Octr 15 1867

Dear Stanley,
I will take my chance of finding you as I pass by & talking over the M. dinner.[1]
Yrs | D.

TO: LORD ROSSLYN   Downing Street [Wednesday] 16 October 1867   **4552**
ORIGINAL: SRO GD164/1832/1
EDITORIAL COMMENT: C of Ex paper.

The | Earl of Rosslyn[1]   Octr 16 1867

My dear Lord,
Alas! all the kindness of our too kind friends in Scotland will be baffled by our adverse fate. Our stay in your / kingdom can only be 8 & 40 hours, for King Theo-

---

Aires 1859 and Rio de Janeiro 1865. Within a few days of his nomination as envoy at Lisbon in September 1867, Thornton had been selected to replace Sir Frederick Bruce, who had died on 19 September, as minister at Washington; he would remain there until appointed ambassador at St Petersburg 1881 and Constantinople 1884, retiring in 1887.

7 On this day (14th) *The Times* had reported as 'premature' the statement that Thornton had been appointed to replace Bruce (n6) at Washington, as he was in Rio de Janeiro and 'it will be some weeks before we can know whether he will accept it or not ... He is a count of Portugal, and has hereditary ties with that kingdom, and it is by no means certain that he will relinquish his new appointment [at Lisbon] for that at Washington, which, for its rank and position, is perhaps the least attractive in the diplomatic service. – *Sunday Gazette*.'

8 John Wodehouse (1826-1902), 3rd Baron Wodehouse 1846, 1st Earl Kimberley 1866, PC 1864 and KG 1885, held office in every Liberal administration from 1852 to 1895: under-secretary of state for foreign affairs 1852-6 and 1859-61, under-secretary of state for India 1864, LL of Ireland 1864-6, lord privy seal 1868-70, colonial secretary 1870-4 and 1880-2, secretary of state for India 1882-5, 1886 and 1892-4, lord president of the council 1892-4 and foreign secretary 1894-5.

9 Stanley on this day (14th) would reply from the foreign office: 'Many thanks for your information. I am disposed to believe it: so far at least, as to assure that there is an understanding, even if no actual treaty has been concluded.' H B/XX/S/785.

---

1 Stanley on 14 October had written to D from the foreign office: 'I am not going out of town till Wednesday night or Thursday morning, for the Manchester dinner. I wish you would tell me what to say!' On this day (15th) he would note that D 'came to discuss various matters. He sketched out to me the outline of his intended speech at Edinburgh.' H B/XX/S/785; *Disraeli, Derby* 319.

---

1 Robert Francis St Clair Erskine (1833-1890), Lord Loughborough until 1866, 4th Earl of Rosslyn 1866, was four times high commissioner to the general assembly of the Church of Scotland and 69th Grand Master Mason of Scotland 1871. On 12 October he had written from Dysart House, Kirkcaldy, Fife, to tell

dore is going to call Parliament together & Queen Victoria has summoned me to Balmoral.

Pray offer our united complimts / to Lady Rosslyn. My wife requests me to say, that she hopes the babe will resemble his father, in manners, mind, & person.[2]

Ever yrs sin[cere]ly | D.

4553 TO: LORD STANLEY   [London, Wednesday 16 October 1867]

ORIGINAL: DBP Box 12/3/40

EDITORIAL COMMENT: Endorsed in Stanley's hand on the second page: 'Mr. Disraeli October 16. 1867 *France & Italy* Telegram from Fane.' *Dating*: by Stanley's endorsement and context; see nn1&2.

½ past 10.

Dear S.

I had not seen it. They don't send me the telegrams now. Its very grave.[1] I will be with you at F.O. at ½ past two, so that we may consult before you see D.'A.[2]

Yrs ever | D.

D he had 'been asked to be V.C. of the Banquet in yr. honour to be held in Edin. on 29th' and to ask the DS 'to honor my poor house with yr. presence if your visit to Scotland was of sufficient duration to permit it but I expect Lady Rosslyns confinement daily & she wd I fear be hardly recovered sufficiently by the 29th to receive visitors.' The vice-chair would be Robert Nisbet Hamilton. H B/XXI/R/169; *The Times* (30 Oct 1867).

2 Rosslyn on 8 November 1866 had married Blanche Adeliza FitzRoy (1839-1933), widow of Col Charles Henry Maynard (d 1865). On 20 October 1867 she would give birth at Dysart House to her first child, Millicent Fanny St Clair Erskine (1867-1955), who would marry, firstly, in 1884, Lord Cromartie Sutherland-Leveson-Gower, Marquess of Stafford and 4th Duke of Sutherland (becoming Marchioness of Stafford 1884-92 and Duchess of Sutherland 1892-1913); secondly, in 1914, major Desmond Percy Fitzgerald (becoming Lady Millicent Fitzgerald 1914-19); and thirdly, in 1919, Col George Ernest Hawes (becoming Lady Millicent Hawes 1919-55). A great beauty and prominent London hostess, her work as social reformer earned her the nicknames the Democratic Duchess and Meddlesome Millie. For her work with the Red Cross during World War I she would receive the French Croix de Guerre, the Belgian Royal Red Cross and the British Red Cross. Her works include the semi-autobiographical novel *That Fool of a Woman* (1924).

1 Stanley had presumably sent D a telegram (see ec) from Julian Fane, most likely about the ongoing uprising by bands of Italian republican insurgents, news of which filled the French and Italian press daily. *La France* on the 13th had reported that the entry of troops into Pontifical territory, 'if it took place as an act of the Cabinet of Florence ... would immediately provoke from France not a protest only, but intervention,' and *L'Univers* estimated 'the strength of the invading Garibaldians at 10,000 men.' Telegrams from Florence on this day (16th) reported that 'The entire Italian press is unanimous in calling for the occupation of the Papal territory. The *Opinione* again urges the Government to take measures to prevent any intervention ... The *Perseveranza* insists upon the immediate occupation of the Pontifical States by the Italian troops ... The *Riforma* states that to-day ... the Pope has convoked the Cardinals to deliberate upon present events.' *The Times* (14, 17 Oct 1867). See 4557&n7.

2 Stanley on this day (16th) noted that D 'came at my request to discuss the Roman trouble, he agreed with me in thinking that interference would be at any rate premature.' Stanley would meet with the Marchese d'Azeglio on 21 and 22 October. *Disraeli, Derby* 320.

TO: [EDWARD STRATHEARN GORDON]   4554

[London?, before 17 October 1867]

ORIGINAL: H B/X/A/13
EDITORIAL COMMENT: *Dating*: by context; see n1.

I have seen Mr Campbell[1] and I think your business is arranged not necessarily to your satisfaction tho to that of

 Yrs faithfully

 D.

TO: MONTAGU CORRY   Downing Street [Thursday] 17 October 1867   4555

ORIGINAL: H B/XX/D/53
EDITORIAL COMMENT: C of Ex paper. Endorsed in another hand on the first page: 'To Rowton Castle.'
Sic: embarassed.

Montagu Corry Esq   Octr 17 1867

My dear Montagu,

The Ld Advocate has sent a packet this morning with all that is needful: including a report of Ld Palmerston's sayings & doings in 1863 – so you need trouble / yourself no more on that head.[1]

 I am very much embarassed by an invitation to ~~Osborne~~ ↑Balmoral↓, & to go from thence to the dinner. I am sure all this is intended by the Queen merely as / personal kindness, & to honor me at this particular moment: but it is very distressing at a time, when one wishes to be quiet & not exhausted. I have made up my mind not to go – but how to extricate oneself from / so gracious an invitation?[2]

---

1 Apparently 'Mr Campbell Swinton' (**4555**n1), probably advocate and jurist Archibald Campbell Swinton (1812-1890), LLB 1843 Glasgow University, LLD 1860 Edinburgh University and professor of civil law there 1842-62, JP and DL for Berwickshire, an active Conservative and author of numerous reports of trials and court decisions.

---

1 Edward Gordon on 17 October had written to Corry from Edinburgh: 'I had the following satisfactory note from the C of E. "I have seen Mr Campbell and I think your business is arranged not necessarily to your satisfaction tho to that of Yrs faithfully D." [*see* **4554**&n1] I wrote a letter yesterday to you, but marked to be opened by the C of E if you were absent. I sent him some suggestions for a speech & also a copy of the [Edinburgh] Courant of 1863 when Ld P. went through the same ordeal as affording a fair indication of the course of procedure on this occasion ... I also sent a Paper with a speech by [Edinburgh MP James] Moncreiff to his constituents reviewing the proceedings of last Session.' In his letter of the 16th, Gordon had specified that he was sending 'the Courant of *Saturday* last, which contains the Final list of the *Stewards*: – and also a Report of *Moncreiffs* Speech in the last Session ... I send also the Courant of April 1863 which contains the report of the meetings for presenting the Freedom of the City to *Ld Palmerston* & of the Dinner to him.' Gordon had enclosed '*Suggestions* as to National, or Local topics – apart from Politics' and '*Memorandum as to Scotch Politics*' (nine pages in total), upon whose cover Corry had written '(prepared by him [*Gordon*] & Mr Campbell Swinton).' H B/X/A/13, 12a,b,c. Palmerston had been installed as Lord Rector of the University of Glasgow on 30 March 1863 and on 1 April had received the freedom of the city of Edinburgh. Corry on 18 October would reply from Rowton Castle, 'But for your letter of yesterday, I should have today sent you the information you wished for [*presumably in a letter (not found)*] as to Lord Palmerston's visit.' H B/XX/CO/29.

2 See **4556**&n1. Corry (n1) hoped that D had succeeded in extricating himself from the invitation. 'But for my confidence in your tact, I should doubt the possibility of so doing, without giving offence. Even the Queen, however, must feel that two or three days perfect repose is not too much to ask before so vast an

I continue in a state of considerable lethargy, & sometimes think I shall never rally.

Yours ever, | D.

4556   TO: CHARLES GREY   Grosvenor Gate [Thursday] 17 October 1867
ORIGINAL: RAC B24 12
EDITORIAL COMMENT: C of Ex paper, seal crossed out and 'Grosvenor Gate' written in. *Sic*: Oct.

Mr Genl | Hon: Chas Grey   Grosvenor Gate | Oct. 17 1867

My dear General,

Your letter followed me unsuccessfully to several places, & at last found me here – I am sorry to say – on my sofa.[1]

The / fall of the leaf always sees my fall, & I came on here, where much is going on, to see if I could baffle the usual effects. How I am to get to Edinbro' I / don't see, except in the way, that troops, that have marched thirty miles with empty stomachs, still fight, & often conquer.

Nothing, especially at this moment, could have / been more gratifying to me, than to have had the honor of being H. M's guest at Balmoral. I wish you would be so kind as to lay my grateful duty at / H. M's feet, & convey to H. M., how sensible I am of Her Gracious kindness, & how deep the disappointment is, on my part, that I must ask permission, for once, to disobey Her / condescending command.

I suppose it would be presumptuous in me to suggest a visit to Balmoral *after* the dinner, for a day – ↑but then I could not come until the 1st Oct. as I have got freedoms to receive &c.↓[2]

It seems to me, that if I can get patched / up to reach H. M's northern capital, I might, then, not despair of reaching Her Palace.

But all this I leave to your real [*illegible deletion*] friendliness, wh: I have / so often proved. At this moment, I can hardly crawl. It's always so every year, but my visitation happily occurs at a time when, generally, no one need hear of it[.]

Ever yours sincerely | D.

4556A   TO: JOHN ROEBUCK   Downing Street [Thursday] 17 October 1867
ORIGINAL: IAA [7]
PUBLICATION HISTORY: International Autograph Auctions Ltd., online at www.autographauctions.co
.uk/; item 500, an image of the first page
EDITORIAL COMMENT: C of Ex paper. *Sic*: Edinbro'.

Private   Oct 17 1867

J.A. Roebuck Esqr | M.P[.]

undertaking as yours of the 29th, and that perfect repose is not normally found by great Ministers in their Sovereign's Palace.'

---

1 Grey on 11 October had written from Balmoral requesting D's presence there prior to D's visit to Edinburgh on 29 October. H B/XIX/D/34.

2 In Edinburgh on the 29th the Ds would attend a Conservative banquet for 1,300 guests at the Corn Exchange. On the 30th at 2 *pm* D would be presented with the freedom of the city in the Music Hall; at 3:30 *pm* an LLD would be conferred upon D in 'the Hotel of the University Library'; at 8 *pm* D would address a working men's meeting in the Music Hall. *The Times* (16, 30, 31 Oct 1867). See **4563**&n3.

Dear Roebuck,

I have sent you, as you wished, a public line to show your friends.[1]

The Queen has been graciously / pleased to let me give the day of my arrival at Bal: but evidently contemplates the visit is to take place before the dinner / at Edinbro'.

That would hardly suit me, as the effort wd. be too shattering in the fall of the leaf, wh: always brings my fall, so I have asked for / an *after* visit, & am in hopes, that the Court may be moving at the time, & so the whole thing may evaporate.[2]

I hope you are well, & that the Dorset breezes have done their duty.

Always yrs, | D.

TO: **LORD DERBY**   Downing Street [Saturday] 19 October 1867   **4557**
ORIGINAL: DBP Box 146/3
PUBLICATION HISTORY: M&B IV 553-4, misdated 18 October 1867, the first (omitting parenthetical matter) to the sixth paragraphs
EDITORIAL COMMENT: C of Ex paper. Endorsed by Derby on the first page: '*Ansd*'. *Dating*: D has written a '9' over the '8' of the day. *Sic*: Edinbro'.

Right Honble | The Earl of Derby | K.G.   Oct 19 1867

My dear Lord,

I congratulate you on the Manchester Demonstration.[1] It will do great good, especially at this moment / (See Morning Advertiser: leading art: of today; funny & true).[2]

And I thank you for the kind manner, in wh: you spoke of myself, & wh: you invariably / do.[3]

I came up to town for change of air, for when the leaf falls, I fall. I never can es-

---

1 This letter has not been found.
2 See **4556** &nn1&2.

---

1 Stanley on 17 October had recorded that at the banquet (that day) in his father's honour in the Free Trade Hall at Manchester, 'About 800 sat down, and 1,200 more looked on', Derby speaking 'about an hour, his voice feeble, but in other respects the speech effective.' This would be Derby's last major public address. Upon departing, he had encountered 'a most enthusiastic demonstration from a large crowd' that followed him to the railway station. *Disraeli, Derby* 319; *The Times* (18 Oct 1867).
2 *The Morning Advertiser* on the 18th had published the same lengthy report of Derby's speech found in *The Times* (see n1). In a leader on this day (19th), quoting Derby's rationale for passing the reform bill – '"That to bring forward a measure short of that which had been produced by the late Government, would have subjected me to an ignominious discomfiture"', the only course being '"to ask the concurrence of the Conservative party in passing a large and liberal measure"' – the paper had noted its own prescience: 'so long ago as in last June or July, before Lord Derby had opened his mouth, we expressed our belief that this would be the plea he would advance in justification of his conduct ... we saw that this was the only, and the obvious explanation ... that a Tory Government should propose and carry an almost Radical measure of Reform.' Recently, the 'Radical Reformers appear to be in a state of perplexity', their speeches 'filled with explanations, justifications, and mystifications', while the 'whole Liberal party seems to be in a state of doubt, distraction, and perplexity.'
3 Derby had begun his speech (n1) by thanking D, 'to whose tact, temper, and judgment it was mainly owing that that arduous undertaking [the reform bill] ... did not result, instead of a triumphant success, in a disastrous failure (Cheers.) ... he will be deeply gratified by seeing the reports which cannot fail to reach him of the manner in which the mention of his name has been received (Loud cheers.).'

cape: luckily my attack is as regular as the trade wind, & occurs at a / time when it little signifies, & can be kept secret.[4]

Unfortunately, this year, I have something to do: the Edinbro' Banquet. How I am to get there I know not, but, I feel, I shall. I think of / troops that have marched thirty miles & then, on empty stomachs too, have to fight. They do fight, & often conquer.

Unfortunately, the Queen, I am sure entirely from kindness, / & to do me honor at this particular moment, has asked me to pay a visit to Balmoral before the dinner, & to fix my time.[5]

This, I feel sure, wd. quite finish me, & I have written to Genl Grey, / & have a hope his friendliness may extricate me from this overwhelming honor.[6]

But the principal, indeed sole, reason for my writing this, is to know how you really feel after yr great exertion. / Stanley cd. not tell me that, tho' he told ⌐me⌐ of the genuine enthusiasm, with wh: you were received.

I hope, therefore, you will let me have a line.

Italian affairs were never so critical! /

The King's Government is really so weak, that they cannot perform the common offices of police; to say nothing of observing conventions. No power in Europe desires war, & / yet this Roman imbroglio may bring it. I shd. be glad if Stanley cd. reap some fresh laurels in its management, but it demands reserve.[7]

Cranborne has amplified / his speech on the third reading into a Quarterly Review pamphlet[8] – & the Edinbro' has also a manifesto.[9] They are, neither of them, very alarming.

Yrs ever, | D.

4 Derby on 20 October would reply from Knowsley that he was also suffering from 'a renewed attack of gout, which however I hope will not be a serious one. Your, and my, periodical attacks in the Autumn are, as long as we are in Office, an additional argument against a November Session, which however this year is inevitable.' H B/XX/S/453.

5 Derby (n4) was 'sorry to hear that you, like myself, are not in the best trim, or, as we say in this Country in "fettle" for receiving the public demonstrations which are being made in our Honor. I do not doubt however but that "pluck" will carry you through, especially if you escape the Balmoral visit.'

6 See 4556&n1.

7 Derby (n4) thought that 'Italian affairs seem to be in a very complicated state; and what with the party of action on one side, and the Pope on the other, the Emperor of the French, and the King of Italy are both of them brought to an "impasse," in which they must act, and yet cannot do so without the gravest danger. The Emperor is at his wits end; and his Ministers, or rather his Advisors, are so divided among themselves, that a break-up seems imminent. This however, where Ministers are impossible Advisors, and where the real Authority rests with one man, is a matter of minor importance.'

8 For Cranborne's speech in the House on 15 July, see 4472n1. In his lacerating essay, 'The Conservative Surrender', published in *Quarterly Review* 123:246 (Oct 1867) 533-65, Cranborne had charged the Conservatives with 'placing a great empire under the absolute control of the poorest classes in the towns' and critiqued 'the project of Tory democracy ... so long and so sedulously concealed' (534, 539). In his speech in Edinburgh on 29 October, D would allude to 'that article ... written by a very clever man who has made a very great mistake'; as a magistrate and inspector of asylums, D found that the most absurd and distressing cases were those 'when the lunatic believes all the world is mad, and that he himself is sane.' Kebbel *Speeches* II 485.

9 The unsigned 'The Session and its Sequel', published in *Edinburgh Review* 126 (Oct 1867) 540-84, had castigated both parties for their handling of the reform bill and charged the Conservatives with 'Unlimited abandonment of principles and policy on Reform, deceit in any quantity, vacillation without end'

TO: [CHARLES RIVERS WILSON] Grosvenor Gate **4558**
[Monday] 21 October 1867

ORIGINAL: NYPL Montague [20]
EDITORIAL COMMENT: C of Ex paper, seal crossed out and 'G.G.' written in. *Sic*: Ratazzi.

G.G. | Oct 21 1867

Do what you think best.[1] I think, like Ratazzi, I must resign.[2]

As the dinner is on the 29th: & I will not consent to any function before it, the rest must, I apprehend, be crammed into the next / day.

The Town Council is at two o'ck: I suppose the University will be at three – & it must be after that.[3]

The astute wisdom of the L. Adv: must settle.

D.

TO: [LORD BARRINGTON?] Downing Street [Friday] 25 October 1867 **4559**
ORIGINAL: BL ADD MS 58210 f5
EDITORIAL COMMENT: C of Ex paper. *Recipient*: by context; see n1.

Octr 25 1867

My dear B.

I return you his letter,[1] wh: I don't much like – but we must hope the best – an original remark!

I will try to think over the meeting of Parlt. / point. It does not seem of much importance.

Ever yours | D.

I go tomorrow morning.[2]

---

and Derby with 'carrying a measure dyed with any shade of Radicalism, however, deep, which might be needed to attain the end in view' (543, 563). D would comment that the article's author 'is rather placed upon a prancing hearse horse, with which he consummates the entombment of Whig principles.' He compared 'these "Edinburgh" and "Quarterly Reviews"' to 'first-rate, first-class post-houses, which in old days, for half a century or so ... carried on a roaring trade' until 'some revolution or progress' occurred and, failing to understand them, 'instead of that intense competition and mutual vindictiveness which before distinguished them, they suddenly quite agree.' Kebbel *op cit* 484-5. The *Wellesley Index* I 516, item 2753, attributes the review to Gladstone.

1 Wilson on this day (21st) had written to D announcing the arrival in London that morning of 'Mr. Charles Scott "Counsel for the officers of State for Scotland" and four Edinburgh Working men' who, according to Scott, 'wish to give a character of importance to the ceremony which they contemplate inflicting upon you' (see **4563**n3). Wilson was expecting Corry at 3 *pm* and had told Scott and his men to come to Downing Street at 4 *pm*. 'I suppose you will receive the address, and that Corry had better arrange with the Ld Advocate [Edward S. Gordon] as to time and place? The address itself is explained to be a conservative lower-class manifestation as a Pendant to the upper-class Banquet.' H B/X/A/16a.

2 Urbano Rattazzi (1808-1873) had held various government posts since 1848 and was PM March-December 1862 and April-October 1867. He and King Victor Emmanuel II had 'hatched an essentially nefarious plan secretly to encourage Garibaldi to invade the Papal States' and gave him arms and money, but under pressure from Napoleon III 'lost their nerve' and had Garibaldi arrested. Rattazzi had resigned on 20 October. Lucy Riall *Garibaldi: Invention of a Hero* (2007) 349-50; *The Times* (21 Oct 1867).

3 See **4556**n2.

---

1 Perhaps Northcote's letter to Derby at **4560**n1.

2 The Ds would leave Euston on the 26th at 10 *am* and arrive in Edinburgh at 9:30 *pm*; see **4544**n1.

4560 TO: LORD DERBY   Downing Street [Friday 25] October 1867

ORIGINAL: DBP Box 146/3
EDITORIAL COMMENT: C of Ex paper. Endorsed by Derby on the first page: 'Put by Private D.' *Dating*: D
has apparently misdated his letter, as the DS would leave for Edinburgh on 26 October ('tomorrow'). *Sic*:
Oct 26; embarassing.

Right Honorable | The Earl of Derby K.G.   Oct 26 1867

My dear Lord,

I think you are doing too much, but we must hope the best; an original remark, you will say.[1]

The / Indian Mail might bring embarassing news. I think we had better adhere to our original day.

I go to Scotland tomorrow. The Duke of Richmond has written to the Committee to say, / that, as the Cabinet meets on the 5th:[2] it would be inconvenient for him to be at Edinbro' on the 29th:, & therefore he does not appear.

It was the only attention he could possibly have / paid me – to say nothing of yourself, & the Ministry, of wh: he is a member! The logic of the excuse is, I think, feminine.

Yours sincerely, | D.

4561 TO: LORD STANLEY   Downing Street [Monday] 4 November 1867

ORIGINAL: DBP Box 12/3/41
EDITORIAL COMMENT: A reproduced circular letter endorsed by Stanley on the second page: 'Mr. Disraeli
Nov. 4. 1867 *Meeting of Parliament* Circular'.

Downing Street | Novr. 4. 1867

My Lord,

It having been deemed necessary to summon Parliament to meet on Tuesday, the 19th. Inst:, for the despatch of business, it is my duty, while I much regret the inconvenience you may consequently experience, earnestly to request your attendance in your place on that day.[1]

I have the honor to be, | My Lord, | Your faithful Servant | *B. Disraeli*

---

1 Derby on 24 October had written to D from Knowsley a letter marked '*Private*': 'I have received the enclosed from Northcote [*not found*] suggesting that Parliament should not meet till the 21st. I do not know whether the reason he assigns is very important; but it would be inconvenient for him to have to dispatch a heavy mail on the day of the meeting. On the other hand the 19th is full late, if we do not wish to run deep into December; and I am afraid that the wording of our last Bill will render it necessary to renew the Irish Insurrection Act during the Novr. Session. I am not sure, *but* I am afraid it was only passed till 21 days after the next meeting of Parliament. But as to the 19th or 21st I am quite ready to be guided by your opinion; and will thank you to settle it with Northcote. I hope you are getting in better trim for your reception at Edinburgh, which, from all accounts, will be on a magnificent scale. I shall look eagerly for the Report of the Proceedings. I had a triumphant reception in Liverpool yesterday, but was very far from being up to the mark.' H B/XX/S/454.

2 The Duke of Richmond and D would attend the cabinet council on 5 November. *The Times* (6 Nov 1867).

---

1 Gladstone would publish a very similar letter dated 7 November. *The Times* (13 Nov 1867). The House would convene at 1:30 *pm* on 19 November. A proclamation by the Queen dated at Windsor on this day (4th), published in the *Gazette* that day and reprinted in *The Times* on the 5th, further prorogued Parliament from 6 to 19 November.

ORIGINAL: H H/LIFE
EDITORIAL COMMENT: From an incomplete manuscript copy headed: '*To Edward Strathearn Gordon* Downing St. S.W. *Nov* 4. 1867'.

You will be glad to hear we made a safe & speedy journey home,[1] tho' really it seems we have scarcely parted; our united names appear so frequently in the newspapers, that I fancy we are still altogether.[2]

The good offices of England were limited to England inducing France not to treat the entrance of the Italian troops into the Papal dominions as a *casus belli*: and, not withstanding the alarm of the newspapers, we have, substantially, effected that.....[3]

TO: EMILY DUNDAS   Downing Street [Monday] 4 November 1867   4563
ORIGINAL: BRS Dundas of Arniston Letterbooks Vol 9 No 167
EDITORIAL COMMENT: C of Ex paper.

Nov 4 1867

Dear Mrs Dundas,

Tho' farewells are always painful, I felt a pang, in leaving Scotland, that I had not said adieu to you, & tried to / thank you for all your kindness to us during our visit.[1]

I often think of it, & of the portraits & glens of your historic home.[2]

I hope Arniston has quite recovered from / what might have been an awkward accident. It was most kind in his coming to the meeting of working men.[3] Pray give

---

1 Gordon on 2 November had written to D at length about Scottish franchise reform, hoping D had had 'a pleasant journey to London' but making no mention of the issues raised by D in the second paragraph (see n3). H B/XI/M/18.
2 *The Times* had reported that on 31 October D had dined at Gordon's Edinburgh residence and that on 1 November the DS, 'accompanied by the Lord Advocate and the Misses Gordon, arrived in a carriage and a pair at the Waverley-bridge terminus' shortly after 10 *am*, where a crowd 'from 200 to 300' had gathered for their departure. The DS reached Grosvenor Gate at 9:55 *pm* on that day (1st). *The Times* (2 Nov 1867); H ACC.
3 *The Times* published dozens of articles on the 'Roman Question' in October and November, including two on this day (4th). On the 3rd, Papal troops had attacked Garibaldi between Tivoli and Monte Rotondo: he was 'arrested upon arriving on Italian territory.' Stanley on the morning of the 5th would receive a telegram announcing the defeat 'and consequent evacuation of papal territory by insurgents.' *The Times* (5 Nov 1867); *Disraeli, Derby* 321.

---

1 See **4544**&n1.
2 Robert Dundas (1685-1753), lord advocate of Scotland, designated Lord Arniston in 1737, had commissioned architect William Adam to design Arniston House, a Georgian mansion located eleven miles from Edinburgh. Built 1726-50 and completed by his son John Adam (brother of famous architect Robert), with a parkland by Capability Brown, its important art collection includes family portraits by Sir Henry Raeburn and Allan Ramsay.
3 Nearly 2,000 members of the working classes had crowded the Music Hall in Edinburgh on 30 October at 8 *pm* to present D with 'a Complimentary Address ... for the noble and successful manner in which he achieved the extension of the Franchise to the Working Men of England, and also for the proposed extension to the Working Men of Scotland.' In a much-cheered speech D had stated how, during a thirty-year career, he had never been hostile to the interests of the working classes and, moreover, during that time thirty-two Acts had been passed, 'laws affecting their wages, their education, their hours of toil,

him my hearty regards, & say kind words / for me to Miss Dundas,[4] & all who may linger round yr happy hearth.

Yours sincerely, | *B. Disraeli*[5]

4564

TO: JAMES HARTLEY   Downing Street [Wednesday] 6 November 1867
ORIGINAL: BRN [30]
EDITORIAL COMMENT: C of Ex paper.

Private   Nov 6. 1867

James Hartley Esqr | M.P.[1]

Dear Sir,

It will be gratifying to H.M. Government if you will honor them by seconding the Address on the approaching meeting of Parliament.[2]

The / speech from the throne[3] will not be confined to the subject of Abyssinia, but I will take care, that you are duly apprised of its contents, & that you shall have every / facility, if you undertake the office, of fulfilling it to your satisfaction.

I have the honor | to remain, dear Sir, | faithfully yours, | *B. Disraeli*

4565

TO: LORD DERBY   Grosvenor Gate [Wednesday] 6 November 1867
ORIGINAL: DBP Box 146/3
EDITORIAL COMMENT: C of Ex paper, seal crossed out and 'Grosvenor Gate' written in. *Sic*: James'.

Right Honorable | The Earl of Derby | K.G.   Grosvenor Gate | Novr. 6 1867

My dear Lord,

I count on getting to the Cabinet tomorrow[1] (D.V), but I shd. like very much to have some talk with / you before we all meet.

---

their means of self-improvement ... I have always looked upon the interests of the labouring classes as essentially the most conservative interests of the country.' H B/X/A/25C; *The Times* (31 Oct 1867).

4 Anne Dundas (d 1917) was Robert Dundas's sister. *The Times* (2 Feb 1917).

5 Emily Dundas on 7 November would reply: 'I am pleased to think that Arniston is connected with your recollections of your visit to Scotland. Mr Dundas ... returned from the Meeting of the Working Men, much pleased with the enthusiastic reception you met with.' She also related that, after attending the meeting, a friend's 'very Radical' butler had declared, '"I came back almost a Tory."' H B/XXI/D/425.

---

1 James Hartley (1811-1886), a glass manufacturer and co-founder (with his brother John) in 1837 of Hartley Wear Glassworks in Sunderland, was a River Wear commissioner, a director of the North East Railway Company, a JP for Durham co and for Sunderland, mayor of Sunderland 1851, 1853, 1862 and MP (C) for Sunderland 1865-8.

2 In the House on 19 November the address would be seconded by Col James Hogg. *Hansard* CXC cols 60-5. See 4575n5.

3 See 4580n1.

---

1 Stanley on 7 November would record: 'Cabinet at 3, Ld D. absent from govt [*mistranscription of 'gout'*]. Sentences of Manchester Fenians discussed, but no final decision. Question raised of prosecuting the *Irishman* newspaper, and certainly the articles produced were treasonable enough: but Naas, Hardy, Disraeli, and I all objected, thinking the risk of failure great, and the advantage small: and it was determined to do nothing at present. The most vehement for prosecuting were Chelmsford and J. Manners.' One article was 'a violent attack on [former Irish sol-gen] Judge [William] Keogh' and another was by [Irish nationalist] 'Isaac Butt: once a Conservative M.P., now a pauper, and with a ruined character.' *Disraeli, Derby* 322.

How shall we manage it?

It wd. rather be an effort for me to disembark in St. James' Sqr, as well as D.S. – but if you / cd. meet me at D.S. some little time before the Cabinet, I have ɨ a room down stairs, wh: wd. save me mounting, &, then, I cd. get to the Cabinet on the same / level.[2]

I am sorry to give you all this trouble.

Yours sincerely, | D.

TO: REGINALD STUART POOLE

Downing Street **4566**
[Wednesday] 6 November 1867

ORIGINAL: BL ADD MS 58079.V.ff.17

EDITORIAL COMMENT: C of Ex paper. *Sic*: Pirke Avoth.

R.S. Poole, Esqr   Nov 6 1867

My dear Sir,

Your volume reached me in busy scenes, but, as I returned to town from Edinburgh, I found the article a most interesting companion.[1]

Pray express to its writer[2] / the entire satisfaction with wh: I read it, & my gratification, that a Semitic subject shd. be treated in a philosophic vein, & in so classical a style.

The matter was not so new to me, as it must prove to the general: for tho' / I never mastered the Talmud, I have read Pirke Avoth,[3] & many other works of that kind, & was familiar with Lightfoot as a boy.[4]

Justice can never be done to the Jewish people, until their literature is viewed completely & comprehensively. There never / was a race, wh: wrote so many books, & wh:, for so continuous a period, formed & affected opinion.

2 These appear to be early signs of D's debilitating attack of lumbago at the end of the month. See **4593**.

---

1 Reginald Stuart Poole had written to D from the British Museum on 22 October enclosing 'a copy of the Quarterly with my colleague Mr. Deutsch's article on the Talmud, which while it opens the way to a new study of that great treasury of Shemitism [*sic*], also offers a link between the two faiths'. H B/XXI/P/400.

2 Emanuel Oscar Menahem Deutsch (1829-1873), a German-Jewish orientalist, had studied under his uncle, distinguished Talmudist Rabbi David Deutsch, before attending the University of Berlin. Appointed first-class assistant in the library of the British Museum in 1855, he would publish articles (many on the Talmud) in Chambers's *Cyclopedia*. His *Quarterly Review* essay of October 1867 created a sensation and 'helped to correct the biased view of the Talmud that many English readers of the previous generation had imbibed from Isaac D'Israeli's dismissive approach in *The Genius of Judaism* (1833)'. The poor working conditions at the museum, which would cause a breakdown in Deutsch's health, would be exposed by Stephan Poles in *The Actual Condition of the British Museum* (1875), in which Deutsch is said to have been '"slowly murdered by the studied malice, and the petty jealousy of officials".' *ODNB*.

3 The Pirkei Avot ('sayings of the elders') is a collection of maxims on ethics and morality from the Talmud.

4 John Lightfoot (1602-1675), BA 1621 and MA 1624 Christ's College, Cambridge, deacon 1622, master of St Catharine's College 1650 and DD 1651, was a prominent Hebraist and Biblical scholar. His books include *Erubhin, or, Miscellanies Christian and Judaicall* (1629) and *Horae Hebraicae et Talmudicae* (1658-78), his most important study. John Rogers Pitman's *The Whole Works of the Rev. John Lightfoot, D.D.* (13 vols) was published 1822-5. Hughenden library has a copy of *Some genuine Remains of the late pious and learned John Lightfoot, D.D.* (1700), ed John Strype.

This article on the "Talmud" is in the right direction, & I hope it will be followed up.

I hope, also, Mrs. Poole is well.[5]

Yours faithfully | D.[6]

4567 TO: MONTAGU CORRY   [London, Friday] 8 November 1867

ORIGINAL: H B/XX/D/54
EDITORIAL COMMENT: C of Ex paper.

Nov 8 1867

I have decided on the Clarendon, & shall call [on] them in my way to D.S. Get your list ready for me.[1]

Mr. Innes an M P.[2] has / an appointment today at ½ past 4.

Sir H.B.[3] at ½ pt 3. What are we to do about the Commission for Campbell?[4]

4568 TO: MARY ANNE DISRAELI   Windsor, Sunday [10 November 1867]

ORIGINAL: H A/I/A/340
POSTMARK: In a circle: 7 | WINDSOR | NO 10 | 67; in a circle: OFFICIAL PAID LONDON | B A | NO 11 | 67
EDITORIAL COMMENT: Windsor Castle paper. *Dating*: by postmark and context; see n1.

---

6 o'ck: Sunday

My dearest wife,

Just arrived & safe, & pretty well.[1] The Queen dines at ½ past 8 – but a message from General / Grey to say, that he is coming to see me immediately.

I thought you would like to hear of
    Your own, | D.

---

5 Poole on 6 August 1861 had married Eliza Christina Forlonge, daughter of politician William Forlonge.
6 Poole on this day (6th) would reply that he had conveyed the contents of D's letter to Deutsch, who thought D 'one of the very few learned men who have every qualification to judge his labours.' The letter had come 'at a turning-point' in Deutsch's life. 'For years he has been hidden in a corner of the Museum Library ... and has never been transferred to his proper field.' There had even been a long-standing memorial 'pressing that Mr. Deutsch should take charge of the Semitic antiquities in the Museum. Yet it has never been acted on ... Had he not been a Hebrew I do not think he would have been kept out of his right so long: were he not a Hebrew he would not be fit to be placed there. I should not have written with this entire frankness were not a duty imposed on me by the concluding words of your letter, in which you express a hope that the article will be followed up ... My Wife begs to thank you for your kind message: she has not forgotten the happy time passed with you and Mrs. Disraeli at Alnwick.' H B/XXI/P/401.

---

1 Possibly a guest list for D's parliamentary dinner at the Clarendon Hotel on 18 November; see **4577**&n1.
2 Arthur Charles Innes (1834-1902), later Innes-Cross, of co Down, Ireland, educated at Eton, a JP for Down 1862, was MP (C) for Newry 1865-8.
3 Presumably Sir Henry Bulwer, MP (L) for Tamworth 1868-71 and the model for Tremaine Bertie in D's novel *Endymion* (1880). See **4218**&n1.
4 Campbell has not been identified.

---

1 D had arrived at Windsor Castle on this day (10th) and would leave on the 11th. *The Times* (12 Nov 1867).

TO: W. COTTER   [Windsor, Monday 11 November 1867] 4569
ORIGINAL: PS 1550
PUBLICATION HISTORY: *The Times* (12 Nov 1867)
EDITORIAL COMMENT: H B/XIII/96a is a heavily corrected draft (docketed '?Nov 1867') in D's hand on
Windsor Castle paper addressed to 'Mr W Cotter.' The text below is from *The Times. Recipient*: see n1.
Dating: by context; see nn1&2.

Sir,[1] –

I regret that I cannot dine with the London and Westminster working men today.[2] I
should have been honoured and gratified by being their guest; but it is impossible.
I approve the purpose of their association,[3] of which you are chairman, and of the
means by which they are effecting it. None are so interested in maintaining the institutions of the country as the working classes. The rich and the powerful will not
find much difficulty, under any circumstances, in maintaining their rights, but the
privileges of the people can only be defended and secured by national institutions.
There is also another reason why I am glad to see among the working classes an
organization in favour of the laws and constitution of the country. There are some
symptoms of a lawless spirit amongst us at this moment which the light-headed may
be inclined to admire as the proofs of the spirit of freedom.[4] Nothing can be more
fallacious. Their tendency is hostile to freedom, and their consequence must be
detrimental to our common rights. In old days it was our pride that the constable's
staff had more authority in this realm than the sabres and muskets of the police of
the continent. It will be bad for us all if that constitutional conviction ceases to influence this country. It was a homage to law, which is the foundation of all freedom. He
who wars against order wars against liberty.

    I remain yours truly,
      B. DISRAELI

1 W. Cotter, signing himself 'chairman' of the London and Westminster Working Men's Constitutional
Association (see **4452**n2), on 8 November had written to D: 'We venture most respectfully but most
earnestly again to approach you to solicit your reconsideration of our invitation ... we do ask that on
this memorable occasion – the first on which the Constitutional Working Men of England have been
honoured by receiving as Guests the Ministers of their beloved Sovereign – you, Sir, to whose wondrous
talent, judgement & temper they feel they are mainly indebted for admission to the full privilege of citi-
zenship may not be Absent.' H B/XIII/96b.
2 On this day (11th) at the Crystal Palace, '2,000 members of metropolitan and provincial Constitutional
Associations' would dine together to celebrate the passing of the Reform Act. 'The centre of the wall
behind the orchestra was decorated with a trophy and the words, "The Altar, the Throne, and the Cottage"'. The main speaker, Lord John Manners, had 'doubtless' suggested that motto, 'for this mysterious
alliance between religion, monarchy, and industry was, as usual, the keynote of his discourse.' After dinner R.N. Fowler, in the chair, would read D's letter. *The Times* (12, 13 Nov 1867).
3 The Association aimed 'to unite the friends of constitutional principles in resisting any attempt to sub-
vert the Protestant faith or the constitution of the country; to protect the prerogatives of the Crown; and
to defend the rights and privileges of the people.' *Dickens's Dictionary of London, 1879. An Unconventional
Handbook* 203.
4 Fenian lawlessness would culminate in the Clerkenwell explosion of 13 December 1867. See **4624**&nn1&2.

4570

TO: [MONTAGU CORRY?]　　　　　　　　　[London] Tuesday 12 November 1867

ORIGINAL: NLC E.A. Petherick MS 760 Series 18 MS71
EDITORIAL COMMENT: C of Ex paper.

Tuesday Novr 12./67

The Postal Contracts must be brought before the Cabinet the *first* matter today.[1]

See Lord Barrington thereon / – & arrange that the Post-Master General & the Secr. of the Treasy are in attendance on the Cabinet.[2]

The matter can't / be delayed. I shall come to D.S. after the Court, if possible.[3]

D.

4571

TO: SIR HENRY STRACEY　　　　　　　　　　　　Downing Street
　　　　　　　　　　　　　　　　　　[Wednesday] 13 November 1867

ORIGINAL: BUL [1]
EDITORIAL COMMENT: C of Ex paper. The addressee line has been cut off and 'Lady Stracey' partly obliterated and written in by a later hand.

[Sir Henry Stracey]　　　　　　　　　　　　　　　　　Nov 13 1867

My dear Sir Henry,

Tho' late, I thank you heartily.

I hope [Lady Stracey] is well – & all your hearth.[1]

Yrs sincerely, | D.

4572

TO: LORD DERBY　　　　Grosvenor Gate [Thursday] 14 November 1867

ORIGINAL: DBP Box 146/3
EDITORIAL COMMENT: C of Ex paper, seal crossed out and 'G.G.' written in.

Right Honble | The Earl of Derby | K.G.　　　　　　G.G. | Nov. 14 1867

My dear Lord,

I have been thinking very much about the Education Par:[1] & have great doubts

---

1 Stanley on this day (12th) recorded a 'Cabinet at 4. Queen's Speech read and partly considered: also the Manchester Fenians: but our chief business was the renewing of the contracts of P. and O. company, which we agreed to, at £400,000 a year for twelve years, and a guarantee of 6%: high terms, I thought, but nobody would compete with them, and they are masters of the market.' *Disraeli, Derby* 322. See **4507**&n3.

2 James Graham, 4th Duke of Montrose, was postmaster-general and G. W. Hunt was treasury financial secretary.

3 D at 2 *pm* would attend the 'Morrow of St Martin', the ancient ceremony of nominating sheriffs, at the Court of Exchequer. *The Times* (13 Nov 1867).

---

1 Sir Henry and Lady Stracey had seven sons and six daughters. Stracey had sent D cygnets in 1862 and 1865; see **3987**&n1.

---

1 The paragraph, extracted from the Queen's speech in the Lords on 19 November (see **4580**n1), would be published on the 20th: '"The general question of the Education of the People requires your most serious attention, and I have no doubt you will approach the subject with a full appreciation both of its vital importance and its acknowledged difficulty."' D would assure the House on the 19th that 'the passage referring to Education is not a rhetorical flourish. Her Majesty's Government have given their most earnest attention to the subject.' *The Times* (20 Nov 1867); *Hansard* CXC col 75.

about its propriety. I do not like in Cabinet / to oppose anyth[in]g you suggest, of any importance, & if you decide upon the par:, I shall support you.[2]

But I have misgivings.

The Public expect a meagre speech, & / the omission of any subjects will not estop our treating them in Feby &c., if we deem it expedient. I don't think our silence will be misconstrued into any / intentional neglect of such subjects.

Whereas, a vague par: leads to criticism & cross-examination, & often induces imprudent, or inconvenient, engagements[.]

Think of this. I would come on, but cannot.

Yrs ever, I D.

TO: [LADY BROWNLOW]   [Downing Street, mid-November 1867] 4573
ORIGINAL: H B/XIII/93
EDITORIAL COMMENT: A draft in D's hand on C of Ex paper. Docketed in another hand on the first page: '?1867'. *Dating*: see n1. *Sic*: Octo 1.

Octo 1

I passed yesterday in the company of a most interesting & charming society, wits & statesmen & delightful women; their manners easy & natural, & all they said or thought wise or witty.[1] / When I closed the volume, it seemed an enchanting dream but there was a reality wh: remained, & wh: consoled me: that she whose hand waved the magic wand of graceful reminiscence / was for our happiness yet spared to us; happy ↑herself↓ & well I hope amid her native rocks & ↑western↓ vistas ~~at at Torquay~~;[2] & not indisposed I hope ↑and fain believe↓ to accept the congratulations & regards of a busy but grateful friend.

D.

TO: MONTAGU CORRY   [Grosvenor Gate, Friday] 15 November 1867 4574
ORIGINAL: H B/XX/D/55
EDITORIAL COMMENT: C of Ex paper, although D is evidently at Grosvenor Gate attending to MA.

Nov 15. 1867

Mrs Disraeli is so seriously unwell,[1] that I much doubt, whether I shall be able to reach D.S. today.

---

2 Stanley on this day (14th) noted a two-hour cabinet at 4 *pm* 'considering the speech.' *Disraeli, Derby* 322.

1 Lady Brownlow on 5 November 1867 had written to D from Lowndes Square, London: 'In obedience to Mrs Disraeli's behest I am going to be presumptuous and conceited enough to send you a copy of my little bantling which is now appearing before the world. Pray be kind & merciful to this unpretending production, for it pretends to be no more than "Slight Reminiscences," but they are *truthful*, & if in an idle half hour they can beguile your thoughts from more serious things, I shall feel very proud.' *Slight Reminiscences of a Septuagenarian, from 1802 to 1815* (1867) would be republished (with additions) in 1940 as *The Eve of Victorianism, Reminiscences of the Years 1802-1834*. H B/XXI/B/1060; *The Times* (14 Nov 1867).
2 Lady Brownlow suffered from chronic attacks of bronchitis and spent much time at Torquay.

1 MA was exhausted from the DS' Scottish tour, and her illness may be connected to the cancer of which she would die in 1872.

You must explain all / this to Mr Roebuck – & my great regret at not receiving him.

If he will extend his confidence to you, I shd. feel obliged / to him.

Things appear to me to be so serious, that I can't make any arrangements about tomorrow, & even must contemplate the / possib[ilit]y of asking Ld Stanley to preside over my dinner[2] – but silence about this at present[.]

D.

4575   TO: [MONTAGU CORRY]   [Grosvenor Gate] Saturday [16 November 1867]
ORIGINAL: H B/XX/D/56
EDITORIAL COMMENT: C of Ex paper. *Dating*: by context; see n4.

Saturday | ½ pt 12

A bad bulletin. Sleepless night[.] Increased suffering & no relief from Remedies.[1]

Cowell[2] has seen her, & / ~~Grey~~ Gull[3] meets him here at ¼ past four.

I think, at her request, that I shall try to walk for an hour or so, & / wd. try to get to D.S. by three, tho' I must leave it then immediately.

I fear you will hardly be able to be my companion, at / such an hour in these busy times.

Tell me, when we meet, what is the dinner hour ~~tomorrow~~ ↑on Monday↓ & remember, in precedence after ~~the~~ Mr Speaker,[4] the mover & seconder[5] come, Dyke on my left[.]

Yr D.

2 See **4577**&nn1&2. In an undated letter docketed 'F.O. 3.30', Stanley would assure D he would 'do anything in my power to help you. Your messenger found me just starting to enquire for the latest reports at Grosvenor Gate & I earnestly hope, and trust, all will go well. In the meanwhile whatever it is possible to do in the way of taking business off your hands, I, and all your colleagues, will be ready to undertake.' H D/VIII/A/42.

---

1 *The Times* on 18 November would report that MA was 'suffering from [a] very serious illness, and was in a condition last evening to cause considerable anxiety.'

2 London apothecary and ophthalmic surgeon George Cowell (1836-1927), educated at St George's Hospital, LSAL and Lic. Midwif. 1858, FRCS 1867. He was a surgeon at the Victoria Hospital for Children 1866-85 and at the Royal Westminster Ophthalmic Hospital and the Westminster Hospital 1869-96, lecturing on surgery at the latter 1873-93. *Medical Register* (1879); *The Times* (19 Nov 1927).

3 William Withey Gull (1816-1890), 1st Bt and Kt 1872, MB 1841 London University, MD and FRCP 1848, FRS 1869, had had a distinguished career at Guy's Hospital, London: medical tutor 1841, medical superintendent of the lunatic ward 1843, lecturer on natural philosophy 1843-7 and on physiology and comparative anatomy 1846-56, assistant physician 1851-6 and full physician 1856-65. He was physician in ordinary to the Prince of Wales, whom he would treat for typhoid fever in 1871. He is credited for having coined the expression *anorexia nervosa* in 1873.

4 House Speaker John Evelyn Denison would be among the thirty-two guests at D's parliamentary dinner at the Clarendon Hotel on the 18th. *The Times* (19 Nov 1867). See **4577**&n1.

5 At the dinner (n4) the mover of the address would be William Hart Dyke (1837-1931), 7th Bt 1875, PC 1880, MA 1864 Christ Church, Oxford, MP (C) for W Kent 1865-8, Mid Kent 1868-85 and Dartford 1885-1906. He would be Conservative whip 1868-74, parliamentary secretary to the treasury 1874-80, chief secretary for Ireland 1885-8 and vice-president of the committee of council on education 1887-92. The seconder would be James Macnaghten Hogg, member 1867 and chairman 1870-89 of the metropolitan board of works.

TO: LOUISA, LADY ANTHONY DE ROTHSCHILD   Grosvenor Gate   4576
Sunday [17] November 1867

ORIGINAL: ROTH BK II 3-5
EDITORIAL COMMENT: C of Ex paper, seal crossed out and 'Grosvenor Gate' written in. *Dating*: by context; see **4575**.

Grosvenor Gate | Sunday ↑evg.↓ Nov 1867

Dearest Lady de Roth[schil]d,

Alas! I can give no good news! Dr Gull was still hopeful when he left ↑us↓ two hours ago, but, / I think, her sufferings increase & her weakness.

Think of me as the unhappiest of men!

D.

TO: LORD STANLEY   Grosvenor Gate [Monday] 18 November 1867   4577

ORIGINAL: DBP Box 12/3/42; H H/LIFE
PUBLICATION HISTORY: M&B IV 570, undated extract from the first paragraph and the last paragraph
EDITORIAL COMMENT: C of Ex paper, seal crossed out and 'Grosvenor Gate' written in.

Right Honorable | Secy Lord Stanley   Grosvenor Gate | Nov 18 1867
Dear Stanley,   3. ock:

I must appeal to you as a comrade in arms, & the friend of my public life, to aid me at this distressful moment, & / take the chair at the Clarendon today in my stead.[1]

The ceremonies are not very elaborate.

After the dessert has been served, you will ask your guests to charge their glasses, & when / that is completed, you will give H.M's health: the only toast. Then, when they are seated, you will, ↑standing,↓ read the Queen's speech,[2] wh: one of my Secretaries, Mr Montagu Corry, will bring / you in a box.

[H H/LIFE:] This has been a critical day in my wife's life, but not a bad one. There seems a favorable turn, and I count almost on being in my place to-morrow.

Ever yours, | D.

TO: [CHARLOTTE, BARONESS LIONEL DE ROTHSCHILD?]   4578
Downing Street [Tuesday 19 November 1867]

ORIGINAL: ROTH RAL 000/848
EDITORIAL COMMENT: C of Ex paper. *Recipient* and *Dating*: by context; see **4579**.

3/ o ck

The symptoms more favorable: the strength not so much impaired by the remedies as was feared this morning: & taking some sustenance: your soup, wh: was approved.

Ever | D.

---

1 On this day (18th) D would give a parliamentary dinner at the Clarendon Hotel but would not attend, 'owing to the serious indisposition of Mrs. Disraeli.' *The Times* (19 Nov 1867).
2 Gathorne Hardy on the 19th would record that 'Stanley read the Speech badly & omitted though he wd. not admit it an important part. He was in a doubtful state!' *Hardy Diary* 54.

4579 TO: CHARLOTTE, BARONESS LIONEL DE ROTHSCHILD

Grosvenor Gate [Tuesday] 19 November 1867

ORIGINAL: ROTH RAL 000/848

EDITORIAL COMMENT: C of Ex paper, seal crossed out and what appears to be a minuscule 'GG.' written beside it. The last sentence is written across the lower left corner of the last page.

GG. | ½ past 10 o'ck: | Nov 19 1867

Dearest Baroness,

Good news. This morning, about two short hours before Lionel called,[1] I was hurried from my bed by Mr Cowell to / break to me the worst news. My wife had had a dreadful night, & there were other reasons, that he felt it his duty to tell me the catastrophe might prove imminent[.]

This will explain why I / seemed to receive Lionel so wildly, & cd. not see him, or even write to him.

I had a consultation with Gull directly, & remedies were applied.

At three o'ck: Dr Gull considered affairs were yet "hopeful", & I / ventured to go down to the House of Commons.

There I received a very favorable telegram, & from three o'ck, there has been a change, & if we can sustain her (but her weakness is terrible) we may yet do.[2]

Give me yr best thoughts

Yr affectionate, | D.

She murmured to me to write this to you.

4580 TO: QUEEN VICTORIA

Downing Street [Tuesday] 19 November 1867

ORIGINAL: RAC B24 29

PUBLICATION HISTORY: M&B IV 571; Sir Charles Petrie *The Carlton Club* (1955) 115, the first paragraph; Weintraub *Disraeli* 457-8, the last paragraph, omitting the final clause

EDITORIAL COMMENT: C of Ex paper.

Nov 19 1867

The Chr of the Excheqr with his humble duty to Yr Majesty:

The Address to Yr Majesty's speech[1] was moved this evening by Mr Hart Dyke in with / grace, & great ability: a young man, good-looking, & very popular. He gained the whole house: M.P. for W. Kent.[2]

---

1 The Lionel, Meyer and Anthony de Rothschilds had called upon or sent inquiries to MA during her illness. *The Times* (21 Nov 1867).

2 *The Times* on this day (19th) reported that Drs Gull and Cowell were 'constantly in attendance.'

---

1 On this day (19th) the session had been opened in the Lords by commission and the Queen's speech read by the lord chancellor. Topics outlined included an expedition to Abyssinia to liberate British subjects held '"in violation of all international law"'; the hope of early withdrawal of French troops from the Papal territory; the intent to quell the Fenians' '"organized violence and assassination"'; upcoming bills '"for amending the Representation of the People in Scotland and Ireland"' and for the prevention of bribery and corruption at elections; a re-tabling of the Public Schools Bill; the '"general question of the Education of the People"'; and, following the decline of the cattle plague, '"permanent enactments [to] facilitate the introduction ... of foreign cattle for home consumption."' *The Times* (20 Nov 1867).

2 William Hart Dyke had dealt with each of the topics in the speech (n1) in turn. He assured the House that the government had no 'wish for territorial aggrandizement' in Abyssinia and that every diplomatic

414

Mr Gladstone rose immediately, & made / a very fair & just speech:[3] & very kind & considerate to the Chr. of the Exchequer, who was much touched by it.[4]

And he begs leave to offer to Yr Majesty his / very grateful thanks for all Yr Majesty's sympathy & gracious kindness in his great sorrow.

Your Majesty is too good[.][5]

This morning, all seemed dark, & he was told / to hope no more; but within three hours of this, there was a change, & everything became hopeful: a state of complete composure but accompanied by increased strength.[6]

TO: LORD BEAUCHAMP   Grosvenor Gate [Wednesday] 20 November 1867 **4581**

ORIGINAL: BCP [38]; now BL ADD MS 61892

EDITORIAL COMMENT: C of Ex paper, seal crossed out and 'G. Gate' written in.

G. Gate | Nov 20 1867

My dearest Beauchamp,

I must thank you for all your considerate kindness.[1]

She also desires me to thank you for remembering her.

There is a ray of hope / under this roof, since the last four & twenty hours.[2]

Yours ever, | D.

---

means had been taken to free the captives. He suggested completing 'the partial settlement we have arrived at' on parliamentary reform; noted the difficulty in defining the exact point at which 'a man, instead of conscientiously canvassing for a vote, is endeavouring to use corrupt influence'; and hoped that the 'urgent' education question would 'soon receive a satisfactory solution.' Hardy would note that 'Dyke moved the address like a gentleman & pleased the House by his unaffected style.' *Hansard* CXC cols 51-60; *Hardy Diary* 54.

3 Gladstone had stated he would adhere to 'the general and prudent rule that excludes controverted matters' from the debate on the address and congratulated Hart Dyke on his 'most intelligent and judicious' speech. He thought the Queen's speech contained 'little, if anything, of which we have reason to complain', but hoped the rumour that the commissioners inquiring into the Established Church of Ireland would not merely collect and examine facts but have the 'authority to propose plans', which should be 'reserved entirely for the discretion of Parliament', would be proven false. *Hansard* CXC cols 65-72.

4 Referring to D's 'domestic circumstances', Gladstone (n3) had assured him 'that he carries with him universal sympathy.' D replied that he was much touched by Gladstone's allusion to his 'domestic affliction, and by the way in which the House has received his allusion to that subject.' *Hansard* CXC cols 72-5. Stanley on this day (19th) noted that in replying to Gladstone's 'temperate and courteous' speech, D 'for the first time since I have known him was unable to speak audibly when he first rose, from emotion.' *Disraeli, Derby* 323. See **4585**.

5 A messenger's note, dated 18 November 1867 on Windsor Castle paper, had informed D that 'Her Majesty would be glad to know by the bearer how [MA] is.' The Queen would send D telegrams on the 20th ('Anxious to hear how Mrs Disraeli is this morning') and 21st ('The Queen trusts that the improvement still continues'). H D/VIII/A/1, 3, 4.

6 MA's health on this day (19th) had been reported as 'not so favourable', her doctors recording that she had had '"a bad night and continues very ill."' Stanley noted his anxiety at having 'to take the lead [in the House on this day], in Disraeli's absence, should Mrs D. die which is thought possible.' *The Times* (20 Nov 1867); *Disraeli, Derby* 323. See **4583**.

---

1 Beauchamp had written to D on 18 November hoping for 'a satisfactory Bulletin of Mrs Disraeli's progress as well as a good report of yourself' and on the 19th had sent D some grapes 'brought up this morning from Madresfield & it will give me much pleasure if they shall prove agreeable to Mrs Disraeli. I need not assure you how much I feel for you in your anxiety.' H D/VIII/A/10, 13.

2 On the afternoon of this day (20th) MA had become 'a little stronger' and on the 21st would show 'a slight improvement'. *The Times* (21 Nov 1867).

4582
TO: PHILIP ROSE   Downing Street [Wednesday] 20 November 1867
ORIGINAL: H R/I/A/202
EDITORIAL COMMENT: C of Ex paper.

Private   Nov. 20 1867

Philip Rose Esq

My dear Rose,

If the greatest of misfortunes had happened to me, wh: 8 & 40 hours ago, threatened, I shd. have sent for you & you only; for / you knew her, & knew all. I cd. have seen no other person – but, thank God, yesterday afternoon, a happy change took place, & she has since continued to / rally: & I have great hopes. If she continues to gain strength, or even to maintain her strength, slight as it is, for a couple of days – they say, all will go well.[1]

So, I write this good news to you, who have ever been to me a faithful friend.

Yrs ever, I D.[2]

4583
TO: EMILY CLUBBE   Grosvenor Gate [Wednesday] 20 November 1867
ORIGINAL: RIC [36]
EDITORIAL COMMENT: C of Ex paper, seal crossed out and 'Grosvenor Gate' written in.

Grosvenor Gate I Nov. 20 1867

Dear Mrs. Clubbe,

We have been in great sorrow, but there is now a ray of hope under this roof.

A favorable change took place ~~last~~ / ~~last night,~~ ↑yesterday afternoon↓ when everything seemed at the worst – & from that moment, my wife has continued to rally.[1]

I know that you will all be happy to / hear this[.]

Yrs sin[cerel]y, I D.

4584
TO: LOUISA, LADY ANTHONY DE ROTHSCHILD   Grosvenor Gate
[Wednesday] 20 November 1867
ORIGINAL: ROTH BK II 3-4
EDITORIAL COMMENT: C of Ex paper, seal crossed out and 'G.G.' written in.

G.G. I Nov. 20 1867

---

1 See **4574**&n1 and **4581**&n2.
2 Rose on this day (20th) would reply: 'Your letter has just reached me. I deeply value the fond feeling which dictated it but it is doubly welcome for the good news it contains of Mrs. Disraelis improvement. We have all been in great distress and anxiety about you and sincerely joined in the universal feeling of sympathy which has showered you on all sides. – It was very kind of you to write to me at such a time and I earnestly pray that your anxieties may soon be still further relieved in seeing one so dear to you gradually restored to health and that you may be spared for many years the heavy blow of parting which at one time we so much dreaded.' H R/I/B/112.

---

1 Emily Clubbe on 21 November would reply from Hughenden vicarage thankful 'to hear a better acct of dear Mrs Disraeli for we have been in great anxiety about her, & sincerely trust she will continue to improve.' H D/VIII/A/18. See **4581**n2.

Dear Lady de Rothschild

There is a ray of hope now under this roof, & if we can maintain her strength, all may yet / be well.[1]

Yours ever, | D.

TO: **WILLIAM GLADSTONE** Grosvenor Gate [Wednesday] 20 November 1867 **4585**
ORIGINAL: BL ADD MS 44413 ff242-3
PUBLICATION HISTORY: M&B IV 570, the second paragraph; Bradford 276, the first two paragraphs; John Morley *The Life of William Ewart Gladstone* (1903) II 546
EDITORIAL COMMENT: Grosvenor Gate paper.

The Right Honorable | W.E. Gladstone   Nov 20 1867
Dear Mr Gladstone,

I was incapable yesterday of expressing to you, how much I appreciated your considerate sympathy.[1]

My wife had always / a strong personal regard for you, &, being of a vivid & original character, she could comprehend, & value, your great gifts & qualities.

There / is a ray of hope under this roof since the last four & twenty hours:[2] round your hearth, I trust, health & happiness will be ever present.[3]

Yours sincerely, | *B. Disraeli*

TO: **PEDRO ROMULO NEGRETE** [London, Thursday] 21 November [1867] **4586**
ORIGINAL: BRN [84]
EDITORIAL COMMENT: Endorsed in another hand: 'General Negrete Salvador Minister'. *Dating*: by context; see n1.

Nov. 21. 11 o'ck

The improvement in Mrs Disraeli's state is maintained.[1]

---

1 Lady de Rothschild on 22 November would reply from Aston Clinton with 'a thousand thanks for your great kindness in sending me those welcome words of hope and our heartfelt congratulations upon the continued improvement in your beloved patient's health.' H D/VIII/A/23.

---

1 See **4580**&n4.
2 See **4583**&n1.
3 Gladstone would reply: '"I have always been grateful for, and have sincerely reciprocated, Mrs. Disraeli's regard, and during the recent crisis I was naturally mindful of it; but, even if I had not had the honour and pleasure of knowing her, it would have been impossible not to sympathise with you at a moment when the fortitude necessary to bear the labours and trials of your station was subjected to a new burden of a character so crushing and peculiar."' Qtd in M&B IV 570.

---

1 *The Times* on 22 November would report that 'the improvement already announced as having taken place in the health of Mrs. Disraeli is still maintained.' On this day (21st) it reprinted from *The Globe* the names of those who had called upon MA on the 20th or sent to inquire about her condition, which included 'all the *Corps Diplomatique*.' General Pedro Romulo Negrete (d 1878), special minister from Salvador 1858 and consul-general of Guatemala July 1867, would be minister plenipotentiary of San Salvador 1869 and of Guatemala 1872. *The Times* (3 Apr 1858, 23 Jul 1867, 15 May 1869, 26 Jun 1872).

4587

TO: [PEDRO ROMULO NEGRETE?]

[Downing Street, Thursday] 21 November [1867]

ORIGINAL: BRN [85]

EDITORIAL COMMENT: C of Ex paper. *Dating*: see **4586**&n1.

Nov: 21. 3 o'ck:

Mrs. Disraeli is gaining strength.

4588

TO: QUEEN VICTORIA   Downing Street [Thursday] 21 November 1867

ORIGINAL: RAC B24 30

EDITORIAL COMMENT: C of Ex paper.

Nov. 21 1867

The Chanr of the Exchequer with his humble duty to Yr Majesty:

In the House tonight, nothing of significance, but a conversation about the Fenian Convicts,[1] arranged / among some Irish members & a few secondrate lawyers.[2] Mr Hardy spoke briefly; but with dignity & decision.[3] Mr Gladstone made a speech, wh: the Att[orn]ey Genl ought to have made;[4] / but the general result was satisfactory.

The Chr of the Excr presumes to ask permission to thank Yr Majesty again for the Expression of Yr gracious sympathy.[5] It had some sustaining power, even in the darkest hour, / & he shall never forget Yr Majesty's goodness to him, wh:, indeed, he has ever proved; & hopes he may some day deserve.

She, in whose welfare Yr Majesty deigned to interest yourself, rallied wonderfully,

1 In the House on this day (21st) debate had centred on the recent Fenian trials in Manchester, where one convict had been pardoned, four sentenced to hanging and, thanks to what MP (L) John Maguire called 'riddled and damaged' evidence, five acquitted. 'These Judges might be very eminent in their profession, but they were not infallible.' Asking the government 'not to perpetrate a legal murder', Maguire moved the adjournment of the House. *Hansard* CXC cols 113-29.

2 MPs John Maguire (Cork), Sir Patrick O'Brien (King's co), Sir George Bowyer (Dundalk), Sir Colman O'Loghlen (Clare co) and John Bagwell (Clonmel) were Irish; Montagu Chambers (Devonport) and Stephen Gaselee (Portsmouth) were barristers. All were Liberals and all spoke in the debate (n1).

3 Hardy (n1), stating that Maguire 'wishes me to take an absolutely illegal course' and show contempt for the judges' decision, refused 'to interfere with the execution'. Maguire would withdraw his motion following Montagu Chambers's assurances to Hardy that the latter would be doing nothing illegal in advising the Queen 'to ask the advice of her Judges ... as to whether there had been a legal or an illegal conviction for murder.'

4 Gladstone, speaking with what he termed 'great deference and humility', did not believe Hardy would 'be offending against the statute or doing an illegal act.' He explained that, according to a recent statute, instead of leaving the matter of the suspicion of an invalid conviction to the Crown's discretion, 'it shall be considered by the Judges who tried the case' and whose judgement was final. Attorney-general Sir John Karslake, speaking last, thought Gladstone had 'stated with perfect accuracy' that prior to the recent statute 'the Crown was in the habit of consulting the Judges upon points of law raised before one of the Judges,' but that since then 'a power has been given to a Judge, if he thinks that a question raised before him is worthy of consideration, to have that question reserved for the solemn argument and decision of the Judges in a Court of Law.' The House had adjourned at 6:15 *pm*.

5 See **4580**n5.

on Tuesday afternoon, at the blackest moment – & there has been no relapse.[6] All is hope.[7]

TO: [PEDRO ROMULO NEGRETE?]   Grosvenor Gate **4589**
Friday [22 November 1867]

ORIGINAL: BRN [88]
EDITORIAL COMMENT: C of Ex paper. *Dating*: see **4586**&n1.

Grosvenor Gate | Friday 3 o'ck.

Mrs. Disraeli continues to improve.

TO: CHARLOTTE, BARONESS LIONEL DE ROTHSCHILD   **4590**
Downing Street [Saturday] 23 November 1867

ORIGINAL: ROTH RAL 000/848
PUBLICATION HISTORY: Weintraub *Charlotte and Lionel* 215, the last sentence
EDITORIAL COMMENT: C of Ex paper. *Sic*: occured.

In Cabinet   Nov 23 1867

Dearest Baroness

I promised my wife to write to you to day – but have been so pressed with affairs from the rising to the setting of the sun, that I must / ask you to forgive these hurried lines in a mysterious place.[1]

She is much distressed at what occured about yr visit yesterday;[2] somebody ought to have written to you who did not. I think, howe[ve]r, tho' I deeply / regret the inconvenience to wh: you were subjected, that it was, on the whole, better you did not meet yesterday, for, from protracted want of sleep, & other causes, she was in a state of great excitement, so that I myself never see her / in the evening now.

She has not yet seen anyone,[3] & still hopes she may see you first; sends you many loves, & will always be ready to greet you after two o'ck:

---

6 MA had been 'progressing favourably' and the improvement in her health was 'still maintained.' *The Times* (22 Nov 1867).

7 On this day (21st) on Clerkenwell green over 20,000 would meet to adopt a petition for clemency to the Queen. On the 22nd a deputation would travel to Windsor only to have the petition returned by General Grey, who (in a note) stated that, since the petition was addressed to Hardy, only he could submit it to the Queen. On the 23rd in Manchester three members of the Irish Republican Brotherhood – William Philip Allen, Michael Larkin and Michael O'Brien (later famously dubbed the Manchester Martyrs) – would be hanged before a crowd of over 8,000, 'the first Fenian executions for murder in Great Britain.' *The Times* (23, 25 Nov 1867); Paul Rose *The Manchester Martyrs: The Story of a Fenian Tragedy* (1970) 95. See **4590**n1.

---

1 Stanley on this day (23rd) noted a 'Cabinet at 3, discussed postal contracts at length, London cattle-market, and prospects of Fenian disturbance in London.' *Disraeli, Derby* 323. Hardy on the 24th would note that the cabinet had decided 'not to interfere with the funeral procession to Hyde Park today' honouring the three Fenians (the Manchester Martyrs) executed on the 23rd. *Hardy Diary* 55. The volatile political situation and fear of reprisals may have prompted the cabinet to meet secretly in an undisclosed ('mysterious') location. *The Times* does not mention a cabinet council on this day.

2 The Baroness on 22 November had written to her son Leopold, 'I went to town on a wild goose chase. Mrs. Dis. was much better, but could not receive me – so I am to call again on Sunday when she will be visible after 2 o'clock; the great man was busy.' ROTH.

3 MA would record on the 29th: 'House one month no company myself very ill.' H ACC.

I wd. also send you my love, but I gave it you long ago.

D.

4591 TO: JOHN BENJAMIN SMITH   Downing Street [Monday] 25 November 1867

ORIGINAL: MPL [5]

EDITORIAL COMMENT: C of Ex paper.

J.B. Smith Esqr I M.P.[1]   Nov 25 1867

Dear Mr Smith,

I have been very much occupied, & could scarcely attend, as I ought to have done, to business: / otherwise, I should have acknowledged before your interesting letter.[2]

The matter is of much importance, & I should like to have an opportunity, some / day, of talking it over with you.

Believe me, I faithfully yours I *B. Disraeli*

4592 TO: QUEEN VICTORIA   Downing Street [Tuesday] 26 November 1867

ORIGINAL: RAC P18 48

PUBLICATION HISTORY: *LQVB* I 470-1

EDITORIAL COMMENT: C of Ex paper.

---

12 o'ck: I Nov. 26 1867

The Chanr of the Exchequer with his humble duty to Yr Majesty:

He introduced tonight, in a very guarded speech, avoiding all points of controversy, *the vote of credit (2 mill:)* for / the *Abyssinian expedition.*[1]

His plan for the battle was, that, when the attack was made & the enemy had betrayed their points of ~~attack~~ ↑assault↓, that Lord Stanley shd. / reply on the *policy*, & Sir S. Northcote on the *administrative* details of the preparations.

These two generals of division realized all his hopes, & gained laurels.

---

1 John Benjamin Smith (1794-1879), a former Manchester cotton merchant, president of the Manchester Chamber of Commerce 1839-41 and first president of the Anti-Corn-Law League 1839 (he was dubbed 'Corn Law' Smith), was MP (L) for Stirling district 1847-52 and Stockport 1852-74. A promoter of free trade, Smith would serve on the royal commission on international coinage in 1868.

2 Smith had written at length on 7 November calling D's attention to the subject of 'an International system of moneys weights & measures' and summarizing previous efforts to this end, including an 1862 Commons committee (on which Smith had served) that had '*unanimously* reported in favour of the adoption of the metrical system of weights & measures.' If D were 'prepared to take the lead ... no time must be lost to be first in the field', Smith suggesting the Government 'immediately invite a Congress of Nations to consider' the matter and offering to wait upon D should he 'wish to talk over the subject with me.' MPL [3Q].

---

1 In the House on this day (26th) in committee of supply D had moved £2,000,000 '"for defraying the expenses of the Abyssinian Expedition, beyond the ordinary expenses of the year 1867."' The motion would be agreed to after protracted debate, the House adjourning at 1 *am.* Ever since the receipt on 13 August of a letter (of 26 July) from colonel William Merewether reporting the King of Abyssinia's rejection of Stanley's mid-April ultimatum, the situation had become, in D's words, 'distressing and scandalous ... intolerable.' A 'recourse to arms' was absolutely necessary, the country 'going to war not to obtain territory, not to secure commercial advantages, but for ... high moral causes alone.' In his concluding remarks he would tell Lowe (n2) that 'the course we took ... was strictly within the limits of Constitutional practice.' *Hansard* CXC cols 182-305 (D 182-93, 303-5).

Mr Lowe opened the / attack with much elaboration, but with less [*illegible deletion*] fire, than fury.[2]

Lord Stanley, not *excited*, but *stimulated* by everything at stake, made by far the greatest, & the most / successful effort he has yet achieved in the House of Commons.

He covered every point of the case, & concluded even with a ~~bo~~ burst of feeling.[3]

The / effect was so great, that the House broke up, tho' it had been well-filled, & never afterwards fairly got together. The understanding for an adjourned debate was relinquished, & the / opposition to the vote took the shape of cavils & petty criticism from secondrate men,[4] Mr Gladstone sending a message, that he shd. probably not speak, & merely on the / financial points. Mr Bright, who came down to speak, left the House.

It was difficult to find an excuse to put up Sir Stafford Northcote,[5] but we contrived to do so. He is now about / to conclude, but there is every prospect of the debate finishing with some remarks from Mr Gladstone.[6]

The 2. Mill: vote will certainly pass tonight[.]

TO: **MONTAGU CORRY**   [Grosvenor Gate] Wednesday [27 November 1867] **4593**
ORIGINAL: H B/XX/D/58
EDITORIAL COMMENT: C of Ex paper, seal crossed out. In pencil. *Dating*: by context; see n1.

Montagu Corry Esq   2 o'ck: | Wednesday

---

2 Lowe (n1) had blamed Stanley's speech of 26 July for inducing 'the House to believe that [the Government] were not going immediately or in a short time to take any decided steps against King Theodore', yet preparations had been made 'as hotly and as fast as they could,' the Government informing the House they were going to war only 'when its powers were in the very act of being suspended by the prorogation of Parliament.'

3 Stanley (n1) had countered Lowe's 'remarkable display of rhetorical ingenuity' by explaining that the Government in April had 'demanded the prisoners in a formal manner' and 'at the same time' began communicating with the India and War Offices about the prospects of an expedition; that it was possible to provide 'for an event which though probable is not certain'; that Abyssinia's terrain was mapped and its climate healthy; that there would be little 'serious military resistance' and (according to Sir Robert Napier, who would lead the expedition) that only a force of 10,000 to 12,000 men would ensure success; that even a few weeks' delay 'would have probably involved the loss of the year'; and that to have 'snatched a hasty Vote' in August from the House in the absence of seven-eighths of its members, those present being 'habitual supporters of the Government, and to have made such a Vote an excuse for putting off all discussion regarding the expedition till February, would have been a far more unconstitutional course than the one which we have pursued. As to evading responsibility, that accusation is childish.' He concluded that 'so far as the weakness of human judgment allows, we have in this painful and difficult matter done neither more nor less than our duty.'

4 Stanley's remarks (n3) were followed by speeches or comments by Liberal MPs Edward Horsman, R. Sinclair Aytoun, captain J.C.W. Vivian, Sir Harry Verney, Henry Du Pré Labouchere, Ralph Osborne and Austen Henry Layard who, speaking at great length, approved of the expedition but not of 'the measures by which it is proposed to carry it out.'

5 Northcote (n1) defended Stanley against Lowe's accusations that he had deceived the House, summarized the sequence of events to date beginning with Stanley's ultimatum and assured the House that in leaving matters to Napier (n3), whose experience and recommendations he detailed, 'we have taken a prudent course'.

6 In a short, deferential speech Gladstone (n1) would make a few critical comments but was 'wholly unprepared to censure or condemn the policy which the Government have pursued' and promised them 'every assistance and support' in obtaining the necessary supplies.

I am prostrate – on my back, & positively cannot move witht. agony – but I have seen Gull & hope to be in my place tomorrow.

There is a Cabinet today at 4 o'ck:[1]

Ask Ld. Barrington who calls it. Tell Ld Stanley, who / knew last night of my attack, that I shd. like to have a line as to what takes place in the Cabinet.[2]

I write this in bed, lying on my back.

It will only be physical imposs[ibilit]y that will prevent my opening the Ways & Means tomorrow.[3] If I find when awake, that it is impossible, I will send the / papers I have to Mr Hunt, & beg him to make the proposal. But see him to day & prepare him for this not absolutely improbable contingency.

What is thought of last night?[4] Send me news.

Yr | D

4594

TO: GEORGE WARD HUNT   Grosvenor Gate [Thursday 28 November 1867]
ORIGINAL: NSR WH223
EDITORIAL COMMENT: C of Ex paper, seal crossed out and 'G.G.' written in. *Dating*: by context; see **4595**&n1 and **4596**&n2.

G. Ward Hunt Esqr | M.P   G.G. | ½ past 11 o'ck

My dear Hunt,

I literally can't move, tho' otherwise well enough.

It is most annoying, but I have the consolation of having a / Lieutenant in whom I have perfect confidence.

Yours ever | D.

4595

TO: LORD BARRINGTON   Grosvenor Gate [Thursday] 28 November 1867
ORIGINAL: BL ADD MS 58210 ff6-7
EDITORIAL COMMENT: C of Ex paper, seal crossed out and 'G.G.' written in.

G.G. | Nov 28 – 67

My dear Barrington,[1]

Notwithstanding Dr Gull & ceaseless remedies, I am on my back & literally can't move. Was ever anything so damnable!

---

1 *The Times* on 28 November would list D as present at a cabinet on this day (27th), but Stanley on the 27th would note, 'Cabinet at 4: Disraeli absent.' *Disraeli, Derby* 323.
2 Stanley on this day (27th) would reply from the foreign office at 6 *pm* enclosing a three-page outline (dated 'NOV.27.1867.' marked 'SECRET' and headed 'CABINET') summarizing discussion of 'a bill to restore the exemption of charities from rating' (the principal question debated), 'Postal arrangements with the United States', 'old ships to be fitted out for training-ships' and Lord Mayo's search (to date fruitless) for a president for his educational commission. H B/XX/S/789, 789a.
3 See **4595**n1.
4 See **4592**.

---

1 Barrington on this day (28th) had written to D, 'I was so very sorry to hear from M. Corry yesterday that you were suffering from lumbago, & that in all probability you wd not be able to go to the House today. I hope I may be able to give the Chief a better account of yr health this morning, as well as of Mrs Disraeli's. I have good accounts of Lady Craven, & my "Grandaughter" [*sic*].' H D/VIII/A/32.

With a budget, tho' a / small one, to launch!

I am now sending to Hunt to be my lieutenant[.]² I am very glad to hear about dear Lady Craven.³

Yours ever | D.

TO: [MONTAGU CORRY]   Grosvenor Gate, Thursday [28 November 1867]   4596
ORIGINAL: H B/XX/D/59a
EDITORIAL COMMENT: C of Ex paper. Docketed in another hand on the fourth page: 'Th: Nov 28'. In pencil. *Dating*: by context; see nn1&2.

Thursday

Alas! Alas! All the doctors & all the remedies, wh: have been unceasing, have done very little. I can't move.

What can be more vexatious! See Mr Hunt directly. He is a Lieutenant I can confide / in, ~~but~~ wh: is something.

But what about Sir S. Northcote's resolution?¹ Are we in danger?

Let me have as much news as you can. And especially later about ~~the~~ what is going / on in the House.²

But at ½ past ten o'ck this hospital, for such it has become, shuts up.

Yr | D.

Mem: Mr Layard's letter.³ Something must be done about Deutsch's appointment wh: is absurd. This is what I T.O. / meant to have prevented the day I did *not* go to Brit: Mus: Nov: 9[.]⁴

---

2 In the House on this day in committee of ways and means, G.W. Hunt, introducing D's supplementary budget, would propose a resolution (agreed to) raising income tax by one penny in the pound during 1867-8 to help raise £2,000,000 to finance the Abyssinian Expedition. *Hansard* CXC cols 339-59. See **4596**n2.

3 Barrington's second daughter, Evelyn Laura (1848-1924), had become Countess of Craven upon marrying George Grimston Craven, 3rd Earl of Craven, on 17 January 1867. On 26 November she had given birth to a daughter, Lady Mary Beatrix.

---

1 See **4597**&n1.

2 Corry on this day (28th) at 7:20 *pm* would inform D that G.W. Hunt, also on this day, had 'made his statement with great clearness and ability, and was cheered from both sides of the House. Gladstone criticized your proposal minutely and very fairly, ending by saying that it could not be pronounced "other than the most just and prudent." ... Northcote has been up 20 minutes. Fawcett intends to divide, but will be opposed by Gladstone. Glyn expects about 50 will follow Fawcett ... [in the Leicestershire s by-election] Majority of 51 for Paget at 5 o'clock has been telegraphed; but there is an outlying Conservative district called Bosworth, from which, they say, it is impossible for the result to have been yet received.' Corry added '7.30. I hear they have telegraphed to get the truth about Leicester. I have told the messenger to wait, and take the answer on to you.' H B/XX/CO/30. See **4600**n2.

3 This letter has not been found. Archaeologist Austen Henry Layard (1817-1894), DCL Oxford 1848 and GCB 1878, had made important excavations in Mesopotamia between 1839 and 1847 (his specimens of Assyrian antiquities are now in the British Museum). He was under-secretary for foreign affairs 1861-6, ambassador to Madrid 1869-77 and Constantinople 1877-80, and MP (L) for Aylesbury 1852-7 and Southwark 1860-70. Although his 'blunt criticism' made him enemies and 'his hatred of subordinate place bordered on the pathological', he had an 'intense sympathy with the oppressed, especially those suffering under clerical rule.' His works include *Nineveh and its Remains* (2 vols, 1849), *Discoveries in the Ruins of Nineveh and Babylon* (1853) and *Autobiography and Letters* (2 vols, 1903). ODNB.

4 On 9 November D had attended the Lord Mayor's banquet at Guildhall, arriving shortly after 6 *pm*. Evidently he had planned to raise the matter of Deutsch's inappropriate appointment at the British Museum on that day. *The Times* (11 Nov 1867). See **4566**nn2&6.

TO: SIR STAFFORD NORTHCOTE   Grosvenor Gate
                                                          [Thursday 28? November 1867]

ORIGINAL: BL ADD MS 50015 f221
PUBLICATION HISTORY: M&B IV 571-2, undated at Grosvenor Gate, with the notation '(*In pencil.*)'
EDITORIAL COMMENT: C of Ex paper, seal crossed out and 'G. Gate' written in. Docketed in another hand
on the first page: '1867', and in a third hand: '[c. 28 Nov 1867]'. *Dating*: by context; see n1 and **4595**&n1.

                                                                            G. Gate

My dear Northcote,

I am obliged to write to you on my back, & can't move, tho' I am otherwise well
enough.

I am clear, that nothing shd. be postponed.

Hunt will find no diff[icult]y: if he do, wh: is impossible, the / House I am sure
will take the division on a subsequent stage.

With regard to India you are quite sufficient to fight the battle. You know the case
thoro[ugh]ly, can speak as often as you like, & will win.[1]

Sooner than have the / business postponed, I will come down & be carried into
the House. I am serious in this, & beg, therefore, that you will let me know, that I
may prepare[.][2]

yrs | D

TO: MARY ANNE DISRAELI   Grosvenor Gate [Friday 29 November 1867]
ORIGINAL: H A/I/A/341
PUBLICATION HISTORY: M&B IV 572, omitting the third paragraph
EDITORIAL COMMENT: The first of a series of undated letters and notes (**4598** to **4608**) preceded by a page
in MA's hand: 'Notes from Dear Dizzy during our illness when we could not leave our rooms – at the end
of the month both quite well. Decr. 1867'. *Dating*: by context; see n3.

My darling, darling –
Being on my back, pardon the pencil.

You have sent me the most amusing, & charming, letter[1] I ever had – it beats Horace Walpole & Md. de Sevigné.[2]

It was most mortifying for the Chr of Exr. to be *hors de combat* the night of the sup-

1 In the House in committee on this day (28th), following the debate over D's budget, Northcote would
   submit (in his words) 'a Resolution authorizing part of the revenues of India to be applied for the ordinary pay of troops chargeable on the Indian revenues, but about to be employed in the hostilities which
   are upon the point of commencing in Abyssinia.' It was agreed to 198 to 23. *Hansard* CXC cols 359-407.
2 Northcote on 28 November would reply: 'On no account dream of coming down. I feel sure we shall do
   very well. I am sorry to find that my case about the 3rd China War is not quite so strong as I thought, but
   it will do.' BL ADD MS 50015 f223.

   ———

1 MA's letter has not been found.
2 Horace Walpole (1717-1797), 4th Earl of Orford, the son of England's first PM Sir Robert Walpole and
   cousin of Horatio Nelson, was Whig MP for Callington (1741-54), Castle Rising (1754-7) and King's
   Lynn (1757-68). He is remembered for his voluminous correspondence and for Strawberry Hill, his extravagant Gothic-style house. Marie de Rabutin-Chantal (1626-1696), marquise de Sévigné, wrote to her
   daughter Françoise for nearly thirty years.

plementary budget! But I had a good Lieutenant, whose ~~account~~ ↑bulletin↓ has just arrived. I send it – quite triumphant.[3]

Grosvenor Gate has become a hospital but / a hospital with you is worth a palace with any body else.

Your own | D.

TO: MARY ANNE DISRAELI   [Grosvenor Gate] Friday [29 November 1867] **4599**
ORIGINAL: H A/I/A/343
EDITORIAL COMMENT: C of Ex paper. See **4598**ec. In pencil. Addressed by D on the fourth page: '*Mrs. Disraeli*'. *Dating*: conjectural. *Sic*: medecine.

Friday

Dearest Darling,

I have not been able to get anything satisfactory out of Gull, except he says that it is not caused by the kidneys, they / being in a state of perfect condition.

Well, then, I suppose it is the Liver.

I have taken a great deal of medecine, all to counteract acidity, & won – but I have found no benefit. /

Your letters are delightful. I can only send you a 1000 loves.

Yr own | D.

TO: [MONTAGU CORRY]   [Grosvenor Gate, Friday] 29 November 1867 **4600**
ORIGINAL: H B/XX/D/59b
PUBLICATION HISTORY: M&B IV 572, the fourth paragraph, omitting the first nine words
EDITORIAL COMMENT: C of Ex paper. In pencil.

Mon très cher   Nov 29. | 67

I am annoyed about a confounded Conscience money ½ 50£ note wh: a lunatic sent here.

I thought it came to day: perhaps it / came yesterday – & I may have sent it you. I can't find it: remind me tomorrow.[1]

I have an idea that Pell has won[2] – because Spofforth is always / wrong.

Gull says now it is Sciatica; wh: frightens me[3] – James, my man,[4] says, his mother has the *sciatics*, & they last a year, at least. But, tho' depressed, I / have still faith in

---

3 This 'bulletin' by G.W. Hunt, who on Thursday 28 November 1867 had introduced the supplementary budget (see **4595**&n2), has not been found.

---

1 D on 2 December would acknowledge receiving 'the second half of a 50*l*.-note from "Alpha" on account of income-tax.' *The Times* (2 Dec 1867). See **4199**n7.
2 Albert Pell (1820-1907), MA 1842 Trinity College, Cambridge, had campaigned in 1865 for the slaughter of animals to wipe out the cattle plague. Member 1867 and chairman 1888 of the Farmers' Club, he would go to the United States and Canada in 1879 as an assistant commissioner to the Duke of Richmond's royal commission on agriculture. Pell would be defeated by Thomas T. Paget (L) on 30 November 1867 by 39 votes at a by-election for S Leicestershire but would be MP (C) for S Leicester 1868-85. See **4596**n2 and **4602**&n1.
3 D was suffering from a severe attack of lumbago. *The Times* (3 Dec 1867).
4 James Foote, D's footman.

my star – I think it wd be a ridiculous conclusion of my career – & after all, ridicule settles nothing & nobody.

Yrs ever | D.

4601 TO: LORD STANLEY   Grosvenor Gate, Saturday 30 November 1867
ORIGINAL: DBP Box 12/3/43
PUBLICATION HISTORY: M&B IV 571, the third paragraph
EDITORIAL COMMENT: C of Ex paper, seal crossed out and 'G.G.' written in. Endorsed by Stanley on the fourth page: 'Mr. Disraeli November 30. 1867 *Still ill* In açcount of Cabinet. letter from *Mr. Clay* as to *E.C. Ker Seymer's* wish for promotion.' *Dating*: by context; see ec and n1.

Secy | Lord Stanley   G.G. | Saturday | Nov 30

Dear Stanley,

I have been three days on my back – in bed, motionless – but feel much relieved this morning – & hope to be in my place on Monday. But I can't manage / the Cabinet this morning. Would you again be kind, & let me know what takes place?

Your precis is always clear, condensed, & dramatic.[1]

When I got home on Wednesday / morning, in the cab in wh: you kindly tumbled me in, I cd. not get out, & the driver, I fancy, thought I was drunk.[2]

I enclose a confid[entia]l letter.[3]

Ever, | D.

4602 TO: MARY ANNE DISRAELI   [Grosvenor Gate, Saturday 30 November 1867]
ORIGINAL: H A/I/A/346
PUBLICATION HISTORY: M&B IV 572, the fourth and fifth sentences
EDITORIAL COMMENT: See **4598**ec. In pencil. Addressed by D on the second page: '*Mrs. Disraeli*'. *Dating*: see nn1,3&5.

My Dearest Love

We have lost the Leicesters[hir]e. election,[1] but the Ld. Advocate will be returned,

---

1 Stanley, replying on this day (30th) that 'not much was done at the Cabinet', enclosed a five-page summary (headed 'Cabinet. Nov. 30. 1867.'). There had been discussion of 'a bill for better collection of statistics relating to cotton', 'educational resolutions to be proposed by Ld Russell on Monday' and the 'possible establishment of a minister of education' (with Derby questioning the 'wisdom of state aid to middle-class schools'). Hardy, believing that 'a revolutionary movement on a great scale is preparing', would propose a bill restricting the carrying of arms. H B/XX/S/790, 790a. Stanley on this day noted that there had been 'much discussion on the Fenian business. Hardy says that arms are being bought in large quantities', mostly Belgian revolvers. 'We were all, however, of opinion that the case was not strong enough to justify us bringing in a bill.' *Disraeli, Derby* 323.

2 Following protracted debate on 26 November, the House had adjourned on Wednesday 27th at 1 *am*. See **4592**.

3 Presumably a letter (see ec) from D's lifelong friend James Clay regarding his son Harry Ernest Clay Ker-Seymer (who had assumed the name Ker-Seymer in 1864). Stanley (n1) would tell D: 'I will send you the letter referred to when Hardy returns it.'

---

1 See **4600**n2.

& it takes a vote from Cranborne.[2] M. Corry gone to the Opera.[3] James is to send me some wonderful dry sherry.[4] We have been separated four days – & under the same roof! How very strange! – I begin to get low. And no charming letters!

1000 loves | yr own | D[5]

TO: MARY ANNE DISRAELI   Grosvenor Gate, Monday [2 December 1867]   **4603**
ORIGINAL: H A/I/A/344
PUBLICATION HISTORY: M&B IV 572, omitting the fourth and fifth sentences
EDITORIAL COMMENT: C of Ex paper. See **4598**ec. In pencil. Addressed by D on the fourth page: 'Mrs Disraeli'. *Dating*: by context; see **4604**n1.

Monday

My dearest Love,

I have had a sleepless night, & in agony the whole time. This morning the pain in the foot became greatly mitigated – & I dozed ↑a little from 6 to 8.↓ I have been nearly a week in bed,[1] & am much worse than when I took to it[.]

Dr Gull mistook my / case. Stimulants were poison to me.[2] My only consolation is, that you are better & stronger. I never felt worse or more desponding. I am so irritated at the blundering manner in wh: I have been treated.

Your own | D

TO: [MONTAGU CORRY]   [Grosvenor Gate] Monday [2 December 1867]   **4604**
ORIGINAL: H B/XX/D/57
EDITORIAL COMMENT: C of Ex paper. *Dating*: by context; see n1.

Monday

I have had a sleepless night from continuous & agonizing pain, wh: is now much mitigated.

---

2 Scottish lord advocate Edward Gordon, who would become MP (C) for Thetford (disfranchised 1868) on 2 December, had stated on 18 November that he wished a seat in the House 'for the purpose of carrying the Scotch Reform Bill'. *The Times* (20 Nov 1867).

3 Her Majesty's Theatre, which presented Mozart's *Don Giovanni* on this day (30th), would burn to the ground on 6 December. *The Times* (28 Nov, 7 Dec 1867).

4 James Disraeli had an extensive wine cellar. H A/I/D/24. See **4608**.

5 In a letter dated 'Saturday night' and docketed in another hand '?1867', MA would reply: 'I am thinking of you my own dearest. It makes me so unhappy not to see you tonight to get stronger. When I change the room I think it will be of service. Your Dear little note revives me. I am glad the Ld Advocate has gained his election & more than glad Ld C will be injured by it. I think the person who wrote sketches from the House could not hear you himself[.] he appears so annoyed by it & angry – thro all he says of you – Send me word by Ann what Dr Gull said today[;] is he coming again? I am glad James is to send you some old sherry – a stronger wine than Amontillado to take for a short time – Pray put a strip of flan[ne]l round yr waist it would not be seen[.] flan[ne]l drawers is not enough when you go out of yr warm room. Princess Mary with her 1 baby, called here to day – how kind they have been. Baroness Mayor [*sic*] very affectionate letter must have cross[e]d mine as I wrote to her yesterday. I shall never get any stronger, constantly in this room & not to even see you. I will try tomorrow after luncheon, & no one with you. Yr loving devoted M.' H A/I/A/509.

---

1 On 27 November (**4593**) D had written to Montagu Corry 'prostrate – on my back'.

2 See **4599**.

But I am too exhausted to see you today.

You must see Lord Stanley, / & tell him, that I shall not be in my place today, &, I fear, not again in the present sitting.[1]

Ever yr | D

4605   TO: MARY ANNE DISRAELI   [Grosvenor Gate, Monday 2? December 1867]
ORIGINAL: H A/I/A/342
EDITORIAL COMMENT: See **4598**ec. In pencil. *Sic*: medecines. *Dating*: conjectural; see n1.

My darling love,

It is gout & I always suspected it. He[1] says it is a better thing than sciatica: but it involves a change of medecines & diet. No meat, at least no roast meats – boiled fish, boiled chicken, farinaceous puddings[2] ↑& so on↓: no wine, a little brandy & water.

After luncheon, I will write again, my darling love.

D.

4606   TO: MARY ANNE DISRAELI   [Grosvenor Gate, Monday 2? December 1867]
ORIGINAL: H A/I/A/345
EDITORIAL COMMENT: C of Ex paper. See **4598**ec. In pencil. Addressed by D on the fourth page: 'Mrs Disraeli:'. *Sic*: medecine. *Dating*: conjectural, but see **4605**.

Dearest,

I did not answer the most important part of yr letter, but I was just going to take my first gout medecine.

I don't think you ought to come down today. It is dripping damp.

Yr own

4607   TO: MARY ANNE DISRAELI

[Grosvenor Gate, about Monday 2 December 1867]

ORIGINAL: H A/I/A/348
EDITORIAL COMMENT: See **4598**ec. In pencil. Addressed by D on the second page: 'Mrs Disraeli'. *Dating*: conjectural; see **4603**.

The Book is Ewald's History of Israel[1] but I can't read, the pain in my foot getting worse every minute but I hope it will cure the other pains.

---

1 Corry on this day (2nd) at 6:30 *pm* would reply that D's letter had reached him just as he was leaving for Grosvenor Gate. 'I think, with a shudder, of the night you must have passed, with those terrible throbs shaking your frame every minute. I have every hope that tomorrow you will be able to see me, – today you were quite right to remain quiet.' H B/XX/CO/31.

---

1 Most likely Dr William Gull. See **4599**.
2 See **4612**.

---

1 Hughenden library has a copy of *The History of Israel to the death of Moses* (1867), translated by Russell Martineau, one of the volumes of *Geschichte des Volkes Israel* (1843-59, 3rd ed 1864-8), by eminent Göttingen orientalist and theologian Georg Heinrich August Ewald (1803-1875). *The Times* on 15 October 1867 had announced publication by Longmans.

TO: MARY ANNE DISRAELI   [Grosvenor Gate, Tuesday 3? December 1867]   **4608**
ORIGINAL: H A/I/A/347
EDITORIAL COMMENT: See **4598**ec. In pencil. *Dating*: by context; see **4605**.

Dearest darling,

James[1] has sent to know how we both are. I reply that I am ɏ as yesterday, & you, thank God, continue to improve. He has sent a bottle of Sherry; it is, I believe, dry. You must have it, as I am not to drink wine.

I have seen no one.

Yr own | D

TO: [MONTAGU CORRY]   [Grosvenor Gate] Wednesday [4 December 1867?]   **4609**
ORIGINAL: H B/XX/D/69
EDITORIAL COMMENT: *Dating*: conjectural; see n1.

Wednesday

I continue very unwell[1] – & tho' I must manage to get out, for ½ an hour, to see my heroine, as the business is important,[2] I shall return / home, & not go to D.S.

I shd. like very much, therefore, to see you any time after ½ past five, or at that hour.

D.

TO: LORD DALMENY   Grosvenor Gate [Saturday] 7 December 1867   **4610**
ORIGINAL: ROSE [38] Dalmeny House Collection
EDITORIAL COMMENT: C of Ex paper, seal crossed out and 'Grosvenor Gate' written in. *Sic*: Chatellaine.

The | Lord Dalmeny   Grosvenor Gate | Decr 7 1867
My dear Dalmeny,

I should have answered·yr kind letter, received some days ago,[1] but have been myself indisposed, tho' / not seriously, severely.

I was quite sure, that you would sympathise with me in the great sorrow, wh: seemed about to engulf my life.

---

1 James Disraeli; see **4602**&n4.

---

1 D in early December 1867 was suffering from gout; see **4605**.
2 Neither this person nor D's business has been identified.

---

1 In an undated letter (docketed by MA '1867 Decbr') on Christ Church, Oxford, letterhead, Dalmeny had written warmly about MA's recovery. 'You must know how I sympathised with you in your trouble, & how delighted I am to see you with a happy prospect of getting rid of this anxiety ... I dined at Blenheim last night ... you have no more devoted adherent than Lady Cornelia Churchill!' On 6 December he had written to D that 'My uncle Mr Primrose who has been in the public service for upwards of 30 years has a very large family & wishes very much to place his second son in the Treasury. But, I am told, the nominations to this are in Lord Derby's own hands. Still, a request from you would of course be complied with: & I wanted to know if you would take the trouble to ask him for a nomination ... Could you tell somebody to send me a line to Blenheim to say whether it be possible or not?' H B/XXI/R/139-40.

I will take care to / ask Lord Derby to place Mr Primrose's name on his list.[2] I fear, however, Mr Primrose may have to wait, as there have been a number of vacancies, much above the average, of late in the / Treasury, in consequence of some arrangements in the Department; &, I shd. think, for the future, there must be ↑many↓ candidates. However, I will do my best for you, & for yr sake.

I send kind words, & kinder thoughts, to the charming young Chatellaine of Blenheim.[3]

Yours ever, I D.

4611   TO: SIR HARRY VERNEY   Grosvenor Gate [Saturday] 7 December 1867
ORIGINAL: VER [3]
EDITORIAL COMMENT: C of Ex paper, seal crossed out, with 'Grosvenor Gate' written in.

Sir Harry Verney I Bart: M.P.[1]   Grosvenor Gate I Dec. 7 1867
Dear Sir Harry,

This is the first day I am again writing letters, & one of the first must be to you; to thank you for yr very kind note, / the thoro' friendship of wh: I quite appreciate, & am grateful for.[2]

My lumbago ended in a rather severe attack of gout, wh:, I suspect, had been threatening / me for several months.

I hope you will have a happy Xmas in yr happy home,[3] & wh: you have the great satisfaction of always feeling, that you yourself make / happy. I fear we shall not get

2 Dalmeny's father, Archibald Primrose, 1st Lord Dalmeny (1809-1851), had one brother, Bouverie Francis Primrose, who in 1838 had married Lady Frederica Sophia Anson; they had four daughters and six sons, the second of which was Henry William Primrose (1846-1923), CSI 1885, KCB 1899, ISO 1904 and PC 1912. He would enter the treasury in 1869, becoming secretary to the office of works 1886-95 and chairman of the boards of customs 1895-9, inland revenue 1899-1907 and Pacific cable 1907-14.
3 Although her mother the Duchess was still alive, this is presumably Lady Cornelia Henrietta Spencer Churchill (1847-1927), daughter of 7th Duke of Marlborough and his Duchess, the former Lady Frances Anne Emily Vane. In 1868 Lady Cornelia would marry Sir Ivor Bertie Guest, 2nd Bt, and from 1880 would be styled Baroness Wimborne of Canford Magna.

---

1 Sir Harry Verney, born Calvert, had assumed the surname Verney in 1827 on the death of his cousin Catherine Calvert ('Mrs Verney') of Claydon House (see n3). He was DL Bucks, MP (L) for Buckingham 1832-41 and 1857-74, Bedford 1847-52 and Buckingham borough 1880-5. In 1858, following the death in 1857 of his wife Eliza (whom he had married in 1835), Verney married Frances Parthenope Nightingale. His devotion to her sister Florence, a frequent visitor to Claydon, earned him the name 'The Member for Florence Nightingale'.
2 Verney on 3 December had written to D from London that he had 'suffered very severely from Lumbago' and that a doctor at Rome had advised him to rub himself with belladonna. Verney also recommended 'a good tea spoon full of a powder, quinine & magnesia, in a wine glass of milk at night or very early in the morning. This is the way that I cure myself, & my poor people at Claydon, of Lumbago – but I believe that both medicines are potent, & not to be used without medical advice – but nothing is so good as to throw a pail of cold water over onself on a morning like this & then to rub onself dry so roughly that the towel becomes hot. Pardon my Doctoring & do not trouble yourself to take any notice of this. You know, so I need not tell you, that both sides rejoice equally that you are relieved of anxiety on the subject of Mrs Disraeli.' H A/IV/L/4.
3 Claydon House (near Middle Claydon, Bucks), the seat of the Verneys since 1620, rebuilt 1757-71 by Ralph, 2nd Lord Verney, would remain in the Verney family until 1956.

to Hughenden, wh: is a great disappointment, but my wife, tho' convalescent, has not yet left her room.

With sincere regard, | Yours, | *B. Disraeli*

TO: SIR STAFFORD NORTHCOTE Grosvenor Gate **4612**
[Saturday] 7 December 1867

ORIGINAL: PS 1548
PUBLICATION HISTORY: M&B IV 572, with the notation '(*In pencil.*)'.

My dinner, consisting, I am sorry to say, of a tapioca pudding, need not have prevented us meeting yesterday; but my butler is a pompous booby....[1]

We shall remain in town at present. Mrs. Disraeli must not leave her room, tho' getting on well.

TO: MARY ANNE DISRAELI [Grosvenor Gate] Sunday [8? December 1867] **4613**
ORIGINAL: H A/I/A/349
EDITORIAL COMMENT: See **4598**ec. In pencil.

Sunday

My dearest,

I am much better. Nothing can have been more successful, than ~~the~~ ↑your↓ pill. I feel a load of misery off me. I shall be in the Blue room in ten minutes.[1]

Your own, | D

I heard you had a very good night[.]

TO: HENRY MANNING Grosvenor Gate [Sunday] 8 December 1867 **4614**
ORIGINAL: MANN A639
EDITORIAL COMMENT: C of Ex paper, seal crossed out and 'Grosvenor Gate' written in.

His Grace | The ArchBp of Westminster Private | Grosvenor Gate | Decr 8 1867
My dear Lord,[1]

We are not going to leave town, as my wife is still a prisoner to her room: therefore, I am at your service on any day convenient to / you, except tomorrow, when there is a Cabinet & I believe, the last before Xmas.[2]

Yours sincerely, | D.

---

1 The DS' butler at this time may have been a Mr Brixy; see **4421**&n1.

---

1 The Blue Room was MA's second-floor boudoir. See IV app X.

---

1 Manning on 6 December had requested a meeting with D prior to his departure from London ('before you return [I] may be called to Rome') and had inquired about MA's health. H B/XXI/M/166.

2 D on the 9th would attend a cabinet, summarized by Stanley on that day: 'Cabinet at 12, sat nearly four hours, wasting time, as I thought, for all but little was settled. We talked of education, and the idea was much discussed of, as it were, turning the flank of the religious difficulty by paying only for results, leaving the school to be set on foot and managed as the parties establishing it may think best. This seemed to be approved by several present. Then arose a discussion on Vancouver's island and British Columbia,

4615

TO: ELIZA SPENCER   Grosvenor Gate [Monday] 9 December 1867

ORIGINAL: GRI 6057

EDITORIAL COMMENT: C of Ex paper, seal crossed out and 'Grosvenor Gate' written in.

Grosvenor Gate | Dec. 9 1867

Dear Mrs. Spencer,

I must thank you for your kind letter,[1] altho' this is the first opportunity I have enjoyed to do so. I much valued your / sympathy, & that of the excellent Bishop,[2] in the great sorrow, wh: seemed about to engulf my life.

Mrs Disraeli's recovery has been almost miraculous. / She is now quite herself again, tho', in obedience to the injunctions of her physicians, she must not leave her room.

If the weather softened, & / your beautiful bay were not so distant, I shd. almost be tempted to persuade her to return to its sunny shores.

She begs me to remember her, very kindly, to yourself, & his Lordship.

Yours sincerely, | *B. Disraeli*

4616

TO: MARY ANNE DISRAELI   Carlton Club
[about Monday 9 December? 1867]

ORIGINAL: H A/I/A/350

EDITORIAL COMMENT: Carlton Club paper. Docketed in another hand on the first page: '1867.' and addressed by D on the second page: '*Mrs Disraeli*'. *Dating*: conjectural; see **4613**. D was housebound with gout 2-8 December 1867.

½ pt 4 o'ck

My dearest,

Send me a couple of dinner pills by the bearer – in a good thick despatch looking letter.

No news.

Yr own | D.

---

and it appeared clear that neither one nor the other could be held against the U.S. in the event of a war, without a totally disproportionate expenditure of force. Then Ireland: question of prosecuting the *Irishman* for an article manifestly seditious, but as usual, no decision come to.' *The Times* (10 Dec 1867); *Disraeli, Derby* 324.

---

1 Eliza Spencer (see n2), having recently heard of MA's illness from one of the Ds' Bucks neighbours, on 20 November had written from Braddon Tor, Torquay with 'deep sympathy with you in your present time of great anxiety ... I think that God will spare her to you, for there never was a more devoted wife, & a husband who so entirely appreciated that great blessing.' H B/XXI/S/391.

2 Bishop Aubrey George Spencer (1795-1872), a great-great-grandson of John Churchill, 1st Duke of Marlborough, deacon 1818, priest 1819 and bishop 1839, had been a missionary of the Society for the Propagation of the Gospel at Newfoundland 1819, archdeacon of Bermuda 1825, first Bishop of Newfoundland 1839 and second Bishop of Jamaica 1843. In 1855 he had retired to Torquay, where he wrote *A Brief Account of the Church of England, its faith and worship: as shown by the Book of Common Prayer* (1867). In 1822 he had married Eliza Musson, daughter of a rich Bermuda merchant.

TO: [MONTAGU CORRY]   [Grosvenor Gate] Tuesday [10 December 1867]   **4617**
ORIGINAL: H B/XX/D/66
EDITORIAL COMMENT: Written on the *recto* and *verso* of an envelope. Docketed in another hand on the second page: 'Autumn of 67'. *Dating*: by context; see n1.

Tuesday.

I don't think I shall go out today, ArchBp Manning comes to me at three.[1]

I shd. like to hear how affairs go on. T.O. /

Mr. Secy Hardy goes out of town today I believe. Ascertain when he returns, as I have to see him immediately on his arrival.[2]

D.

TO: PHILIP ROSE   Grosvenor Gate [Wednesday] 11 December 1867   **4618**
ORIGINAL: H R/I/A/204
EDITORIAL COMMENT: C of Ex paper, seal crossed out and 'Grosvenor Gate' written in. *Sic*: checque.

Phil: Rose Esq   Grosvenor Gate | Dec 11 1867

My dear Rose,

I enclose you a checque for £1500: I will send you another in a few days, wh: will square our acct.

I shall be at the office to day, & if you cd. call, betn. ½ pt. 3 & 5 o'ck, shd. be glad to see you.

Ever yours | D.

TO: CHARLES CLUBBE   Grosvenor Gate [Wednesday] 11 December 1867   **4619**
ORIGINAL: RIC [37].

Grosvenor Gate | Dec. 11 1867

Dear Clubbe,

The doctors won't let Mrs. Disraeli come down to Hughenden at present, &, therefore, I send you a cheque for school & working club.[1]

My wife is quite herself again – with all her energy, but she has not yet left her rooms.

With kind regards to all,

Yrs sincerely | D

---

1 See **4614**n1.

2 Hardy had left for Staplehurst on 9 December and would return to London on the 13th. *The Times* (11 Dec 1867); *Hardy Diary* 58. See **4623**&n1.

---

1 For the National school at Hughenden (opened 1862), see VIII **3725**&n3. D probably means a working men's club, of which there were many in England.

4620

TO: SIR JOHN PAKINGTON
Grosvenor Gate
[Thursday] 12 December 1867

ORIGINAL: H B/XX/D/60a

EDITORIAL COMMENT: C of Ex paper, seal crossed out and 'Grosvenor Gate' written in.

Right Honorable | Sir Jno Pakington   Grosvenor Gate | Dec. 12 1867
My dear Pakington,

Could you call here (G.G.) before you go to yr office? I wish to consult you on very important & / urgent matters[1] – & wd. come on to you but the gout keeps me a prisoner.

Yrs sincerely, | D.

4621

TO: THE DUKE OF CAMBRIDGE
[Downing Street, Thursday] 12 December 1867

ORIGINAL: RAC VIC ADDL MSS E/1 5629

EDITORIAL COMMENT: C of Ex paper. *Sic*: Fielding.

Confidential   Decr 12 1867
H.R.H. | The Commander in Chief
Sir,

With reference to the confidential letter of Lord Derby to Yr Royal Highness on Monday evening last,[1] I / have, now, on the part of H.M. Government, to request, that Yr Royal Highness will have the goodness to direct, that the services of Colonel Fielding should be placed at the disposal / of the Secy. of State for the Home Department for special service.[2]

The Secretary of State is absent from town[3] & the matter is urgent, otherwise I / would not have taken the liberty of thus troubling Yr Royal Highness.

I have the honor to remain, Sir, | with great consideration | Yr Rl Hss's faithfl Servt | *B. Disraeli*

4622

TO: [MONTAGU CORRY]   [London] Thursday 12 December [1867]
ORIGINAL: H B/XX/D/60

EDITORIAL COMMENT: *Dating*: by context; see n1.

Confidential   Thursday | Decr. 12.
Read Lord Mayo's letter & enclosures.[1] I sent off immediately to Sir Jno. Pakington,

---

1 See **4622**&n1.

---

1 After a 9 December cabinet, Derby had met with D to discuss the formation of a detective force which he called, in his letter of that day to the Duke of Cambridge, commander-in-chief of the military, a '"separate and secret organization."' Kennedy 110.

2 William Henry Adelbert Feilding (1836-1895), younger (fourth surviving) son of the late William Basil Percy Feilding, 7th Earl of Denbigh, was lieut-col 1860 and gen 1893 Coldstream Guards and inspector general of recruiting at headquarters 1891-4. He had for some years investigated Fenianism in the army in Ireland. *The Times* (26 Mar 1895). See **4629**.

3 See **4617**n2.

---

1 Mayo on this day (12th) had written from Dublin Castle to inform D that he had seen Feilding on the 11th to offer him the command of a secret London-based detective force but had 'received the enclosed

who left town last night, & will not return till Saturday night! / What on earth are we to do?

I think ~~the pres~~ the letter & enclosures must be sent to Lord Derby tonight – to show the deadlock.

Can you suggest anything?[2] /

D.

TO: GATHORNE HARDY   Downing Street [Friday] 13 December 1867   **4623**
ORIGINAL: ESU [1]

EDITORIAL COMMENT: C of Ex paper. Endorsed by D on the fifth page: '*confidential*'.

---

confidential   Decr 13 1867

Right Honorable | Mr. Secy. Hardy

My dear Hardy,

I came down to D.S. the moment I received yr note, & so found you were in town.[1]

I was greatly vexed to have / missed you.

I would not disturb you at Hemsted, particularly as I heard, that you had interesting occupations there; but on Monday, after the dispersion of the Cabinet,[2] Ld. Derby received information, wh: determined him to / take immediate steps for establishing some organisation for looking after English, & especially, London, Fenianism.[3]

---

from F. to-day. I think however some temporary official position might be given him either in the War or Home Office which would enable him to overcome his Scruples which are to a certain extent well founded.' Feilding on the 11th had written to Mayo from the Royal Barracks, Dublin, twice. His first letter declined Mayo's offer because the position, not being '*officially* and *openly* recognised ... would suggest the insinuation, to the existing police authorities, that they were either not trustworthy, or incapable – & in either case my employment wd not only be resented: but every effort made by me would be partially paralysed, if not wholly neutralised by the means at their disposal.' In addition, he 'shd be liable to be treated as a spy.' His second letter stated his wish to serve the Government 'if I can do so without bringing into jeopardy my character as an officer of H M Army. If I were made a Temporary Under Scy at the Home Office or given *any* official position I would undertake what you wish'. H B/XX/BO/42, 42a,b,c. See **4627**&n2.

2 Mayo on the 13th would inform D that he had seen Feilding, who was leaving for London that evening. 'As his position will now be officially recognized his scruples have disappeared ... Let him choose his own Staff and give him none but *general* instructions. Tell him what you want and he will find means to do it.' H B/XX/BO/43.

---

1 Hardy on this day (13th) had written from the home office: 'My absence from town has prevented my coming to enquire but I have been glad to hear good reports [of MA's and D's health] from other sources. Mayo has sent me the enclosed & begs me to forward it to you. I think that they have done right under the circumstances. The same question is arising at Glasgow & Liverpool & will I imagine be similarly dealt with by the local authorities.' Mayo on the 12th had written to Hardy from Dublin Castle enclosing a proclamation, adopted that morning, outlawing 'Rebellious and treasonable assemblies ... if we had allowed them to go on we should have had a Fenian display ... in Every Village in Ireland.' H B/XX/HA/12, 12a.

2 See **4614**n2.

3 Hardy on 15 December would write to D from Hemsted Park (near Staplehurst, Kent) on the necessity of creating a 'detection organisation', cautioning that 'if a department were permanently established it could hardly be done without parliamentary cognisance. Under present circumstances there could be no difficulty in avowing the need of secret service funds. As such a department should be the centre for secret information from all parts of the United Kingdom & indeed the continent it could not form a part of the Metropolitan police at all events while on its present footing. In fact its universal superintendence forms ample ground for detaching it altogether from the sway of the Commissioner.' H B/XX/HA/13.

He conferred with me, & we saw Lord Mayo, about to depart to Ireland / that evening. Our arrangements were all made on the assumption, that you were, or would be, in town, & that a certain person from Ireland, who would probably undertake the chief management of / the enterprise, wd. be able to report himself on his arrival to you. He has not yet come, as there are always difficulties at the commencement of these matters, & as I am obliged to remain in / town at present, I would not have you wantonly & unnecessarily disturbed. I think, however, it now looks, that he will arrive here tomorrow, or Monday at the latest, & I think, therefore, / you ought to know what is going on.

My best compliments to Mrs Hardy.

Always yrs sin[cere]ly | D.

4624   TO: [MONTAGU CORRY]   [Grosvenor Gate] Saturday 14 December [1867]
ORIGINAL: H B/XX/D/61
EDITORIAL COMMENT: Endorsed in Corry's hand on the third page: 'The Clerkenwell Explosion'; he has also added '/67' to the date. *Dating*: by context; see nn1&2.

Saturday | Dec 14

What an event![1]

When our mind was on the very subject! How is this: the catastrophe happens at ¼ pt. *4* o'ck: & I am at D.S. till ½ past five, & in constant communication with the / Home Office & hear nothing?

I desire to know when the Home Office was informed – *precisely*.

I suppose they have telegraphed for Mr Secy. Hardy.[2] When he arrives, I shd. wish to / see him & cd. come on to D.S. as more convenient for all parties.

Otherwise, I had not intended to move out today.

D.

1 On 13 December there had been a failed attempt to help two Fenian prisoners escape from Middlesex House of Detention at Clerkenwell in central London. The explosion had demolished a large section of the prison wall and a row of nearby working-class houses, killing twelve people and severely injuring and mutilating more than 100, resulting in widespread outrage. According to an early report, 'the devastation has been beyond belief ... The conspirators have to no purpose committed a crime which will bring down on themselves and their scheme the execration of the world ... Some 40 persons are dead or wounded ... the Fenians have shown that they shrink not from bloodshed ... Their object is now apparently to create a terror throughout the United Kingdom ... the time is past for clemency and forbearance.' *The Times* (14 Dec 1867).
2 Hardy on the morning of the 15th would record that 'At 4 [on Friday] occurred the explosion of wh. we had been warned *from Ireland* (!) & [permanent under-secretary at the home office Adolphus] Liddell had warned prison authorities & [police commissioner Sir Richard] Mayne ... the police allowed the [gunpowder] cask to be brought placed & lighted at the very hour & place notified. Strict inquiry is needed.' *Hardy Diary* 57. In the House on 9 March 1868, Hardy would quote a message dated 11 December 1867 and, he said, received at the home office around noon on the 12th: '"I have to report that I have just received information from a reliable source to the effect that the rescue of Richard Burke from prison in London is contemplated. The plan is to blow up the exercise walls by means of gunpowder; the hour between three and four p.m.; and the signal for 'all right,' a white ball thrown up outside when he is at exercise."' *Hansard* CXC col 1215.

ORIGINAL: DBP Box 146/3
PUBLICATION HISTORY: M&B IV 573
EDITORIAL COMMENT: C of Ex paper. *Sic*: Fielding.

Confidential   Dec. 14 1867

Right Honorable | The Earl of Derby | K.G.

My dear Lord,

Affairs here are very serious.

I have contrived to get Col. Fielding over, tho' after inexpressible difficulties, & even now doubt, whether I shall be / able to set him to work: so great are the obstacles at every step; but it must be done.[1]

I have not been able to see Hardy until today, &, unfortunately, he has gone out of town again, but will / be here on Monday.[2]

It is my opinion, that nothing effective can be done, in any way, in these dangers, if we don't get rid of Mayne. I have spoken to Hardy, who says he "wishes to God he wd. resign:"[3] but, / surely, when even the safety of the State is at stake, there ought to be no false delicacy on such a point?[4]

I am too harassed to go into detail, wh: wd. require a volume on these matters. I think you ought to interfere.

I took upon myself to send Govt. aid to the Clerkenwell sufferers.[5]

Yours ever, | D.[6]

1 Derby on 15 December would reply from Knowsley with a letter marked '*Private*': 'You do not state what have been the difficulties you have had to contend with in availing yourself of Col. Fielding's [*sic*] services; but I have written to Hardy to say that if any obstacles have been thrown in your way by any jealousy on the part of Sir R. Mayne, he must be given to understand distinctly that nothing of that nature can be allowed to interfere with what the Government may think necessary for the public service.' H B/ XX/S/456.

2 See **4617**n2.

3 Metropolitan police commissioner Sir Richard Mayne, who apparently had prior knowledge of the Clerkenwell attack (**4624**n2) and who would offer to resign on several occasions, would die on 26 December 1868 while in office.

4 Derby (n1) would 'write today to Hardy, and press upon him the necessity of a strict enquiry into the precautionary measures taken, (or neglected,) in consequence of the information received from Ireland; to which source, if our detectives were worth their salt, we ought not to have been indebted for it. But having obtained it, it was so precise as to time, place, and modus operandi, that the accomplishment of the plot ought to have been impossible. I am much inclined to think that Sir R. Mayne is no longer equal to his post; from which however it could be very difficult to dismiss him, after so many years' service, without some flagrant proof of incapacity.'

5 Corry on this day (14th) at 8:30 *pm* would inform D that he had 'just come home after a tremendous day's work – with [John] Lambert. We have relieved nearly a hundred families, and done infinities of good. The distress is awful.' D had given them 'unlimited powers' to relieve the distress, Corry carrying 'a leather bag containing money, and visiting the poor, homeless people in the neighbourhood for the purpose.' H B/XX/CO/33; *The Times* (16 Dec 1867).

6 Derby (n1) thought D had 'done quite right in sending aid, on the part of the Government, without delay, to the Clerkenwell Sufferers. I should be obliged by your letting me know to whom you have entrusted it, and whether there is any person, or body of persons, authorised to receive private contributions.'

4626

TO: [MONTAGU CORRY]   Downing Street [Saturday 14 December 1867]

ORIGINAL: H B/XX/D/62

PUBLICATION HISTORY: C of Ex paper. Docketed in another hand on the first page: '*Dec 67.*' *Dating*: by context; see n1. *Sic*: Fielding.

½ past 4 o'ck:

I am now going home – having seen Mr Secy Hardy & Col: Fielding[1] – & put things in some train, tho not, as yet, at all to my satisfaction.

I am convinced, that unless we get rid of / Sir Rd. Mayne, we shall never be able to sa steer the ship in these dangers.

Let me have a box with yr last news.

Yrs ever | D.

4627

TO: LORD MAYO   Downing Street [Saturday] 14 December 1867

ORIGINAL: INL Mayo Papers MS 11,150

EDITORIAL COMMENT: C of Ex paper.

Right Honorable | The Earl of Mayo   Dec 14 1867

My dear Mayo[1] –

I have seen (& we have seen, Hardy & myself) your friend, who seems the right man & anxious to help / us, but nothing can be done satisfactorily & efficiently, unless we get Whelan – all the rest we can manage.[2]

It is impossible for the Home Governmt to make the arrangement wh: Whelan insists on. We / have very limited control over the Police here, & really only the Metrop: Police under any circumstances. What we want you to do, is to let Whelan go on halfpay or sell out, & provide for him in / the Irish Constaby, & then send him over here.[3]

The urgent state of affairs justifies such an act on the part of yr Governmt.

Pray answer by return.[4]

Yrs ever, | D.

---

1 D had apparently met with Hardy and Feilding on 14 December, Hardy noting on the 15th that 'More detective force & skill is imperatively needed.' *Hardy Diary* 57. See **4625**.

---

1 See **4622**&nn1&2.

2 Feilding had written to Mayo on this day (14th) that he could not do justice to the Government's '"expectations & anticipations of results unless I have a co-adjutor in whom I have the greatest possible confidence."' This was William Whelan, capt 8th Regiment, who had helped Feilding root Fenianism out of the army in Ireland. Hardy in March 1868 would offer Whelan a position within the London Metropolitan Police, 'presumably as head of the new detective force Hardy expected the Home Office Committee would recommend', but Whelan instead accepted Mayo's original offer of a Resident Magistracy in Ireland. Kennedy 114, 104, 120.

3 Whelan not only wished his position to be officially recognized but 'insisted on a permanent law enforcement post', which would require parliamentary approval. Hardy appealed to Mayo, who promised Whelan the first vacancy among the Resident Magistrates in Ireland. Whelan would take leave of his regiment and join Feilding in London just before Christmas 1867. *Ibid* 114.

4 The next extant communication to D from Mayo is a telegram received in London on the 15th: 'All quiet no processions anywhere.' H B/XX/BO/44.

TO: LORD DERBY   [London, Monday] 16 December 1867 4628

ORIGINAL: DBP Box 146/3

PUBLICATION HISTORY: M&B IV 574, '*Most secret*' and the next three paragraphs

EDITORIAL COMMENT: C of Ex paper, seal crossed out on the first page. *Sic*: Fielding [*four times*].

Confidential   Dec. 16 1867

Right Honorable | The Earl of Derby | K.G.

My dear Lord,

I have just received yours,[1] & am now going to D.S. to meet Hardy, & shall write to you again at the close of the day;[2] / but think it best at once to jot down some memoranda as to the Fielding plan wh: I was too ~~wearied~~ tired & worried to do on Saty. night.

1st Diff[icult]y: Fielding objected to the equivocal position in / wh: the acceptance of our offer would place him: fatal to his professional status & prospects: in order to undertake it, must have an avowed & responsible post; suggested, of course, a new / U.S. at the War office, at least for the time, & so on.[3]

Pakington out of town. After reflection, I thought it best to consult the commr. in Cf, as he was already partly in the affair, & I suggested that F. might be appointed to / enquire into Fenianism in the army &c., but the Duke thought this wd. not do, as he did not think that Fenm. was ↑at all↓ widespread in the army, & it might alarm: then he said that F. might be appointed to a "special service" / in connection with the Home Office, if I would write a letter expressing the confidl. opinion of this Governm[en]t. This I did; adverting at the commencement to yr confidl. note written to / H.R.H. after the Cabinet on Monday, ↑,in order to show the unity of the business.↓[4]

In consequence of this, F., after full interview with Ld. Mayo, came over on Saturday.[5] He seems to me a man equal to the occasion: young, resolute, full of resource, & master of / the subject.

He wanted two things:[6]

1st. That he shd. have the power of appointing ~~to~~ an individual to serve under him in whom he had entire confidence:

2nd. That at least three detective officers of our Police shd. be placed under his command & / to report to him & not to Mayne, with whom he declined to act in any way, as he said, from ~~exp~~ experience, that Mayne would thwart everything.[7]

1 See **4625**nn1,4&6.

2 See **4629**&n2.

3 See **4622**n1.

4 See **4621**n1.

5 Feilding had arrived in London on the morning of Saturday 14 December, the day after the Clerkenwell explosion.

6 Feilding on 15 December had written to D outlining the 'reasons for urging the expediency of this somewhat extraordinary measure' – the formation of 'a permanent central Police Force ... under the direct control of an official in The Home Department' – and had included a list of positions and salaries, including 'A Permanent U[nde]r. Secy of State for the Home depart whose duties shd. resemble that of the Prefet de Police in France' at £1,000 per year. H B/XXI/F/66.

7 'Mutual jealousy and mistrust had led to clashes between Feilding and Dublin detectives during the army investigations' of 1866, when William Whelan had met Mayne 'and found him dismissive and uncooperative.' Kennedy 112.

The individual he wanted was Captain Whelan, at present, I believe, on the Staff at Dublin, who / had worked with him in Ireland in detecting Fenianism in the army: he describes him as a first-rate man for this business, & Fielding said, that if Whelan were appointed, he (F) cd. work the thing for two months, go over to Paris & other places, wh: is / absolutely necessary, & then ↑, quitting altog[ethe]r at the end of the two months,↓ leave the department organised, & matured in Whelan's hands: & we shd be well served.

But Whelan has the same objection to the employment as Fielding: its equivocal nature is fatal, professionally.

But / he offers to go on half pay, if we appoint him to some ostensible post connected with the police, wh: will bring him in an income wh: will supply the deficiency occasioned by his retirement from such active profess[iona]l duties:

or he will sell out altog[ethe]r if / we can make it square.[8]

Mayo, who has all the Police of Ireland under ↑him↓, says he can't arrange it: Hardy has only the metrop: police over wh: he has any influence.

I could make temporary arrangements as to the pecuniary part, & even for / more than a year; but if there is to be a permanent post, the salary must, sooner or later, come before H of Comm:

However, I am to see Hardy upon this & many other points in an hour or so, when I shall write again.

With respect to / the next point, Hardy says that Mayne will not consent to any of his force reporting to any one but himself; but on this point, I think we ought to insist upon what is necessary, & if Mayne chooses to resign / in consequence, let him.

Most secret

You remember Mrs. Montgomery & her strange, but now not improbable, information a year ago.[9]

She now informs me, that on Saturday morning last, a dying Irishman in one of the London Hospitals / confessed that, early in the Session, there was a plot, quite matured, to blow up the Houses of Parliament by gunpowder introduced thro' the gas-pipes: but it failed thro' the Houses being too well-watched. / They are going however to blow up another prison: but wh:, he tho' pressed, he refrained from declaring.[10]

I have sent this information to Hardy, tho' silent as to the source. Gunpowder thro' / gaspipes is a new idea, & worth attention.

8 Whelan, noting his status as 'an officer in the Army as well as having regard to my position as a gentleman', had outlined these conditions in a letter to Feilding on 11 December. H B/XXI/F/65.

9 Fanny Charlotte Wyndham Montgomery (1820-1893), wife of Alfred Montgomery, published novels as 'the Hon Mrs Alfred Montgomery'. On 12 September 1865 she had sent D her first novel, *The Bucklyn Shaig: a Tale of the Last Century* (2 vols, 1865). D replied on 15 October with (in her words) 'flattering expressions' about it. On 4 August 1866 she had written to D with 'something very important' to tell him that 'affects the government, and the whole country generally. I must not write it.' H B/XXI/M/471-3. See note 10.

10 Montgomery on 15 December had written to D on 'Irish Office' paper ('I write from Mayo's house'), recalling their meeting the previous year 'in Brook Street No. 38' and relating the dying Irishman's information. The prisons targeted were 'either Westminster or Millbank ... It is probably which ever Prison Fenians are detained in.' H B/XXI/M/474.

I sent Montagu Corry & Lambert to Clerkenwell: representing Treasury & Poor Law Board.[11]

I doubt, whether any public subscriptions are necessary: the sufferers are not paupers, but, generally speaking, reputable mechanics, with their homes suddenly ravaged; their furniture & tools destroyed.[12]

Immediate aid was the great thing, & it has done ~~great~~ ↑vast↓ good.

Lambert & Corry were there yesterday, & they are there this morning.

Ever yrs, | D.

TO: LORD DERBY   Downing Street [Monday] 16 December 1867   4629

ORIGINAL: DBP Box 146/3

PUBLICATION HISTORY: M&B IV 573-4, omitting the second paragraph and last sentence

EDITORIAL COMMENT: C of Ex paper. *Sic*: Fielding [*three times*].

---

confidential   Dec 16 1867

Right Honorable | The Earl of Derby | K.G.

My dear Lord,

I will not trouble you with all the schemes, conferences, hopes, & disappointments, of this busy day. The result / is that Colonel Fielding, who has just left my room, has undertaken to ascertain, if possible, the relations between the Fenians in England & the Revolutionary societies abroad. /

He had much greater plans, but his operations will be limited to this head.[1] His greater plans, wh: wd. involve a discovery of the Incendiaries & the Incendiary / plots in this kingdom, must be renounced, from the absolute impossibility of furnishing him with competent agents. This morning, Mr Secy. Hardy settled with me, that he ↑(F)↓ shd. certainly have / three or more detectives at his disposal, but Mr Hardy is of opinion ~~th~~ from his subsequent inquiries, that there are really no men in the force, who, either from lack of honesty or intelligence, can / be trusted.[2] Col:

---

11 See **4624**n1 and **4625**n5.

12 On 17 December, the Rev Robert Maguire, incumbent of Clerkenwell, would acknowledge receipt of sums for a 'special fund now being raised for the sufferers. Our working committee will be formed tonight.' According to Maguire, nearly all of the victims were watchmakers and jewellers. 'In the immediate ruins much gold is buried, and other valuables that the men were working with.' *The Times* (17 Dec 1867). See **4636**n3.

---

1 Derby on 17 December would reply from Knowsley with a letter marked '*Confidential*': 'I have to thank you for two long and interesting, but thoroughly unsatisfactory, letters received this morning. If I rightly understand the situation Col. Fielding's [*sic*] operations will be confined to endeavouring to trace a connexion between the disturbers of our peace at home, and the revolutionists abroad. In this I fear he will fail; as from what Mayo told us in Downing Street, I very much doubt the existence of any concert between them. Even should he be able to establish it, it would be much less effectual towards our immediate object of preserving the public safety, than an accurate knowledge of the plots and intentions of Conspirators and Incendiaries at home. It is really lamentable that the peace of the Metropolis, and its immunity from wilful devastation, should depend on a body of Police, who, *as Detectives*, are manifestly incompetent; and under a Chief [*Mayne*] who, whatever may be his other merits, has not the energy, nor, apparently, the skill to find out, and employ, men fitted for peculiar duties.' H B/XX/S/457.

2 Hardy on 18 December would note that on this day (16th) he had spent 'a long day at the H.O. & with Disraeli. Constantly new information all of the same stamp – incendiarism.' *Hardy Diary* 58.

Fielding says his conversation with the Secy. of State was the most despairing & unsatisfactory one (as regards the position of the country) he ever knew.

There is no doubt, that there is a system of organised / incendiarism afloat, & we
credibly hear of men coming from America, who are to take empty houses in various parts of London, & set them on fire; probably simultaneously.

Col. Fielding wd have / wished to have grappled with these impending calamities.

Many of the miscreants who are to perpetrate these crimes, are ↑now↓ here, & are
known – & we can't touch them.

I think the Habeas Corpus ought to be suspended.[3] / However, the Colonel undertakes the original purpose. *But we hear nothing of our Swiss correspondent!*[4]

Yrs ever, | D.

4630 TO: LORD STANLEY   Grosvenor Gate, Monday 16 December [1867]
ORIGINAL: DBP Box 12/3/44; H H/LIFE
EDITORIAL COMMENT: Endorsed in Stanley's hand on the third page: 'Mr. Disraeli December 16. 1867
Supposed implication of U.S. consul in Fenian plots Letter from Mr. Greenwood to Mr. Hardy. Enc. copied &
original returned to Mr. Hardy Dec 17'. *Dating*: by context; see n1.

[DBP:]
Confidential   Grosvenor Gate | Dec. 16. Monday eve.
Right Honorable | Secy. Lord Stanley
Dear Stanley,
The enclosed letter, just received from Hardy, is most important, & demands the
gravest attention.[1]

Sir John Pakington, who has returned to town, has requested, / [H H/LIFE:] in
unison with the Duke of Buckingham, that the members of the Cabinet in town shall
meet to-morrow morning and confer on the present critical state of the Metropolis.

---

3 Derby (n1) would reply that 'There is no doubt that the public are sufficiently alarmed; but not so much,
I think, as to tolerate the Suspension of the Habeas Corpus Act in England. We must trust to the operation of the ordinary law, at all events unless, and until, we are able to bring before a Secret Committee,
impartially composed, such evidence as shall satisfy all of them as to the necessity of some exceptional
measures ... *If* we can bring forward all the evidence which we have of what is going on at home, irrespective of any concert with foreign Revolutionists, we *may* establish a case strong enough to induce Parliament to sanction some exceptional measures, applicable to particular districts, equivalent to the case of
the proclaimed districts in Ireland. But this Greek fire is a new and formidable element, which will not
be affected by any Registration of Arms Bill, or any measures of that description. Let me say that I think
you are quite right in acting at once for the relief of the Clerkenwell Sufferers, and also in consulting the
Cmr. in Ch. as to employing Col. F.' For Greek fire, see **4643**&n1.
4 Emile Van Quellin, a Swiss-American living near Berne who had arrived in London shortly after the
Clerkenwell explosion, had abruptly disappeared following his first interview with Feilding. Hardy on the
13th had left at daybreak to see him, but Van Quellin never appeared. Kennedy 109, 116; *Hardy Diary* 57.

---

1 Hardy on this day (16th) had written to D, 'This note is very important & I think we should know Stanley's
opinion – will you send it on to him ... & write to him what you consider it would be right to do.' H B/XX/
HA/14. In H H/LIFE is Stanley's copy of a letter dated 16 December 1867 to Hardy from treasury solicitor
John Greenwood: 'Something has fallen from a witness, examined here, tending to shew that the American Consul ([Benjamin] Moran) was in frequent communication with Fariola and Cluseret – shortly
before the intended rising in March /67 – and we have a letter from the Consul to Fariola, (found in his
house). Nothing of this has come out in Court – and before making further enquiries, I should like to
know whether the Government would like us to meddle with such matters.'

And I believe it is arranged, that we are to meet at my office to-morrow at one o'clock.[2]

I trust you will be there, tho' the enclosed refers to a matter on which we should perhaps consult in a more limited circle.

Hardy begs, that I would request you /[DBP:] to return the enclosed to him. Yours ever | D.

TO: SIR THOMAS PHILLIPPS   Downing Street [Tuesday] 17 December 1867   4631
ORIGINAL: BODL MSS Phillipps-Robinson [1]
PUBLICATION HISTORY: Alan Noel Latimer Munby, *The Dispersal of the Phillipps Library* (Cambridge 1960) 11-12
EDITORIAL COMMENT: C of Ex paper.

confidential   Dec 17 1867

Sir Thos: Phillipps | Bart:

Dear Sir Thomas,

I have given great consideration to your noble purpose respecting your Library & collections, & altho' I greatly sympathise with your / intentions, I cannot hold out any prospect of my being able to induce Parliament to co-operate with you in the plan as, at present, proposed.[1]

The House of Commons, I feel sure, will never recognise, / & confirm, the trusts of a will not in existence at the time the Act passes,[2] or wh:, if in existence, might be altered at any moment before your death. They will sanction no / arrangement, I am persuaded, where the nature of the trusts, the conditions of donation, the site & extent of the houses & lands to be appropriated, & to be freed from the operation of the / Mortmain Act, would be wholly unknown to Parliament.

I am sorry to throw difficulties in the way of plans of so elevated and commendable a character, as those on / wh: you have done me the honor of consulting me, but I should still more regret to be the means of deceiving & disappointing you.

If I can be of any further use, command me / at all times.

---

2 See **4632**n1.

---

1 Munby (ph) quotes Phillipps's 3 December letter to D: 'I do not see the necessity of consulting Legal Authorities, because I hope Parliament will *make a Law* for this particular Case. I offer to make my Library a permanent one to which the Public will have access under certain reservations & after a certain time & subject to such rules as I may lay down. I conceive the Act may be framed thus "Whereas Sir Thomas Phillipps is desirous that his Library of MSS & Printed Books shall not be dispersed for 500 years be it enacted that the said Library shall be so founded & established according to such Rules & Conditions as the said Sir Thomas Phillipps shall by will lay down for the Government of it & the said Library shall be supported by such Funds and Property as the said Sir Thomas Phillipps shall appoint notwithstanding any Act of Mortmain or any other Act limiting the disposition of Property now made or hereafter to be made. And to encourage the foundation of the said Library it is hereby enacted that the said Library Houses & the Grounds attached to it shall be free from the Legacy Duties & Succession Duties & from all Property Taxes, & all Parochial Rates and Taxes whatsoever now or hereafter to be imposed upon any Property in Great Britain." I hope this will meet with your cordial approbation.' See **4476**&n1.

2 Phillipps would sign his will, 'drafted and redrafted for over fifty years', on 1 February 1872, five days before his death. *ODNB.*

I trust you have recovered from your indisposition, & I remain, with great consideration, | faithfully Yours, | *B. Disraeli*[3]

4632 TO: LORD DERBY Downing Street [Tuesday] 17 December 1867

ORIGINAL: DBP Box 146/3
PUBLICATION HISTORY: M&B IV 574-5, omitting the last three paragraphs
EDITORIAL COMMENT: C of Ex paper. *Sic:* expence.

Confidential
Right Honorable | The Earl of Derby | K.G.   Dec. 17 1867
My dear Lord,

Affairs appear to be so serious, that, last night, the Cabinet in town (seven strong) agreed to meet & confer – mainly on the / critical condition of the Metropolis. For[eig]n Secy. of State (Northcote away) myself, the Ld Chanr & Corry. Hardy's bulletins, some received this morning, were of a most anxious & menacing character:[1] but the chief feature was / a telegram from Ld. Monck[2] informing the D of Bucks that some eight days past, a Danish Brigantine left New York with a band of thirty men sworn to assassinate H. M. & her Ministers.

Ld. Monck is not / an alarmist & particularly deprecates the expence of Trans-Atlantic telegrams – but, in this instance, he requests a telegram of rec[eip]t.

We have no powers to cope with such circumstances as these, & others wh: are / taking place under our nose.

The Duke of Bucks has ascertained, that on the day named, such a ~~sh~~ vessel did leave New York, & with the prevailing westerly wind may / be expected to arrive in 4 or 5 days.

3 In the Corry papers in H is a letter from Phillipps, presumably to D, writing from Thirlestaine House and dated 9 December (instead of '19' perhaps): 'I did hope you could have passed a Short act to enable me to establish the Library subject to no jurisdiction of Chancery, Charity Commissioners or any other Power except those Trustees that I should appoint. It is absurd to make *Libraries* subject to *Mortmain*!!! A certain Income is all that is necessary to maintain the Building & provide the Salary for the Librarian and a small sum may be set apart for printing the rare unpublished MSS. say £100 or £200 pr anm untill [*sic*] all were printed. A foreign Library has expressed a wish to have my Library, but I am too patriotic to let it go elsewhere, if I can fix the foundation here according to *my own* laws.' H B/X/C/2.

1 Stanley on this day (17th) would record: 'At 1 p.m. met Disraeli, Hardy, the Chancellor, Pakington, [H.T. Lowry-] Corry and D. of Buckingham: called together by Hardy, who has received a multitude of Fenian communications. One informant speaks of 155 Fenian and republican clubs in London alone, all unknown to the police.' Their schemes included blowing up Parliament, burning packed theatres, kidnapping the Prince of Wales, even assassinating Hardy, Derby and Stanley. Stanley did not 'attach much importance to any of these stories, but no doubt they justify some precautions. Hardy says we have no detectives, and that a new force will require to be organised, independent of Sir R. Mayne. We agreed to hold a cabinet on Thursday.' *Disraeli, Derby* 324-5.

2 Charles Stanley Monck (1819-1894), 4th Viscount Monck of Ballytrammon 1849, Baron Monck (UK) 1866, BA 1841 and hon LLD 1870 Trinity College, Dublin, an Irish barrister (King's Inns 1841), MP (L) for Portsmouth 1852-7, a junior lord of the treasury 1855-8, gov-gen of British North America 1861-7 and of Canada and Prince Edward Island 1867-9, GCMG and PC 1869, member of the Church Temporalities and National Education commissions 1871-81, commissioner of the Irish Lands Act 1882-4 and LL of Dublin co 1874-92. In 1864 he had urged the formation of the Great Coalition (which had led directly to Canadian Confederation) and had taken part in the debate on the British North America Act in the Lords in February 1867.

444

Ostensibly chartered for Dieppe, it is to land its passengers in the Bristol Channel.[3]

What are we to do?

If they land, & are seized, Habeas Corpus will immediately / release them. If stopped on the high seas, we may be involved in a war with America.

For my part, I shd. not hesitate advising seizure, & trusting to a parliamentary indemnity; but it seems that Hab: Corp: is too strong even for / such daring; & that we shd. violate the law without gaining our purpose.

If we call Parlt. tog[ethe]r –, the object will be apprehended by these miscreants & their like, & during the interval that must elapse before the meeting / of Parlt, every crime & plot will be stimulated [*illegible deletion*] & encouraged to avail themselves of the vanishing opportunity.

In this state of affairs, & the great alarm & indignation of the public / mind, there seemed an unanimous opinion, that the ↑real↓ Cabinet shd. ~~really~~ meet with[ou]t loss of time, & Mr Secy Hardy says the Queen expects it.[4]

I lament this for your sake: / ↑greatly.↓

You will hear about it from others, but I thought I wd. send you these few & hurried lines.

Yrs ever I D.[5]

TO: MARY ANNE DISRAELI   Carlton Club, Tuesday [17 December? 1867]   **4633**
ORIGINAL: H A/I/A/351

EDITORIAL COMMENT: Carlton Club paper. Docketed in another hand on the first page: '?1867'. *Dating*: conjectural; D was housebound with gout 2-8 and 10 December, but attended a cabinet on 17 December.

Tuesday I 7 o'ck.

My dearest

Pray send me, by bearer, an easy pair of boots. I suffer much now, / & can't attend to my work.

Your own I D.

3 The Duke of Buckingham on this day (17th) wrote to D that 'The "*Mercury*" is on her way from N. York stated to be freighted with *Petroleum* for the Bristol Channel or Cork', confirming Monck's 'unpleasant telegram'. H B/XX/BO/45.
4 After speaking with Hardy on the 18th, General Grey on the 19th would inform the Queen of Hardy's fears for her safety following reports of a planned attempt on her life. The Queen, much alarmed, would write to Hardy on the 19th suggesting a three-month suspension of the Habeas Corpus Act. On that day, following a three-hour cabinet, Derby would write to her at great length that such a course would be a 'serious infraction of the liberty of a whole people for the sake of punishing a few desperate conspirators', and that it had been decided instead to focus on 'measures of increased precaution', including 'a separate and secret' detective organization. She would reply on the 20th that Windsor was '*not at all safe*', that 'to London *nothing* will make her go' and that '*Such* precautions are taken here [Osborne] that the Queen will be little better than a *State* prisoner.' LQVB I 477-84.
5 'The Canadian story [in Monck's telegram] turned out to be a hoax, and the Queen chaffed the Cabinet and Hardy for paying any attention to it.' M&B IV 575.

4634 TO: LORD STANHOPE   Downing Street [Wednesday] 18 December 1867
ORIGINAL: H H/LIFE
EDITORIAL COMMENT: From a typescript headed '*1867*.'

The Earl Stanhope.   C. of E., Dec. 18. '67.
My dear Lord,
If the Fenians spare me, which is doubtful, I will take the chair as you wish, and on any Wednesday in May agreeable to the Society.[1]

I should have treated the promise of '52 only as an after-dinner indiscretion, if I had not, at the same time, spoken of your Lordship in so sensible and accurate a manner.[2]

I accept cordially your truly obliging offer to be present, and I feel sure, that I shall not be able to steer the ship without your aid.

Pray offer, for me, the kindest compliments of the season to Lady Stanhope, and to the charming daughter of your house and heart.[3]

Yours sincerely, D.

4635 TO: LORD JOHN MANNERS   Downing Street [Saturday] 21 December 1867
ORIGINAL: BEA [93]
EDITORIAL COMMENT: C of Ex paper.

Private   Dec 21 1867
Right Honorable | Lord John Manners
My dear J.M.
The Duke of Bucks informs me, that the Governmt. of Tasmania is vacant, £3000 p ann:, & that / he must be a House of Commons man, accustomed to public business & the art of government.[1]

No governors used to Crown Colonies wd do for the post.

Would / it suit Cochrane? The Duke leaves the appointment ↑to me↓. Let me

1 Stanhope on 14 December had written to D from Chevening enclosing a resolution adopted at a meeting of the committee of the Royal Literary Fund (Stanhope was president) inviting D to '"take the Chair at the Anniversary Dinner"' of the Fund in May. Stanhope offered to relieve D of 'any of the subordinate or unimportant Toasts.' D would chair the dinner on 6 May 1868. H B/XXI/S/492, 492a; *The Times* (7 May 1868).
2 Stanhope (n1) had enclosed 'a Report of the Anniversary of 1853 when you last presided. You will see if you refer to page 25 that you are understood to have said: "My friends may rest assured that if I be again a Minister of the Crown I shall be only too proud to fill the Chair again." And I cannot myself turn to that passage without noting the very graceful & only too obliging expressions which in the very next sentence to that which I have quoted you applied to me', for which he offered his 'sincere acknowledgments.'
3 See **4069**n4.

1 The Duke of Buckingham had been colonial secretary since March 1867. *The Times* on 30 July 1868 would report that Charles Du Cane (C) 'has accepted the Government of Tasmania', succeeding Aylesbury-born career soldier colonel Sir Thomas Browne (who would remain governor until 30 December 1868) on 15 January 1869.

know, as soon as you can, as I have others in my eye,[2] but this is the first / offer I have made of it.[3]

    Yrs ever I D.

TO: GATHORNE HARDY   Grosvenor Gate [Thursday] 26 December 1867 **4636**
ORIGINAL: ESU [2]
EDITORIAL COMMENT: C of Ex paper, seal crossed out and 'Grosvenor Gate' written in.

Right Honorable I Mr Secy Hardy   Grosvenor Gate I Dec 26 1867
My dear Secretary,
The inclosed, from the opposite side of the House, may be useful to us, in case you have to reconstruct your / Police force.[1]

    Mayo writes to me, that you will probably receive Fariola's report today, wh: he wishes me to see as soon as convenient to yourself.[2]

    I / shall be at the office rather early, having a Clerkenwell Deputation at three o'ck:[3]

    Yours, I D.

TO: SIR WILLIAM STIRLING MAXWELL   Downing Street **4637**
      [Thursday] 26 December 1867
ORIGINAL: STCL 17/21
EDITORIAL COMMENT: C of Ex paper. *Sic*: Anne.

Sir. W. Stirling Maxwell I Bart: M.P.   Decr 26 1867

---

2 *The Times* on 12 March 1868 would report that 'Sir James Elphinstone, M.P. for Portsmouth, will not be Governor of Tasmania, as has been generally stated.'

3 In a letter of 22 December 1867 from Cadland, Southampton, marked '*Private*', Manners would inform D that he had discussed D's letter with Alexander Baillie-Cochrane. Although grateful for D's confidence, Baillie-Cochrane could not 'reconcile himself to the idea of relinquishing public life in England'. H B/XX/M/149.

---

1 Hardy on this day (26th) had written to D from the home office: 'I have read the enclosed [*not found*] cursorily. It is of the past but some parts [are] interesting. Will you let me have it again as soon as you have read it that I may go through it again for names, dates &c.' H B/XX/HA/17.

2 Mayo on the 25th had written to D from Dublin Castle that 'General Fariola's Statement [*not found*] went to London last night. Hardy will have it tomorrow. You should see it without delay.' Belgian-born Fenian Octave Louis François Étienne Fariola de Rozzoli (1839-1914) had served in the American Civil War (capt 77th US Colored Infantry and lieut-col 96th US Colored Infantry) and honourably discharged in 1866. Arrested in London in July 1867 and incarcerated in Dublin's Kilmainham Gaol, he had offered in early December to exchange information for passage to Australia. He would become a planter in Queensland and a civil engineer in Australia and Borneo, and claim an invalid pension in Virginia in 1905. He is buried at Arlington National Cemetery. H B/XX/BO/47; 'Belgians in the American Civil War, 1840-1865' online; *The Times* (19 Jul 1867).

3 On this day (26th) D would discuss indemnification with a deputation from the Clerkenwell Relief Committee. According to the Rev Robert Maguire, who introduced the deputation, 200 houses containing 600 families had been affected and damages had been estimated at between £12,000 and £15,000. D replied that the need for funds had 'never yet been really put before the country, nor has any adequate idea yet been given of the actual amount of damage done.' He wished to know 'what amount you would be likely to require before we come forward with Governmental assistance', suggesting that a 'general statement of the effects of the calamity' would 'bring you all the assistance in the shape of funds you may require.' *The Times* (27 Dec 1867). See **4638**&n3.

My dear Stirling,

I hear with great concern of your relapse. Let me have some news of you! And if too languid / for such an office, perhaps Lady Anne will deign to let me hear of one, whom everybody respects & regards.

The Fenians / keep me in town, as well as Hardy. So much for a merrie Xmas!

It is one of the most singular conspiracies in history. On Xmas eve, London was / to have been fired in many places.[1]

ArchBp Manning very wisely forbad the midnight masses,[2] wh: helped us: but all the public buildings are full of police & soldiers.

Yours sincerely, | D.[3]

4638   TO: [CHARLES RIVERS WILSON?]

[Grosvenor Gate]
Friday [27 December 1867]

ORIGINAL: NYPL Montague [27]
EDITORIAL COMMENT: *Dating*: by context; see nn2&3.

Friday

I think that blundering booby, Maguire,[1] in his report of what took place yesterday, has repeated ~~the~~ his original mistake, by circulating a perfectly erroneous & unauthorised notion, that, if the public won't subscribe further, / the Govt will supply ~~further~~ funds.[2]

Of course, no one will subscribe with such an alternative.

I think it might be desirable to send to the Journals a paragraph such as I / have sketched, or like it.[3]

---

1 According to Stanley, writing on 17 December, Gathorne Hardy had received numerous Fenian communications from informants, including one about 'an association whose object is to hire houses in various parts of London, fill them with combustibles, and set them on fire at the same time.' *Disraeli, Derby* 325. See **4629**.
2 There had been 'no high mass at the Roman Catholic chapels at midnight on Christmas-eve ... in consequence of Archbishop Manning's prohibitory edict'. *The Times* (27 Dec 1867).
3 Stirling Maxwell on 29 December would reply from Keir that he was now 'able to be up for a few hours every day.' He 'was glad to learn by the newspapers' of MA's 'complete recovery ... & that your indisposition had also passed off ... Fenianism is indeed a curious madness. We ought to be more grateful than some of us are to those who are ready to meet the responsibilities & the dangers of power during the continuance of the mania.' H B/XXI/M/294.

---

1 The Rev Robert Maguire (1826-1890), MA and DD Trinity College, Dublin, rector of St James's, Clerkenwell 1857 and of St Olave's, Southwark 1875, was chairman of the Clerkenwell Relief Committee. See **4628**n12.
2 D appears to have read the report in *The Times* on this day (27th) (see **4636**n3) and may allude to remarks by churchwarden F.W. Willcocks: 'Private benevolence had its limits; besides which many persons were of the opinion that either the Government or the country were liable for the amount of damage done ... [and] that the Government should come forward and assist the committee with funds, if such assistance should be required.' *The Times* (27 Dec 1867).
3 A press release, signed 'C. Rivers Wilson' and dated 27 December, published in *The Times* on 30 December, would correct 'the erroneous impression which, in consequence of the absence of reporters, has transpired of what took place at his interview yesterday with the Clerkenwell deputation. Mr Disraeli expressed his opinion that if a complete statement, on the responsibility of the relief committee, were made of all the legitimate claims on their consideration, national sympathy alone would be found ad-

I shall be at D.S. about three, if the fog does not increase, & we can ↑then↓ consult together about it: but if the fog increases I shan't come. So you must do what you think / best anent.[4]

Yrs | D.

TO: GATHORNE HARDY   Grosvenor Gate [Friday] 27 December 1867   4639
ORIGINAL: ESU [3]
EDITORIAL COMMENT: C of Ex paper, seal crossed out and 'G. Gate' written in.

Right Honorable | Mr Secy Hardy   G. Gate | Dec 27 1867
My dear Hardy,

I return Fariola's statement.[1] It is a most interesting & invaluable document, because it is the only complete account of the plans & / resources of the Fenian conspiracy. They do not seem essentially formidable, tho', no doubt, if treated with negligence, might perpetuate immense mischief, & / called into operation at an apropos moment, achieve some public disaster.

I enclose also an anonymous letter,[2] because there are one or two details, as to names of persons, wh: / appear to me not altog[ethe]r contemptible.

Did you capture your Pole?[3]

Yours ever | D.

If the fog ~~des~~ does not get worse, I shall be at D.S. in afternoon[.]

TO: HENRY MANNING   Grosvenor Gate [Friday] 27 December 1867   4640
ORIGINAL: MANN 641
EDITORIAL COMMENT: C of Ex paper, seal crossed out and 'Grosvenor Gate' written in.

His Grace | The ArchBp of Westminster   Grosvenor Gate | Decr 27 1867

---

equate to satisfy them; but, if not, that it might then be advisable to hold a public meeting on the subject *out* of Clerkenwell. The Chancellor of the Exchequer gave no prospect of any further assistance from the Government, which was afforded in the first instance because it was deemed desirable, under the peculiar circumstances, that instantaneous relief should be secured to the sufferers.' This is followed by a letter from Maguire, dated the 27th, outlining the damages as suggested by D in **4636**n3, and one by Robert Paget, dated the 28th, referring to Wilson's letter and stating that 'a professional reporter' had in fact been present on the 26th. 'This, however, only became known to the deputation and myself on quitting the room, and was, of course, unknown to the Chancellor of the Exchequer.'

4 Dense fog continued to blanket London on the 27th and 28th. *The Times* (27, 28, 30 Dec 1867).

---

1 Hardy on the 28th would note that Fariola's statement 'is not I think the *whole* truth as to the past & all informers fall short.' *Hardy Diary* 59.
2 This letter has not been found.
3 This Polish informant, who spoke no English, 'turned out to be a woman venting her anger toward a previous employer by accusing him of plotting with the Fenians.' Kennedy 166.

My dear Lord,

The Fenians give me so much trouble, & take up so much time, that, I fear, I have seemed to neglect your letter. Would / tomorrow suit Yr Grace at two o'ck?[1]

Yours sincerely | D.[2]

4641   TO: MONTAGU CORRY   Downing Street [Saturday] 28 December 1867
ORIGINAL: H H/LIFE
EDITORIAL COMMENT: From a typescript headed: 'C. of E. Downing St., Dec. 28. '67.'

Montagu Corry, Esq.

My dear Montagu,

No news of importance. The Martello Tower affair maintains the fever in the public mind; and every hour Fenianism more and more absorbs public sentiment.[1]

Lord Mayo sent me Fariola's secret report: nothing can be more interesting. It is the first, and only, document, which gives us some general view of the plans and the resources of Fenianism. They are not essentially formidable; but if neglected, great public inconvenience may be occasioned, and perhaps some public disaster achieved.

No news yet of the Pole.

Victor Yorke, reciting Shakespeare on Monday last at Aston Clinton, fell down dead! I only heard of it this afternoon! Strange, that it was never in the papers.[2] Lord and Lady Hardwicke have gone to Aston: amid immense sorrow and consternation.

Ever, D.

4642   TO: LORD STANLEY   Grosvenor Gate [Tuesday] 31 December 1867
ORIGINAL: DBP Box 12/3/45
EDITORIAL COMMENT: C of Ex paper, seal crossed out and 'Grosvenor Gate' written in.

Rt Honorable | Secy Lord Stanley   Grosvenor Gate | Dec 31 1867

---

1 Manning on 22 December had written to D with a request to discuss a letter he had received from Cardinal Cullen. He would reply on this day (27th) that he would see D on the 28th. H B/XXI/M/167-8.
2 Manning would read to D portions of Cullen's letter (n1) on the 28th. On 3 January 1868 D would tell Mayo that he inferred from the letter 'that there would be no question about endowment in case we granted a charter to the R.C. University.' INL Mayo Papers MS 11,164 (to be published in *Benjamin Disraeli Letters: 1868*).

---

1 On 26 December at about 5 *pm* a Martello tower at Fota, near the entrance to Cork harbour, had been raided and a quantity of arms and ammunition stolen. *The Times* (30, 31 Dec 1867).
2 Victor Alexander Yorke (1842-1867), third son of the Earl of Hardwicke and a lieutenant in the Royal Horse Artillery, had been staying at Aston Clinton, Sir Anthony de Rothschild's estate. On 23 December Yorke was taking part in 'an entertainment given to the villagers in Lady de Rothschild's Girls' Schoolroom' when, during a reading of Tennyson's 'The Grandmother', at the words 'He stood like a rock', he fell from his platform, expiring at about 11:15 *pm*. *The Times* (31 Dec 1867) reprinting from the *Bucks Advertiser*.

Dear S.

I have just come up from Quart. Sess:[1] but find here strange accounts from Paris.[2] I will try to see you in / the course of the day:

about three o'ck: in my ~~day~~ way to D.S.:

if you are then engaged, we might meet / for ten minutes later.

Yrs ever, | D.

TO: MONTAGU CORRY   Downing Street [Tuesday] 31 December 1867   **4643**
ORIGINAL: H B/XX/D/63
EDITORIAL COMMENT: C of Ex paper.

Private   Decr 31 1867

Montagu Corry Esq

My dear Montagu,

I went down to Q. Sess: yesterday morning, & slept at Aylesbury, so I could not write to you.

I have just returned / but have no news: tho' with Abyssinia, a declining revenue, an European war, & a Fenian conspiracy, one should have some.

I ~~have~~ sent over to the For. Secy., but he is at / Hatfield, wh: the messengers at F.O. always mention, as if he were at home.

We were obliged to discharge our Fenian prisoners in Bucks, tho' they have been night-drilling at Wolverton & / experimenting in Greek fire, but the intimidation was so severe, that our witnesses became panic-struck.[1]

Sir Jenkinson has written to me,[2] & Lady J. to my wife.[3] This is my merrie Xmas, & these are my new Year's gifts.

---

1 D on the 30th had attended the Quarter Sessions at Aylesbury. *The Times* (31 Dec 1867); BH (4 Jan 1868). See **4643**n1.

2 According to *The Times*'s Paris correspondent, the Paris newspaper *La Liberté* on the 29th had called the Clerkenwell explosion the work of 'a lower class of Fenians, who were paid by the agents of the Government in order to throw discredit on Fenianism! These poor creatures ... were merely serving as the instruments of secret police agents ... At any rate, whether the paragraph proceeds from ignorance or from malice, it deserves to be noticed, and so I do notice it, and claim for it the contempt it deserves.' *The Times* (31 Dec 1867).

---

1 At the Quarter Sessions on the 30th there had been discussion of enhanced security measures at Aylesbury jail taken prior to the arrival of suspected Fenians James Connerby, a fitter, and Gladwin Meehan, a coach body maker, both later discharged due to insufficient evidence. They had been arrested on the 24th at Wolverton and charged with having, on the 17th, 'compassed and intended to levy war against our Sovereign Lady the Queen.' BH (4 Jan 1868); *The Times* (27 Dec 1867). Greek fire (or 'liquid fire') was a potent incendiary mixture first used by the Byzantine navy in the seventh century.

2 Sir George Samuel Jenkinson (1817-1892), 11th Bt, capt 8th Hussars, DL of Gloucestershire 1855 and high sheriff 1862, had unsuccessfully contested N Wiltshire in 1865 and Nottingham in 1866. He would be MP (C) for N Wiltshire 1868-80. On 29 December he had written from Eastwood Park, Berkeley, to thank D for his 'kind note & good wishes of the Season' and invite him for a visit, expressing disappointment 'that all my efforts have hitherto failed to enable me to range myself on your side in Parliament. I fully hoped that my good fight at Nottingham, a year & half ago, would have resulted in procuring me a Seat before now, especially as your Party have remained in office.' H B/XXI/J/32.

3 Jenkinson in 1845 had married Emily Sophia Lyster (d 1892), daughter of Anthony Lyster of Stillorgan Park, co Dublin. Lady Jenkinson on 26 December had written to MA asking her and D to visit her in

Yours, I trust, are more bright & lively.

D.

Gout much better.

4644

TO: JOHN WILLIAM FANE   [London, Tuesday] 31 December 1867

ORIGINAL: COR Rare PR 4581 f73+V.2(35)

EDITORIAL COMMENT: C of Ex paper, seal crossed out.

Col: Fane M.P.   Decr 31 1867

Dear Fane,

I had heard from your brother before I received yr. letter, &, by return of post, applied to / Colonel Wilson Patten.

Here is his reply, wh: is not a refusal, but is very diplomatic in its tone. It is evident he is not, or was not, aware of / the impending vacancy.

Will you let yr brother know all this, & send him the letter. I said all I could.[1]

yrs sincerely, | D.

4645

TO: MONTAGU CORRY   [London? 1867?]

ORIGINAL: H B/XX/D/68

EDITORIAL COMMENT: Docketed in another hand on the first page: '?1867'.

Montagu Corry | Esq   6 o'ck

My dear Montagu,

I think, I have arranged it all – & very well.

I was looking for you to tell you, that you might have a good nights / rest, & send this to D.S., with the same hope.

Adieu! | D

4646

TO: [MONTAGU CORRY]   Downing Street
                                    Sunday [July 1866-February 1868]

ORIGINAL: H B/XX/D/333

EDITORIAL COMMENT: C of Ex paper.

                                                        Sunday

Don't be later than three o'ck: as I want to see you very much.

Yrs | D.

Bristol on 21 January 1868: 'I think the mild air of this part of the country would do you good. I suffer so much myself from a delicate chest ... & I am also *so much of an invalid that my guests need never exert themselves more than they like*'. H D/III/D/314.

---

1 John William Fane had one surviving brother, the Rev Frederick Adrian Scrope Fane (1810-1894), vicar at Norton Mandeville, Essex. Fane's letter, his brother's letter, D's letter to John Wilson Patten and Patten's reply have not been found.

TO: [MONTAGU CORRY]·   Downing Street [July 1866-February 1868]   4647
ORIGINAL: H B/XX/D/366
EDITORIAL COMMENT: C of Ex paper. *Sic*: Skeg.

Remember the letter wh: came from Mr Skeg, the surgeon.[1] You have it. It requires some *attention*. You / did not mention it yesterday – & I miss some other letters. Perhaps they may all be in one of yr boxes unopened?

TO: [MONTAGU CORRY]   Downing Street   4648
Thursday [July 1866-February 1868]

ORIGINAL: H B/XI/J/44
EDITORIAL COMMENT: 11 Downing Street paper.

Thursday

There are a good many troublesome questions today; look after them, as I shall not be at the office till late[.]
     D.

TO: [MONTAGU CORRY]   Grosvenor Gate   4649
Wednesday [July 1866-February 1868]

ORIGINAL: H B/XX/D/381
EDITORIAL COMMENT: C of Ex paper, seal crossed out and 'Gros: Gate' written in. *Dating*: speculative; see n1.

Wednesday | Gros: Gate

I shan't go out this morning, until the Temple Dinner:[1] there is, however, much that requires immediate attention & I shd. be glad to see / you here at ½ past twelve o'ck: or about that time.
     D.

TO: [MONTAGU CORRY?]   [1866-8; 1874-80]   4650
ORIGINAL: PS 1517
PUBLICATION HISTORY: Richard Ford (Bookseller inventory #2537) at AbeBooks.com. Undated letter described as: '1 page, 8vo ... Docketed at head in pencil: "The Rt. Honble. B. D'Israeli."'

From the Rector of Chalfont[1]
     Will you ask whether, [he] can have this second delivery.

1 Evidently John Joseph Skegg, Lic R Coll Phys Edinburgh 1860, member R Coll Surg England 1860, house-surgeon at Charing Cross Hospital 1861. *Medical Register* 1879; *The Times* (15 Jul 1861). Skegg's letter has not been found.

1 Possibly one of the annual dinners to the Auditors of the Inner Temple, at which 'a numerous and distinguished company is expected.' *The Times* (17 Jun 1865).

1 This letter from the Rev Charles Lloyd has not been found.

I think I tried for it in vain when we were in opposition.[2]

Yrs

D.

4651   TO: LORD BARRINGTON   [London] Monday [Feb 1867-Aug 1876]
ORIGINAL: DUL [4]
COVER: The | Viscount Barrington | M.P. | D
EDITORIAL COMMENT: *Dating*: conjectural; see cover and n1.

Monday.

Thanks! Very good! Shall be at the Carlton in an hour.

Yrs | D.[1]

2 Lloyd had written to D on 4 October 1860 asking for help in obtaining a second postal service for Chalfont St Giles, 'as all the letters from the North of the county are now two days in coming here.' Similar
letters had followed on 30 October and 1 November 1860 and on 28 January 1861. None of Lloyd's letters
(eight to D and one to Corry), written 1862-76 from the Chalfont St Giles rectory, mention the postal
service. H B/XXI/L/229-40, 246.

---

1 George Barrington became 7th Viscount Barrington in February 1867; D would become Earl of Beaconsfield in August 1876.

APPENDIX I

PRE-1865 LETTERS NEWLY FOUND

These are letters that properly belong in the previously published volumes, but which came to light or were correctly dated too late for inclusion there.

The 'x' following a letter number indicates a new letter to be inserted into the sequence following the letter identified by the number only. The 'R' following a letter number indicates a letter that now replaces the letter with that number which was previously published in part for reasons stated in the headnote for that letter. The letter thus superseded may, however, still contain extracts from other letters not yet found. The 'A' following a letter number indicates an additional new letter to be inserted into the existing sequence.

NO	DATE	TO	PLACE OF ORIGIN	LOCATION OF ORIGINAL
264XR	16 APR '33	WILLIAM J. FOX	DUKE STREET	JWA
414X	[8 AUG '35]	SARAH DISRAELI	[LONDON]	MAB
535X	[30?] OCT ['36?]	FRANCIS BONHAM	BRADENHAM	MAB
1033X	[17? JAN '40]	WILLIAM L. MABERLY	H OF COMMONS	PS
1094R	[29 SEP '40]	SARAH DISRAELI	[LONDON]	CRA
1315XA	19 JUL '43	MARIE É.F. BAUDRAND	LONDON	PS
1487X	18 MAY '46	[UNKNOWN]	GROSVENOR GATE	PS
1511XA	14 OCT '46	THOMAS BAILEY	CARLTON CLUB	WIL
1643AR	4 MAY ['48]	HENRY DRUMMOND	GROSVENOR GATE	DUP
1923R	21 NOV '49	LORD MALMESBURY	GROSVENOR GATE	MAB
1929X	4 DEC '49	[LORD MALMESBURY]	HUGHENDEN	MAB
1949R	1 JAN '50	LORD MALMESBURY	HUGHENDEN	MAB
2202XR	3 DEC '51	SPENCER WALPOLE	GROSVENOR GATE	MIL
2480R	26 JAN '53	LORD MALMESBURY	FRYSTONE	MAB
2645X	28 MAR '54	LORD GALWAY	GROSVENOR GATE	PS
2797R	30 NOV '55	LORD MALMESBURY	HUGHENDEN	MAB
3035X	[26 FEB '58]	SIR WILLIAM JOLLIFFE	[LONDON]	SCR
3362X	6 JUN '5[9?]	[WILLIAM RAINGER]	GROSVENOR GATE	UO
3481A	[30 JUN? '60]	LORD DERBY	CARLTON CLUB	DBP
3567R	24 MAR '61	HENRY ALMACK	GROSVENOR GATE	JWA
3764R	28 DEC '62	[JOHN SKELTON]	TORQUAY	PS
3887A	14 DEC ['63]	JOHN F. MAGUIRE	GROSVENOR GATE	PS
3924X	16 MAY '64	[JOHN SKELTON]	GROSVENOR GATE	PS

TO: WILLIAM J. FOX   35 Duke Street [Tuesday] 16 April 1833
ORIGINAL: JWA [8]
PUBLICATION HISTORY: From John Wilson Manuscripts (www.manuscripts.co.uk), item 24724. See VI
264X&nn1&2.

35 Duke St. St James | Ap. 16th 1833

My dear Fox,

This is the fifth day of my influenza, & I can just scrawl you a line to thank you for your kind note. I send you something short, if not sweet, apropos to "Insincerity." Certainly the popular party seem~~ed~~ determined to make me a Tory, w[hi]ch I regret, as my talents are all the other way. But in this damned hereditary country, every body believes that you are indebted to your father for your politics as well as yr. [*illegible deletion*] property. Vale! I can scarcely see.

D. /

Postscriptum

The party I wish to influence are the persons who brought in Whalley a mere tool. The chiefs are *Potter* not the Belgian, but I believe a Political Unionist, as great a rebel. Wilson whom I do *not* know. Could Place influence these? Very likely.

TO: SARAH DISRAELI   [London] Saturday [8 August 1835]
ORIGINAL: MAB [1]
COVER: Miss Disraeli | Bradenham House | *High Wycombe*
POSTMARKS: (1) A large numeral 2; (2) in a circle: EX | 8 AU 8 | 1835; (3) in a lozenge: NIGHT | AU 8 | 1835.

Saturday

Dearest,

Ld. L. has received your cheese which pleased him very much: I am sorry to say he is very unwell to day, so that he cannot go to the Lords whence he ought not to be absent a moment, as all depends upon him. Peel has gone into the country. I cannot write particulars; but this I say that at / *no time have affairs ever looked so well, or L. himself personally been of more importance.* I think nothing can be better in every respect & for every person for whom we are interested, but if Ld. L. is seriously ill, I think its all over with us.[1]

In gt haste | BD /

I forgot to say Brougham came home in the carr[iag]e with L. after the debate.[2]
Immense store of silks coming for mere[.][3]

---

1 For Lord Lyndhurst's illness and his crucial role in the Municipal Corporations Bill, see II **416**&nn1-3 and **419**n1.

2 In the Lords on Friday 7 August 1835, rivals Lyndhurst and Brougham had spoken very briefly. *Hansard* XXX cols 136-9. See II **413**&n5 and **419**n1.

3 Sarah would reply from Bradenham on the 9th: 'We are much concerned to hear of Ld. Lyndhurst's illness. I fear it is much more than prudence that would keep him from the house on Saturday ... Immense number of thanks, & love, & regards comes to the proper quarter in return for the promise of immense store of silks, which promise is most gratefully received & most fully appreciated. The first article of the last Edinbro' [Review] is the first fruit of Macaulay's literary lecture in India, & a splendid article it is; but I suppose you have no time for it.' H A/I/B/561.

TO: **FRANCIS BONHAM**   Bradenham, Sunday [30?] October [1836?]   535X

ORIGINAL: MAB [2]

EDITORIAL COMMENT: *Dating*: If D's '1' is a compressed '0', Sunday 30 October 1836 is a possible date. However, none of the years in which 31 October is a Sunday fit the context; see n4. *Sic*: Sunday Oct 31; Neal [*twice*]; electioneerer.

---

private   Bradenham | Sunday Oct 31

My dear Mr Bonham,[1]

The influence & co-operation of Lord Carrington, if active & hearty, would, I believe, secure the seat. As a matter of duty to the party I would not shrink, but should be unwilling to come forward without / a moral certainty of success. Mr. Neal, Lord Carrington's steward, is a man of considerable talents & the most skilful electioneerer in this part of the world.[2] I have the utmost confidence in his skill & judgment; I believe that he could manage the affair. It should be kept quiet, & there should be no / forwardness on my part. In short it would require generalship; but I repeat Mr Neal is the man, & without his advice & assistance, I would not move. I am led to believe that the vast majority of my former friends are all staunch, & that the rest might be easily revived. The ↑present↓ residence of Lord Home[3] in our neighbourhood is in our / favor; & Sir W. Young & Mr. Norris have greater influence at present than during the last election.[4] But with all this, George Dashwood will be a formidable opponent, & unless I am returned, depend upon it he is the winning horse.[5]

Ever Yours | B DISRAELI

TO: **WILLIAM LEADER MABERLY**   House of Commons   1033X
                                              Friday [17? January 1840]

ORIGINAL: PS 1535

PUBLICATION HISTORY: A catalogue page received from Donald Mopsik, with item 31 described as 'Autograph Letter Signed, 4 pages 8vo, House of Commons, "Friday", no date but ca 1840 ... to [William Leader] Maberly ... marked "private".' Matter after the page break (the letter's fourth page) is courtesy of International Autograph Auctions Ltd., online at www.autographauctions.co.uk/; item 750.

EDITORIAL COMMENT: *Dating*: by context; see nn1&2.

As members of parliament have been deprived of their privilege of receiving letters free,[1] it seems to me but just, that they should at least be placed on an equality of convenience with the rest of the Public & that they should enjoy the common advan-

---

1 Francis Bonham was the unofficial Tory party organizer for elections; see, for example, II **473**&n4.
2 John Neale was an agent for Lord Carrington.
3 Alexander Ramey Home, 10th Earl of Home (1769-1841), LL of Berwickshire 1794-1841, col Berwickshire Militia, Representative Peer (Scotland) 1807-41, in 1814 had assumed the additional surname of Ramey.
4 Sir William Young had been elected Tory MP for Bucks in 1835; Mr Norris may be John Norris of Hughenden House. At the 10 January 1835 Bucks elections, the Marquess of Chandos, Sir William Young and James Backwell Praed had defeated Liberals George Henry Dashwood and Dr John Lee.
5 In a 20 February 1837 Bucks by-election occasioned by Praed's death on 13 January 1837, George Simon Harcourt (C) would defeat Dashwood (L) 2,233 to 982. In the 1837 general election, Dashwood and another Liberal on 24 July would be unopposed at Wycombe; he would represent it until his death in 1862.

---

1 Prior to the introduction of uniform penny postage and the abolition of free franking on 10 January 1840, MPs had the right to frank and receive a number of letters gratis.

tage of having their letters delivered according to the direction these letters bear. Mine are all forwarded according to the direction which I was obliged to register with compliance / with the old system.

Might I take the liberty of calling your attention to this suggestion?

I have the honor

to be, Sir,

your faithful s[ervan]t | *B. Disraeli*[2]

1094R TO: SARAH DISRAELI [London, Tuesday 29 September 1840]

ORIGINAL: CRA [1]

EDITORIAL COMMENT: See III **1094**. D has used the convention of representing an upper case 'F' by 'ff' in script in 'LaFarge'. *Sic*: acknowlege. *Dating*: by the show of hands on 29 September; see n2.

½ pt 4

My dearest Sa,

I have just recd. yr. letter – which ~~com~~ arrives always abt this hour. I have heard from Jem since I last wrote, but he says nothing of his health tho' of his intended movements.

Devonport burned but / whe[the]r by Jack the Painter I dont know[1] – Alderman Harmer[2] this morning had the show of hands in his favor – & they say will be returned in spite of Publicola, the Voltaire of the back slums.[3]

Peace still continues the / order of the day.[4] I didn't read the trial of Madame LaFarge with any attention – which I regret – but it seemed to me that the French do not acknowlege any of our principles of the law of evidence – the mysteries of Orfila & the cadaverous smell remind one of a procés in the middle ages. I met a lady / a few days back who knew Madle – not pretty, but *bien gentille* in her appearance. There is a portrait of her in the Charivari which has an p̶ arsenic look – taken

---

2 This is evidently the letter D had mentioned on 15? January to Sarah ('I shall write to Maberly') in III **1031**. Maberly's reply (if he wrote one) has not been found. For D's use of the Carlton Club as a confidential venue for some of his correspondence, see IV **1214**n1.

---

1 The Devonport dockyard had been extensively damaged by a fire apparently deliberately set on Monday 28 September. *The Times* (29 Sep 1840). James Hill (with several aliases), known as Jack the Painter, in 1776 with French backing to aid the American colonists had set fire to the Portsmouth, Bristol and Plymouth dockyards, failing only at Plymouth. He was hanged in 1777.

2 James Harmer (1777-1853) was alderman of the ward of Farringdon Without 1833-40, sheriff of London and Middlesex 1834, president of the Newsvendors' Benevolent Providential Institution and member of the Guild of Spectacle Makers. An influential lawyer and vocal advocate for reform of criminal law, he investigated in particular cases where he considered that prisoners had been wrongly committed.

3 See III **1096**&n2. The election began on 29 September with a show of hands for the three candidates marginally in Harmer's favour, resulting in a call for a poll. Harmer's *Weekly Dispatch* regularly published controversial articles (advocating very advanced liberal religious and political views), among the most contentious being ones signed 'Publicola' (Publius Valerius Publicola was a Roman consul who died in 503 BCE). These evoked outraged letters and leaders in the press and induced a successful movement to block Harmer's election. *The Times* (25, 29 Feb, 4, 11, 12 Mar, 21, 29, 30 Sep 1840). MP in a 30 September 1840 leader summed up Harmer's offences: 'he permits the columns of [his] newspaper ... to be constantly devoted to the purpose of ... converting the humbler classes of society into a reckless and profligate multitude of Deists and Atheists.'

4 See III **1093**&n2.

in court. Walpole has no doubt of her guilt & thinks she took the idea of the white powder from Vivian Grey.[5]

On dit the Cabinet are united in rejecting the French propos[iti]ons.[6]

1000 loves!

D

TO: MARIE ÉTIENNE FRANÇOIS BAUDRAND · London **1315**XA

[Wednesday] 19 July 1843

ORIGINAL: PS 1533

PUBLICATION HISTORY: Maggs catalogue 1418 (2008) item 46, described as 'Autograph Letter Signed ("D") to General Baudrand ... 3 pages 4to with integral address leaf, London, 19 July 1843.'

By this post, I send you a copy of the "Times". I beg to call your attention to the letter of Mr. Smythe, which you will there observe.[1] That party of the youth of England, of which, many months ago, I apprised you & others, are now attracting very great attention in our Parliament, & throughout the country. The speeches of Mr. Smythe, Lord John Manners, Mr. Cochrane, & others, in the late debate on Ireland, have arrested public attention in the highest degree. In consequence of some attacks, Mr. Smythe through the medium of an address to his constituents, has put forth this morning a programme of these new, or rather revived, opinions. You will observe well how the alliance with France is definitely advanced as a political principle;[2] you will appreciate our courage & determination in doing this at a moment when we understand that considerable disagreement exists between the Cabinets of the two countries. I write in great haste, but wished to lose no time in drawing your attention, & that of one whom I never remember but with profound respect & affection,[3] to this very interesting & important document. If you can find a good occasion to write to me about Spain, I should be glad.[4]

---

5 See III **1094**nn1-3.

6 The cabinet had met on 28 September for the first time since the summer. Ridley *Palmerston* 236. There was at this time much cabinet division over the threat of war with France, but at this meeting, at which Palmerston updated cabinet on the state of affairs and ranted against France, no resolution was reached because of Lansdowne's absence, and the discussion was adjourned. For an account of the meeting, see Greville IV 320–2, quoted in Bell *Palmerston* I 310.

---

1 'To the Electors of Canterbury', a letter by George Smythe dated 18 July. *The Times* (19 Jul 1843).

2 Smythe (n1) reminded his constituents that he 'believed that the principles advocated by "the old Tory" party, now more than a century ago ... were still ... the soundest principles of Government.' He thought with 'the patriots of that day ... that in foreign policy the French alliance is the best guarantee for the peace of Europe and the prosperity of England ... and therefore my humble confidence is with a Ministry which is pledged to that alliance.'

3 Most likely King Louis Philippe of France.

4 Baudrand would reply from Paris on 5 August very pleased to see that D had managed to instil 'le parti de la jeune Angleterre' with his views, 'non seulement sur les affaires de l'intérieur; mais encore sur les importantes questions de la politique éxtérieure' [not only on domestic matters but also on important questions of foreign policy]. Baudrand said King Louis Philippe had maintained a policy of 'Simple Spectatrice' [mere onlooker] concerning 'les affaires d'éspagne' in the interest of 'le repos, la prospérité et le bonheur de la France, et la paix de l'europe' [the tranquillity, prosperity and happiness of France and the peace of Europe]. H B/II/101. *The Times* (n1) had carried the latest news on the ongoing Spanish civil war: a report from Madrid dated 10 July announced that the capital was now 'altogether dependent for its security and defence upon the National Guard ... Strong patrols perambulate the city'.

1487X TO: [UNKNOWN]   Grosvenor Gate, Monday 18 May 1846
ORIGINAL: PS 1531
EDITORIAL COMMENT: Black-edged paper. Text taken from an eBay online photograph of the single-page original.

Grosvenor Gate | Monday May 18 ⁄46

Dear Sir:[1]
If you could call upon me this morning, I should be glad to see you.
    Your faithful sert | *B Disraeli*

1511XA TO: THOMAS BAILEY   Carlton Club [Friday] 14 August 1846
ORIGINAL: WIL [1]

T. Bailey Esq.   Carlton | Aug 14. 1846

My dear Sir
Herein I send you £500 – Altho' the letter be registered, have the / kindness to acknowledge its receipt.[1]
    Yours faithfully | *B Disraeli*

1643AR TO: HENRY DRUMMOND   Grosvenor Gate [Thursday] 4 May [1848]
ORIGINAL: DUP [2]
EDITORIAL COMMENT: First page on black-edged paper. *Dating*: by context; see V **1643A**n1.

H. Drummond Esqr   Grosvr Gate | May 4
Dear Sir,
I have little doubt, that his Lordship is himself the correspondent of the "Post". If I remember right, it / is not the first time, that his Manifestoes have appeared in that Journal.
    I return you his letters, & the copy of / his resolutions. When Chaos comes, & we have an opportunity of creating order, we may set about working in this way; at present, we must be less methodical; a / little more bungling & practical.
    Ever yours faithfully | D.

1923R TO: LORD MALMESBURY   Grosvenor Gate [Wednesday] 21 November 1849
ORIGINAL: MAB [4]
PUBLICATION HISTORY: See V **1923**ph.

Grosvenor Gate | Nov. 21. 1849

---

1 Possibly publisher Richard Bentley, to whom D had been writing at this time. See IV **1486**, **1487**, **1488**.

---

1 D is paying the £500 bill mentioned by Bailey on 31 July (IV **1501**n4) as being due on 19 August. D on 6 September would describe it to Bailey as 'due 17th. Augt. & wh: was met' (IV **1518**). For the background to D's debt, see IV **1329**n1.

My dear Lord,

It is most vexatious, that we shd have missed each other, as there was no one with whom I more wished to confer than yourself, having every confidence in your intelligence and firmness, & shd., long ago, have written to you on many affairs / had I not found it impossible to write on subjects so complicated.

I probably leave town tomorrow, & have no prospect of being here again on the 2nd. Decr, as on the 5th. I have a Bucks meeting, wh:, in the present awkward condition of affairs, I must attend.

The / state of our Press is deplorable. I approve of your suggestion respecting the "Post" – but it would be as ↑well↓, I think, previously to communicate with Knox, with whom, I only, some months ago, had a casual conversation on the subject in the hall of the Carlton.

With respect to other matters, the scandal of our / provincial movement is great & flagrant, but I hope the evil is more superficial than it seems, & that, with tact & temper, the ship may be righted. I have spared no effort, nor has Beresford, but we have had to deal with a wrongheaded man.

Ever yrs sincerely, | *B. Disraeli.*[1]

TO: [LORD MALMESBURY]   Hughenden [Tuesday]4 December 1849   1929X
ORIGINAL: MAB [5]
EDITORIAL COMMENT: Docketed in another hand at the top of the fourth page: 'Decr 4. /49'.

Hughenden Manor | Dec. 4: /49

My dear Lord,

I have just received yr. packets: we are this moment going off on a run of visits in the north of the County & Bedfor[d]sh[ir]e, & I have only time to write briefly. My packet was carefully sealed, & never reopened by me.[1]

Nobody / has seen the letter to Christopher, *ex[cep]t yourself & Ld Henry Bentinck.* I did not send it to Ld Stanley, for I thought he was bored by the whole affair, & rather disgusted, as I was myself, a little.[2]

I send you back the copy, wh: you may keep, & use / according to your discretion, in wh: I have complete confidence. I shall shape my discourse at Newport Pagnell tomorrow in a way suited to the times, & I hope ~~to~~ in a manner to put everything very straight.[3]

I hope to have the advantage of conferring personally / with you either in town, or at Heron Ct., before the meeting of Parlt[4] – but I don't, at present, see my way very clearly about moving.

Yours sincerely | D.

1 See V **1923**&nn1-5.

---

1 Mamesbury's and D's packets have not been identified.
2 According to M&B (III 232), at about the time of D's 21 November letter to Malmesbury (see V **1923**), D 'also wrote a letter to Christopher, explaining his views in a conciliatory manner.' This is presumably Robert Adam Christopher. For the background to 'the whole affair' and the role of arch-protectionist George Frederick Young, see V **1902**&nn1&2, **1917**&n5, **1921**n2 and M&B III 232-3.
3 For D's speech at Newport Pagnell on 5 December, see V **1930**&n1.
4 Parliament would meet on 31 January 1850.

1949R

TO: LORD MALMESBURY   Hughenden [Tuesday] 1 January 1850
ORIGINAL: MAB [6]
PUBLICATION HISTORY: See V **1949**ph
EDITORIAL COMMENT: D has written his 'PS' at the top of the first page. Docketed in another hand at the top of the last page: 'Jan 1, 1850'.

Hughenden Manor| Jan: 1. 1850

My dear Lord,

My absence at Quart: Sess: prevented my receiving your very kind letter until today. I am very sorry indeed, that it is not in my power to have the pleasure of becoming your guest, as you propose, but I have engagements at home, from wh: I cannot extricate myself. /

Sir Robert's letter is pompous & trite. There is really nothing proposed in it, wh: might not have been done with equal propriety, if the Corn Laws had not been repealed, but he has succeeded in conveying an impression, that his estate is in bad condition, & that / he is conscious he has led his friends into a hopeless scrape. He always writes about agriculture like a cockney.[1]

I think Sidney Herbert is in a pretty scrape, 35,500[2] needlewomen to be deported at 15£ apiece (his own estimate) wd. take upwards of £600,000. He shd have subscribed at least one years income, as an example, / and if he succeeds in his object, wh: is impossible, he will do no good.

I am sure you will make a capital speech at Salisbury; but I wish the movement was not merely agricultural. Where are the other great interests (in buckram) that yr friend, G.F. Young, talked so much of?[3] Why does not Limehouse at least stir?

Ever yr ffl, | D.

PS. *Let nothing prevent you looking at the last art: in Blackwood on high farming in Scotland.*[4]

2202XR

TO: SPENCER WALPOLE   Grosvenor Gate [Wednesday] 3 December 1851
ORIGINAL: MIL [1]
EDITORIAL COMMENT: A letter pasted in M&B I, previously owned by the Holland family.

S.H. Walpole Esq MP.   Grosvenor Gate | Dec. 3. 51

My dear Walpole,

I will meet you at the Carlton tomorrow (Thursday) at ½ past four o'ck.[1]

Yours sincerely | D.

---

1 This sentence is omitted in Malmesbury I 256.
2 This figure is 35,000 in Malmesbury I 256.
3 This sentence begins 'There' and omits the question mark in Malmesbury I 256.
4 See V **1949**&nn1-3.

---

1 See VII **2202X**, V **2201**&n1 and **2204**&n1.

Private confidential   Frystone, Ferrybridge | Jan 26. 1853
The Rt Hon | The Earl of Malmesbury
My dear M.

I have not been equal to the task of drawing up the New Pragmatic Sanction, wh: is
to reconcile town & country, & lay the foundation of a National party – but I / have
tried some of its points & tendencies on some of our friends here, & they bite.

We must have our eyes opened at last to the futility of attempting to govern this
country ~~by~~ merely by the landed interest, & not even by its complete power.

All democratic elements have / gradually seceded from our party; the Reform Bill
took away the Freemen; the Repeal of the Navigation Laws, the great ports.

Hitherto the Whigs, by pretending to lead the towns, have never given us an opportunity of conciliating / them. In their eagerness for place, they have thrown over
the urban interest, wh: is panting for revenge.

There is no longer any ~~material~~ difference in the material interests of town &
country.

From all I can learn from the best authorities in / this district, there is no real
democratic virus.[1]

The only change that cd. injure us is disturbance of the balance by disfranchisement & the formation of new electoral districts. It is not the multitude who care
for this: the most they care for is to have a vote: / those who urge the alteration, or
disturbance, of the balance, are the town leaders, who, under the territorial constitution, are excluded from power. Admit them, & they will be quite content with the
territorial constitution.

But none can do this so easily, & so effectively,[2] / as the patrician party. ~~It wd. be~~

FitzRoy Kelly says, that with respect to the suffrage he can prepare a measure, wh:,
while it wd.[3] be very popular, wd. consolidate & confirm our power.

These are rough suggestions, but they are / pregnant.

Direct to me after tomorrow at
    Viscount Galway, M.P.
      Serlby Hall
        Bawtry
          Yorkshire
where I shall be a short week.
    Ever yrs[4]
    D.[5]

1 VI **2480** has 'vivus'.
2 Stanley has transcribed the word as 'effectually'.
3 Stanley has transcribed this as 'should'.
4 Stanley has omitted the passage from 'Direct' to 'yrs'.
5 See VI **2480**&nn1&2.

2645X TO: LORD GALWAY Grosvenor Gate [Tuesday] 28 March 1854

ORIGINAL: PS 1539

PUBLICATION HISTORY: From Julian Browning Autographs (London) online, item 6556, described as 'autograph letter signed "Ever yours, D", to Viscount Galway M.P., regretting that he is unable to be present at the opening of the New Hall of the Sheffield Institute, because he will be spending Easter at home ... Grosvenor Gate, 28 March 1854.'

I hope to pass my Easter, tranquilly at home,[1] where I have not found myself for some months; & indeed, generally speaking, I have not time, or strength, to attend public assemblies without the precincts of my own county.[2]

2797R TO: LORD MALMESBURY Hughenden [Friday] 30 November 1855

ORIGINAL: MAB [8]

PUBLICATION HISTORY: See VI **2797**ph

EDITORIAL COMMENT: *Sic:* reigns; *Waleski.*

Confidential[1] Hughenden | Nov. 30. 55

The Rt Hon | The Earl of Malmesbury

My dear M.

It is very provoking to have missed you, & only by an hour!

It seems to me, that a party, that has shrunk from the responsibility of / conducting a war, would never be able to carry on an opposition against a Minister for having concluded an unsatisfactory peace, however bad the terms.

We are off the rail of politics, & must continue / so, as long as the war lasts, & the only thing that can ever give us a chance, is that the war should finish, & on the terms wh: may be now practicable. Then, we shall, at least, revert to the position / we occupied, before the fatal refusal to take the reigns last February, wh: lost us the heart & respect of all classes.

As a general rule, silence & inactivity shd be our tactics, but anything wh: indicates a desire to / conclude the war on honorable terms in this country assists the Emperor, & distracts & enfeebles Palmerston, who cares for nothing but his immediate career.

I shd. like very much to know, *whether the opinion you have formed as to the probable result of / the negotiations is shared by Waleski & Co.* Send me a line if you can.

Yours ever, | D.[2]

---

1 Parliament would adjourn from 12 to 26 April for Easter (16 April) recess, which the DS would spend at Hughenden (until the 27th). See VI Chronology.

2 Ebenezer Elliott had set up the Sheffield Mechanics' Institute in 1832; the foundation stone was laid on 1 September 1847 and the building opened in 1849. The 'opening of the New Hall' may be related to a 60-foot long frieze designed for the Institute in 1854 by Godfrey Sykes.

---

1 This word is omitted in Malmesbury II 37.

2 See VI **2797**&nn1&2.

TO: SIR WILLIAM JOLLIFFE · [London] Friday [26 February 1858] **3035X**
ORIGINAL: SCR DD/HY C/2165 [82]
EDITORIAL COMMENT: *Dating*. by context; see n2. *Sic*. Blackburne.

Friday

Sir W. Jolliffe

My dear Jolliffe,

When I left Ld Derby, affairs stood thus: If Ld. Lovaine did not take the Lay Lordship, H. Lennox was to go to the Admiralty & the Treasury ~~was~~ wd. then still remain unfilled. In that / case, we thought of putting Blackburne to the Treasury – vice Lennox[.] But a most important consideration remains. Nothing has been done for a powerful & discontented Clique – the Durham Clique.[1]

On the whole, I am of / opinion, that office shd. be offered to Vane Tempest in preference to Blackburn, if we have the opportunity.

Let Lord Derby know all this, & tell his Lordship that I fear the Ho: of Comm: is rather undermanned in these arrangements.

The / Chancellorship of the Duchy ought to have been in the Lower House.

We have lost the *Duchy* the ↑U.↓ Secretary of State – *Colonies* & *Lord in* waiting. ↑& *India*↓ [.]

It is fatal policy to starve the Commons.

We have gained nothing, for tho we have War Secy. we have lost War *U* Sec.

Yrs ever | D.

And we have lost India. Pray look to your list. I am alarmed[.][2]

TO: [WILLIAM RAINGER] Grosvenor Gate [Monday] 6 June 185[9?] **3362X**
ORIGINAL: UO [46]
EDITORIAL COMMENT: C of Ex paper, seal crossed out and 'Grosvenor Gate' written in.

Grosvenor Gate [Monday] June 6 185[9?]

The | Secrety; Carl: Cb.[1]

Sir

Mr Earle's address is No. 10 Downing St[.] He is still desirous of becoming a member of the Carlton Club[2] & / his political opinions are the same, as those, wh: the Club was founded to maintain, & wh: are, I trust, upheld by all its members. /

I am, Sir, | yr obedt Sert | *Disraeli*

---

1 Possibly a group of followers of the late 1st Earl of Durham, known as 'Radical Jack'. The Durham region was also home to some 'progressive' Liberals.

2 For the list of the Derby government of 25 February 1858 to 18 June 1859, see VII app II.

---

1 William Rainger, of 6 Evury Street, Pimlico SW, was secretary of the Carlton Club 1846-62. He had written to MA from the Carlton on 3 June 1859 vouching for the character of the person he had sent to manage her dinner party on 6 June. *LPOD* (1859); Sir Charles Petrie *The Carlton Club* (1955) 216; H D/III/D/840.

2 D has apparently given Rainger a 10 Downing Street address because Ralph Earle, who would become a member of the Carlton Club, was often abroad.

3481A TO: LORD DERBY   Carlton Club, Saturday [30 June? 1860]
ORIGINAL: DBP Box 146/1

EDITORIAL COMMENT: Carlton Club paper. Endorsed by Derby on the last page: 'Disraeli B.' *Dating*: Although the letter has in another hand been dated 'May 12', a not impossible date (see VIII **3470**&n1), the more likely date is 30 June 1860; see n1.

Saturday 6 o'ck

I have just seen Cairns, who seemed a little perplexed last night, but who came up to me today, to say, that he had, since fully considered / the objections of the enemy, as to privilege &c, in all their hearings, & was convinced they were "a complete mare's nest".

The fallacy was ~~to~~ confusing annual taxation with / permanent ~~ways & mea~~ revenue.[1] I urged him to call on you, wh: he did – in vain – but will see you on Monday at your Comm[itt]ee, being himself / engaged in the Ho: of Lords.

D.

3567R TO: HENRY ALMACK   Grosvenor Gate [Sunday] 24 March 1861
ORIGINAL: JWA [47]

PUBLICATION HISTORY: John Wilson Manuscripts (www.manuscripts.co.uk) item 24288, described as 'Autograph Letter Signed ("B. Disraeli") ... 3 pages 8vo on black-edged paper, Grosvenor Gate, 24 March 1861.'

The | Revd. Dr. Almack Grosvenor Gate | March 24, 1861 Sir,

I ought before this, to have informed ↑you↓ that I received, & duly presented to the Ho: of Commons, the petition from the parish of Fawley against the / unconditional abolition of Church Rates, and the great pressure of public business must be my excuse.

This is a great crisis in Church Affairs, for the Bill of Sir Jno. Trelawny is only part of a concerted movement, comprising other / measures against the union between Church & State: but I am hopeful as to the result, & have confidence in the awakened energies of the Country.[1]

Believe me, | Sir, | faithfully yours, | *B. Disraeli*

3764R TO: [JOHN SKELTON]   Torquay [Sunday] 28 December 1862
ORIGINAL: PS 1557

PUBLICATION HISTORY: *Contemporary Review* 39 (1881) 974; *Littell's Living Age* 35 (1881) 30-1. D's letter is quoted in Skelton's essay, 'A Last Word on Disraeli'. Stewart *Writings* 196 (#1441). See VIII **3764**&n1, a draft dated 'December 1862' and published as '[London, early-January 1863?]'.

Torquay, Dec. 28, 1862.

Dear Sir,

I am honored and I am gratified by the dedication of "Thalatta."

I entirely sympathize with the object of the work, which gracefully develops a tone

---

1 See VIII **3481**&n3. In his 5 July speech, D would use this distinction in his argument.

---

1 See VIII **3567**n1.

of thought and sentiment on the prevalence of which the continued greatness of this country depends.

Believe me, | Your obliged servant, | B. DISRAELI.

TO: JOHN FRANCIS MAGUIRE   Grosvenor Gate 3887A
[Monday] 14 December [1863]

ORIGINAL: PS 808

PUBLICATION HISTORY: Paul C. Richards Autographs catalogue 191 (1984) item 2, described as 'Autograph Letter Signed "B. Disraeli", on black-bordered mourning stationery. 3 pages, 8vo. Grosvenor Gate, [London] December 14, 1865. To Francis Maguire, M.P.'

EDITORIAL COMMENT: *Dating*: Richards evidently mistook D's '3' for '5', as D used black-edged stationery following SBW's death on 11 November 1863; see also n1, *Father Mathew* (1863). *Sic*: Matthew.

I am indebted to your kindness for a real accession to my library, & have seldom read a more animated & interesting piece than your biography of the admirable Father Matthew. I congratulate you on your renewed honors as Mayor of your ancient and celebrated city....[1]

TO: [JOHN SKELTON]   Grosvenor Gate [Monday] 16 May 1864 3924X
ORIGINAL: PS 1558

PUBLICATION HISTORY: *Contemporary Review* 39 (1881) 975-6; *Littell's Living Age* 35 (1881) 32-3. D's letter is quoted in Skelton's essay, 'A Last Word on Disraeli'. Stewart *Writings* 196 (#1441). See VIII **3331X**&nn1-4, an undated draft dated '[London, Thursday 7 April 1859]' to '[T.E. KEBBEL]'.

EDITORIAL COMMENT: Discrepancies between draft and published version include: Reform as 'a burning question with the Tories after the Rev of 1688' instead of (below) 'a living question with the Tories for the quarter of a century, at least, that followed the Revolution of 1688'; 'measures' instead of 'remedies'; 'scandal' instead of 'affair'; and 'accomplished' instead of 'nearly accomplished'. *Sic*: Hinde.

Grosvenor Gate, May 16, 1864.

Dear Sir,

I thank you for your article, which I received this morning.[1] I read your criticisms

---

1 John Francis Maguire (1815-1872), proprietor and founding editor of the *Cork Examiner* 1841, mayor of Cork 1853 and 1862-4, was MP (L) for Dungarvan 1852-65 and Cork 1865-72. His *Father Mathew, a Biography* (1863) is the story of Capuchin friar Theobald Mathew, founder in 1838 of the Knights of Father Mathew, a Catholic temperance society promoting complete abstinence from alcohol.

---

1 Skelton's 'A Campaigner at Home. V.–Politics: the Old World and the New', published anonymously in *Fraser's Magazine* 69.413 (May 1864) 591-600, would be republished (omitting the last section, 'Party Government', pp 597-600, from which the extract below is taken) as 'IV. Commodore Diamond' (pp 70-85) in *A Campaigner at Home* (1865); see **4029A**&n2. In 1881 (see ph), Skelton would write that D's letter 'throws a curiously direct light upon certain ambiguous incidents of his life. In an article in *Fraser* for May, 1864, the controversy between Lord Macaulay and Earl Stanhope (then Lord Mahon) had furnished the text for a discourse on the historical antecedents of our political parties'. He proceeds to quote a lengthy passage (pp 598-9), of which the following is a brief extract (with omissions in brackets): 'The *gage d'amour* which Lord Mahon undertook to defend against all comers was a somewhat startling paradox. "I cannot but pause to observe," he said, "how much the course of a century has inverted the meaning of our party nicknames – how much a modern Tory resembles a Whig of Queen Anne's reign, and a Tory of Queen Anne's reign a modern Whig." Mr. Macaulay lifted the glove. The modern Tories resembled the Whigs of Queen Anne's reign because the principles which these Whigs announced had been accepted by the Tories. The Whig had remained consistent; the Tory had come over to the enemy. [Mr. Disraeli, during the great Peel battle, illustrated the same proposition by a homely figure and in

always with interest, because they are discriminative, and are founded on knowledge and thought.

These qualities are rarer in the present day than the world imagines. Everybody writes in a hurry, and the past seems quite obliterated from public memory.

I need not remind you that Parliamentary Reform was a living question with the Tories for the quarter of a century, at least, that followed the Revolution of 1688. Not only Sir William Wyndham and his friends were in favor of annual parliaments and universal suffrage, but Sir John Hinde Cotton even advocated the ballot. These were desperate remedies against Whig supremacy. It appeared to me in 1832 that the Reform Act was another 1688, and that influenced my conduct when I entered public life. I don't say this to vindicate my course, but to explain it.

So, also, I looked then – as I do now – to a reconciliation between the Tory party and the Roman Catholic subjects of the queen. This led, thirty years ago, and more, to the O'Connell affair, but I have never relinquished my purpose; and have now, I hope, nearly accomplished it.

If the Tory party is not a national party, it is nothing.

Pardon this egotism, which I trust, however, is not my wont, and believe me,

Dear sir, with respect, | Faithfully yours, | B. DISRAELI.[2]

familiar phrase. Sir Robert had found the Whigs bathing and had run away with their clothes.] It may be questioned whether [Macaulay's] retort ... is entirely satisfactory. Is it fair to assume that a party must be inconsistent because it adopts a policy which, fifty years before, it had opposed? During these fifty years the world has altered. Truth, in a political sense, is a relative term ... Lord Bolingbroke correctly described the duty of a practical statesman when he said to Sir William Windham, "It is as much a mistake to depend upon that which is true, but impracticable at a certain time, as to depend on that which is neither true not practicable at any time." In this view the Tory who votes against an extension of the franchise during one century, and who votes in favor of its extension during the next, may be acting not only with sagacity but with consistency.'

2 Skelton would reply from 20 Alva Street, Edinburgh, on the 18th: 'I am very grateful for the kind expressions you apply to my desultory & fragmentary efforts. No one knows better than I do how very imperfect they are: but – amid the engagements of a laborious profession – it is difficult so to concentrate the mind upon literary work as to be able to produce anything permanently valuable. But ever since I began to think & write on political subjects I have been struck by what appeared to me your consistent & liberal conception of the nature & functions of the Tory party, & I have done what I could in different ways to support & disseminate similar views. I am inclined to believe that within a few years a great change in intelligent public feeling on this matter will be seen: & that you will find that the influence of your opinions has been greater than you at present imagine. I speak with special reference to our younger men, – whose repugnance to what they considered the narrow & selfish spirit of Toryism has been already removed. Let me add (if you will pardon the observation) that for my own part I have never doubted that there has been a real & vital consistency in your political views – the only consistency which sensible & honest men can value – & I am convinced that this is every day becoming more visible to those who choose to open their eyes, & who are not blinded by passion or spleen.' H B/XXI/S/277.

The following is a list of the Derby government of 28 June 1866 to 25 February 1868, including some of the permanent office-holders:

THE CABINET

First Lord of the Treasury	Earl of Derby PC (28 Jun 1866)
Chancellor of the Exchequer	B. Disraeli PC (6 Jul 66)
Lord President of the Council	Duke of Buckingham PC (6 Jul 66)
	Duke of Marlborough PC (8 Mar 67)
Lord High Chancellor	Lord Chelmsford PC (6 Jul 66)
	Lord Cairns PC (29 Feb 68)
Lord Privy Seal	Earl of Malmesbury PC (6 Jul 66)
Secretaries of State	
Home Affairs	S.H. Walpole PC (6 Jul 66)
	G. Hardy PC (17 May 67)
Foreign Affairs	Lord Stanley PC (8 Jul 66)
Colonial Affairs	Earl of Carnarvon PC (6 Jul 66)
	Duke of Buckingham PC (8 Mar 67)
War	J. Peel PC (6 Jul 66)
	Sir J. Pakington PC (8 Mar 67)
India	Viscount Cranborne PC (6 Jul 66)
	Sir S. Northcote PC (8 Mar 67)
First Lord of the Admiralty	Sir J. Pakington PC (12 Jul 66)
	H.T. Lowry-Corry PC (8 Mar 67)
President of the Board of Trade	Sir S. Northcote PC (6 Jul 66)
	Duke of Richmond PC (8 Mar 67)
President of the Poor Law Board	G. Hardy PC (12 Jul 66)
	Earl of Devon (21 May 67)
	[*not in cabinet*]
Minister without Portfolio	S.H. Walpole (17 May 67-1 Dec 68)
First Commissioner of Works and	
Public Buildings	Lord J. Manners PC (6 Jul 66)
Secretary to the Poor Law Board	R.A. Earle (2 Jul 66)
	G. Sclater-Booth (1 Mar 67)
Chief Secretary for Ireland	Lord Naas (later Earl of Mayo)
	PC (10 Jul 66)

CHIEF OFFICERS OF STATE NOT IN CABINET

Commander-in-Chief	Duke of Cambridge PC
Paymaster-General	S. Cave (10 Jul 66)
Quartermaster-General	Sir J.H. Grant (1865-70)
Judge-Advocate General	J.R. Mowbray (12 Jul 66)

Attorney-General	Sir H.M. Cairns (10 Jul 66)
	Sir J. Rolt (29 Oct 66)
	Sir J. Karslake (18 Jul 67)
Solicitor-General	Sir W. Bovill (10 Jul 66)
	Sir J. Karslake (29 Nov 66)
	Sir C. Selwyn (18 Jul 67)
	Sir W. Brett (10 Feb 68)
	Sir R. Baggallay (16 Sep 68)
Junior Ministers	H. Whitmore (12 Jul 66-1 Dec 68)
	Lord C. Hamilton (2 Nov 68-1 Dec 68)
Chancellor, Duchy of Lancaster	Earl of Devon (10 Jul 66)
	J. Wilson-Patten (26 Jun 67)
	Col T.E. Taylor (7 Nov 68)
Postmaster-General	Duke of Montrose (19 Jul 66)
President, Poor Law Board	Earl of Devon (21 May 67)
Parliamentary Secretary	R.A. Earle (12 Jul 66)
	G. Sclater-Booth (1 Mar 67)
	Sir M. Hicks-Beach (28 Feb 68)
Education	H.T. Lowry-Corry (12 Jul 66)
	Lord R. Montagu (19 Mar 67)
Lord Lieutenant of Ireland	Marquess of Abercorn (13 Jul 66)
Board of Trade (vice president)	S. Cave (10 Jul 66)

THE PRIVY COUNCIL

President	Duke of Buckingham (1866-8 Mar 67)
	Duke of Marlborough (8 Mar 67-9 Dec 68)
Clerk in Ordinary	A. Helps
Chief Clerk	E.S. Harrison
Vice President for Education	Lord R. Montagu
Science and Art Department	H. Cole

THE PRIVY SEAL

Lord Privy Seal	Earl of Malmesbury (6 Jul 66)
Chief Clerk	W. Goodwin

THE TREASURY

First Lord	Earl of Derby
Private Secretary	G.W. Barrington
Chancellor of the Exchequer	B. Disraeli (6 Jul 66)
Private Secretaries to Disraeli	M. Corry
	C. Fremantle
	C.R. Wilson (Aug 67-Feb 68)
Chancellor of the Exchequer	G.W. Hunt (29 Feb 68)
Private Secretaries	Lieut-Col T.E. Taylor (14 Jul 66)
	G.J. Noel (11 Nov 68)
First Secretary	G.W. Hunt (11 Jul 66)
	G. Sclater-Booth (4 Mar 68)
Assistant (Permanent) Secretary	G.A. Hamilton
Junior Lords	G.J. Noel (12 Jul 66-2 Nov 68)
	H. Whitmore (12 Jul 66-1 Dec 68)
	Sir G. Graham-Montgomery (12 Jul 66-1 Dec 68)
	Lord C. Hamilton (2 Nov 68-1 Dec 68)
Messengers to the Chancellor of the Exchequer	H. Gabbitas (1860)
	T. Turner (1864)
Solicitor	J. Greenwood

EXCHEQUER (RECEIPT OF)

Comptroller-General	Sir W. Dunbar
Assistant Comptroller	W.G. Anderson
Chief Clerk	H.W. Chisholm
Superintendent, Weights and Measures	H.W. Chisholm (1866)

SECRETARIES OF STATE'S OFFICES

Home Affairs – Principal Secretary	S.H. Walpole (6 Jul 66-11 May 67)
	G. Hardy (17 May 67-3 Dec 68)
Under-Secretary	Earl of Belmore (10 Jul 66)
	Sir J. Fergusson (1 Aug 67)
Permanent US	A. Liddell
Private Secretary to Liddell	E.A. Perceval
Foreign Affairs – Principal Secretary	Lord Stanley PC (8 Jul 66-9 Dec 68)
Under-Secretary	E.C. Egerton (6 Jul 66-12 Dec 68)
Permanent US	E. Hammond
Private Secretary to Hammond	T.H. Sanderson
Assistant US	J. Murray (1858-4 Jul 69)
Colonial Affairs – Principal Secretary	Earl of Carnarvon (6 Jul 66-8 Mar 67)
	Duke of Buckingham (8 Mar 67-1 Dec 68)
Under-Secretary	C.B. Adderley (6 Jul 66)
Permanent US	Sir F.L. Rogers
Assistant US	T.F. Elliot (to 1868)
Private Secretary to Elliot	H.S. Bryant
War – Principal Secretary	J. Peel PC (6 Jul 66-8 Mar 67)
	Sir J. Pakington PC (8 Mar 67-1 Dec 68)
Under-Secretary	Earl of Longford (7 Jul 66)
Private Secretary to Longford	S.G. Osborne
Permanent US	Sir E. Lugard (1862-71)
Private Secretary to Lugard	W.R. Buck
Assistant US	Capt D. Galton
India – Principal Secretary	Viscount Cranborne (6 Jul 66)
	Sir S. Northcote (8 Mar 67)
Private Secretary to Northcote	W.S. Northcote
Under-Secretary	Sir J. Fergusson (6 Jul 66)
	Lord Clinton (31 Jul 67)
Permanent US	H. Merivale
Assistant Secretary	J.C. Melvill

SCOTLAND

Lord Advocate	G. Patton (12 Jul 66)
	E.S. Gordon (28 Feb 67)
Solicitor-General	· E.S. Gordon (12 Jul 66)
	J. Millar (6 Mar 67)

IRELAND

Lord Lieutenant	Marquess of Abercorn PC
Lord Chancellor	F. Blackburne PC
Chief Secretary	Lord Naas (later Earl of Mayo) PC (10 Jul 66)
Attorney-General	J.E. Walsh PC (25 Jul 66)
	M. Morris PC (3 Aug-1 Nov 66)
	H.E. Chatterton PC (8 Nov 66-1867)
	R.R. Warren PC (1867)
	J.T. Ball PC (1868)

Solicitor-General	M. Morris (3 Aug 66)
	H.E. Chatterton (8 Nov 66)
	R.R Warren (1867)
	M. Harrison (1867)
	J.T. Ball (1868)
	H. Ormsby (1868)

THE ARMY

Commander of the Forces	Duke of Cambridge
Military Secretary	Maj-Gen W.F. Foster
Private Secretary to Foster	Col J. Macdonald
Adjutant-General	Maj-Gen Lord W. Paulet
Quarter-Master General	Lieut-Gen Sir J. Hope Grant
Judge-Advocate General	J.R. Mowbray
Chaplain-General	Rev G.R. Gleig
Director-General of Medical Dep	J. Brown Gibson

THE NAVY

Admiralty – Lords Commissioners	Vice-Adm H.J.L. Corry
	Vice-Adm Sir A. Milne
	Vice-Adm Sir S.C. Dacres
	Rear Adm G.H. Seymour
	Rear Adm Sir J.C. Dalrymple-Hay
	C. du Cane
First Secretary	Lord H. Gordon-Lennox (16 Jul 66)
Second (Permanent) Secretary	W.G. Romaine
Surveyor-General of the Ordnance	*vacant*
Hydrographer	Capt G.H. Richards
Astronomer Royal	G.B. Airy
Chief Constructor	E.J. Reed
Civil Departments	
Accountant-General	J. Beeby
Comptroller	Rear Adm R.S. Robinson
Storekeeper-General	R. Dundas
Comptroller of Victualling	C. Richards
Director-General of Medical Dep	A. Bryson, MD

COMMITTEE OF COUNCIL ON EDUCATION

President of the Council, Lord Privy Seal, First Lord of the Treasury, Foreign Secretary, Home Secretary, First Lord of the Admiralty, Chancellor of the Exchequer, President of the Board of Trade, President of the Poor Law Board

Vice President	H.T. Lowry-Corry (12 Jul 66-19 Mar 67)
	Lord R. Montagu (19 Mar 67-1 Dec 68)
Secretary	R.R.W. Lingen

BOARD OF TRADE

President	Sir S. Northcote (6 Jul 66-6 Mar 67)
	Duke of Richmond (8 Mar 67)
Private Secretary to Richmond	C.L. Peel
Vice President	S. Cave (10 Jul 66)
Private Secretary to Cave	W.W.E. Tennent
Permanent Secretary	T.H. Farrer (2 Jan 67)
Chief of Statistical Department	A.W. Fonblanque

Ass Secr of Commercial Business	L. Mallet
Ass Secr of Railway Business	R. Herbert
Ass Secr of Harbour Business	C.C. Trevor
Ass Secr of Marine Business	T. Gray
Railway Department Inspectors	Capt Tyler
	Col Yolland
	Col F.H. Rich
	Col Hutchinson
Registrar, Designs Office	W.W. Robertson
Registrar, Joint Stock Companies	E. Curzon
Registrar-General of Seamen	J.J. Mayo

DUCHY OF LANCASTER

Chancellor	Col J. Wilson-Patten
Vice Chancellor	W.M. James
Attorney-General	H.W. West

WORKS AND PUBLIC BUILDINGS

Commissioner	Lord J. Manners (6 Jul 66)
Secretary	A. Austin
Assistant Secretary	G. Russell
Solicitor	J. Gardiner
Architect and Surveyor	J. Pennethorne
Surveyor of Works	H.A. Hunt

WOODS AND FORESTS

Commissioners	C.A. Gore
	J.K. Howard
Solicitor	H. Watson

ROYAL MINT

Master	T. Graham
Deputy and Comptroller	W.H. Barton
Chief Medallist	L. Wyon

POST OFFICE

Postmaster-General	Duke of Montrose
Private Secretary to Montrose	J.L. Du Plat Taylor
Secretary	J. Tilley
Assistant Secretaries	F. Hill
	F.I. Scudamore
Secretary in Edinburgh	F. Abbott
Secretary in Dublin	G.C. Cornwall

BOARD OF CUSTOMS

Commissioners	Sir T.F. Fremantle (chair)
	F. Goulburn-Grenville (deputy)
	C.L. Berkeley
	R.W. Grey
	Col F. Romilly
Secretary	G. Dickins
Solicitor	F.J. Hamel

BOARD OF INLAND REVENUE

Commissioners	W.H. Stephenson (chair)
	C.J. Herries (deputy)
	A. Montgomery
	H. Roberts
	Sir A.C. Duff Gordon
	J. Disraeli
Joint Secretaries	T. Sargent
	W. Corbett

POOR LAW BOARD

President	Earl of Devon
Secretaries	G. Sclater-Booth
	H. Fleming
Assistant Secretaries	W.G. Lumley
	F. Fletcher

AUDIT OFFICE (*terminated 1 April 1867*)

Commissioners	Sir W. Dunbar (chair)
	R.V. Davis
	W.L. Maberly
	C.Z. Macaulay
	W.G. Anderson

REGISTRAR-GENERAL'S OFFICE

Registrar-General	G. Graham
Secretary	E. Edwards
Superintendents	Dr Farr
	J.T. Hammick
	W.H.W. Tytheridge
	W. Clode
	T.Oakes
	J. Shoveller
Registrar-General for Scotland	W. Pitt Dundas
Registrar-General for Ireland	W. Donnelly

LOCAL GOVERNMENT ACT OFFICE

Secretary (under Home Department)	T. Taylor
Med Inspector (under Privy Council)	J. Simon

STATIONERY OFFICE

Comptroller	W. Rathbone Greg

THE QUEEN'S HOUSEHOLD

Hereditary Joint Great Chamberlain	Lord Willoughby D'Eresby
Secretary	R. Burrell
Hereditary Earl Marshal	Duke of Norfolk
Secretary	W.A. Blount
Deputy Earl Marshal	Lord E.G.F. Howard
Private Secretary to the Queen	Lieut-Gen C. Grey (30 Apr 67)
Lord High Steward	Duke of Marlborough (10 Jul 66-22 Mar 67)
	Earl of Tankerville (22 Mar 67)
	Lord Ossulston (19 Mar 67)

Treasurer	Lord Burghley (10 Jul 66)
	Col P.E. Herbert (27 Feb 67)
Comptroller	Viscount Royston (10 Jul 66)
Master of Household	Major Sir J.C. Cowell
Sec to Board of Green Cloth	E.M. Browell
Paymaster of Household	W. Hampshire
Hereditary Grand Almoner	Marquess of Exeter
Lord High Almoner	Bishop of Oxford
Secretary	J. Handby
Sub-Almoner	R.W. Jelf (1846-71)
Clerk of the Closet	Bishop of Worcester
Deputy Clerks of the Closet	Rev E.S. Keppel
	Dean of Westminster
	Rev Lord W. Russell
Dean of the Chapel	Bishop of London
Domestic Chaplain	Dean of Windsor
Sub-Dean	Rev F. Garden
Coroner	W.T. Manning
Lord Chamberlain	Earl of Bradford (10 Jul 66)
Vice Chamberlain	Lord C. Hamilton (10 Jul 66)
Comptroller of Accounts	S.C.B. Ponsonby
Keeper of Privy Purse	Maj-Gen Sir T.M. Biddulph (30 Apr 67)
Lords in Waiting	Viscount Strathallan (13 Jul 66-1 Dec 68)
	Viscount Hawarden (13 Jul 66-1 Dec 68)
	Lord Bagot (13 Jul 66-1 Dec 68)
	Lord Polwarth (13 Jul 66-16 Aug 67)
	Lord Crofton (13 Jul 66-1 Dec 68)
	Lord Skelmersdale (13 Jul 66-1 Dec 68)
	Lord Raglan (13 Jul 66-1 Dec 68)
	Earl of Haddington (7 Sep 67-1 Dec 68)
	Lord Torrington
Extra Lord in Waiting	Lord Byron
Grooms in Waiting	H.J.W. Bentinck (1859-67)
	Sir H. Seton
	Col J.C. Murray
	Lieut-Col C.H. Lindsay
	Rear-Adm Sir W. Hoste
	Lieut-Col M. Sackville-West (1852-76)
	Lieut-Col W.H.F. Cavendish
	Col A.F. Liddell
Extra Grooms in Waiting	Maj-Gen F. Seymour (1 Jun 67)
	Sir C.A. Murray
	Lieut W.C. Stirling
Master of Ceremonies	Gen Sir E. Cust
Poet Laureate	A. Tennyson
Examiner of Plays	W.B. Donne
Principal Portrait Painter	Sir G. Hayter
Librarian	B.B. Woodward
Capt Gents at Arms	Lord Ossulston (10 Jul 66)
	Marquess of Exeter (20 Mar 67)
Capt Yeomen of Queen's Guards	Earl Cadogan (10 Jul 66)
Mistress of the Robes	Duchess of Wellington (25 Apr 61-1868)
Ladies of the Bedchamber	Duchess of Atholl (1854-97)
	Duchess of Roxburghe (1865-95)
	Dowager Marchioness of Ely (1851-89)
	Countess of Caledon (1858-78)
	Viscountess Jocelyn (1841-67)
	Viscountess Clifden (1867-72)
	Lady Churchill (1854-1900)
	Lady Waterpark (1864-90)

Extra Ladies	Viscountess Jocelyn (1867-80)
	Dowager Duchess of Norfolk (1843-70)
	Countess of Mount Edgcumbe (1865-81)
Bedchamber Women	Lady Caroline Barrington (1837-75)
	Viscountess Forbes (1837-74)
	Mrs George Campbell (1837-73)
	Viscountess Chewton (1855-1901)
	Lady Hamilton Gordon (1855-1901)
	Lady Codrington (1856-85)
	Lady Lindsay (1859-90)
	Mrs Robert Bruce (1866-89)
Extra Bedchamber Women	Mrs Pratt (1839-88)
	Lady Augusta Stanley (1863-76)
	Lady Charlotte Copley (1866-75)
Honorary Bedchamber Woman	Lady Biddulph (1857-1901)
Maids of Honour	Lucy Maria Kerr (1844-72)
	Caroline Fanny Cavendish (1847-81)
	Emily Sarah Cathcart (1855-80)
	Horatia Charlotte Stopford (1857-77)
	Harriet Lepel Phipps (1862-89)
	Florence Catherine Seymour (1864-70)
	Mary Louisa Lascelles (1865-81)
	Flora C.J. Macdonald
Gold Stick in Waiting	Lord Gough
	Earl of Lucan
Master of the Horse	Duke of Beaufort (18 Jul 66)
Chief Equerry and Clerk Marshal	Col Lord A.H. Paget (1 Jul 59)
Crown Equerry and Secretary	Lieut-Col Sir G.A. Maude (1859-94)
Equerries in Ordinary	Lieut-Gen C. Grey
	Lord A.C.L. FitzRoy
	Maj-Gen A.N. Hood
	Maj-Gen F.H.G. Seymour
Extra Equerries	Maj-Gen Sir T.M. Biddulph
	D.C. Fitzgerald de Ros
	Lieut-Col C.T. du Plat
	Col H.F. Ponsonby
	Col A.E. Hardinge
Honorary Equerry	Col A. Hamilton-Gordon
Master of Buckhounds	Lord Colville of Culross (10 Jul 66)
Hereditary Grand Falconer	Duke of St Albans
Physician to Household	F. Hawkins
Physicians	Sir J. Clark
	Sir H. Holland
Physician in Ordinary	Sir W. Jenner
Physicians Extraordinary	P.M. Latham
	N. Arnott
	Sir T. Watson
Physician-Accoucheur	Sir C. Locock
Surgeons Extraordinary	J. Hilton (14 Oct 67)
	P.G. Hewett (14 Oct 67)
	J.M. Arnott
	R. Quain
Serjeant-Surgeons	Sir W. Lawrence (d 5 Jul 67)
	Sir W. Fergusson (1867)
	C.H. Hawkins
Serjeant-Surgeons Extraordinary	J. Paget
Apothecaries to the Person	E.D. Moore
	C.F. du Pasquier

PRINCE OF WALES'S HOUSEHOLD

Groom of the Stole	Earl Spencer
Lords of the Bedchamber	Viscount Hamilton
	Lord A. Hervey
Extra Lord of the Bedchamber	Earl of Mount Edgcumbe
Comptroller and Treasurer	Lieut-Gen Sir W. Knollys
Grooms of the Bedchamber	C. Lindley Wood
	A. Temple-Fitzmaurice
Equerries	Maj C. Teesdale
	Maj G.H. Grey
	Lieut-Col F.C. Keppel
Private Secretary	H.W. Fisher
Honorary Chaplains	Dean of Westminster
	Rev C. Kingsley
	Rev H.M. Birch
	Rev C.F. Tarver
Physicians in Ordinary	Sir W. Jenner
	E. Sieveking
Surgeons in Ordinary	J. Paget
	G. Pollock
Surgeon Extraordinary	J. Minter
Honorary Physicians	T.K. Chambers
	W.H. Acland
	A. Armstrong
Lord Warden of Stannaries	Lord Portman
Secretary to the Duchy of Cornwall	J.W. Bateman
Keeper of Privy Seal	H.W. Fisher
Attorney-General	Sir W.J. Alexander

PRINCESS OF WALES'S HOUSEHOLD

Chamberlain	Lord Harris
Ladies of the Bedchamber	Marchioness of Carmarthen
	Countess of Morton
	Countess of Macclesfield
	Viscountess Walden
Bedchamber Women	Mrs Stonor
	Mrs W.G. Grey
	Mrs E. Coke
	Mrs A. Hardinge
Extra Bedchamber Woman	Mrs R. Bruce

APPENDIX III

The following is the text of an undated draft (in DBP Box 146/2) in D's hand published in *Hansard* as 'REPRESENTATION OF THE PEOPLE. THE RESOLUTIONS *referred to by the Chancellor of the Exchequer, on the 11th February*' (see Appendix IV).

RESOLUTIONS

This House, having in the last Session of Parliament assented nem: con: to the second Reading of a Bill entituled "A Bill to Extend the right of voting at Elections of Members of Parliament in England & Wales", is of opinion:

1st: That the number of Electors for Counties & Boro[ugh]s in England & Wales ought to be increased[.]

2nd. That while one of the principal objects of such increase should be / to give adequate & more direct Representation to the labouring classes, it is contrary to the Constitution of this Realm, that any one class or interest should exercise a predominating power over the rest of the Community.

3rd. That the occupation franchises for Counties & Boro[ugh]s should be based on the principle of rating[.]

4th: That it is expedient to revise the existing distribution of Seats[.] /

5th. That it is not expedient absolutely to disfranchise any Boro, except on proof that corrupt practices have extensively prevailed therein.

6th: That in revising the existing distribution of seats, this House will acknowledge, as its main consideration, the expediency of supplying representation to places not at present ~~dis~~ en-franchised, & wh:, from their population & property, or from special circumstances, may be considered entitled to that privilege. /

7: That it is expedient that the system of Registration of voters in Counties should be revised, & assimilated, as far as possible, to that wh: prevails in Boro[ugh]s.

8: That it shall be open to every parliamentary voter, if he think fit, to record his vote by means of a polling paper, duly signed & verified.

9: That provision be made, by means of additional polling places, for greatly diminishing the distance wh: voters have to travel for the purpose of recording their votes. /

10: That a Humble Address be presented to H.M., praying H.M. to issue a Royal Commission, to enquire to what extent the wage-paid class of the population is in possession of the Parliamentary Franchise, both in Boro[ugh]s & Counties; how far persons in the ~~same r~~ receipt of the same rate of wages, as those now possessed of such franchise, are excluded from it, & the causes thereof: To consider the changes that have taken place in / the relative value of money & property in so far, as they bear on the electoral qualification: To enquire how far, without giving undue preponderance to any one class of the population, the parliamentary franchise can be beneficially extended: To investigate the operation of the Laws relating to Bribery & Corrupt Practices at Elections, & to suggest such alterations thereon, as / may appear to them expedient: And, lastly, to revise the boundaries of all Parliamentary Boro[ugh]s, so that, where the population has outgrown the limits assigned to them by the Reform Act, a scheme for new & enlarged boundaries may be prepared for the consideration of Parliament, &, subject to such consideration, to fix the limits of all Boro[ugh]s not represented in Parliament, wh: possessed, according to the Census of 1861, a population of not less than ten thousand (10,000) souls.

APPENDIX IV

'REPRESENTATION OF THE PEOPLE. THE RESOLUTIONS *referred to by the Chancellor of the Exchequer, on the* 11*th February*' published in *Hansard* CLXXXV (February-March 1867). There are significant differences between these resolutions and D's draft (see Appendix III).

In Committee on the Act 2 and 3 William IV., on the Representation of the People, to move the following Resolutions:–

This House having, in the last Session of Parliament, assented to the Second Reading of a Bill, intituled "A Bill to extend the right of Voting at Elections of Members of Parliament in England and Wales," is of opinion,

1. That the number of Electors for Counties and Boroughs in England and Wales ought to be increased.

2. That such increase may best be effected by both reducing the value of the qualifying Tenement in Counties and Boroughs, and by adding other Franchises not dependent on such value.

3. That, while it is desirable that a more direct Representation should be given to the Labouring Class, it is contrary to the Constitution of this Realm to give to any one class or interest a predominating power over the rest of the Community.

4. That the Occupation Franchise in Counties and Boroughs shall be based upon the principle of Rating.

5. That the principle of Plurality of Votes, if adopted by Parliament, would facilitate the settlement of the Borough Franchise on an extensive basis.

6. That it is expedient to revise the existing Distribution of Seats.

7. That in such revision it is not expedient that any Borough now represented in Parliament should be wholly Disfranchised.

8. That, in revising the existing Distribution of Seats, this House will acknowledge, as its main consideration, the expediency of supplying Representation to places not at present represented, and which may be considered entitled to that privilege.

9. That it is expedient that provision should be made for the better prevention of bribery and Corruption at Elections.

10. That it is expedient that the system of Registration of Voters in Counties should be assimilated, as far as possible, to that which prevails in Boroughs.

11. That it shall be open to every Parliamentary Elector, if he think fit, to record his vote by means of a polling paper, duly signed and authenticated.

12. That provision be made for diminishing the distance which Voters have to travel for the purpose of recording their votes, so that no expenditure for such purpose shall hereafter be legal.

13. That a humble Address be presented to her Majesty, praying Her Majesty to issue a Royal Commission to form and submit to the consideration of Parliament a scheme for new and enlarged Boundaries of the existing Parliamentary Boroughs where the population extends beyond the limit now assigned to such Boroughs; and to fix, subject to the decision of Parliament, the Boundaries of such other Boroughs as Parliament may deem fit to be represented in this House.

APPENDIX V

The following is the text of a memorandum (RAC F15 23) in D's hand published in *LQvB* I 396-9, the first three paragraphs and paragraphs twenty-seven to forty-two, omitting matter following 'The probable result', and in M&B IV 495-7 as 'some rough notes for a letter to Her Majesty,' omitting paragraphs fifteen and sixteen, the text ending at the end of paragraph twenty-eight with '[The rest is missing].'

Memorandum of an Audience granted by Her Most Gracious Majesty to the Chancellor of the Exchequer at Osborne, on Sunday, Feby. 17th. 1867

On the preceding day, Saturday the 16th, the Cabinet having been summoned to sanction the definitive propositions to be made on the subject of Parliamentary Reform to the House of Commons by the C. of Er. on Monday the 25th: Inst:, General Peel, after the propositions had been unanimously adopted by his colleagues, & after they had been modified in the interval since the preceding Cabinet to / meet his views, announced his inability to sanction any reduction of the Borough franchise & his intended resignation in consequence.

The confusion & embarassment [*sic*] of such a proceeding, at such a moment, were extreme, & as, by a fortunate chance, the C. of Exr had received Her Majesty's gracious commands to repair to Osborne on the following day, Lord Derby was of opinion, that it was an occasion to appeal to Her Majesty for Her aid & influence, & authorised the C of Exr to confer fully / & freely with Her Majesty on the subject[.]

The Chr of Exr. arrived at Osborne on Sunday the 17th, & had the honor of an audience of Her Majesty on the same day at 7 o'ck:

Her Majesty, who had been apprised of the resignation, in the interval that had elapsed since the arrival of the Cr. of Exr, expressed Her great regret at the loss of General Peel's services: he had been a faithful servant to H. Majesty, was an able Minister, & one personally very acceptable to Her Majesty, but, Her Majesty added "the / Reform Bill is more important than General Peel"[.]

Rumors had reached H.M. of the probability of some secessions of this kind; but they were not confined to one: Lord Cranborne had been mentioned; even Mr Hardy.

The C. of Exr. assured Her Majesty that Lord Cranborne & Mr Hardy had made the most earnest appeals in the Cabinet to General Peel to reconsider his course.

The C of Exr. then described to Her Majy. General Peel's conduct during the various phases of the policy of the Cabinet on the subject of Parliamentary Reform, from the re-assembling of the Cabinet in November / until the present time.

In Novr., Lord Derby proposed to proceed by Resolutions, pledging the House of Commons, in the first Resolution, to reduction of County & Boro' franchises, & ending with address to the Crown for a Royal Commission of Enquiry.

After Xmas, & as the period for the re-assembling of Parliament approached, it gradually developed, that the Country expected settlement, & that it required legislation & not enquiry. After much discussion, the Resolutions were re-modelled, the proposition of enquiry omitted, & they were to be brought forward as the basis of a bill.

Then / came the decision as to the notice of Parliamentary Reform in Her Majesty's speech from the Throne.

During the whole of this period, General Peel's demeanour was that of dogged silence. It alarmed the Ch of Exr, but Lord Derby felt certain of the General's standing by him. Lord Derby was alarmed about Lord Cranborne; the Cr of Exr not so; because Lord Cranborne talked, argued, & sometimes conquered in discussion.

After the Royal Speech, Lord Derby called the attention of the Cabinet to the final revision of the Resolutions, & proposed, that if the principle of plural voting, in the shape he recommended, was / adopted, the Cabinet sho[ul]d recommend that the Boro' franchise shd. be extended to every occupier rated to the poor, & who paid his rates. The Cabinet unanimously adopted this with the exception of General Peel, who said nothing beyond requesting, that a copy of the Resolutions sho[ul]d be sent to him. This was done, & the next day (Friday the 8th.?) he returned them to the Cr. of Exr. with a dry note; identical with one addressed, at the same moment, to Lord Derby; announcing that he could not support Household Suffrage, altho the difference between Household Suffrage, & Rating Suffrage, is quite as great as the difference between the Sun & the Moon.

The / Cr. of Exr. saw the General that afternoon at the House of Commons, & had a private interview with him. The Cr of Exr said that every possible concession shd. be made to retain him as a Colleague, & finally proposed that the line shd. be drawn at a £5 nominal rating. The General said he was perfectly satisfied.

This modification greatly marred Lord Derby's original ~~sol~~ scheme, & really was not nearly so conservative, as, to be practical, it involved considerable tampering with the Law of Rating, wh: is really the true Conservative principle of all franchises.

Her Majesty, here, requested some / details to be given Her Majesty on these plans, but, ultimately commanded the Cr of Exr to draw up a memorandum on the subject, wh: is, consequently, annexed to this note.

On Saturday the 16th, as before stated, the modified proposition was brought before the Cabinet for final sanction, when the General made the declaration before quoted.

Every argument was used, & every appeal was made to him, but in vain.

Lord Derby reminded him, that for many months, he had repeatedly sanctioned their first Resolution, wh: pledged the Cabinet to reduction.

Her Majesty / here intimated, that the retirement of the General, on this particular question, might not perhaps be so injurious to Her Government, as it wd. seem at the first glance, & that when the question of Reform was settled, he might yet return to Her service. Her Majesty then graciously invited the Cr. of the Exr to discuss this point before Her.

The Cr of the Exr, encouraged by Her Majesty's kindness, then put the ~~oppositi~~ opposite views before Her Majesty, for Her Majestys consideration.

On the one side, the greater chance of success in carrying the Reform Bill in consequence of the General's secession:

On the other, the advantage of / having a homogeneous Cabinet, & the weakness & injury, wh:, generally speaking, secessions at critical moments occasion – & he concluded by humbly offering his opinion, that, on the whole, it was more prudent, if possible, to retain the General.

Her Majesty then, most graciously said, She was willing & prepared to do anything in her power to support Her Ministry, as She desired, above all things, that the Reform Question should be settled, & added, that, if Lord Derby wished it, She would, certainly, write to General Peel.

C of Exr. said, that he might presume to answer for Lord Derby's wishes on this / head, as there was entire confidence between them, &, at the time of the first resignation, the C of Exr had suggested to Lord Derby to appeal to Her Majesty, but Ld. Derby, then, said he was reluctant to press too much on the Queen, whose personal interposition sho[ul]d be reserved for other quarters, &, he thought, he ought to keep his Colleagues in order. But this second resignation had changed Lord Derby's views.

Her Majesty then entered into the enquiry as to the kind of letter, wh: Her Majesty sho[ul]d write, & encouraged the C of Exr to offer his suggestions on that head. He presumed to / observe, that it did not appear to be a case for argument, or reference to details of measures, but rather for an expression of Her Majesty's deep interest in the question, & a declaration of Her Majesty's desire that a measure of Parly. Reform shd. be passed: but mainly an appeal to the personal devotion of the General, wh: was, no doubt, very great to Her Majesty.

Her Majesty deigned to listen to these suggestions ~~to~~ [*illegible deletion*] with interest, & mused as they were made.

Her Majesty then opened, with great frankness, on the delicate question, as to what was to be done in case of the General's persistance [*sic*]. What wo[ul]d Ld. Derby do?

The / Cr of Exr observed, that Ld Derby might, probably, try to obtain some additional strength, & as he was in communication with Ld. Grosvenor, might perhaps appeal to him.

Her Majesty did not seem to think, that young men of no official experience, & of no shining abilities, were fitted for such offices, as Secretary for War. Her Majesty said, that in her present state of health, she really had neither inclination, nor energy, sufficient, to educate boys for such offices, as War & Admiralty. She did not appear to believe, that Lord Grosvenor wo[ul]d accept the / office, feeling he was not equal to it. What then? Had Lord Derby none, among his own friends, on whom he could ~~reply~~ rely? Surely, he must have touched on this subject with the Chr of Exr?

Chr of Exr admitted some conversation had passed between Ld. Derby & himself on this head, tho' he feared it might be deemed ⸶presumption⸷ in him to touch upon it to Her Majesty, but, with Her Majesty's ~~op~~ permission, he would venture to observe, that the name of Sir John Pakington had been mentioned, as one qualified for the War / Department: official experience, great personal respectability & repute; & power of clear expression in the House.

Her Majesty seemed highly to approve of this suggestion: but such a step would vacate the Admiralty, a department not less important, than that of War, & one also in intimate relation with the Sovereign. Had Lord Derby any one among his colleagues of competent character & experience for such a post?

The Chr of the Exchequer suggested the name of Mr Henry Corry, as one not unworthy of / Her Majesty's consideration. Mr Corry, tho' not an old man, had been forty years in Parliament; had been Sir Robt. Peel's Secy to the Admy.; then Lord Derby's; a firstrate administrator, popular in the House, & beloved by the Service, to wh: he had once belonged – & he could speak.

The Queen highly approved of these names, &, with much feeling, directed the Chr of the Exchequer to express to Lord Derby the complete satisfaction, wh: Her Majesty experienced at these prospects[.]

Her Majesty then opened on the greatest question of all: Her / hope, that Lord Derby would not allow the defection of one, or even more than one, of his colleagues to induce him to resign his trust. She expressed Her hope & wish, that he would resolve to proceed until the great enterprise in wh: he had embarked was concluded, for, in Her Majesty's opinion, the highest interests of the State were involved in its settlement. Her Majesty thought the time favorable, & the occasion ripe, & believed, from what Her Majesty heard, that the / Opposition would not be of an extreme character. The question, Her Majesty repeated, must be settled. There was a lull now, but if the opportunity was not seized, there would be a revival of discord.

The Chr of the Exchequer felt justified in assuring Her Majesty, that Lord Derby was prepared to effect Her Majesty's wishes at every sacrifice, & was resolved not to quit the helm, until the settlement was concluded.

Her Majesty then, playfully, expressed a hope, that there would not be another Crisis. It was an incident Her Majesty particularly disliked. / And, then, a Crisis always came in May. Her Majestys health required frequent change of air, & she was then absent. Her Majesty had no wish again to be hurried from her Highland Home.

The Chr. of the Excheqr thought he could undertake, that there wo[ul]d be no Crisis, & then Her Majesty graciously dismissed him.

In the evening, General Grey received a box from Her Majesty, wh: he opened, & then beckoning to the Chanr of the Exr, they withdrew to the end of the room. The Genl. said "Here is the / Queen's sketch of her letter to General Peel, & Her Majesty says, it may be shown to the C of Er. & he ⸶may⸷ suggest any alteration that he likes.["]

The C of Exr read the letter twice with deep scrutiny. So much was at stake, that he wd. not have hesitated in making a criticism, had he deemed it necessary: but the letter appeared to him, both in conception & expression, perfect – & when he returned it to Genl Grey he said "on my word as a gentleman, I would not change the dot of an i."

Next morning, the Chanr left / Osborne, was obliged to repair to a busy House of Commons immediately on his arrival in town, but had instantly forwarded the box to General Peel.

The Chr. of the Exchequer cd. not reach Ld. Derby at his house in St. James' [*sic*] Sqr. until ½ past nine ⸶that evening,⸷ & remained with him till midnight.

The next morning, immediately after breakfast, Genl. Peel called on Ld. Derby, & withdrew his resignation & expressed / his determination to support *any* measure of Reform wh: Ld Derby might introduce. /

The Plan of Lord Derby for the Borough Franchise.

Lord Derby proposes to create four new Franchises.

1 Educational

2. Savings Bank qualification

3. Funded Property D[itt]o.

4. Payment of 1£ of direct taxation

And he further proposes, that any Borough occupier, qualified to vote for a member of Parliament, should, if he possess any one of the foregoing franchises, enjoy a second vote; but, under no circumstances, more than one.

If The House of Commons agreed / to this, every occupier in a Borough to have a vote, who was rated to the Poor, & who himself paid the rates.

The probable result would be this

Present Boro' ⎡Household⎤ Constituency, of whom 128,000 are now working men, 488,000 – therefore 360,000 propertied class.

	Propertied Class	Working Men at present
	360,000 Householders	128,000
2nd. Vote	271,000 Direct taxation	400,000 – General Rating Franchise
	50,000 Education	
	20,000 Savings Bank	20,000 Savings Bank
	701,000	548,000

Funded
  Propy   150,000
          851,000 /

No working man pays £1. pr annm. direct taxation, because, as the Income Tax is now drawn, ~~In~~ incomes of £100 pr annm. are not assessed on the first sixty pounds.

This plan would give a vote to every bona fide Householder – the needy & the migratory would alone be excluded.

The present qualification as to residence: in practice about one year & a half; would be retained.

APPENDIX VI

D's memoirs, written in the mid-1860s, contain some interesting descriptions of people and events from that period. The only year covered in this volume for which there are extracts is 1865. H A/X/A/73-76, 72. For the complete text, see DR 135-43.

1865

At Court; a renewed rumor that the Emperor of the French was seriously ill. Some one said to Brunow [*sic*] "But what is his complaint?" "That" replied the Russian Ambassador, "wh: ~~has~~ killed my late master, & so many of his predecessors. ↑No one can stand it.↓ The responsibility of arbitrary power."

I heard ↑him say↓ this. /

1865

At the meeting of the House this year when I went up to salute the Speaker, I asked part[icula]rly after his health: he had had a severe attack in the autumn. "I am all right" sd the Speaker "but how is your great man? How is Lord Derby? I dined with the other yesterday, according to custom, as you know. I have had the honor ↑too↓ of dining at yr right hand. Well yesterday, there was a young man (he is coming into the house now in scarlet uniform ↑*↓) who sate on my left _____ & [*written at the bottom of the page*] *Hanbury Tracy, who was to second the address. / and ↑at the end of the dinner↓ I said to him "Now you are a very young man, & if I were you when I went home tonight I would make a memorandum of what happened to day; something in this fashion "Mem: dined with the Prime Minister, who ↑is↓ was upwards of 80 years of age. He ate for dinner two plates of turtle-soup; ↑he was then served very amply to a plate of cod & oyster sauce;↓ he then took a paté; afterwards he was helped to two very greasy-looking entrées; he then / despatched a plate of roast mutton; there then appeared before ↑him↓ the largest, & to my mind, the hardest, slice of ham that ever ~~appeared~~ ↑figured↓ on the table of a nobleman, yet it disappeared, just in time for him to answer the enquiry of his butler "Snipe, my Lord, or pheasant?" He instantly replied pheasant: thus completing his ninth dish of meat ↑at that meal.↓ I need not now tell you what is the state of his health." This is a literal report of an anecdote told by the Speaker with much grave humor. ~~a few months~~

A few weeks afterwards: it was after / his first levée, he said to me "↑I know↓ you remember a little trait or two I gave you of our friend's health on the Treasury bench, because I believe you have been ↑pleased to↓ ~~mentioned it~~ what I said on that occasion. Now I will give you another bulletin. "He ↑did me the honor of↓ attend**ed**'g my levée last night, wh: by the bye the leader of the Oppos[iti]on did not do, & ↑was↓ graciously pleased to enquire after my health. "That" I said "was really / of very little importance: but yours, my lord, is a national affair. I venture to hope you have not entirely ↑dis-↓ regarded my representations to you on that head, & that you take a little more care of yourself than heretofore[.] "Oh! I do indeed" he replied "I very often ~~go home in~~ ↑take↓ a cab ↑at night↓, & if you have both windows open, it is almost as good as walking home" ~~at night~~ "Almost as good!" exc[laime]d: the valetudinarian Speaker with a rueful expression. "A thorough draught & a north-east wind!, And in a hack cab! What a combination for health." /

Dissolution of 1865. July.

The state of Lord Palmerston's health is really this. The gout, from wh: he never suffered much, is a pretence. The real complaint is an irritation in the bladder. Probably, there is nothing in itself fatal or dangerous, but its consequences are serious at his time of life in this respect; he is obliged to give up riding; his favorite & principal exercise; & the complaint breaks his ↑faculty of↓ sleep, wh: was his forté, & carried him thro' everything. Dr. Ferguson [*sic*] just before he died ↑(this spring)↓, said that six months must elapse before he / cd. decide, whether Ld Palm: co[ul]d recover from this complaint, but Dr Ferguson [*sic*], tho' a very clever man, is always an alarmist. His reign was the reign of terror. /

1865.

31st Augt. Mary Anne & I went to Raby & stayed a week. I believe it was the first reception of the Harry Vanes', since their accession. Raby a real castle – & vast: & tho' occasionally altered & "improved", not substantially changed in character. The general effect feudal & Plantagenet. Tho' the country in the vicinity not beautiful, the immediate domain well wooded: a herd of 400 deer, & red deer also: but they never blend physically & socially; they live apart.

The Duchess a brilliant woman; sister of Ld. Stanhope: she has the ↑quickest, & the↓ finest, perception of humor I know, with extraordinary power of expression; & the Stanhope wit; her conversation unceasing, but never long or wearying: a wondrous flow of drollery, / information, social tattle, ↑taste,↓ eloquence: such a ceaseless flow of contemporary anecdote I never heard. And yet she never repeats.

The Duke ↑makes↓ a very good Duke: tall & dignified, but very natural, & tho' not exactly good-looking, a good presence & a good expression of countenance, kind eyes.

Affectionate to his step-children. Hers by her former marriage with Ld Dalmeny, eldest son of Earl of Rosebery. The grandfather yet living.

Her eldest son, Dalmeny, seemed to me very intelligent & formed for his time of life (not yet of age) & not a prig, wh: might be feared.

His younger brother, Everard Primrose, 17, very promising.

Two sisters: one handsome, & both pleasing. /

Then we went from the ancient to a modern Castle, Lowther: a splendid domain: parks & deer, mountains & lakes. The house convenient, & handsome in the interior, but the exterior deplorable, as might be expected from the Gothic of 1800 & Sir Smirke.

As my Lord receives no ladies, but would receive my wife, a female cousin, Lowther, & her brother, were present, & the rest a silent, but not scanty, court of retainers.

Then we returned to the South, to Ashridge Castle, Lord Brownlow's; also a modern erection by Wyatt, but gorgeous, & in a vast ↑park↓ of wonderfully sylvan beauty.

Lord Brownlow, a good deal beyond six feet high, slender, rather bent, with one lung already lost, & obliged to pass the winters at Madeira, intellectual, highly educated, with a / complete sense of duty, & of soft & amiable disposition: living, as it were, on sufferance, but struggling to perform his great part. A devoted mother watches every glance & every wind; shares his ↑annual↓ exile ~~to Madeira~~, where she actually has not a single companion.

Brownlows upper part of the face, the brow, the eyes, very fine; his fatal deficiency, the absence almost of chin: the distinctive mark of man, for animals have no chin: so he was thought always ill-looking – but since beards have become the fashion & he has become old eno' to grow one, & that a famous one, he has turned out quite handsome. As Bernal Osborne said of a ↑once-ill-looking↓ ~~man~~ fellow ↑who became passable by being very hirsute,↓ "He has planted out his face."

Adalbert Cust, B's only brother, has both his lungs, is as tall, ↑well-formed↓ & one of the handsomest young fellows in England. The day he came of age, his brother ~~gave~~ ↑presented↓ him / with the title deeds of an estate of 6000£ pr. ann: in the north of England. Winston (I think) near Raby: I went to see it with D[uche]ss of Cleveland. The brothers were always devotedly attached ↑to each o[the]r↓ – naturally affectionate, their mother has studiously developed their mutual love.

Lady Marian a woman of commanding ability. Above the common height, a fine figure, but a countenance of animation & intelligence marred by a red & rough complexion. She always reminded me of Lady Blessington in face, when Lady B's beauty had departed – the eyes were the same, ↑extremely sparkling.↓ Lady Marian had also, like Ly. Blessington, very pretty hands, wh: tell ~~well~~ particularly in a large woman; well-shaped, & small, & plump, & white.

From ~~Ra~~ Ashridge we went to Woburn Abbey, & paid a visit of several days to Hastings Russell & his wife Lady Elizabeth, sister of Lady Salisbury. The present Duke of Bedford, lives / in perfect solitude, & fancies himself unable to encounter the world. I am told his abilities are good. He believes that his health is very bad: some say this is entirely imagination. Lord Carington, who knew him when he was a youth, told me, that he always hated his position, & shrunk with horror from its representation & responsibility. He detests the country, & country life: especially the provincial magnificence of grand seigneurs. "Let me live always among chimney pots" he says. ·

When he was of age, he was returned to the House of Commons, & I remember him there for a session: he soon retired. A handsome man: with regular features & fine complexion, something of the beauty of the Stanhopes (his mother was dau[ghte]r of Lord Harrington) & thin gold spectacles.

He must be now nearer sixty than fifty; nor is it probable, he will ever marry. He has two mistresses: one is his nurse; the / other he visits daily & dines with her. She is not faithful to him: That's now wonderful, perhaps not necessary. The only person in society he ever sees except Hastings Russell is Poodle Byng, who recommended him to marry ↑& get heirs.↓ "Why should I" sd the Duke. "Could I have a better son than Hastings?"

Hastings is his cousin, & will be, in all prob[abilit]y, the future Duke: a young man, at least he looks young, tho' he has been married twenty years – ~~very~~ good-looking, graceful, tho' ~~not above~~ ↑hardly↓ the middle size, very intelligent, well informed & well-meaning. The Duke gave him Oakley & £6000 a year, & expressed his wish also, that he wd. receive every year his friends at Wooburn [sic], wh: is kept up exactly as if His Grace resided there. Hastings has the entire management of the property; it is a principality. He prepares his budget every / year like a Chanc[ello]r of the Ex[cheque]r: all the expenditure estimated in detail, the proposed improvements, alterations, repairs; farm-buildings, churches, schools, cottages. The Duke goes thro' every item in his solitary London house with scrutiny, & intention. The Duke builds cottages wh: cost 240 or 250£ a piece to wh: 30 pr Ct. as Mr Bright ↑says↓ ought to be added for the expence of the plant in Wooburn [sic] Park where all the materials for all the operations of the estate are prepared, & wh: is an establishment as large as the hugest factories & workshops in the North. Hastings objects to these costly cottages wh: are let to peasants receiving at the most 10/ pr week at rents of 1s/ or 1/6 per week, so that they are to live with all these conveniences, even luxuries, with incomes necessarily inadequate to their dwellings & the tastes wh: they produce. /

Hastings showed some of them to Sir Edward Kerrison, a thorough country-gentleman, experienced in rural life. Kerrison was indignant. "These are not cottages" he sd "these are villas[.]"

Wooburn [sic] is fine from its greatness & completeness: everything that the chief seat of a princely English family requires. The house tho' not beautiful in its exterior is vast: ~~a~~ ↑the↓ great quadrangle when lit up at night with its numerous & flashing windows reminded Bright, he said when on a visit there, of a factory. Then there are stables not unworthy of Chantilly, a riding house, a gallery of sculpture, the finest private one perhaps in the world. A mass of choice & rare collections of all kinds wh: have been accumulating for centuries: splendid books, rare MSS:, ~~many~~ ↑some↓ fine, many interesting pictures. A park of 3000 acres, with great variety, & undulation ↑& wild scenes↓ you would / not expect in Bedfordshire: splendid oaks, unrivalled cedars; ornate gardens & wilderness drives[.]

And all this only 40 miles from town!

The Salisburys, our dear friends, & the Caringtons were there, & Cte. Pahlen, who gives the results of a life experienced in society with taste & terseness, & Odo Russell just arrived from Rome (where he is our Minister) viâ Paris.

He brought the new toy; Pharoah's [sic] serpent. Quite a miracle! A most agreeable party, wh: it cd. not fail to be with such guests, & such a host & hostess, for Lady Elizabeth is quite worthy of her husband.

The ↑predominant feature &↓ organic deficiency of the Russell family is shyness. Even Hastings is not free from it, tho' he struggles to cover it with an air of uneasy gaiety. /

1865

Lady Marian Alford (Ashridge) said "~~an author is never bored~~ "Posterity remembers only one work of an author, but what that work shall be, Posterity alone can decide."

1865.

Some incomes of our Nobility – authentic.

The Duke of Northumberland recently deceased had more than 150,000 pr. ann:.

The present Duke of Cleveland (Harry Vane) has £120,000. pr. ann: aggregating in himself the three fortunes. 80,000 pr ann: the Cleveland Duchy, enjoyed by his elder brother, who died less than two years ago: the Powlett fortune enjoyed by his second brother, Ld. Wm. Powlett (Duke William of less than a year) & his own considerable appanage, wh: was nearly half a mill: & wh: he had increased, previous to his accession, by economy. /

Lord Derby has £110,000 pr. ann:

Lord Lonsdale has about 60,000 pr ann:.

[*inserted below.* Note 1872. Lord L. died & left exactly double this.]

Lord Brownlow has 90,000 pr ann.

all these incomes clear.

The late Lord Beauchamp left Elmley, after very amply providing for the junior members of the family, £45,000 ↑pr ann:↓, clear. This family had a great talent for amassing. "It will soon be £50,000 pr. ann:" Ld.

St Germans, who was Elmley's uncle, said, when it was first mentioned, & ⌐who⌐ knew the Lygons well. I have heard, that the late Lord left Elmley £100,000 Bank St[ock], worth more than a quarter million sterling. Elmley was very proud of his personal property. Landed prop[ert]y was all show, he used to say.

The present Duke of Bedfords income is £220,000 pr. annm. & he allows £40,000 pr. ann: for repairs & agency. Duke of Cleveland / told me this, & said, that he knew it as [a] matter of business. Hastings Russell told me, that from his experience of the management of great estates (& he managed this), taking tithes into consideration, wh: he did, he did not think that more than 50 pr Ct. came net to the Proprietor.

Duke of Cleveland said that "notwithstanding all the stories about["], he thought Palmerston's affairs must be pretty well. He got nothing from Broadlands: that only kept itself up; but he had other property in Ireland & Yorkshire; tho' to be sure they might be mortgaged. Then there was Lady Palmerston's considerable fortune: a life interest in Lord Melbourne's estate not less than £12,000 per ann: & her Cowper jointure; at least 3000 per ann: & he always in office – & no children. Yet there always had / been these odd stories. But why he (Duke of C) thought he must be well off now was this. ["]Palmerston" he said "~~was~~ had been always a great speculator["], & some years ago he got hold of some slate quarries in Wales, & worked them with a couple of friends, one of whom was ~~his~~ ⌐the Duke's⌐ brother William (William Powlett, late Duke of Cleveland). Now he had to settle his brothers affairs on his decease; & he found to his astonishment that his brother was getting 5000£ per ann; at least for his share in these quarries, & his share was a very small ⌐one⌐ compared with that of Ld Palmerston.

2nd. D. of Wellington used to say with regard to Palm's ⌐embarassed⌐ [*sic*] affairs "The explanation is Hush Money."

~~September~~ ⌐October⌐ 1865
Lord Palmerston's last joke.

Lord Granville (Lord President) had a dairy farm near London: 100 cows, & they all died from the pestilence, now raging. And early in Octr., Ld. Granville suddenly married, a very young lady indeed, "sweet seventeen", he himself being upwards of 50 (tho' very young looking, & quite adapted to captivate the youngest). When told, P. said "So, having lost his cows, Granville has taken a heifer[.]"

Ld. P. died on the 18th. Octr.

His decease was quite unexpected by Lady Palmerston, who thought it possible, that he might not be able to bear the late hours of the Ho: of Comm: another Sess: but was resolved he shd. meet the ⌐new House of⌐ Commons in 1866 as their leader, because as the majority was returned as a demonstration of / confidence in him, he was bound not to retire. If, however, the late hours were found too great a trial, Ld. P. was to go to the Ho: of Lords, remaining Premier. And Lady Palmn. thought, that this arrangement might go on for years.

This may be quite relied on.

Almack, Henry 3567R
Austin, Alfred 4020
Baillie-Cochrane, Alexander 4129
Bailey, Thomas 1511XA
Bain, James 4177
Barrington, Lord (George) 4310, 4559, 4595, 4651
Baudrand, Marie Étienne François 1315XA
Baxter, Robert Dudley 4093, 4095
Beauchamp, 5th Lord 3996, 4042, 4046, 4050, 4057
Beauchamp, 6th Lord (Frederick Lygon) 3995, 4000, 4012, 4026, 4061, 4130, 4192, 4267, 4414, 4581
Bentinck, George Cavendish 4132
Bigg, Lionel Oliver 4005
Blewitt, Octavian 4032
Bonham, Francis 535X
Brixy, Mr 4421
Brownlow, Lady 4573
Buckingham and Chandos, Duke of 4189
Bulwer, Sir Henry 4218
Burdett-Coutts, Angela 4104
Cairns, Lord (Sir Hugh) 4182, 4486
Cambridge, Duke of 4621
Carrington, Lord 4253
Cattle Insurance Association 4067
Cleveland, Duchess of 4034
Clubbe, Charles 4016, 4066, 4070, 4619
Clubbe, Emily 4583
Coleman, Edward 4035, 4072, 4077, 4487, 4499
Conservative MPs 4068, 4303, 4314, 4401
Copeland, William Taylor 4014
Corry, Montagu 4137, 4143, 4147, 4150, 4164, 4172, 4183, 4184, 4187, 4188, 4190, 4191, 4194, 4195, 4196, 4198, 4199, 4203, 4204, 4206, 4208, 4209, 4215, 4217, 4220, 4221, 4223, 4224, 4225, 4226, 4227, 4230, 4233, 4235, 4236, 4237, 4238, 4240, 4242, 4243, 4244, 4250, 4255, 4256, 4260, 4264, 4270, 4271, 4272, 4282, 4284, 4285, 4289, 4296, 4304, 4306, 4307, 4308, 4309, 4311, 4313, 4315, 4319, 4325, 4327, 4330, 4336, 4360, 4361, 4362, 4364, 4365, 4367, 4368, 4371, 4375, 4378, 4379, 4386, 4392, 4393, 4397, 4402, 4406, 4407, 4415, 4422, 4426, 4427, 4430, 4432, 4435, 4443, 4445, 4446, 4447, 4450, 4457, 4477, 4481, 4483, 4496, 4500, 4505, 4510, 4512, 4523, 4527, 4531, 4544, 4546, 4547, 4555, 4567, 4570, 4574, 4575, 4593, 4596, 4600, 4604, 4609, 4617, 4622, 4624, 4626, 4641, 4643, 4645, 4646, 4647, 4648, 4649, 4650
Cotter, W. 4569
Cranborne, Lord 4292, 4358
Cruikshank Committee 4109
Dalmeny, Lord 4201, 4509, 4514, 4610
Delane, John 4021
Denison, Alfred 4434

Denison, John Evelyn 4051

Derby, Lord 3481A, 4009, 4027, 4030, 4033, 4038, 4060, 4081, 4085, 4103, 4116, 4117, 4118, 4119, 4121, 4123, 4124, 4135, 4140, 4142, 4146, 4152, 4154, 4175, 4202, 4207, 4212, 4216, 4228, 4229, 4246, 4249, 4261, 4262, 4263, 4266, 4274, 4288, 4291, 4293, 4298, 4302, 4305, 4316, 4317, 4318, 4320, 4322, 4323, 4338, 4341, 4343, 4344, 4345, 4346, 4347, 4348, 4350, 4351, 4353, 4354, 4355, 4356, 4357, 4366, 4369, 4373, 4376, 4381, 4382, 4384, 4387, 4391, 4404, 4413, 4452, 4456, 4461, 4463, 4473, 4478, 4482, 4485, 4492, 4494, 4501, 4518, 4526, 4530, 4545, 4557, 4560, 4565, 4572, 4625, 4628, 4629, 4632

Dick, William W.F. 3994, 4091

Dickens, Charles 4455

Disraeli, Mary Anne 3991, 3993, 3998, 3999, 4002, 4007, 4110, 4111, 4158, 4160, 4167, 4185, 4268, 4333, 4339, 4399, 4417, 4425, 4439, 4459, 4466, 4471, 4474, 4542, 4568, 4598, 4599, 4602, 4603, 4605, 4606, 4607, 4608, 4613, 4616, 4633

Disraeli, Ralph 4394, 4408

Disraeli, Sarah 414X, 1094R

Drummond, Henry 1643AR

Dundas, Emily 4563

Dundas, Robert 4525

Earle, Ralph 4045, 4049, 4054, 4098, 4102, 4105, 4120, 4125, 4138, 4165

Editor of *The Times* 4144

Edwards, Sir Henry 4193, 4520

Egerton, Algernon 4540

Elcho, Lord 4006, 4096, 4214

Electors of Bucks 4013, 4019, 4024, 4127

Fane, John William 4644

Fane, Victoria Temple 4205

Fell, George 4200

Forsyth, William 4276

Fox, William J. 264XR

Fremantle, Charles 4169, 4176, 4286, 4290, 4295, 4300, 4410

Fremantle, Thomas 4281

Gainsborough, Lady 4420, 4429

Galway, Lord 2645X

Gladstone, Sir Thomas 4128, 4537

Gladstone, William 4064, 4585

Gleig, C.E.S. (Edward) 4018, 4036

Gordon, Edward Strathearn 4554, 4562

Grey, Charles 4232, 4372, 4412, 4479, 4484, 4541, 4556

Grey, Lord 4106, 4107

Grote, George 4265

Hamilton, George Alexander 4156

Hannay, James 4134

Hardy, Gathorne 4283, 4403, 4418, 4438, 4623, 4636, 4639

Hartington, Lord 4087

Hartley, James 4564

Hay, Sir John Dalrymple- 4241

Hennessy, John Pope 4028

Hepburn, B. 4076

Heytesbury, Lord 4063

Hill, Alsager Hay 4108

Houghton, Lord 4040

Hunt, George Ward 4507, 4594

Hunt, James 3979

Hylton, Lord (Sir William Jolliffe) 3035X, 4100, 4495

Kebbel, Thomas 4332

Kelly, Sir Fitzroy 4073

Lambert, John 4497

Lee, Frederick George 3983, 4003

Lee, Thomas Faulkner 4533

Lennox, Lord Henry 3989, 4092

Leslie, William 3988

Liddell, Henry 4114

Lonsdale, Lord 3997, 4039, 4044, 4052, 4126, 4133, 4389, 4437, 4502

Lowther, William 4506

Maberly, William Leader 1033X

Maguire, John 3887A

Malmesbury, Lord 1923R, 1929X, 1949R, 2480R, 2797R, 4470

Manners, Lady John 4383

Manners, Lord John 4122, 4179, 4635

Manning, Henry 4409, 4441, 4614, 4640

Marlborough, Duke of 4442

Maxwell, Sir William Stirling 4534, 4637

Mayo, Lord (Naas) 4141, 4178, 4254, 4489, 4490, 4503, 4508, 4532, 4627

McKenna, Joseph Neal 4115

McLagan, Peter 4337

Michell, Amelia 4136

Montagu, Andrew 4170

Negrete, Pedro Romulo 4586, 4587, 4589

Nevill, Lady Dorothy 4001

Newdegate, Charles 4335

Newton, Charles Thomas 4275

Northcote, Sir Stafford 4074, 4082, 4084, 4234, 4247, 4287, 4301, 4352, 4363, 4475, 4522, 4539, 4597, 4612

Padwick, Henry 4528

Pakington, Sir John 4251, 4257, 4620

Palk, Sir Lawrence 4010

Panizzi, Anthony 4273

Parrott, Joseph 4197

Peel, Jonathan 4222

Phillipps, Sir Thomas 4476, 4631

Plunket, David 4090

Poole, Reginald Stuart 4566

Potter, Thomas Bayley 4149

Powell, William 4173

Rainger, William 3362X

Rennie, Charles Colleton 4094

Ridley, Sir Matthew 4538

Ridgway, Robert 4062

Roebuck, John 4548, 4556A

Rogers, James Thorold 4097

Rose, Philip 3980, 3982, 3985, 3990, 4008, 4037, 4041, 4058, 4078, 4079, 4080, 4099, 4101, 4326, 4329
    4517, 4549, 4582, 4618

Rosslyn, Lord 4552

Rothschild, Charlotte, Baroness Lionel de 4062A, 4297, 4390,
4578, 4579, 4590

Rothschild, Juliana, Baroness Mayer de 3986, 4112, 4113

Rothschild, Louisa, Lady Anthony de 4131, 4239, 4252, 4576, 4584 Rothschild, Leopold de 3984

Ryde, Henry Thomas 4031

Salisbury, Lord 4017, 4043

Shaftesbury, Lord 4004

Skelton, John 3764R, 3924X, 4029A

Smiles, Samuel 4065

Smith, John Benjamin 4591

Smith, William H. 4023

Spencer, Eliza 4615

Spofforth, Markham 4025, 4071, 4089, 4180, 4245

Stanhope, Lord 3992, 4011, 4069, 4083, 4171, 4634

Stanley, Lord 4048, 4053, 4055, 4056, 4059, 4075, 4139, 4174, 4258, 4259, 4294, 4299, 4395, 4396, 4411,
    4419, 4513, 4515, 4521, 4529, 4550, 4551, 4553, 4561, 4577, 4601, 4630, 4642

Stracey, Sir Henry 3987, 4571

Synge, William Follett 4029

Unknown 1487X, 4015, 4022, 4088, 4145, 4231

INDEX TO VOLUME NINE

The references in this index are to letter numbers; bolded numbers denote main notes for persons; numbers ending in 'x', 'xA', or 'R' refer to letters in appendix I unless preceded by a roman numeral denoting a previous volume.

4222n6, 4262, 4340&n4, 4343&nn3&5, 4377&n3, 4383n1, 4386n3, 4387n1, 4403&nn1&4, 4433&n2, 4447n1, 4454, 4465, 4542n5, 4592

Bright, Priscilla 4447n1

Brighton 4089&n3

Brill, Bucks 4197&n1

Bristol 4465n1

Bristol, Marquis of v **1675n8**, 4478

Bristol Channel 4632&n3

British Almanac 4290&n6

British Army 4480&n1; in India 4293n3; purchase system 4424&nn2&4; in Abyssinia 4482n3

British Columbia 4614n2

British Gold Coast 4209n4

British Museum 3992&nn1-4, 4085, 4269&nn2-5, 4275&n2, 4279, 4476n3, 4479&nn1&4, 4482, 4566nn1&2&6, 4596&nn3&4

British North America Bill and Act (1867) 4222n5, 4261n2, 4632n2

Brixy, Mr (butler or valet) **4421&n1**, 4612n1

Bromley, Davenport 3988n2

Brontë, Charlotte 4029An1, 4032n2

Brooks, Robert 3988n2

Brooks's Club 4505&n4

Brougham and Vaux, 1st Baron I **105n1** 414x&n2

Brown, George 4004n1

Brown, Lancelot 'Capability' 4496n2, 4563n2

Browne, Lord John Thomas (4th Marquess of Sligo 1896) **4141&n6**

Browne, Sir Thomas 4635n1

Brownlow, Dowager Countess (1st Earl) II **408n17** 4573&nn1&2

Brownlow, 2nd Earl VII **2968n1**, 4326&n2

Brownlow, 3rd Earl **4526&n5**

Bruce, Sir Frederick 4196n4, **4529&n2**, 4550nn6&7

Bruce, Sir James Knight- 4228nn2&3, **4234&n2**

Brunel, Isambard 4508n2

Brunnow, Philip Ivanovich, Baron (later Count) v **1675n5**, 4419&n6

Buccleuch, 5th Duke of I **306n5**, 4184n1, 4512n1

Buchan, Dowager Countess of VIII **3862n5**, 4045&n6

Buckingham 4062, 4089n3, 4124

Buckingham and Chandos, Duchess of (3rd Duke) III **936n2**, 4120n3, 4124&n4, 4195n2, 4197n1, 4632n1, 4635&n1

Buckingham and Chandos, 2nd Duke of I **352n3**, 4199&n6, 4219n1, 4341, 4385n8

Buckingham and Chandos, 3rd Duke of III **936n2**, 4058n2, 4062n3, 4117, 4189&nn1&3&4, 4191&n5, 4195n2, 4198, 4229n2, 4249n5, 4359n2, 4377&nn6&7, 4381&nn3&4, 4415n3, 4438, 4485, 4630, 4632&nn1&3

Buckingham Palace 4233

Buckinghamshire 1923R, 1929X, 3987&nn1&3, 4013, 4021, 4023, 4024, 4067&ec, 4124n4, 4127, 4189, 4224, 4229, 4253&n1, 4254, 4295&n1, 4499, 4503&n5, 4520, 4643

Buckland, F. 4067ec

Bucks Chronicle 4144n2

Bucks Herald 3988n2, 4031&nn1&2, 4068ec, 4198n3, 4200n1, 4215n1; reports D's address to the Crown (6 May 1865) 4002n1; D's letter to Bucks electors (8 Jul 1865) 4013n4; D's nomination speech (14 Jul 1865) 4021n1; Aylesbury meeting about cattle plague (18 Nov 1865) 4058n2; rinderpest commissioners' report (18 Nov 1865) 4052n1

the Budget: (Oct 1866) 4251&n5, 4257&n1, 4299n2; (Apr 1867) 4391&nn2&3, 4398&n1; (Feb 1866) 4398n1; (Apr 1852) 4398&n2; (Apr 1853) 4398n2; (Nov 1867) 4595&n1, 4597&n1, 4598&n3

Buenos Ayres 4506&n2, 4529n1

Bulley, John F. 4187n3

Buloz, François 4519n2

Bulstrode Park 4001&n2

Bulwer, Sir Henry (1st Baron Dalling and Bulwer 1871) I **107n3** 4218&n1, 4567&n3

Burghley, Baron. *See* Exeter, 3rd Marquess of

Burghley, Baroness. *See* Exeter, Marchioness of (3rd Marquess)

Burghley House 3982&n2, 3986

Burke, Thomas 4444n3

Burke, Viscount (2nd Marquess of Clanricarde 1874) 4503n1

Burlington House 4179n1

Burnet, Gilbert **4015&n1**

Bushy Park 4169&n2

Butt, Isaac v **1936n4**, 4565n1

Buxton, Charles 4150n3, 4163n1

Byron, 7th Baron III **909n5**, 4015&n3, 4383n2, 4509

Cadogan, 4th Earl VII **2998n5**, 4495n2

Cairns, Baroness (1st Baron) (Countess Cairns 1878) **4182&n5**

Cairns, Lady (Sir Hugh). *See* Cairns, Baroness (1st Baron)

Cairns, Sir Hugh. *See* Cairns, 1st Baron

Cairns, 1st Baron (Earl Cairns 1878) VII **3048n1**, 3481A, 4140n4, 4148&n3, 4152n2, 4163&n2, 4182&nn1&5, 4228&nn2-6, 4234, 4238&n12, 4241, 4249n5, 4259n5, 4261, 4317n2, 4332n2, 4415&n4, 4424n5, 4430&n3, 4485&n3, 4486&n1, 4491n3, 4492n3

Caithness, 14th Earl of (Baron Barogill UK) 4145n2

Caledon, Dowager Countess of (3rd Earl) **4268&n6**

Caledon, 3rd Earl of 4268n6

California 4079&n1

Calne, Wilts 4089n3, 4291n5

Cambridge, Duchess of (1st Duke) III **973n3**, 4039nn3&6, 4492n4

Cambridge, 2nd Duke of V **2020n2**, 4474&n3, 4621&n1, 4628, 4629n3

Cameron, Charles Duncan 4482n3, 4515n2

Campana, Giovanni Pietro 4269n3

Campana Collection 4269&n3

Campbell, John McLeod **4543&n5**

Campbell, Mr (unidentified) 4567&n4

Campbell, T.M. 4244n3

Campden, Viscount. *See* Gainsborough, 2nd Earl of

Campden, Viscountess. *See* Gainsborough, Countess of (2nd Earl)

Canada: defences of 3999n1, 4251, 4257n1; deputation to London 4004&n1; defences of 4108n2; Fenian attacks 4127n3; reinforcements for 4191&n5; defences and Fenians 4216&nn6-9&11; confederation 4222&nn2&3&5; governor-general 4268n5, 4417n2; Stanley Cup (hockey) 4424n3; Grand Trunk Railway 4432nn1&3; railways 4488&nn1&3; Great Coalition and Confederation 4632nn2&5

Canning, George I **21n7**, 4238&nn3&4, 4491

Canning, 1st Earl VI **2387n7**, 4091n3

Canning Club, Oxford 4136n1

Canterbury, Archbishop of. *See* Longley, Charles Thomas

Capital punishment 4444&n3

Cardiff 4549&n1

Cardigan, 7th Earl of II **652n6**, 4207n6

Cardigan, 14th Earl of 4496n2

Cardwell, Edward (1st Viscount Cardwell 1874) V **2113n8**, 4104&n2, 4163&n3

Carleton, Dudley 3998n1

Carleton, Mrs Dudley 3998n1

Carlton Club 1033xn2, 1923R, 2202xR, 3362x&nn1&2, 3989, 4018ec, 4026, 4077&n1, 4078, 4124, 4300&n1, 4341&n7, 4345&n3, 4346&nn2&4&6, 4349, 4651

Carlton Terrace 4437&n1

Carnarvon, 4th Earl of VII **3033n7**, 4047n1, 4137&n2, 4198, 4322n1, 4340, 4341&n4, 4344n2, 4359n2, 4381n4, 4473nn1&3, 4478, 4542&n6; reactionary approach 4082&nn1&2; colonial secretary 4120n3; purchase of arms from US 4222n2; resignation 4338nn1&2, 4352n1, 4355n2, 4356nn2&4, 4358n1, 4376n1

Carrington, Baroness (2nd Baron) III **1082n5**, 4253

Carrington, Edmund **4536&n1**

Carrington, G.H. Hill 4543n2

Carrington, Mr (son of Edmund Carrington) **4536&n1**

Carrington, Sir Codrington Edmund 4536n1

Carrington, 2nd Baron I **134n1**, 535x&n2, 4253&ec&n1

Cartier, George-Étienne 4004n1, 4432n1, 4488n1

Cartwright, Mr 3981n1

Catholic Relief (Emancipation) Act (1829) 4238n7

Catholics and Catholicism 3924X, 4140&n1, 4167, 4207n7, 4216, 4226nn3&4, 4236&n1, 4438n4, 4490, 4640n2; temperance 3887An1; journals 3983nn1&2; Irish universities 4060&nn1&4; converts 4085n3, 4242n2; toleration of 4121n1; mixed education 4148n2; education of poor 4154&nn1-3&5&6; Jesuits 4238&nn6&14; Irish 4254&nn5&6; mayors 4362n2; Fenianism 4409nn1-3; Catholic University of Ireland 4441n1; Ireland 4501n4; midnight masses cancelled 4637&n2

Catholic University of Ireland 4060n4, 4441n1, 4640n2

Cattle Association, Buckingham 4062&n3

Cattle Diseases Prevention Act Amendment (No. 2) Bill (1866) 4045n5, 4189n1

Cattle plague. *See* Murrain (or rinderpest – cattle plague)

Cattle Plague Bill (1866) 4045n5

the Cave. *See* Adullamites

Cave, Stephen VIII **3653n4**, 4111n2, 4135&n9, 4191&n3, 4222&n1, 4274&n1, 4341

Cecil, Lady Robert. *See* Cranborne, Viscountess (4th Viscount)

Cecil, Lord Edgar Algernon Robert 4195n1

Cecil, Lord Eustace VIII **3833n4** 4369&n6

Cecil, Lord Robert. *See* Cranborne, 4th Viscount

Cecil family 4124&n3

Ceeley, Robert 4052n1

Census (1861) 4106, 4293, 4435n1

Census (1871) 4106

Central Anti-Malt-Tax Association 4074n2

Chalfont St Giles 4650&n1

Chambers, Montagu 4588nn2&3

Charivari 1094R

Charles I 4247n4

Charles II 4124n5, 4247n4

Charlotte, Queen VII **2948n2**, 4280n3

Chatham, 1st Earl of (Pitt the Elder) IV **1396n1** 4419&n8, 4513

Chatterton, Hedges Eyre 4444n1

Chelmsford, 1st Baron III **863n5**, 4120n3, 4219n3, 4227&n1, 4238&n11, 4286&n1, 4289, 4359n2, 4450, 4489n4, 4492&n3, 4565n1, 4632&n1

Cheltenham 4347&n1

Cheshire 4251&n2

Chevening House 4069&n1, 4171n3

Childers, Hugh VII **3393n1**, 4135&n1, 4142n2, 4313n3, 4373n2

Chile 4258n1

Chiltern Hills 4195&n3

China 4196n4, 4507nn1&2

China War 4597n2

Christian, Jonathan 4178n1

Christian, Prince of Schleswig-Holstein 4126n2, 4268&n3, **4417&n1**

Christian, Princess of Schleswig-Holstein VIII **3810n3**, 4126n2, 4268&n3, 4337n2, 4417n1, 4541&n1

Christian August, Duke of Schleswig-Holstein-Sonderburg-Augustenburg 4417n1

Christie, Manson & Woods (autioneers) 4517n1

Christopher, Robert Adam (later Nisbet-Hamilton) III **891n2**, 1929x&n2

Chronicle 4091n5

Church and State Gazette Office 4194n4

Church and State Review 4026n5, 4061&n3

Churchill, Baroness (2nd Baron) VII **3085n2**, 4417

Churchill, Lady Cornelia Spencer (Lady Cornelia Guest 1868; Baroness Wimborne 1880) 4509n1, **4610&nn1&3**

Church of England 3567R, 4000n3, 4013, 4014n1, 4048n3, 4097n1; benefactors 4104n1; appointments 4121&n1; education 4148n2; ecclesiastical commission 4211n2; 'Ritualistic Commission' 4527n3

Church Rates Abolition Bill (1858) 4013&n1

Church Rates Abolition Bill (1866) 4083n1, 4151&n3

Church Times 4000&n3

Churchward, Joseph George **4286**&ec&nn1&2

Cicero 4276&n2, 4415&n5

Cipriani, Giovanni Battista 4442n1

Clanricarde, 1st Marquess of V **2137n6**, 4091&n3, 4111, 4118&n3, 4142&n2, 4146, 4503n1

Clarendon, 1st Earl of 4060&n5, 4116n1, **4247&n4**

Clarendon, 4th Earl of III **1113n3**, 3980&n3, 4045&nn1&6, 4053n1, 4110&n2, 4119&n3, 4174n2, 4190n1

Clarendon Hotel 4567&n1, 4577&n1

Clarke, Seymour **4508**&nn1&2&6, 4532&nn1&5

Clay, James I **97n16**, 4381, 4400n1, 4415n8, 4601ec&n3

Clay, Sir William, 1st Bt III **747n5**, 4443&n3

Claydon House 4611&nn1-3

Clay's Act. *See* Compound Householder's Act (1851)

Clayton, Arthur John **4543&n3**

Clayton, Francis Edmund **4543&n3**

Clayton, George Augustus **4543&n3**

Clayton, Maria Amelia V **2190n4**, 4543n3

Clayton, Rice Richard V **1909n1**, 4543n3

Clayton, Richard Nugent **4543&n3**

'Clerical' (insurance company) 4080&ec&n1

Clerical Disabilities Act (1870) 4097n1

Clerkenwell explosion 4304n1, 4569n4, 4624ec&n1, 4625&nn3&6, 4628&nn5&12, 4629nn3&4, 4636&n3, 4638nn1-3, 4642n2

Clermont, Baron 4145n2

Cleveland, Duchess of (4th Duke) III **748n9**, 4034&nn1&2, 4201n1, 4506, 4509&n8

Cleveland, 4th Duke of VI **2664n8**, 4034&n1, 4201n1, 4509&n8; D's description of 4038&n2

Clifton 4039&n1

Clinton, Lord Albert Sidney Pelham- 4216n4

Clinton, Lord Arthur Pelham- 4216n4, **4256&n2**

Clinton, Lord Edward William Pelham- 4216n4

Clonbrock, 3rd Baron VII **3357n2**, 4503n1

Clubbe, Charles V **2149n1**, 4016, 4066, 4070&n1, 4195n2, 4527

Clubbe, Emily V **2168n2**, 4583&n1

Cluseret, Gustave Paul 4630n1

Cnidus (or Knidos) 4417n4

Cobbold, John VII **2921n1**, 3988n2, 4074n2

Cobden, Richard IV **1224n3**, 4108n2, 4149n1

Cobden Club 4149n1

Coburg, Duke of 4039n6

Cochrane, Alexander Baillie- (1st Baron Lamington 1880) III **1032n4**, 1315XA, 4128n2, 4129&nn1&2, 4133n2, 4635&n3

Cockburn, Sir Alexander V **2132n2** 4243&n3

Cogan, William Henry Ford **4377&n2**

Colebrook, Sir Edward 4444n1

Colebrooke, Sir Thomas Edward, Bt 4545n4

Coleman, Edward John **4035**&nn1&3, 4072&n1, 4077&n1, 4487, 4499

Coleman, Gertrude **4035&n4**, 4072, 4077, 4487, 4499

Colenso, John VIII **3741n4**, 4104n2

Coleridge, John Duke (Kt 1868; 1st Baron Coleridge 1874) 4382n4, 4400nn1&2, **4401&n3**

Collett, Mr (unidentified) 4143&n2

Collier, Edward M. 4258n1

Colonial Bishops Bill (1866) 4104&n2, 4137n2

Colville of Culross, 10th Baron (Scotland; UK 1885) VIII **3841n2**, 4495n2

Committees: on British Museum building (1865) 3992; on Jamaica (1866) 4163n1; on Statute Law (1868) 4260&n1, 4261n2

Commons, House of 3567R, 4092, 4103, 4104, 4106&nn2&5, 4111&n1, 4119, 4127&n1, 4147, 4152&nn1&2, 4224, 4235, 4238, 4266, 4290, 4291&nn1&5, 4319, 4326&n1, 4334&nn1&4, 4335&n1, 4339&n1, 4343, 4373&n3, 4374&nn1&5, 4377, 4378, 4379, 4382, 4405&n1, 4415, 4428&nn1&2&4, 4436&nn1&2, 4453, 4466&n1, 4474, 4476, 4596&n2, 4597&n1; 'fatal policy to starve the Commons' 3035x; parliamentary petition 3992&n3; hour of adjournment 3993n1; 'great & serious confusion on both sides' 3999&n1; disorder 4007n1; opinion of franchise enquiry 4009&n2; retirement of member 4020; W.H. Smith's leadership 4023&n1; 1865 dissolution 4027&n2; confidence in Hennessy 4028; D's leadership 4030; concessions needed to pass a bill 4055; Gladstone's leadership 4060; election of Speaker 4068&n1; 'probable temper' 4074; brief meeting 4078n3; parliamentary oaths 4085&nn1&2; 'shy of long & complicated amendments' 4096&n2; following 1865 and 1868 elections 4107&nn1&2; 'fortunately expired' 4113&n1; leadership 4116&nn1&2, 4315; members qualified for administration 4128&nn1&2, 4129; morning sitting 4142&n3; defeat of franchise bill 4148&nn1&6; surprised by Cranborne's speech 4151&n1; Stanley's inaugural speech as foreign secretary 4153&n1; 'very thin ... but ... agitated' 4155&n1; 'discussion ... highly, & unexpectedly, satisfactory' 4157&n1; prorogation 1866 4161&nn1&3, 4172&nn1&2; petition to 4162&nn5&6; 'good effects of parliamentary discussion' 4163&n4; 'dreary debate' 4166; 'special ... knowledge' 4204; support for Derby 4210; Scottish members 4225&n3; 'first man' 4228&nn2&4; Stanley's opinion of 4229; 'opposed to any violent reform' 4262; chancellor of the exchequer's title 4264; salaries for private secretaries 4280; parliamentary reform 4302&n1; parliamentary dinner 4314&n3; 'most serene' 4321&n6; 'curiosity' about reform 4328&nn1-3; packed for D's speech 4340&n3; 'expects "compensation"' 4341; 'agitated & disturbed' 4342&n1; reform bill 4350&nn1&2, 4355; 'bad night' 4356&nn1&2; ministerial resignations 4358&n1; 'agitated & excited' 4359&n1; 'cheers from all sides' 4370&nn1&5; gallery 4372&nn4&5; 'contemplated tactics' 4381; 'wearied' then 'rallied' by reform speeches 4385&n1; D's room in 4386&n3; 'representative character' 4387n1; 'patriotic sentiments' 4392n1; 'almost ... enthusiasm' for budget 4398&n1; 'party revolution' 4400&n1; attendance 4401&nn1-4; 'wearied of the eternal partridge' of D 4419&nn2&9; 'affairs ... nervous' 4424&n2; 'in favor of Peace' 4431&n3; visitors 4434&nn1-3; 'quite alone on our bench' 4438&nn2&5&6; 'loud cheers, from both sides' 4440&n1; 'four sittings pr week' 4444&nn1&2; 'a good report' 4448&nn2&5&7; 'thin' attendance 4451&nn1&2; ladies' gallery 4454&n2; 'progress of ... Bill ... expedited' 4464&nn1&2; 'conclusive on all matters' 4465&n1; 'debate ... brilliant & interesting' 4467&n1; 'more than four hundred members' 4468&n1; 'great cheering from both sides' 4469&n1; 'Proxies of an Estate' 4470&n1; 'universal sympathy'

4472&nn1&2; reform bill amendments 4473&n1; 'wants the plot ... decided on' 4479&n4; 'scraped up from every corner' 4491&nn1-3; end of session 4498&n1; objections to foreign mail services 4507&nn1&2; relationship with government 4535; telegraphs to 4579; 'nothing of significance' 4588&nn1&4; 'broke up' 4592&nn1&2&5; 'art of government' 4635; 'opposite side' 4636. *See also* Parliament

Compound Householder's Act ('Clay's Act,' 1851) 4386&n2, 4443&n3

Congress of Paris (1865) 4110n2

Connemara, Baron 4035n4

Connersby, James 4643n1

Conolly, Thomas V **1818n2**, 4545n2

Conservatives 264XR, 4071&nn3&4, 4347&n1; electoral reform 3924X&nn1&2; efforts in opposition 4013; majority on registers 4017&n2; 1865 elections 4020n3, 4022n1, 4023nn3&4; 1865 elections compared to 1857 and 1859 4025&ec&nn2&4, 4026&nn1&2&4, 4027&n1; possibility of coalition 4033&n1; would accept Stanley as leader 4055&n4; Carnarvon's reactionary approach 4082n2; meetings on reform 4083n2, 4346nn2&6; internal jealousies 4106; 1865 and 1868 election results 4107; destructive effect of reform bill 4114&n1; leadership 4116&n2; in Oxford 4136n1; electoral reform 4144&n1; purchase of *Globe* 4180n1; 'Societies' 4194; Canadian policy 4222; 'true Tory principles' 4223; election results 4225&n3; Roman Catholics 4236, 4238; *Globe* aids cause 4245n2; Derby addresses whole party 4340; 'tho' slow ... always accurate' 4342; will support Derby 'as a mass' 4372&n3; 'rallied' 4374; 'rallied' by reform speeches 4385; 're-establishing Toryism' 4414&n2; 'united ... to a man' 4448; 'vindicated' 4472&n1; party meeting 4486&n2; Irish 4490&n1; Scottish 4525n1; Manchester banquet for Derby 4540&n1

Constantinople 4419&n4

Constitutionnel 4423n1

Cooke, William Henry **4186&n1**

Cookesley, William Gifford IV **1341n3**, 4211&nn1&3&4

Cooper, Lady Charlotte Ashley- **4505&n2**

Cooper's Road 4304

Cope, Francis 4292n2

Cope, George 4292n2

Copeland, William IV **1241n3**, 4014&ec&n1

Copthall Court, London 4233

Co Cork, Ireland 4242&n2, 4254n6

Cork Examiner 4415n3

Corn Laws 1949R, 4056&n2

Cornwall 4372&n2, 4485

Cornwallis, 2nd Marquess I **189n2**, 4280n3

Corry, Alice Charlotte Mary Lowry- **4233&n6**

Corry, Henry Thomas Lowry- VI **2402n5**, 4308n3, 4313&n1, 4370&n1, 4459n1, 4505&nn1&6, 4632&n1

Corry, Lady Harriet Anne Lowry- 4217n2

Corry, Montagu Lowry- (1st Baron Rowton 1880) 4009n1, 4143, 4147&n1, 4164n1, 4169n1, 4171n1, 4172, 4183, 4190, 4191&nn4&7, 4200&ec, 4203, 4208&ec, 4220&ec, 4225, 4228n5, 4229n3, 4230, 4231, 4242, 4244, 4254, 4255, 4260&n1, 4284, 4285, 4289, 4296, 4304, 4308&n3, 4309, 4311, 4313, 4319, 4327&n1, 4330, 4332, 4336&n2, 4337nn2&4, 4338n1, 4339n1, 4341&n5, 4359n2, 4360, 4361, 4362, 4364, 4365, 4367, 4368, 4369n3, 4371, 4375, 4378, 4379, 4392, 4393, 4397, 4402, 4406, 4407, 4415&nn1&4&9, 4435, 4439n1, 4443, 4445, 4446, 4447&n3, 4450, 4477, 4481, 4483, 4489nn2&3, 4495n4, 4500&ec, 4504, 4505&nn1&2&6, 4510, 4512&nn1&3, 4523&nn1-3, 4527&n1, 4531&n1, 4542&n3, 4543&n3, 4544&n2, 4547, 4555&nn1&2, 4558n1, 4567, 4570, 4574, 4575, 4577, 4593, 4600, 4609, 4617, 4622, 4624, 4626, 4631n3, 4641, 4643, 4645, 4646, 4647, 4648, 4650; hired as D's private secretary **4137&n1**; assumes duties as D's private secretary 4138n1; advises D re Hamilton's trustees 4184&n2; prepares list of reform speeches 4187&nn3&4; explains compares to D 4188&n2; obtains information re wine duties 4191&nn4&7; digests New Forest brief 4194&nn1&2&4&5; visits Hughenden 4195&nn2&6, 4204&n6; reassures D about wine duties 4196&n2; forwards Stanley's letters to foreign office 4198; advises D about Wolowski's articles 4199&nn1&4&14; paper and ink for D 4206; 'vacant hours' employed with D's pens and papers 4209; estimates of reform meetings 4213n6; pays bills for D 4215; despatch for Derby 4217&nn2&4; 'row' with Anderson 4221&nn1&3; advises D re Canadian policy 4222ec&n3; proud to be editor of reform speeches 4223&nn3&7&10; Strange case 4224&n1; 'Irish news' 4226&n2; opinion of Kenealy 4227&n3; sister's health 4233&nn4&6; edition of D's speeches 4235&n1, 4256, 4270&n4, 4271, 4272&n2, 4306&n1; keeps letters in his 'archive' 4236; receives papers re Portuguese treaty 4237&n1; sends D specimen page of speeches 4238&nn1&2&4&9&15; sends D £100 4240&n1; deters Kenealy 4243&n4; 'Shropshire home' 4250&nn3&4; illness 4264&nn1-3, 4282&n4; outlines report on Portuguese treaty 4295n4; 'My dear Mr Editor' 4307; makes copies of throne speech 4315; reform papers to cabinet 4325&n1; reports to MA on D's reform bill speech 4374n7; receives journals at Rowton

4386&n1; sends a budget to D 4422&n1; prepares memorandum on residence 4426, 4427&ec&n1; 'great praise' 4430&n1; reads 'Watkiniana' 4432; reform bill 4457; assists MA 4466&n2; visits Savernake Forest 4496; meets D at Blenheim 4546&n1; reports debate to D 4596&n2; attends opera 4602; sympathizes with D's suffering 4604&n1; delivers relief money to Clerkenwell victims 4625n5, 4628&n9

Cother, Dunbar John, Jr **4285**&ec&n**n1**&2

Cother, William **4285**&n**n2**&**3**

Cotter, W. **4569&n1**

Cotton 4601n1

Cotton, Sir John Hynde-, 3rd Bt VIII **3331xn2**, 3924X

Coulton, David VI **2551n2**, 3980&nn1&4

Coulton, Sarah 3980nn1&5

Coulton, Sophia **3980**&n**n1**&5

County Cattle Insurance Company of Hertford 4043&nn1&2, 4058n2, 4062

Courtenay, Lord (12th Earl of Devon 1888) VIII **3940n3**, 3988n2

Court of Exchequer 4570&n3

Courts of Justice Building Act (1865) 4479n2

Coutts, Angela Georgina Burdett- (Baroness Burdett-Coutts 1871) III **748n8**, 4104&nn1&2

Coward, Thomas (coachman) **4005**&n**n2**&3

Cowell, George **4575&n2**, 4579&n2

Cowley, Countess (1st Earl) VIII **3547n1** 4414&n3

Cowley, 1st Earl VI **2358n1**, 4174&n1, 4396n2, 4414&n3

Cowper, Countess (6th Earl) **4045&n3**, 4046, 4062An1

Cowper, William Francis (1st Baron Mount-Temple 1880) II **408n27**, 4157&n5

Cowper, 6th Earl 4045n3

Cox, Edward William II **409n2**, 4020n4

Cracherode, Clayton Mordaunt **4476&n3**

Crampton, John 4174n2

Cranborne, Viscountess (4th Viscount; Marchioness of Salisbury 1868) 3998n1, 4185n1, **4187&n4**, 4190&n3, 4191, 4195&nn1&2, 4205

Cranborne, 4th Viscount (3rd Marquess of Salisbury 1868) VI **2650n1**, 3998n1, 4052n1, 4120n3, 4151&n1, 4187&n4, 4195nn1&2, 4198, 4202&n1, 4205, 4212, 4229n5, 4238n15, 4292&n1, 4301n1, 4322n1, 4336n1, 4340, 4341&nn4&5&7, 4342, 4602&nn2&5; resignation 4338nn1&2, 4352n1, 4355n2, 4356&n4, 4358&n1, 4359nn1&2, 4372, 4376n1; 'denounced' 4454; 'vindication' 4458&n2; 'great bitterness' 4472&n1; Grey's amendment 4473n3; resignation 4557&n8

Cranworth, 1st Baron II **572n3**, 4259n5, 4489n4

Craven, Countess of (3rd Earl) **4595&n3**

Dickens, Charles: appeals to D on friend's behalf 4455&nn1-3; *All the Year Round* 4519n2

Dickerson, Mr 4130n1

Dickson, Alexander **4286**&ec**&n3**

Dieppe 4632

Dimsdale, Baron 4369n6

Disraeli, Benjamin: 'determined to make me a Tory' 264XR; 'affairs [n]ever looked so well' 414X; 'I would not shrink' from standing for election 535X; abolition of free franking 1033X&n2; 'Peace ... order of the day' 1094R; alliance with France 1315XA&n4; 'glad to see you' 1487X&n1; morning caller 1487Xec&n1; sends £500 by registered letter 1511XA&n1; 'When Chaos comes' 1643AR; confidence in Malmesbury 1923R; 'bored ... & rather disgusted' 1929Xnn1-3; Peel's letter 'pompous & trite' 1949R; meets Walpole 2202XR; 'material interests of town & country' 2480R; declines Galway's invitation 2645X&ec&n1; 'off the rail of politics' 2797R; 'alarmed' by affairs 3035X; recommends Earle for Carlton Club 3362X; Lords and privilege 3481A&n1; 'crisis in Church Affairs' 3567R; thanks Skelton for dedication in 'Thalatta' 3764R; thanks Maguire for book 3887A&ec; thanks Skelton for article 3924X&nn1&2; thanks Hunt for book 3979&n2; recommends assistance for Coulton's widow 3980&ec&nn4&5; poaching at Hughenden 3981&n1; 'large balances' for investments 3982&n1; thanks Lee for journal 3983&n2; letter for Leopold de Rothschild's collection 3984&nn1&2; returns paper to Rose 3985; thanks Juliana de Rothschild for pâté 3986; thanks Stracey for cygnet 3987&nn2&3; at Carlton Club 3989; 'can't annex an idea' 3990&n1; asks MA for 'an easy pair of boots' 3991&n1; petition re British Museum building 3992&n1; advises MA of late House 3993; meets with Derby 3994&n2; corrects proofs for Lygon 3995&n1; offers Mt Braddon to Beauchamp 3996&nn1&3-5; agrees to meet Lonsdale 3997; invites Stanley to dinner 3998; 'great & serious confusion' 3999&ec&n1; approves Lygon's corrections to ecclesiastical speeches 4000&nn1-3; visits Bulstrode Park 4001&nn1&2; 'sate down with great cheering' 4002&nn1&2; agrees to meet Lee 4003; declines invitation to meet Canadian deputation 4004&n2; seeks reference for coachman 4005&n2; cautions Elcho about electoral reform 4006&nn1&2; 'a heavy & anxious night' 4007&n1; returns horses to jobmaster 4008&n1; unable to support Elcho's motion 4009&ec&nn1&2; asks to see Palk 4010; 'interview ... not satisfactory' 4011; thanks Lygon for edition of speeches 4012&n1; letter to Bucks electors

4013&nn2&4, 4019, 4024&n1; 'order & propriety of Life' 4014&ec; instructions for binding and selling books 4015&ec; asks for Clubbe's help 4016; asks Salisbury for 'a moderate subscription' 4017; supports Gleig's candidacy 4018&ec&nn1&3; supports Austin's candidacy 4020&n4; Bucks nomination 4021&n1; anxious about Wilts elections 4022; supports W.H. Smith's candidacy 4023&nn2&4; compares 1865 polls to 1857 and 1859 4025&nn2&4, 4026&nn2&5; Conservative over-confidence 4027&nn1&2&4; concerned about Hennessy's defeat 4028; thanks Skelton for book 4029A&n3; unable to meet widow of Hawaiian king 4029&n3; offers to resign as leader of opposition 4030&nn1-5; unable to assist *BH* 4031&n3; attempts to help female author 4032&nn1&3; acknowledges Derby's letter re coalition 4033&n1; 'dreams & visions' 4034&nn1&2; thanks Coleman for birds 4035&n1; asks Gleig not to publish his letter or a pamphlet 4036&n1; notices mistake in Rose's calculations 4037nn1-3; rumours of reform measures 4038&nn1&2&7; news of European royalty 4039&nn1&3; declines Houghton's invitation 4040&n1; meets with Rose 4041&n1; death of Beauchamp's sister 4042&nn2&3&5; asks Salisbury about cattle insurance 4043&n1; foresees 'tempestuous times, & great vicissitudes' 4044&nn1&3-8; 'political gossip & excitement' 4045&nn1&4&6; *carte de visite* with photograph 4046&n3; prefers murrain to meeting of parliament 4047&nn2&3; invites Stanley to Hughenden 4048&nn1&3; invites Earle to Hughenden 4049; invites Beauchamp to Hughenden 4050&n2; alarmed by rumours of early meeting of parliament 4051&n4; advises Stanley to be reserved about reform 4053&nn1&2; thoughts on new government 4054&n1; 'position of affairs ... ricketty' 4055&nn1&4-6; reminds Stanley of Russell's 1845 attempt to form government 4056&nn3&4; anticipates Beauchamp's visit 4057; attends Aylesbury meeting about cattle plague 4058&nn1&2; conversations with Stanley 4059&nn1&2; comments on government appointments 4060&n1; 'dunned ... intolerably' by Adams 4061; advises Buckingham cattle association 4062&n3; 'agreeable note'; quarrel amongst servants 4063; asks Gladstone about throne speech 4064; thanks Smiles for book 4065; contributions to Hughenden school 4066&n1; mutual cattle insurance associations 4067&ec; circular letter to MPs 4068&ec&n3; thanks Stanhope for library catalogue 4069&n1; Hughenden school matters 4070; Goschen's promotion 4071&n3; thanks Coleman for game

Sultan 4475; Phillipps's library 4476&n1, 4631&nn1&3; stationery supplies 4477&n1; new county seats 4478&ec&nn1&2&5; S Kensington plan 4479&nn1&4; army of reserve 4480; *Saturday Review* articles 4481&n1; reports cabinet meeting to Derby 4482, 4485; reform bill in Lords 4483&nn1&2; 'entire confidence' in Grey 4484&nn1&3; party meetings 4486&n4; thanks Coleman 4487; proposes Watkin for knighthood 4488&n1; Irish appointments 4489&nn2-4, 4490; 'difficult to get men together' 4491&n3; 'lose my temper' with Chelmsford 4492&nn2-4; expenses of entertaining Sultan 4493&n2; prorogation 4494; 'anxious to serve Rose' 4495&nn1-4; love of forests 4496; thanks Lambert for help with reform bill 4497&nn1&3; concludes business in the House 4498; thanks Coleman for venison and birds 4499; McKenna's knighthood 4500&ec&nn1&2, 4501&nn2&4; declines invitation to Lowther 4502&n1; first letter to Rivers Wilson 4504&nn1&2&4; 'beginning to enjoy Hughenden' 4505&nn1&3&5&6; appointment for Lowther 4506; tenders for postal service 4507&n1; railway commissioners 4508, 4532; 'pure democracy' 4509&nn1&5&9; needs paper and pens 4510; instructs Rivers Wilson 4511&nn1&4&5&7-10; confidence in Corry 4512&nn1&3&5; European affairs 4513&n1; invites Lady Holland to Hughenden 4514&nn1&2; Abyssinian news 4515&nn1&3; education in Scotland 4516&n1; thanks Rose for inkstand and friendship 4517&n1; advises Derby to summon parliament 4518&n4; journal subscriptions 4519&n3; thanks Edwards for grouse 4520&n1; need to summon parliament 4521&nn1&2&4; 'this Abyssinia mess' 4522&nn1&2; invites Corry to Hughenden 4523&nn1&2; accepts invitation to Edinburgh 4525&nn1&2; 'my career will terminate with' Derby's 4526&nn3&6; ritualistic commission 4527&n1; lord lieutenants 4528&n1; death of US envoy 4529&n1; prorogation or adjournment 4530; summoned to Knowsley 4531; coat of arms 4533&n2; Stirling Maxwell's library 4534&nn1&5; 'this absurd Council' 4535&nn1-3; the 'Millenium' 4536&nn1&2&4; declines invitation to Fasque 4537&n1; declines invitation to Blagdon 4538&n1; 'inability of letter-writing' 4539; declines invitation to Manchester 4540&n1; 'summoned to Knowsley' 4541&nn1-3; 'Reform banquet ... ludicrous failure' 4542&nn3&4; favourable articles in *Manx Sun* 4543&nn3&6; 'unprecedented ... fate' of Derby's red deer 4545&nn2-4&7; declines master cutler's invitation

4546&nn1&2; 'Abyss: papers' 4547&n1; 'great function' in Edinburgh 4548&n1; interest on Welsh investments 4549; secret treaty 4550; discusses Edinburgh speech with Stanley 4551&n1; declines Rosslyn's invitation 4552&n1; Italian uprising 'very grave' 4553&nn1&2; Gordon's business 4554; 'how to extricate' himself from Victoria's invitation 4555&nn1&2; honoured in Edinburgh 4556&nn1&2, 4556A; congratulates Derby on 'Manchester Demonstration' 4557&nn3&5&8&9; 'I think ... I must resign' 4558&n1; 'we must hope the best' 4559&n2; 'logic of the excuse is ... feminine' 4560&ec&n2; summons parliament 4561; invasion of Rome 4562&nn1&2; 'a pang, in leaving Scotland' 4563&n3; downstairs at Downing Street 4565&nn1&2; 'a Semitic subject' 4566&nn1&6; parliamentary dinner at Clarendon 4567&nn1&3; dines with Victoria 4568&n1; sends regrets to working men 4569&nn1&2; postal contracts 4570&n3; thanks Stracey 4571&n1; education in speech from the throne 4572&n1; praises Lady Brownlow's book 4573&n1; attends to MA during illness 4574&n1; 'Dr Gull still hopeful' 4576; asks Stanley to chair dinner 4577&n1; MA's 'symptoms more favorable' 4578; 'catastrophe might prove imminent' 4579; 'much touched by' kindness of Gladstone and Victoria 4580&nn4&6; 'a ray of hope' 4581&n1, 4583; 'great hopes' re MA 4582&n2; 'all may yet be well' 4584&n1; Gladstone's 'considerate sympathy' 4585&n3; MA's 'state is maintained' 4586; MA 'gaining strength' 4587; 'All is hope' 4588; MA 'continues to improve' 4589; 'hurried lines in a mysterious place' 4590; international system of money, weights and measures 4591&n1; Abyssinian expedition for 'high moral causes' 4592&n1; misses cabinet 4593nn1&2; asks Hunt to be his 'Lieutenant' 4594, 4595&n1; asks Corry to report from House 4596&n4; 'nothing should be postponed' 4597; 'pardon the pencil' 4598&ec; 'a great deal of medecine' 4599; 'faith in my star' 4600&nn1&3&4; 'separated [from MA]... under the same roof' 4602&n5; 'irritated at the blundering' 4603&n1; 'not ... in my place today' 4604&n1; 'always suspected' gout 4605; 'dripping damp' 4606; cannot read for pain 4607; sherry from James 4608; 'must manage ... to see my heroine' 4609; patronage appointments 4610&n1; 'again writing letters' 4611&n2; 'my butler ... a pompous booby' 4612&n1; 'a load of misery off me' 4613; agrees to meet archbishop 4614&nn1&2; 'the great sorrow' 4615&n1; 'No news' 4616; meets with archbishop

on representation of the people (res 5) (11
Feb 1867) 4320n1, 4328&n1; on representation of the people (25 Feb 1867) 4331n2,
4340n3; on reform bill (4, 5 Mar 1867)
4356nn1-3; ministerial explanations (5 Mar
1867) 4359&n1; Scotland – representation
of the people (14 Mar 1867) 4365n2; navy
estimates (14 Mar 1867) 4370n1; Fenianism
(15 Mar 1867) 4372n5; Ireland – railways
(15 Mar 1867) 4373n2; Reform Bill (18 Mar
1867) 4374&n1, 4438n5; on Reform Bill
(1 Apr 1867) 4382n4; Reform Bill (26 Mar
1867) 4385n1, 4387&nn1&3, 4390n1; at
Institute of Civil Engineers' dinner (8 May
1867) 4386n3; second reading of reform
bill (25 Mar 1867) 4386n3; on the budget (4
Apr 1867) 4391n2, 4398&nn1&2, 4418n2; to
deputations from reform league and societies (2 Apr 1867) 4392n1; on the budget (30
Apr 1852) 4398; Reform Bill, Ministerial
Statement (3 May 1867) 4401n4; Reform Bill
– cl 3 (12 Apr 1867) 4403n1; Reform Bill, cl
3 (11 Apr 1867) 4404&n3; Reform Bill – cl
3 (2, 3 May 1867) 4428nn1&4; Reform Bill
– cl 3 (6 May 1867) 4431n3; Reform Bill,
Hodgkinson's amendment to clause 3 (17
May 1867) 4438nn2&8; Reform Bill – cl 34
(27 May1867) 4443n1; on the Fenian convict
Burke (27 May 1867) 4444n3; disfranchisement of certain boroughs (30 May 1867)
4445n3; Reform Bill – cl 9 (13 Jun 1867)
4451&n1; Reform Bill (13 Jun 1867) 4452;
Reform Bill (27 Jun 1867) 4462n2; Reform
Bill (24 Jun 1867) 4462n3; Reform Bill – cl
9 (13 Jun 1867) 4463n3; Reform Bill – new
clause (1 Jul 1867) 4464&n1; postponement
of review (4 Jul 1867) 4466n1; on reform
bill – 3rd reading (15 July 1867) 4472&n1;
3rd reading of reform bill; household suffrage (15 Jul 1867) 4478n2; S Kensington
plan (29 July 1867) 4479n4; Reform Bill
(8 Aug 1867) 4491n3; comments on supply, entertainment of Sultan (9 Aug 1867)
4493n2; at Hughenden harvest home (19
Sep 1867) 4514n2; at Edinburgh (29 Oct
1867) 4551&n1, 4557nn8&9; at working
men's meeting in Edinburgh (29 Oct 1867)
4556n2; to working men in Edinburgh (30
Oct 1867) 4563&nn3&5; speech from the
throne (19 Nov 1867) 4572n1; 'unable to
speak audibly ... from emotion' (19 Nov
1867) 4580&n4; on Abyssinian expedition
(26 Nov 1867) 4592&n1
– works: *Vivian Grey* 1094R; *Progress of Jewish
Emancipation Since 1829* 3984n2; "*Church
and Queen*": *five speeches ...* 3995&n1,
4000&n2, 4012&n1; *Henrietta Temple*
4001&n2; article for *Church and State Review*
4026n5; *The Young Duke* 4103n3; *Constitutional Reform* (1866) 4187&n1; *Parliamentary*

Reform (1867) 4187&n1, 4306&n3; *Mr Glad-
stone's Finance* 4238n5; *Endymion* 4512n5,
4567n3
Disraeli, Coningsby Ralph 4394n1,
4408&nn1&2
Disraeli, Dorothy (Dolly) 4408n1
D'Israeli, Isaac I **4n2**, 4069ec&n3, 4476, 4533;
Curiosities of Literature 4174n6; *The Genius of
Judaism* 4566n2
Disraeli, James I **12n5**, 1094R, 4602&n4,
4608
D'Israeli, Maria I **1n1**, 414x
Disraeli, Marion Grace (née Silva) 4408n2
Disraeli, Mary Anne I **169n5**, 3986, 3993ec,
4002&ec, 4051, 4072&n1, 4120n2, 4121n3,
4158, 4167, 4217, 4265ec, 4339&n1, 4374n7,
4383n3, 4399&ec, 4417, 4425, 4471,
4514nn1&4, 4566n6, 4573n1, 4607; hires
manager for dinner party 3362x; stationery 3982&ec&n2; account books 3988n2,
4008n1; sale of Mount Braddon 3996n4;
Stanley's visit 3998&ec; dines with Mayer de
Rothschilds 3999&ec&n1; opinion about
coachman 4005n2; attends Lady Derby's
assembly 4007&n3; regrets not meeting
Hawaiian queen 4029; family 4035; news
from Charlotte de Rothschild 4040; visit
at Wrest 4045n3; planting at Hughenden
4046n2; 'no company' 4048nn2&3; quarrel amongst servants 4063n2; Cecil Jolliffe's wedding 4100&nn1&2; bronchial
attack 4110&ec&n1, 4112; 'already better'
4111&ec; 'extreme debility' 4113&n2; pensions 4185&ec; no company except dinner
party 4195&nn2&6; introduces Roseberry
to Hannah de Rothschild in 1875 4201n1;
invites Lennox to Hughenden 4202n2;
buys ink for D 4206; 'engaged in colossal
works' 4239&n1; receives money from D
4240n1; brother's debts 4244&n2; handwriting cheers D 4268&n1; receives 'impudent
letter' 4285ec&n2; waits for D at Southsea
4333; attends Mrs Gladstone's assembly
4365ec; champagne and pie for D's reform
success 4405n1; childlessness 4408&n1; con-
fers with D on affairs 4439&n1; tickets for
'two humble country friends' 4450; invited
to tour Royal Academy library 4459&nn1&2;
postpones morning party 4466&ec&nn1&3;
Sultan's reception 4474&n4; clippings file
4481n1; invitation to Knowsley 4501n2;
friendships 4509&n1; subscription to
journal 4519; visit to Edinburgh 4525n2,
4534&n1, 4538&n1; 'heiress of the Vineys
of Gloucestershire' 4533; 'dearest Love'
4542; business interests in Wales 4549n1;
Lady Rosslyn's baby 4552&n1; 'Your own' at
Windsor 4568; 'seriously unwell' 4574&n1;
'increased suffering' 4575&n1; 'Dr Gull
still hopeful' 4576; 'a critical day' 4577&n1;

Irish church 4362n2; 'great fight ... against real rating' 4369&n1; 'never spoke more ably' 4374&nn2&3&5&7; advises voting against reform bill 4377&nn1&3; 'more violent than ever' 4381; 'abstract resolution' 4382&nn3&4; poem about his reform speech 4383nn1&3; 'too committeeish' 4384&n1; 'wearied the House' 4385&nn2&3; objections to reform bill 4386; 'so very excited and so alarming' 4387n1; 'a moderate measure' 4389n2; payment of debt 4391n3; alterations to reform bill 4393&n1; resolution on reform bill 4398&nn1&2; 'retreat' of members 4400&nn1-3; amendments 4401&nn1&2, 4402n2, 4405n1; 'not in his best style' 4403nn1&2; Manning's pastoral letter 4409n3; 'laid ... on his back' 4415n9; 'at a discount' 4419&n6; 'acting from pique' 4420&n2; 'at the head of Vestries and "Civilization"' 4438&nn5&6; high commissioner Ionian Islands 4448n8; 'spoke with former fire' 4454; 'cannot rally more than 120 men' 4465; 'beaten by a majority of 29' 4468&n1; proxies in Lords 4470n1; 'taking copious notes' 4472&n2; Irish Catholic votes 4501n4; Abyssinian war 4518&n2, 4521; does not attend reform banquet 4542n5; sends regrets to Reform Banquet 4542n5; review of the session 4557n9; November meeting of parliament 4561n1; 'kind & considerate' to D 4580&nn3&4; 'great gifts & qualities' 4585&n3; 'speech ... satisfactory' 4588&n4; 'probably not speak' 4592&n6; pronounces D's budget 'most just and prudent' 4596n2
Glasgow Chamber of Commerce 4146n4
Glasgow University Library 4534n2
Gleig, C.E.S. (Edward) VII **2994n4**, 4018&ec&nn1&3, 4036&n1
Glenluce, NB, Scotland 4225
Globe 4069n2, 4180&n1, 4245&nn1&2, 4586&n1
Glorious Revolution of 1688 3924x&n1
Gloucester 4080&n2, 4285&n2
Gloucestershire 4533
Glyn, George Grenfell 4596n2
Godolphin, 1st Baron 4044n1
Goldsmid, Sir Francis, 2nd Bt II **450n3**, 4168n2
Goliath (Bible) 4102n2
Goodwin, Mr (unidentified) 4187&n7
Gorchakov (Gortchakoff), Prince Alexander Michaelovich VII **3208n1**, 4513
Gordon, Edward Strathearn (Baron Gordon of Drumearn 1876) **4365&n1**, 4430, 4445&n4, 4527n1, 4554, 4555&n1, 4558&n1, 4562&nn1&2, 4602&nn2&5
Gordon, George William 4150n2, 4163nn1&4
Gore, Mr (Woods & Forests) 4545n2
Goschen, George Joachim (1st Viscount Goschen 1900) **4060&nn**1&**2**, 4069&n2, 4071&nn2&3, 4075&n5

Goulburn, Frederick 4313n4
Goulburn, Mr (Custom House) 4164n1
Goulburn, Mr (Fishery Commissioner) 4313n4
Gower, Lord Cromartie Sutherland-Leveson-Gower (Marquess of Stafford 1884; 4th Duke of Sutherland 1892) 4552n2
Graham, Sir James, 2nd Bt II **516n3** 4194
Grand Trunk Railway 4432n1
Grant, Sir John 4163n3
Grant, Sir Robert 4038n5
Granville, 2nd Earl II **676n1**, 4045&nn2&6, 4118&n3, 4119&n3, 4470n1, 4473&n3, 4478
Graves, Samuel Robert **4314**&n**n2**&3, 4319, 4320, 4321n6, 4345n3, 4372
Gravesend 4463&n3
Gray, Sir John 4254n6
Great Brickhill Manor 4536
'Greek fire' 4629n3, 4643&n1
Greenwood, John 4630n1
Greg, Percy **4284**&ec&n**n2**&3
Greg, William Rathbone VII **3371n3**, 4284&nn1&2
Gregorian calendar 4101n1
Gregory, William (Sir William 1876) VII **3355n2** 3992n4, 4091, 4116n1, 4212&n4
Grenville, Baroness (1st Baron) V **2169n1**, 4508n5
Grey, Charles I **201n5**, 4103n3, 4159, 4233, 4302&ec&nn1&3, 4328n3, 4333n1, 4334n2, 4341n7, 4349n1, 4350&nn1&2, 4352n1, 4369n7, 4370&n4, 4372&n4, 4374n1, 4377n7, 4380n1, 4400n3, 4412&nn1&3, 4413, 4417, 4419n1, 4428n2, 4431n1, 4479&n1, 4484&nn1&4&5, 4541&n1, 4556&n1, 4557, 4568, 4588n7, 4632n4; personally delivers Victoria's letter to Derby 4120&n2; sends Gladstone's estimates to D 4160&n1; private secretary to Prince Albert 4232&nn1&2; delivers Victoria's letter to Northcote 4247n1; recalls 'first acquaintance' with D 4268; remuneration as private secretary 4280&n1; considered for reform committee 4291n1; memoir of Albert 4422nn2&3
Grey, Major (unidentified) 4501n2
Grey, Sir George, 2nd Bt III **713n2**, 4002&nn1&2, 4038n5, 4157&n4, 4498&n3
Grey, 2nd Earl I **122n7**, 4038n5, 4353&n1, 4527n2
Grey, 3rd Earl II **379n1**, 4106&ec&n1, 4107&n1, 4246&n1, 4247&n1, 4291&nn1&5, 4317, 4318&ec, 4473&nn1-3, 4478&n5, 4485&n2
de Grey, Thomas (6th Baron Walsingham 1870) **4314**&n**n1**&3, 4319, 4321&n6, 4379&n2
de Grey, 2nd Earl 4045n3
de Grey, 3rd Earl and 2nd Earl Ripon (Marquess of Ripon 1871) VII **3124n1**, 4075ec&n3
Griffith, Darby 4224n2
Grosvenor, Earl (3rd Marquess of Westminster

1869; 1st Duke of Westminster 1874) 4091,
4098&nn**1**-3, 4102&nn1&7, 4111, 4116&n1,
4316n1, 4340, 4343&n3, 4346, 4349, 4366n1,
4369, 4372, 4377n1

Grosvenor, Robert Wellesley 4023n3

Grosvenor Gate 3982&n2, 3986, 4041&n1,
4045&n4, 4150, 4160, 4256, 4405n1, 4410,
4421&n1, 4441, 4486&n3, 4620; parliamentary dinner 3988; stationery 4206, 4209;
housekeeper 4519; a 'hospital' 4596, 4598

Grosvenor Street 4308&n3 .

Grote, George II **558n1** 4265&nn1&2

Guest, Sir Ivor Bertie, 2nd Bt 4610n3

Gull, William Withey (1st Bt and Kt 1872)
4575&n**3**, 4576, 4579&n2, 4593, 4595, 4599,
4600, 4602n5, 4603, 4605&n1

Gunnersbury Park 3986&n1, 4297

Gurney, Russell **4150**&n**2**, 4448&nn7&9

Guy, William Augustus V **2206n2**, 4089n3

Habeas Corpus Act (1679) 4629&n3, 4632&n4

Habeas Corpus Suspension (Ireland) Act Continuance Bill (1866) 4166&nn2&4

Halifax, 1st Viscount V **1624n3**, 4029An3,
4075&ec&n3, 4119&n3, 4145n2, 4309&n2,
4331n1

Halifax, 2nd Viscount 4529n4

Hamersley, John William **4543**&n**4**

Hamilton, Charles Baillie-. *See* Lord Jerviswoode

Hamilton, Duchess of (11th Duke) 4184n1

Hamilton, George Alexander V **2165n1**, 4156,
4221&n3, 4225, 4263n1, 4289, 4504n1,
4521n2

Hamilton, Lord Claud John **4523**&n**3**

Hamilton, Mr (unidentified) 4015

Hamilton, Robert Nisbet- III **891n2**, 4552n1

Hamilton, 11th Duke of VI **2392n4**, 4184n2

Hamilton, 12th Duke of (8th Earl of Selkirk
1886) **4184**&nn**1**&2, 4528nn1-3, 4542&n4,
4545&n4

Hampshire 4187, 4190, 4194n2

Hams Hall 4040&n3

Hancock, Neilson 4503n1, 4508n6, 4532n5

Hannay, James VIII **3752n1**, 4134&n1

Hansard 4092n1, 4187, 4204&n1, 4223n10,
4308&n2, 4309&n2

Hansard, Thomas Curson, Jr V **1806n1**, 4530

Harcourt, George Simon II **577n1**, 535Xn5

Harcourt, William George Venables-Vernon-
(Sir William 1874) **4259**&nn**1**&2&5

Hardwicke, Countess of (4th Earl) III **770n3**,
4641

Hardwicke, 4th Earl of I **192n3**, 4641&n2

Hardy, Gathorne (Viscount Cranbrook 1878;
Earl of Cranbrook 1892) VII **3033n3** 4026n1,
4120n3, 4154&nn1&2, 4283&nn1&2,
4359n2, 4366, 4370&n3, 4376&n5,
4377&nn6&7, 4378, 4384&ec&n1, 4387n2,
4414n2, 4418&nn1&3, 4438&nn3&11,
4444n1, 4485, 4527n3, 4565n1, 4580n2,

4588&nn3&4&7, 4617&n2, 4621,
4623&nn1&3, 4624&n2, 4627&nn2&3, 4628,
4636&nn1&2; dual voting 4380n1; 'full of
sense & spirit' 4385&n3; secret cabinet
4402n2; D 'unscrupulous' 4403&nn1-2;
'summoned to a Cabinet' 4404n4; Derby's
explanations to party 4429n4; approves of
amendment 4439n1; East Surrey representation 4452; withdraws parks bill 4498n1;
execution of Manchester Martyrs 4590n1;
bill restricting carrying of arms 4601nn1&3;
Clerkenwell explosion 4625&nn1&4; secret
police 4626&n1, 4629&nn2&4; Fenian plots
4630&n1, 4632&nn1&4&5, 4637, 4637n1;
informers 4639&n1

Hardy, Jane (Viscountess Cranbrook 1878;
Countess of Cranbrook 1892) **4418**&n**3**,
4623

Hardy, Thomas Duffus **4248**&n**1**

Hare, Thomas 4415n8

Harmer, James **1094R**&n**n2**&3

Harness, Henry Drury VII **2437Xn1**, 4189n2

Harrison, Michael **4490**&nn**1**&2

Hart, Solomon Alexander **4459**&nn1&2

Hartington, Marquess of (8th Duke of Devonshire 1891) VII **3360n2**, 4071n2, 4087&n1,
4216&n11, 4222&n3, 4224&n2

Hartismere, Lord. *See* Henniker, 4th Baron

Hartley, James **4564**&n**1**

Hartley, John 4564n1

Harvey, William Henry VIII **3937n1**, 4078&n2

Hatfield House 4643

Hatsell, John VI **2752n1**, 4530&n2

Hawes, George Ernest 4552n2

Hawkes, Alderman (Birmingham) 4329n1

Hay, Lord William Montagu 4020n4

Hay, Sir John Dalrymple-, 3rd Bt VIII **3790n2**,
4202n1, 4216&n14, 4220&ec&nn1&2,
4225&n1, 4241&nn1&2

Hay, William 4304n1

Haydon, Frederic VII **2974n1**, 4175n1

Hayter, Arthur Divett (2nd Bt 1878; Baron
Haversham 1906) 4096n2, **4102**&n**n3**&4-7,
4103&n1, 4105&nn1&2, 4106&n5

Hayter, Sir William Goodenough, 1st Bt VI
2524n1, 4102&n5, 4103

Heathcote, Gilbert (not same as Sir Gilbert)
4116n1

Heathcote, Sir William III **917n4**, 4026n1,
4102n7, 4210&n2, 4291&n2, 4372&n3, 4374

Helena, Princess. *See* Christian, Princess of
Schleswig-Holstein

Helps, Arthur (Sir Arthur 1872) VIII **3813n1**,
4051n4, 4156&n2, 4535&nn1&2

Hemsted Park 4623&n3

Henley, Francis George 4381, **4492**&n**n2**&4

Henley, Joseph John **4492**&c**n1**

Henley, Joseph Warner V **1936n7**, 4124&n1,
4148n4, 4291n5, 4372&n3, 4374&n4,
4477&n2, 4478&n2, 4492&nn1&2&4

Ink 4206&n4

Inkerman, Battle of 4454

Inner Temple 4649&n1

Innes, Arthur Charles (later Innes-Cross) **4567&n2**

Institute of Civil Engineers 4386&n4

Ireland 1315XA, 4090&ec&n1, 4133, 4199&n9, 4209&n5, 4215&n6, 4222, 4226&nn2-5, 4335n2, 4614n2; elections (1865, 1866) 4028&nn1&2; church 4059n2; church and universities 4060&nn1&4; Fenians 4068n2, 4127n3, 4279n3, 4331&n3, 4444n3, 4628&n7; home rule 4091&n6; finances 4115ec&nn1&4; difficult for new government 4123nn1&3; lords of treasury 4129; treasury appointments 4135&n1; chancellorship 4140&n1-3&6; government 4141&nn3&4&7&8; railway loan 4142&n2, 4373n2; university education 4148&nn2-5; government appointments 4165&n1, 4178&n1, 4489&nn2-4; habeas corpus 4166&nn3&4, 4167n3; Derby's 'Irish Government' 4212&nn3&4; Fenianism 4216&n7, 4277n1, 4623&n1; postal service 4220nn1&2; elections 4236&nn1&2, 4254&nn3&5&6; journalists 4238n6; railways 4251, 4444n1, 4503&n1; 'difficult ... questions' 4262n3; education 4298n6; famine (1847) 4308n1; church and land bills 4362n2; 'adequate policy for' 4409nn1-3; Catholic education 4441n1; railroads 4485&n1; legal appointments 4490&nn1&2; electoral reform 4500n1; 1868 election 4501&n4; railway commissioners 4508&nn1&2&6, 4511&nn5&7, 4532&nn3&5, 4546; proposed visit by Queen 4545nn1&2; established church 4580n3; Irish Republican Brotherhood 4588&nn2&7; army 4621n2; Clerkenwell explosion 4624n2, 4625n4; police 4627&nn2&3

Irishman 4565n1, 4614n2

Irish Railway Directors' Conference 4142n2

Irish Times 4165n1, 4256n2

Ironclads 4125n2, 4550&n3. *See also* Shipbuilding

Isham, Arthur V **2175n3**, 4199&n1

Isham, Mr (son of above) 4199&n1

Isle of Man 4543&n1

Israel 4607&n1

Italy 4153nn3&5, 4515n3, 4550&n1, 4557&n7, 4562&n3; finance 4524&n1; republican insurgents 4553n1

'Jack the Painter'. *See* Hill, James

Jacob (Old Testament) 4545n5

Jacobites 4033n2

Jamaica 4068n2, 4150nn2&3, 4163&nn1-4

Jamaica Royal Commission 4163nn1&4

Japan 4068n2, 4410, 4524&n2

Jenkinson, Lady (Sir George 11th Bt) **4643&n3**

Jenkinson, Sir George Samuel, 11th Bt **4643&nn2&3**

Jersey, Countess of (5th Earl) III **719n6**, 4044&n7, 4156&n1, 4225&n5, 4254, 4312&nn1&2&4; death 4313&ec&n5

Jersey, 5th Earl of III **719n6**, 4312nn2&4

Jersey, 6th Earl of III **1172n7**, 4312n3

Jersey, 7th Earl of **4312&n3**

Jerusalem 4104n1

Jervis, Ernest Scott 4491n1

Jerviswoode, Lord VII **3243n2**, 4542&n4

Jews and Judaism 3983n2; emancipation 3984n2; first member of Royal Academy 4459n2; disabilities 4478n4, 4492n3; anti-Semitism 4566&nn1-4&6; Ewald's *History of Israel* 4607&n1

Johann I, King of Saxony VIII **3774n2**, 4541n1

John Bull 4026&n6

Johnson, Samuel VIII **3942n3**, 4015&n4

Johnstone, Christopher 4503&n1, **4508&nn1&6**

Johnstone, Henry Butler- VI 2680n2, 4387&n2

Jolliffe, Cecil Emily. *See* Sefton, Countess of (4th Earl)

Jolliffe, Sir William, 1st Bt. *See* Hylton, 1st Baron

Jones, Bence 4052n1

Jones, J. Winter **4275&n2**

Julian calendar 4101n1

Julian the Apostate (Flavius Claudius Julianus) **4419&n4**

Junior Carlton Club 4025n2, 4086&n1

Juvenal 4194&n5, 4196

Kamehameha IV, King of Hawaii 4029n2

Karslake, Sir John Burgess 4228n7, 4379, **4385&n5**, 4588&n4

Kavanagh, Arthur MacMurrough 4236n1, 4242n3, 4254n6

Kebbel, Thomas Edward VIII **3467n1**, 4306&n4, 4332&n2, 4369

Keighley 4463&n3

Keir House 4534&nn1&2

Kelly, Sir Fitzroy VI **2234n3**, 2480R, 4073&nn1-3, 4074&nn2&7, 4075&nn1&7

Kempson, Mr (unidentified) 4536n4

Kendall, Henry Edward 4223n9

Kendall, Nicholas **4372&n2**

Kenealy, Edward IV **1496n3**, 4227&ec&nn1-3, 4238, 4243&nn1-4

Kenry, Baron. *See* Dunraven, 3rd Earl of

Kensington 4269&n4, 4304, 4479&n1, 4482

Kensington Museum. *See* Natural History Museum

Kent 4580

Keogh, William V **2133n1**, 4565n1

Kerrison, Sir Edward, 2nd Bt VI **2504n1**, 4142n1, 4311ec&nn1&2, 4349&n3

Keyworth, John 4199n7

Liverpool, 2nd Earl of IV **1320n5**, 4135n1

Lloyd, Charles V **1877n7**, 4650&n1

Locke, John 4483n2

Loftus, Lord Augustus VIII **3921n1**, 4174&n3, 4294&n5, 4419n12, 4511&n1

London 4190, 4431, 4526, 4532; weather 3996&n2; 1865 election results 4026&n4; Liberal stronghold 4027&n6; 'bill-discounters' 4199; poor relief 4283&nn1&2; police force 4304&n1; work houses 4370&n3; Fenianism 4623&n3, 4629&n1, 4630, 4632&n1, 4637&n1

London, Chatham and Dover Railway Bill (1866) 4495&nn1-3

London and Westminster Bank 3985&n2

London and Westminster Working Men's Constitutional Association 4452n2, 4569&nn1-3

Londonderry, Dowager Marchioness of (3rd Marquess) II **408n9**, 4509&nn4&5

Londonderry, 3rd Marquess of II **389n5**, 4509n4

London Gazette 4209n5, 4412n3; notice to holders of exchequer bills (4 Sep 1866) 4187n6

London University 4478nn1&5

Long, Charlotte Anna 4346n3

Long, Mary Anne III **1072n6**, 4505&nn5&6

Long, Richard Penruddocke **4346&nn3**&4

Long, Walter III **922n2**, 4346n3, 4505&n5

Longfield, Mr 4508n6

Longfield, Robert **4141&n8**

Longfield, Samuel Mountifort **4532&n2**

Longford, 3rd Earl 4222n2

Longley, Charles Thomas 4527n3

Longman, Thomas VII **2165xn1**, 4223&nn1&9&10, 4264, 4282&n1, 4306

Longman, William 4223n1, 4264n3

Longman & Co (publishers) 4223&nn3&10, 4235, 4238, 4282&n3

Longmans, Green & Co (publishers) 4187&n3

Lonsdale, 2nd Earl of II **426n4**, 4047n2, 4128n2, 4218n2, 4263, 4376&n3, 4389&nn2&3, 4437&n1, 4486&n6, 4502&n1, 4506n2; Middlesex election 3997, 4017; invites DS to Lowther 4039&n1; letters to his ancestor 4044&nn1&3-5&8; chronic illness 4052&n3; recommends nephew to D 4126&nn1&3; application to D misunderstood 4133&n1

Lonsdale, 6th Earl of 4044n3

Lord Clyde (ironclad) 4372n5

Lords, House of 3481A, 4323, 4356&n2, 4448, 4454, 4481, 4491&nn2&3, 4498; parliamentary petition 3992&n3; neutrality re Civil War 4002&n3; Granville's leadership 4045&n2; cabinet members 4060&n5; 1866 reform bill 4106; Roll of the Lords 4145n2; health and reformatory school bills 4166; 1867 reform bill 4440&n2, 4444, 4483n1, 4485&n2;

proxies 4470&nn1&2; 1867 reform bill 4473&nn1-3. *See also* Parliament

Lorne, Marquess of 4268n5

Louise, Princess (Marchioness of Lorne 1871; Duchess of Argyll 1900) **4268&n5**

Louise Margaret, Princess of Prussia (Duchess of Connaught and Strathearn and Countess of Sussex 1879) 4417n2

Louise Sophie, Duchess of Schleswig-Holstein-Sonderburg-Augustenburg 4417n1

Louis Philippe of France II **413n1**, 1315XA&nn3&4

Lovaine, Lord. *See* Northumberland, 6th Duke of

Lovegrove, Joseph V **1776n5**, 3990n1, 4080&n2, 4285

Lovell, William IV **1235n1**, 3996n4, 4080&ec&n2, 4199&nn2&4&5, 4295

Lovett, Mr (woodman) 3981&n1

Lowe, Robert (Viscount Sherbrooke 1880) VI **2734n2**, 4340&n4, 4374, 4376, 4383n1, 4386n3, 4387n2, 4433&n2, 4440n1, 4504n1, 4592&nn1-3&5; cattle plague commission 4052n1; *Times* articles 4054&nn1&2; 'offered Lancaster & the Cabinet' 4071; 'clear majority against' reform bill 4074; leader of Adullamites 4102n2; 1865 speeches 4108n2; 'Adullamite co-operation' 4116n1; Adullamite followers 4118n3, 4291; opposition to reform 4324&n1; cumulative voting 4467&n1, 4481n1; 'great bitterness' 4472&n1; Grey's amendment 4473n3

Lowndes, Richard William Selby-, Jr **4536&n4**

Lowndes, Richard William Selby-, Sr 4536n4

Lowndes, William IV **1576n2**, 4031n2

Lowther, James 4369n6, **4389&nn1&2**

Lowther, William VII **3184n5**, 4506&n1, 4513n1, 4529n1

Lowther Castle 4039n1, 4040, 4218n2, 4502&n1; D's description of 4044&nn1&3&5

Lucas, Frederick **4238&n7**

Lucas, Samuel (editor of *Morning/Evening Star*) VIII **3452n1**, 4238n7

Lucas, Samuel (editor of *Press*) VI **2331n1** 4075&nn1&2

Lumley, John Savile 4550n5

Luton 4452n3, 4463&n3

Luxemburg 4396nn1&2, 4411n1, 4419&nn1&5&12, 4420n1, 4431nn1&2, 4484&nn1&5, 4491

Lygon, Frederick. *See* Beauchamp, 6th Earl

Lyndhurst, 1st Baron I **338n6**, 414x&nn1-3, 4219n1

Lyster, Anthony 4643n3

Lyster, Henry 4250n4

Lyster, Lady Charlotte 4250n4

Lytton, Sir Edward Bulwer-, 1st Bt. *See* Lytton, 1st Baron

Lytton, 1st Baron I **83n1**, 4111&n2, 4145n2

Lyveden, 1st Baron IV **1255n2**, 4485&n2

Maberly, William Leader III **1012n2**, 1033x&n2

Macaulay, Charles Zachary **4263&n1**, 4291n1, 4330n1

Macaulay, Thomas Babington (Baron Macaulay of Rothley) I **233n3**, 414xn3, 3924xn1

Macclesfield, 6th Earl of **4268&n2**

Macdonald, John A. 4004n1

Macfarlane, Duncan **4337&nn1&2&3**-4

Macnabb, James Monro 4449n2

Madresfield Court 4414ec

Madrid 4198

Maguire, John **3887A&n1**, 4091&n2, 4588nn1-3

Maguire, Robert 4628n10, 4636n3, **4638&nn1-**3

Mahaffy, Sir John Pentland **4090**ec&**n1**

Mahon, Lord. *See* Stanhope, 5th Earl

Mahon, Viscount (6th Earl Stanhope 1875) **4142&n1**

Maidstone Journal 4180n1, 4245n2

Major, Mr 4270&n1

Mallet, Louis 4191nn2&7, **4196**&nn1&**2**, 4237&n1, 4295&n5

Malmesbury, 3rd Earl of III **1067n11**, 1923R, 1929x&nn1&2, 1949R, 2480R, 2797R, 4310n1, 4346n2, 4402nn1&2; refers Birch to Rose 3980n4; dines with DS 3998n1; lord privy seal 4120n3; scheme of making Salisbury a duke 4124; worst appointment 4174n3; 'memorialists' 4194n2, 4340n2, 4438n3, 4485; foreign secretary 4259&n4; police magistrate idea 4263; D's reform plan 4331n2; proxies in Lords 4470&nn1&2; reform bill 4483ec&n1

Malone, Edmond **4015&n7**

Malt tax 4073&nn1-3, 4074n2, 4075, 4204, 4232, 4237&n2, 4251, 4391&n4, 4418n2

Manchester 4089n3, 4146n4, 4149&n1, 4213&n4, 4464, 4465n1, 4512&n2, 4540&n1, 4547, 4551&n1, 4557&nn1&4, 4570n1, 4588nn1&7

Manchester Courier 4144n2

Manchester Guardian 4144n2

'Manchester Martyrs' 4588n7, 4590n1

Manchester school 4149n1

Manners, Lady John (Janetta, 2nd wife) VIII **3722n1**, 4179, 4383&nn1&3

Manners, Lord John (7th Duke of Rutland 1888) III **1129n2**, 1315XA, 4340n2, 4346n2, 4359n2, 4463, 4485, 4565n1, 4569n2, 4635&n3; commissioner of works 4120n3, 4157n5; summoned by D 4122; suggested as ambassador 4123&nn1&3&4; damage to parks by rioters 4161n2; Burlington House reconstruction 4179&nn1&3; dual voting 4380n1

Manning, Henry V **2069n5**, 4085&n3, 4154&n2, 4238n6, 4409&nn1-3, 4441&n1, 4614&n1, 4617, 4637&n2, 4640&nn1&2

Mansel, Henry Longueville 4266n2, **4267&n2**

Mansfield, Sir William 4491n1

Mansfield Street 4190

Manx Sun 4543&n1

Marlborough, Duchess of (7th Duke) V **2000n16**, 4217n2, 4509n1, 4610n3

Marlborough, 1st Duke of 4615n2

Marlborough, 4th Duke of 4217n2, 4442n1

Marlborough, 7th Duke of V **1995n15**, 4217n2, 4359n2, 4377, 4438n3, 4442&n1, 4500n2, 4516&n1, 4535, 4610n3; Fenian convicts 4444n3

Martello tower 4641&n1

Martin, Philip Wykeham **4105&n1**

Martineau, Russell 4607n1

Martinez, Manuel Alonso 4190n1

Martynov, Solomon Mikhailovitch 4039n4

Mary, Queen (George V) 4039n3

Mary Adelaide, Princess of Cambridge. *See* Mary Adelaide, Princess of Teck

Mary Adelaide, Princess of Teck (Duchess of Teck 1871) V **1794n6**, 4039&nn3&6, 4602n5

Mary II 4015n1

Mathew, Theobald **3887A&n1**

Maunsell, Henry **4489&nn1**-4

Mauritius 4244nn1-3

Mauroy, Prosper 4519n2

Maximilian I, Emperor of Mexico 4466n1

Maxwell, Lady Anna **4534&n4**, 4637

Maxwell, Sir William Stirling VIII **3579n1**, 4068ec, 4534&nn1&2&4&5, 4637&n3

May, Sir Thomas Erskine (1st Baron Farnborough 1886) 4501n2, **4530&n2**

Mayall, J.E. 4046n3

Maynard, Charles Henry 4552n2

Mayne, Sir Richard 4155n2, 4157nn2-4, 4162n6, **4304&n1**, 4624n2, 4625&nn1&3&4, 4626, 4628&n7, 4629n1, 4632n1

Mayo, Countess of (6th Earl) VI **2618n1**, 4141&n2, 4178, 4254

Mayo, 5th Earl of 4503n1

Mayo, 6th Earl of V **2000n15**, 4143ec, 4298n6, 4331&n3, 4441, 4485, 4489&nn3&4, 4490, 4500n1, 4503&nn1&3&5, 4508&nn1&6, 4511&n4, 4532&n5, 4565n1, 4593n2, 4622&nn1&2, 4623&n1, 4627&nn2-4, 4628&n10, 4629n1, 4636&n2, 4640n2, 4641; dines with DS 3998n1; Irish secretary 4120n3; Irish appointments 4141&ec&n1; Napier's withdrawal 4152n1; Napier's rumoured appointment 4165n1; habeas corpus suspension 4166n2; mastership of the rolls 4178&n1; chief secretary for Ireland 4212&n3; absent from cabinet meeting 4229n2; 'most able, sensible, & enlightened' 4236; 'clerical party indignant' 4242n3; Tipperary election 4254&nn1&6&7; Irish government breaking up 4279&nn3&4; Irish railways 4444n1; Fenian convicts 4444n3

McKenna, Sir Joseph Neal **4115**&nn1&3&4,

4373n2, 4500ec&nn1&2, 4500&ec&nn1&2, 4501&n1

McLagan, Peter **4337**&nn**1**&4

McLaren, Duncan **4447**&nn**1**&2

M'Clean, Mr 4051n4, 4052n1

McNeile, John 4182n4

Measom, Sir George 4536n2

Meehan, Gladwin 4643n1

Meetings in Royal Parks Bill. *See* Parks Regulation Bill (1867)

Mellor, John William **4307**&n**2**

Mellor, Sir John VIII **3586n1**, 4307n2

Mellor, Thomas Walton **4307**&n**2**

Mentmore Towers 3986n2

Mercury (ship) 4632&n3

Meredyth, Baron. *See* Athlumney, Lord

Merewether, Charles George 4503n1, 4508n1

Merewether, William 4592n1

Merthyr Tydvil 4463&n3

Merton, Lewis 4037n1

Metropolitan Police Force 4304n1

Metropolitan Poor Bill (1867) 4283n1, 4362n2, 4370&n3, 4438n4

Michell, Amelia **4136**&n**1**

Michell, Edward Blair 4136n1

Michell, Richard 4136n1

Middlesex 4017&n1, 4044&n5, 4067ec, 4300&nn1&2

Middleton Stoney, Oxon 4313&n5

Mill, John Stuart VII **3289n6**, 4023n3, 4150&n3, 4157&n6, 4283n2, 4291&n5, 4447n2; in 'profound slumber' in House 4162&nn5&6; women's suffrage 4440n1; Fenian convicts 4444n3

Mills, Arthur **4020**&nn**1**&**3**

Milne, Sir Alexander VII **3239n2**, 4202n1, 4216&n14, 4251&n1, 4257n1

Minto, 3rd Earl of 4174n5

Monck, Baron 4145n2, 4222n2, **4632**&nn**2**&**3**&5

Moncreiff, James Wellwood (Baron Moncreiff 1874; 11th Bt 1883) **4445**&n**1**, 4555n1

Moniteur (Paris) 4182n2

Monk, Charles J. 4160n2

Monmouth, Duke of 4124n5

Monsell, William (Baron Emley 1874) VIII **3496n3**, 4085, 4165n1, 4236&n5

Montagu, Andrew VIII **3683n1**, 4170&n1, 4505n1

Montagu, Lord Robert VIII **3837n13**, 4263&n1, 4291n1, 4376&n4, 4535&nn1&3

Montefiore, Emma V **1997n7**, 4239n1

Montefiore, Henrietta Francisca **4239**&n**1**

Montefiore, Joseph Mayer **4239**&n**1**

Montefiore, Nathaniel Mayer V **1997n7**, 4239n1

Montgomery, Fanny (Hon Mrs Alfred) **4628**&nn**9**&10

Montrose, 4th Duke of III **961n13**, 4570&n2

Monypenny, W.F. 4506ec

Moran, Benjamin 4630n1

Morier, Robert (Sir Robert 1885) **4174**&ec&n**4**

Morning Advertiser 4557&n2

Morning Herald 4144n2, 4174&n3, 4284n2

Morning Post 1643AR, 1923R, 4075&n1, 4144n2, 4215n4, 4386&n3; London mayoralty election (30 Sept 1840) 1094Rn2; reviews Napoleon's *Histoire de Jules César* (6 Mar 1865) 3996n6; D's letter to Bucks electors (7 Jul 1865) 4013n4; inauguration of statue of Prince Albert at Coburg (30 Aug 1865) 4039n6; MA's 'recent indisposition' (3 Jul 1866) 4113n2

Morning Star 4144n2, 4447&n2

Morris, Michael (1st Bt 1885; Baron Morris of Spiddal 1889; 1st Baron Killanin 1900) **4140**&n**1**, 4141&nn1&5

Morris, William **4091**&n**4**

'Morrow of St Martin' 4570n3

Mortmain Act (1279) 4476n1, 4631&nn1&3

Mount Braddon 3985n3, 3996&nn3-5

Mount Edgcumbe, Countess of (4th Earl) VIII **3780n7**, 4512n4

Mount Edgcumbe, 4th Earl of VIII **3743n3**, 4512&n4

Moustier, marquis de **4232**&nn**5**&6, 4294&nn4&10, 4297, 4420n1, 4515n3, 4529n1

Moxon, Thomas **4233**&nn**3**&4

Mozart, Wolfgang Amadeus: *Don Giovanni* 4244n3, 4542n5, 4602n3

Mulcahy, Denis Dowling 4141n8

Mulholland, John (1st Baron Dunleath of Ballywalter 1892) 4503n1, **4508**&nn**1**&4&6, 4511&n5, 4532n5

Munby, Alan 4476n1, 4631ph&n1

Municipal Corporations Bill 414xn1

Murrain (or rinderpest – cattle plague) 4043n1, 4045&n5, 4047&nn1-3, 4051&n4, 4052&n1, 4058&n2, 4062&nn3&5&6, 4067, 4068n2, 4127n3, 4189&nn1&2&&4, 4197&nn1&4, 4198n3, 4251&n2, 4535nn1-3, 4580n1, 4600n2

Murray, J.W. 3996nn4&5

Murray, Robert 4286ec

Murray, Sir Charles Augustus I **261n3**, 4550n5

Museum of Natural History 4269

Music: opera 4244n3, 4542n5, 4602&n3

Musson, Mr 4615n2

Naas, Lord. *See* Mayo, 6th Earl of

Napier, Joseph V **1818n6**, 4148n5, 4165&n1

Napier, Sir Robert 4521n4, 4592nn3&5

Napoleon III, Emperor of the French III **971n7**, 2797R, 4302n3, 4396&nn1&2, 4419n1, 4423n1, 4515n1, 4557n7, 4558n2; *Histoire de Jules César* 3996&n6; assassination conspiracy 4110n2; war with Prussia 4139n1; Bowyer's tirade against 4153n4; illness 4174n1, 4182&n2, 4232&nn5&6; proposal to annex Belgium 4294&nn1&10; speeches 'reassuring' 4513&n1; secret treaty between Prussia and Italy 4550&n1

National Club 4372&n2

National Gallery 4442n1, 4479

National Gallery of Naval Art 4459n2

National Portrait Gallery 4171&n1

National University of Ireland 4060n4

Natural History Museum 4479n1, 4482

Navigation laws 2480R

Neale, John I **359n3**, 535X&n2

Neate, Charles V **2135n1**, 4220n2

Neeld, Sir John, 1st Bt IV **1558n1**, 4022&n1

Negrete, Pedro Romulo **4586**&ec**&n1**, 4587, 4589

Nelson, 1st Earl VIII **3505n4**, 4194n2

Nelson, 1st Viscount VIII **3505n3**, 4598n2

Nevill, Lady Dorothy IV **1589n1**, 4001&n1

Nevill, Viscount (5th Earl of Abergavenny 1868; Marquess of Abergavenny 1876) VIII **3969n1**, 4025&n2, 4027&n3

Newberry, Charles (under-butler) **4063&n2**

Newbury, Berks 4250, 4255

Newcastle, 5th Duke of I **324n7**, 4488&n2

Newcastle, 6th Duke of **4207&n7**, 4216&n4, 4256n2

Newcastle Weekly Chronicle 4061n2

Newdegate, Charles Newdigate IV **1511n3**, 4335&n2

New Forest, Hants 4194&nn1&2, 4204&n5

New Forest Poor Relief Bill 4194n2

Newman, John Henry V **2122n5**, 4060n4, 4441n1

Newport, Viscount. *See* Bradford, 3rd Earl of

Newport, Viscountess. *See* Bradford, Countess of (3rd Earl)

Newport Pagnell 1929xn3

Newton, Charles Thomas **4269&n**n1**&5**, 4275&n2, 4417&nn3&4

New York 4543&n3, 4632&n3

New Zealand bonds 4187&n5

Nightingale, Florence 4611n1

Nigra, Constantino (Count Nigra 1882) **4550&n2**

Noel, Gerard VIII **3837n7**, 4226n2, 4341&n5, 4485&n5

Noel, Lady Blanche 4429n1

Norfolk 4319

Normanby, Marchioness of (1st Marquess) **4512&n5**

Normanby, 1st Marquess of **4512&n5**

Normandy 4199&n11

Norris, John I **191n3**, 535X&n4

North America 4410, 4524&n2

Northbrook, 1st Baron III **1046n2**, 4293n2

Northcote, Henry Stafford (9th Bt 1887; 1st Baron Northcote 1900) 4366, 4381&n4, 4477n1, 4543n3

Northcote, Sir Stafford Henry, 8th Bt (1st Earl of Iddesleigh 1885) VI **2838n4**, 4073n3,

4228n5, 4246&nn1&2, 4287&ec, 4301&n1, 4341, 4343, 4345, 4352&n1, 4359n2, 4363, 4474n2, 4475&n1, 4482&n3, 4522, 4526n1, 4539, 4542n6, 4545n3, 4559n1, 4560n1, 4592&n5, 4596&n2, 4597&nn1&2, 4612, 4632; cautions D against 'false moves' 4074&ec; supports Carnarvon on railway bills 4082; Lady Salisbury's views 4084; president of board of trade 4120n3; purchase of gun metal 4159n2; board of trade 4191; duties on Portuguese wine 4196n1; banquet at Liverpool 4207n2; friend of Gladstone 4221&n2; railway companies bill 4233n5; financial state of railway companies 4234; Portuguese treaty 4237&nn1&2; reform question 4247&nn1&2; cattle plague in Cheshire 4251n2; plan for board of trade 4274&n4; seat in Devon 4289&n4; elected to Trinity House 4293n2; position on reform 4377&n7; dual voting 4380n1

Northumberland, 5th Duke of VII **2998n6**, 4038n5, 4351nn1&2

Northumberland, 6th Duke of VI **2818n3**, 3035X, 4351&nn1&2

Norwich 4347&n2

Nugent, Sir George, 1st Bt IV **840Rn6**, 4543n3

Oath of Abjuration Bill (1858) 3984n2

O'Brien, Michael 4588n7

O'Brien, Sir Patrick, 2nd Bt VII **3350n5**, 4028n1, 4588n2

Observer 4258n1

O'Connell, Daniel I **198n1**, 3924X

Odger, George **4415&n**n8&9

O'Donoghue, Daniel VII **3348n4**, 4060n4

Old Broad Street, London 4233n3

Oliphant, Laurence 4157n3

O'Loghlen, Sir Colman 4588n2

Olympus 4377

O'Mahony, John 4216n7

Oram, Richard Bennett **4461&n2**

Orange Order 4490

Orfila, Matthieu III **1094n1**, 1094R

Orford, 1st Earl of IV **1391n4**, 4044n2, 4598n2

Orford, 3rd Earl of IV **1503n3**, 3988n2

Orford, 4th Earl of III **720n1**, 4598&n2

Orr, James 4418n3

Osborne 4330, 4334&nn1&2, 4438&n3, 4501

Osborne, Catherine Isabella Bernal V **1401Xn2**, 4382&n8

Osborne, Grace (Duchess of St Albans 1874) 4527n2

Osborne, Lady (Sir Thomas, 9th Bt) 4382n8

Osborne, Ralph Bernal III **1182n2**, 4148n5, 4157&n3, 4166&n3, 4356n2, 4374&n6, 4382&n8, 4400n1, 4527n2, 4592n4

Osborne, Sir Thomas, 9th Bt 4382n8

Ossington Holy Rood 4292n2

Oswald, M. Alexander 4184n2

Ottoman Empire 4294n9. *See* Turkish Empire

Otway, Arthur John 4356n1, 4491n1

Overend, Gurney & Co (bankers) 4125nn1&2
Oxford 4186&nn1&2
Oxford Street 4304
Oxford University 4026&n1, 4265n1,
    4266ec&n2, 4369
Paddington Station 4201
Padwick, Henry Sr VII **2895n1**, 4528&nn1&3
Paget, James VII **3430n3**, 4052, 4299n2
Paget, Lord Alfred III **900n8**, 4268&n9
Paget, Robert 4638n3
Paget, Sir Augustus Berkeley 4515n3, **4524&n1**
Paget, Thomas Tertius 4596n2, 4600n2,
    4602n1
Painted Hall. *See* National Gallery of Naval Art
Pakington, Sir John, 1st Bt (1st Baron
    Hampton 1874) III **713n4**, 4207&n3, 4250,
    4316n1, 4330, 4341&n2, 4351n2, 4356&n1,
    4359n2, 4402n2, 4434n2, 4620, 4622,
    4628, 4630, 4632n1; first lord of admiralty
    4120n3; inspects Portsmouth dockyard
    4175&nn1&6&7; inspection of ships
    4202nn1&2; reorganization of admiralty
    4216&n14; reserves of navy 4229&n4; pur-
    chase of 'most powerful ship' 4249&nn1&5,
    4257&nn1&3; ironclads 4251&nn1&5; Irish
    papers 4277n1, 4279n4; re-election speech
    4373&n3, 4374&n2; 'Army of Reserve'
    4480&n1
Palk, Sir Lawrence, 4th Bt (1st Baron Haldon
    1880) VI **2666n2**, 4010, 4341, 4342
Pall Mall 4304
Pall Mall Gazette 4263n1, 4537n3
Palmer, Sir Roundell (1st Baron Selborne
    1872) V **2113n10**, 4238&n12, 4387&n2
Palmerston, 3rd Viscount II **668n14**, 1094Rn6,
    2797R, 4029An3, 4060n6, 4315, 4518n4; 1857
    dissolution 4025, 4027; death anticipated
    4030n1; illness and death 4038&nn7&8;
    death 4044n8, 4045&nn1&2, 4051, 4052&n2;
    1859 government 4056n3; 1865 speeches
    4108n2; 'Palmerstonian sympathies & influ-
    ences' 4121&n1; Irish MPs 4135&n1; Albert
    memorial 4160n2; anniversary of death
    4204n3; non-confidence motion 4236; 1863
    speeches 4555&n1
Panama Star and Herald 4029n2
Panizzi, Anthony VIII **3820n1**, 4074, 4273&n1
Paris 4125, 4269&n1, 4297&nn4&6,
    4419&nn4&12, 4529nn1&4, 4550, 4628&n6,
    4642&n2
Paris International Exhibition 4313n3
Park, Frederick William 4256n2
Parker, Sir William (Admiral) 4293n2
Parker, William (Major) 4074n2
Parkes, E.A. 4052n1
Parks Regulation Bill (1867) 4483n2, 4494&n2,
    4498&n1
Parliament 1315XA, 4055, 4216&n3, 4449,
    4631&n1; meeting (1850) 1929X&n4; dis-
    solution (1865) 4013, 4019&n1, 4038&n7;

meeting (1866) 4045&n5, 4064&nn2&3,
    4068, 4222; November meeting doubtful
    4047&nn1&3; rumoured meeting 4051,
    4052; 'Irish Church ... unpopular' 4060;
    ministerial resignation 4115&n2; proro-
    gation (1866) 4167n3, 4168n3; opening
    (1866) 4190; meeting (1867) 4290&n5,
    4291&nn1&5, 4303; opening (1847) 4308n1;
    prorogation (1867) 4494&n1; summoned
    re Abyssinian war 4518&nn2-4, 4521&n3;
    'difficulty' 4522&n2; autumn session
    4526&nn1&3; distinction between proro-
    gation and adjournment 4530&nn1&2;
    November meeting 4534, 4537&n3, 4538,
    4545&n3, 4552, 4559, 4561&n1, 4564&n2;
    plot to blow up 4628, 4632&nn1&4. *See
    also* Commons, House of; Lords, House
    of
Parliamentary Oaths Amendment Bill (1866)
    4078n3, 4085&nn1&2&4
Parliamentary Voters (Ireland) Bill (1850)
    4223n10
Parrott, Joseph VIII **3706n1**, 4189n3,
    4197&nn1&4
Partridge, William Edwards III **830n3**,
    4219&nn1&3
Paternoster Row 4223&n1
Patten, John Wilson (Baron Winmarleigh
    1874) VI **2360n2**, 4381, 4644&n1
Paull, Henry 3988n2
Peacocke, George Montagu. *See* Sandford,
    George Montagu
Peel, Archibald **4354&n2**
Peel, Edmund Yates **4354&n2**
Peel, John **4354&n2**
Peel, Jonathan VI **2402n4**, 4123n5, 4123&n5,
    4155n1, 4223, 4296, 4323&n2, 4331n2, 4340,
    4341&nn4&5, 4342, 4354&nn1-3, 4480n1;
    war secretary 4120n3; 'take ... on his own
    terms' 4124; defence of Canada against
    Fenians 4216nn7&11; purchase of rifles for
    Canada 4222&nn2&3&6, 4251; Irish papers
    4277n1, 4279n4; opposition to household
    suffrage 4322&n1; withdraws resignation
    4334&n2; resignation 4338n1, 4352n1,
    4355n2, 4359nn1&2, 4376n1; army estimates
    4351n2, 4357&n1; army estimates postponed
    4356&n1
Peel, Sir Robert, 2nd Bt I **188n3**, 414x, 1949R,
    3924xn1, 4029An3, 4074n3, 4238n4, 4270n1,
    4304n1; 1845 resignation 4056; 'parsimoni-
    ous' in distribution of honours 4146
Peel, Sir Robert, 3rd Bt V **2113n3**, 4148&n2
Peel, William Augustus **4354&n2**
Pell, Albert **4600&n2**, 4602n1
Peninsular and Oriental Steam Navigation
    Company 4507&n3, 4570n1
Pennant, Edward Douglas-. *See* Penrhyn, 1st
    Baron
Penrhyn, 1st Baron VI **2598n4**, 4145n2, 4448n7

Percy, Countess (Duchess of Northumberland 1899) 3998n1

Percy, Earl. *See* Northumberland, 6th Duke of

Percy, Earl (7th Duke of Northumberland 1899) 3998n1

Percy, Lady Josceline **4038&n5**

Percy, Lord Josceline William VII **3249n5**, 4038n5

Peto, Sir Samuel VII **3360n3** 4054&n3, 4055&n3

Phillimore, Sir Robert Joseph VIII **3505n6**, 4482&n5

Phillipps, Sir Thomas IV **1262n3**, 4476&n1, 4631&nn1-3

Phillipps de Lisle, Ambrose 3983n1

Phipps, Sir Charles VIII **3662n1**, 4081&n1

Piccadilly 4304

Pim, Jonathan **4090**&ec**&n1**

the Pirkei Avot 4566&n3

Pitman, John Rogers 4566n4

Pitt, William (the Younger) IV **1320n4**, 4044n1, 4238n4

Pius IX, Pope IV **1548n2**, 4236n4, 4553n1, 4557n7

Place, Francis VI **264xn2**, 264XR

Playfair, Lyon 4052n1

Plunket, David Robert **4090**&ec**&n1**

Plunket, 1st Baron **4140&n3**

Poland 4470, 4639&n3, 4641

Poles, Stephan 4566n2

Police 4155nn2&4, 4157nn2-5&7, 4159&n1, 4162n6, 4636; secret service 4621&n1, 4622n1, 4623&n3, 4626n1, 4629&n1, 4642n2; Clerkenwell explosion 4624n2, 4625nn3&4; London Metropolitan 4627&n2, 4637; London and Ireland 4628&n6; London Metropolitan 4632n4

Poole, Eliza **4566&n5**&6

Poole, Reginald Stuart VIII **3822n3**, 4566&nn1&5&6

Poor Law Amendment Act (1834) 4007n1

Poor Law Amendment Bill (1866) 4154&nn3&6

Poor Law Board 4372, 4628

Pope, Alexander 4015&n5

the Porte 4232&n6

Portpatrick, Scotland 4220nn1&2

Portsmouth 4330, 4333&n1

Portugal 4298&nn3&6, 4299&nn1&2, 4313&n2, 4316&n1, 4504&nn2&4, 4511; high customs tariff 4191&nn1&2&7; commercial treaty with Britain 4196n1, 4203, 4237&nn1&2, 4293, 4295n4

Postal service 4196, 4204, 4526, 4527; abolition of free franking 1033X&n1; registered letters 1511XA; night post 4048, 4230; 'second post' 4060, 4249; to Stowe 4124; 'first post' 4195; instead of government boxes 4198; to Balmoral 4206, 4233; mail train 4210n1;

between London and Knowsley 4217; railway postal subsidy 4220nn1&2; between Hughenden and Knowsley 4246; to Strathfieldsaye 4271; Dover to Calais 4286n2; purchase of telegraph companies 4293&n4; post office packets 4485&n1; to China and India 4507&nn1-3; 'leathern covers' 4524; Indian 4560; P&O contracts 4570&nn1&2; with United States 4593n2; second delivery 4650&n1

Potter, Richard VI **264xn2**, 264XR

Potter, Thomas Bayley 4093n2, **4149&n1**, 4383n1

Powell, William VI **2421n1**, 4173

Praed, James Backwell II **625n2**, 535X&nn4&5

Prescott, William **4002&n5**

Press 3980&n1, 4075n1; reprints D's speeches from *The Times* 3995

the press 1923R, 4110&n2, 4489&n1; opposition from 4522; 'always speak truth' 4537&n3, 4538; alarmed at invasion of Rome 4562&n3

Preston 4526

Price, Councillor (Leeds) 4329n1

Primrose, Archibald William (5th Earl of Rosebery, 1868). *See* Dalmeny, 2nd Lord

Primrose, Bouverie Francis 4610nn1&2

Primrose, Everard Henry 4509n1

Primrose, Henry William **4610&nn**1&**2**

Primrose, Lady Frederica Sophia 4610n2

Primrose, Mary Catherine 4509n1

Princes Gate, Knightsbridge 4098&n1

Prisons 4219&n1, 4233n1

Protestants and Protestantism 4372, 4569n3

Prowett, Charles Gipps VIII **3482n2**, 4026n6

Prussia 4395&n1, 4396n1, 4411&nn1&2, 4419nn1&12, 4420n1, 4484&nn1&2&5, 4491&n4, 4513&n1, 4515nn1&3, 4529n1, 4541n1, 4550&nn1&3; advance on Vienna 4139n1; war with Austria 4153nn1&3; 'most powerful ship' 4249n5, 4251n5; ironclads 4257&nn1&2; division of Germany 4294&nn3&10

Public Health Bill (1848) 4162n2

Public Health Bill (1866) 4161&n1, 4162&n2, 4166n1

Publicola, Publius Valerius **1094R&n3**

Public Schools Bill (1867) 4580n1

Punch 4029An3

Punnett, P.S. 4074n2

Purcell, Mr 4490nn1&2

Puseyites 4060

Quain, Richard 4052n1

Quakers 4075n6, 4090n1

Quarterly Review 4557&nn8&9, 4566nn1&2

Quarter Sessions, Aylesbury 1949R, 4233&n1, 4253&n1, 4294&n8, 4297, 4642&n1, 4643&n1

Queen's Gate 4304

Queen's Hotel, Portsmouth 4333&n1

Queen's University of Ireland 4060n4,
4148&nn2-4, 4254n6
Quin, Frederic II **494n6**, 4542&n1
Raby Castle 4034&n1, 4038&ec, 4040n1,
4509&n1; D's description of 4037&n2
Radcliffe, Ann I **57n2:** *Mysteries of Udolpho*
4509&n2
Radicals 4262, 4284, 4347, 4372
Raeburn, Sir Henry 4563n2
Raglan, Baroness (2nd Baron)
4042&nn**1**&3&5
Raglan, 2nd Baron 4042n1, 4474n3
Railway Bills (1866) 4082n2
Railway Companies Arrangements Bill (1867)
4233n5
Railway Companies (Ireland) Temporary Advances Act (1866) 4226n5, 4373n2
Railways 4001, 4226&nn1&5, 4268, 4333; expansion in 1860s 4125n2; Ireland 4142&n2,
4251, 4485&n1, 4503nn1-3, 4511&n5,
4532n3, 4546; mail trains 4210n1; Portpatrick, Scotland 4220n1; Great North
and South of France 4233n3; London and
North Western 4233n3; financial state
4233&nn3-5, 4234; Grand Trunk (Canada)
4432n1; Ottoman 4474n2; Canada 4488;
1866 bill 4495nn1&3; Wellington and Market Drayton 4505n2; railway commissioners
4508&nn1&2&6; timetables 4536nn2&4;
Wales 4549n1
Railways (Ireland) Temporary Advances Bill
4142&n2, 4161n1
Rainger, William **3362x**&nn**1**&2
Ram, Mr 4236n1, 4242n1
Ramsay, Allan 4563n2
Randolph, J.W. 4290ec&n2
Ranelagh, 7th Viscount IV **1347n5**, 4017&n1,
4044n5, 4300&nn1&2
Rattazzi, Urbano **4558&n2**
Ravensworth, 1st Baron II **410n4**, 4512n5
Read, Clare Sewell 4074n2
Read, Mr 4052n1
Redesdale, 2nd Baron (1st Earl Redesdale
1877) II **514n6**, 4495n3
Redistribution of Seats Bill. *See* Reform Bill
Reeve, Henry VII **3371n3** 4282&n3
Reform Act (1832) 3924x, 4144&n1, 4302,
4327&n1, 4378n1, 4385n8
Reform Act (1867) 4293n7, 4317n2, 4351,
4452n3, 4505n1, 4569n2; 10th resolution
4301n1; 'Reform banquet' at Crystal Palace
4542&n5
Reformatory Schools Bill (1866) 4161&n1,
4166n1
Reform Bill (Ireland 1867) 4580nn1&2
Reform Bill (Scotland 1852) 4365n2
Reform Bill (Scotland 1860) 4365n2
Reform Bill (Scotland 1866) 4365n2
Reform Bill (Scotland 1867) 4435n1, 4436&n1,
4580nn1&2, 4602n2

Reform Bill (1832) 2480R, 4093n2, 4291
Reform Bill (1854) 4375, 4378&n1
Reform Bill (1858) 4013&n2
Reform Bill (1859) 4013&n2, 4038n4,
4056&n3, 4089n3, 4187&n4, 4238&nn2&4,
4328n3
Reform Bill (1860) 4054&n2, 4187&n4
Reform Bill (1865) 4115n4, 4438n4
Reform Bill (1866) 4038&n3, 4044&n8,
4054n1, 4059n2, 4074&n6, 4075, 4083n2,
4090n1, 4091&nn1&2&7, 4094n4, 4095n1,
4098n1, 4102n2, 4104&n3, 4105&nn1-3,
4106, 4107&n1, 4110nn3&4, 4111n1,
4114&nn1&3, 4115&n2, 4148n1, 4151&n1,
4152, 4187, 4206&n3, 4228n4, 4238nn4&8,
4261&n2, 4292n1, 4343n3, 4346n4,
4350&n1, 4428n2
Reform Bill (1867) 4093n1, 4304,
4321&nn2-4&6, 4328&nn1-3, 4341n2,
4355, 4356&nn1-3, 4366&n1, 4367, 4390n1,
4397&n1, 4415&nn1&7&9, 4434n3, 4459n1,
4474, 4476, 4478&nn1&2&5, 4481&n1,
4519n3, 4534n5, 4557nn3&9; resolutions 4 and 5 4320nn1&3; resolution 5
4322&n2; resolutions 4325&n1; plural
voting 4331&n1; 'thoroughly conservative measure' 4334&n4; 'Ten Minutes Bill'
4340&nn2-4, 4373&nn1&3; 'will be accomplished' 4342&n1; resolutions 5 and
6 4343&nn2&3; occupation franchise
4344&n1; £6 or £5 rating 4345&nn1-3;
ratepaying principle 4346&nn1-4&6;
Horsman's bill 4349&nn1&3; £6 rating
4350&nn1&2; household suffrage (res 5)
4359&n1; statistics re compound householders 4362n2; redrafted 4368&n1; printed
for Cabinet 4369&nn1-3&5-7; copy to
Queen 4370nn4&5; franchise statistics
4372&nn3&4; introduced 4374&nn1&3-7;
second reading 4377&nn1&5&6,
4380&nn1&2, 4384&n1, 4386&n3; dual voting 4381&n3; personal rating and dual voting 4382&nn3-5; second reading, first night
4385&nn1-5&7-8, 4389&nn1&2; second
reading, second night 4387&nn1-3, 4388;
objections to 4392n1; clause 7 (second vote)
4393&n1; 'a trial of strength' 4398; use of
voting papers 4399n1; 'safe' 4400&nn1-3;
Gladstone's amendments 4401&nn1-4;
clause 3 4403&nn1&2&4, 4404n1, 4405&n1;
'in a canter' 4419&nn9&10; residence qualifications 4426; clause 3 (borough franchise)
4428&nn1-4; 'an Armageddon' 4429&n4;
compound householders 4430; clause 3
'now safe' 4431&nn1&3; clause 3 'result
overwhelming' 4433&nn1&2; 'considerable progress' in committee 4436&nn1&2;
amendment clause 3 4438&nn2&5-9&11;
Hodgkinson's amendment 4439n1; clause
3 agreed to without division 4440&nn1&2;

911n5, 4131&n1, 4239&nn1&3, 4252&n1, 4576, 4579n1, 4584&n1, 4641n2

Rothschild, Sir Anthony de, 1st Bt III **730n10**, 4579n1, 4641&n2

the Rothschilds 4075n8, 4396, 4513&n1; 'confident of peace' 4484n3

N.M. Rothschild & Sons (bankers) 4125

Rouher, Eugène 4507n1

Rowan, Charles 4304n1

Rowton Castle 4250n4, 4505&nn1&2

Royal Academy 4430&n3, 4459n2

Royal Agricultural Hall 4162&nn3&6

Royal and Central Bucks Agricultural Association 4200

Royal Bucks Agricultural Association 4535n2

Royal Courts of Justice 4479&n2

Royal Literary Fund 4032n1, 4634&nn1&2

Royal Navy 4257n2

Royal University of Ireland 4060n4

Rumpenheim Castle 4039&nn5&6

Russell, Francis Charles Hastings (9th Duke of Bedford 1872) **4385&n6**, 4448&n3

Russell, 1st Earl I **141n4**, 4029An3, 4316n1, 4317n1, 4328n3, 4343&n3, 4378&n1, 4385&n8, 4412n3, 4415n8, 4478, 4601n1; Lincoln's assassination 4002n3; premiership 4038&nn3&8, 4044&n8, 4060&n5; discusses reform with Clarendon 4053n1; 'has ... a reform Bill' 4054n1; offers Stanley Duchy of Lancaster 4055n5; 1845 attempts to form government 4056&n2-4; Gladstone's scheme to promote Goschen 4071&nn2&3; quarrel with Delane 4074n5; 'Goschen fiasco' 4075; resignation delayed 4081&n1; resignation 4111n1; ministerial resignation 4115nn2&4; protection of Hyde Park 4159n1; brother-in-law 4174n5; 1860 reform bill 4187&n4; Victoria's opinion of 4216n3; arms to Canada 4222n3; reform bill (1866) 4228n4; Irish opposition 4238n6; reform 4247n1; 'Finality Jack' 4272&n1; speech on ways and means (18 Feb 1848) 4308, 4309; speech from the throne 4315n1; 1866 reform bill 4346n4, 4428n2; 'in a precarious state' 4545n7

Russia 4419nn6&12, 4484, 4515n1

Russo-Turkish War (1877) 4104n1

Rutland, 6th Duke of III **1032n1**, 4123&n4

Rutlandshire 4207&n8

Ryde, Henry Thomas II **557n8** 4031&nn1-3

Ryland, Alderman (Birmingham) 4329n1

Ryley, Edward **4238**&nn**6**&8&9

Rymer, Thomas 4248nn1&2

Sabouroff, Peter Alexandrovich 4195n2

Sadler, Mrs William 4087n2

Sadler, Pte 4087&ec&n2

Sadler, William 4087n2

St Albans, Duchess of (10th Duke) 4523n2, **4527&n2**

St Albans, 10th Duke of 4523n2, **4527&n2**

St Anne's Hill, Chertsey 4514&nn1&3&4

St Clair Erskine, Lady Millicent Fanny (Mss of Stafford 1884; Dss of Sutherland 1892; Lady M Fitzgerald 1914; Hawes 1919) **4552&n2**

St George's Church, Hanover Square 4100n1

St James's Square 4059&n2, 4117, 4146, 4307, 4404, 4565

St Martin's le Grand Street 4206

St Martin's Summer 4057&n1

St Stephen's Chapel 4505&n4

Salford 4463&n3

Salisbury 1949R

Salisbury, Marchioness of (2nd Marquess) v **1845n11**, 4084

Salisbury, 2nd Marquess of III **730n5**, 3988n2, 4017&ec&n2, 4035n1, 4043&nn1&2, 4062, 4083n2, 4124&nn2&3, 4363n1

Sandford, George Montagu v **1861n7**, 4105&n1, 4373n3

Sandwich Islands 4029nn1&2

Sanitary Act (1866) 4162n2

Saturday Review 4235, 4481&n1

Saul (Bible) 4102n2

Saunders, Otley & Co (publishers) 4187n3

Savernake Forest 4496&n2

Savings banks 4038&n4, 4287&n2, 4291n1

Saxony 4541nn1&3, 4550&nn4&5

Scanes, A.E. 4545n1

Schleswig-Holstein 4484&nn2&3, 4491&n4

Schreiber, Charles **4347&n1**

Scotland 1949R, 4030n1, 4133, 4179&n3, 4221, 4225&nn1-3, 4263, 4372&n4, 4511&n4, 4512&n1, 4525&nn1&2, 4537&nn1&2, 4542&nn3&4, 4546, 4552&n1, 4560, 4563&nn2&3&5; 1865 elections 4025, 4026&nn3&4; Liberal stronghold 4027&n6; MPs 4085; lords of treasury 4129; treasury appointments 4135&n1; electoral reform 4365nn1&2, 4447&nn1&2; population statistics 4435n1; reform bill 4436&n1; education 4516&nn1&2

Scotsman 4218n2

Scott, Charles 4558n1

Scott, Lord Henry 4369n6

Scrope, William III **801n6**, 4035&n3

Scudamore, Frank Ives **4287&n2**, 4293n4

Seaham Hall 4509&n5

Sefton, Countess of (4th Earl) VIII **3658n3**, 4100&nn1&2

Sefton, 4th Earl of **4100&n1**

Ségur-Dupeyron, P. de 4519n2

Selkirk, 6th Earl of 4486n4

Serlby Hall 2480R

Servants 4421&n1, 4519&n1, 4526, 4602n5, 4612&n11; annual wages for coachman 4005n2; 'blunder' 4045; quarrels amongst 4063&n2; footman 4185

Seven Weeks War. *See* Austro-Prussian (Seven Weeks) War

Sévigné, Françoise de **4598&n2**

Mayor of Dublin (21 May 1867) 4335n2; list of Conservative supporters (26 Feb 1867) 4340n2; leader on Reform Bill (27 Feb 1867) 4344&n1; Derby's plan to reintroduce original reform plan (5 Mar 1867) 4356&n2; Conservative party meeting (16 Mar 1867) 4372nn1&5; Pakington's indiscretions (15 Mar 1867) 4373n3; announces appointment to poor law board (22 Mar 1867) 4376n6; Liberal party meeting (22 Mar 1867) 4377n1; Russell's speech on reform (6 Feb 1867) 4385n8; civil engineers' dinner (9 May 1867) 4386&n4; French-Dutch negotiations (30 Mar 1867) 4396n1; Gladstone's amendments (10 Apr 1867) 4401n1; appointments of Grey and Biddulph (1 May 1867) 4412n3; Derby's gout (1 Apr 1867) 4413n4; Hennessy's appointment to Labuan (11 May 1867) 4415&nn3&7&8; Hyde Park proclamation (2 May 1867) 4416n2; praises D for Blacas collection (8 Feb 1867) 4417n3; Prussia and Luxemburg (20 Apr 1867) 4420nn1&2; announces publication of Grey's and Victoria's memoir of Albert (27 Jul 1867) 4422n2; Conservative party meeting (6 May 1867) 4429n4; approves of D accepting Hodgkinson's amendment (18 May 1867) 4439n1; leader on reform (15 Jun 1867) 4454&n1; supports amendment to reform bill 4473n3; army of reserve (27 Jul 1867) 4480n1; French interference in Prussian affairs (29 Jul 1867) 4484n2; meeting of the House (10 Aug 1867) 4486n2; Walpole's resignation (10 May 1867) 4498n2; D's harvest home speech (20 Sep 1867) 4514n2; Abyssinian captives (13 Sep 1867) 4515n2; elephants in Abyssinia (3 Sep 1867) 4516n4; anxieties about Abyssinian campaign (11 Sep 1867) 4522&n3; D's invitation to Edinburgh (14 Sep 1867) 4525n1; ritualistic commission (24 Jun 1867) 4527n3; meeting of parliament (24 Sep 1867) 4537n3; letters of regret from Gladstone and Bright (1 Oct 1867) 4542n5; letters of regret re reform banquet (1 Oct 1867) 4542n5; diplomatic appointment to Washington (14 Oct 1867) 4550&n7; Derby's Manchester speech (18 Oct 1867) 4557n2; prorogation of parliament (5 Nov 1867) 4561n1; the 'Roman Question' (4 Nov 1867) 4562nn2&3; MA's doctors in attendance (19 Nov 1867) 4579n2; improvement in MA's health (22 Nov 1867) 4586&n1; error re D's attendance at cabinet (28 Nov 1867) 4593n1; announces new governor of Tasmania (30 Jul 1868) 4635nn1&2; Clerkenwell relief (27 Dec 1867) 4638nn2&3; Paris report of Clerkenwell explosion (31 Dec 1867) 4642n2
Tinsley, Annie **4032**&ec&n**n2**&3
Tinsley, Charles 4032nn2&3

Tipperary, Ireland 4226nn2&4, 4236&n1, 4254&nn5&6
Tomline, George III **1158n3**, 4074n2
Tornado (ship) 4258&n1
Toronto Globe 4216n7
Torquamada, Tomàs de **4085&n3**
Torquay 4075&n7, 4573&n2, 4615&nn1&2
Torrens, William Torrens McCullagh **4419&n9**, 4458n2
Tower Hamlets 4291
Towneley, Charles 4039n4
Townley, James 4174n4
Trades's Unions 4305n2, 4346
Trajan, Emperor 4297n2
Treaty of London (1867) 4396n2
Treherne, Morgan 3988n2
Trelawny, Sir John, 9th Bt VIII **3567n1**, 3567R
Trevelyan, George Otto (2nd Bt 1886) **4424**&nn**1**&2
Trevelyan, Sir Charles, 1st Bt VI **2225n3**, 4424&n1
Trinitarians. *See* Trinity House
Trinity College, Dublin 4148n2
Trinity House 4268&nn7&8, 4286&n4, 4290n3, 4293&n2, 4425
Trollope, George Francis **4305&n2**
Trollope, Sir John, 7th Bt (1st Baron Kesteven 1868) V **1761n5**, 4372
Tuileries 4294&nn2&10
Turkish Empire 4232&nn5&6, 4249nn1&5, 4251&n5, 4257&n1, 4297, 4532
Turkish loans 4037n1
Turner, H.J. 4178n4
Turville, Bucks 4087&n2
Tweeddale, 8th Marquess of 4164n1
Twiss, Sir Travers V **1656n1**, 4482&n5
Ulrich, Prince of Saxe Weimar (unidentified) 4039&n3
Ultramontanism 4226&n3, 4236, 4254
Unicorn divisions 4485&n3, 4491n3
Union Chargeability Bill and Act (1865) 4007nn1&2
Union Review 3983&n2
United Church of England and Ireland 4527n3
United States 4614n2; Civil War 4002n2, 4196n4, 4259n1, 4289, 4550&nn3&6&7, 4636n2; congressional elections (5 Nov 1866) 4216&nn5&11, 4222; diplomats 4529&nn2&4; Fenians 4629, 4632; consul 4630n1
Universities (Scotland) Act (1858) 4225n2
University Education (Ireland) Act (1879) 4060n4
Vance, John VI **2460n2**, 4027&n1
Vancouver Island 4614n2
Vane, 2nd Earl (5th Marquess of Londonderry 1872) III **874n1**, 4207n7, 4509&n7, 4514n1
Van Quellin, Emile **4629&n4**